Also Available:

THE NEW INTERPRETER'S® BIBLE:
A COMMENTARY IN TWELVE VOLUMES

THE NEW INTERPRETER'S® BIBLE INDEX

THE NEW INTERPRETER'S® STUDY BIBLE

THE PASTOR'S® BIBLE STUDY:
A NEW INTERPRETER'S® SERIES

THE NEW INTERPRETER'S® BIBLE
OLD TESTAMENT SURVEY

THE NEW INTERPRETER'S® BIBLE
NEW TESTAMENT SURVEY

THE NEW INTERPRETER'S® DICTIONARY OF THE BIBLE

THE NEW
INTERPRETER'S®
HANDBOOK
OF
PREACHING

EDITORIAL BOARD

THE NEW INTERPRETER'S® HANDBOOK OF PREACHING

ABINGDON PRESS

Nashville

THE NEW INTERPRETER'S® HANDBOOK OF PREACHING

Copyright © 2008 by Abingdon Press

Library of Congress Cataloging-in-Publication Data

The new interpreter's handbook of preaching / [Paul Scott Wilson, general editor].
 p. cm.
Includes bibliographical references.
ISBN 978-0-687-05556-2 (binding: casebound-cloth binding : alk. paper)
1. Preaching—Handbooks, manuals, etc. I. Wilson, Paul Scott, 1949-

BV4211.3.N49 2008
251—dc22

2008024712

08 09 10 11 12 13 14 15 16 17—10 09 08 07 06 05 04 03 02 01

MANUFACTURED IN THE UNITED STATES OF AMERICA

CONTRIBUTORS

O. WESLEY ALLEN JR.
Lexington Theological Seminary
Lexington, KY
Revelation

RONALD J. ALLEN
Christian Theological Seminary
Indianapolis, IN
*Conversational Preaching; Form Criticism;
Lectio Continua; Listening and Observation Skills;
Part 10 Introduction; Teaching*

DALE P. ANDREWS
Boston University, School of Theology
Boston, MA
*African American Apprenticeship;
African American Biblical Interpretation*

JEFFREY D. ARTHURS
Gordon-Conwell Theological Seminary
South Hamilton, MA
Proverbs

RAYMOND H. BAILEY
Seventh & James Baptist Church
Waco, TX
Baylor University School of Law
Waco, TX
Retired, The Southern Baptist Theological Seminary
Louisville, KY
Stories, Ethics in Use of

DAVID L. BARTLETT
Columbia Theological Seminary
Decatur, GA
Allegory, Allegoresis; Historical Criticism; Typology

CASEY BARTON
Ph.D. Candidate
Emmanuel College, School of Theology
Toronto, ON, Canada
The Big Idea

CHARLES L. BARTOW
Princeton Theological Seminary
Princeton, NJ
Homiletical (Theological) Criticism; Word of God

DIANNE BERGANT, C.S.A.
Catholic Theological Union in Chicago
Chicago, IL
Esther; Song of Songs

DAVE L. BLAND
Harding University Graduate School of Religion
Memphis, TN
Deductive

CHARLES E. BOUCHARD, O.P.
Aquinas Institute of Theology
Saint Louis, MO
God, Ethics and

ROLF T. BOUMA
University of Michigan
Ann Arbor, MI
Environmental Ethics

MICHAEL A. BROTHERS
Princeton Theological Seminary
Princeton, NJ
Appearance; Inductive

CAROLYN C. BROWN
Certified Christian Educator
Presbyterian Church USA
Charlottesville, VA
Preaching to Children

SALLY A. BROWN
Princeton Theological Seminary
Princeton, NJ
Soteriology

JEFFREY F. BULLOCK
University of Dubuque
Dubuque, IA
Structuralism

CHARLES L. CAMPBELL
Columbia Theological Seminary
Decatur, GA
Part 3 Introduction; Preaching, Ethics of

WILLIAM J. CARL III
Pittsburgh Theological Seminary
Pittsburgh, PA
Preacher's Week

JERRY CARTER
Calvary Baptist Church
Morristown, NJ
Conclusions

BRYAN CHAPELL
Covenant Theological Seminary
St. Louis, MO
Christology

JANA CHILDERS
San Francisco Theological Seminary
San Anselmo, CA
*Part 6 Introduction; Preacher's Creative Process;
Pulpit, Use of; Weekly Sermon Preparation Using the
Handbook of Preaching*

JAMES M. CHILDS JR.
Trinity Lutheran Seminary
Columbus, OH
Doctrines and Biblical Texts

LINDA LEE CLADER
Church Divinity School of the Pacific and the Graduate
Theological Union
Berkeley, CA
*Anxiety; Holy Days and Holidays;
Metaphor and Figures of Speech*

ROBERT E. CONOVER
Presbytery of the Redwoods,
Presbyterian Church (USA)
Napa, CA
Identification

ROBERT B. COOTE
San Francisco Theological Seminary and the Graduate
Theological Union
San Anselmo, CA
Geography

DAVID A. DAVIS
Nassau Presbyterian Church
Princeton, NJ
Exegetical; Sermon Research

SCOTT K. DAVIS
Lehigh Valley Hospital and Health Network
Allentown, PA
Healing and Exorcism

KENDA CREASY DEAN
Princeton Theological Seminary
Princeton, NJ
Preaching to Youth

MARK DEVRIES
Youth Ministry Architects
Nashville, TN
First Presbyterian Church
Nashville, TN
Youth Ministry

THOMAS B. DOZEMAN
United Theological Seminary
Trotwood, OH
Canonical Criticism

MICHAEL DUDUIT
Preaching Magazine
Graduate School of Ministry at Anderson University
Anderson, SC
Illustration and Stories; Preparation; Sermon Series

PATRICIA DUTCHER-WALLS
Vancouver School of Theology
Vancouver, BC, Canada
Literary Criticism

TERRY W. EDDINGER
Carolina Evangelical Divinity School
High Point, NC
War, Preaching during

O. C. EDWARDS JR.
Emeritus, Seabury-Western Theological Seminary
Evanston, IL
Puritan Plain Style; Style

DAVID ALBERT FARMER
Silverside Church
Wilmington, DE
Palmer Theological Seminary
Philadelphia (Wynnewood), PA
Wilmington University
New Castle, DE
Time Management

STEPHEN FARRIS
St. Andrew's Hall
Vancouver, BC, Canada
*Bridging Then and Now; Exegesis of Self; Exegesis of
the Congregation, Denomination; Hermeneutics;
Part 1 Introduction*

AL FASOL
B. H. Carroll Theological Institute
Arlington, TX
Evangelistic Preaching

GORDON D. FEE
Regent College
Vancouver, BC, Canada
Contextual Epistles

PETER W. FLINT
Trinity Western University
Langley, BC, Canada
Apocrypha, Deuterocanonicals

SCOTT M. GIBSON
Gordon-Conwell Theological Seminary
South Hamilton, MA
Missiology; Point Form

KENYATTA R. GILBERT
Howard University School of Divinity
Washington, DC
Suspicion

FRANCISCO JAVIER GOITÍA-PADILLA
Iglesia Luterana Del Buen Pastor
San Juan, PR
Evangelical Seminary of Puerto Rico
San Juan, PR
Bilingual Setting

MIKE GRAVES
Saint Paul School of Theology
Greater Kansas City Christian Church
(Disciples of Christ)
Kansas City, MO
Comparison; Rhetorical Criticism

DAVID M. GREENHAW
Eden Theological Seminary
St. Louis, MO
Call

JOEL C. GREGORY
George W. Truett Theological Seminary
Baylor University
Waco, TX
Expository

SIDNEY GREIDANUS
Emeritus, Calvin Theological Seminary
Grand Rapids, MI
Moralism

DAVID P. GUSHEE
McAfee School of Theology,
Mercer University
Atlanta, GA
Individual Ethics

ADAM HAMILTON
The United Methodist Church of the Resurrection
Leawood, KS
Controversy

PAUL D. HANSON
Harvard University
Cambridge, MA
Apocalypticism

RICHARD B. HAYS
The Divinity School
Duke University
Durham, NC
Resurrection

SUSAN K. HEDAHL
Gettysburg Lutheran Theological Seminary, ELCA
Gettysburg, PA
Ordination

GREGORY HEILLE, O.P.
Aquinas Institute of Theology
St. Louis, MO
Daily; Lay Preacher; Part 4 Introduction

ALFRED J. HOERTH
Emeritus, Wheaton College
Wheaton, IL
Archaeology

LUCY LIND HOGAN
Wesley Theological Seminary
Washington, DC
*Learning Styles; Part 5 Introduction;
Persuasion*

JOHN C. HOLBERT
Perkins School of Theology
Southern Methodist University
Dallas, TX
*Job; Laws and Regulations; Levitical
Holiness Codes; Pathos/Feeling*

DAVID E. HOLWERDA
Emeritus, Calvin Theological Seminary
Grand Rapids, MI
John

ROBERT R. HOWARD
formerly at Louisville Presbyterian Theological Seminary
Louisville, KY
*Internet Preaching Databases; Internet Preaching
Forums; Technology and the Sermon*

JAMES C. HOWELL
Myers Park United Methodist Church
Charlotte, NC
Duke Divinity School
Durham, NC
Exodus

MARY S. HULST
Calvin Theological Seminary
Grand Rapids, MI
Part 7 Introduction

F. GERRIT IMMINK
Protestant Theological University
Utrecht, The Netherlands
Part 11 Introduction

DAVID SCHNASA JACOBSEN
Waterloo Lutheran Seminary
Waterloo, ON, Canada
Apocalyptic

JOSEPH R. JETER JR.
Brite Divinity School
Texas Christian University
Fort Worth, TX
Crisis; Part 8 Introduction

PABLO A. JIMÉNEZ
Consultant Editor, Chalice Press
Vega Alta, PR
Liberation Criticism; Missional Preaching

CHERYL BRIDGES JOHNS
Church of God Theological Seminary
Cleveland, TN
Eschatology; Holy Spirit and Preaching

JAMES F. KAY
Princeton Theological Seminary
Princeton, NJ
Theology of Proclamation

MICHAEL P. KNOWLES
McMaster Divinity College
Hamilton, ON, Canada
Miracles

PAUL E. KOPTAK
North Park Theological Seminary
Chicago, IL
Application

HENRY J. LANGKNECHT
Trinity Lutheran Seminary
Columbus, OH
Introductions; Literal Sense

CLEOPHUS J. LARUE
Princeton Theological Seminary
Princeton, NJ
*African American Preaching Perspectives;
Preaching Out of the Overflow*

THOMAS G. LONG
Candler School of Theology
Emory University
Atlanta, GA
*Authority (Theology); Exegesis; Funeral; Radio;
Sermonic, Theological Epistles*

JENNIFER L. LORD
Austin Presbyterian Theological Seminary
Austin, TX
Sacraments, Preaching and Teaching of

DAVID J. LOSE
Luther Seminary
St. Paul, MN
*Sermon as Proclamation;
Systematic, Constructive Theology*

EUGENE L. LOWRY
Emeritus, Saint Paul School of Theology
Kansas City, MO
Arrangement; Narrative Preaching

BARBARA K. LUNDBLAD
Union Theological Seminary
New York, NY
Feminist Criticism; Narrative Theory

DUNCAN MACPHERSON
University of Wales
Lampeter, Wales
College of Preachers
United Kingdom
Doctrinal; Holy Land Tours; Mystagogical Preaching

BRUCE J. MALINA
Creighton University
Omaha, NE
Social Scientific Criticism

RAY JOHN MAREK, O.M.I.
Oblate School of Theology
San Antonio, TX
Television

J. CLINTON McCANN JR.
Eden Theological Seminary
St. Louis, MO
Psalms

JOHN S. McCLURE
The Divinity School
Vanderbilt University
Nashville, TN
Collaboration; Deconstruction

ALYCE M. McKENZIE
Perkins School of Theology
Southern Methodist University
Dallas, TX
*Ecclesiastes; Formalist Criticism; Popular Psychology
and Preaching*

MARVIN A. McMICKLE
Antioch Baptist Church
Cleveland, OH
Prophetic Message

HENRY H. MITCHELL
Emeritus, Colgate-Rochester-Crozer Divinity School
Rochester, NY
Celebration

WILLIAM S. MORROW
Queen's Theological College and Department of
Religious Studies
Queen's University,
Kingston, ON, Canada
Laments

BRENDAN MOSS, O.S.B.
St. Meinrad School of Theology
St. Meinrad, IN
Lectio Divina

MARC T. NEWMAN
MovieMinistry.com
Vista, CA
Video Clips

JAMES R. NIEMAN
Hartford Seminary
Hartford, CT
Career Path/Life Stage; Theology in the Sermon

JAMES A. NOEL
San Francisco Theological Seminary
San Anselmo, CA
Politics, Ethics and; Revivals

DENNIS T. OLSON
Princeton Theological Seminary
Princeton, NJ
Pentateuchal Narratives

DEBORAH A. ORGAN
The Saint Paul Seminary School of Divinity
Saint Paul, MN
Cultural Hermeneutics

EUGENE EUNG-CHUN PARK
San Francisco Theological Seminary
San Anselmo, CA
Philosophical Hermeneutics

AMY PLANTINGA PAUW
Louisville Presbyterian Seminary
Louisville, KY
Anthropology

MARY MARGARET PAZDAN
Aquinas Institute of Theology
St. Louis, MO
Luke/Acts; Passion Narratives

CORNELIUS PLANTINGA JR.
Calvin Theological Seminary
Grand Rapids, MI
Novels

LUKE A. POWERY
Princeton Theological Seminary
Princeton, NJ
Holy Spirit/Passion; Postcolonial Criticism

B. KEITH PUTT
Samford University
Birmingham, AL
New Historicism

MICHAEL J. QUICKE
Northern Baptist Theological Seminary
Lombard, IL
Trinity

G. LEE RAMSEY JR.
Memphis Theological Seminary
Memphis, TN
Self-Disclosure

BARBARA E. REID
Catholic Theological Union
Chicago, IL
Parables; Synoptic Gospels

ROBERT S. REID
University of Dubuque
Dubuque, IA
Part 9 Introduction; Rhetorical Devices

ANDRÉ RESNER
Hood Theological Seminary
Salisbury, NC
Character; Ethos; Logos; Social Justice

CHARLES L. RICE
Emeritus, Drew University
Madison, NJ
Authority (of the Preacher); Wedding

CYNTHIA L. RIGBY
Austin Presbyterian Theological Seminary
Austin, TX
Sin and Evil

JEFFREY S. ROGERS
First Baptist Church
Greenville, SC
Conquest Narratives

THOMAS G. ROGERS
Pacific Lutheran Theological Seminary
Berkeley, CA
Emerging Church Preaching

JOHN M. ROTTMAN
Calvin Theological Seminary
Grand Rapids, MI
*Concerns of the Text and Sermon; The Four Pages of
the Sermon; How to Use the Handbook of Preaching
in the Homiletics Classroom; Part 2 Introduction*

TEX S. SAMPLE
Saint Paul School of Theology
Kansas City, MO
Film; Worship Style

CLAYTON J. SCHMIT
Fuller Theological Seminary
Pasadena, CA
Manuscript

QUENTIN J. SCHULTZE
Calvin College
Grand Rapids, MI
Technology

MARY J. SCIFRES
Ordained Elder, The United Methodist Church
Gig Harbor, WA
Seeker Messages

EDWIN SEARCY
University Hill Congregation of the
United Church of Canada
Vancouver, BC, Canada
Shaping Congregational Identity

GARY V. SIMPSON
The Concord Baptist Church of Christ
Brooklyn, NY
Drew Theological Seminary
Madison, NJ
Gender, Race, and Ethnicity; Testimonial

CHRISTINE M. SMITH
United Theological Seminary of the Twin Cities
New Brighton, MN
Feminist Perspectives; Social Justice Networks

ROBERT SMITH JR.
Beeson Divinity School
Samford University
Birmingham, AL
Call and Response; Topical

SARAH J. SMITH
Middleton, WI
Reader/Listener Response

RAQUEL A. ST. CLAIR
St. James A.M.E. Church
Newark, NJ
Womanist Criticism

RICHARD C. STERN
Saint Meinrad School of Theology
St. Meinrad, IN
Plagiarism

LAURENCE HULL STOOKEY
Emeritus, Wesley Theological Seminary
Washington, DC
Asbury United Methodist Church
Allen, MD
*Lectionary and the Christian Year;
Worship Environment*

TERESA LOCKHART STRICKLEN
Pittsburgh Theological Seminary
Pittsburgh, PA
Definition; Moves

BARBARA BROWN TAYLOR
Piedmont College
Demorest, GA
Columbia Theological Seminary
Decatur, GA
Devotional Life/Life-Style

JOHN V. TORNFELT
Evangelical Theological Seminary
Myerstown, PA
Leadership

THOMAS H. TROEGER
Yale Divinity School
Yale University
New Haven, CT
Arts; Imagination/Creativity

PATRICIA K. TULL
Louisville Presbyterian Theological Seminary
Louisville, KY
Jewish/Christian Perspectives

MARY DONOVAN TURNER
Pacific School of Religion
Berkeley, CA
Narrative Form; Prophetic Preaching; Ruth

HOWARD VANDERWELL
Calvin College and Calvin Theological Seminary
Grand Rapids, MI
Long-Range Sermon Planning

RAYMOND C. VAN LEEUWEN
Eastern University
St. Davids, PA
Prehistory

CALVIN P. VAN REKEN
Calvin Theological Seminary
Grand Rapids, MI
Ethical Methods

ARTHUR VAN SETERS
Emeritus, Knox College
Toronto School of Theology
Toronto, ON, Canada
Corporate Ethics; Globalization

JAMES A. WALLACE, C.Ss.R.
Washington Theological Union
Washington, DC
Special Occasion

RICHARD F. WARD
Iliff School of Theology
Denver, CO
*Oral/Aural Communication; Performative Language;
Performing the Manuscript*

DON M. WARDLAW
Emeritus, McCormick Theological Seminary
Chicago, IL
Focus and Function Statements

JOSEPH M. WEBB
Gardner-Webb University
Boiling Springs, NC
Memory; Without Notes

MICHAEL E. WILLIAMS
First United Methodist Church
Hendersonville, TN
Contemporizing

WILLIAM H. WILLIMON
Resident Bishop, North Alabama Conference of
The United Methodist Church, Birmingham, AL Area
Duke Divinity School
Durham, NC
Ecclesiology

PAUL SCOTT WILSON
Emmanuel College
University of Toronto
Toronto, ON, Canada
*Four Senses of Scripture; Fusion; Magnification;
New Homiletic; Theme Sentence*

BEVERLY A. ZINK-SAWYER
Union Theological Seminary and the Presbyterian
School of Christian Education
Richmond, VA
Women

CONTENTS

General Editor's Preface xxv

How to Use the *Handbook of Preaching* in a Homiletics Classroom xxvii

Weekly Sermon Preparation Using the *Handbook of Preaching* xxix

1. BIBLE

Introduction: Choosing and Delimiting the Text 1

African American Biblical Interpretation 3
Allegory, Allegoresis 5
Apocalypticism 9
Archaeology 13
Canonical Criticism 15
Exegesis 17
Form Criticism 24
Four Senses of Scripture 28
Geography 29
Hermeneutics 31
Historical Criticism 37
Liberation Criticism 45
Literal Sense 49
Literary Criticism 51
Philosophical Hermeneutics 53
Suspicion 55
Typology 57

2. BIBLE GENRES

Introduction: Literary Forms 65

Apocalyptic 67
Apocrypha, Deuterocanonicals 69
Conquest Narratives 71
Contextual Epistles 73
Ecclesiastes 75
Esther 76
Exodus 77
Healing and Exorcism 79
Job 81
John 82

Laments 85
Laws and Regulations 86
Levitical Holiness Codes 88
Luke/Acts 89
Miracles 91
Parables 92
Passion Narratives 94
Pentateuchal Narratives 95
Prehistory 98
Prophetic Preaching 101
Proverbs 103
Psalms 104
Resurrection 106
Ruth 108
Sermonic, Theological Epistles 110
Song of Songs 112
Synoptic Gospels 113

3. ETHICS

Introduction: Ethics and Preaching 115

Controversy 117
Corporate Ethics 119
Environmental Ethics 121
Ethical Methods 122
God, Ethics and 124
Individual Ethics 126
Moralism 127
Plagiarism 128
Politics, Ethics and 129
Preaching, Ethics of 131
Self-Disclosure 133
Social Justice 135
Stories, Ethics in Use of 137

4. LITERARY CRITICISM

Introduction: Subjectivity and the Sermon 141

Cultural Hermeneutics 143
Deconstruction 146
Feminist Criticism 149
Formalist Criticism 151
Homiletical (Theological) Criticism 154
New Historicism 157
Postcolonial Criticism 159
Reader/Listener Response 161
Rhetorical Criticism 163
Social Scientific Criticism 165
Structuralism 167
Womanist Criticism 170

5. POETICS

Introduction: Poetics and the Context of Preaching 173

Application 176
Arts 177
Bridging Then and Now 179
Concerns of the Text and Sermon 181
Contemporizing 182
Film 185
Focus and Function Statements 187
Fusion 188
Illustration and Stories 189
Imagination/Creativity 191
Magnification 193
Metaphor and Figures of Speech 193
Moves 199
Narrative Preaching 201
Narrative Theory 203
Novels 204
Theme Sentence 207
Video Clips 209
Worship Environment 210

6. PREACHER

Introduction: The Preacher's Performance 213

African American Apprenticeship 215
Anxiety 217
Appearance 218
Authority of the Preacher 219
Call 223
Character 225
Devotional Life/Life-style 227
Leadership 229
Learning Styles 231
Listening and Observation Skills 232
Long-range Sermon Planning 232
Performative Language 234
Performing the Manuscript 236
Preacher's Creative Process 239
Preacher's Week 241
Preaching Out of the Overflow 243
Sermon Research 246
Time Management 247
Women 249

7. SOCIAL LOCATION

Introduction: Identity and Communication 253

Bilingual Setting 255
Career Path/Life Stage 257

Collaboration 258
Crisis 262
Exegesis of the Congregation, Denomination 266
Exegesis of Self 267
Gender, Race, and Ethnicity 269
Globalization 272
Lay Preacher 274
Missional Preaching 276
Preaching to Children 279
Preaching to Youth 281
Pulpit, Use of 284
Sacraments, Preaching and Teaching of 284
War, Preaching during 285
Worship Style 286

8. EXPERIENCE

Introduction: Preaching in a Diverse World 291

African American Preaching Perspectives 293
Call and Response 297
Celebration 297
Emerging Church Preaching 298
Evangelistic Preaching 300
Feminist Perspectives 302
Holy Days and Holidays 304
Holy Land Tours 306
Holy Spirit/Passion 308
Internet Preaching Databases 310
Internet Preaching Forums 313
Jewish/Christian Perspectives 315
Lectio Continua 318
Lectio Divina 319
Lectionary and the Christian Year 321
Radio 326
Revivals 328
Social Justice Networks 330
Technology 332
Television 336
Youth Ministry 337

9. RHETORIC

Introduction: Seeking a Response 343

Arrangement 346
Comparison 348
Definition 349
Ethos 350
Identification 350
Logos 353
Memory 354

Oral/Aural Communication 356
Pathos/Feeling 358
Persuasion 360
Rhetorical Devices 362
Style 364
Technology and the Sermon 366

10. SERMON

Introduction: Seeking to Be Heard 369

Conclusions 372
Conversational Preaching 372
Daily 373
Deductive 375
Doctrinal 377
Exegetical 380
Expository 381
(The) Four Pages of the Sermon 384
Funeral 385
Inductive 390
Introductions 392
Manuscript 394
Mystagogical Preaching 395
Narrative Form 396
New Homiletic 398
Point Form 401
Popular Psychology and Preaching 404
Preparation 406
Prophetic Message 408
Puritan Plain Style 410
Seeker Messages 411
Sermon as Proclamation 414
Sermon Series 416
Shaping Congregational Identity 418
Special Occasion 419
Teaching 420
Testimonial 423
The Big Idea 424
Topical 425
Wedding 426
Without Notes 429

11. THEOLOGY

Introduction: Bearer of the Word 433

Anthropology 435
Authority (Theology) 440
Christology 444
Doctrines and Biblical Texts 448
Ecclesiology 452

Eschatalogy 456
Holy Spirit and Preaching 460
Missiology 465
Ordination 469
Revelation 473
Sin and Evil 477
Soteriology 481
Systematic, Constructive Theology 486
Theology in the Sermon 489
Theology of Proclamation 493
Trinity 498
Word of God 502

ALPHABETICAL LIST OF ARTICLES

African American Apprenticeship 215
African American Biblical Interpretation 3
African American Preaching Perspectives 293
Allegory, Allegoresis 5
Anthropology 435
Anxiety 217
Apocalyptic 67
Apocalypticism 9
Apocrypha, Deuterocanonicals 69
Appearance 218
Application 176
Archaeology 13
Arrangement 346
Arts 177
Authority (Theology) 440
Authority of the Preacher 219
Bilingual Setting 255
Bridging Then and Now 179
Call 223
Call and Response 297
Canonical Criticism 15
Career Path/Life Stage 257
Celebration 297
Character 225
Christology 444
Collaboration 258
Comparison 348
Concerns of the Text and Sermon 181
Conclusions 372
Conquest Narratives 71
Contemporizing 182
Contextual Epistles 73
Controversy 117
Conversational Preaching 372
Corporate Ethics 119
Crisis 262
Cultural Hermeneutics 143
Daily 373
Deconstruction 146
Deductive 375
Definition 349

Delivery (See Performing the Manuscript)
Devotional Life/Life-style 227
Doctrinal 377
Doctrines and Biblical Texts 448
Ecclesiastes 75
Ecclesiology 452
Emerging Church Preaching 298
Environmental Ethics 121
Eschatology 456
Esther 76
Ethical Methods 122
Ethics
    Corporate 119
    Environmental 121
    God, Ethics and 124
    Individual 126
    Personal (See Individual Ethics)
    Politics, Ethics and 129
    Preaching, Ethics of 131
    Stories, Ethics in Use of 137
Ethos 350
Evangelistic Preaching 300
Exegesis 17
Exegesis of the Congregation, Denomination . . 266
Exegesis of Self 267
Exegetical 380
Exodus 77
Expository 381
Fallen Condition Focus (See The Big Idea)
Feminist Criticism 149
Feminist Perspectives 302
Figures of Speech (See Metaphor and
   Figures of Speech)
Film 185
Focus and Function Statements 187
Form Criticism 24
Formalist Criticism 151
(The) Four Pages of the Sermon 384
Four Senses of Scripture 28
Funeral 385

Fusion 188
Gender, Race, and Ethnicity 269
Genre Criticism (See Form Criticism)
Geography 29
Globalization 272
God, Ethics and 124
Healing and Exorcism 79
Hermeneutics 31
Historical Criticism 37
Holy Days and Holidays 304
Holy Land Tours 306
Holy Spirit and Preaching 460
Holy Spirit/Passion 308
Homiletical (Theological) Criticism 154
How to Use the *Handbook of Preaching* in the
   Homiletics Classroom xxvii
Identification 350
Illustration and Stories 189
Imagination/Creativity 191
Individual Ethics 126
Inductive 390
Internet Preaching Databases 310
Internet Preaching Forums 313
Interpretation (See Hermeneutics)
Introductions 392
Introductions to Parts
   1—Choosing and Delimiting the Text 1
   2—Literary Forms 65
   3—Ethics and Preaching 115
   4—Subjectivity and the Sermon 141
   5—Poetics and the Context of Preaching ... 173
   6—The Preacher's Performance 213
   7—Identity and Communication 253
   8—Preaching in a Diverse World 291
   9—Seeking a Response 343
   10—Seeking to Be Heard 369
   11—Bearer of the Word 433
Jewish/Christian Perspectives 315
Job 81
John 82
Johannine Epistles (See Contextual Epistles)
Laments 85
Laws and Regulations 86
Lay Preacher 274
Leadership 229
Learning Styles 231
Lectio Continua 318
Lectio Divina 319
Lectionary and the Christian Year 321
Levitical Holiness Codes 88
Liberation Criticism 45
Listening and Observation Skills 232
Literal Sense 49

Literary Criticism 51
Logos 353
Long-range Sermon Planning 232
Luke/Acts 89
Magnification 193
Manuscript 394
Memory 354
Metaphor and Figures of Speech 193
Miracles 91
Missiology 465
Missional Preaching 276
Moralism 127
Moves 199
Music (See Arts)
Mystagogical Preaching 395
Narrative Form 396
Narrative Preaching 201
Narrative Theory 203
New Historicism 157
New Homiletic 398
Novels 204
Oral/Aural Communication 356
Ordination 469
Parables 92
Passion Narratives 94
Pastoral Epistles (See Contextual Epistles)
Pathos/Feeling 358
Pentateuchal Narratives 95
Performative Language 234
Performing the Manuscript 236
Persuasion 360
Petrine Epistles (See Contextual Epistles)
Philosophical Hermeneutics 53
Plagiarism 128
Poetics (See Part 5 Introduction:
   Poetics and the Context of Preaching)
Point Form 401
Politics, Ethics and 129
Popular Psychology and Preaching 404
Postcolonial Criticism 159
Preacher's Creative Process 239
Preacher's Week 241
Preaching, Ethics of 131
Preaching Out of the Overflow 243
Preaching to Children 279
Preaching to Youth 281
Prehistory 98
Preparation 406
Prophetic Message 408
Prophetic Preaching 101
Proverbs 103
Psalms 104
Pulpit, Use of 284

Puritan Plain Style 410
Radio 326
Reader/Listener Response 161
Resurrection 106
Revelation 473
Revivals 328
Rhetoric (See Part 9 Rhetoric. Introduction:
   Seeking a Response)
Rhetorical Criticism 163
Rhetorical Devices 362
Ruth 108
Sacraments, Preaching and Teaching of 284
Seeker Messages 411
Self-Disclosure 133
Sermon as Proclamation 414
Sermon Research 246
Sermon Series 416
Sermonic, Theological Epistles 110
Sexuality (See Anthopology)
Shaping Congregational Identity 418
Sin and Evil 477
Social Justice 135
Social Justice Networks 330
Social Scientific Criticism 165
Song of Songs 112
Soteriology 481
Special Occasion 419
Stories, Ethics in Use of 137
Structuralism 167
Style 364
Suspicion 55

Synoptic Gospels 113
Systematic, Constructive Theology 486
Teaching 420
Technology 332
Technology and the Sermon 366
Television 336
Testimonial 423
The Big Idea 424
Theme Sentence 207
Theology in the Sermon 489
Theology of Proclamation 493
Time Management 247
Topical 425
Trinity 498
Typology 57
Verse by Verse (See Exegetical;
   Puritan Plain Style)
Video Clips 209
War, Preaching during 285
Wedding 426
Weekly Sermon Preparation Using
   the *Handbook of Preaching* xxix
Wisdom (See Ecclesiastes; Esther;
   Preaching, Ethics of; Proverbs)
Without Notes 429
Womanist Criticism 170
Women 249
Word of God 502
Worship Environment 210
Worship Style 286
Youth Ministry 337

GENERAL EDITOR'S PREFACE

Ever since the events described in Nehemiah 8, people have gathered to hear the Word of God read and interpreted, "So they read from the book, from the law of God, with interpretation. They gave the sense, so that the people understood the reading" (8:8). These words mark the beginning of both hermeneutics and preaching as we know it. The serpent in the Garden of Eden may have claimed, "What God said is not what God meant," but in Nehemiah we have the first plain distinction between what a text says and what it means. From this early time, theology, biblical studies, and homiletics have been interrelated, in part because all are needed for the pulpit. At least until recent decades, each discipline understood its purpose as serving the preaching of the church, for the Word was understood as central to all other aspects of the church's life and ministry. Today other purposes abound: theology may not always be concerned to bring God to voice, biblical studies seems loyal to history and often mute on revelation and God's Word, and homiletics may too easily forget to be practical. When these disciplines are at their best, as is seen in these pages, they function not in isolation, but as three areas of conversation that complement one another in the service of God to strengthen the church.

From the beginning of this project two goals have been foremost. The first was in keeping with the New Interpreter's® imprint, to present the best and most recent scholarship, in this case on nearly every facet of sermon preparation and delivery, including theology of the Word. Second, each author was asked to pay special attention to practical matters like, how will this preach? The practical component was to focus on repeated tasks the preacher might normally engage, not esoteric or idiosyncratic practices. The many scholars represented here come from diverse denominational and discipline backgrounds and in addition to Christian faith share in common a high regard for preaching, most often as a vocation.

As a result the *New Interpreter's® Handbook of Preaching* is a unique resource that presents the state of the art of homiletics in this new millennium; it also sets new benchmarks for preaching in the coming years. In fact, it could provide the basic reading material for several courses in homiletics, and some sample courses are outlined in the introductory materials. Also in those materials is reflection on how to use this volume as a resource for weekly preaching.

This handbook represents many perspectives, not any one particular school of homiletical or theological thought, although it generally encourages preaching that is biblical and centers on God and humanity in relation to God. It is interdisciplinary and develops theory/theology geared to practice. Its theory arises from study of excellent preaching past and present and of actual sermon preparation and composition. Authors were encouraged where possible to include sermon extracts. When theory and practice critique each other in this manner, the resulting guidelines typically assist greater quality and economy in preaching the gospel. The practices recommended in these pages are of the "here is something that works well" variety, rather than the more whimsical "here is something to try."

The practical component here makes it possible to recommend this volume for a place on the reference shelf of the preacher's library marked Used Most Often. If a preacher for some unimaginable reason had to own only one resource beyond the Bible, a commentary, a volume of systematic or constructive theology, and the news, this might be it. Preachers will find a wide range of topics, along with examples, suggestions, and brief bibliographies referring readers to key books and articles. Here are essays that range in subject matter from anxiety in the pulpit, to exegesis, preaching various kinds of biblical literature, the uses of technology including the Internet, and the place of revelation. Sermon forms range from deductive and expository to inductive and conversational; they are for occasions as diverse as regular services, revivals, youth ministry, funerals and weddings, and television.

Readers may access articles in several ways. The Contents is broken down into nine sections that correspond to tasks the preacher normally engages, for example, Bible, theology, rhetoric, social location, and so forth. Immediately following the Contents is an alphabetical listing of entries to assist readers in quickly locating articles by topic of interest. There is also an index of authors. Articles are themselves cross-referenced to provide related reading within the handbook.

Thanks are due in particular to many members of the Academy of Homiletics who have shared their encouragement and insights, and especially to those who gave particular guidance concerning topics and authors to pursue. The Editorial Board is most grateful to the contributors for their willingness to write and for the opportunity of getting to know them better, or some of them for the first time, through the process of correspondence and editing. That has been a deep personal joy made all the richer by the privilege of being exposed to various thoughts and perspectives on preaching. Some of the writers were under constraint by word limits we assigned to them and we are grateful for their understanding and efforts to comply even though significant aspects of their topics sometimes could not be fully developed. Contributors were selected for their expertise and have more than lived up to our expectations; they demonstrate a wonderful ability to distill subjects that are often difficult into clear and concise overviews, informed analysis, proposals, and guidelines. The contributors are the ones who truly offer this volume.

Finally I thank professors Jana Childers, Cleophus J. LaRue, and John M. Rottman, whose wisdom and selfless work for this project were essential to its success. Our meetings and conversations together were enriching at many levels and added a lot of fun to the process. They join with me in expressing our gratitude to the people of Abingdon Press, Dr. Paul Franklyn, who first envisioned the project and got it off the ground, and Dr. Robert Ratcliff, who ably took over mid-project and saw it to completion. Both have been helpful and supportive guides and their insight and friendship have meant much not only professionally in these pages but personally as well. To Dr. John F. Kutsko, project director, and the Abingdon staff who managed the invitation and collection of articles and who helped throughout the editing and publishing process, we offer our sincere thanks. Without them, gathering these materials would have been an even larger undertaking than it was, and much less enjoyable.

Of course any project of this sort has many articles that overlap and provide richness and inevitably has many gaps as well. Some of the gaps have to do with topics that we imagined might be covered under a different heading but in the end were not, and some have to do with people who were on our lists but were somehow overlooked. The project is less rich for these lacunae. We do not claim that all of the important preaching topics have been covered, just that these have importance. Some of the gaps have to do with limitation of space. For example, partly because of the practical emphasis, we requested most articles to have a historical component but beyond this we made no attempt to cover the history of preaching or biographies of important preachers. Further, preaching looks different in many parts of the world and in different cultures. Literature in these areas is only starting to grow and is underrepresented here. Some of the gaps are simply due to error (we hope they are few) and belong to us and not to any of those who were our advisors. In any case, this handbook is offered in humility to those who preach, in the hope that the combined efforts of many people make for a worthy contribution to a field that is essential for the ongoing health of the church. It is our hope that the collective effort here may strengthen proclamation of the gospel of Jesus Christ.

PAUL SCOTT WILSON, GENERAL EDITOR

HOW TO USE THE *HANDBOOK OF PREACHING* IN A HOMILETICS CLASSROOM

The *New Interpreter's® Handbook of Preaching* provides a wonderful resource for those who teach and learn preaching. Often those who teach preaching already have a favorite textbook that they use to anchor their introductory course material. The choice of a single text with a single method often works well to introduce fledgling preachers to a basic homiletic from which they might later branch out. A single, usable, tried-and-true foundational method for the beginning preacher is usually well advised. Unfortunately, an introductory text invariably omits or skims over important issues. No text can do everything. For example, a text may be very good on homiletical method, but provide little or no theology of proclamation. Another textbook choice may offer fine direction for preaching biblically, but almost omit issues surrounding what has traditionally been called delivery, the various aspects in which the preacher embodies the sermon. In order to address these deficiencies, the preaching teacher often feels the need to supplement the primary text with additional resources. Requiring a large number of additional books can be an unwelcome expense for students. Collecting supplementary articles or book chapters with the requisite permission forms takes time and effort on the part of the professor and student.

In the face of these challenges this handbook provides a welcome resource for a variety of reasons. First, the *Handbook of Preaching* is the kind of resource that new and experienced preachers will want to own; it is the best single resource on homiletics today and sets new standards for the coming years. Second, it is a resource that has enough variety and specialization to provide reading for several courses in preaching. Third, if the *Handbook of Preaching* is not the primary text for a course, the teacher nonetheless can use individual articles, written by recognized experts in their field, to expose the student to approaches that differ from the primary text without requiring too much additional reading or trouble. If the primary text is weak on artistic aspects of preaching, articles in PART 5, POETICS, may be helpful. Sometimes a particular student needs more help in a particular area than the class as a whole. In such a case individual articles provide tools for remediation. For example, if students are tied or even shackled to their manuscripts, the article WITHOUT NOTES may prove to be the proper prescription, or if students lack background in the church, articles on APPEARANCE or WORD OF GOD might be needed. Students writing essays on topics in preaching can be pointed to the *Handbook of Preaching* as a starting place, using related articles to gain various perspectives and the bibliographies for more in-depth reading.

The *New Interpreter's® Handbook of Preaching* also provides resources around which one is able to structure entire courses. Some sections in their entirety could serve as reading material for a course. For instance, a course on Sermon Form and Structure could be based on PART 10, where nearly all aspects of both the old and NEW HOMILETIC are discussed.

If one wished to teach a course on Preaching Old Testament Genres, the BIBLE GENRES section offers particular resources. One might think of a semester-long course divided roughly in half with the first half focusing on theory and the second half spent preaching and discussing sermons that put the course theory into practice. One might choose to follow the genres in the order that they roughly appear in the Bible, beginning with the article on PREHISTORY in the book of Genesis. After that the articles on PENTATEUCHAL NARRATIVES and EXODUS might provide the next two foci for the course. While the Common Lectionary treats them rather scantly, the course could include a session on preaching CONQUEST NARRATIVES, using that article and perhaps supplementing it with the article on ETHICS, GOD AND. Preaching the Psalms could be handled in another session or two, making use of the article on LAMENTS in attending to psalms of lament. The articles on LAWS

AND REGULATIONS and LEVITICAL HOLINESS CODES will allow the class to focus on large chunks of the OT that are often neglected. The articles on MORALISM and THE FOUR PAGES OF THE SERMON would help prevent the student from preaching sections of this genre as a big "to do" list. And one might conclude by using the article on PROPHETIC PREACHING, which will allow the student to consider preaching prophetic literature, and the entry on SOCIAL JUSTICE, which may help the student see the implications of this genre for the present.

Alternatively, the above course on biblical genre might consider narrative preaching in the first part of the theory section of the course using articles on PENTATEUCHAL NARRATIVES, CONQUEST NARRATIVES, EXODUS, RUTH, ESTHER, SYNOPTIC GOSPELS, and LUKE/ACTS as a guide to narrative preaching. Then the second half might consider non-narrative genres using articles on LAWS AND REGULATIONS; PSALMS; SERMONIC, THEOLOGICAL EPISTLES; and APOCALYPTIC.

A course on Preaching and Pastoral Ministry is another possibility. Since the rise of popular psychology, one may be inclined to think of pastoral care as pastoral counseling, but in larger congregations individual contact with every member happens most often through preaching. Hence the necessity for pastors to handle pastoral care issues in the pulpit. Articles across several sections could be gleaned for this purpose, perhaps starting with CONTEXTUAL EPISTLES. AUTHORITY OF THE PREACHER, CHARACTER, EXEGESIS OF SELF, ETHOS, LEADERSHIP, and LISTENING AND OBSERVATION SKILLS would ground class discussion on issues concerning the preacher. EXEGESIS OF THE CONGREGATION, DENOMINATION would assist discussion of the congregation, along with COLLABORATION; IDENTIFICATION; and GENDER, RACE, AND ETHNICITY in preaching. When one considers preaching at critical junctures of people's lives, articles such as those on preaching the WEDDING and the FUNERAL will need to be consulted in the classroom. Pastoral care at the beginning of a marriage relationship and for those left after the death of a loved one includes critical areas of pastoral ministry to which the student needs to be exposed. Articles on CRISIS and CONTROVERSY will allow other salient issues to be treated and can be supplemented with the articles in PART 3, ETHICS.

If one wished to organize a course on Preaching Doctrine, PART 11 provides rich resources for guiding students and stimulating discussion. One might choose articles on core doctrines such as the ones on CHRISTOLOGY, SOTERIOLOGY, TRINITY, WORD OF GOD, ECCLESIOLOGY, and ESCHATOLOGY and so follow an almost classic loci pathway. The fine article on preaching RESURRECTION from the BIBLE GENRES section should also be included in such a course. Doctrines could be examined in relationship to the LECTIONARY AND THE CHRISTIAN YEAR and LONG-RANGE SERMON PLANNING. How doctrines fit into the sermon planning process can draw upon PREACHER'S CREATIVE PROCESS, PREACHER'S WEEK, SERMON RESEARCH, and TIME MANAGEMENT. Pairing the articles on doctrines with traditional denominational doctrinal statements or topics in an introductory systematic or constructive theology textbook will train the future pastor to cultivate the habit of thinking about the faith in the course of preaching the weekly sermon.

The above examples are simply meant to demonstrate what is possible. Any number of courses can be assembled using the articles in the *Handbook of Preaching*, depending upon the needs of the churches and the students for whom they are being educated and trained. Should the focus of the classroom be continuing education for pastors, the *Handbook* offers review modules that will refresh and extend those things learned in seminary. With its useful bibliographies, this volume also provides a resource for preachers who have begun to take responsibility for their own post-seminary education.

The editors are confident that the *Handbook of Preaching* makes a unique academic and practical offering that will assist not only preachers in their pulpits but also professors and students in their classrooms and places of study.

JOHN M. ROTTMAN, EDITORIAL BOARD

Weekly Sermon Preparation Using the *Handbook of Preaching*

The *New Interpreter's® Handbook of Preaching* is designed to assist the preacher in preparation of weekly sermons. It provides resources for every major category of preaching endeavor, whether it is biblical, theological, homiletical, or related to a number of other issues pertaining to preachers' regular tasks and duties. For those seeking inspiration, the articles here provide practical suggestions and/or examples designed to get the preacher's juices flowing. Those seeking clarity will find definitions, background materials, explanations, and bibliographies for some of preaching's most important methods and topics. Others will use the *Handbook of Preaching* to help stretch themselves, trying out new homiletical forms or tackling parts of the Bible previously unexplored. Still others will need a bit of this and a bit of that and will dip into the *Handbook's* resources throughout the sermon creation process.

As long as there have been preachers, there have been sermon handbooks, oral and printed, Scripture-based and theological, formal and informal. Currently, there is nothing on the market that comes close to this resource in terms of the range of its subjects and their practical application to preaching. Since most human beings have no more than eight or nine ideas on any given subject, good preachers naturally turn outward for help. Whether they call it "stirring the pot" or "priming the pump," the need for conversation partners, reference materials, and handbooks is a given.

Different preachers find different kinds of resources useful. Some need help thinking up the sermon; others need help thinking about the sermon. There are preachers who need help writing the sermon and preachers who need help delivering it. Some people could use support to make more careful hermeneutical decisions about the text; some need resources to help them parse the listeners. It goes without saying that needs differ not only from preacher to preacher but also from sermon to sermon. One way to use this handbook is by free association, letting one article lead you to another by following cross-references. Below are examples of how I might use this volume on a couple of occasions.

EXAMPLE: RESOURCES FOR AN ANXIOUS PREACHER

Some preachers need the most support at the beginning of the process. When I sit down to begin working in earnest on a sermon, the sort function of my brain kicks in. First, I think about the e-mail cluttering my inbox and the thank-you notes burning a hole in my to-do list. I calculate how long I have to stare at the blank screen before I can get up and move the washed clothes to the dryer. How close to the cookie jar will I pass on the way? How many Oreos could I justify? I let my gaze roam over the text. There is a verb that needs parsing, a nail that needs filing, a place name that needs identifying. Finally, I make a list of the questions the text raises, offsetting the impossible ones slightly onto the side margin of the page.

Before I have even written my opening sentence, I am looking for support. The article on ANXIETY adjusts my perspective. There are other preachers like me. Several practical methods for managing anxiety are recommended; I try the deep breathing. SERMON RESEARCH further reassures me. I have done the work I need to do on the text. The article suggests one more avenue to explore. From FEMINIST PERSPECTIVES I learn that my initial thoughts about the text are not harebrained and are instead possibly related to women's experience in the world. Finally, I turn to the article on LUKE/ACTS. It is the last thing I read before I start to write. It reminds me of my passage's larger context and stirs me to feel again the power of Luke's stories. It makes me want to start writing.

Though the sermon introduction jumps out onto the page, the question of its connection to the heart of the sermon begins immediately to plague me. My sort function has gone wild again. There are several rough outlines on my scratch paper, but none of them seems to hang together. I thumb through PART 10, looking for myself. Am I a FOUR PAGES preacher or a PURITAN PLAIN STYLE? Shall I try something new? The article on INDUCTIVE sermons describes familiar terrain. I feel that someone has given me permission to write a sermon in a style that might actually work for me. I set aside the outlines and try out THEME SENTENCEs, carefully following the article's suggestions. Finally, using the recommendations made in focus and function statements, I discover the red thread that holds my disparate ideas together. I am off and writing.

EXAMPLE: RESOURCES FOR A CHALLENGING BIBLICAL TEXT

Of course, not everybody writhes through the process of sermon creation. Some people pace. Others soar. Some (virtually) skip. Not all preachers are plagued by writer's block. But all preachers, happy and tortured alike, wrestle.

Sometimes it is the exegetical and hermeneutical issues that keep us up at night. The problem with waffling, niggling, and being torn over a text's interpretation is that it can really slow down the process of sermon preparation. For some of us slowing down is akin to losing momentum, which is akin to stalling, which is a short step from a surfeit of Oreos. But even for confident preachers, finding answers to the questions that arise during the preacher's exegetical and hermeneutical process can be challenging. And no matter how happy a preacher you are, if you are still struggling over the interpretation of the text on Thursday or having second thoughts on Friday, you are in trouble.

For my Isaiah sermon, the support I need most is found in PARTS 1 and 2, but I start with PART 4, just to be sure. I want to compare HOMILETICAL (THEOLOGICAL) CRITICISM with RHETORICAL CRITICISM, to be certain I remember the differences correctly. I make my choice and proceed to a quick review of HERMENEU-TICS in PART 1. From there I make a more leisurely study of ALLEGORY, ALLEGORESIS, being fully aware that I have been flirting with that category. Satisfied that I have not veered into heresy yet, I read the articles on PROPHETIC PREACHING and METAPHOR AND FIGURES OF SPEECH. Isaiah's world begins to take shape for me.

Launching into the body of the sermon leaves me wondering about some of the interpretations of this text I have heard over the years. The article on MORALISM helps separate the voice of the text from the voice of modernist preachers. That leads to a bit of confusion over the nature of sin as Isaiah understands it, and I read the SIN AND EVIL article with a sense of growing clarity. Although the sermon is humming along nicely now, I find myself distracted by the thought of putting some of Isaiah's images on our church's screen. TECHNOLOGY AND THE SERMON lays out several options. Finally, I am facing my last set of questions. EXEGESIS OF THE CONGREGATION, DENOMINATION suggests a way forward. The article on preaching during war (WAR, PREACHING DURING) offers practical advice that probably keeps me from putting my foot in it with congregants on both sides of the issue.

PREACHERS ON PREACHING

Certainly, one of the best things about doing any reading in the field of homiletics is that homileticians are generally a pithy tribe. They often write like they speak. Everything reminds them of a story. Fresh images, powerful metaphors, and the felicitous turn of the phrase—these are their bread and butter. But the preachers whose work fills the pages of this volume have a particular advantage—they are preachers writing to other preachers. For them a chance to talk frankly about the field to its practicing artists is the best of all possible assignments. It brings out the best in them, producing ideas that make a difference and insights that sing. For homileticians and for working preachers, for the calm and the nervous, for novices and old hands, and for all who have not retained every last fact they learned from the institution that provided their fine theological education, conversation with other preachers is essential.

Whether you have a particular question to answer or a perception to check or you are just grazing for inspiration, The *New Interpreter's® Handbook of Preaching* has something to offer every preacher interested in the opinions of other preachers. Here you will find not only salient facts, trenchant analysis, and practical advice to feed your sermons but also people. Nowhere on earth can you find a better combination of living preachers to "talk" with about the art and craft of preaching. The editors and contributors thank you for your interest and invite you further up and higher into this conversation.

JANA CHILDERS, EDITORIAL BOARD

PART 1 INTRODUCTION: CHOOSING AND DELIMITING THE TEXT

Stephen Farris

In some Christian traditions it is common for preachers to read texts in church but to preach on something entirely different with little or no use of any scriptural text. Whatever the merits of such preaching, the focus of this entry is the pattern of preaching on some part of one or more texts read aloud during the liturgy. In such preaching the sermon grows out of the preacher's study of the text. Here the importance of choosing and delimiting the text cannot be overstated. It is the primary step in responsibly interpreting that text for preaching. A preacher who irresponsibly chooses and delimits the text can make the text say what it was never intended to say. By contrast, the preacher who carefully chooses and delimits more likely allows the text to speak its own word rather than a word imposed upon it.

Though choosing and delimiting a text are two aspects of the same process and frequently happen simultaneously, they will be treated here as separate steps. First, there is the matter of choosing a text. A traditional method is to search in Scripture until one finds a text that seems appropriate to the situation of the congregation or season. The possible advantages of this method include relevance to the contemporary context and the room it may give to the work of the Holy Spirit. (Though surely, the Holy Spirit can also work through a more disciplined method!) In practice, however, preachers may lose precious time vacillating among texts or may choose texts they like or ones that seem to say what they have already decided they want to say. There is the possibility of creating over the years a personal mini-lectionary of texts that say only what the preacher already knows and believes.

A better choice is to follow a lectionary of the wider church, the *Revised Common Lectionary*. (*See* LECTIONARY AND THE CHRISTIAN YEAR.) Although the selection of texts in the lectionary has been criticized, it covers a wide variety of texts, and its christological and seasonal focus is as likely to be as acceptable as anything else that could be devised. In many denominations it can be used simply as a

tool to facilitate the choice of lessons. There are considerable advantages to preaching the lectionary. The preacher need not waste time wandering through Scripture in desperate search of a likely text for the coming Sunday. Moreover, the lectionary forces one to study and preach on texts that one would not willingly choose. The spiritual discipline of preaching difficult texts may lead to the perception of more light and truth. Furthermore, there are many lectionary-based resources available in books and journals and online. Those resources often provide prayers, other elements of the liturgy, children's stories, and appropriate hymns for the service. There are even lectionary-based Christian education curricula. Many communities have lectionary study groups, and if these are lacking locally, they can be found online. There is an embarrassment of riches available for the lectionary preacher.

A choice still faces lectionary preachers: Which of the four texts will they preach from, or will they attempt to preach upon a link among two or more texts for the day? Finding a link among all four texts is often difficult. Connections that may be identified among four texts often seem forced. Moreover, attempting to address four texts in the sometimes brief span allotted to the sermon may mean that none of these texts is treated adequately. It is frequently the case, however, that there is an obvious and compelling connection between two readings for the day. To address the connection between these readings can be a valuable option. To preach entirely from one of the texts remains the primary option for most preachers; however, in some circles there appears to be an expectation that the sermon will be preached on the Gospel text. To preach the Gospel text invariably or nearly so may leave the congregation ignorant of the rest of Scripture. It may even turn preachers into practical Marcionites. Marcion was a 2nd-cent. heretic who repudiated the authority of the OT for Christians. Never or rarely to preach on a section of Scripture is effectively to deny its authority. Moreover, the psalm for the day, though sometimes passed over even by lectionary resources, ought not to be ignored. Psalms, with their raw human emotions and sometimes disturbingly direct language, can be marvelous preaching material.

The lectionary is not the only disciplined approach to choosing a text. Another practice, *LECTIO CONTINUA*, has an ancient history in the church and, before it, in the synagogue. (Although patterns of reading Scripture in the synagogues of NT and earlier times cannot be fully determined, it seems likely that *lectio continua* was a common practice.) This is the practice of reading and preaching through a biblical book in order. This approach enables the congregation to hear the preaching text in its canonical context. Texts are always heard and interpreted in relation to their contexts. The lectionary creates its own context because each text is inevitably heard by worshipers in relation to the other lections of the day that are read aloud with it. This process may do particular damage to OT texts that may be radically reinterpreted, not always for the better, in light of the christological context in which the lectionary generally places them. A fair and sustained treatment of OT texts on their own terms may sometimes require abandonment of the lectionary. Another advantage of *lectio continua* is that the preacher may be able to amortize the investment of time and energy in understanding the background and situation of a biblical book over a number of preaching Sundays. *Lectio continua* may deepen the congregation's knowledge of and respect for Scripture. Some *lectio continua* is present in the lectionary itself at certain times. Where this is the case, the advantages of *lectio continua* belong to the lectionary also.

Preachers may also organize their work around doctrinal series, such as a study of the Apostles' Creed or another summary of Christian doctrine. Some preachers choose to begin with human need, popular questions of the day, or contemporary social issues. The number of potential organizing principles for a sermon series is limited only by the creativity of the preacher. In all these cases, the choice of the text is a secondary task. A text is chosen primarily because of its apparent relation to the topic of the day. A common variant of this approach is to select from the reading a particular verse or portion of a verse and to preach not so much the text itself, but the doctrine addressed in the verse. In such sermons the preacher is likely to move to other texts throughout Scripture that address the same doctrine

rather than to consider extensively the canonical context of the verse in question. Doctrinal preaching probably requires some such use of Scripture. Biblical preaching ought not to be conceived so narrowly as to prevent the preacher from addressing doctrines in their wider biblical context. The doctrine addressed, however, ought to be a major concern of the text, not something touched on in passing. The question here is whether the preacher has misrepresented the meaning of the text that is the starting point for the doctrinal reflection. In preaching as in systematic theology, good doctrine does not grow from bad exegesis.

Once a text is chosen, it must be delimited. If not adhering rigidly to the lectionary, the preacher must decide where to begin reading and where to stop. Where there is an identifiable pericope, as is often the case in the SYNOPTIC GOSPELS and in the prophetic books, the pericope ought generally to be the unit read and preached. Pericopes may be identified by their form, such as miracle stories, pronouncement stories, parables, and laments. Where this is the case, the delimiting of the text is easy. Pericopes usually have a clear beginning and end; the preacher should respect these. A number of markers may be noted in determining the limits of a text. A time marker may appear at the beginning of a text, such as "On a Sabbath" or simply "Then." There may be a change of scene, characters, or subject matter. If the passage is a story, one may easily observe plot features such as the problem, increasing tension, and denouement. Where such characteristics are present, the preacher should typically begin at the beginning, carry on to the end without leaving anything out, and stop reading and preaching at the end of the unit.

Sometimes, the boundaries of texts are fluid and unclear, as is often the case in Paul's letters or in collections of sayings. In other cases, such as the discourses of the Gospel of John, the limits may be clear but the individual units too long to be easily read aloud in most contemporary churches. Practical considerations ought not to overrule integrity of interpretation, but they certainly have their place. Wise preachers respect the limits of their listeners' capacity to hear intelligently. One may distinguish here between the "read text" and the "effective text." The "read text" is the one read aloud in church. The "effective text" is the text that is actually preached. The two should overlap but need not be identical. In some complex passages, the preacher may rightly concentrate on one aspect of the text. In other cases, the preacher may preach on the connection between neighboring texts or on a theme that connects a series of texts in a book. In some cases, it is impossible to preach a sermon on a specific text within a longer story without retelling the story as a whole. One cannot, for example, preach on Nathan's rebuke to King David without also recounting the story of David and Bathsheba. The principle here is that the preacher need not be strictly limited to the text that is read aloud. In earlier generations the effective text seems often to have been a verse or part of the verse. In contemporary preaching the effective text seems to be growing longer, approaching the length of the text as it is read aloud.

This matter takes us back to the lectionary. The weakest feature of the lectionary may be the way it delimits texts. It often leaves out parts of texts or even parts of verses. Similarly, the lectionary may omit the end of a story. These excisions are often of materials that are trouble. In these excisions the texts may express anger, hatred, self-righteousness, or perhaps anti-Jewish sentiments. To edit out trouble is, however, not only a misrepresentation of the text; it is homiletically disastrous. People can most often connect to the text precisely in the trouble. Some homiletical theorists suggest that identifying trouble in the text may be the first move in effective preaching. Moreover, if one is to address anger, hatred, or self-righteousness in the contemporary world, it is probably best not to cut it out of the word from the ancient world. The uniformly and obviously edifying is usually boring. The solution to difficult or disturbing feelings in the text is not excision but intelligent preaching. Where the tradition of the church allows some freedom with respect to the lectionary, the preacher might consider restoring the excisions. Where the tradition is to follow the lectionary exactly, the effective text of the preacher may well include the material omitted in the lectionary. Whether using the lectionary or not, the primary concern in delimiting a text must be to avoid misrepresenting its contents with artificial or tendentious boundaries. Choosing and delimiting a text is, like all other aspects of interpretation, an art rather than a science. There is no sure way to tell when the preacher has got this process right. But it is usually obvious when the preacher gets it badly wrong. (*See* DOCTRINAL; EXEGESIS; THE FOUR PAGES OF THE SERMON; LECTIONARY AND THE CHRISTIAN YEAR; TOPICAL.)

Bibliography: Stephen Farris. *Preaching That Matters: The Bible and Our Lives.* (1998); Eugene Lowry. *Living with the Lectionary: Preaching Through the Revised Common Lectionary.* (1992).

❖   ❖   ❖   ❖

AFRICAN AMERICAN BIBLICAL INTERPRETATION
Dale P. Andrews

The tasks of biblical interpretation in preaching involve core beliefs that determine the mission and ministries of the black church. For black preaching traditions, as with most Christian traditions, the obvious sources of authority are centered in theological claims concerning sacred Scripture and divine inspiration. Scripture is both a historical and a metahistorical deposit of divine revelation that the church discerns with some difficulty. Divine inspiration functions as authoritative revelation specific to the activities of preaching, inclusive of sermon preparation and the preaching event itself. Mirrored in the divine sanction of Scripture, then, are theological claims of God's activity in preaching that seek to interpret Scripture for contemporary life. Herein lie critical questions for preachers.

Whether churches have been formed in response to crises or out of inherited traditions depicting God's engagement with humanity, black churches approach biblical interpretation from and in response to distinctive black experience or exigencies upon black life. Black preaching hermeneutics builds upon at least two predominant ways of employing biblical texts: first, to discern the ways of God; and second, to discern God's presence in our midst. These elements provide for a pastoral-prophetic dialectic in black preaching as sharing in the Word of God and telling the story. The Bible is the Word of God because it gives witness to God's activity in human history. It witnesses to the character and faithfulness of God. The Bible's power in black preaching is as a living Word. With the essential tools of modern exegetical studies (i.e., historical, source, literary, rhetoric, etc.) in hand, we meet the God of the Bible in our preaching events because of God's self-disclosure in our unfolding history. The Bible has its heritage and its future as the

Word of God living among the people of God. While the significance of human experience in the formation of churches is certainly not unique to black churches, the starting point of black experience in biblical interpretation cannot be overstated. How do black humanity and the black community encounter God and respond? This question is as much pastoral as it is prophetic.

From the perspective of pastoral biblical interpretation a primary task is the development of faith identity. The pastoral preacher is deeply committed to the interpretation and formation of meaning in the lives of believers and seekers. The tasks of preaching along these lines may involve interpreting theological doctrine, historical traditions, and the symbols of faith that connect people and therefore shape community. Pastoral leadership, though, is not limited to framing discipleship; it also engages ultimate questions that challenge us in times of crisis. African American preaching seeks also to tell the story of God's care for all humanity, which gives expression to faith identity in our specific human contexts. Storytelling in black preaching offers an important point of pastoral agency to biblical interpretation. Storytelling requires reconstructing redemption history within the lives of persons gathered in community. The task is to interpret life within a meaning-making process. The dialogical nature of the preaching event cannot help but to focus upon human struggles for meaning in life and the need for community.

From the perspective of prophetic biblical interpretation a primary task is to expand the preaching enterprise more deeply into meaning and relationships. God's care for humanity and response to human need are communal as much as personal. The community of faith is called to respond no less than the individual person. In turn, prophetic preaching attempts to address social contexts of human need and God's care communally. The prophetic enterprise engages the world with God's care; therefore divine self-revelation is evidenced through that care. It speaks from God's unfolding story with humanity through the community of faith. Beyond the formation of the church, this story is God's encounter and care for the world. Biblical interpretation in preaching participates in the divine encounter and care for the world. That care for the world pursues liberation in justice and relief from suffering.

African slaves and early African Americans faced immediate demands to reinterpret their encounter with brutal slavery and Western racism. Theological worldviews were at the core of the clash and were central to reinterpreting African American history in terms of God's interests and involvement with humanity. With the destruction of African oral folklore, sacred ancestry, proverbial wisdom, and religious practices, the Bible became a resource that provided familiar worldviews and spiritual values. In short, the ancestral faith narratives and wisdom literature from the Hebrew Bible and the gospel narratives from Christian Scripture were integral to interpreting African American history and reinterpreting Western Christianity. Black preaching appropriated biblical traditions and sacred heritage. The Bible, with its own historical oral culture, functioned as the living Word of God. Continuity between the Bible and the strongest assets of African oral culture and spirituality allowed the slaves and early African Americans to bridge the chasms created by the prohibitions to education or even literacy. African Americans learned and reinterpreted biblical narratives and teachings through the oral and aural encounter of worship. Biblical interpretation would translate central narratives or sacred themes into formulae for the preaching event, as well as for singing spirituals, relating God's faithfulness to and on behalf of an oppressed people of faith.

Two hermeneutical principles are key: the personhood of black wholeness and a sense of peoplehood or community within God's values of freedom and social justice. Black preaching highlights core biblical, theological tenets to interpret the Word of God in black life. These core tenets include creation in the image of God, the sovereignty and historical commitments of God evidenced in events like the exodus/liberation from slavery, the suffering of Jesus in solidarity with black humanity, the gospel of salvation and conversion, and the in-breaking eternal reign of God. The tasks of interpreting the Bible reinterpreted the faith and transformed the church. Black preaching thereby took on the mantle of pastoral care and prophetic reform in both personal wholeness and communal agency.

Pastoral interpretation is concerned with the ministry of care that has to do with spiritual and communal values. Prophetic interpretation is the ministry or faith consciousness that insists uncompromisingly upon social justice, whether it is interpersonal, cultural, political, or economic. It is focused upon the relationship between historical values of liberation and the liberation of spiritual values that might otherwise rest content with personal thriving. It is an intentional or purposeful consciousness that addresses the needs and concerns of persons living under oppressive conditions.

Black preachers used biblical traditions and stories to transform American Christianity and defy the destructive capacities of slavery and the living legacy of racism. Even the institution of black churches stemmed directly from these racist practices impinging upon faith communities and worship itself. Black wholeness and freedom would endure in preaching, navigating through storms of oppression and intrinsic needs for survival and liberation.

A fragile balance exists between the pursuits of wholeness and historical liberation. In the balance, African American hermeneutics relies heavily upon the rhetorical strategies of black preaching. The pastoral-prophetic dialectic sustains biblical interpretation within the context of oppression and the quest for wholeness and freedom. At risk is loss of the dialectic, wherein the predominant rhetoric of wholeness loses sight of the quest for freedom and its social obligations. Conversely, if the pursuits of historical liberation neglect the gospel of God and attendant spiritual values, preaching loses sight of the vital liberation of the soul from the ravages of oppression. Black preaching and biblical interpretation therefore necessarily involve interpreting faith in terms of survival, restoration, self-help, and liberation. Black preaching seizes upon biblical narratives and the gospel message in nurturing black wholeness and clarifying the divine call for black sociopolitical and economic freedom. Survival and liberation, wholeness and freedom—the poles of the dialectic are variously depicted. Through pastoral care for black wholeness and the prophetic consciousness of social justice, the transformation of American Christianity continues. *See* AFRICAN AMERICAN APPRENTICESHIP; AFRICAN AMERICAN PREACHING PERSPECTIVES; LIBERATION CRITICISM; POSTCOLONIAL CRITICISM; SUSPICION.

Bibliography: Dale P. Andrews. *Practical Theology for Black Churches.* (2002); Lawrence W. Levine. *Black Culture and Black Consciousness.* (1997); Gayraud S. Wilmore. *Black Religion and Black Radicalism.* (1973, 1998); Vincent L. Wimbush, ed., with Rosamond C. Rodman. *African Americans and the Bible.* (2000).

ALLEGORY, ALLEGORESIS
David L. Bartlett

Allegory is a literary device that makes a comparison between two sets of relationships. Where simile and metaphor usually compare one vehicle with one idea (i.e., this is like this or this is this), allegory compares more than one vehicle (e.g., Hagar and Sarah) with more than one idea (e.g., old covenant, new covenant). Allegory says this means this, on the basis of an appeal to spiritual truth or earthly reality. Allegorical interpretation can be dangerous; at the same time, many interpretations the church makes concerning Christ have allegorical roots, and allegory continues to have importance for the church.

A. What Is Allegory?
   1. Allegory vs. Typology
   2. Allegory vs. Allegoresis
   3. Allegory and Prophecy
B. Allegory in the Bible
   1. Old Testament
   2. New Testament
C. Allegory in the Early Church
   1. Precedents
   2. Christians and Allegory
D. Advantages and Drawbacks of Allegory for Preaching
E. Guidelines for Allegorical Preaching
F. Examples of Allegorical Preaching

A. What Is Allegory?

The etymological root of *allegory* is the Greek *allos* (another) and *agoreuein* (to speak). Allegorical interpretation provides "another way of speaking" about what may appear to be the plain sense of a passage.

Allegory, like other figural speech (metaphor, simile, parable, typology), juxtaposes a narrative and another reality. This reality provides the real or hidden meaning for the allegory.

Allegories compare a number of features in the narrative to corresponding features in the reality. The interpretation is always multifaceted.

Classical allegory usually takes putatively historical narratives and interprets them non-historically. Allegory finds spiritual, ideal, or religious meanings behind the stories. However, as we shall see, biblical allegory is often prophetic or historicized—it often takes the features of the original narrative to refer not to a spiritual truth, but to some kind of intra-historical fulfillment.

Often allegory suggests that the historical meaning of the narrative is not important because the function of the narrative is to point to the true meaning beyond it.

1. Allegory vs. Typology

Though allegory and typology are very similar and sometimes indeed overlap, the following distinctions can be made:

Typology presupposes the historical reality and theological importance of both terms of the comparison. Allegory may deny the historical reality of the first narrative or may argue that it is either the spiritual or the newly applied interpretation that is the real meaning of a text.

Typology compares one feature of each narrative to one feature in the other. Allegory compares multiple features.

Typology usually holds that both type and antitype are significant indicators of God's activity. Allegory usually holds that the narrative (type) exists largely as an opportunity for its explanation.

2. Allegory vs. Allegoresis

Literary theorists have made a useful distinction between allegorical texts and the method of allegoresis. Allegorical texts are those that indicate in themselves that they are to be interpreted figurally. (See Ezek 17; Mark 4; *Pilgrim's Progress*.) Allegoresis is the method by which any text can be read to reveal hidden spiritual meanings. Philo's readings of the patriarchal narratives in Genesis are an excellent example of allegoresis.

3. Allegory and Prophecy

Like allegory, prophetic literature often points beyond itself, but like typology, prophecy usually points to a future event. Prophecy is usually non-narrative and often includes only one or two terms for interpretation rather than the plethora of terms found in allegory.

B. Allegory in the Bible

1. Old Testament

The OT clearly contains numerous metaphors and similes, but in a few places the language takes on the shape of a full-fledged allegory. Ezekiel 17:1-21 is explicitly allegorical:

The word of the LORD came to me: O mortal, propound a riddle, and speak an allegory to the house of Israel. Say: Thus says the Lord GOD:
> A great eagle, with great wings
>   and long pinions,
>   rich in plumage of many colors,
>   came to the Lebanon.
> He took the top of the cedar,
>   broke off its topmost shoot;
> He carried it to a land of trade,
>   set it in a city of merchants.
> Then he took a seed from the land,
>   placed it in fertile soil;
> A plant by abundant waters,
>   he set it like a willow twig. (Ezek 17:1-5)

The commentaries tell us that the great eagle is Nebuchadnezzar, the top of the cedar is the house of David, the city of merchants is Babylon, and so on. This is obviously a kind of historicized allegory, that is, the features of the allegory point not to spiritual truths but to historical fulfillments, appropriate for prophecy.

Hosea 2 is an elaborate allegory in which the story of Hosea's wife and her prostitution is a sign of what God intends for Israel's apostasy and a portent of God's intended punishment. Not only the narrative of Hosea's marriage but also the names of his children ("No pity" and "Not my people") have a second meaning pointing to the refusal of Israel to obey and of her people to repent.

Isaiah 5:1-10 provides both an allegory and its interpretation: "Let me sing for my beloved, / my love-song concerning his vineyard. . . . / For the vineyard of the LORD of hosts / is the house of Israel, / and the people of Judah / are his pleasant planting." The allegories of Ezekiel, Hosea, and Isaiah are interpreted as being descriptions and prophecies concerning Israel. The allegory of 2 Sam 12 points directly at King David. Nathan tells the allegory of the rich man and the poor man, their flocks and their ewe. When David finally understands the allegory, with considerable help from the prophet, he realizes that the rich man is a figure for him, the poor man a figure for Uriah, and the ewe is Bathsheba. Reading the other meaning of the narrative, he pronounces judgment on himself.

2. New Testament

The most discussed allegory in the NT is probably that found in Mark 4:1-12, 13-20, and parallels. New Testament scholars have often argued that Mark or someone in the early church has added an allegorical interpretation to Jesus' own fairly straight-forward parable about the growth of the kingdom.

Whatever its editorial history, the canonical passage is read allegorically. Different kinds of soil are figures for different kinds of people as they respond to the gospel. The features of the story that detail the forms of resistance to the seed can be read allegorically for different kinds of resistance to Jesus', or to the church's, preaching. The birds are like Satan. The thorns are the cares of the world. As in the OT, this kind of allegory does not move so much toward spiritual truths as toward realities in the life of the community that are figured and pre-figured in the parable.

Mark 12:1-12 (and parallels Matt 21:33-44; Luke 20:9-19) represent an allegory on the allegory of Isa 5:1-10. The image of Israel as a vineyard is now expanded to indicate the different kinds of tenants who have misused the vineyard. The "slaves" who are sent certainly represent the prophets—and the last one, who is "killed," may represent John the Baptist. Certainly, the "beloved son" is a figure for Jesus himself, though the allusion is particularly rich because it can also refer back to Isaac as the beloved son almost sacrificed in Genesis and ahead to the Beloved Son sacrificed in Mark 15.

John 15:1-11 is certainly also allegorical and may also represent a kind of interpretation of Isa 5. Now Christ is the true vine in Israel's vineyard. The allegorical details correspond to a theological discussion of the role of God, Christ, and believers in the life of the church.

In Gal 4 Paul uses typology and allegory, and he uses both terms to describe what he is doing. Typologically, the story of the children of Sarah and Hagar points ahead to the stories of Jews under the law and Gentile believers freed from the law. However, the interpretation of the Hagar story is also full of allegorical features: "Now Hagar is Mount Sinai in Arabia and corresponds to the present Jerusalem, for she is in slavery with her children. But the other woman corresponds to the Jerusalem above; she is free; she is our mother" (Gal 4:25-26). The injunction from Gen 21:10 ("Drive out the slave and her child") is read allegorically as an exhortation to the Galatian churches to drive out the false teachers in their midst.

First Corinthians 10:1-13 is mostly a typological comparison between the children of Israel as they pass through the sea and eat manna and the Corinthian Christians as they experience baptism and the Lord's Supper. However, the passage also includes allegorical features, especially 10:3-4: "And all ate the same spiritual food, and all drank the same spiritual drink. For they drank from the spiritual rock that followed them, and the rock was Christ" (similarly see 1 Pet 3:20-22).

C. Allegory in the Early Church

1. Precedents

In the world of Greek philosophy allegory emerged as a way to interpret classic works of poetry—especially Homer. The purpose of allegory was to interpret what might seem superstition in ways that were more rational, what might seem contradictions in ways that were more consistent, and what might seem primitive in ways that were more modern and sophisticated. Philosophical allegorical interpretation of Homer flourished as early as the 5th cent. BCE and continued up to the time of the NT.

One of the most prolific allegorists and the one who had the most influence on early Christian preaching was Philo of Alexandria. Philo provided allegorical interpretations not of Homer, but of the Greek translation of the Hebrew Scriptures. (Clement of Alexandria and Origen, both Christian allegorical interpreters, were also Alexandrian.)

2. Christians and Allegory

Allegorical interpretation was a major feature of preaching from the 3rd cent. until at least the Enlightenment. It seems clear, however, that allegorical interpretation was not limited to the interpretation of allegorical biblical texts.

In the very early generations of Christian writing, the Epistle of Barnabas, probably written toward the beginning of the 2nd cent. CE, is full of allegorical interpretations of the OT. Origen (d. ca. 254) was the early theologian who most relied on allegorical interpretation. He apparently knew Philo and Alexandrian exegesis, and he was also influenced by some of the Gnostic allegorical interpretations of Scripture. Origen states the theological reason for his allegorical interpretations and sermons: "The Scriptures were written by the Spirit of God and have a meaning, not only such as is apparent at first sight, but also another, which escapes the notice of most. For those words which are written are the forms of certain mysteries, and the images of divine things" (Greidanus 1999, 84).

Augustine (d. 430) famously preached allegorically: "Samson was kept in a millhouse, he was blinded, he was imprisoned. The prison and the millhouse indicate the toil of this life. The blinding of Samson is a sign for those who, blinded by faithlessness, have not known Christ, nor His might, nor His ascent into heaven" (Howe 1967, 124).

D. Advantages and Drawbacks of Allegory for Preaching

There are both advantages and drawbacks to allegorical preaching. Among the advantages are these:

1) Allegory provides a way of preaching on the OT in ways that can claim OT texts for Christian congregations. Allegory provides one way to avoid the kind of Marcionism that simply avoids OT texts. It also provides a legitimate way to use OT texts in the service of NT and Christian claims. The fact that Mark 12 and John 15, for example, are both allegorical interpretations of Isa 5 and that Gal 4 is an allegorical interpretation of the story of Hagar indicates that there is intra-biblical precedent for this kind of OT interpretation. The attempt of 20th-cent. parable criticism to rescue the parabolic Jesus from the allegorical early church is questionable methodologically and highly tendentious theologically. For whatever reasons, we have been taught to love the aphoristic teacher and suspect the allegorical one. The NT itself gives us a Jesus who is perfectly capable of both rhetorical strategies.

2) Allegory provides a way of acknowledging the unity of the canon. Old Testament and NT texts alike can be used as pointers to broader theological claims that the two Testaments have in common.

3) Allegorical preaching was a standard homiletical tool for a millennium and a half of Christian preaching. It is one thing to say that we cannot preach allegory in just the way that Chrysostom and Augustine did, and quite another thing to say that unlike Chrysostom and Augustine, we cannot preach allegory at all.

4) Allegorical preaching is an elaborate rhetorical strategy that enables the preacher to acknowledge two fundamental gifts of preaching:

  a. Allegory stresses the use of imagery in preaching. It can be concrete and not always propositional and abstract.

  b. Allegory insists that texts should be applied and not simply rehearsed or paraphrased in preaching.

Among the disadvantages of allegorical preaching are these:

1. By seeking to find a more general (usually Christian) truth behind every OT story, the preacher tends to treat the OT more as a puzzle to be solved than as a witness to be heard. The reality of Israel and Israel's people drops from view as they become a cipher for some other, later, truth.

2. Allegorical preaching (or at least preaching according to the mode of allegoresis) often fails to note the diversity of the canon. Because almost any text can be allegorized, almost any text is allegorized. This encourages preaching that ignores the differences between narrative and poetry, allegory and parable.

3. Allegorical preaching is often far too busy metaphorically and conceptually for a congregation to hear. This may well be a sign of how far we have fallen in our ability to juggle a variety of concepts and images all at once, but most contemporary preachers would do well to acknowledge the fall.

4. Allegorical preaching can undervalue the gifts provided by the historical-critical method. Before we try to discover what a text might mean, most preachers will want to get some understanding of what meaning(s) the text had in its earliest historical and literary context. Mark, Paul, Chrysostom, and Augustine did not live with the post-Enlightenment disciplines of historical criticism, but we cannot pretend that they are our contemporaries. Furthermore, for all its problems, historical criticism has helped preachers attend more carefully to the rich diversity of canonical texts. And by honoring what Mark said rather than what we can make him say, we practice a kind of intellectual love of the neighbor—separated from him by time and space though we may be.

5. Allegorical criticism, or at least allegoresis, sometimes seems to soar free of any constraints. If the preacher decides that the story of Jacob and Esau and the birthright is an allegory of the political struggle for the hearts and minds of 21st-cent. North Americans, it is hard to find in the allegorical method by itself a reason to rein in the preacher.

6. Allegorical criticism easily turns into moralism. This is perhaps especially true in the phenomenon of the children's sermon where any text, no matter how theologically deep or historically problematic, can be enlisted to remind the boys and girls that they had better be good.

E. Guidelines for Allegorical Preaching

On the whole the best allegorical sermons will be sermons based on allegorical texts. This is a subsidiary principle of a more general rule that on the whole the best narrative sermons will be on narrative texts and the best meditative sermons on psalms. The advantage of preaching allegorically on John 15, for example, is that the text invites, indeed almost requires, us to do so. The further advantage is that the text gives us some guidelines and imposes some limits on the directions the allegory can go. John 15 is not an allegory about the Christian family or the nation-state, for example.

On the whole the best allegorical sermons will pay attention to what we learn from historical criticism. Whether or not the preacher says everything she knows, she should know that the roots of the vineyard allegories in the NT are found in the vineyard allegory of Isa 5, and she should know what Sarah and Hagar are doing in the Genesis story before preaching about what they are doing in Gal 4.

Allegorical sermons will probably not try to draw theological or moral connections for every feature of the day's text. That kind of allegory usually presupposes both more biblical background and more retentive memories than we are apt to find in our congregations.

Allegory will be one rhetorical and hermeneutical strategy among many that the faithful preacher will employ.

If one is preaching an allegorical sermon, one should sustain the allegory through the sermon. Occasionally, a mixed genre sermon is effective, but almost never if one of the genres is allegorical.

Normatively, preaching holds forth Christ. Therefore, allegorical preaching is still always gospel and seldom—even for children—simply a lesson on good behavior.

F. Examples of Allegorical Preaching

One contemporary allegorical sermon based on this text distinguishes more simply between those who are the early workers and those who are the late, and then seeks to find in both groups a clue to the lives of the gathered congregation: "All of us came to the vineyard early . . ."; "All of us came to the vineyard late."

Katie Geneva Cannon preached a sermon on Gen 21:1-21 and provided a different allegorical interpretation from that in Gal 4. Those in the congregation were urged not to follow the Abraham syndrome of pleasing people or the Sarah syndrome of trespassing on God's territory. They were urged instead to be "sisters of Hagar." Then the preacher drew from the story features of Hagar's narrative that are appropriate guides today (Cannon 1985, 43–50).

A sermon on the dry bones of Ezek 37 did allegory mostly by interpreting and expanding the refrain: "We are without hope; our bones are clean dried up." The refrain was applied personally, to the congregation, and to the nation.

In these cases the preacher practiced a kind of chastened allegory. More generally, as suggested here, most good preaching draws in analogy, image, and metaphor. Sometimes the metaphor shapes the whole sermon. More often the metaphor or image shapes one move within the sermon. Seldom will the careful or caring preacher pile on the metaphors so thick that the congregation feels more bombarded than illumined. *See* FOUR SENSES OF SCRIPTURE; HISTORICAL CRITICISM; TYPOLOGY; WORD OF GOD.

Bibliography: "Allegory." *The New Princeton Handbook of Poetic Terms.* (1994) 7–12; Augustine. *Selected Sermons of St. Augustine.* Translated and edited by Quincy Howe Jr. (1967); Katie G. Cannon. "On Remembering Who We Are." *Those Preachin' Women.* Edited by Ella Pearson Mitchell. (1985) 43–50; Sidney Greidanus. *Preaching Christ from the Old Testament.* (1999); Paul Scott Wilson. *God Sense: Reading the Bible for Preaching.* (2001).

APOCALYPTICISM
Paul D. Hanson

Like the prophet, the apocalyptic seer delivers words and visions derived from the divine realm designed to guide individuals and communities through the issues they face. Normative in both cases is a notion of divine purpose and corresponding standards of justice and mercy against which humans are to be judged. Prophecy and apocalyptic diverge, however, in mode of address and sphere of application: whereas the message of the prophet is public and aims at mundane institutions and structures, the apocalyptic message tends to be esoteric and focuses on transcendent realities.

A.   The Contemporary Problem Posed by Apocalypticism
B.   The Roots of Biblical Apocalypticism
C.   From Prophecy to Apocalypticism
D.   The Era of Full-Blown Apocalypticism
E.   Applying Apocalyptic Texts in Preaching

A. The Contemporary Problem Posed by Apocalypticism

Apocalypticism is a mysterious and complicated phenomenon, marked by belief that the end times are imminent. The media reverberate with apocalyptic notions: "The Great Satan," "An End to Evil," "Armageddon." It is tempting to dismiss all things apocalyptic as a distraction, yet of all forms of religion, this one has the greatest chance of self-fulfillment that could mean the destruction of the world as we know it.

Understanding the contemporary significance of any artifact of the past begins with seeking to grasp its original meaning in its historical setting. Examples of the violation of this principle are many: Ezek 38–39 is used to predict an attack on the state of Israel by Russia and China; a religious fanatic gathers followers behind the walls of a compound in anticipation of the opening of the seventh seal of the book of Revelation. Examples of adherence to this principle are not lacking: Hans Lilje writes a commentary on the book of Revelation as a source of guidance and comfort for Christians suffering under the Third Reich; the tradition of the antichrist informs Dietrich Bonhoeffer and fellow members of the Confessing Church in their painful deliberation over action to be taken against Hitler.

Inferences from biblical apocalyptic texts are being drawn in our world today, whether by Osama bin Laden, Pat Robertson, or those in high political office. It is a responsibility of the church to clarify the guidelines that lead to a faithful and responsible reading of those texts.

B. The Roots of Biblical Apocalypticism

While various influences, some native, some foreign, were in play over the century of the development of Jewish and Christian apocalypticism, in the first instance it is a phenomenon growing out of biblical prophecy. If one compares the prophet Isaiah (7th cent. BCE) with the seer of Dan 7–12 (2nd cent. BCE), both derived their authority to address their communities from the experience of being called by God. In considering God's governance of creation, Israel's prophets and seers believed that a special role had been assigned to Israel, namely, to bear witness to God's compassionate justice as codified in the Torah. They understood their calling in relation to the conditions inherent in the covenant binding God and people: obedience would lead to peace and well-being, while perfidy would incur divine judgment. Prophet and seer can thus be understood as heralds of divine intention, and whether their message was one of blessing or curse depended on the conduct of the people in relation to the Torah.

The main difference between prophecy and apocalypticism now comes into view: the interaction between prophet and people occurred within a setting recognizably historical, involving the stuff of every society. Businessmen cheated customers, landlords oppressed tenants, judges accepted bribes, and reformers spoke out on behalf of the oppressed, even as they announced impending punishment in the form of invading armies and natural disasters or promised the restoration of the nation under just rulers. Though often opposed and even persecuted, prophets persisted in the conviction that they were acting on behalf of God's purpose, and from that perspective they identified the instruments of divine blessing and punishment within the realm of history and everyday life.

In contrast, the descendants of the prophets, the seers, envisioned the struggle between good and evil in a transcendent realm: the forces wreaking havoc on earth reflected heavenly adversaries, and salvation was awaited in the form of direct divine intervention. God's commissioning words reveal the shift of the herald's role from public reformer ("Go and say to this people" [Isa 6:9]) to revealer of esoteric knowledge to the elect ("Daniel, keep the words secret and the book sealed until the time of the end" [Dan 12:4]).

C. From Prophecy to Apocalypticism

What led to this shift from a this-worldly to an otherworldly perspective? Changing circumstances encouraged either a positive attitude toward the amenability of society and world to divine commandments and purpose or a bleak assessment of earthly institutions and their leaders. Neither an ineluctable process nor a single influence (such as Israel's contact with Zoroastrianism) can be found; since the shift occurred amid the "thickness" of historical experience, it is safest to look for clues in actual texts.

Historically, a major threshold was crossed with the fall of Jerusalem to the Babylonians in 587 and the ensuing exile. In Isa 40–55 an anonymous prophet (Second Isaiah) sought to explain the intractable paradox of the destruction of God's dwelling place and the conquest of the land by the Babylonians by enlisting imagery from the ancient myth of cosmogonic conflict (Isa 51:9-11). The later apocalyptic writings are marked by this dualism, with its division of eras, a past dominated by chaos and a future promising universal peace and prosperity (Isa 43:18-19). But the tilt toward apocalypticism remains restrained, since with the identification of a historical figure, Cyrus, as God's anointed deliverer (Isa 45:1), the message retained its prophetic perspective, though the historical mooring becomes tenuous.

Further fraying can be observed following the edict of Cyrus in 538. Isaiah 59 begins in classic prophetic style; a divine spokesperson indicts a nation, but in place of the struggle of the prophets for repentance, indictment leads directly to the announcement of direct divine action: "[The Lord] saw that there was no one, / and was appalled that there was no one to intervene; / so his own arm brought him victory" (Isa 59:16).

We get a glimpse of the situation that was abetting this switch from human agency to unmediated divine intervention in Isa 65–66. The restoration community had become rent by division, with a minority, claiming to be faithful servants oppressed by their leaders, abandoning the prophetic mode of struggling for reform and awaiting the ultimate source of vindication: "And it shall be known that the hand of the LORD is with his servants, / and his indignation is against his enemies. / For the LORD will come in fire, / and his chariots like the whirlwind. . . . / For by fire will the LORD execute judgment, / and by his sword, on all flesh; / and those slain by the LORD shall be many" (Isa 66:14-16).

These late 6th-cent. BCE texts can be designated proto-apocalyptic, for while features like dualism and a mythic orientation anticipate the world of apocalypticism, the historical orientation of prophecy has not been abandoned completely. Full-blown apocalyptic will be characterized by greater complexity. In Isa 56–66, for example, the bleak conditions abetting recourse to otherworldly redemption are internal to the Jewish community, whereas in the 2nd cent. BCE the threat of foreign enemies adds to the flames of apocalyptic fervor. John J. Collins (1988, 5–7) identifies that "historical apocalypse" combines in later texts with "otherworldly journeys" (e.g., 1 En. 17–36).

Other texts that plot the transition from prophecy to apocalypticism are Isa 24–27, Zech 12–14, and Ezek 38–39. In each, the shift from historical to transcendent salvation is apparent. The Ezekiel passage bears the marks of a later addition, since Gog of Magog's attack on hapless Israel, followed by the Divine Warrior's fierce counterattack culminating in a banquet consisting of the flesh of the slain, disrupts the continuity from the vision of national renewal in ch. 37 to the program of restoration in chs. 40–48. Here the threat originates not within the Jewish community, but from the outside, more specifically in the form of the Persian Empire whose imperium derailed the vision of glorious restoration found in the visions of Haggai and Zechariah.

D. The Era of Full-Blown Apocalypticism

Jewish apocalypticism flourished in the last two centuries BCE and the first two centuries CE, though there is evidence of it earlier. The book of Malachi (mid-5th cent. BCE) is notable not only for its announcement of the coming of the Lord in judgment preceded by his "messenger" but also for pronouncement of God's curse on the (Zadokite) temple priesthood contrasted with description of God's "covenant with Levi" as exemplary of reverence and blessing. Herein lies a clue to the inner-community strife reflected in the earliest parts (late 3rd–early 2nd cent. BCE) of 1 Enoch, where the Second Temple is depicted as defiled from its inception

(89:72-77). The antediluvian Enoch in turn was esteemed by the Essenes of Qumran, for they, too, regarded the Jerusalem Temple as defiled and administered by an illegitimate priesthood. Considering themselves persecuted by fellow Jews and foreigners (especially the Romans) alike, they practiced strict adherence to Torah in sacramental anticipation of the heavenly banquet that would follow the victory of their Divine Warrior in an end-time battle in which they would fight cheek by jowl with angels.

We turn now to the classic expressions of apocalyptic in the Bible. Daniel 7–12 was written between the desecration of the Temple by Antiochus IV and its rededication after the victory of the Maccabeans (167–64 BCE). The daunting magnitude of the Seleucid threat and the utter dependence on God of those remaining faithful to Torah find expression in the apocalyptic imagery of mythic monsters, battles between contending angels in heaven, and a divine judgment hall where the Ancient of Days delivers the kingdom into the safekeeping of the Son of Man. To the martyrs, who through their witness unto death preserved the cause of righteousness, is promised eternal life.

Apocalyptic elements in the NT are so numerous as to have led one scholar to identify apocalyptic as the "mother of Christianity." Mark 13, likely reflecting the destruction of Jerusalem in 70 CE, draws upon a vast repertory of apocalyptic themes and images. Second Thessalonians illustrates the Apostle Paul's familiarity with this mode of expression. But pride of place belongs to the book of Revelation.

Revelation 13–22 illustrates the appropriation of apocalyptic themes and symbols by a Christian community suffering under the absolute claims of the Roman imperial cult. Apocalyptic images alone seem adequate to express the gravity of the crisis: a beast from the sea entices the inhabitants of the earth to worship it, but the beast's reign of terror is limited, for in heaven a drama unfolds in which the angelic hosts faithful to Christ the Lamb succeed in defeating the beast and its host and in raising up the fallen faithful to the eternal peace of the new Jerusalem. Woven into this scenario are numerous images from Ezekiel, Daniel, and other apocalyptic writings, many of which in turn can be traced to myths of the 2nd millennium BCE (e.g., the 14th-cent. myths of Ugarit).

E. Applying Apocalyptic Texts in Preaching

One must caution against the cobbling together of apocalyptic texts to produce elaborate timetables for predicting the end of the world (e.g., dispensationalism and millennialism). The authors of apocalyptic writings were persons of faith responding to a call from God to make sense of adversity and dissonance within the specific concrete social and historical circumstances of their day. They betray remarkable freedom in rearranging images into new patterns (e.g., Revelation's reapplication of the images of Ezek 38–39 and Dan 7–12) and manifest no compunction in correcting earlier predictions (e.g., the seventy years of Jer 25:11-12 are adjusted to seventy weeks of years in Dan 9:20-27). They function to provide comfort and hope to believers who see nothing in their world that supports the claim that God remains steadfast to those who worship no other God and remain faithful to the covenant.

Another hermeneutical principle applies: the meaning of a specific text must be sought with awareness of its place within the overall message of Scripture. That message has at its center the God who created all there is. Jesus Christ upholds the moral structure of the world through judgment and mercy and guides that world toward its final goal, which is not annihilation from which a few will be snatched, but redemption from decay and restoration to wholeness in the form of universal peace, justice, and healing.

In asking what relevance the apocalyptic texts have for preaching, we must remember that they were meant to provide courage and hope for a community enduring severe suffering specifically because they refused to acknowledge any authority other than God's. With the rare gift of piercing through the misery of persecution and tumult of war, the seer drew on a rich repertory of images to distinguish clearly between the true God and every impostor and to dramatize the ultimate triumph of God's reign and the vindication of those who resisted the lure of apostasy, even unto death. Preachers therefore will be wise to use such texts not to predict the future but to affirm the faithfulness of God no matter how bad things may be.

Preachers might also remember that the apocalyptic mode of expressing the truths of Scripture is provided by Judaism and Christianity alike. Faithful

Jews anticipate the day when perfect obedience to Torah will herald the coming of the Messiah to establish the kingdom of eternal peace and justice. Jesus' words and deeds were understood by the early church as signs of the kingdom of God, and Mark 13 draws freely from antecedent apocalyptic texts to portray the final triumph of God's reign.

At a time when the fear-induced, death-wish sensationalism of *Left Behind* (Tim LaHaye and Jerry B. Jenkins, 1995–2006) defines apocalypticism for most people and distortions of the political implications of apocalyptic texts such as dispensationalism nudge the world toward the fiery abyss of Hal Lindsey's *Late, Great Planet Earth* (1970), it is important that preachers possess sufficient knowledge of Scripture to reclaim Ezekiel and Daniel and Revelation for the proclamation of good news to those most sorely in need of hope and comfort, those suffering ridicule and persecution for their faith. Even in times when faith communities are not experiencing persecution, it is our responsibility to keep vividly in our minds the portrait of a moral universe that is placed in jeopardy not only by the assaults of Satan but also by those lured through comfort and luxury into a moral numbness incapable of distinguishing between good and evil. *See* APOCALYPTIC.

Bibliography: John J. Collins. *The Apocalyptic Imagination.* (1988); Paul D. Hanson. *Old Testament Apocalyptic.* (1987); Paul S. Minear. *New Testament Apocalyptic.* (1983).

ARCHAEOLOGY
Alfred J. Hoerth

Archaeology can aid preaching because it examines the past through excavation and interpretation of the data recovered. During the mid-decades of the 20th cent., it was seen as an invaluable bridge into the world of the Bible. Since then a number of archaeologists have shifted their emphasis from text and history to anthropology and the natural sciences, creating a tension over the appropriateness of the term *biblical archaeology* (see Davis 2004). In 1998 the long-standing periodical *Biblical Archaeology* changed its name and focus to *Near Eastern Archaeology.*

Attempts to enlist archaeology to prove the Bible should be avoided; archaeology can speak to the historicity of some events, but not to their underlying theological message. Further, this use generally overlooks instances where archaeology has uncovered textual puzzles that would not otherwise have been recognized. In fact, some scholars argue that archaeology contradicts portions of the biblical account. Little of what was made or written in antiquity can be expected to have survived to this day; and a fraction of what is potentially recoverable has even been found, let alone published for scholarly evaluation. Therefore, using archaeology to determine which portions of the Bible are historical is seldom useful.

Interpreting Archaeological Finds

Interpretation is the key word when it comes to utilizing archaeological finds, and depending on a person's perspective, archaeologists can reach different conclusions. For example, in 1979, two amulets were found in a tomb in the Hinnom Valley south of Jerusalem. They contain an abbreviated version of Num 6:24-26, and are evidence that this priestly blessing and the wearing of amuletic texts were in use at least as early as the 6th cent. BCE. Some believe this is evidence supporting the early composition of the Pentateuch. For others, however, the benediction is only a blessing, which was incorporated into the book of Numbers when it was subsequently written. For more examples of how different interpretations can derive from the same archaeological data, see William G. Dever (2001) and Kenneth A. Kitchen (2003). Among their many disagreements, for Kitchen the patriarchal age is a reality; for Dever it is not.

Simply put, it is best not to use archaeology to bolster any theological position. The separation between archaeology and theology can be illustrated through the words of a prominent archaeologist, William F. Albright. Decades ago he acknowledged that archaeology was making him respect the historicity of the Bible more and more, but at the same time he clearly saw himself becoming theologically more liberal (Albright 1963).

Illumination

What can archaeology do then, and of what use is it in preaching? Most important, archaeology illuminates the biblical text; it enlarges our understanding of many biblical episodes. It also fleshes out many of the people of the Bible, so that we can better understand why they acted as they did and wrote as they did. We can see what they saw. In these ways archaeology helps convey the context of the theological message.

Despite the small percentage of the ancient world recovered thus far, much is known in the material realm. Plans, monuments, restorations, and even "virtual tours" are available for the cities and terrains of the Bible. The horned altars of the OT (e.g., Exod 29:12), the grain ships that figured in the travels of Paul (e.g., Acts 27)—archaeology has made them, and so much more, visible to us. Computers and presentation software are becoming increasingly a part of sermon delivery, and thousands of archaeological images are available, either for free downloading (www.HolyLandPhotos.org) or for purchase by churches (www.Bibleplaces.com).

Beyond the simply visual, commentaries that integrate archaeological insights can be useful tools (e.g., the Anchor Bible commentaries). For example, commentaries on Romans should include archaeological information that illuminates Rom 16:23. Paul makes the passing comment that "Erastus, the city treasurer, . . . [greets] you." A thorough commentary will include information on the pavement inscription found at Corinth, which reads, "Erastus, for the office of *aedile*, laid [the pavement] at his own expense." The pavement dates to ca. 50 CE, and an *aedile* included financial affairs in his job description. Various evidences point to this inscription as being commissioned by the Erastus mentioned in Romans. Paul's seemingly unimportant comment takes on added significance when it is realized that Erastus was possibly the highest ranking Roman to be converted in NT times. It was not just the common people who were attracted to the gospel. In the pavement, a bit of Erastus's activity remains from when he focused on making his mark in this world. Such insights should be weighed to see what might add interest and understanding to a sermon.

Turning to the OT, in recent decades much has been learned about the Philistines, and some of this information can be applied, for example, to the confrontation between David and Goliath. Goliath's spear is likened to a "weaver's beam" (1 Sam 17:7). The Philistines came from the Aegean where "rifling cords" gave a spear greater stability and distance. To the biblical writer, the loops tied to a weaver's beam were a way of describing such an attachment. A good commentary may also make

use of ancient reliefs, which allow us better to visualize Goliath's armor. Additionally, slingers, like David, did not wear body armor; their mobility was their defense. The effective range of a sling was in excess of one hundred yards—farther than any weapon Goliath carried—and a sling stone, many of which have been uncovered by archaeologists, could be propelled at a speed of more than one hundred miles an hour. Despite the bravado of 1 Sam 17:43-44, and however much hyperbole is granted Judg 20:16, Goliath was a more stationary target, and David carried a lethal weapon. Archaeology can rescue this well-known story from the grip of the animated video cartoon.

Archaeology has made it possible to plot on a map many of the places mentioned in the Bible. That ability does more than fill Holy Land tour buses; it also enriches the exposition of passages preached from the pulpit. Current Bible atlases make great use of archaeology, and they should be consulted for possible insights whenever biblical places or geography is involved. According to Acts, when Paul was in Lystra, people came from Antioch in Pisidia and Iconium, and stirred up the crowds so that Paul was nearly stoned to death (14:19). Little archaeological work has been done at these specific cities, but being able to locate them on a map reveals a religious zeal that would otherwise be missed. The people from Antioch and Iconium committed themselves to travel about one hundred miles to reach Lystra in hopes that they could silence Paul (it would take several days of normal travel to make a round trip). In the next verse Paul and Barnabas have moved farther east to Derbe. From there they are not far from Tarsus, Paul's hometown, and from Tarsus to Antioch where this first missionary journey would end. Instead of continuing east, Paul and Barnabas retraced their steps, revisiting the churches they had just established. From a purely physical perspective they took a dangerous and needlessly long route home. That choice signals the depth of Paul's concern for the new congregations. A sermon lurks within.

Sometimes archaeology and geography combine to enhance an episode. Ezra 5–6 tells of a letter sent from Jerusalem to King Darius hundreds of miles to the east. The Persian archives were searched, and a response was sent back. It is not uncommon for people to assume that one or more years passed before a reply reached the beleaguered residents of

Jerusalem. The internal chronology in the book of Malachi requires a time span of under four months, but archaeology suggests that the wait time was considerably less than that. The Persians put great emphasis on communication, and their Royal Road stretched some 1,700 miles from Susa to Sardis. "Pony express" posts at regular intervals enabled a message to travel from one end of that Royal Road to the other in a week. The road network from Susa to Jerusalem covered a shorter distance. The 5th-cent. BCE historian Herodotus was so impressed by the Persian mail system that he wrote, "Neither snow nor rain nor heat nor gloom of night stays these couriers from the swift completion of their appointed rounds" (*Hist.* 8.98). *See* GEOGRAPHY; HOLY LAND TOURS.

Bibliography: William F. Albright. *Christianity Today.* 7/8 (1963): 3–5; Amnon Ben-Tor, ed. *The Archaeology of Ancient Israel.* (1994); James H. Charlesworth, ed. *Jesus and Archaeology.* (2006); Thomas W. Davis. *Shifting Sands: The Rise and Fall of Biblical Archaeology.* (2004); William G. Dever. *What Did the Biblical Writers Know and When Did They Know It?* (2001); Alfred J. Hoerth. *Archaeology and the Old Testament.* (1998); Philip J. King and Lawrence E. Stager. *Life in Biblical Israel.* (2001); Kenneth A. Kitchen. *On the Reliability of the Old Testament.* (2003); Amihai Mazar. *Archaeology of the Land of the Bible: 10,000–586 BCE.* (1992); John McRay. *Archaeology and the New Testament.* (1991); Alan Millard. *Treasures from Bible Times.* (1985); Anson F. Rainey and R. Steven Notley. *The Sacred Bridge: Carta's Atlas of the Biblical World.* (2006).

CANONICAL CRITICISM
Thomas B. Dozeman

Canonical criticism is a historical-critical methodology focused on the late formation and preservation of biblical texts by religious communities who attributed divine authority to the literature. Thus, canonical criticism is concerned with the dynamic relationship between an authoritative text and the faith community on the journey to preserving texts as canon. The methodology investigates the unique literary features and the social function of the genre, canon, paying particular attention to the way in which once historically conditioned literature is given a new authoritative function as the comprehensive word of God to later communities of faith.

The Social and Theological Background for the Rise of Canonical Criticism

The modern and postmodern study of biblical literature confronts the preacher with two fundamental challenges in proclaiming Scripture as the authoritative word of God for all people, in all places, and at all times. The two related problems are the lack of theological unity to biblical literature and the diverse communities of faith who read and hear Scripture differently in light of their unique social experience.

1. Canon and Historical Criticism in the Modern Era of Interpretation

The rise of historical criticism in the modern period uncovered the multiple, historically conditioned, and conflicting voices within the Bible. The book of Isaiah presents a more distinct theology of God, worship, and community than Jeremiah. The same problems arise from a comparison of the Priestly and non-Priestly literature in the Pentateuch, or the Gospels. The fragmentation of Scripture into multiple authors presented a direct challenge to the belief that Scripture contained one, authoritative word of God. The hermeneutical problem for preachers and theologians throughout the modern period has been to reconcile the multiple voices of Scripture into a single, divine truth. Is there a center to canon? If there is not a theological center, should the preacher pick one biblical voice over others, and thus create a canon within the canon? Yet is not the very authority of canon lost if the interpreter can pick and choose favorite texts, while ignoring others? The modern period of biblical interpretation accentuated the pluralism within Scripture and thus pressed the question of how interpreters are able to hear the voice of the same God through historically dissimilar traditions.

2. Canon and Diverse Communities of Faith in the Postmodern Era of Interpretation

The postmodern period of interpretation intensified the problem of an authoritative canon by introducing the formative role of experience in the appropriation of Scripture as the Word of God. The modern period confronted the interpreter with multiple voices within the canon, which could not be harmonized into a single truth. Yet in the modern period, interpreters assumed that multiple readers of the same text could arrive at a similar interpretation. Interpreters in the postmodern period remove even this limited view of hermeneutical unity by stressing the formative role of experience in interpretation, which prompted distinct communities to read the same text in a different way. In the postmodern period factors such as gender and social location fragmented interpretation even further. A woman will read a text differently from the way a man will read it. A South American church will read a text differently from the way an African community of Christians will read it. The postmodern period of biblical interpretation accentuated the pluralism of the readers and hearers of Scripture in addition to the multiple voices within canon. The formative role of experience in the interpretation of any text intensified the problem of canon, when it was viewed as containing a single truth.

The Goals and Methodology of Canonical Criticism

Canonical criticism addresses the authority of Scripture in a pluralistic world. Brevard S. Childs provided guidelines for the preacher to reevaluate the nature of an authoritative canon, not as representing a single truth, but as providing the boundaries of truth (Childs 1979, 83). James. A. Sanders explored the dynamic relationship between a fixed canon and the ever-changing communities of faith, who appropriate and adapt Scripture through their unique experience (Sanders, 1987, 65–66).

1. Brevard S. Childs and the Shape of the Canon

Childs opened a new phase in the theological interpretation of Scripture by focusing on the genre of canon. Childs emphasized two hermeneutical principles in the study of canon, which are important for preaching.

First, a central feature in the formation of canon is its religious use by the community of faith who formed the text (Childs 1979, 58). Thus, faith becomes an important hermeneutical component in the critical interpretation of canonical literature. The Gospels of Jesus in the NT provide an example. The Gospels contain glimpses of the life of Jesus. But the religious authority of the Gospels does not arise from

their historical reliability. As canonical literature, it would be a mistake to interpret the Gospels as though they were shaped simply to preserve the life of Jesus. They are constructed, instead, to speak directly to future readers about the power of God in Christ. The early church was certainly interested in the life of Jesus, but the active role of faith in the composition of the literature necessarily loosened the Gospels from the past so that they could function as canonical literature in the future. The Gospels illustrate that the authority of Scripture cannot be confined to the past. Such a limited historical-critical reading of the Gospels would ensure their misinterpretation as canonical literature.

Second, the canon represents a hermeneutic of controlled pluralism (Childs 1979, 83). The historical-critical period of interpretation firmly established the theological pluralism within the literature of Scripture. The multiple voices in Scripture provided the starting point for Childs. His focus, however, was not on the distinct traditions, but on their present relationship in the formation of a religiously authoritative canon. Thus, canon is a chorus of voices for Childs and not a solo performance; it provides the boundaries of possible interpretations rather than the one acceptable truth.

Childs looked for literary features in the shape of canon, which provide the reader with a road map on how to relate historically dissimilar traditions into a holistic reading. Historical-critical interpretation of the political setting of biblical books aids in identifying the parts of Scripture, and it even safeguards against an artificial unity to the literature (Childs 1979, 127). But the poetics of canon looks for the relationship of the parts into a larger literary corpus, in which historically dissimilar texts qualify and complement each other.

For example, an interpretation of the social and political background of First Isaiah (Isa 1–39) does not adequately interpret the book of Isaiah in its present canonical shape. The interpreter of Isaiah must also explore the literary features, which relate First, Second, and Third Isaiah into a single complex corpus. The poetics of canon can branch out even further, leading interpreters to identify innerbiblical devices that bring Isaiah into conversation with Jeremiah. Rather than harmonizing Isaiah and Jeremiah, the poetics of canon would explore the relationship between the distinct books and, in the process, heighten the demand for the interpretative community to fashion a broad and coherent theology that can embrace the distinct messages of the two books.

2. J. A. Sanders and the Function of the Canon in Faith Communities

Sanders shares many of the hermeneutical insights of Childs regarding canon, including the diversity of traditions within the text, the need to interpret canon holistically, and the dynamic relationship between the formation of canon and the community of faith. His interpretation of canon also branches out in a different direction to explore in more detail the function of the canon within faith communities (1987, 19–20). Thus, in contrast to Childs, who concentrated on the unique literary features within canon, Sanders focuses on the nature of the community of faith, who embraces the canon through time in different social contexts. Sanders wanted to know how a fixed, stable text, like a closed canon, was able to remain dynamic and adaptable through time. The adaptability of canon lay in its reuse by the ever-changing communities of faith, who seek identity and an ethical vision from its stories.

When the canon is embraced as the authoritative Word of God, a community of faith cannot help but adapt its message to their particular social setting and life experience. In the process, the canon becomes a "book of life." Its stories remain constant, but they take on the color and the hues of the community, which has chosen to remember them and to live by them. Thus, the one story of the exodus will be adapted in different ways by European, African American, or Asian communities of faith. The formative role of experience in the appropriation of the canon results in a broad pluralism among distinct faith communities, even though they read the same text. An important quality of any faith community, which lives by the canon, is the goal of social harmony and peace—a quality that Sanders describes as the quest to "monotheize" (Sanders 1987, 30). The function of canon in different faith communities alerts the preacher to the important task of interpreting the faith experience of congregations as well as biblical texts.

Preaching the Canon with Authority in a Pluralistic World

Canonical criticism is an essential hermeneutical tool for proclaiming the gospel in a pluralistic world. It is a self-critical methodology because it rejects the notion of a canon within the canon, and thus forces the preacher to interpret voices in the canon that he or she may instinctively reject. At the same time, the methodology frees the interpreter from searching for a single unifying message either in the canon or in the congregation. In this way, canonical criticism advocates a range of authoritative interpretations in Scripture, which are able to support a diverse community of faith.

Bibliography: B. S. Childs. *Introduction to the Old Testament as Scripture.* (1979); B. S. Childs. *Biblical Theology of the Old and New Testaments.* (1993); J. A. Sanders. *Torah and Canon.* (1972); J. A. Sanders. *Canon as Paradigm: From Sacred Story to Sacred Text.* (1987).

EXEGESIS
Thomas G. Long

Competent exegesis in preparation for preaching involves crafting a synthetic exegetical procedure from many of the exegetical methods and then weaving this procedure into the regular pattern of the preacher's schedule.

  A. Exegesis and Eisegesis
  B. Exegetical Methods
    1. Historical Criticism
    2. Literary Criticism
    3. Theological Criticism
    4. Canonical Criticism
    5. Sociological Criticism
    6. Highly Contextualized Exegesis
    7. Prayerful and Meditative Exegesis
  C. The Exegetical Habit

Exegesis, when the term is used in relationship to preaching, normally refers to the act of interpreting a biblical text so that the meanings of the text can be understood and the present-day import of those meanings can be expressed in sermons. Exegesis for preaching, then, requires a careful attention to the nature and character of the biblical text itself as well as a discerning attention to the contemporary context in which that text is read and preached.

A. Exegesis and Eisegesis

Exegesis done as a part of the creation of a sermon builds upon—and challenges—a distinction often made between exegesis and eisegesis. The English word *exegesis* is derived from the Greek exēgeomai, meaning "to lead out" or "to draw out," while the word *eisegesis* is a compound Greek term meaning "to lead into." Exegesis, construed as a good thing, occurs when the interpreter draws out only those meanings that are truly inside a text, in sharp contrast to eisegesis, a more negative term, in which the interpreter imposes meanings on the text from the outside. In this sense, exegesis is seen as objective and true to texts, while eisegesis is viewed as subjective and a misreading of texts.

Today, while able biblical preachers would surely wish to avoid a clumsy form of eisegesis, namely, a twisting of biblical texts and a forcing on them of alien readings, most would acknowledge that purely objective readings of ancient texts are neither possible nor desirable. Biblical texts are seen not as jars with eternal meanings inside, but as interactive fields of meaning. Contemporary readers and interpreters do not don sterile gloves to withdraw uncontaminated meanings from texts. They instead interact with texts, drawing the questions and issues of their own situations to the encounter. What one brings to the text affects what the text means in every new context. Texts are independent of readers and exert force on the interpretive process, but only in relation to the worlds of each new wave of readers.

Consider, for example, Paul's advice to the church at Corinth about eating meat offered "to idols" (1 Cor 8:1-13). In its original setting, this passage offered very specific advice about a hotly debated ethical issue. A common religious practice in the city of Corinth was to place freshly cut meat on the altar of some local divinity as an offering, and then, after a proper time, to remove the meat and use it for human consumption. The question was, Could Christians in good conscience eat such meat? Was it ethically acceptable for them to buy this meat in the market or eat it at the tables of their non-Christian neighbors?

Some Corinthian Christians said no. Eating meat offered to another god was, they argued, tantamount to idolatry, and they would have nothing to do with it. Others in the congregation, however, probably the more educated elite, pooh-poohed this attitude as ignorant and superstitious. "We all know there is only one God," they argued. "Sure, other people in town are not so enlightened. They believe in dumb idols and offer meat to them, but we know these idols do not really exist. So, since none of these other so-called gods is real, putting a piece of meat on a stone altar somewhere means nothing; it is an empty gesture with no religious power or impact. Why not eat this meat and enjoy it without a ripple of regret?"

Paul begins by taking the side of the educated elites. "You are theologically right," he says. "There is only one God. You are perfectly free to eat meat wherever it comes from. You get an A for knowledge." But then he changes the equation by trumping sheer knowledge with love. "Knowledge puffs up, but love builds up," he says (v. 1).

The Corinthians want to be right, but Paul suggests that being right pales before another goal: building up the community through love. He then takes the elites to task. "Your knowledge about the non-existence of idols may be correct, and your attitude about eating this meat may be absolutely right," he says, "but your attitude toward your brothers and sisters in this church is pompous and arrogant. Not everybody in this church has grown to your level of knowledge, and there are members of this congregation, people for whom Christ died, who have just barely cut themselves loose from the worship of other gods. Their Christian faith is young and fragile, and they will be damaged if you continue to assert your superior knowledge. If you love them, you will not act so hastily." Paul then gets to the punch line, which he expresses in terms of his own ethical choice: "I may have the freedom to eat whatever I want, but freedom in Christ is always the servant of love. If eating this meat would cause one of these others to fall, I will never do it."

In its historical context, then, the meaning of this text is clear and concrete. If exegesis is determining only the meaning of a text in its first context, then this passage is historically interesting, but mainly irrelevant to most contemporary settings. While there are still a few Christians in the world for whom the question of "meat offered to idols" is a literal and live issue, this is not the case for most. When the text is seen not simply as a vessel containing an idea, but as an interactive field of meaning, it projects a world in which commitment to Christ brings freedom, knowledge, and love into dynamic relationship. This world has the power to engage and to affect the world of contemporary readers across a wide range of issues and concerns. The text's claim that Christian love values theological knowledge and ethical freedom, but weaves these goods into the larger fabric of building up the community and encouraging the weak, has the capacity to affect readers in every new context.

B. Exegetical Methods

Exegeting, that is to say, interpreting a biblical text for preaching, involves more than the simple act of reading. Over the centuries, the church has developed and adopted many tools and methods of approach designed to allow intelligent and pertinent interpretations of texts. The history of this development is marked by many twists, turns, and debates, from the figurative exegesis of Augustine to the spiritual multileveled interpretation of Origen to the grammatical analysis of the Reformation period to the scientific methods of modern exegesis. Essentially, though, the development of the church's exegesis for interpretation and preaching is marked by the gradual acceptance of all of the methods of analysis that any scholar, religious or not, would use to study ancient texts, while at the same time holding to some understanding of the Scripture as the source for a word from God that transcends the words on the page.

Sandra Schneiders helpfully describes the two overall objectives of biblical interpretation as *information* and *transformation*. The goal of information turns the interpreter toward the past, seeking to discover such facts about the text as authorship, date, circumstance, theological positions, and relationship to the social world in which it was created. The goal of transformation, however, turns the interpreter to the present, asking about the truth of the text for contemporary readers and the consequences of the text for these new readers. While interpreters can, if they wish, seek only information and not transformation, the converse, Schneiders claims, is not true. Anyone "interested in the existential aspect of the text has no choice but to become seriously involved with its informational aspects" (Schneiders 1991, 14).

Among the primary methods of exegesis employed by preachers to achieve this integration of information and transformation are the following:

1. Historical Criticism

The method of historical criticism recognizes that biblical texts were created by human beings at a particular time and in specific circumstances. The goal of historical criticism is to discover the conditions under which a text was created and the relationship of a text to its own historical setting. As such, historical criticism is concerned with history in two senses: the history *in* the text and the history *of* the text (Hayes and Holladay 1987, 45).

The history *in* the text essentially consists of historical information that can be derived from the details of the text. For example, when Ps 24 provides the picture of worshipers ascending "the hill of the LORD" singing, "Lift up your heads, O gates! / and be lifted up, O ancient doors!" (v. 7), this may well be based upon the actual liturgy for an ancient ritual of entrance, in which pilgrims climbed the hill to the Temple in Jerusalem. When Paul, writing to the Galatians, charges, "I am astonished that you are so quickly deserting the one who called you in the grace of Christ and are turning to a different gospel" (Gal 1:6), the historical critic tries to reconstruct the nature of the conflict between Paul and his readers and to determine what "different gospel" is attracting them.

The history *of* the text concerns itself with questions of authorship, date, vocabulary, grammar, and the circumstances of composition and preservation of the text. For example, when historical criticism is employed to examine the story of the woman caught in adultery in John's Gospel (7:53–8:11), a number of questions and issues are raised. The story is not included in the vast majority of the oldest Greek manuscripts of John, and the vocabulary and style of the text are quite different from the rest of John. What is more, it seems to interrupt the natural flow of John's narrative. For all of these reasons, most historical critics are persuaded that, while the story probably comes from the authentic oral tradition about Jesus, it was not originally in John's Gospel and may have been originally a part of Luke or one of the other Gospels.

2. Literary Criticism

The method of literary criticism does not step away from the concerns of authorship, circumstance, and grammar that are the focus of historical criticism; instead, it adds to those concerns an awareness that texts are poetic and artistic creations. They employ language in ways that generate meanings, emotions, and responses in readers.

For example, the account of the dialogue between Jesus and Peter in John 21:15-19 is obviously no mere straightforward journalistic report, but a quite artfully constructed literary artifact. Three times Jesus asks Peter, "Do you love me?" and three times Peter responds, "You know that I love you." The threefold question and affirmation pattern corresponds to the threefold denial of Jesus described earlier in John's Gospel (13:38; 18:17; 18:25-27), and as such, the narrative serves as a story of the restoration of Peter. The connection between the denials and affirmations is reinforced by the fact that the final two denials and the threefold restoration take place around a charcoal fire (18:18 and 21:9), which in a literary sense functions symbolically to join the two moments.

Another example of the usefulness of literary criticism can be seen in the analysis of Ps 19. In terms of historical criticism alone, this psalm is something of a crazy quilt, being patched together from three different sources and genres. The first portion of the psalm (19:1-6) is based on a Near Eastern nature hymn in praise of the sun. It has been changed into a tribute to the glory of God in creation, but it still bears the markings of its nature-worship origins. The second section of the psalm (19:7-10) is a piece of wisdom poetry, and the meter, the vocabulary, and even the Hebrew name of God change from the first section. This section describes in rhythmic fashion the attributes of the teachings and commandments of the law of the Lord (the Torah): "perfect," "sure," "right," "clear," "pure," "true," and desirable. The final section of the psalm (19:11-14) shifts the genre again, this time to a personal lament in which the psalmist cries out, asking God, "Let the words of my mouth and the meditation of my heart / be acceptable to you, / O Lord, my rock and my redeemer."

From a historical point of view, then, this psalm is a confusing jumble of genres, moods, audiences, and circumstances. But when the psalm is seen through a literary lens, the various parts come together as a unified whole. What unites the psalm is the metaphor of speech; the creation is speaking, the Torah is speaking, and finally, the psalmist is speaking. The psalm can even be heard as a kind of incipient narrative, as the psalmist moves from nature to Temple to self (Fishbane 1988, 84–90).

The story begins with the psalmist walking around in the world of nature, overwhelmed by seeing the magnificence of the heavens and hearing the firmament sing the great hymn of creation. But for all of this ecstasy, the psalmist is also experiencing alienation. Nature is singing, but the psalmist is unable to decipher the words of the heavenly hymn or fathom its full meaning ("There is no speech, nor are there words; / their voice is not heard" [19:3]). He moves from nature to the Temple, and there he hears the wise speech of the Torah. The law of the Lord, the great speech event of Scripture in decree and commandment, names the God whose glory is being sung by the heavens. Torah refracts the sense of God's presence in nature, bringing it into clear focus, giving it shape and substance. Now the psalmist can be gathered up personally into this event of speech, pleading to God, "Let the words of my mouth . . . be acceptable to you." Historically, Ps 19 is a glued together pastiche of materials. Literarily, it is a powerful description of the move from voiceless wonder to personal praise.

Or consider the story of the healing of Jairus's daughter in Mark 5:21-43. The story begins when Jesus, who was being mobbed by the crowds as he taught and healed in the region around the Sea of Galilee, was approached by a man named Jairus, an official of the local synagogue. Jairus's twelve-year-old daughter was critically ill, and he begged Jesus to come and lay hands on her. Jesus decides to accompany Jairus to the bedside of his child, eventually arriving at Jairus's home, only to find that the little girl has already died. "Your daughter is dead," say some members of the household sadly. Jesus enters the house, takes the little girl by the hand, and says to her, "Little girl, get up!" Amazingly, she does, to the astonishment of everyone in the house.

What is disclosed to the eye of literary criticism is the way that Mark, as a narrator, interrupts the story of Jairus's daughter with another narrative, the account of a desperate woman whose illness, a hemorrhaging of blood that has lasted twelve years, has exhausted her physically, emotionally, and financially. As Jesus is making his way to Jairus's house, this woman emerges from the crowd following Jesus and reaches out and touches Jesus' clothing. Immediately, she is healed. An exchange occurs between Jesus, his disciples, and the woman, at the end of which Jesus tells the woman, "Daughter, your faith has made you well; go in peace, and be healed of your disease" (Mark 5:34).

This insertion of one narrative (the healing of the woman with the flow of blood) inside another longer narrative (the healing of Jairus's daughter), which some commentators call Mark's sandwich technique, is a literary device employed by Mark to create interaction and resonances between the two stories. Each story expands and interprets the other. One of the most significant overlaps comes right at the hinge between the two stories, when Jesus says to the woman, "Daughter, your faith has made you well." Mark informs the reader that, while Jesus "was still speaking," in other words while these words were still in the air, the mourners from Jairus's house announce, "Your daughter is dead." Daughter is well . . . daughter is dead—these simultaneous and opposite proclamations are not simply stray pieces of dialogue from two independent narratives; they are instead symbols of the two worlds that the text intends to place on collision course: the world of death and the world of life in the reign of God.

3. Theological Criticism

Theological criticism seeks to discover the convictions about the character of God that lie at the heart of the text. Sometimes these convictions are explicitly stated in the text, and sometimes they are implied. For example, Paul's discussion of spiritual gifts in 1 Cor 12 ("To each is given the manifestation of the Spirit for the common good" [v. 7]) is aimed at overcoming internal rivalries and jealousies in the Corinthian community, but it also conveys an implicit theology of the church. The church, theologically speaking, is not a collection of intrinsically spiritual persons, but a community of believers through whom the Spirit of God expresses the life of God in gifts and manifestations. By being open to the working of the Spirit, and by celebrating the various manifestations of the Spirit in the gifts and ministries of the congregation, the church is drawn deeper and more fully into the life of God.

Or again, the account in Mark 4:35-41 about Jesus' stilling the storm on the sea is not simply a story of Jesus the miraculous wonder-worker. Theologically, the wild, storm-driven sea evokes the chaotic and demonic powers that threaten human life and rival the reign of God. Jesus' command to the seas, "Peace! Be still!" is not simply a quieting of the storm but a proleptic announcement of God's eschatological *shalom*, the great calm that will ultimately prevail in a creation where God is all in all.

4. Canonical Criticism

Canonical criticism is a method of interpretation that focuses its attention on the text as Scripture as received and read by the church, that is, the Bible as the church's canon. As such, canonical criticism is somewhat in tension with historical criticism, which tends to rank of most importance the oldest version of a text rather than the final, received version.

The parable of the Wise and Foolish Maidens in Matt 25:1-13 tells the story of ten bridesmaids, five of them wise and five of them foolish, who were waiting for the delayed arrival of a bridegroom. The wait dragged on, the hour grew late, and all of these women became drowsy and dropped off to sleep. At the stroke of midnight, though, a shout went up that the groom was at last arriving, and the startled women woke up to trim their lamps and to prepare for the bridegroom's arrival. But the foolish maidens realized they had a problem; they hadn't brought enough oil with them, and their lamps were already flickering out. They tried to bargain with the wise maidens for some oil, but there was not enough in reserve to share, so the foolish maidens had to hotfoot it to the market to buy more oil and ended up missing the big wedding banquet.

Jesus ends this parable in Matthew by saying, "Keep awake therefore, for you know neither the day nor the hour." This is admittedly a very strange lesson for Jesus to draw from this parable, since in the story itself *all* of the bridesmaids—the wise and the foolish alike—fell asleep. Historical critics point out that it is very likely that Matthew added this ill-fitting tag line to the parable, perhaps even mangling the story and missing Jesus' point in the process. The original parable, some of them suggest, had to do with the ethical task of the church, the oil being symbolic of good works, and the line about keeping awake is Matthew's attempt to retrofit the parable into his own context, a church grown weary of waiting for the arrival of the kingdom. Canonical critics, however, refuse to slice off the final line since it belongs to the received, canonical version of the text. Whatever else the parable may say about discipleship and good works, canonical critics want to add the element of vigilance and watchfulness to the equation.

5. Sociological Criticism

Sociological methods of exegesis seek to discover the relationship between a biblical text and its political, cultural, and social environment. In the same sense that no future scholar could fully understand the text from our own culture "Thank you for not smoking" without being aware of the social and medical developments about smoking in our time, just so, readers of biblical texts need to be aware of the social and political contexts in which they were created.

For example, in Mark 9:33-37, Jesus tells his disciples, "Whoever wants to be first must be last of all and servant of all." Then he takes a small child and places that child among the disciples. "Whoever welcomes one such child in my name welcomes me." Later in Mark, people hold out their children for Jesus to bless with a touch. When the disciples try to shoo these people away, Jesus rebukes them: "Let the little children come to me; do not stop them" (Mark 10:14), and then he adds, "Truly I tell you, whoever does not receive the kingdom of God as a little child will never enter it" (Mark 10:15).

Many foolish and sentimental sermons have been preached on these and the other "child" passages in the NT. Naive interpreters of these texts import into them contemporary images and attitudes toward children from our child-centered society. Children are seen as sweet, trusting, innocent, loving, and pure, and sermons based on such assumptions become verbal equivalents of the pious Sunday school art showing Jesus in the middle of a crowd of cute, smiling children, just like we imagine the kids in our neighborhood. When sociological tools are employed to study these texts, however, a very different picture emerges. Children in Jesus' day had virtually the same status as a slave. Children were weak and vulnerable, and as many as 60 percent of them died by age six. Childhood was "a time of terror," and when people held out their babies for Jesus to touch, they were fully aware that many of these infants would soon be dead (Malina and Rohrbaugh 1992, 238, 243). Instead of symbolizing sweetness and innocent trust, a child was the very embodiment of need and low status.

6. Highly Contextualized Exegesis

Every act of biblical interpretation is contextualized in the sense that the interpreter stands here and not there, in this time and place and social setting and not somewhere else. It is a mark of contemporary hermeneutical understanding to expose as an illusion the idea of a neutral interpreter, float-

ing above all social commitments, free of all biases, and able to look clearly and objectively at texts.

Many methods of exegesis bring the social, political, and theological location of the interpreter into full view in order to temper its influence somewhat. The interpreter may stand with both feet in a rational, scientific world with certain standards of truth, but this reader should not assume that this is the world of the text. The interpreter cannot shed his or her worldview, like taking off a coat, but texts come from different worldviews and should have a chance to have their say.

Other methods of exegesis, however, emphasize the social location of the interpreter in a more positive way, employing the vantage point of the interpreter as a way to see aspects of the text overlooked by other readers who stand in different places. Mary's words in the Magnificat, "[God] has brought down the powerful from their thrones, / and lifted up the lowly; / [God] has filled the hungry with good things, /and sent the rich away empty" (Luke 1:52-53), may come across as a lullaby in Beverly Hills, but when they are heard by impoverished people in Solentiname, they have a hopeful, even revolutionary, political edge.

In the last several decades many methods of exegesis have been developed that emphasize reading and interpreting texts from social vantage points often overlooked by the kind of exegetes who have produced the bulk of biblical commentaries (educated, mostly male, mostly European and North American, mostly economically well off, etc.). Liberationist methods explicitly view texts from the perspective of poor and politically powerless people. (See LIBERATION CRITICISM.) Feminist and womanist methods take the vantage points of women. (See FEMINIST CRITICISM; WOMANIST CRITICISM.) Asian, African, Latino, and other ethnically and geographically situated methods lift up the ways that racial and cultural identities give access to often neglected dimensions of biblical texts.

Sometimes highly contextualized exegetical methods emphasize strands in a text that might otherwise be muted. One feminist exegete, for example, finds great power and meaning in Paul's use of the metaphor of childbirth in Galatians ("My little children, for whom I am again in the pain of childbirth until Christ is formed in you" [Gal 4:19]), calling Paul "mother to the Galatian Christians" (Newsom and Ringe 1998, 426). On other occasions, such exegetical methods correct mis-readings of texts. The assumption that the Samaritan woman whom Jesus encountered at Jacob's well was necessarily a woman of low morals and a serial divorcée ("you have had five husbands, and the one you have now is not your husband" [John 4:18]) is challenged by many feminist interpreters. There are other plausible explanations for her marital history than moral looseness (e.g., levirate marriage), and to preach about her as a "tramp" or a "five-time loser" says more about the prejudices of the preacher than the claim of the text (Newsom and Ringe 1998, 384). Finally, highly contextualized methods of exegesis can sometimes provide leverage for a critique of the commitments of the biblical writers themselves. For example, in 1 Kgs 16–21 and 2 Kgs 9, Jezebel, a Phoenician princess who married King Ahab of Israel, is portrayed not as a strong woman or a political leader but as a vain, conniving, manipulative seductress, a symbol of all that threatens Israel's fidelity to God. Feminist commentators point out that this assessment of Jezebel may have more to do with male fears of female power and with anxiety about "foreignness" than with any historical reality about Jezebel (Newsom and Ringe 1998, 110).

7. Prayerful and Meditative Exegesis

All of the above methods of exegesis are, technically speaking, *critical* methods, not in the sense of being negative but in the sense of being analytical. In all of them, biblical texts, at least for a phase of the interpretive process, become objects of scrutiny and inquiry. These methods serve well the objective of *information*, but the goal of *transformation* can be missing or muted. Recently, and partly in reaction to the technologizing and objectifying of texts that can occur in many of the current, more scientific exegetical methods, older, deeply reflective practices of biblical interpretation have been recovered. These methods focus not on analysis and deconstruction of biblical texts but instead on prayerful meditation upon passages of Scripture.

Perhaps the best known of these reflective methods is *lectio divina*, an ancient process of slowly praying the Scriptures that has roots in the early church and that took specific shape as early as the 12th cent. in *The Monk's Ladder* by Guigo II, a Carthusian monk. (*See* LECTIO DIVINA.) *Lectio divina*, which can be done by oneself or in groups, generally involves four steps or moods of encounter with biblical texts: *lectio*, *meditatio*, *oratio*, and *contemplatio*. In *lectio*, the interpreter simply reads the text very slowly, listening attentively and in openness for whatever the passage may wish to say. Such listening involves both a readiness to empty oneself before the text and a willingness of heart to hear God's voice speaking in and through the text. In this step, the reader stays alert to any word or phrase in the text that seems, in this moment, to have particular significance or meaning.

In *meditatio*, the reader focuses on the phrase or section of the text that seems to speak most personally and meaningfully. The reader does not seek to analyze or even to understand this portion of Scripture as much as to meditate on it, allowing the text to draw the reader into its rhythms. As is the case in each of the four steps, *meditatio* cannot be rushed. The slow repetition of reflecting again and again on the same portion of Scripture allows it to work its way into the consciousness of the reader.

The third step is *oratio*, a prayerful conversation with God. In the step *meditatio*, the reader listens for the particular word that God speaks to the heart, and now, in this third step, the reader speaks in response, offering to God those cries, confessions, and concerns that have been stimulated by the Word.

The last step is *contemplatio* in which the one who has read words, meditated on words, and spoken prayer words now seeks to move beyond words and into a peaceful and restorative relationship with God. The process of *lectio divina* seeks to bring the interpreter not into the presence of the text but into the presence of God, and this final phase of process allows the reader to dwell in that presence.

C. The Exegetical Habit

Doing competent exegesis in preparation for preaching involves crafting a synthetic exegetical procedure, drawing from many of the exegetical methods, and then weaving this procedure into the regular pattern of the preacher's schedule. Exegesis is best done as a matter of habit, a predictable practice and discipline.

A typical exegetical procedure would involve four phases. First, the preacher selects the text for the sermon (using a lectionary or other method) and does some preliminary study of the text, simply ensuring that the basic vocabulary and background of the text are understood. Second, the preacher engages in a creative, prayerful, perhaps even play-ful conversation with the text, collecting all of the insights that occur in this phase. Third, the preacher specifically employs the technical methods of exegesis—historical, literary, sociological, and so on—both as a way of discovering additional insights and as a means of testing the insights already found. Finally, the preacher seeks to name the claim of the text, that is, to identify, out of all of the exegetical process, what most compelling word from God for this day and for these hearers is heard in the text. This becomes the central force and purpose of the resulting sermon.

Such a process takes time, of course, which is often in short supply for practicing pastors. Many pastors have found that breaking the process into measured portions and spreading them out in a reg-ular and routine pattern across the length of a week or more is the best plan. Also, the involvement of others, either an exegetical study group of pastoral colleagues or a "feed in" group of parishioners, enriches the exegetical process and makes it more efficient. *See* EXEGESIS OF SELF; EXEGESIS OF THE CONGREGATION; EXEGETICAL; EXPOSI-TORY; HERMENEUTICS; HISTORICAL CRITI-CISM; LITERARY CRITICISM.

Bibliography: Michael Fishbane. *Biblical Text and Texture.* (1988); John H. Hayes and Carl R. Holladay. *Biblical Exegesis: A Beginner's Hand-book.* Rev. ed. (1987); Bruce J. Malina and Richard L. Rohrbaugh. *Social Science Commentary on the Synoptic Gospels.* (1992); Carol A. Newsom and Sharon H. Ringe. *Woman's Bible Commentary.* Expanded ed. with Apocrypha. (1998); Pontifical Biblical Commission. "The Interpretation of the Bible in the Church." *Origins* 23 (January 6, 1994) 497–524; Sandra M. Schneiders. *The Reve-latory Text: Interpreting the New Testament as Sacred Scripture.* (1991).

FORM CRITICISM
Ronald J. Allen

Form criticism, an older discipline of the criti-cal study of the Bible, sought to show how the gospel writers join with other disciplines in help-ing preachers consider how the form and function of a biblical text can suggest a form and function for the sermon.

A. Early Aims of Form Criticism
B. Forms and Life Settings in the Two Testaments
  1. Old Testament
  2. New Testament
C. Interaction with Other Criticisms
  1. Redaction Criticism
  2. Literary and Rhetorical Criticism
  3. Studies in Oral-Aural and Rhetorical Cultures
D. An Approach to Using Form Criticism in the Service of Preaching
E. Examples of Form Criticism in the Service of Preaching

A. Early Aims of Form Criticism

Form criticism emerged after the First World War. The form critics focused on the period of oral tradition before the materials in the Bible were written down. These scholars had two primary aims. First, they believed that many individual pieces of biblical material originated in oral form in specific life settings and circulated in oral form before being written down and joined with other pieces of material. By "setting in life" (*Sitz im Leben*), the form critics meant particular, repeated occasions in the life of the community, such as set-tings for worship, teaching, or dealing with legal matters. The form critics sought to recover the his-tory of pieces of material; they were particularly interested in identifying the original form of the text, that is, the text as it existed before subse-quent layers of interpretive details were added to it, as well as in subsequent development. The form critics gave little attention to how the forms were used by the writers who put together the docu-ments in the Bible as we now have them, a turn that awaited redaction criticism.

Second, a further basic work of form criticism was to identify the characteristic literary elements in each of the different forms, and how these elements contributed to the function of the forms in their life settings. By focusing on the literary composition of the forms, the form critics modestly anticipated aspects of literary criticism. In a methodologically unsophisticated way, the form-critical focus on oral tradition also anticipated interpretation of biblical materials from the points of view of oral-aural and rhetorical cultures.

B. Forms and Life Settings in the Two Testaments

The general concerns of form criticism are similar in the study of both the OT and the NT. However, the life settings and the forms differ in the worlds of the two Testaments. Such a short article cannot catalog all the life settings and forms, but can indicate some representative ones and how awareness of them is valuable to the preacher.

1. Old Testament

Worship is the easiest setting in life to identify in the world of the OT. Many of the psalms (and some other materials) derive from worship, especially in the Temple. Form criticism continues to be helpful to the scholar and preacher in this regard. While many of the psalms cannot be dated to particular historical moments, knowledge of their uses in worship makes them accessible for preaching. The law court is another easily identifiable setting, and it gave birth to the *rib* or controversy form that depicts dialogue among judge, plaintiff, prosecutor, defendant, and witnesses. The prophets (and other writers) employ call stories, as well as oracles of judgment and salvation. The wisdom literature brings into play different kinds of proverbs and many other forms, often for use in educational settings.

2. New Testament

In earlier years, form criticism has been most evident in the NT in connection with the synoptic Gospels, for they are so obviously composed of short pieces of material that have been joined together. Among the many forms that scholars identify are parables, miracle stories, and controversy stories. Scholars are also interested in the preexisting forms that Paul and other writers incorporated (and adapted) in their writings. Such materials include the letter form itself, as well as lists of virtues and vices, household codes, hymns, and creeds. The book of Revelation (itself an apocalypse) makes use of multiple forms.

Few contemporary preachers or scholars of preaching practice form criticism as an exclusive approach to a biblical text. Due to reasons associated with studies in oral-aural and rhetorical cultures, interest in form criticism of the Gospels is waning.

C. Interaction with Other Criticisms

1. Redaction Criticism

Redaction criticism began to emerge after World War II and made extensive use of the results of form criticism. The redaction critics sought to account for the biblical documents as we now have them by reconstructing what was happening in the historical circumstances of the communities to whom the documents were written and noting how the ancient authors shaped those documents to influence the communities. Where form criticism is interested in the history of individual forms, redaction criticism focuses on how the biblical authors wove together the discrete pieces of material (as identified by form criticism) to make the new whole document with its distinctive message. For example, the redaction critic might ask, "How did the writer of Mark change a preexisting exorcism story, and how do those changes reveal Mark's purpose in using the story?" The redactors (the biblical authors) were not merely editors who strung together existing materials but were creative theologians. From this point of view preachers are often instructed by noticing how the final authors reshaped earlier materials in order to serve the purposes of the new document.

2. Literary and Rhetorical Criticism

While literary criticism and rhetorical criticism are distinct endeavors, they share the common concern of aiming to describe how the text in its present mode of composition affects the reader or listener (*see* LITERARY CRITICISM; RHETORICAL CRITICISM). The term *literary criticism* refers not to a single approach to biblical exegesis but to a family of diverse approaches (e.g., New Criticism, narrative criticism, reader-response criticism). Where form and redaction criticism were very interested in how biblical materials addressed particular historical circumstances, the literary and rhetorical critics have often had relatively less interest in how the text addressed a community in the past and more interest in the text itself as a mode of communication. Though occasional literary critics altogether eschew interest in how the text addressed ancient contexts and focus entirely upon how the text creates an imaginative world into which the reader enters, most literary and rhetorical critics think that some knowledge of ancient assumptions and history can help us understand the text.

Form criticism intersects with these develop-ments in a way that is promising for preaching. As noted above, the form critics seek to name the ele-ments that are characteristic of the various forms. While the literary and rhetorical critics are particu-larly interested in the biblical documents as wholes, they must also take account of how specific pas-sages contribute to the whole, and how awareness of the whole enriches our understanding of indi-vidual texts. Literary and rhetorical criticism often adapts categories reminiscent of form criticism to discuss individual passages and how these passages function in the document in which the text is found and also in the larger world of consciousness beyond the text. Literary and rhetorical approaches also pay attention to how the elements of the text work together to create the text's effect upon read-ers and listeners (ancient and modern).

3. Studies in Oral-Aural and Rhetorical Cultures

In the last twenty-five years, many biblical schol-ars have come to see biblical worlds as oral-aural or rhetorical in culture (see PERFORMING THE MANUSCRIPT, ORAL/AURAL COMMUNICA-TION). While the form critics spoke of a period of oral tradition, they did not identify the characteris-tics of oral-aural culture, a phenomenon that per-tained during much of the period of the OT. To characterize the world of the NT, scholars increas-ingly use the expression *rhetorical culture*, that is, a community in which oral-aural and written modes of communication mutually influence one another but with written modes still largely serving oral-aural purposes. In rhetorical culture, a written text (such as a letter or a Gospel) is often a prompt for oral performance in the community.

In oral-aural and rhetorical cultures storytellers did not simply pass along stories verbatim (as sup-posed by many form critics) but expressed creativ-ity in retelling the stories for new audiences. Many scholars now conclude that the form critics' view of transmission during the period of oral tradition was too limited. The new scholarship raises the pos-sibility that differences in the synoptic tradition may result not from the Gospel writers intentionally changing wording they found in written sources but because the Gospel writers drew from different storytellers who told the stories differently.

The preacher is advised to approach the biblical passage less from the perspective of print-based cul-ture and more as an oral-aural or rhetorical per-formance expressed in the medium of print. The preacher should read the passage aloud and, even more important, listen to the text as performed on tape or by a live performer. By so doing, the preacher is more likely to experience the text as oral-aural/rhetorical event similar to the ways peo-ple in antiquity would have experienced it. Fur-thermore, these studies remind the preacher that the sermon itself should be oral in character. The sermon is not simply a report on a piece of written sediment from the past, but can do for our time what the storytellers of antiquity did for their times: speak the text and its interpretation in an oral-aural/rhetorical way that gives the story a fresh shape for the contemporary situation.

D. An Approach to Using Form Criticism in the Service of Preaching

Most preachers and scholars of preaching recog-nize values and limitations in both historical-critical methods (e.g., form criticism, redaction criticism) and literary and rhetorical approaches. Moreover, the preacher can integrate insights from studies in oral-aural and rhetorical cultures into aspects of these methods and into preparing the ser-mon itself. An approach to utilizing these ap-proaches in the service of preaching follows. The approach is framed as a series of questions that the preacher might ask of a particular biblical text.

The first two questions are derived from the methodologies of biblical interpretation discussed in this article. The last two questions arise from hermeneutical reflection on the text, especially the hermeneutic of analogy, and presume that what the text asks the community to believe and do is theo-logically and morally appropriate.

1. What form is the passage? If this information is not immediately evident to the preacher, it will likely be available in Bible commentaries and dictionaries and in specialized studies of forms and genres in the Bible.
2. What was the function of the passage in the ancient community (or in the document of which it is part)? The preacher wants to know what effect the text was intended to have on the listening community. This is easiest to determine at the level of the document in which the text appears, and the situation of

the community to whom that document was written. Again, the preacher may be helped in these regards by the biblical commentaries or by the specialized studies of forms and genres such as the ones noted in the bibliography. Oral-aural/rhetorical culture studies may further help the preacher discern how the passage functioned in some performance settings prior to being incorporated into the document, and can often help the preacher sense how the community to whom the document was written might have received the performance of this passage.

3. What are the elements of the passage, and how do these elements help the passage carry out its function? The preacher first wants to identify the characteristic elements of the form. The preacher then needs to describe how the elements work together to help the passage perform its function. The preacher explores the movement of the passage and what happens when that movement takes place in the minds and hearts of the listening community.

4. Does the function of the passage suggest a similar function for the sermon? The minister needs to reflect on similarities and differences in the ancient and contemporary contexts. If the situation of the contemporary community is similar or analogous to that of the ancient community, the function of the passage may suggest a similar function for the sermon. If the situation of today's congregation and world is not similar, or if the passage is theologically or morally inappropriate, the preacher should explore these matters with the congregation.

5. Does the form itself—its characteristic elements and movement—suggest a form or movement for the sermon? If the function of the passage does suggest a similar function for the sermon today, the preacher can, of course, simply explain the function of the passage in antiquity and how the passage performs a similar function today. However, as numerous writers in contemporary preaching suggest, the preacher might also consider letting the movement of the sermon follow the movement of the form. If the form of the passage does not seem to serve as a direct model for the sermon, the preacher might consider shaping the ser-

mon so as to achieve a similar effect as the text though through a different literary structure and movement. For example, a proverb that seeks to shock the listener into becoming aware of some aspect of God's purposes for human life may be only two lines long. While the specific form may be too short to provide a model for the sermon, the pastor may be able to construct a sermon whose effect is to shock the listening community in a way similar to the shock provoked by the proverb.

E. Examples of Form Criticism in the Service of Preaching

The following discussion uses the five questions just articulated to show form at work. The text under discussion is Ps 13, which the NRSV titles "A Prayer for Deliverance from Enemies."

1. What form is the passage? Psalm 13 is an individual lament.

2. What was the function of the passage in the ancient community (or in the document of which it is part)? Individual laments were composed by people in difficult circumstances. The individual laments her or his situation. Going beyond lamentation, however, the individual turns to God for help in rectifying the situation. The function of the lament is thus to give the individuals an opportunity to express their sorrow to God, to seek God's assistance, and to pledge to serve God when the season of difficulty has passed and the individual is restored. While the lament unflinchingly acknowledges difficulty, it offers the individual hope by reminding the individual that God is present and can restore. In the case of Ps 13, the individual feels beset by unnamed enemies.

3. What are the elements of the passage, and how do these elements help the passage carry out its function? Individual laments typically contain the following elements, all of which are found in Ps 13: (1) opening address to God, Ps 13:1 a, (2) description of the circumstances of difficulty, Ps 13:1 b-2, (3) petition to God for help, Ps 13:3-4, (4) affirmation of trust in God, Ps 13:5, (5) vow to praise God in anticipation of restoration or in thanksgiving for it, Ps 13:6.

4. Does the function of the passage suggest a similar function for the sermon? This psalm could help individuals who are experiencing intense difficulty to name their difficulties and to recognize that they are not alone; God is with them as a source of encouragement and help. Some preachers believe that God can directly intervene and change situations. Other preachers believe that God has more limited power and cannot simply intervene, but that God is constantly present to lure all involved toward restoration. Regardless of the preacher's view of divine power, the sermon can help the congregation confront their difficulties and live in the hope that God is with them to help them make their way through the season of trouble.

5. Does the form itself—its characteristic elements and movement—suggest a form or movement for the sermon? The form does suggest a movement for the sermon. While the sermon (1) is addressed to the congregation and not to God, (2) the preacher could help the congregation identify present circumstances of difficulty, and remember previous situations of distress, and could help listeners name their feelings of loss and fear during such times. (3 and 4) The sermon could help the congregation recognize how God is present during difficulty and (5) could help the congregation commit itself to a life of thanks and faithfulness in response to God's providential presence.

Bibliography: Ronald J. Allen. *Contemporary Biblical Interpretation for Preaching.* (1984) 49–59; James L. Bailey and Lyle D. Vander Broek. *Literary Forms in the New Testament: A Handbook.* (1992); Donald E. Gowan. *Reclaiming the Old Testament for the Christian Pulpit.* (1980); Michael Graves. *The Sermon as Symphony: Preaching the Literary Forms of the New Testament.* (1997); Holly E. Hearon. "The Implications of Orality for the Study of the Biblical Text." *Performing the Gospel: Orality, Memory and Mark.* (2006) 3–20; Werner H. Kelber. *The Oral and Written Gospel: The Hermeneutics of Speaking and Writings in the Synoptic Tradition, Mark, Paul and Q.* (1997); Rolf A. Knierim, Gene A. Tucker, and Marvin A. Sweeney, eds. *Forms of the Old Testament Literature.* 17 vols. (1983ff.); Thomas G. Long. *Preaching and the Literary Forms of the Bible.* (1988); Bruce E. Shields. *From the Housetops: Preaching in the Early Church and Today.* (2000).

FOUR SENSES OF SCRIPTURE
Paul Scott Wilson

The early church devised four ways to mine sacred texts for theological meaning, and these are called the four senses of Scripture. A text may be read for what it says about the historical event it describes, the literal sense; theological doctrine in connection to Christ, the allegorical sense; how life is lived, the moral (tropological) sense; and the next life, the prophetic or soul (anagogical) sense. John Cassian in his *Conferences* took the word *Jerusalem* to mean literally the geographical city, allegorically the church, morally the human soul, and prophetically the heavenly city of God.

These senses undergirded biblical interpretation and preaching for the first fifteen hundred years of the church and beyond. They allowed preachers to discover what can be said about a biblical text. The fall prevented humans from fully comprehending what is written (see Isa 6:9-10), and the four senses were understood to be God's means of restoring to humans the ability to comprehend God's saving purposes. Historically, these senses contributed to the preservation of the OT as Christian Scripture, to the affirmation of the unity of both Testaments, and to the development of systematic theology.

The Reformers affirmed the literal sense as the only legitimate sense of Scripture. Preachers are wise to remember, however, that Luther's and Calvin's literal sense was a late medieval double literal sense, a lower one concerned with grammar and history, and a higher one concerned with God that was primary for preaching. Recent historical criticism affirms only the first, but preachers need both.

Some preachers unfortunately spend most of their preparation time doing historical-critical study and never get to theological and homiletical interpretation. The result can be sermons that do not give life. Preachers have ways of reading Scripture that are distinct from the work of many scholars upon whom they rely. The goal can be to (a) use the best available historical-critical tools to ensure an informed and scholarly reading of the biblical text in its own time, culture, and context, and

(b) use that as a basis for subsequent theological interpretation.

Our age can learn from our preaching ancestors not by copying their allegorical methods but by striving for their theological goals. Preachers rightly never stopped using a moral sense, though it is not acknowledged. When a sermon provides instruction for right living, a moral sense of the text is often invoked. Preachers can learn from the allegorical sense the importance in the sermon of connecting the biblical text to the larger gospel story, and from the anagogical sense the importance of speaking about God's larger purposes. In this way preachers may more effectively and faithfully communicate God, God's action in the past and present, and the promise of God's actions in the future. *See* ALLEGORY, ALLEGORESIS; HERMENEUTICS; HOMILETICAL (THEOLOGICAL) CRITICISM.

Bibliography: John Cassian. *Conferences;* Henri de Lubac. *Medieval Exegesis: The Four Senses of Scripture.* Vol 1. Translated by Mark Sebanc. (1998); James Samuel Preus. *From Shadow to Promise.* (1969); Paul Scott Wilson. *God Sense: Reading the Bible for Preaching.* (2001).

GENRE CRITICISM
See FORM CRITICISM.

GEOGRAPHY
Robert B. Coote

Preaching requires a sense of place and space. The church began as a Jewish sect but gradually cast off prevailing Jewish significations of space, in which the Temple, Jerusalem, and the land of Israel represented centers from which most of the nation had been dispersed. Jesus Christ represented the new center, embodied in churches, congregations, and church heads wherever they might be, and before long also disembodied through a commanding philosophical idealism. Modernism brought both intensification of the church's spatial idealism, through a decentering of authority and a pervasive individualism, and paradoxically, a rediscovery of the specificity of place. The contemporary church's sense of place depends on several factors that go beyond mere issues of land.

Biblical Geography and Mythic Space

Landscape geography played an important role in the history of Palestine and the Fertile Crescent in the biblical period. Both Egypt and Mesopotamia had great river valleys and irrigation agriculture while Palestine lay at the edge of a zone of productive rainfall agriculture. It supported a comparatively small population and was nearly always dominated by outside powers. Imperial supremacy is prominent in the Bible, from the Egyptians, Assyrians, Babylonians, and Persians to the Greeks and Romans.

The main topographical feature of Palestine is its four north-south zones: the Mediterranean coastal plain and foothills, central Cisjordanian highland, Jordan Valley and Dead Sea depression, and Transjordanian tableland. The central highland offered refuge from monarchic oppression; hence, God is called "rock." To come "up" from Egypt was to ascend into this highland. Early Israel formed a village-based society there for more than a century. When the Israelite monarchy emerged during the 11th and 10th cent. BCE, the highland terrain contributed to its continual instability, and most Israelite dynasties were overthrown in a generation or two. The house of David survived longer, in the highland backwater of Judah. Israelite, Samaritan, and Jewish kings or governors rarely controlled the coastal lowland.

The Jordan Valley did not form a social or political boundary before the Assyrian period and rarely afterward. The Jordan as a boundary was probably introduced by the Assyrians and consequently adopted as an administrative and symbolic innovation by the house of David. It played a significant role in the retrospective history of Davidic sovereignty found now in Deuteronomy through 2 Kings. In the 20th cent. it was adopted by the European powers to define the British mandate in Palestine and became an indelible component of the modern image of the land of Israel.

Until recently, it was widely held that the desert played a seminal role in the shaping of the religious and ethical values of Israelites in contrast to Canaanites. This view can still be found in popular works, but most scholars regard it as invalid. ANTHROPOLOGY, ARCHAEOLOGY, LITERARY CRITICISM, RHETORICAL CRITICISM, and the history of scholarship have shown that Israel formed primarily in settled territory, that Israelites were themselves mostly Canaanites, that camels were not used to survive at the desert edge until long after Israel originated, that nomadism as ceaseless wandering never existed in the ancient Near East, that the supposedly formative "wandering" in the desert of Sinai represented, despite its forty-year duration, a migration, that the "return to the desert" envisioned in the Prophets was a negative, not a positive, ideal, and that the notion of the unspoiled desert as the womb of the nation was rooted in the romantic myth of the wholesomeness and purity of the uncivilized.

Political geography distinguishes three levels of sovereignty—local, intermediate, and imperial—and this structure applies to the biblical world. As few people at the local level could read or write documents of more than a few lines, the Bible usually represents the interests and perspectives of the intermediate level, either the government of Jerusalem for the OT or prevailing church authorities for the NT. Because such governments and authorities were concerned about threats to their power from peer opponents, the Bible is filled with texts, both short and long, that justify intermediate powers, privileges, and prerogatives. At the same time, they were concerned about their relationship to both imperial and local sovereignties, and most biblical texts appeal, directly or through selected denunciations, to contemporaneous imperial overlords above and local chiefs, peasants, and other poor people below. In the biblical world, boundaries of sovereignty were extremely variable, contrary to the impression often conveyed by maps of the biblical period. Sovereignty was marked by, among other things, shrines to the sovereign deity, which were established not just at the center of territory held but also at the periphery.

A critical social geography of the biblical world is in its infancy. In the biblical world, social and political identity was universally kin-based, in conceptuality if not always in actuality. Thus, ethnicity was usually conceived in terms of kin, occasionally in terms of locality, and rarely, if ever, in terms of cultural pattern or distinction. This represents a profound difference from modern experience, with implications for preaching in today's world. Interpreters are increasingly aware that modern concepts of state, nation, and culture-linked ethnicity do not apply to the biblical world. However, to represent truthfully the social geography of the biblical world in the face of today's ethnic diversity and multiculturalism has proved difficult.

The construction of temple and cult in biblical Palestine inevitably entailed concepts of symbolic space typical in the ancient Near East, which find clear, if sporadic, expression in the Bible. The temple was founded by God as the victorious storm deity, on a high mountain and over the subdued subterranean sea. At the temple, God presides. From there God supplies the land with fructifying rain, and from there a freshwater stream emerges to refresh the land. Should the temple be destroyed, God can rebuild it by again splitting the great sea dragon and reconstructing God's abode over its remains. The temple replicates the divine palace; on earth the temple sits adjacent to the royal palace, while next to both lies the palace garden, the biblical Eden, planted by the reigning divinity, watered by cosmic springs, and tended by earthly royalty. Perhaps the most complete conceptual geography of Israel is found in the latter part of Ezekiel, especially its last nine chapters, an idealistic account in which some elements of this standard myth are repeated while others are undermined.

Values Inherent in Geographical Settings

In the wake of the romanticizing and politicizing of nature in the 19th and 20th cent., modern interpreters have inherited an assortment of vibrant geographical impressions and associations. Mountains mean fresh water and air, a sublime encounter with the Creator, proximity to God. The desert is the arena of freedom and spontaneity. The seashore connotes the energetic, the liminal, the limitless. Uninhabited or sparsely inhabited nature epitomizes the harmony of God's creation—easier to imagine in the absence of people. Geographical catchphrases bolster political assumptions, as in the United States: "from sea to shining sea," "Mason-Dixon line," "north of the Rio Grande," "Third World," "North-South divide." Some truth resides in all such associations, but a moment's reflection reveals how tenuous they can be. They must be approached critically, without weakening responsible environmentalism and advocacy.

Variable Perspectives of Social and Cultural Location

The contingency of location is a truism of contemporary modern and postmodern consciousness—what you perceive depends on where you stand. The preacher is challenged to hold this insight together with the formulas of faith inherited as universals and absolutes, and together with the experience or expectation of surety that comes with faith. The geographical metaphor—our location in an expansive, complex, and differentiated world—can be the most welcome and effective one for thinking through the implications of inevitable partiality. We become aware of many overlapping locations—wealth, status, age, gender, nationality, ethnic culture, regional background, language, education, family, denomination, and much more. The spatial notion of location encourages us to see ourselves in relation to others, and it puts our place in relative perspective.

Local Context

Geography reminds the preacher to take seriously the particularities of congregation or audience. All local contexts differ from one another in important ways. Every church differs from the one up the street, every neighborhood from the one a few blocks away, every town from the others in the county. Often such differences spring from geographical features: What are the local economy, local demography, local climate, local landscape, local patterns of transport and communication?

The *Stasis* of the Homiletic Argument

There are many kinds of sermons, and only some involve rational argument. Preachers eschew argumentation for its own sake and instead favor indirection, inference, evocation, and invitation. With respect to decision making, they prefer consensus building, and with respect to dispute, avoidance or harmonization. But people of faith are encouraged to reason, and communities of faith are shaped to support people in their disagreements as well as agreements. Nearly all preachers at some point responsibly take a position on a contested issue, while providing a forum for all views to be heard and taking care not to abuse the privilege of the pulpit. The rhetorical concept of *stasis*, the location

where opponents in an argument arrive at a standstill, refers to the focal point of a disagreement, the place where contending arguments directly encounter each other. Insofar as argumentation is a valid means for disputants to move forward, it is essential to identify what exactly is at issue in the dispute to prevent a stalemate. Thinking about the sermon in terms of argumentation is worthwhile even if the sermon does not overtly include an argument, since preachers are as prone as others to let partiality in through the back door. Thinking about argumentation in geographical terms and the importance of different perspectives gives the point at issue the prominence it deserves.

Bibliography: Colin Flint and Peter Taylor. *Political Geography.* 5th ed. (2007); Steven L. McKenzie and Stephen R. Haynes. *To Each Its Own Meaning.* Rev. ed. (1999) 230–306; J. Maxwell Miller and John H. Hayes. *A History of Ancient Israel and Judah.* 2nd ed. (2006) 1–29; Kurt L. Noll. *Canaan and Israel in Antiquity.* (2001); Anson F. Rainey and R. Steven Notley. *The Sacred Bridge: Carta's Atlas of the Biblical World.* (2006).

HERMENEUTICS
Stephen Farris

The *Compact Edition of the Oxford English Dictionary* defines hermeneutics as "the art or science of interpretation, particularly of Scripture, esp. as distinguished from exegesis or practical exposition." Though the word is plural in form, it is usually treated as a singular noun. The primary focus of hermeneutics is the theory that undergirds the EXEGESIS and application of a biblical text, though in practice it is difficult to be precise about the distinction between exegesis and hermeneutics. Hermeneutics, however defined, is about the preacher's central task, namely, interpretation. Indeed, the word *hermeneutics* comes from the Greek verb *hermeneuo* (to interpret).

A. The Development of Hermeneutics
B. Contemporary Hermeneutics for the Preacher
 1. The Preacher's Lenses
 2. The Hermeneutical Circle
 3. Moving from Then to Now

4. The Location of Meaning
5. The Right Use of the Text
6. Transformation through the Text

A. The Development of Hermeneutics

The problem of interpretation may be as old as speech itself. But as long as one could simply ask the speaker, "What do you mean?" there was no need for hermeneutics as such. The problem became real with the advent of writing. Once the author was no longer present to be interrogated, the difficulty of interpretation was raised to a new level. That difficulty became particularly pressing when the writing that needed interpretation functioned as a community's scripture or was understood to be a word from a god or gods. (Hermes, whose name is obviously related to our topic, was the messenger of the Greek gods.) In Christianity also, the Scriptures require interpretation, precisely so that a word from God can be heard from them. For example, the risen Christ must interpret the Scriptures of Israel in the new situation after the resurrection for the disciples: "Then, beginning with Moses and all the prophets, he interpreted to them the things about himself in all the scriptures" (Luke 24:27). Relating the old Scriptures to the new situation may be the right way to describe a form of hermeneutics that is particularly vital for preachers.

In the history of Christian interpretation of Scripture, the church was first compelled to address the challenge implied by the Lukan text, that is, finding the presence of Christ in the OT. It then was challenged by texts, chiefly in the OT but also in the NT, which seemed to violate the insistence that the God made known in Christ is a God of love. (The problem of interpreting "texts of terror" is by no means new.) But hermeneutics is not quite interpretation itself but reflection on the principles, processes, and methods of interpretation, and it is at this point that the practice of conscious reflection on the interpretation of Scripture may be said with confidence to have begun. Reflection of that sort goes back at least to the early 3rd-cent. theologian Origen. The contribution of Augustine of Hippo must also be mentioned. His work, *De Doctrina Christiana*, is sometimes called the first textbook on preaching, but it might also be described as a study of practical hermeneutics. Reflection on methods of interpretation was not only the province of individuals. In classical times, schools of interpreta-

tion emerged, such as the school of Alexandria, which advocated more figurative modes of reading Scripture, and that of Antioch, more literal. Various methods of interpretation were adopted to meet the challenges faced by interpreters. Old Testament figures or events were treated as types of Christ or of events in the Gospels. Problematic passages were interpreted allegorically seeking a higher, spiritual sense beyond the literal. Eventually, a fourfold method of largely allegorical interpretation became common. Though these specific interpretive strategies may not be employed today (*see* ALLEGORY, ALLEGORESIS; FOUR SENSES OF SCRIPTURE), the same challenges remain for the contemporary preacher as, for example, when preaching the OT texts for Advent or when approaching difficult passages such as descriptions of the conquest of Canaan.

With the Protestant Reformation, the need for an appropriate hermeneutics became much more apparent. The Reformers substituted the authority of Scripture itself for the authority of the Magisterium of the Roman Catholic Church. To oversimplify a complex debate, Scripture no longer meant what the church declared; its meaning was to be discovered by faithful readers equipped with the appropriate skills for reading the texts. Once that meaning was discovered, it was to be applied, ordering the doctrine and the life of church and society. The Reformers were concerned with determining not only the right sense but also the right use of texts. The right use of texts remains a preoccupation of preachers to the present day. Furthermore, the Reformers and their heirs affirmed the clarity or perspicuity of Scripture. The texts of the Bible, at least insofar as they teach the way of salvation, are transparent, unambiguous, and coherent. Moreover, this clarity resided not in a higher spiritual meaning discovered by the use of allegory but in the plain and literal meaning of the text. It quickly became apparent, however, that readers could understand these transparent and unambiguous texts in very different ways. In this new situation, reflection on the proper methods and principles of interpretation became a matter of prime importance.

One ought not suppose, however, that hermeneutics was an exclusively theological task in the post-Reformation period. In the same era legal theorists reflected on the proper methods of interpreting statutes and codes of law, and classical philologists sought the right ways of reading ancient Greek and Roman texts. Shortly after the Reformation, it became clear that hermeneutics is the province of scholars in various fields but of critical concern to students and preachers of the Bible. That remains the situation to the present day. Hermeneutics relates closely to almost everything in theology and is also a central concern of many other disciplines. Through and since the Enlightenment, scholars of many fields have contributed to the study of hermeneutics, with their own ends in view. The preacher has much to learn from these studies, but one must confess that the variety of approaches can be daunting to the non-expert. Nor is it only the variety of approaches that can intimidate the preacher. Where hermeneutics touches philosophy or literary theory, its concepts are sometimes couched in dense and difficult prose that may also daunt the preacher. The preacher may not master the technical language of hermeneutics but is not thereby excused from reflection on the processes of interpretation.

B. Contemporary Hermeneutics for the Preacher

At this point it may be profitable to abandon a historical overview of the development of hermeneutics and to turn more specifically to those issues in hermeneutics that most affect the preacher. Certainly, more recent developments in hermeneutics may emerge in such a study. Whether or not preachers can master the various theories of hermeneutics, they must become at least moderately skilled in understanding the processes of interpretation. At the very least, they must understand the interpretive principles they bring to Scripture. All preachers have interpretive principles. It is chiefly a matter of being clear about what they are. In the absence of conscious reflection on such matters, preachers may victimize their listeners with prooftexting.

It is not only fundamentalists who may misuse Scripture; preachers of any sort may force Scripture to say what their presuppositions and prejudices conspire to make it say. The answer to this problem may seem at first sight to be an attempt to put aside all prejudices and preconceptions when reading a text. From the Enlightenment until very recent times it has been assumed that the ideal interpreter of any text is objective and unbiased, bringing no prejudices but only reason to the text. This ideal has been questioned in recent years. An objective reading of texts may be neither possible nor desirable. There may even be an unconscious exercise of power in any reading of an authoritative text. The claim to read Scripture without prejudice or bias may, on this understanding, have been an exercise of power by white male intellectuals who arrogated to themselves the role of arbiters of the meaning of Scripture.

1. The Preacher's Lenses

The reader always brings a pre-understanding to the text. In its simplest form we bring to the task of reading a text some notion of what the text is. We read texts differently depending on what we think the text is and does. For example, we read the Yellow Pages differently from the way we read a novel and, in turn, from the way we read the Bible. We expect different things from each form of reading. Very quickly, however, hermeneutics moved beyond that straightforward point. It was recognized that readers, including preachers, are shaped by their social location, class, race, gender, sexuality, and so on, and their readings are inevitably shaped by their standpoints. Moreover, interpreters stand within a tradition of interpretation. These standpoints function as hermeneutical lenses through which we look at Scripture. Preachers, in other words, practical interpreters of Scripture, have a responsibility to identify the lenses they bring to Scripture. They must consider their social location as interpreters and its effect on their reading of the tradition of interpretation in which they live. All this is a part of a turn to the interpreter and a turn to the context that has been so pronounced a feature of recent biblical interpretation.

The interpreter's social location is not the only lens brought to the text, however. For the purposes of preaching it may be more important to note that certain fundamental notions about the nature of Scripture also function as lenses. Here we may return to St. Augustine and the problem of texts that do not promote love. Such texts, he argued, must be interpreted in light of the *regula fidei*, or the rule of faith, which represents the plainer parts of Scripture and the common understanding of the Christian church. For Augustine, the rule of faith leads to a reading that increases our love for God or for the neighbor and that makes the reign of love draw nearer (*Doctr. chr.* 3.2.2, 3.10.14–3.10.17).

Augustine's lens of love is not, of course, the only possible one. Martin Luther read all Scripture in light of a strong distinction between law and gospel and with a christological lens, seeking that which "pushes Christ" in whom the gospel is made known. In various liberation and feminist theologies (*see* LIBERATION CRITICISM; FEMINIST CRITICISM; WOMANIST CRITICISM), Scripture may be read with a view to the liberation and equality of all human persons. In Latin American theology, for example, Scripture is to be read in light of God's preferential option for poor people. In ecological theology a reader might seek a reading that tends toward the well-being of Planet Earth. Sometimes liberation and feminist critics are accused of imposing an alien ideology on Scripture. The real question is not whether readers and preachers bring a lens to Scripture; it is whether they will allow Scripture to judge the sufficiency of their lens. This brings us to an important concept, the hermeneutical circle.

2. The Hermeneutical Circle

There are several forms of the hermeneutical circle. In its simplest form, the concept of the hermeneutical circle reminds us that one cannot understand the whole of a text without understanding its individual parts nor can one understand the individual parts without the whole. That is to say, one cannot, for example, understand what the whole of a text is about without understanding the individual words; equally, one cannot understand the meaning of the original words apart from their relationship to the entire text. That concept has been extended in several important ways. An interpreter must take certain presuppositions to the text, read the text in light of those presuppositions, and then return to the presuppositions to judge their sufficiency in light of reading the text. Other scholars argue that an element of praxis needs to be included in the hermeneutical circle. Here one is more likely to speak of a community rather than an individual as the interpreter. The interpretive community reads the text, reflects on its meaning, usually in light of some form of social analysis, acts on the basis of that understanding, reflects on the value of the action in light of the text and whatever other theory may be brought to the circle, returns to the text, and so on. It is sometimes suggested that the phrase "hermeneutical spiral" would better describe this process since that suggests the kind of movement that would result from such a process. Christian hermeneutics aims at movement or, more exactly, transformation, a matter to which we must return at a later point in this entry.

3. Moving from Then to Now

Preachers must also develop a comprehensible method of moving from "then" to "now." In precritical times, it was assumed that the meaning of a text then is also its meaning now. By careful exegesis, the preacher determined as nearly as possible the text's sense in its original context and then expounded and applied that sense in preaching. It is possible to understand the sense of a text, that is, to understand all its words and sentences, but not recognize in that text any significance for one's life. A text may be understandable but irrelevant. If there remains a valid distinction between exegesis and hermeneutics, it lies at this point. Exegesis lays bare, insofar as this is possible, the historical sense of the text, and hermeneutics describes the process of naming the contemporary significance of the text. The preacher cannot rest content with only the historical sense of the text. The meaning of a text for preaching is the combination of sense and significance. The process of moving from then to now can be described metaphorically in several ways. With respect to preaching, the metaphor of bridge building is often employed (*see* BRIDGING THEN AND NOW). In more theoretical hermeneutics, one might speak of horizons of the text and of its interpreter. In the process of interpretation there occurs a fusion of horizons. In all this, there is the assumption that the text is an "other." The text has a horizon different from that of the interpreter. It has an independence from the interpreter, an independence that has the capacity to surprise and transform.

4. The Location of Meaning

The preacher must also ask the question, Where does meaning lie—behind, in, or in front of the text? In traditional historical-critical study of Scripture (*see* HISTORICAL CRITICISM), meaning was to be found behind or even underneath the text. Meaning existed in something that happened before the text was composed. It might be found primarily in events that could be reconstructed through a careful study of the history of the development of the text. (It is no accident that the German term used for the various forms of historical-critical interpretation of Scripture, *Geschichte*, actually means not criticism but "history.") The process of determining meaning has sometimes been likened to archaeology, digging back through the layers of tradition deposited in the text to some original reality. The hermeneutical assumption here is that the interpreter is a particular kind of historian. Meaning might not reside in events, however, but in the theological insights of the author or in the adaptation to various life situations of the community that collected, expanded, and preserved the texts. The first task of the interpreter in this understanding is to engage in the most careful historical and philological study of the text possible. That alone is insufficient, however. The interpreter must enter by an act of the imagination, even divination, into the mind of the author or of the community. This act requires a posture of openness to the "other" represented by the text. The assumption that a text means what an author intends it to mean has been strongly challenged in recent decades. Paul Ricoeur has argued that once a text has been written down and the author is no longer available for interrogation, a "surplus of meaning" develops in the text (1976, 29–30). That is to say, there is meaning in the text that the author may not have known was there or that may be developed in the history of interpretation. Nevertheless, the posture of openness to an "other" one encounters in the act of reading is vital for the hermeneutics that can inform preaching.

If meaning is not confined to the intention of the author, it may be found not behind the text but within it. Meaning may reside within the text itself in a narrative world that the text creates and into which the interpreter may enter. In such a hermeneutical understanding the interpreter most resembles a literary critic, observing literary patterns, storytelling techniques, repeated use of symbols, and so on (see LITERARY CRITICISM). Historical questions are likely bracketed out in such an approach. In another key insight, Paul Ricoeur proposed an understanding of the nature of symbols, which may be applied also to the reading of texts. A reader may experience a three-stage understanding. One begins with a childlike "first naiveté," understanding a text as a literal description of reality. Then the reader goes through a stage of "critical distance," noting the problems and discrepancies of the text. Finally, one returns to the text with a "second naiveté," understanding it at the level of symbol and hence deeper meaning (Ricoeur 1967, esp.

349–55; Thiselton 1992, 344–59). This is a way of reclaiming texts that skeptical contemporary listeners may otherwise dismiss. Preachers may even structure their sermons around this very process. There is nevertheless a problem here. Is there a referent outside the world of the text to which the text points? Christianity is an irretrievably historical faith, and the question of a reality in a world outside the text, a world in which the listeners reside, cannot be indefinitely evaded.

Meaning may also reside in a world in front of the text, that is, a world created by the reader or by the reader's interpretive community. Clearly, the preacher's denomination and theological tradition can function as an interpretive community. Meaning is not merely discovered in texts; it is created by the interaction of interpreter and text. Much of the "surplus of meaning" described above is created in this manner. Though the role of the interpreter and the interpreter's community in creating meaning is undeniable, several interconnected questions immediately arise. Is the reader sovereign over the text? Is there any control over the subjectivity of the interpreter? Are there an infinite number of possible readings of the text?

Almost all scholars and most preachers have abandoned the notion that there is only one right understanding of a biblical text. Anything but the simplest text of any sort is polyvalent, and biblical texts are never simple. Indeed, it may be that the very ambiguity of texts creates meaning by provoking the mind to consider many new possibilities. But not all readings of a text are possible. It is impossible, for example, to read the parable of the Good Samaritan as authorizing the reader to hate the neighbor. Such a reading would simply not persuade listeners with any competence in the use of language. The grammar, vocabulary, and syntax of a text, understood in its historical context by interpreters possessing competence in the necessary skills of interpretation, still function as a control, permitting many interpretations but ruling out others. This is not far from the LITERAL SENSE of the text so prized by the Reformers.

5. The Right Use of the Text

To continue to borrow traditional language, preachers ought to consider not only the right sense of the text but also its right use. This brings us close to something vital; study of the Bible as Scripture has a purpose. The Bible is not only the specimen on the slide under the microscope, the thing to be examined through lenses. The Bible itself is a lens and must be used as such. The right use of a lens is not to look at it but to look through it. It is entirely possible to study the writings that make up the Christian Bible out of purely scholarly interest, and the discoveries of scholars who do so are often of immense value to the people who use the text. There is a greater and more significant truth about the Bible, however. The most important and also the most obvious reality about the Bible is that its writings form the Scriptures of a great world religion. As such, it is used for theological reflection, ethical decision making, education of children and adults, and (most important for our purposes) preaching. In preaching we look through the lens of Scripture to see more clearly God and God's world. The concept of the right use of Scripture therefore remains of first importance for preachers.

6. Transformation through the Text

There still remains the matter of transformation. Some words have so profound an effect that they are the equivalent of actions, changing the state of the speaker or the listener. "With this ring, I thee wed" may be considered a prime example. This kind of language is called performative, and the study of such words and language is called speech-act theory. Not only spoken but also written words can become speech acts. All texts that possess any significance have some effect on the reader, and in certain cases that effect is so life changing that it may be called transformation. The aim of both Christian biblical interpretation and Christian preaching is transformation.

It is questionable, however, if words themselves, either written or spoken, can effect the kind of transformation that is the goal of preaching. In this connection there arises another fundamental hermeneutical question. What does the preacher expect to encounter in the text, a proposition or a person? When reading the Scripture of the Christian church, the effect desired is an encounter with a person. To use trinitarian language, that encounter is with the God and Father of our Lord Jesus Christ through the power of the Holy Spirit. The reality outside the text to which it points as referent is God. The other to which the interpreter must remain open is not simply the text itself but the Holy Spirit who speaks through the text. To turn too easily to the work of the Holy Spirit as an expla-

nation for interpretation is methodologically lazy; to ignore that work altogether is theological folly (see HOLY SPIRIT AND PREACHING; HOLY SPIRIT/PASSION). The goal of Christian interpretation and of preaching is not only understanding the meaning of the text as such, though understanding is always worthwhile; it is a transforming encounter with the other who speaks through the text.

All this clearly relates closely to the interpreter's core theology, particularly the theology of Scripture. If one's theology of Scripture includes the understanding that God speaks through Scripture to address us in our need and our rebellion and to promote growth toward personal and social righteousness, then the process of interpretation is not a one-way street. We do not operate on the text like a pathologist dissecting a corpse. We do not even simply look through it, as through a lens. Nor do we merely interpret the Word; the living Word judges and interprets us. One temptation of hermeneutics, with its concentration on procedures and principles, may be excessively to focus our minds on the human part of interpretation to the exclusion of the divine freedom to address humanity. The reader-preacher is not the only partner in the conversation that is the church's reading of Scripture. The turn to the interpreter and the context must not preclude a turn to God in our reading. Or more precisely, the turn to the interpreter has already been made by God. In most Christian theologies, revelation involves a self-disclosure on the part of God; the sovereign God interprets Scripture and makes the divine self known. For communities that profess such a theology, hermeneutics is always limited. Truly transforming interpretations occur only when the Holy Spirit works through the interpreter and the community. When this happens, however, the walk to Emmaus is repeated. The hearts of listeners burn within when the Word is read and interpreted. See CULTURAL HERMENEUTICS; NEW HISTORICISM; PHILOSOPHICAL HERMENEUTICS; SUSPICION.

Bibliography: Augustine. *De Doctrina Christiana; Compact Edition of the Oxford English Dictionary,* s.v. "hermeneutics"; Ellen F. Davis and Richard B. Hays, eds. *The Art of Reading Scripture.* (2003); Richard Lischer. *The Company of Preachers: Wisdom on Preaching, Augustine to the Present.*

(2002); Donald K. McKim. *A Guide to Contemporary Hermeneutics: Major Trends in Biblical Interpretation.* (1986); Kurt Mueller-Vollmer. *The Hermeneutics Reader.* (1997); Paul Ricoeur. *The Symbolism of Evil.* (1967); Paul Ricoeur. *Interpretation Theory: Discourse and the Surplus of Meaning.* (1976); Anthony C. Thiselton. *New Horizons in Hermeneutics: The Theory and Practice of Transforming Biblical Reading.* (1992).

HISTORICAL CRITICISM
David L. Bartlett

Historical criticism is the practice of reading the Bible with a view to reliable manuscripts and translations, original forms, sources, author/editor intentions, historical settings, and culturally conditioned meanings. It is an essential foundation for biblical preaching in helping to establish what a text does and does not say.

A. What Is Historical Criticism?
B. A Brief History of Historical Criticism
C. Modes of Historical Criticism
    1. Philology
    2. Textual Criticism
    3. Source Criticism
    4. History of Religions
    5. Form Criticism
    6. Redaction Criticism
    7. Rhetorical Criticism
    8. Social Scientific Criticism
    9. History of Effects (*Wirkungsgeschichte*)
D. The Advantages of Historical Criticism for Preaching
    1. The Inevitability of Historical Criticism for Preaching
    2. The Value of Historical Criticism for Preaching
E. Drawbacks of Historical Criticism for Preaching
F. Guidelines for the Use of Historical Criticism in Preaching
G. A Model of Preaching from a Historical-Critical Perspective

A. What Is Historical Criticism?

The distinguished NT scholar and Lutheran bishop Krister Stendahl provided a kind of mission statement for historical criticism: "From the point of view of method it is clear that our only concern is to find out what these (biblical) words meant when uttered or written by the prophet, the priest, the evangelist, or the apostle—and regardless of their meaning in later stages of religious history, our own included" (Stendahl 1962, 422).

Historical criticism is not so much a method as a strategy that employs a variety of methods. The goal of the strategy is to understand as thoroughly as possible the meaning of a text in its original historical, social, and religious context. Early and eager practitioners of historical criticism often refer to their task as the "scientific study of the Bible," and their hope is clearly to follow the model of the sciences: propose a hypothesis, test it on the basis of the evidence, and seek to win broad consensus from other biblical "scientists."

B. A Brief History of Historical Criticism

There is general agreement that the Renaissance's interest in returning to classical sources and the Reformation's insistence on the right of the individual or the congregation to interpret Scripture without approval from a centralized church authority helped pave the way for historical criticism.

However, historical criticism in its full attention to the study of the original context of biblical material was a child of the Enlightenment. Not without considerable opposition, a number of Enlightenment philosophers, historians, and philologists sought to bring the same criteria of rationality celebrated elsewhere in intellectual circles to bear on the study of religion and in particular the study of Scripture.

Not surprisingly, much of the Enlightenment agenda in biblical studies—from the first day until now—was focused on trying to recover either the true history of Israel (for OT scholars) or the true biography of Jesus (for NT scholars).

In England in 1695 John Locke wrote *The Reasonableness of Christianity, as Delivered in the Scriptures* and sought to distinguish the true and necessary preaching of Jesus and the apostles from the accretions of later dogma. A number of rationalist Christian scholars and Deists followed in Locke's wake.

More thoroughgoing historical analysis of the NT emerged in Germany in the mid-18th cent. in the work of J. S. Semler (d. 1791) and J. D. Michaelis

(d. 1791). Semler states the goal of biblical scholarship: "An interpreter ought not to interject anything of his own ideas into the writing he wishes to interpret, but to make all he gets from it part of his current thinking and make himself sufficiently certain concerning it solely on the basis of its content and meaning" (Kummel 1972, 66). Semler sought to distinguish Scripture (which is human) from the Word of God, which speaks through Scripture. Michaelis tried to determine what books were genuinely canonical, by which he meant genuinely written by an apostle, and ended up with a canon much reduced.

Herrmann Samuel Reimarus (d. 1768) was a near contemporary of Semler and Michaelis. He was the first scholar who sought entirely to separate the teaching of Jesus from that of his followers. Jesus was entirely a Jew and entirely to be understood in the Jewish context. Ideas of atonement and redemption were foisted onto his story by later believers (Kummel 1972, 89–90).

The father of OT historical criticism was J. G. Eichhorn (d. 1827), who wrote a three-volume introduction to the OT in which he employed the canons of humanistic scholarship to try to put the OT writings in their original context (McKim 1998, 312–31).

In the 19th cent. the two great exponents of a historical-critical approach to the NT were David Friedrich Strauss (d. 1874) and Ferdinand Christian Baur (d. 1860). Strauss (Kummel 1972, 120–27) was the first to argue that the bulk of NT material was "mythical"—the result of the poetic impulse of early believers (Kummel 1972, 128–43). That is, the NT did purvey a number of viable spiritual truths, but it did not convey "real" history.

Baur undertakes a historical-critical understanding of the development of the church. For him the book of Acts represents a fairly late attempt of the author to reconcile Paul's and Peter's quite different visions of Christian faith (McKim 1998, 287). In that book the conflicting tendencies of Jewish Christianity (represented by Peter) and Hellenistic Christianity (represented by Paul) are brought together. Behind this development of the church—sometimes far behind it—lies the purer moral teaching of Jesus, not yet sullied by the arguments of faction or dogmatics.

In OT studies perhaps the most influential 19th-cent. critical scholar was Julius Wellhausen (d. 1918). Wellhausen began with textual study and proposed the still-prevalent four-source theory of the development of the Pentateuch. He combined his textual study with historical reconstruction to write a major study of the history of Israel, *Prolegomena to the History of Israel* (1878), considered from a historical, not a dogmatic, perspective. Wellhausen's near contemporary in England, Samuel R. Driver (d. 1914), began his scholarly work as a philologist whose work has influenced the teaching of biblical Hebrew to this day. He then wrote *An Introduction to the Literature of the Old Testament* (1891), which presented the results of historical criticism, including the source hypothesis, to English-speaking people in a way that combined both rigorous scholarship and evident piety.

Albert Schweitzer (d. 1965) stands as a kind of bridge between the 19th and the 20th cent. in NT studies. In his book *The Quest of the Historical Jesus: A Critical Study of Its Progress from Reimarus to Wrede* (1910) Schweitzer argues that the quest for the historical Jesus always reveals more about the one who does the seeking than about the one who is sought. In that sense he seeks to bring an end to the kind of historical self-confidence of his predecessors. At the same time he does sketch a vision of the historical Jesus as one who is thoroughly apocalyptic in his preaching and self-understanding. In this way Schweitzer seeks even more thoroughly than his predecessors to place Jesus in the social and religious context of his own time.

Throughout the 20th cent. historical criticism was the foundation of biblical studies at most mainline universities and seminaries in Europe and North America, and by the mid-20th cent. this was true for both Protestant and Roman Catholic schools.

The varieties of historical criticism multiplied as the century progressed. The next section of this article discusses some of the manifestations of historical criticism practiced in the 20th and into the 21st cent.

C. Modes of Historical Criticism

1. Philology

The most widespread and inescapable use of historical criticism is translation. From Jerome's Latin translation of the Greek and Hebrew texts in the 4th cent. through the most recent revision of the New Revised Standard Version Bible biblical scholars depend on historical criticism. They study the variety of usages of a word within the canon, but they range far beyond the canon to discover in a whole range of ancient literature clues to the appropriate translations for any word or phrase or paragraph. Translators of Hebrew texts rely not only on extra-canonical Hebrew literature but on the study of a whole range of cognate languages, and translators of NT texts have to consider the possibility of Aramaic traces or Latin loanwords. In this sense every student of the Bible from the most secular to the most literal depends utterly on historical criticism.

2. Textual Criticism

Most modern translations of the Bible are the work of committees pondering "critical" texts, which are also the work of committees. The more contemporary NT translations are all translations of a NT text that never existed in antiquity but that represents the educated hypotheses of scholars trying to determine in a multitude of cases which ancient manuscript most likely has the most accurate reading. The job of the text critic is to look at the remarkable number of variants in Hebrew, Aramaic, or Greek texts of Scripture and to decide which is most likely close to the (also hypothetical) original. Again no preacher of any theological commitment can do without this paradigmatically historical-critical research.

3. Source Criticism

Critical study of the Pentateuch was transformed by the work of Julius Wellhausen who argued that the canonical Pentateuch had been woven together from four sources, a Yahwist (J), an Elohist (E), a Deuteronomic (D), and a Priestly (P) source (1878). From that day until now OT scholars have argued about the sources and composition not only of the Pentateuch but of the historical writings and the Prophets—most notably Isaiah and Jeremiah.

In NT studies the two-document hypothesis posits that Matthew and Luke had two primary sources for their writings, Mark and a hypothetical document called Q that consisted mostly of sayings material. Scholars have also suggested that the Fourth Gospel, Mark, and Acts are edited versions of earlier sources.

4. History of Religions

As scholars became more aware of the variety of religious options in the ancient world, studies of such disparate topics as Near Eastern enthronement rites, Gnosticism, and the Isis and Osiris cults of Egypt were used to find analogies that could help explain the origin and function of religious practices both in Israel and in the churches.

5. Form Criticism

Among OT scholars Herman Gunkel led the way in moving beyond the question of literary sources for the biblical books to ask about the oral traditions—songs, stories, legends, sagas—that preceded the written text (McKim 1998, 487–91).

Drawing on Gunkel's insights Rudolf Bultmann and Martin Dibelius were the most influential pioneers of NT form criticism (Kummel 1972, 330–41). They asked two questions. First, what were the different forms of oral literature that lay just behind the written texts of the Gospels? Second, what *Sitz im Leben* (setting in life) accounted for the transmission of such literary forms? They were engaged not in a quest for the historical details of the life of Jesus, but in a quest to reconstruct the social practices of the early church. In what circumstances did Christians tell miracle stories or relate tales of Jesus' controversy with his opponents?

6. Redaction Criticism

Redaction criticism was both an extension of form criticism and a corrective to its single-minded emphasis on the creative role of early communities. Redaction critics asked about the creative, theological work of the authors of the Gospels. The evangelists were no longer seen largely as collators of earlier material but as creative redactors with particular perspectives. In NT studies Matthew and Luke provided particularly fertile ground for redaction criticism since there was general agreement that part of what they had done was to edit and reinterpret the material in Mark (and Q). However, there are also important redactional studies of Mark and John, somewhat trickier because they depend on first reconstructing the sources and then discussing the redaction of that hypothetical material. Recent work on Isaiah in its present canonical form is an example of a kind of OT redaction criticism. How has an editor brought together the material, and what does this arrangement suggest rhetorically and theologically?

7. Rhetorical Criticism

In NT studies, and perhaps especially in Pauline research, the 20th cent. represented a flourishing attention to the rhetorical practices of the Greco-Roman world in which the NT was written. The forms that orators, letter writers, philosophers, poets, and historians used in non-Christian literature helped to explain the rhetorical function of a wide variety of passages in the NT. Often the discussion of the forms of non-Christian literature shaded over into a discussion of its content. In what way did Paul borrow from the Stoics, for instance, not only the form of his argument but also some of its content?

8. Social Scientific Criticism

As a logical extension of the interest in the history behind biblical texts, many scholars have applied the insights of sociology, social psychology, and anthropology to a study of biblical texts. Some scholars have provided a kind of "thick" description of the social world of various biblical communities. Others have drawn on particular models from the social sciences for a kind of cross-cultural analysis of sectarianism or apocalyptic expectation. Some have been influenced by particular economic and political theories (loosely Marxist) to propose particular ideological agendas behind many biblical texts.

9. History of Effects (*Wirkungsgeschichte*)

The meaning of the term meaning is notoriously slippery, but a number of interpreters of texts have suggested that part of the meaning of a text is not just what it meant originally but how it has been used and interpreted through the years. Certainly, within the context of communities of faith part of the significance of a text is how it has been used through the years. Ulrich Luz has been the most thoroughgoing proponent, including in exegesis a "history of effects"—arguing that sometimes the meanings that a text has accrued through centuries of interpretation enrich its possibilities of significance for present readers and hearers (Luz 2005, 349–69). A sermon on being justified by faith, for instance, may want to ask not just what Paul meant by justification (in each particular circumstance) but what Luther thought Paul meant by it and why. If Luther was wrong exegetically, is he therefore useless theologically and pastorally?

D. The Advantages of Historical Criticism for Preaching

1. The Inevitability of Historical Criticism for Preaching

If we preach from biblical texts, we are stuck with the historical-critical method. It is obvious that the translations we use are the products of centuries of historical-critical work. Less obvious perhaps is the fact that the Hebrew, Aramaic, and Greek editions of Scripture that serve as the source for our translations are also the products of extensive research, scholarly argument, and tenuous consensus. The editions of the Greek NT that we use in seminary classes and that stand behind our contemporary translations are themselves compilations from a variety of early manuscripts. The job of compiling, choosing, and criticizing is done by text critics.

The job of translating depends absolutely on the historical-critical discipline of philology and may be strengthened and deepened by rhetorical or social scientific research as well. How can the translator tell whether Paul is being sarcastic? In part by looking at the rhetorical strategies of other ancient writers. How do we know whether 1 Cor 1:26 should be translated, "Consider your own call, brothers and sisters, not many of you were wise by human standards, not many were powerful, not many were of noble birth," or should be translated, "Consider your own call, brothers and sisters, were not many of you wise by human standards, were not many powerful, were not many of noble birth"? The Greek text makes either translation possible. The translator's decision depends in part on the whole context of 1 Corinthians, but it also depends on hypotheses about the social structure of early Pauline house churches.

Literary readings of texts seek to understand internal structure of the narrative and not the world behind it. Yet even such interpretation requires attention to the history behind the text. The parable of the Good Samaritan loses much of its meaning and all of its power if we are ignorant of the troubled relationship between Samaritans and Jews in the 1st cent.—a historical-critical issue.

Furthermore, for all the useful talk of postmodernity, we are all still modern enough to want to know what really happened. Of course that is a naive question, but it is a naive question driven by the legitimate concern about whether the Bible portrays the relationship of a real God to a real world through the lives and words of real people. More traditional Catholic and Protestant preachers may be bemused by the endless quest to pin down the real Jesus—or the real Mary Magdalene, or the real Judas. But behind the quest lies the inevitable human concern that these texts—and our sermons—are about something beyond themselves.

Put differently, for all the disputatious puzzlements about how God might act in history and what it might mean to say that Jesus Christ is God incarnate, the texts we preach are steeped in both those claims. To be stuck with this God is to be stuck with history, and to serve this Christ is to be stuck with stuff—material, social, psychological, cultural. Historical criticism helps us deal with that.

2. The Value of Historical Criticism for Preaching

To a large extent historical criticism lies behind the sermon as history lies behind the scriptural text. The preacher will want to engage in considerable historical research, but not every insight that helps get us to the sermon belongs in the sermon. With that caveat in mind, here are some ways in which historical criticism helps preaching.

Source criticism can provide insights into the particular tendencies of a text. Sermons on J, D, E, and P seem doomed to failure, but the insight that Gen 1–3 presents two different creation stories from two different sources helps the preacher think about the differences in the texts, about the similarities, and about the fact that whoever put Genesis together thought that the J, E, and P stories belonged together too. The power of the two-document hypothesis (that behind Matthew and Luke lie Mark and Q) is not only that the theory seems to work better than other theories statistically but also that it works better homiletically. To see Matthew and Luke as early interpreters of Mark provides a way into their texts.

Form criticism provides the reminder that biblical texts grew out of actual communities and their practices. Since we preach to communities, a sense of the liturgical and practical settings that helped birth our texts may enrich the way we can understand our own liturgical and practical settings. With the proliferation of books and articles on Christian practices as a clue to the shape of faith we are invited to find in and behind our texts signs of very early Christian practices that could help us reshape our own.

Redaction criticism is an invaluable tool for trying to understand the theological convictions and homiletical strategies of the biblical writers. Those who preach from the lectionary would do well to spend some time before Year C begins studying some of the redactional studies of Luke's Gospel, for instance. Those who are not committed to the lectionary could do a series on one of the Gospels. The series could highlight texts that are key to the claims of that particular Gospel writer. One does not need to fall into the seminarian locution "Mark's Jesus tells us" in order to pay attention to Mark's particular—redactional—way of dealing with Jesus' story.

Rhetorical criticism is a tool for asking the invaluable question, What is the author doing here? Why does Paul argue this way in this text? The comparison with other authors contemporary to Paul helps gives us some clues to the answer to those questions. Furthermore, there is much to be said by letting the rhetorical function of a sermon be guided by the rhetorical function of the passage. What then should we say? Should we let the diatribe style of Rom 6 suggest a similar style for a sermon on that text? Maybe so.

Social scientific criticism helps preaching in at least two ways. Biblical studies that include thick descriptions of ancient communities can provide lenses with which to do thick descriptions of our own communities. Reading the background of a text with care, we are inspired to read the background of our congregations with care. Preaching improves as insight deepens. Biblical studies that draw on anthropological or sociological models of behavior presuppose cross-cultural links. Studies of contemporary social practice provide a lens to help us interpret social practice in the Johannine communities, and then we read our churches through the Johannine texts. The use of models may sometimes depend on overconfident correlation between contemporary status anxiety, for instance, and that of the Corinthians—but preaching takes the same risks.

History of effects helps to bring preacher and congregation into a conversation that long precedes us. The meaning of a text is, in part, the meaning the text has had through the centuries, from the 1st cent. till the 21st cent. Our reading is enriched by knowing about Martin Luther's reading and

Martin Luther King Jr.'s. Our congregations are enriched by realizing that the Christian story does not simply leap from Jesus to us without intermediaries, witnesses.

All the varieties of careful historical-critical methodology have the useful function of checking our hypotheses and reining in our imaginations. Good preaching seldom starts with the commentaries, but the careful preacher will check out his or her insights against the insights of the experts. They will disagree with each other, and the preacher may disagree with all of them, but if that interpretation has never appeared in the long, rich history of exegesis, it may be a sign of extraordinary genius or a sign that imagination has flown a bit too high.

Finally, the historical-critical method is an essential aid to obeying the second half of the great commandment. The obligation to love the neighbor as we love ourselves extends to those who are our neighbors chronologically as well as geographically. We owe it to Paul to try to get what he was getting at, though we will not want or need to say exactly the same thing in our different context. Of course, we will never get him exactly right, but we owe him the attempt to do it as well as we can.

E. Drawbacks of Historical Criticism for Preaching

Professor Mark Douglas suggests that the historical-critical method is like methadone. The method proved exceedingly useful in helping break preachers of addictions to a variety of abusive treatments of the text. But then historical criticism became its own addiction, and preachers got hooked again (pers. comm.).

This suggests one drawback to the historical-critical method as a basis for preaching. Its paradigmatic status may become tyrannical. The historical-critical method can close us off from other methods—literary, liberationist, metaphorical—that also provide for rich readings. And the attention to history may divert attention from the other ways in which Scripture figures God—poetry, metaphor, wisdom, Torah.

A second drawback to preaching in the historical-critical mode is that it may simply misread or ignore the quite appropriate theological, existential, and social concerns of the congregation. Harry Emerson Fosdick famously observed that members of his con-

gregation were not "desperately anxious to discover what happened to the Jebusites" (Crocker 1971, 30). But in some ways that is a question of perspective rather than methodology. Left to themselves, not many congregations care about the Galatians, either. However, if the story of the Galatian churches helps us think about issues of striving and cultural anxiety today, then the Galatians are both pertinent and interesting.

The third drawback is that the easiest way to present historical-critical material is to do so pedantically. Having read the commentaries, we begin to sound like them. Or we assume that the only way to do historical-critical work in a sermon is to do it in a great undigested lump at the beginning. "Let us review all the problems that Paul was having with the church at Corinth, and let us also say a bit about the cultural and economic features of that ancient city."

The fourth drawback is that preaching that attends to historical-critical questions is always open to revision. Preachers who went to school toward the middle of the last century and tried to keep up with the literature started out thinking of the Gospel of John as the most "Greek" of the Gospels and are now cautioned to think of it as the most "Jewish." A little humility in presentation helps. "It seems likely that John's church was facing a feud with the synagogue" is better than "It is now established beyond a doubt that John's church was facing a feud with the synagogue." One can also say that this is part of the fun of the historical-critical paradigm; new evidence provides new exegesis. God is still God, and Jesus is still Lord, but we do not read Romans just the way we read it in 1965.

The insight about shifting historical hypotheses reminds us that while history provides a useful and perhaps even necessary background for our preaching, and a corrective to our wildest guesses, it is not the history behind the text that we preach. We preach the text and the God to whom the text bears witness. We do not need to change fundamental allegiances every time the scholars change their mind about the Epistle to the Romans or revise our christology with each new quest for the elusive historical Jesus. The more we read and the more we preach, the more modest our claims about what Paul really meant—or who the "real" Jesus must have been—but that does not mean that our claims about who God really is or about what Christ does wobble and weaken along the way. For the Reformers *sola scriptura* and *sola gratia* were two ways of saying the same thing. *Sola historia* was never really an option.

F. Guidelines for the Use of Historical Criticism in Preaching

The first guideline is really a question of good faith. All preachers should acknowledge our dependence on historical-critical research. The pretense that we preach the pure Word of God uninterpreted and unfiltered by human scholarship is just that—pretense. We do not have to say this every time we get up to preach, but our overall preaching needs to make clear our dependence not only on the Holy Spirit but on the communion of (scholarly) saints.

The second guideline is that the preacher needs to make the distinction between what goes into the preparation for a sermon and what goes into the sermon itself. In the sample sermon below, the preacher may have some sense of how Johannine studies moved from the work of Rudolf Bultmann to that of J. Louis Martyn, and a fairly clear idea of some of the objections that have been brought to some of the details of Martyn's reconstruction, but that is more than the congregation needs or probably wants to know. It is a matter of judgment how much historical detail needs to go into the sermon in order to make the point. The point, of course, is the gospel exhibited by the text, not the erudition exhibited by the preacher (compare Bultmann 1971; Martyn 2003).

Closely related, if the question is how often one should quote the Greek or Hebrew word in a text in order to make a point, the answer is that one should do so just as often as that foreign word is absolutely essential to making the point. The answer to that thought experiment will be closer to "never" than "frequently." It may be that the only way to preach about *shalom* is to say "Shalom," but that is definitely the exception.

Third, some texts beg for historical-critical exposition in the sermon, while other texts suggest leaving that exposition in the silent footnotes. It is hard to imagine doing a very helpful sermon on many texts in Galatians without having to talk about the controversy about circumcision; but one could preach a good sermon on the talents without a long excursus on the actual monetary value (adjusted for inflation) of five, three, and one talents, respectively.

If the text is about history (1 and 2 Sam), it is a good rule of thumb that the sermon should pay attention to its historical claims. If the text is a poem about shepherding, even if the text is attributed to King David, it is not clear that much of the sermon needs to go into the plausibility of the shepherd boy doing in Goliath with that sling.

Fourth, the greatest advantage of historical criticism is often not in shaping the sermon as in checking it. Commentaries are more useful at the end of the process of sermon preparation than at the beginning. Can that word really mean what you say it does? Who was that king Isaiah was referring to? Closely related to this is the proposal that the best way to do historical-critical reading for preaching is to take on major studies over a period of time rather than hurried reads of six commentaries on Saturday. If the preacher has summertime to read, or a sabbatical, let the preacher read up on Isaiah or the Gospel of John. That way a good deal of the historical-critical work is done before one ever sits down with this text.

Fifth, there is nothing wrong with taking a few sentences before the scriptural reading to set the text in its canonical and historical context for the congregation, so that not all that work happens in the sermon itself. There is a great deal right with having Bible study as a regular part of congregational life, at a time other than the worship service.

Sixth, there really are more and less interesting ways to provide historical information. Preaching uses oral language and relies heavily on narrative. Which first sentence is more promising for a sermon on Galatians? "Paul's letters usually begin with prayers of thanksgiving for the churches, but in Galatians the opening words are not of praise but of astonishment." Or "Paul has been hearing about the Galatians, and is he annoyed." Too many sermons move from flat exposition to flashy application. History, even biblical history, perhaps especially biblical history, can be lively history.

G. A Model of Preaching from a Historical-Critical Perspective

Here are the first paragraphs of a sermon preached at Battell Chapel, Yale University, for the university's Good Friday service on April 10, 1998:

Notice that in John's Gospel, Good Friday is not a tragedy, it's a triumph. In Mark's and Matthew's

Gospel Jesus cries the awful cry of abandonment: "My God, my God, why have you forsaken me?" In John's Gospel he cries the cry of victory: "It is finished," which means, "I did it."

Even the small details play the note of victory. In the other Gospels, the tired Jesus has Simon of Cyrene carry the cross up the hill. In John's Gospel the determined Jesus carries it all by himself. In going to Calvary he does just what he wants to do just when he intends to do it: "It is finished."

J. Louis Martyn has written a good deal about John's Gospel and helps us understand why this journey from Bethany to the top of Calvary is presented without the slightest sign of Jesus' wavering or doubting. When John's Gospel was written, there was a struggle going on in the synagogues of John's community. For years Jews who believed that Jesus was God's Son and Jews who doubted it had worshiped side by side. They worshiped the same God, after all, and there were all those years of shared stories, and shared aunts and uncles. Then there was some kind of crisis, and the leaders of the synagogue decided that followers of Jesus were not good Jews after all, so they excommunicated Christians who were openly Christian, kicked them out of the synagogue.

This helps explain why some of the language about Jewish people in John's Gospel is so intemperate. It was a family feud between one group of Jews and another, and you know how it goes in family feuds. The rhetoric escalates, and charity goes by the board.

The synagogue crisis also helps explain why John tells the story of the crucifixion the way he does. Jesus is a sign of all the good that God promises to those who have the courage to confess Jesus and follow him. Jesus is also a sign of what courage looks like. You may have to give up everything you've cherished to be a Christian (just as Jesus has to lay down his very life). But the wonder is this: that when you are willing to give up everything you will also gain everything—purpose, hope, comfort, confidence—life that is really life.

Look at Jesus. He lost it all; he found it all. The cross, which looked like defeat, was really victory. "It is finished," he cries. "I won." (Bartlett 2003, 124-25)

Implicitly, this sermon depends on a hypothesis from source criticism—that the author of John's Gospel knows and "corrects" the traditions of Jesus' crucifixion represented most clearly in Mark's Gospel. Also behind the sermon lies a fair amount of research on the social setting of John's community as a sectarian group seeking to find its identity over against its Jewish neighbors. In a more unusual move the sermon cites the work of a particular scholar and his reconstruction of the historical setting for John's Gospel. This is in part because Martyn's work has

been central to a kind of paradigm shift in Johannine studies and in part because many in the congregation know Martyn as a friend and neighbor.

The hypothesis about the origins of John's Gospel does at least two things. It provides the opportunity to try to defuse some of what seems to be painfully anti-Jewish in this Gospel. And it provides a social context for the fundamental theological claim of the sermon: on Golgotha God asks everything and gives everything. The rest of the sermon uses that social context to present the stories of Nicodemus, the Samaritan woman, and Jesus' mother and disciple at the foot of the cross as paradigms for the struggles and possibilities of losing and gaining for Christ's sake.

The preacher's hope was that historical criticism illumined not just the world behind the text but the text itself, and through the text, the lives of the members of the congregation. The attempt was to use language that was careful but accessible and not unduly professorial. Though illustrative allusions were drawn briefly from contemporary circumstance, for the most part the stories from John's Gospel carried the narrative movement of the sermon. *See* EXEGESIS; HERMENEUTICS; PHILOSOPHICAL HERMENEUTICS.

Bibliography: David L. Bartlett. *Between the Bible and the Church: New Methods for Biblical Preaching.* (1999); David L. Bartlett. *What's Good About This News?* (2003); Rudolf Bultmann. *The Gospel of John.* Translated by G. R. Beasley-Murray. (1971); Lionel Crocker, ed. *Harry Emerson Fosdick's Art of Preaching.* (1971); Werner Georg Kummel. *The New Testament: The History of the Investigation of Its Problems.* Translated by S. McLean Gilmour and Howard Clark Kee. (1972); Ulrich Luz. "Hermeneutics of 'Effective History' and the Church." *Studies in Matthew.* Translated by Rosemary Selle. (2005) 349–69; J. Louis Martyn. *History and Theology in the Fourth Gospel.* 3rd ed. (2003); Donald K. McKim, ed. *Historical Handbook of Major Biblical Interpreters.* (1998); Albert Schweitzer, *The Quest of the Historical Jesus.* (1910); Krister Stendahl. "Biblical Theology, Contemporary." *IDB.* Vol. 1. (1962) 419–32; Julius Wellhausen. *Prolegomena to the History of Israel.* (1878); Paul Scott Wilson. *God Sense: Reading the Bible for Preaching.* (2001).

INTERPRETATION
See HERMENEUTICS.

LIBERATION CRITICISM
Pablo A. Jiménez

The second part of the 20th cent. saw the emergence of several methods of biblical interpretation that intended to transcend the traditional historical criticism. Liberation criticism is one of those methods. Liberation criticism blends historical, literary, and ideological analysis of the Scriptures. The goal of this method is to place the Bible in the hands of the people, particularly those who are oppressed, highlighting its message of solidarity, freedom, and liberation.

A. Latin American Roots
B. The Latin American Hermeneutic Circle
C. See-Think-Act
D. Hermeneutical Mediation
E. A Correspondence of Relationships
F. Key Contributors
G. Liberation Criticism and Preaching

A. Latin American Roots

Although today authors related to different minority communities employ the principles of liberation criticism, the method originally emerged in Latin America. In the 1960s several South American theologians developed a new theological movement that sought to unmask the ideological forces that kept poor people oppressed and to proclaim God's solidarity with those who suffer. The movement was called liberation theology (Gutiérrez 1973).

From the beginning, the Bible occupied a central place in Latin American liberation theology. On the one hand, the Bible had been used as an oppressive tool in the conquest of America. Christendom, as a whole, employed the Bible as a legitimizing tool for the colonial enterprise. This situation forced the Latin American church to read the Bible anew. On the other hand, oppressed people found a counterhegemonic and, therefore, liberating message in the Bible. Through the new readings of the Bible, it truly became a faithful ally in the struggle for liberation.

B. The Latin American Hermeneutic Circle

Juan Luis Segundo made a decisive contribution to liberation criticism when he developed what is known as the Latin American hermeneutic circle.

This is a heuristic device that attempts to relate the critical reading of reality to the reinterpretation of sacred texts, discerning their liberating message (Míguez 2003). Based on the contributions of Bultmann, Gadamer, and Ricoeur, among many others, the hermeneutic circle links the world of the reader with the world proposed by the text, seeking a fusion of horizons that may further understanding.

Segundo proposed a circle that entails four stages. First is social analysis. The interpreter becomes aware of the way he or she interprets reality. This step requires social analysis, using preferably Marxist categories for both economic and ideological research. Second is critique. The interpreter critiques the ideological superstructure that legitimizes the oppressive system. The economic system develops the ideological superstructure in order to attain, legitimize, and sustain hegemony over the people. The term *superstructure* comes from the particular brand of Marxism developed by Antonio Gramsci. Third is a hermeneutic of suspicion. The interpreter applies a hermeneutic of suspicion, understanding that the traditional interpretation voices a discourse that legitimizes oppression, misrepresenting the liberating message of Scripture. Usually, the interpreter concludes that the traditional interpretation of the Bible has not taken into account important pieces of the data. Fourth is a new hermeneutic. The interpreter develops a new hermeneutic, a new way of reading the text that leads to an appropriation of the Bible in a liberating way (Segundo 1976, 7–38).

Liberation criticism understands that interpreters always come to the text with biases and presuppositions that affect their way of reading the Bible. There is no such thing as objectivity. All interpreters are conditioned by their ethnicity, race, social status, religious background, and sexual orientation, among other situations. Therefore, practitioners of liberation criticism are usually related to a particular oppressed group and come to the Bible seeking its liberating message for their oppressed people.

Although the use of Marxism analysis is indeed polemical, liberation criticism sees it as a useful tool for understanding society. Practitioners of this theological method point out that traditional theologies respond to the interests and values of the dominant classes, those who exert hegemony over others. They analyze society using categories that respond to liberal capitalism. The problem is that these traditional interpreters are blind to their own political commitments. Liberation criticism affirms that those biblical interpreters who claim to be objective or apolitical are either deluded or dishonest. All readings of the Bible are political because they envision a particular way of using power in society. All readings of the Bible are partisan because interpreters cannot extricate themselves from their social and political reality.

The hermeneutic circle is open-ended and evolving. For this reason, some theologians prefer to use the term *hermeneutic spiral*. This means that no reading of the Bible will exhaust the meaning of the text. The biblical text has a "reserve of meaning" that makes its message valid in different historic, social, and cultural settings.

C. See-Think-Act

Another model of biblical interpretation calls the interpreter to engage in a three-tier process (Boff and Boff 1987, 11–21). The first step is the observation and analysis of reality. Once again, interpreters will necessarily use tools for social analysis, preferably Marxist analysis. The second step involves the biblical and theological reflection upon reality, as discerned through the first step. As interpreters judge reality, they will develop strategies to address the social problems that plague their respective communities. The third step is the implementation and performance of specific actions in favor of oppressed persons. After taking action, the observation and reflection process starts all over again.

The see-think-act model is also called the action/reflection method. It calls the church to develop a particular practice of the faith and to reflect theologically upon it. As the hermeneutic circle, this is also an open-ended and evolving process.

Latin American liberation theology prefers the word *praxis* over the term *practice*. They are not synonyms. While any action can constitute a practice, praxis refers to politically aware actions. Ministers engaged in praxis intend to change the oppressive reality, debunking and unmasking the ideological superstructure. Praxis requires a commitment with a community of oppressed people, a commitment to struggle for social, economic, and political change.

In this sense, it is wrong to speak about Jesus' praxis. In spite of his commitment to poor people, Jesus had no access to the contemporary tools for social analysis needed to critique and debunk the ideological superstructure that supports hegemony and legitimizes oppression.

D. Hermeneutical Mediation

Liberation theology understands that God has taken the side of poor and oppressed persons in the world. The life, death, and resurrection of Jesus of Nazareth exemplify God's preferential option for poor people. Therefore, in order to fully comprehend the message of the Bible, an interpreter must either belong to or be in solidarity with an oppressed community. This option for the oppressed gives access to the liberating message of the Bible.

Liberation criticism, thus, reads the Bible from the perspective of poor and oppressed persons (Richard 1988a, 113–33; Tamez 1982, 57–74). Of course, this is not the only possible reading of Scripture. However, it is the preferred one. The goal of liberation criticism is to participate in God's liberating project for society, in particular, and for the world, in general. In this sense, the application of the biblical message is more important than its explanation. Oppressed communities search in Scripture for the strength to continue their struggle for life. For this reason, liberation criticism reads the "Bible in life and life in the Bible" (Mesters 1984, 89–93).

Liberation theology also understands that the message of the Bible is powerful. Scripture can help transform individuals and societies. When such transformation occurs at the personal level, it is called conversion. However, the transformation of society as a whole is a revolution. Here liberation theology affirms the messianic and eschatological character of the Christian faith.

This reading of the Bible relates the Christian story with the story of poor people. In particular, it highlights the political aspects of the death of Jesus of Nazareth, at the hands of the Roman Empire. For this reason, liberation theology celebrates the lives of the modern martyrs who have died struggling for justice against hegemonic and colonial forces.

In general, liberation criticism sees the Bible as an ally in the struggle for life, freedom, and self-determination. However, while some theologians affirm that Scripture as a whole is liberating, others use a canon-within-the-canon approach. The latter method allows interpreters to distinguish between different layers of Scripture. They can deconstruct texts that manifest imperialistic or even sexist tendencies, expounding on the texts that clearly affirm God's option for poor and oppressed persons. Liberation criticism privileges the study of five biblical traditions. The exodus, with its story of liberation from oppression, offers an important hermeneutical key for liberation criticism. The prophets, with their defiant attitude against oppressors, affirm and embolden those who are seeking liberation. The Gospels contain both the anti-hegemonic teachings of Jesus and the story of his assassination by the imperial army. The book of Acts describes the efforts to create a new egalitarian and free community of faith. Finally, Revelation describes in poetic language the struggle of those persecuted for their commitment with a new order of justice.

E. A Correspondence of Relationships

An often neglected aspect of liberation criticism is that it seeks to establish a "correspondence of relationships" between the social location of the oppressed community and the social location of the Bible. This method of interpretation draws a formal analogy between the relationship of the Bible to its social context and the relationship of the Christian community to its own social location (Segovia 1992, 45–46).

Clodovis Boff explains that the model of "correspondence of relationships" goes farther and deeper than the model of "correspondence of terms" (also called "hermeneutics of analogy") employed by traditional historical criticism. The latter seeks to establish the meaning of a biblical concept, the significance of narrative, or even the implications of a historical event based on linguistic correlations. Once a conclusion is reached, the model calls the Christian community to apply these findings (1980, 275).

The many studies devoted to determine whether Jesus was a pacifist or a Zealot are good examples of the hermeneutics of analogy. While some interpreters try to demonstrate that Jesus was a Zealot, others try to prove that he was a pacifist. The implications are obvious. If Jesus was a Zealot, then Christians can participate in revolutionary processes. However, if he was an avowed pacifist, then revolutionary Christianity is illegitimate.

For its part, the model of correspondence of relationships seeks to establish a correlation between the relationships that exist between the different terms of Scripture. The correlation is not between the words of the text, not even between experiences depicted in biblical narratives that may be similar to ours. The correspondence is between the social relations that underlie and therefore shaped the biblical text and the social relations that underlie and shape our experience.

The model of correspondence of relationships—in contrast to the correspondence of terms—does not yield formulas to be copied or techniques to be applied. It is much more subtle in its approach to the Bible. This reading offers orientations, models, types, directives, and inspiration. The aim of such reading is to give us elements to be used as tools in the interpretation of our current reality and the possibilities that the future will bring. The purpose of this reading is to provide part of the criteria that will help us to move along our hermeneutic circle.

Going back to the example provided earlier, liberation criticism concedes that Jesus was not a revolutionary in the contemporary sense. However, Jesus' discourse was indeed counterhegemonic. That is why the occupation army that ruled Judea finally assassinated him. Therefore, although Jesus was not a revolutionary or a Zealot, he did oppose Roman hegemony. His example calls the church to engage in anti-hegemonic practices here and now.

F. Key Contributors

Hans de Wit highlights the contributions of three outstanding Latin American biblical scholars to liberation criticism (2002). José Severino Croatto blended liberation criticism with the European hermeneutic and literary theory. Carlos Mesters' writings exemplified the use of the Bible in Latin American base communities. Finally, Pablo Richard (1988a; 1988b) systematized Latin American hermeneutic theory, emphasizing its theological import.

Although liberation criticism originated in Latin America, different oppressed communities have adopted and adapted its hermeneutical principles, developing, thus, their own methodologies. In particular, liberation criticism attracts theologians and hermeneutists from developing countries, where the church is still dealing with the colonial legacy, and from minority groups in developed nations, where racial-ethnic communities still confront oppression, racism, and discrimination. (*See* AFRICAN AMERICAN BIBLICAL INTERPRETATION; FEMINIST CRITICISM; GENDER, RACE, AND ETHNICITY.)

G. Liberation Criticism and Preaching

The impact of these studies for preaching is clear. For example, Hispanic theology responds to the pastoral needs of the Latino/a people in the United States. Inspired by Latin American theology, Hispanic biblical scholars have developed their own hermeneutic circle (González and Jiménez 2004; Jiménez 1997). It also has four steps:

1. Understanding that marginalization is the entry point. The first step is pondering the social situation of the Latino people in the United States. The experiences of marginalization, oppression, and discrimination endured by the Latino people serve as the point of entry to the liberating power of the Bible. The particular social location of the Latino people makes possible a liberating dialogue with Scripture. When a Hispanic person reads the Bible, he or she finds a message written by and for marginalized and oppressed persons. This grants Latinos and Latinas a unique access to the core of the biblical message.
2. Seeking points of contact. With the above-mentioned social analysis at hand, we then read to seek in the Bible different points of contact between the social location of the Hispanic community and the biblical narrative.
3. Correlating social locations. After finding such points of contact, the model calls us to compare the social location of the Latino community and the social location of the Bible. Justo González provides an excellent example of this methodology in one of his sermons on Josh 4:1-7. Commenting on the narrative of Israel at Gilgal, he considers the reaction of a Canaanite "spy" to the arrival of the Israelite "migrants":

> I can imagine that spy from Jericho running back to his city. We are much bigger than they—so much so, that next to us they look like grasshoppers. But these people have come to stay! Build the walls higher! Close the gates! Call up the army! Or, if it were today, I can imagine the same panic: Close the border! Call the Migra! Require them to have work permits! Apply Proposition 187! These people are here to stay. They are talking about writing their history, about raising a monument for their children, and for their children's children. (1996, 130)

The text does not offer a perfect parallel with the situation of the Latino people. González does not imply that the United States is the promised land—actually, elsewhere in the sermon he clearly says it is not—nor does he imply that the Latino people must take over that land by force. Yet the text gives him the opportunity to establish a correlation based on society's resistance to change. Both the ancient Israelites and the contemporary Hispanics faced forces that opposed their migration to a new land; both groups share a particular social location. On this basis, González explores the measures devised to keep the feared "newcomers" out of the land.

4. Employing key metaphors. Hispanic theology employs different metaphors to communicate the implications of the correlation between the social location of the text and the social location of the Latino community. Such metaphors embody its findings, functioning as a paradigm. In a way, the metaphor summarizes the whole hermeneutical process. Then, the metaphor-turned-paradigm is used to exegete both the Bible and the Hispanic reality. The two key metaphors employed by Latino and Latina theologians are marginality and *mestizaje*. These metaphors evoke the correspondence of relations between the social location of the Bible and the social location of the Latino people discussed above.

Liberation criticism can make a decisive contribution to contemporary homiletics. People who belong to oppressed groups and communities find in these hermeneutical principles solid guidelines for researching, designing, and preaching sermons to those who suffer. Those who belong to dominant groups find in liberation criticism a methodology that challenges their privileged place in society (González and González 1994, 24–29).

Leonardo Boff (1986) asks how it is possible to preach the cross in a continent of crucified people. This question summarizes the challenge and promise of liberation criticism. *See* CULTURAL HERMENEUTICS; SUSPICION.

Bibliography: Clodovis Boff. *Teología de lo político: Sus mediaciones.* (1980); Leonardo Boff. "Cómo predicar la cruz en una sociedad de crucificados?" *Desde el lugar del pobre.* (1986); Leonardo Boff and Clodovis Boff. *Introducing Liberation Theology.* (1987); José Severino Croatto, *Biblical Hermeneutics: Toward a Theory of Reading as the Production of Meaning.* (1987); Hans de Wit. *En la dispersion el texto es patria: Introducción a la hermenéutica clásica, moderna y posmoderna.* (2002); Catherine G. González and Justo L. González. *The Liberating Pulpit.* (1994); Justo L. González. *Santa Biblia: The Bible through Hispanic Eyes.* (1996); Justo L. González and Pablo A. Jiménez. *Púlpito: An Introduction to Hispanic Hermeneutics.* (2004); Gustavo Gutiérrez. *A Theology of Liberation: History, Politics and Salvation.* (1973); Pablo A. Jiménez. "The Bible: A Hispanic Perspective." *Teología en Conjunto: A Collaborative Protestant Theology.* Edited by José D. Rodríguez and Loida Martell-Otero. (1997) 66–67; Carlos Mesters. *Flor sin defensa: Una explicación de la Biblia a partir del pueblo.* (1984); Nestor O. Míguez. "Hermeneutical Circle." *Dictionary of Third World Theologies.* Edited by Virginia Fabella and R. S. Sugirtharajah. (2003); Pablo Richard. *La fuerza espiritual de la iglesia de los pobres.* (1988a); Pablo Richard. "Lectura popular de la Biblia en America Latina: Hermenéutica de la liberación." *Revista de Interpretación Bíblica* (RIBLA) 1 (1988b) 31; Fernando F. Segovia. "Hispanic American Theology and the Bible: Effective Weapon and Faithful Ally." *We Are a People: Initiatives in Hispanic American Theology.* Edited by Roberto S. Goizueta. (1992) 21–49; Juan Luis Segundo, S.J. *The Liberation of Theology.* (1976); Elsa Tamez. *Bible of the Oppressed.* (1982).

LITERAL SENSE
Henry J. Langknecht

The "literal sense" has been a key interpretive category throughout the church's history, though there is neither historical nor contemporary consensus about its precise meaning or application. Embedded within various formal uses of the phrase and also in such idiomatic expressions as "taking the Bible literally" are implicit, habitual, and complex criteria for combining a passage's literal sense with various modes of reference. Most formal historical and contemporary uses of the phrase favor one of five such constructions:

1. Literal sense assumes whatever mode of reference the community customarily considers sensible and authoritative for that passage. This understanding is rooted in the Hebrew plain sense (peshat); is operative in most devotional and non-technical readings; and spontaneously employs whatever theological, cultural, or commonsense filters render the text accessible or relevant.

2. Literal sense assumes direct reference to ostensive historical entities and events. In premodern interpretation this sense was commonly eclipsed by figurative—or spiritual—modes of reference. In its most severe modern form (literalism) this sense eschews figurative reference.

3. Literal sense assumes whatever mode of reference points toward major canonical themes or the Bible's essential subject matter (e.g., for Luther the literal sense reveals Christ).

4. Literal sense assumes the mode of reference intended by the historical human author (the dominant formal understanding of Protestantism since the 19th cent.).

5. Literal sense insists on no fixed mode of reference but refers in whatever way the Holy Spirit guides it through the hearing community. Here we might also include the *double literal sense of history*, which while valuing the grammatical or historical sense adds the stipulation that God may intend or empower new reference in new contexts. (Calvin gave precedent to this meaning.)

There is a further way to understand the literal sense. It is, narrowly and literally, the capacity of the letters (Latin, *littera*) of a text—as arranged into words, syntax, paragraphs, and literary units—to be perceived in intelligible, coherent, and potentially meaningful (Latin, *sensus*) ways. The literal sense establishes (a) a configured world of the text consisting (in English) of entities and their character (nouns, pronouns, adjectives), (b) activity or states of being and their nature (verbs, adverbs), (c) relationships between entities (prepositions, conjunctions), and (d) development of these elements and their interrelation (argument, plot). Although texts are customarily intended by authors and understood by readers to make reference to the real world (the ostensive historical world of people and events or the internal world of ideas and emotions), the literal sense of the text is pre-referential and potentially multi-referential; it is the fundamental configuration from which all reference and subsequent meaning are derived.

In biblical interpretation, it is crucial to distinguish between sense and reference. First, because the Bible is confessed to be God's Word and authoritative Scripture, how it refers to the real world shapes doctrine, attitudes, practices, and preaching. Claiming the literal sense powerfully connotes access to a text's essence—even in traditions where authority is shared between Scripture, tradition, reason, and experience. By insisting that the move from literal sense to reference be as transparent as possible, we have means to hold interpreters to account for clear and consistent meaning and interpretation.

Second, the church reads its Scripture in many settings and for various appropriate purposes (e.g., private devotion, historical or literary study, worship, preaching). Most readings comprise less than the whole canon, Testament, or book, and are sometimes merely portions of verses, so context has considerable impact on the literal sense. The literal sense even of a short reading configures a world of the text and provides a ground for reference—though most would agree that longer readings enrich configuration and strengthen the persuasiveness of reference. Nearly all understandings of the literal sense consider a passage's nested biblical contexts (e.g., chapter, book, author's corpus), though opinions vary as to how much context is necessary and how that context is to be weighted. Many passages taken out of context (that is, their literary context) have been accommodated profitably by the church into contexts where they yield new and often unexpected revelation. Undisclosed assumptions about the breadth, depth, or nature of Scripture's proper context muddle clarity about the literal sense, modes of reference, and textual meanings. Distinguishing sense from reference helps to isolate the assumptions and criteria used in correlating the literal sense with the real world. We can see how these various assumptions about sense, reference, context, and interpretive filters interact by considering the church's deliberation about homosexuality focused on Lev 20:13 ("If a man lies with a male as with a woman, both of them have committed an abomination; they shall be put to death; their blood is upon them").

The pre-referential literal sense of this verse is reasonably clear. Some take the verse as a discrete unit (i.e., considering no broader textual context), take the words *man* and *male* to refer unambiguously to all men in all circumstances, and thereby condemn all male homosexual behavior (even while employing filters that allow "they shall be put to death" to refer hyperbolically to the severity of the offense or metaphorically to eschatological judgment). Some might take the verse as a discrete unit, refer the described *action* directly to today's world while allowing *man* and *male* to refer by analogy to any same-gender couple, thus also condemning female homosexual behavior. Some place the passage into its historical-cultural context and assert that the verse condemns pederasty and therefore does not refer to consensual adult homosexual behavior. Some may place the passage into the historical-literary context of the Holiness Code in Leviticus; consider the code's exigencies (e.g., the need for the Hebrew people to be set apart from indigenous Canaanite practices); honor habitual analogical references (Hebrew people = contemporary Christians; Canaanites = secular culture); and then qualify the reference to homosexual behavior by asserting that the prohibition of a different contemporary secular cultural practice would more effectively honor the sanctifying intent of the code. Still others place the passage into broad canonical context and assert that any condemnation of contemporary actions is chronologically and theologically superseded by such dominant scriptural themes as the prophetic shift from holiness to mercy or Paul's proclamation of our freedom from the law. Some would conclude that the plain sense is clear and contemporary homosexual behavior is condemned because that is how the church has customarily understood the reference from the passage. Each of these various interpretive moves can credibly claim to be the literal sense of the passage.

Interestingly, though no consensus exists in the church about the literal sense of Scripture's literal sense, there is agreement about why the concept is important. First, the literal sense honors that the Bible is a literary text. Even given the wide variety of interpretive practices, the agreed-upon text of the Bible provides a relatively fixed artifact in relation to which conversation about reference, meaning, doctrine, and practice can occur. Because the literal sense includes the Bible's unique elements and the world they configure, it preserves the Bible's express voice in conversation with other sources of church authority.

Second, because the literal sense of the text configures the world of the text by establishing that world's entities, images, relationships, themes, and plots, it constrains—according to the logic appropriate to any given stipulations about context or reference—what the text can refer to and ultimately mean. If the words of the text were different or were configured differently, the reference or meaning derived from even the most fanciful allegorical interpretation would have to be different in some corresponding way.

Third, the literal sense is the Bible's public sense. The church has the right to stipulate how its Scripture is read and interpreted. But the Bible is also a cultural artifact and is read and heard in uncatechized ways in unexpected contexts by those to whom the church must present a persuasive case from the text in real-world evangelism, apologetics, and preaching.

The literal sense's gift for preachers is its focus on the elements of the text and the worlds they configure. Here preachers will find a treasure of vocabulary, imagery, and themes for preaching—and those able to defer or resist habitual reference will find fresh and surprising insight for sermons. The challenge for preachers is to respect the complex assumptions under which audiences hear the text—each exerting influence on hearers' wagers about reference. As preachers strive to be faithful to the influence on the literal sense of theological commitments, customary interpretations, literary context, and history, they may hold supremely to the belief that the church reads Scripture in worship expecting it to refer principally to God, human relation to God, and God's action in our world. *See* ALLEGORY, ALLEGORESIS; FOUR SENSES OF SCRIPTURE; HERMENEUTICS.

Bibliography: Brevard Childs. "The Sensus Literalis of Scripture: An Ancient and Modern Problem." *Beiträge zur Alttestamentlichen Theologie: Festschrift für Walther Zimmerli.* Edited by Herbert Donner, Robert Hanhart, and Rudolf Smend. (1977); Sandra Schneiders. *The Revelatory Text: Interpreting the New Testament as Sacred Scripture.* (1999). Paul Wilson. *God Sense: Reading the Bible for Preaching.* (2001).

LITERARY CRITICISM
Patricia Dutcher-Walls

Literary criticism refers to a wide range of methods that take seriously the literary expression and artistry of biblical texts. Use of these methods can help preachers pay attention to the passages they use for preaching and be aware of their own interpretive strategies in reading those passages.

In the modern era, literary criticism developed as a part of historical-critical study of the Bible that looked at how texts were written in their historical contexts, the faith communities of ancient Israel and the early church. Historical-critical literary methods used a diachronic perspective, studying such matters as the written sources of texts, the forms or genres of texts, the setting and intention of the authors, and editing or redaction by later writers.

Since 1965, influenced by the study of literary method in other fields, literary criticism in biblical scholarship has developed methods that investigate the narrative and poetic artistry of texts, examining such things as plot, character, imagery, emotion, genre, effect, and the like. In contrast to the diachronic (through time) perspective of historical criticism, these literary methods use a synchronic (at the same time) perspective. Passages are treated as having a unity in themselves and are often seen as capable of communicating meaning, independent of history. Some practitioners assume that this meaning is independent of the original (and unrecoverable) intentions of the author. These narrative and poetic methods concentrate on a close reading of texts to observe artistic elements such as structure or characterization and literary devices such as metaphor that help create meaningful and beautiful writing.

In recent decades, various types of literary criticism developed in interaction with fields such as literary theory, structuralism, philosophy, rhetoric, feminist and ideological hermeneutics, and deconstruction. These interactions have produced a wide range of literary methods, for example, some

1. emphasize deep narrative structures underlying a story,
2. question the possibility of specifying one single meaning of a text,
3. identify the ideological commitments that shape authors and readers, or

4. consciously deconstruct the apparent commitments of the author in a text.

As with all critical biblical study, literary criticism has also been influenced by a paradigm shift associated with postmodern perspectives. While many interpreters assume that a text itself communicates a variety of meanings, reader-response criticism says that what any one interpreter finds significant is valid. Clearly, the starting points of the reader and the reading community—their assumptions, faith or doctrinal commitments, and social and political location—need to be taken into consideration.

Practical Implications

For preachers who want to ground a sermon in careful observation of how literary criticism helps discern meaning, several types of questions can guide study of a passage.

1. Literary Features

What does a passage emphasize through its literary aspects? For example, in Isa 40–55, repetition of titles for God (Holy One of Israel, Redeemer, Creator) helps convey the prophet's theology. Such repetition of words and phrases, or even elements like repeated character traits or imagery, is perhaps the best indicator of a passage's key concerns. Other elements that slow down the pace of a passage (e.g., dialogue or accumulation of detail) also help communicate significance. Likewise, elements that catch a reader's attention (e.g., dramatic action, emphatic language, or persuasive argumentation) express a passage's interests.

2. Form and Movement

How do form and movement in a passage add to its impact? Wisdom literature (e.g., Prov) often makes its points through the form of short pithy statements; apocalyptic writing (e.g., Rev) uses imaginative and symbolic formats operating on several levels of meaning. In a narrative, the movement of the plot from conflict to turning point to resolution creates interest and meaning. In a poem, both structured forms (e.g., a judgment oracle) and movement within a poem (e.g., from despair to hope) help express messages that a reader can identify. In a letter format, noting the use of a familiar form can help one understand what the writer communicates.

3. Patterns

Does a passage create patterns or expectations that are then completed or disrupted? The fulfillment or disruption of expectations can work to persuade or dissuade a reader about elements in the passage. For example, after two questioners dispute with Jesus, a scribe agrees about the great commandment (Mark 12:13-34); this sequence favorably highlights both the commandment and the scribe who breaks the expected pattern of controversy. One particular sequence often seen in biblical narrative is that of command-enactment-report. When Samuel commands Saul to utterly destroy Amalek, and Saul's enactment of the command spares the livestock, Samuel's reaction in the report serves to discredit Saul (1 Sam 15).

4. Characterization

How does characterization convey significant interests of a passage? Lacking the fullness of modern character description, biblical narrative nonetheless creates vivid characterization. Phrases of direct characterization (Jesus was "deeply moved" [John 11:33]) are infrequent and highly important. Dialogue carries much of the weight of character portrayal in what characters say and in what is said about them (Ahab said to Elijah, "Have you found me, O my enemy?" [1 Kgs 21:20]). A biblical author's shaping of character is often disclosed by narrative actions ("So Abram went, as the Lord had told him" [Gen 12:4]). Analysis of characterization provides significant insight into a passage's concerns.

5. Gaps

What gaps does a passage leave unexplained? Are there missing explanations or connections? Temporary gaps are made clear later in the passage (What does "the kingdom of heaven has come near" mean [Matt 4:17]?). Permanent gaps are never explained (How does the woman know what God said about the tree [Gen 2:16; 3:2-3]?). A temporary gap helps a writer increase suspense and emphasis, while a permanent gap indicates that the issue was not of concern to the writer or was left open to tease out complexity or ambiguity. In either case, how readers try to fill in an unexplained element helps identify their own presuppositions and commitments, which influence the meanings they find in a passage.

Literary criticism is a basic tool of sermon preparation. Careful literary analysis helps preachers identify the literary elements and artistry of a passage and their own values and presuppositions, all of which contribute to the identification of meaning and significance of biblical texts. *See* EXEGESIS.

Bibliography: Robert Alter. *The Art of Biblical Narrative.* (1981); Yairah Amit. *Reading Biblical Narratives.* (2001); Tom Long. *Preaching and the Literary Forms.* (1989); Paul Wilson. *Practice of Preaching.* (2007).

PHILOSOPHICAL HERMENEUTICS
Eugene Eung-Chun Park

Hermeneutics is an academic discipline that deals with theories of interpretation primarily, if not exclusively, for written texts. Etymologically, the term derives from the Greek god Hermes (Hermēs), who appears in Homer (*Odyssey* 5.28) and Hesiod (*Theogony* 938) as a messenger of the gods to humans. His task is both pronouncing the divine message and interpreting it; hence the meaning of *hermeneia* (hermēneia) as "interpretation" or "translation."

Various rules of interpretation existed in antiquity mostly for religious texts, but it was not until Friedrich Schleiermacher (1768–1834) that the so-called general hermeneutics was conceived as an art of understanding that could be applied to any type of text. For Schleiermacher, the meaning of a text is what the author had in mind at the time of composition, and therefore interpretation is a matter of finding the authorial intent (*intentio auctoris*) through reexperiencing the mental process of the author in composing the text. In Schleiermacher's hermeneutics, interpretation has two stages: grammatical and psychological. The former has to do with the general linguistic analysis, while the latter deals with the specificity of the author as an individual. Even though the reader starts with a given sentence and moves on to penetrate the mental world of the author, these two stages are not strictly linear, but they constantly intersect with each other. Similarly, Schleiermacher speaks of the hermeneutical circle, in which parts are understood only in reference to the whole and vice versa. This inherent circularity in understanding requires intuition on the part of the reader and makes hermeneutics an art rather than a scientific method.

Since Schleiermacher's hermeneutics makes the information about the author's life and historical background necessary for recovering the authorial intent, it became the foundation for HISTORICAL CRITICISM, in which the following exegetical principle is upheld: *sensus non est inferendus sed efferendus* (meaning is not to be brought in [to the text] but to be brought out [of it]). Also called romantic hermeneutics, Schleiermacher's interpretive theory influenced Wilhelm Dilthey (1833–1911), who wanted to formulate an objective and universally valid method of interpretation, and Emilio Betti (1890–1968) and E. D. Hirsch (1928–   ), who continued Schleiermacher's legacy to identify the meaning of the text with the authorial intent. With the presumption of objectivity in historical research in the Enlightenment era, this author-oriented hermeneutics has long been highly influential in LITERARY CRITICISM, legal interpretation, and biblical interpretation.

With the rise of phenomenology and existential philosophy, there was a radical shift in hermeneutics. Phenomenology rejects the Kantian dichotomous notion that the object (*re*) exists out there in the external world independently of the subject and therefore can be observed objectively. Instead, it recognizes that the object can be perceived only as what appears to be (to phainomenon, hence the term *phenomenology*) to the subject, not as what really is (to on) in the language of Plato's dualistic epistemology. All realities should be regarded as phenomena, and these phenomena are the only data from which we can deduce meaning. On the existentialist side, it was Martin Heidegger (1889–1976) who elevated hermeneutics from method of interpretation to an ontology of understanding. He starts with the notion of the irreducible givenness of human existence (*Dasein*) and declares that understanding (*Verstehen*) is a fundamental dimension of *Dasein*, and as such, it is the power to grasp one's own possibilities for being. Since *Dasein* is necessarily historical, understanding is also radically historical/existential. It is always caught up with the concrete situation in which one finds oneself. Therefore, there is no such thing as a transcendental subject who could rise above historical particularities to attain to pure objectivity, nor is there such a thing as pre-suppositionless interpretation.

Understanding happens always in terms of the concrete existential reality, in which the subject encounters the object.

This recognition of the existential nature of understanding is further articulated by Hans-Georg Gadamer (1900–2002) in the form of "philosophical hermeneutics," which is a *terminus technicus* he used in the subtitle of his *Truth and Method* (*Wahrheit und Methode*, written in 1960). In this book Gadamer criticizes the premise of romantic hermeneutics that defines the meaning of a text as a reproduction of the author's mind and the original conditions in which the work was created, and he calls such an attempt a "futile undertaking in view of the historicity of our being." Gadamer says it was not until the Enlightenment that the concept of prejudice acquired a negative connotation. Then he redefines prejudice as a judgment rendered before all the elements that determine a situation have been finally examined and on that basis rehabilitates prejudice as a necessary condition of understanding. In the process of interpretation, the prejudices of the interpreter create certain anticipations that will be affirmed or revised to produce the meaning. This affirmation of the inevitability of prejudice on the part of the interpreter leads Gadamer to regard the hermeneutical event as a dynamic encounter between the past and the present, which is famously articulated as the "fusion of horizons" (*Horizontverschmelzung*). A horizon is the range of vision within which a particular standpoint allows one to perceive reality. For Gadamer, both the horizon of the past and the horizon of the present are always in motion, because the historical movement of human life is never bound to any one standpoint and therefore can never have a closed horizon. Moreover, the horizon of the present is not formed without being connected with the past and vice versa. Therefore, understanding is always the fusion of these horizons.

This recognition of the encounter between the past and the present in Gadamer's philosophical hermeneutics laid the foundation for reception aesthetics and reader-response criticism (*see* READER/LISTENER RESPONSE), which are different versions of the same hermeneutical theory in the late 20th cent. that legitimizes the role of the reader in literary criticism. According to this theory, the meaning of a text is not something that is permanently fixed at the time of composition but is a result of concretization of some potential meanings of the text through negotiation between the artistic pole of the author and the aesthetic pole of the reader throughout the process of reading. Therefore, meaning is not a static entity that can be extracted from the text but a dynamic one that comes into being only when the text is being read. Then every act of reading generates a new meaning. This new hermeneutical movement has been influential and popular in literary criticism, especially in America. On the one hand, it bestows all readers, educated or not, with a liberating power to construe a meaning of the text that is relevant and meaningful to their existential realities, but on the other hand, it causes anxieties about the danger of hermeneutical anarchy. Various theories have been proposed to solve the problem of arbitrariness of interpretation, such as the concept of an informed reader who is equipped with adequate linguistic and cultural knowledge about the text or an interpretive community that provides norms and standards for the range of legitimate interpretation.

From antiquity, hermeneutics has been closely related to religion, as the etymology of the term testifies. Qumran literature, Philo of Alexandria, rabbinic Judaism, and different schools in early Christianity developed distinctive hermeneutical rules for scriptures. In modern times, the rise of historical criticism and its establishment as the primary mode of inquiry in biblical interpretation were, at least, partially indebted to the hermeneutics of Schleiermacher that focused on the authorial intent and the historical circumstances in which a text was written. Schleiermacher's contention that there is no distinction between hermeneutics of sacred texts and hermeneutics of secular texts also helped. With the prevailing notion of EXEGESIS (exēgesis) as the legitimate way of interpreting the Bible by bringing out (ex̂ hēgeomai) the authentic meaning from the text, as opposed to eisegesis (eisēgesis) as a wrong way of interpreting a biblical text by bringing (eiŝhēgeomai) a subjective meaning into it, the basic premises of romantic hermeneutics of Schleiermacher still seem to be upheld.

However, biblical scholars have also been informed of the new insights from philosophical hermeneutics and have thus become sensitized to the issues of the presumption of objectivity and the limitations of one's interpretive perspective. This awareness has led many biblical scholars to reassess the nature and scope of historical criticism. Also the hermeneutical theory that focuses on the role of the reader opened up possibilities for various new interpretive perspectives in biblical criticism, such as DECONSTRUCTION, FEMINIST CRITICISM, LIBERATION CRITICISM, POSTCOLONIAL CRITICISM, and WOMANIST CRITICISM, to mention only a few.

In romantic hermeneutics, there is a sharp distinction between interpretation of the text and its practical application, but according to philosophical hermeneutics of Gadamer, such a distinction is rather arbitrary and application is an integral part of interpretation itself, not an afterthought. The distinction between the exegesis of a biblical text and its homiletical application should perhaps not be drawn too sharply. This does not mean that the exegetical part can be haphazardly subjective. The distance between the past and the present should still be recognized and honored. Ultimately, a good preacher should be able to interpret a biblical text in its own terms and from an existentially defined perspective so that its homiletical outcome may do justice to the biblical text as well as to the preacher and the community she or he is called to serve. *See* CULTURAL HERMENEUTICS; HERMENEUTICS.

Bibliography: A. K. M. Adam. *Faithful Interpretation: Reading the Bible in a Postmodern World.* (2006); Josef Bleicher. *Contemporary Hermeneutics: Hermeneutics as Method, Philosophy and Critique.* (1980); Hans-Georg Gadamer. *Truth and Method.* (1975); Martin Heidegger. *Being and Time.* Translated by John Macquarrie and Edward Robinson. (1962; retranslated by Joan Stambaugh, 1996); E. D. Hirsch. *Validity in Interpretation.* (1967); Richard E. Palmer. *Hermeneutics: Interpretation Theory in Schleiermacher.* (1969); Petr Pokorny and Jan Roskovec, eds. *Philosophical Hermeneutics and Biblical Exegesis.* (2002); Friedrich Schleiermacher. *Hermeneutics and Criticism and Other Writings.* Translated by Andrew Bowie. (1998); R. S. Sugirtharajah. *Asian Biblical Hermeneutics and Postcolonialism: Contesting the Interpretations, the Bible and Liberation.* (1998); Anthony C. Thiselton. *The Two Horizons: New Testament Hermeneutics and Philosophical Description with Special Reference to Heidegger, Bultmann, Gadamer, and Wittgenstein.* (1980); Jane P. Tompkins, ed. *Reader-Response Criticism: From Formalism to Post-Structuralism.* (1980).

SUSPICION
Kenyatta R. Gilbert

Suspicion asks by what authority the preacher's words and interpretation of Scripture should become guidelines for one's speaking and acting. A hermeneutics of suspicion finds entrance into the potential meaning of biblical texts by questioning the authority behind these texts and the assumptions of those who interpret them. Suspicion coincides with understanding, which is intrinsically tied to language and history. Thus, one should be suspicious that certain modes and conclusions in the practice of reading and interpreting Scripture may reinforce oppression, illegitimate uses of power, and unjust social arrangements.

A hermeneutics of suspicion cautions preachers to be mindful about the historical and sociocultural distance that exists between postmodern preachers and past events recorded in Scripture. Here lies the hermeneutical problem. If biblical books had authors whose intentions were to engage specific auditors in their distinct social environments, at what point(s) do postmoderns also listen as intended recipients? Paul Ricoeur affirmed that the meaning of a text is never a function purely of facts about the author and his or her original public (Ricoeur 1981, 139). So the question then becomes, How do these ancient sacred texts speak, and what do they mean for us today?

A hermeneutics of suspicion also insists that Christian preachers take nothing for granted. Accordingly, preachers do not get to delve into the past as disinterested interpreters but unavoidably come to the exegetical and hermeneutical process tainted by presuppositions at the very beginning. Hans Gadamer rightly claimed that some creative synthesis occurs in our attempts at understanding the meaning of texts (Gadamer 2000, 306). We are always connecting our horizon of assumptions, culture, and tradition to the horizon of the text. It is therefore important for preachers to enter the process of biblical interpretation soberly and illumined by humility.

The preacher who goes to Scripture never stands above the Word she proclaims. As a safeguard, hearing communities become lead appraisers of a preacher's message. Postmodern listeners, says Robert Stephen Reid, are highly suspicious of preaching characterized by the three *c*'s—closure, certainty, or control (Reid 1995, 1–13). At the risk of exercising a hermeneutics of suspicion in preaching at least two things will be evident: (1) the task itself will be branded a subjective enterprise, and (2) professed truth claims will always be subject to challenge.

An African American Preaching Touchstone

If one considers the subversive power of symbol and story in African American preaching, one notices the crucial importance of questioning authority behind biblical texts. One could not underestimate the pervasive distrust that blacks had for whites who professed Christian love and liberty, on the one hand, while justifying through Scripture black subjugation and social inferiority as God's will, on the other. David Walker's *Appeal,* an antislavery tract published in 1829, called for slaves to revolt against their masters. Naturally, questions about the misuse of Scripture for Walker were tantamount. Even traditional texts such as Matt 7:12, the Golden Rule, claimed Walker, required reconsideration in light of black life in antebellum America. Because every slaveholder had violated the "do unto others, as you would have others do to you," one scholar notes that Walker rendered the Golden Rule for slaves to read something like this: "Don't take the abuse from others that you would not expect them to take from you." Walker's hermeneutic supplies a significant early source where suspicion and militancy become the means for drastic social change.

Albert Raboteau describes the type of sermon that slaves heard repeatedly:

> You slaves will go to heaven if you are good, but don't ever think that you will be close to your mistress and master. No! No! there will be a wall between you; but there will be holes in it that will permit you to look out and see your mistress when she passes by. If you want to sit behind this wall, you must do the language of the text "Obey your masters." (Raboteau 1978, 213)

As a result, most slaves wanted to hear from their own black preachers. Despite their illiteracy in most cases, slave preachers rejected such idiotic interpretations of the Bible and, through personal magnetism and natural eloquence, possessed the capacity to organize and effectively lead religious communities to become framers and innovators of an indigenous Christianity.

More contemporarily, a sermon preached by Rev. Dr. Jeremiah Wright Jr. reveals the lack of suspicion in many present-day African American churches across the country where the "prosperity gospel" is preached. In a sermon titled "Reclaiming Prophetic Ministry," based on Mark 1:14 and Isa 61:1-4, he invited listeners to ponder the leitmotif of John the Baptist's wilderness preparation as emblematic for prophetic ministry. Juxtaposing his ministry with today's preachers of health and wealth, Wright moves from suspicion to unashamed indictment:

> Today's prosperity preachers count as their claim to fame that they have access to the White House. As Esau sold his birthright for a mess of pottage these folks have sold their souls and their people out for a mess of money. Hush mouth benefits or tax cuts from the President and you get them free and with lock jaw. They can't open their mouths to speak the truth in the presence of such high profile liars. They see no evil and hear no evil . . . look at the victims of Katrina. They see no evil . . . our megachurch ministers hear no truth because the . . . dog can't howl when he's got a bone in his mouth. They have access to the White House but have lock jaw in the process. (Wright 2006, 179)

Not long after this scathing rebuke, Wright's preaching reveals suspicion chastened by a hermeneutics of trust:

> Mark writes: a lone voice crying out in the wilderness preaching the baptism of repentance, and the forgiveness of sins. . . . It is that proclamation which is the final reason it is hard out here for a prophet . . . because of what we have to preach. Proclamation leads one into the process of transformation . . . restoration, wholeness for God's purposes. (Wright 2006, 180)

A Paradigm Shift in Homiletics

The work of Fred Craddock has become synonymous with suspicion. His groundbreaking book *As One without Authority* (1971) outlined his homiletical method of inductive preaching. (*See* INDUCTIVE.) Typically, the inductive sermon forms through a series of anecdotal illustrations that move with minimal abstract reflection to a point at which hearers must draw their own conclusions and make their own decisions. The preacher makes it possible for listeners to actively participate in the creation and affective experience of the sermon. Craddock and others of the new homiletic believed three-point deductive sermons violated the fundamental movement of thought and conversation—"telling too much too soon." By contrast, inductive sermons are shaped by the preacher's existential encounter with the biblical text and his or her recontextualized experience of the text's meaning. For a culture desensitized to the Christian message, Craddock worked out his distinctive approach "to effect a new hearing of the gospel in a culture suspicious of authority." Pulpit authoritarianism has outlived its usefulness for today's visually oriented, socially active pew, says Craddock (Craddock 1971, 56–59, 62). The goal is to enable congregations to participate actively in the movement and meaning of the sermon, and the power of story in effect becomes an evocative medium for revelation. The governing consideration of inductive preaching is "creating an experience," and the primary resource for the sermon is the audience's imagination. But what remains less clear is how new homiletic practitioners define the nature of this experience.

Some attention must be paid to the theology upon which the new homiletic is built. Gerhard Ebeling's new hermeneutic theology undergirds the new homiletic's "turn to the hearer." In contrast to Barth's emphasis that the locus of preaching's authority—and the requisite accountability of the preacher—derives not from the congregation but from the Word of God, which God alone speaks, in Ebeling's post-Bultmannian theology the hearer of the Word is part of revelation. If one uses suspicion, a danger of the new homiletic is that it has no inherent social gospel. One is helped toward more biblically focused preaching, which emphasizes narrative communication and the oral, evocative, and performative power of language. Inductive preaching may indeed prompt a new hearing of the gospel, yet more may be needed.

Preaching Payoffs

There are a number of practical ways that a hermeneutics of suspicion aids preaching. Let us consider some of them. Suspicion (1) supports the preacher's recognition of the importance of context (historical, sociocultural, and ecclesial) and the many complex forces at work in biblical interpretation and proclamation of the Word; (2) helps preachers see sermonic conclusions as acknowledged beliefs that ultimately rest on eschatological hope rather than clear-cut judgment; (3) flouts "spotlight preaching" but upholds preaching viewed as shared experience between preacher and congregation; (4) fosters creative sermon development with its explicit interest in symbol, metaphor, and story; (5) helps preachers establish a useful framework for raising critical questions that involve the biblical, theological, and cultural substratum that orients and gives shape to sermonizing; and (6) urges preachers to appreciate the fact that biblical texts can supply a fecundity of meaning without univocal limitation. *See* HERMENEUTICS; LIBERATION CRITICISM; NEW HISTORICISM; POSTCOLONIAL CRITICISM.

Bibliography: F. B. Craddock. *As One without Authority.* (1971); H. G. Gadamer. *Truth and Method.* 2nd ed. (2000); A. J. Raboteau. *Slave Religion.* (1978); Robert Stephen Reid. "Postmodernism and the Function of the New Homiletic in Postmodern Christendom Congregations." *Homiletic* 20 (1995); Paul Ricoeur. "The Hermeneutical Function of Distanciation." *Hermeneutics and the Human Sciences.* Edited by John B. Thompson. (1981); Jeremiah Wright. "Reclaiming Prophetic Ministry." In K. R. Gilbert, "A Time to Preach, a Time to Cry: An Investigation into the Nature of Prophetic Preaching in Black Churches during the Great Migration Period 1916–1940." PhD diss., Princeton Theological Seminary. (2006).

TYPOLOGY
David L. Bartlett

Typology is a method of comparison between two actions or people or groups of people that traditionally has been used as a way to claim prophecy fulfilled. Typology can still provide an effective way for the preacher to proclaim the relationship between two texts and between what God has done and is doing now. Types allow Scripture to be interpreted by Scripture and may be conceived as echoes or conversations between texts.

A. What Is Typology?
B. Typology in the Bible
  1. Typology in the OT
  2. Christological Typology
    a. Explicit typology
    b. Implicit typology
  3. Ecclesial Typology

C. Typology in Early Christian Interpretation
D. Preaching Typologically Today
  1. Possibilities of Typological Preaching
  2. Problems with Typological Preaching
  3. Guidelines for Typological Preaching
E. Examples of Typological Preaching

A. What Is Typology?

Both allegory and typology are interpretive methods that find behind a text meaning that points beyond the text. The distinction between allegory and typology is not altogether clear. Paul refers to his imaginative interpretation of the story of Hagar in Gal 4 as an allegory (4:24), while he says that in a similar interpretation of the exodus story in 1 Corinthians, he is using "types" (1 Cor. 10:6; "examples," NRSV).

For the purposes of this article, I propose the following distinctions between typology and allegory:

1. Typology compares two real sets of events while allegory compares the real/material/physical to the spiritual/ideal, or the earthly to the divine.
2. Typology compares one feature of each story to one feature in the other: as Joshua entered the promised land as pioneer, Jesus enters heaven as pioneer (Heb 12:2); as in Adam all die, in Christ all shall be made alive (1 Cor 15:22). Allegory compares multiple features. (Note, for example, the different kinds of soil in the explanation of the parable of the Sower, Mark 4:13-20.)
3. Typology moves from past to present or future while allegory moves from immanent to transcendent.
4. Further, often, typology presumes that the second instance is greater than the first (see Rom 5:17).

In NT writings and in Christian preaching, typology has most often been used to draw a line between the OT and Christ, but typology can also draw the line between the OT and 1st-cent. believers.

B. Typology in the Bible

1. Typology in the OT

The story of the exodus and the trip to the promised land function typologically as a word of comfort to the people in exile. Sometimes the promise of return recapitulates the story of the first exodus:

> And the LORD will utterly destroy
>   the tongue of the sea of Egypt;
> and will wave his hand over the River
>   with his scorching wind;
> and will split it into seven channels;
>   and make a way to cross on foot;
> so there shall be a highway from Assyria
>   for the remnant that is left of his people,
> as there was for Israel
>   when they came up from the land of Egypt.
> (Isa 11:15-16; see also Isa 51:9-11; Jer 16:14-15)

Sometimes exodus and return function in a contrasting way. The second exodus will be both like and unlike the first:

> Thus says the LORD,
>   who makes a way in the sea
>   a path in the mighty waters. . . .
> Do not remember the former things
>   or consider the things of old.
> I am about to do a new thing;
>   now it springs forth, do you not perceive it?
> I will make a way in the wilderness
>   and rivers in the desert. (Isa 43:16-19)

Like the first exodus, the second will bring God's people to a promised homeland. But where in the first exodus God made dry land in the midst of the waters, now God will bring forth water in the midst of the dry land. The second miracle both continues and reverses the first (see also Jer 31:31-34).

2. Christological Typology

a. Explicit typology. Jesus provides a typological exegesis of his coming resurrection: "For just as Jonah was three days and three nights in the belly of the sea monster, so for three days and three nights the Son of Man will be in the heart of the earth" (Matt 12:40).

In Rom 5 Paul presents a complicated typological contrast between Adam and Christ; the key typological verses are 18-19: "Therefore just as one man's trespass led to condemnation for all, so one man's act of righteousness leads to justification and life for all. For just as by the one man's disobedience the many were made sinners, so by the one man's obedience the many will be made righteous." First and Second Adam are both compared and contrasted—Christ is other than Adam because he is obedient; Christ is greater than Adam because his obedience overcomes the consequences of Adam's sin.

The passage from Romans implies an eschatological dimension to Paul's typology that 1 Cor 15 makes even clearer:

But in fact Christ has been raised from the dead, the first fruits of those who have died. For since death came through a human being, the resurrection of the dead has also come through a human being; for as all die in Adam, so all will be made alive in Christ. (vv. 20-22)

There are really two typological moves here. The christological move is from Adam as death-giver to Christ as life-giver. The anthropological move is from Christ as "first fruits" of the resurrection to the resurrection of all. In both cases the claim is that Adam prefigures the eschatological redemption that has come in Jesus Christ and that is to come.

In Heb 7, Melchizedek, the somewhat mysterious figure from Gen 14:18-20, is typologically compared both to the Levitical priests and to Jesus. Unlike the Levitical priests, Melchizedek's priesthood is without beginning and without end. As Melchizedek is greater than the Levitical priests, Christ is like Melchizedek but greater yet. He is truly priest forever.

Furthermore, a reading of the whole Letter to the Hebrews suggests that there is an elaborate typological exposition of the story of Joshua in the OT. For those like the readers of Hebrews who knew the OT in Greek, Joshua's name was Jesus, and for Hebrews both the first and the second Jesus replace Moses and lead God's people to the promised rest—only the second Jesus does so effectively and eternally.

b. Implicit typology. One could suggest that the whole theme of messianic anticipation in the OT, in 1st-cent. Judaism, and especially in the NT is itself an example of typological exposition. The great "anointed" king, David, anticipates the greater anointed "Messiah" who will both succeed and surpass his reign.

The NT is full of claims of prophecy fulfilled and of allusions to OT texts. Sometimes the range of allusion is rich enough to suggest a comparison between two different narratives—and thus moves toward the typological.

In Matthew's Gospel, for instance, Joseph, Mary's husband, is typologically related to the Joseph of Genesis. He dreams and interprets dreams; he travels into Egypt. He claims and adopts Jesus, who in some ways typologically reenacts the Moses story, providing a new law on the Mount and leading God's people to redemption.

In John 3:16 where God "gave his only Son," one hears echoes of Gen 22 and Abraham's near sacrifice of his only son. Though the typology is represented here only by an allusion, it provides rich possibility for understanding something of the meaning of God's gift and Christ's death in John's Gospel.

In John 1:51 Jacob and his ladder are cited as types of the Son of Man (see Gen 28:10-17). Jesus here is the means by which God's messages come to earth and human petitions ascend to God. In John 3:14 the story of Moses and the serpent in Num 21:9 prefigures the story of Jesus' crucifixion. The typology works in at least two ways. Jesus will be lifted up as the serpent will be lifted up. Jesus will bring life to those who believe in him as the serpent brought healing to those who beheld it.

3. Ecclesial Typology

Qualitatively, we may want to say that christological typology is the paradigmatic form of NT figurative interpretation, but quantitatively, ecclesiological typology seems almost as prevalent.

In 1 Cor 10:1-6 Paul argues typologically from the children of Israel to the Christians of Corinth:

I do not want you to be unaware, brothers and sisters, that our ancestors were all under the cloud, and all passed through the sea, and all were baptized into Moses in the cloud and in the sea, and all ate the same spiritual food, and all drank the same spiritual drink. For they drank from the spiritual rock that followed them, and the rock was Christ. Nevertheless, God was not pleased with most of them, and they were struck down in the wilderness.
Now these things occurred as types for us, so that we might not desire evil as they did.

In this last verse the NRSV translates typoi—types—as "examples," rightly noting that we have here in part the use of typology for exhortation; those who precede the Corinthians are not only like them, but they also serve as a strong (negative) example. Nonetheless, types they are, because they have participated in the foreshadowing of the sacraments and their participation did not save them from evil, any more than sacramental worship in itself will save the Corinthians.

Galatians 4 includes the elaborate typological discussion of Abraham's two children. The slave child of Hagar foreshadows those who have submitted to the yoke of the slavery of the law. The free child of Sarah foreshadows those who are born according to the Spirit, the Galatian Christians who do not submit to the law and its demands, especially the demand for circumcision.

C. Typology in Early Christian Interpretation

The theological and hermeneutical presuppositions for the development of typology are found in the work of Irenaeus of Lyons (d. ca. 200). Irenaeus holds that the purpose of the whole biblical story is to tell the story of Christ, but he also holds that the OT is an essential part of that story. It is true in itself and in what it prefigures.

For Irenaeus the story of the Bible is the story of God's progressive revelation. It is progressive because it reaches its climax only in Christ and its consummation only in the final age, but it is revelation from Gen 1:1 all the way through (Kugel and Greer 1986, 156).

It is a useful oversimplification to suggest that after Irenaeus, Christian theologians were divided between those who read the OT texts allegorically and those who read the texts typologically. Origen (d. 254) is the clearest representative of the first school, and Theodore of Mopsuestia (d. 428) is the clearest representative of the second (*see* ALLEGORY, ALLEGORESIS).

Theodore's devotion to typology grew in part from his sense that Origen too often neglected the narrative meaning of a text in order to discern its spiritual meaning. Furthermore, Theodore understood that God had so designed the history of the world that time was divided into two eras—the OT and the NT. The OT tells real historical events and needs to be understood on its own terms. Nonetheless, one can also find in those events some foreshadowing of the NT narratives. On the whole, Theodore wanted to stress those typological interpretations that the NT writers themselves discovered in the OT (Greidanus 1999, 92–94; Kugel and Greer 1986, 182–83).

John Chrysostom (d. 407), too, drew heavily on typological interpretations of texts. Chrysostom affirms two theological and hermeneutical claims. First, any text must be understood in its own historical and literary context. Second, the whole reading of Scripture is governed by the central story of

Christ, and therefore, it is appropriate to see in the OT foreshadowing of Christ, both in prophecy and in narrative—in typology (Greidanus 1999, 94–96).

D. Preaching Typologically Today

1. Possibilities of Typological Preaching

One theological presupposition of typological exegesis is that God is the author of history, and like any good novelist, God uses events in ch. 3 to foreshadow events in ch. 11 and uses events in ch. 12 to recall events in ch. 2. Typological preaching bears witness to a coherent canon. The Bible, for all its diversity, tells one story.

The other theological presupposition of typological exegesis is that God is at work in history, and that therefore the events of the remote past (the OT) help us to understand the events of the more recent past (the NT). For the typological preacher, there is the further conviction that God works in history now in ways that both fulfill and surprise our expectations. Both OT and NT provide clues to our present situation and promises for the world's eschatological future.

To stake these theological claims is to begin to answer the question of how and why typological preaching is appropriate for contemporary preachers. Typological preaching can help us to attend to the complicated unity of the canon. Typology protects us from implicit Marcionism. Typology affirms the authority of both Testaments.

Typology also protects us from a kind of biblical balkanization. One of the great gifts of historical criticism is that it helps us to see the diversity of Scripture. One of its drawbacks is that it may seduce us to such affection for the diversity of witnesses that we neglect the One to whom the witnesses testify.

Further, typological preaching at its heart is christological preaching. For all the varieties of types we find in Scripture and beyond Scripture, typological preaching is based on the fundamental christological claim: "Long ago God spoke to our ancestors in many and various ways by the prophets, but in these last days he has spoken to us by a Son, whom he appointed heir of all things, through whom he also created the worlds" (Heb 1:1-2).

Appropriately, these verses form the prologue to the most thoroughly typological book in the NT—and the book as it develops shows not only that God spoke to the prophets in various ways but also that

God acted with God's people in various ways. These OT activities are congruent with God's great christological intent.

There is a further, practical advantage to typological preaching. On many Sundays, typology provides a biblically and theologically coherent way for the preacher to bring together OT and NT texts.

Typological preaching helps, too, in deepening and broadening faith. It breaks down the easy and confused cultural distinction between the "OT God" and the "NT God." Typological preaching lets preachers do what the church fathers and the Reformers urged us to do—to interpret Scripture in the light of Scripture.

Finally, thinking typologically may help the preacher to think imaginatively. Bracket for this week the lectionary decision: which OT text is assigned to go with this NT text. Look at one or the other bearing in mind the richness and diversity of the canon. What other conversations between texts might the preacher suggest?

It may seem at first that typological preaching is doomed by the "modern" inability to think typologically. Yet even in contemporary America we think more typologically than we know. We hear echoes in history. The story of Europeanized America begins with the typological claim that the Massachusetts Bay Colony is a city set on a hill, and for good and for ill, that typological confidence has continued to this day. As this article is being written, both the Iraq War and the debate about its value continue to rage. The debate is partly typological: is this like World War II with the danger being a new Munich, or is this like the Vietnam War with the danger being a new quagmire?

Furthermore, if postmodernity turns out to be a movement and not just an intellectual photo op, we may discover that the richest opportunities for interpretation lie precisely in our freedom to find in one story a clue or a foil to another. That is, if the appropriate intellectual quest is not so much for universal truth as for narratives that interpret us and interpret other narratives, typology provides one way of continuing that hermeneutical pilgrimage.

2. Problems with Typological Preaching

Problems with typological preaching are both theological and practical. Theologically if we always preach the OT texts typologically, we can fall into a more subtle but nonetheless pervasive kind of triumphalism. Sometimes the story of Jacob wounded in his wrestling can lead to the wounds of Christ, and sometimes the story of Moses can lead to the story of the new lawgiver and the better covenant, but the God who is named or adumbrated in these stories is still the real God, and we can diminish their power if we call the congregation to presume that we always tell them as a lead-in to the real story—Part 2: Jesus. Such practice can also be heard to diminish the Jewish faith (see JEWISH/CHRISTIAN PERSPECTIVES).

Similarly, constant typological preaching may suggest that the only way to acknowledge the unity of the canon or to bring OT and NT together is typological. There are other ways to bring together two texts. Note, too, that the line from problem to solution does not always run from OT to NT but sometimes in the opposite direction. How does one deal with what sometimes looks like the total privatization of ethics in the Pauline epistles? Look at Amos.

Often the best way to preach a text is to preach that text. Sufficient to the day is the exegesis thereof. It may be that a sermon on John 3:16 is greatly enriched by a typological reference to Gen 22, but sometimes John 3:16, all tied up with Nicodemus, is enough for one sermon, and then some.

This points to a practical problem with preaching typologically. Given the pervasive complaint that Christians do not know the Bible as we used to, it may be more than one sermon can do to bring people on board both with Abraham and Isaac and with Jesus and Nicodemus.

3. Guidelines for Typological Preaching

Nonetheless, the gifts of typological preaching are sufficiently rich that typology should provide one way in which the gospel is preached. There are guidelines, not necessarily rules, for how typological preaching can best proceed.

Most typological preaching will show forth Christ. The centrality of incarnation for typological preaching was clear in the church fathers. Even in Paul, where typology is sometimes ecclesiological, the underlying assumption is that the past points us to Christ's people as Christ's people.

On the whole, simple typology works more effectively than allegorized typology. Again, if one is preaching John 3:16 in the light of Gen 22, one might stress the giving up of the only son without also drawing analogies between Abraham's faith and that of the church (there are other texts for that) or between the ram caught in the bush and Jesus as the sacrificial Lamb of God. Practically, typology in preaching often works better as allusion or conclusion than as the grounds for an elaborate correspondence.

It is probably better not to overload the oral exegesis of two texts. Preachers should make a distinction between what we put into our preparation and what we put into our sermons, but certainly when dealing with two texts, one should not overestimate the historical-critical curiosity of the congregation.

Usually, the best texts to preach typologically are themselves typological. It is hard not to preach Isa 43 without reference to the exodus story, and it is impossible to preach Rom 5 without attention to Gen 2–3.

Typological preaching presupposes the importance of both narratives or figures in the typology. The "real" meaning of Moses' story is still in part the story about Moses, not just the way in which Moses' story is continued and transformed in Christ.

In preaching typologically, the preacher should pay attention to the canonical, historical, and cultural context of each text. Do not preach all this, but think about it. Know what Isaiah was doing in Isa 7:14 as well as what Matt 1 was doing with what Isaiah was doing (*see* HISTORICAL CRITICISM).

There is considerable biblical precedent for preaching typologically about the community of faith as well as preaching about Jesus. Both 1 Corinthians and Hebrews use the children of Israel as types for which the church is anti-type; therefore, there is biblical precedent for using the Corinthians as type for your own congregational anti-type. Indeed, in some ways the presupposition of most preaching is typological, and in most cases we and our congregations are the anti-type. Even the most orthodox christocentric sermon tends to move beyond the person of Christ toward the reasons why Christ is important for me, or for us, or for the contemporary world.

So the rules of typological preaching become a guide for most preaching. Be fair to the text in its original context. Be open to analogies. Do not take on too much, or at least do not talk about everything you have taken on. Avoid too much allegory (too many comparisons). Preach Christ.

E. Examples of Typological Preaching

Here is a brief list of typological strategies used in actual sermons.

One of the most clearly typological sermons I have heard drew on John 1:51 and Gen 28:10-17. The conclusion to which the sermon drove was that for the Gospel of John, Jesus Christ is Jacob's ladder. He is the means by which God condescends to dwell with humankind and by which humankind is lifted up into the presence of God. The sermon worked reasonably well in a seminary setting. It would be harder if the preacher had to take time to explain both the Jacob story and John's Gospel at length.

A sermon on John 3:16 and Gen 22 worked better for a more general congregation because the preacher could simply tell both stories as part of the sermon and suggest ways in which the gift of God's Son was an anti-type of—fulfillment and surpassing of—the near sacrifice of Isaac.

A sermon on Rom 5 simply took Paul's typology head-on. The first and most complicated part of the sermon talked about the ways in which we still use representative figures in our time. Then the sermon dwelled briefly on Adam's disobedience and at greater length on Christ's obedience. The sermon was tough going for preacher and congregation alike, but Rom 5 is also tough going, and once in a while it may be all right for a sermon to ask everyone to think hard.

A sermon on Isa 43:16-19 talked about Isaiah's use of typology without using the term. With a nod to Irving Berlin, the preacher said that God's refrain in this text is: "Anything I can do, I can do better." The sermon moved from the new exodus to the communion table and the new covenant.

A sermon on Elijah's distress in 1 Kgs 19:1-18 used a double typology. The preacher moved from Elijah's distress to Martin Luther King Jr.'s distress when opposition to his ministry grew especially threatening to the less dramatic difficulty of members of the congregation keeping faithful during tough times.

Countless sermons use biblical communities as types for which our congregations are anti-types. Every preacher has preached to contemporary Corinthians who love the former preacher far better than the present one, and to Galatians who are striving mightily to show some fleshly mark of their worth before God. Implicitly, these are all typological sermons.

Good typological preaching is not easy, in part because preachers and congregations do not easily think typologically. For those who seek biblical models for the homiletical task, typology provides an intriguing model for showing both the consistencies and the surprises of the biblical story. *See* CHRISTOLOGY; ECCLESIOLOGY; WORD OF GOD.

Bibliography: David L. Bartlett. *Between the Bible and the Church: New Methods for Biblical Preaching.* (1999); Sidney Greidanus. *Preaching Christ from the Old Testament.* (1999); James L. Kugel and Rowan A. Greer. *Early Biblical Interpretation.* (1986); Paul Scott Wilson. *God Sense: Reading the Bible for Preaching.* (2001).

PART 2 INTRODUCTION: LITERARY FORMS

John M. Rottman

Literary forms or genres are typical patterns of written communication that conform to recognizable conventional patterns. The Bible contains a variety of such literary forms: history writing, praise, lament, letters, apocalyptic, prophecy, law, proverbs, and parables are among those most broadly recognized. Admittedly, categories of classification are somewhat arbitrary. Mike Graves identifies such minor forms as genealogy, diatribe, and speeches as those important in NT studies, but unworthy of extended treatment (1997, xviii). Whether a particular form constitutes a form in its own right or stands as a sub-form of a broader one is debatable, but the presence of distinct literary forms in the Bible seems obvious. The key issue for preaching is how the form of the biblical text relates to (1) the meaning of the text and (2) the form of the sermon.

Ignoring matters of form portends trouble. At the level of exegesis misidentifying or ignoring the form of the preaching text threatens to derail the sermon at the onset. For instance, if a sermon uses Prov 22:6, "Train children in the right way, and when old, they will not stray," and preaches about God's promises for parents, the preacher has misidentified the form of the preaching text. Such a sermon misidentifies this proverbial wisdom form as a promise. As wisdom, Prov 22:6 means only to observe a general creational pattern, one in which a child's ways of behaving tend to be set at a young age and persist into adulthood. The text makes no promise, but when preached as if it does, it leaves parents of errant children wondering what they did wrong or why God has not been faithful. In such a case, the form of the text figures prominently in determining the misguided content of the sermon.

Another example of insufficient attention to the form of the preaching text comes when the preacher supposes that attitudes or activities described in narrative texts are normative for the contemporary hearer. For example, the preacher might choose 2 Sam 6 and observe that David dances in his undergarments ("a linen ephod") before the Lord, concluding in the sermon that one's undergarments are the proper dancing attire for contemporary liturgical dancing. Such exegetical moves misidentify a historical narrative form as an example story. Misidentifying or ignoring the form of the preaching text risks sending the sermon off into confusion early in the preparation process. Respecting the form of the text is part of the initial exegetical process.

HISTORICAL CRITICISM has been instrumental in helping preachers see the importance of form in the biblical text. FORM CRITICISM in particular looks to identify oral and literary forms that preceded the biblical text in its final form. Particularly in the Gospels, form critics seek to identify the *Sitz im Leben* in which smaller parts of the text such as collections of sayings or parables might have been used and preserved. Their efforts have helped preachers to see forms within the biblical text that might not otherwise be immediately obvious. But once identified, the precise nature of the relationship of the form of the text to the form of the sermon still remains to be specified.

Prior to the emergence of the new homiletic in the late 1950s and 1960s, rhetorical considerations largely dictated the form of the sermon. (*See* RHETORICAL CRITICISM.) The actual form of the biblical preaching text influenced the form of the sermon very little, if at all. If the preaching text were a narrative text like the prodigal son from Luke 15, the parable story would not necessarily even be retold in the sermon. The sermon would simply make three observations about the parable, usually three points. Those observations were typically ordered not according to their appearance in the story but according to their perceived strength as arguments. The second strongest point came first, the least strong came second, and the strongest was offered last. No matter what the text, the sermon typically came packaged in three or so points. Those points in some respect or other derived from the content of the text, but the text's form hardly came into it. Only when the preaching text offered an additional point beyond the usual three might the form of the sermon be affected.

With the rise of the new homiletic, a new appreciation for the integral relationship between form and content arose. Scholars sensed that the form of the preaching text ought not to be extraneous to the sermon, but they struggled to articulate exactly what the relationship between the two might be. There was some early appeal to the suggestion that the form of the text ought to follow the form of the sermon. Some recommend, for example, that narrative sermons ought to take a narrative form. Although there is an initial plausibility to this tactic, one encounters problems when trying to generalize this relationship with respect to other biblical forms. For instance, a sermon using a proverb as a preaching text needs to be something more than proverbial in form with respect to its length and to the extent of its explanation.

Hans Frei was particularly instrumental in prompting preachers to treat narratives as more than sources for propositional truth. Although Frei himself was interested in narrative not as a genre but as a category of witness, his work inspired preachers to take narratives themselves seriously as an avenue for ushering readers/hearers into a world in which they could be shaped and formed (1974). Charles Campbell teases out some implications of Frei's ideas for post-liberal homiletics. He points to the value of the gospel forms "that render the identity of Jesus of Nazareth, who has been raised from the dead and seeks today to form a people who follow his way" (1997, 190).

All those who have thought more deeply about the relationship between the form of the biblical preaching text and the form of the sermon recognize the pitfalls of making too easy of an equivalence between the form of the text and the form of the sermon. They have tried to articulate the nature of this relationship in various ways. Thomas Long, for instance, proposes that the sermon ought to unfold in such a way that the focus of the text, what the biblical text is talking about, also be the focus of the sermon. He further specifies that the function of the text, what the text does, also needs to be done by the sermon. He says that "what the text intends to say and do governs what the preacher hopes to do and say in the sermon" (2005, 108). Said another way, the preacher extends the impact of the text into the sermon (1989, 33). Here the rhetorical function of the form of the text comes into play because certain forms are designed to do certain things better than

other forms (1989, 26). Along similar lines, Graves advocates that the mood of the text or series of shifting moods associated with the text, its emotional impact, be replicated by the sermon (1997, 20). He further enjoins that along with the mood, the sermon ought to say what the text is saying and do what the text is doing (1997, 18). He calls this "form-sensitive" preaching (1997, 22).

While these suggestions offer helpful direction, they also point to certain questions in specifying the relationship between sermon form and the form of the text. Texts themselves, of course, do not focus on anything, even though those who wrote them did. Furthermore, preachers consistently disagree about the precise focus of particular texts. Texts are multivalent. Even after identifying a possible function of the text in its historical setting, the preacher may still be left wondering whether the function identified is the right one, or whether that text still functions or ought to function in the same way for contemporary listeners. Since the text does not stand alone, how does that larger form to which it belongs impact what is said about its particular form?

Speaking about the function of a text may gloss over a fair bit of complexity. Texts do not function apart from a human producer or user of the text. Neither do they have moods or authorize anything by themselves. To complicate the problem still further, the church has recognized the hand of God in the biblical text, both in its initial composition, its canonical shaping, and in the ways that the Holy Spirit prompts the preacher to use it to speak God's word in the sermon.

Perhaps one way to move beyond these complexities is to recognize that every preaching text is, in fact, a text fragment. Taking this approach, the most basic preaching text is the whole Bible and not some part of it. Arguably, if a preacher calls upon a particular text fragment to guide the form of the sermon without taking Scripture as a whole into account, difficulties can ensue.

Suppose the preacher were to choose Eccl 10:19 for the Sunday sermon: "Feasts are made for laughter; / wine gladdens life, / and money meets every need." At first glance the text seems to advocate or authorize a hedonistic life-style. Of course on most readings considered within the context of Ecclesiastes, this text does not advocate hedonism at all. And certainly as a part within the whole of Scripture, the text cannot finally be read to authorize a libertine ethic. But speaking only of what an isolated text authorizes or how it functions stands in danger of giving inadequate attention to the whole Bible as it functions within the community of faith to inform the meaning, shape, and function of the sermon.

The Bible as a whole is read by the church as revealing a God who created a very good world, saw it fall into sin, and responded by moving to save, restore, and redeem it. The Bible tells the story of a world in trouble and infected by sin, and how God comes to rescue those who could never rescue themselves. In this approach, the sermon form needs to mirror this broad sweep of Scripture. It needs to move from fall to redemption, from captivity to liberation, from wilderness to promised land, from cross to resurrection, from dying with Christ to rising with him. In short, the biblical text as a whole prescribes the form of the sermon. In this sense the Christian gospel itself has a form, and if this is true, the form of the gospel could be said to take precedence over the form of the biblical text in finally shaping the sermon (Wilson 2007, 39–53, 157–83). Like Scripture as a whole and in its major themes, the biblical text authorizes the sermon to move from trouble to grace. (*See* THE FOUR PAGES OF THE SERMON.)

The contributions to this section seek to assist the preacher in seeing how a particular genre or form within the biblical text necessitates particular exegetical insights in pursuit of constructing the sermon. *See* NARRATIVE FORM; STYLE.

Bibliography: Charles Campbell. *Preaching Jesus.* (1997); Hans Frei. *The Eclipse of Biblical Narrative.* (1974); Mike Graves. *The Sermon as Symphony: Preaching the Literary Forms of the New Testament.* (1997); Thomas G. Long. *Preaching and the Literary Forms of the Bible.* (1989); Thomas G. Long. *The Witness of Preaching.* 2nd ed. (2005); Paul Scott Wilson. *The Practice of Preaching.* 2nd ed. (2007).

❖   ❖   ❖   ❖

APOCALYPTIC
David Schnasa Jacobsen

Apocalyptic texts pose interpretive problems for the preacher. The strange symbolic language of beasts, fire, and mysterious numbers set in narratives that blur the lines between heavenly and earthly realities makes them problematic for contemporary proclamation. Although some less scrupulous preachers use apocalyptic texts uncritically to point to contemporary events as harbingers of a literal end of the world, most contemporary North American preachers choose to remain silent about them because of their strangeness or the violence they portray.

Any homiletical silence about apocalyptic texts must contend with a Bible that contains various apocalyptic materials. Although Dan 7–12 and Revelation represent the only full-blown biblical apocalypses, apocalyptic scenes and motifs appear in other canonical writings, especially in the Synoptics (Matt 24; Mark 13; Luke 21) and in Paul's letters (1 Cor 15; 1 Thess 4–5). Moreover, the core proclamation of the Christian faith, Jesus Christ crucified yet risen, centers on an apocalyptic motif: the resurrection of the dead. Therefore, whether out of pastoral concern for the effects of literalistic misinterpretation on parishioners or out of a need to rearticulate core apocalyptic traditions, preachers require ways of faithfully preaching such texts.

The problem is not new. Within the canon there are attempts to temper overconfidence about apocalyptic timetables (Mark 13), modify end-time expectations (John 11:24-26), and even reframe Jesus' imminent return (2 Pet 3:8-10). Competing ways of proclaiming apocalyptic faith continue into early Christianity and beyond. Some, like the 2nd-cent. Montanists, held to a literal view of end-time scenarios. Occasionally, such views resurfaced in fiery sermons like Savonarola's preaching in Medici Florence or the Millerites' in 19th-cent. North America. Others, however, interpreted apocalyptic texts figuratively. Augustine, for example, viewed apocalyptic texts like Mark 13, which urged people to watch for signs of Jesus' return, as inculcating in hearers the virtue of patience.

With the rise of historical-critical approaches to biblical texts, the problem sharpened. Although the precise historical referents of bestial symbols and numbers in Daniel and Revelation proved difficult to ascertain, scholars clearly grounded these texts in the historical contexts that produced them. Yet if the meanings of apocalyptic texts were closely bound to specific historical contexts, the homiletical question remained open. How might they continue to mean something to hearers today? (*See* APPLICATION.)

Lately, homiletical approaches have developed along three lines: liberationist, translational, and Barthian/post-liberal. Despite their differences, all three have developed in response to challenges posed by the historical-critical interpretation of apocalyptic texts.

A. Liberationist
B. Translational
C. Barthian/Post-liberal

A. Liberationist

The liberationist approach argues that the most fitting interpretations of apocalyptic texts today come from analogous historical contexts of oppression. Although Elisabeth Schüssler Fiorenza and Pablo Richard represent this view in biblical scholarship, preachers like Allan Boesak in South Africa embody it in the pulpit. For them, bestial forms of evil that apocalyptic texts decry in their own historical context find fitting resonance among those who struggle today against evil in its many guises: racism, sexism, and economic or political oppression. Liberationist interpretation does not hide the fact that apocalyptic texts were a word for communities in an earlier context of oppression, yet that word in context offers a typological analogy for interpreting today. In his sermon "The Finger of God," Boesak links the metaphor of God's finger from Exod 8:19 to the revelation of the rider "Faithful and True" on the white horse in Rev 19:11. He then uses that metaphor typologically to illumine a revelatory moment where corruption was exposed in 1970s apartheid South Africa:

> And it will get far worse. As did the pharaoh, government officials will harden their hearts and they will refuse to listen until the rider on the white horse appears. What we are seeing now is the beginning of God's judgment on those who have long-trampled his righteousness underfoot.
> Believers see: this is the finger of God! But they see yet more: they see the rider on the white horse, the Lord, the Kyrios, the victor. It is he who rises above the powerlessness of his people and strikes the enemy with the judgment of his mouth. (Rogers and Jeter 1992, 157).

Boesak's words represent no end-of-the-world literalism, but envision typologically the transformation of an oppressive order by God's intention for justice.

B. Translational

A second approach to preaching apocalyptic texts relies on the possibility of translating their claims into contemporary thought and language. This finds its contemporary roots in the work of Rudolf Bultmann. Bultmann argued that mythological elements of ancient worldviews could not be represented plausibly in a scientific world. For this reason, Bultmann proposed to "demythologize" biblical texts by shearing them of their pre-scientific worldview and subsequently "remythologize" in terms of existentialist self-understanding. Bultmann's translation approach sounds like this in his sermon on Mark 13:31-33:

> Whether this end be near or far, the terrible thing is really not that our surrounding world will pass away, but that we ourselves who are framed and enclosed by it are frail perishable mortals; that our lives will reach their term, when heaven and earth will in any case pass away for us, even though they continue to subsist for a time as far as coming generations are concerned. (Bultmann 1960, 239)

Nonetheless, one limitation to Bultmann's view is an individualism that ensures that much of what is meaningful in apocalyptic texts is "left behind."

In the 1980s homiletician David Buttrick offered an important corrective to Bultmann's overly individualistic translation. For Buttrick, apocalyptic texts proclaim a theological structure: an "old age" passing away and a "new age" emerging in our shared consciousness. It sounds like this in his sermon on the Holy City in Rev 21:

> Now, do you want to know a secret? *Making new: that's what's going on in the world*; that's what's happening. The Holy City is not future perfect, it's present tense. (Check out the Greek verbs in the text!) Now the Holy City is descending. Now God is making things new. Right now God is wiping tears and easing pain and overcoming the power of death in the world. Now! There's nothing otherworldly about the vision; it's happening now in the midst of our worn, torn, broken world. (Rogers and Jeter 1992, 163f.)

In the late 1990s this author sought to translate apocalyptic texts into contemporary understanding with greater variety than Buttrick's single structure, old age/new age. The argument was that apocalyptic texts allow at least three ways of understanding ourselves theologically in a social-symbolic world: "destruction" of an old social order, "creation" of a new social-symbolic world, or "maintenance" of a world. By doing so, it was hoped preachers could account theologically for an even greater diversity of apocalyptic texts.

C. Barthian/Post-liberal

The Barthian/post-liberal option proceeds from a decidedly different starting point. Instead of trying to translate apocalyptic texts into modern worldviews, those who adhere to this approach argue that modernity is the problem. With Barth, they view "the strange world of the Bible" positively. For them, the proper conversation partner for apocalyptic texts is not a broadly conceived contemporary "world" in terms of which hearers need to understand, but the church. This church/Scripture relationship is foundational for preaching apocalyptic texts.

In the 1980s homiletician Tom Long contended that the content and form of apocalypses work to undermine in their own communicational context any settled understanding of "world." Apocalyptic texts are designed to guide hearers to make the fantastic realms of the heavenly world and the earthly world we know (including the liturgy and context of early Christian communities) "mutually interpretive." Long's sermon about the troublesome seven bowls of wrath of Rev 16 exemplifies this. Although we may be tempted to domesticate the seven bowls with theological moves that translate divine wrath into a "slap on the wrist" or a "dab of castor oil," Long wants hearers to allow the pouring out of the bowls to unsettle our context:

> It is in response to these cries that John speaks the word of our text. It is—and can only be rightly heard as—a promise from beyond all human time to the prayers of victims for whom the passing of time only confirms their fate and deepens their hopelessness. The God of the hopeless hears their cries and stirs in heaven. A loud voice from the messengers of unyielding mercy, "Go and pour out on the earth the seven bowls of the wrath of God." (Rogers and Jeter 1992, 137)

For Long, the apocalyptic symbols possess a performative force in their own context that can be partially replicated in our own.

Larry Paul Jones and Jerry L. Sumney echo similar themes in their work. Although they argue for a historical-critical view of apocalyptic texts and against uncritical literalism, they share the view that a contemporary church community experiencing an exile of being "out of sync" with the world is most likely to hear and understand apocalyptic's radical claims. Recently, a more thoroughgoing post-liberal position has been articulated in the work of Charles Campbell. He views Revelation in particular as an example of "resistance literature." The goal of a sermon on such a text is to form the church into a community of resistance. For Campbell, preaching has no need to translate an apocalyptic text for the sake of a broad, worldly understanding of its meaning. Instead, sermons on apocalyptic texts exist to form God's people, the church, in discipleship.

Of course, these approaches are not exhaustive. Yet despite these promising approaches, the above questions about analogous situations of interpretation, the possibility of translation, and the issue of the strange otherness of apocalyptic texts remain. Still, something unites all those who struggle with such questions. For all there is a call to proclaim anew a gospel that begins with decidedly apocalyptic news: "He is risen!" *See* ESCHATOLOGY.

Bibliography: Rudolf Bultmann. *The Word and the Beyond.* (1960); David Jacobsen. *Preaching in the New Creation.* (1999); Dorothy Jonaitis, O.P. *Unmasking Apocalyptic Texts.* (2005); Larry Paul Jones and Jerry Sumney. *Preaching Apocalyptic Texts.* (1999); Cornish Rogers and Joseph Jeter, eds. *Preaching through the Apocalypse.* (1992).

APOCRYPHA, DEUTEROCANONICALS
Peter W. Flint

Apocrypha is a plural word (singular: *Apocryphon*) that literally means "hidden or secret writings," which were to be read only by initiates into a given Christian group. The term was eventually used for works that were similar to biblical books in content, form, or title, although not accepted into a particular canon of Scripture.

Defining the Apocrypha/ Deuterocanonicals

In the most common, narrow sense, Apocrypha denotes the seven books and parts of two more books that appear in Roman Catholic Bibles but not in Jewish or Protestant ones: Tobit, Judith, the Additions to Esther, the Wisdom of Solomon, Ecclesiasticus, Baruch (including the Letter of Jeremiah), the Additions to Daniel, 1 Maccabees, and 2 Maccabees.

These books were included in the Septuagint (Greek Bible), but were not accepted by the rabbis who finalized the Jewish canon or by the church leaders who fixed the Protestant canon during the Reformation. For Catholics and Orthodox Christians, however, these writings qualify as Scripture and are known as the deuterocanonicals (i.e., belonging to a second canon).

In a less common, broader—and more ecumenical—sense, *Apocrypha* can include further ancient books found in the Bibles of various Orthodox churches. When these books are included, the term *Apocrypha* may be more broadly defined as "Jewish works of the Second Temple period that are excluded from the Jewish Scripture but are included in the OT of some but not all churches."

For those who accept the Apocrypha as Scripture—and call them deuterocanonicals—these books carry the same authority as other biblical books. For Protestants, too, the Apocrypha can be helpful; Martin Luther recommended that they be read "for edification." Moreover, the common lectionary includes some apocryphal passages in its weekly roster of Sunday texts. For biblical scholars and clergy, the Apocrypha/deuterocanonicals should be especially important because they cover the years and events between the OT and NT.

Apocrypha/Deuterocanonicals in the Traditional Sense

1. Tobit (4th or 3rd cent. BCE) relates the sufferings of the pious Jew Tobit in Nineveh and raises the issue of theodicy, the vindication of God's justice. Among other events, the angel Raphael, disguised as a human, tells Tobit's son, Tobias, how to cure his father's blindness.

2. Judith (2nd or 1st cent. BCE) deals with the military and religious crisis facing the Israelite town of Bethulia, which was besieged by the Assyrian army and its general Holofernes. Judith, a God-fearing woman, makes herself beautiful in order to gain access to Holofernes, who desires to sleep with her. But Judith beheads the Assyrian general, which throws his army into panic. Bethulia is thus rescued from disaster.

3. Additions to Esther (2nd or 1st cent. BCE). These are found in the Greek (Septuagint) translation of Esther, but not in the Hebrew. Addition A (before Esth 1:1) concerns Mordecai's dream and a plot against the king; Addition B (after 3:13) details the king's letter authorizing Haman to destroy the Jews; Additions C and D (after 4:17) present the prayers of Mordecai and Esther in the face of imminent destruction of their people, and describes Esther's reception by the king; Addition E (after 8:12) gives the contents of Artaxerxes' decree favoring the Jews after Haman was hanged; and Addition F (after 10:3) describes how the deliverance of the Jews from Haman fulfills an earlier dream of Mordecai, and closes the book with a postscript.

4. The Wisdom of Solomon (ca. 40 CE or earlier) was written in Greek by an Alexandrian Jew in praise of wisdom, or Sophia, which is portrayed in feminine terms. The reader is exhorted to uprightness; the life of the wicked is described, as well as the destinies of the righteous and the wicked. The book places much emphasis on King Solomon's prayer for Wisdom and his love of Wisdom, which is a gift from God. The work and presence of Wisdom are then described, from Adam to the exodus and the crossing of the Red Sea.

5. Sirach (ca. 180 BCE; prologue ca. 132 BCE). Also known as Ecclesiasticus or the Wisdom of Jesus ben Sira, this book of wisdom was widely used in antiquity in educational and instructional settings, and was copied many times in its Hebrew and Greek forms. The fifty-one chapters of Sirach combine the learning of Israelite wisdom traditions with the law of Moses found in the Torah, placing emphasis on the "fear of the Lord."

6. Baruch (between 200 and 60 BCE) purports to be a letter sent by Baruch, Jeremiah's scribe, from exile in Babylon to the priests and people of Jerusalem. Three originally independent compositions—a prose prayer, a wisdom poem, and a poem of consolation—have been joined together and given an introduction. Baruch 6 contains the Letter of Jeremiah (4th to late 2nd cent. BCE), which is addressed to the Jews deported to Babylon by King Nebuchadnezzar, most likely in the first exile of 597 BCE.

7. The Additions to Daniel are in three sections (all 3rd to 2nd cent. BCE). The Prayer of Azariah (= Abednego) and the Song of the Three Jews while they were in the furnace are inserted between Dan 3:23 and 3:24. Susanna (ch. 13 of the Greek version of Daniel) details how Daniel rescued the

beautiful and godly woman Susanna after she had been unjustly accused by two elders who tried to seduce her. Finally, Bel and the Dragon (ch. 14 of the Greek version) highlights Daniel's opposition to idolatry and the priests of Bel, and relates how he killed a great dragon that the Babylonians worshiped.

8. First Maccabees (late 2nd or early 1st cent. BCE) describes the origin and course of the Maccabean revolt against the oppressive Syrian king Antiochus Epiphanes. Initiated by the Jewish priest Mattathias, the revolt was carried on by his five sons and grandson. The family came to be known as the Maccabees (literally hammerers; see 1 Macc 2:4) and also as the Hasmoneans. The Maccabees are portrayed as God's instruments in retaking Jerusalem and bringing about Jewish independence.

9. Second Maccabees (124 BCE) furnishes important details for the events leading up to the Maccabean revolt, and follows the subsequent exploits of Judas Maccabeus, leader of the revolt, until 161 BCE, when he defeated the Syrian general Nicanor.

CONQUEST NARRATIVES
Jeffrey S. Rogers

Few sequences of biblical narrative appear to have fallen any farther out of favor in the pulpit than the conquest narratives in the book of Joshua. Historical-critical and archaeological investigations have eroded confidence in these narratives' picture of a comprehensive conquest of the land. Sociopolitical interpretations have soundly criticized the ethnocentrism, militarism, and nationalism reflected in them. Horrific modern examples of genocide, ethnic cleansing, and wartime atrocities have contributed to making the wholesale eradication of indigenous peoples (Josh 10:40), the slaughter of innocents (Josh 6:21; 10:28-40), and the murder of prisoners of war (Josh 10:22-26) offensive even to battle-tested sensibilities. In addition, because the *Revised Common Lectionary* (*RCL*) conveniently averts its gaze from these narratives, preachers in liturgical settings in particular have had few opportunities to make sense of them in the context of proclaiming the gospel. Nevertheless, open doors for vital proclamation remain.

In the two passages from Joshua in the RCL that mention the Israelites' settlement, this conquest is referred to as an act of God on Israel's behalf rather than as a military operation by invading Israelites (Josh 3:10; 24:18; see also 13:6). In fact, Israel's emergence in the land as a gift instead of a taking is the dominant inner-biblical understanding. The conquest was celebrated as God's victory, not Israel's, and remembered as a testimony to God's grace and power, not the Israelites' prowess (Pss 44:1-8; 68:12-14; 78:54-55; Acts 7:45). Some readers may reasonably object that this understanding only shifts the interpretive problem of these narratives from the injustice of the invaders to the thornier question of the justice of God. But the underlying theological dilemma posed by the conquest is precisely its depiction of a divine choice *for* Israel and *against* "the nations," the reverse image of the quandary that Paul negotiates in Rom 9–11 by shifting the focus from "the problem of Israel" to the question of the righteousness of God. Theological reflection on the ways of God in the world is at the heart of the proclamation of the gospel, which sooner or later must engage the persistent conundrums of the mystery of "God's purpose of election" (Rom 9:11), the enigma of "the kindness and the severity of God" (Rom 11:22), and the inscrutable intent of God "to be merciful to all" (Rom 11:32). One need not be an allegorist to agree with Origen that effective preaching of these narratives requires that the interpreter "ascend from history to a higher understanding" (Franke 2005, 3).

In an otherwise amiable encounter, an American suburbanite announced to a professor of religion, "When is the church going to start preaching the whole Bible and not just part of it? I'm fed up with all this 'love-your-enemies' and 'turn-the-other-cheek' garbage. When is the church going to start preaching that to save this country, we need to make like Joshua and drive out all the unbelievers?" Stunned for a moment by the unexpected specter of fascism in biblical garb, the professor responded, "Well, I have always thought that being a Christian was about 'following Jesus' rather than 'making like Joshua.' I guess that's why 'love your enemies' and 'turn the other cheek' make sense to me. I follow Jesus, not Joshua." In confronting the conquest narratives and inappropriate appropriations of them, it is worth recalling that not every citation of Scripture was met with Jesus' approval, "Do this, and you will live" (Luke 10:28), and not every parable of Jesus ended with the approbation, "Go and do likewise" (Luke 10:37). Sometimes the most appropriate hermeneutical model (*see* CULTURAL

HERMENEUTICS) is found in the gospel tradition's words of Jesus: "You have heard that it was said to those of ancient times. . . . But I say to you . . ." (Matt 5:21-22, 33-34). Indeed, no passage in the Bible calls on ancient Israel to recapitulate or repeat the conquest. Ritual reenactments of creation (new year's festival), the exodus from Egypt (Passover), the wilderness wandering (Feast of Booths), and the giving of the law (Pentecost) are well attested in biblical and later Jewish traditions. But nowhere is a conquest day or a season of conquest affirmed as a sacred ordinance, nor is conquest a mission that biblical Israel was ever again called to fulfill.

Centuries of sermons have vilified the inhabitants of the land and treated them as foils for the church's reputed religious, political, and cultural enemies. At the same time, however, a well-attested avenue of interpretation has been to understand the adversaries in the land not as historical peoples but as the vices, temptations, and undisciplined passions of the faithful against which it is necessary to struggle always. This is the Pogo interpretation of the conquest narratives, after the great Walt Kelly's cartoon character's deft malapropism, "We have met the enemy, and he is us." While some interpreters may dismiss such readings as flights of allegorical fancy, they are nevertheless thematically in keeping with the Deuteronomistic agenda in Joshua through 2 Kings that insisted that Israel's favor in God's eyes was a function of God's grace and Israel's faithfulness, not the faithlessness of "the other." According to the Deuteronomists, God's people have always been their own worst enemy in their relationship with God.

The battles in the land have also been interpreted as depicting the terrors and trials that every person may face sooner or later in living or dying. Even the most irenic pastor who has walked with congregants down the dark roads of addiction, abuse, mental illness, or destructive or self-destructive behavior resonates with the battle imagery: "You are in a fight for your life. 'Put on the whole armor of God, so that you may be able to stand'" (Eph 6:11). "'Be strong and courageous; do not be frightened or dismayed, for the Lord your God is with you wherever you go'" (Josh 1:9). To "proclaim the gospel of peace," it is necessary to take up the "sword of the Spirit," according to the writer of Ephesians (6:15, 17). A symbolic sword also appears in the gospel tradition's transmission of words of Jesus that sound too much like Joshua to suit some readers: "Do not think that I have come to bring peace to the earth;

I have not come to bring peace, but a sword" (Matt 10:34). Even that saying is easy to swallow compared to the apocalyptic appropriation of the sword and conquest imagery in Rev 19:11-21. The shameful examples of literal and homicidal interpretations of passages such as these do not justify suppressing them. Valid and effective proclamation of the conquest narratives and related passages requires the interpreter to plumb the depth of the symbolic power of the biblical images of violence and redemption, friend and foe, and self and other, in order to reappropriate and reapply them creatively.

Creative proclamation often derives from "listening for countervoices as well as dominant themes" (Pressler 2002, 5). Christian interpreters from the earliest centuries of the church have been captivated by the character of Rahab, who sheltered and protected "the other" in the person of the Israelite spies sent to Jericho (Josh 2:1-7, 12-16; 6:25; Heb 11:31). In reaction in part to Protestant preaching that insisted Rahab's faith, not her works, saved her, pluralistically minded interpreters have objected that Rahab was deemed worthy of mercy only because she abandoned her religion and culture to embrace the Israelites'. However, both readings ignore the explicit statement of the text that her hospitality was her salvation (Josh 6:25; Jas 2:25). The countervoice of hospitality to strangers (Rom 12:13; Heb 13:2) sounds beneath the prevailing din of armed conflict. The spies who promised Rahab and her family safekeeping extended a preemptive word of peace in obvious contradiction of the rules of engagement laid out in Deut 20:15-18, with the result that the countervoice of the Golden Rule (Matt 7:12; Did. 1.2) resounds in the midst of a deadly clash of cultures. Similarly, the courageous unnamed "leaders of the congregation," who along with Joshua resisted the "murmuring" of the people who wanted to eradicate the Gibeonites who had tricked the Israelites into thinking they were a people from outside the land, model honoring a good-faith commitment of peace to persons that supersedes a draconian enforcement of the law (Josh 9:26-27, in contrast to Lev 27:29). Elsewhere in the book of Joshua (and in Judg 1), it is possible to hear a recurring countervoice attesting to the ongoing coexistence of Canaanites and Israelites in the land (13:1-6; 15:13-17, 63; 16:10; 17:12-13). By listening to these countervoices, a strong interpretive case can be made that the conquest narratives of Joshua are more about the exceptions in mercy than they are about the rules of wrath, a gospel motif if ever there was one. *See* ALLEGORY, ALLEGORESIS; GENDER, RACE, AND ETHNICITY; GOD, ETHICS AND.

Bibliography: Jerome D. Creach. *Joshua.* (2003); John R. Franke, ed. *Joshua, Judges, Ruth, 1–2 Samuel.* (2005); Carolyn Pressler. *Joshua, Judges, and Ruth.* (2002).

CONTEXTUAL EPISTLES
Gordon D. Fee

All of the NT epistles are historically conditioned (i.e., ad hoc to some degree), yet some of them are more specifically so than others. The historical situations into which they speak are often quite foreign to those of the contemporary preacher and his or her congregation. But in all cases, at issue for the preacher is how to move from the then and there to the here and now, and to do so in such a way as to keep integrity with both contexts.

Defining the Problem

The simplest description of a *contextual epistle* is one that was occasioned from the recipient's end, to which the author is responding, rather than one initiated by something the author wanted to say to the persons or churches to whom he was writing. At least ten of the letters in the Pauline corpus (excepting Rom, Eph, and Phlm) are contextual in this sense—some more intensely so than others (e.g., 1 Cor and Gal)—while Hebrews and the so-called General Epistles are less so. And since the ten are occasioned by a communication of some kind to Paul (written or oral), the exegetical task always involves an attempt to determine the situation in the church to which Paul is speaking, while the preaching task is to apply the meaning of the text to comparable situations in today's church.

However, even the more intensely occasional letters, such as 1 Corinthians and Philippians, have different kinds of occasionality when it comes to the hermeneutical/preaching task. Consider the genuine historical/cultural differences between 1 Cor 1–4 and 11:2-16. In the first instance, the task of translating from culture to culture is more minimal: internal squabbles within the community of faith continue to arise; and the church still needs to hear

Paul's threefold concern about the basic gospel (of a crucified Messiah; 1:18-25), the role of leadership (3:1-15), and the true nature of the church (God's temple, indwelt by the Spirit; 3:16-17). In the second instance (11:2-16) we have almost nothing that compares culturally with the issue of head coverings. The difficulty in this case comes when the preacher tries to make theological gain out of the ad hoc supporting arguments that Paul offers, because even these are contextually conditioned to some degree.

Defining the Task

The first task of preaching from the contextual epistles is careful exegesis of the passage at hand. The preacher must think not only about the meaning of specific words and phrases, but especially about what might have occasioned these words, written in this specific way for this specific context. And here is where one should consult the better commentaries (for such a list, see Fee 2002, 173–77).

The second task is the primary one of all preaching: to translate the meaning of the text in its original setting into a word for God's people today in their own contemporary setting. The authority of the sermon rests with the preacher letting the biblical text set the agenda for the sermon; the integrity of the sermon rests with the preacher's ability to bridge the historical distance in a way that makes the point of the biblical text relevant to a comparable situation in today's world.

Thus, for example, if one were to preach from 1 Cor 1:18-25 about the ultimate oxymoron of the Christian faith—a crucified Messiah as the heart of the Christian gospel—one needs to ask why such a concern comes up first in response to the matter of divisions within the community where different leaders are the focal point of the divisions. It will not take long to recognize that a serious misconstrual of the gospel itself lies at the heart of the problem. The task of preaching, then, is to expound the significance of the passage not only for Corinth but as a crucial word for all churches in all times and settings.

Preaching from Contextually Comparable Texts

In many ways this is the easiest of all preaching tasks. At issue for the preacher is making sure he or she has done careful exegesis in order to avoid

(1) assuming a contemporary context that ultimately would deflect the meaning of the Pauline text itself or (2) missing the possible potential of the text for a contemporary congregation by preaching what seems to be plain on the surface but, in fact, misses the significance of the original context.

As an example of the first matter, note the significant contemporary possibilities of the three paragraphs in 1 Cor 3:5-17. In the first paragraph (vv. 5-9) Paul is trying to retool their minds regarding the role and significance of the leaders over whom they are at odds. Their role is one of servanthood only; they neither own the church nor are they to be exalted in the church. Church leaders are simply servants of the farm; everything (both church and leaders) belongs to God (v. 9).

In the second paragraph (vv. 10-15) Paul turns his attention to the leaders themselves, not himself and Apollos but those currently in Corinth responsible for "building the church." At issue is how, and therefore with what, one builds the local church. If they "build" in ways that focus on the leaders rather than on Christ, the foundation, they are in danger of building a church that cannot withstand the test of time. After all, they are building God's "temple" in Corinth (note that "gold, silver, precious stones" come from texts in 1 and 2 Chronicles regarding building Solomon's Temple).

And that is the singular concern of the third paragraph (vv. 16-17), where Paul tries to get them to rethink about who and what the church is—God's temple in Corinth. In fact, there is not another text in the NT that speaks so strongly about God's view of the nature and significance of the local church, so that those who would destroy it are in danger of eternal judgment.

As to the second matter, one of the pitfalls to avoid in preaching from the contextual epistles is the temptation to preach from well-known passages apart from their original context. A common example is to preach from the "acropolis of the Pauline letters," Phil 2:5-11, without recognizing that Paul tells the Christ story precisely to curb some festering disagreements in the Philippian community. Thus in his appeal to unity in 2:3, he isolates the twin evils: "Do nothing from selfish ambition or conceit." The two sentences in vv. 6-8, which speak of the divine humiliation of the eternal Son, speak directly to these two evils. In contrast to "selfish ambition," Christ did not regard his equality with God as "something to be exploited" but "emptied himself" by "taking the form of a slave." And in contrast to "conceit," Christ in his humanity "humbled himself" by becoming obedient to death on the cross. The second paragraph (vv. 9-11) then indicates the divine vindication of such self-emptying and obedience. What follows (vv. 12-16) is the Pauline application of Christ's example to their own situation.

Preaching from Contextually Non-comparable Texts

In some ways this might seem to be the more difficult task; in fact, such texts can usually be translated into a different, but relatively comparable context so as to keep integrity with both contexts. A case in point would be the Corinthians' insistence on continuing to attend the feasts in the idol temples (1 Cor 8 and 10:1-22), which Paul forbids absolutely. While such matters still have considerable significance in some Asian cultures, they have very little significance for those in the West. One would need to identify what is truly idolatrous in one's own cultural setting, meaning worship of a deity other than the living God. But one must take care to avoid applying the text in such a way that a person who is merely offended by, but would not participate in, the action of another sits in judgment of the person who is free to participate.

Some Abuses to Avoid

The most common abuse in preaching from the contextual epistles is something endemic to the church of the West, namely, to individualize texts that were intended only for the Christian community as a whole. A classic example of this abuse occurs when one individualizes 1 Cor 3:10-15, 16-17. A second common abuse is to go to some Pauline texts for their wording and to preach from that wording with total disregard for the context in which that wording appears. Such preaching is not at all biblical, as has been defined above. So the rule of preaching from the contextual epistles is to remember the context—both Paul's and one's own—and to translate meaningfully from the one to the other. See APPLICATION; BRIDGING THEN AND NOW; SERMONIC, THEOLOGICAL EPISTLES.

Bibliography: G. D. Fee. *New Testament Exegesis.* 3rd ed. (2002).

ECCLESIASTES
Alyce M. McKenzie

Many preachers skip over Ecclesiastes, assuming it to be a depressing, pessimistic book. In reality, it is the work of a wise teacher whose insights can strengthen us to face both the tedium of everyday life and the sting of sudden tragedy. Though often characterized as dismal and dark, Ecclesiastes contains a realistic message of gratitude to God and joy in the gift of life.

The preacher or teacher (Qohelet) who wrote and/or collected the wisdom teachings in the book of Ecclesiastes was probably a sage writing in Palestine in the 5th cent. BCE, a time during which Persian kings ruled over the people. This insecure, oppressive time seems to have shaped Qohelet's view, both of God and of life. It seems to have contributed to his disillusionment with the traditional, optimistic wisdom of the book of Proverbs. For Qohelet, God is transcendent and mysterious. Like the Persian kings who doled out portions of land, some larger and more fertile than others, God is responsible for enjoyment and injustice alike. This God is to be revered and not challenged (5:2). In relation to this distant God, human wisdom is severely limited (8:17).

Qohelet characterizes human life as hevel, which though often translated as "vanity" has no true English equivalent. Its literal meaning is "breath" or "breeze." Qohelet uses hevel not to describe God but to describe situations in life in which the expectations of traditional wisdom (a good life equals a fortunate life) are disappointed. He uses it to speak of the ephemerality of life (6:12; 7:15; 9:9), joy (2:1), human accomplishments (2:11; 4:4), and youth and the prime of life (11:10). While traditional wisdom asserted with confidence that good acts lead to good consequences, Qohelet saw that it did not always work out that way. Traditional wisdom distinguished between the wise person and the fool, but Qohelet felt that grounds for commending wisdom over folly had been swept away by the fact that misfortune and death afflict the wise person as surely as they do the foolish one (2:14, 16; 6:8, 11).

Ecclesiastes challenges us to face the facts of life that we would prefer to ignore. Life is unpredictable, God is inscrutable, and death is inevitable. Once we face these facts, this wise teacher advises us to live each moment aware of our human limitations and appreciative of the precious, if precarious, joy that God has granted us as our portion in this unpredictable life (3:9-14).

Hopeful Themes in Ecclesiastes

The hope in Ecclesiastes is played in the minor key, but it is hope nevertheless. One hopeful theme is the acceptance of our human limitations (3:9-22; 5:1-7; 8:16-17). We are all limited in time, energy, life span, control of circumstances, and knowledge of God. Qohelet believes that true wisdom lies in acknowledging our limitations and turning to the One who put them there in the first place (3:9-11). We are limited because this is the way God has set things up. We stand before God with humility and allow God to be God (5:7).

Another hopeful theme is the expectation of disappointment. A sermon on this theme might be called "When We Don't Get the Rose Garden We Were Never Promised." Qohelet's list of disappointments includes the fact that death comes to the wise just as it does to the fool (2:12-17), the fact that present toil does not lead to lasting profit (2:18-23), the uncertainty of life (6:1-6; 9:11-12), and the oppression of the weak by the powerful (4:1-3). This does not mean we should preach to people that they should expect the worst so they will never be disappointed. The implications of Qohelet's outlook have a potentially liberating effect. Ecclesiastes frees us to live our lives realizing that our tidy human constructs and unfounded expectations are often inadequate to withstand the broader realities. The book of Ecclesiastes frees us to live our lives disabused of the fantasy that misfortune will come to everyone but us. Qohelet's themes free us to live our lives open to the growth that comes from both tragedy and triumph.

A third hopeful theme from Ecclesiastes is that we can enjoy our "portion," Qohelet's word for our lot in life, and be grateful for the blessings of food, drink, work, and love it contains (2:10; 3:22; 5:18; 9:7-9). Why? Because our portion, taking its joy and sorrow together, is a gift from God. Qohelet repeatedly exhorts us to enjoy our portion and be grateful for its blessings. He also repeatedly urges us to remember the inevitability of our own death. He wants us to focus on the joy in our portion, finding it all the more precious because it is precarious. Focusing on the joy we have at hand is far better, in his view, than underestimating our blessings as we focus on ambition, endless toil, and the gains we think these will bring us (9:7-10).

Ecclesiastes in Context

Any text from Ecclesiastes ought to be preached in light of the concerns and context of the book as a whole. This will prevent preachers from lifting out poetic, inspirational-sounding passages, such as 3:1-8 and 12:1-8, and misinterpreting them as straightforward exhortations to praise the orderliness of the seasons of life or to be religious when you are young. (*See* WISDOM, PARANESIS.) Passages from Ecclesiastes need also to be preached in the context of the other wisdom books of the OT, especially Job and Proverbs. Qohelet's melancholy vision of a distant God is balanced by Job's angry knocking on heaven's door. Job is met by a God who is by no means distant, especially in times of suffering. Job's God is a God who, like Qohelet's, does not fit into our neat, cause-and-effect rubrics. Ecclesiastes also needs to be preached in the context of the more optimistic book of Proverbs. Ecclesiastes' insistence on the limitation of human wisdom needs to be balanced by Proverbs' confidence that the one who seeks wisdom will find a great deal of joy and insight in life. Ecclesiastes, with its stress on a distant, unknowable God before whom we are to tremble, needs Proverbs' assurance that when we trust in the Lord with all our heart, we will find wisdom and life (1:7; 3:18; 4:13; 9:10; 10:27; 14:27). Qohelet needs Proverbs' depiction of the fear of the Lord as a radical reverence that leads not only to a recognition of the divide between humanity and God but also to a considerable degree of insight about how best to live one's life (3:5-8). Ecclesiastes, with its social passivism and resignation, needs the passion for social justice of the Hebrew prophets.

From the perspective of the Christian canon, a sermon on Ecclesiastes views the book's unique themes in the larger context of God's revelation in Jesus Christ. Several of Qohelet's themes—God as distant, God as responsible for justice and injustice alike, resignation toward the oppression of the weak by the powerful, death as the end of life, and God as the determiner of the timing of life events—need to be supplemented and corrected by being put in dialogue with NT texts and themes.

Bibliography: Alyce M. McKenzie. *Preaching Proverbs: Wisdom for the Pulpit.* (1996).

ESTHER
Dianne Bergant, C.S.A.

Esther may conjure up images of both Cinderella and Joan of Arc for the modern reader. In this story, a young girl from an obscure family becomes the queen of Persia and risks her life to save her people. The story has come down to us in two major forms, a shorter Hebrew version and a longer Greek text. The Jewish community and the Protestants who chose their canon accept only the Hebrew text. The Roman Catholic version includes Greek additions as well. Despite these textual differences, the structure of the story remains basically the same.

Although a remnant of the exiled Jews returned to the land of Israel as a consequence of the edict of Cyrus (2 Chr 36:22-23), a large community remained in Persia. Many of them seem to have prospered in this Diaspora, but they were often treated as a marginal people and sometimes they suffered persecution, as reflected in the story of Esther, which takes place in the Persian city of Susa. There an orphaned Jewish girl named Hadassah is brought into the harem of the Persian ruler after Queen Vashti refuses to follow a royal order and, as a consequence, is banished. Hadassah—a woman of exceptional beauty, known now as Esther—is made queen in Vashti's place. She is elevated to this position without revealing her Jewish identity. Some time later, Mordecai, Esther's cousin who had adopted her as his daughter, refuses to accord public homage to a Persian official named Haman, claiming that such behavior would violate his Jewish sensitivities. Enraged by this, Haman concocts a plot to have Mordecai hanged and the entire Jewish community exterminated.

Mordecai turns to Esther for help. But what is she to do? If she enters the presence of the king without being summoned, she risks incurring his displeasure and suffering the same punishment as did her predecessor, Queen Vashti. If she pleads the cause of her people, she reveals her Jewish identity and risks the same death that Haman has planned for her people. However, if she does nothing, their fate is sealed.

While this story is a wonderful, suspenseful tale, for centuries both Christians and Jews questioned its religious value because God plays no part in the drama. How can such a story be considered sacred? This is remedied somewhat in the Greek version, which states that both Mordecai and Esther turn to God in prayer. However, the account's value as a story of political intrigue is beyond question. In fact, when the Jewish community finally accepted it, it became the festal legend behind the celebration of the Feast of Purim, commemorating the deliverance of the Jewish people from threatened extinction.

The artistry of this story is evident in the way the storyteller weaves in various themes important to the Jewish community in the Diaspora. First and foremost is the theme of deliverance. In many ways this story line resembles the much earlier account of the exodus. In both instances, the people are disadvantaged in a land not their own. Though they appear to prosper there (see Exod 1:7), eventually, their uniqueness is resented, and their very existence is in jeopardy. Then, against all possible odds, the people are saved. Furthermore, the events unfold in a land presumably under the jurisdiction of other gods. This element of the story lays bare the universal dominion of the God of Israel. In other words, God's power is not confined to one land, but is able to overcome the domestic powers of another nation.

Second, the people's deliverance is accomplished through the agency of a woman, someone least expected to take this role. Along with the other stories of women deliverers, notably Jael (Judg 4:21) and Judith (Jdt 13:8), the account of Esther's courage reveals how God performs wonders through the weak and vulnerable of the world. In this way, no doubt remains regarding whose power is really at work.

Finally, this story illustrates a very important message for people living in the Diaspora. God enables God's people to live devout and faithful lives outside the land of promise. It assures them that in circumstances where they may be vulnerable, marginal, or otherwise discriminated against, they can still depend upon the promises of protection and blessing made by God to their ancestors long ago.

These are themes cherished by the Jewish community and Christian believers. This theological message is well suited to both communities, both the theme of deliverance in times of peril and the universal dominion of God, and God's choice of vulnerable people to confront those who typically exercise power. Moreover, both communities highly value individuals who are willing to place themselves in jeopardy for the sake of the community.

Feminists of both religious bodies recognize the complexity of the image of the heroine. On the one hand, they applaud Esther's courage in interceding for her people, even in the face of possible repercussions for herself. However, they may be troubled by the way she manipulates the king with her beauty. They may see this as reinforcing a stereotypical feminine ploy. On this point, many of them prefer Queen Vashti, who refused to parade her beauty for the enjoyment of a drunken crowd. However, Esther's actions are in keeping with the biblical characterization of other disadvantaged individuals who make use of whatever is at their disposal to accomplish their goals. (Many cultures tell stories of the trickster who outwits those in authority and averts some pending disaster.) In Esther's case, the goal was the deliverance of her Jewish community. And in this she was eminently successful. *See* GENDER, RACE, AND ETHNICITY.

Bibliography: L. Allen and T. Laniak. *Ezra, Nehemiah, Esther.* New International Biblical Commentary. (2003); Carol M. Bechtel. *Esther.* Interpretation: A Bible Commentary for Teaching and Preaching. (2002); Michael V. Fox. *Character and Theology in the Book of Esther.* 2nd ed. (2001); Eugene F. Roop. *Ruth, Jonah, Esther.* Believers Church Bible Commentary. (2002).

EXODUS
James C. Howell

Origen and Augustine, Luther and Calvin, Whitefield and Brooks, King, Romero and Taylor all preached Exodus. Exodus may be preached in our time since God still aims to free the people of God. The secret to preaching this ancient narrative is this: instead of rummaging around, digging up some shiny nugget from the past, which is quickly retrieved for the present situation, the preacher must linger back then, letting herself be "astonished" by the text, which is utterly compelling and not merely "useful" (Davis 2005, 2).

The preacher might begin by reading Exodus through in a single sitting. Feel Pharaoh's whip and the sand under your feet. Imagine faces. Tremble at the foot of the mountain. Hear the commandments as if for the very first time. Notice yourself murmuring and partying around the golden calf. Superb commentaries (Childs, Sarna, Brueggemann,

Meyers, and Durham) from Jewish, Christian, and clinically historical angles may prod the imagination. (*See* IMAGINATION/CREATIVITY.)

Exodus forms a people. Our imaginations are reshaped by the story of people in bondage who are set free, receive God's commands, find themselves on a journey, and must humbly admit at every turn that they are a stiff-necked people, ungrateful, hardly zealous for the God who saves them in spite of themselves—and the climax of this part of the story is worship at the mountain as the tabernacle is being constructed. Exodus presents variations on a single melody: "Let my people go, so that they may worship me" (Exod 8:1).

Sermon Temptations to Resist

If the preacher settles into Exodus instead of lunging too swiftly toward the NT, or toward relevance—me and my life today—the interpreter will have a chance to resist several homiletical temptations. We might spiritualize or psychologize the text: I wander through the desert of my life, and I hope God delivers me from the oppression of my anxieties. But the exodus actually happened to real people; the lashes to their backs were not spiritual!

We are tempted to co-opt the exodus for political purposes. Liberation themes are resident throughout—but if Exodus is about freedom, it is a different sort of freedom. God did not open the Red Sea, shuttle the people through, and then say, "Bye! Have a fun life!" Moses knew where they were heading: "Let my people go, that they may serve me" (Exod 8:20 RSV). Me, and no one else. Freedom is not autonomy but service to the delivering God who liberates Israel, but then hurries them along to Mount Sinai where they are given hundreds of laws. Freedom is not me doing as I wish, but letting myself be set free to live in total obedience to God.

A political dimension is undeniably present in Exodus. But we must take care not to project our agenda where it does not belong. Exodus is not about class struggle. Many who were poor did not successfully exit Egypt, and the Israelites themselves had slaves. Egypt was not overthrown. The text is very clear that God chose Israel, not poor people in general. Love is always particular like this, is it not? Love is not the recognition of value; rather, the beloved acquires value because it is loved. We can love something that is totally lacking

in virtue! To rediscover the dynamics of how Israel was loved, and so how we are loved by God, helps us take a deep breath, and instead of using the Bible as a weapon against others, the preacher can make a bridge.

Preaching Exodus is delicate for Christian speakers, for this is actually the story of someone else, too. Long before Jesus appeared, and to the present day, Exodus is the story for the Jews. We are tempted to snatch it from them, as if it were a mere dress rehearsal, a code, a crystal ball in which we see what the story is really about. But Exodus is not really about Jesus, the resurrection, or the eucharist. It is about what God did for the Israelites. For Jews, Exodus is the story of Passover, and for Christians, Jesus is the Paschal Lamb. Christians believe that whoever delivered Israel through the sea is the same one who raised Jesus from the dead.

Where do we find ourselves in the Exodus story? This poses a treacherous question especially for Americans and Europeans, who frequently think that "we" refers to us as a nation and not to we as Christians: Are we Israel or Pharaoh? If Christians imagine themselves as the "Exodus church" (Moltmann 1967, 304), then Christians are not the powerful: an exodus movement consists of the pilgrim people on the way, unsettled, not getting enmeshed in the powers of this age. If the notion that America resembles ancient Egypt, that the United States is mighty and can force others to bend to its will, then in all humility, Christians must be willing to let a word of judgment fall, perhaps to rediscover the relevance of Exodus for the church even as they hold out for a hermeneutic of divine electing love.

The Subject of the Story

Of course, the story is about God, not about us. We cannot argue that the OT God is wrathful and legalistic, while the NT God is kind and gracious. In Exodus we find that God's grace is not a novelty that Jesus introduced. How gracious is God in Exodus! What are new in the NT are the incarnation, crucifixion, and resurrection. We understand the consistency of God's patient endeavors in the face of the embarrassingly habitual feebleness of human response to God. God makes and keeps promises. In the language of Exodus, echoed in the Nicene Creed's description of Jesus, God "comes down." Salvation is not something we accomplish. God is the powerful savior: God rescues people who in their hearts are much like the "reluctant . . . prodigal . . . brought in kicking, struggling, and darting his eyes in every direction for a chance of escape" (Lewis 1955, 229).

The drama in Exod 32 unveils a God who negotiates, listens, blazes, aches, and grows tender. God's power is manifest in compassion. In Exodus God is not abstractly defined by philosophical adjectives (such as *infinite, ineffable, impassible*), but is revealed in the story of Scripture, and in ways that offend philosophical sensibility. "Omnipotence is never loved; it is only feared" (Moltmann 1993, 223)—and the God of Exodus would be loved. This God can rage in anger, but God's heart is melted by Moses' desperate pleas. God's mind can change and exercise compassionate restraint. Such a God is not removed from the vicissitudes of history; Exodus portrays a fiercely partisan God who sides with God's people with a vengeance.

Exodus provides us with a panoply of texts to become more intimately acquainted with God, and thereby to be remolded as God's people. The narratives are utterly absorbing, and the preacher will need to remember not to leap prematurely to the story's point. A painting, a symphony, or even my life cannot be reduced to a point. The story itself is the meaning.

Yet we can relish stories so much that we miss the other literary types that speak so powerfully in Exodus. The laws unveil a God who commands; yet hidden inside those very commandments are God's mercy and a powerful promise. (*See* LAWS AND REGULATIONS.) "Moses lifted the freshly chiseled tablets of stone in his hands and gazed down the mountain to where Israel waited. He knew a great exultation. Now men could be free. They had something of the essence of divinity expressed. They had the chart and compass of behavior. They need not stumble into blind ways and injure themselves. This was bigger than Israel. It comprehended the world. Israel could be a heaven for all men forever, by these sacred stones. With flakes of light still clinging to his face, Moses turned to where Joshua waited for him. 'Joshua, I have laws. Israel is going to know peace and justice'" (Hurston 1939, 233).

Exodus sings and dances with poetry and music (Exod 15). Finally, we have the most remarkable liturgical readings: the detailed directions for the observance of Passover (Exod 12) can help us reflect upon the theological life of the Jewish people, and upon the significance of the Lord's Supper, which is how Jesus and the earliest Christian preachers understood the significance of his sacrificial death and our deliverance from bondage.

Bibliography: Walter Brueggemann. "Exodus." *New Interpreter's Bible.* Vol. 1. (1994); Brevard Childs. *The Book of Exodus.* Old Testament Library. (1974); Ellen Davis. *Wondrous Depth: Preaching the Old Testament.* (2005); John I. Durham. *Exodus.* Word Biblical Commentary. Vol. 3. (1987); Zora Neale Hurston. *Moses, Man of the Mountain.* (1939); C. S. Lewis. *Surprised by Joy.* (1955); Carol Meyers. *Exodus.* New Cambridge Bible Commentary. (2005); Jürgen Moltmann. *Theology of Hope.* (1967); Jürgen Moltmann. *The Crucified God.* (1993); Nahum Sarna. *Exodus.* JPS Torah Commentary. (1991).

HEALING AND EXORCISM
Scott K. Davis

The healing ministry of Jesus was connected integrally to his authority in preaching and teaching concerning the kingdom of God: "Jesus went throughout Galilee, teaching (didaskō) in their synagogues and proclaiming (kēryssō) the good news of the kingdom and curing (therapeuō) every disease and every sickness among the people" (Matt 4:23). Jesus' healing acts provided visible credibility of word with deed regarding the transformed living of the great commandments of loving God and neighbor in anticipation of the eschatological vision of creation's irenic restoration to wholeness. There is an eschatological correlation with Jesus' healings of illness and the resurrection life: while all healing is transitory, the mortality rate remains 100 percent; Jesus' healing power points to the final resurrection and consummation of all things. Compassion was not the sole distinguishing mark of Jesus' healing ministry: there was an emphasis on the liberation of persons once sick and alienated, and their restoration into worshiping communities and social relationships, attesting to the welcoming blessing for all within the kingdom of God. The Gospels are more interested in healing illness than in defining health; more concerned about how Jesus' healings pointed to present and future realities of transformed thinking and living before God and within human community than in disease processes or the physiological and hamartological etiologies of sickness; more concerned about the social dimension of healing than individual cures.

Healing and curing are to be distinguished. Curing as a modern biomedical concept focuses on individuals and treatment of disease (defined broadly as some causative, functional abnormality within the body). Healing is also directed toward a social effect of illness (defined as the experiencing of disease or sickness), providing social meanings, resolutions, and restorations to a broad range of somatic and relational problems related to the sickness. As finding meaning and purpose, healing is possible even when cure is not an outcome. Jesus did more than cure; along with preaching and teaching, the healing offered restoration to individuals broken and to social systems divided by sickness.

Three key words in the biblical Greek that carry different connotations and contextual meanings not fully communicated in modern translations and interpretations make healing a complex dynamic in the Gospels. The Gospels of Matthew and Mark generally use therapeuō in reference to Jesus' healing ministry and the commissioning of disciples to engage in healing, pointing both to the medical intervention of curing (physical aspect) and to a sense of persuasion toward a continuing change or transformation of one's life (spiritual aspect) in service. For a more Hellenistic audience, iaomai becomes a favorite in Luke, carrying a connotation of the healing activity of God or a God-appointed agent. With sōzō and its cognates, the reader and preacher will need to discern whether the context is about healing, saving, or both. Jesus is the subject when sōzō is used in healing narratives, with a result of full and holistic participation in community of the person who by pistis (faith) or by haptos (touch) has been healed, and who may be moved to follow Jesus as a disciple.

Exorcism is presented as another dimension of Jesus' healing ministry in the SYNOPTIC GOSPELS, limited to six specific cases and their parallels: Matt 9:32-33; Mark 1:21-28, 32-34; 5:1-20; 7:24-30; 9:14-29. In Mark's Gospel exorcism is Jesus' first act of public ministry. Contemporary Christians may tend to be more comfortable with Jesus the healer than Jesus the exorcist, but Jesus' exorcism ministry supports the gospel intent to point to Jesus' authority as God's agent over all forms and powers of evil. The distinct pattern of exorcism of those whom Jesus encountered ends with Jesus calling upon the demon to come out (exerchomai) or by summary statement having cast the demon out (ekballō).

Preachers will want to explore their personal and reference-group understandings of illness and healing regarding social relationships as they engage biblical texts with a goal to discern, correlate, and distinguish the disparate biblical and modern worldviews for themselves and the hearers of sermons on biblical healing narratives. While modern culture focuses on curing diseases affecting an individual's body by eradicating biomedical causes so that the individual might function well and self-sufficiently within the social order once again, the Gospels are concerned with healing illness that by its social interpretation has marginalized a person from being fully present within community that is capable of restoring the person in relationships. The narratives about Jesus' healing ministry do not provide unequivocal diagnostic criteria about illnesses encountered by Jesus to provide clear and direct correlations to modern understandings of diseases, causes, and symptoms. For instance, the Gospels offer a tripartite metaphorical zonal understanding of bodily dysfunctions with social relationships and functioning: hearts-eyes correlate to emotion-fused thinking; mouth-ears to self-expressive speaking; and hands-feet to purposeful functioning. As interesting as dynamics of sickness, illness, and healing may be for the modern preacher, it is the Gospels' interests that Jesus' healing ministry pointed beyond the moment to a truth about his divine authority as one inaugurating the very kingdom of God proclaimed and present in his word and deeds and the eschatological healing of a groaning creation.

Determined partially by the witness of the scriptural narrative and partially by the preacher's understandings of God and of biblical and theological interpretations, sermons about Jesus' healing ministry will be preached somewhere on a continuum between "zap" and "zero": between proclamations of immediate, complete, miraculous cures dependent on a faith element in Jesus as Lord and rationalized, scientific explanations limiting biblical accounts to traditional folk medicine cures. From one perspective, sermons might teach that persons need to be cured to enter a body/spirit wholeness and right relationship with God, focusing on the dynamics of a determinant faith to effect the overcoming of sin to receive divine salvation in miraculous fashion. From another perspective, sermons might sidestep any focus on both the malady and the possibility of miraculous cures in order to see a bigger picture of divine mysteries of saving activity that transcend healing narratives. Between these perspectives, preachers might want to interpret healing narratives metaphorically, identifying the maladies of a few with the moral faults of many. Such direct connections to physical conditions of persons in the biblical narrative with moral faults of the person then or persons today fail to acknowledge the differences in understandings of disease and cause. The healing narrative of the blind man in John 9 and its "blind . . . see" image repeated in the familiar hymn "Amazing Grace" is one example of this hermeneutic hazard connecting illness and moral fault that even John 9 downplays.

The following excerpt is from a sermon of mine connecting Matt 10:5-16 (Jesus' commissioning of disciples to preach, heal, and perform exorcisms) with a congregation's experience of healing:

Years of acute care and rehabilitation hospitalizations still left Vic with major physical, mental, and emotional deficits: he was not the same self-employed back-hoe operator whose graceful hands and feet were one-with-machine in excavating agility. Vic's heart still grieved his wife's death in that highway accident. And the pastor's voice that prayed constantly at bedside still traumatized his ears so that Vic responded with angry rants when the pastor spoke.

Physical and emotional cures were continuing . . . slowly. But healing was both imminent and yet to be that first Sunday when his nurse assisted Vic into the front pew for worship. Congregants murmured from their seats around and behind Vic; but none dared approach him to welcome him back. Then there were Vic's unbridled outbursts responding to the pastor's sermon; but none dared reproach Vic's behavior. At the usher's invitation, his nurse assisted Vic forward to receive the Eucharist. After all they had seen and heard, no one in the congregation dared to kneel beside Vic. Welcomed at the Lord's Table, the congregation could not yet welcome Vic.

Without hesitation—disregarding the ushers' sense of orderliness—the congregational matriarch and patriarch arose, came forward, and knelt, one on either side of Vic, to receive with Vic the Lord's body broken, the Savior's blood poured. . . .

No one comprehended the meaning of that moment until the pastor's voice quivered and stuttered over the prayed phrases before falling silent: "We give you thanks . . . / that you have refreshed us through the healing power of this gift of life / . . . in your mercy . . . strengthen us . . . / in faith toward you / and in fervent love toward one another . . . ." (Collect #241, *Lutheran Book of Worship*, p. 74). And in hushed awe the people said, "Amen."

Bibliography: Kathy Black. *A Healing Homiletic: Preaching and Disability.* (1991); J. Keir Howard. *Disease and Healing in the New Testament: An Analysis and Interpretation.* (2001); *Lutheran Book of Worship.* (1978); John J. Pilch. *Healing in the New Testament: Insights from Medical and Mediterranean Anthropology.* (2000); Louise Wells. *The Greek Language of Healing from Homer to New Testament Times.* (1998); John Wilkinson. *The Bible and Healing: A Medical and Theological Commentary.* (1998).

JOB
John C. Holbert

Perhaps no book of the OT is more difficult to address from the pulpit than the book of Job. It is a lengthy, poetic discourse, framed by a narrative prologue (chs. 1–2) and epilogue (42:7-17), written in a rich and complex Hebrew style, addressing some of the most contentious subjects that theology faces in any age. (*See* SIN AND EVIL.) The book grapples with the purposes and meanings of suffering, issues of righteousness and justice in a world too often lacking both, and the identity and purposes of God, among many others. To address the book from the pulpit, the preacher must make at least two critical choices about the text's meaning.

First, the preacher must decide if the book can be read as a whole piece: Can all forty-two chapters make sense as they stand? Many readers have found the answer to be no and have offered myriad textual reconstructions, additions, and subtractions, to make what they think is better sense of the book. Questions include: Can the portrait of Job in the prologue and epilogue be understood as consonant with his picture found in the poetic dialogue? How are the two speeches of God to be understood as answers or responses to the preceding dialogues between Job and his four partners? Does the epilogue represent a retreat from one of the dialogue's major concerns to deny that God rewards and punishes?

Second, among those questions, the most important one appears to be what to do with the speeches of God. The main discussion of the book before the appearance of God seems clear enough. Job is introduced as a perfectly righteous man, called "blameless and upright" both by the storyteller (1:1) and by God (1:8). But at the end of the prologue he is alone, seated on the city dump, scraping himself with a broken piece of pottery. His three friends appear and in turn claim that Job must have done something altogether evil to have ended up in his condition. For them, the universe is easily understood; the righteous are always rewarded, and the wicked are always punished. Job has been punished, so he must be wicked. The evidence sits in agony before them. Examples of this belief may be found in the speeches of Eliphaz (4:7), Bildad (8:3-4), and Zophar (11:5-6).

To their assaults Job responds that if he has done something he should not have done, surely, it was not so heinous as to deserve this massive divine attack. Job very early in his speeches blames God quite directly for his ash heap home (6:4; 7:12; 9:21-24, among many others). Job never claims complete innocence, but he does reject completely the friends' beliefs. He blames God for making a mistake in his case (7:12)! Job is evil! say the friends. God is wrong! says Job. And the friends are no friends at all (6:14-27)! And so it goes from chs. 3 to 31.

After the intrusion of the speech of the fourth friend, Elihu, a speech that many find of little help to the book, God appears. Job had in many ways called for God to come and straighten out the mess of the dialogue, since he realized that his head-knocking debate with the friends was leading nowhere. But the speeches of God are in many ways very surprising and have been understood in several ways.

1. God puts the haughty Job in his place. In response to Job's blasphemous ranting about God as beast (16:12-14), amoral monster (9:21-24), and confused tyrant (7:12), God tells Job to shut up. "Where were you, little man, and just who do you think you are in the face of my divine creation and work," could be a summary of the speeches of God. And in the face of this divine anger, Job first shuts up (40:3-5) and then changes his mind, or repents (42:1-6).
2. God announces in the speeches that the friends and Job are completely wrong about the activity of God in the universe. They think that the world revolves around human justice and injustice. But God has far larger concerns than that. The fact is that God is not in the business of rewarding the righteous and punishing the wicked. God is creator and sustainer of a universe of deep complexity and rich mystery. Not only does God bring rain on places devoid of human life (38:26), not only is God concerned about the sustenance of creatures completely separate from human life (lions, ravens, eagles, ostriches), but God is also creator of those great creatures, Behemoth and Leviathan (40:15-41), monsters of chaos in the Canaanite pantheon of gods. Since God creates Behemoth "just as I made you, [Job]" (40:15), the universe is not a place to be reduced to the simplicity of a bumper sticker. God is concerned and involved with all of God's creation, even the parts of it not readily understood or controlled by humans.

3. The speeches of God do not answer the problem of human suffering because that is finally not the real question of the book of Job. The real question is: Just who is this God? And the answer is that God is holy, mysterious, surprising, not to be reduced to any sort of human formula.

How the preacher answers the question of the purposes of the speeches of God will determine how the preacher will use Job in preaching. The shape of that preaching can be narrative, telling the dramatic story through. Or the preacher can choose a more topical approach, focused on one of the subjects raised by the book for this day's sermon. Always, it is imperative that the questions raised above be addressed and answered before any sermon from Job is attempted. Each preacher will need to have in mind his or her understanding of the whole story before Job can offer its unique power to 21st-cent. hearers.

Bibliography: Norman C. Habel. *The Book of Job.* (1985); John C. Holbert. *Preaching Job.* (1999); Carol A. Newsom. "Job." *New Interpreter's Bible.* Vol. 4. (1995).

JOHANNINE EPISTLES
See CONTEXTUAL EPÍSTLES.

JOHN
David E. Holwerda

The Gospel of John confronts the preacher with a fascinating combination of simplicity and mystery.

The mystery lies in the depth created by the Word become flesh. The preacher must recognize that the descent into its depth is a call to faith in the astonishing richness of Jesus' identity and mission.

A. The Purpose of John's Signs—Gospel
B. The Christology of John
   1. Announced in the Prologue
   2. Shaped by OT Institutions and Festivals
   3. Revealed in Symbols
     a. Universal symbols
     b. Symbolic actions
C. Christology and Discipleship
   1. A Trajectory of Faith
   2. Following Jesus as the Way, the Truth, and the Life
   3. Disciples as Bearers of His Glory

A. The Purpose of John's Signs—Gospel

The first preacher of this Gospel gives his purpose for recording these signs. His selection of signs from Jesus' ministry "are written that you may believe that Jesus is the Christ, the Son of God, and that believing you may have life in his name" (John 20:31 RSV).

The first sign at the wedding in Cana is a good example of John's purpose and method, for it reveals basic perspectives that shape the entire Gospel. The preacher should note that the focus does not fall on the miraculous as an act of power, as it does sometimes in the other Gospels, because in this Gospel faith in Jesus based merely upon the miraculous is considered to be insufficient (John 2:23-25; 3:1-5). Instead, this sign reveals the mystery of Jesus' identity and mission in the following ways:

   a. Jesus fulfills and thereby displaces the OT and Jewish waters of purification with the wine of the new era.
   b. This miracle anticipates the true cleansing and renewal that occur through the "hour" of Jesus' death.
   c. The sheer abundance of the choice wine reveals his glory because it is a sign of the presence of the God who promised to make the earth overflow with good wine (Joel 3:18; Amos 9:13).
   d. If weddings are ongoing symbols of God's first act in establishing humanity as a community, Jesus' presence and special gift at this wedding

celebration point to his renewal of and his making possible all forms of true and lasting community (John 13:34; 15:1-9).
   e. Thus, this first sign reveals the glory of the Word made flesh who, by his actions, reveals that the promised era of salvation is being inaugurated by the God who is full of grace and truth (John 1:14; Exod 34:6-7).

B. The Christology of John

1. Announced in the Prologue

John's use of Logos (Word) recalls the creative and redemptive Word of God in the OT (Gen 1; Isa 45:22-25; 55:10-11). Like Wisdom and Torah in the OT and Jewish traditions, the Word is the preexistent mediator of creation, the source of light and life, truth and salvation, and the revelation of the presence (glory) of God. Hence the Word become flesh embodies and fulfills all prior words and promises of God by revealing in his person and actions the grace and truth or faithfulness of God. By making his dwelling place among his people, the Incarnate Word fulfills God's ultimate covenant promise (Ezek 37:27; 43:7; Zech 2:11). Now the one who truly sees Jesus "has seen the Father" (John 14:9). Therefore, salvation or life ("walking in the light") and judgment or death ("walking in darkness") are tied to belief in or rejection of Jesus' name (John 3:16-21). Such claims offend many, and conflicts over these claims fill the pages of this Gospel.

2. Shaped by OT Institutions and Festivals

Frequently, John mentions OT institutions and festivals not merely for historical or chronological reasons, but to reveal how Jesus displaces them by fulfilling their essential meaning: for example, water for ceremonial cleansing displaced by the new wine and the Temple as the symbol of God's dwelling place and of access to his presence displaced by the temple that is his body (John 2), the Sabbath fulfilled by Jesus' healing on the Sabbath (John 5), the Jewish expectation of new manna restored at the Feast of Passover fulfilled by Jesus as the Bread from heaven (John 6), the symbols of light and living water associated with the Jewish celebration of the Feast of Booths fulfilled in Jesus as the Light of the World and the source of life-giving water (John 7–8). Thus, the preacher must become acquainted with these institutions and festivals as they functioned both in the OT and in Jewish hopes and expectations in order to understand the nature of their fulfillment in Jesus.

3. Revealed in Symbols

a. Universal symbols. Since symbols are borrowed from created reality, they are accessible to persons of various cultural backgrounds. Hence in form and content John's Gospel is a universal address to the world (John 3:16; 10:16). This symbolic christology functions on three levels: Jesus as a human being, as Messiah, and as God himself.

For example, the symbol of water flows through this Gospel as a refreshing stream. Its source is Jesus, not John the Baptist, because Jesus baptizes with the life-giving Holy Spirit (John 1:33; 7:39). This metaphor of living water once applied to Wisdom and Law in the OT finds its fulfillment in Jesus' words and his gift of the Holy Spirit (John 4:14; 7:39). The water flowing from his side on the cross continues this symbolic meaning (John 19:34). This water symbol also reflects three dimensions of Jesus' identity: (1) as a teacher and prophet greater than the OT prophets, his words are spirit and life (John 3:35-36; 6:63); (2) as the one who was pierced and became the fountain to cleanse from sin, he is the promised Davidic Messiah (Zech 12:10; 13:1); (3) as the fountain or spring of living water, he is God himself (Jer 2:13; 17:13).

b. Symbolic actions. The symbolic deeds of Jesus, his works and miracles, are specifically called signs. They are signs not only because they reveal Jesus' identity but also because they manifest the new redemptive rule (kingdom) of God that is coming and is already present in Jesus. Just as the first snowflake is a sign of winter and the first flower a sign of spring not merely by giving information about the coming future but by being already ahead of a new reality that is coming, so Jesus' signs reveal by being a manifestation of the new redemptive reality that is coming and is already present in Jesus. Traditionally, scholars have spoken of seven signs: turning water into wine (John 2:1-11), healing the nobleman's son (4:46-54), healing the lame man (5:1-18), feeding the multitude (6:1-15), walking on water (6:16-21), giving sight to the man born blind (9:1-14), and raising Lazarus (11:1-57). Each of these signs reveals the significance of the Word become flesh who already is the presence of God in time and history renewing life and giving eternal life.

For example, the cross and resurrection function as sign. Even though the cross and resurrection are not specifically called signs, they are filled with symbolic significance and, when viewed as two parts of a single event, may well be considered as the climactic sign. As such, this event reveals the true nature of the glory of God, full of grace and truth, for it makes specific and completes the redemptive action signified in the prior signs. Here also there are three levels of meaning: Jesus is crucified as God's obedient Son/servant, as the messianic King defeating the people's enemy (Satan), and as the divine bearer of the glory of God who defeats the powers of evil (John 3:14; 8:28-29; 12:23-26; 13:31-34). For these reasons the cross is viewed in this Gospel as glorification, not humiliation.

C. Christology and Discipleship

1. A Trajectory of Faith

In John's Gospel the acquisition of faith is a journey of plumbing the full depths of Jesus' identity and mission. While faith on a more superficial level may be accepted as a temporary stage on the journey, Jesus challenges his disciples again and again to acknowledge the deeper dimensions of his identity. Surprisingly, the language of faith is used to describe even those who believe because of Jesus' miracles (John 2:23), yet Jesus withholds himself from them and challenges Nicodemus, who voices the same kind of faith, to accept the necessity of a new birth from above, a birth related to the lifting up of the Son of Man (John 3:1-21). Many of Jesus' disciples, when challenged by his "hard" teaching, turn away and no longer follow after him (John 6:60-66 RSV). Later many who had believed reject the necessity of receiving from Jesus freedom from sin and receive instead Jesus' harsh judgment, a judgment that echoes the OT language of God's lawsuit against God's disobedient people (John 8:31-58).

The positive narrative symbol of one who completes John's trajectory of faith is the story of the man born blind who acknowledges Jesus first as a man, then as a prophet, and finally worships the divine Son of Man as Lord (John 9). Faith that perceives the true depth of Jesus' identity echoes Thomas's confession, "My Lord and my God" (John 20:28).

2. Following Jesus as the Way, the Truth, and the Life

The truth claims made by Jesus in sign and word are a challenge and an invitation to believe in him as the only source of genuinely free human life (John 3:16; 8:31-32; 20:31). The truth revealed in Jesus is not only to be believed but walked in (2 John 4-6) because Jesus as the Way and the Truth reveals the way to live and walk in this world. His Way is an ancient path marked out by the Creator (Jer 6:16) and now revealed and made accessible by Jesus' life and teaching. The essence of walking in the truth is to love one another (John 13:34-35; 1 John 4:8). To those who walk in this Way of love and truth, Jesus gives through the Holy Spirit a life filled with his love (John 15:9), his joy (John 15:11), and his peace (John 14:27); in fact, he gives eternal life that cannot be canceled by death (John 11:25-26). While this life is given to individual believers, its essence requires that it be lived in community with other believers.

3. Disciples as Bearers of His Glory

Disciples are like their Master: "As the Father has sent me, I am sending you," and "whoever accepts anyone I send accepts me; and whoever accepts me accepts the one who sent me" (John 20:21; 13:20 NIV). Thus, the life of true discipleship continues the presence and witness of Jesus in the world: as Jesus witnessed to himself, so now his disciples equipped with the Holy Spirit as their advocate are called to be his witnesses (John 15:26-27); as Jesus was hated by the world, so his disciples are called to the same possibility (John 15:18); and as Jesus was the revealer of the glory of God (John 1:14; 13:31-35), so the disciples because of their unity with the Father and the Son have become the bearers of the glory of God in the world (John 14:23; 17:21-23). The church as the body of Christ's disciples has the high privilege of being the visible sign of the presence of the Father and the Son in the world, provided they live in unity with Christ and with one another by keeping his commandment (John 13:34-35; 17:23).

This new community of love and service is now the chief sign to the world of the ongoing presence of the God who is full of grace and truth. In fact, just as the Word become flesh was God's appointed means to overcome evil, so now the community indwelt by the living Lord is God's chosen means in the present time to resist and overcome the evil that is in the world by its life, its deeds, and its witness (compare Rev 12:10-11). In this way the church continues to manifest the present redemptive rule of God and to prepare the world for the final arrival of God's kingdom. *See* HISTORICAL CRITICISM.

Bibliography: R. E. Brown. *The Gospel According to John.* 2 vols. AB 29, 29A. (1966–70); D. A. Carson. *The Gospel According to John.* (1991); C. S. Keener. *The Gospel of John.* 2 vols. (2003); C. R. Koester. *Symbolism in the Fourth Gospel: Meaning, Mystery, Community.* (1995); A. Lincoln. *Truth on Trial: The Lawsuit Motif in the Fourth Gospel.* (2000).

LAMENTS
William S. Morrow

Preaching from the tradition of lament provides support to the life of faith by providing words for bringing human troubles before God. Other names for lament include complaint prayer and the arguing-with-God tradition.

Prayers of lament are cries for justice. Complaint prayer assumes that divine providence is always potential but not always realized. For God has not eliminated chaos, but eliminated it by thrusting it to the margins of the created order. Nevertheless, agents of chaos can temporarily gain the upper hand, just as storms may flood the dry ground or brigands invade the land of the king. Lament serves notice of these compromises of divine sovereignty and pleads for the righteous judge to act on behalf of God's good, created order, which typically includes the petitioners themselves.

Complaint psalms belong to a pattern of liturgy and theology that reflects the movement from lament to thanksgiving, from suffering to salvation—from crucifixion to resurrection. Nevertheless, lament refuses to exalt the hope of Easter to the point of trivializing the Good Friday moments in people's lives. Individual complaint psalms express the shame, grief, and fears of persons who are deathly ill or victims of adverse social circumstances. Typically, these prayers were performed in family services or in semipublic venues on an ad hoc basis under the guidance of a liturgical expert. Significant national threats such as drought or military defeat were met by proclamations of a day of prayer and fasting on which a community lament was used. Serious conflict within the congregation was also an occasion for lament (e.g., Pss 9–10). The book of Lamentations points to periodic services for remembering and processing experiences of profound trauma in the life of the community. Such observances still continue in Judaism.

Recent work on the application of lament to pastoral care emphasizes its usefulness for addressing the effects of grief and trauma. Such ministry is often directed at individuals, but collective crises such as church closings and social disasters can also be comprehended by lament. (*See* CRISIS.) Contemporary pastoral usage will often correspond to ancient practice, drawing on complaint prayer for ministry with suffering persons on an ad hoc basis. But there are important reasons to bring awareness of lament into public worship.

First, participation in the ordered grief signified by the structure of complaint psalms benefits from public proclamation. Otherwise, persons and congregations needing to avail themselves of this tradition may not know how one can grieve faithfully. There is a strong strain of Christian theology that suggests expressions of grief and doubt are signs of unfaithfulness. Lament is good news because it allows for honest mixtures of faith and doubt, of hope and despair in prayer. Lament legitimizes strong expressions of anxiety in the midst of suffering. It also communicates the normative nature of a spiritual paradox characteristic of biblical faith: confidence in the care of a just and loving Creator in a world that is often terribly unfair.

Second, sermons in the arguing-with-God tradition help worshipers challenge inadequate understandings of God while preparing the way for new understanding. Job's arguments with God, for example, oppose a retributive theology that explains human suffering as punishment for sin. The result is a fresh vision of God in Job 38–41. According to Gen 18:16-32, YHWH all but invites Abraham to question the Lord's justice. Their dialogue casts new light on the righteousness of God.

Third, complaint prayers "stand alongside other texts of the Bible that struggle against violence and in reaction to it" (Zenger 1996, 85). Preaching lament helps victims of violence to deal with feelings of anger and revenge—not by denying or censuring them, but by attempting to give them a proper focus. It is noteworthy that the petitions for revenge (imprecations) in the complaint psalms almost never seek strength from God so that victims themselves can redress the violence; rather, they give the role of avenger to God. In fact, behind the imprecations is a fierce desire to refuse to be the kind of person who perpetrates violence. These prayers are, in their own way, pleas to be liberated from a violent world.

Finally, preaching lament communicates the church's solidarity with those who suffer. Lament is good news because it underscores a pastoral purpose of the congregation. Part of the goal of lament psalms was to restore sufferers to a community of support that was tempted to ostracize or disown them. Because suffering leads to experiences of isolation, the prayers of lament are literally forms of community making in situations where community is lacking. Lament indicates to the church an essential part of its divine vocation: "to bind up the brokenhearted" and so on (Isa 61:1-2; compare Luke 4:18-19). Daring to preach the stories of the oppressed and abused is a witness to the mission of Christ.

Sermons drawing on the spirituality of lament do not necessarily have to be based on a text of complaint prayer either. Whenever injustice is challenged from the pulpit, some kind of complaint is presupposed. In fact, "the cry to God and the response of God are a fundamental theme of the whole of Scripture" (Brown and Miller 2005, 16). For example, the sermons of Martin Luther King Jr. often responded to the realities signified by lament, even though they were seldom based on complaint prayers.

Bibliography: Kathleen D. Billman and Daniel L. Migliore. *Rachel's Cry: Prayer of Lament and Rebirth of Hope.* (1999); Sally A. Brown and Patrick D. Miller, eds. *Lament: Reclaiming Practices in Pulpit, Pew, and Public Square.* (2005); Anson Laytner. *Arguing with God: A Jewish Tradition.* (1990); Erich Zenger. *A God of Vengeance? Understanding the Psalms of Divine Wrath.* (1996).

LAWS AND REGULATIONS
John C. Holbert

As a Christian preacher seeks to use the laws and regulations of the OT responsibly in a sermon, two related dangers must be avoided. Only by misreading them could the laws and regulations ever be employed as a foil for the grace of the NT; they may not be used as examples of the so-called legalism of the OT from which the NT comes to free us. And second, they should never be ripped from their contexts as free-standing laws, readily adaptable to a 21st-cent. context. These laws and regulations have a long history in Israel and a specific purpose in that history.

The laws and regulations of the OT include laws of demand (e.g., the Ten Commandments at Exod 20 and Deut 5), usually called apodictic; and laws that, when followed, promise certain results ("if this, then this"), usually called casuistic. There are hundreds of regulations concerning appropriate behavior in the community, which address wide-ranging issues from child rearing to idolatry and from agriculture to poverty. Some seem quite time bound (e.g., the warning not to boil a lamb in the milk of its mother [Exod 23:19]), while others seem quite immediately relevant for us (e.g., love your neighbor as you love yourself [Lev 19:18]). There are always a danger and a temptation to find an ancient regulation and attempt to fit it to a modern context without first taking its theological context with utmost seriousness.

A Christian preacher who desires to address this material in the OT will do well to ponder Deut 6:20-25. The book of Deuteronomy is the most important book in the OT for the ongoing survival and significance of Judaism. It was in Deuteronomy that the rabbis found the richest reflections on God's gift of torah (teaching) to God's chosen people. A careful reading of Deuteronomy can help a Christian preacher understand the crucial significance of torah for Judaism, and can further lead him or her to grasp the content and purposes of torah in that tradition. This passage from ch. 6 will begin to make it plain.

In the context of a liturgy of the exodus celebrated in a family setting (see also the Passover celebration of Exod 12:26-27), the child asks the adults: "What is the meaning (the word could also be read witness or purpose) of the decrees and statutes and ordinances that the Lord our God has commanded you?" (Deut 6:20, author's trans.). Anytime that specific laws are discussed, it is crucial to ask after the purpose of those laws before considering the meaning of those laws themselves. The answer to the child's question is surprising. The purpose of the laws is not first that if we follow them, we will be better, or that our community will be

stronger, or that our God will shower us with divine favor. No, the purpose of the laws is, first and foremost, a reminder of the basic story of God with us. "We were Pharaoh's slaves in Egypt, but the Lord brought us out of Egypt with a mighty hand" (v. 21). "[God] brought us out from there in order to bring us in, to give us the land" (v. 23). The laws themselves are a gift of God calling people into a life-sustaining relationship, not primarily a list of regulations designed to keep them under control.

Then the preacher who chooses to preach these texts may be led to reflect on Deut 7:7-8 to fix this connection between law and redemption forever in our minds: "It was not because you were more numerous (or greater) than all the nations that YHWH desired you and chose you—you were the least of all the peoples! No, it was YHWH's loving of you" (author's trans.). This central Deuteronomic claim, that YHWH's choice of Israel was born in and driven by divine love, stands at the heart of our appropriation of the laws and regulations of the OT.

Deuteronomy 6:24 states, "YHWH commanded us to observe all these statutes, to fear (or worship or stand in awe of) YHWH our God for our continuous good, to keep us alive as we are now" (author's trans.). It is only after we have remembered and celebrated the inexpressible gift of our freedom from YHWH that we turn to follow the laws of YHWH for our continuous good. The law of YHWH is nothing less than the fulfillment of God's plan of redemption for us. The gift of our freedom can have no lasting significance if not ordered by YHWH's further gift of divine regulations: "It will be for us righteousness when we strive to keep this entire commandment before YHWH our God just as we were commanded" (v. 25, author's trans.).

The Ten Commandments are a classic case in point. Both the Exodus and the Deuteronomy versions begin with a sentence that is not a commandment at all, but a statement of divine fact: "I, YHWH, am your God, who brought you out of the land of Egypt, out of the house of slavery" (Exod 20:2; Deut 5:6, author's trans.). This statement is followed by ways that we human beings deny the freedom that God has so graciously given to us. We choose other gods, making some we would rather have; we blaspheme God's mighty name and make God's time our own by refusing Sabbath's gift. Our stories feature those times when we kill, steal, commit adultery, and spend more time desiring other people's things than loving these people. In all these ways we prefer slavery to freedom, and we thereby deny God's desire to complete our redemption from slavery that God wants to make complete.

God creates, frees, and offers the law as the completion of God's desires for us. This law is God's torah, a word that more properly means "teaching." The torah of God includes not only laws and regulations but also prayers, hymns, stories, and parables. So when a Christian preacher confronts OT law, let her remember that God's law is gift, and through it, God also moves to complete our acceptance of that gift. *See* LEVITICAL HOLINESS CODES.

Bibliography: Graeme Goldworthy. *Preaching the Whole Bible as Christian Scripture.* (2000); Gordon Wenham. *Leviticus.* (1979).

LEVITICAL HOLINESS CODES
John C. Holbert

In a day when many Christian worshipers know little of basic Christian belief and practice, why should Christian preachers worry about such arcane texts as the Levitical Holiness Codes? Did not the Acts of the Apostles declare that God has made all things clean (10:13-16), hence Christians are no longer bound by former commands against eating certain foods or acting in certain ways? Have not these old laws been rendered obsolete and unimportant for Christians since in Christ all things have become new? (*See* LAWS AND REGULATIONS.)

Although such beliefs are common in many Christian communities, it remains equally clear that many OT laws, including many from the Holiness Code (Lev 17–26 is technically the code, but much Levitical material may be found in Exod, Num, and Deut), are quoted as still having universal applicability. Many sexual proscriptions, those against incest, adultery, and bestiality (Lev 20), continue to inform modern practice. Also, deep concerns for the care of poor and oppressed persons of the land (19:9-10) are still quoted as goads for modern behavior in the sight of God. At least some of these old laws still seem to contain power for us now.

However, such selective use of portions of the Holiness Code runs the risk of prooftexting, choosing only the laws that fit some predetermined understanding of modern behavior. Do the food laws (Lev 11; Deut 14), for example, have no

contemporary relevance? To answer that sort of question, we must search for some more basic sense of the ancient codes.

The anthropologist Mary Douglas has offered much help in this regard. She argues that the Holiness Code is held together by the central idea of purity that in the code is characterized by physical perfection and wholeness, both in individuals and in species or categories. Things are then pure if they are appropriate to their class. For example, "everything in the waters that has fins and scales" (Lev 11:9) may be eaten, because that is "normal." So lobsters, shrimp, and crabs may not be eaten since they are not "normal," and are hence impure and unclean. Priests may not serve at the altar if they are not physically perfect, since only those physically perfect can by definition be clean, pure, and whole.

Such a way of construing reality raises serious moral questions. By such a definition, my blind friend, who is a pastor, would never have been ordained. Thanks to Acts 10, I, as a Christian, can happily eat shrimp. Still, why should having fins and scales determine what is normal? This entire worldview runs headlong against other biblical views that are far more inclusive (e.g., Isa 56:3-5). By quoting passages from Leviticus, the preacher runs the risk of bringing this particular view of reality along, one that is a too-simple accounting of what is normal or pure in the world.

So should we then avoid this odd material altogether? Or can we find value in these texts without buying into the ancient worldview that spawned them? The priests of ancient Israel were searching for a way of being holy, just as the Lord their God was holy, a phrase used again and again in this literature. The Christian preacher should note several important conclusions that may be drawn from the priests' diligent search for holiness.

1. The possibility of my holiness is first a gift from God. God has created the world and the creatures in it, one of which I am. My goal is to become holy, as God is holy. Just as God loves the creatures God has made, so I am called to do the same (Lev 19:18). Just as God has made an ordered and stable world, so I must search for order and stability in the world of God. God has set me apart for this work, a work that goes far beyond right eating and right worship. Such order must be sought

in every area of existence, including personal and social behavior.

2. No ancient priest would have ever imagined that obedience to the law of God would earn God's favor. This pernicious idea has been kept alive in Christian pulpits for centuries and needs to be rejected as the complete misunderstanding that it is. Far too many Christian preachers have made fun of these ancient laws as silly and/or narrow attempts to buy the favor of God. Our search for holiness is undertaken only in the light of God's holiness.

3. Following the dietary and other ancient laws was a constant reminder that God was in the community, calling it to holiness. In a time when idolatry was always a great temptation, when the high gods of Canaan or Egypt or Babylon seemed to be all-too-present alternatives to the God of Exodus and Sinai, a life lived from the dinner table to the most complex moral choice helped keep idolatry at bay. In our time when gluttony and obesity seem too common, and diet crazes consume billions of dollars, a rediscovery of the direct connections between God and our food might be a way that we could avoid more modern idolatries.

4. When the priests devised the code, they said in effect that all of us are finite. We cannot simply do, cannot simply eat, anything we want. Whether we eat or drink or whatever we do, we do it in relationship with God. Is this call to recognize human finitude, to limits, not a crucial call for our time? As the oil drains away, as the atmosphere warms up, as the species disappear, our finitude under the command of the infinite God becomes more real each day. Christian preachers could learn from the priests of old that restrictions could, in fact, be very good news for those of us who think we are, in fact, not finite at all.

No Christian preacher is likely to use such texts regularly, but they need to appear in every preacher's repertoire. The Levitical Holiness Codes comprise a huge block of material in the OT and remain important for modern Judaism. And they can still speak God's word for us Christians.

Bibliography: Mary Douglas. *Leviticus as Literature.* (1999); Gordon J. Wenham. *The Book of Leviticus.* (1979).

LUKE/ACTS
Mary Margaret Pazdan

For lectionary preachers, Luke occurs in the Cycle C series of Gospel readings, while Acts appears at Easter, Ascension, and Pentecost (*RCL*); in two instances lections appear together (*ABC*). (*See* LECTIONARY AND THE CHRISTIAN YEAR.) Bibles and lectionaries separate Acts from Luke and make visual/auditory recognition of their unity less obvious. However, lectionary severance of the two should not prevent preachers from preaching sermons that consider this amazing two-volume narrative as a whole. It offers multiple responses to an essential question: How can persons follow Jesus amid living in a reign of God and an empire of extraordinary religious, political, economic, and geographical diversity?

While Luke uses historical references to situate Jesus and the disciples in the 1st cent. of the Roman Empire (e.g., Luke 1:5; 2:1-2; Acts 4:5, 27), his purpose is to present a theological, Greco-Roman biography and history that convinces hearers of God's presence to Jesus, the Jewish people, and the early church. By using clear, parallel structures, the narrator offers a continuous story with specific markers:

1. Prologues (Luke 1:1-4; Acts 1:1-5)
2. Coming of the Holy Spirit (Luke 1:5–2:52; Acts 1:2–2:41)
3. Baptism (Luke 3:1-22; Acts 1–2; 8–11)
4. Journeys: Galilee to Jerusalem (Luke 9:51–19:27) and Jerusalem to Rome (Acts 8:1–28:16)
5. End of journeys: Jerusalem (Luke 19:45–24:53) and Rome (Acts 28:17-31)

The narrator prompts hearers to connect with their experiences and dreams. For Jewish believers, there are multiple characters and references to the OT, prophets, and the Temple in Jerusalem. For Gentile believers, there are multiple characters and plots, especially Paul and his adventures through Asia Minor, as well as the Council of Jerusalem (Acts 15). There are also a distinctive theological vision and emphasis upon the reign of God within the empire that embrace basic convictions:

1. God desires all persons to be saved (3:6). For example, dual witnesses long for redemption (Zechariah and Elizabeth; Simeon and Anna).

Angels announce Jesus as the Savior. Jesus recognizes his vocation: "I *must* proclaim the good news of the kingdom of God" (4:43); I *must* be on my way, because it is impossible for a prophet to be killed outside of Jerusalem" (13:33); "Was it not *necessary* that the Messiah should suffer these things and then enter into his glory?" (24:26; Acts 17:3). In these verses, the verb "it must happen / it is necessary" (δει) indicates God's agency through Jesus.

2. God reverses expectations. The Beatitudes (6:20-23) identify persons who receive God's blessings: poor, hungry, weeping, excluded, reviled, and defamed. In contrast, empire persons (rich, full, laughing, and accolade seekers) receive God's woes (6:24-26). It is significant that poor persons (v. 20) are not spiritualized (compare Matt 5:3). They constitute more than 80 percent of the empire. But the calling of Levi (5:27-32) suggests that the Lukan community embraced a wide diversity of persons. Both volumes draw attention to care for poor persons in the reign of God through stories, miracles, and teaching. It is not an abstract, general appeal; rather, it is rooted in the very real needs of specific communities that mirror the realities of the neediest within the empire.

3. The Holy Spirit is a dynamic presence that fills, directs, and empowers characters (e.g., Mary, as well as Jesus, the disciples, and crowds). The Spirit's multiple activities in Luke continue in Acts. A clear parallel exists between the speech and deeds of Jesus and the disciples after Pentecost. The Holy Spirit exhorts preachers and congregants to continue the ministry of Jesus in our empire today. (*See* HOLY SPIRIT AND PREACHING.)

4. Prayer is essential for Jesus, the disciples, and believing communities. The Lukan Jesus is praying when the Holy Spirit anoints him (3:21). He prays, which deepens his sense of identity as he seeks the guidance that directs his words and deeds. Prayer enables Jesus to be alert, decisive, and compassionate. Likewise, prayer sustains others in this Gospel in the Temple and synagogues.

5. Meals are important in Luke/Acts. They symbolize God's providence on multiple levels (e.g., feeding on the hillside, meals with Pharisees and disciples, the Lord's Supper, the broken bread at Emmaus). Preachers can draw from those pericopes to bless and challenge congregations with fundamental questions: Who is invited to the table? Who comes? Who stays?

6. Stories involving women are numerous and significant. Women function in pairs with men. Jesus restores life to a centurion's servant at Capernaum and a widow's son at Nain (7:1-17). When Jesus teaches in parables, there is a man who searches for sheep and a woman who looks for a coin (15:3-7, 8-10). In the Acts of the Apostles, there are references to couples. Ananias and Sapphira belong to an early Christian community (5:1-11) while Priscilla and Aquila are missionaries (18:1-4, 18-28). Luke also includes nineteen stories of women that are not found in the other Gospels. (*See* FEMINIST PERSPECTIVES.)

However, critical feminists writing since the 1990s ask another question. "Do you see this woman?" (7:44). Preachers need to reexamine these stories to see how Luke may have respected the social mores of the empire because he wanted to protect the Christian community from persecution.

In this Gospel a limited character analysis is useful to uncover what is happening: Who speaks and is spoken to? Who acts and is acted upon? When Luke develops a story common to all the Gospels, he portrays a Pharisee in his status as host vis-à-vis "a woman in the city, who was a sinner," a double generic name (Luke 7:36-50; compare Matt 26:6-13; Mark 14:3-9; John 12:1-8). Her sin, as well as her religious and political impropriety, labels anyone who had anything to do with her a potential traitor. Yet Jesus affirms the woman's new status as one who has come to Jesus when he tells the debtors' story. He praises the woman as a grateful, forgiven servant and addresses her directly, "Your sins are forgiven" (v. 48).

Preachers can engage Luke/Acts with the assurance of the Spirit who ensures the continuity between the story there and the preaching and life today.

Bibliography: Paul Borgman. *The Way According to Luke: Hearing the Whole Story of Luke–Acts.* (2006).

MIRACLES
Michael P. Knowles

Preaching about scriptural and post-scriptural miracles poses in compelling fashion the question of divine intervention in human affairs. Yet by testifying to God's saving activity, all Christian preaching describes and to some extent participates in the miracle of salvation.

Whether in the history of Israel, the life of Jesus, or the ministry of the early church, miracles do not stand alone but serve to express God's gracious purpose and saving intervention in situations of acute human need. Jesus thus feeds the hungry, heals the sick, casts out demons, and calms the storm in order to demonstrate the practical and operative dimensions of God's reign. Although early apologists distinguish between miracles and magic (Justin Martyr, *1 Apol.* 30; Origen, *Cels.* 6.41), and the Talmud later denies that miracles can serve as proof (*b. Bava Metzi'a* 59b), both Jews and Gentiles of Jesus' day acknowledge the possibility of miraculous occurrences. Miracles must therefore first be understood within the worldview of their original cultural and religious contexts. Jesus' actions cannot be interpreted apart from his teaching about the establishment of God's kingdom (Matt 12:28; Luke 11:20), or from the earliest confession of his followers that he is "Messiah," "Savior," and "Lord." His miracles (as well as those of his disciples, accomplished on his authority) are intended to reflect his identity and communicate the nature of his mission.

While patristic writers affirm that miracles serve both to convince and to confirm faith (especially Augustine, *Civ.* 22.5.8) and medieval apologists see miracles as testifying to the intercessory power of the saints (e.g., Gregory of Tours' *Eight Books of Miracles*), the Reformers emphasize the relationship between the miracles of Scripture and the preaching of Christ and his apostles (John Calvin, "Dedication," *Institutes of Religion*). In a post-Enlightenment setting, preachers must weigh the prevailing skepticism of scientific rationalism against the claims of Pentecostal and charismatic Christians in particular that God continues to grant miracles in our day. But whatever a preacher's background, denomination, or piety, claims of miraculous occurrences (past and present alike) pose the challenge of the metaphysical realm, and of a reality that is more than a material or merely human construct.

Faithful preaching—especially on the subject of miracles—thus resists the impulse to reduce God to comfortably human dimensions. By definition, Christian preaching remains open to the reality, presence, and saving initiative of God, and thus also to the possibility of miracle. In this sense, preaching about the miracles of Scripture provides a classic case of the reader being "read" by the text: such preaching is diagnostic with regard to its hearers, revealing the contours and limitations of their philosophical presuppositions. This is especially important for postmodern perspectives, which acknowledge the limits of scientific rationalism and are increasingly open to mystery, wonder, and the possibility of God.

Scripture expressly challenges all perspectives other than its own, critiquing our assumptions and commanding our allegiance. For this reason, instead of simply asking, Can contemporary audiences accept the miraculous? or Are such occurrences possible today? the preacher does better to consider, If God does provide miracles, what then? and Who is this unchanging God, who acts decisively to save people like us? While Christian preaching always points beyond itself and its immediate context to the person and purpose of Jesus, preaching about miracles in particular points ultimately to the gracious character, generous provision, and saving power of God.

On the other hand, scripturally faithful preaching on this subject needs to be as forthright as is Scripture itself, which testifies to the frequent inability of the disciples to perform miracles (Mark 9:17-19) and to the persistent incredulity of some, even in the presence of the risen Christ (Matt 28:17). Jesus himself refused signs to those who demanded them (Mark 8:11-12), insisting that the ability to perform "mighty works" in his name was no indication of true piety or faithfulness (Matt 7:22-23 RSV).

It is not the task of the preacher to prove (or disprove!) miracles, much less produce them, any more than preachers are either obligated or able to generate faith on the part of their hearers. Rather, preaching is itself an act of trusting dependence upon God, relying on God to convince, convict, and console hearers. Even for preachers or congregations who find it easier to read scriptural miracles as evidences of God's general intent (e.g., to liberate from oppression, answer prayer, or alleviate human need) than as accurate historical records, the issue of direct divine intervention and its manifestation remains paramount. Preaching about miracles calls for faithful anticipation on the part of every hearer that God will also remain faithful in providing for human need and in testifying—with or without miracles—to the validity of the preached Word (Acts 14:3, 17).

In arguing that Jesus' resurrection provides the basis for Christian preaching (1 Cor 15:14), Paul implies that God's miraculous intervention does not depend on faith so much as inspire it, as was the case with the initially skeptical apostles. (*See* RESURRECTION.) Similarly, that "Jews demand signs and Greeks seek wisdom, but we preach Christ crucified" (1 Cor 1:22-23 RSV) implies that neither preaching nor miracles can satisfy our desire for power and certainty, but that the most profound evidence of God's work is the response of faith itself. Thus, according to Augustine, the conversion of the preacher's audience is the most convincing miracle: "We are still left with the one stupendous miracle, which is all we need: the miracle of the whole world believing, without benefit of miracles, the miracle of the Resurrection" (*Civ.* 22.5).

Bibliography: Augustine. *The City of God: An Abridged Version from the Translation by G. G. Walsh, et al.* Edited by Vernon J. Bourke. (1958); Wendy Cotter. *Miracles in Greco-Roman Antiquity: A Sourcebook.* (1999); Eric Eve. *The Jewish Content of Jesus' Miracles.* (2002); Graham H. Twelftree. *Jesus the Miracle Worker: A Historical and Theological Study.* (1999).

PARABLES
Barbara E. Reid

If we had only the SYNOPTIC GOSPELS, we would think that Jesus preached exclusively in parables (Matt 13:34; Mark 4:34). This kind of preaching drew varied reactions. There were those who were puzzled by what he meant or by what response was demanded, including his closest disciples (Mark 4:10-12). There were others who understood the point perfectly well and who plotted to do away with this preacher (Mark 12:12). By examining some dynamics of the parables and analyzing how parables function, contemporary preachers can learn to emulate Jesus' manner of storytelling and proclamation, and so engage their listeners more effectively with the gospel message.

One of the ways in which Jesus used parables was to address a sensitive topic in a manner that was not confrontational, thus disposing his listeners to be more receptive to the challenge in his message. For example, in Luke 7:36-50, where Jesus is dining at the home of Simon, instead of directly confronting his host about his misjudgment of himself and of the woman who anoints his feet, Jesus instead tells a parable about two debtors. In the story world, Simon quickly sees Jesus' point. The question remains at the end of the incident whether Simon will be able to move to a correct perception of the woman and of Jesus. Likewise, contemporary preachers may be able to more easily convert hearts and move congregations to action by engaging them with parables than by direct confrontation.

Another characteristic of Jesus' parables is his use of vivid images from everyday life. His listeners knew what happened when a sower sowed seed on various types of soil (Mark 4:1-9), or when a woman put leaven into bread dough (Matt 13:33 // Luke 13:20-21). Everyone knew what it was like to search for a lost sheep or a lost coin (Luke 15:3-10). This is not only an important attention-getting device at the outset of the preaching, but it communicates an important theological message about incarnational faith: the stuff of daily life is where God is encountered each day. In the style of parables, effective preachers avoid abstract verbiage, and they use colorful, familiar language and down-to-earth examples to bring alive the message.

One problem for contemporary hearers is that the imagery in the gospel parables, while very familiar to 1st-cent. hearers, is not so understandable for 21st-cent. believers in industrialized, technology-driven societies. Those in present-day agrarian settings might find the world of the Gospels more familiar, but urban dwellers may need a good deal of explanation to understand the metaphors and images. But having to explain a parable risks ruining its rhetorical impact. It is like telling a good joke and then having to explain the punch line. One technique that can be effective is to construct a modern-day parable that replicates the dynamics and message of the gospel story, but with contemporary language and imagery. This is very tricky to do well, however, since parables are complex and ambivalent, and it may not always be possible to preserve crucial characteristics in a modern version. (*See* CONTEMPORIZING.)

Jesus' parables do not stay on the level of the mundane. While the story is told in terms of recognizable everyday realities, there is always a deeper meaning, having to do with God or life in the realm of God. A shepherd looking for a sheep or a woman searching for a coin can speak of God's seeking out the lost through the ministry of Jesus. Discovering a buried treasure or a pearl of great price can lead to reflection on how one becomes a disciple and at what cost.

The familiar world with which gospel parables start is usually shattered, as there is often a twist that turns the story upside down. Like a boomerang, such parables can turn back on the hearer in unexpected ways. Parables are not pleasant stories meant to entertain; they are startling and confusing. The function of parables is to unsettle, to open up the hearer to conversion. By shattering the structures of the accepted world, they penetrate our defenses and make us vulnerable to God. Parables do not necessarily reassure; they do not typically reinforce life as it is—that is the function of myth. When contemporary preachers are being parabolic, they are seeking not to console, but to invite the hearers to conversion of heart and to subsequent action.

One of the most difficult characteristics of Jesus' parables is that they are in some ways open-ended, which makes them subject to a variety of interpretations. For example, at the end of the story of the father and two sons (Luke 15:11-32), the father is still pleading with the elder son to come in to the party. Does he? That is for the hearer to decide. Moreover, the message of the parable can depend on the character with which the hearer identifies. From the younger son's perspective, the parable is an invitation to accept the gratuitous love of God, which is never earned or deserved, as the first step toward repairing broken relationships. If the hearer identifies with the elder son, the invitation is to let go attitudes of slavish obedience and joyless resentment, to move to a spirit of rejoicing with God over all who are brought into the divine embrace—including oneself! From the perspective of the father, the parable invites persons in authority to allow themselves to be so filled with love for those under their care that they would go to extraordinary lengths to seek out all the lost ones, both those who are lost while at home and those who have gone away.

These three different perspectives do not exhaust the meaning of this parable. With parables there is not one stable meaning for all times and places. Some preachers make the mistake of thinking that once they know the meaning of a gospel parable, the task is simply to replicate that meaning with modern examples. Instead, the preacher's task is to study the parable intently to ferret out the diverse possible meanings, then to discern, in light of the contemporary situation of her or his congregation, which is the message that is most needed at this time and place for this particular congregation. Of course, the needs of diverse members of the congregation vary.

One other caution: just because parables can have more than one meaning, it does not mean that a parable can mean anything we want. Nor are all interpretations equally valid. Preachers must employ tools of critical biblical interpretation to determine possible meanings in the original context before bridging to the contemporary situation of the hearers. (*See* BRIDGING THEN AND NOW.) When one's interpretation of a parable moves in the direction of offering good news to those most downtrodden, and a word of challenge to those with power, privilege, and status, then its interpretation is likely to be closer to that intended by Jesus. There is a further challenge to preachers who like to give neat answers and tidy conclusions. Parabolic preaching invites the hearers into a world of mystery, paradox, and ambiguity. Jesus points the way to the truth, but invites the hearer to figure out how to embark upon that path. Parabolic preaching makes the hearer an active participant in determining the meaning of the text and acting upon it.

One final characteristic of Jesus' parables: they are short and to the point. Their brevity and vivid imagery make them easy to remember and enhance their impact. So, too, contemporary preachers would do well to master the art of pithy expression. Along with this is the skill for elaborating only one powerful point. Homilies that have one clear message proclaimed in vivid language are those that are longest remembered.

In the late 19th cent. the German biblical scholar Adolf Jülicher revolutionized the study of parables by arguing that a parable has only one main point, and that it must be sought in the historical context of the teaching of Jesus (1899). Prior to Jülicher, many exegetes approached parables as allegories (*see* ALLEGORY, ALLEGORESIS), in which every detail of the story had a symbolic meaning. Two good examples of allegorical interpretation can be found right in the biblical text, at Mark 4:13-20 (and parallels) and Matt 13:18-23, in which the parables of the sower and the weeds among the wheat are explained. Most scholars agree that these allegorical interpretations represent the voice of Jesus from early Christian communities. Since the time of Jülicher, there has been much debate over the degree to which parables invite or allow allegorical interpretation. Even though Jülicher's "one point" conclusion is now recognized as extreme, this challenge does not give license to a strategy of rampant allegorization.

Finally, an effective preacher may become a lived parable as her or his very life becomes more and more conformed to that of Jesus, and so both instructs and puzzles the wider society. Parabolic living and witnessing to the gospel in the pulpit and beyond give power for transformation to the preaching.

Bibliography: John R. Donahue. *The Gospel in Parable: Metaphor, Narrative, and Theology in the Synoptic Gospels.* (1988); William R. Herzog II. *Parables as Subversive Speech.* (1994); Adolf Jülicher. *Die Gleichnisreden Jesu.* 2nd ed. 2 vols. (1899); Barbara Reid. *Parables for Preachers.* 3 vols. (1999, 2000, 2001); Luise Schottroff. *The Parables of Jesus.* Translated by Linda M. Maloney. (2006); Klyne Snodgrass. *Stories of Intent.* (2008).

PASSION NARRATIVES
Mary Margaret Pazdan

On Passion Sunday and Good Friday, Christians gather to listen to the story of Jesus' betrayal, arrest, suffering, and death. Often individuals assume the roles of characters in the Passion Narrative (PN). The congregation, too, is encouraged to become the crowd that condemns Jesus, "Crucify him. Crucify him." Many are uncomfortable. They do not want to be identified with the Jews. Seldom do we hear vivid, strong acclamations to condemn Jesus.

Preachers struggle with the culture of congregations that assume the PN is a historical account. An insert in the church bulletin can help the congregation to contextualize the PN. Reconstructed 1st-cent. history indicates that Judea was under Roman rule. Caiaphas and Pilate were responsible

for peace in Jerusalem. Caiaphas, overseer for the Temple and guards, was a Roman appointee. Pilate and his soldiers visited Jerusalem during annual pilgrimage festivals to handle crowds. Jewish leaders and people had no authority to put Jesus to death, but Pilate executed individuals for threatening Roman dominion. Jesus' words and deeds about the kingdom of God made him popular among the crowds. His crucifixion was a general, political punishment of the empire that religious authorities endorsed.

Another challenge is how to use the theological story of Jesus' suffering and death. The Gospels express early Christian communities' understanding about why Jesus died as well as their experience of Jewish people and life in the empire. Conflicts between Christian minorities and a majority of Jewish communities influenced the evangelists' descriptions of Jewish characters. Threats of persecution and living peacefully affected Roman characters. Additionally, these narratives carry the conviction that God acted decisively in the death and resurrection of Jesus to save God's people and the whole world.

Character analysis offers preachers insights into the story.

1. *Jesus* is protagonist, not victim, in Matthew. He announces his death and interacts with Jewish and Roman characters. Many characters conspire to betray and publicly humiliate Jesus before the Sanhedrin, in Pilate's court, at the cross. However, enemies fail to alter his status before crowds because they ask about identity claims using titles of honor: king of the Jews, Son of God, king of Israel (27:37, 40, 42). Ironically, hearers/readers know these titles are true. At the last supper Jesus' speech about a new kingdom and resurrection (26:29, 32) is confirmed in post-resurrection narratives (28:1-20), a vindication of his honor. In John, Jesus' love for "his own" to "the end" brackets events from the last supper to his final words on the cross (13:1; 19:30). When arrested, Jesus takes initiative, "I am he"; replies to Annas and Caiaphas about his teaching; and dialogues with Pilate, his colleague. On the cross, the trilingual inscription identifies Jesus as king of the Jews (27:37).

2. *Disciples* share the Lord's Supper and flee Gethsemane. In Matthew, Judas conspires to betray Jesus; he gives money back and repents. He is a literary foil for Jewish authorities, whereas in John, he accompanies a crowd with lanterns to arrest Jesus. Many women followers witness his

crucifixion. Joseph of Arimathea provides for his burial. John adds the Beloved Disciple who appears at supper, in the courtyard, at the foot of the cross with Jesus' mother. There, Jesus gives them into one another's care, thereby creating a new family of disciples in light of Jesus' cross.

3. *Religious authorities*, often stereotypical characters, deliver Jesus up to death. In Matthew, chief priests and elders plot his death with Judas. They persuade the crowd to ask for Barabbas's release and demand Jesus' crucifixion. Caiaphas affirms Jesus' false witnesses and surrenders power to chief priests and elders, a historical improbability. In both Gospels, Jewish police, a literary fiction, carry out the chief priests' orders.

4. *The Jews* (hoi Ioudaioi) appear thirty-one times in John where roles of religious authorities and Jewish people blur. Their declarations to Pilate shift quickly from a law forbidding execution (18:31) to one demanding execution for Jesus because he claims to be Son of God (19:7). Pilate's response, "Here is your King!" is met with "crucify him" and "we have no king but the emperor" (19:14-15).

5. *Roman characters*, often stereotypical characters, are not innocent according to history. Pilate, a wavering prefect, finds Jesus innocent and attempts to free him from the people's demand, "Let him be crucified!" (Matt 27:23). His public hand-washing ritual before a rioting mob is scarcely tenable. Contrastingly, a subject people curses, "His blood (haima) be on us and on our children!" (Matt 27:24-25).

Pastoral praxis challenges preachers with two questions. (1) Who was responsible for Jesus' death? Jewish culpability appears in the texts if interpreted literally without nuance. Historically, the Romans were ultimately responsible for Jesus' death with a few Jewish leaders' initiative. Theologically, deicide and the blood curse (see above, numbers 4 and 5) were interpreted to include God's rejection and punishment of the Jews as the chosen people, interpretations that led Christians to acquiesce and even cooperate with the Holocaust. (2) Why did Jesus die? Although various Christian communities will provide many interpretations, basically Christian faith has affirmed the saving character of Jesus' death.

Recent films, for example, Mel Gibson's movie, *The Passion of the Christ*, challenge preachers with a new context of the PN. Communities want to hear the truth about Jesus' suffering and death. They listen to these narratives as eyewitness, historical accounts of Jesus and his opponents. Such movies claim to portray Jesus and his opponents literally. Some characters are agents of Jesus' death; others are disciples, crowds, individuals. Mel Gibson's film of Jesus' violent suffering appeals to some audiences that identify with the violence to experience the saving event of Jesus' death in new ways.

Nonetheless, emphasizing the violence of the PN does not emphasize its theological significance. By focusing on the emotional impact of such violence, preachers can obscure the deeper theological meaning and disregard the minimal violence of the PN.

Many denominations and interreligious groups have seen clear anti-Semitism in portrayals such as *The Passion of the Christ*. Preachers need to be aware of how to retell the PN with sensitivity about any anti-Semitic language. Some preachers have responded by using lections lacking polemical Jewish verses. Since preaching cannot include every interpretation, congregational education and gatherings are essential. *See* LITERARY CRITICISM.

Bibliography: Paul Fredricksen and Adele Reinhartz, eds. *Jesus, Judaism and Christian Anti-Judaism: Reading the New Testament after the Holocaust.* (2002); *Perspectives on the Passion of the Christ: Religious Thinkers and Writers Explore the Issue Raised by the Controversial Movie.* Foreword by Jonathan Burnham (2004).

PASTORAL EPISTLES
See CONTEXTUAL EPISTLES.

PENTATEUCHAL NARRATIVES
Dennis T. Olson

The narratives of the Pentateuch provide the biblical preacher with engaging and theologically rich stories of ancestors in the faith that, with some guidance, can resonate with contemporary hearers as truthful and compelling witnesses to the God of Jesus Christ.

"A Wandering Aramean Was My Ancestor": Claiming the Bible's Foundational Stories as Our Own

The ancient narratives of the Pentateuch (Gen–Deut) tell the Bible's foundational stories of God, Israel, and the world, stretching from the two creation stories in Gen 1 and 2 to Moses' last words to a new generation of Israelites on the edge of the promised land of Canaan in Deuteronomy. Jewish tradition regards the Pentateuch (or Torah) as the most authoritative part of its Hebrew Scripture, and the exodus story (Exod 12–15) as the essential master narrative for Jewish identity and vocation. The Christian tradition has always (except for a few heretics like Marcion) regarded the stories of the Pentateuch as an authoritative witness to the God of Jesus Christ, seeing in Israel's stories a mirror of the church's hopes, fears, failures, and promises (1 Cor 10:1-13). The pentateuchal story of Adam and Eve in the garden of Eden (Gen 1–3) has played an especially important role in the Christian master narrative of sin and redemption in the history of Christian biblical interpretation and preaching.

Ancient Israelite worshipers brought their offerings to the altar in worship and recited their tradition's creedal narrative confession of what God has done for God's people, claiming it as their own: "A wandering Aramean was my ancestor" (Deut 26:4-11; 6:20-25). At the annual festival of Passover, worshipers celebrate "because of what the Lord did for me when I came out of Egypt" (Exod 13:8). The pentateuchal narratives are meant to be recited and reclaimed as our stories in the context of the worship of God. In reclaiming these stories as ours, Christian preachers remember that these OT stories are first of all the heritage of historical Israel and people of Jewish faith. However, in Christ, Gentile Christians and the church have been grafted or adopted into the covenantal story line of God and God's people. Thus, Christians have a humble but rightful claim to these stories as belonging to them as well (Rom 11:17-20; Gal 3:27–4:7).

The preacher will at times need to help the congregation understand some of the ancient cultural background so as to get to the enduring human issues of life, death, and faith that these stories embody. (*See* BRIDGING THEN AND NOW.) Each pentateuchal text should be studied carefully within its OT cultural and literary context as a first step in order to acknowledge the OT witness's integrity. As a second step, the interpreter should put the pentateuchal text in dialogue with other OT voices and then in dialogue with the theological witnesses of the NT when appropriate and helpful (e.g., compare Gen 15:1-6; Rom 4:9-15; Jas 2:14-26).

"And So They Plundered the Egyptians": The Pentateuch, Preaching and Adapting the Resources of Our Culture

When the Israelite slaves left Egypt in the exodus from bondage, they asked for and received gold and silver jewelry from the Egyptians. The precious jewelry helped to furnish God's holy tabernacle in the wilderness (Exod 35:20-29) but was also used to construct the idolatrous golden calf (Exod 32:1-6). The story is a commentary on the necessity of relying on and using whatever resources are available in the culture in which we are embedded while, at the same time, critically assessing and adapting those resources in light of the church's scriptural traditions and theology. Thus, the early church mined the treasures of ancient Greek philosophy and rhetoric to shape its theology, creeds, and proclamation, citing the Israelite plundering of the Egyptians as a model.

The development of the pentateuchal narratives themselves illustrates this borrowing from the wider culture. Many pentateuchal stories arose and were adapted from traditions of the wider ancient Near Eastern cultural context in which ancient Israel emerged. Examples include the creation stories of the Babylonian *Enuma Elish* (Gen 1), the flood story of the Babylonian Epic of Gilgamesh (Gen 6–9), the case law of the Code of Hammurabi (Exod 21–23), or the heroic legend of the Babylonian king Sargon (Exod 2). However, Israel adapted these resources that often originated in polytheistic contexts to conform to their theological, ethical, and social norms shaped by Israel's distinctive faith in one God who was sovereign over all the earth (Exod 19:5-6; 20:3; Deut 32:39).

In this way, the pentateuchal narratives themselves authorize and guide the biblical preacher to place the Bible's distinctive stories and witness in dialogue with the contemporary issues, language, images, media, and methods that make the biblical word persuasive, compelling, relevant, and engaging to contemporary rhetorical contexts and audiences. Effective proclamation of the Word made flesh will seek to strike a delicate balance between adapting to the rhetorical culture and audience being addressed, on the one hand, and being faithful to the distinctive and often countercultural voice of Scripture, on the other.

"I Will Be Who I Will Be": The Unfolding Revelation of God's Character and Name in the Pentateuch

Part of the preacher's task is a gradual, week-by-week unveiling of God's deeper character and activity to a congregation through engagement with particular texts of Scripture and particular contexts of the community in which the preacher ministers. In the book of Exodus, the name of God unfolds in various stages throughout the narratives of Exodus, moving from the mysterious "I Will Be Who I Will Be" (Exod 3:14, author's trans.) to the newly expanded name of "the Lord your God, who brought you out of the land of Egypt . . . a jealous God, punishing . . . to the third and the fourth generation . . . but showing steadfast love to the thousandth generation of those who love me and keep my commandments" (Exod 20:2, 5-6).

The crisis of the near fatal rebellion of Israel's worship of the golden calf (Exod 32) required yet another and deeper revelation of God's name and character in Exod 33–34. In a dramatic reversal, God is no longer first of all a "punishing" God (Exod 20:5-6) but a God who is above all "merciful and gracious, / slow to anger, / and abounding in steadfast love and . . . forgiving iniquity" (Exod 34:6-7). Consequences of disobedience will remain ("by no means clearing the guilty" [Exod 34:7]), but the judgment of God is moved to a secondary and muted position. God's overriding mercy, love, and forgiveness will have the final word.

Significantly, all five books of the Pentateuch conclude their major narrative arcs with definitive assurances of God's positive blessing, promise, or presence after a period of judgment or conflict: Jacob's blessing of the twelve sons in Gen 49:1-27, God's restored presence in Exod 40:34-38, the assurance of forgiveness after exile in Lev 26:40-45, the rise of a new generation of hope in the wilderness after the death of the older generation in Num 26–36, and Moses' blessing of the twelve tribes in Deut 33:1-29 in spite of their disobedience (Deut

31:29). The overarching message of the Pentateuch's narratives resonates with the rest of the Bible, including the NT: God's love and mercy will in the end triumph over the powers of chaos, sin, and death.

"I Have Let You See It . . . But You Shall Not Cross Over There": The Enduring Realism of the Stories of Genesis–Deuteronomy

Even as the pentateuchal narratives offer genuine hope and promise, they are at the same time profoundly realistic. There is no Pollyannaish "happily ever after" ending. The blessings are temporary (Gen 3; Exod 1:8). The fulfillments are partial and often endangered (Gen 15; 22:1-19). In the concluding narrative of the Pentateuch, God allows Moses to see only a glimpse of the promised land of Canaan before he dies; Moses can see it but not enter it (Deut 34:1-12). In the story of God's people, glimpses of the promised land are sometimes all that can be hoped for in this life. God's people will continue to sin (Judg 2:11-23). Tragedies will occur (Ps 13; Job 1–2). At times God will seem absent (1 Sam 3:1). Thus, the Pentateuch points forward in hope and expectation to the rest of the biblical story, including the stories of Jesus and his earliest followers. Even in light of genuine Christian hope in the God of Jesus Christ, however, the ancient stories of the Pentateuch retain their relevance. Like their pentateuchal ancestors, the lives of post-NT Christians continue to experience similar trials, tribulations, and tragedies as well as genuine glimpses of God's promised land. The pentateuchal narratives thereby endure as faithful and compelling resources for Christian preaching in our contemporary world.

Bibliography: J. P. Fokkelman. *Reading Biblical Narrative: An Introductory Guide.* (1999); Terence Fretheim. *The Pentateuch.* (1996); Steven Mathewson. *The Art of Preaching Old Testament Narrative.* (2002).

PETRINE EPISTLES

See CONTEXTUAL EPISTLES.

PREHISTORY
Raymond C. Van Leeuwen

Primeval history in the Bible designates the first eleven chapters of Genesis, encompassing creation, rebellion in the garden, fratricide, the rise of the arts of creation (Lamech's sons), earth corrupted and filled with violence, judgment by flood, a new beginning with Noah, leading to the "tower of Babel" (= Babylon), and concluding with an incomplete genealogy that stops with barren Abram and Sarai. Chapter 12 thus begins God's new initiative in the call and promises to Abram that lead to Israel and the Messiah.

A. Modern Expectations Cause Confusion
B. Texts Address Worldview Questions
   1. Our Lived Environment
   2. All Creatures Are God's Subjects
   3. Sin and Evil Are Not Natural
C. Relations among Different Creatures
D. Human Harmony Is Broken

A. Modern Expectations Cause Confusion

Scholars use the term primeval or *prehistory* because the realities portrayed here predate writing. They are inaccessible to normal historical research, and the genres used are more "mythic" than historical. (Mythic here does not mean "false," but a way of portraying reality.) These chapters describe pre-historical divine actions (the creation) that set the conditions for nature and history. The human actions depicted are also of a foundational, archetypal sort, condensing long historical and cultural developments into genealogies and parable or myth-like genres (compare Gen 11:1-9 with Isa 14:4-20; Gen 3 with Ezek 28).

Today these chapters cause confusion, even for preachers, largely because we bring modern expectations to texts whose issues and means of communication are different than ours. In particular, both "liberals" and "conservatives" have brought scientific issues to the Prehistory. The former conclude that the texts are scientifically and historically deficient, while the latter strive to defend the Bible's "literal truth" in the face of scientific evidence for the processes of cosmic development, and the great antiquity of creation and humanity. Both approaches disrespect the text and fail to hear its message.

This article means to help preachers and laypeople understand the message of the Prehistory and the means by which it is communicated. These texts, for all their strangeness, are God's word about reality, also for us.

When we compare the stories of Gen 1–11 to the tales most like them from the ancient Near East (such as *Atrahasis, Enuma Elish,* and *Gilgamesh,* tablet 11), we see that they are in the genres of myth and legend. Israel used the literary resources of its day to speak truth about God and reality, in opposition to the polytheistic worldviews of Mesopotamia, Egypt, and Canaan. The genres and topics are similar, but the message is different. This message is especially important in our time of destroyed natural resources, global warming, widespread violence, national and ethnic enmity, and injustice. In an age of pluralism, it also makes the radical claim that Israel's God, the Father of Jesus Christ, is the only Creator, Judge, and gracious Redeemer of all things.

B. Texts Address Worldview Questions

Like the NT book of Revelation, these stories do not so much give us the detailed facts (compare Revelation 12's story of the birth of Jesus and the church), as the true meaning of cosmos and history, either in broad outline or in archetypal stories. Using the tools of their day, these texts address "worldview questions," such as all thoughtful societies ask. N. T. Wright has suggested they are as follows: (1) "Where are we?" (2) "Who are we?" (3) "What is wrong?" (4) "What is the solution?" (Wright 1996, 121–44; sequence modified).

1. Our Lived Environment
The first question concerns our lived environment, in two senses: What sort of reality do we live in? And where in the history of that reality are we? It is clear that the Prehistory begins with an elaborate answer to this question. The God of Israel made all that is, so that there exist only *Creator, Creation* with its diverse *creatures,* and the relations among them. Creator is not Creation, and vice versa. Outside of Israel, the gods are at the same time creators and (powers within) creation. But in Israel's "Priestly" account (Gen 1:1–2:3/4a), God is presented in the implicit metaphor of a King with his royal court (Gen 1:26, "Let us make…"), who builds for himself a cosmic "house" (see Prov 3:19-20; 24:3-4). Following a

common ANE pattern, in the first three days of creation God builds the "rooms" of the cosmic house by making (walls of) separation. In the corresponding three days, each room is filled with the appropriate creatures: (4) heavenly lights, (5) sky creatures (birds) and water creatures, and (6) land animals and "Adam." On the seventh day, God, as it were, relaxed and celebrated the completion of his house (compare Exod 31:17). This world is God's "house" or temple/palace where he intends to dwell with us his royal human servants (see Rev 21–22).

Several points are crucial to preach here, for they help us know who God is and how God relates to everything in the world. First, God creates by giving the cosmos order by God's word of command. Contrary to modern worldviews, humans do not own the world or anything in it. God does. Nor do we give meaning or purpose to reality. God does. God's order encompasses not just "nature," but also the "cultural" order of society and history. Thus, God gives sun, moon, and stars to set humanity's cultural calendar (Gen 1:14b), and plants "for food." The distinctions of plants and animals "according to their kind" will be used by historical Israel to determine things holy, clean and unclean, edible and inedible (Leviticus; Wenham 1987, 169-70).

2. All Creatures Are God's Subjects

Second, all creatures are God's servants, subject to God's will and order. God commands and they exist. The sun and moon, which the ancients worshiped, are not even named. They are merely servants assigned a function in God's great house. God makes light without them (Day 1); God does not need them, but humans do (Day 4). God's servants are not slaves: both animals and humans receive the King's blessing of life and fruitfulness. They are to "fill" the house with their offspring, and for humans, this means to fill it with the King's glory embodied in themselves as servant-kings made in God's image (see Ps 8; 1 Cor 11:7; 15:35-49). This blessing is also a task. To be human (image of God) is to rule as a minor king on God's behalf, as a responsible servant, each of us, with our own little kingdom or "garden" to care for, according to the good purposes of God. These principles apply also to social institutions and organizations.

3. Sin and Evil Are Not Natural

Third, God's creation and God's creatures are simply good. Sin and evil are not "natural," but are distortions of creation. Thus, Genesis opposes "Gnostic" worldviews that downplay "material" things in favor of "spiritual" things. Created entities are spiritual entities—including our bodies, sexuality, and "material" things (see Col 2:20-23; 1 Tim 4:3-5). Biblically, all things are seen in relation to the Creator and thus, as spiritually consequential, whether for good or evil. To see anything merely as "secular," apart from this relationship to God, is to see it abstractly and falsely. Like God's tabernacle house (Exod 40), all the earth is filled with God's glory (Isa 6:3). All things are spiritual, so that our material bodies are God's temple (1 Cor 6:19-20), or are subject to spiritual forces that Paul names "the flesh." All this can and should be preached as aspects of biblical wisdom about our bodily life in the creation. But more than this, one can proclaim the wisdom of God, who made all things good and filled the earth with splendor. Faith believes in a good Creator, even when tragedy or sin seems to call that belief into question.

C. Relations among Different Creatures

While Gen 1 focuses on distinctions and diversity of kinds, ch 2, usually ascribed to the Yahwist writer (J), focuses on the relations among different creatures. Even wordplay is enlisted to make this point: ʾadham is made from the ʾadhamah, "human from the humus." That is, to be human is to be made of cosmic stuff and, like other "living creatures" (nefesh khayyah in 1:20 and 2:7), a part of the cycles of nature. The animals are brought to Adam because he is a social creature, someone who needs an ʿezer keneghdo, "a counterpart to help" in the human task. As this partner in the human task, "woman" is made from "man" (ʾishah from ʾish).

God gives humans great freedom to know and shape reality, as shown in the naming of the animals. This naming is a sort of secondary creation, for in the ANE, to name things is to know them and determine their function and destiny—is a plant for food, making flax, creating a watershed, making money, or building a church? All are possible. By "naming," humans can develop creation in ways that glorify God and bless creatures, or destroy and corrupt. Thus this freedom is placed within reality limits: they may not eat of the tree of the knowledge of good and evil, lest they die (2:17). They may not take the Creator's place and determine for themselves what is good or bad.

So Gen 2 complements the account of human-ness given in ch 1, where Adam, male and female, is made as the "image of God" (lit. "statue of God"). This royal language (compare Ps 8) means that humans are God's representatives on earth, given the task of ruling and serving the earth on God's behalf, according to God's purposes. King-like authority and power are given only to serve God and the creatures entrusted to the human king's care (compare 1 Kgs 12:7). Thus Genesis 1–2 answers also the question, "Who are we?" and related questions, like what is our purpose on earth? To preach this fact of God-given identity and purpose in secular America is both necessary and liberating.

D. Human Harmony Is Broken

Chapter 3 introduces the problem in the cosmic metanarrative: humanity's rebellion against the word and order of the heavenly King for creation. Here humanity rejects God's word about reality (eat of this tree and die) and, listening to the snake's alternate word (eat and be like God), decides to determine the meaning and goodness of reality by itself! By eating of a tree that is good (as Eve's experience rightly tells her), but not good for her, Eve and Adam step outside the created conditions that make life possible. They are driven from the garden of Life in God's presence, and begin to die in the midst of life.

God responds to human rebellion with grace and judgment. Judgment, in that humans now die, struggle for life in a creation subjected to futility (Rom 8:18-23), and struggle with enmity even in the intimacy of marriage. Mutual blame is the first response of Adam and Eve to their "exposure." Grace, in that God covers their nakedness and shame and, in spite of sin, preserves them in life with much good to enjoy, including children. Indeed, even the judgments of God are merciful. Both sin and suffering are cut short by death, so that the truly evil cannot triumph forever. More profoundly, suffering and death confront us: we are mere "breath" (Abel's name in Hebrew), and must flee to God for mercy and life.

Vertical rebellion against God soon leads to horizontal sin: brother kills brother. But God's common grace preserves Cain alive, and from his line comes the city and other gifts to society (4:20-22). The genealogies sum up God's grace and judgment.

There is birth, life, death, and a new generation. God is not yet through with creation.

As "mythic" narrative, the flood story portrays the reality of God's cosmic judgments. Floods did happen in the ANE, as tsunamis happen today. Ultimately, every generation dies completely. This is simply our human condition. The story represents this truth through its cosmic scope. (In the Joseph story, the famine, by lack of water, also covers the entire earth; Gen 41:54, 56-57). As sin (ch 6) ruined and undid the creation, so the flood undoes the creation, especially the separations of Gen 1. God's judgments sometimes appear as interventions; more often they are simply the cosmic consequences of human behavior. We reap what we sow. The flood story forces us to contemplate God's hand in that reality. There is also grace: Noah and his family preserve all living creatures, and there is a re-creation of life-giving order as the waters recede. Now, sacrifice for sin, as a means of grace, is more clearly basic to continued human existence. God makes a covenant with Noah and with all creation and its creatures, promising never to totally destroy the earth.

In spite of grace, Noah abuses the gifts of creation and human labor (wine!), leading to a curse that prefigures Israel's later conflict with Canaan (not Ham!). The story of the Tower of Babel (actually Babylon), takes sin from the primeval rebellion of Adam and Eve to the edge of history. Babylon, throughout the Bible, is both a literal, historical city, and also the city symbolic of human civilization arrayed against God. (Jerusalem will be its positive historical and symbolic counterpart.) Here the collective power of sin, through organized wealth, commerce, and technology is portrayed as an attempt to storm heaven and take God's place as ruler of the universe (see Isa 14:4-20; Rev 17–19). In judgment and grace, God once again inhibits the power of sin. He divides human unity: language against language, culture against culture, race against race, and nation against nation. The world cannot be wholly united in its opposition to God and the good. But human harmony in God's service is also broken, until the nations at Pentecost begin to undo Babel through the Holy Spirit of Christ (Acts 2).

The Prehistory ends in ambiguity. The nations are scattered, Abram's line of blessing-to-be is barren. Is the story one of failure? No matter how much grace God gives, humanity always rebels again, destroying life? Is the story one of success? No matter how much humans sin, God graciously makes new beginnings? The story here is unfinished. With the command and promises to Abram, God makes a new start (Gen 12:1-3). *See* LITERARY CRITICISM.

Bibliography: Walter Brueggemann. *Genesis.* (1982); David J. A. Clines, *The Theme of the Pentateuch.* (1978); Gordon J. Wenham. *Genesis 1–15.* WBC 1 (1987); N. T. Wright. *The New Testament and the People of God.* (1996).

PROPHETIC PREACHING
Mary Donovan Turner

Prophetic preaching is a form of proclamation that critically questions the status quo, offers theological insight into the current situation, and challenges people to repent by performing God's justice and extending God's compassion. This understanding of prophetic preaching is rooted in the collected and edited words recorded for us in the OT. There, particularly in the words of the latter prophets, major (Isa; Jer; Ezek) and minor (Hos; Joel; Amos; Obad; Jonah; Mic; Nah; Hab; Zeph; Hag; Zech; Mal), we come to know something of the times, missions, and life experiences of those chosen to deliver a message from God. Their recorded words, which collectively make up one of the three sections of the OT, provide for us the locus for our thinking.

The prophets bring a particular word to their communities, depending upon the political and social circumstances of their places and times. Thus, the language and metaphors used by each prophet are distinctive, and the issues named reflect their observations of the daily living of the Israelites and the national, political situation of their rulers. As with all metaphors, they are constrained by the situations that give them rise. At the same time, the prophetic language paints for us vivid portraits of what was happening in the community.

Some prophets describe for us their call into such a vocation. In the collective portrait painted of the prophets' calls and ministries, we are made aware that the tasks of the prophet are challenging, often excruciating. The prophets are called to be change makers, to shake the community out of its complacency and apathy. They describe an alternative to the world's ways of living. The words that the prophet speaks can be harsh and fall upon deaf ears. Jeremiah particularly describes the prophetic life as a lonely and dangerous one.

Although it is difficult to generalize the prophetic message, for most, the prophetic task begins with a careful observation and naming of the realities of the people's living. The prophets then put these observations into theological perspective by asking discerning questions. Where have the people gone wrong? How have they turned away from God? Where have they strayed from covenant living? What can they do to restore a fractured relationship with the God who created and called them? The prophets mince no words. Generally, the false prophet brings a whitewashed word, one that is compromising and superficial. The words of the true prophet, however, call the people out of their idolatries and false confidences. The words often demand a return and embrace of justice (a concern for society's most vulnerable) and righteousness (a call to right relationship with neighbor and with God). While the prophets were critical of Israelite ways of living, the purpose of their speaking was not simply to reprimand or criticize, though the people's choices were often destructive and led them toward spiritual death. The prophets' purpose for speaking was redemptive. They hoped to pull people forward out of what was restrictive and limited into a God-given, rich, and free existence. Although the prophets were not fortune-tellers, God gave them eyes to see that the people's patterns of living were not leading them toward peace, health, and a promising future. They could see that the people were living in a way that eventually would bring destruction and death. In that way, they knew what the future would inevitably bring.

The prophets were rooted in their communities and their traditions. Through the centuries (the first writings are located in the 8th cent BCE), the prophets spoke a word from the God who called them. Theirs was not a remote God, uncaring or unfeeling about the plight of the people. Theirs was a God who had a word for them and a personal claim upon them. The prophets spoke of a God who could be known, a God who could be trusted. The prophets helped the community make connections between its past, its present, and its future. They brought perspective and dimension to the ancient question, How shall we live? The prophets were wrapped up, restless in, and wrestling with God's word. They were not passive. They were active in the prophetic event, bringing heart and mind to the tasks of bringing a word from God. The prophets asked questions about human living that stand the test of time, questions that live in the heart of our own wonderings about how to go about faithfulness. Micah, asks, for instance, What does the Lord require? As do other prophets who follow him, he wonders whether God is concerned with right ritual or with the ways we treat others.

The prophetic word in the OT holds an important place in the life of the Christian community. From the prophet Isaiah Jesus quotes a prophetic word to begin his ministry:

> The Spirit of the Lord is upon me,
>   because he has anointed me to bring good news
>   to the poor.
> He has sent me to proclaim release to the captives
>   and recovery of sight to the blind, to let the
>   oppressed go free,
> to proclaim the year of the Lord's favor.
>   (Luke 4:18-19; see Isa 61:1-2)

Jesus locates his mission and call fully in the words of the prophets before him. His ministry is for poor, captive, blind, oppressed, and disinherited persons. Thus, this call to prophetic ministry and preaching is passed on to his disciples. As the anointed prophet, Jesus' prophetic authority and power are made known through his voice. His prophetic identity is known when he silences oppression and when he liberates the oppressed.

Understanding the growth and development of prophetic preaching in the canon invites three important questions for consideration as we think about preaching and proclamation in the 21st cent. The first question has to do with the authority of the prophet. The second has to do with the content of the prophetic message, and the third with the challenge of prophetic preaching.

One of the most frequent prophetic utterances in the OT is: Thus says the Lord (AUTHORITY OF THE PREACHER). This introduction to the message that follows serves to credential the prophet. The word comes from God; the prophet is God's messenger. How do we understand the authority of today's preacher? When the preacher speaks, is this a word from the Lord? Is this God speaking? Or is this a woman or man bringing to the community her or his provisional and time-limited understanding of what God is saying to a particular community at a specified time and place? And why does this question matter? Our understanding of the authority of the preacher informs the content of our preaching, how we prepare, what we claim, and how we live in relationship to the community that has called us.

The second important question deals with prophetic preaching's content. Often prophetic preaching is defined as preaching that is harsh and critical. It is preaching that deals with difficult social issues and calls members of the community to accountability in light of their relationship with the God who created them. This preaching is often defined in contrast to pastoral preaching, which is thought to be comforting, affirming, loving, and caring—but not challenging. These distinctions are artificial and misleading. A return to the Hebrew prophets helps us see that the distinctions between prophetic and pastoral preaching must, of necessity, remain ambiguous. The prophets did call their communities to accountability by bringing accusations and oracles of doom. If the people did not repent and return to a dependence on God, the future was uncertain. Juxtaposed to these same words of accusation, however, are often found words of hope and redemption. There are strong, grace-filled words from a God who is willing, again and again, to welcome back a wayward people. Prophetic preaching is filled with grace, coming from a prophet who loves the community and hopes for it a new future. The pastoral preacher is also not afraid to bring to the community words that will truly feed and nourish its members. These words may challenge, correct, guide, and educate. A pastoral word brings what nourishes the community, even when that word is difficult to hear.

The third important question for the preacher is this: How do we as preachers keep ourselves open to a word from God without becoming arrogant and self-righteous, on the one hand, or guilt ridden, on the other? (*See* PREACHING, ETHICS OF.) It is easy to be seduced by the world's priorities and values so that we bring a compromised, flat word to our communities. Preachers often wonder how to open their congregations and communities to a new and challenging word. Yet an equally important challenge is for the preacher to stay open to a radical, life-changing word from God. To which voices does the preacher listen? In a noisy and crowded life, how do preachers know that the voice they are hearing is the voice of God? *See* PROPHETIC MESSAGE.

Bibliography: Walter Brueggemann. *The Prophetic Imagination.* (2001); Charles Campbell.

The Word Before the Powers: An Ethic of Preaching. (2002); Linda Clader. *Voicing the Vision: Imagination and Prophetic Preaching.* (2004); André Resner. *Just Preaching.* (2006); Philip Wogaman. *Speaking the Truth in Love: Preaching in a Broken World.* (1998).

PROVERBS
Jeffrey D. Arthurs

Sensitivity to three issues of genre suggests homiletical options when preaching from the book of Proverbs.

The Issue of Pericopae

The homiletical truism counsels biblical preachers to preach units of thought, but following this directive can be tricky when preaching from the book of Proverbs. While the long poems of chs. 1–9 and 30–31 contain self-evident units, the other chapters appear to be a catalog of maxims. However, within this catalog, the redactor(s) supplied some context by grouping sayings by topics, such as the drunkard (23:29-35), the king (25:2-7), and the sluggard (26:13-16). Context can also be present on a more subtle level. Catchwords and inclusio sometime indicate the boundaries of a thought unit. At first glance proverb x may seem to be unrelated to proverb y, but look again. Expect unity. It is often possible to preach thought units of multiple verses even from the catalog.

Having said that, a topical approach can also be a genre-sensitive way to preach Proverbs. Preachers can gather all the proverbs on a theme, such as old age, gossip, laziness, or humility, to preach a message or a series of messages on that theme.

The Issue of Wisdom

Proverbs transfer wisdom to the naive. In the Hebrew Bible wisdom is a teachable skill. Authorities such as parents or teachers transfer distillations of cultural values, which are phrased as observations of repeated phenomena. These observations are stated in present tense, indicative mood. The intention behind the book of Proverbs is, of course, admonitory, but it often makes its admonitions by observing classes of behavior and types of people. Behind each proverb are hundreds of case studies: the contentious wife is irksome; the hotheaded man makes enemies; the gossip loses friends; and so forth. These sayings warn and counsel, but didacticism does not burst through the front door. It comes through the back door and invites contemplation before action.

Genre-sensitive preaching from Proverbs makes observations. With statistics, examples, current events, and stories, preachers can show the truth as well as tell it. For example, with contemporary case studies, preachers can show the congregation the results of cheerful words or the results of alcohol abuse. When preaching from Proverbs, we encourage and warn by describing the way things are.

Responsible preaching from Proverbs handles the sayings as generalizations, not promises. The sage knows how to apply a proverb, but the fool does not. That is why a proverb in the mouth of a fool is as useless as a "lame man's legs that hang limp" (26:7 NIV). Proverbs distill many experiences, but they do not include all experiences. They should not be applied everywhere and at all times. For example, the biblical sage has observed that the fear of the Lord adds years to life (9:11), but presumably, the same sage would not deny the reality of martyrdom. Preachers of Proverbs should rove mentally through society, searching for situations illumined by a particular proverb.

Of special concern, when interpreting proverbs as wisdom, is the foundation of that wisdom—the fear of the Lord. Reverencing God is the "beginning" of wisdom (1:7; 9:10). In the Hebrew tradition, skillful living arises from recognition of our finitude and God's infinity. This world is imbued with the presence of God, and the presence of God infuses daily experience. Thus, fools come to harm because they are unaware or uncaring of God's law. Preaching Proverbs as mere self-help literature without regular reference to theology spins the truth (MORALISM). These maxims must be understood as humble responses to the King's decrees. Proverbs may sound like the grist of inspirational speakers, but their theological underpinning distinguishes them from mere humanistic advice.

The Issue of Style

The most obvious stylistic feature of these pithy sayings is that they are short. An entire literary unit can be as few as six words in Hebrew and not many more in English. A proverb's compact nature helps the sage assert confidently, not qualify or expound at length. Proverbs look us in the eye to declare that specific consequences follow specific acts.

Even though proverbs can be quite short, they are still poems. They utilize figurative language, hyperbole, irony, and other features of Hebrew poetry, including all types of parallelism. Like all literature, proverbs comment on the universal by way of the particular. They utilize synecdoche even more than metaphor so that the tent stands for the family unit, a *faithful witness* stands for the whole class of truth-telling folk, and the tongue stands for the awesome power of language.

As brief poems, the aural qualities of proverbs exhibit their roots in orality. Rhythm and rhyme, alliteration and assonance help proverbs lodge in memory, and tight convergences of sound and sense contribute to proverbs' rhetorical effect. They sound right. To reproduce those effects, preachers can employ some techniques common in African American preaching, such as rhythm, repetition, and metaphor.

Another homiletical response to proverbial style would be to phrase the sermon's central idea like a proverb, with brevity, balance, image, or sound values. A sermon centered on one provocative, well-phrased idea speaks as the sages spoke. Often a proverb itself can become the sermon's central idea. A statement such as "death and life are in the power of the tongue" (18:21) is concise and striking. Preachers can also coin new proverbs or rephrase current ones. Instead of proclaiming, "Seeing is believing," we might proclaim, "Believing is seeing."

To preach Proverbs well takes wisdom. It takes skill to speak about skill. *See* CHRISTOLOGY.

Bibliography: Jeffrey D. Arthurs. "Short Sentences Long Remembered: Preaching Genre-Sensitive Sermons from Proverbs." *Journal of the Evangelical Homiletics Society* 5 (2005); Thomas G. Long. *Preaching and the Literary Forms of the Bible.* (1989); Alyce M. McKenzie. *Preaching Proverbs: Wisdom for the Pulpit.* (1996); Raymond C. Van Leeuwen. "Proverbs." *NIB* 5. (1997).

PSALMS
J. Clinton McCann Jr.

From the first recorded Christian sermon (Acts 2:14-36), which was based in part on Pss 16, 110, and 132, the church has maintained a rich history of preaching the psalms. Even so, some contemporary homileticians and biblical scholars counsel against preaching the psalms. Their logic is unflinchingly form-critical; they argue that because the psalms originated primarily as the prayers and praises of ancient Israel, the psalms should continue to be prayed and sung, not preached. This logic ignores the process that led to the formation of a canon of Scripture. Material that originated as human response to God in prayer and praise was received and transmitted as Scripture—God's word to humankind. In fact, as James L. Mays points out, the psalms "contain more direct statements about God than any other book in the two testaments of the Christian canon" (Mays 2006, 69–70). Thus, the psalms virtually beg to be preached, as they have been for centuries.

The Psalms and Jesus Christ

As Peter's sermon in Acts 2 demonstrates, the NT writers understood the psalms as prophecies concerning Jesus; however, contemporary interpreters and preachers need not adopt this perspective in order to put the psalms in fruitful conversation with the NT. In short, the psalms do not speak predictively of Jesus as the Christ, but they do speak frequently of the Judean king, each one of whom bore the titles of God's "anointed" (Ps 2:2; Hebrew, messiah [mashiakh]; Greek, christ [christos]) and God's "son" (Ps 2:7). In this sense, the psalms are frequently about "Christ." Because so many psalms are attributed to David, especially in Books I–II (Pss 1–72), and because royal psalms are located at crucial junctures (see Pss 2; 72; 89), recent Psalms scholarship speaks of the messianic orientation of the psalter in its final form. The intent of this conclusion is not to say that the psalms predict Jesus as the Messiah, but this conclusion does suggest that Christians can learn from the psalms what we mean when we say Jesus Christ.

In particular, the psalms connect the office of Christ with the enactment of God's justice and righteousness toward the establishment of the peace that God wills for the world (Ps 72:1-7). This peace has everything to do with the protection of and provision for poor, weak, and needy persons (Ps 72:12-14). To hear Ps 72 in conversation with the NT is to be reminded that when we say Jesus Christ, we ought to have clearly in view Jesus' ministry of compassion to the poor, the least, and the lost. (*See* SOCIAL JUSTICE.)

Reflecting the crisis of exile, the psalter in its final form recognizes and articulates the demise of the Judean monarchy by way of the content of Ps 89 (especially vv. 38-51) and its placement at the end of Book III. The psalter's "answer" to this crisis is its portrayal of God's kingship in Book IV (Pss 90–106), especially Pss 93; 95–99. This collection of enthronement, or God-reigns, psalms is often described as the psalter's central theological affirmation. While the focus here is God's reign, not that of the earthly Messiah, it is still fruitful to put these psalms in conversation with the NT. The central affirmation of the psalter, "God reigns," turns out to be virtually synonymous with the core of Jesus' teaching and preaching: "The time is fulfilled, and the kingdom of God is at hand" (Mark 1:15 RSV).

What God as "coming" king will do is the same thing with which the earthly Messiah was entrusted: "He [God] will judge the world with righteousness" (Pss 96:13; 98:9, in which *judge* could be understood as "establish justice"). When the royal psalms and enthronement psalms are put in conversation with the NT, they help the church proclaim the good news that the fully human Jesus of Nazareth was also the one who fully embodied God's purposes for the world. Psalms 96 and 98 are psalms for Christmas Day, not because they predict the birth of Jesus, but because they provide the language to affirm what the birth of Jesus means. As Mays puts it in a sermon on Ps 98:

> For with its words we take up a liturgy that lifts our eyes to behold the mighty acts of God who comes into time and space for our sakes. Divine love and power have invaded our world. The mystery of righteousness has struck from above into the below . . . and at the climax of the invasion of the divine is the child in the manger. (2006, 176)

While the psalms enable the church to understand and proclaim more fully the significance of Jesus' birth, the core of his teaching, and the content of his work as Messiah or Christ, they were also employed by the Gospel writers to narrate and explicate the significance of Jesus' passion. Since the psalms feature the affirmation of God's sovereignty or power, it is especially important to observe that from the beginning of the psalter, God and God's "anointed" have enemies (Ps 2:1-3). And throughout the psalter, "the righteous" are constantly surrounded and opposed by "foes" (Ps 3:1) and "enemies" (Ps 3:7). Indeed, this is precisely what the psalmists regularly lament

or complain about, and the implications are profound. Suffering cannot be construed simply as punishment or a sign of alienation from God. Rather, God is with afflicted, poor, and needy persons (see Pss 22:24; 40:17; 109:31). And given the preponderance of laments in the psalter (LAMENTS), one must conclude that God's power does not consist of sheer force against God's enemies. The groundwork is laid for a Messiah whose royal status does not involve immunity from suffering, one who exercises power as self-giving love rather than enforcement, one whose crown will be a crown of thorns. Not surprisingly, the most intense of the laments—Pss 22, 31, and 69—figure prominently in the portrayal of Jesus' suffering in the Gospels. Again, the point is not that these psalms predict Jesus' passion, but that they provide language for the church to articulate the meaningfulness of Jesus' death.

The Spirituality of the Psalms

Recent work on the psalms has relativized the importance of genre and setting, highlighting instead the content and theology of the psalms. In addition to the theological content suggested above, the following aspects of the spirituality of the psalms offer directions for proclamation.

1. Happiness

The very first word of the psalter is *happy*, and the remaining twenty-four occurrences construct a portrait of the happy or righteous person. Happiness involves constant attention to God's teaching or will (Ps 1:1-2; "law" in NRSV), dependence upon God rather than self (Ps 2:12), and embodiment of God's values (Ps 41:1). Such submission to God is the essence of praise, which the psalms portray not only as a liturgical response but as a lifestyle (see Ps 100:2, where NRSV "worship" can also be translated "serve," as in RSV). The lifestyle of praise is a powerful alternative to cultural definitions of happiness that center on self-aggrandizement and purchasing power. Not coincidentally, Jesus pronounces "happy" or "blessed" precisely the categories of persons who pray the laments—those who are poor, humble/humiliated, afflicted, meek, and persecuted (Matt 5:3-11; Luke 6:20-22).

2. The Agony and the Ecstasy

The psalms affirm the exalted status of humankind (Ps 8:3-8), but in the context of consistent recognition of human finitude, fallibility, and neediness. In fact, with the exception of Ps 88, each of the laments articulates both hurt and hope, pain and praise, suffering and glory. As such, the laments have profound implications not only for understanding how God exercises power (see above), but also for understanding human identity and vocation. Mays summarizes the lesson in a sermon on Ps 13: "The agony and the ecstacy belong together as the secret of our identity" (2006, 169). Or in explicitly Christian terms, we live simultaneously as people of the cross and people of the resurrection (see Mark 8:34-35).

3. Thy Will Be Done

Because the presence of enemies is a pervasive feature of the psalms, it is not surprising that there are frequent requests that God dispose of them. These violent-sounding requests seem quite unchristian and are often excised by the lectionary; however, if we take seriously that the psalmists have really been victimized, these prayers may be understood not as requests for personal revenge, but as urgent pleas for justice—something like "thy will be done." If we were to attend to these pleas more carefully instead of quickly dismissing them, we might be led to confront the violence and extent of victimization in our world; and we might be led to pray for and work with God toward the justice, righteousness, and peace that God wills.

4. Waiting for the Lord

Because the psalms simultaneously affirm that God reigns and that God's purposes are opposed, they suggest that faithfulness inevitably involves waiting. Such hope is articulated in the opening line of Ps 40, "I waited patiently for the LORD"; but as Ellen F. Davis points out in a sermon on Ps 40, a better translation is, "I waited tensely for the LORD" (2006, 4). Given the brokenness and chaos of our world, Davis suggests, we cannot but wait anxiously and urgently for God. (*See* ESCHATOLOGY.) We cannot be optimistic; but neither can we fail to hope, given God's commitment to humankind and to the cosmos. The psalms commend a posture not unlike that of the NT, which invites us simultaneously to live in the realm of God as a present reality and to actively and fervently await its consummation.

Bibliography: Dave Bland and David Fleer, eds. *Performing the Psalms.* (2005); Ellen F. Davis.

"Demanding Deliverance." *Preaching from Psalms.* Edited by R. Alling and D. J. Schlafer. (2006); James C. Howell and J. Clinton McCann. *Preaching the Psalms.* (2001); James L. Mays. *Preaching and Teaching the Psalms.* (2006).

RESURRECTION
Richard B. Hays

Christian preaching proclaims the bodily resurrection of the crucified Jesus as the act of God that has defeated the power of death and transformed the world. As a result of Jesus' resurrection, all who are in Christ experience new life in the present time and look with hope to their own resurrection at the last day.

The Resurrection of Jesus

The early Christians strongly proclaimed, as the Apostles' Creed affirms, that after Jesus was crucified, dead, and buried, he arose from the dead on the third day. The earliest witnesses are insistent that this was not merely a visionary experience but a bodily resurrection that left Jesus' tomb empty. As N. T. Wright has shown, the term *resurrection* in 1st cent. Judaism was understood to refer to the raising of a physical body, not merely a spiritual exaltation to heaven or a mystical visionary experience by Jesus' followers (Wright 2003, 129–206).

Paul insists in 1 Cor 15 that the resurrection of Jesus stands at the heart of Christian preaching. He quotes a foundational confessional formula that he "handed on" to the Corinthians, proclaiming that Jesus "was raised on the third day in accordance with the scriptures" (1 Cor 15:3-5, perhaps alluding to Hos 6:2). Paul goes on to refer to a large group of "more than five hundred" witnesses to the risen Christ, including himself as "last of all." He is adamant that the truth of the gospel hinges on this claim: "If Christ has not been raised, your faith is futile and you are still in your sins" (1 Cor 15:17).

All four canonical Gospels reach their climax in the resurrection of Jesus, but each nuances the resurrection message differently. Mark maintains the solemn, mysterious character of his Gospel by omitting any direct narrative of Jesus' resurrection appearances, but his proclamation of the resurrection remains explicit and emphatic (Mark 16:6-7). Matthew's account of the resurrection highlights

Jesus as the triumphant Son of Man who has received "all authority in heaven and earth" and who sends his disciples out on a mission to declare his authority to the whole world (Matt 28:16-20; compare Dan 7:13-14). Luke's account emphasizes the mysterious presence of the risen Jesus with the disciples at table (Luke 24:30-31, 41-43), highlights his role in teaching his followers how to read Scripture (24:25-27, 44-47), and foreshadows the giving of the Spirit to the community (24:49). John links Jesus' resurrection with the disciples' mission, with the bestowal of the Spirit, and with forgiveness of sins (John 20:21-23). He also adds the distinctive stories of Jesus' appearances to Mary Magdalene (20:1-18) and Thomas (20:24-29); the latter narrative underscores both the bodily character of Jesus' resurrection and its pertinence to future generations "who have not seen and yet have come to believe."

Rather than explaining away these early accounts with demythologizing or rationalizing theories, the role of Christian preaching is to carry forward faithfully what was handed on by these traditions, and to reaffirm these stories as the true source of our hope.

Roots of Resurrection Hope: The Jewish Apocalyptic Tradition

Christians sometimes fail to realize that the hope of resurrection of the body is a distinctively Jewish idea. To be sure, there are only a few references in the OT to the hope of resurrection; the most important texts are Ezekiel's vision of the valley of bones (Ezek 37:1-14), Isaiah's vision of a great eschatological banquet after God has swallowed up death forever (Isa 25:6-10a), and Daniel's portrayal of Israel's final deliverance when "many of those who sleep in the dust of the earth shall awake" (Dan 12:2-3). Nonetheless, by the 1st cent. CE, the hope of resurrection was widespread in Jewish culture. (For a good illustration, see the story of the seven martyred brothers in 2 Macc 7.) Belief in resurrection was embraced by the Pharisees, but rejected by the Sadducees. This intra-Jewish dispute is clearly reflected in Acts 23:6-10, where Paul defends himself before the Jewish council in Jerusalem by declaring, "Brothers, I am a Pharisee, a son of Pharisees. I am on trial concerning the hope of the resurrection of the dead" (see also Mark 12:18-27). Of course neither the Pharisees nor any other Jewish group was expecting a

crucified and resurrected Messiah, whose own resurrection would be a singular event apart from a general resurrection and final judgment; this was a distinctively Christian development, grounded in what actually happened to Jesus.

The Jewish origin of resurrection hope is important for two reasons: (1) it reminds us that resurrection must be understood as God's eschatological re-creation of the body, not as an escape from the body; and (2) it reminds us that resurrection language is linked strongly with God's restoration and final vindication of Israel. It is not merely a matter of individual life after death, but of God's faithful fulfillment of the covenant promises made to God's elect people Israel, God's fixing of all that has been broken. (See ESCHATOLOGY.) Keeping these roots of resurrection language in mind will help the preacher guard against inappropriately spiritualized and individualistic interpretations of the promise of resurrection.

Participation in Christ's Resurrection: The Form of Christian Hope

The basic form of early Christian hope for the future was that believers would share ultimately in Jesus' resurrection. Paul expresses this hope by describing Christ as the "first fruits of those who have died," anticipating the final great harvest: "For as all die in Adam, so all will be made alive in Christ. But each in his own order: Christ the first fruits, then at his coming those who belong to Christ" (1 Cor 15:20-23; compare Phil 3:20-21).

Christian preachers, then, should never lose sight of the distinction between resurrection of the body and the idea of the soul going to heaven. Justin Martyr, the great 2nd-cent. Christian apologist, observed that there are "some who are called Christians . . . who say that there is no resurrection of the dead, and that their souls, when they die, are taken to heaven." Justin sternly labeled such people as "godless, impious heretics" and insisted that authentic Christian preaching proclaims a future bodily resurrection, not disembodied immortality (Dial. 80). Why was Justin so insistent on a resurrection of the body? Because it is a sign that God the Creator intends to redeem the created world. Anyone who preaches that salvation entails an escape from the body, an ascent to an ethereal realm, is in effect denying that God will redeem and restore what God has made.

This point was highlighted by the recent discovery and publication of a 2nd-cent. Gnostic text—roughly contemporary with Justin Martyr—called *The Gospel of Judas*. In this ancient text Jesus is portrayed as contemptuous of the physical body in which he is trapped ("the man that clothes me"); he wants Judas to betray him to death so that he can escape from his bodily confinement in the evil material world. This is a serious distortion of the early Christian understanding of Jesus' death and resurrection: the denial of resurrection of the body goes hand in hand with the denial that God's creation is good. By contrast, Christian teaching affirms that those who have the Spirit groan in the present time along with the suffering of creation, while awaiting "the redemption of our bodies" (Rom 8:18-23).

Resurrection and Ethics

Because Christians are united with Christ's death in baptism and share the hope of his resurrection life, they already live now in the power of the resurrection. They are freed from the ruling power of sin and empowered to live a new life of obedient freedom (Rom 6:1-14; 8:1-11). Christ's resurrection turns the world upside down and proclaims that the old oppressive powers no longer hold sway, that we are living already within a new politics, a new world (Acts 17:6-7). We are therefore called, in Wendell Berry's apt phrase, to "practice resurrection" (Berry 1984, 152): we are called to order our practices in such a way that the church's life embodies a foretaste of the resurrection life of the world to come, a world of new creation in which there is "neither Jew nor Greek, there is neither slave nor free, there is neither male nor female" (Gal 3:28 RSV).

Even in the gloomiest moments of adversity and suffering, Christians can hold on to hope because we have read to the end of the book: we know that finally God will wipe away every tear and "death will be no more" (Rev 21:4). Those who belong to Christ will be made alive together with him. That is the hope that sustains us. That is why Paul ends his long discussion of the resurrection of the body in 1 Cor 15 with a warm word of encouragement to his brothers and sisters at Corinth. Despite their struggles and failings, the truth is that death has been swallowed up in victory. And so he writes to them: "Therefore, my beloved, be steadfast, immovable, always excelling in the work of the Lord, because you know that in the Lord your labor is not in vain" (1 Cor 15:58). That is what God says to all of us. In Christ all shall be made alive. And so, in the present time, we are empowered and called to practice resurrection.

Bibliography: Dale C. Allison. *Resurrecting Jesus: The Earliest Christian Tradition and Its Interpreters.* (2005); Wendell Berry. "Manifesto: The Mad Farmer Liberation Front." *Collected Poems, 1957–1982.* (1984) 151–52; Oscar Cullmann. *Immortality of the Soul or Resurrection of the Dead? The Witness of the New Testament.* (1958); Brian E. Daley. "A Hope for Worms: Early Christian Hope." *Resurrection: Scientific and Theological Assessments.* Edited by T. Peters, R. J. Russell, and M. Welker. (2002); Rowan A. Greer. *Christian Life and Christian Hope: Raids on the Inarticulate.* (2001); Richard B. Hays. "Reading Scripture in Light of the Resurrection." *The Art of Reading Scripture.* Edited by Ellen F. Davis and Richard B. Hays. (2003) 216–38; Jon D. Levenson. *Resurrection and the Restoration of Israel: The Ultimate Victory of the God of Life.* (2006); Claudia Setzer. *Resurrection of the Body in Early Judaism and Early Christianity: Doctrine, Community, and Self-Definition.* (2004); Rowan Williams. *Resurrection: Interpreting the Easter Gospel.* (1994); N. T. Wright. *The Resurrection of the Son of God.* (2003).

RUTH
Mary Donovan Turner

The author, time of writing, and various purposes of the book of Ruth remain in some dispute, yet the story holds enormous promise for the preacher. Was this story a polemic against the regulations in the time of Ezra and Nehemiah that demanded a Jewish man divorce his foreign wife? Was the story an attempt to justify the Davidic line? It is not possible to know for sure. The deceptively simple narrative is replete with subtle theological themes and affirmations that inspire us, while the story line itself is bound in social and cultural norms that challenge us.

In the Christian canon, the book of Ruth is the narrative bridge between the rule of the judges and the beginnings of the Israelite monarchy. The serene story of Ruth provides a sharp contrast with the book of Judges, which precedes it; the latter is filled with violence and bloodshed. In the Hebrew canon, the book finds its home in the Writings. Ruth is one of five Festival Scrolls that are designated for reading on the holy days throughout the Jewish year. The book of Ruth is to be read at the Feast of Weeks because of its emphasis on the harvest season. In its four brief chapters, it recounts the story of Naomi and her daughter-in-law Ruth. In a close reading of the text, the preacher will be attentive to the plot's geographical movement as Naomi and Ruth make their way through wilderness to Bethlehem (house of bread). There is other movement as well. Naomi, who is "empty," becomes "full." Naomi, who was "bitter," becomes "pleasant" once again. Two vulnerable women who have no husbands to provide food, security, or name are, in the end, blessed with child and grandchild and become part of the lineage of David.

Three brief texts from Ruth are included in the *Revised Common Lectionary.* The first, 1:1-18, includes the identification of the story's characters and the first scene where Naomi returns to Bethlehem with her daughter-in-law Ruth, who vows faithfulness to her. The second, interestingly, recounts Naomi's sending Ruth to the threshing floor to meet Boaz and secure their well-being (3:1-5). The third chapter of Ruth includes language and imagery that are playful and replete with sexual innuendo. The third lectionary reading relates the story's conclusion where the child is born, and Naomi and Ruth once again have found their place in a society that does not value them. The preacher cannot preach from these texts apart from their context in the larger narrative. The story's introduction informs the way we interpret its ending. And knowing the ending of the story in some measure fashions how we read its beginning. This does not mean, of course, that the preacher must tell the entire narrative in every sermon. Restraint is key, and the preacher must make important decisions about what information is necessary for the congregation to travel along on the sermon's journey.

The four chapters in the book of Ruth provide an interesting but simple story line:

Chapter/Scene 1: In the introduction of characters and their plight, Ruth accompanies her mother-in-law from Moab to Naomi's native land. (Her expression of faithfulness to Naomi is often repeated in wedding homilies as expressions of faithfulness between husband and wife.)

Chapter/Scene 2: Ruth goes out into the fields to glean and gather grain for Naomi and herself.

Chapter/Scene 3: Ruth goes to the threshing floor to meet Boaz.

Chapter/Scene 4: Ruth and Boaz marry, and their son, Obed, redeems Naomi from her childless state.

The preacher can profitably explore the important theological themes running through these four chapters. The most prominent is redemption (forms of this word occur approximately twenty times in the book's eighty-five verses). In Israelite society, a man's nearest relative (brother, uncle, cousin, or another kinsman) must restore for his kindred what has been lost. In this story, Boaz is the redeemer, a close relative of Naomi's deceased husband. He is willing to buy back property for Naomi, and he then marries Ruth. Together, Boaz and Ruth provide Naomi with a grandchild and renewed standing in the community. The preacher will notice that just as Boaz has delivered and redeemed Naomi and Ruth, God in the OT redeems people from evil, violence, oppression, enemies, distress, danger, illness, death, and sin (SIN AND EVIL). How does the preacher—and how does the community—know God as one who draws us out from whatever confines, oppresses, frightens, or destroys us? That is redemption.

Another theological thread in Ruth emerges from the word translated "loving-kindness." This word is often used to describe the never-ending, steadfast love of God. But in this story, men and women show that they, too, are capable of this love (1:8; 2:20; 3:10). The story demonstrates that people can show extraordinary care and concern for each other. In day-to-day activity, the characters are aware of God and pray to God. Redemption or deliverance, however, comes about through the loving and heroic actions of its human characters.

There are other interesting dimensions of the story for the preacher. Ruth is from Moab; she is a foreigner. The story helps us explore issues of hospitality in the face of difference and hostility. Moabites were fierce enemies of the Israelites. Their country was known as a place of lewdness and idolatry (see Gen 19:30-38; Num 22–24). Ruth finds a place in her mother-in-law's country of Israel, but not wholly. She continues to carry the title of "Ruth the Moabite." She is identified as an outsider. And at the end of the story, as the birth of her son is recounted, she becomes virtually invisible. Does the title "Ruth the Moabite" remind the community that good deeds are being done by a foreigner? Or is the phrase a reminder that Ruth never really becomes a member of the Israelite community? Through dialogue, the book explores issues of Ruth's identity in a land not her own: "To whom does this young woman belong?" "Who are you?" Ruth is destitute; she is a foreigner with no power or privilege, and she depends on those who would take notice of her. The book of Ruth can help us explore theological issues of ethnic difference and of inclusion and exclusion in our congregations, communities, and nation. Who is in our notice? Who is not?

The book of Ruth is, in large measure, about Naomi, though she is forgotten in its title. It is her complaint that initiates and propels the story's plot. In the beginning, she is bereft, with no children or grandchildren; her economic survival is largely in doubt. She is destitute and community dependent. She has experienced famine, loss, and grief because "Yahweh's hand has gone forth against [her]" (1:13b, author's trans.). Like Job, she believes God has caused her bitterness. The story gives the preacher and community an opportunity to explore their understandings of misfortune and tragedy. Are these at the "hand of God"?

There are no allusions to the book of Ruth in the OT canon. Ruth's name, however, is included in the genealogy of Jesus as it is recounted in the Gospel of Matthew. She is mentioned along with a group of women that includes Tamar, Rahab, Bathsheba, and Mary (the mother of Jesus), though it is not entirely clear why. Is it because they are Gentiles or have connections with Gentiles and Matthew is signaling the inclusive nature of the gospel? Are they included because they have unusual stories related to the conventional, patriarchal norms of their day? Or are they included because they show extraordinary strength and faithfulness to bring about God's purposes? Perhaps the answer lies in a combination of all of these.

Bibliography: Pui-lan Kwok. "Finding Ruth a Home: Gender, Sexuality and the Politics of Otherness." *Postcolonial Imagination and Feminist Theology.* (2005); Jacqueline Lapsley. "Seeing the Older Woman: Naomi in High Definition." *Engaging the Bible in a Gendered World.* Edited by Linda Day and Carolyn Pressler. (2006) 102–13; Eunny P. Lee. "Ruth the Moabite: Identity, Kinship and Otherness." *Engaging the Bible in a Gendered World.* Edited by Linda Day and Carolyn Pressler. (2006) 89–101; Katharine Doob Sakenfeld. *Ruth. Interpretation.* (1999); Katharine Doob Sakenfeld. *Just Wives? Stories of Power and Survival in the Old Testament and Today.* (2003); Mary Donovan Turner. "Redemption." *Old Testament Words: Reflections for Preaching.* (2003) 36–38.

SERMONIC, THEOLOGICAL EPISTLES
Thomas G. Long

Preachers sometime shy away from preaching on the letters of the NT. There are a number of reasons why this is so. The lectionary tilts toward the Gospels, or it may seem easier and more inviting to preach on biblical narratives, or perhaps the sometimes dense argumentation of the Epistles appears daunting, even boring. Chrysostom said that hearing the Epistles was "like a spiritual trumpet" (cited in Cousar 1996, 15), but sometimes the trumpet is muted. For example, the rousing voice of the Letter to the Romans, once the call to arms of the Reformation, has in recent times often quieted to a whisper in the pulpit.

Reasons for Epistolary Preaching

Although the popularity of preaching on the NT Epistles rises and falls on rhetorical, cultural, and theological tides, there are several good reasons to revive the practice of epistolary preaching:

1. Preaching on the Epistles helps to correct the overreliance on narrative preaching. A steady diet of narrative preaching can produce an episodic understanding of the Christian faith. There is this story and there is that story, but what about the relationships among the central scriptural narratives? The Epistles are more focused on the ligaments and connections of the gospel, and they represent a move from narrative immediacy to the posture of theological and ecclesial reflection. Humanity does not live by narrative alone, but by every word that comes from God. (*See* DOCTRINAL.)

2. Preaching on the Epistles allows the sermon to depict the Christian faith not simply as a series of experiences or a collection of doctrinal affirmations, but as a way of life grounded in specific and coherent practices. The emphasis in the Epistles on such

everyday matters as money, gossip, jealousy, hospitality, religious pluralism, and marriage underscores that the Christian life has a lived-out shape.

In his book *Religious Experience in Earliest Christianity*, NT scholar Luke Timothy Johnson contrasts the front and the back of a typical Catholic church. At the front, he says, everything is "orderly and correct." Up at the front are the furniture and art of the church's neatly arranged power, but in the back of the church things are a good bit messier. In the back is a bulletin board with brochures, news clippings, announcements—a pilgrimage here, a sighting of Mary there, a charismatic prayer meeting elsewhere. In the front is correct doctrine, but in the back is Christianity as it is actually lived out on the ground. The Epistles provide superb access to the back of the church, to the messy attempts to find a coherent way of belonging to the faith, to the often fragmented attempts to discover a shape of living that gives form to the promises of the gospel, hammered out amid the conflicts and ambiguities that mark any human endeavor.

3. Preaching on the Epistles allows sermons to help hearers in their quest to find meaning in the relationships and commitments of their lives. The NT Epistles are quite theological, but they are not doctrinal in the systematic sense. The authors of the NT letters wrestle with the theological claims of the gospel in the cauldron of real-life conflicts and experiences. It is one thing to talk abstractly about Christian freedom or justification by faith; it is quite another to see these claims struggled through by Paul in the Letter to the Galatians, with people who are suffering a loss of zest and meaning in life because they have lost their nerve, have been willing to trade identity in Christ for conventional religious marks of status, and have drawn back from the strong winds of freedom and love in the gospel.

Characteristics of the Letters

When preaching on a text from the NT letters, preachers should be mindful of certain key characteristics of epistles:

1. The orality of letters. The very idea of a letter can be misleading to contemporary interpreters and preachers because we tend to think essentially of a *written* document. The letters of the NT, however, were largely intended to be read aloud in worship. They were not conceived as essays that would be inserted in a file folder or posted on a corkboard

somewhere. They were written for the ear, and the markings of orality can be seen all over them.

For example, when Paul concludes Philippians by saying, "I urge Euodia and I urge Syntyche to be of the same mind in the Lord. Yes, and I ask you also, my loyal companions, help these women" (Phil 4:2), these words were read in the assembly during worship. We do not know the nature of the dispute between these two, but we can be assured that these women flinched a bit to hear their names spoken out loud in the presence of the community.

2. The "map" of the letters. Just as is the case with letters today, the ancient Hellenistic letter was constructed according to a customary pattern. And also as is the case today, NT letter writers conveyed meaning by filling and by subverting the customary form. The basic structure of the NT letters is as follows (Roetzel 1998, 51–66):

a. Salutation, which includes the signature, the names of the recipients, and the greeting. One can tell much about the letter from these seemingly formulaic elements. For example, the signature on a letter can reveal information about the character of the author and of the letter. When Paul signs Philippians "Paul and Timothy, servants of Christ Jesus" (Phil 1:1), the breeze of humility has already begun to blow through this epistle, in contrast to the more brash signature of Galatians: "Paul an apostle—sent neither by human commission nor from human authorities, but through Jesus Christ and God the Father" (Gal 1:1).

b. Thanksgiving. Many NT letters include a thanksgiving section, often phrased in terms of prayer. Notice how the prayer of thanksgiving that opens 1 Corinthians (1:4-9) includes on the prayer list all of the problems that will be addressed later in the letter, as if to imply that the grace and faithfulness of God will shine through the broken places in Corinth.

c. Body. The body of Paul's letters, at least, is generally divided into two sections: a discussion of the issues at hand, and specific ethical instructions. No neat distinction between theological issue and ethical discourse can be made, however, since these are interpenetrating realities. The preacher should attend to the often skillful use of rhetorical forms (such as the diatribe and the autobiographical trope) and strategies in the body of letters. For example, in 1 Corinthians, Paul begins the body of the letter by addressing the most embarrassing, touchy, and painful problem in the congregation, namely, the fact that they are bitterly divided into vicious little cliques. "For it has been reported to me by Chloe's people," he begins, "that there are quarrels among you" (1 Cor 1:11). But as soon as Paul raised this explosive issue, he seems suddenly to drop it and to launch into a long excursus on the nature of the cross of Jesus and the contrast between human and divine wisdom. It would be as if a preacher today had said, "I have heard a rumor that there is adultery going on among choir members. Now, as for the cross of Jesus . . ." But this apparently abrupt change of subject is actually a brilliant rhetorical strategy. While the Corinthians wait for the other shoe to drop, Paul is making claims about the cross and divine wisdom, and by the time he returns to the issue of church divisions, it has been transformed by the word of the cross.

d. Closing, including greetings and a benediction. Even this seemingly ritualistic element of epistles can be theologically and homiletically fruitful. For example, NT scholar Peter Lampe has done a careful analysis of the twenty-six names mentioned by Paul in Rom 16. He uncovers such insights as the fact that approximately a dozen of the names are described as being hard workers or especially active in the church, and that the majority of these are women (Lampe 1991, 222).

When preaching takes up the Epistles as a source, the chances are good that sermons will be rescued from being either abstract theological essays or op-ed pieces on the cultural issues du jour. They will address the great questions that have always troubled the human heart, and they will do so in ways that build up real churches facing concrete problems and trying to heal actual conflicts. *See* CONTEXTUAL EPISTLES.

Bibliography: Charles B. Cousar. *The Letters of Paul.* (1996); Luke Timothy Johnson. *Religious Experience in Earliest Christianity: A Missing Dimension in New Testament Studies.* (1998); Peter Lampe. "The Roman Christians of Romans 16." *The Romans Debate.* Edited by Karl P. Donfried. Rev. and expanded ed. (1991); Calvin J. Roetzel. *The Letters of Paul: Conversations in Context.* 4th ed. (1998).

SONG OF SONGS
Dianne Bergant C.S.A.

The following quotation seems curious when we remember that the erotic character of the Song of Songs, or Canticles, has not always been appreciated in its literal sense: "All the world is not worth the day that the Song of Songs was given to Israel; all the writings are holy but the Song of Songs is the holy of holies" (*m. Yad.* 3:5). However, Rabbi Akiba had no misgivings regarding its matter-of-fact meaning. He scathingly condemned its use as a drinking song, but never the poems themselves: "Whoever trills his voice singing the Song of Songs in a banquet hall, regarding it a common song of praise, has no part in the world to come" (*Sanh.* 12:10; compare *b. Sanh.* 101a).

These sentiments clearly indicate that from earliest times the poems were considered sacred. The question remains: Why has the sensual character of these poems traditionally been interpreted allegorically while much of the Bible has been understood literally? Some argue that the explicit erotic imagery troubled demure readers. Whatever the case may be, various methods of interpretation have been employed for reading this intriguing book.

Four basic approaches developed over the centuries: (1) a literary reading argues that the book is a collection of love poems; (2) speeches of the woman, the man, and an apparent chorus identified as "the daughters of Jerusalem" have led some to view the book as a dramatic performance; (3) numerous references to the new growth of springtime and the bounty of harvest suggest ancient fertility rites; and (4) traditionally, the poems have been read as an allegory describing the love relationship between God and Israel, Christ and the church, or God and the individual soul.

Each of these approaches opens up distinctive facets of the Song of Songs that yield corresponding possibilities for understanding its message. Despite this, few people today view the book as either a dramatic performance or a reenactment of fertility rites. However, they continue to read it either as a form of allegory or as a collection of erotic poems. In these two instances, the individual songs are read first as love poems, and only then is the character of the love determined. Is it human/human or divine/human?

The love relationship is depicted from the point of view of the woman. She describes recurring cycles of mutual longing (Song 2:16), aroused anticipation (2:8), exhilarating satisfaction (5:4), and despairing loss (5:6). The nature imagery that characterizes these emotions appeals to each of the senses. The man's kisses intoxicate like wine (1:2);

his voice calls to the depths of her soul (2:10); his scent captivates her (3:6); his touch makes her swoon (2:6); the sight of him thrills her (5:10). The crowning feature of this all-encompassing love is found at the end of the book:

> Love is strong as death,
>   passion fierce as the grave.
> Its flashes are flashes of fire,
>   a raging flame.
> Many waters cannot quench love,
>   neither can floods drown it. (Song 8:6-7)

Death, the grave, and fire are unrelenting. So is love! It can even withstand the waters of chaos.

Mystics like Bernard of Clairvaux, Teresa of Avila, and John of the Cross considered the book a metaphor for the mystical marriage between God and the individual soul. Such readings are popular in spirituality circles even today. Here, the eroticism is interpreted as profound spiritual devotion, the woman characterizes the soul, and God is the ever-elusive lover who calls and ultimately satisfies human yearning. Such an interpretation has a long history in Christian tradition. It explains the deep longing in all of us, a longing of which Augustine spoke: "You have made us for yourself, O Lord, and our hearts are restless until they find their rest in you" (*Conf.* 1.1.2). The courage of the woman might symbolize the courage we all need for overcoming the obstacles we will face as we both wait for and go out in search of God.

There are limitations to such allegorical interpretation. First, it perpetuates gender stereotypes, characterizing God as male and the human soul as a receptive, if not passive, female. Many English translations reinforce this perception by calling the man the "lover," the active partner, and the woman, the "beloved," the one who is loved. Furthermore, this interpretation focuses exclusively on the relationship of the couple and overlooks the communal implications of spirituality rooted in the Bible. Unlike contemporary emphasis on individualism even in spiritual matters, the Bible always reminds us of our obligations toward others. It identifies us as "the people of God," "the body of Christ." It reminds us that we are part of a community with responsibilities toward other community members.

A literal reading of the poems provides the preacher a very different interpretation. It showcases the dignity and profound beauty of erotic love between a man and a woman. The ebb and flow of absence, longing, presence, and absence again aptly describe the intricacies of that love. Furthermore, it is the woman's voice that is heard throughout the poems. Her passion is unabashed. Though she is the primary figure in the poems, the woman and the man share a mutual love. They are both lovers; they are both beloved. The exquisite nature imagery places human love squarely within the context of the gift of the mystery of life itself. This kind of reading can demonstrate how the human heart is in tune with the heart of the natural world.

The preacher might develop various themes: the intimate and passionate relationship between God and human beings; the sacredness of human love; and human attraction as an expression of natural creation. See ALLEGORY, ALLEGORESIS; FEMINIST PERSPECTIVES.

Bibliography: Augustine. *Confessions*; Dianne Bergant. *Song of Songs: The Love Poetry of Scripture.* (1998); Marcia Falk. *The Song of Songs.* (1990); Robert W. Jenson. *Song of Songs. Interpretation: A Bible Commentary for Teaching and Preaching.* (2005); Roland Edmund Murphy and Elizabeth Huwiler. *Proverbs, Ecclesiastes, Song of Songs.* New International Biblical Commentary. (1999).

SYNOPTIC GOSPELS
Barbara E. Reid

When preaching from the synoptic Gospels, there is a temptation to conflate the three distinct portraits of the Markan, Matthean, and Lukan Jesus. Skilled preachers know the importance of attending to the differences in these three presentations of Jesus. Although many passages in the Synoptics are almost identical in wording, they do not always have the same function in their respective Gospel contexts. Subtle differences in wording and context can have important theological and pastoral implications for preaching. Use of literary and narrative criticism is essential to understand the development of the plot and characters in each of the Gospels. As well, source and redaction criticism, along with social science analysis, are indispensable tools for preachers to understand the text in its original historical and literary contexts before looking for how it can illumine contemporary situations. Liberation perspectives (*see* LIBERATION

CRITICISM), such as feminist and postcolonial, are equally important lenses with which the preacher will want to read the text.

One example of parallel passages with important differences is the story of the arrest of Jesus (Matt 26:26-56; Mark 14:32-52; Luke 22:39-53). Each of the three evangelists tells the story with a slightly different christological emphasis and with subtly different pastoral implications. In Mark's version, Jesus is cast in the mold of a righteous sufferer, whose words echo those of the lament psalms. He is greatly distressed and troubled, begging Abba Father three times to remove the cup from him (recalling Jesus' challenge to James and John, 10:38-39, and his words over the cup at the Last Supper, 14:24). Mark emphasizes the disciples' frailties, as they fail to understand, repeatedly fall asleep, and finally all flee, with the exception of a young man, clad in white, who tries to follow, but who runs away naked after being seized. Mark highlights the humanness of Jesus, who is in the depths of distress, yet goes forward into the unknown with utter trust in God.

Matthew's account is similar to Mark's but has significant differences. Unique to Matthew's version is that Jesus addresses Judas directly as friend. The one who draws his sword is not a bystander but one of Jesus' companions, whom he admonishes, "Put your sword back into its place; for all who take the sword will perish by the sword" (26:52). Matthew links the Gethsemane scene with the temptation account, adding a saying of Jesus concerning his refusal to appeal to his Father to send legions of angels (26:53; compare 4:6) and a clear statement that Jesus' arrest occurs to fulfill Scripture. Matthew's account places more emphasis on the person of Jesus, and the disciples are not as unknowing as they are in Mark. Just as Jesus, the Teacher, has been schooling his disciples, so he himself is being schooled in prayer to know and do God's will.

When Luke tells the story, Jesus does not fall prostrate on the ground, but kneels upright, praying only once. He is in agony, a word only Luke uses, and one that speaks of a struggle, like a wrestler. The term agōnia does not refer to emotional tur-moil or anguish of soul. Like an athlete, Jesus' effort is so intense that his sweat falls like great drops of blood. There is an angel who strengthens Jesus, signaling the importance of this episode, as do the angels at the annunciation of John's and Jesus' births, the two heavenly messengers at the transfiguration, the two at the empty tomb, and those at the ascension. Luke is gentler toward the disciples and excuses them for sleeping "because of grief." Judas does not complete his kiss of betrayal. In Luke's account those who were around Jesus ask if they should strike with a sword. And one of them does before Jesus responds, "No more of this!" Only in Luke's Gospel does Jesus heal the ear of the man. In the arresting party, Luke separates the leaders from the people, keeping the latter still open to Jesus and his teaching (22:52). For Luke's Hellenistic readers Jesus is cast as a true prophet and philosopher: he does not exhibit the vices of fear or grief. It is not Jesus who is sorrowful, but his disciples. In the midst of the chaos, Jesus is confident and unafraid.

As a preacher attends carefully to each of the differences in synoptic accounts, a rich mosaic emerges of a Jesus who is complex and multivalent. Attending to the diversity of the varied accounts, preachers draw their hearers deeper and deeper into the mystery of the One who stands at their center and whose life we embody in our own. *See* CHRISTOLOGY.

Bibliography: John R. Donahue and Daniel J. Harrington. *The Gospel of Mark.* Sacra Pagina. (2002); Daniel J. Harrington. *The Gospel of Matthew.* Sacra Pagina. (1991); Luke Timothy Johnson. *The Gospel of Luke.* Sacra Pagina. (1991); Sharon H. Ringe. *Luke.* Westminster Bible Companion. (1995); Donald Senior. *Matthew.* Abingdon New Testament Commentaries. (1998); Bonnie Bowman Thurston. *Preaching Mark.* (2002).

WISDOM

See ECCLESIASTES; ESTHER; PREACHING, ETHICS OF; PROVERBS.

PART 3 ETHICS. INTRODUCTION: ETHICS AND PREACHING

Charles L. Campbell

Ask someone about the relationship between preaching and ethics, and the conversation almost immediately turns to a discussion of preaching on ethical issues. Many people assume that ethical sermons either speak prophetically to a specific moral concern, such as war, or help congregations make decisions on controversial issues, such as abortion or euthanasia. As a result, preachers and homileticians have often neglected the larger ethical dimensions of the weekly sermon, which only occasionally addresses specific ethical dilemmas.

In addition, the topic of preaching and ethics often raises the specter of moralistic preaching (MORALISM). Wary preachers and congregations conjure up visions of authoritarian preachers issuing rigid, non-negotiable moral absolutes from the pulpit. Preaching and ethics thus have often been uneasy partners because of the fear that ethics in the pulpit will replace the good news of God's grace with some form of works-based righteousness.

In examining the relationship between preaching and ethics, then, preachers will need to consider three specific areas: (1) the role of ethics in preaching on moral issues or quandaries; (2) the broader ethical dimensions of sermons that weekly form the community of faith; and (3) the relationship between grace and ethics.

In dealing with these matters, preachers need to be clear about the use of the term *ethics*. One way to clarify this term is to say that ethics is to the moral life as homiletics is to preaching. That is, ethics involves second order, critical reflection on moral concerns; it is a discipline that examines the various factors that shape moral decisions and the moral life. As such, ethics is rarely the direct focus of preaching. Rather, ethical frameworks and convictions shape sermons related to moral decisions and the moral life.

A. Preaching on Moral Issues
B. Beyond Quandaries and Decisions
C. Ethics and Grace

A. Preaching on Moral Issues

One of the greatest challenges for preachers when preaching on moral issues is the variety of ethical frameworks that congregation members bring to bear on these issues. As Alasdair MacIntyre has argued, there is currently no common ethical framework, but a "conceptual incommensurability" and a "private arbitrariness" to moral arguments. As a result, people often talk past each other and cannot even agree on a framework for discussion and disagreement. Moral arguments become interminable and increasingly shrill (MacIntyre 1984, 6–8). This confusion presents a major challenge for preachers when they seek to preach on moral issues (CONTROVERSY).

Within this context, the discipline of ethics can help preachers in two ways. First, ethical reflection can help preachers discern and clarify the ethical frameworks and convictions that they bring to an issue. Second, and equally important, such reflection, combined with a knowledge of the congregation, can clarify the tensions that the preacher may have with the people who come to worship on Sunday morning.

The classical distinction between deontological ethics and consequentialist ethics may reveal the way in which ethical reflection can help the preacher at this point. According to deontological ethics, often associated with Kant, there are absolute moral norms or rules that are always in place. Some actions, such as lying, are wrong, and they are always wrong—no exceptions. On the other hand, consequentialist ethics focuses on the consequences of a moral act as the key component in ethical decision making. Within this framework, an ethicist explores not simply moral absolutes, but whether or not an action, such as a lie, will have morally positive consequences and possibly lead to some greater good.

This simple ethical distinction reveals the kinds of challenges faced by the preacher who wishes to address a moral issue. The preacher, for example, may think consequentially and stand for choice in the matter of abortion because abortions are often necessary for the life or well-being of the mother. On the other hand, some members of the congregation may think deontologically and conclude that abortion is killing, and killing is always wrong. Because of these significantly different ethical presuppositions, discussion of this issue may first need to engage the ethical frameworks within which various people are operating. At the very least, clarity about these differences will help the preacher as he or she seeks to explore a moral issue from the pulpit.

In addition to the deontological-consequentialist issue, other critical ethical concerns further complicate the situation. For example, what are the sources of authority on which ethical decisions are based? Do people turn first to Scripture? And if so, do they view Scripture as a prooftexting document that delineates moral rules and absolutes directly applicable to contemporary life? Or do they approach Scripture more broadly, seeking the way of Jesus or more general principles that require creative interpretation for the contemporary situation? And what role do other sources of authority, such as reason, experience, tradition, and the sciences, play? In addition, different theories of justice may be a source of conflict. For example, a liberation approach to justice, which emphasizes a preferential option for poor persons, will probably lead to different conclusions than a procedural approach to justice, which simply requires fairness in the procedures by which decisions are made.

Exploring these and other ethical concerns when preaching on difficult issues, preachers may find that the discipline of ethics can play a helpful role. Not only can ethics help preachers clarify their convictions that lead to specific decisions on difficult issues. Possibly even more important, ethical reflection can help preachers examine and clarify the areas of difference—and even of disconnect—between the preacher and the congregation, which often contribute to the conflictual nature of such preaching.

B. Beyond Quandaries and Decisions

Preaching on difficult issues represents only one small aspect of the relationship between preaching and ethics. The ethical dimensions of preaching are much broader and deeper than the occasional sermon dealing with challenging moral quandaries. In fact, every sermon has important ethical dimensions because every sermon contributes to the formation of a people. Every sermon, even if not focused on an explicit ethical issue, helps to form the way that people see, imagine, and negotiate the world. And at the deepest level, such formation is central to the work of ethics.

The ancient tradition of character or virtue ethics, which has played a central role in the Roman Catholic tradition and has been renewed in Protestant ethics in recent years, explores this deep dimension of the moral life. Character ethics focuses not primarily on ethical quandaries and decision making, but on the kinds of people we are—on ethical character. According to character ethicists, the issues and decisions we encounter are inseparable from the kinds of people we are. Prior to any quandaries or decisions, there are people who seek to negotiate the world in particular ways and seek to live out certain virtues. Decisions, these ethicists remind us, are shaped as much by the kinds of people we are as by any set of rules or guidelines for decision making.

Within this framework, the fundamental ethical challenge for the Christian pulpit has little to do with preaching on moral issues—though that will occasionally be necessary. Nor does the fundamental ethical task involve providing principles or guidelines to help individuals make decisions. Rather, preaching seeks to build up the community of faith to see and live in the world in distinctive ways. Ethical preaching functions more at the level of imagination than at the level of decision making. For ethical issues, as well as the decisions that people confront, are fundamentally shaped by the kinds of communities of which they are a part, the kinds of people they are, and the way they see, imagine, and live in the world. Consequently, the most important ethical work of preaching takes place at this deep level prior to the focus on issues or the moments of decision.

At this deep level every sermon has ethical dimensions. People who have hope, for example, will see and live in the world differently from people who have no hope. They will probably have more energy to work for change as well as more patience for the journey. Similarly, people shaped by grace will live in the world differently from those who do not know grace, possibly being more open to outsiders and more forgiving of the failings of others. And people formed by Jesus-shaped love will see and live in the world in distinctive ways. They will confront certain ethical issues (e.g., the death penalty, homelessness) that may not even appear to people not formed by Christian love. In short, people formed by the story of Jesus will see, imagine, and live in the world differently from people shaped by other stories. Consequently, every sermon that helps to build up people in this story, every sermon that nurtures the Christian virtues of hope and love, has profound ethical implications.

Preachers, then, need to attend to the ways in which all of their sermons are helping to form the character of congregations and individuals. They need to explore the distinctive virtues that are shaped by the Christian narrative as well as the ways in which these virtues empower believers to negotiate the world in distinctive ways. Helping to build up the character of the church within the story of Jesus is one of the most profound ethical challenges of preachers. And this process occurs over time through every Sunday sermon, not just on occasional Sundays when the preacher addresses a particular controversial issue.

C. Ethics and Grace

In this sense, ethical preaching is not in conflict with the gospel of God's grace, for the proclamation of that gospel helps form people to see and live in the world in distinctive ways. The good news of the gospel is that we have been redeemed from the powers of sin and death so that we might freely live in the world in new and faithful ways. As Paul put it in Rom 6, "Do you not know that all of us who have been baptized into Christ Jesus were baptized into his death? Therefore we have been buried with him by baptism into death, so that, just as Christ was raised from the dead by the glory of the Father, so we too might walk in newness of life" (vv. 3-4). Grace sets us free for newness of life. The gospel of grace and the call to the Christian life are inseparable.

In fact, the relationship between grace and the Christian life is complex. It is not simply the word of grace that empowers discipleship. Rather, the efforts to live as faithful disciples may actually draw people more deeply into the reality of grace. Jesus, after all, first calls the disciples to follow him. And only as they seek to follow Jesus do the disciples recognize their deep need for grace—grace as forgiveness, as empowerment, and as sustenance.

Indeed, people may come to know the necessity and reality of grace only as they seek to live the Christian life. As Dietrich Bonhoeffer noted, only those who have left all to follow Jesus have the right to say they are justified by grace alone (Bonhoeffer 1959, 43). In this sense, inviting a congregation to live more faithfully is not at odds with the gospel of God's grace, but an invitation to discover and live into that grace more fully. From this perspective, the moral life is an integral aspect of the gospel and a critical dimension of the good news that the church proclaims.

Bibliography: Dietrich Bonhoeffer. *The Cost of Discipleship.* Translated by R. H. Fuller and Irmgard Booth. 2nd ed. (1959); Charles L. Campbell. *The Word before the Powers: An Ethic of Preaching.* (2002); James H. Harris. *Preaching Liberation.* (1995); Stanley Hauerwas. *A Community of Character: Toward a Constructive Christian Social Ethic.* (1981); Alasdair MacIntyre. *After Virtue: A Study in Moral Theory.* 2nd ed. (1984); John S. McClure. *Other-Wise Preaching: A Postmodern Ethic for Homiletics.* (2001); Christine M. Smith, ed. *Preaching Justice: Ethnic and Cultural Perspectives.* (1998); Arthur Van Seters. *Preaching and Ethics.* (2004); J. Philip Wogaman. *Speaking the Truth in Love: Prophetic Preaching to a Broken World.* (1998).

CONTROVERSY
Adam Hamilton

When preaching on controversial issues, every preacher must decide whether the aim is to influence her or his hearers, or simply to irritate them. The latter is easy, requires no skill, and is certain to shrink one's congregation into a body of only like-minded people. But for those who desire to influence their parishioners, there are several important ideas that can help build a strong, healthy congregation while inviting persons to take seriously the position of a pastor advocating on a given controversial issue.

What should the members of your congregation believe about embryonic stem cell research? U.S. immigration policies? The policy of waging a preemptive war? Euthanasia? Late-term abortions? Homosexual marriage? Most people will not take the time to understand the various sides in these complex moral issues. So who will shape their views? Politicians? Hollywood? Friends? The media?

The church is meant to play a critical role in helping congregants reflect upon complex moral issues in the light of their faith. Pastors do this routinely at the hospital when important medical decisions are being made, or in the counseling setting when parishioners are facing situations that require an immediate decision about a moral issue. But these are typically reactive situations. It is important that the church take a proactive role in helping parishioners as they wrestle with the controversial issues of our time.

While forums and small group studies of such controversies will likely draw a significant number of people, they are unlikely to reach more than half of the typically worshiping congregation. In most cases the number will be significantly smaller. Yet there are issues that are so important, so urgent, or so pressing that pastors will feel led to address them with the entire congregation (or at least those who attend worship). In addition, the pastor may find that addressing the controversial issues, if handled appropriately, will actually draw a significant number of people to worship—both members and seekers. (*See* INDIVIDUAL ETHICS.) Finally, if preaching is aimed at forming authentic and mature disciples of Jesus Christ, then teaching congregants how to do Christian ethics during weekend worship would seem to be significant. (*See* CORPORATE ETHICS.)

When preaching any given sermon on a controversial issue, one must first consider the aim. You must decide if your desire is simply to express your views on the issue, or if there is a higher calling to help parishioners understand both sides of the issue, dialogue with others about the issue, and reach their own conclusions about how to think theologically about the issue. If your aim is to influence your flock and encourage them to bring Scripture, tradition, reason, and experience to bear in their own ethical thinking, you'll likely find your congregation and people in the community interested in hearing what you have to say.

This is the approach I have used in preaching on controversial issues:

First, I try to remember that controversial issues are controversial precisely because thinking people of faith have been able to make a reasonable and often impassioned case for various sides of the issue. Hence I assume that thinking, reasonable, and committed Christian people are to be found on all sides of today's controversial issues. If not, the issue is not controversial.

Second, I endeavor to be as informed as possible about all sides of the issue. I seek the best and most objective information on the issue (it is difficult, perhaps even impossible, to find absolutely unbiased and objective information on these kinds of issues). I also read or talk to the most passionate proponents of various positions on the issue. The Internet is an invaluable tool for finding such proponents. On the most controversial issues, my aim is to be among the best-informed persons in our congregation. These issues require more sermon preparation time than ordinary sermons require. It is likely that you will devote twenty hours just to reading and interviewing experts on the subject before beginning to write your message.

Third, I aim to understand with both my head and my heart why people on different sides of the controversy hold the position they do. This helps me formulate my views more clearly, but it also plays a key role in earning the trust of the congregation. In my preaching on the controversies, I start with the position that is least like my own, presenting it as persuasively as possible. I follow with the position closest to my own, presenting it equally as persuasively. Doing that allows the congregants who hold a view other than the one you will conclude with to feel that their view was taken into account, respected, and seriously presented. I have had parishioners who ultimately disagree with my conclusions thank me for presenting their own position in a stronger way than they could have articulated it. In the end, parishioners will allow you to disagree with them and will even respect you for it if you demonstrate that you can understand and fairly represent their position.

Fourth, while I approach the controversial issues with my own preconceived ideas, I aim to reflect upon those issues with an openness to the idea that my conclusions may be faulty and the possibility that God will move me to a different place. Hence in my study, prayer, and reflection, I am open to the possibility of changing my mind. Only as you are willing to consider such a move can you lead a congregation to be willing to reconsider their own views as they listen to you preach on a particular topic. When I preached on the death penalty several years ago, my views actually changed as a result of my study. My preconceived ideas on several controversial issues gave way to new conclusions as a result of my study of these topics. When a pastor can stand in the pulpit and say, "I have really struggled this week studying this issue. I began my study with one opinion, and partway through, as a result of my reading, prayer, and reflection, my views changed," the congregation will be all ears to hear what the pastor has to say.

Fifth, it is critical to demonstrate humility, respect, kindness, and love when preaching on controversial issues, and particularly when revealing your conclusions. At the end of sermons on controversial subjects, I will say something like, "Having wrestled with both sides of this issue, I would like to share with you my own conclusions. I am not suggesting that mine is the only position a Christian could hold, nor that I feel any less love for those who disagree. Please know that you are welcome to disagree. But as I have reflected on this issue in the light of Scripture, tradition, experience, and reason, God has led me to conclude that . . ." Presenting your conclusions with humility, respect, kindness, and love will lead persons to take seriously your position and, for many, to make it their own.

Finally, when preaching on a controversial issue, it is helpful to provide some setting for parishioners to ask questions and challenge the views presented in the sermon. Following worship, we have offered sessions at which parishioners were able to ask questions and express their frustration or disagreement. These have led to greater understanding and allowed persons to have an outlet to state their views (*See* READER/LISTENER RESPONSE).

Our faith is meant to inform and shape how we approach complex moral issues. It is the role of pastors to teach and model for their congregants how to think theologically about these issues *and* how to do so with respect, humility, and love. There are a variety of venues in which the controversial concerns can be addressed. When approaching them through preaching, a pastor can increase the likelihood of positively influencing congregants and creating healthy and mature disciples of Jesus Christ. (*See* SOCIAL JUSTICE.)

Bibliography: Ronald Allen. *Preaching the Topical Sermon.* (1992); Adam Hamilton. *Confronting the Controversies.* (2005); William H. Willimon. *Preaching about Conflict in the Local Church.* (1987).

CORPORATE ETHICS
Arthur Van Seters

Decisions made in corporate boardrooms have implicit ethical implications for many areas. Management behavior and investor relationships are obvious ones, but so are those implications for individual workers, local communities, national economies, and the environment. Churches often have expressed concern over such issues as sweatshop factories, job loss due to outsourcing, and ecological disasters arising from industry. But preaching on corporate ethics has often seemed inaccessible or shrill.

Until about thirty years ago, corporate ethics focused primarily on internal accounting of what was acceptable, and business tended to resist external influence on its accountability. So, even though business ethics has been broadening, it would still likely feel unusual for a preacher to address the theme of corporate ethics in a sermon. Not only do many preachers feel ill prepared to do this, but listeners, especially those involved in the world of business, might be surprised that a preacher would even attempt such a sermon.

Add to this the widespread assumptions that the market operates according to its own laws and is value free, natural, and the most efficient way of distributing resources fairly. Market structures have always been human constructs, though this is not universally recognized. Philip Wogaman describes a conversation in which an economist challenged him to name any values that they would not hold in common. Some values may be shared, but which particular values should be highlighted in a given situation and what is the ultimate source of the good upon which lesser goods or values are dependent carry no such consensus. For Christians, this ultimate good is God (Wogaman 1986, 1–8).

Preachers, of course, know that congregational members in business share the conviction that God is the ultimate good and may also want the church to address corporate ethics. Tom Chappell, president of Tom's of Maine, told his pastor one day that he was tired of just creating new brands and making money. He was successful but felt empty. He wondered about his purpose in life. He concluded that he needed to study theology. After a year at Harvard Divinity School, he realized that previously he "hadn't had the intellectual confidence to question some of the standard way of doing business" (Chappell 1993, 8, 18).

In seeking to bring their responsibility as investors into harmony with their social teachings, churches have worked ecumenically for more than a decade to analyze how corporations behave across a comprehensive range of corporate responsibility expectations. They have sought to move beyond internal business ethics to explore a larger corporate social responsibility (CSR) that includes a triple bottom line: monetary, social, and environmental. Outside the church this CSR movement has been growing rapidly. What the church contributes (in addition to a rationale) is spiritual motivation to achieve sustainable CSR goals. This process also helps Christians to clarify the meaning of their discipleship in the arena of corporate ethics. Moreover, church position papers on CSR can be an important resource for preachers.

William Schweiker argues that part of the mission of the church is to articulate that in all spheres of society (including the economy), persons are treated as having intrinsic value. They are never to be viewed as mere instruments in a system (i.e., as commodities). Reality exists in relation to God as creator, redeemer, and sustainer. Therefore, human beings have inviolable worth because God became incarnate in Jesus Christ and because the Spirit of Christ is communicated through the Christian community and its practices. Having faith in God means interpreting and evaluating the world. Indeed, Christian discourse can work like a curative computer virus within the moral code of civilization to rewrite that code to make dignity of persons and demands of justice basic in a vision of life (Schweiker 2004, 128, 132–34).

Preaching is essentially theological discourse, and ethics is too often rooted in theology. Because we are people of faith, our basic convictions shape our individual and corporate discipleship. An important way of helping Christians reconstruct a new vision of corporate ethics would be to focus on the doctrine of God as Trinity. Katherine Tanner (2004) spells out an economy of grace arising from the reciprocal self-giving of the members of the Trinity to each other. This economic arrangement is marked by three principles. The first, obviously, is *unconditional giving*. The whole of what creatures are is based on grace. Union with Christ is maintained by God in spite of our not reflecting God's self-giving. God gives without measure, without calculus. Debts in the Jubilee tradition (Lev 25) are freely forgiven so that genuine economic restoration and renewal are possible. This has nothing to do with being or not being deserving.

Second, unconditional giving leads to *universal inclusion*. All have been created by God, and all can be redeemed through Christ regardless of race, gender, social status, or particular circumstance. God gives purely on the basis of need, and no one is without need. Gifts are never the exclusive possession of anyone. All have the right to livelihood and dignity.

Finally, an economy of grace is *non-competitive*—in the sense that it does not come at the expense of others. Market economies pervasively cause some to lose in order for others to win. But gift arrangements are based on non-exclusive owning. Property is shared according to need, not for its own sake.

After exploring Catholic social teaching on economics (among other areas), Walter Burghardt asks whether, "by all that is holy and good," this social teaching can be preached. He answers affirmatively with the qualification, *if* the preacher has first been "filled with the gospel message." He adds that this gospel must pulse through one's flesh and put fire into one's belly (Burghardt 1998, 53). Implicit in these words is the sense that a theological approach to corporate ethics is overwhelmingly countercultural. Those who receive the proclaimed word may seek to be shaped by the gospel, but they can also be profoundly "economized" by the world. So preaching needs to include the Apostle Paul's call to be transformed by the renewing of the mind (Rom 12:2). The chief motivation for such cutting-edge economic preaching is God's infinite love and grace. This grace includes those congregants within the business world and also for many others (near and far) affected by corporate practices. The controversial nature of such preaching needs to be admitted, and the preacher will want to invite listeners to give candid feedback, perhaps even invite them to explore further the shape of their discipleship. In the process, preaching on corporate ethics may respond to the longing of many to have the gospel fully (and concretely) proclaimed. Many businesspeople with whom this alternative vision resonates earnestly need sermons that support them as they struggle to live out what they believe. See GOD, ETHICS AND; READER/LISTENER RESPONSE.

Bibliography: Walter J. Burghardt, S.J. *Preaching the Just Word.* (1998); Tom Chappell. *The Soul of a Business: Managing for Profit and the Common Good.* (1993); William Schweiker. "Responsibility in the World of Mammon: Theology, Justice and Transnational Corporations," *Religion and the Powers of the Common Life*, Max L. Stackhouse, ed. with Peter J. Paris, vol. I (2000), 105 39; William H. Shaw, ed. *Ethics at Work: Basic Readings in Business Ethics.* (2003); Katherine Tanner. "Economies of Grace." *Having: Property and Possession in Religious and Social Life.* Edited by William Schweiker and Charles Mathewes. (2004) 353–82; Arthur Van Seters. "Economy according to the Trinity—A Particular Challenge for Preaching." *Academy of Homiletics* (December 2006); J. Philip Wogaman, *Economics and Ethics: A Christian Inquiry.* (1986).

ENVIRONMENTAL ETHICS
Rolf Bouma

Christian preaching has often utilized the doctrine of creation and its affirmation of God's attention to the natural world. St. Augustine penned no less than five expositions of the first chapters of Genesis. Luther and Calvin illustrated divine providence using God's orchestration of winds and waves. Puritan divine Jonathan Edwards saw creation as littered with types or symbols of divine realities: deep spiritual truths could be discerned in the ways of creation and its creatures.

Nature as an arena of human moral responsibility, however, is a relatively recent phenomenon, coincident with the dawning cultural awareness of the environmental crisis and our fragile place within nature. So the basic questions of environmental ethics are these: Is nature endlessly resilient, no matter what humans do to it? Are human interests the only interests worth considering, or are animals, plants, and ecosystems valuable in themselves? Are species worth saving from extinction? Is it possible for humans to live sustainably on the earth? How should we live?

A danger lurks in thinking that preaching on the environment and Christian ethics is a concession to modernity, merely a trendiness that imposes a foreign and contemporary agenda on biblical and theological material. Since when did Earth Day become a Christian holy day? Accentuating the unease is the famous allegation of historian Lyn White in a 1967 *Science* article that Western Christianity, the "most anthropocentric religion that the world has ever known," is a root cause of our environmental crisis. Electing to preach on the environment can seem like an act of contrition—an attempt to redress past wrongs by finding something of relevance to the environment within the Christian tradition.

The saving grace of preaching on ecological issues is that it relies upon foundational, oft-repeated biblical themes. One only need read the sermons of the late Lutheran theologian Joseph Sittler, whose sermons from the 1940s and 1950s on human out-of-sortness with creation pre-date the cultural awareness born of Rachel Carson's *Silent Spring* (1962), to recognize the reality that one cannot love God with heart, soul, mind, and strength without similarly loving the creation.

Humanity's Place in the Cosmos

The Christian faith begins by affirming God as creator of heaven and earth. The Nicene Creed nicely summarizes the trinitarian involvement in creation: the Father is Maker of heaven and earth; the Son is the one through whom all things were made (John 1; Col 1:15-20); and the Spirit is the Lord and giver of life (Ps 104). It is axiomatic that the earth is not ours to do with as we please; the earth is the Lord's (Pss 24; 50; Exod 9:29). The creation so witnesses to God's glory (Ps 19) that to defile creation is, as Christian ecologist Calvin DeWitt puts it, to mute creation's evangelical witness to God as creator (1994, 53–54).

So what is humanity's place? We are, by God's primordial commission, caretakers and stewards of the earth and its creatures. While the traditional translation of our original task on earth is to "till and keep" the garden (Gen 2:15), a straightforward translation of the Hebrew verbs 'abad and shamar is "to serve and protect." While given dominion over the earth and its creatures (Gen 1:26-28; Ps 8), humans are called as persons in the *imago Dei* to represent God to the rest of creation by serving and protecting it. When done well, creation sings a ceaseless song of praise to its Maker, with humans adding the libretto to creation's orchestration (Ps 148). Andrew Linzey, an Anglican theologian, has noted that Christians need not shrink from affirming the elevated status of humans (1995, 56–58). The genius of the Christian faith, however, is that the greater serves the lesser. People are *for* creation as caretakers in an even more fundamental sense than creation being *for* humans.

Wisdom and Folly

Creation is the arena in which divine wisdom finds room for play. At the dawn of creation, wisdom toiled by God's side as God constructed a world of intricacy and delight (Prov 8:22-31). The diversity of creation's forms makes the psalmist exclaim, "How manifold are your works! / In wisdom you have made them all" (Ps 104:24). Intimate knowledge of earth's creatures is a principal form of wisdom (1 Kgs 4:29). One can likewise argue that Adam's task of naming the creatures (Gen 2:19) is not just appending a name, but coming to understand the place and purpose of each living thing. Wisdom protects God's creatures in the time it takes for us to understand their purpose and place; folly pushes them into extinction unnamed and unknown.

Human folly risks the undoing of creation. Jeremiah 4:22-28 is a prophetic metaphor for environmental calamity: human sin decreases the cosmos as the earth again becomes waste and void, the lights of the heavens are extinguished, birds no longer grace the sky. Similarly, Lev 24–25 suggests that failure to treat the promised land with respect and to extend Sabbath rest to God's creatures will result in the rebellion of the earth against its oppressors.

Humility

Pride joins folly as the primary human contributors to ecological tragedy. Pride manifests itself in thinking that we are the only species that matters, or that whatever damage we inflict can be countered by human ingenuity. The indictment par excellence of human pride is the last chapters of Job (chs. 38–42) in which God speaks out of the whirlwind, using those elements in creation that have nothing to do with humans to put Job in his rightful place. Creation is not about us, but about God's glory. Much of creation has to do with God's relationship with creatures that have little or nothing to do with humans.

Valuing Creation

Christian theology, in its early struggles with Gnosticism, insisted that the material world was good, the inevitable conclusion drawn from God's declaration of creation's goodness apart from human presence and its very goodness with humans present (Gen 1). God so values the creation that, following the flood, God covenants with both humans and the earth (Gen 8–9). The promise of continuing seasons and harvests is as much a promise for all God's creatures as it is for humans.

Humans may be of greater value than sparrows and flowers (Matt 6), but it should not be forgotten that God values them, too. Environmental ethics in the Christian community is nothing less than learning to love and value the creation the way that God loves and values it. *See* GOD, ETHICS AND.

Bibliography: Steven Bouma-Prediger. *For the Beauty of the Earth: A Christian Vision for Creation Care.* (2001); Calvin DeWitt. *Earthwise: A Biblical Response to Environmental Issues.* (1994); Andrew Linzey. *Animal Theology.* (1995); Bill McKibben. *The Comforting Whirlwind: God, Job, and the Scale of Creation.* (1994); Joseph Sittler. *Evocations of Grace: Writings on Ecology, Theology, and Ethics.* Edited by Stephen Bouma-Prediger and Peter Bakken. (2000); Lyn White. "Historical Roots of Our Ecological Crisis." *Science* 155 (1967) 1203–7.

ETHICAL METHODS
Calvin P. Van Reken

Preachers frequently engage in ethics at some level. They do so in the assessment of the ethical issues at play both in the text being preached and in the lives of their listeners. Many sermon texts teach or entail not only some doctrine (viz. what one should believe), but also some ethical precepts (viz. how one should act). When preachers properly identify the ethical implications of a text, they are able to speak truthfully. When preachers grasp something of the personal and communal ethical struggles of those listening, they are able to speak relevantly. So for preachers to speak truthfully and relevantly on ethical matters, they must understand the ethical implications of the sermon text and the ethical issues in the lives of the listeners.

Ethical Implications
of the Sermon Text

Three problems are common in trying to understand the ethical implications of the sermon text.

The first is attempting to extract a binding moral precept from a text that does not (directly) teach one. (*See* MORALISM.) Many passages of Scripture describe situations without either endorsing or condemning them. For example, in Acts 4:32 the early church in Jerusalem is described: "Now the whole group of those who believed were of one heart and soul, and no one claimed private ownership of any possessions, but everything they owned was held in common." The temptation for a preacher reading this text is to conclude: persons in churches ought to hold all their material possessions in common. Yet the text is not prescribing a precept for all churches; it is describing a situation. The text clearly is commending the Jerusalem church for this situation, yet it does not teach that such conduct is obligatory for all churches. (In the same way, one could commend someone for enlisting in the air force without implying that all persons eligible for such service ought to do so.) To avoid finding moral precepts in the text where there are none, preachers must be vigilant in distinguishing what the text *describes* and what the text *prescribes*. For example, when David fought Goliath, he chose not to wear Saul's armor. Is there some hidden moral precept here? Does the text teach that God's people should not trust in armaments? Preachers need to be careful not to read into the sermon text moral lessons that are not intended by the text.

A second error of preachers is the opposite of the first. It is entirely missing the ethical implication of a text. John 13 describes Jesus washing the feet of the disciples, after which he says, "So if I, your Lord and Teacher, have washed your feet, you also ought to wash one another's feet. For I have set you an example, that you also should do as I have done to you" (vv. 14-15). This is not just a description of something Jesus did in the course of his earthly ministry; the text clearly teaches that it was an object lesson to teach that Christians should serve one another (even in menial ways). To miss this ethical teaching would be to miss a central part of the text. When the text prescribes something, a preacher should note it.

A third error of preachers is getting the moral implication wrong. Some preachers have mistakenly found precepts about proper parenting in the parable of the Prodigal Son. Some preachers recommend that Christians should on occasion imitate Gideon in putting out a fleece, although the text in Judges depicts Gideon doing so out of a weak faith.

In 2 Chr 7:14 we read, "If my people who are called by my name humble themselves, pray, seek my face, and turn from their wicked ways, then I will hear from heaven, and will forgive their sin and heal their land." Some preachers have applied this text directly to the United States, even though it is addressed to ancient Israel. It is a mistake to apply directives from the OT intended solely for ancient Israel to the United States or any other nation today, including modern-day Israel. Preachers need to be alert to the ethical implications of the text and must not too glibly or readily jump to conclusions about what a text is saying.

Ethical Issues in the Lives of Listeners

When preachers avoid these three errors, they are equipped to preach sermons that encourage moral conduct. To couple this with preaching sermons that are morally relevant, the preacher needs to understand something about moral issues in the lives of listeners. There is no method that ensures acquiring this understanding, but some practices can help. First, a preacher should personally know a substantial number of his or her listeners. One cannot remain aloof and distant from the everyday world of the listeners and successfully understand the challenges of that world. So a preacher who wants to be relevant works at knowing the names and occupations of regular listeners, visits them in their homes and places of work, and speaks one-on-one with them about issues in their lives when the opportunity arises. (*See* EXEGESIS OF THE CONGREGATION, DENOMINATION.)

Second, preachers need to pay attention to the moral struggles in the community, nation, and world. Some ways of doing this include reading the daily newspaper, reading news on the Internet, listening to radio, watching television news reports and documentaries, and subscribing to journals and weekly news magazines (*see* CONTROVERSY). Preachers need to be sensitized to the ever present struggle between the old and the new, the traditional ways and the changes that are occurring. Preachers who are morally relevant know the world they are preaching to and the people and problems that inhabit that world.

The truth is that most people have a reasonably good grasp of how a person ought to live. This knowledge is instilled through parents, teachers, laws, and peers. However, despite this knowledge, many people simply do not choose to live consistently in this way. To be sure, good preaching can clarify what moral living looks like. More important, it can inspire people to choose to live in this way and to encourage them to access the power of God that make such ethical living possible. *See* GOD, ETHICS AND.

Bibliography: Catholic Church. *Catechism of the Catholic Church.* Pt. 3. (1994); Richard B. Hays. *The Moral Vision of the New Testament.* (1996); Westminster Assembly. *Westminster Larger Catechism.* Question and Answer 99.

ETHICS, PERSONAL
See INDIVIDUAL ETHICS.

GOD, ETHICS AND
Charles E. Bouchard, O.P.

Morality and ethics are often associated with faith or religion, but it is important to note at the outset that ethics can also be autonomous, that is, undertaken without explicit reference to theology, faith, or religion. Autonomous approaches to ethics tend to rely on reason, emotion, or intuition. Immanuel Kant's categorical imperative is a good example of a moral system ostensibly derived solely from logic and reason (1992 [1785], 30). Preachers inadvertently tend to preach autonomous ethics when they preach what humans are to do without reference to God or to the help that God provides in living lives modeled on Christ.

Preachers are primarily concerned with theonomous ethics, which derives its norms (*nomos*) from God. There are at least two kinds of theonomous ethics. They are distinguished by preachers' understanding of Christian anthropology, especially the relationship between nature and grace and the extent to which God's will is mediated through created reality and human nature. Some traditions give relatively more weight to the effects of original sin and de-emphasize mediation and immanence. Some tend to see God as more distant and other and stress the difference between the divine and human realms, the righteousness of God and the depravity of human beings, the completeness of the fall and the necessity of grace for redemption and salvation, and the initiative for the latter lying entirely with God in Christ

Another approach is more often characteristic of Catholic theology, which views human nature as capable of integrating grace or being perfected by grace. This is the source of the scholastic axiom "grace builds on [or perfects] nature" (Aquinas 1947–48, 1, q. 1, a. 8). This means that grace and nature, while distinct from each other, are relatively more compatible. Unlike the dialectical approach, this sacramental view understands that even after the fall, elements of divine goodness remain in creation and human beings, that it is possible for human beings to initiate acts of goodness, that the church serves in a mediating role in offering the sacrament of salvation, and that one finds within society certain aspects that anticipate the realm of God.

Mary Catherine Hilkert uses the categories of dialectical and sacramental imagination to build a theology of preaching. She shows how the preacher's stance on these fundamental issues will shape his or her understanding of ethics and convictions about the sources of moral or ethical knowledge (1997, 15). A more dialectical view leads to stronger or even exclusive reliance on Scripture and on obedience to the command of God. The Reformation insistence on sola scriptura comes to mind here.

A more sacramental view allows that God's will for us is mediated through created reality and even through human experience. The Catholic moral tradition might be described as semiautonomous. This view accepts the primary role of Scripture and revelation, but believes that God's will is also mediated, to some extent, through creation and experience, that it can be known through reasonable reflection. For Catholics, Scripture serves more as a moral reminder that illuminates and deepens our rational understanding of God's law.

The process of reflection on nature and experience and the norms that are derived from this reflection are known as natural law. Widely misunderstood as having something to do with laws of nature (which govern physics and animal behavior), natural law is actually more a process of discovering God's plan for creation through the use of reason than it is a set of propositions or invariable conclusions.

St. Thomas Aquinas describes natural law as rational participation in the eternal law. This suggests that because it is rational, natural law is uniquely human, and it is autonomous in the sense that it can be known in principle by any rational person. It is "natural" only in the sense that it pertains to human nature, and it is "law" only in the sense that it is an ordinance of reason (Aquinas 1947–48, 1–2, q. 94).

While thinkers in the Lutheran and Calvinist traditions often find the idea of natural law incompatible with their understanding of the effects of original sin, we do find something similar in the Wesleyan "quadrilateral." Wesley allows for rationality and experience as sources of moral knowledge; these are similar to the Catholic understanding of natural law. In practice, theological presuppositions about Christian anthropology and the way in which God's will is known will shape preaching in at least three ways.

The Role of Experience

There are only two places to begin preaching: with the Word of God, or with human life and experience. Generally, the more sacramental a preacher's imagination is, the more readily she or he will begin with experience as revelatory of God's plan for us. This leads to an inductive approach to preaching, one where evidence is gradually built up that leads to a conclusion. The inductive or narrative approach to preaching may be criticized as too fragmented, too personal, and as nothing more than a string of disconnected stories. This is certainly a danger; all of us have heard narrative in which the preacher's own stories or concerns obscure the gospel.

However, *inductive* can also mean beginning with human experience as illustrative of grace, using the familiar starting point of human life. This approach leads listeners to a fuller understanding of God's plan by allowing them to identify it in their own experience.

Focus on Character and Affection

Preaching that flows from a dialectical imagination tends to focus heavily on the virtue of obedience. God's word is spoken definitively in the Scriptures, and our duty is to listen and obey. Dialectical preaching begins with the command of God as a judgment upon our sinfulness; that judgment brings us to our need for faith and acceptance of grace in our lives. Grace is never possessed or owned or presumed; it saves us but remains radically other.

A more sacramental approach employs the idea of mediation; in this view, grace is understood to permeate human life and is even able to be appropriated into a life of holiness. This is understood as virtue in the Catholic tradition and as sanctity in the Wesleyan view. A preacher will have to be very clear about the extent to which grace and nature are compatible as he or she preaches. Is the goal to call believers to judgment and despair, or to call them to feel and name the grace that is already present in human life and experience? Both elements are essential to the Christian life, of course, but our theological convictions will lead us more in one direction than another.

Public Policy and the Reign of God

Robin Lovin says there are a number of reasons why a preacher would bring the language of religious conviction to bear on public policy issues. The primary purpose might be proclamation (proclaiming the truth of the gospel at a distance with little or no hope that society will be moved to embrace it); conversion (proclaiming the gospel with the intention of converting society to it); or articulation (articulating basic gospel truths in non-religious language with a view toward collaboration). Each view represents a different theological/ethical stance the preacher might take (1989, 15–23).

Some churches are public churches in the sense that they understand preaching to extend beyond the faith and morals of individual believers and even beyond a specific community of faith. Christopher Mooney notes that these churches

> face toward both the private and the public spheres. They give a measure of stability to the former by explaining for their members the meaning of life and transcendence, as well as by providing them with personal identity and belonging in a community.
>
> In the public sphere, on the other hand, churches act as agents for transmitting (not uncritically) the operative values of society, formulating the moral aspects of political questions and seeking to interpret the biblical message for today's world. (1986, 3)

The problem with public preaching is that it always carries the risk of compromise; in preaching to "the world out there," we risk partial acceptance of our message, or having to settle for less than 100 percent of the gospel.

Let us say that because I am a preacher, my faith leads me to reject capital punishment as entirely immoral. As a preacher, I can keep my convictions pure by driving a wedge between faith life and public life; I can proclaim the truth of my position, rooted in Scripture, but refuse to engage in public discourse for fear of compromise. Or I can wade into the waters of pluralism and dialogue. I can contribute to the public policy conversation knowing that I will probably not have the final word, but hoping that I can present my convictions persuasively enough that I will gain some ground. The preacher does this, in the words of Bryan Hehir, by "creating space in the public argument for explicit moral analysis" (1985, 7).

As preachers approach the text, they must be aware of their tradition's stance toward the world and the way in which they understand God's action, or grace, in the world.

Bibliography: Thomas Aquinas. *Summa Theologica.* Translated by Fathers of the English Dominican Province. (1947–48); Bryan Hehir. "Preaching and Public Policy: The Parish and the Pastorals." *Church* (Fall 1985) 3–7; Mary Catherine Hilkert. *Naming Grace: Preaching and the Sacramental Imagination.* (1997); David Hollenbach. "Preaching and Politics: Consistency and Compromise." *Church* (Summer 1987) 11–20; Immanuel Kant. *Grounding for the Metaphysics of Morals.* Translated by James W. Ellington. (1992 [1785]); Robin Lovin. "Perry, Naturalism and Religion in Public." *Tulane Law Review* 63 (1989) 15–39; Christopher Mooney. *Public Virtue: Law and the Social Character of Religion.* (1986); Albert Outler. "The Wesleyan Quadrilateral—in John Wesley." Wesley Center Online. http://wesley.nnu.edu/wesleyan_theology/theojrnl/16-20/20-01.htm; Ronald F. Thiemann. *Religion and Public Life: A Dilemma for Democracy.* (1996).

INDIVIDUAL ETHICS
David P. Gushee

Preachers need to address the entire range of issues raised by Scripture, which includes sensitive matters of individual ethics. Such issues include diet, finances, sex, divorce, anger, and other behaviors that occur within the private sphere.

Many preachers shy away from addressing ethical matters of personal morality, and it is not hard to identify reasons for this reticence. One concern is the fear of giving offense. This is especially the case in a time when many churchgoers have abandoned recognizably biblical standards of personal behavior. To address such matters invites the rejection of the preacher and the church.

Another factor is a fading degree of confidence in the biblical moral witness. Whether biblical teachings are viewed as simply erroneous, or as so culturally bound as to be of little contemporary applicability, the Bible often ceases to serve as a source of concrete guidance for the preacher or the congregation.

A third hindrance is the preacher's fear of personal scrutiny or embarrassment. Once sensitive matters of personal behavior are put on the table, especially if listeners believe themselves to be addressed with uncomfortable directness, the preacher might have reason to fear that her or his personal choices will become the object of scrutiny and discussion before too long.

The primary cost of a silent pulpit on matters of individual ethics is the moral malformation of the community of faith. Christian people and all others who will listen need to be exposed to the whole counsel of God as revealed in the Scriptures. If the Bible addresses an issue, especially if it does so frequently, in various genres, and with a consistent message, then that issue must be addressed from the pulpit as well.

Certainly, there is the possibility that listeners will resent such direct treatment of sensitive moral issues germane to their daily lives. They may question the authority of the church or of the preacher to treat such issues. The foundation of an adequate response to such concerns must be the church's wholehearted commitment to the authority of God's inspired Word in every area of life. A congregational climate must be created in which each person, the preacher included, stands under the authority of the Scriptures and is prepared to be shaped by biblical teachings. The question then becomes not whether the church has the authority to offer moral guidance for individual life, but whether the congregation acknowledges the authority of God via the Scriptures.

Once the fateful but necessary decision has been made to end the silence of the preacher on matters of personal ethics, a whole host of other questions arise (*see* AUTHORITY OF THE PREACHER). One of the most important is the issue of what types of moral norms are offered to the listening congregation (Stassen and Gushee 2003, 99–124).

For example, the broadest and most abstract level of moral norm can be called basic convictions. These include our core understandings of the character, activity, and will of God, and also our other fundamental theological convictions about such matters as human nature, the possibility of personal change, and the reality of evil. These basic convictions are acutely relevant to individual ethics but do not generate specific guides to personal action. Certainly, such concerns deserve regular pulpit treatment. They are in a sense pre-ethical.

At the next level of abstraction, moral principles are broad statements of moral obligations such as "tell the truth," "love your neighbor," "care for poor people," "keep your promises," and "exercise self-control." For Christians, these principle-norms usually emerge from specific biblical teachings or are deduced from basic convictions about God and the world. Moral principles point people toward specific moral trajectories, or toward patterns of desirable action and character, but they do not tell listeners specifically what they must do in every case.

Moral rules tell us directly and concretely what we must do—or more often, what we must not do. They apply to all relevantly similar cases. They bind more tightly than moral principles because they are so much more concrete. Examples include, "Do not commit adultery," "Do not eat gluttonously," "Do not curse other people," "Give a tithe of your money to God's work," "Do not divorce"—or "Do not divorce for any but the following reasons . . ." One can easily see that the preacher who offers such direct moral exhortation risks offending. But one can also sense in many congregations a hunger for precisely this kind of concreteness in moral teaching. The Bible itself is full of such direct moral rule-exhortations.

A final and even more direct level of moral instruction is also possible from the pulpit—particular judgments. These are moral declarations about what is morally obligatory in one particular case. A preacher might offer such a particular judgment, say, upon discovering that some in the congregation are not welcoming persons of other races: "We must and we will throw our doors and our hearts open to all people." All moral address will want to strike a balance between imperatives that place responsibility upon the listener and a recognition of the power of God that enables those who follow Jesus to embrace and keep those moral imperatives.

Beyond this, it is probably not appropriate for the preacher to offer a particular judgment from the pulpit about what a specific congregant is doing. However, preachers do need to be prepared to offer such concrete moral guidance in private pastoral conversation.

Ultimately, it may be that there is no such thing as individual ethics. There is no part of life exempt from Christ's rule. And Christians are a community, the body of Christ, so what affects one part of that body affects all the rest. Our contemporary notion of the "individual" and the "private" sphere owes more to secular than to Christian sources. Preachers who address sensitive matters of personal morality with humility, honesty, compassion, and boldness are desperately needed among us today.

Bibliography: David P. Gushee and Robert H. Long. *A Bolder Pulpit: Reclaiming the Moral Dimension of Preaching.* (1998); James William McClendon. *Systematic Theology: Ethics.* (1986); Glen H. Stassen and David P. Gushee. *Kingdom Ethics: Following Jesus in Contemporary Context.* (2003).

MORALISM
Sidney Greidanus

Merriam Webster's dictionary defines *moralism* as "the habit or practice of moralizing." In preaching, *moralizing* is a pejorative term; it means "to draw a moral from" the preaching text when such was not intended by the author of the text. Of course, frequently the biblical authors teach morals, that is, right conduct. The OT legal genre, such as the Decalogue, teaches right conduct. So does a wisdom book like Proverbs as well as a prophetic book like Amos. In the Sermon on the Mount and elsewhere in the Gospels, Jesus teaches right behavior. And Paul concludes every one of his letters with a section of exhortations—exhorting us to right conduct. When the author of the preaching text intends to teach morals, the contemporary preacher should naturally follow suit. But when the author does not intend to teach morals and the preacher still seeks to draw a moral from the text, the result is moralizing.

Preachers usually fall into the trap of moralizing because of a valid concern for preaching relevant sermons. Their assumption is that a sermon is not complete until they have admonished the congregation to do something or not to do something. Preachers therefore tend to read the text through moralistic glasses, asking the text what it says about right conduct or wrong conduct. But not every biblical text speaks to the issue of conduct. For example, to read a biblical narrative as if it were law is a genre mistake, and the preacher ends up drawing morals from the text counter to the text's intention. In the process the real relevance of the passage is lost. The original author may have written this passage not with the goal to urge Israel to do something, but with the goal to teach Israel about God's faithfulness, to comfort Israel in exile, to call the early Christians to faith in their risen Lord, or to give hope to persecuted Christians. The real relevance of the sermon is found not in adding things to do or not to do, but in discerning the original relevance of the text and transmitting this relevance to the church here and now.

Moralizing is a virus that inclines to infect especially sermons on biblical narratives. Instead of listening for the point (theme) of the narrative, some preachers immediately zero in on the biblical characters whom they view as ethical models, heroes for emulation, or villains for warning. Hence, they freely attach do's and don'ts to arbitrary elements of the narrative. This virus is frequently tagged with the words *like* and *unlike*. For example, "Like David, we should all bravely fight our Goliaths"; "Unlike David, we should avoid temptations that lead to adultery"; "Like Simeon, we should look forward 'to the consolation of Israel'" (Luke 2:25); "Unlike Thomas, we ought not to doubt Jesus' resurrection." The biblical author's descriptions of biblical characters are too easily turned into prescription for the congregation. And in so doing, preachers risk missing the point of the text. If the biblical author's intention was to sketch a biblical character as a model of conduct for Israel or the early church, preachers today can follow suit. But if this was not the biblical author's intention, preachers today ought to avoid imposing their moralistic views on the text.

Moralizing preaching distorts the message of the text, it weighs down the congregation with tiresome do's and don'ts, and it conceals the gospel. Preachers would serve their congregations better if they would inquire first about the Bible's good news that "in Christ God was reconciling the world to himself" (2 Cor 5:19), and next about the text's original relevance: What was the author's message (theme), and why did the author write this at that time (goal)? This lays the biblical foundation for preaching relevantly to the church today.

Bibliography: Sidney Greidanus. *Sola Scriptura: Problems and Principles in Preaching Historical Text.* (1970).

PLAGIARISM
Richard C. Stern

Plagiarism is one of the most likely factors to be included on a list of ethical practices for preachers, and yet it is also the one most likely to be violated. Plagiarism, which comes from the Latin word for *kidnapper*, is the use of resources without proper acknowledgment. In preaching it is manifested in the use of someone else's specific, personal, copyrighted, or unique ideas as though they originated with the preacher. It also includes claiming the experiences of others as though they were the preacher's own, for example, using others' stories as though they happened to the preacher. Finally, it can include using the basic outline or thrust of someone else's preaching as though it were one's own.

With the proliferation of readily available homiletic resources such as books, periodicals, and the Internet, plagiarism has become easier and more common. Plagiarism can be blatant or subtle, intended or unintended. Nevertheless, commentators seem to agree that it is a clear breach of ethics. A preacher can appropriately use copyrighted material without disruption of the sermon's flow. One does not need, for example, an author's permission to use material from sermon helps marketed and sold precisely for use in preparing to preach. However, the matter of plagiarism comes into play when a preacher uses this material without credit or acknowledgment, acting as though she or he created, imagined, or experienced it firsthand.

Standards are understandably more rigorous and the consequences more dire for plagiarism in other arenas and disciplines. Academic scholarship usually passes scrutiny over a longer time, while preaching is, in one sense, a disposable medium intended for one people, place, and time. But the repercussions for plagiarism in preaching can be severe. In recent years, some preachers have resigned or have been removed from their positions because of plagiarized sermons. This situation would suggest that most members of the congregation assume that preachers do not flagrantly or intentionally plagiarize. A preacher's credibility rests in part on this assumption.

None of this is to deny that good ideas can come from others and can be useful in one's preaching. Most certainly this is the case. What is at stake is the honesty of the preacher and the integrity of the preacher and the word preached. Are the ideas of others subverting or preventing the preacher from developing his or her ideas, or are the ideas enhancing, supporting, or even correcting his or her ideas? Ethos, personal credibility, is one means of PERSUASION. The congregation presumes the preacher to be a person of faith, someone who strives to practice the ethical dimensions of that faith. Using the work of others as though it were one's own certainly compromises the preacher.

There have been times in church history when preaching was so poorly practiced that some preachers purposefully prepared sermons for others to use. Even today, with clergy who are more likely to have seminary training, there is a resignation or a rationalization among some preachers that their parishioners would be better served by a well-crafted but plagiarized sermon than by more mediocre fare prepared by the local preacher. This is, at best, an unfortunate attitude accommodated because of the increasing demands on and diminished morale of many clergy. As administrative and other demands increase, time to devote to preaching decreases. Other causes of plagiarism seem to be poor time management, misplaced priorities, lack of discipline or interest, and overcommitment. An occasional lapse slips into a permanent practice in one's (lack of) preparation. (See PREACHING, ETHICS OF.)

To be sure, there is a gray area where it may be difficult to assess whether a sermon or portion thereof is a product of plagiarism. Preachers are encouraged to research biblical passages for the levels and range of meaning, history of interpretation, and relevance to the current situation. Does every idea garnered from research need to be documented in the sermon? Probably not. However, as slight a nod as, "I came across this story . . . ," "The newspapers have been claiming that . . . ," "One commentator notes . . . ," or "Luther once wrote . . . ," seems to be sufficient acknowledgment that the idea or story was not original to the preacher. When done appropriately and sparingly, such attributions suggest support for one's sermonic claims. If one biblical commentator proposes an idea that is significantly out of the mainstream of interpretation, that should be noted: "Most commentators seem to agree, but Fenstermacher claims that . . ."

Richard L. Johannesen's discussion of communication ethics within a religious perspective asserts four principles: (1) "Humans deserve full respect as reflections of God's image." (2) "Honesty should be practiced in all aspects of persuasion." (3) "Only the best language should be used." (4) "The genuine needs of an audience should be determined and an attempt made to meet those real needs" (Johannesen 1983, 78). In this instance preaching can be considered as a form of persuasive speaking. Using other people's materials, ideas, and experiences as though they were one's own clearly violates all of the above principles. Even using "the best language" means more than simply using dazzling words. The best language is that which fits the situation of the congregation, and the local preacher would be the best judge of that.

Bibliography: Richard L. Johannesen. *Ethics in Human Communication.* 2nd ed. (1983); Richard L. Johannesen. "Perspectives on Ethics in Persuasion." *Persuasion: Reception and Responsibility.* Edited by Charles U. Larson. 5th ed. (1989) 28–55.

POLITICS, ETHICS AND
James A. Noel

All preaching is political, but preaching should not be limited or reduced to politics. The way one thinks about preaching and politics is related to the way one thinks about the church and politics. Some, like the clergypersons who took out an ad critical of Martin Luther King's protest against racial segregation in Birmingham, Alabama, during the civil rights movement, argue that the church should not be politically involved. It follows from such a stance that sermons should not be political. But this seemingly non-political stance is also political. Moreover, the issue for the preacher is not one of deciding whether or not to preach a political sermon. The preacher's challenge is to develop a hermeneutical method that enables him or her to identify, remain conscious of, and negotiate among the political contexts of the text, the congregation, and himself or herself. This is somewhat tricky, and an effort to do so is well served by an artful combination of historical and reader-response criticism (See READER/LISTENER RESPONSE.).

There are several reasons why it is impossible for a sermon not to be either explicitly or implicitly political. By its very nature the sermon has to take into account the contexts of the original writers, redactors, and readers. The preacher must also seek to bridge the gap between those contexts and the one wherein the sermon will be delivered. It is only by doing extreme violence to the text that the preacher will be able to ignore the political aspects of its original context. Indeed, the original context most often was one wherein the social, political, and religious realms of human endeavor were not viewed as being discrete. One can see in even a cursory reading of the prophetic books in the OT or Hebrew Scriptures that God's admonition to the economic elites and kings of Israel and Judah very often pertained to foreign policy and the treatment of poor and oppressed persons. Political motives can be discerned in passages that seemingly advocate a non-political stance, such as in the NT letters when slaves are admonished to be obedient to their masters. Therefore, any examination of these texts that does not analyze their political content and contexts does not qualify as adequate exegesis. Identifying the biblical text's political dynamics by no means exhausts its meaning because numerous dimensions must also be included in one's interpretation, such as the spiritual, cultural, psychological, and social.

The notion that preaching should not meddle in political matters is a recent one in the church's history. The Roman Church did not have this understanding of preaching, nor did the Protestant. The ability to conceptualize the political realm as one that is distinct from those of religion and culture did not arise until after the American War of Independence and the French Revolution. One outcome of these events was that people could conceive of the secular, in terms of the separation of church and state, and the notion of the private sphere. But even then sermons continued to address political themes.

The political continued to insinuate itself in sermons perhaps because the term freedom became the root metaphor that moderns used to define the nature, meaning, and deepest aspiration of the human. But this term was already operative in the Protestant church in terms of its understanding of grace as freedom from the law. Thus, the locus of human freedom became situated in three realms: the political, the religious, and the private.

Explaining how humans can exercise their God-given freedom while dwelling simultaneously in these three realms has been the underlying problematic of political sermons—especially in the U.S. where at one point humans were considered private property. Thus, the language about freedom always masked the reality of the un-freedom undergone by some. American preachers in the 18th cent. regarded political freedom as a fundamental perquisite to religious freedom. The law existed to protect human freedom, maintain justice, and coerce evil people into acting rightly.

We can witness this problematic being variously addressed in the Declaration of Independence, election sermons, the artillery sermon, the jeremiad form, and the sermons preached on special days of thanksgiving during the colonial period. Although these preaching forms grew rarer after the War of Independence, they did not disappear entirely. There were anti-slavery sermons, and during the Civil War, both Northern and Southern clergy preached sermons describing God as the vindicator of their cause, the cause being the cause of freedom in both cases. The Social Gospel, of which Walter Rauschenbusch was the chief advocate, came later. During WWI and WWII, American clergy described God as being on the side of human freedom and democracy—the side of the U.S. and its Allies.

After WWII the U.S. was confronted with the problem of actualizing freedom for its African American citizens. Martin Luther King Jr. drew from the language of the Declaration of Independence to legitimate the demands of the civil rights demonstrators. Because the laws of various southern states had been used to deny freedom to African Americans, King pointed out in his "Letter from Birmingham City Jail" (1963) that certain laws are just and others are unjust. King's critique of racial injustice in the U.S. did not exempt its victims, whose cause he championed. In *Where Do We Go from Here? Chaos or Community?* (1967) he wrote that for him, freedom from suffering came only with struggle, and he believed that not even the African American community had paid freedom's full price.

From King's preaching and writings, we can see that the preacher need not downplay his or her political commitments if he or she demonstrates thereby a sensibility about God's kingdom as being an eschatological reality that critiques all human material and ideational constructs. Today the American church's political context is one where U.S. military intervention in foreign non-Christian lands is being justified in the name of freedom. The church must comment on this claim because this term continues to reside in the three realms of the secular, the religious, and the private. See PREACHING, ETHICS OF; SOCIAL JUSTICE.

Bibliography: Hannah Arendt. *Between Past and Future.* (1968); Bernard Bailyn. *The Ideological Origins of the American Revolution.* (1967); Eric Foner. *The Story of American Freedom.* (1998); Ellis Sandoz, ed. *Political Sermons of the American Founding Era: 1730–1805.* (1991); James Melvin Washington, ed. *A Testament of Hope: The Essential Writings of Martin Luther King, Jr.* (1986).

PREACHING, ETHICS OF
Charles L. Campbell

What makes preaching ethical or unethical? What should preachers ethically do or not do in the pulpit? The ethics of preaching focuses on these kinds of questions and examines the ethical dimensions of the preaching occasion.

Answers to these questions—and consequently one's ethic of preaching—will be shaped by one's understanding of preaching itself. Preaching, like ethical actions, involves both ends and means. These two dimensions of preaching take different forms within different understandings of preaching, and each dimension requires serious ethical reflection. For example, if the purpose of preaching is to convert people at all costs, then one might argue that the end of conversion may justify any number of means that the preacher decides to employ. When these include the use of threats, manipulation, guilt, or even verbal abuse, profound ethical questions arise in relation to both the end sought and the means employed. Similarly, preachers who understand the purpose of preaching as persuasion or transformation will need to examine not only these homiletical ends themselves, but also the ethically appropriate means for achieving them.

More open-ended approaches to preaching, such as some forms of conversational preaching, inductive preaching, or story preaching, also require serious ethical reflection. These approaches may generally (though not always) avoid domination and manipulation, but they nevertheless can bring another set of ethical issues with them. For example, is the preacher under an ethical obligation to stand somewhere, to share convictions, and to make moral claims based on the gospel rather than leaving the sermon open for every individual to draw his or her own conclusions? Both the ends and the means of thoroughly open-ended sermons raise questions about the ethical challenges of the gospel and their role in preaching. Every understanding of preaching thus carries with it implicit ethical convictions and issues that need to be critically examined by preachers.

A second area that calls for ethical reflection involves the language of the sermon. As has been suggested, preachers should always examine whether their language is manipulative or even abusive. In addition, preachers need to pay attention to the illustrative material in their sermons, the stories, metaphors, and examples they employ. Does this material demean or exclude certain people? For example, are blindness and darkness, even with biblical support, always presented in negative terms, thereby demeaning people who are visually impaired or people of color? Are the positive examples of discipleship in the sermon always male, thereby suggesting that women have no significant role as disciples and potentially excluding women in the congregation from genuine participation in the sermon? Do the illustrations always focus on adults, thereby leaving youth and children out of the sermon altogether? An ethic of preaching examines these linguistic challenges faced by all preachers.

A third area requiring ethical reflection is the character of the preacher, including his or her relationship with the congregation. The ethics of preaching examines the virtues required of preachers—such as integrity, truthfulness, and humility—and how these virtues are embodied in sermons. More broadly, an ethic of preaching will reflect on the character of the relationship between the preacher and the congregation. Various kinds of relationship are possible, from authoritarian domination to parental direction to mutual friendship to pastoral shepherding, and all carry with them important ethical implications.

At this point, the ethics of preaching becomes quite expansive, moving far beyond a narrow understanding of the preaching occasion to include the life of the preacher and congregation, which always contribute to that occasion. How one preaches and how one lives are intimately and inseparably related. Indeed, the character of the preacher and the nature of his or her relationship with the congregation often qualify other ethical dimensions of the sermon mentioned earlier. For example, if the preacher's relationship with the congregation is characterized by friendship, then a deductive sermon that makes specific claims may not come across as dominating or authoritarian, but may be heard as the direct, honest speech of one friend to another—or even as part of a larger conversation among friends in the congregation. Similarly, if the preacher's relationship with the congregation is characterized by manipulation or deceit, even a seemingly open-ended, conversational sermon may be heard as underhanded or manipulative. The ethics of preaching covers much ground indeed!

Finally, in the contemporary context, reflection on the ethics of preaching must wrestle with the question, Who is allowed to preach? This question focuses significant issues related to the ethics of preaching. Silencing people, as many have noted, is an act of violence, and violence is one of the enormous ethical issues of our time. Consequently, when certain marginalized people are silenced in the pulpit so that their voices cannot be heard, the pulpit itself can become a place of violence. This critical ethical issue in the church today calls for serious reflection within any ethic of preaching. (*See* GENDER, RACE, AND ETHNICITY.)

How do preachers ethically adjudicate these and other matters? The phrase *ethics of preaching* provides preachers with at least two options. On the one hand, preachers can begin with ethics and explore the ways that ethical reflection informs the ethics of preaching. In this sense, ethics is the subject, and preaching is the object. Preaching becomes the recipient of the wisdom of ethical reflection, which shapes our understanding of ethical preaching. For example, one might turn to the long tradition of CHARACTER (or virtue) ethics to explore the virtues necessary for the preacher, as well as the appropriate means that preachers might use to nurture the character of the congregation. Or one might develop the implications of liberation ethics

for the practice of preaching. In these instances, one begins with insights from the field of ethics and then applies them to preaching.

On the other hand, one might ask whether the practice of preaching itself contains implicit or explicit ethical guidance for preachers. In this approach, preaching is the subject, and ethics is the object. The question becomes, Does the practice of preaching itself embody a particular ethic? Rather than preaching simply being informed by the field of ethics, the ethics of preaching grows out of the character of preaching itself. For example, one might ask, "What is the ethical significance of the fact that Jesus 'came . . . preaching'?" (Mark 1:14 RSV). And one might argue that Jesus' choice of preaching is ethically significant. Jesus did not choose coercion. He did not choose weapons or war, though some apparently hoped he would. He did not choose the way of domination, though he was tempted with this option in the wilderness. In short, Jesus did not choose violence. From the temptation to the cross, Jesus did not remain silent, but he actively challenged the powers of domination and death in the world. Nevertheless, the only sword that Jesus wielded was "the sword of the Spirit, which is the word of God" (Eph 6:17). One might conclude, then, that Jesus' choice of preaching involved a distinctive ethical option: nonviolent resistance to the powers of domination and death. Other approaches would have been at odds with the end for which Jesus was working—the *shalom* or reign of God.

Within this framework, an ethic of preaching would involve actively challenging the powers of domination and death, but seeking to do so nonviolently. Preachers would not remain silent, but at the same time they would avoid coercion and verbal abuse. Preachers would seek sermon forms and language that actively stand somewhere and challenge the powers that be, while also seeking to avoid domination and manipulation. The relationship between preacher and congregation, likewise, would not be one of domination, but one closer to friendship. Finally, such preaching would resist the violence of silencing marginalized voices by excluding them from the pulpit.

This ethical understanding of preaching is only one example of the way in which an exploration of the ethical dimensions of the practice of preaching itself may shape an ethic of preaching. It does suggest the numerous dimensions—far beyond the actual sermon—that such an ethic will include.

Every preacher has an ethic of preaching, which becomes implicit or explicit in his or her sermons and life. Critical reflection on this ethic of preaching and intentional efforts to conform this ethic to the gospel are critical tasks for both preachers and congregations.

Bibliography: Charles L. Campbell. *The Word before the Powers: An Ethic of Preaching.* (2002); James H. Harris. *Preaching Liberation.* (1995); John S. McClure. *Other-Wise Preaching: A Postmodern Ethic for Homiletics.* (2001); Christine M. Smith. *Preaching as Weeping, Confession, and Resistance: Radical Responses to Radical Evil.* (1992); Arthur Van Seters. *Preaching and Ethics.* (2004); J. Philip Wogaman. *Speaking the Truth in Love: Prophetic Preaching to a Broken World.* (1998).

SELF-DISCLOSURE
G. Lee Ramsey Jr.

Self-disclosure in preaching refers to those elements within the sermon in style and substance that disclose the personhood of the preacher and that selectively incorporate the preacher's life experiences, for example, personal stories, anecdotes, and testimonies, for the purpose of elucidating the gospel.

Background and Context

At least since the Apostle Paul, preachers have stitched parts of their personal stories into the proclamation of the larger story of the gospel. In his preaching and teaching, Paul refers to his conversion (1 Cor 15) and feelings of affection for co-laborers in ministry (Phil 1:3-11), and offers an intriguing but ambiguous self-disclosure about a "thorn" in his flesh (2 Cor 12:7). Paul lays before his hearers how faithfulness to Jesus Christ impacts his life, whether at the level of thinking, feeling, or believing. More important, he shows how allegiance to the dying and resurrecting Savior directs his ongoing commitments in the world.

Preachers since Paul (some more than others) have attempted through the sermon to align themselves, the messenger, with the message in the hope of delivering a sermon marked by integrity. In the North American context, preaching as a form of personal testimony received a great boost after the First Great Awakening and on through the 19th cent. as Protestant evangelicalism spread across the country. (*See* REVIVALS.) As Christine Heyrman documents, many preachers, both Caucasian and African American, and increasingly in the southern United States, used their personal conversion narratives as a touchstone for weekly preaching (1997, 232ff.). In various forms, the tradition continues today.

Recent homiletic theory has struggled to delineate the appropriateness of self-disclosure in contemporary preaching. In the wake of Karl Barth's thunderous "No" to human experience as a trustworthy source of Christian revelation, even preachers within traditions that value self-disclosure from the pulpit have rightfully questioned the approach. On the one hand, David Buttrick argues that virtually no self-reference has a place within Christian proclamation (1987, 141–43). On the other, Fred Craddock demonstrates how a lively incorporation of personal experience, especially through the artful use of stories, can enliven the preaching of the gospel (1985, 208).

Within the topic, usually addressed under the rhetorical category of ETHOS (the character of the preacher), a number of questions—theological, psychological, and practical—merit consideration.

Theological Considerations

The primary theological question is whether the preacher's self-disclosure within the sermon serves or hinders proclamation of the gospel. There is a theological content to Christian preaching, a *kerygma*, as the NT scholar C. H. Dodd identified it (1937), that lies at the center of Christian proclamation. In one way or another, Christian sermons point toward the saving grace of God through the life, death, and resurrection of Jesus Christ. This does not mean that sermons based on the OT necessarily end at the foot of the cross. But there is a core theological content within Christian proclamation that coheres around the creating, redeeming, and sustaining grace of God most fully expressed through Jesus Christ. The question is, Does the preacher's life help to illuminate or obscure that good news? Recognizing the distance between ourselves and God, and the human propensity for sin, Buttrick cautions that "all in all we are a poor substitute for the gospel" (1987, 106). Eager to connect with the congregation, some preachers are unaware that shining the spotlight upon themselves through a dramatic event in their lives can cast the gospel into the shadows. The hearers see the preacher just fine, but Jesus remains standing in the wings. Such sermons are full of anthropology, particularly the human situation as expressed through the life of the preacher, but nearly devoid of theology.

The underlying theological concern is the incarnation. Dietrich Bonhoeffer claimed that "the proclaimed word is the incarnate Christ himself" (1991, 176). The act of preaching reveals Christ among us, palpably, truthfully. But most preachers, if we are honest about our sinfulness, recognize that our lives fall pitifully short of the glory of God in human flesh. Theologically speaking, we may hold God's power as treasure in clay jars (2 Cor 4:7) as surely as Jesus Christ, but when the sermon places too much attention on ourselves, the listeners usually see shards and scattered pieces of clay rather than a worthy vessel. As Will Willimon says, "Thank God we preachers have something to preach other than ourselves" (1981, 61).

Psychological Considerations

Beginning in the early 1960s, a spate of pastoral literature emerged that attempted to harvest the insights of humanistic psychology for the benefit of preaching. (*See* POPULAR PSYCHOLOGY, RECOVERY OF.) Preachers were encouraged to be genuine, authentic, and vulnerable in the pulpit as a way to strengthen identification with the hearer and gain adherence for the message. Many seminary students and seasoned preachers got the message that the preacher needed to learn to "be himself or herself" in the pulpit. Self-disclosure by the preacher was not only acceptable but also encouraged as a primary means of creating the preacher-listener relationship.

The move was partly in reaction to authoritarianism within preaching. The goal was to get the preacher out of the elevated pulpit from where he or she delivered the message from on high and to stand in human solidarity among the people. Insofar as it checked unbridled clerical authority in the pulpit, the move provided a helpful corrective.

But several precautions ensue. As already noted, preaching is foremost a theological endeavor and an act of scriptural interpretation that reveals God with us. Sermons that emphasize self-disclosure as a means to strengthen listener identification run the risk of becoming something else entirely. Namely,

the pastor may subtly or not so subtly use the pulpit as a way to gain ego satisfaction for himself or herself. Rather than a moment of gospel proclamation, the sermon becomes a moment of pastoral confession, attention seeking or, worse yet, psychological exhibitionism.

Some argue that a measured level of self-disclosure during the sermon strengthens pastoral relationships as the sermon invites the congregation to see the pastor as a human being among human beings. In this case, a limited gain may accrue for some preachers and congregations. But the risk here is still a reduction of the gospel to human relationship. It courts the real possibility that constructing preaching upon the pastor-parishioner relationship will produce sermons filled with relational planks but short on theological and biblical substructure.

So we are still left with the initial question: How does self-disclosure by the preacher elucidate the gospel, and in what ways is it a hindrance?

Practical Resolutions

The matter can be resolved through theological and self-awareness by the preacher. It requires homiletical discipline and restraint. In one sense all sermons involve the self-disclosure of the preacher (EXEGESIS OF SELF). Style, delivery, content, and organization of the sermon all say something to the congregation about the preacher. Studies by Mary Alice Mulligan and Ron Allen verify the significance of self-disclosure for sermon listeners (2005). It is not a matter of whether the preacher discloses herself or himself to the congregation, but how. When it comes to selecting and editing the specific content of the sermon—biblical and theological interpretation, stories, examples, analogies, and so forth—preachers may find the following considerations helpful:

1. If the sermon includes personal material, evaluate who is the focus of the material—the preacher, another character, or God? As Barbara Brown Taylor points out, Jesus "did not star in his own stories" (1998, 76).

2. Before including personal material in the sermon, no matter how compelling, consider whether another story or example will accomplish the same homiletical goal without directing attention to oneself.

3. Avoid using the pulpit for achieving pseudo-intimacy with the congregation as a proxy for the lack of intimacy in other parts of your life. In other words, create and sustain healthy emotional relationships outside the pulpit so that the sermon event does not become a substitute.

4. Avoid revealing pastoral confidences or including others—spouse, children, and friends—without their knowledge and consent.

5. Most important, consider who is being served. What is the intent of the self-disclosure within the sermon? Is the personal story self-serving, gratuitous, or being used for some other purpose than directing the listener toward service of Jesus Christ?

Awareness of these and similar guidelines can assist preachers who recognize that occasionally our modest and restrained self-disclosure may reflect, however dimly, the full self-disclosure of God through Jesus Christ. *See* CHARACTER; DEVOTIONAL LIFE/LIFE-STYLE.

Bibliography: Dietrich Bonhoeffer. *Worldly Preaching: Lectures on Homiletics.* Edited by Clyde E. Fant. (1991); David Buttrick. *Homiletic: Moves and Structures.* (1987). Fred Craddock. *Preaching.* (1985); C. H. Dodd. *The Apostolic Preaching and Its Developments.* (1937); Christine Leigh Heyrman. *Southern Cross: The Beginnings of the Bible Belt.* (1997); Thomas G. Long. *The Witness of Preaching.* (1989); Mary Alice Mulligan and Ron Allen. *Make the Word Come Alive.* (2005); G. Lee Ramsey Jr. *Care-full Preaching.* (2000); David Switzer. *Pastor, Preacher, Person.* (1979); Barbara Brown Taylor. *When God Is Silent.* (1998); Richard Thulin. *The "I" of the Sermon.* (1989); William Willimon. *Integrative Preaching.* (1981).

SOCIAL JUSTICE
André Resner

Justice may be thought of as words and actions taken to close the gap between God's vision for healthy, loving, and harmonious community life and the reality of a broken, violent, and fearful world. Preaching social justice moves from the exposure and indictment of violations to the presentation of God's vision for healthy, whole, and peaceful life in community.

Memory and Hope

Memory and hope are the poles between which the banner of social justice hangs. To *re-member* is to recollect, to reassemble a fragmented and dis-membered body. Repeatedly in Scripture, God appeals to memories of God's people of having been the vulnerable and often abused stranger. Deuteronomy is a reiteration of the Torah with a sustained accent on the necessity to remember God's identity, especially highlighting their common work of doing justice on behalf of the most vulnerable (Deut 4:9; 6:1-6; 8:2-20; 10:12-22; 16:18-20). From childhood, all members of the community were to be told the story of their identity and mission so as to imprint it upon their minds, hearts, and dwelling places. Some key, humbling realities were to be constantly recalled in order to shape them into a community of mutual care: they were stewards, not owners; they were a free people by the delivering power of God, agents of light not because of any special characteristic of their own, but because God chose them. They were aliens in a foreign land and were never to forget that in relation to any future stranger they met. To mistreat, exploit, or neglect any human in need is to violate the Creator through the means of the created. In turn, whenever poor and oppressed persons are taken up into the compassionate care of the community, God is honored.

To preach social justice is to call the community back to its original purpose and destiny. The dead end of forgetfulness is amnesia, the loss of one's past and thus one's identity, self, and future. Preaching either contributes to the community's memory loss or counters it by casting the biblical vision for who its God is and who it is as God's people in the world.

To Know God Is to Do Justice

Doing justice is a sine qua non of being God's people. It is part and parcel of the reign of God. Doing justice means rightly knowing God: "Justice, and only justice, you shall pursue, so that you may live and occupy the land that the LORD your God is giving you" (Deut 16:20); "Strive first for the kingdom of God and his [or its] righteousness" (Matt 6:33).

Many read the Bible and preach a derived gospel that does not serve the memory of the liberating God who set apart a people to be a blessing, a light for justice and righteousness. Satan's use of Scripture to tempt Jesus from his mission is a reminder that Scripture can be used to deceive as well as remind (Matt 4:1-11).

Forms that such misuses take include (1) creating a false dichotomy between saving souls for eternity vs. meeting temporal needs, (2) reducing spirituality to a private kind of sequestered piety, and (3) selling out to greed by shaping one's message according to the materialistic culture of health and wealth. (*See* LIBERATION CRITICISM.)

Biblical notions of justice include but go beyond retributive and distributive to restorative justice. The latter takes seriously the *social* part of social justice with specific reference to those who are most vulnerable. Forgetfulness will obscure the mirror that the vulnerable are to be for Israel. Justice carried out with compassion and with a view to peaceful and peaceable relations depends upon memories of Israel's oppression and vulnerability. "There is a profound injustice about the God of the biblical tradition. It is called grace" (Volf 1996, 221). For Micah (6:1-8), the profound injustice was khesed (mercy, covenant faithfulness, or loving-kindness) received and given in the practice of doing justice. Only a people humbled by their relationship with God given as a free gift could be in a position to do that kind of justice in relationship with God. Justice done without the temper of mercy results in everyone getting what he or she deserves, something no one really wants. The ability to hold concrete deeds of justice in the creative, imaginative, and liberating frame of mercy requires the humble memory of an undeserved walk with God made possible by God's profound suspension of retributive justice and instantiation of restorative justice. The early church perpetuated this vision through its continuation of the ministry of Jesus. His stated mission was to proclaim the coming of God's kingdom, a reign embodied in Jesus' healing of the sick, freeing of the oppressed. The earliest church embodied his presence (Acts 2:43-47; 4:32-37), proclaimed the reign of God, shared a common life together, and even obliterated notions of private ownership of possession in order to care for whomever had need (Acts 4:32).

Preaching Social Justice as Bad News and Good News

Preaching social justice is the hopeful declaration of both bad news and good news. The good news consists in God's desire and promise to fulfill God's vision for a whole and harmonious community life. The fulfillment of the vision for a complete, just social realm is ultimately an eschatological reality. This does not excuse God's people from both announcement and the enactment of that realm or living into its reality in concrete form in the here and now. Such announcement and instantiation are a foretaste of the ultimate fulfillment. God sustains hope by such just proclamation.

The prophetic act of naming, exposing, and indicting is both bad news and good news since revelation of the truth, even when that truth is a difficult and demanding word, is always better than a continued deception. Preaching social justice is not mere indictment and judgment, however, and a failure of much preaching on justice is that it attempts to motivate primarily by guilt and fear. Sustained preaching ministries on social justice are fueled by the same compassion, mercy, and hopeful vision that make the biblical notion of justice more than punitive. True preaching offers a vision of the peaceful and peaceable realm that God alone can create and preaches the resources of God that empower the community of faith to rise above its failures to echo God's redemptively creative and prophetically caring, long-suffering presence.

Preaching Social Justice in Unjust Social Realms: Preaching as Prophetic Care

The real reason for silence on social justice issues in the pulpit may be that preachers do not trust in God enough to preach biblical justice in a corrupt land where too many laws are made by the wealthy who are lobbied by corporations; where the judges and juries are swayed not by the truth but by the best rhetorical performance that defendants can buy; where the poor, who own no land, fight the wars for the rich, who own all the land, in order to keep the homeland safe; where our media embraces the idea that everything in America is for sale and everybody is sold out to the false gods of agelessness, beauty, and sensuality; where fear of losing paycheck, place, or pension outweighs conviction about the true and weighty concerns of God and humanity. Preachers have often found convenient excuses to avoid the harsher side of the prophetic because of the need to give their communities pastoral care. What preachers need is a sense of call to prophetic care within community. Preachers have a clear and bold moral compass that empowers them to care enough about God's vision for community to say "No!" when that vision is being compromised in safe and sequestered, even seemingly pious and orthodox, church environments and to point them to the resources for change that God offers.

Though inherently controversial (CONTROVERSY), preachers of the gospel do not have the luxury of keeping the church's conversations about its life separate from social concerns that are created by economic and governmental practices that perpetuate and widen the gap between the vision of the peaceable kingdom and reality. In so doing, they are to be suspicious of any governmental or economic system since such systems are so frequently manipulated in order to benefit those who have power and privilege. For God's people, this world's ideologies must always be held accountable to God's vision for human beings in community.

Just preaching accomplishes at least four things:

1. Awareness and attitude. Preaching social justice is an act of raising awareness and working to adjust community attitudes to the biblical and theological imperatives of just living and just compassion in the face of concrete injustices.
2. Assessing and assembling assets. Preaching social justice helps people assess the assets that each person in the community has for helping address the problems. Community assets need to be identified and pooled so that actions that do the work of "jubilee" occur (i.e., setting those who are captive and oppressed free to the life for which God made us all).
3. Genuine accompaniment. Preaching social justice motivates genuine, non-condescending accompaniment with persons who are victims of poverty, oppression, and the many isms that perpetuate hatred and violence. True accompaniment is the connecting of human to human by the power of God across all "natural" barriers of race, gender, economics, and nationality in the mutual building up of one another in the common cause of community building. Genuine accompaniment occurs when names become known, faces are recognized, stories are told, and bonds are created.
4. Advocacy. Just preaching accesses the power of God to motivate and activate those in positions of power, influence, and lawmaking to make systemic changes to our political and economic structures that work against just, compassionate, loving, and whole community.

See CORPORATE ETHICS; SOCIAL JUSTICE NETWORKS.

Bibliography: Joseph Grassi. *Informing the Future: Social Justice in the New Testament.* (2003); André Resner Jr. *Just Preaching: Prophetic Voices for Economic Justice.* (2003); Miroslav Volf. *Exclusion and Embrace: A Theological Exploration of Identity, Otherness, and Reconciliation.* (1996).

STORIES, ETHICS IN USE OF
Raymond Bailey

A few preachers possess the talent to create stories with intellectual and emotional appeal, but the average preacher will be relegated to interpreting and applying the creations of others and events re-created from life experience. Reading sermons by the great preachers of other centuries, one is often struck by their literary knowledge and stories and allusions drawn from classical works of fiction and the histories and biographies of the past. Writers such as Frederick Buechner, Richard Lischer, Dan McAdams, William J. Bausch, Anne Lamott, and Madeleine L'Engle have demonstrated that the most effective preaching in our time is found in the stories of human struggle told in poetry, drama, novels, plays, and movies. A preacher's skillful reading or retelling can bring a hearer and text into a context of revelation.

Movies and television provide common types and themes of contemporary culture. Films based on religious classics by such authors as C. S. Lewis and J. R. R. Tolkien make the religious imagination of these Christian writers accessible to central audiences less inclined to read. Scenes from these movies are a rich resource for the creative preacher. Scripts written with no religious intent often raise ultimate questions to which the Scriptures offer solutions.

Fairy tales and children's stories are excellent sources of illustrative material. From *Aesop's Fables* to contemporary cartoons, moral themes are to be found in new fantasies. All comedy is based on human discomfort, and these stories of self-inflicted trouble and injustice can track lessons of sin and grace. *The Ugly Duckling, The Frog and the Prince, The Wizard of Oz,* and *Pinocchio* are only a few such tales that have found their way into sermons. While such stories have obvious appeal to children, adults also find them amusing and subtle sources of universal themes.

Personal experience provides the most common source for illustrative vignettes. Care must be taken to keep the focus on God rather than the preacher, but that is true for all material. Narratives of personal experiences should never claim experiences of others as their own. If a preacher wants to draw on the experiences of others, he or she should introduce the tale as read or heard from another. The preacher should also beware of presenting himself or herself as a model of morality, always making the right choice or decision. The most effective personal stories are often those that expose the preacher's vulnerabilities or depict the preacher in a humorous situation. Good humor is based on human discomfort resulting from flawed character. The gospel again and again reveals humans caught in dilemmas produced by their foolishness. The preacher who confesses his or her struggles will greatly enhance credibility with the congregation. *Here is a person, they will think, who can understand my struggles.* Personal stories should be occasional devices. The weekly sermon should not be the latest entry in the minister's journal.

The same rules applied to personal stories should apply to those about one's family with additional precautions. Having a bit of fun at one's own expense is quite different from telling family stories about spouse, children or parents, and siblings. There are enough difficulties for the minister's spouse and children without public humiliation from the pulpit. Stories told from the pulpit about young children may haunt them when they grow up. Any vignette about a family member should be cleared with the individual before use. A spouse or child should not be blindsided on Sunday morning. Do not think it permissible to share stories away from home either, because the disrespect and possible embarrassment exist wherever the forum. If children are too young to make a decision, discuss the matter with the other parent who is not desperately seeking a sermon illustration. One's family should not be presented as perfect, and attempts to do so often lead to great embarrassment when one slips; this is particularly true of adolescents. The

congregation may wonder how the preacher with a perfect family can possibly understand what goes on in their households.

Ethics require the same respect be accorded the church family as is accorded one's nuclear family. Members of the congregation should not be attacked from the pulpit or embarrassed. Personal conversations about families should not find their way into a sermon unless all parties give their permission. The Protestant pastor's study should be as sacrosanct as the Catholic confessional. Under no circumstances should a matter or event disclosed in a counseling session be used as a sermon illustration. Changing the names or location of the story still violates trust of the party or parties. Stories from previous places far removed from a present charge and some distance in time may be permissible with changed names, but great care must be exercised even here.

Preachers are notorious borrowers. Wise is the preacher who keeps a notebook to record interesting stories that may appear in short story, novel, newspaper, magazine, or the sermons of others. Most preachers are flattered to have illustrations taken from their presentations and used by others in the service of the gospel. Originality is difficult for the preacher as she or he retells the old, old story and its role in shaping human events. The creativity of the preacher is usually demonstrated in the arrangement of the sermon, the adaptation of material for a particular audience, language, and delivery. The preacher should not hesitate to use the material of others, but only with integrity. Credibility is the most important virtue for the preacher. A preacher who plagiarizes (*see* PLAGIARISM) uses the material of others without ascription, risks the loss of credibility, and disgraces the art of preaching. A sermon is a special form of rhetoric, and the preacher must maintain integrity of attribution without surrendering to boring, detailed documentation. Often in a sermon it is enough to note that "a biblical scholar has written" or "the story is told" or "I once heard a tale." A rule of scant attribution serves as a good rule of thumb for the sermon.

Let it also be noted that a good story is worth hearing more than once. Some preachers are reluctant to use a story that they have used before with a particular congregation. Churches sing the same hymns over and over without less power. A good story may be used in different contexts with great effectiveness. See APPLICATION; SELF-DISCLOSURE.

Bibliography: William J. Bausch. *Storytelling: Imagination and Faith.* (1989); Thomas E. Boomershine. *Telling the Truth: The Gospel as Tragedy, Comedy, and Fairy Tale.* (1977); Fred B. Craddock. *Overhearing the Gospel.* (1978); Anne Lamott. *Traveling Mercies: Some Thoughts on Faith.* (1999); Madeleine L'Engle. *Penguins and Golden Calves: Icons and Idols.* (1996); Eugene L. Lowry. *The Homiletical Plot: The Sermon as Narrative Art Form.* (1980); John Shea. *Stories of God: An Unauthorized Biography.* (1987).

Part 4 Literary Criticism.
Introduction: Subjectivity and the Sermon

Gregory Heille, O.P.

Some years ago, University of Toronto homiletician Paul Scott Wilson mentioned in a letter, "I used to think (when I graduated from seminary) that biblical exegesis took the preacher 80 percent of the way into the pulpit; I am still convinced that the exegetical work is fundamental and essential, but that it takes the preacher only 30 to 40 percent of the way. (Of course, without it one would be nowhere.)" If Wilson's instinct rings true, it may be because the remaining 60 to 70 percent has something to do with the preacher's internal authority as guided by the Holy Spirit and grounded in spiritual, theological, and pastoral practice. As with the practices of writing, distance running, or medical diagnosis, there is a rigorous subjective component to the practice of preaching, and even to biblical interpretation that is to be desired and best not escaped if we truly desire to serve the revelatory purposes of God.

Longing to Become the Good News We Preach

Benedictine monk David Steindl Rast once wrote about the Grimm's fairy tale Snow White and the Seven Dwarfs in terms of life in a monastery—making note of their refectory, their dormitory, and their work, commenting on monastic life as a "Path with a heart" that approximates the "Great Path" (*Parabola* 5:3, 33). Medieval monastics spoke of the impulse that first brought them to the convent or monastery door as being spousal, and I think it is this same spousal impulse to follow the Great Path with a Heart that first brings most contemporary men and women to the seminary door. As ministers in the making, we approach our formative years with hope and love. Most often, however, as beginners we are naive to the ways in which theological studies, seminary and denominational systems, and our initiation into ministry will test our faith and challenge us beyond our first vocational naiveté to ever deeper integrity and surrender to the gospel path.

Most of us come to seminary as novices to the rigorous practices that comprise graduate study for ministry—practices such as close reading of texts, social analysis, theological reflection, written and oral communication, spiritual formation, and collaboration.

Whereas in the medieval monastery theology and ministry were holistically experienced as an integrated way of living and being, this has not so much been the case since the Enlightenment. In what Edward Farley of Vanderbilt University calls a clerical paradigm of ministerial education (and which he considers in reference to preaching), seminary curricula have been compartmentalized into a standard fourfold division of professionalized and often competitive disciplines—including biblical studies, church history, systematic theology, and pastoral ministry (2003). Historical-critical method has held pride of place, and spirituality and especially spiritual formation may be included minimally or not at all.

It can be granted that in the best of worlds we must expect students for ministry to experience some measure of distanciation as they learn the skills for critically receiving and thinking the faith. Yet if it is true that most fledging ministers still come to the seminary door with a certain inchoate spousal impulse for ministry as a *habitus* or practice of discipleship, is it not a pity that so many beginning ministers leave seminary disillusioned by theological education and surprisingly unprepared for ministry as a reflective practice of the heart? For many pastors, ministry has become a professional pastiche of management, social service, and—in terms of preaching—formulaic speech and mass entertainment. For those trained under the Enlightenment paradigm, the historical-critical method learned in the ivory tower of seminary can seem virtually irrelevant to the clerical practice of professional ministry. Sadly, as ministry is besieged by mounting pressures of work and an erosion of public trust, many trained ministers do not begin to know how to be theologically reflective practitioners.

Any busy preacher might read Marilynne Robinson's extraordinary second novel, *Gilead*. Today's preacher might well feel nostalgia for a simpler time when reading about the ministry of the Reverend John Ames, the elder Protestant pastor at the center of this story of rural Iowa in the 1950s. Reverend Ames has attained the personally enriching pastoral ethos that many of us originally sought and may still long for—a theological *habitus* formed by lifelong preaching and studious reflection. By virtue of his authenticity as a reflective practitioner and pastoral theologian, this rural preacher exemplifies for us what it might mean to become the good news we preach.

From Theory-Application to Engaging the Worlds of Experience and of the Text

To a great extent, most seminary-trained preachers have been formed in a theory-application approach to theology, ministry, and preaching. In this, the Scriptures and doctrines and teachings are assumed to convey objective truths that are accessible to historical-critical method and then applicable to parishioners' lives through instruction, storied examples, and admonition. Often, however, preaching in this mode of building a bridge from Scripture to life is perceived as formulaic and out of touch with life as people experience it. For many, a more practicable and gospel-oriented approach to preaching and Christian life is called for.

The Roman Catholic bishops of the United States, in their internationally regarded *Fulfilled in Your Hearing: The Homily in the Sunday Assembly*, have put preaching in perspective by speaking first of the assembly, then of the preacher, and only finally of the homily and homiletic method. Here, preaching is a communicative act in which the preacher mediates meaning, not so much by expounding upon and then applying the scriptural and liturgical texts as (and this is a subtle distinction) by reflectively interpreting people's lives through a contemplative and studious engagement with the texts.

Preaching, when well served by academic theology, can itself be a theologically imaginative and authentic call to action for Christian discipleship in the midst of the real experiences of a graced and broken world. In this vein, a literature by Don S. Browning of the University of Chicago and others in the academic field of practical theology offers a new way to think about what many ministers instinctively are doing—letting go of a false dichotomy of theory and application in favor of a habitus of engaged reflection in dialogue with the personal, ecclesial, and cultural experiences that inform our world. In this approach, preaching mediates meaning less through abstraction and application and more through engaged dialogue, principled reflection, and faith-filled action.

Practical theology challenges a separation between theological theory and ministerial practice and invites us to return to a vision of ministry as inseparable from theology and in which all theology—even in the academy—is grounded in the subjectivity of lived experience.

In *Method in Ministry*, James D. and Evelyn Eaton Whitehead have called for a correlation or critical dialogue among three relevant worlds of experience, which may be paraphrased as the experience of believers (of faith—of personal and communal Christianity); the experience of the Christian tradition (of church—of historical and institutional Christianity and the Scriptures); and the experience of institutions and systems (of culture—of Christianity in the context of the larger society). It is akin to the see-judge-act practical model for engaged discipleship that was practiced by generations of workers, students, families, and activists since first posed by the Belgian priest Joseph Cardijn in the 1930s. However, the Whitehead model is an action-oriented, value-directed interpretation of personal, ecclesial, and cultural worlds of experience on behalf of the gospel vision of the reign of God.

Whereas it is good that all preachers receive training in the historical-critical appropriation of the privileged texts and practices of the tradition, a certain postmodern skepticism regarding the operative assumptions of modernity is leading ministers to question whether they can continue to base scriptural preaching purely on a theory-application, diachronic approach that portends to represent the minds of the inspired authors of received texts in terms of objective truths to be applied to lives today. A solid grasp of historical-critical method remains indispensable, but today's preacher deserves and needs also to acquire basic familiarity and skill in more synchronic, literary-critical interpretive approaches to texts.

Two works giving a solid orientation to contemporary biblical interpretation for preachers are

Sandra M. Schneiders's *The Revelatory Text: Interpreting the New Testament as Sacred Scripture* and Robert Kysar and Joseph M. Webb's *Preaching to Postmoderns: New Perspectives for Proclaiming the Message*. Both organize their explication of differing hermeneutical approaches according to the standard principle of the three worlds of the text: *the world behind the text* (*see* HISTORICAL CRITICISM, with attention to NEW HISTORICISM and to very preacher-friendly SOCIAL SCIENTIFIC CRITICISM), *the world of the text* (the several literary critical methods so influential on recent homiletical instincts to let preaching follow the form and function of the texts being preached: STRUCTURALISM, READER-LISTENER RESPONSE, RHETORICAL CRITICISM, HOMILETICAL [THEOLOGICAL] CRITICISM), and *the world in front of the text* (FEMINIST CRITICISM, CULTURAL HERMENEUTICS, POSTCOLONIAL CRITICISM, WOMANIST CRITICISM, and emerging postmodern DECONSTRUCTION perspectives on Scripture—each in its own way begging careful consideration by preachers).

First Contemplation and then to Study

Scholars are learning, even if reluctantly, that there is an inextricably subjective dimension to reading, interpreting, and receiving Scripture. It would be dualistic and somewhat simplistic to identify the historical-critical interpretation of the world behind the text as objective and the literary critical interpretations having to do with the worlds within and in front of the text as subjective. The same is true of the implied suggestion of privileging the so-called objective interpretation of texts.

To get at the constitutively subjective dimension of all preaching and of all scriptural interpretation for preaching, it helps to keep the role of the Holy Spirit in mind. It is no secret that Spirit-guided preaching must begin with prayer. Yet in the hurly-burly of ministry the instinct, despite seminary training, can be (all too easily) to reach first for a commentary or a website and to let an expert explain what the text means. One can give preference to human expertise over the contemplative practice of allowing the Holy Spirit to engage the reader in his or her first encounter with the text. More and more preachers are faithfully employing the time-honored Benedictine practice of *lectio divina,* a step-by-step contemplative reading of the

text, as explained for example by Thelma Hall in *Too Deep for Words: Rediscovering* Lectio Divina.

Like Jacob wrestling with the angel, we are invited to wrestle personally, which is to say subjectively, with the text. Can we dare to let the Holy Spirit engage us contemplatively with the text—and only then to take Spirit-guided doubts, questions, and concerns to a critical appropriation of the worlds of the text, of the sort that happens with the help of the best commentaries and websites and the fullest repertoire of interpretive approaches we can muster? Having first contemplatively and only then studiously engaged the text, we are positioned from a necessary stance of internal spiritual authority grounded in reflective practice to surrender to the revelatory power of Scripture—today, for this community, in this preaching. *See* CHARACTER; DEVOTIONAL LIFE/LIFE-STYLE; ETHOS; EXEGESIS OF SELF; SELF-DISCLOSURE.

Bibliography: Bishops' Committee on Priestly Life and Ministry, National Conference of Catholic Bishops. *Fulfilled in Your Hearing: The Homily in the Sunday Assembly.* (1982); Edward Farley. *Practicing Gospel: Unconventional Thoughts on the Church's Ministry.* (2003); Thelma Hall. *Too Deep for Words: Rediscovering* Lectio Divina. (1988); Robert Kysar and Joseph M. Webb. *Preaching to Postmoderns: New Perspectives for Proclaiming the Message.* (2006); Marilynne Robinson. *Gilead.* (2004); Sandra M. Schneiders. *The Revelatory Text: Interpreting the New Testament as Sacred Scripture.* (1999); David Steindl-Rast. *Parabola* 5:3 (Fall 1980); James D. Whitehead and Evelyn Eaton Whitehead. *Method in Ministry: Theological Reflection and Christian Ministry.* Rev. ed. (1995).

❖   ❖   ❖   ❖

CULTURAL HERMENEUTICS
Deborah A. Organ

Cultural hermeneutics is the intentional use of cultural context, both of text and of contemporary reader, in the interpretive process. Cultural hermeneutics and related philosophical studies offer preachers and communities new possibilities for responsible and faithful engagement with biblical texts.

A. Biblical Interpretation and Culture
  1. Authorial Intent and the Perspective of the Contemporary Reader
  2. Characteristics of a Valid Interpretation
  3. Integration and New Possibilities
B. Drawing Us Beyond Ourselves: The Parable
  1. Life in Chiapas
  2. The Parables Alive
  3. The Parable of the Lost Coin
C. The Contributions of Cultural Hermeneutics to Preaching: Toward the Future

A. Biblical Interpretation and Culture

Biblical interpretation is central to preaching, and cultural hermeneutics has significantly expanded the horizons for interpretation, particularly over the last twenty years. Scholars and communities of faith have begun to interpret Scripture out of their specific cultural contexts, yielding new and varied interpretations that enrich community life as well as introduce the possibility of reading the Bible together out of diverse cultural contexts. Many preachers have recognized that they interpret and preach through their own cultural lens, and that the Word of God truly comes alive for congregations when it is preached in their cultural idiom and interpreted from within their specific cultural contexts.

Along with this new richness and cultural diversity in biblical interpretation, with all of their implications for congregational life and preaching, questions have arisen. How diverse can biblical interpretations be and still be valid? What constitutes a valid interpretation for preaching?

For more than fifty years, the discipline of hermeneutics within the field of philosophy has grappled with these and other questions related to interpretation of texts. Hermeneutical theorists Hirsch, Gadamer, Fish, and Ricoeur, whose main works were published primarily in the 1970s, made significant contributions to biblical interpretation and helped form the basis for the development of the New Homiletic over the last fifty years.

1. Authorial Intent and the Perspective of the Contemporary Reader

E. D. Hirsch's research was primarily concerned with the role of the author's intent and context in the interpretation of a written work (1967). For Hirsch, an interpretation is valid to the degree that it is consistent with what can be known about the author's intention. An important assumption that seems to follow from Hirsch's position is that of the existence of one normative interpretation of a biblical passage.

Hans-Georg Gadamer countered the author-centered approach of Hirsch and others by pointing out the new possibilities for interpretation of a text by contemporary readers in diverse cultural contexts (1977). He believed that valid interpretation occurs whenever a reader interprets a text. Thus, all interpretations are valid for Gadamer. Though both Hirsch and Gadamer were concerned with true interpretation, they were at opposite poles about what should form the basis of that interpretation. Should it be the intentions of the author (as far as they can be determined) or the experience of the contemporary reader?

2. Characteristics of a Valid Interpretation

Stanley Fish contributed to the dialogue about valid textual interpretation by acknowledging the existence of a variety of interpretations of any given text (Saye 1996). He emphasized, however, that some interpretations are more valid than others and that an interpretation is only correct or incorrect relative to the assumptions underlying the interpretation. Fish believed that there are many sets of assumptions (or, one could argue, cultures) from which a text can be interpreted, but that the validity of the interpretation is dependent on the authority of the interpretive community from which a set of assumptions comes.

A valid critique of Fish's theory is that it lacks clarification on what constitutes authority in an interpretive community, and that speaks directly to the concerns of cultural hermeneutics. Cultural hermeneutics often produces interpretations from cultural contexts that may be perceived as marginalized rather than powerful. Fish's approach could potentially invalidate interpretations of marginalized communities and endorse the hegemony of powerful and dominant cultural perspectives in biblical interpretation. Cultural hermeneutics arose in part to allow previously marginalized people to interpret the Bible from their contexts.

While Fish and others attempted to hold in some kind of critical tension a variety of interpretations, arguably Paul Ricoeur made the greatest contribution to depolarizing the debate about text and context.

3. Integration and New Possibilities

Uncomfortable with the inherent subjectivity of Gadamer's approach, yet believing that the cultural context and concerns of the reader play an important part in the interpretive process, Paul Ricoeur established the interpretive act in the encounter between text and reader (1980). Ricoeur identified the text as "other," with a life of its own worthy of attention and study. It was in the encounter between the contemporary reader, within a cultural context, and the text, with its own identity and context, that meaning and new possibilities emerged for Ricoeur.

Ricoeur recognized, then, that a variety of valid interpretations of a text are possible and necessary, as long as they are authentic encounters between text and reader. Furthermore, he emphasized that focusing only on the contemporary reader's concerns might merely accommodate the text to the reader's worldview. Ricoeur argued that serious engagement with the world of the real text, because of its very difference from the world of the reader, could draw the reader into new possibilities that transcended his or her current context.

Ricoeur's new possibilities have clear implications for cultural hermeneutics and preaching. Engagement with a text from various cultural perspectives yields new meaning within a given cultural context and between cultural contexts as communities read the Bible together. The role of the preacher is to interpret the Word and preach in the cultural idiom(s) familiar to the congregation so that the community can recognize the Word alive in their midst. But the responsibility of preacher and community does not end there. Preachers also have the sacred task of engaging the biblical text in their own lives in ways that lead to personal transformation, and then preaching in a way that calls people to transformation.

In order to illustrate the potential of the kind of textual encounter envisioned by Ricoeur, as well as such an encounter's power to inspire and enrich the preaching ministry, let us turn to a community of indigenous Mayan women in the highlands of Chiapas, in southern Mexico near the Guatemalan border.

B. Drawing Us Beyond Ourselves: The Parable

Sixty women gathered on an unseasonably cold and rainy day in January 2006 in the public hall of a small Tzotzil Mayan community called Las Llagas (the Wounds of Christ). The women ranged in age from fifteen to sixty-five, and about 85 percent were monolingual Tzotzil speakers. More than 60 percent were illiterate, and 80 percent were married, with the remaining women widows or young unmarried women. For at least half of the women, the three-day retreat was the first time they had been away from home and family overnight. Some women brought their small children with them. The meetings of the retreat took place in the public hall, with benches arranged in a three-quarter round with a beautiful display of candles, fresh pine needles, and rose petals in the middle of the room. Women and children shared meals around a roaring wood fire in a small building across the village plaza from the hall.

The women came from roughly twenty-five poor farming communities in the highlands region of Chiapas. Many came in groups escorted by spouses, while some walked or took public transportation to get as close to the village as possible. They engaged in a process that began with exploration of their context, which was followed by a study of parables and then by imaginative work around interpretation and new possibilities.

1. Life in Chiapas

The retreat leader worked with a Tzotzil-Spanish interpreter and began the retreat by asking the women to introduce themselves and say a little about their lives. What followed was a four-hour conversation about suffering, alcoholism, poverty, migration, deaths of small children, domestic violence, and other misuse of power. The patient listening and length of the conversation were typical of the Mayan cultural context. What was unique, according to the interpreter, was the immediate depth of the conversation. One of the women, whom the retreat leader judged to be in her thirties, indicated that this was the first time she had ever known that other women had experiences similar to hers.

Following this conversation and another focused on what gave the women the strength to persevere in their situations, the women turned to the Bible and to the study of parables. Because so many of the women could not read, each group of six had a reader.

2. The Parables Alive

The retreat leader began the conversation with an introduction to Jesus' use of parables in his teaching. She reflected on how he used everyday objects, stories, and images that would have been very familiar to the ancient listeners but often gave them unexpected twists that encouraged the listeners to new ways of thinking and being.

Each group of women was then assigned a parable to read. First, the groups discussed what they thought Jesus was trying to do with the parable in the ancient community, based on the introduction to ancient Mediterranean cultural context they had heard. Second, the retreat leader asked the women to create a dramatic representation of what that parable would look like in their Mayan cultural context. Specifically, the women were asked to visualize and then represent the direction they thought the parable might be calling their own communities to move.

The exercise freed the women to go beyond traditional or normative interpretations of parables with which some were familiar to an authentic encounter between their community and the ancient text. The results were amazing.

3. The Parable of the Lost Coin

One small group focused on the parable of the Lost Coin (Luke 15:8-9). As they reflected on the importance of searching for and finding something precious in the ancient world, they realized that as women they had, in many cases, lost a sense of their inherent human dignity. They considered factors such as sexism, family history, and responsibility for children as instrumental in the subsuming of their own identities and dignity. They then opened their imaginations to the implications of and possible ways to accomplish the "sweeping out the house" of their local communities in order to find and restore the dignity of women.

The drama that this group presented posed the question of lost and potentially found dignity in their cultural context. The drama opened the listeners' hearts and minds to their losses and to the possibilities for their empowerment of one another.

When talking about the potential of biblical hermeneutics for transformation, Ricoeur argued that the parables specifically allow readers (and preachers) to engage a metaphoric process and bridge into new possibilities. This clearly happened with the Mayan women on retreat. They did not merely reduce the biblical text to their context, but engaged the text in such a way that it spoke to their context and opened new possibilities.

C. The Contributions of Cultural Hermeneutics to Preaching: Toward the Future

The story of these women points to what can happen when preachers lead their communities to real encounters with the biblical texts out of their own contexts.

The Chiapas experience indicates that preachers and communities can clearly make use of cultural hermeneutics and the insights of Ricoeur and other philosophers to engage biblical texts so that they come alive in community cultural contexts and yield new meaning and possibility.

The contributions of Ricoeur, Hirsch, Fish, Gadamer, and others in the area of hermeneutics can help preachers responsibly and faithfully engage the biblical interpretive process through their cultural lenses and those of the communities they serve. The result of such engagement is not only potential transformation of local communities, but also increased richness and texture in the biblical interpretations that come from a variety of cultural contexts. *See* GENDER, RACE, AND ETHNICITY; FEMINIST PERSPECTIVES.

Bibliography: David L. Bartlett. *Between the Bible and the Church: New Methods for Biblical Preaching.* (1999); Musa Dube, ed. *Other Ways of Reading: African Women and the Bible.* (2001); Hans-Georg Gadamer. *Philosophical Hermeneutics.* (1977); E. D. Hirsch Jr. *Validity of Interpretation.* (1967); Morny Joy. *Paul Ricoeur and Narrative: Context and Contestation.* (2001); Bruce J. Malina and Richard L. Rohrbaugh. *Social-Science Commentary on the Synoptic Gospels.* (1992); Daniel Patte, ed. *Global Bible Commentary.* (2004); Paul Ricoeur. *Essays on Biblical Interpretation.* (1980); Scott Saye. "The Wild and Crooked Tree: Barth, Fish and Interpretive Communities." *Modern Theology* 12 (October 1996).

DECONSTRUCTION
John S. McClure

Deconstruction is a form of text criticism designed to uncover binaries (male-female, white-black, speech-writing, one-many, totality-infinity, etc.) in which one term is privileged and depends upon the suppression or exclusion of the other term for its identity. Deconstructive critique proceeds by arguing that, in fact, primacy belongs to the excluded or hidden term. The fundamental deconstructive strategy, therefore, involves the reversal and rewriting of a textual hierarchy.

Background

The idea of deconstruction is attributed to the French philosopher Jacques Derrida (1930–2004). Although Derrida applied deconstruction primarily to Western metaphysical texts, deconstruction has been applied broadly to texts within many academic fields today, including biblical studies, sociology, political science, cultural criticism, psychology, and cinema. Sometimes criticized as parasitic, nihilistic, or relativistic in nature, deconstruction is essentially an ethical practice, insisted Derrida. Although some have attempted to elevate deconstruction to a worldview, Derrida saw it as a critique and as therapeutic in nature, not meant to replace constructive ontological reflection, but to keep ontological constructions open, honest, and changeable in the face of human suffering (1998, 21–24, 184–91).

Derrida's idea of deconstruction was made possible by the structural linguistics of Swiss linguist Ferdinand de Saussure (1857–1913). According to Saussure, the meaning of a word is not constituted by its realistic representation of an actual thing. Rather, the word gains its meaning because it is arbitrarily chosen to refer to something, and because it is different from other words designating other things (1998, 11ff.). For instance, the word *tree* gains its meaning by virtue of its participation in a set of binary relationships with words that are not *tree*, such as *shrub, bush,* or *flower*. The meaning of *tree* is dependent on its being different from other words. Language creates meaning, therefore, through a play of differences. Although most of these differences are benign in nature, involved in constantly shifting hierarchies of relationships, some differences, especially those that are written into texts that become cultural classics (the Bible, great literature, great philosophical texts), can produce closed systems of meaning and formal hierarchies that can support oppression, violence, and even war. Deconstruction is designed to pry these binary oppositions open, demonstrating that what seems like a fixed hierarchy of meaning within a text is, in fact, arbitrary, creative, and interpretive at best, and should not be set in stone.

Method

Deconstructive critics stress that deconstruction is not something they do. Rather, deconstruction is something that texts do to themselves. Even though a text may seem to operate naively, privileging one term over another in order to promote a set of meanings, inevitably, the text always allows hints that this privileging cannot be consistently maintained. In perhaps the most obvious example, in the story of creation in Gen 2, the text asserts that the first woman comes forth from Adam's side. Not only does the prior version of the creation story in Gen 1 directly contradict this story, but throughout the remainder of the biblical narrative, women consistently give birth to men (as one might expect). At the same time, Adam's name is a masculine form of the feminine term 'adhamah. The deconstructive critic will accentuate the fact that the story of woman's derivation from man is sandwiched between the contradictory witness of the larger biblical narrative and this etymology in which the term for *man* is female-dependent. The biblical text, then, actively deconstructs itself, or undermines the very premises upon which it tells us it stands. The deconstructionist critic will then highlight other ways in which the biblical narrative attempts (unsuccessfully) to suppress or exclude the term *woman* in order to promote a fixed hierarchy of meaning in which *man* is privileged.

Seen in this light, deconstruction seems to undermine the authority of the biblical text by highlighting its internal contradictions, making a definitive interpretation *undecidable*, to use one of Derrida's favorite terms (1988, 116). This, however, would be to misunderstand Derrida's idea of the *undecidability* of the meaning of texts. For Derrida, texts display a kind of authority that is disseminated, bound neither to an author behind the text, theological or confessional assumptions brought to the text by believers, nor the contextual decisions of readers within what literary critic Stanley Fish calls "interpretive communities"(2005). Instead, the authority of a text emerges only through a complex midrashic conversation between a multiplicity of interwoven voices within and beyond the text.

Homiletic Implications

What are the implications of deconstruction for homiletics and preaching?

1. Challenges Oppressive Forms of Authority

Deconstruction presents a significant challenge to the authority of preaching as it has been traditionally conceived. Most of the authorities for preaching have been undergoing deconstruction for nearly forty years. The Bible, theological tradition, experience, and reason have been deconstructed and shown in many ways to repress difference, novelty, relativity, and openness. Although deconstruction does not necessarily undermine these authorities (deconstruction must have something to deconstruct!), it does keep preachers ever mindful of the ways in which each of these authorities can engender closure, oppression, and suffering if hierarchies of meaning are left relatively settled.

2. Accentuates the Bible's Rhetorical Power

Deconstruction invites preachers to begin to see the Bible not only as a historical community's witness to God's unchanging revelation in history, but also as a rhetorical and persuasive form of cultural and social literature, exerting tremendous force within human discourse as a whole. Deconstruction should make preachers profoundly aware of the ways in which biblical texts shape and promote the ongoing binaries and hierarchies that exist within societies today, for better or for worse.

3. Encourages Openness

Preachers challenged by deconstruction will experience a new spirit of generosity concerning the pulpit ministry. They will be concerned to invite the usually excluded "other" into exegetical and homiletic practices. The preacher influenced by deconstruction will find ways to subvert fixed hierarchies between preacher and listener, systematic theology and local theology, insider and outsider, churched and unchurched, tradition and local practice, and so forth, in order to open preaching to new insights, experiences, and perspectives. Some preachers will find ways to invite a broader range of voices into the sermon brainstorming process, listening to interpretations of texts by those within their own faith communities and by strangers beyond. They will also read and interpret texts from other social and experiential locations, intentionally purchasing commentaries written by women, racial-ethnic minorities, and global partners. Models of preaching rooted in collaboration and conversation suggest ways to invite this kind of expansive "otherness" into preaching.

4. Accentuates the Role of Countertestimony

Deconstruction underscores the dynamic rhythm between testimony and countertestimony throughout the history of Israel and the church. Both Derrida and his constant conversation partner, Lithuanian-born Jewish philosopher Emmanuel Levinas (1906–95), asserted that testimony is the quintessential act of "faith" (Ricoeur 1995, 118). Whenever we address someone, whether from the pulpit or otherwise, the listener is being asked to "believe me" or "trust me." This testimony might be credible and faithful; it may, however, contain untruth or be either wittingly or unwittingly false. This, then, calls forth the need for a deconstructive form of countertestimony in order to reopen a question and encourage the pursuit of truth. Paul Ricoeur, Walter Brueggemann, Rebecca Chopp, and Anna Carter Florence have seized on this rhythm between testimony and countertestimony as fundamental to thinking about proclamation in a postmodern context.

5. Encourages Ethical Communication

Deconstruction reminds preachers of the inadequacies of their words. In fact, it reminds preachers of the inadequacies of all language. This reminder refers preachers inevitably to the ethical underpinnings of preaching, whereby preaching seeks, in whatever ways possible, to purify itself as a form of speech relative to other forms of public rhetoric. Deconstruction encourages preachers to come clean, and to speak in ways that might escape the totalizing and stratifying effects of words, so that their preaching can become an ethical form of communication.

6. Suggests the Rebirth of Homiletic Spiritualism

Pentecostalist theologian Cheryl Bridges Johns encourages a deconstruction of homiletics, suggesting the possibility of a rebirth of homiletic spiritualism (2003, 45–49). Johns suggests that the Pentecostalist tent of meeting could be a model for a deconstructed, radically decentered form of preaching in the postmodern context. Like Moses' face-to-face meeting with God in the tent at Horeb, preachers and hearers might find themselves deconstructed or anointed in the Spirit when preaching is done in a way that invites God's interruptive Spirit into the closest possible proximity to the event itself.

7. Reminds of Preaching's Subversive Nature

Deconstruction reminds preachers that preaching has always been a decentered, interruptive, world-subverting form of speech. Preachers have always dwelt in the desert spaces between metanarratives and worldviews—not entirely happy with settled hierarchies or relationships. They sense that God is beyond all settled patterns and binaries and always constitutes something of a deconstructive presence in our midst. *See* AUTHORITY OF THE PREACHER; COLLABORATION; SUSPICION; TESTIMONIAL.

Bibliography: Walter Brueggemann. *Theology of the Old Testament: Testimony, Dispute, Advocacy.* (1997); Rebecca Chopp. *The Power to Speak: Feminism, Language, God.* (2002); Jonathan Culler. *Deconstruction: Theory and Practice.* 3rd ed. (2002); Jacques Derrida. "Afterword: Toward an Ethic of Discussion." *Limited, Inc.* Edited by Gerald Graff. (1988) 111–60; Jacques Derrida. *Of Grammatology.* Translated by C. Spivak. (1998); Stanley Fish. *Is There a Text in This Class? The Authority of Interpretive Communities.* (2005); Anna Carter Florence. *Preaching as Testimony.* (2007); Cheryl Bridges Johns. "What Makes a Good Sermon: A Pentecostal Perspective." *Journal for Preachers* (Pentecost, 2003) 45–54; John S. McClure, *Other-wise Preaching: A Postmodern Ethic for Homiletics.* (2001); Stephen D. Moore. *Poststructuralism and the New Testament.* (1994); Paul Ricoeur. "Emmanuel Levinas: Thinker of Testimony." *Figuring the Sacred: Religion, Narrative, and Imagination.* Edited by Mark I. Wallace. Translated by David Pellauer. (1995) 115–35.

FEMINIST CRITICISM
Barbara K. Lundblad

Feminist criticism is an approach to the Bible that honors women's experience as an interpretive lens; in particular it focuses on elements that contribute to violence toward women and their alienation, oppression, and disempowerment.

Founding Voices

Before the word *feminist* was ever used, women were engaged in feminist criticism of Scripture and theology. Abolitionist Sojourner Truth and other African American preachers such as Jarina Lee and Julia Foote read the Bible through the lens of their own experience. These women preached with the strong conviction that God had called them in spite of violent opposition from men who quoted Scripture to deny their calling. In North America, one of the early efforts to apply later feminist principles to the interpretation of Scripture was Elizabeth Cady Stanton's *The Woman's Bible* published in 1895 and 1898.

Almost sixty years passed between Cady Stanton and women who claimed the term *feminist* for their reading of the Bible. At the core of feminist criticism are at least the following convictions: women's experience is an essential source of knowledge and guide for theology and biblical interpretation; women are created fully in the image of God (Gen 1:26-27); the Bible was shaped primarily by men and remains an androcentric text in which women's lives are under-represented and often demeaned; though written primarily by men, the Bible is also the history of women who responded to God.

Feminist criticism borrows from movements in the larger culture and from historical-critical tools of biblical interpretation. Mary Daly was one of the earliest contemporary voices to bring secular feminist theories into conversation with theology and biblical studies. In her groundbreaking book *Beyond God the Father* (1974), she boldly stated that if God is male, then male is God. Daly's charge was aimed at the long road of Christian tradition, a road that led back to the Bible in which the dominant texts name God solely in male language and call for the submission of women.

Various Emphases of Feminist Criticism

Some feminists have focused their energies on retrieval of neglected stories of women in Scripture: the heroic women of the OT, women who stayed with Jesus at his death and became the first resurrection preachers, and women named as leaders of the early church in Acts and in Paul's letters. Resources were developed to include every story about women in both Testaments, including unnamed women. Because most of these efforts do not challenge the biblical texts directly, the work of retrieval is often least threatening to church traditions. But retrieval is not an adequate feminist response to the biblical texts. Stories of women's leadership in Scripture are few compared with stories of male leadership. Furthermore, texts remain within the canon that deny women's experience and prove dangerous and demeaning to women's survival and well-being.

Honoring women's experience as a critical lens, feminist biblical scholars interpret biblical texts with a hermeneutics of suspicion, questioning what has been left out and analyzing the narrator's viewpoint in relationship to women. Texts that seek to silence or control women are understood as evidence that women were indeed speaking and acting as subjects, not complying with the rules. Feminist criticism claims that any textual mention of women represents a more extensive presence of women that history does not record. Biblical texts that deny life experience of women, diminish their created worth, or perpetuate violence against them are judged to be non-revelatory. For some feminists this means distilling a canon within the canon, acknowledging only libratory texts as "Word of God." Others insist that the whole Bible is women's history. Stories of victimization as well as stories of courage and survival need to be remembered, interpreted and, when necessary, challenged. Critical feminist evaluation uncovers and rejects elements within Scripture that perpetuate violence, alienation, and patriarchal subordination. At the same time, a feminist critical hermeneutic recovers those elements within biblical texts and traditions that articulate the liberating experiences and visions of the people of God, including women (Schüssler Fiorenza 1983).

Feminist criticism has been challenged by women of color whose experiences are not the same as white women. Delores Williams focuses on the stories of Hagar and Sarah as a tragic metaphor for the oppression of African American women by white women. Asian, Latina, and Native American women hear biblical texts through life experiences that cannot be subsumed within the term *feminist.* The lively conversation among women from diverse racial and cultural communities raises new questions and offers new insights about texts that have been read from the social location of white women. Texts about poor widows, sojourners, aliens, surrogate mothers, concubines, and prostitutes require analysis that is serious about issues of class and economics, as well as gender.

Implications of Feminist Criticism for Preaching

1. Value Women

With women's experience as a core value, preachers will listen attentively to the stories of women in the congregation and community. The life experience of women becomes a resource for interpreting all texts of Scripture, not only texts about women. "Do no harm" becomes an oath of the preacher, a commitment to value the lives and well-being of women in every sermon. Thus, it is never faithful to affirm biblical texts that disparage women, or to tell contemporary stories that stereotype or demean women. At times this will mean preaching against the biblical text or against traditional interpretations that force women to be silent and submissive. "Texts of terror" that are neutral or permissive about rape, incest, and physical abuse can no longer remain hidden, but must be brought into the light of day, calling forth condemnation where Scripture and church tradition have condoned such violence through silence or neglect (Trible 1984).

2. Question Biblical Texts in Relation to Women

Trusting women's experience, preachers will dare to raise questions about texts that have shaped Christian theologies over the centuries, including central teachings such as the necessity of sacrificial suffering, the dualism between body and spirit, and pride as chief among all sins. Abused women who have been told to stay with a violent husband in order "to bear the cross" need to hear sermons that reframe the meaning of Jesus' death on the cross. Women whose bodies and sexuality have been disparaged as negatively opposed to spirit need to hear that their bodies and their sexuality are indeed part of God's good creation. Women who have been taught to have low self-esteem need sermons that beckon them to speak up rather than scold them for pride they have never known.

3. Include More Texts with Women

Preachers will also enlarge the storehouse of texts to include more women. Whether being guided by the lectionary or choosing texts by some other pattern, preachers need to map out a plan ensuring that women are fully present rather than erased. When following the lectionary, this means moving beyond the cycle of readings to include women who have been left out, such as the persistent Shunnamite woman of 2 Kgs 4 or the courageous stand of Vashti in the book of Esther. Mary Magdalene's presence in all four resurrection stories needs to be remembered as evidence of her prominence in the early church.

4. Consider Sermon Guidelines

Preachers are guided by questions such as these:

- If the biblical text focuses only on male characters, what stories from literature, the newspapers, or congregational life will give women a voice?
- How and when can I intentionally make time to preach a sermon series on the forgotten women of the OT and NT?
- Are there any stories about women during the season of Lent? The anointing at Bethany (John 12) or at the house of Simon the leper (Mark 14) should be considered as the starting point in framing the whole passion story.
- How can I shift women from the margin to the center of interpretation in order to reverse the centuries-long marginalizing perspective of patriarchal tradition and interpretation?
- Even if the liturgy printed in the worship book offers only male language for God, how can my sermon include more expansive, explicitly female images and metaphors for God?

5. Incorporate New Forms

New forms of preaching are also called for, forms that are more collaborative and less hierarchical, even when only one person is speaking. Listening to women and trusting women's wisdom are critical for men and women alike in preparing sermons. The preacher needs to be intentional in seeking women's perspectives on texts and bringing these perspectives into sermons. Forms such as conversational preaching invite listeners to respond to the sermon itself or to participate in conversation that shapes the sermon (Rose 1997). The authenticity of the preacher is at least as important as the preacher's authority. Women listeners will be hard pressed to give authority to sermons that deny the authenticity of their experience as women.

Preaching that is shaped by feminist criticism is not for its own sake or for the sake of women alone. Such preaching is grounded in the theological affirmations that women and men are created in the image of God; that God's desire is justice for all people, especially those who have been and continue to be oppressed; that the body of Christ is more than a spiritual metaphor: there is flesh on that body, flesh of many colors, and Christ's body is incomplete without women and men of every race. *See* FEMINIST PERSPECTIVE; GENDER, RACE, AND ETHNICITY; SUSPICION; WOMANIST CRITICISM; WOMEN.

Bibliography: Mary Daly. *Beyond God the Father.* (1974); Elisabeth Schüssler Fiorenza. *In Memory of Her.* (1983); Lucy Atkinson Rose. *Sharing the Word: Preaching in the Round-Table Church.* (1997); Phyllis Trible. *Texts of Terror: Literary-Feminist Readings of Biblical Narratives.* (1984); Delores Williams. *Sisters in the Wilderness.* (1993).

FORMALIST CRITICISM
Alyce M. McKenzie

Formalist criticism is a way of reading a text with regard only to its current form, paying particular attention to how its parts make a whole and removal of any of its parts affects its meaning. When used in conjunction with historical and reader-oriented criticisms, formalist criticism can be instructive to preachers both in interpreting texts and in shaping sermons.

Distinguished literary scholar M. H. Abrams helpfully grouped theories of textual interpretation under four headings: "Audience" (reader-centered theories), "Artist" (author-centered theories), "Work" (text-centered theories), and "Universe" (world-centered theories). Audience-centered theories include impressionistic criticism, rhetorical criticism, and reader-response criticism. Artist-centered theories include expressive, psycho-biographical, and psychoanalytic schools of criticism. Work-centered theories of interpretation include formalism, New Criticism, structuralism, Russian formalism, postmodernism, post-structuralism, and deconstruction. Universe-centered schools of criticism include archetypal (Jungian) or mythic, historical, history of ideas, sociopolitical, new historical, feminist, race (minority studies), queer theory, and cultural studies (Gannon).

Formalist criticism is a work-centered approach to literature that developed and thrived from the 1940s to the 1960s, first in Europe and then in the United States, where it was referred to as New Criticism. Biblical scholar Terence J. Keegan defines New Criticism as "a methodology associated with the program announced in John Crowe Ransom's book *The New Criticism* (1941), aiming at scientific objectivity by avoiding both the impressionism of reader-oriented criticism and the intentionalism of literary-historical scholarship" (Keegan 1985, 169). Formalist criticism is interested in the text itself, in the formal, technical properties of the work of art. Wimsatt and Beardsley (1946, 466–88) argue that texts do not allow one to say anything about an author's intention, a practice they call intentional fallacy. Detailed analysis of the language of a literary text can reveal layers of meaning in that work that are independent of the effect of the work on the readers. Formalist criticism viewed attempts to understand the mind and times of the author as reductionistic and attempts to understand it by exploring the historical setting and impact of a work as irrelevant. Critics such as I. A. Richards and Robert Penn Warren are commonly associated with formalism.

For formalist criticism, what mattered was the work itself: its technical or formal properties of language, structure, and tone; the relationship between form and meaning in a work, focusing on how a work is arranged; matters such as diction, irony, paradox, metaphor, and symbol; and broader factors such as plot, characterization, and narrative technique. Since formalist critics read a literary text as an autonomous work of art, they generally do not examine anything outside the work, including historical influences.

Biblical scholars of the first half of the 20th cent. or so operated largely from the perspective of historical criticism; their major concern was to recover the original author's historical meaning. They discovered that, many times, that original meaning was beyond their grasp. Formalism and its American school, New Criticism, began to see this phenomenon not as a problem to be solved, but as an opportunity for interpretive creativity (Kaiser and Silva 1994, 239). Instead of asking, "Does the text mean this or that?" says G. W. Turner, critics began

to ask, "Can the text mean this or that?" (Turner 1973, 100–101). Formalist approaches became dominant in American literary criticism in the 1940s and 1950s, though the impact on biblical scholarship was slower in coming. While earlier biblical scholarship was criticized for focusing too intently on historical questions, the formalist, new critical perspective can accurately be described as ahistorical. It considered the Bible as literature, the biblical text as a literary object to the exclusion of historical context.

Recent Developments

In the 1970s literary-critical approaches began to influence works in biblical studies. Formalist and new critical approaches were first applied to the parables and then, in the early 1980s, to the Gospels. Some biblical scholars began to use the term *narrative criticism* for the types of literary approaches to the NT they were employing. Literary-critical works on the OT also began to be written, but the term *poetics* was often used instead of narrative criticism. The focus was the text itself, the play of its language, the styles, patterns, and narrative techniques evident in the text's final form (Gowler 2000, under "From New Criticism to Narrative Criticism"). By the end of the 1980s, other developments in literary theory began to influence biblical studies: the plurality of interpretations and the roles of readers in creating meaning in dialogue with texts. For the 21st cent. preacher approaching a text(s) for sermonic interpretation, close attention to the world of the text itself remains an important emphasis, along with analyses that highlight the historical context and the context of contemporary readers.

The Value of Formalist Criticism for Preachers

The benefit of the formalist perspective in biblical study is that it has taught us to pay attention to the texture of biblical literature. As preachers, we can appreciate that gift while still paying attention to the historical character of the text, since its roots in historical contexts are an essential characteristic of biblical religion. We are also interested in the theology of the text, which cannot be separated from its quality as a text arising from a historical context. Use of formalist analysis, with its attentiveness to the composition of the literary text, also helps us access the theological perspective and intent of the text. The theological perspective of the biblical authors is seldom expressed in explicit terms, but it is often reflected in their composition of the text (Kaiser and Silva 1994, 240).

As preachers, we need to employ historical criticism to explore the world behind the biblical text; we need to employ formalist criticism to explore the world of the text; and we need to employ contextual and reader-response criticism to explore the world in front of the text. An exegesis for preaching that focuses on one of these arenas (behind, in, and in front of the text) to the exclusion or neglect of the other two will produce one of three phenomena. It will produce a historical lecture on the ancient Near East, a literary treatise on the texture of a discrete text, or a catalogue of the needs of the congregation.

Practical Formalist Tools for the Preacher

Formalism's gift to preachers is its instruction in analysis of formal features of the text itself and how they contribute to its meaning. This approach can be helpful in analyzing an individual biblical passage as well as the larger book within which it appears. The preacher, approaching a text for sermonic interpretation, might ask some of the following questions.

What is the play of language, its uses and meanings, in the text? This question encompasses the following: imagery, figures of speech, and diction (word choice). It also touches on syntax (how the words are structured and grouped to form meaningful thought units) and word use, both conventional meanings (denotations) and additional suggested meanings (connotations).

As applied to various texts, here are some typical questions that formalist criticism would encourage a preacher to ask: Why would the life devoted to God be conveyed using the image of a tree planted by streams of water in Ps 1? Why does the book of Proverbs refer to foolish people as those who are "wise in their own eyes" (3:7; 26:12)? What is the meaning of the term Jesus uses only in Matthew to describe the disciples—"little faith ones" (Matt 6:30; 8:26; 14:31; 16:08, author's trans.)? Why does Ecclesiastes juxtapose conventional proverbs that promise rewards for a wise life with sayings that undercut that promise (Eccl 2:13-

14; 7:1-2)? What is the connotation of Jesus' reference to God as "Abba" (Mark 14:36), a strangely intimate address to God for a Jew of his day? Are there distinctive phrases or key words? What is signified by Proverbs' repeated equation of wisdom with life (3:21-22; 8:35; 10:2; 13:3, 14; 16:17; 19:16; 21:21; 22:4)?

With regard to the matter of form, formalist criticism would advise preachers to examine how the work is structured to express the meaning. Why does Matthew present Jesus' teachings in five major groupings? What pattern of development was used within the structure of the work? Does it build to a climax? With regard to many psalms, the structure follows a plot of descent into despair, recognition of God's presence, and ascent to praise. Does the text have separate parts? In many of Luke's parables, for example, the parts of the story are action by protagonist, crisis, inner dialogue that sums up the character's plight, and new resolve. Are there patterns within the text? The risen Christ in John's Gospel asks Peter three times, "Peter, do you love me?" (John 21:15-17). Romans 8:31-37 proceeds by a forward momentum created by a series of questions: "What then are we to say about these things?"; "If God is for us, who is against us?"; "Who will bring any charge against God's elect?"; "Who will separate us from the love of Christ?"

These formal features we have considered with regard to literary texts can help the preacher shape the sermon based on them, with regard both to what it says and how it says it. Asking literary questions often surfaces theological insights that shape the theme the preacher chooses for the sermon. Instructed by formalist criticism, the preacher can use imagery, figures of speech, diction, syntax, distinctive phrases, key words, structure, and repetition to shape the sermon to maximize its impact. *See* FORM CRITICISM; LITERARY CRITICISM.

Bibliography: Thomas C. Gannon. TCG's Literary Criticism and Critical Theory Page. http://www.usd.edu/~tgannon/crit.html; David B. Gowler. "Heteroglossic Trends in Biblical Studies: Polyphonic Dialogues or Clanging Cymbals?" *Review and Expositor* 97 (2000) 443–66. http://userwww.service.emory.edu/~dgowler/RE article.htm; Walter C. Kaiser Jr. and Moisés Silva. *An Introduction to Biblical Hermeneutics: The Search for Meaning.* (1994); Terence J. Keegan, O.P. *Interpreting the Bible: A Popular Introduction* *to Biblical Hermeneutics.* (1985); G. W. Turner. *Stylistics.* (1973); W. K. Wimsatt and M. Beardsley. "The Intentional Fallacy." *Sewanee Review* 54 (1946) 468–88.

HOMILETICAL (THEOLOGICAL) CRITICISM
Charles L. Bartow

Homiletical criticism is the theological practice of assessing preaching in relationship to theory or developing theory in relationship to it. It is of three types: pedagogical, professional, and scholarly. The pedagogical type is the theory-based critique of student preaching by seminary homiletics instructors, focusing, though not exclusively, on sermon delivery (Bartow 1995). The professional type is a preacher's week-by-week practical theological assessment of his or her own sermonic efforts (see Bartow 1997, ch. 5). The scholarly type of homiletical criticism is critical research undertaken in order to discover implications for preaching theory from a rigorous study of exemplary practice (see Childers 1992; Prakash 1991; Saldine 2004). Here we will concentrate on the theological underpinnings of homiletical criticism in general, its nature, purposes, and methods.

A. The Theo-logic of Homiletical Criticism
B. Biblical Authority and Homiletical Criticism
C. Imagination in Biblical Preaching
D. Incarnation and Synesthetic Speech in Preaching
E. Summary
F. Conclusion: Thought Made Flesh in Service to the Word Become Flesh

A. The Theo-logic of Homiletical Criticism

What makes these three types of criticism homiletical—and not strictly rhetorical or performative, that is, exclusively an act of sermonic speech criticism—is their theological groundedness. Rhetorical and performance norms clearly are consulted, but they are interpreted and implemented under the guidance of a theological understanding of the nature and purpose of preaching. Homiletical criticism thus has to do not simply with performance

(the artful use of verbal, vocal, and physical gesture) and rhetoric (the discovery and use in any given situation of the available means of persuasion). More significantly, it has to do with theo-rhetorical and theo-performatory assessment of proclamation—assessment, that is, of the preacher's act of bearing witness to that to which the Bible itself bears witness, namely, Jesus Christ, crucified, risen, regnant, the eternal Son of the Father, identified in the Nicene Creed as "God of God, light of light, very God of very God."

By the Holy Spirit, vouchsafed to the church in word, sacrament, and prayer, Christ Jesus himself may be believed to be speaking the words of Scripture that, through his speaking of them, make them, *pro nobis*, for us, the very word of God written. So also Christ Jesus himself may be known in the proclamation of the gospel as the true, acting Subject in preaching (Kay 1994, 113–17). A theologically normed public reading of the Holy Scriptures, therefore, would have those Scriptures heard and received in the present not as dead letter but as living, contemporaneously God-breathed literature.

So also a theologically normed proclamation of the gospel would have purely human words, spoken in attempted fidelity to the scriptural attestation to Christ, received in the church as God's own human speech. Bernard Manning put it this way: "the incarnate Word through the written word by the spoken word" (Maxwell 1993, 4). The theologic of Scripture reading and of preaching, and of critical study of those practices of the church, is God in Christ in the power of the Spirit disclosing the holy triune Divine Self to anyone who has ears to hear—or eyes to see, or a tongue to taste, or flesh to feel—"what the Spirit is saying to the churches" (Rev 2:7, 11, 17, 29; 3:6, 13, 22).

B. Biblical Authority and Homiletical Criticism

Just so then does the Holy Bible function authoritatively in the church. The Bible, that is, functions for faith as a means of grace. It is not some power latent in the texts themselves that leads the church to regard its canon, its rule of faith and practice, as unique and authoritative, as the Confession of 1967 states (*Confessions* 1996, 265). Instead, it is God's scripturally attested holy use of them that brings the church, in faith, to receive them as unique and authoritative, holy, set apart to the purposes of God.

The Bible is received according to the church's faith as the peerless inscripted witness to divine self-disclosure in the history of Israel, in the history of the church itself, in the midst of the created order's natural history, and in the stormy history of peoples and nations.

In worship, in the prayer for illumination, worshipers ask God to inspire their hearing of the Scriptures and of sermonic interpretation of the Scriptures. They do this in anticipation that their hearing may be inspired by God just as surely as, in faith, they understand God to have breathed divine guidance into the hearing, the seeing, and the speaking of prophets, sages, psalmists, evangelists, and apostles whose witness, even in the present, is received among believers as God's very own word written. For worshipers of the triune God, in their own time and place, must come to grips with more than the sense of texts, the sense of texts being their conceptual content (i.e., what is asserted in them). Worshipers also must come to grips with those texts' present significance: the questions God may raise in would-be faithful hearers of the Scriptures to trouble the answers they hold dear, until those worshipers confess as their only comfort in life and in death, their belonging—"body and soul, in life and in death"—not to themselves but to their "faithful Savior, Jesus Christ" as the Heidelberg Catechism expresses it (*Confessions* 1996, 29).

The Bible, then, is not the believers' way of getting hold of God. It is God's way of getting hold of them. The Bible is, as has been said, living literature pressed into the service of a living God. It is Holy Writ by means of which God makes them holy who, in receiving it and seeking to understand it, are received by God as God's own. Thus being received by God, they also are called by God to hear and obey God. Obedience, as understood here, is not a cowed will. It is a fired imagination.

C. Imagination in Biblical Preaching

According to Luke, for instance, John the Baptist said of Jesus: "He will baptize you with the Holy Spirit and fire" (Luke 3:16). Luke, in his second volume, Acts, says how the Holy Spirit descended upon the apostles with "a sound like the rush of a violent wind. . . . [And] divided tongues, as of fire, appeared among them, and a tongue rested on each of them" (Acts 2:2-3). As is indicated in the text itself, what is said in this passage is to be read and heard as a figure of speech; it is to be imagined and lived. But a figure is not a fiction. A figure is a linguistic event, a statement of fact or experience plus interpretation of the fact or experience. And the fact or experience—so faith regards it—is God's own instancing of a proclamation of the gospel. So is that proclamation apostolic, authoritative. And the authoritative, apostolic proclamation, as already has been noted, is Christ Jesus, crucified, risen, regnant. Obedience, therefore, is imaginative engagement with Scripture.

Christ is at the center of imaginative obedience. This apostolically attested Christ is preached in accordance with the Scriptures. In the case of the proclamation of the gospel in Acts 2—and throughout the NT—the Scriptures in accordance with which Christ is proclaimed are, of course, the OT. According to apostolic testimony, those Scriptures are fulfilled in Christ and by Christ as he is preached. In other words, in the apostolic preaching of him, Christ fills full with fresh significance the OT witness to the judging-saving action of God. He does this as he fills full of contemporary significance his own apostles' witness to him inscripted in the NT.

God's promises to Israel, then, are not superseded and rendered of no continuing import in the apostolic witness to the crucified, risen, regnant Christ. Instead they are confirmed in it and given fresh, contemporary significance as, by the apostolic witness to Christ Jesus, and through it, Gentile believers who, through Christ entrust themselves to the God of Israel, now are made to participate in the coming to fruition of Israel's hope. That hope itself, according to Holy Scripture, is grounded in Yahweh's promise to Abraham that through his offspring "shall all the nations of the earth gain blessing for themselves" (Gen 22:18).

D. Incarnation and Synesthetic Speech in Preaching

There is an interaction of the senses in preaching and hearing the Word. In Christ Jesus, so the Apostle John records it, the eternal Word, which from the beginning was with God and was God, became for us not mere words but flesh (John 1:14). The Word of God, that is to say, the everlasting Son through whom everything came into being and without whom "not one thing came into being" (John 1:3), himself engaged and, by his Spirit, engages still, in oral-aural, face-to-face, synesthetic human speech.

Here we see what the Word means to us. Here we taste the Word's goodness to us. Here we feel the Word's quickening of our own heart's dead beat. Synesthetic speech, oral-aural, face-to-face human speech, divinely lived, is speech that stirs all our senses, all at once, even as words come to us in sequence, one at a time. So, as has just been indicated, the Word, addressing itself to us as human speech, can touch us and move us deeply.

As a result, the Apostle Paul can speak of the Word of God on his lips and in the ears of his listeners as something other than a rhetoric displaying mere human wisdom. Paul can speak of it as "a demonstration of the Spirit and of power" (1 Cor 2:4). It does not seem appropriate then to speak of the Bible as containing God's Word, for God's Word of Spirit and of power cannot be contained, fully, exhaustively, finally stated in a sequence of words on a page. It is more appropriate to speak of the Bible as God's word, God's own human speech written, yet gathered into, contained as it were within, the human event of divine self-attestation found in Jesus Christ. To put it another way, Jesus Christ, by the Spirit and in regnant power, ever and always addresses the church, and through it all humankind, with the biblical word. The Bible thus is set to a holy use. It is appointed by God to be a means of grace. Further, in receiving the Holy Scriptures as divinely authorized human speech, the church, with Scripture, itself is gathered into the event of God's self-attestation in Jesus Christ. The church thereby is empowered to proclaim the Word of God afresh in every generation.

This incarnate, synesthetic speech act of divine self-disclosure is what Calvin and others referred to as God's accommodation to our human capacity. Through the written word becoming a spoken word, we are made to hear the Incarnate Word of God. And as stated in the Theological Declaration of Barmen, this Incarnate Word, namely, "Jesus Christ as he is attested for us in Holy Scripture, is the one Word of God which we have to hear and which we have to trust and obey in life and in death" (*Confessions* 1996, 257).

E. Summary

In light of the foregoing discussion we move now to a summation of the nature, purposes, and methods of homiletical criticism, what it looks for, and how it gives account of what it sees.

First, homiletical criticism endeavors to see how any given instance of preaching evidences responsiveness to Holy Scripture as the unique and authoritative witness to Jesus Christ in the church catholic and God's word to preachers and their congregants in particular locales of ecclesial faith and action.

Second, homiletical criticism will look at preaching in terms of its gospel content, its witness to the rectifying or "setting things right" action of God in Christ through the power of the Holy Spirit in the midst of the world as it is—in its sin and rebellion against God—and in the church as it is—all the more itself of the world as it attempts to be otherworldly, all the more itself against God as it presumes to have God on its side in its controversies with itself and in its controversies with worldly powers.

Third, homiletical criticism will look for preaching's affirmation of the presence and purpose of God in the here and now, which presence and purpose is not only to "comfort the afflicted and afflict the comfortable" but also to raise the dead, bring to newness of life in the divine presence those inclined to absent themselves from that presence. Homiletical criticism thus will evaluate sermonic discourse for its articulation of good news—not bad news—its articulation of the faith of Christ and not merely its call to persons to put their faith in Christ. It is, after all, the faith of Christ that elicits faith in Christ. At the most profound theological level, we therefore must say that preaching is "through faith for faith" (Rom 1:17).

Fourth, homiletical criticism will attempt to provide a critique of preaching in terms of its oral-aural, face-to-face, synesthetic eventfulness. Preaching may be artistic, but it is not, per se, art. It is not illusional, virtual life. It is actual life. It is life at the very height of actuality. It is here and now encounter with God. And it is encounter with God not despite, or without, human rhetorical effort and performatory discipline, but in them, with them, and through them.

F. Conclusion: Thought Made Flesh in Service to the Word Become Flesh

Speech communication concerns consequently cannot be dismissed as irrelevant. It does matter that homiletical speech is suasory and not utterly unpersuasive. It does matter that, as Tillich famously observed, persons are confronted with the offense of the gospel and not with the sheer offensive, obtrusive rhetorical and performatory incompetence of the preacher. A sermon, after all, is not a manuscript left to posterity to dissect. It is, rather, a moment of face-to-face discourse and lasting significance even as the preaching moment itself passes into history and, in passing, is forgotten in many, if not all, of its particulars.

Theory-based critique of student sermons in the seminary or divinity school thus will be theo-rhetorical and theo-performatory. A preacher's practical theological self-assessment likewise will be observant of more than the particular pleasing or not so pleasing (to the preacher) rhetorical turns of phrase or speech mannerisms. These observations, instead, will be taken account of in terms of the preacher's understanding of what preaching is and what the preacher is to be about. It is, in fact, the preacher's obligation to develop and preach from a sound theology, and from that theological perspective, to make rhetorical and performatory judgments. So also scholarly assessment of exemplary homiletical practice, undertaken with a view to the reformulation of preaching theory, will be theo-rhetorical and theo-performatory. Invention, arrangement, style, memory, and delivery—the classical canons of rhetoric—thus will be implemented in a critique of preaching that is informed by the canon of Scripture: that is, Jesus Christ as the Holy Bible bears witness to him and as he bears witness to the Bible as unique and authoritative in its witness to himself. From the written word become a spoken word, preachers and congregants alike are brought face-to-face with, and within earshot of, the Incarnate Word of God.

Let us close with a concrete illustration of this last thought. If the Word preaching attests is incarnate, should not the thought of the preacher itself take on flesh and blood and muscle? Clearly, it should. And it does in this sermonic moment from decades now long spent. George A. Buttrick, in one of his Harvard sermons, speaks incarnationally of God's name at Christmas, not giving illustrations to enliven an abstract thought, but expressing his thought itself illustratively, as a poet might craft not merely a line, but a life.

> God has many names. . . . [God's] name is "Mystery," for the heavens were not emptied when Jesus came; and if God were not Mystery, [no one could ever] have worshiped. His name is "Power": [God] lifts the cosmos and will not let the name of Jesus die. [God's] name is "Judgment," for our life is not a jaunty affair in which Jacob-deceit goes unnoticed after twenty years, in which God casually wipes [divine] lips of our wantonness, saying, "Oh, don't mention it"; life is a momentous once for all encounter. God's name is "Holiness": people who glibly wish they might meet Jesus forget that once his friends cried out in agony: "Depart from me, for I am a sinful man, O Lord" (Luke 5:8). [God's] name is "Enigma": we simply cannot construe the plan which includes earthquakes and maniacs, and should not pretend that we can. But the central name, if only because it starts our tears and joy and deepest resolve, is Jesus: "for he will save his people from their sins" (Matthew 1:21). (Buttrick 1959, 170)

See IMAGINATION/CREATIVITY; SYSTEMATIC, CONSTRUCTIVE THEOLOGY; WORD OF GOD.

Bibliography: Charles L. Bartow. *The Preaching Moment: A Guide to Sermon Delivery.* (1995); Charles L. Bartow. *God's Human Speech: A Practical Theology of Proclamation.* (1997); George Arthur Buttrick. "The Name of the Nameless." *Sermons Preached in a University Church.* (1959) 164–71; Jana Lynn Childers. "A Critical Analysis of the Homiletical Theory and Practice of Brown Barr: First Congregational Church, Berkeley, 1960–1977." Ph.D. diss. (1992); James F. Kay. *Christus Praesens: A Reconsideration of Rudolf Bultmann's Christology.* (1994); Jack M. Maxwell. "Why Preaching?" *NSPC Pulpit.* Newtown Square Presbyterian Church, Newtown Square, Pa. (1993); Perumala Surya Prakash. *The Preaching of Sadhu Sundar Singh: A Homiletic Analysis of Independent Preaching and Personal Christianity.* (1991); Presbyterian Church (U.S.A.). *The Book of Confessions.* (1996); Kristin Emery Saldine. "Preaching God Visible: Geo-Rhetoric and the Theological Appropriation of Landscape Imagery in the Sermons of Jonathan Edwards." Ph.D. diss. (2004).

NEW HISTORICISM
B. Keith Putt

New historicism (NH) is a critical strategy of interpretation that acknowledges the inseparability of texts and history. NH extends interpretation theory beyond a narrow attempt to discover the sense of literary documents to the broader implications of how documents manifest and manipulate social and political forces. It first rejects all purely formalistic theories of literary interpretation, such as New Criticism, because such theories consider texts to be ahistorical aesthetic objects whose meaning can be ascertained without any consideration for their historical and communal genesis. Instead, NH insists that texts simply do not spontaneously generate nor do they develop within environments devoid of prejudicial values, expectations, and presuppositions. In other words, texts can never be immune to the influences of the historical, social, and political contexts within which they were composed. At this point, NH relies heavily upon the sociologist Clifford Geertz's notion of "thick description," whereby one can begin to understand the meaning of social expressions only by situating them within their cultural and historical contexts.

Second, NH does not adhere to a naive positivistic theory of historiography. It refuses to believe that an interpreter can approach texts as transparent windows through which to comprehend clearly and confirm precisely the truth of their original historical milieus. Whatever history one encounters through texts is always a history that has been vetted according to criteria established by some socially dominant theory. Written texts do not merely reflect a culture's worldview or system of values but are constructed within complex networks of economic, political, and social intrigue and may actually be co-conspirators in those networks, quite often spinning their own webs of deception and domination. Here NH channels the critical spirit of the post-structuralist thinker Michel Foucault. Foucault investigates how structures of power compete within cultures to establish social homogeneity and to demonize any theory or group different from the status quo. NH is particularly sensitive to Foucault's explanation of how systems of power and prejudice explicitly and implicitly insinuate themselves into certain types of discourse in order to hide behind a false facade of rationality and logic.

Finally, NH insists that interpreters themselves never exist in an intellectual and existential vacuum. Readers are finite, limited human beings who are embedded within various histories, who speak particular languages, and whose ideas and intentions have been formed within the crucibles of distinct cultural contexts. As a result, NH denies that readers of texts can ever be successfully inoculated against the potential hermeneutical infections of traditional, dogmatic, and ideological pretexts. Interpreters are not objective, value-free investigators who analyze documents and seek only to discover their textual facts. On the contrary, texts, histories, and readers always bear the marks (wounds?) of cultural conflicts, of multiple heterogeneous traditions that clash over intellectual differences and that condemn every hermeneutical process to the all-too-human struggle over power and control. Furthermore, given their cultural embodiment, readers will inevitably connect their interpretations of texts to their contemporary sociopolitical contexts and risk contaminating their interpretations with, and conscripting the texts for, their self-serving strategies.

The significance of NH for homiletics obviously concerns how its critical perspectives on historical, literary, and cultural interpretations may benefit biblical hermeneutics. Sacred texts do not differ appreciably from secular texts with reference to processes of composition and traditions of reception; therefore, the historical, cultural, and ethical sensibilities of NH may be a hermeneutical gift to those who proclaim messages based on the Hebrew and Christian Scriptures. Undoubtedly, anyone whose chief interest lies not only in explaining and understanding the meaning of the Scriptures but also in communicating that meaning so as to affect individuals and societies should appreciate how NH enhances the practical application of biblical truths. One might say that NH contributes to the preacher's intent that people not only be hearers of Torah or of the gospel but doers also.

Ministers who seek through their sermons to translate biblical texts into contemporary situations and idioms can discover provocative insights in the work of scholars who approach Scripture with NH sensitivities. For example, Harold Washington's investigation into the gender bias of biblical language as it relates to war, specifically how it often analogizes military action with rape (compare Deut 20 and 21), can profoundly affect how one preaches on violence and military conflict (*Biblical Interpretation*). One might also consider Elizabeth Castelli's fascinating Foucaultian study of St. Paul's discourse on imitation. She meticulously details how Paul uses such language not only to evoke his readers to follow Christ but also to acknowledge his own ecclesiastical power and the need for them to act and believe according to his model. Such a work might remind the preacher to be vigilant against the temptation to use Scripture as self-serving evidence for pastoral superiority. Also, Yvonne Sherwood's rich study of the history of commentaries of Jonah manifests how each generation of preachers can reinterpret biblical texts to suit their ideological and political agendas. Her book may act as a prophetic warning against a homiletical blindness to one's personal desires and cultural loyalties.

Although NH can enhance the exegesis of individual passages in Scripture, perhaps its most redemptive contribution to biblical homiletics is to remind the preacher not to assume a false formalism when it comes to proclaiming God's written Word. The Bible did not drop out of heaven unscathed as an alien work but developed through muddled human processes of history and culture. It also does not come down to the preacher untouched by previous interpreters who shaped how it should be read. Finally, the preacher does not proclaim the Bible outside social and psychological situations that impact its contemporary comprehension and communication. A sensitivity to NH, therefore, may well induce homiletical humility and the recognition that biblical proclamation should consistently be done with fear and trembling. *See* HERMENEUTICS; HISTORICAL CRITICISM; LITERARY CRITICISM.

Bibliography: Elizabeth A. Castelli. *Imitating Paul: A Discourse of Power.* (1991); Gina Hens-Piazza. *The New Historicism.* (2002); Yvonne Sherwood. *A Biblical Text and Its Afterlives: The Survival of Jonah in Western Culture.* (2000); H. Aram Veeser. *The New Historicism.* (1989); Harold Washington. "Violence and the Construction of Gender in the Hebrew Bible," *Biblical Interpretation* 5 (1997).

POSTCOLONIAL CRITICISM
Luke A. Powery

Postcolonial criticism analyzes texts from the perspectives of colonial exploitation and domination, revealing the pervasiveness in global societies and the unfortunate impact on the colonized. It deconstructs Western imperial history, which undermines the voice and identity of colonized peoples. It attempts to construct a response to the oppressive legacy of colonial empires by liberating the silenced and marginalized through textual cultural interpretations and just sociopolitical actions in the world. There is much debate over the history, meaning, and scope of postcolonialism and its development as criticism.

Questioning Colonial History of Domination

Even as postcolonialism takes different shapes throughout history, its questioning of colonial power does not wane. Some view postcolonialism as beginning in the 1960s after the fall of formal European colonialism, following struggles for independence by colonized peoples. Others view it as creative literature and resistance discourse within former colonies of the Western empires. A critical work that paved the way for the introduction of postcolonialism into academic circles within the United States is Edward Said's *Orientalism* (1978). In it, Said connects the production of academic knowledge with colonialism; therefore, orientalism was the Western way of dominating, restructuring, and having authority over the Orient. He demonstrates that the West's key to power was knowledge, which it used to promote the idea that rulers knew better than the ruled and that the rulers' actions benefited the ruled, though this was not necessarily the case. The rise of postcolonialism in academe continued in the 1980s with the emphasis on theorizing and literary analysis. With the entrance into the academy, postcolonial studies emerged as a way of engaging the historical, textual, and cultural expressions of societies shaped by the reality of colonialism; thus, these studies address and interrogate the legacies of colonialism and imperialism.

Postcolonialism can be viewed to have two major foci: historical and discursive. The historical refers to colonized aesthetic production, and some assert that as a hyphenated word, *post-colonialism* refers to the historical period after colonialism. Sans hyphen, *postcolonialism* represents the discursive trajectory that is discourse resistant to colonialism, practiced through radical interrogation of dominant knowledge systems; its purpose is to recover the past from Western imperial propaganda and to critique neo-colonizing tendencies, even after so-called independence. The discursive focus provides a means of critically reflecting on situations where one group is dominated by another. In this form, postcolonialism is criticism, and as such it is always an oppositional, contextual, sociopolitical, life-enhancing task through its resistance to domination and abuse. Postcolonial criticism is concerned with human freedom and upholds the cause of the marginalized and oppressed other. Postcolonial thought arises and grows from the interaction between the colonizer and the colonized, indicating its hybrid nature. As a hybrid critical discourse, it employs particular and diverse ways of reading life and texts.

Practicing Critical (Re)Reading Strategies

Reflecting its hybrid character, postcolonial criticism is not monolithic because it incorporates various concerns and stances, differing between locations and disciplines in terms of application. It draws on post-structuralism, Marxism, cultural studies, linguistics, and literary studies to name a few of its conversation partners; yet some practices are key. Through a postcolonial lens, one analyzes the methods used by colonizers to create images of the colonized. Also, one studies how the colonized used these methods and moved beyond them to empower themselves by reclaiming their identity and self-worth. Furthermore, postcolonialism introduces power and politics into literary criticism, revealing how literature has been linked to European colonialism. A postcolonial critic rereads Western canonical texts in order to identify explicit or implicit traces of colonialism in them. The critic searches literature and other texts such as historical and official documents, and missionary reports, to determine how the colonized were represented and how they resisted or accepted colonial values. Furthermore, postcolonial literary analysis of colonial texts can be a way of writing back to the center by challenging colonial perspectives while producing a new form of representation. It foregrounds marginal elements of a text, giving voice to the silenced and subjugated, and subverts traditional perspectives.

In biblical interpretation, this hybrid reading method embraces a multidimensional approach through sensitivity to culture, race, class, age, and gender as opposed to a single axis myopic reading. While becoming aware of one's own colonization, a postcolonial reader cannot ignore the colonized in the text or promote interpretations that erase their existence. Biblical scholars, such as R. S. Sugirtharajah (2003), argue that the aim of postcolonial biblical criticism is to situate colonialism at the center of the Bible and its interpretation by focusing on issues of expansion, domination, and imperialism as central forces that obliterate any presence of hegemonic totalizing biblical interpretations. Through this awareness of the pervasiveness of colonialism, a postcolonial critic may expose the latent cultural biases of canonical texts and then construct decolonizing interpretations. With this understanding, postcolonial criticism is deconstructive and constructive in ways that are transformative and life-giving, especially for the colonized, not only in terms of textual interpretations but also in terms of social actions in the world.

Preaching Under the Postcolonial Influence

The deconstructive and constructive nature of postcolonial criticism can impact preaching in negative and positive ways. One may view the deconstructive inquiry of postcolonial criticism as detrimental to the act of preaching because it may question the preacher's authority. Preachers could be viewed as colonialists in that they have the power to speak while others sit, listen, and obey, without a voice. Postcolonial critics realize that someone in authority gives power to particular people to become preachers while others may not be given the same opportunities (e.g., women of color), portraying the preaching enterprise as an imperial and patriarchal educational tool, as evident in the past. Postcolonialism could be a force to destroy preaching, even criticizing the Bible as a colonial resource to perpetuate imperial domination and abuse. The authority of Scripture can be undercut to such an extent that the Bible is viewed as irrelevant for Christian living, thus, inappropriate to be used as a source of revelation for Christian preaching. This could lead to preaching ourselves rather than the gospel of God expressed in Jesus Christ. In some biblical interpretations, Jesus may even be criticized for operating like a superior colonial officer when he calls the Syrophoenician woman a "dog" (Mark 7), though he too is colonized, revealing the impact of colonial thinking on his mind. In addition, a postcolonial reading of Mark 5:1-20 is sensitive to the fact that a man is deemed different, which may be why he is called "unclean" by Mark, who was a Jew with power even if only by his act of writing the life history of another. One could also question why there are only men in this biblical narrative. On many levels, a postcolonial interpreter can highlight views that may seemingly hinder the preaching of the gospel due to a hermeneutics of suspicion that (re)reads texts in unconventional ways. This could be viewed as weaknesses of postcolonial criticism because there does not appear to be a hermeneutics of trust, which is necessary for preaching. However, there are strengths to postcolonial criticism that may help preaching.

In fact, the suspicious impulse of this kind of criticism can aid a preacher in becoming aware of the colonial influence in texts and in the world, causing preachers to aim for life-giving decolonizing interpretations and actions. Postcolonial influences can give preachers insight into the global sociopolitical realm and dissatisfaction with the status quo, which may lead to effective prophetic preaching. A realistic view of a complex world, via postcolonialism, will allow sermons to incorporate true pictures of trouble in the world and not just in an individual's life. A constructive interpretation of Mark 5:1-20 may deconstruct colonial tendencies in society by demonstrating how humans demonize difference and are afraid of the other, revealing a colonial legacy. Yet in the end, the colonized Jesus liberates the man who was colonized by the Roman Empire, indicated by his name, "Legion." The marginal demoniac becomes a preacher to the colonized, deconstructing ideas of who should speak for God. In this way, the colonized demoniac is liberated by Jesus to speak for all who are ostracized, giving the silenced license to talk back in resistance. This kind of postcolonial interpretation calls individuals and societies to new ways of life and proclaims the need for justice at all levels of society, condemning spirituality that is only concerned with personal piety and oblivious to the sociopolitical implications of religion. Furthermore, preachers can be opened to the other, possibly leading sermons to include diverse voices and experiences through stories and sermon illustrations, reflecting postcolonial hybridity. It should be clear that postcolonial criticism does not have to hinder the proclamation of the gospel but can be used to help incarnate the liberating gospel for the colonized and the colonizer in word and deed. *See* DECONSTRUCTION; LITERARY CRITICISM; NEW HISTORICISM.

Bibliography: Homi K. Bhabha. *The Location of Culture.* (1994); Laura Donaldson. *Decolonizing Feminisms: Race, Gender, and Empire Building.* (1992); Edward Said. *Orientalism.* (1978); R. S. Sugirtharajah. *Postcolonial Criticism and Biblical Interpretation.* (2002); R. S. Sugirtharajah. *Postcolonial Reconfigurations: An Alternative Way of Reading the Bible and Doing Theology.* (2003).

READER/LISTENER RESPONSE
Sarah Jane Smith

Reader-response criticism is an approach to texts using the response that texts generate as a valid point of departure for interpretation. Also known as *reception aesthetics* or *reception theory*, it studies the relationship between the reader and the text. It addresses the reader, the process of reading, and the response generated by reading. Reader-response's emphasis on the reader's role marked a new approach to literary analysis. Romanticism of the 19th cent. emphasized the primacy of the author, whereas the New Criticism of the early to mid-20th cent. focused on the unity of the text. With the introduction of reader-response criticism in the 1960s, attention was now directed toward the reader.

The exploration of the role of the reader was long overdue. If no reader exists to interpret the author's words, no text exists: "A work of literature . . . has no objective existence: it only exists when it has entered the mind of a particular reader" (Bonnycastle 1996, 174). The danger of reader-response criticism is that a text can be made to say anything; the strength is that readers participate in the creative act.

Reader-response theory has been applied homiletically to the process of listening. Though the medium changes from printed to spoken word, the central idea remains: the sermon comes into existence when it is preached and interpreted through the hearing of its message.

Listener-response theory suggests that while preachers can lead listeners in certain directions, they cannot totally control the listening process (i.e., how listeners interpret what is heard, make meaning, etc.). Because listeners shape the hearing of the sermon in significant ways, they are, in effect, the sermon's co-creators.

Key Principles and Homiletical Tools

Five key characteristics of listener-response theory can be derived from the work of reader-response proponents Stanley Fish (1980; interpretive communities), Norman Holland (1968; identity themes), Wolfgang Iser (1978; literary framework influences the making of meaning and reading produces new understandings and reinterpretation), and David Bleich (1975; reading facilitates transformation). These theories generate the key principles of listener-response theory, which can be paired with corresponding homiletical tools to enable the preacher to construct a sermon that addresses the role of the listener in the homiletical process:

1. The interpretive community of the church shapes the hearing of and response to the preached word (Fish 1980). Listeners' interpretive communities are diverse. They are the political, theological, and social camps with which they align themselves, guiding their philosophies about business, people, worldviews, and money. Interpretive communities are ethnic in nature. Listeners belong simultaneously to a wide variety of interpretive communities. The sermon locates listeners within their various interpretive communities, which, in turn, enables identification with the sermon. **Identification** as a homiletical tool involves using points of view from various interpretive communities to foster identification and facilitate change.

2. Homiletical interpretation is a function of one's personal identity (Holland 1968). Listeners bring to the task of listening their identity themes. Sociological, economic, gender, race, educational, religious, and historical backgrounds impact identity. They influence how we make meaning out of what we have heard. Identity is not permanently fixed or predetermined. As we move through life, we add experiences and knowledge to our identity banks. When listeners are exposed to new concepts, they filter what is heard through a system of familiar defenses or adaptive strategies, and based on this, they make decisions about what has been presented. In essence, listeners establish a **connection.**

Connection encourages selecting sermon material that is polyvalent and thus provides various points of connection with individual listeners. Polyvalent material allows the story or illustration to produce a multiplicity of meanings as it meets listeners in their unique places. It comes in many forms: images that ring true to life experiences; descriptive language that brings back familiar smells and sounds (such as the blast of the school bus horn

or the antiseptic smell of the doctor's office); a story told so well that listeners feel they have seen it. Polyvalent material speaks to each person in unique ways, yet it speaks to many people at the same time. Listeners can apply what they hear to their specific contexts as they bring information from their identity banks to bear on what is presented.

3. Listeners interact within the framework of sermon structure and content to make meaning (Iser 1978). Preachers can identify listeners' reactions to the text/topic of the sermon through the use of the implied listener, a homiletical construct anticipating the presence of listeners but not necessarily defining specifically who they are. The implied listener serves as a diagnostic tool that helps preachers address better the situation of listeners.

The corresponding homiletical tool is **anticipation**. This principle suggests that preachers anticipate the implied listeners' potential reactions to the ideas and images of the text/topic and create a sermon structure that responds to them. The sermon can be constructed to enable listeners to move past their stereotypes and preconceived notions and to create space for hearing what the message has to offer. The implied listener helps the preacher anticipate a wide range of listener perspectives and potential responses and thus generate a sermon structure that artfully addresses these concerns.

4. Homiletical listening makes possible new understandings (Iser 1978). A homiletical tool that helps listeners arrive at new understandings is **reinterpretation**. It pairs familiar feelings/ thoughts with theological insights that offer a new approach or a surprising twist, thereby creating the potential for modification in listeners' attitudes. Listener-response theory engenders listener recognition in three ways, which, ultimately, enables reinterpretation: wandering viewpoints, blanks, and negations.

a. Wandering viewpoints. With wandering viewpoints, listeners' past memories are recalled within their specific contexts and then paired with newly presented ideas. This interaction between new and old produces the potential for reassessment or reinterpretation. The preacher uses wandering viewpoints to engage past memories about our personal situations and to point listeners toward new theological insights about God and a life of faith.

b. Blanks. Blanks are places in which just enough is said about a subject for listeners to fill in the empty space and to come to their own conclusions as they interact with the sermon's content and structure. Blanks are found throughout the sermon and appear in various forms: they may be well-placed questions; statements empowering self-discoveries; options for handling a situation that one has encountered; and wording that allows listeners to draw personal connections with the biblical text. Structurally, blanks are important because they leave open places within the sermon and give the listener an opportunity to connect with the message, making it personal.

c. Negations. Negations are homiletical constructs whereby the preacher brings into focus the familiar only to cancel it, but what has been canceled remains in view and causes the listener to contemplate a new way of living. Negations work by first striking a familiar chord with the listener before introducing the new. With artful words, the preacher selects a story or uses descriptive language that builds in listener recognition. Soon listeners are nodding in mental agreement, *Yes, I know that feeling.* The familiar is clearly in focus, and listeners are not just hearing it, but experiencing it and siding with what is presented. Then, with what is generally a quick twist, the tables turn.

Theologically, wandering viewpoints, blanks, and negations empower listeners to reconsider inadequate or destructive beliefs about God and life and to look at the situation with new eyes of faith. In this way, they fulfill a theological role of pointing listeners toward God or drawing them into a deeper faith relationship. This new perspective paves the way for transformation.

5. Homiletical listening facilitates transformation. Christian tradition reminds us that we are invited to experience ongoing transformation as we strive to become more Christ-like in our lives, thoughts, and actions.

And so the fifth homiletical tool is **transformation** (Bleich 1975). It helps preachers to provide listeners with examples of a transformed life to which they may respond in transformed ways. Listener-response theory suggests that space be created for listeners to interact with and respond to the message throughout the sermon. Some form of an invitation invites listeners to make decisions about transformed living. An invitation does not require exclusively a public call to accept Christ at its close; it does suggest, however, that the sermon be crafted so that listeners examine their lives in relation to biblical precepts and then respond

in their hearts and minds by making appropriate discipleship decisions.

The use of these listener-response theory tools—identification, connection, anticipation, reinterpretation, and transformation—aids preachers in developing sermons that homiletically engage listeners in practical and theological ways. The benefit of these tools is that they ride alongside any sermon construction method the preacher employs. With their use, listeners are invited to be co-creators in the homiletical process. Listener-response theory recognizes and invites the unique contribution each listener has to make to the event of hearing the preached Word. *See* FORMALIST CRITICISM; LITERARY CRITICISM.

Bibliography: David Bleich. *Readings and Feelings: An Introduction to Subjective Criticism.* (1975); Stephen Bonnycastle. *In Search of Authority.* (1996); Stanley E. Fish. *Is There a Text in This Class?: The Authority of Interpretive Communities.* (1980); Norman H. Holland. *The Dynamics of Literary Response.* (1968); Wolfgang Iser. *The Act of Reading.* (1978); Sarah J. Smith. *Hearing Sermons: Reader-Response Theory as a Basis for a Listener-Response Homiletic.* Ph.D. diss. (2002); Jane Tompkins, ed. *Reader-Response Criticism: Formalism to Post-Structuralism.* (1980).

RHETORICAL CRITICISM
Mike Graves

As one of many critical lenses through which to study Scripture texts, rhetorical criticism analyzes how structure and content artfully work together in communicating meaning. Use of this method has implications not only for the interpretation of ancient texts but also for proclamation today.

Although scholars typically cite James Muilenberg's 1968 address to the Society of Biblical Literature ("After Form Criticism What?") as the beginnings of rhetorical criticism, the method had been the focus of Amos Wilder's classic work, *Early Christian Rhetoric,* published in 1964. Concerned with the quality of preaching in his own day, Wilder noted that the *form* and *content* of the NT writings could not be viewed separately, that they worked together in not only the writings of the early Christians (*see* LITERARY CRITICISM) but their speaking as well. Wilder believed the implications of the rhetoric used by early Christians have a profound effect on preachers today.

And although Wilder may have overestimated the novelty of the NT's forms as well as their extemporaneous nature, he was a pioneer in pointing to the artistry and power of such forms. He noted four types of literature—gospel, acts, letter, and apocalypse—all of which were comprised of smaller rhetorical patterns or genres such as poetry, parable, doxology, prayer, and so forth. Each of these patterns, he noted, employs a range of rhetorical techniques.

Muilenberg's address picks up similar themes, noting the artistry and rhetorical intentions of the biblical authors. This appreciation of rhetoric's role in shaping texts stood in contrast to the often authorless and ahistorical approach of form criticism. But neither Wilder's approach nor Muilenberg's approach, helpful as each was in moving scholarship from form criticism to rhetorical criticism, was the final word. Rhetorical criticism did not emerge in its present form until the early 1970s when scholars began to see rhetoric as something less concerned with ornamentation—as Quintilian had stressed—and more concerned with argumentation or proofs—as Aristotle had emphasized.

The history of biblical studies in relation to rhetorical criticism can be seen largely as a division over different emphases. For instance, while some scholars claim that the Apostle Paul's disregard for rhetoric is evident most particularly in his letter to the Corinthians in which he claims not to have come proclaiming "in lofty words or wisdom" (1 Cor 2:1-5), others regard this passage as pure irony, noting the lofty language that Paul uses in this very passage. Thus, the debate about the relative importance of rhetoric continues among interpreters.

The debate also continues among homileticians, ever since St. Augustine's endorsement of rhetoric in what is widely regarded as the first homiletics textbook, *On Christian Teaching* (Book 4). Among contemporary teachers of preaching who have claimed rhetoric for preachers is Fred Craddock, who asked a seminal question in his 1971 volume, *As One Without Authority.* Examining the Bible's rhetoric, he asked, if on most pages of Scripture one finds a whole range of literary forms and rhetorical strategies employed, why do so many of our sermons sound the same (37–38)?

Over the decades that followed, homileticians explored the question. Most notably, Thomas Long published *Preaching and the Literary Forms of the Bible* in 1989, showing how the rhetorical strategies of the biblical authors could suggest ways for preachers to craft their own sermons. He listed five questions to be asked of texts: (1) What is the genre of the text?; (2) What is the rhetorical function of this genre?; (3) What literary devices does this genre employ to achieve its rhetorical effect?; (4) How in particular does the text embody those rhetorical characteristics?; and (5) How may the sermon say and do what the text was saying and doing in its original setting? (24). In other words, Long sought to explore what it might mean for preachers to pay attention to the myriad ways that biblical texts function rhetorically and to how preachers might learn from those techniques.

Several examples are worth mentioning, one of which comes from Long's work. For instance, biblical scholars have long noted the call and response pattern of the Gen 1 creation story. During the six days of creation, God is portrayed more than a dozen times as saying, "Let there be. . . ." Everything from light to humankind takes shape with the divine words, "Let there be. . . ." What is particularly fascinating from a rhetorical criticism standpoint, however, is the permissive nature of the language as opposed to declarative. Rather than command light, God says, "Let there be light." Rhetorical scholars point out how the language seeks for the created order to participate with God in creation.

On one level, the interpretation is obvious enough: we are invited to participate with God in the ongoing work of creation—in issues of soteriology, ecology, justice, and the like. But are there other homiletical implications? What difference does it make, for example, that the text employs call and response? To ask this is to delve into another layer of rhetorical analysis. Such exploration might result in the preacher's building a sermon's rhetorical strategy upon that found in the text (i.e., employing repetition and inviting congregational response in a variety of ways).

Long considers an example from the Psalms, a most underused resource in Christian preaching, perhaps due in part to a misunderstanding of the form and rhetorical strategy of the Psalms. Psalm 1 is wisdom poetry, contrasting the ways of the righteous and the wicked. The psalmist, however, does more than say what those differences are; the psalmist highlights them by poetic means. The wicked, for instance, are described as frenetic, moving here and there in unstable ways, like wind-blown chaff. The righteous, however, are described as settled and sure; the only verb used to describe them is *meditating*. In working with this text most preachers would note the psalm's content, the contrasting life-styles of the righteous and the wicked. But aided with insights from rhetorical criticism, the sermon could also seek to re-create the contrast in terms of pacing and the imagery used.

In the NT we find rhetorical strategies at work as well, in the evangelists' telling of the Christ story and the letters of Paul, which together constitute the bulk of the Christian literature. For example, Luke tells about Jesus' parable commonly known as the Prodigal Son (Luke 15:11-32), but what are often overlooked are the context of that telling and the rhetorical strategy employed by the evangelist. The entire chapter forms a fascinating example of rhetorical criticism at work. The well-known parable follows two other parables, the Lost Sheep (vv. 3-7) and the Lost Coin (vv. 8-10), all of which come on the heels of Jesus' encounter with the scribes and Pharisees (vv. 1-2). Having been asked why he eats with sinners, Jesus tells three stories, each inviting a positive response on the part of the Pharisees (and Luke's hearers/readers): when a lost sheep is found, celebration is in order; when a lost coin is discovered, celebration is in order; but what about when a lost son is found? What then? The third parable challenges this notion, introducing the older brother who must wrestle with celebration when applied to wayward people. This pattern not only belongs in the sermon's content; it suggests a strategy whereby today's preacher might weave a narrative sermon, initially inviting agreement and then challenging notions of religious propriety.

Or consider the rhetorical strategy behind one of Paul's many letters, which were aural in nature, intended to be read aloud in the Christian community. In Phil 2 he urges the congregation to get along with one another (vv. 1-4), a common theme in Pauline writings. But in addition to his customary use of parenesis and imperatives, Paul includes a hymn about Christ (vv. 5-11). Rhetorical critics have surmised that the use of the hymn may have invited the Christians to recall times of worship when they were gathered together, singing praises to God. The hymn, then, would be a rhetorical reminder drawn from their common experience, in addition to Paul's imperatives. This would likewise suggest a strategy for today's preachers, calling on the church to get along but also reminding them of their common worship experiences in the past.

Rhetorical criticism continues to explore the Bible's diverse forms and rhetorical techniques, even as homiletics continues to explore a diversity of sermon forms and techniques. *See* HISTORICAL CRITICISM; LITERARY CRITICISM.

Bibliography: Augustine. *On Christian Teaching.* Translated by R. P. H. Green. (1997); Fred B. Craddock. *As One Without Authority.* (1971; rev. ed. 2001); Mike Graves. *The Sermon as Symphony: Preaching the Literary Forms of the New Testament.* (1997); George A. Kennedy. *New Testament Interpretation through Rhetorical Criticism.* (1984); Thomas G. Long. *Preaching and the Literary Forms of the Bible.* (1989); James Muilenberg. "Form Criticism and Beyond." *Journal of Biblical Liberature* 88 (March 1969); Amos N. Wilder. *Early Christian Rhetoric.* (1964).

SOCIAL SCIENTIFIC CRITICISM
Bruce J. Malina

Social scientific criticism is a type of historical reading of the Bible carried out with an awareness that the Bible is a collection of books from the past (history) as well as from alien cultures (social system). This form of biblical study is motivated by the desire to avoid anachronism and ethnocentrism, that is, to avoid imagining the people portrayed in the Bible as though they lived in the 21st cent. with the understandings, concerns, and problems shared today. For example, historically, Jesus was a Jewish holy man and prophet who proclaimed the kingdom of heaven to his fellow 1st-cent. Jews. Within his social system, Jesus proclaimed the forthcoming advent of a new theocracy, a political religious order for 1st-cent. Judea. Social scientific criticism looks into the significance of theocracy in antiquity: What sort of social structure was political religion; what were the statuses and roles available to political religious personnel; why could Jesus not speak of religion at all without at the same time speaking of politics; and why was Jesus crucified with the accusation that he was a political religious ruler of the Judeans?

Along with historical awareness, the basis for social scientific criticism is the insight that meaning in language and behavior comes from the social system of speakers and writers. Language consists of three levels: markings or soundings, wordings (patterns), and meanings that come from the social system in question. Reading involves letting the patterned sounds or markings evoke images that are shared by those communicating. Learning a foreign language for the most part entails learning the patterns of the sounds and markings of that language. But without an understanding of the social system of native speakers, language learners can insert meanings only from their own society, not from the writers of foreign documents, whether it be the Bible or any other non-Western writing. Social scientific criticism attempts to take ancient social systems seriously in order to understand biblical writers.

According to historically oriented anthropologists, culture areas are rather stable around the world. Scholars learn ancient social systems in the same way scholars have pieced together ancient languages, that is, they begin with modern descendants in a specific culture area. They then go back through the ages and stages of development that led to the various forms found in history until they get to the period they search for. Biblical writings come from the eastern Mediterranean culture area. A study of the social system of native peoples of those regions (this excludes Khazar Jews in "Israel") traced through the various, significant historical stages up to the period one searches for yields a useful approximation of what ancient social systems were like. For example, it is common historical knowledge that separation of government and religion into two freestanding social institutions happened in Europe in the 18th cent. CE (the so-called separation of church and state). Nowadays political science and religion are two distinct subjects. However, before the 18th cent., they were not distinct. The same is true of government and economics. The present arrangement of the separation of bank/market and state likewise occurred in the 18th cent. CE. Before that there was only political economy. In the same way, there was domestic religion and there was domestic economy with no distinct institutional arrangements. In other words, in the biblical periods, there were two main or focal social institutions: kinship (family) and politics (government). To talk about religion, one necessarily talked of family and government; the roles, statuses, and values of family and government were used to express religion. God was king, father, of a people consisting of brothers and sisters or children.

Along with different institutional arrangements, social systems have various clusters of values. Value in this context means a general quality and direction of behavior. Values always inhere in value objects. For example, the value *goodness* always inheres in some good persons, good foods, good housing, and the like. Goodness is a value, a general quality. In the world of the Bible, the focal value was *honor*, some quality and direction of behavior that is judged to be of social worth. Honor is ascribed or acquired when people judge another person's standing or behavior as of social worth. God is honorable, that is, judged by those who worship God as of eminent social worth—"our God, God of power and might." Values inhere in value objects, which include selves, others, nature, time, space, and God (or gods). Next to honor, the main value inhering in persons is their gender: selves are always males or females (no middle ground) and are honorable if they express their gender according to social norms. Males represent the family and group to the outside of the group; females represent the family and group on the inside. The lineage tracing through the father has entitlements—this is patriarchy.

The value object called *others* deals with the worth attached to ingroup over against outgroup. Ingroup included one's immediate household, wider kin group, neighborhood or village (city) section, village, region or tribe, and people. The boundary around the ingroup shifts according to one's interacting partner. A Bedouin proverb says: "I against my brother; I and my brother against our cousin; I and my brother and my cousin against our village," and so forth, in ever expanding circles. The outgroup is always secondary, and often without entitlements at all when some limited good was at issue.

Nature refers to every entity in one's social environment aside from people. Non-human person-like beings included the denizens of the sky (stars, spirits, demons, angels; storms, winds, rainfall), animate beings, trees and plants and special stones (meteorites), and everything else. Many of these entities behaved just like humans. The people who populated the Bible believed humans were subject to nature, unlike God. Hence they had behavior forms that attempted to protect them from the impact of nature. Along with demon-caused drought and windstorms, there were various illnesses and social calamities.

Time as value object was concerned with assessing change: seasonal change that was circular and repetitive, and biological change that was linear from birth to old age. People in the Bible were concerned mostly with the present and the past insofar as it had shaped the present. They planned for the forthcoming: the birth of a baby, a new crop after planting. They had little or no concern for any abstract future. Biblical people had no eschatology, although they did believe the social environment was running down: crops were fewer, children were smaller, and the like. Hence they believed in a sort of devolution and a *worse-ology*. Israelites expected the God of Israel to intervene and stop the trend with a renewed world and a revived people.

Space, both sky space and earth space, was marked off as territory belonging to someone. A sky segment and the land below were in the control of non-human celestial entities such as constellated stars. People born in some divinely owned territory believed that their ancestors, they, and their households were part of that land, although more powerful elites sought to steal their birthright, either by extorted purchase or by simple theft. The purpose of the elite annual activity called war was to divert peoples and their lands to elite purposes and enrichment.

Along with value objects, social systems likewise consist of person types. After gender and kin group, the sense of who one was derived from a socially rooted psychological perspective that covered a range from individualistic self to collectivistic self. Individualistic cultures expect children to learn how to stand on their own two feet, to think of themselves and their own well-being first, to distance themselves from family in the pursuit of success. Collectivistic cultures expect children to live for the well-being of their ingroup, to support and maintain the group and its members at all costs, with success being defined as group rather than individual well-being. Most cultures in the world today are collectivistic (80 percent), and so were the people whom we confront in the Bible.

The purpose of social scientific criticism is to develop scenarios or frames of reference built of the aforementioned institutional, cultural, and person-type dimensions to enable Bible readers to bring such scenarios to their Bible reading. Biblical texts come alive not in writing, but only in the minds and imaginations of Bible readers. Outfitted with a set of useful social scenarios, the modern Bible reader or preacher—an alien in time and culture to the world of the Bible—can read what the biblical authors meant in a fair and insightful way. If contextualization of the biblical message entails reading the Word of God with its original meanings and proclaiming that Word in a way that can resonate with contemporary Christians, then an appreciation of the social system that filled the biblical documents and the people they portray with meaning and feeling is a fundamental tool (see Pilch 1995–2004). *See* ARCHAEOLOGY; GEOGRAPHY; HISTORICAL CRITICISM; NEW HISTORICISM; POSTCOLONIAL CRITICISM.

Bibliography: Bruce J. Malina. *The New Testament World: Insights from Cultural Anthropology.* 3rd ed. (2001); Jerome H. Neyrey. *Render to God: New Testament Understandings of the Divine.* (2004); John J. Pilch. *Cultural World of Jesus [. . . of the Apostles; . . . of the Prophets].* (1995–2004); John J. Pilch and Bruce J. Malina, eds. *Handbook of Biblical Social Values.* (1998); Richard L. Rohrbaugh. *The Social Sciences and New Testament Interpretation.* (1996).

STRUCTURALISM
Jeffrey F. Bullock

Structuralism is a school of language theory that posits that underlying structures (i.e., *parole* and *langue*) create meaning and cause communication. Its founder, Ferdinand de Saussure, argued that language is a closed system of signs that is determined by society; it has no necessary connection to the world of things, and no necessary connection to truth. Signs mean what they mean not because they are connected to objective reality but because they are different from other signs in the same system (1916). Structural theorists argue that language, at its most elementary level, operates as a system; meaning is discerned by studying the hidden structure. The kind of analysis practiced by structuralists generally includes who says what to whom, when it is said, why it is said, through what sign or symbol, and to what effect. Structuralism is not concerned with the author since all that one has is the text; it looks for patterns (e.g., abc, abc) or structures (e.g., polarities) beneath the surface of language to help explain or critique texts.

Though structuralism is a much more complex and highly nuanced approach to language theory than described here, at its core it rejects the family of theory known as representationalism or the symbol model of communication. Practitioners of representationalism or the symbol model of communication theory posit a view of language where "this means that" or symbol = thing, where language represents one world to another world. Language is a tool, and human beings use that tool to signify or represent one world to another.

Structuralism and Exegesis

In the Christian tradition, the words and meaning of the Bible are represented to the modern world through the process of exegesis, a disciplined interpretive technique by which the interpreter breaks down the grammar, syntax, and structure of a passage and represents that meaning, that interpretation, to a contemporary audience of receivers. In the modern era, the German theologian Friedrich Schleiermacher is sometimes credited with being the father of exegetical method. Schleiermacher argued that understanding requires that the interpreter must have some kind of internal connection with that which is being understood. Through proper exegetical method, interpreters ostensibly get back to what the author originally intended and thereby enable the text to be understood by a new generation of believers. Such an interpretation can happen only if the grammar, syntax, and structure of a passage are known in its original meaning and as the original author intended it to be understood. Structuralist criticism by contrast is interested in the text only as a system of signs, not as a vehicle of truth. While this flies in the face of much Christian understanding, preachers can still benefit from some structuralist understandings. A rejection of diachronic (through history) understandings of texts opened up ways of reading them synchronically (at the same time), that is, texts did not depend for meaning on returning to the historical author. Biblical studies began to see the value of synchronic approaches to texts in a wide array of literary criticism.

A brief sample of a structuralist rendering of the parable of the Prodigal and His Brother (Luke 15:11-32) might look like this: bad son leaves, hits bottom, returns good; good son stays, works hard, turns bad. Laying out the basic polarity (bad son/good son) reveals a pattern in the action that generates meaning for the preacher to explore.

A More Adequate Theory of Language

Structuralism arose because a number of theorists began to ask the question, Do we, as human beings, really communicate using representational signs and symbols, or is it more complicated than that? Is our calling as preachers really as simple as uncovering the deep symbols of what Paul meant by justification in Rom 5? Do we only need to master an interpretive technique perfected these last several centuries, and then accurately represent that intention to a modern audience, or is something else happening? Kierkegaard once suggested that, in a Christian land, he was tired of hearing "Sunday babbling" about Christianity's "priceless and glorious truths." What was missing in this "history lesson" format, he said, was the one thing that could not be directly communicated from one person to another (Kierkegaard, 35). In Kierkegaard's opinion, direct communication, whether that be through a history lecture or a sermon, apparently did not necessarily translate into comprehension and understanding.

It is in response to this notion of direct communication and an abiding sense that, as human beings, we do not really communicate that way, that structuralist and other post-structural models arose. Theorists in this group are trying to get at that which Kierkegaard once said could not be directly communicated from one person to another. Rhetorical, reader-response, hermeneutical, and deconstructive theorists, feminists, and liberationists were largely influenced by Derrida, who spoke of what is absent in a text not as sheer negativity, but as leaving a "trace" of a presence (1967). Things otherwise not seen (e.g., the role of women; the place of poor people) now became the subject of focus often through what was not said or was left out. Human beings in communication are much more complex than sending and receiving vessels. Sermons are much more complicated than the representation of external data characteristic of the epistemological hermeneutics of the modern era; "this" does not always mean "that," in other words.

The Task for Theology

According to Hans-Georg Gadamer, Martin Heidegger turned away from reading texts in a way that was dominated by methodological rigor and the foundations of scientific method. The problem in theological and biblical inquiry was not one of "mathematical formula" or "infinitesimal method"; rather, it was a problem of "unstable linguistic shapes" or, as he was quoted, a "problem of language." For the "true task of theology—a task that theology must find its way back to—[is] to search for the word that was capable of becoming one to and preserving one in the faith" (Gadamer, 1994, 30). Theological hermeneutics had been about the methodological acquisition and the homiletical disputation of objective facts, and Heidegger introduced an alternative approach to language and even homiletics; one where understanding, as Gadamer put it, "is the original characteristic of the being of human life itself" (Gadamer, 1993, 259) Gadamer's philosophical hermeneutics describes how language forms or constitutes human reality. This perspective claims that words, that is, talk, conversation, dialogue, question and answer, produce worlds. This alternative hermeneutic posits that a human being is not first and foremost a *cogito* employing reason to connect and disconnect with objects around it, but is first and foremost an interpreter, understander, or sense maker engaged in everyday coping, and the primary site of that coping is conversation and interpersonal communicating.

Implications for Preaching

Structuralism and post structuralism have had considerable impact on preaching. The representational school of thought still underlies much propositional point-form preaching, where it is often assumed that the communication of information is communication of faith. By contrast, the New Homiletic conceives of the preacher as more of a conversational partner with Scripture, tradition, and the congregation than an expositor of Scripture who imposes his or her exegesis on the receiving congregation. He or she is a participant in the play of meaning rather than the creator of meaning; a homiletician whose first move is to listen rather than to speak, both to Scripture and to the persons making up his or her community of faith. This homiletician learns to be subject to the power of the message rather than the object of a message that is considered to be powerful. As subject to Scripture, the preacher is acted upon as much as he or she is an actor. He or she also practices ministry within the to-and-fro, give-and-take of congregational community life, a community that is also subject to that which presents itself in Scripture. The homiletician who practices this kind of ministry, who is in conversation with the everyday events of his or her congregation, is similar to the two *homileuing* (conversation) partners in Luke's Gospel. As the two partners on the road to Emmaus discovered, it is through this give-and-take of talk that the risen Christ is recognized (Luke 24:13-35).

Structuralism and post-structuralism in all of their iterations inform a different kind of approach to preaching, an approach acknowledging that every sacred text has a synchronic dimension—it has meaning in the present. It must be encountered again and again as it intersects with the actual living out of community life. Therefore, to be meaningful, to be understood, to be fully and completely experienced, each tradition-bound text must be applied or field-tested; must be in conversation with the diverse members and groups of the community of faith as it endeavors to live out its faith. Each group brings its own perspective to the text that renders meaning, and not all meanings are in harmony. The preacher is a conversation partner, an attuned participant whose sermons incorporate elements of interpretation and application and manifest themselves as articulated practice. So what do these sermons look like, maybe even sound like? How do we know when our preaching is more than about the transfer of information as in a history lesson or the "Sunday babbling" about Christianity's "priceless and glorious truths"? There are many preachers today who, perhaps unknowingly, practice a kind of post-structural homiletics. They allow for different viewpoints, often valuing testimony over logical proofs. Narrative, story, first-person presentations, drama, music, interpretive dance, and interactive media are all ways to get at the "trace" of something absent for which Derrida was searching; or the *erfahrung* (experience) of meaning unlike that of the lecture or history lesson that Kierkegaard rejected. Contemporary homiletical theorists argue that something unique happens when preachers function more as Socratic *maieuts* (midwives) than experts in control; a something that may have less to do with our hermeneutical skill and abilities than the persuasive power of the Holy Spirit. *See* LITERARY CRITICISM; PHILOSOPHICAL HERMENEUTICS.

Bibliography: Jeffrey Francis Bullock. *Preaching with a Cupped Ear.* (1999); Fred Craddock. *Overhearing the Gospel: Preaching and Teaching the Faith to Persons Who Have Already Heard.* (1978); Jacques Derrida. *Of Grammatology.* (1967; English 1974); Hans-Georg Gadamer. *Philosophical Hermeneutics.* (1976); Hans-Georg Gadamer. *Truth and Method.* (1993); Hans-Georg Gadamer. *Heidegger's Ways.* (1994); Søren Kierkegaard, *Practice in Christianity,* ed. and trans., Howard V. Hong and Edna H. Hong. (1991); Frank Lentricchia. *After the New Criticism.* (1980); Ferdinand de Saussure. *Course in General Linguistics.* (1916); John Stewart. *Language as Articulate Contact.* (1995).

WOMANIST CRITICISM
Raquel A. St. Clair

In 1983, Alice Walker coined the term *womanist* and defined it as a "black feminist or a feminist of color" (Walker 1983, xi). By so doing, she provided the nomenclature for academic and grassroots reflection that took seriously the experiences of African American women by simultaneously analyzing the trifold oppression of racism, sexism, and classism. The antecedents of womanist thought are found in the civil rights movement of the 1950s and early 1960s and the second wave of feminism in the 1960s. Although these liberation movements fought against racism, classism, and sexism, they did not address these societal ills concurrently. In other words, the civil rights movement focused on racism but not sexism in the African American or wider community while the feminist movement focused on sexism but not the racism that affected African American female life. Womanist thought, on the other hand, provides African American women the opportunity to occupy their particular gender, racial, and economic spaces without denying or subordinating any aspect of who they are. Womanist theologians used Walker's definition to create a space in which Christian theology and the experiences of African American women could connect. This theological reflection led to womanist biblical criticism that seeks to "discover the significance and validity of the biblical text for black women who today experience the 'tridimensional reality' of racism, sexism, and classism" (Jones-Warsaw 1994, 22, 30).

Womanist biblical criticism utilizes a "hermeneutics of wholeness" that employs four basic principles: (1) it promotes the wholeness of African American women without oppressing others; (2) it is grounded in the particularities of African American female life; (3) it affirms that God supports African American women in their struggle for wholeness and freedom from oppression; and (4) it affirms that Jesus' life and ministry are significant for African American women and the means by which African American women understand his suffering and death (St. Clair, 2007, 59–60). A preacher may employ these interpretive principles by posing them as questions to examine their exegetical conclusions and the resulting sermon.

First, the preacher would ask whether his or her exegetical conclusions or sermon points promoted the wholeness of African American women. One would try to determine whether the message and practical response encouraged by the sermon would help or hinder African American women in embracing their full humanity as persons created in the image of God *and* whether non–African American female persons would be encouraged to acknowledge and treat them as the same. The goal is not to prioritize the wholeness of African American women above that of others but to create sermons that encourage the wholeness of the entire human family including African American women.

Second, one would ask whether one's interpretation was grounded in the reality of African American female life. To state it another way: Has the preacher at the very least acknowledged within himself or herself the nature of African American women's oppression and sought to include them as a part of the congregation who will hear this word? This does not mean that the sermon would have to be geared specifically to African American women but that the preacher has considered the social location of persons who are affected by racism, classism, and sexism and is making a conscious effort not to proclaim a message that might perpetuate these evils. In short, this question is designed to help the preacher recognize that the sociocultural location and existential experience of African American women differ from those of both African American men and women from other racial/ethnic groups in noteworthy ways.

Third, the preacher would ask whether his or her interpretation affirms that God supports African Americans in their struggle for wholeness and freedom from oppression. In other words, does the message proclaimed inspire, persuade, and/or encourage African American women to recognize, name, and fight against oppressive systems or simply support a status quo that neither includes nor benefits them? Moreover, the preacher who preaches to a congregation in which there are no African American women could ask, Does my sermon inspire, persuade, and/or encourage my congregation to recognize, name, and fight against oppressive systems or simply support a status quo that excludes others, even though it may benefit them?

Fourth, the preacher would ask whether the sermon affirms Jesus' life and ministry as significant for African American women and the means by which African American women understand his suffering and death. By employing this fourth principle, the preacher seeks to avoid making suffering the goal of discipleship. One's faithfulness to Jesus becomes predicated upon following him in ministry rather than suffering like him on the cross. Suffering becomes a possible consequence of discipleship rather than a condition of it. This final question ensures that suffering is not lifted up as a model for suffering people (St. Clair 2008).

Womanist criticism gives a preacher a different set of questions and another cultural lens though which to examine the biblical text as well as develop sermons. It enables one to consider alternate ways of hearing and understanding the gospel. In short, it sensitizes the preacher to his or her use of language. For example, the use of a phrase like "servant/slave of God" is heard differently by persons who have a history of being enslaved and relegated to positions of servitude. Jacquelyn Grant notes that African American women historically have been the "servants of servants." Therefore, a preacher would need to contemplate how and if such phrases are to be used so as not to euphemize servitude by equating it with Christian service (Grant 1993, 199-218).

Womanist criticism also causes one to take into account how traditional theological concepts may be understood from different sociocultural spaces. Delores Williams notes that what distinguishes African American women's oppression from that of other women is the experience of surrogacy. She argues that historically African American women have been forced to take others' places for the benefit of others. During slavery and after slavery, they were forced by law or economic necessity to do the domestic and manual work in the place of and for white people. Therefore, atonement theories that present Jesus as a surrogate or substitute for humanity who dies in our stead on the cross to save us from our sins can serve as theological justification for the historical oppression of African American women (Williams 1999). This interpretation of the work of Christ runs the risk of making the suffering of African American women sacred by virtue of its parallels to Jesus' salvific work. One might conclude that it is beneficial, if not a fundamental Christian tenet; that suffering for the benefit of others is good. A preacher would thus need to reflect upon how to preach about salvation and how it is achieved through Christ in a way that does not encourage people to accept surrogacy roles passively as a means of emulating Jesus.

Womanist criticism compels the preacher to exercise consistency in biblical interpretation and proclamation. Clarice Martin provides a clear example. She notes that in Col 3:18–4:1; Eph 5:21–6:9; and 1 Pet 2:18–3:7, slaves are to submit to their masters, and women are to submit to their husbands. Yet slavery is not something Christians affirm, and persons have applied various hermeneutical principles to disavow its practice. However, these same principles are not as consistently applied to the portion of the pericope that admonishes wives to submit to their husbands. Somehow, the slaves are freed, but the women remain subordinated (Martin 1991). Womanist criticism challenges such inconsistent interpretation and its resulting subjugation of women. It seeks to find more egalitarian and uniform ways of exegeting the Scripture.

By employing these interpretive principles, preachers, regardless of their gender, race, or class, can examine Scripture and interpret it in ways that are salutary not only to African American women but to society as a whole. She or he can adopt a cultural lens that considers the trifold oppression of African American women so as not to perpetuate these ills through the proclamation of God's Word. The preacher can use womanist criticism to consciously consider and include persons often relegated to the status of the least of these within one's exegetical and homiletical practices and create more wholistic, empowering, and inclusionary sermons that benefit all hearers. *See* AFRICAN AMERICAN BIBLICAL INTERPRETATION; FEMINIST CRITICISM; SOTERIOLOGY; SUSPICION.

Bibliography: Jacquelyn Grant. "The Sin of Servanthood and the Deliverance of Discipleship." *A Troubling in My Soul: Womanist Perspectives on Evil and Suffering.* Edited by Emilie M. Townes. (1993) 199–218; Koala Jones-Warsaw. "Towards Womanist Hermeneutics: A Reading of Judges 19–21." *Journal of the Interdenominational Theological Center* 22 (1994) 18–35; Clarice Martin. "The Haustafeln (Household Codes) in African American Biblical Interpretation: 'Free Slaves' and 'Subordinate Women.'" *Stony the Road We Trod: African American Biblical Interpretation.* Edited by Cain Hope Felder. (1991) 206–31; Raquel A. St. Clair. *Call and Consequences: A Womanist Reading of Mark's Gospel.* (2008); Raquel A. St. Clair. "Womanist Interpretation." *True to Our Native Land: An African American New Testament Commentary.* Edited by Brian Blount. (2007) 54–62; Alice Walker. *In Search of Our Mothers' Gardens: Womanist Prose.* (1983); Delores S. Williams. *Sisters in the Wilderness: The Challenge of Womanist God-Talk.* (1999).

PART 5 POETICS. INTRODUCTION: POETICS AND THE CONTEXT OF PREACHING

Lucy Lind Hogan

"What language shall I borrow to thank thee, dearest friend, / for this thy dying sorrow, thy pity without end?" Paul Gerhardt voices a central question for preaching with these words from his famous hymn, "O Sacred Head, Now Wounded." Poetics helps to answer such questions about the language we might borrow to proclaim the good news. The language we borrow is neither neutral nor ornamental. It has the profound potential to shape our experience, our reality, our world, and our being. Poetics comprises the theory of language use, figures of speech, strategies of form, arrangement, and performance. Preachers must decide not only what they will say but also how they will say it, and it is here that poetics both assists and challenges.

Biblical Roots

Here we are not able to turn to a systematic analysis of biblical poetics comparable to those we will find in the classical philosophy and literary theory. Nevertheless, Scripture seems to bear witness to the understanding that we are able to do things with words and that different words, structures, and forms do different things.

Literary theorists describe genres, or categories of literature, that achieve different ends by different means—poetry, drama, novels. The Scriptures are composed of a variety of genres. There are narratives or stories that unfold over time and space with characters and plot. Whether it is the story of Moses leading the children of Israel dry footed through a sea bottom, Jesus encountering a sinful fisherman, or the tale of a father who gave his two sons their inheritance long before he died, the stories draw us in and pique our curiosity. Who are these people? What will happen to them? The poetry of the Psalms may sing God's praises or lament God's absence. Paul's letters, one of yet another genre, contain arguments seeking to convince his readers that the Jewish rabbi who was executed by the Roman officials was none other than God himself. And the apocalyptic visions of Daniel and John, like science fiction, give us visions of alternative worlds and ways of being.

Classical Roots

The concept of poetics as a discipline has its roots in the classical world where it stood over and against rhetoric. Rhetoric provided the theories and strategies of preparing speech that would be persuasive. It treated the rational, intellectual, and logical dimensions of speech and language. Poetics dealt with poetry, drama, and literature; with the aesthetic and emotive or affective dimensions of language and form.

In his *Republic*, Plato observed that poetry and theater produced only an imitation (*mimesis*) of life, which itself is a shadow of the eternal forms. Poetry and drama, therefore, would be an inadequate means to knowledge and truth and consequently would not have a place in his ideal state.

Aristotle, in the *Poetics*, set out to argue the opposite. It was his contention that the arts, tragedy in particular, had the potential to lead people to make judgments. In this unfinished work, Aristotle identified the significant genres: comedy, epic, and the most important, tragedy. He examined the elements of character development and diction, but viewed the most important poetic element to be plot. By careful arrangement of the events in a drama, the author will seek to lead the audience to a cathartic experience. And in that experience the audience will be led to proper judgments.

Another significant debate occurred around whether people are led to knowledge and judgment by logic and reason or by the eloquence and sublimity of the presentation. Which will be more important: the arguments that one constructs or the beauty of one's words, the creativity of one's images, and the liveliness of one's delivery? While rhetoric was originally conceived as the preparation of persuasive arguments, it eventually came to be equated with a more poetic disposition. As one 20th-cent. rhetorician observed, it is the "artful presentation" of the truth (Weaver 1970, 15). The belles lettres approach to rhetoric featured language and literature, and it was this school that would dominate the end of the 19th and beginning of the 20th cent. Oratory was no longer viewed as political persuasion; rather, it was seen as a fine art, as poetics.

Preaching and Poetics

In spite of Augustine's observation that preachers were not only to teach and move, but were also to delight (*Doctr. chr.* 4.27), the relationship between poetics and preaching has been a tensive one for a number of reasons. One was the perception that the truth of the gospel did not need artful presentation. The truth would be compelling in and of itself. Therefore, theology is more important than aesthetics.

Second was a distrust of imagination and creativity. Much of the preaching tradition was grounded in a theological anthropology that viewed the input of the preacher with suspicion. The preacher is a fallen creature using fallen language. We are not to trust imaginative leaps. Likewise, iconoclasm and rejection of the image meant that illustrations, images, and figures of speech were to be kept to a minimum.

Finally, the attention to the listener, so important in both poetics and rhetoric, was viewed as contrary to REVELATION. Revelation was from God, and consequently, the preacher was not to be concerned with shaping a message for a particular congregation at a particular time.

Yet despite these concerns, preachers continued to be confronted with the questions of deciding not only what they were to say, but also how to say it. They thought about the words they would use. And they thought about the order and structure of their sermon. Whether they knew it or not, they were thinking in the categories and strategies of poetics.

A New Hermeneutic and New Homiletic

Much of traditional homiletics assumed a rational and logical dissemination of knowledge and information about Scripture and the doctrines of the church. It was rooted in the understanding that it was the preacher's role to study the Scriptures and determine the idea or theme contained in a particular passage. The preacher would then preach that idea to the waiting but passive congregation. But are listeners passive? Should they be passive? What might be the role of the congregation, the listener in the sermon?

In the mid-20th cent., biblical scholars sought to develop a hermeneutical approach that would make the Scriptures come alive for the listener or reader. The new hermeneutic, grounded in the writings of Gerhard Ebeling and Ernst Fuchs, sought to bridge the apparent gap between the ancient text of Scripture and the contemporary reader. Could the Testaments, written for people two thousand years ago, speak a fresh word for people living today? How might biblical scholars or preachers approach the Scriptures in such a way that the contemporary audience would understand that they were included and there was a message for them as well? (*See* APPLICATION; BRIDGING THEN AND NOW; CONCERNS OF THE TEXT AND SERMON; CONTEMPORIZING; FOCUS AND FUNCTION STATEMENTS; FUSION.)

The new hermeneutic was grounded in an understanding of the eventfulness of language and the importance of the reader. The meaning of the text is not a static treasure to be unearthed by the preacher, like the pearl of great price, and then displayed to the listeners. Rather, the meaning grows out of a relationship between the text and the listeners, and it is the preacher along with the Holy Spirit who makes that relationship possible. The preacher does not so much ask, "What does the text mean?" as "What is the text saying to us?" and "How might I shape a message that will engage the community in exploring this question?"

In his book *The Renewal of Preaching*, David Randolph described the possibilities for preaching inherent in this new hermeneutical understanding and approach, which he identified as a New Homiletic. Grounded in the understanding that preaching is an event, Randolph argued that it was more important to think about what a sermon does than what it is or says: "The homily must then be understood in its uniqueness as the form of discourse designed to bring the word of God to expression in the concreted situation of the hearers" (Randolph 1969, 19).

Likewise, in *As One Without Authority*, Fred Craddock sought to provide a counterbalance to the DEDUCTIVE, logical, rational, propositional approach of the old hermeneutic and homiletic with a more INDUCTIVE and experiential approach. He observed, "The sole purpose [of preaching] is to engage the hearer in the pursuit of an issue or an idea so that he will think his own thoughts and experience his own feelings in the presence of Christ and in the light of the Gospel" (Craddock 1978, 157).

The Poetic Turn

Affection, emotions, passions, imagination, and poetics began to make a return to homiletics in the 19th cent. through the influences of romanticism. But it was not until the mid-20th cent. that we begin to see significant attention paid to poetic elements. Preaching began to focus not so much on the content, what the sermon said, as much as on what it did. Preaching was seen as creating an experience much the same way that Aristotle observed that the goal of tragedy was to create catharsis.

As we have already noted in the discussion of the New Homiletic, the listener came to occupy a more significant role in the preaching event. What will the listener think? How will the listener be affected by the sermon? What does the preacher need to say and do that will encourage the listener's involvement? To explore these questions, preachers and homileticians have turned to poetic elements.

1. Language

The nature and use of language pose a significant question in poetics. Preachers have come to understand that language is culturally grounded and shaped. Language choices, and the use of figures of speech, are essential dimensions of preaching as opposed to frivolous ornamentation. Postmodern theory has helped us to understand that language constitutes and shapes reality. (*See* METAPHOR AND FIGURES OF SPEECH.)

2. Form and Arrangement

Another important poetic turn has focused on the narrative and the plotting of sermons. The form a sermon takes is not to be viewed as an empty vessel into which one pours the content of the message. Rather, homileticians such as Eugene Lowry have reminded us that we can never separate content and form; how we say something is as essential to the experience as what we say (Lowry 2000, 6). Likewise, narrative does not serve solely as illustration and example in preaching; narrative is a legitimate alternative to rational or discursive argu-

mentation. (*See* MOVES; NARRATIVE PREACHING; NARRATIVE THEORY.)

3. Imagination

Thomas Troeger has helped preachers understand the importance of the imagination. In what he describes as "imagination theology," he "employs the visionary and integrative capacities of the mind to create theological understanding" (Troeger 1990, 26). The poetic turn has encouraged preachers to appreciate and use a variety of artistic and literary dimensions in preaching. It has also challenged them to develop their creative, storytelling capabilities. (*See* ARTS; FILM, ILLUSTRATIONS AND STORIES; IMAGINATION/CREATIVITY; NOVELS.)

4. Emotion

While Jesus may have reminded us to love God with all our heart, soul, strength, and mind, most preaching traditionally was directed to the mind, the logical and rational. The poetic turn has reminded preachers that preaching must incorporate the rational with the affective.

The Call for Poets

In his book *Finally Comes the Poet*, Walter Brueggemann argues that preaching has become so "twisted, pressed, [and] tailored" that the shocking challenges of the gospel have been domesticated and distorted. In place of this reduced prose, he urges preachers to recover the poetic voice. The speech of the poet is "counter speech" that leads to the "counter life." Poetic preaching, he claims, has the potential to be "dramatic, artistic," and is that which is "capable of inviting persons to join in another conversation" (Brueggemann 1989, 3). Although language alone will not do it, God's use of the preacher's full-orbed poetic offerings make this conversation with God a possibility. See NARRATIVE FORM; NEW HOMILETIC; POINT FORM.

Bibliography: Augustine. *Christian Instruction*; Walter Brueggemann. *Finally Comes the Poet: Daring Speech for Proclamation*. (1989); Fred Craddock. *As One Without Authority*. (1978); Eugene Lowry. *The Homiletical Plot*. (2000); David Randolph. *The Renewal of Preaching*. (1969); Thomas Troeger. *Imagining a Sermon*. (1990); Richard Weaver. *The Ethics of Rhetoric*. (1970).

❖   ❖   ❖   ❖

APPLICATION
Paul E. Koptak

Application is the process by which preachers demonstrate the contemporary significance of biblical teaching in a particular context. Put more directly, application grows out of the preacher's desire to speak words that will be used by the Holy Spirit to bring about changes in the lives of believers and believing communities. Application and life change are shared concerns of preacher and congregation. When asked, many who listen to sermons say that they want their preachers to show how the ancient words of the Bible offer guidance for living today. They do not appreciate sermons that leave them stranded thousands of years in the past or lost in abstraction.

The sermon should, like the Bible itself, speak a word that is both timeless and timely. The "so what?" of a sermon begins in the study of the text; it is not a step added as the sermon is written. Three typical approaches, each with their particular emphases, share important features with the others.

First, for preachers who take the biblical principle approach, the goal of the sermon is to teach Scripture's original meaning and then generalize, looking for the principle operating in the text that can be used to speak to a new situation. Jack Kuhatschek (1990, 31) shows how Paul used the older legal prohibition against muzzling the ox to argue the principle that workers are worth their hire, even preachers (1 Cor 9:7-14). Application questions can also ask: Does the text have a command to obey, a promise to trust, an example to follow or avoid, a reason to praise God? Haddon Robinson (2002, 102–3) looks for a central truth that will lead to questions that listeners might ask: What does this mean? Is it true? What difference does it make? Bryan Chapell speaks of three preaching strategies: explain, illustrate, and apply (2005, 103–4).

The method lends itself to expository preaching and its strengths in teaching. Some prefer topical sermons that draw together multiple scriptures to point more directly to life lessons. Others put application at center stage by writing the main points as life lessons.

Second, a preacher can use the biblical dynamic of trouble and grace as a guide. Paul Scott Wilson recommends a theological grammar of movement between human need or failure (trouble) and God's work of provision, empowerment, and forgiveness (grace). Once the preacher identifies the trouble and grace in the text, he or she draws parallels in each of these areas for the contemporary listener. The sermon will have at least two sections of application, one of trouble and another of grace. For Frank Thomas, preaching gives listeners an "experience of the assurance of grace" that overcomes evil (1997, 18). Like Wilson, Thomas asks preachers to offer good news, both in the text and our time, as an answer to the bad news of sin, oppression, or adversity. A behavioral purpose statement clarifies the preacher's theme ("I propose . . .") and the intended outcome ("to the end that hearers will . . ."), leading to a set of strategies for celebration of that good news in contemporary terms (*see* CELEBRATION). The joyful celebration of the way things can and will be reinforces the impact of the good news so that listeners receive it with mind and emotion (1997, 1–11).

Third, good preaching highlights the sense of identification that readers and hearers experience with the Bible, sermons, and preachers. As rhetorical symbols, sermons are most effective when their description of lived experience overlaps with that of listeners. Symbolic resolutions, such as reconciliation in Joseph's family, can help listeners move toward resolution in their own conflicted situations. Moreover, preaching as an act of narrative imagination links the stories of Christian people and congregations back to the larger story of God's work of kingdom and *shalom*. Craig Loscalzo shows how this disposition toward the listener communicates care, standing with the listeners instead of over or against them (1992, 77).

In sum, attention to application in biblical interpretation will point the way to the sermon's evocation of God at work in daily life. For that reason preachers will look over their sermons to be sure that at least some of the illustrations resemble the lives represented in the seats, not just those of the heroes of the faith. The time-tested advice of looking at life through the eyes of others can be enhanced by visits to homes and workplaces. Leonora Tubbs Tisdale recommends that pastors become exegetes of text and congregation, paying close attention to local cultural assumptions and modes of communication (1997, 30). Sermon study/planning groups also give preachers a window into their listeners' lives as well as their reactions to the sermon text.

Careful listening to the desires, cares, and hopes of the congregation not only communicates interest, but it also enhances variety, as does preaching from a variety of biblical texts and looking for the concrete implications of the common themes they address. For example, drawing out the various aspects of forgiveness (acknowledging emotions, seeking reconciliation, wiping accounts clean) can keep preachers from repeating themselves.

How much of the sermon ought to be application? Although no numerical guideline will serve the variety of sermon styles in use today, the methods outlined here imply a 50/50 balance of time spent in the ancient and contemporary worlds. Robinson's rule of thumb says that a sermon will include only enough explanation to help listeners understand the message of the gospel in the text(s) of the day (2002, 42–44). The guiding concern is faithfulness to the message of Scripture as well as the lives of listeners. *See* BRIDGING THEN AND NOW; THE FOUR PAGES OF THE SERMON; THE BIG IDEA; THEME SENTENCE.

Bibliography: Lori Carrell. *The Great American Sermon Survey.* (2000); Bryan Chapell. *Christ-Centered Preaching: Redeeming the Expository Sermon.* 2nd ed. (2005); Paul Koptak. "Rhetorical Identification in Preaching." *Preaching* (November/December 1998) 11–18; Jack Kuhatschek. *Taking the Guesswork Out of Applying the Bible.* (1990); Craig A. Loscalzo. *Preaching Sermons that Connect: Effective Communication through Identification.* (1992); Mary Alice Mulligan and Ronald J. Allen. *Make the Word Come Alive: Lessons from Laity.* (2006); Haddon W. Robinson. *The Development and Delivery of Expository Messages.* 2nd ed. (2002); Frank A. Thomas. *They Like to Never Quit Praisin' God: The Role of Celebration in Preaching.* (1997); Leonora Tubbs Tisdale. *Preaching as Local Theology and Folk Art.* (1997); Paul Scott Wilson. *The Four Pages of the Sermon.* (1999).

ARTS
Thomas H. Troeger

The first step in effectively employing the arts in preaching is realizing the artistry of the biblical writers. Consider the marching cadences of the prophets, the poetic beauty of the psalms, the narrative eloquence of Luke, the imagistic splendor of John, and the rhetorical flourishes of Paul. The art of the biblical writers is an essential part of what makes their proclamation engaging and transforming. (*See* IMAGINATION/CREATIVITY.) When preachers realize the artistry of the biblical writers, they are less apt to think of art as ornamentation or enrichment. Instead, art represents the disciplined use of our creative powers to fashion something that expresses the wonder and beauty of God.

Since the Bible exists in the form of a written text, one might conclude that it gives warrant to use artistic language but not other art forms, such as sculpture, pictures, and dance. There have been theologians and movements in Christian history that have eschewed the arts in worship and preaching, but there are others who have celebrated them. Centuries of Christian art in a multitude of forms give witness to something irrepressible in the human heart: the need to employ every possible means in expressing to God our faith and our gratitude, our joy and our grief, our hope and our yearning.

Even traditions that are iconoclastic often end up developing their own visual aesthetic. For example, the Congregationalists of New England rejected the use of physical images in their worship space, but ended up building churches that engage the eye with clean angular lines, proportion and balance, and a sense of airy spaciousness and light. It is as though the great artist who fashioned creation built into our very being a need for art that one way or another finds expression.

Because theological education is overwhelmingly verbal, some preachers feel uncertain about using any of the arts other than those that are written, such as poetry, drama, or fiction. Others feel comfortable drawing upon movies, television, and video because, like the people to whom they minister, they are immersed in the multimedia culture of our age. Although electronic media provides effective resources for preaching, a narrow focus upon it can obviate our drawing upon the church's vast treasury of art. Sticking exclusively with our own generation of audiovisual productions has two deleterious consequences for the life of faith. First, the bombardment of images and sounds can dull our capacity to probe the spiritual depths of any work of art. Second, art from the past can help us reclaim ways of seeing the gospel that are full of wisdom and insight. Just as the Bible preserves for us truths about the human condition that contemporary culture may ignore to its own detriment, so too art often gives witness to the glory of God in ways that reveal the distortions and inadequacies of our own passing moment in history.

These may sound like grandiose claims for the use of art in preaching, but let me offer an illustration of a sermon I heard that drew upon a great piece of art, and that has stayed with me for more than thirty years, even though I have heard thousands of sermons since then. The preacher employed a technique common to the classical rhetoric that St. Augustine inherited from Cicero. Ancient rhetorical training included an exercise that required the student to study a picture or scene in minute detail and then to describe it as graphically and precisely as possible. The image gives birth to the language.

The sermon I heard was preached at a Christmas midnight service and was based on a nativity scene engraved by the renowned artist Albrecht Dürer (1471–1528). The preacher had photocopied the scene onto the front of the bulletin. The holy family was at the center of the etching. On the right-hand side of the picture was a classical building in disrepair. On the left was a medieval building in the same state of decay. Above the holy family and bridging the two buildings were some rough sawn planks with a small tree growing out of them. The preacher asked the congregation to look at the picture and then described the details I have related. The preacher explained that Albrecht Dürer lived when the synthesis of classical and Christian thought was breaking down. The artist portrayed that breakdown through the decaying buildings that framed the nativity of Christ. The Incarnate Word was born as "love among the ruins." The preacher then talked about the ruins of human life in individuals and in communities. The sermon ended with an affirmation that through the birth of Christ, love is born among the ruins, and like the little tree sprouting at the top of Dürer's etching, life and hope spring up anew.

Nowadays the preacher might employ Power-Point®, though in some ways the use of the bulletin cover was more effective because members of the congregation could take it home and put it on the refrigerator and remember the sermon every time they opened the door. (*See* TECHNOLOGY.) The great strength of this homiletical method is the fusion of language and image to make an unforgettable proclamation of the gospel. The image reinforces the language, and the language moves our vision to a deeper level of spiritual insight. The

danger in such preaching is that one might deliver an art lecture instead of a sermon. But the preacher can avoid that by giving only as much background as the congregation needs to enter the theological and pastoral depths of the image.

Notice also how this single picture and its organizing visual focus/theological concept, "love among the ruins," give us a center point to which members of the congregation can bring their stories of brokenness and restoration. The narrative and dramatic action of the sermon take place in the human heart as it is engaged both visually and conceptually. (*See* ILLUSTRATIONS AND STORIES.)

Moving beyond this one example, we can name the following principles for employing art in our sermons. The power of the art is not automatically present in the sermon, any more than the power of a biblical text is. Just as the text requires exposition, so too does the art. The effectiveness of a sermon using art results from the synergy of several elements working together:

1. seeing or hearing the art itself;
2. calling attention to details that the uninformed eye or ear would otherwise miss;
3. presenting the preacher's theological interpretation of the work;
4. using the first three elements to illumine the congregation's life and faith.

When all of these come together without any one of them dominating, the sermon can be a vital and transforming witness to the gospel of Christ.

These principles for the use of art in preaching extend not only to graphic, plastic, and musical masterpieces from the treasury of Christian art, but also to the art that parishioners may supply, especially as more and more churches feature religious arts festivals as part of their educational programs and worship services. I think, for example, of sermons I have done using children's art that interpreted select passages from the Bible. The children drew pictures with brilliant, bold markers. Subsequently, a member of the congregation took digital photos and downloaded them for a PowerPoint® presentation that I accompanied with a sermon. I used the same principles to interpret the children's work that we saw at work in the sermon on Albrecht Dürer's etching. One sermon featured two pictures of the temptation of Jesus in the wilderness. A five-year-old had drawn a stick figure Jesus with his mouth wide open, speaking a single gigantic word that dominated the picture: "No!" The next picture of the same scene by another child was an abstraction: two free-floating amoeba-like forms intermingled, their colors running together. I preached that sometimes temptation is crystal clear and we can speak a loud and certain "No!" but other times it is much less clear because good and evil flow together and our choices are more ambiguous. The use of the children's art was able to hold the attention of the children, while the verbal interpretation simultaneously spoke at a more adult level. (*See* PREACHING TO CHILDREN.)

If preachers feel uncertain about employing art in the creation of sermons, they could share this article and ask for help from members of their congregation who are artistically gifted. Just as Bible study groups often give a pastor new insights into what to preach, so artists can help to open new wellsprings to the living Spirit of God and to create a witness to the gospel that is alive with beauty, wonder, and grace. (*See* FILM; VIDEO CLIPS.)

Bibliography: David Brown and David Fuller. *Signs of Grace: Sacraments in Poetry and Prose.* (1995); Othmar Keel. *The Symbolism of the Biblical World: Ancient Near Eastern Iconography and the Book of Psalms.* Translated by Timothy Hallett. (1997); Margaret R. Miles. *Image as Insight: Visual Understanding in Western Christianity and Secular Culture.* (1985).

BRIDGING THEN AND NOW
Stephen Farris

In pre-Enlightenment times there was little awareness of a need to bridge then and now since it was assumed that the text was capable of speaking directly to the hearers of the preached word. To be sure, commentators carried out careful exegeses of their texts to clarify the grammatical sense of the text. Particular Jewish customs or practices in both OT and NT passages were also explained. Moreover, there was awareness, sometimes vivid, of the problem of relating OT texts to the NT, but by the use of allegory, typology, or a promise and fulfillment scheme, these challenges were met. Thorny texts in both Testaments that did not obviously promote the love of God or neighbor were wrestled with, and higher "spiritual" senses of the text were

sought. Once those tasks had been carried out, the resulting word, it was assumed, spoke directly to its new hearers. Nothing further remained but to express the text's meaning clearly and eloquently. The meaning "then" was, for the most part, the meaning "now." There is no need for a bridge when there is no distance to be spanned.

Pre-Enlightenment interpreters certainly understood that texts grew out of specific historical situations. It was assumed, however, that the contemporary church stood in continuity with its NT ancestor and that a word to one could be directly transferred to the other. With the Enlightenment, two major factors arose that made the task of bridging then and now a critical one. First, there was a sharpened awareness that biblical texts arose from specific historical situations. Such texts, more daring scholars claimed, must be interpreted in the same way as other texts from the ancient world. Second, scholars increasingly experienced a sense of distance between the biblical texts and their new world ruled not by inherited dogma or by the superstitions they were growing to despise, but, they believed, by reason. In a world lit by reason, the direct intervention of God, in creation and resurrection or miracles, seemed problematic. Interpreting texts written in what now seemed a distant world demanded a bridge.

Since the Enlightenment, preachers have employed many bridge-building techniques. Here we may briefly consider three general strategies that contemporary homiletics has adopted in order to create a bridge between then and now. One widely practiced solution is to identify a theological truth, theme, or big idea within the text and to bring that forward into our world. Most churches consider themselves to be in some sense apostolic in their doctrine. Whatever the distance in time or circumstance, it is argued, churches maintain or ought to maintain the doctrine of the early church. The big idea method of bridging then and now attempts to identify in the text the doctrine that represents this continuity. This method may work best in churches where revelation is understood to be propositional in nature. In this understanding the biblical preacher's task is to identify and convey those truths about God and humanity, the knowledge and acceptance of which lie at the heart of Christianity. Other churches, however, do not understand revelation as primarily propositional. Preaching's task is not primarily to convey truths but to point to the one who is truth, the loving God made known in Jesus Christ through the Holy Spirit. This doctrinal understanding has a homiletical equivalent. In the New Homiletic, preaching aims not to instruct in Christian doctrine but to evoke an experience of the gospel.

The New Homiletic may not sufficiently appreciate the need for doctrinal preaching. Moreover, some texts do seem to have been written precisely to convey truths about God or humanity. Nevertheless, one aspect of the New Homiletic's critique of propositional preaching ought not be ignored: the big idea method of bridging then and now does not adequately take into account the form of the biblical text. In such preaching it matters not whether a text is a parable, a hymn, a lament, or anything else. The form is ignored as the text is boiled down to a simple declarative proposition. Meaning is conveyed in the union of content and form, but here content is divorced from form. Much of the vigor of the text is lost in the process. Contemporary homiletics has urged, therefore, that attention be paid to the form of the text. This is more than a matter of labeling the genre of the passage in question. Identifying the form of the text is helpful in determining the function of the text. All texts were intended to do something in their original settings. A hymn of praise gave voice to the joy of the people, a lament to their sorrow, and so on. The function of the text becomes the second method of bridging then and now. The preacher asks whether the sermon can do in its new setting what the text did in its original setting.

This brings us to the third general method of bridging then and now, the use of analogy. The preacher looks for some analogy between the situation of the ancient text and the situation of the hearers of the text. Analogy is not identification but the perception of similarity. Our situation is not the same as that of the first readers or hearers of a text. It may be similar, however. The potential analogy does not merely lie in the function of the text. There may be persons or groups in the text to whom persons or groups in our world are similar. Listeners may be similar to either the younger son or the older son in the parable of the Prodigal Son, to give one example. Those persons or groups may not be within the text; they may be behind it. The similarity on which the analogical bridge rests may be the need or the trouble of the people to whom the text was written. So, for example, we may be similar to the troubled

and conflict-ridden church in Corinth. The primary analogy may be an analogy of need. The analogy may also rest on a movement or experience or transformation in a text. For example, there may be an analogy in contemporary experience not simply to the figure of the younger son but to the "lost and found" transformation he experienced. In the end, any analogy that rests purely on similarities in human experience is incomplete. In a gospel sermon, there must also be an analogy of grace. The Bible as a whole points to God's gracious involvement in the world. The preacher's task is to testify that the God who acted graciously in the world of the text continues to act graciously in the world of the new listeners. This method of bridging then and now may be called a hermeneutic of analogy.

Some scholars have recently challenged the concept of bridging then and now. The bridge metaphor breaks down the process into three discrete tasks: (1) determining the meaning of *then*, (2) transferring that meaning into our world (the bridge), and (3) declaring it in our world. Reality is more seamless; the interpreter swings dynamically between worlds. Moreover, it is claimed that the preacher ought to preach not a nugget of truth contained in an individual text but the gospel.

The bridge problem remains particularly acute if meaning is primarily to be found behind the text, in the setting in life of the communities that produced the texts or in the theology of the authors as seem widely assumed by those who practice the historical-critical method. The hegemony of that method has been shattered, however. It is now possible to conceive of meaning residing in the texts in a literary world into which it is possible to enter while bracketing out historical questions that had long preoccupied scholars. Meaning may also be found in a world in front of the text. Meaning is created within the reader/hearer by the interaction of the interpreter or the community with the text. In either the world "in" or "in front of" the text, there may be no need of a bridge.

These objections are useful but overstated. There is no free-floating gospel divorced from the thorny specificity of texts. The Christian gospel is incarnate in a person and in the texts that bear witness to him. In a religion of the book, preachers will always use texts. Careful explanation of the text can elucidate the historical background, explain key words, and identify literary strategies or power struggles (*see* EXEGESIS). It can even show why the text used to matter. Such explanation does not automatically show why the text still matters now or even that it should matter. Uncovering meaning is also an identification of the significance now of texts and indeed of the gospel that they proclaim. If the significance of the text is not necessarily its significance for its first hearers, surely some movement from then to now is necessary. It is undeniable that many listeners do experience a distance from these ancient texts, whether from the texts' patriarchy, pre-scientific worldview, or their anthropology. As long as there is a sense of distance, something like a bridge is necessary. The metaphor of the bridge may be abandoned; the need for the movement that it expressed remains as real as ever. *See* APPLICATION; CONCERNS OF THE TEXT AND SERMON; FOCUS AND FUNCTION STATEMENTS.

Bibliography: Ronald J. Allen. *Contemporary Biblical Interpretation for Preaching.* (1984); Edward Farley. "Preaching the Bible and Gospel." *Theology Today* 51 (1994) 90–103; Stephen Farris. *Preaching that Matters: The Bible and Our Lives.* (1998); Nancy Lammers Gross. *If You Cannot Preach Like Paul.* (2002); Thomas Long. *Preaching and the Literary Forms of the Bible.* (1989).

CONCERNS OF THE
TEXT AND SERMON
John M. Rottman

Concerns of the text and concerns of the sermon are the bridges that preachers use between the biblical text and today within the sermon. They are terms that operate in the homiletic of Paul Scott Wilson (Wilson 2007, 76–105). Simply stated, concerns of the text are those things that the text states directly or are implied by what is stated, and concerns of the sermon are those ideas to which they lead. Every text gives rise to multiple sorts of concerns. Some of these concerns are intended by the biblical author, others perhaps not. If the chosen preaching text can be thought of as a quilt, concerns of the text are those individual pieces of cloth that make up the quilt.

Concerns of the text ordinarily emerge as a product of the preacher's exegesis of a preaching text, the pericope selected as the primary focus of the sermon. The preacher asks various questions of the

text in order to prompt it to reveal its concerns. These questions may arise on a variety of levels and give voice to any number of possible concerns. At the basic grammatical level, the preacher may ask about the meaning of a particular word or phrase. On the historical level, the preacher will voice the questions most often asked by historical critics, for example, where does the conquest of Palestine in Josh 5 fit into the political history of the ancient Near East? At other levels, the preacher will raise questions from a sociological or theological perspective. The answers to these exegetical questions and others like them will give rise to concerns of the text.

Many concerns of the text can be identified by questions that can be posed and answered in the course of merely reading the text. Others will surface in the later process of consulting commentaries, pursuing grammatical/linguistic clues, or engaging in further theological reflection.

Wilson further suggests that concerns of the text be expressed in short, simple sentences having a single subject and predicate. The preacher needs to pay particular attention to what God is doing in and behind the text since these concerns are some of those that often prove to be most homiletically fruitful. For example, if the preacher were to begin to identify the concerns of the text from Mark 1:1-11, she or he would be able to list quite a number of possibilities in only the first few verses. Among them might be included:

1. Mark refers to Jesus as Christ.
2. Christ means anointed one, Messiah.
3. God brings good news via Jesus.
4. Mark sees Jesus' ministry foreshadowed in Isaiah.
5. Isaiah is an OT prophet.
6. Jesus' gospel begins with John the Baptist.
7. Mark identifies John as a voice in the wilderness like the one in Isaiah.
8. God sends John as a messenger.
9. John is a voice.
10. The voice calls from the desert.
11. John comes to straighten the way for Jesus.
12. John comes baptizing.
13. John preaches repentance.
14. John preaches that repentance and forgiveness result in the forgiveness of sins.

Making such a list also slows the preacher down, allowing him or her to examine the text in greater depth and detail.

Once identified and added to a gross list, the concerns need sorting. Some will already seem more homiletically promising than others, tending toward trouble or grace. Trouble might be thought of as the burden that the text references or places upon the readers, and grace or good news can be conceived as God's action in addressing this burden to ease or remove it.

Concern #13 seems to raise the specter of trouble or judgment, the need for repentance. Concern #14 seems to move in the direction of hope, the possibility of the forgiveness of sins. Other concerns, such as concern #9, seem more theologically and homiletically inert. Concerns that embody echoes of trouble or grace will often be especially conducive to helping the preacher focus and preach the larger themes of the gospel. The preacher will look for grace concerns among those concerns that speak of God's saving and sustaining activity. Such concerns will have God (or one of the divine persons) as their subject, and when possible, the preacher will work to formulate concerns of the text in a way that makes the activity of God obvious. Concern #8 might in the first instance be formulated as "John is a messenger," but making the activity of God explicit (God sends John as . . .) keeps the theological purpose of the sermon in the foreground. The preacher will also wish to pay special attention to concerns that seem especially troubling, interesting, or puzzling since these concerns, too, are likely to be homiletically evocative. The preacher should not be surprised to find that the Holy Spirit uses this sorting of the concerns to help him or her see more precisely what in the text might be calling for attention on a particular Sunday.

While concerns of the text emerge from exegeting the biblical text, the preacher generates concerns of the sermon by transforming concerns of the text into statements of contemporary application. The preacher produces these transformations by playing with the concerns of the text under the direction of the Holy Spirit. Practically, the preacher transforms concerns of the text by replacing several words or a phrase in it in order to make an analogous concern that speaks about the contemporary world.

Changing the word *John* to *God* and *preaches* to *demands* in concern of the text #13, "John preaches repentance," yields an analogous concern of the sermon, "God demands repentance from us." Similarly, concern of the text #14 can be transformed into "God promises that our repentance and forgiveness result in God's forgiveness of our sins." Transforming concerns of the text into concerns of the sermon is a practical way for the preacher to begin to bridge the gap between the ancient text and the contemporary situation. While the preacher will initially wish to entertain any number of transformations, concerns of the sermon also will need to be sorted. Concerns of the sermon that make the grade will both speak of the contemporary situation and speak of it truly. This is to say that the preacher is guided by theology and by common sense in making the needed transformations.

Preachers already employ concerns of the text and sermon every time they move from the biblical text to today; they just may not know the terminology or have control of the process to harness creative tension (Wilson 1988, 88).

For a particular sermon, Wilson suggests that a trouble-tending concern of the text be paired with its transformed concern of the sermon to guide the first half of the sermon. The second half of the sermon would be guided by one of the gospel-tending concerns of the text paired up with its analogous concern of the sermon (Wilson 1988, 115–21). In Wilson's homiletic the good news always features the action of God through which God addresses the trouble identified and explored in the first half of the sermon. God, after all, is the one who lifts the burden from God's people, who are unable to save themselves. Using concerns of the text and concerns of the sermon to shape one's homiletical efforts helps to ensure that the sermon focuses upon something important in the biblical text and that it is applied effectively to the world of the hearers. *See* BRIDGING THEN AND NOW; FOUR PAGES OF THE SERMON.

Bibliography: Paul Scott Wilson. *Imagination of the Heart: New Understandings in Preaching.* (1988); Paul Scott Wilson. *The Practice of Preaching.* Rev. ed. (2007).

CONTEMPORIZING
Michael E. Williams

Contemporizing is the recasting of a biblical passage in contemporary language and imagery so that those hearing the sermon may enter into the world of that text with greater freshness and immediacy. Contemporizing may be as brief as a phrase or as extensive as an entire book. The process requires the preacher to identify analogies from the world of their hearers that embody and express the characters, places, objects, or events in the biblical text. Contemporizing calls upon the historical curiosity of the preacher because proceeding demands discovering the most accurate historical context the preacher can discern. It also calls on the poetic sensibilities of the preacher because it requires the preacher to discover modern analogies to portions of the biblical text that the preacher shares with those who will hear the sermon. Finally, it calls upon the imaginative discernment of the preacher to engage the imaginations of the hearers so that they may participate in the world of the text as if it was their own life experience.

Midrash and Contemporizing

One source of contemporizing for preaching today is the ancient Jewish interpretive art of midrash. The word *midrash* comes from another Hebrew word **darash** which means "to go in search of something." When ancient rabbis sought insights in a passage, they assumed that the scripture held such an all-encompassing view of the world that its wisdom could be applied in any possible human situation (*see* BRIDGING THEN AND NOW). To find that application, however, the rabbis had to find points of connection between the world of the text and the world of the listeners.

The rabbis' need to find points of connection led them to ask a question of the text. They asked, "To what shall we compare this (person, place, thing, or event) in our lives and the lives of our listeners?" Jesus asked this question in teaching his disciples: "To what shall we compare the reign of God? The reign of God is like . . ." Then Jesus would present an image or story from the world of his listeners that allowed them to experience a glimpse of the reign of God in their own world.

Historical Context

In order to find appropriate analogies for biblical settings, characters, objects, and language, the preacher must first establish an accurate historical context for the biblical passage. Bible dictionaries and books on the culture and customs of the world of the Bible are often more helpful in setting that context than commentaries, unless a commentary exhibits a particular concern for this area.

To establish the setting of a text, it is also important to understand the geography, vegetation, animal life, or architecture of the area in which the passage takes place. To portray properly the characters who appear in a text, the preacher needs to establish how each character would have been viewed in his or her own time and cultural setting. Objects that appear in the text may no longer be identifiable in our time, or they may have had specific practical or ritual functions in their own time that we would no longer recognize. Finding the expressions in modern language that approximate those of the ancient text is another important feature of this process. The historical context of these concrete elements of a biblical passage helps set appropriate parameters within which the preacher can choose their counterparts in the contemporary world.

Poetic Sensibilities

Contemporizing calls upon the poetic/cultural sensibilities of the preacher because it requires choosing settings, characters, objects, or language analogous to those that appear in the biblical passage.

The general question when beginning to look for contemporary analogies for an ancient text is, When have my listeners experienced something analogous to the events of the text? The preacher further asks questions about the concrete elements of the passage. The setting of the text prompts the question, What environment in the world of my hearers' experience most closely resembles the setting of the text? Or the preacher might ask, In the world of my hearers, who would most closely resemble the characters in the passage? For objects in the passage, the question would be, What thing in the experience of my hearers might serve the same or similar practical or ritual function as the object in the text? With respect to language, the question is, What words would express the sentiments of the text today?

The success of any attempt to contemporize a text lies in the appropriateness of the contemporary analogies to the elements of the original text in its historical context.

Imaginative Discernment

Since one purpose of contemporizing is to allow the hearer to experience the world of the text with immediacy, the preacher works to choose analogies from the contemporary world that are specific to the world of those who will be listening. Consequently, the preacher who would contemporize the biblical text must be as knowledgeable of the congregation who will hear the sermon as of the historical context of the text. The choice of the most appropriate analogy depends to a degree on an intimate knowledge of the world of those who will be hearing the sermon. Pastors are called upon to develop such familiarity with the congregations they serve.

Strengths and Weaknesses of Contemporizing

A strength of contemporizing the biblical text is that it allows hearers to experience the world of that text with presence and immediacy. They can, with the help of analogies chosen by the preacher, walk through the text as if it were taking place today in a world with which they are familiar.

A weakness implicit in contemporizing is that its specific analogies may not apply closely enough in other cultural settings and once constructed will become outdated. The images that produce the immediacy of experience of the text in this place will not fit as precisely in other places either.

Examples

Translation/paraphrases of biblical texts by Clarence Jordan and Eugene Peterson offer two recent attempts to contemporize the text. Jordan, a Southern Baptist preacher and biblical scholar, was known for his experiment in interracial community at Koinonia Farms in Georgia. Jordan published his "Cotton Patch Versions" of Matthew and John, Luke and Acts, and various Pauline and non-Pauline letters in the 1960s and 1970s. Jordan grounded his work in his knowledge of Greek, history, and formation of the text, and of his own cultural location as a product of the segregated American South. Jordan chose analogies that were powerful and challenging to Christians who lived in a culture in which separation of the races had been justified by the Bible. An example is his substitution of *lynching*

for *crucifixion.* He exchanged place names of cities from the Bible for those in his native region and chose contemporary characters to replace biblical figures. Rome became Washington and Corinth became Atlanta in his rendering of the letters. Today, however, many of Jordan's analogies seem dated. For example, in his almost exclusive emphasis on racial issues, he inevitably exchanges *white man and Negro* for *Jews and Gentiles.*

In the 1990s and into the 21st cent., Eugene Peterson, a Presbyterian pastor and biblical scholar, took on the task of "translating" the entire Bible into contemporary language. In *The Message: The Bible in Contemporary Language*, Peterson took a very different approach from that of Jordan. Rather than replace the names of ancient cities and the race of biblical characters with modern counterparts, he chose to leave those elements of the biblical text, while changing the idiom in which the texts are expressed. Peterson's contemporizing focuses on finding a current idiomatic expression for the phrasing in each ancient text. For example, when St. Paul chastises the Galatians at the beginning of ch. 3, Peterson translates, "You crazy Galatians! Did someone put a hex on you? Have you taken leave of your senses?" While Jordan places emphases on setting and characters, Peterson turns his attention to the language of the text. Jordan wants his readers to identify with the modern places and people that correspond to those in the ancient texts, while Peterson seeks to have his readers recognize the contemporary idiom of the language that refers to the ancient places and people of the texts. Peterson renders John 3:17 this way: "God didn't go to all the trouble of sending his Son merely to point an accusing finger, telling the world how bad it was. He came to help, to put the world right again."

Each writer's approach to contemporizing features a different sense of immediacy for the reader or hearer. Jordan's approach to setting and character creates an environment in which the story is transported into the present-day setting, while Peterson's focus on language moves to transport the reader or hearer into the past. *See* APPLICATION; ARCHAEOLOGY; HISTORICAL CRITICISM; HOLY LAND TOURS.

Bibliography: Clarence Jordan. *The Cotton Patch Gospel.* Vols.1–4. (2004); Eugene H. Peterson. *The Message: The Bible in Contemporary Language.*

(2002); Michael E. Williams and Dennis E. Smith. *The Storyteller's Companion to the Bible.* Vols. 1–13. (1991–2006).

FIGURES OF SPEECH
See METAPHOR AND FIGURES OF SPEECH.

FILM
Tex S. Sample

The coming of electronic culture, with its offering of an increasing range of technologies for worship, brings with it new possibilities for preaching as well. Certainly, one of these is the use of film, especially now that digital form makes for ease of use and high quality of presentation. Our focus here is upon the use of film or video for the preaching task. The suggestions only touch on the range of uses that will likely emerge in the near future.

God's Story

The first consideration for the use of film in preaching is one of priority. That is, the task is to place the film clip in God's story. Film is not to be used simply because it is interesting or entertaining or popular at the time. The purpose of a clip in a sermon is to serve God's story. To fulfill this purpose, it needs to fit into a larger context of worship and proclaiming good news. To be sure, the film itself may be bad news or nihilistic and/or contradictory to Christian faith, but its use in the sermon is there to achieve the more encompassing task of proclaiming God's story.

In his book *Improvisation,* Samuel Wells uses the practice of improvisation in theater as a metaphor for doing ethics. For example, in theatrical improvisation one actor says or does something that is then followed by another actor whose comment or action places this previous comment or action in some larger, more compelling setting that completely changes the meaning and impact of the former. This is a good direction for the use of film in preaching.

Crucifixion and resurrection are a basic way to understand improvisation. Jesus was betrayed, arrested, sent before a kangaroo court, tortured, beaten, mocked, and executed in a public display of his utter powerlessness and agonizing vulnerability. And God answered with history-altering improvisation, with the resurrection. This is the central way of placing the world's story in God's story, although not the only one. A movie clip can be the first move in such improvisation, or it can be in some instances the follow-up move. With this orientation, we can examine some common issues in film use in preaching.

Referentiality in Film

Perhaps the most frequently used format for film in preaching is that of illustration, when a clip from a film makes a point in the sermon. This is a good use of film but also carries with it a problem to be avoided. A sermon can be too preachy, and the film can be as well.

Here it is important to keep in mind the best practice of imagination in the use of images and film. Often scholars complain that film, in contrast to print, takes away one's creative imagination; that is, the viewer does not get to create his or her own images, but these are displayed for the viewer, making him or her a passive recipient of the film. Print, in contrast, allows the reader to create images.

Although the kind of imagination that characterizes reading is important, this view misses the creative practice more associated with film. It misses the fact that the creative impact of film is in the referentiality of images and stories. It is not that the viewer creates images as in print, but that film or images trigger a host of references in the viewer's mind. Herein is the creativity. It is important, then, for the preacher to consider the issue of referentiality.

This is one reason why a preachy use of film is to be avoided. A preachy point can end or short-circuit referentiality or, worse, take it in the direction of referencing the hearers'/viewers' experience with moralizers in their lives, the people who were always spouting "musts" and "shoulds." (*See* MORALISM.)

This raises a related point. Gene Lowry and I have worked on storytelling for more than twenty-five years. One of our conclusions about the use of narrative fits well with the use of film; that is, the redemptive person or current of a story or a movie must be flawed. If the word tries to make use of "Miss Goody Two-shoes" or "Mr. I'm Always Right," it loses gravity and authenticity. An even worse risk occurs when the word comes from a story in which the preacher is the hero. Thus in a movie clip, the most powerful expressions of the word will come from employing the character or event from whom one does not expect it. It is a cinematic version of a Christ showing up where no one anticipates it.

Placement

One of the common complaints about the use of film clips is the difficulty of getting the congregation back to the sermon after the clip is shown. The film tends to overpower the sermon. A basic way to address this problem is through placement. Three suggestions can be made. First, preachers often use clips in the middle of the sermon that should be placed at the end; that is, some scenes are so powerful, so compelling, and so conclusive that there is nothing to be said after they are shown. Move them to the end of the sermon. When the clip ends, the sermon may be over without further comment.

Second, some clips are best used at the beginning of a sermon. The sermon then becomes a commentary on the clip, placing it within God's story as suggested above. In cases like these, the clip begs for comment, for implication, and for connection to the gospel.

Third, other clips can be used in the middle of the sermon. In these cases it may help to give the viewing congregation an assignment, that is, something to look for in the clip. This creates anticipation for what happens after the clip. Thus, when the clip ends, the congregation anticipates a next step. If a congregation is not too large, a preacher can invite comments from the congregation, although this is not necessary to evoke a sense of expectancy beyond the film. Suggestions like these are not exhaustive but indicate directions for using a film in a way that does not lose the congregation.

Congregational Production

Use of film need not be restricted to the use of commercial cinema. Involvement of the congregation in making a film of its own is another possibility. Not only does this bring high motivation to the congregation for the use of a video in worship or preaching, but it also engages the congregation in learning how to use, "read," and view film. In a world of virtual reality, it is important that congregations not simply be passive recipients of film but

learn the ways it is produced. There is perhaps no better way to learn such things than to become producers themselves. This also trains a congregation on the orientations and techniques for placing video in God's story. Testimonies by church members or others, church mission ventures, important moments in the church's life, and many more video possibilities provide an array of resources for use in the homiletic effort. Furthermore, the preacher who has these video creations at his or her disposal in the preaching moment may anticipate a highly motivated congregation who no longer only hears the sermon but becomes active contributors to it.

Some will object that a congregation can never provide video of the quality of motion pictures or television. This is not a disadvantage in the experience of preachers who have made use of it. They suggest that movies and TV always have the problem of being slick. People become used to these offerings. (Notice the ability of people now to turn off hi-tech, quality ads.) Yet because of the sense of ownership by the church and because they are local, congregational productions not only do not suffer from such a lack of technological sophistication but actually benefit from it. Of course, attention to quality is important for local productions, but Hollywood would love to have the devotion of an audience that a congregational effort typically has.

A Few Do's and Don'ts

First, pick a good film and then trust it. The temptation for many preachers is to overexplain or tell the congregation too much about a film. There is hardly anything worse than a sermon that dwells on the obvious after a film has said it quite well.

Second, do not moralize with a film. Avoid showing a video for the sole purpose of telling people what they ought to do. Video can be quite powerful in describing situations and circumstances that are, for example, destructive and harmful. A moralizing comment often works to take away the energy and moral vitality of a well-chosen film.

Third, remember that sometimes a film does not make a point; it is the point. When the preacher then also uses words to make the point, the more fully orbed impact of the movie is often reduced. *See* IMAGINATION/CREATIVITY; TECHNOLOGY; VIDEO CLIPS.

Bibliography: Samuel Wells. *Improvisation: The Drama of Christian Ethics.* (2004).

FOCUS AND FUNCTION STATEMENTS
Don M. Wardlaw

Focus and Function Statements are technical terms devised by Thomas G. Long to ensure that preachers are guided by the biblical text in determining sermon direction. Homileticians have long insisted on the critical importance of the theme sentence as a sermon-planning tool. The theme is a sentence that condenses what the sermon seeks to say. For instance, a theme for a sermon on the prodigal son might read, "God waits for the joyous moment when we return to God." The clearer, the better chance the sermon follows suit. Long's two-sentence approach is one of a number of recent double-barreled approaches to theme sentences (Wilson, 15).

Long's approach is related to that of Fred Craddock. Both identify the biblical text as the source of the theme sentence and they rely in part on rhetoric to establish it. Craddock asks, "What is the text saying? In one sentence, and as simply as possible, state the message of the text." (1985, 122) This is what Tom Long calls a "focus statement." (1989, 86) Craddock also wants the sermon to accomplish something of the original purpose the text had in its original setting; thus he also asks, "What is the text doing?" Tom Long identifies this second sentence the "function statement".

Craddock and Long use these two questions to orient the sermon away from being simply an intellectual venture that explores an abstract principle, a danger with the classical understanding of a theme sentence. They believe that the sermon should perform something of the rhetorical function of the text, whether it is to praise, persuade, encourage, lament, or whatever. The text's meaning, form, and function are linked. The sermon has intellectual and affective dimensions.

Before the NEW HOMILETIC, preachers assumed that a cogent, reasoned appeal was the most dependable way to present the faith. Poesis, metaphor, and story, as imagistic ways of perceiving, served primarily to garnish the argument. Today the logical consistency of the sermon is no less important, but we now gaze with different optics upon the use of theme sentences. Homiletics has shifted from deductive toward inductive, from static toward tensive, from denotative toward connotative.

Sermon Implications

These new slants on homiletical perception make themselves felt even in sermon planning. The sermon function statement has a broader agenda than the sermon focus statement, suggesting not only the focus of the sermon-in-planning, but also the *why* and the *how* of the prospective homily.

The sermon might open with the situation in the congregation's life that elicits this sermon at this time. For instance, a sermon on the prodigal son might identify as the focus statement that "All are in need of generous forgiveness. The pastor might be concerned about the extent to which many in the well-to-do flock are pouring themselves into self-serving pursuits, behavior akin to the prodigal itching for the far country. Early in the sermon preparation, this pastor employs the sermon focus statement in shaping sermon direction, "In view of the extent to which many here are preoccupied with feeding their hedonistic appetites . . ." Such a clause helps the preacher keep in mind why this particular flock needs to hear this sermon.

One might now come to the function statement: the text convicts listeners of self-serving pursuits. The word *focus* customarily implies a concentration on content, on what the text says and the sermon wants to say. On the other hand, the function statement centers on what the sermon wants to happen in the consciousness of the hearers. The sermon function is experiential. It wants the hearers not just to reason together, but more important, to travel together from one place to another, and to feel engaged, heart and soul, as well as mind, in the journey.

This shift in emphasis owes much of its impetus to the New Hermeneutic, a postmodern approach to biblical texts. Such an orientation to interpretation seeks to connect with the life and drama inherent in the language of the biblical text or in the events that gave rise to the text. Here the text assumes the air of a transformative presence, working in dynamic interaction with the interpreter. Text is as text does. And if Scripture is as Scripture does, then the sermon is as the sermon does.

Rhetorical Strategy

Now we are ready to consider *the rhetorical means*. If the sermon seeks to move the hearers from the far country of self-indulgence to the waiting arms of God, what kind of sermon rhetoric might induce that experience? Given our commitment to the eventfulness of Scripture, we know that the parable of the Prodigal Son begs not so much to be defined as to be enacted, not so much to be discussed as to be experienced. Our preacher, therefore, intends not to speak about but from the parable, from the far country of empty indulgences, and from the homecoming of God's embrace.

In this approach, the cognitive is reframed and retrained to write scripts rather than essays, to make of sermons moving pictures rather than lectures on still life. Such will take all the gray matter the preacher can muster to bring as much integrity as possible to the sermon's faithful cultural translation of the biblical text. Maybe the preacher will create a contemporary narrative that reprises Luke's parable. Or maybe the preacher will hold up to the light of God's revelation some image from the prodigal story and slowly turn that image like a diamond in the sun. Or maybe the preacher will string together several seemingly unrelated, contemporary events, all of which, as the sermon plays out, come into focus as the prodigal makes his way home to the waiting father. The way the preacher holds these images to the light can either make or break the sermon. While it calls for a rich, playful imagination, it just as surely calls for careful reflection that can discipline that creativity to serve faithfully the intent of the biblical text. *See* INDUCTIVE; THE BIG IDEA; THEME SENTENCE.

Bibliography: Fred B. Craddock. *Preaching.* (1985); Thomas G. Long. *The Witness of Preaching.* (1989); Paul Scott Wilson. *Preaching and Homiletical Theory.* (2004).

FUSION
Paul Scott Wilson

Fusion is a practice in sermons that attempts to establish a seamless unity between the biblical text and the congregation such that listeners discover their own reflection in the text and experience themselves to be enrolled in the biblical story. The term is adapted from Hans-Georg Gadamer, who said the goal of hermeneutics is a "fusion of horizons" (Gadamer 1975, 273), an overcoming of the gap between the biblical text and contemporary time such that the two horizons unite. His metaphor speaks of understanding a text in its own time and culture before venturing what it means for today.

Fusion has distinctive features in homiletics: (1) Fusion is related to the purpose and function of God's Word as revelation and appropriately takes place in the sermon, not as a private act of interpretation. (2) Fusion points to something discernible in sermon language, not primarily to the phenomenon of understanding a text. The story of people in the biblical text becomes the story of the listeners through the two being brought together with the temporal and cultural gap between them dissolved. As in cooking or music, the two separate identities are not lost in fusion; rather, each is enhanced by the presence of the other. The preacher shows listeners their own reflection in the mirror of the text. (3) Whereas analogy treats the text as simile using *like* or *as* ("We are like the people in the text"), fusion is extended metaphor; the listeners need to enter the story in order to understand. (4) Fusion ideally brings listeners into relationship with God in the text. Biblical people are portrayed as having faith issues concerning doubt, sin, waywardness, injustice, and so forth, of the sort that most people experience. For all the real and important differences that separate them and us, for the preaching moment these are transcended and overcome. With fusion, faith unites then and now.

Fusion happens for David when Nathan tells him the story of a rich man who stole a poor man's lamb to feed to his visitors and adds, "You are the man!" (2 Sam 12:7). Fusion happens when a child hears Jesus' words as personal address: "Let the children come to me . . . for it is to such as these that the kingdom of God belongs" (Luke 18:16). Fusion is found in medieval art when biblical people are painted in costume of the day, yet fusion is more than just making a text contemporary: the focus is the listener's life before God. Fusion is the creation of "then as now" or "now as then" when the focus is theology, matters of faith, and Israel as church.

Fusion happens in every tradition, for instance, when the words of annunciation spoken to Mary are heard by listeners as addressed to themselves or when Jesus' road to Jerusalem (beginning in Luke 9 and ending on the cross) is portrayed as a road we know well—the road to all of our disappointments including our denial of Christ. The preacher's challenge is to discern how the text's story is the listeners'. To tell it so that "they are there" or "there is here" can be accomplished best if no scenery change or bridging words are used.

Richard Lischer notes that in much African American preaching the hearers are "enrolled in the world of the Bible." The Bible mirrors their lives, even as life "mirrors or replicates the figures and stories of the Bible" (Lischer 1995, 201). Moses is not only a historical person, but he is also the present leader (e.g., Martin Luther King Jr.'s "I have been to the mountaintop") leading them to liberation. Pharaoh lived in Egypt, but he also lives in the big plantation house.

In preaching about Naaman (2 Kgs 5:1-14), Carolyn Ann Knight moves seamlessly from his story to now; in other words, she does not suspend the story to talk about the congregation but leaves it in place so that listeners are present in the story:

> [His assistants pleaded,] "You have been washing in the waters of Damascus all your life, but you have not been cured."
> Part of our problem, as we survey this sick situation, that has saturated our society, is that we have been washing in rivers where there is no healing and no power. We have been associating and aligning ourselves with people who cannot help us. You can wash in political rivers if you want, but that is not where your healing can be found. You can wash in economic rivers if you want, but that is not where your healing can be found. You can wash in sexual rivers if you want, but that is not where your healing can be found. You can wash in the biggest river, the pretty river if you want, but that is not where your healing is.
> "Captain Naaman, why not follow these simple instructions and go wash in the Jordan?" (Knight 2001, 49–50)

Fusion recovers for preaching something like a naive reading of the biblical text. What is its value? Does analogy not accomplish the same thing? Fusion treats the entire story as a metaphor of contemporary experience instead of one aspect of it, as is the case with analogy. Fusion can seem more imaginative and involving and may communicate the text at a deeper level. Finally, faith issues are the immediate topic with fusion. The preacher needs to make no special transitions to approach them. *See* APPLICATION; BRIDGING THEN AND NOW; CONTEMPORIZING.

Bibliography: Hans-Georg Gadamer. *Truth and Method.* (1975); Carolyn Ann Knight. "A Simple Solution to a Complex Problem." *Outstanding Black Sermons.* Edited by Walter S. Thomas. Vol. 4. (2001); Richard Lischer. *The Preacher King: Martin Luther King Jr. and the Word That Moved America.* (1995); Paul Scott Wilson. *Broken Words: Reflections on the Craft of Preaching.* (2004).

ILLUSTRATION AND STORIES
Michael Duduit

"Once upon a time . . ." There is something about those words that grabs our attention and makes us anticipate what is about to come. That is because we love stories. And that is why stories are such a vital tool in the preacher's hands: because they can engage both the heart and the mind in driving home biblical truth.

As Bryan Chapell has observed, illustrations "are integral to effective preaching, not because they entertain, but because they expand and deepen the applications the mind and heart can make" (2001, 13).

What Is an Illustration?

To *illustrate* literally means "to put light on a subject." Just as you might focus additional light on an object in order to better see it, so an illustration is used by the speaker to enable the listeners to better "see" the truth or idea being presented. Thus, an illustration is a rhetorical tool used to aid the listener in understanding the truth being presented, in connecting emotionally with that truth, and/or to motivate the listener toward some action or decision based on that truth. Illustrations are a venture from the abstract concept to the tangible example. They are a move from the theoretical to the particular and familiar. The preacher uses illustrations to make clear or understandable some theological or biblical idea or application. They are not used for their inherent value, merely to entertain, to impress, or to fill in time in the sermon. If they do not help the listener better understand something you are trying to communicate, they do not belong in the sermon.

Haddon W. Robinson notes that illustrations are used in the sermon to "restate, explain, validate, or apply ideas by relating them to tangible experiences. . . . An illustration, like the picture on television, makes clear what the speaker explains" (2001, 149).

But not only do illustrations aid in understanding an idea; they also help the listener emotionally and spiritually connect with that idea in a way that can lead to life change. Propositions are an important element of preaching, but they rarely do the job on their own; an effectively chosen illustration can engage the emotions and motivation in a way that a proposition alone often fails to do.

That is why Chapell asserts, "Illustrations are not supplemental to good exposition; they are a necessary form of exposition in which biblical truths are explained and applied to the emotions and the will as well as to the intellect. Illustrations will not allow mere head knowledge. They exegete Scripture in the terms of human experience to create a whole-person encounter with God's Word" (2001, 13).

Illustrations have a unique power to drive home a message. No wonder Jesus used them regularly, as have most of the great preachers in Christian history.

Types of Illustrations

Illustrations can take various forms, from a vivid restatement to an apt play on words to a gripping story. Among the most frequently used types of illustrations are comparisons. Direct comparisons include simile (a brief comparison expressing the similarity between two things) and analogy (which is a lengthier comparison). Indirect comparisons include metaphor (a statement that implies one thing is like another without explicitly stating so, such as "You are the salt of the earth") and allegory (which operates like an extended metaphor). (*See* METAPHOR AND FIGURES OF SPEECH.)

In the contemporary church, visual illustrations are increasingly used, whether as a physical object woven into the sermon or a short film or movie clip. Testimonies and interviews are also increasingly popular illustrative forms; within sermons they are sometimes presented live and sometimes on video.

Yet the most common form of illustration in preaching is the story or narrative. At the heart of our Christian faith is a story—the story of God's creation, humanity's fall, and Christ's redemptive action. Within God's inspired Word, that larger story is told by the use of a multitude of stories—Adam and Eve in the garden of Eden (Gen 2–3), Abraham leaving home at the call of God (Gen 12), Moses leading his people out of bondage in Egypt (Exod 3–15), David facing the giant Goliath with just a sling and five stones (1 Sam 17), and on it goes. The major element of Jesus' teaching consists of stories—parables about a lost coin and a lost son, about a sower and a persistent widow. God has revealed truth to us again and again in story.

There is power in story, as preachers have known over the centuries. There is an old saying among preachers that the congregation may forget the outline but will remember our stories. Indeed, many contemporary preachers have discovered that one of the most effective methods for preaching to postmodern audiences is the retelling of biblical stories. (*See* EMERGING CHURCH PREACHING.)

Stories are a valuable tool for the preacher because they not only shed light on the biblical truth being presented but they also engage the listeners and allow them to imaginatively enter into an experience in which that truth can make a powerful impact on their emotions and their will. In fact, well-chosen stories often carry much of the force of the sermon. Fred B. Craddock observes, "In good preaching what is referred to as illustrations are, in fact, stories or anecdotes which do not illustrate the point; rather they are the point. In other words, a story may carry in its bosom the whole message rather than the illumination of a message which had already been related in another but less clear way" (1990, 204).

A biblical example is the story of the prophet Nathan confronting King David (2 Sam 12). Rather than initially confronting David with his sin, Nathan tells the king a story about a wealthy man and a poor man and his precious lamb. By the time the story is over, David is so emotionally involved that he is ready to execute the wealthy man who took the poor man's lamb. How much more powerful, then, was Nathan's moment of confrontation when he looked at David and pronounced, "You are the man!" (v. 7). Stories have the power to change lives.

There are different approaches to the use of story in sermons. One is the biblical story, in which the preacher uses a narrative drawn from the pages of Scripture to illustrate some truth. Another approach is the personal story, in which the preacher shares an anecdote from his or her life to shed light on the idea being discussed. Preachers also use historical stories, or stories drawn from literature or popular culture (such as television or film), or even fictional stories created specifically to illustrate the truth being preached.

While preachers use stories primarily as illustrative tools within the sermon, sometimes the sermon itself takes the form of an extended narrative. And even when such an approach is not taken, homileticians like Eugene Lowry have emphasized the need to "plot" or craft the sermons much as one would create a narrative.

Where Can a Preacher Find Illustrations?

The effective preacher is always on the hunt for powerful stories that will make a difference in sermons. Illustrations and stories are found in many places, including:

1. personal experience or that of family and friends;
2. experiences of members of the congregation or community;
3. books, magazines, and newspaper articles;
4. movies or television shows;
5. historical and current events;
6. sermons of other preachers;
7. preaching periodicals and website resources;
8. published collections of illustrations. (This is the least desirable source, but one most preachers nevertheless turn to from time to time.)

There are some cautions to keep in mind in selecting illustrations. One is to seek illustrations and stories to which your listeners can relate. Though we may wish otherwise, it is a reality that illustrations drawn from Shakespeare and ancient history will likely not engage a listener as well as a story from a popular television show or the events in yesterday's newspaper. In that same vein, make sure the illustration you use does not require explanation; if you have to explain how the story illustrates the truth you are explaining, then it did not really illustrate. Look for one that will do the job on its own.

Another caution is to know your sources. In an age when stories fly through cyberspace into millions of e-mail inboxes, be sure that you do not too quickly share one of those stories as an illustration without trying to verify its authenticity. Many such stories are distributed as true when, in fact, they are not. Before simply lifting a story from an e-mail or website and using it, take advantage of some of the Web resources (such as Snopes.com) to check out the accuracy of stories. Your credibility as God's messenger is too valuable to risk for the sake of an illustration that is not what it appears to be.

Illustrations help us to engage our listeners and help them better understand the biblical truth that is being presented in our sermons. That makes them a vital tool in the minister's toolbox.

Bibliography: Bryan Chapell. *Using Illustrations to Preach with Power.* (2001); Fred B. Craddock. *Preaching.* (1990); Eugene Lowry. *The Homiletical Plot: The Sermon as Narrative Art Form.* (2000); Haddon W. Robinson. *Biblical Preaching: The Development and Delivery of Expository Messages.* (2001).

IMAGINATION/CREATIVITY
Thomas H. Troeger

An imaginative preacher can take a biblical text and create a sermon that sets the Word of God singing and dancing in our hearts, empowering us to live the gospel more completely.

Common American speech often uses *imagination* and *creativity* as synonyms, but both terms repel precise definition. We describe people who are creative as "imaginative" because they have the capacity to envision, to "image" something new and to present it in a way that engages and delights us with fresh insight. Preachers, however, often resist the use of the imagination in their sermons because *imagination* is an ambiguous word. Although it is often synonymous with creativity, it also can be equated with pure fantasy, as when we dismiss someone's fear, saying, "It is all in your imagination." Furthermore, theologians have sometimes attacked the imagination for creating idolatrous understandings of God. But since the imagination, like all the faculties of the human mind, is a gift from God, we should not ignore it simply because it can be misused.

When preachers faithfully use their imaginations in the pulpit, they are doing far more than making their sermons captivating. They are demonstrating to their listeners what it means to be made in the image of God, for the very first act of God that appears in the Bible is that of Creator (Gen 1). To be made in the image of God, then, is to be created to create, to use one's imagination. Preachers manifest the divine image whenever they employ the imagination to create sermons that are in harmony with the infinitely imaginative God. This God created fifty billion galaxies, this blue green mossy marble on which we live, and a macramé multiplicity of DNA patterns. This God redeems the whole broken creation through an itinerant rabbi from the wrong side of the tracks who was killed and yet lives, and who is the very Word through whom everything was made in the first place! Biblical preaching is imaginative because the Bible gives witness to an imaginative God.

In the 19th cent. homileticians began to appreciate imagination as an essential gift for preaching. By the end of the 20th cent. liberation theologies amplified imagination's creative role as homileticians worked to re-imagine (re-image) God, the church, and the global community in ways that more fully embody a generous and inclusive vision of the Christian gospel. Homileticians encouraged preachers to develop their imaginations in order to communicate more effectively with people raised in a multimedia electronic culture and to provide alternatives to the imagined world of a consumer society that thrives on images of gratuitous sex and violence.

Preachers need at least three kinds of imagination in order to exercise their creative gifts in ways that are theologically sound: the conventional, the empathic, and the visionary.

The conventional imagination employs the world of Scripture, symbol, and religious practice that is alive in the congregation. Effective preachers honor the conventional imagination of the people to whom they preach because they realize it is the congregation's imaged/imagined world of holy meaning. It is a world filled with memory and spiritual power.

The empathic imagination is the capacity to step into another's shoes, to entertain experiences and perspectives unlike the preacher's own. The empathic imagination empowers preachers to help their people stretch their hearts beyond their own concerns to those of God, the larger world of the human family and of Planet Earth. (*See* EXEGESIS OF THE CONGREGATION, DENOMINATION.)

The visionary imagination is deliberately attentive to the fresh and unexpected movement of the Spirit so that the preacher is given to see new ways of understanding the Bible and tradition, new worlds, new language for articulating faith in Christ and identifying the holiest dreams of the heart of God.

Creative preaching interrelates these three forms of imagination so that each can enrich, challenge, and correct the other. For example, when the conventional imagination enshrines prejudices and practices that are at odds with the gospel, the empathic imagination can awaken our feeling for those who have been injured by our distorted beliefs, and the visionary imagination can picture what a new church and a new community of healing and hospitality would look like.

On the other hand, the conventional imagination may preserve values and insights that can help us test if it is indeed the Spirit of the living God who is moving us to preach some new vision or insight.

It is helpful in the creation of sermons to view a passage of the Bible from the perspective of each kind of imagination. Consider, for example, Luke 15:11-32, traditionally titled the parable of the Prodigal Son. The conventional imagination treasures this story as a quintessential image of the grace of God. A preacher would want to honor the pastoral and theological significance of that image for the congregation. At the same time, the empathic imagination might ask what is missing from the image for girls and women, and the visionary imagination might ask how to expand the conventional imagination to make it more inclusive of all people (*see* FEMINIST PERSPECTIVES).

None of this imaginative work precludes doing careful scholarly work: looking at the passage in its context, finding out what exegetes have to say about the parable, reading it in Greek, Hebrew, and various translations, and using all the scholarly tools at one's disposal. Far from being antithetical, scholarship and imagination feed and stimulate each other. Preachers blend them together in the act of creating the sermon so as to engage the imaginations of the listeners in ways that renew their faith in Christ and their gratitude for "the depth of the riches and wisdom and knowledge of God" (Rom 11:33a).

Bibliography: Gregor T. Goethels. *The Electronic Golden Calf: Images, Religion and the Making of Meaning.* (1990); Richard A. Jensen. *Envisioning the Word: The Use of Visual Images in Preaching, with CD-ROM.* (2005); David H. Kelsey. *Imagining Redemption.* (2005); Thomas H. Troeger. *Imagining a Sermon.* (1990).

MAGNIFICATION
Paul Scott Wilson

Magnification is the homiletic practice of enhancing God's action in or behind a biblical text in order that God may have significant focus in the sermon. This practice presumes that (1) historical criticism does not necessarily concern itself with God and matters of revelation, (2) one of the purposes of preaching is to speak about God and God's will for humanity and creation, and (3) not all biblical texts focus in significant ways on God. David and Goliath becomes a text for preaching only if one assumes that God guided the stone that David shot (1 Sam 17); the book of Esther does not mention God, and to preach it, one needs to assume that Esther is God's representative. One could preach on Noah and never mention God, since only two verses out of four chapters mention God as the author of the flood (Gen 6–9). Excellent preachers learn magnification, both in the biblical sense of praising God (Ps 34:3; Luke 1:46) and in the contemporary English sense of making great or enlarging the focus upon God's action.

Among the practices that preachers may try are the following: (1) Make God's action the subject of the theme sentence of the sermon. God's actions are always significant, but biblical texts and sermons do not always render them so. (2) If God's action is barely mentioned in the biblical text, retell the text in the sermon so that God's true role is front and center. Take time with Moses' burning bush for God to set it on fire, add the smoke, add the crackling sounds, and create the heat. (3) Reflect on the biblical scene theologically, bringing church teachings about God to bear on it. (4) Take advantage of sermon references to God as opportunities to offer even brief praise. The purpose of magnification is not to entertain through sustained development of Scripture but to proclaim the wonders of God's name.

Bibliography: Paul S. Wilson. *God Sense: Reading the Bible for Preaching.* (2001).

METAPHOR AND FIGURES OF SPEECH
Linda Lee Clader

Metaphor and other figures of speech lend emotional and intellectual impact to preaching, involve the listener in the creation of the sermon, encourage a community's openness to mystery, and invite the Holy Spirit to inspire faith and action. Figurative language's power to influence listeners demands that the preacher attend not only to the enrichment it offers, but also to its dangers.

A. Introduction: The Power of Figurative Language
B. Metaphor and Imagination
   1. Metaphor
   2. Metaphorical Figures
       a. Simile
       b. Metonymy
       c. Image and symbol
C. Other Figures of Speech and Rhetorical Techniques
   1. Figures That Aid Memory
       a. Formula
       b. Refrain
       c. Alliteration
       d. Anaphora
       e. Homoioteleuton
       f. Rhythm and rhyme
   2. Other Figures and Techniques
       a. Tricolon
       b. Antithesis and parallelism
       c. Personification
       d. Direct speech
   3. Techniques with a Twist
       a. Hyperbole
       b. Irony, puns, and wordplay

A. Introduction: The Power of Figurative Language

Public speakers, poets, and other writers have always taken care to arrange language in ways that please the ear, arouse emotion, excite the imagination, or otherwise draw attention to something the author wishes to emphasize. In addition, those who compose for the ear rather than for the eye must find ways to aid the memory of both the speaker and the listener. These aspects of public speaking have been the subject of a vast literature, beginning with the works of Greek philosophers Plato (e.g., *Gorgias*) and Aristotle (*Poetics, Rhetoric*) and Roman rhetoricians Cicero (e.g., *The Orator, Brutus*) and Quintilian (*Institutio Oratoria*) and continuing to the present. The literature on metaphor, in particular, has burgeoned in recent years, as cognitive linguists have begun to explore this aspect of language as a fundamental element in how human beings think.

Because preaching is an oral/aural form of communication (*see* ORAL/AURAL COMMUNICATION), preachers have easily applied techniques derived from the rhetorical tradition to their work. In spite of some suspicion that a too artful sermon may lack authenticity, most preachers have understood that care in construction, delivery, and choice of words is an appropriate concern in proclaiming the gospel. But preaching is not only a rhetoric of persuasion; it is also an art. Thus, preachers have drawn from theories of language related to classical rhetoric and from techniques developed by poets and dramatists. As Paul Ricoeur states, "[P]oetry and oratory mark out two distinct universes of discourse. Metaphor, however, has a foot in each domain" (1977, 12). The same can be said of other figures of speech.

A preacher's goals are not usually restricted to conveyance of information, but include a desire to excite listeners' imagination or open their hearts to receive direction from the Holy Spirit. Meeting these goals depends on a preacher's comfort with the realms of ambiguity and mystery, areas in which poetry, more easily than prosaic discourse, makes its home. Indeed, much of theological thought is heavily dependent on poetic or metaphorical speech, so preachers and other theologians need to become conversant with the technique of using figurative language and also with the aesthetic, linguistic, psychological, and philosophical theories about how figurative language functions.

As homiletical theory has turned toward the listener in exploring the dimensions of preaching, it has become more and more obvious that preachers need to attend to the way not only the speaker but also the listener uses figurative language. Preachers can take great care in choosing words or expressions to fit their purpose, but if listeners make associations that conflict with those expressions, the preachers have not communicated what they intended. Recent scholarship on figurative language has focused on aspects that are intrinsic to language at its most basic—even unconscious—level. Most preachers are aware that listeners may have hot buttons that a word or image may trigger without the preacher's awareness, but many do not realize that the highly metaphorical content of all language is likely to trigger a multitude of associations that

shape or color how the most common discourse is heard. The bibliography at the close of this article will direct preachers to a few of the basic works that explore this aspect of figurative language.

B. Metaphor and Imagination

1. Metaphor

Metaphor is a linguistic phenomenon in which two words or concepts are juxtaposed to create a tensive relationship. Through most of history, metaphor has been understood primarily as a literary tool, a technique that writers or speakers use intentionally to enliven or inject ambiguity into their expression. Metaphor requires some effort of the listener to receive and process the energy created by the "not quiteness" of the implied comparison or juxtaposition. Metaphor has therefore been associated with poetic diction because poets often use it to imply more than they appear to say.

A metaphorical statement can be as simple as two single words held up next to each other: "*The LORD is my rock, my fortress . . . / my shield,* and the *horn* of my salvation, my *stronghold*" (Ps 18:2). We understand that the psalm is not saying God is literally a rock or a shield, and yet we also understand that it is saying something beyond "God is really strong." This tension between literal identification and mere coloration is where the power of metaphor resides.

A metaphor can be extended, however, far beyond just a pair of words. The psalm quoted above goes on to describe God as an erupting volcano, riding on a cherub, bowing down the heavens, thundering, flashing lightning, and reaching down and pulling the psalmist out of waters. The simple equation "God is my rock" has been expanded to an entire story, but the medium is still basically metaphor. Upon reading the psalm, we do not find ourselves envisioning God as a volcano, but we have a vastly richer vision of the psalmist's experience, perhaps one that enriches our theological imagination.

Indeed, metaphor is fundamental to theological thought. Since no one has seen God, all our language about God must be in some way metaphorical (e.g., *Father, Shepherd*, even the title *Lord*). Jesus himself has been called "the metaphor and symbol of God incarnate" (Avis 1999, 111). Throughout history, some of the most vexing theological questions have arisen from attempts to translate metaphorical concepts from one language or culture to another (e.g., *Son of God*); and amid the current tensions within and between Christian communities today, a significant factor is the level of comfort with metaphorical language.

Christian hymns offer a treasury of theological metaphor and are a good place for preachers to turn to sensitize themselves to how metaphor rules our tradition. A prime example is the familiar Easter hymn of John of Damascus, translated by John Mason Neale as "Come, Ye Faithful, Raise the Strain." This hymn identifies resurrection with spring and with bursting from prison; death with sleep; Christ with light and rising like the sun; and sin with a long, dark winter. Most fundamentally, the entire first verse implicitly identifies the resurrection of Christ with Israel's miraculous liberation from bondage and passing through the sea. A worthwhile exercise might be to play with a single one of the identifications: In what ways is Christ light? What does that metaphor convey? What might be its limitations? Does it always work, or can it be problematic for someone?

The Christian tradition of reading the OT typologically is also fundamentally a metaphorical process. Israel's exodus from Egypt is not literally the same as the resurrection of Jesus, nor is Israel literally the forebear of most Gentile Christians. Abraham's sacrifice of Isaac is an imperfect analogue for the saving work of Christ. The story of the flood contains colorful elements that have little to do with resurrection or baptism. But the presence of the OT story next to the NT one creates tension or generates an electrical current that enhances the meaning of an individual story and enriches the Christian tradition.

Recent scholarship, primarily by cognitive scientists and linguists, claims that metaphor is not just a decorative figure used intentionally by an artist, but is also inherent in the way human beings think, having its origins in our very existence as embodied creatures. Our language, these scholars argue, is built on a basically physical foundation, and we are hard-pressed to avoid using vocabulary and expressions that are not grounded in concepts arising from common, embodied experience. For example, note the idea of building a foundation, with a base in physical reality—expressions that are so familiar to us that we may be hard-pressed to notice that they are metaphorical. Some common conceptual metaphors are: "Life is a journey" (*You're making progress; she has reached adulthood; I'm on my way*), "Emotion is heat" (*He was boiling with rage; my heart burns with love*), and "Happiness is up" (*I'm on cloud nine*). Specifically religious applications of these might include "Jesus is the Way," Wesley's strange "warming of the heart," and Isaiah's "Arise, shine; for your light has come" (Isa 60:1).

Preachers need to be aware of both aspects of metaphor: how they can use it consciously to extend meaning, arouse attention, or excite the imagination, and how it may be operating at an unconscious level among listeners and speakers. A further concern is the fact that metaphorical language may be heard differently by different communities or individuals. In some cases, what the speaker considers metaphorical shorthand (referring to mental illness as "demonic") might be interpreted literally by a listener (the suffering individual is possessed by a personalized, superhuman being). Another case would be the classic problem of identifying light as good and dark as evil, an ancient and common identification that has been seen as racially charged. (*See* GENDER, RACE, AND ETHNICITY.) But every preacher has had the experience of unintentionally offending—or inspiring—someone who experienced a strong reaction to an image or an expression that the preacher thought harmless or a throwaway line. The power of metaphor lies in the very ambiguity that can open hearts—and also confuse or wound them.

2. Metaphorical Figures

All of these techniques and linguistic figures, whether applied intentionally or unconsciously, create the kind of gap between ideas, or between the familiar and the unfamiliar, that Paul Scott Wilson has represented with his image of a spark flying between two electrodes (1988, 33f.). They excite the imagination, involve the listener in the creation of the message, and offer space for the action of the Holy Spirit.

a. Simile. Metaphor is often contrasted with simile, a figure that also holds two entities close for comparison, but without the tension that arises from metaphor's ambiguity. "God is *like* a rock, God is *like* a shield" does not have the force of the language in Ps 18, cited above. In general, a simile depends on some quality or trait that the two entities have in common: God is strong or immovable or hard like a rock; God stands between me and an enemy, like a shield. The comparison may be a long enough stretch to be almost outlandish, once the reader starts to think about it: "[Those who delight in the law] are like trees planted by streams of water, / which yield their fruit in its season" (Ps 1:1-3), and yet it is still clear that the psalmist is not saying that a human being is a tree. The force of poetry is there, but the reader or listener is not challenged to determine whether the statement is true or *how* it is true. The ambiguity is resolved.

b. Metonymy. Another type of metaphorical figure is metonymy, where a part is used to stand for the whole, or a substance for the entity made of it, or a container for the entity it contains. Scripture offers a wealth of examples: "Your *hand* will find out all your enemies" (Ps 21:8); *Jacob* or *Israel*, the proper name of the patriarch, standing for the whole of the people; the *Temple* as shorthand for the presence of God; *tongues* for language; *gold* for wealth. Such expressions are so familiar as to have lost their impact, but creating a new one may excite quick interest.

c. Image and symbol. Metaphorical language is also fundamental to the power of image. People tend to visualize what they are hearing, probably on account of language's basis in embodied existence. Imagery is the deliberate creation of a verbal picture, an intentional challenge to listeners to "see" with their ears in order to enliven discourse. It is not a long stretch from here to the use of symbol, which is a visual image that represents something abstract, but in a conventionalized way, such as the cross representing the passion of Jesus, the banner of Christianity, defense against death or evil, and so on. Another fruitful exercise for a preacher would be to dig into some familiar symbolic language of the faith and follow the strings of mental associations that symbol can produce.

C. Other Figures of Speech and Rhetorical Techniques

If metaphor operates to open windows and leaves room for the imagination to play, speakers have found a variety of techniques to aid in directing that imagination. The most obvious way to arouse interest in listeners is to appeal to their emotions—fear, sorrow, pride, gratitude, shame, and so on—but artful speaking can also arouse interest by its cleverness of expression and even by the music

of the language. The basic impulse is to find ways to make a specific aspect of the composition stand apart from the rest. Students of cognitive poetics call this foregrounding (Stockwell 2002, 13–25).

One purpose of such foregrounding is to make the content memorable. Any speaker intends for his or her speech to make enough of a difference that it will be remembered, either long enough to effect a change in the listener or the community, or long enough to participate in the development of an argument or line of thought. In addition, preachers speaking without written prompts will find techniques to help them retain the content or the structure of their preaching. Although various figures of speech may have that practical function, they can also function as pleasurable forms of speaking and engage the interest of the listener simply by their artfulness.

1. Figures That Aid Memory

Simple repetition is foundational to the retention of information. Many figures of speech and rhetorical techniques, therefore, are in essence variations on modes of repetition. Even a single sound, repeated over several words or phrases, can make an expression memorable.

a. Formula. Speakers who operate in a truly oral style—that is, speaking without any notes and composing, to some degree, in the very act of speaking—depend on formulas and other kinds of repetition to keep their ideas in mind and give themselves time to remember the next phrase or topic. The formulas may be short expressions echoing biblical or hymnic material (e.g., *daily bread, God's steadfast mercy, amazing grace*), full phrases or sentences, or formulas the speaker has developed over years of such discourse (e.g., Martin Luther King Jr., "I have a dream"). African American preaching, in particular, has been characterized by forms of repetition that reveal its foundation in truly oral composition and delivery. (*See* AFRICAN AMERICAN PREACHING PERSPECTIVES.) Whether or not they compose and preach their sermons using a written manuscript, most preachers understand that in order for an idea to stick with their listeners, the idea needs to be offered more than once, preferably in a variety of modes. They may repeat the idea, or they may attach the idea to a word or expression that is then repeated.

b. Refrain. Many hymns make use of a repeated refrain, offering the singer a respite perhaps from intense concentration on remembering the words, or simply the pleasure of familiarity. Some psalms (e.g., Ps 136), similarly, employ refrains that may reflect a dialogic liturgical performance. Preachers sometimes adopt this pattern of verse and refrain, training the listeners to chime in at a chorus or to anticipate the repetition. The use of repetition can thus function as a pleasurable source of suspense.

c. **Alliteration.** Repetition of single sounds can also serve as memory devices, for the speaker and for the listener. For example, alliteration refers to the practice of beginning a series of words with the same sound. Its prevalence in popular culture—comic names, clichés, and slogans—is evidence of its relationship to memory: *Donald Duck; baby blues; fatal flaw; God, guns, and guts.* Preachers may develop formulas that are more memorable on account of this kind of repetition (e.g., *bear our burdens; times of trial; repentance, reconciliation, and renewal*), and may find that their congregations are thus enabled to recite the compositions—and the ideas—in response.

d. **Anaphora.** Anaphora refers to the repetition of either an entire word or a series of words at the beginnings of phrases. In arguably his most poetic (and probably most often recited) passage, St. Paul uses several forms of repetition, including anaphora: "*Love* is patient; *love* is kind; *love* is not envious or boastful or arrogant or rude" (1 Cor 13:4-5). And in his 1963 speech at the Lincoln Memorial in Washington, D.C., Martin Luther King, Jr. introduced a series of prophetic visions with the words, "I have a dream," which he later turned into a refrain, "I have a dream *today!*"

e. **Homoioteleuton.** The passage from 1 Corinthians cited above goes on to use anaphora's opposite, *ending* sentences or phrases with the same word or sound (homoioteleuton): "It bears all things, believes all things, hopes all things, endures all things. . . . When I was a child, I spoke like a child, I thought like a child, I reasoned like a child" (1 Cor 13:7-11). This form of repetition also has the effect of emphasizing the part of the expression that is *not* repeated: "bears . . . believes . . . hopes . . . endures; spoke . . . thought . . . reasoned."

f. **Rhythm and rhyme.** In his Gettysburg Address, Abraham Lincoln combined anaphora with other forms of repetition: "We cannot dedicate, we cannot consecrate, we cannot hallow this ground." This statement not only repeats "we cannot . . . ," but also uses words with parallel rhythm

and rhyme: "dedicate" and "consecrate." In the face of competing renderings, the familiar King James translation of the Lord's Prayer may attribute some of its resiliency to echoes of sound and rhythm: "Thy kingdom come; thy will be done." Again, if a preacher wishes to develop the ability to use rhythm and rhyme, there is no better place to begin looking than the hymns and prayers of our tradition.

2. Other Figures and Techniques

a. **Tricolon.** Lincoln's speech, cited above, also employs tricolon, or the use of three of any expression. Sets of three are frequent in oratory as well as European and American popular culture, and seem to be the longest series the memory can retain easily (*blood, sweat, and tears*). The elements in a tricolon, as in Lincoln's example, often grow longer as they proceed, to create a climax.

b. **Antithesis and parallelism.** More often than groups of three, speakers depend on pairs of ideas, sounds, or images. Possibly because human beings are binary—two eyes, two legs, and so on—there seems to be a natural or innate tendency to think in binary oppositions: *black and white, up and down, dead or alive, more or less.* An extension of this tendency results in antithesis. Built on the concept of *on the one hand . . . on the other*, antithesis can be as simple as a balanced contrast between two objects or as elaborate as whole sentences or arguments, paired through sound, rhythm, structure, or similar content.

Biblical poetry offers countless examples of parallel structure without the sharp contrast that creates antithesis (e.g., "I will not accept a bull from your house, or goats from your folds. / For every wild animal of the forest is mine, / the cattle on a thousand hills. / I know all the birds of the air, / and all that moves in the field is mine" [Ps 50:9-11]). A preacher may use a similar structure, elaborated to the level of illustration or story. Parallelism creates for the listener a sense of balance and control. Used too often, like any of the figures described here, it could turn preaching stale by giving it a static quality.

c. **Personification.** A speaker can attract sudden attention to an image or idea by the use of personification, presenting an inanimate object or animal as if it were capable of thought, intentional action, or speech. Jesus' proclamation, "If these were silent, the stones would shout out" (Luke 19:40), is memorable in part because of the shocking idea of shouting stones. Wisdom literature, likewise, offers a mine of examples, from personified maxims such as "Wine is a mocker" (Prov 20:1), to the elaborate personification of Wisdom in Sirach (Ecclesiasticus) 15 and elsewhere.

d. Direct speech. A related rhetorical technique is for the preacher to impersonate a character or idea in a sermon by using direct speech in the voice of that character. Speaking in the voice of the character rather than simply reporting events enlivens a narrative and contributes to emotional impact by bringing that character into direct contact with the listener. A particularly powerful version of this technique is when the preacher quotes God or Christ speaking to the congregation: *You are my child, in whom I am well pleased.* Because the impact can be so strong, the potential for manipulation is also strong, and such direct speech is therefore a tool that must be used with caution.

3. Techniques with a Twist

a. Hyperbole. When speakers intentionally exaggerate beyond what is normal or credible, they are engaged in hyperbole. Colloquial expressions using hyperbole are common (*He is about a million years old; I thought I would die laughing*) and frequently carry a comic tone. Often, too, hyperbole results from a desire to express a strong visceral reaction or emotional condition metaphorically, and people attempting to describe spiritual experiences often resort to hyperbolic metaphor ("I know a person in Christ who fourteen years ago was caught up to the third heaven" [2 Cor 12:2]; compare also the imagery in Ps 18). Prophetic literature operates consistently in the realm of hyperbole as the writers struggle to express in words ineffable visions and truths (e.g., "I looked, and lo, the fruitful land was a desert, / and all its cities were laid in ruins / before the Lord, before his fierce anger" [Jer 4:26]), and poets in general use it as a way to elevate the tone (e.g., "A thousand may fall at your side, / ten thousand at your right hand, / but it will not come near you" [Ps 91:7]).

Preachers often move easily between conversational and poetic registers, and may adopt hyperbolic speech as a way to build emotional energy or move into the climax to a sermon. Like metaphor, however, hyperbolic speech carries the risk of misunderstanding if it is heard too literally. It also sits perilously close to caricature, for language that goes over the top today will often elicit a laugh, and a preacher who engages in hyperbole too consistently can be dismissed as a blowhard.

b. Irony, puns, and wordplay. Verbal irony is intentionally saying something that is the opposite of what is actually meant. A speaker often reveals the presence of irony with vocal cues or physical gestures—a wink, a tilt of the head, a smile, or an exaggerated intonation (e.g., a person exclaiming, "Oh, great!" as he or she drops or breaks something). Like most kinds of humor, irony depends for its effect on the confidence that speaker and listener are truly operating in the same language and cultural assumptions; otherwise, the listener may take the expression amiss, and the confusion will cause a breach of trust or understanding. Sarcasm, irony with a caustic or pejorative thrust, should almost always be avoided.

A preacher needs to exercise caution, too, when engaging in playful manipulation of the language itself. Most puns and word games require deep familiarity with the common speech of a community, including anomalies of spelling, dialect, and contextual and cultural references. Any humor that depends on insider knowledge risks excluding a newcomer or visitor. Too much wordplay may also brand the preacher as a performer, more interested in exhibiting linguistic prowess than proclaiming the gospel. *See* IMAGINATION/CREATIVITY.

Bibliography: Paul Avis. *God and the Creative Imagination: Metaphor, Symbol and Myth in Religion and Theology.* (1999); Linda L. Clader. *Voicing the Vision: Imagination and Prophetic Preaching.* (2003); Zoltán Kövecses. *Metaphor: A Practical Introduction.* (2002); George Lakoff and Mark Johnson. *Metaphors We Live By.* (1980); Richard A. Lanham. *A Handbook of Rhetorical Terms.* 2nd ed. (1991); Andrew Ortony. *Metaphor and Thought.* (1993); Paul Ricoeur. *The Rule of Metaphor: Multi-disciplinary Studies of the Creation of Meaning in Language.* Translated by Robert Czerny with Kathleen McLaughlin and John Costello. (1977); Sheldon Sacks, ed. *On Metaphor.* (1979); Peter Stockwell. *Cognitive Poetics: An Introduction.* (2002); Paul Scott Wilson. *Imagination of the Heart: New Understandings in Preaching.* (1988).

MOVES
Teresa Lockhart Stricklen

Moves are oral units of unified meaning sequenced in such a way that together they form a sermon designed to move hearers deeper into life in Christ. The concept of moves is based upon a theology of the Word of God, so an understanding of moves requires a discussion of the nature of God's Word and REVELATION.

David Buttrick coined the term *moves* to contrast with the static nature of preaching points in the classic three-points-and-a-poem sermon (1987, 23). Such static preaching has a tendency to analyze Scripture and then present its distilled meaning to a congregation like a lecturer presents information at a seminar. This homiletic method distorts the nature of Scripture and betrays God's Word as divine self-disclosure. It contains an implicit belief that conversion happens through consideration of informational knowledge given to us from a human authority figure. In this view of revelation, the preacher tends to stand over against the congregation as the possessor of the truth, which is dispensed on God's behalf to those who would learn of the preacher. This skews the nature of preaching as God's Word speaking through the words of a sermon.

Since God's Word is alive and happening, working to create, judge, and bless us, sermons need to reflect the same kind of movement in language that calls us into new life. God's Word is not an object for our manipulation. We do not handle the Word; it handles us. Under the authority of the living Word that continues to speak as it did to ancestors of faith, preachers shape their Spirit-gifts of thoughts and words into a sermon that serves as a sluice through which the ever-flowing stream of living Word can move in a powerful way to enliven a particular people at a particular period in time.

Since the Word fosters experiential knowledge of God, it is the preacher's job to shape language to promote such knowledge. Although it is not the only way that God's Word comes to us, oral language is perhaps the medium that best reflects the ephemeral nature of God's Word. Delivered out of a person's being using nothing but breath forced over flesh, oral language embraces all within its hearing. Oral language is something that happens without leaving anything but a trace of its happening in memory. In the end, nothing remains for us to grasp and control, only something that moves us to follow. (*See* ORAL/AURAL COMMUNICATION.)

Preachers are called by the community of faith to work in accord with God's creative, redeeming, and sustaining Word. (*See* WORD OF GOD.) They preach out of the church's memory of God's speaking through the ages. Thus, preachers use the hearing aid of Scripture to amplify God's eternal Word still calling us to participate in God's sovereign work of transforming the world into what the Lord created it to be. The Bible's linguistic structures of our ancestors' expressive testimonies to God's happening Word supply clues as to how the dynamic Word happens to shape faith. These linguistic structures also provide pathways that preachers can follow to shape current faith consciousness in contemporary language that testifies to the same divine reality. Therefore, Buttrick's homiletic of moves and structures requires careful exegesis of the structured movement of Scripture's imaged thought. Using analogous contemporary language and similar biblical linguistic structures of meaning, sermons can do the same things that Scripture itself intends to do—proclaim God's good news.

The constraints of human understanding through oral speech require that meaning unfold gradually, step by step by step, or move by move by move. Although the language of preaching is conversational, it is not a conversation. Whereas people can cover a series of subjects with rapid succession in a conversation, public speaking requires the focusing of a group's consciousness on a single assertion before focusing on something else. If we talk about too many things in too little time, all that people will experience is a blur of language without being able to focus on much of anything, much like what happens when someone tries out a new movie camera for the first time and does not dwell long enough on each subject. Just as it takes a while for the auto-focus on the lens of a camera to adjust to form a focused picture, it takes a while for us to focus on what the speaker is trying to tell us. A move focuses language around a single assertion that is explored through illustrations, analogies, examples, images, affective attitudes, and concepts, in accord with the move's focus and the hearers' lived experiences and attitudes. If hearers have no understanding of the theology, explanation may need to occur. Mistaken notions will need to be countered. Oppositions to the theological affirmations will need to be acknowledged and overcome.

Exactly how a move is developed is determined by where the hearers are with regard to its assertion as well as what each move needs to do in relation to advancing the sermon's overall gospel.

Moves are connected by some sort of logic of movement that parallels the way we naturally think. Together, a sermon's moves form an on-the-move rhetorical journey. For example, in a sermon on 2 Cor 5:17-21, the moves might be logically sequenced in accord with Scripture in this way:

Move 1: We like to keep accounts so we know we are in the clear.

Move 2: But in Christ, God has torn up all the account books, reconciling all debts in Christ.

Move 3: So you know what this means? We are already a part of God's new creation in Christ.

Move 4: So is it not about time that we quit trying to earn God's favor and just enjoy living in the free and clear grace of God?

Move 5: Then we can be Christ's ambassadors, spreading the good news so others can get in on the grace of God's new life, too.

This structure starts where a congregation may be with regard to the theology of grace by acknowledging the world's way of thinking that affects our existence. The moves could be organized in different ways using the same rhetoric of Scripture, depending upon where the preacher discerns the congregation is in the process of detaching from sin and adhering to Christ at a particular time.

Based on his field research of good preaching, Buttrick has fairly strict prescriptions for a move: its first two or three sentences should assert one central idea that the move will explore for about three minutes. These opening sentences are crucial in that they need to focus hearers' attention quickly, show the connective logic to the last move while yet distinguishing it as another move, indicate the perspective from which we will be exploring the assertion, and set the mood of the move. The development of a move needs to demonstrate the assertion in accord with a logical, experiential pattern, and the move should end by reiterating the focal idea before pausing to go on to the next move (1987, 23–79).

Buttrick says nothing new in one sense. Good preachers and speakers have always used focused units of unified language in order to unfold the meaning of a sermon. What is new is the emphasis on the movement of God-talk so that the language can do what Scripture does instead of merely talk about God from a distance. Most homiletics today consist of narrated plots of meaning. Eugene Lowry, for instance, talks about the narrative movement of a sermon's words unfolding in time like scenes in a drama (2001, 12–87). Whereas Lowry's homiletic demands a set movement of form, however, Buttrick's moves are more flexible in the sermonic patterns they can unfold. Moves can be put together in a variety of ways, depending upon the function and overall goal of the sermon, which follows not dramatic theory, but Scripture's imaged theology and the movement of life in Christ.

Buttrick's insistence upon the importance of a move's focal sentences is helpful in orienting listeners as to which aspect of the multiple meanings of illustrations, images, analogies, and examples they are to focus upon. (*See* FOCUS AND FUNCTION.) Without such focal sentences at move openings, a sermon can seem like a string of unrelated stories with no coherence. The closing sentence that reiterates the focus of a move helps hearers easily follow the preacher without having to work so hard to figure out where they are on the rhetorical journey of the sermon. Slavishly followed without internal variety of development, moves can sound mechanical. Done well, however, moves focus oral language in such a way that hearers feel as though the preacher is speaking their thoughts for them in holy conversation with the living Lord Jesus Christ who calls us to participate in the divine work of transforming us and the world to the glory of God.

Bibliography: David Buttrick. *Homiletic: Moves and Structures.* (1987); Richard Eslinger. *The Web of Preaching.* (2002); Thomas G. Long. *The Witness of Preaching.* (2005); Eugene Lowry. *The Homiletical Plot.* (2001); Lucy Rose. *Sharing the Word.* (1997).

MUSIC
See ARTS.

NARRATIVE PREACHING
Eugene L. Lowry

The term *narrative preaching* has come to include several kinds of quite similar sermons—linked together by the fact that all involve some kind of procedural plot. The term *narrative*, however, is not as self-explanatory as it might seem.

Any story sermon is, of course, a form of narrative preaching, but a narrative sermon does not necessarily include a story. Toni Craven, professor of OT at Brite Divinity School, speaks of narrative as temporal sequence (source or presentation) (1996, 4). Hence, by this definition any sermon that is shaped by means of temporal sequence is a narrative sermon. Bishop Gerald Kennedy once published a book of sermon manuscripts based on several parables of Jesus (1960). Some were traditional three-point sermons. One might say that Kennedy took a narrative text (source) and turned it into a non-narrative sermon (presentation). On the other hand, a narrative preacher, for example, will turn a non-narrative Pauline text into the shape of a plotted sermon—moving from issue to resolution. Any narrative-style preacher utilizing the parable known as the story of the Prodigal Son will shape a narrative, narrative sermon. That is, the text (source) was of narrative shape, and the sermon (presentation) also was of narrative shape.

More important—and often ignored by writers in the field of preaching—the central consideration of narrative preaching goes far beyond and deeper than the matters of form or shape reductionistically considered.

One cannot speak of form outside the larger question of substance or meaning. H. Grady Davis makes it clear that there is no such thing as substance without form (1958, 1–17). Indeed, form is the shape that substance takes. One cannot have an idea without its being embodied, or have a completely unformed thought. It may be a poorly formed thought, which may drastically violate one's intention. We all can recall a moment in conversation when we offered our view on a matter and then declared, "No, that's not what I mean at all. Let me try that again." All of which is to say that substance/form is one entity. This may in part be what Craddock meant when he said that how one speaks is considered by hearers to be what one speaks (1974, 145).

So when sermon form is changed, substance changes. Gospel claims muted by dry, suspenseless recital are utterly different in meaning, substance, and power from a decisive, even surprising turn from hopelessness to grace. So, for example, when followers of the lectionary preach their once-every-three-years sermon on Jonah by beginning with 3:1—the second call of Jonah—they miss the powerful meaning of Nineveh's repentance as well as God's. Left out altogether is the rebellion of the first call; missing is the incredible grace offered when judgment literally threw Jonah into the water. Formed that way, the story ends with an empty resolution because it lacks the prior irresolution that gives the story its anticipation, tension, pleasure, and power. This is not just minor tampering with homiletical form. It may be the difference between report and proclamation. No wonder Jesus used parables.

Moreover, narrative preaching takes seriously the fact that a sermon is not an object in space but an event in time. Hence, one does not construct a sermon like putting together a brick wall. To do so is to reify the gospel. The intent is not to make a piece of the gospel for Sunday but to effect an event. Said H. Grady Davis: "The proper design of a sermon is a movement in time. It begins at a given moment, it ends at a given moment, and it moves through the intervening moments one after another" (1958, 163). He compared a sermon to music, "not music in the score but in the live performance . . . bar . . . . after bar . . . never all at once" (1958, 163). Hence, "If we wish to learn from other arts," he admonished, "we must learn from . . . arts based on a time sequence" (1958, 164).

Indeed, we might learn from the writing of Jeremy S. Begbie, Cambridge theologian and professional musician, who clarifies music's time as something that involves "an integral relational order . . . driving toward rest and closure . . . leading to some kind of goal or 'gathering together'" (2000, 38). In our context, a narrative sermon is any sermon in which the arrangement of ideas takes the form of a plot involving a strategic delay of the preacher's meaning. Otherwise put: the narrative sermon moves from "itch to scratch." It is an ordered form of moving time.

The roots of all this in the Western world go back at least as far as Aristotle's *Poetics*. His view of narrative plot involves four steps along the way, moving from conflict to complication to peripeteia to denouement (1949). That is, a narrative sermon (tightly defined) begins with an issue, born of the biblical text's inclusion of some kind of disjuncture, that then becomes further complicated. This conflict and complication intensifies by means of logic, image, or story—depending on the text, purpose, and occasion. The decisive central shift, typically coming in the final third of the sermon, has been called the peripeteia, reversal, or sudden shift—one that makes possible a resolution born of the gospel.

For example, the Martha and Mary story in Luke experiences this sudden shift when Jesus says that Mary has chosen the better part (Luke 10:42). This story is not an anti-kitchen story but an anti-exclusion story. The point is not to lecture Martha about priorities but to assert that for all disciples the highest good is time at the feet of Jesus.

With this shift leading to, facilitated by, or arising out of the good news, the sermon has found the grounds for resolution—pointing toward a new future for the people of God. All of which is to suggest that the imperative of the gospel's claim is not reducible to some kind of ethic of obedience, but is undergirded by the good news. In the illustration of Martha and Mary, the biblical story carries the theological freight—the message through the concluding stages of the plot. A sermon on Ps 23 will more likely utilize the biblical images to carry the thread of thought. A sermon based on Romans concerning the grounds for salvation more likely will feature ongoing logical engagement of the issues at stake. What this means for preparing the sermon is clear. The narrative preacher's first question of the text is not finding the sermon's final point or resolutional "answer." Rather, the first question has to do with discovering the disjuncture, issue, juxtaposition, or context that reveals the conflict calling for resolution by means of the good news.

Generally, such disjuncture is found within the text itself—perhaps in an apparent conflict among several texts or between the context of the text and that of the congregation. Looking for such conflict quickens the mind, first of the preacher and then of the congregation. As a result, sermon preparation finds both focus and efficiency.

Note, too, that this means that narrative preaching should not and cannot be reduced to an older topical style of preaching based on what often are called felt needs.

This sermonic disjuncture, the conflict needing resolution, must not only be sustained; it should also become further complicated. Often preachers feeling called to provide sermonic/liturgical answers succumb to the temptation to resolve the matter quickly without deeper exploration. The results are that the congregation loses interest as the quick resolution retires the tension and anticipation, and that the power of the real gospel becomes stunted by superficial answers offered too quickly.

Regarding jazz improvisation, Leroy Ostransky noted that the difference between great and ordinary musicians has to do not with the eloquence of the final resolution but with the profundity of the prior irresolution (1960, 83). In preaching, therefore, the opening disjunctive conflict must not be allowed to vanish; it must continue, with even greater complication prior to resolution born of the gospel.

Commitment to "maintaining the 'not yet' of resolution," notes Begbie, "is generally reckoned to be one of the crucial skills to be learned by any composer" (2000, 100). Accomplishing this in preaching is crucial but not all that difficult. The most significant key is the preacher's mind-set—allowing the issues to deepen rather than reaching for quick, superficial moves of do's and don'ts that tend to resolve issues by means of admonition. Strategic delay of the sermon's conclusion is the means. Moreover, there is good reason to believe that the Holy Spirit can work better with us in the context of ambiguities raised by the biblical issues than with the firmness of our certainties brought to the text in advance.

Finally, there are variations of this narrative-based sermon model. Craddock once called it inductive preaching (1974), Buttrick spoke of patterned moves (1987), Rose named confessional preaching (1997), Mitchell called it celebration (1990), and Troeger utilizes episodal form (1990). The designation utilized for this larger grouping—often known as the New Homiletic—might be plotted preaching. Note that there are substantive differences in these various approaches. Yet, at the same time, they all share commitment to forms of sermonic shape that intend toward a corporate event of the good news. *See* INDUCTIVE; MOVES; NARRATIVE FORM; NARRATIVE THEORY; NEW HOMILETIC.

Bibliography: Aristotle. *Aristotle's Poetics.* (1949); Jeremy S. Begbie. *Theology, Music and Time.* (2000); Walter Brueggemann. *Finally Comes the Poet.* (1989); David Buttrick. *Homiletic.* (1987); Fred Craddock. *As One*

Without Authority. (1974); Toni Craven. "An Introduction to Narrative." Paper presented at Society of Biblical Literature. Irving, Tex., March 16, 1996; H. Grady Davis. *Design for Preaching.* (1958); Gerald Kennedy. *The Parables.* (1960); Eugene L. Lowry. *The Sermon: Dancing the Edge of Mystery.* (1997); Eugene L. Lowry. *The Homiletical Plot.* Expanded ed. (2001); Henry H. Mitchell. *Celebration and Experience in Preaching.* (1990); Leroy Ostransky. *The Anatomy of Jazz.* (1960); Lucy Atkinson Rose. *Sharing the Word.* (1997); David J. Schlafer. *Surviving the Sermon.* (1992); Thomas H. Troeger. *Imagining a Sermon.* (1990).

NARRATIVE THEORY
Barbara K. Lundblad

Narrative theory describes one way of knowing. Psychologist Jerome Bruner says that human beings come to know the world and express what they know in two very broad ways. The first way is "logico-scientific," conveyed through logical propositions. The second way of knowing is conveyed through narrative. Bruner claims that narrative is the most basic way in which people give meaning to their experiences, a way of knowing that crosses cultures and time periods (1986, 11–14). For many years preaching fell primarily within the way of knowing through propositions: statements of meaning distilled from biblical texts, spoken as truth and supported by sub-points that substantiated the primary propositional claim. The Bible itself was viewed as a deposit of truths that interpreters and preachers could mine through careful excavation.

Narrative theory suggests a different way of knowing, a different way of interpreting texts, and a different way of preaching. This methodology has reshaped preaching, especially since the 1970s with the publication of Fred Craddock's book *As One Without Authority.* Craddock turned propositional preaching upside down, encouraging preachers to move through the same process in the pulpit that the preacher uses in engaging the text. Rather than beginning with a proposition, the sermon moves inductively toward the discovery of meaning by preacher and listener together. Others expanded on the work of Craddock and his predecessors, focusing on narrative movement rather than propositions in what has come to be known as the New Homiletic.

One key aspect of narrative is movement through time or temporal flow. Even mundane stories that describe getting up in the morning begin at a point in time and move on through time to an ending. People also tell stories in the present that recall events that happened in the past and that have a part in shaping the future. The Bible itself can be read as such a story, remembering the past, shaping the present, and calling the community of faith into the future. Through the lens of narrative theory, the Bible is viewed as one encompassing narrative, including not only those passages identified as stories, but non-narrative passages as well. Songs, proverbs, letters, apocalyptic visions, and Levitical codes are all set within the larger canonical frame of narrative. Some narrative interpreters see the Bible as the normative story that provides the grammar for the Christian community, claiming that the biblical narrative shapes the consciousness of those in the believing community. Feminists and persons of non-dominant cultures question such a claim since the experiences of women and those seen as "other" have not been fully included in the biblical narrative and have often been neglected in the church's narrative both past and present. (*See* FEMINIST CRITICISM.) Yet when feminists emphasize women's experience as a source of wisdom and as a hermeneutical guide, it is the narratives of women's lives that become the critical lens for reading Scripture.

A narrative approach to biblical interpretation insists that the narrative form itself is essential to the text's meaning. Rather than extracting a proposition from a narrative, the narrative itself holds the meaning, and that meaning cannot be separated from the form.

Thus, a parable does not simply have a point—the parable itself is the point, and its narrative quality invites the reader's participation. While historical-critical tools may be involved in setting a particular narrative in a historical time frame, it is the narrative itself that is most important. Other disciplines come into play in engaging narratives and responding to them. In *The Art of Biblical Narrative*, Robert Alter uses literary criticism to engage biblical texts with methods applied to non-biblical literature (1981, 12–13). Phyllis Trible explores the narrative through rhetorical criticism, paying close attention to repetitions, patterns, and movements within the narrative passage itself (1978, 10–11). These and other methodologies within the umbrella of narrative theory have in common a deep trust that the narrative form cannot be separated from its content.

Implications for Preaching

If the community of faith is shaped by the biblical narrative, people need to know that narrative. For preachers this means retelling biblical stories in ways that invite people to experience these narratives and connect them with the narratives of their lives. Retelling is not the same as repeating. Preachers in the historic black churches are especially gifted in retelling the narrative in an imaginative way that invites the community to enter into the story. The preacher often pauses in retelling the biblical story, turns in a direct aside to the congregation to lift up a contemporary situation, then returns to the biblical narrative. (*See* CONTEMPORIZING.) Sometimes the sermon encourages people to keep on keeping on; at other times retelling the story calls people to let God turn their lives around and enable them to live in more faithful ways. The preacher may use what Richard Eslinger calls "contemporizing cues" by adding a word or an image that brings the biblical narrative into the present (1995, 155–56) as in Barbara Brown Taylor's description of Naaman: "He was a national hero, for goodness' sake. He had an office with a view of the Aramean Pentagon" (1999, 156). The biblical narrative may also be framed or set up by a non-biblical narrative, a kind of parable that leads into the biblical story. Such a frame might come from a movie or a play, from the newspaper or a story created by the preacher.

Narrative sermons pay special attention to plot and movement. Whether preaching on a biblical narrative or creating a narrative to put flesh on a non-narrative text, the preacher plans the flow of the sermon with care. For Eugene Lowry, a narrative sermon begins with a discrepancy, something that upsets the equilibrium. The sermon moves downward to a point where preacher and listeners discover the good news in the text, then upward to experience implications of that good news and perhaps even celebration. In Lowry's shorthand, the sermon moves from oops to ugh to aha, then up toward whee and yeah! (2001, 26). David Buttrick describes the sermon as a series of "moves" like the frames of a film. Each move is crafted to hold the attention of listeners within that frame, then carefully connected to the next frame to create the

narrative flow of the sermon (1987, 23–24). (*See* MOVES.)

Narrative preaching considers separate stories as part of the larger canonical whole. Rather than focusing on how the text came into its present form, narrative theory attends to the current shape and placement of the text. Preachers watch for canonical interruptions and interpolations. In 2 Kgs, four stories of *shalom* interrupt holy war (ch. 3) and the story of a warrior (ch. 5). In the synoptic Gospels, a nameless bleeding woman interrupts Jesus on his way to heal Jairus's daughter. Narrative interruptions hold clues to meaning.

Provocative proximity offers other clues. The story of Herod's gruesome banquet is told almost in the same breath as the story of Jesus' feeding the five thousand. One narrative is the feast of empire, while the other is Jesus' vision of the commonwealth of God. John's Gospel ends twice, but we do not notice unless we read the end of John 20 and the beginning of John 21 together. When the narrative seems to be over, the story begins again, and people are invited to live in the postscript, which never ends.

Narrative theory encourages preachers and listeners to trust that the story holds the meaning. Narrative preaching is experienced rather than explained. See INDUCTIVE; NARRATIVE FORM; NARRATIVE PREACHING; NEW HOMILETIC.

Bibliography: Robert Alter. *The Art of Biblical Narrative.* (1981); Jerome Bruner. *Actual Minds, Possible Worlds.* (1986); David Buttrick. *Homiletic: Moves and Structures.* (1987); Fred Craddock. *As One Without Authority: Essays on Inductive Preaching.* (1974); Richard L. Eslinger. *Narrative & Imagination: Preaching the Worlds That Shape Us.* (1995); Eugene Lowry. *The Homiletical Plot: The Sermon as Narrative Art Form.* Expanded ed. (2001); Barbara Brown Taylor. *Home by Another Way.* (1999); Phyllis Trible. *God and the Rhetoric of Sexuality.* (1978).

NOVELS
Cornelius Plantinga Jr.

Preachers may undertake a program of general reading for various reasons, including sheer guilty pleasure, but most of the reasons have to do with respect for listeners. Respectful preachers do not assume that their own life experience is rich enough soil for growing every sermon, and so they import nutrients from others. Preachers read poetry, for instance, to tune their ear for language, their first tool. Preachers read biography to acquire good judgment, especially of human character. Meanwhile, journalism strengthens the preacher's grasp of contemporary trends and events. Essays teach preachers to focus their thought (many of Orwell's essays are about exactly one thing). And children's literature ("They say Aslan is on the move" [Lewis 1978, 67]) gives the preacher a model of prose style, one that can be described as "noble simplicity."

Fiction for adults offers many of the same treasures and several of its own, which have little to do with making sermons lush. Not every congregant wants to hear that "the sky was blushing pink behind the hills of Moab." Or that "the apostle's wings were furled as his feet paced the beaten causeway of life." After all, who talks like that?

Nor does the preacher read fiction just to quote it in sermons—which is, in any case, a tricky business. Big quotations are big risks: they may overwhelm the rest of the sermon. Small quotations, if snipped from their context in the novel, may puzzle listeners, and the preacher who attempts to rebuild the context for them will need time and skill. In general, highly literary preachers, whether employing their own language or someone else's, can sound effete.

Still, there are mighty reasons for the preacher to read fiction and to paraphrase or even quote it occasionally. For one thing, preachers are always on the prowl for illustrations. So the preacher pondering Paul's glad counsel, "Clothe yourselves with . . . humility" (Col 3:12), wants to know Marilynne Robinson's preacher, John Ames, in *Gilead*, who incarnates genial self-irony, an appealing species of humility. Ames tells us one of his dreams: "I was preaching to Jesus Himself, saying any foolish thing I could think of, and He was sitting there in his white, white robe looking patient and sad and amazed" (Robinson 2004, 68). The preacher of patience will remember John Steinbeck's Ma Joad from *The Grapes of Wrath*, a woman of immense capacity for absorbing irritants, even injustices, without becoming paralyzed by them.

Where successful illustrations from fiction are concerned, much depends on the preacher's judgment. How apt is this illustration? How fancy? How tight is the fit between it and what it illustrates? How useful would this illustration be to a general audience?

But no veteran preacher reads fiction just for its ability to illustrate pre-established themes. For one thing, reading novels merely for illustrations is too much like work. For another, reading with so narrow an aim distracts the preacher from a bigger and more general advantage, namely, that a well-chosen program of reading tends to make the preacher wise. After all, fiction abounds in revealing incidents, images, character sketches, phrases, and observations about everything under the sun, including life, death, sin, grace, pilgrimage, patience, God, aging, rejoicing, longing, going home, and reaping what you sow. Preachers address the same themes in Scripture and have an advantage if they do so with minds already rich in understanding of them.

Take one example out of thousands. In Steinbeck's *East of Eden*, Samuel and Liza Hamilton, husband and wife, lose their eldest daughter, Una. In telling us of this loss, Steinbeck makes us see how death is differently received by one human soul than by another: "Una's death cut the earth from under Samuel's feet and opened his defended keep and let in old age. On the other hand Liza, who surely loved her family as deeply as did her husband, was not destroyed or warped. Her life continued evenly. She felt sorrow but she survived it" (1952, 336). Why such difference? Samuel did not really believe in death. To him, it was "an outrage, a denial of the immortality he deeply felt" (ibid.). But in Liza's world death is inevitable: "She did not like death, but she knew it existed, and when it came it did not surprise her" (ibid.).

The thoughtful preacher will ponder this difference and compare it to biblical attitudes toward death. Is death an outrage ("the last enemy to be destroyed" [1 Cor 15:26]), a phenomenon that never should have entered our world? Or is death a natural part of the rhythm of life, in which there is "a time to be born, and a time to die" (Eccl 3:2)? Or both?

The preacher's gift and calling is wisdom. Without it, who could stand under the Sunday assignment to teach, caution, inspire, and encourage a congregation? With it, the preacher may hope at least that the congregation will not sit there looking "patient and sad and amazed." Preachers know that with just a few shelves of novels, they have a hundred possible worlds to enter and dwell in for a time, each a revelation. Inside one of these worlds, preachers store up "middle wisdom," the insights that range in the center of the spectrum from trivia to profundity. For example:

1. Human compassion is often just under the surface, and if a tough person shows it first, then it becomes contagious as others take permission.
2. But compassion can feel less like a gift than a load when the compassionate person wants to be good to you on his or her own terms.
3. Anger can destroy and corrupt, but when it is aimed at injustice, anger can quicken people and make them purposeful.
4. Silence is the natural context from which to speak, and it is the natural context from which to listen. The rhythm of silence, sound, and silence is built into creation by God, and when we break the rhythm, we become disoriented.
5. Under the pressure of sin, love can take unthinkable forms, even ones that look like betrayal.

Beyond the pursuit of wisdom, preachers also want a little help with the dynamics of their sermons. According to the homiletics of such writers as Fred Craddock (1971), Eugene Lowry (1997), David Buttrick (1994), Richard Eslinger (1996), and Lucy Atkinson Rose (1997), sermons should sound less like essays and more like odysseys. They should sound like stories, poems, parables, "plotted narratives," or even conversations, and thus follow the shape of the non-discursive genres of Scripture. In a much-discussed option, David Buttrick wants a sermon to zig and zag as a human consciousness does when reacting to a significant event (Buttrick 1994, 80).

In any case, the idea is that sermons need to move, and not by argument or by application of a thesis. Instead, sermons might tell us what happened, and what happened next, and who said or did what to make things happen. They might also suggest what it felt like to experience the things that happened. Otherwise put, a well-made sermon would typically display a dynamic sequence of linked "frames" or scenes that remind us more of a film-strip than of a still photo (Buttrick 1994, 83, 95, 98; Eslinger 1996, 64; and Paul Scott Wilson 1999, 84).

Here fiction is a preacher's friend, filled with motive, dialogue, action, and consequence, all inside a narrative arc. Does the preacher want to learn some beginnings ("In our family there was no clear line between religion and fly fishing" [Maclean 2001, 1])? Or some endings that feather everything out and make people ache ("I'll pray and then I'll sleep" [Robinson 2004, 247])? Does the preacher need to create tension and resolve it, but not wholly? Will the preacher want, like Jesus in some of his parables, to build a timed-release mechanism into his or her sermon, so that the sermon finishes in people's hearts several hours after the service?

For all these things the preacher will want short fiction as well as novels. Some of the best fiction writers (John Cheever, John Updike, Graham Greene, William Maxwell) did some of their best work in short stories. Moreover, the shortness is itself instructive. The stories of Alice Adams, for example, sometimes begin, develop, and end in just nine or ten pages. Everything happens in a story that is roughly the same size as a sermon. The best stories can also help the preacher learn such powerful devices as foreshadowing, flashback, and surprise. In this connection, maybe the wise preacher will reread Edith Wharton's "Roman Fever" once a year.

Why preach Scripture instead of just reading it? Is not preaching fallible and inefficient? Are not the preacher's words a pitiful vessel for carrying the majesty and mystery of the gospel?

Yes. And yet, said Jonathan Edwards, we preach because this is how God chooses to move human hearts, softening them toward mercy and stiffening them against injustice (Edwards 1959, 115). A final reason that preachers ought to read, say, The Grapes of Wrath, is not only for its illustrations, wisdom, and structural genius. Preachers read about Ma Joad because they know they have no hope of being used by God to move other people's hearts unless they are vulnerable to the miracle. See FILM; IMAGINATION/CREATIVITY; INDUCTIVE; NARRATIVE FORM.

Bibliography: David Buttrick. *A Captive Voice: The Liberation of Preaching.* (1994); Fred Craddock. *As One Without Authority.* (1971); Jonathan Edwards. *The Works of Jonathan Edwards.* Vol. 2, *Religious Affections.* Edited by John E. Smith. (1959); Richard Eslinger. *Pitfalls in Preaching.* (1996); C. S. Lewis. *The Chronicles of Narnia.*

Book 2, *The Lion, the Witch, and the Wardrobe.* (1978); Eugene Lowry. *The Sermon: Dancing the Edge of Mystery.* (1997); Norman Maclean. *A River Runs Through It and Other Stories.* (2001); Marilynne Robinson. *Gilead.* (2004); Lucy Atkinson Rose. *Sharing the Word: Preaching in the Roundtable Church.* (1997); John Steinbeck. *East of Eden.* (1952); Paul Scott Wilson. *The Four Pages of the Sermon: A Guide to Biblical Preaching.* (1999).

THEME SENTENCE
Paul Scott Wilson

The theme sentence of a sermon is a statement of the idea that the sermon intends to communicate or explore. The standard rule in rhetoric is that the theme be a simple (not compound) declarative sentence in the indicative mood; not only ought it state a subject, but it ought also make a claim about the subject. In topical sermons the theme sentence is an umbrella or unifying statement; in biblical preaching this sentence is usually derived from exegetical study of the biblical text. Since an entire biblical pericope or unit cannot meaningfully connect with all aspects of contemporary life, some aspect of the text needs emphasis in order to link with some dimension of life. Choice of a theme sentence can be among the most important steps a preacher makes toward constructing the sermon.

The notion of a theme sentence goes back to before Cicero in classical rhetoric and has changed little over the centuries. Until recently, typical homiletic understanding held that the theme sentence arises from a biblical passage and presents the key thought of a text, the idea that offers the text its unity and is intended by God. This theme was a propositional statement and was understood to make a universal truth claim that represented an unprejudiced interpretation of the text's singular meaning. Exegesis was conceived as a scientific process that asks two kinds of questions: What is the historical origin of the biblical text, and what is its objective meaning?

Not until the 1950s did these ideas begin to be seriously challenged. Scholars now generally accept the idea that texts have multiple meanings and interpretation is a process fraught with bias and dependent upon perspective; interpreters, like their texts, are located in specific historical settings and are affected by the particularities of their expe-rience. Universal claims with regard to religious experience are now generally considered as suspect, as is the attempt to reduce a biblical text to a propositional statement. The postmodern milieu requires all assumptions to be subject to critical examination; claims need to be tentative, culturally and historically limited, with no single point of view claimed as "right." It is now common to speak of biblical texts having an arena of legitimate interpretations that are dependent upon perspective; thus, many kinds of criticism each yield meanings. The perspective of the listener has become central. A question that preachers now need to address is: Which perspective(s) best serve the purposes of the sermon as the Word of God?

Three Camps

Homileticians contributed to these new understandings. Today, there are three camps advocating in favor of a theme sentence and one against. The camp closest to the traditional theme sentence is led by scholars who argue that it represents a synthesis of textual and authorial intent. It thus answers the question, What is the intended meaning of this biblical passage?

Two other camps emerged in the wake of H. Grady Davis's 1958 *Design for Preaching.* He perceived that the two questions guiding biblical exegesis (i.e., origin and meaning) are not those that shape the sermon. For him the theme is theological and concerns some aspect of the gospel of Christ. It is an idea that grows, guided by these questions: "What am I to talk about?" and "What does this mean / What must be said?" (43–44). The theme sentence became organic and double-barreled instead of static and propositional. He thought both theologically and rhetorically (i.e., how to be persuasive), and partly due to him two camps have emerged, each using a double-barreled organic approach. The rhetorical camp (e.g., Fred Craddock, Thomas Long) claims that the sermon should do now what the biblical text did then; the sermon should be responsive to the needs of the listeners in the same manner that the biblical text anticipated its hearers. An advantage of this approach is that it gives priority to preaching what the biblical text says.

Another double-barreled approach is the theological camp (e.g., Bryan Chappell, Paul Wilson); it gives priority to developing the good news in the biblical text. Sermons in this camp tend to focus first on some trouble or sin in the biblical text and then on some grace in the text that addresses the trouble. The theme statement is developed in the second half of the sermon and answers the question, What is God doing in or behind this text and in our world? The first half of the sermon is guided by the inverse or human side of the theme sentence and answers the question, What need (or sin) in the text and our world does God address? An advantage of this approach is that it guards against anthropocentric preaching and guides the sermon toward both demand and good news.

Both the rhetorical and the theological double-barreled approaches assume that the sermon is not just ideas and that it communicates using argument (LOGOS), feelings (PATHOS/FEELING), and character (ETHOS). It employs, as does the Bible, various devices including images, metaphors, stories, symbols, hymns, prophecies, histories, laws and dilemmas, propositions, and ideas. The theme sentence is no longer a static proposition to be broken down into points (though it can be) and is rather an organic idea that grows, providing movement and assisting plot.

Opposition to a Theme Statement

A significant number of teachers of homiletics speak against a theme statement. To them it implies an idea-driven homiletic. David Buttrick conceives of the sermon as an instrument that shapes consciousness, moving people to think in images or pictures. He is against preaching in points that develop a single proposition and advocates instead a series of moves that bring a statement of a move—or meaning—into focus. No more than five moves would be in a fifteen-minute sermon (Buttrick 1987, 25), each having its own statement, each moving logically to the next.

Others (like Eugene Lowry) have argued against the notion of a single idea governing the sermon, often with good reason. The theme sentence in traditional homiletics commonly was derived from outside the text itself. These critics propose preaching a form that is episodic and mobile: a series of shifting textual images, or following a story line, or a mixture. The closest thing to a theme sentence in this approach is the determination of a difficult situation that the sermon will work through (Lowry 1997, 107). Sermons will be evocative and open-ended, tentative in their truth claims, making proposals or wagers.

Some scholars advocate that the sermon arise from a roundtable discussion within the congregation and propose that the sermon is a communal venture in which the preacher has no special corner on meaning, but that meaning arises out of the community and the sermon explores various interpretations. The sermon is multifocused and invites members of the community to listen for the divine.

Sermon Practice

Whether or not one uses a theme statement is related to one's entire homiletic and concerns large issues about the form and substance of sermons, the authority of the Bible, the office of the preacher, the role of the hearers, the nature of the gospel, theology of the Word, the goal of preaching, and the like. How is a preacher to proceed in the face of these often conflicting approaches? His or her tradition may give guidance as some of the above camps are closely aligned with various denominational teachings.

From a practical perspective, every sermon must be about something and have some unity. It must be structured to communicate something and be heard to communicate something. Essentially, a theme sentence is no more than a disciplined attempt on the part of the preacher or hearer to summarize the sermon and to use this summary in shaping what is said. This summarization can be done no matter what the sermon genre, whether a narrative plot, argument, or some other form. To some extent, the avoidance of a theme sentence on the part of the preacher ignores the evaluative process of the discerning listener and may be a recipe for poor communication.

Critics of a theme sentence respond to the traditional propositional approach without acknowledging the double-barreled changes to a theme sentence. Both the rhetorical and the theological approaches listed above seem to present viable routes for preachers to follow. Both honor the text (the one honors the text's rhetorical intent in doing something while the other honors the text's theological intent as a dimension of the gospel), the sermon as an organic instrument that has its own life, the listener as a communication partner, and the double-barreled theme sentence as an essential tool in bringing the potential sermon to expression. *See* FOCUS AND FUNCTION STATEMENTS; READER/LISTENER RESPONSE; THE BIG IDEA.

Bibliography: David Buttrick. *Homiletic: Moves and Structures.* (1987); Bryan Chappell. *Christ-Centered Preaching: Redeeming the Expository Sermon.* (2005); Fred Craddock. *Preaching.* (1985); H. Grady Davis. *Design for Preaching.* (1958); Thomas G. Long. *The Witness of Preaching.* (1989); Eugene L. Lowry. *The Sermon: Dancing the Edge of Mystery.* (1997); Paul Scott Wilson. *Preaching and Homiletical Theory.* (2004).

VIDEO CLIPS
Marc T. Newman

When discussions arise about whether preachers should incorporate video clips into their sermons—particularly clips from popular films—detractors often respond with some version of "can any good thing come out of Hollywood?" Supporters immediately appeal to Acts 17, arguing that the Apostle Paul made good use of Athenian religious, philosophical, and literary culture in leading others to Christ. We might add that Paul's reference to "the games" in 1 Cor 9:25 used a cultural example of organized sport—probably the Olympics—to teach spiritual lessons. Jesus told fictional stories in the parables and used physical visual aids, such as the fig tree, to illustrate truth. Video clips are merely a more technologically dependent form of an already acceptable source for sermon-supporting material: storytelling.

Liabilities

The two major liabilities associated with using video clips in sermons occur when clips subordinate the text or are used excessively. Clips can become a gimmick—something used primarily to show a congregation that the pastor is culturally relevant or cool. Clips should play a supporting role in sermon development. Like all other visual aids, sermon video clips should be used to show a congregation something that would otherwise be difficult to verbally describe or mentally imagine. Additionally, clips can serve as a unique attention-getting device at the beginning of a sermon in order to draw on shared cultural experience. They should never be used as a time-filling substitute for the difficult task of biblical exegesis. The text is foundational, and clips should support the text.

Additionally, just like any other visual aid, video clips can get in the way of the message if overused. Preaching is primarily an oral art. But with the advent of easy-to-construct visuals, some preachers think that if a sermon sub-point does not have an accompanying slide or clip, then they are under-utilizing the available technology. The overuse of visual support can be a distraction if congregations are constantly shifting their attention from speaker to screen and back again.

Advantages

Humans are visual creatures. Even when stories are communicated orally, they "appear" in the mind's eye. The chief advantage of video clips is their ability to take abstract ideas and incarnate them in an emotionally moving way. In 1580, Sir Philip Sidney's essay "The Defence of Poesie" (spelled several different ways) made the claim that fictional literature is superior to both philosophy and history because it can provide an ideal example and make it appear in a historical setting. Sidney's claim is equally applicable to film. Movies can create characters that embody biblical ideals, as well as those that serve as cautionary tales.

Selecting Clips

A potential hazard that accompanies the use of clips from Hollywood films is that even when pastors are using only a clip, they may appear to be endorsing the entire film. R-rated films should be avoided as a source of sermon clips for a general congregational audience that includes children. Preachers should use the same discretion in selecting a video clip that they would exercise when selecting any supporting material: it should be meaningful to and accessible by everyone. Since the clip is designed to draw on the collective cultural consciousness of the congregation, popular films work best. Outstanding older films can serve as well as recent movies, and have the added benefit of working cross-generationally.

The large number of films available can make clip selection time-consuming. For people seeking clips from Hollywood films, MovieMinistry.com has a large searchable database to make selection easier. For those seeking clips created mostly by small Christian studios, specifically for illustration purposes, services such as SermonSpice.com might be consulted.

Ideal Length and Number

Most video clips should be between thirty seconds and four minutes in length, though allowances can be made for particularly well-crafted, moving scenes. Lengthier scenes work best as attention-getting devices in the introduction or as concluding devices, assuming the clips are able to capture the sermon's full intent. As supporting material in the middle of a sermon, limiting the clip to a couple of minutes keeps audiences from being carried away by the story (and being disappointed when it stops). Whenever clips are used as supporting material, they should be preceded by the theological teaching they are to illustrate.

Preachers can use as many clips as needed to illustrate the text. However, unless multiple, sequential scenes from a single film are used to exemplify a particular biblical text, clips should be limited in order to create maximum impact. Congregations appreciate variety, and since not all films will be widely known, mixing illustration types is the best way to make an impression on everyone.

Legal and Technological Constraints

As this article goes to press, the status of using film clips in congregational settings appears in flux. Historically, showing clips in church requires a license made available through organizations such as Christian Video Licensing International. However, some studios have recently been making downloadable clips available for church use without the need for separate permissions. Eventually, a wealth of downloadable clips from Hollywood films may be freely available. Until that time, licenses are appropriate.

Beyond the legal constraints of using video clips are the technological requirements. For very small congregations, a laptop computer with a DVD player and a couple of monitors might be sufficient. Larger congregations will need drop-down or permanently installed screens accompanied by mounted projection units. Such units should be purchased through reputable professionals willing to allow the church to test the equipment.

Video clips can create a sense of reality unavailable through any other illustrative medium. Selected and used wisely, they can incarnate biblical texts and allow audiences to see principles in action. By adhering to the law regarding the fair use of video clips, pastors set a good example for their parishioners. By selecting appropriate equipment, they can maximize the impact of a good clip. Ultimately, the value of a video clip will be determined by its ability to assist and enhance the Word of God. *See* ARTS; FILM; TECHNOLOGY.

Bibliography: http://www.MovieMinistry.com; http://www.SermonSpice.com; Quentin J. Schultze. *High-Tech Worship.* (2004); Philip Sidney. "The Defence of Poesie" (1580, 1595).

WORSHIP ENVIRONMENT
Laurence Hull Stookey

Anyone attending a funeral in a school gymnasium or an ordination in a concert hall becomes aware of the importance of environment for worship. Although it is notoriously difficult to define what makes a space suitable for worship, certainly there are environments that to most people seem utterly unsuited. (Consider the oppressively low-ceilinged space of an empty public parking garage at a busy intersection!)

Just as the surroundings affect the worshipers, so also can they affect the preacher. A room that is dingy, poorly maintained, and lacking in any hint of transcendence can take the wind out of the sails of a preacher, even one who has prepared well for the occasion. The problem is compounded if the lighting is such that the preacher cannot clearly see the faces of members of the congregation, so that they appear only as silhouettes, not real human beings.

Some environmental factors can be anticipated and dealt with. If asked to preach at an out-of-doors sunrise service, the wise preacher will carry everything in a ringed notebook (so that there are no books and papers to juggle, since what passes for a lectern may be scant). Anyone who anticipates possible difficulties at such an event will place in plastic sleeves anything produced on an inkjet printer, lest on a slightly damp morning, everything literally begins to run off the page.

Some situations cannot be changed or even anticipated. A guest preacher has no way of altering the height of the pulpit or the amount of illumination available (PULPIT, USE OF). Those who preach in five-thousand-seat arenas where worshipers primarily view the proceedings on video monitors cannot look individuals in the eye, as can those who preach to fifty people in a small room.

A matter crucial in almost any setting is the sense that the people assembled are a part of the body of Christ on earth, not just assorted strangers who happened to show up. In particular, when placed behind the pulpit and table and facing the congregation, choir members seem to be less a part of the community than they appear to be a performing ensemble that entertains an audience. Further, it is neither easy to preach nor to listen to someone who is facing the same direction you are facing. Perhaps the anthem can be sung early in the order of service so that choir members can join their families in the nave seating area before the Scripture readings and sermon occur.

In churches that wish to retain historic traditions, the worship environment will usually include three furnishings, which together set forth crucial theological tenets:

1. a baptismal area, which may be near the main entrance to remind us that we enter the church through this rite; alternatively, it may be at the front of the congregation to signify that baptism is a public act done in the midst of the body of believers. Even on non-baptismal occasions, the baptistery should be readily seen by the people. A pool should not be hidden behind a drapery except when in use. A bowl should not be stored in a closet or be used as a repository for books of matches for the convenience of the acolyte.

2. a Lord's table (or altar), to signify that those to whom God gives birth, God nourishes. It is not a flower stand, thus never should it be hidden behind or beneath masses of poinsettias, lilies, or tulips. It is a place for the meal that sets before us the promise of the great feast of heaven.

3. a pulpit, to proclaim that the Scriptures are to be read and interpreted to those who are preparing for baptism and to members engaged in their mission as disciples. The Scriptures are read from the pulpit, not from a separate lectern (which suggests that the reading of the Word and its interpretation are unrelated events). For those who wish to remain firmly within the Reformation tradition, the preacher does not abandon the pulpit during the sermon, for an empty pulpit is as hobbled a furnishing as a baptismal bowl hidden in a closet or a table that could not

possibly be used for a meal because it has become a shelf for seasonal floral displays.

Those who work within a tradition in which the sermon is given while walking throughout the congregation need to note well that without realizing it, most of us do some lipreading. Those with impaired hearing may need more than a public address system in order to understand the preacher; they may need to see the preacher's face, which is very difficult if the preacher moves around.

Still, staying within the pulpit can present its own kind of challenges, as follows.

A massive pulpit may suggest not the authority of preaching so much as an authoritarian approach to preaching. A tiny pulpit, particularly in a large space, can seem to trivialize the preacher's task. A pulpit whose design is too elaborate can draw attention away from proclamation, while an acrylic pulpit that exposes the entire body to view can seem to lionize the preacher—or can distract the congregation when the preacher unconsciously does a tight little dance while preaching, or removes her or his shoes.

The worship environment can itself provide opportunities for preaching themes such as the meaning of font, table, and pulpit; and the meaning of symbols prominently displayed within the worship space such as the sacred monograms, especially those used on a Chrismon Tree at Christmas (IHS = Jesus; Chi Rho = Christ; ICXC NIKA = Jesus Christ Conquers; INRI = Jesus of Nazareth, King of the Jews). Stained glass windows that depict biblical or historical persons and events can be the basis of sermons and, in some cases, may be appropriate for instructing children during what is commonly called the children's time.

Preachers who have served two or three small churches at the same time can attest that the difference in the buildings can suggest varying styles of preaching even when the sermon itself is basically the same. The size, the acoustical properties, the amount of symbolism in place—all of these can call for variations of presentation. In the 4th cent., St. Augustine taught preachers to distinguish between three basic styles of preaching: the subdued, the moderate, and the grand styles (*Doctr. chr.* 4). The Bishop of Hippo was a wise man who still has much to teach us. *See* WORSHIP STYLE.

Bibliography: Augustine. *Christian Instruction.*

PART 6 PREACHER. INTRODUCTION: THE PREACHER'S PERFORMANCE

Jana Childers

Recovering Performance

Delivery is the word most often used to describe the public part of the preaching process. If you have a compliment to give or a complaint to make about a preacher's pulpit manner, you approach her or him about the sermon's delivery. "Did you know you hold your head to one side when you preach?" you say, imitating the look. "When I think of your preaching, I will always think of the way you tuck your hair behind your ear," you comment, hand looping wildly at the side of your head. Or "you certainly have a powerful delivery style."

Everybody knows that what the human being in the alb contributes to the preaching moment is called the delivery. What do preachers do? They use their muscles—literal and spiritual—to ensure the message's delivery, to make sure the message gets across or comes through. It is a clear concept. As a term, *delivery* may have its downside depending as it does on a mechanical understanding of communication—that is, the transportation of goods through space—yet for many it is vastly to be preferred to the artifice, manipulation, and sham associated with a word like *performance*. *Delivery* is, at least, a dignified word.

Euphemisms are revealing, are they not? We would rather imply that preaching is like trucking dry goods across Kansas than like the transaction that happens across the footlights. We are more comfortable with comparisons to UPS than to Carnegie Hall. We are happy to let the suggestion hang in the air that the preaching moment is like the moment FTD reaches across the threshold and lays the roses in your arms. It is better than letting people think that preaching has anything to do with pretending. Perhaps it is not surprising that the people who take delivery on our sermons have such a sense of ownership. In the delivery model of preaching, the satisfaction of the receiver is the point of the enterprise. The customer is always right.

Of course, it is also true that people have a right to be leery of artifice and concerned about sloppiness in the pulpit. The people of God should give schlocky, hammy, or insincere preaching a wide berth. We are right to demand authenticity from our preachers and their sermons. We are right to think that trickery and manipulation have no place in the pulpit. We are right that deception and pretense are preaching's natural enemies. But we are not right about the word *performance*.

Performance is a better word than *delivery* for what the preacher contributes to preaching. It is better because it is a bigger word. It more accurately represents the aspect of preaching that is derived from and dependent upon lived experience. It is a word that means more than we give it credit for. *Performance* is a broad, strong word that deserves to be used more widely among preachers. It may not be realistic to imagine that it will ever gain wide acceptance among the folks in the pews. The negative connotations that cling to the popular use of the term are tenacious. But preachers know that we do not actually deliver sermons any more than we receive them from God's hand. We know we perform them the way C. Everett Koop does surgery, the way Dorothy Hamill pulls off a triple toe loop, the way an Elvis impersonator unites two gamblers in marriage. People perform surgery, jumps, and marriages. And people perform sermons, starting on Monday in the study and finishing Sunday just before the noon bell.

If we are to reclaim the power of this word for contemporary use, examining the original meaning of the word would be a start. *Performance* has Old French and Latin roots dating to the 14th cent. *Fournir* (to furnish or provide) was the basis of the word. To perform meant to furnish or provide a way for a task to be accomplished. The term did not begin to be used in the theatrical sense until centuries later. Even today, "to carry out," "to execute," and "to accomplish" are among the word's most popular usages.

What better image for the preaching moment can we offer than that of furnishing or carrying through to completion? The preacher furnishes the word or the message or the image with the vehicle it needs (human consciousness, body, voice) to carry it through to completion. What better understanding is there of the human and divine creative process that is preaching? *Performance* is a term that neatly encompasses both the mechanical and the organic aspects of the preaching moment, both the human and the divine. It is the perfect street language equivalent of the theological term *incarnation* or the philosophical term *entelechy*. Alla Bozarth refers to the kind of thing we do in preaching as "bodily entelechy." *Entelechy* refers to an entity that has the potential for coming into being coming into being, according to Bozarth. Calling preaching "bodily entelechy" is a way of acknowledging that preaching is a certain kind of performance—the kind where a preacher offers his or her body to bring into being something that wants to comeinto being.

Self-Performance

Performance provides an apt description not only of the preaching moment, but of a number of other aspects of the preaching process as well. It is a broader term than it first appears. In the most contemporary uses of the term (associated with the academic field of performance studies) a wide variety of everyday events are analyzed for the clues they yield on how human beings perform themselves. In this section of *The New Interpreter's Handbook of Preaching*, articles on the preacher's character, leadership style, time management program, research, and devotional life provide examples of this analysis. These aspects of the preaching task are examined to show something of how preachers present or use themselves—something of their self-performance. That knowledge, in turn, tells us something about the dynamics that undergird sermons or at least about the phenomena that accompany them.

The traditional language for this area of the pastoral task is "the preacher's use of self." It is a softer, less objectionable phrase than the term *self-performance*. Interesting, too, that it does not seem to matter much how modest or narcissistic the nomenclature is. This aspect of preaching has never been a popular focus of homiletical research—not in previous generations or this one. Theologians P. T. Forsyth, Phillips Brooks, and H. H. Farmer touched briefly on its subjects. In more recent years, one lone volume, Richard Thulin's *The "I" of the Sermon*, has appeared. But though nearly all introductory preaching texts give the subject lip service ("it is essential that the preacher have a rich devotional life"), few examine the subject further. (*See* DEVOTIONAL LIFE/LIFE-STYLE.)

It takes little imagination to understand the homiletical hesitation. Preachers are not psychologists, after all. When it comes to talking about themselves, focusing on themselves, examining their own experience and evaluating the role that ego, character, skills, and appearance play in the effectiveness of their preaching, preachers are torn. Many of us are at the same time fascinated and repulsed by the prospect. On the one hand, the voices of our mentors come back to us, "Never talk about yourself in the pulpit"; "Never make yourself the hero of the story"; and "Avoid the first person singular pronoun." On the other hand, feminist theology and other liberation theologies press us to examine personal experience. "What do we have to offer but our own witness? How can we speak authentically without acknowledging the limits of our own context? Isn't testimony important to preaching?" they ask.

They have a point. In the contest between our mid-20th cent. professors and our early 21st cent. colleagues, the voices speaking up for the use of personal experience have prevailed. And they have left us with a couple of challenging questions. Is there any such thing as preaching that does not involve the self-presentation (self-performance) of a human being? And if all preaching does involve a human being, is it not better to have in mind some guidelines to govern the use of that person's experience than to leave it to chance?

Performing the Sermon

More recognizable as performance are those aspects of preaching that occur just after a preacher steps into the pulpit. But it might be instructive for us to ask ourselves what we are seeing in even such a familiar moment as this. Are we seeing the Prince of Denmark mourning? A white-faced mime juggling? Houdini prestidigitating?

No, the performance we see in the pulpit is something quite different. The preacher mounts the steps, turns on the lectern light, takes a breath, and . . . merges. The entity that is the preacher merges with the entity that is the sermon-as-planned to produce a third entity, the sermon-as-received. Sermon performance is an incarnational event, and a more exquisitely appropriate medium for the propagation of the Christian gospel would be difficult to imagine.

The preacher is not an imposter or poser or pretender in such an event, but a participant—a player in the ongoing incarnating of the gospel message. Preachers do not put on an identity; they offer theirs up. They do not accept another's view or serve another's word; they collaborate with the congregation to create one that is shared. Performing a sermon differs from performing Shakespeare in any number of ways. But perhaps first and foremost, in preaching the performer retains his or her integrity. In preaching, the integrity of the performer is an important part of the mix.

There are other ways to conceive of the shape of the event, of course. The text merges with the preacher to produce the message, some might say. Or the preacher's interpretation of the sacred text merges with the congregation's understanding of the text to produce the message-as-heard. Or the Holy Spirit's gracious energies merge with the preacher's and congregation's to produce the sermon. But all of it describes incarnation—the merging of two distinct entities to produce a third entity in which the integrity of the first two is still preserved and to which the human being called the preacher is essential.

The incarnation or performance view of preaching contributes to homiletics in several ways. It links the pattern of the gospel's propagation to its origin. It describes the preacher's role in preaching in a healthy, legitimate way (neither denying the importance of that role nor leaving it without parameters). It even makes a place for all those people who want to tell you how often you scratch your nose when you preach or how distracting your earrings are. A performance view of preaching makes it clear that sermons are the result of collaboration. Preachers are not delivery persons or wait staff, but co-creators. God uses human beings and the very stuff of their lives to make a sermon and perform it among us. (*See* PERFORMING THE MANUSCRIPT.)

Bibliography: Charles L. Bartow. *God's Human Speech: A Practical Theology of Proclamation.* (1997); Alla Bozarth-Campbell. *The Word's Body: An Incarnational Aesthetic of Interpretation.* (1979); Jana Childers. *Performing the Word: Preaching as Theatre.* (1998); Richard F. Ward. *Speaking of the Holy: The Art of Communication in Preaching.* (2001).

AFRICAN AMERICAN APPRENTICESHIP
Dale P. Andrews

African American preachers often go through a valuable period of apprenticeship that involves learning from and with an experienced preacher in a covenantal relationship. Many traditions provide opportunities for field education and placement opportunities for student ministers that serve as a kind of apprenticeship for ministry, but few go so far as to provide such a profoundly interpersonal apprenticeship in preaching throughout the formative years of ministry. Learning and teaching black preaching are dialogical processes that thoroughly interweave tasks for both the apprentice and the mentor. Apprenticeship involves reciprocal learning strategies of the mentor that are embedded in the pedagogy itself. A mentor engages an integral task of understanding or learning the apprentice, which involves the person's spiritual development and intensely explores the person's familiarity with the preaching event and intricate facets of preparing a sermon. The intensity or pace of learning arises from an interpersonal exchange that evolves into a process of praxis. Praxis involves a reflexive conversational enterprise between experience, practices, theological studies, and critical reflection in preaching strategies.

Needed skill sets are determined pragmatically by the apprentice as much as by the mentor. While a mentor may have a strong sense of the skills necessary for effective preaching, the potential and actual gifts of the apprentice along with one's needs for growth determine the focus of teaching and learning. An apprentice enters an unending adventure of self-discovery and excavation of the preaching event. Typically, the process begins with exploring the apprentice's discernment of calling to the preaching ministry. Although apprenticeship usually begins with acknowledgment of one's calling and the confirming process of an ecclesial community, one may enter an apprenticed relationship with a mentor at intermediate levels of experience in preaching. The needs of the potential apprentice and the availability or suitability of a particular mentor determine the entry and length of apprenticeship. When an apprentice moves into one's own church or independent ministry, the mentoring relationship may continue, but the apprenticeship likely ceases formally. This maturation may even occur within a lengthy association of both mentor and apprentice within the same church ministry. As important, however, throughout the apprenticeship years and beyond, a mentor may provide spiritual support in addition to teaching the art of preaching. Unfortunately, this is not always the case. Still, a guided process into self-discovery helps an apprentice discern the spiritual, intellectual, and practical gifts one may build upon early in learning to preach.

An apprentice never really enters the learning process without at least some familiarity with the preaching event. Although the experience with preaching as a hearer involves quite a different form of participation from actually preaching, an apprentice begins with impressions and perceived exigencies of the preaching enterprise. The mentor begins teaching by helping to identify those perceptions held by the apprentice. Mentoring someone immediately enters a parallel process. The apprentice learns through discovery and a critical process of praxis nurtured through preaching opportunities, and the mentor learns how best to teach the apprentice in a parallel process of discovery and critical reflection on that person's experiences of/within the preaching event, current comprehension, gifts, and needs.

A mentor's experiences with preaching obviously comprise a core resource for the mentor in discerning the gifts and needs of the novice preacher. The temptation is to rely too heavily on one's own styles and strategies, which may risk imaging oneself in the apprentice. The danger may increase because an important learning experience for many novice preachers is to emulate beloved mentors or those esteemed preachers reaching eminent stature among church circles. Emulation may even take the form of play among apprentices who gather informally or at church programs, but play remains an intricate learning practice of preaching dynamics and strategies. This play reflects the learning process. The mentor does not attempt to squelch this play or other efforts to simulate skills from renowned preachers. Instead, experimentation with preaching strategies, both in the art of oratory and various methods of composing sermons, offers teaching moments. Many preachers can recall that early occasion when after preaching, they were confronted with the question from the mentor, "Who was that?" There was no confusion over what the mentor meant. The lesson behind the question guided

the apprentice into deciphering one's desired nuance in the preaching strategy. God calls each one of us with gifts possessed, with foibles to overcome, and a learning curve in acquiring skills of the craft.

The parallel process of mentoring extends beyond the preaching pastor to include the faith community. Because preaching and worship in black churches typically incorporate high degrees of congregational participation, the faith community often willingly adopts some mentoring agency. The community mentors through participation in the preaching event. For example, one may witness congregational mentoring occurring in the dynamics of CALL AND RESPONSE during the preaching event in black churches. The oral-aural exchange translates the faith and the message. As the apprentice seeks to break forth from the experience as hearer into creating an experience of hearing for others, the feedback of communal responses nurtures the learning process of the novice preacher. In the exchange between preacher and community, the novice gains insight into what gifts of preaching the community may affirm or confirm as blessings received in the preaching moment. Since this exchange is not restricted to the preaching moment in worship, the novice is nurtured similarly in preparation for preaching and well into the informal fellowship (feedback) after the service. Some congregations, in partnership with their pastors, underscore that a significant mark of their local church ministry is to help train preachers. An astute mentor may indirectly employ the congregation as a critically reflective or dialogical partner in exploring the gifts and needs of the apprentice.

Acquiring assigned skills is not always embraced without questioning in apprenticeship. Mentors will at times require novice preachers to wrestle with various unfamiliar preaching strategies or methods of constructing sermons. Even when teaching efforts employ more academic methods, the pedagogy remains inductive. While most homiletic methods have relied upon deductive pedagogy requiring a mastery of reproduction, apprenticeship pedagogy relies more heavily upon the apprentice's actual struggles and mastery of integration, even if incremental, as the form of teaching and learning. The apprentice's guided experiences in sermon preparation and the preaching event conscientiously become the virtual classroom or studio. Study and practices come together when a mentor guides the novice into trying on a new preaching garment. At risk of stretching the metaphor, the mentor becomes a tailor, helping the preacher find not only the best suits, but also the optimal fit with each change of fabric. One size never fits all!

Ultimately, the partnership between mentor, apprentice, and congregation centers in the divine promise of encounter with sacred revelation. Anticipation of this spiritual encounter in the preaching event is guide and goal for the apprentice and the mentor alike. It is an anticipation of a spiritual experience—an encounter with the Spirit. This anticipation becomes a teaching tool as much as it is intrinsic to the worship ethos. A mentor helps the apprentice seek the encounter in sermon preparation. This spiritual encounter becomes part of the pedagogy in the convergence of discernment in God's Word, homiletic methods, preaching strategies, and poetic practices. The apprentice builds upon experiences as a hearer in encountering the Spirit. The apprentice also learns from the sermon preparation process the capacity to anticipate and be open to sacred revelation. That capacity is then translated into sermon composition in order to re-create the spiritual encounter for the worship community within the preaching event, as much as this is humanly possible. The apprentice discerns how to "co-re-create" with the help of the Spirit that encounter with God.

Both the apprentice and the mentor test how to balance exegetical studies of Scripture, homiletic methods of sermon construction, rhetorical strategies for composing an argument, and artistry in creating a persuasive hearing. An apprentice works with the mentor to grasp the Word, the theological traditions and doctrines of the faith, as well as the anticipated needs of the anticipated congregation. The world of a congregation's needs for wholeness, liberation, and social justice is never far from the mentoring tasks. The in-breaking of God's self-revelation in sermon preparation is a guide itself in re-creating the encounter within the preaching event. A mentor navigates the apprentice into and through these learning experiences, never aside from congregational life. African American apprenticeship relies upon experiencing the grace of God's self-revelation and the gifts of many guides into the preaching event. *See* AFRICAN AMERICAN BIBLICAL INTERPRETATION; AFRICAN AMERICAN PREACHING PERSPECTIVES; DEVOTIONAL LIFE/LIFE-STYLE; LEADERSHIP; PREACHING OUT OF THE OVERFLOW; TEACHING.

Bibliography: Dale P. Andrews. "Teaching Black Preaching." *African American Pulpit* 9 (Fall 2006) and 10 (Winter 2006–2007); Dale P. Andrews. "Black Preaching Praxis." *Black Church Studies.* Edited by Stacey Floyd-Thomas et al. (2007); James Earl Massey. *Designing the Sermon.* (1980); Henry H. Mitchell. *Celebration and Experience in Preaching.* (1990); William H. Pipes. *Say Amen, Brother! Old-time Negro Preaching.* (1992).

ANXIETY
Linda Lee Clader

Preachers may take comfort in the fact that anxiety about public speaking has been well attested from earliest times. Moses famously tried to back out of confronting Pharaoh, objecting that he was "slow of speech and slow of tongue" (Exod 4:10). Jeremiah protested, "Truly I do not know how to speak, for I am only a boy" (Jer 1:6). In contemporary terms, a recent Internet search for the topic "public speaking anxiety" yielded more than ten million results.

Some causes of anxiety may be peculiar to preachers, and it is a worthy spiritual exercise for a preacher to try to uncover which sources are particularly troublesome. Beginning preachers may lack facility with the language of the faith and may fret about knowing enough to proclaim God's Word. They may also misunderstand Jesus' command not to worry about speaking before hostile authorities ("for the Holy Spirit will teach you at that very hour what you ought to say" [Luke 12:11-12]); assume that true, Spirit-filled preaching must be extemporaneous; and worry that their inability to preach confidently without a manuscript reveals their unfitness to be preachers.

Preachers should reflect on whether their anxiety betrays the appropriate nervousness of inexperience, the performance anxiety that can energize a speaker, or an urge to compete. (*See* EXEGESIS OF SELF.) Indeed, St. John Chrysostom connects anxiety with the preacher's taste for applause (*Priesthood* 5.5.6). The antidote, he says, is to spurn the approval of the human congregation and preach for God as audience.

Some forms of anxiety are valid signs of the magnitude of the task. Moses and Jeremiah were called to put their lives on the line in service to God. Anxiety about standing up to Pharaoh is an appropriate human response to actual danger, and could be a natural mechanism reminding a preacher to think and pray before speaking a prophetic word (*see* PROPHETIC PREACHING). In fact, a preacher's ability to challenge authority or the complacence of a congregation without feeling anxious may be evidence of arrogance or folly.

Likewise, preachers are right to tremble at the responsibility of their sacred office. Martin Luther offers this colorful caveat: "How difficult an occupation preaching is. Indeed, to preach the Word of God is nothing less than to bring upon oneself all the furies of hell and of Satan, and therefore also of . . . every power of this world. It is the most dangerous kind of life to throw oneself in the way of Satan's many teeth" (Campbell 2002, 69).

A natural component of the preaching life, anxiety should move preachers to continue study of Scripture and reflection on their craft as well as upon their relationship to their community. But a preacher needs to be able to use his or her whole body as a musical instrument, and extreme anxiety can literally cut off one's ability to breathe. In cases of this kind of paralysis, preachers may want to take on a discipline of breathing techniques, seek professional coaching, or undertake simple aerobic exercise. Focusing on the physical manifestations of anxiety can actually work to address the spiritual and social causes that underlie the physical symptoms. *See* CHARACTER; ETHOS.

Bibliography: Charles L. Campbell. *The Word Before the Powers: An Ethic of Preaching.* (2002); St. John Chrysostom. *Six Books on the Priesthood.* (1984).

APPEARANCE
Michael A. Brothers

Consulting a ministerial manual in mid-20th cent. America, the preacher was advised to garb and groom like a "minister and a gentlemen" with practical aphorisms, such as "a good gown covers a multitude of poor tailoring." The preacher's appearance, both in and out of the pulpit, was a matter of gender-specific social status, etiquette, and good taste.

By contrast, contemporary homiletics regards appearance as part of the embodiment of the sermon through non-verbal communication in diverse contexts and communities (*see* PERFORMING THE MANUSCRIPT). Influenced by communication theory, this broader understanding of appearance includes not only apparel and adornment but also the movement of the body, including gesture (kinesics); the relationship of the body to space, objects, and architecture (proxemics); facial expression including eye contact; and the negotiation of the physical and psychological space between the preacher and the hearers (aesthetic distance). Rules and norms of appearance, once determined by position and etiquette, are now considered expressions of the interplay between theological and cultural worship traditions, occasion, congregational context, gender, and the role and identity of the preacher (*see* EXEGESIS OF SELF).

What Should I Wear to Preach?

The dynamics of tradition (or anti-tradition), context, and identity help to answer this question. For liturgical churches, prescribed vestments are pedagogical symbols of the sacraments, ordination, and the traditions of the church. A white alb, stole, and chasuble remind the congregation of their baptism, the ordained responsibilities of administering sacraments and preaching, and the hope of the eschatological banquet. In congregations where the wearing of such vestments is not prescribed, the preacher may still be faced with the choice of whether or not to robe. The black robe or Geneva gown, originally an academic gown worn by various professionals, is another common garment for ordained ministers leading worship. In its plainness, the robe deemphasizes symbols as well as the peculiarities of everyday dress, thereby focusing attention to the hearing of the Word of God read and proclaimed. For yet other communities and occasions, the presence of the robe represents an institutional formality that is incongruent with the congregation, worshiping space, role or personality of the preacher, and the message proclaimed. In such contexts, professional or casual dress creates the least distraction and best facilitates the hearing of the sermon.

In choices involving appearance, a question worth asking is: How is the gospel best proclaimed to these people in this particular context? For some, what is seen enhances what is heard. For others, what is not seen directs attention toward the evocative power of the spoken word. *See* CHARACTER, ETHOS.

Bibliography: Linda B. Arthur, ed. *Religion, Dress and the Body.* (1999); Charles L. Bartow. *The Preaching Moment: A Guide to Sermon Delivery.* (1989); Nolan B. Harmon. *Ministerial Ethics and Etiquette.* (1950); Mark L. Knapp and Judith A. Hall. *Nonverbal Communication in Human Interaction.* (2006); Celeste Marie Nuttman. "Vesting the Church," *Liturgy: Dressing the Church* 5, no. 4 (1986).

AUTHORITY OF THE PREACHER
Charles Rice

The authority of preaching resides in the community to whom the sermon is addressed, in its texts, history, liturgy, values, and corporate life. The preacher exercises the authority of the pulpit in organic connection to Scripture, teaching, presiding in liturgy, pastoral care, prophetic leadership, and daily life among the people.

A. The Book: Beginning from the Biblical Text
B. The Pulpit: Sunday after Sunday
C. The Baptistery and Table: Word and Sacrament
D. The Words: The Ring of Truth
E. The Speaker: Authentic and Available

A. The Book: Beginning from the Biblical Text

Martin Marty introduces the film *Protestantism* in the BBC series *The Long Search* by taking us to a plain New England meetinghouse, with its high pulpit and open Bible. This, he says, is the essence of American Christianity, a community gathering to read the Bible and to listen to the preacher. In earlier times there was a pulpit Bible, most often in the King James Version—the common text of home, Sunday school, and worship—from which the preacher read and preached. When the preacher mounted the pulpit, opened the book, and laid a finger on the text for the day, the starting point of preaching could not be missed.

The pulpit Bible is less common today. The visible connection between the community's book and the sermon is not as clear as before. It is still true, nonetheless, that there is a continuing expectation that every sermon will somehow connect with a biblical text. Remnants of the majestic image of the preacher opening the book, reading from it, and beginning there persist among virtually all congregations, of whatever denomination. When the Bible is read with the expectation that a respected and qualified person is about to say something about the reading, the congregation falls silent, and in that silence there is the unmistakable recognition of preaching's authority.

We see this in the account of Jesus' own preaching: "And he stood up to read; and there was given to him the book of the prophet Isaiah. He opened the book and found the place. . . . And he began to say to them . . ." (Luke 4:16ff. RSV). This image continues to define preaching and to assert that in the biblical text we hear the authoritative voice that emboldened the prophets and apostles: "Thus says the Lord." However variously the Bible may appear in sermons, the expectation remains: authoritative preaching begins with the community's texts.

The ecumenical lectionary has strengthened this connection between the church's texts and the sermon. Consistent use of the lectionary reminds the preacher—and the congregation—that preaching is not merely a matter of the preacher's opinion or current interests. The sermon springs from the common reading of texts that have been chosen not by the preacher but by the community's accumulated experience. Preaching becomes, then, not a matter of private interpretation or the preacher's "thing," but a community's assent to Holy Scripture.

Setting biblical preaching in the context of Buber's I-Thou relationship, H. H. Farmer grounds its authority in the preacher's life in the congregation (1942, 84–92). In a more recent book, Ronald Allen sees authoritative preaching as promise: "Contemporary preachers speak authoritatively when they show how the gospel . . . offers the community a word of promise that emerges from a genuine conversation among gospel, tradition, and contemporary experience" (1998, 37–38).

This suggests that the preacher is first of all a listener, a listener with the congregation. It begins with the liturgical moment when the Bible is read. On a Sunday morning, the layperson reads from Ephesians with understanding and measured passion. In that moment—so close to his or her standing up to preach—the preacher of the day hears in the emphasis given to a word, in subtle inflection, something that reshapes the sermon then and there. This moment of hearing the text is so powerful that the preacher lays aside the prepared text, goes to the pulpit with only a Bible, puts a finger on the piece of the text that had leaped out, and starts right there. For the preacher, no less than for the congregation, the sermon begins in hearing the biblical language. (*See* ORAL/AURAL COMMUNICATION.)

For this reason—the close connection between reading the Bible and preaching—Karl Barth has discouraged introductions to sermons, especially when they are so elaborate or clever as to obscure the text (1991, 121–25). For the same reason, hymns and anthems between reading and sermon—even prayers before preaching—can unnecessarily break the connection. The authority of preaching begins in faithful attention to the church's book.

B. The Pulpit: Sunday after Sunday

The large stone church whose doors open out onto Main Street speaks, just by its architectural weight and beauty, of the past. Simply walking into this dark and cool building, the illumination from its stained glass windows changing like the hours of prayer from morning to evening light, evokes a storied past meeting the present. Those who worship there base belief and practice in what has been called the "three-legged stool": Scripture, tradition, and reason. The edifice itself embodies this and communicates to the congregation, and even to the casual visitor, something of what is meant by the authority of tradition.

The high pulpit of this church is made entirely of stone, the lectern atop the pulpit carved by some fine artisan into the shape of an open book. That symbol reminds the preacher of the starting point of preaching in Holy Scripture. But what the preacher is most likely to notice is that the limestone steps leading up to the pulpit are beginning to wear down: How many preachers have hiked up their vestments and climbed up here? Then the preacher lays hands on the cool stone wings of the pulpit: How many hands have braced themselves here, seeking words, seeking connection with each unique congregation? The stone is worn smooth, down to a patina of the constant, faithful preaching of the gospel that has not failed here in a hundred years.

The word *tradition* has its roots in the hands: the idea is that we hand over what has been put into our hands. Before the preacher says a word, the very presence of this person standing where so many have stood before speaks. Even beyond that, the moment the pastor arrives in town, moves into the manse, and appears in vestments, authority is announced. Here, in the titles and trappings of the office, an unmistakable and powerful authority resides. Much depends upon the capacity to wear and to use this gift gracefully. This is not an authority to be wrested: it comes from taking one's place in history. Joseph Sittler puts this well: "The act of preaching is organic to . . . the rich magnitude of the historical life of the catholic church in such a way as both to illuminate the particularity of this time, this place, this people—and to gather that particularity up into the prodigious pattern of the past" (1966, 8).

The pulpit itself, where preachers have stood Sunday after Sunday, speaks of authority. Recognizing that, the preacher should have good reason for choosing another place to stand. (*See* PULPIT, USE OF.) The Sunday sermon never begins from scratch, and the preacher does not stand alone. Every Sunday has a number, in the long line of faithful Sabbaths. Taking one's place in that line, standing in the pulpit one more time, grounds preaching in the authority of the church moving faithfully through time. The place itself and the gathered people remind us of the ground of all that the preacher declares: the gospel and the church as its evangel. This, said P. T. Forsyth, is the ultimate ground of the authority of preaching: the grace of God declared and embodied in the church (1907, esp. chs. 2, 3, 6, and 9).

C. The Baptistery and Table: Word and Sacrament

This continuity with the ongoing life of the church becomes clear in the context of the liturgy. David Bartlett writes, "It is not in the sermon alone but in worship, including word and sacrament, that the promise of God's presence is fulfilled. The preacher here may also be priest, the authority of preaching derived in part from presiding at the table and at the baptismal font" (1995, 23). The sacramental life of the community surrounds the preacher's language. (*See* SACRAMENTS, PREACHING AND TEACHING OF.) Baptism and eucharist reveal the deeper meaning of the preacher's words. In the words and actions of priest and preacher, the congregation hears the same Word.

As the preacher stands between baptistery and table, we see preaching's organic connection to the sacramental life of the church, holding the sermon close to the essentials of what the community believes and proclaims. There is no place in which preaching is so enabled or validated as in the presence of the sacraments. At the table in the presence of the baptistery, the preacher will stay closer to that which gives preaching its true authority: Christ is present among his people, speaking in sermon and sacrament the saving Word. Keeping the sacraments in view keeps the preacher from drifting into moralizing, promotion, and propaganda, diversions from proclamation that erode its authority (compare Rice 1991, 54–56).

Even when the sacraments are not being celebrated, preaching can make this liturgical connection. The preacher can point to baptistery and table, reminding the people of the base lines of our faith: we are Christ's people, by water and the Spirit. Sermons can rely on the sacraments as exhibits of what we are always proclaiming: we are God's people, always striving to be more truly God's people. This is what the community deeply believes and asserts, in all its liturgical action. Baptism and Holy Communion reiterate this faith and body it forth. The more the preacher—in word and gesture, in the images and allusions of the sermon—connects with palpable liturgy, the more irresistible will be the authority with which she or he speaks.

D. The Words: The Ring of Truth

The authority of preaching comes also from the simple fact that the preacher speaks the truth. The hearer responds to speech that is reasonable, clear, and true to experience. Preaching that describes recognizable human experience carries the weight of truth. We see this in the parables of Jesus: images of family life, business, nature, and so on engage the hearer's imagination and challenge calcified ideas. Confronted by the self-evident truth of human experience, those who heard the parables were called to a new level of thinking and living.

At the end of the Sermon on the Mount, Matthew writes, "And when Jesus finished these sayings, the crowds were astonished at his teaching, for he taught them as one who had authority, and not as their scribes" (7:28 RSV). In that sermon, and in the quintessential teaching of his parables, Jesus relies upon language that has the ring of truth. He does not argue or cajole. Rather, he asks them to open their eyes and see what is there in plain sight, as he lures the imagination and teases the recalcitrant will. From this Fred Craddock takes his homiletic of inductive speech and the title of his groundbreaking book, *As One Without Authority* (1971).

Paul Tillich preaches a sermon on the grace of God as *acceptance*, and he speaks from what we now know was his own experience. He paints a picture of walking the dark path of alienation, and goes on to describe finding acceptance, grace. This sermon has the clear ring of truth, relying as it does not so much on theological language—though that is obviously important to Tillich—but on deeply human expression (1948).

David Bartlett says that the sermon has authority because it is "intellectually compelling." He adds, "The preacher is not only an interpreter of scripture but commentator on the dilemmas and puzzles of contemporary life. The biblical model for such preaching may rest in the Proverbs . . . the authority of the sage rests in the ability to see how the world is going and how the structures of the world relate to the wisdom of God" (1995, 23). Sermons whose content reveals that the preacher inhabits the same world as that of the congregation—the world of books and the media, newspapers and the arts—will command attention and gain authority.

The preacher's authority depends also on personal resonance. Edmund Steimle said that at some point in the sermon the listener should be saying: "That preacher knows what it is like to be me" (1970). His ability to accomplish this made Steimle one of our greatest preachers, especially on the radio. When the National Broadcasting Company chose him as preacher on *The Protestant Hour*, an executive wrote to the United Lutheran Church in America that Dr. Steimle had that most prized gift, "intimacy with the listener" (Stanley 1955). Even on the air Steimle gave the listener the impression that he was speaking directly to that person. This, he thought, was a characteristic of all authoritative preaching:

> I understand the preacher to be simply one member of the community of faith who is given biblical and theological training and is then called by the community (and ordained) to do on their behalf what the training has made it possible to do: to interpret the biblical story in terms of their world and their stories. The preacher does not preach at them but talks with them. (Steimle, Niedenthal, and Rice 1980, 38)

In this respect, the attitude and technique of the preacher imitate the incarnation, in which God "takes the plunge" into the middle of the human situation (Steimle 1970). Pastors make the best prophets. In the pastor's prophetic call people can see the connection of the issues to their lives. Propaganda, self-promotion, and all forms of partiality are excluded. The prophet's watchword is "Thus says the Lord": that authoritative pronouncement is completely dependent upon the transparency of truthful speech in the context of a community's shared faith and its genuine concerns. (*See* PROPHETIC MESSAGE.)

This does not mean that the preacher will avoid speaking against the community. The office of preacher includes reminding the congregation of a larger world and of the teaching of "the one, holy, apostolic and catholic church." The timeless play *Inherit the Wind*—a story of bigotry and ignorance in religious garb—reminds us that Christianity is not necessarily what goes on among the holy people of Hillsboro (Woods 1995, 15–68). The pastor/prophet tries to find the words that can speak the truth in love, even the hard truth.

Prophetic speech finds its authority in both ability and humility. The preacher seeks words and images that connect with a particular community and also challenge its complacency. Success depends upon humility that avoids condescension, veiled anger, and cheap shots. The goal is a community acting responsibly, and the way toward that is speech that has the ring of truth. This demands both theological and pastoral insight, along with imagination. The prophet, no less than the artist, seeks to bring people to a moment of recognition: this is the truth.

E. The Speaker: Authentic and Available

Phillips Brooks defined preaching as the communication of truth through personality (1877, 5). The authority of preaching does not rest primarily on the preacher, but the life of the one who speaks plays its role. Joseph Sittler writes, "Preaching is not merely something a preacher does; it is a function of the preacher's whole existence concentrated at the point of declaration and interpretation" (1966, 8). This, Sittler says, includes the preacher's own life of faith—"as believer, doubter, sinner, aspirer"—in the context of life in a particular community.

This is not a call to moral perfection or superior piety. Rather, it is the recognition that the Word of God, known in Christ, provides the clearest example of a speaker's integrity. In Jesus Christ there is a complete congruence of words and the Word: in him, act and being coincide. Jesus taught that words come from the depths of a person's being, from the heart. As one teacher of homiletics put it: "You must preach from the soles of your feet." The integrity of preaching rests inevitably on the authenticity—the true personhood—of the preacher. This means honesty, courage, and a frank humanity.

Such a person can be truly available to the community, both in daily living and in the Sunday sermon. When Jesus stands to preach in the synagogue in his hometown, they know who he is. His words are congruent with what they know, even though they may take offense at what he says. This must be what both preacher and congregation hope for—even when words are troubling or challenging: a recognizable human being who without pretense exhibits in word and deed our dependence upon the grace of God.

By integrity and availability, the preacher's authority grows. Ezekiel sits with his people by the river, trying to sing their song with them, and Jeremiah buys land in his hometown when everything seems to be falling apart. Both understood what it is to be honestly among the people and truly available. A sage pastor was once asked by a novice, just beginning his first parish: "I wonder if a new pastor should be like a new broom; just get in there and make some real changes." The older pastor answered: "I suggest that you don't use your influence until you get it." As has been said, before the new pastor does anything—hangs a diploma on the wall, preaches a sermon, or counsels anyone—she or he has authority. Just walking into the pulpit and opening the Bible announce this authority. What follows and surrounds that action, however, enhances authority, to the point that Sunday after Sunday the people hear in the recognizable language of their ordinary lives and in the person and ministry of the preacher the Word of God. *See* AUTHORITY (THEOLOGY); CALL; WORD OF GOD.

Bibliography: Ronald J. Allen. *Theology for Preaching: Authority, Truth, and Knowledge.* (1998) 37–38; Karl Barth. *Homiletics.* Translated by Geoffrey Bromiley and Donald Daniels. (1991) 121–25; David Bartlett. *Concise Encyclopedia of Preaching.* (1995) 23; Phillips Brooks. *Lectures on Preaching.*

(1877) 5; Fred Craddock. *As One Without Authority.* (1971); H. H. Farmer. *The Servant of the Word.* (1942) 84–92; P. T. Forsyth. *Positive Preaching and the Modern Mind.* (1907); Charles Rice. *The Embodied Word.* (1991); Joseph Sittler. *The Anguish of Preaching.* (1966); Edward Stanley, director of Public Service Programs, NBC. Letter to the United Lutheran Church in America, August 9, 1955; Edmund A. Steimle. "The Involvement of the Preacher." Recorded lecture. Princeton Theological Seminary, September 11, 1970; Edmund A. Steimle, Morris J. Niedenthal, and Charles L. Rice. *Preaching the Story.* (1980) 37–42; Paul Tillich. "You Are Accepted." *The Shaking of the Foundations.* (1948); Alan Woods, ed. *The Selected Plays of Jerome Lawrence and Robert E. Lee.* (1995) 15–68.

CALL
David M. Greenhaw

Call is one of the most important symbols in the Christian faith and provides a central category for understanding both the preacher and preaching. Divine call assumes there is a caller, God, who invites or enlists human beings to share in God's intentions. The mechanism of the call is not a simple conduit—God speaks in my ear, and I then speak to the congregation—but a complicated process of discernment, of perceiving a need and a will for change and a capacity to make a difference. For the preacher, the preached word is authorized by a correspondence of the word preached and the call to preach. The preacher does not merely share her or his opinion, but speaks on behalf of God. For the hearers, the word preached is received largely as a word that transcends the intentions of the human preacher and points to the God who saves and sends.

The Symbol of Call

A call is a symbol, and like all symbols, it invites thought. The symbol has a literal pole, the image of an actual voice, the voice of God speaking to a human. As a symbol, however, it also has a figurative pole, an understanding that transcends the literal and figuratively names a reality beyond the literal. To think through the symbol of call, consider a narrative of a literal call—that of Samuel in 1 Sam 3:1-9. The boy Samuel awakens in the middle of the

night to the sound of his name. He rises and goes to Eli, the aged priest whom he serves and whom he presumes has called out his name. The priest, who has not spoken the boy's name, sends him back to bed. Again the boy hears his name spoken, and again he goes to the older man. Only after a third time does Eli discern that God is calling the boy and then instruct him on how to respond. In this narrative a call from God is an audible word spoken from God's mouth to the ear of the one called.

If a call comes only as a spoken word from God, then a call barely or rarely comes, since few people actually hear the literal voice of God. Taken as a literal exemplar of divine call, this narrative would exclude almost all from having received a call. However, when read another way, moving beyond the literal to the figurative, this passage indicates that a call is difficult to hear and is greatly helped by another's interpretation. In this case, the other is one deeply embedded in the religious tradition, the priest Eli. In many ways the role of the preacher is like that of Eli. A preacher is a person deeply embedded in a religious tradition that helps others discern and respond to a call from God.

Divine Intentions and Human Agency

The numerous biblical narratives of God's call are exemplars for the contemporary experience of call. They include the call of Abraham to journey to a foreign land (Gen 12:1-3), Moses to lead a people to freedom (Exod 3:7-12), Samuel to anoint a monarch (1 Sam 8:22), Huldah to judge the meaning of God's word (2 Kgs 22:14-20), Isaiah to prophesy in humility (Isa 6), and Jeremiah to pronounce with great reluctance the end of a regime (Jer 1:4-19). In the NT, the call of the disciples (Matt 4:18-22; 9:9; Mark 1:16-20; 2:14; Luke 5:1-11; John 1:35-43) and the call of the baptized (Acts 2:37-42) form the foundation of the church. The very word for church, ekklesia, means "those called out." In each of these stories is a commitment to a divine will at work in the world.

These biblical calls are rooted in the notion that God enlists human agents to share in the fulfillment of divine intentions. That is, God has projects and purposes in which human beings have a role to play, and God calls persons to respond according to their gifts. Said differently, God has a will and utilizes human beings in accomplishing that will. God calls women and men to do God's work in the world.

Modern theology has been reluctant to attribute a will to God. In part, this reluctance stems from the abuse of the idea of the "will of God"—that is, its use as an excuse for much of the suffering and evil in the world. As the will of God has fallen out of use as a theological category, so has the notion of divine call. Malcolm Warford notes this trend away from a divine call in a revision of the Episcopal *Book of Common Prayer*. The 1928 prayer book reads: "Deliver us, we beseech thee, in our several callings . . ." (44) while the 1979 revision reads: "Deliver us in our various occupations . . ." (Warford 1990, 17). This shift from "several callings" to "various occupations" represents a tragic diminishment. "Several callings" suggests an understanding that God has plans and projects in which human beings are called to serve. "Various occupations" implies that time is merely filled with activity: occupations that keep us busy.

The Call of the Preacher

The preacher is not merely interested in preaching, but is called to preach. Preaching is in response to God's call; it is to accomplish something that God intends. Not merely a little talk on Sunday morning, preaching is efficacious speech, speech to accomplish a divine purpose:

So shall my word be that goes out from my mouth;
    it shall not return to me empty,
but it shall accomplish that which I purpose,
    and succeed in the thing for which I sent it.
                                        (Isa 55:11)

Inasmuch as the preacher says something that accomplishes what God intends, it is faithful preaching. The discernment and verification of God's call are at the heart of the truth of preaching and the integrity of the preacher. Some aspects of this discernment and verification are open to ecclesiastical scrutiny; other aspects are not. H. Richard Niebuhr's classic fourfold form of divine call clarifies this; he identifies a Christian call, a secret call, a providential call, and an ecclesiastical call. The Christian call is a call to discipleship issued to all the baptized. The secret call is an inner persuasion or experience of God's call. The providential call is a matching of one's talents to the needs or circumstances of the world. The ecclesiastical call involves the church community inviting one to serve on its behalf. This latter call represents the special calling

of the clergy and other church leaders (Niebuhr 1956, 64).

If a preacher claims to have been called by God to say or do a particular thing, it is beyond the ability of others to confirm or deny this experience. However, the church has long avoided the singular authority of such a calling and has instead placed the authority of such private experiences alongside the discernment of tradition, Scripture, and reason. The preacher is called by God to preach a word, even a disturbing word, but such a calling occurs in a richly formed context.

Thomas G. Long's much used textbook on preaching, *The Witness of Preaching*, describes the movement from the pew to the pulpit. He says,

We who preach get up from our place in the midst of the congregation, and then we walk to the pulpit and stand in front of the people. There is a distance between us and them, and often we feel this distance keenly. We want to speak the gospel to them, the gospel of grace and demand, and yet we are standing there looking out at people who could hardly seem less receptive. Because we come from them we know them, know their apathies and divisions, know their broken places and their dull ears. (Long 1989, 5)

This movement out of the congregation in order to say a word to the congregation involves a longer journey than that from pew to pulpit. It involves a struggle to discern God's call, a discernment steeped in the study of Scripture, tradition, and the contemporary context. It tries to find words that will name the experience of the listeners and help them discern God's purposes and plans for them. Like Eli, the preacher becomes a person deeply embedded in a religious tradition. From such a position, he or she can participate in the discernment of God's call to this generation.

The Call of the Congregation

The Apostle Paul described the various gifts of those God calls as the parts of a body performing different functions; so too those whom God calls play different roles in God's world. Finding one's role, discerning one's call, can be a source of great joy. As Frederick Buechner has said: "The place God calls you to is the place where your deep gladness and the world's deep hunger meet" (Buechner 2004, 405). *See* AUTHORITY OF THE PREACHER; CHARACTER; ETHOS.

Bibliography: Frederick Buechner. *Beyond Words: Daily Readings in the ABC's of Faith.* (2004); Thomas G. Long. *The Witness of Preaching.* (1989); H. Richard Niebuhr. *The Purpose of the Church and Its Ministry: Reflections on the Aims of Theological Education.* (1956); Malcolm Warford. *Our Several Callings.* (1990).

CHARACTER
André Resner

A key concept in both ethics and rhetoric, character refers etymologically to an indelible mark, engraving, or imprint from external pressure or force that changes the shape, orientation, and manifestation of one's self, soul, identity.

As an ethical category, character has to do with the true nature of a person beneath all the masks that are projected from that person or are veneered onto a person by observers. The nature and shape of a person's character are an amalgam of a number of factors from family of origin matters to gender, ethnicity, nationality, and religious orientation, as well as one's psychological and emotional makeup. A person's character becomes known through the actions and words that make up that person's life (i.e., in the habitual ways that person leaves his or her mark on events and people). Ultimately, no one knows a person's true character, not even the person himself or herself, but only God who knows the human heart beneath all of a person's historically and socially fluctuating life events.

"Good" or "bad" character is a socially negotiated reality. (*See* INDIVIDUAL ETHICS.) Out of a shared life and history, life practices, beliefs, values, choices and uses of classic texts, images, narratives, and metaphors, a community produces a working understanding of what constitutes good character. The more consistent a person's words and actions are with a particular community's values, the more a person is said to have good character. There are always some, usually political and religious leaders, who are expected to demonstrate exceptional character (i.e., to live out the prized community values in an exemplary way). Though it is debated whether it is possible to differentiate the person from the office in politics, few would claim that it makes no difference what kind of character ministers have so long as they perform their ministerial duties well. For most ministers, the exercise of exemplary character is one of the chief duties of office. And though ministers are just as human, historically situated, and subject to the accidents of everyday living as anybody else, preachers are generally held to higher standards of certain community valued norms and virtues and their character is judged more quickly, sharply, and publicly. Who and what, however, determine the guidelines for what is to be considered good character in the Christian community? Numerous voices vie for the authoritative role in defining Christian, and more specifically ministerial, character.

One such voice is pop culture, especially as it converges with a moralistic version of Christianity that owes its moorings to puritanical notions of morality—"the minister should be just as good as any good person, only better." Media caricatures of Christianity and ministers (compare Sinclair Lewis's *Elmer Gantry*, Steve Martin in *Leap of Faith*, Robert Duvall in *The Apostle*) put certain perspectives and expectations regarding (especially poor) ministerial character in many people's minds. The very visible moral failures of some real-life celebrity preachers, as well as the seeming successes of others, cause many to have culturally driven expectations for ministers.

In a society enamored with celebrity, many wish for a minister who has a character that the surrounding culture finds appealing, even though such character is not necessarily consistent with the call of discipleship. And all things being equal, who would not want a minister who was tall, thin, athletic, well-dressed, good-looking, game-show-host-gregarious, permanently smiling (with really straight, white teeth), positively peppy and never sad or negative, with a good sense of humor, nice and friendly to children, older people, and animals, and always available for a chat, a cup of coffee, a tee time (or tea time), or to be a reassuring shoulder to cry on—oh, yes, and non-judgmental of our greed, prejudices, and any other glaring ways in which we are inconsistent with the gospel? Show me such a person, add a soothing, upbeat message of health, wealth, and happiness, and I will show you someone whom American Christianity will reward generously. American pop culture triumphs when the mind-set of churchgoers increasingly turns from understandings of church as a community of disciples formed by its prophetically cruciform-shaped beliefs and practices and instead reflects a consumer's mind-set where people's unreflective appetites and felt needs are fed, entertained, even pampered, and whose cultural prejudices are tolerated and even reinforced, if necessary, so long as they attend and give money. This is a picture of church and ministerial character sold out to culture.

Another voice comes from theological ethics. With specific regard to ministerial character, Stanley Hauerwas (Willimon, Lischer, and Campbell, too) focuses his attention on the nature of the minister's office and its functions. Brushing aside moralistic construals of character, Hauerwas (drawing from Aristotle and MacIntyre) argues for a character that manifests itself in wise actions and words regardless of the situation (2003). Ministers of good character have the sustenance, constancy, vision, and focus to carry out over a lifetime the tasks for which they were ordained, and in so doing, they function to form and sustain communities of like character.

A voice that has been almost completely missing comes from a theologically informed understanding of the use of rhetoric in preaching. This approach turns on the way in which the gospel is understood to be constitutive of the church, its ministry, its mission, and its message. Ministerial character is derivative ultimately of one's understanding of what God has said and done, is saying and doing, and has yet promised to say and do. How God has spoken and "done" the gospel in the person, works, and words of Jesus and Paul is just as important in reflecting on how we continue to do the same thing as today's disciples.

The word and deed of the gospel is the most profound impression on the character of a person and a people. That gospel, heard and lived together in habitual community practices that reflect that word and deed, continues to shape and mold the community into the peculiar and often misunderstood vessel for God's prophetic gospel. That vessel is always fragile, earthen, and inadequate to the task but for God's grace. Any evaluation of character has the prophetically cruciform gospel as its reference point.

Something "real" goes on in character transformation of those who speak and hear the gospel, but in daily life and in worship leadership and preaching all that we have is a perception of character based on what people say and do. Aristotle was helpful in describing the nature of perceived character and its influence in rhetorical situations. His suggestion that the perceived character of the speaker (ethos) was the most influential factor in whether hearers were persuaded (as opposed to

logos or pathos) influenced homiletical theory from Augustine to the present. Because of this insight, speakers are encouraged to know their audience—its values, dispositions, and prejudices and especially its criteria for character and credibility. Adopting those same values and criteria in the speech puts speakers in a better position to win hearers over. Conversely, consciously (or unconsciously) violating the character and credibility standards of one's hearers was tantamount to committing rhetorical suicide.

Ironically, for Paul (as for Jesus), rhetorical suicide for the sake of faithful proclamation of the gospel's vision of kingdom was the price to be paid for being a servant of the Word and a steward of God's mysteries. Rather than using the culture's perceptions and standards for character and credibility, Paul named them as idolatrous and as obstacles to the gospel being rightly heard. He swore off using any culturally prized means to proclaim the gospel of Jesus Christ crucified and risen. In so doing, Paul was severely criticized and misunderstood. But the criticisms levied against him were due to his hearers' perspective on legitimacy. To be thrown in jail, shipwrecked, beaten, and in constant danger meant, for Paul's audience, that humanity and also the gods were against such a cursed person. To hang on a tree meant the same thing.

To preach a scandalous gospel of a crucified Messiah with people judging our credibility as an integral aspect of their acceptance or rejection of the message requires a certain approach to character, one that works seemingly opposite of Aristotle's worldly wise advice. Yet for a community that is being formed and re-formed by the prophetic word of the cross and resurrection, only an enigmatically cruciform character will do for the preacher.

Jesus' own death and resurrection were a prophetic undoing of the seen and unseen powers that stood against God's vision for the kingdom of shalom. As the community continues to live out that prophetic discourse, it does so in often violent opposition to this world's standards and values. A rhetoric and character consistent with the message look weak and inane to those whose ideas about strength and vitality are defined in other ways. The gospel's core criteria for credibility constrain followers of Jesus to bear the same identifying marks of authenticity for gospel ministry as were engraved on Jesus and his apostle (2 Cor 4:1-12; Gal 6:17). The gospel gains no momentum or cachet from our living embodiments of it. Our character does not make efficacious the word. Insofar as such embodiment takes place, it is Christ living in and through such persons that gives it its power or impotence, its life-or-death character; we are not sneaking Donatism in the back door (Gal 2:20; 2 Cor 2:14 18). If such embodiment repels some, it is because such revulsion is at the heart of our message and mission. To portray it any other way in order for it to be more acceptable to a people who want something more than or just different from what the gospel has to offer is to turn ourselves into salespeople and negotiators trying to close a deal. So, rather than ethos appeals for the gospel, it might be more useful to speak of ironic or even reverse ethos appeals that embody the bizarre and continuously offensive word of the gospel for the purpose of faithful witness to our prophetically cruciform gospel.

Hauerwas echoes Osborn and voices the concern for ministers everywhere: What criteria ought churches and ministers to have in evaluating faithfulness and effectiveness in ministry? Returning to our core message and mission, the answer becomes clearer if not more difficult. But the difficulty of being a prophetically cruciform people whose character is continuously stamped by Christ's call and the Spirit's empowerment to such an ironically good news presence in the world, and led by culturally misunderstood preachers of Jesus' kingdom vision, at least restores the right difficulty for the people of God. *See* ETHOS; GOD, ETHICS AND; LOGOS; PATHOS/FEELING; WORD OF GOD.

Bibliography: Charles Campbell. "More Than Quandaries: Character Ethics and Preaching." *Journal for Preachers* 16 (1993) 31–37; Stanley Hauerwas. *The Peaceable Kingdom.* (2003); Stanley Hauerwas. *Christian Existence Today: Essays on Church, World, and Living in Between.* (1988); Stanley Hauerwas. "Clerical Character: Reflecting on Ministerial Morality," *Word and World* 6 (1986) 181-93. Richard Lischer. "Before Technique: Preaching and Personal Formation." *Dialog* 29 (1990) 178–82; Ronald E. Osborn. *Creative Disarray: Models of Ministry in a Changing America.* (1991); André Resner Jr. *Preacher and Cross: Person and Message in Theology and Rhetoric.* (1999); William H. Willimon. *Pastor: A Reader for Ordained Ministry.* (2002a); William H. Willimon. *Pastor: The Theology and Practice of Ordained Ministry.* (2002b).

DEVOTIONAL LIFE/LIFE-STYLE
Barbara Brown Taylor

The preacher is a living word about God's Word before the preacher ever says a word. When the preacher speaks, every word reveals the preacher's way of life. Devotion to God and neighbor is the primary prerequisite for preaching the gospel.

While the subject of devotion may conjure images of saintly characters on their knees with their hands clasped in prayer, the devotional life encompasses a far wider range of activities than that. To devote oneself to any task, person, community, or ideal is to give oneself wholly to that object of desire. Johann Sebastian Bach was as devoted to making music as Martin Luther King Jr. was devoted to making justice. Dorothy Day's devotion took her into the streets of lower Manhattan, while Jonas Salk's devotion tethered him to his laboratory. Mother Teresa's devotion to the poor people of Calcutta kept her going to a ripe older age, while Oscar Romero's devotion to the peasants of El Salvador cut his life short.

In the case of religious devotion, the object of desire is God, and yet even here great variety emerges. Abraham and Sarah, our earliest biblical exemplars, embody their devotion by packing up and leaving home to travel toward the promise of a God whose name they do not know. Abraham's devotion does not prevent him from arguing with God, just as Sarah's does not keep her from laughing with disbelief, yet their hit-and-miss journey ripens their faith even before their son arrives.

When Isaac finally does arrive, his mother, Sarah, turns against Hagar, the mother of Abraham's first son, Ishmael. While Hagar's devotion is often overlooked in this story cycle, she is the forerunner of all biblical women who appeal directly to God after the men in their lives have abandoned, betrayed, or consigned them to death. Hagar's single-hearted desert prayer not only saves her son's life but also brings her face-to-face with God.

Such biblical exemplars of divine devotion are often found in the shadows of their more famous kin. One can only imagine what it took for Leah to keep living into God's promise while her husband, Jacob, gave his heart to her more beautiful sister Rachel. Likewise, look for Miriam in Moses' shadow, Boaz in Ruth's shadow, and even Baruch in the shadow of Jeremiah, laboring over his manuscript pages so that the fiery prophet's oracles would be recorded for all time. More often than not, those who devote themselves wholeheartedly to God can do so only because someone else is devoted whole-heartedly to them.

In the NT, Mary is perhaps the most popular icon of the devotional life. Although she has few spoken lines in the Gospels, they hinge on her reply to the angel Gabriel. "Here am I, the servant of the Lord," she says, "let it be with me according to your word" (Luke 1:38). With far more at stake in her honor-shame culture than most present-day believers can grasp, Mary devotes herself body and soul to God's purpose. While she tends to fade from view after the annual Christmas pageant is over, she is revered not only for her mothering skills but also for her inti-macy with her divine Lover. Again, look for Joseph in her shadow, both protecting her and legitimating her son by making the boy his own.

If Moses embodies engaged devotion to God in the OT, Jesus is the embodiment of that devo-tion in the NT. God calls Mary's son to a singular purpose, and he responds by donating himself wholly to that purpose. His devotion is not merely spiritual but also physical, emotional, intellectual, and relational. From his devil-wrestling days in the wilderness, through his boundary-breaking ministry, to his self-emptying death on the cross, he holds nothing back. Those who despair of following such an example may still look to the outspokenness of Peter, the zeal-ousness of Paul, the studiousness of Mary, or the servant-mindedness of her sister, Martha, for NT models of devotion to God.

While the historical traditions of Judaism and Christianity are rich with exemplars as different from one another as Rabbi Akiva and the Baal Shem Tov, the desert fathers and Marguerite Porète, preachers will also find models of devotion in their denominational traditions, especially among those who supported losing causes. John of the Cross spent the better part of a year in a dungeon for his devoted efforts to reform his Carmelite order. While Thomas Müntzer's story is eclipsed by that of Martin Luther, his opposition to Luther in the Peas-ants' War of 1525 was born of his devotion to the cause of the uneducated laity.

George Fox's vivid experience of what he called "the inner light," or "Christ within," led him to speak out against the Anglican Church of his day, and especially against its clerics. His rebellion led to the formation of the Society of Friends, whose devotion to ministries of peace and justice remains vivid to this day.

In these cases and many more, the point is that true devotion to God does not require withdrawal from the world but more often involves active participation in it.

Whatever form the preacher's devotional life takes, sermon preparation will benefit from a bal-ance of the active and receptive modes of atten-tiveness to God. Bible study, journal keeping, spiritual direction, and centering prayer are all time-tested ways of attending to God, but so are garden-ing, dancing, fishing, and flying kites. The point is to enter a space of conscious availability to the Holy Spirit, where one is more likely to notice the Pres-ence that is always present though often ignored. Whether or not the preacher is involved in full-time parish ministry, the wish to be all things to all peo-ple can pull the human heart in so many directions at once that it becomes difficult to find the way home again. One of the chief virtues of a receptive devotional life is the opportunity to spend time attending to one thing instead of everything, to give the self wholly to God instead of bits and pieces.

Such receptive time need not be directly related to sermon preparation. It needs to be directly related only to God for the fruits of this devotion to ripen in the sermon by and by. An often overlooked step in the creative process is called incubation. After a preacher has read and studied, taking copi-ous notes without yet discovering what the sermon will be about, it is time to go for a walk—not to think about the sermon but to listen to the birds. During this fallow time, which may also be described as devotional time, the Holy Spirit works while the preacher is not working, creating the conditions for inspiration to occur. If preachers find themselves short on inspiration, this may be their best indication that they are also short on devotional time.

Because it is important to preach what one prac-tices as well as to practice what one preaches, both the fruits and the general contours of a preacher's devotional life will show up in the sermon from time to time. One good rule is to include only enough detail to spike the listener's appetite for closer intimacy with God. Another is to keep the focus of the sermon on the divine object of devo-tion and not on the self. Preachers who wish to keep a lower profile may also make free use of bib-lical and historical models of the devotional life, while making clear how many traditional and non-traditional devotional paths are open to those who wish to walk more closely with God.

Preachers who speak the language of devotion may find themselves better equipped to address those who consider themselves spiritual but not religious. At least some who describe themselves in such a way are declaring their hunger for a direct experience of God that eludes them in institutional settings. Preachers with firsthand experience of devotional practice are in the best position to invite such seekers into closer intimacy with God, in the church and in the world.

One pursues the devotional life not to get anything for the self but to give the self away. Busy preachers do not have time to skip the regular practice of devotion, for it is only in this way that they may cease being useful to God long enough to enjoy being loved. *See* CHARACTER; ETHOS; EXEGESIS OF SELF; LECTIO DIVINA.

Bibliography: Dorothy C. Bass, ed. *Practicing Our Faith: A Way of Life for a Searching People.* (1997); Abraham Joshua Heschel. *The Sabbath.* (2003); Thomas Keating. *Intimacy with God: An Introduction to Centering Prayer.* (1994); Jon M. Sweeney. *Praying with Our Hands: 21 Practices of Embodied Prayer from the World's Spiritual Traditions.* (2000).

LEADERSHIP
John V. Tornfelt

Preaching and leading are interrelated responsibilities. While leadership skills may prompt a greater responsiveness to a minister's preaching, competence in communicating God's Word can enhance his or her ability to lead.

What should a sermon accomplish? Answers might include inspiration for daily living, growth in love for God, hope in the midst of personal difficulties, or answers to complex global issues. Preaching may address such topics, yet sermons also provide clergy with opportunities to exercise leadership in their congregations. Although pastors often acknowledge a connection between preaching and leadership, it is not well understood. The two disciplines have their differences. Preaching is more theological, with its focus on biblical interpretation and doctrinal truths. Leadership is more

pragmatic and concerned with purpose, strategy, and achievements. Consequently, clergy whose sense of call focuses on communicating God's Word may be inclined to set aside leadership functions to craft sermons. Individuals who are energized by organizational matters and are skillful in leadership responsibilities may not be disposed to devote their best efforts to sermon preparation.

Ideally, preaching and leading should be viewed not as discrete tasks but as integrative responsibilities. Without question, pastors will gravitate toward the tasks they enjoy or have expertise in, but to consider preaching and leading as distinct functions is unwarranted. Hebrews 13:7 instructs believers: "Remember your leaders, those who spoke the word of God to you; consider the outcome of their way of life, and imitate their faith," and 1 Tim 5:17 states: "Let the elders who rule well be considered worthy of double honor, especially those who labor in preaching and teaching." Near the end of his life, the Apostle Paul encouraged Timothy as he assumed leadership to "rekindle the gift of God [leadership] that is within you through the laying on of my hands" (2 Tim 1:6). But he also exhorted Timothy to declare the Scriptures when he wrote: "Proclaim the message; be persistent whether the time is favorable or unfavorable; convince, rebuke, and encourage, with the utmost patience in teaching"(2 Tim 4:2).

Preaching and leading are not only interrelated, but they also mutually enrich and protect each other. Leadership needs theologically informed preaching to keep it from adopting secular models that are devoid of spiritual understanding. While the effective use of leadership skills can achieve significant results in a congregation, outcomes can be misleading and are not necessarily of God. Similarly, preachers need the pragmatic realism that the world of leadership can offer. Without knowledge of organizational culture and the essentials of leadership, preaching becomes naive and unrealistic.

Furthermore, separating preaching and leading undermines the potential effectiveness of both. The ability to skillfully communicate God's Word can prompt a congregation's willingness to trust a pastor's leadership. Messages characterized by clarity, conviction, and truthfulness enable clergy to gain the confidence and support of parishioners. If a pastor can preach, people are more inclined to follow in other aspects. Similarly, as clergy demonstrate aptitude and wisdom in various leadership capacities, congregations may be more receptive to vision, goals, and objectives proposed from the pulpit. A pastor who leads well is more likely to receive a fair hearing from parishioners when she or he deals with controversies from the pulpit (*see* CONTROVERSY). As financial challenges are placed before their congregations, people may be more willing to respond generously. In other words, a reciprocal and reinforcing relationship exists between preaching and leading. While competence in communicating God's Word enhances pastors' ability to lead, skillfulness in organizational matters inclines churches to favorably respond to their preaching.

So in what ways does the pulpit ministry affect a pastor's capacity to lead a body of Christians? What is the relationship between preaching and providing vision, establishing goals and objectives, garnering support, and dealing with resistance? Several ideas merit consideration.

Preaching can inspire a vision for kingdom ministry. Prone to be comfortable and self-protective, God's people need continual reminders of their missional calling and responsibility to engage the world and make disciples (Matt 28:19-20). Unfortunately, time has a way of eroding a congregation's sense of purpose. Apathy is pervasive. Trapped in paradigms from previous generations, parishioners are often unable to envision a future that differs significantly from the past. This was true of ancient Israel when the people returned to Jerusalem to find themselves surrounded by ruins, uncertain about where to begin. But their leader, Nehemiah, provided them with a vision and inspiration to rebuild. Similarly, preachers today have the opportunity to speak prophetically, cast vision, and offer hope. Sermons can provide examples of how congregations with renewed visions have been able to impact their communities. Inspiring yet realistic accounts of other believers fulfilling their God-given callings and achieving results can be encouraging for everyone.

After establishing a clear vision, pastors can become more specific in fleshing out goals and objectives. People need to hear more than a general plan; they need details of how plans will be fulfilled. Although leaders often work diligently to develop master plans with long- and short-term goals, they sometimes give less thought and energy to explaining the plan to the congregation. They too readily assume that the plan will be accepted. But people respond in various ways to changes. Through their

preaching, clergy can share not only the rationale but also the details of a vision. Preaching helps congregations envision positive outcomes. Sermons can help people see with greater clarity the significance of beginning a new ministry or how hiring a staff person might impact their community.

Sermons are a means of achieving consensus when decisions must be made but opinions differ significantly. While it can be frustrating to deal with widespread points of view, a preacher must respect varying perspectives. Change takes time. Some individuals are quick to adopt new approaches and strategies; others are more cautious and likely to lag in their support. Churches are also characterized by people who seem to resist any innovation or departure from the status quo. Through preaching, clergy can exercise considerable power and persuasively achieve a congregation's acceptance and support. Yet while not shrinking from personal convictions and sense of God's leading, pastors must be careful not to impose their own agendas on their congregations. They must not be coercive or manipulative but must give sufficient time to the process in order to achieve support that is heartfelt, sustainable, and consistent with the values of the kingdom of God.

Preaching can mobilize parishioners for ministry. Whether motivating individuals to serve for the first time or to maintain their long-term commitment, preachers face the ongoing challenge of mobilization. There are numerous excuses not to serve, and indifference pervades. For this reason, preachers should exercise leadership as they articulate biblical and theological grounds for responsible service. Efforts to mobilize people should sound not like desperate cries for workers but like invitations to participate in God's kingdom. While clergy should not be demanding, neither should they shy away from reminding the congregation of the satisfaction derived from ministry. Without being contrived or manipulative, preachers can solicit new volunteers, reconnect with members who have withdrawn for various reasons, and encourage individuals to continue in faithful service.

Preaching can force a church to move beyond denial and face existing controversies. While wanting to avoid multifaceted and complex issues, leaders should utilize their sermons to deal with matters that can potentially confuse, immobilize, or even split their congregations. Whether the concerns seem innocuous or insurmountable, clergy must be balanced, sensitive, and judicious in their dealings.

Personal convictions should be evident while remaining respectful of the inevitable differences in a congregation. Though parishioners may disagree, clergy who are forthright in handling complex issues actually exercise significant leadership and, in the end, gain greater respect and influence among their people.

While good preachers are not always competent leaders, effective leaders are by necessity good communicators. They recognize the importance of preaching and the influence of their words. And when both preaching and leading are done with integrity of heart, the work of God is advanced. *See* EXEGESIS OF THE CONGREGATION, DENOMINATION; LEARNING STYLES.

Bibliography: William E. Hull. *Strategic Preaching: The Role of the Pulpit in Pastoral Leadership.* (2006); John S. McClure. *The Roundtable Pulpit: Where Leadership and Preaching Meet.* (1995); Michael J. Quicke. *360-Degree Leadership: Preaching to Transform Congregations.* (2006).

LEARNING STYLES
Lucy Lind Hogan

Through the use of sight, sound, and movement, preachers seek to communicate the good news of the gospel. The ways that people interpret and respond to that communication are, in part, influenced by their preferred learning styles. As a result of both nature and nurture, theorists argue, people learn and respond to the world differently. Learning styles provide a way to recognize the complexity of the manner in which humans perceive and process information.

Some learning style theories are based on personality type. Using various assessment tools, such as the Myers-Briggs Type Indicator, they describe and define different personality types that, in turn, influence learning. Personality-based learning styles include the following: analytic, global, abstract, concrete, and the approaches of the reflector, the theorist, the pragmatist, or the activist. Some people, for example, prefer to process information in a sequential, orderly, systematic way; some prefer to do so intuitively; others prefer unstructured, creative environments (Armstrong 2000, 2).

In the early 1980s Howard Gardner (1983), reacting to the concept that there is only one way of measuring a person's intelligence, identified several intelligences: linguistic, logical-mathematical, musical, bodily-kinesthetic, spatial, interpersonal, intrapersonal, and naturalist. Mozart was a musical genius, and Michael Jordan is a bodily-kinesthetic genius. If traditional preaching is understood to appeal primarily to those of linguistic and logical-mathematical intelligence, how might preachers reach the other intelligences? One way is to use the VAK theoretical approach of neuro-linguistic programming, which stresses the sensory receivers: visual, auditory, and kinesthetic (Jeter and Allen 2002, 70ff.). Some people are visual learners. They like to see an image or the written words on a page. They will respond to seeing key words or images projected on a video screen or perhaps simply to the opportunity to take notes. An auditory learner will prefer to hear those words spoken in the sermon or even in a small group discussion. And kinesthetic learners need touch or movement. A preacher who moves will capture their attention.

There are numerous ways of describing how people receive and process information, but a question remains: How might the concept of different learning styles affect and alter preaching? Most preachers do not subject their congregations to the Myers-Briggs personality assessment or analyze the multiple intelligences represented among their listeners. But it is still important to remember that people are different. They have different needs, and they respond in different ways to the same stimulus. Variety must therefore be a mark of good preaching—that is, preaching that will have the potential to connect with different listeners. Images, either verbal or projected, will reach some people. Abstract concepts will appeal to others. Movement will appeal to still others. Finally, we must also remember that no one sermon reaches everyone's preferred learning style. The sermon is a part of the larger worship service, and it is in and through the multisensory nature of worship that we reach the wide variety of learning styles represented in the congregation. *See* EXEGESIS OF THE CONGREGATION, DENOMINATION; LEADERSHIP; TEACHING.

Bibliography: Thomas Armstrong. *Multiple Intelligences in the Classroom.* (2000); Howard Gardner. *Frames of Mind: The Theory of Multiple Intelligences.* (1983; 1993); Howard Gardner. *Intelligence Reframed.* (1999); Joseph R. Jeter and Ronald J. Allen. *One Gospel, Many Ears.* (2002).

LISTENING AND OBSERVATION SKILLS
Ronald J. Allen

Listening is foundational to preaching. To listen is to perceive an other—for example, a person, a community, a text from the Bible or another source, a practice, or a historical event—in ways that respect the integrity of the other. Listeners seek to avoid projecting their own values on the other; they aim to hear the other in the other's own right. At the basic level, the listener seeks to understand the other in ways that the other would recognize as consistent with how the other would like to be perceived. At deeper levels, the insightful listener may discern dynamics in the other about which the other may be unaware. The listener wants to understand the world from the point of view of the other.

Using the various disciplines of critical interpretation, biblical exegesis (EXEGESIS) is listening to a biblical text to ascertain what the text sought for people in antiquity to believe and do. Eisegesis is reading one's image into the text by failing to honor the text as other.

The preacher also seeks to listen to the voices of all who may help preacher and congregation come to an adequate interpretation of the purposes of God (e.g., the voices of people and texts beyond the Bible, social movements and events, contemporary theologies and theologians, and the Holy Spirit). In all cases a preacher needs criteria by which to distinguish the leading of the Spirit from other impulses (HOLY SPIRIT/PASSION).

Preachers tend to listen to congregations in two ways as part of preparing particular sermons as well as gaining more general insight into how the congregation listens to sermons. (1) Preachers try to pay attention to the congregation's values, perceptions, and feelings as preachers observe them in the everyday course of life; and (2) recently, some in the preaching community have stressed the possibility of the preacher listening to the congregation by interviewing. Preachers increasingly meet with members of the congregation in small groups (or interact with the congregation through other means) to ascertain how the congregation perceives the subject of the sermon. Preachers can also interview members of the listening community to determine qualities that the community finds engaging when listening to sermons. *See* CHARACTER; ETHOS; PREACHER'S CREATIVE PROCESS.

Bibliography: Ronald J. Allen. *Hearing the Sermon: Relationship, Content, Feeling.* (2005); John S. McClure. *The Roundtable Pulpit: Where Leadership and Preaching Meet.* (1995); John S. McClure, Ronald J. Allen, Dale P. Andrews, L. Susan Bond, Dan P. Moseley, and G. Lee Ramsey Jr. *Listening to Listeners: Homiletical Case Studies.* (2004); Mary Alice Mulligan, Diane Turner-Sharazz, Dawn Ottoni Wilhelm, and Ronald J. Allen. *Believing in Preaching: What Listeners Hear in Sermons.* (2005); Mary Alice Mulligan and Ronald J. Allen. *Make the Word Come Alive: Lessons from Laity.* (2006).

LONG-RANGE SERMON PLANNING
Howard Vanderwell

A cartoon appeared in one of the early issues of *Leadership*, poignantly portraying the common panic of preachers. The preacher sat behind a pile of books, eyes wide with fright. On the wall was a unique calendar, the Preacher's Calendar, in which every other column was labeled "Sunday" while the alternate ones were labeled "Monday-Saturday" ([Summer 1983] 103).

I remember the feeling all too well from my early years in ministry. Every other day seemed like Sunday. I began the week with the panic of, *What in the world am I going to preach on this week?* The panic increased geometrically if my uncertainty carried into Tuesday and Wednesday (ANXIETY). But the scenario changed. Instead of running out of ideas, I soon had so many, I could not find enough Sundays to preach on them all. Discovering the value of planning ahead was the key.

Long-range sermon planning refers to a full calendar season, from September to August. Some preachers resist the idea of planning ahead. Perhaps it is the fear of not having enough ideas, or perhaps it is a personality or work style that makes it hard for them to think and project ahead. But more common is the fear that long-range planning means pre-empting the Holy Spirit, losing spontaneity and the ability to respond freshly to current needs. There is no need for such a fear. Those who plan ahead are often surprised at how, in the planning process, the Holy Spirit has gone ahead of us and anticipated needs. In addition, we give ourselves permission to interrupt a planned sermon if something else presses for urgent attention.

Careful thinking about the preaching task will show us there is good reason for planning ahead. Preaching is a task that demands our best, not our leftovers. It is a task so high and noble that it rightly requires the highest priority on our list of duties. Haphazard planning is beneath the dignity of a sound preaching ministry. When it becomes clear to others that we plan ahead (and it will become clear), it tells them that since their preacher takes the task seriously, they should listen in that same spirit. Paul looked back on his ministry at Ephesus and could, with a clear conscience, say, "I have not hesitated to proclaim to you the whole will of God" (Acts 20:27 NIV). The healthy nurture of a congregation over a period of time requires that a full balance of types of biblical literature, issues, and dimensions of doctrine be presented to them. Only a balanced diet will nurture a church well, and long-range planning gives the best assurance that the diet will be balanced.

Benefits

Those who practice long-range sermon planning have discovered a number of benefits.

1. *Panic is replaced with satisfaction.* Many preachers initially find weekly anxiety to be a negative influence on their love for preaching. Planning ahead not only removes the anxiety, but it also makes sermon writing and preaching much more fascinating and rewarding— a Spirit-led adventure!

2. *The quality of preaching is upgraded.* Who of us does not want, and need, higher quality preaching? No one would deny that preaching is a difficult task, especially when done well. So how can we be sure we have caught the core idea of our passage, found its clear application to our hearers, or discovered the best way to communicate it? Many of our messages would be of higher quality if we let them incubate for a number of weeks instead of writing and preaching against tight deadlines.

3. *Our study is more directed.* Preaching requires study, but the press of pastoral duties often competes with study time. Inadequate planning usually eliminates serious study of a passage. We often have to go with what we have on hand because deadlines are approaching. Advanced planning helps us anticipate the subjects and passages we ought to be studying, thereby giving us the opportunity to plan our personal reading diet to complement our preaching schedule.

4. *We get a broader view of our preaching ministry.* If we are preoccupied only with the immediately approaching Sunday, we do not get the chance to step back and take an overall look. Yet healthy preaching requires times to look at the big picture and ask ourselves questions such as: How balanced is this diet of preaching? What percentage of sermons is based on the OT, Gospels, and NT letters? What evidence exists that I may be pushing my pet peeves? What Christian doctrines have I been avoiding?

5. *We can collect better illustrative material.* No one can overestimate the power of a good illustration strategically placed in a sermon. But most of us know the frustration of uncovering the perfect illustration—three days too late! How much better to have in mind the material that is scheduled for months ahead, with files set up for each, and then be able to drop a good illustration in the file so it is there when we need it in a month or two.

The benefits of long-range sermon planning are so outstanding that many preachers say they would never go back to any other way.

Method

How do we approach this task? What methods shall we use? Each preacher must develop a method that fits her or his work patterns, but it is possible to identify a few common, overlapping steps that have helped many preachers.

1. *Create a general hopper.* Many preachers make use of a filing system. One I found useful was to label a large file folder "Hopper for Preaching" and then toss in ideas for sermons and series that came to mind in my reading, devotions, pastoral work, conversations, and so on. This bulging hopper became a vast resource for sermon planning. Preachers

today might want to set up a file of ideas on the computer, including all references, and scan in pages with special ideas for sermon starters.

2. *Pray.* Throughout the course of a year, there will be many needs and considerations of which the Spirit alone is aware. Preachers will make crucial choices in planning that will affect congregational life, so they need discernment. That means preachers must surround all planning with prayer. Prayer for sermon planning must be a part not only of a pastor's personal prayers but also of the prayers of the church staff, elders, and congregation.

3. *Analyze.* Preaching involves careful study of the Word, but it also must involve a careful study of the congregation to discern the needs that ought to be addressed. Those who preach must know the Bible, their parishioners, and the world they live in. They must review impressions gained in pastoral work, personal conversations, and observations. They must also consult with the church staff and the worship committee about the needs they see in the congregation. One suggestion is to include an insert in the weekly bulletin that invites the congregation to offer ideas for matters that ought to be addressed or passages that ought to be studied during the coming year. Doing so helps to accumulate many impressions that feed planning.

4. *Chart the year.* A preacher might design a chart for the fifty-two Sundays and special weekdays for worship, noting the seasons of the Christian Year from Advent through Pentecost season as well as local special observances. Then he or she might chart in vacation times and blocks for series of sermons planned for each season. Those who follow the lectionary will have great help in making these choices. (*See* LECTIONARY AND THE CHRISTIAN YEAR.) For those who regularly preach from one of the confessions of the church, the structure of the confession will serve as a guide.

5. *Flesh it out.* When the chart is blocked for each season or series, the preacher can begin breaking down each season or series into weekly segments, including the Scripture passage and theme or title. The farther out the week, the more general is the planning. For example, if a preacher does his or her planning during the summer, then he or she may flesh out September through January with a specific passage, theme, and title and only generally sketch the next six months (February through August), waiting to plan them more specifically after the first of the year.

6. *Share it.* Most of the work to this point will have been private. But it must be shared with others in order for collaborative worship planning to begin. It is good for preachers to share their master preaching calendar with the church staff and other key individuals and committees for their information and planning.

Preachers who have developed a planning method that works for them often say they find that sermon preparation goes more easily. When preachers plan in advance, their preaching is of a better quality, and the whole experience of worship planning is more satisfying for all. *See* PREACHER'S CREATIVE PROCESS; PREACHER'S WEEK; SERMON SERIES.

PERFORMATIVE LANGUAGE
Richard F. Ward

Performative language is a phrase that arises out of a theory about how language works in human communication, particularly when the speaker is in place in her or his role as pastor, preacher, or liturgist. Based in speech-act theory and performance studies, the theoretical framework that supports the term is a way of understanding the power of words by demonstrating how they function in the interactions afforded in ritual settings and in everyday life. It is also a way to draw distinctions and display interdependence between the semantic content of words or phrases and their use in social interaction.

Traditional studies of language use focused upon its capacity to make statements of truth or falsity, exploring, for example, whether a word was a "true" reflection of reality. How statements were uttered, and under what circumstances, was assumed to be the province of rhetoric or poetic and therefore out of the reach or beneath the concern of philosophy or theology. Such a view could not adequately take into account the interactions where participants make promises, wagers, or declarations—places where spoken language was doing something in the saying. Such doing-something genres of speaking could not be judged as being true or false simply by looking for referents in the world in which these transactions take place. In fact, given the traditional view of language, how was one to understand the preaching of a sermon? Did a sermon reflect only the truth of the preacher's intent? Was it simply an incident where propositions are made and where truth and falsity are revealed and explained? Such queries begged for fresh approaches to understanding human speech.

Recent theories of language have puzzled over whether language as such has the capacity to bear meaning of any kind other than the meaning that a speaker and a listener agree upon. Christian homiletics senses that something other than propositional reasoning is happening in the preaching of a sermon, something that can be attributed to the work of the Spirit in the preacher's relationship to the community being addressed but that is difficult to define (HOLY SPIRIT/PASSION). This experiential dimension of preaching calls for a deeper understanding of how language works. It is important that such an approach also reflect Judeo-Christian understandings of Word (WORD OF GOD) and its efficacy in the performance of faith in worship and in the world.

Christians and their Jewish forebears and counterparts have experienced Word as rich with meaning; it is a mode of action that is inseparable from content. Both Israelite and Christian narratives testify to the power of an utterance to bring something into being that was not so before the utterance was made. Such utterances had a public character. Indeed, in the OT in particular, God is not known apart from God's speech, God's Word. When God speaks through one of God's prophets or through the sacred literature and ritual practices, something uniquely transformative occurs in the life of the community.

Christian tradition (especially that arising from the Johannine community) bears witness to Jesus Christ as the embodiment of God's Word. His life, ministry, death, and resurrection are symbolized in Christian memory as an extended divine utterance that continues to address Christians through the risen Christ. In other words, for Christians, Jesus Christ is God's performative utterance not only in faith history but also in the ongoing shared life of Christian community.

Performative utterances show how words can do more than make statements or convey information.

The term reflects the view that speaking is also a mode of action; it is a doing, not simply a report of a doing. The opposite of performative utterance is constative speech. The two kinds of speech are distinguished from each other by intent and by the attitude in the intending, that is, by what the speaker hopes to accomplish in his or her transaction with listeners.

When a speaker makes a statement, offers a prediction, or answers a question, he or she is using constative speech. The truth that is referenced in constatives does not depend on the saying of it. For example, if the pastor says during announcements, "The supper was on Wednesday night, and eighty-nine people attended it," then the pastor and the congregation are acknowledging that the supper happened. The pastor's reporting of it does not alter that truth. In a similar way, when the pastor says, "Carol Atkins and William Bole were married here yesterday," she is giving an account of a significant change that occurred in the lives of two people known to the congregation—the reality of their lives was transformed. Two different people became bonded in the covenant of marriage, which is understood by the community as a new act of creation. The utterance involved in making that announcement was not performative but constative.

Performative utterances can punctuate the flow of constative speech by injecting elements of transformative action, that is, when the reality of the situation is made or transformed in and by that act of speaking. For example, once the baseball leaves the pitcher's hand and arrives at the plate in the catcher's mitt, the pitch becomes a ball or a strike by means of the umpire's utterance or call. The umpire, playing an authoritative role in the game, makes a call that determines whether the pitch is good, whether a runner is safe or out or takes a base. Until the umpire makes the call, the pitch has no meaning for the game. Of course the umpire's call can be and often is contested by the coach or player, but once it is performed, it stands as reality.

The typical marriage ceremony offers good examples of how different kinds of performed utterances appear in a ritual setting. Words and participants' utterances of them in the ceremony have the power to change the status of two persons into the single entity of "married couple." The entire marriage service hinges on that one sacred moment when the pronouncement is made. In that moment the minister is not simply making the report that a marital bond has been made, but actually by means of a performed utterance makes it so. Along the way, the couple, their families, friends, and colleagues also make performed utterances as they promise support and fidelity and make declarations about what they can expect from one another in the future.

The marriage ceremony also reveals other conditions that are necessary for the efficacy of the performed utterance. For one, the performed utterance must be a part of an accepted procedure; one does not make a performed utterance in a social vacuum. The procedures that call for performed utterances are evoked by appropriate circumstances. For example, in the wake of a tragic event in the community, the public acknowledges a radical change in the status quo of that community. The people recognize a communal need for the kinds of performances that will carry the burden of shared fears, outrage, and grief and offer not only statements of what has happened but also utterances that offer hope, encouragement, and promises of support. The tragic circumstances give great weight to the spoken word and the enacted gesture; they call for procedures that, if properly carried out, will make performed utterances efficacious.

A speaker's attitude and intentionality are crucial to effective performative utterances. Imagine a situation where one person has wronged another and an apology is called for. Both parties would deepen the power and the value of the necessary encounter if they would agree on some acceptable procedure for issuing the apology and words of forgiveness. Yet if the one saying, "I am sorry, and I apologize for my action," comes without any evidence of contrition or intention, then the utterance hardly changes anything, no matter how well the participants have followed the procedure they agreed upon.

Christian worship originated with the need for those who had experienced the appearance of the risen Christ to perform their utterances of praise to the God who in Christ claimed them as God's own. Our forebears created liturgical language, forms, and structures that give shape and direction to our performances of faith and those of our descendants. For the performance of both worship and service to have transformative power, leaders and participants need to be clear about intentions, be effective in their execution of rites and rituals of worship, and sustain the attitude that faithfulness affords. When we perform utterances that invoke the Spirit; confess corporate and individual sins; give our thanks; offer our pleas, petitions, and intercessions; announce good news; pronounce both judgment and forgiveness; and send the community forth to collaborate with God in the redemption of the world, we are creating the truth of our witness and character of our community. *See* PERFORMING THE MANUSCRIPT.

PERFORMING THE MANUSCRIPT
Richard F. Ward

Performing the manuscript is a larger term than what used to be called sermon delivery and describes how language written for the sermon comes to life in the preaching event. The burden of those preachers whose preparation for preaching includes written material is to translate that language—that form of thought—into ORAL/AURAL COMMUNICATION. The phrase *performing the manuscript* conjoins two concepts that require further explication: first, *performance* as it relates to the study of preaching, and second, *manuscript* or the role that writing plays in the preparation and presentation of a sermon. Together they speak of the oral dynamics of preaching.

A. Performance
B. Manuscript
C. Performance as Three Acts
   1. Preparation
   2. Creation
   3. Incarnation

A. Performance

Performance has a new role in the study of preaching, a role that will enable the student of preaching to associate the values of sincerity and authenticity with the vocal and physical behaviors a preacher uses to bring thought to expression. More often than not, *performance* has had pejorative connotations in homiletics. For example, if one wanted to demean or devalue presentational behaviors, one could borrow from the language of the theater. A preacher who used a highly expressive style might be evaluated as just acting or as being overly dramatic. Even in everyday life such behaviors that are experienced as manipulative might be described as playacting, making a scene, or grandstanding. Indeed, the

English language upholds *performance* as an epithet by associating its usage with sham or pretense. In this sense, performance has suffered the same kind of burden that the word *rhetoric* has had in the intellectual history of the West. Those who sought truth in philosophy, science, or theology have traditionally treated both performance and rhetoric with suspicion and have been quick to associate them with distraction and deceit in the quest for truth.

With the rapid rise in the technology of advertising, the language of corporate and consumer culture has lifted performance out from the aesthetics of communication to use it in a different way. When one wants to speak of a worker's efficiency, one comments on the quality of that worker's performance. A person trying to sell a car, a bicycle, or some other machine will comment on the quality of that machine's performance. To bring that set of connotations into a discussion of the preaching event would be absurd. It would turn preaching into a matter of mere technique, with little attention given to the sermon's dynamic and aesthetic qualities.

Communication and cultural studies have uncovered and employed fresher, richer usages of *performance* that are more suggestive for homiletics. Derived from the Old French *par* and *fournir*, *performance* literally means "to perfect" or to "carry through to completion." These connotations suggest that performance describes a coalescence of thought and enactment within a communicative event that is charged with liveliness and engagement. This would situate performance at the very heart of human interaction, since thought is not fully realized until it is embodied and enacted through expression. A sermon is not a sermon until it is performed, that is, until its thought expressed as language is carried through to completion through a set of vocal, physical, and behavioral conventions that a particular worshiping community understands as preaching.

B. Manuscript

A manuscript is a tool that some preachers employ to prompt the performance of the sermon. The word's origins in Latin give us a picture of how the manuscript was created; the manuscript's origin in oral cultures helps us see how it functioned in relation to speech. *Manuscript* is a conflation of the Latin words for "hand" (*manus*) and "writing"

(*scriptum*). Its creation is the culmination of a process that transcribes the sound of words into their representation in writing and requires the competence of a scribe. The scribe was essentially a media specialist of his time, that is, the scribe made use of the technologies of stylus, pen, and papyrus to translate the medium of speech into the medium of writing. In doing so, scribes transferred the fluidity and complexities of remembered oral traditions into written artifacts that represented (and also privileged) aspects and elements of those remembered traditions for a given community. They also made sure that some oral traditions and their interpretations survived in time.

Manuscripts were designed as prompts for communal memory and for speaking. Manuals of rhetoric in the early days of a manuscript culture even provide the rules and norms for holding a manuscript during a presentation. Initially developed as aids to the spoken word, they were not designed to be read in silence. As the art of transcription developed, manuscripts were illuminated with elaborate penmanship to appeal not only to the ear but also to the eye. Even still, the entelechy of the manuscript was in the sound of human speech, not the silence of solitary reading.

This brief background is suggestive for the contemporary preacher. Unlike the medieval scribe, the preacher is not making use of writing to transcribe oral speech or make a copy of something else. The preacher uses writing in a more inventive way, that is, writing becomes a way of discovering and shaping what the preacher wants to say. Writing for preaching offers several advantages. It allows the preacher to become the audience for language selection and arrangement of thought. One is able through writing to get some critical distance from impulsive and germinal impressions in order to shape a more distinct and clarifying word. At other times, writing for the sermon arises out of silent contemplation. In any case, writing may enable the preacher to find the form for congregational address. The form that the sermon will take is what the manuscript holds.

C. Performance as Three Acts

The process of performing a manuscript looks like a drama in three acts: (1) preparation, (2) creation, and (3) incarnation, followed by reflection. Unlike a conventional drama, however, the pattern of movement between them looks more like an ellipse than a straight line. In this drama, voice and body are going to join writing as central players in all three acts; they do not just make their entrance at the end. The first act of any drama is primarily devoted to exposition of the characters, their apparent relationships, the setting, and the situations and predicaments in which they find themselves.

1. Preparation

The first act of performing is preparation. Preachers assess what they have to work with and begin to discover what the material has to say. The eye and the ear work in tandem to guide the preacher through the material. One is looking and listening for God's redemptive action in the world of human affairs. What does one see in the lines of homeless poor persons outside the shelter or between the lines of a biblical text? When the preacher reads the text aloud for the first time, what words stand up to be counted? What turns of phrase turn the gut upside down? What echoes, resonances, dissonances, and harmonies does one hear between the world of the text and the world the preacher lives in? What does everyday speech sound like? Writing the impressions of the senses into a journal or notebook will feed the language that one will choose for the manuscript.

Effective preaching performance employs language that aims at the senses; the discipline of journal writing gives the preacher practice in using concrete imagery, descriptive language, dialogue, and conversation for use in the sermon.

During preparation, the preacher realizes that he or she is part of an ensemble, a think tank. The preacher's role is to first invite other voices into the conversation around a text, topic, justice issue, or pastoral concern and then discover his or her perspective. Here is where scholars bring the wisdom from tradition and careful, thoughtful reading, where artists bring their visions of human experience, where intellectuals bring their ongoing debates, and where a congregant brings a question or a cry of the heart. To find one's voice, the preacher becomes both host and student, serving the conversation by taking copious notes, translating as one goes what one is hearing into the language of everyday speech.

2. Creation

The challenge the preacher faces in act 2—creation—is to find the form and movement that will suit the purposes and goals for the sermon. Without these elements, a preacher cannot take one's proper place at the center of the stage. It helps at this point to have an image of what kind of manuscript one will begin to prepare. Is it a script? An outline? A blueprint? Or a prompt? The preacher will create a design for the sermon, a plan for the event of preaching. Where will the preacher place particular elements that create flow in the sermon? Where in the design will there be pauses and transitions? Here the ear and the eye work together. Sounding out an argument, speaking a story, reading a text aloud again for nuances and different inflections—all contribute to the orchestration of the sermon's elements. The ear will teach the eye and the hand what to write and how to arrange the language on a page. Even as one is writing, one is getting freer from the controlling influence of the page; writing is taking its place in the drama as having a supportive role to play.

The body is at work during creation in other ways as well. The body is thinking too. It is offering responses to the material that the preacher is planning to use (or omit) in the design. What is the effect of this story as I tell it? What emotive qualities of the text am I sensing? What is my gut telling me about what is right and wrong about this topic? What does dislike of this part of the text feel like, and what language does that emotion offer me? The body is getting up and moving around during creation, responding, discovering what items and elements to emphasize through gesture, what images to describe, what position it wants to take in relation to the congregation when something is said.

The outcome of this part of the process is the creation of a form that carries the content of the sermon to the inner ear of the listener. Whatever pattern of arrangement the preacher chooses to use, the primary consideration is whether the manuscript is shaped for oral communication. The preacher takes care to write the sermon in order to speak it aloud. A good test is giving voice to the sermon as it is being shaped. Practicing the parts of the sermon that feel congested and dense will help the preacher with flow, transitions, word choice, and effect.

3. Incarnation

The final phase of the process—incarnation—is actually the beginning of a new one: the live interaction between the preacher and the congregation. The sermon will come through the preacher's voice, body, speech, and gesture. It is by God's grace and the work of the Holy Spirit that the sounding of a preacher's soul becomes the bearer of the Word of God. Embodying the sermon means three things: rehearse; rehearse; rehearse. The point of the rehearsal is not to tighten the preacher's control over the event so that there is no room for interaction with the listener. It is, rather, to prepare the voice and the body for the movement of the sermon in the moment of performance. Vocal exercises, relaxation techniques, and prayer help the preacher become available to the design of the sermon and to the Word emerging through it. The rehearsal process is a trust-building exercise, trust in the work the preacher has done to the best of her or his ability, trust in the Spirit of God to bring that work to completion, and trust in the congregation to collaborate in making meaning of the event itself. In the end, the sermon in performance is an offering to God and to the congregation the preacher is called to serve.

Sermon performance is a journey from the preacher's ear, across the landscape of the soul, and to the voice. Writing serves the process by becoming the preacher's companion. Speech and gesture transform the writing into lively, expressive speech that becomes an action of a loving God toward God's people. Performance of the manuscript bears witness to God's self-performance through the means God has appointed: human reason and imagination, natural revelation, Scripture, and tradition. *See* MANUSCRIPT; MEMORY; PERFORMATIVE LANGUAGE.

Bibliography: Charles L. Bartow. *The Preaching Moment: A Guide to Sermon Delivery.* (1980); Jana Childers. *Performing the Word: Preaching as Theatre.* (1998); Mitties McDonald de Champlain. "What to Do While Preaching." *Best Advice for Preaching.* Edited by John S. McClure. (1998) 99–116; G. Robert Jacks. *Just Say the Word!: Writing for the Ear.* (1996); Richard F. Ward. *Speaking of the Holy: The Art of Communication in Preaching.* (2001); Paul Scott Wilson. *The Practice of Preaching.* (1995) 37–60.

PREACHER'S CREATIVE PROCESS
Jana Childers

The experience of creating a sermon may be understood in spiritual, psychological, or physiological terms or in terms of academic theories of creativity. Preachers who choose to analyze their creative work generally do so by careful observation of the distinct elements of their process and comparison with others. Such self-knowledge identifies opportunities for growth—especially growth of the ability to generate new ideas and make new connections between ideas. In addition, many preachers and artists acknowledge a larger purpose. The study of creativity can be "an attempt to penetrate the mystery of self and perhaps the even greater mystery of Being" (Barron, Montuori, and Barron 1997, 2).

The history of formal academic interest in human creativity is a short one. Though the ancients had their muses and romanticism espoused an interest in imagination, it was not until the early 20th cent., after Freud and Jung introduced the notion of the unconscious, that systematic investigation of the subject began. One of the earliest models of creativity was proposed by Graham Wallas in 1926. He described four stages:

1. Preparation: the stage in which the problem or issue is defined.
2. Incubation: the stage in which the problem or issue is laid aside.
3. Illumination: the moment in which the new idea emerges.
4. Verification: the stage in which the solution is tested (Wallas 1926, 80).

Of particular note is the balance of activities described by Wallas. His model is composed of more or less equal parts of rational (primarily seen in stages 1 and 4) and imaginative (primarily seen in stages 2 and 3) activity.

In the years following the publication of Wallas's model, theorists' focus shifted from rationality's role in the process to the role played by unconscious processes and uncontrollable events. Human creativity began to be understood along Darwinian lines as a function of random variation and natural selection. So it was pointed out that though Alexander Fleming "discovered" penicillin, there was an important element of chance in the way it showed up in the petri dish. Yes, theorists acknowledged, George de Mestral invented Velcro, but it was a walk in the woods and the cockleburs that adhered to his cuffs that "gave" him the idea. By mid-century when Alex Osborn introduced the notion of "brainstorming," the unconscious and the random were held in such high esteem that creativity began to be seen as something quite outside the control of human beings.

World War II provoked the first round of real funding for and serious interest in creativity research. The U.S. Department of Defense anted up, hoping for better technology and more effective leaders. However, the 1950s and 1960s saw little advancement in creativity theory, and by the mid-1970s, academic interest had become focused on empirical methods and measurable phenomena. Social scientists distanced themselves from the seemingly subjective field of creativity, reinforcing the popular belief that the study of creativity was both fuzzy and futile.

Also during this time, a young University of California, Berkeley, psychologist named Frank Barron undertook an ambitious project, which was ultimately to help reestablish the field. His research focused on interviews with well-known artists, scientists, and other creative geniuses. The resulting model, published in 1988 after decades of research, employs the birth metaphor and describes the creative process in four stages:

1. Conception: a prepared mind receives the problem.
2. Gestation: the process develops on an intricate timetable.
3. Parturation: the new idea or solution is born.
4. Bringing Up Baby: a period of further development (Barron, Montuori, and Barron 1997, 2).

On one level, in Barron's echo of Wallas, the field comes full circle. At the end of the first century of study, the creative process is understood once again as a blend of both rational and more-than-rational activities and as an experience over which human beings exercise some control. Also during this period, a flow of interest and funding from corporate and federal sources demonstrated the field's viability. Finally, several promising physiological studies were carried out during this time, suggesting the likelihood that one day science would be able to observe creativity's very roots. In a few decades of study, human creativity was shown to be a worthy subject for scientific and social scientific inquiry. No longer the province of mystery, human creativity turned out to have plottable, measurable, and investigatable aspects. Patterns of the process were found to be describable—eight to ten major models and scores of minor ones were proposed for the task.

Today preachers appropriate the insights of creativity theorists in different ways, with pneumatological differences accounting for the most significant variances. The question of how much of a preacher's creativity is attributable to the Holy Spirit's inspiration and how much to human perspiration is a real one. Some preachers would say "all" that is imaginative, new, or generative in their preaching is a gift of God. Some would say "most," and some would equivocate. Many would agree on a statement something like the following: "The sermon is both all up to God and all up to me." Regardless of how the Holy Spirit's role in the creative process is understood, few experienced preachers would discount the importance of developing skills and spiritual disciplines that cooperate with the Spirit's work. (*See* HOLY SPIRIT AND PREACHING.) The following are examples of ways that preachers apply theorists' findings about human creativity in the quest to be faithful preachers:

1. Accept the reassurances that the field offers. Studies have shown that creativity occurs in several varieties and that it is possible to develop the skills underlying them. Originality, fluency, adaptive flexibility, spontaneous flexibility, sensitivity to problems, and expressional fluency are all aspects of what is commonly called creativity. Most preachers excel at some and not others, but those who are willing to build the concentration, imagination, and observation skills that undergird them all may reasonably expect some growth. Similarly, creative people have been shown to have certain common characteristics, some of which preachers may cultivate. These characteristics include the ability to work independently, high energy, flexibility, an introverted and intuitive nature, and the desire to create. Desire and openness are key characteristics of preachers who pursue creativity.

2. Establish and maintain the conditions that support creativity. A richness of life experience, time set apart to do one's work, and the ability to operate outside the reach of society are among the conditions shown to be important to creative people. There are, of course, any number of preachers who find each of these conditions elusive. However, the most significant environmental factor affecting creativity is one that is in one way or another in most every preacher's grasp. Creative people say that most important among all the conditions supporting creativity is the experience of freedom. Preachers who can achieve a sense of freedom by dint of spiritual discipline or theological rationale will find themselves in the one state considered essential for creative work.

3. Make use of juxtaposition to create space. Holding elements of experience or thought in tension creates the essential condition for creative insight—psychic, psychological, spiritual, and emotional space. This is the phase of the creative process often described with gestation imagery—thoughts are *incubating*, insights are *born*, and ideas *hatch*. The creative preacher can create space anywhere and often with the small blocks of time available by performing pieces of the biblical text and juxtaposing character, voice, context, and rhetorical situation one against the other. The space produced fosters new ideas or deeper engagement on the part of preacher and listener. A preacher can ask, What happens to this line of the text if I say it in this tone of voice? Or this? What happens to this character if I picture him face-to-face with Jesus or with his back turned? What happens to this truth claim if I plop it into my situation? How does this line of dialogue sound if I picture saying it to Mrs. Young or Elder Kim?

Fred Craddock practices a kind of juxtaposition that might be called reverse anachronism in a sermon on Mark 1:1-8, "Have You Ever Heard John Preach?"

Oh a lot of people came. I'm sure some of them came out of curiosity. I can imagine the teenagers in that country sitting around on the hoods of their camels, nothing to do. "Have you heard of John?" "No." "Well, let's go out there." (Long and Plantinga 1994, 38)

The sermon shows more than the preacher's ability to play with juxtaposed images, though. In Craddock's preaching it is also possible to catch a whiff of the inner freedom and a glimpse of the undergirding skills so important to creativity.

The Bible calls it a new birth. You've been to that window, haven't you? The maternity ward, the nursery, and all that stuff up there in that big window? And all the men outside trying to figure out which one she is? You know, Julie is in there somewhere and I know she's the prettiest one, and you can't read those little old bands where the arm comes down and the hand joins and there's a deep wrinkle and there's that band, and it's so small and you say, "Well I think that's. . . ."And the Bible says, That's what it is, that is it. (Long and Plantinga 1994, 43)

See IMAGINATION/CREATIVITY; LECTIO DIVINA; PREACHER'S WEEK; PREPARATION.

Bibliography: Frank Barron, Alfonso Montuori, and Anthea Barron, eds. *Creators on Creating: Awakening and Cultivating the Imaginative Mind.* (1997); Jana Childers, ed. *Birthing the Sermon: Women Preachers on the Creative Process.* (2001); Thomas G. Long and Cornelius Plantinga Jr., eds. *A Chorus of Witnesses: Model Sermons for Today's Preacher.* (1994); Graham Wallas. *The Art of Thought.* (1926).

PREACHER'S WEEK
William J. Carl III

Because by nature ministry is messy, no two weeks are ever the same. The most effective pastors/preachers are those who learn to manage the messiness. Preachers try to establish a sense of order with a daily schedule, only to discover that it works just fine until the interruptions begin. Eventually, the preacher realizes that real ministry often occurs in the interruptions. The story of the woman with the issue of blood who confronts Jesus on his way to heal Jairus's daughter (Mark 5:21-43) shows Jesus' discovery of this fact.

Jesus was constantly being pulled this way and that, and yet he established a healthy rhythm of reflection/action, research, and praxis. He experienced all the pressures of a modern pastor and yet managed to keep his sanity by establishing a regular pattern of prayer and preaching. With all the administrative, pastoral, and community responsibilities on their plates these days, 21st-cent. clergy would do well to follow Jesus' disciplined practice of study and service. Today's preacher also needs to be something of a juggler, keeping numerous balls in the air simultaneously through effective multitasking. Thus, we see the need for a long-term planning process, a regular weekly schedule, and daily prayer and study to deal with the relentless regularity of Sunday morning. (*See* DEVOTIONAL LIFE/LIFE-STYLE; LONG-RANGE SERMON PLANNING.)

Long-term Planning

Sermon planning textbooks and homileticians recommend spending time planning your sermons. The reason is simple: if you do not plan ahead, the weekly demands will eventually wear you down and leave you exhausted. I recommend that you carve out at least a week away from the church, phones, and meetings to plan a year or at least six months of sermons. This homiletical preparation may involve the use of the lectionary (LECTIONARY AND THE CHRISTIAN YEAR) or a mix of lectionary texts and sermon series texts. You may also use LECTIO CONTINUA, starting with the first verse of a biblical book and marching through that book pericope by pericope.

The purpose of getting away is to assure a week of uninterrupted time for study and reflection. It can be at a retreat center, a cabin in the woods, a theological seminary library—you choose. Just get away. The object is not to drill down deeply into each passage, but to do your initial, spiritual reading of the text and brief study of a commentary or two to get a glimpse of an idea that might lead to a sermon. Try to develop a theme and even a possible sermon title or two. You are also deciding whether you are going to preach from one passage or more. One note of advice for your church board: you should not count this week of planning as continuing education because it represents a crucial part of your work as a preacher.

Once you have returned to your church, you might print the results of your research for the director of music. Doing this will certainly make the choosing of hymns and anthems easier and ensure a better fit between your sermon topics and the music. Whether you are serving a larger or smaller church, the entire staff will appreciate seeing where you are going in the upcoming sermons.

Such long-range planning starts the incubation process. By this point, you have dropped the seeds or, thinking of the annunciation, the Holy Spirit has planted the seeds in you, and sermons are beginning to form in your heart and mind. Throughout the year, you are thinking homiletically. What this means is that every time you read a book, watch a movie, hear a story, see something unusual, or just have a fleeting thought that in any way relates to texts or themes you will be addressing, you pull up the file for that sermon and add that thought to it. All year long you keep adding to those files new inspirations that come to mind. Thus, months later when you begin working on the sermon, you have already done lots of research.

A Typical Week (If There Ever Is Such a Thing)

It is Monday or Tuesday morning, and you are ready to sit down and work on your sermon for the coming Sunday. Inevitably, there will be an interruption—a death in the parish, some brush fire to put out. But because you have done your sermon planning, you are ahead of the game and ready for occasional intrusions. Some pastors study at home and come into the office later. You will have to find your rhythm for study and leadership. If you are always available with an ever-present open-door policy, you may never have time to work on a sermon. On the other hand, if you set up your administrative assistant as a bodyguard to block the door all the time, few people may want to come on Sundays and hear what you have to say about Jesus' love for the people. It is a delicate balance.

If the old rule of one hour of study for every minute in the pulpit still holds true, then you are going to have to spend significant time preparing. Otherwise, you will end up like the pastor who said, "I could whip a sermon together in thirty minutes and think nothing of it," and one parishioner replied, "Yes, and we wouldn't either." Lawyers know that cases are won in chambers.

As you sit down with the text, you approach it first as a believer. What does this text say to you spiritually? See your life reflected "in the mirror of the text," as Paul Ricoeur used to say (1974, 385). Otherwise, your sermon can easily slip into a heady, exegetical paper with no traction in people's daily lives. Emotional investment on your part in this sermon will engage the congregation's attention even more on Sunday. This is the initial stage of creativity where, like a composer putting hands to the keyboard, you are beginning to make music. Aaron Copland reminds us that composers are professionals (1957, 24–25). They must create every day; so also preachers. (*See* PREACHER'S CREATIVE PROCESS.) We write sermons every week, whether we feel like it or not.

Once you have a sense of the text, you check commentaries to make sure that gut feeling is on the right track. You also exegete the congregation by asking what certain parishioners, differing age groups, and stations in life might be asking about this text. Some pastors use Bible studies on their sermon passages to get input from congregants and avoid the lone ranger approach to preaching. Suddenly, a direction begins to emerge, a trajectory if you like, a place you want your people to be when you come to your conclusion. This is the "so what" of the sermon. Remember that Augustine insisted that great sermons should do three things well: teach the mind, touch the heart, and move the will.

By Tuesday or Wednesday, you are thinking of illustrative material and the beginnings of a structure. The day before you write the sermon, you should have the outline ready to go, whether you use a traditional point sermon, a problem-solution approach, or a Buttrickian move-system (Buttrick 1987, 23–79). The outline must be so complete that you could almost get up and preach it as is. If it is not that complete, writing it the next day will be a nightmare. By the day you write it, the sermon should flow easily because you know where it is going and how you are going to get there. Whether you write it on Thursday or Friday, you need to let it sit for a day or an afternoon before looking at it again.

Saturday morning is for revisions and learning the sermon, which may take three to four hours of preparation. It is your professional responsibility to internalize the sermon so well that you can look at the congregation when you preach it. Whether or not you carry a manuscript or outline into the pulpit with you is not the point. The point is not to read whatever you have up there with you.

Remember the Sabbath Keep it Holy

In the rhythm of the preacher's week, it is extremely important to allot time for daily prayer and study as well as a breathing space away from the rough-and-tumble of parish life. Otherwise, you will burn out spiritually, reducing your homiletical effectiveness. Since prayer is a way of delegating worries to God, a disciplined spiritual life virtually eliminates any worry a preacher might have about preaching. All preachers, planners and non-planners alike, ultimately rely on God's grace.

Bibliography: David Buttrick. *Homiletic: Moves and Structures.* (1987); Aaron Copland. *What to Listen for in Music.* (1957); Paul Ricoeur. *The Conflict of Interpretations: Essays in Hermeneutics.* (1974).

PREACHING OUT OF THE OVERFLOW
Cleophus J. LaRue

Preaching out of the overflow refers to a sermon practice that arises from a lifetime of reading widely, studying deeply, and reflecting continuously on what will be preached. It has to do with cultivating appropriate study habits and attitudes in contrast to preaching that is shallow or overworked. Overflow preaching is practiced in many African American and evangelical churches and is related to the Reformed notions of an educated ministry and to sermon preparation as spiritual discipline.

   A. Three Kinds of Preachers
   B. Habits of Reading
   C. Having More Ideas than One Can Use
   D. Short-haul Reading
   E. Long-haul Reading
   F. Recommendations

Effective preachers read! And they read a lot. In order to preach with depth and profundity the preacher needs to be on a steady diet of good literature. How one accomplishes this task may vary, but that one *must* accomplish it is of the utmost necessity. A well-read person is a full person.

A. Three Kinds of Preachers

William Stidger, in a work titled *Preaching Out of the Overflow*, claimed that while writing his book on preaching, his train was passing through one of the oil fields of Kansas. This experience led him to compare preaching to the different types of oil wells he saw on his trip. He noted three types: dry holes, wells that have to be pumped, and wells that overflow. Accordingly, he asserted that there are three kinds of preachers and three kinds of preaching. First, there are the preachers whose preaching amounts to a dry hole. Absolutely nothing is there. Their content and style are dry, barren, lifeless, and non-edifying.

Second, there are the preachers who have to pump themselves up—literally force the sermon out each week. These preachers strain, battle, sweat, and worry themselves and their families into misery over the sermon. Each week the production of a sermon is an arduous, gut-wrenching affair.

Third, there are the preachers who preach out of the overflow. These preachers do not have a panic attack each week over the sermon, nor do they scrape the bottom of the barrel for the last kernel of good news. Rather they preach out of the abundance of their reading and research. Overflow preachers preach from a wealth of materials, knowledge, disciplined insight, and rich experiences gained from diligent study and conscious reflection on God's presence in the world.

B. Habits of Reading

Some preachers are morning people. They read in the calm and quiet of a brand-new day. Something about the early morning and its promise of new mercies helps them to retain more of what they consume from the written page. Other preachers are night hawks. Their powers of retention are keenest when burning the midnight oil. They read with great profit when their home is undisturbed, their world is quiet, and the only noise about them is the rush of their own creative process.

Other preachers read on the fly. They catch-as-catch-can. They grab a read here and there—between meetings at the church, a little downtime in the afternoon, on the road during revivals and guest appearances, or some unexpected free time made possible through a cancellation in the schedule. While their reading approach requires them to hustle, the realization that their time is limited seems to help them absorb more on the fly. Be it morning, noon, or night, or on the run, preachers have to read in order to remain fresh, vibrant, interesting, creative, and faithful.

C. Having More Ideas than One Can Use

The best preaching is never worked up but is worked out. Good sermons stem from the natural flow of a ripe mind, an informed intellect, creative thought, and expressions of growth through varied life experiences. Real joy in preaching depends on our having more ideas and suggestions for preaching than we can ever use; and this fine joy, akin to elation, comes only when our minds and our notebooks are crammed full. Stidger listed several areas of human existence where overflows could be nurtured and harvested. Among them were physical fitness, ideas, life experiences, religious experiences, and Christian love. He further noted that an overflow of ideas comes through expansive reading that is initially intended for self-edification.

D. Short-haul Reading

Some reading must be done with intentionality and immediacy. That is the reading one does in preparation for the Sunday sermon. This reading requires initial reflection on the biblical text (lectionary or preacher's choice) and the employment of the rudimentary tools of preparation, such as a concordance, a Bible dictionary, word study, and devotional and critical commentaries that assist the preacher in drawing out the meaning of the passage. The immediacy of this reading is intentional in the sense that it has to be done within a certain amount of time. Every pastor is conscious of the growing roar of next Sunday's fast-approaching train.

E. Long-haul Reading

However, preaching out of the overflow is preaching that grows out of reading for the long haul—reading with no immediate use or specified purpose in mind. Too many preachers scan the shelves of bookstores, libraries, and the Internet with an eye toward the immediacy of next Sunday. If they pick up a book that seems to have little use for the upcoming preaching assignment, they all too often put that book aside in favor of another that appears to provide immediate help for next Sunday. That is shortsighted reading that seems more like pumping the bottom of the well than taking advantage of the gushing oil from the overflow.

Effective preachers learn early to read for the long haul. Long-haul reading is broad, expansive, and enriching, though not necessarily immediately applicable. Initially, it does more for the preacher than for the congregation. But ultimately, the congregation benefits immensely from the rich rewards of the preacher's sustained labor.

F. Recommendations

Several admonitions are in order as one prepares to engage in long-haul reading that will enable one to preach out of the overflow of disciplined study.

1. Do not bite off more than you can chew. Lots of preachers have starting power, but they lack staying power. When it comes to disciplined study, every preacher needs to remember that the race is not given to the swift. Start small and allow yourself room to grow in your reading. Incremental learning is best.

2. Begin with the familiar and ease yourself into the deeper, uncharted waters of more complex theological thought. For example, one could begin with a chapter-by-chapter reading of the entire Bible. Such reading could be a part of one's daily devotional reading, or it could simply be reading that one does fifteen or thirty minutes each day. A systematic, daily reading of the Bible may seem to be a waste of time for those who must turn to it on a weekly basis for sermon preparation. But sadly enough, it is the case that all too many preachers have yet to read in full those words by which they claim to live and in which they claim to have some specialty—the Scriptures.

In addition to the Bible, commentaries and other monographs on Scripture can be immensely helpful in broadening the preacher's intellectual and spiritual horizons. The commentaries that one chooses to read could be on the text one is mulling over for the week, or they could be reading intended to strengthen a planned preaching series in the near future. Many experienced preachers warn against purchasing complete sets of commentaries since the writing and scholarship tend to be uneven. The best way to purchase a commentary is to scan several from a particular book of the Bible with a passage in mind that you have been considering for a sermon. Consider purchasing those that do the best job of challenging and clarifying the critical and the devotional elements at stake in the text. Commentaries can also be a part of one's daily devotional reading.

3. Place good reading materials within your reach. Subscribe to journals and magazines that will allow excellent reading materials to come directly to your home or study on a regular basis. While there are many on the market, one could not go wrong by subscribing to those that have a reputation for intellectual rigor. Among the many are *Theology Today* (theologytoday.ptsem.edu); *Interpretation: A Journal of Bible and Theology* (www.interpretation.org); and *The Christian Century* (www.ChristianCentury.org).

These publications contain excellent articles on theology, biblical studies, and contemporary religious concerns. Also included are outstanding book reviews that allow the preacher to keep up with the most recent publications on the market. More important, it puts the preacher in conversation with the latest in theological thought and the best minds in biblical studies. Moreover, it allows preachers the opportunity to broaden their intellectual circle from the comfort of their home or study.

In addition to journals that help them stay abreast of the latest in theological thought, preachers should avail themselves of non-religious reading materials. Subscription to a regional, statewide, or national newspaper on the order of the *New York Times* or the *Los Angeles Times* can be quite helpful. One should also subscribe, through the mail or online, to weekly news magazines like *Time* or *Newsweek.* It is not that one is expected to read all these publications in full, but the conscientious preacher should at least have an opportunity to thumb through them in search of items of interest. Some news item, feature story, or interesting statistic will inadvertently catch the preacher's eye and can be stored away for future use.

4. Broaden your reading circle. Begin reading in small increments the systematic theologies of theologians past and present. Readers and compendiums on the great theologians abound. Read the sermons of effective preachers, as well as the biographies and autobiographies of great preachers and theologians. For example, read Robert Miller's *Harry Emerson Fosdick* (1985); Eberhard Busch's *Karl Barth* (1976); Charles E. White's *Beauty of Holiness: Phoebe Palmer as Theologian, Revivalist, Feminist, and Humanitarian* (1986); Richard Fox's *Reinhold Niebuhr* (1985); and Samuel DeWitt Proctor's *The Substance of Things Hoped For* (1996).

5. Read things that are not religious on the surface but speak in meaningful ways to our lived

experience. Subscribe to the *New York Times Book Review*, and keep up with the latest in fiction and non-fiction alike. (The best sellers' list with its one-sentence description of what each book is about will teach the preacher brevity if nothing else.) Poets, novelists, playwrights, and biographers have insight into the human situation that many preachers lack. Immerse yourself in the novels of John Grisham, Flannery O'Connor, Frederick Buechner, William Faulkner, Toni Morrison, and many others. Novels enlarge our experience of life because they enable us to live vicariously a much wider range of experience than is normally open to us. They help us to see more deeply into the complexities of the human situation, and they illumine our understanding of complex moral and theological issues.

Read the poetry of Browning, Tennyson, Frost, and Longfellow. Preachers struggle constantly with words, trying to make them describe the essentially indescribable—the nature and love of God. The poets have much to teach us here. Read as widely in this area as you can. It was said of Vernon Johns, Martin Luther King's predecessor at the Dexter Avenue Baptist Church in Montgomery, Alabama, that he would recite poetry while plowing the fields and scrounge around the rest of the day looking for books to read at night. He was seldom at a loss for words.

Preachers who desire to speak out of the abundance of the overflow learn early on to immerse themselves in good literature and a healthy reading regimen. Long-haul reading and broad exposure to many different types of literature will inevitably make a person a more effective preacher. One's reading will determine the height and the depth of one's preaching. *See* AFRICAN AMERICAN PREACHING PERSPECTIVES; DEVOTIONAL LIFE/LIFE-STYLE; SERMON RESEARCH.

Bibliography: Mike Graves. *What's the Matter with Preaching Today?* (2004); John S. McClure, ed. *Best Advice for Preaching.* (1998); Cyril Rodd. *The Pastor's Opportunities.* (1990); William Stidger. *Preaching Out of the Overflow.* (1930); Gardner Taylor and Samuel D. Proctor. *We Have This Ministry: The Heart of the Pastor's Vocation.* (1996).

SERMON RESEARCH
David A. Davis

Sermon research is most often grounded in the preacher's exegetical work with a particular biblical text. In the study and interpretation of biblical texts, exegesis requires attention to language, word studies, history, theology, literary form, and cultural context (EXEGESIS). Given the breadth of these areas of study and the time limitations that come with weekly preaching pastoral ministry, a preacher should develop exegetical tools and a consistency of method. Experienced preachers may follow that method intuitively as they move through the steps of interpretation. When faced with difficult texts or when inspiration seems slow to come, all preachers benefit from the return to a step-by-step engagement with Scripture.

Secondary resources for biblical exegesis exist in abundance. Early on in the preparation process, preachers may consult Bible dictionaries, explanatory notes in annotated Bibles, and texts that give history and background. It is important, however, to allow room for the preacher's imaginative encounter with a particular passage (IMAGINATION/CREATIVITY). Scholarly work in commentaries can sometimes squelch the pastor's voice. Before being too quick to preach the insights of a commentator, preachers should learn to trust their own efforts. When consulted a bit later in the exegetical process, biblical scholars become conversation partners rather than repositories for sermon ideas.

When a preaching ministry is rooted in a congregational context, biblical research is foundational but may not represent the first steps of sermon research. Every sermon is part of an ongoing conversation in the community of faith. Pastors draw upon the theological traditions in which they have been trained. In that sense, research for a given sermon probably starts with one's theological education. The pastoral context of parish ministry plays a necessary part and should be included in the research for or reflection on every sermon. And current events and the complexities of contemporary culture require the preacher's attention as well. Though the Bible may be the primary text to be researched, the preacher is exegeting congregational, cultural, and pastoral contexts on a weekly basis.

"One hour of research for every minute in the pulpit." Every preacher has come upon that old bit of wisdom. The advice must have taken shape back in the day of the great pulpiteer, where pastors had the luxury of endless hours in the study. Contemporary models for pastoral ministry place many more demands on the preacher's time, and in most cases the image of the great pulpiteer who knows a lot about everything has now been lost. Nonetheless, disciplined preparation is essential for faithful preaching and healthy ministry. Effective preachers find a system of preparation that works for them: a couple of hours every morning, a day and a half reserved, or time carved out for study at home. Planning more than a week ahead allows for a sense of ongoing research. Whether actively or subconsciously, pastors are usually working on more than one sermon at a time (*see* LONG-RANGE SERMON PLANNING).

Internet tools are dramatically altering the way a preacher does research. Of course, not all of these changes are good ones. Sites that easily provide illustrations cannot possibly help the preacher with the necessary contextual discernment. Sermon sites make it way too easy for preachers to cut corners in their work or, even worse, to plagiarize. On the other hand, pastors no longer have to sift through old newspapers looking for that one article they remember reading a while back. Research on public issues is easier than ever before. Preachers sitting in their offices now have access to theological libraries of information (*see* INTERNET PREACHING DATABASES).

Certain kinds of sermons require different approaches to research. A preacher who is preaching through a particular book of the Bible can take advantage of the accumulation of relevant research from week to week. A preacher who is tackling a particular public issue that is confronting a congregation will want to plan far enough ahead to allow the time to gather information and exegete the issue. A sermon series approach certainly provides the chance to streamline research, whether preaching a series on the parables of Jesus or a series on prayer in the life of the believer.

When it comes to current events and popular culture, preachers should not apologize for the necessity of research. Having regular subscriptions to newspapers and magazines is almost a given. Taking trips to see films and attend concerts is work related in terms of inspiration and illustrative material. A pastor must take the time to learn where the congregation turns for enjoyment, news, and information.

For those who preach on a regular basis, sermon research becomes something of a way of life.

Pastors are always thinking about sermons and looking for sermon material. For some, that means holding on to a notebook all the time. Others try to develop a filing system or use other means of remembering. More important, sermon research depends upon having the eyes to see the very presence of God in the ordinary places of life. Yes, preachers must be diligent in their work with Scripture, their reading of theology, and their desire to be current in terms of news and culture. But at the end of the day, preachers are also called to look into the world and see sure and certain signs of the kingdom of God in our midst. Researching and witnessing to the presence of God are the harder parts of proclaiming the gospel in the community of faith. *See* PREACHER'S WEEK.

Bibliography: Interpretation: A Bible Commentary for Teaching and Preaching. Series edited by James Luther Mays, Patrick D. Miller, Jr., and Paul J. Achtemeier; *Preaching the New Common Lectionary.* Series edited by Fred B.Craddock, et al.; *Texts for Preaching: A Lectionary Commentary Based on the NRSV.* Series edited by Walter Brueggemann, Beverly R. Gaventa, et al. "The Text This Week: Lectionary, Scripture Study and Worship Links and Resources." Online: http://www.textweek.com; Leonora Tubbs Tisdale. *Preaching as Local Theology and Folk Art.* (1997).

TIME MANAGEMENT
David Albert Farmer

The main reason that most preachers who need a time management plan lack one is that they have never required themselves to make any system their system. Often a simple lack of consistent self-challenge compounds the problem—having found a workable plan, they fail to follow through.

In the classic homiletics textbook, *Preaching the Good News*, George E. Sweazey relates the preacher's problem with time management to laziness: "Preachers may be obscure because they are lazy. It is hard work to translate from the expressions that first come to mind to the way they should be put to an audience. So the minister may say what comes [naturally] to him [or her] and shirk the difficult next step" (1976, 131). Here is a very serious preaching fault: the preacher has not followed through with the hermeneutical and application tasks, and as a result, the sermon is delivered prematurely. The preacher has satisfied herself or himself only with first thoughts and has not taken the extra pains to craft the message in language that can be heard and understood by a particular audience. Though Sweazey suggests that the problem might be understood in terms of laziness, most preachers today are anything but lazy. Instead, they are much more likely to be poor time managers. Fortunately, there are a number of ways a preacher may improve the stewardship of his or her time.

First, never apologize to a congregation for taking the time necessary to prepare consistently excellent sermons. If parishioners do not want trite, simplistic words or some other preacher's warmed up leftovers, then they are going to have to let their pastor work on sermons and bless her or his efforts.

Even more important is planning. The preacher must have a plan, process, or procedure in mind that can be shared with congregational leaders (LONG-RANGE SERMON PLANNING). At the very least, the preacher will prioritize how she or he plans to deal with the multiple demands of ministry. Preaching is only one of several heavy demands in a typical week for the majority of preachers who are also pastors. The average parishioner often does not realize how many varied tasks that a pastor must tend to day by day and week by week. Unless the preacher helps parishioners to understand the demands placed upon him or her, they will never know, and the probability of conflict between pastor and parish about ministry management will escalate exponentially.

A ministry priority list can be an excellent foundation for maintaining pastor-parish harmony and for establishing a time management plan that ultimately will protect preaching preparation time. Generally, a congregation is comforted to know that members in crisis (experiencing critical illness, confronted with bad relationship or employment news, in need of rapid referral to mental health professionals, etc.) get the pastor's immediate and uninterrupted attention. After that, the pastor is going to see to or share with other staff members and/or lay leaders the following, for example: non-crisis counseling (including premarital consultations), communication (returning calls, e-mails, and so on), non-sermon study (staying informed about world issues, ongoing skill development, midweek Bible

study preparation), administrative tasks and staff relations (committee meetings and the like), community ministries, and denominational responsibilities. Indeed, the preacher is learning a great deal about her or his congregants and fellow citizens during the meeting of these responsibilities. In addition to all of these important obligations, though, a pastor must prepare sermons, and this task must be a high priority.

Before the wide availability of personal computers, one pastor had an agreement with her congregation that Tuesdays were her study days. She would not come into the office that day; instead, she would visit the library and possibly a bookstore (even before the advent of coffee in-store!). Every Tuesday she would get her Sunday sermon well on its way. She could be reached only in case of emergency through the church secretary, who was the only person who knew where the pastor would be during her study day.

Another pastor had an agreement with his congregation that he would study first thing every day without any contact short of an emergency, keeping at it until he reached a significant milestone in the sermon preparation process. On some days that meant he had made an interpretive breakthrough with his sermon text and was ready to give attention to other pastoral duties by ten o'clock in the morning. On other days he pressed himself to find his key sermon illustrations and would not be ready to leave his sermon work until sometime after lunch. In both instances, a major part of the preacher's success had to do with the fact that the respective congregations understood how their pastor managed ministry time in the overall scheme of things, and preaching preparation time in particular.

Harry Emerson Fosdick told his Riverside Church congregation and his students at Union Seminary that he needed a good hour of preparation time for every preaching minute (Miller 2001, 353). He was such a superb preacher and homiletician—not to mention a masterful time manager—it seems doubtful that anyone would have argued much with him on that matter.

The single most important step a preacher can take to manage ministry and preaching time effectively is to take care of herself or himself, doing everything possible to enhance physical, emotional, and spiritual health. A close second on the list of requirements for effective ministry time management is the nurturing of relationships with spouse/partner/significant other, family members, and close friends. Somehow, there must be a protective line drawn between these dimensions of oneself along with one's personal life and all things professional, regardless of how compelling work demands may be.

We preach in a high-tech era. Many high-tech tools at our disposal save us an incalculable amount of time, but some of them can, at points, become time-stealers too (*see* TECHNOLOGY).

The Internet is amazing. We can do a major portion of our research at the office, at home, anywhere we have computer access, which saves both time and money. The same computer, though, on which so many of us have grown completely dependent, can fail. We can lose important, even vital, files. Constant backup becomes a way of life, and even with that we may be reloading programs from time to time or fighting off a virus until the wee hours of the morning.

Cell phones have allowed us to be in touch with practically anyone in the world at any time. With a hands-free device, we may choose to return calls while we are driving a distance or stuck in traffic. That is a huge potential time-saver. Cell phones may become tools of intrusion and constant interruption, though, for those who do not discipline themselves to master them. Preachers who have problems setting appropriate professional boundaries find themselves at the beck and call of anybody and everybody who has access to her or his telephone number.

Consider some other time-stealers that may not be obvious to us because we often lack objectivity when looking at our good and bad habits. Two enormous time- and energy-stealers are unaddressed conflict and procrastination. Learning to deal with the former is beyond the scope of this article, but the latter can be easily combated with as much advance preparation as a preacher can demand of herself or himself.

Lectionary preachers have the advantage of a choice of scriptures for any Sunday's sermon text. Why wait until Monday morning to choose them? Why not, instead, take study time—during summer months perhaps—and commit to at least a sermon text or texts as well as a working title for every Sunday in a half- or full-year preaching program? Monday mornings will be transformed! No more blank tablets or solid white word processing screens! At the very least, you will have a sermon title and scripture with which to work. As you become more skilled at such planning ahead, you may even have thought well in advance of Monday morning about the perfect illustration or an exceptionally creative approach to presenting a text's truth that might not have come to you if you had left everything to the few days before a given Sunday. Your music ministry partner will sing your praises because of the opportunity for more careful planning you are affording her or him too. The likely result is a more unified worship service in which music and sermon themes are connected.

Preaching with excellence and effective time management go hand in hand. You will be less stressed when you require yourself to manage your time. You, your colleagues, and your congregants all benefit. *See* INTERNET PREACHING DATABASES; PREACHER'S WEEK.

Bibliography: David Baron. "Establish Creative Down Time." *Moses on Management.* (1999) 176–80; Harry Emerson Fosdick. "Learning to Preach." *The Living of These Days: An Autobiography.* (1956) 83–112; Robert Moats Miller. *Henry Fosdick: Preacher, Pastor, Prophet.* (2001); George E. Sweazey. "The Time for Sermon Preparation." *Preaching the Good News.* (1976) 105–13.

WOMEN
Beverly A. Zink-Sawyer

A tradition of women's public proclamation extends back to the earliest days of Judeo-Christian history. Although not always preaching in the formal, liturgical understanding of the modern church, women have conveyed a word from the Lord to their communities of faith in a variety of ways. The OT names several women who served in leadership or prophetic roles at critical times in the history of the nation of Israel. Miriam, the sister of Moses and Aaron, proclaimed the defeat of Pharaoh's army by raising a tambourine and leading the community n song and dance (Exod 15:20-21). Deborah, a prophet and judge of Israel, and Barak sang in celebration of their triumph over the Canaanites (Judg 5:1-31). Huldah the prophet offered confirmation of the authenticity of the "book of the law" that served as the basis for King Josiah's religious reform (2 Kgs 22:14-20). Other brief mentions of female prophets in the OT include Noadiah, who is named among a group of prophets seeking to intimidate

Nehemiah during his rebuilding of the wall of Jerusalem (Neh 6:14), and an unnamed woman, who may be the wife of Isaiah (Isa 8:3).

NT women continued the Hebrew tradition of female proclamation through song and prophecy. Like Miriam, Mary offered a song of praise in response to the salvific work of God when she received the news that she would bear the Christ child (Luke 1:46-55). After Jesus' presentation in the Temple and blessing by Simeon, the elderly prophet Anna proclaimed the coming of the child "to all who were looking for the redemption of Jerusalem" (Luke 2:38), thus continuing the Hebrew tradition of prophetic women. A number of women, both named and unnamed, are mentioned in the Gospels as bearing public witness to Jesus and his message. The Samaritan woman whom Jesus met at Jacob's well (John 4:7-42) returned to her home city of Sychar and told others of her transforming encounter with Jesus, convincing many to believe in him because of her testimony (v. 39). Arguably, the first Christian preachers were the women who found the empty tomb on Easter morning and were commanded to "go, tell" the other disciples the good news of the resurrection (Matt 28:1-10; Mark 16:1-8; Luke 24:1-12; John 20:1-18). The names of the specific women who went to the tomb at dawn on the first day of the week vary among the Gospel writers, but all four writers report a clear command from an angel or from the risen Christ himself to the women named to proclaim the resurrection to others.

Several women are mentioned in the letters as leaders of the NT church. By virtue of their ecclesiastical responsibilities, they were most likely preachers as well. Lydia, who was converted by the Apostle Paul (Acts 16:11-15), is believed to have established a house church at Philippi, where it can be assumed that she preached. Priscilla and her husband, Aquila, preached "the Way of God" to Apollos of Alexandria (Acts 18:26) and ministered alongside Paul. In the final greetings of several of his letters, Paul thanks women who have been coworkers with him in ministry (Rom 16:1-16; Col 4:15; 2 Tim 4:19). The prophetic work of women also continued in the NT church as indicated by references to the four daughters of Philip the evangelist "who had the gift of prophecy" (Acts 21:9) and to women prophets in the church at Corinth who created controversy by prophesying with their heads uncovered (1 Cor 11:5).

There are glimpses of women's preaching in the early centuries of the church. Perpetua, a late 2nd-cent. prophet and martyr from Carthage, left an autobiographical account of her imprisonment and trial for refusing to renounce Christianity. Through that account, she continued to preach long after her death as her testimony was circulated and read in liturgical settings. Other women preached in the context of house churches and through their work as deacons. As the church became more hierarchical and institutional, however, women were shut out of the ecclesiastical roles they had enjoyed in the earliest centuries of the church. It was not until the late Middle Ages that women preached in greater numbers, occasionally with ecclesiastical sanction. Female mystics and abbesses, such as Hildegard of Bingen (1098–1179), Mechthild of Hackeborn (1240–1298), Julian of Norwich (ca. 1342–after 1413), Catherine of Siena (1347–1380), and Teresa of Avila (1515–1582), preached by virtue of divine revelations they had received.

The Reformation of the 16th cent. gave rise to instances of women preaching in Protestant churches in Europe and England, especially in sectarian movements. Groups that officially sanctioned women's preaching included the Society of Friends and German Pietist traditions such as the Moravians. While the religious and political climate of Puritan America prohibited women's public participation in church or society, some women, including Anne Hutchinson and Sarah Osborn, garnered reputations—and reprimands—for teaching and preaching in their homes. It was not until John Wesley began his Methodist movement in 18th-cent. England, however, that women preachers became prominent in significant numbers. As that movement spread around the world, most notably to colonial America, so, too, did broader acceptance of women's religious leadership, including preaching. In America, women preachers were encouraged by the Great Awakening that swept through the colonies in the mid-18th cent. The Awakening was based on the spiritual empowerment and responsibility of all believers, including women, to testify to the work of the Spirit in their lives. A similar religious movement in the early 19th cent. coincided with expanded roles for women and a proliferation of new religious traditions in the United States, giving rise to many itinerant women preachers. To women preachers in the already established Quaker and Methodist traditions were added women from the African Methodist Episcopal Church, the Shaker community, the Salvation Army, and several Holiness and Freewill Baptist groups. Some women preachers, including the well-known African American abolitionist Sojourner Truth, were independent of any denomination or sectarian group. Others preached in conjunction with their work in overseas missions.

From biblical times until the mid-19th cent., women preached, for the most part, with little or no ecclesiastical sanction and often at risk of severe reprimand. They proclaimed the Word of God in response to personal spiritual visions and divine inspiration despite the condemnation of church and society. When Protestant denominations began ordaining women as clergy in the middle of the 19th cent., women received official sanction for their preaching, adding to that inner spiritual call the blessing of the community. At the beginning of the 21st cent., most Protestant denominations around the world ordain women as clergy, and there are a number of women preachers in traditions that do not ordain women, such as the Roman Catholic Church, increasing the familiarity and acceptance of women's preaching.

An examination of the style and content of women's preaching across the centuries reveals some identifiable characteristics. Both medieval and contemporary women preachers have used more expansive imagery for God and have emphasized feminine dimensions of the divine. They traditionally have illustrated their sermons with images drawn from nature and domestic life and with stories from their life experiences or the life experiences of others. They have not been hesitant to use self-disclosure in their sermons, often using their experiences of faith as testimony to biblical truth. (*See* TESTIMONIAL.) Contemporary women preachers have tended to be more creative in their approach to preaching, preferring narrative sermon designs to more traditional didactic styles. (*See* NARRATIVE FORM.) They make use of feminist and other contemporary hermeneutical approaches in interpreting biblical texts, often leading them to address biblical themes of suffering, oppression, and injustice. (*See* ANTHROPOLOGY; FEMINIST CRITICISM; WOMANIST CRITICISM.) Women tend to regard the sermon as a collaborative effort or conversation between preacher and congregation. As the numbers of women studying and teaching in seminaries and preaching in pulpits increase, however, gender differences in preaching style are becoming less evident.

Through the centuries of Judeo-Christian history, women have found a way, with God's help, to proclaim their faith even when religious establishments rejected their gifts. They have sung, prophesied, witnessed, and preached in response to the work of God in their lives and in the world. At the beginning of the 21st cent., preaching in many traditions embodies the completeness of God's intention for creation with both male and female preachers proclaiming God's Word. Nevertheless, women continue to struggle to find a voice in some traditions and to be granted full acceptance as preachers and pastors in others, longing for the day when all are one in Christ Jesus.

Bibliography: David Albert Farmer and Edwina Hunter. *And Blessed Is She: Sermons by Women.* (1990); Eunjoo Mary Kim. *Women Preaching: Theology and Practice Through the Ages.* (2004); Leonora Tubbs Tisdale. "Women's Ways of Communicating: A New Blessing for Preaching." *Women, Gender, and Christian Community.* Edited by Jane Dempsey Douglass and James F. Kay. (1997).

PART 7 SOCIAL LOCATION.
INTRODUCTION: IDENTITY AND COMMUNICATION

Mary S. Hulst

A preacher looks out over the congregation and views a wide assortment. The older couple, faithful for fifty-two years and still very much in love. The twenty-something, there for his parents but completely unconvinced about the validity of the gospel. The middle-aged widow who harbors deep anger at God for taking her husband. The children, scattered among the crowd, wondering how much of this is for them. Teenagers slouching, new converts leaning in eagerly, elders with arms crossed, newlyweds still glowing—and all of them looking back at the preacher, who looks at them.

Add to all of this ethnic diversity, theological disagreement, socioeconomic variety, and various levels of acceptance of the Bible as the Word of God, and the preacher of the 21st cent. may easily—understandably!—feel overwhelmed and underqualified.

A preacher can no longer presume uniformity among the flock. No longer can assumptions be made about either belief or background. How then to preach? How can an identity for preaching be established? How can a preacher communicate effectively when the touchstones of commonality seem few and far between?

Communication theorists have long known that the best communication takes place when the sender is as aware of the beliefs and biases of the receiver as he or she can be. Knowing more about the receiver allows the sender to tailor the message to fit the one who will receive. "Preach as if there is a broken heart in every pew," advised D. L. Moody years ago, and his words continue to ring true. Marriages running rough, addictions unspoken, diseases tearing apart bodies, children disobeying, and even the simple everyday annoyances of cold and flu season or bad traffic take their toll on us all.

Although you may not know the story behind each broken heart, and in some cases you may not even know the names of all who sit in the pews, you do know that in the reality of human existence every person is looking for comfort. Every heart is hoping for healing. This is one commonality amid the diversity of those who sit in our pews.

But there is a deeper connection that we share, preacher and pew-sitter alike. We are not first joined together through shared heartache and a longing for hope. If we were, we would have little to offer beyond any community twelve-step group. Here is what is unique about the church; here is what pulls us together: we are baptized into the triune name of God.

Not unlike a family reunion in which members of various clans wear color-coded T-shirts to identify them to each other, our baptism marks us as belonging to this family. When we spot a fellow believer across the sanctuary, in Christ we see not single or married, rich or poor, well-dressed or sloppy, but *brother* or *sister*. As you will see, despite the differences that separate one pew-sitter from the next, there are weighty things that draw them together. And laying down some of our assumptions about our congregants may actually lead us to become more effective preachers. Why? Because when we lay down our assumptions, we cease to appeal to ethnic ties or inside jokes, and appeal to that which most deeply defines us: our baptism into the triune name of God.

Whatever the makeup of our congregation or denomination, and whatever the joys and heartaches that sit in our pews, all of us—women and men, toddlers and teens, black, brown, and white—are called to a life of discipleship and are baptized into Father, Son, and Holy Spirit. This identity is first and foremost. I am not first of all a thirty-something white American woman. You are not first of all black or an older person or a Canadian or a jazz lover. All of those other identities—some of which could pull us apart from each other—matter less inside the church. What matters most in the church of Jesus Christ is Jesus Christ, and my first identity is as a disciple of his and a servant of the Most High God. Race matters less; wealth matters less; status matters less. The imitation of Jesus matters most.

Because this is true, we preachers occasionally have to be reminded to get out of the way. We need to be called back to *our* first identity, which is not preacher but Christian. The first article in this section walks us through the life stages of a preacher and alerts us to patterns in our own preaching that may create distance rather than bridge it. When our pulpit ministries subtly shift to solving our problems or working through our developmental issues rather than preaching the gospel to God's people, we not only stop serving our congregants as best we should, but we also allow other identities (parent, spouse, middle-aged North American white male, twenty-something coffee shop lover) to co-opt our baptismal identity.

Preaching out of our identity in Christ also allows us to reach across divides of age or experience. Our North American culture tends to highlight divides between age groups, naming different generations and labeling their differences. We will be reminded in this section of the importance of preaching well to our younger members. This does not and will not happen if we believe that we have nothing to say or that they are not willing to listen. It will not happen if we look down on them and simply wait to preach to them until they grow up. Preaching from and to our identity as Christ-followers enables us to connect with our younger members on the matters that are so important to them: Who am I? Why am I here? What is the world about? Does my life have meaning? Indeed, simply in listing these questions we preachers can see that our younger members may well be our most interested audience. Connecting them to our shared identity in Christ may well be the most important work we do.

I recently interviewed a candidate for ministry. I asked him to describe a pastoral situation that had been challenging for him and how he faced it. He spoke at length about a heartbreaking situation at the church he was pastoring, how it split the congregation, and how he worked hard to make the matters of the gospel—forgiveness, reconciliation, unity—most important. In a situation in which he could have picked sides and fought for a cause, he was instead embodying his baptismal identity and calling his congregants to do the same. This is what sees a church through a crisis—not great leadership, first of all, or extended governing board meetings, but a pastor-preacher who lives out of his identity in Christ. You'll see this discussed further in the article on preaching in times of crisis.

With increasing diversity in North American society and increasing diversity within congregations and denominations, how can identity for preaching be established? By turning again—repeatedly, weekly—to the identity of our baptisms. This unites us to each other: we have been baptized into the triune name of God. We have our identity in Christ. We all wear the same color T-shirts.

And we all share the same story. Our identity brings us together and our stories keep us together. Just like an extended family gathering may always include telling the story of "Uncle Don and the sweet potatoes," our family gathering includes telling the stories of Jesus, and in particular how his story has changed our stories.

Preaching specifically to the congregation that is before us will help us do this effectively and well. We are not called, or hired, to preach generic sermons. We are called to bring God's word to *this* people in *this* place on *this* Sunday. The best sermons are local—sermons that refer to this congregation's trials and triumphs, sermons that weave their stories into the Story. If we first address the diversity within the pews by reminding ourselves of our baptismal identity, we next address it by gathering up the people before us into a remembering of their shared experience as members of that particular local church. Nora Tubbs Tisdale's important work in this section on exegeting the congregation reminds us that we preach to a specific audience in a specific place.

While the articles contained in this section may illuminate practices in the local church, the authors do not know the history of your congregation with particular songs or prayers. Another preacher does not know the weight that certain hymns have for your people. Another preacher does not know the unique expressions that surround baptism in your church. You know these things, and to be a faithful preacher for your time and place is to weave these particulars into the universal narrative of the Christian life. This is what will give you listeners who lean in as you preach. *Hey*, they may think, *he's talking about* us!

The shift that takes place in those instances is the shift from the individual to the group, from the one to the many. The *I* becomes *we;* the *me* becomes *us*. We move from merely existing as individuals who happen to be in the same place at the same time on Sunday mornings to thriving as a church *family*. When we share a common story, we are drawn together. It is this shared story of the local congregation woven into the preached word that draws the hearers together. It is this shared story that bridges gaps between age, economics, and ethnicity.

The shared identity of baptism and the shared story of Jesus move beyond congregational connection to denominational vibrancy. Some bemoan the loss of denominational loyalty, while others consider it an opportunity to present the specifics of their doctrine in fresh ways. It is the latter that should intrigue us. John McClure and James Nieman explore collaboration as a way not only to build bridges between denominations but also as a way to deepen appreciation for our own theological traditions. Some denominations report that congregants are asking publishing houses for more doctrinal materials. Some preachers report that those same congregants are eager for doctrinal sermons.

This may seem countercultural as people seek out experiential worship and appear to be less concerned with theology. But the generation that has now been raised on praise and worship music is starting to read the works of the early Christian writers. They are hungering after knowledge. They want to know what they believe and why. They want to know their denominational story.

Our hearers would not be surprised if we explained the Reformed perspective on baptism, for example, or the Arminian understanding of the end times. In fact, the word from many in the pew is that they would welcome it. It reminds them that they stand as part of a long history and that they do not stand alone. It also reminds us as preachers that we do not preach alone, we do not teach alone. It reminds us that these doctrines that shape us have also shaped those who have gone before us, and that we can lean on their work and thank God for this inheritance. Understanding our work as preachers as that of family storytellers helps us see our work within its broader context.

As preachers, we tell these stories as servants of Jesus Christ, we preach out of our baptismal identities, and we preach to invite others into the great narrative that God is acting out in history. All that we address in the following sections, from COLLABORATION to CRISIS, from GLOBALIZATION to MISSIONAL PREACHING, flows from this identity: we are disciples of Jesus Christ. We are servants of the Most High God. This is who we are. This is how we preach. *See* ECCLESIOLOGY; GOD,

ETHICS AND; IDENTIFICATION; SHAPING CONGREGATIONAL IDENTITY.

BILINGUAL SETTING
Francisco Javier Goitía-Padilla

Is bilingual preaching possible? The first thing to note about bilingual preaching, especially in the Hispanic/Latino(a) community, is that this kind of preaching happens outside the center of church and society. Bilingual preaching is part of the proclamation of the gospel that occurs at the periphery, at the borderlands of the centers of power and culture in the United States. As such, it is part of a permeable and fluid context in which the Spanish-speaking Latin American, Caribbean, and Hispanic/Latino(a) cultures of the American continent encounter, struggle with, and relate to the dominant English-speaking culture of this country. It is a space where linguistic friction, overlapping, and crisscrossing happen not only within language but also between languages.

There are different approaches to bilingual preaching. The most common form of this kind of preaching is to translate the whole sermon and intermittently switch from one language to the other. A second way is to preach in one language—for example, Spanish—and provide a written manuscript of the sermon—in English—to the English-speaking parishioners and guests present at church. A third approach is to insert short paragraphs of a second language—let us say Spanish—that summarize the English sermon up to that point. The premise behind all these attempts is the presence of at least two monolingual audiences listening to the sermon. This presupposition, in my opinion, is misleading. There are occasions where monolingual persons attend worship services conducted in a second language not of their own. But these are exceptions. These are special occasions in which the center of the matter is not bilingual preaching but an interest in inclusiveness, the affirmation of diversity, and the like.

On these special occasions when monolingual persons attend worship together, the assumption of two audiences is correct. Here we have a dominant culture and language that struggle to receive and incorporate a second one. Both peoples and cultures are part of the body of Christ. In this context we need to remember that the sermon is part of the whole worship experience, that proclamation is more than preaching, and that preaching is more than human words. The whole worship experience needs to assume the weight of the juxtaposition of languages and cultures. At this juncture, the strategies and delivery of the sermon have some space for experiment and innovation. Rosa María Icaza offers us advice when attempting bilingual preaching that can be useful for these circumstances. She affirms, first of all, that bilingual preaching is no translation. One needs to know both cultures and manage fairly well the languages of those cultures. Using an article by Bishop Ricardo Ramírez, she proposes the following: (1) repeat the sermon if it is short; (2) give a summary of the sermon at the end of the sermon in the other language; (3) provide a second person to present a synchronized non-literal interpretation of the sermon; and/or (4) supply simultaneous translation using electronic equipment. Icaza finally recognizes that if the sermon is to be preached in a truly bilingual and bicultural congregation, it is perhaps wise to preach a different sermon for each group (Davis and Presmanes 2000, 29).

Bilingual preaching, different from the special circumstances just described, is every-Sunday preaching. It is the preaching that happens in a community that talks, lives, loves, and worships in a bilingual world. Here the preaching experience needs to proclaim the gospel in such a way that everybody understands all the time. As such, the need is to see how this kind of preaching can be efficacious. By far the most effective bilingual preaching that I have heard occurred at a funeral home in Chicago. Both young and old were gathered, and they listened carefully to a young Pentecostal preacher who, speaking as he speaks every day, went fluidly and naturally from one language to the other, sometimes in whole sentences, sometimes in phrases and even inserting words. His primary language was Spanish, the mother tongue of the older persons gathered. Nevertheless, all the younger English-speaking persons also followed him and understood him perfectly. In that funeral home, where the older Spanish-speaking persons understood some English, and where the younger, mainly English-speaking persons knew the core of their mother tongue, the friction, crisscrossing, and overlapping of words produced meaning for all those gathered. This meaning was produced by threading both languages. This particular way of using words and language overlapping at the permeable border of church, culture, and society was the means used by the Word to proclaim the gospel.

A linguistic study done in a Puerto Rican community in Long Island, for example, discovered that younger Puerto Ricans, English dominant speakers, were able narrators when speaking Spanish. They utilized loanwords, borrowing from English. This borrowing was done, nevertheless, preserving the integrity, structure, and syntax of the Spanish language. The author concluded that the innovations and mixing of languages need to be seen "as resources rather than handicaps" (Torres 1997, 123). The use of language at the borders of church and society points to a hybrid space where the gospel is preached and heard in unexpected ways. A homiletical theory that values narrative and plot, for example, needs to note and further explore the possibilities and challenges posed by bilingual preaching.

What can we learn from all this? I believe the presence of bilingual preaching in the North American context invites us to consider the following: (1) recognize the permeable, hybrid, and contested nature of the space in which bilingual preaching occurs; (2) acknowledge the need to become competent in the cultures present in that space; (3) affirm and study further the use of language and the fluidity of oral language—preaching included—in this context; and (4) investigate how the innovations and juxtaposition of languages at this juncture may be a resource for the development of narrative in our homiletical theories. After all, this is nothing new; at Pentecost, everyone listened in his or her own language (Acts 2:7-8). *See* GLOBALIZATION; IDENTIFICATION.

Bibliography: Nestor García Canclini. *Hybrid Cultures: Strategies for Entering and Leaving Modernity.* Translated by Christopher L. Chiappari and Sylvia L. López. (1995); Kenneth G. Davis and Jorge L. Presmanes, eds. *Preaching and Culture in Latino Congregations.* (2000); Daniel Rodríguez and Rodolfo Espinosa, eds. *Púlpito Cristiano y Justicia Social.* (1994); Lourdes Torres. *Puerto Rican Discourse: A Sociolinguistic Study of a New York Suburb.* (1997); Ludwig Wittgenstein. *Philosophical Investigations.* Translated by G. E. M. Anscombe. (2001).

CAREER PATH/LIFE STAGE
James R. Nieman

The shape of one's pastoral life over the years naturally affects what is preached and, when faithful proclamation remains the aim, promises a deeper connection with listeners. When undisciplined or misdirected, however, reference in sermons to these experiences can be self-serving and lead to pandering or pretension. How we think about the nature of ministerial work determines whether its place in preaching will be healthy or spurious. Such reflection also suggests how to stay engaged and enlivened during a lifelong journey as a preacher.

Much turns on whether preachers use conventional terms about our working and living. To speak of ministry as a "career" seductively whispers of professionalism and the self-directed trajectory of achievement in a guild. What do we then make of Paul's career path, his unlikely descent from confident zeal to utter loss for those he rarely saw (Phil 3:4-11)? To speak of life in its "stages" depicts a confident, diagnostic clarity about sure growth from one phase to the next. What can we then say of Mary's life stage, who of meager age and humble account bore a daring song of God's reversal (Luke 1:46-55)? We cannot rightly sense how our ministry should contribute to our preaching while retaining terms that fail to include the messiness of Paul and Mary, let alone the smudged and shaky line our ministry may also have traced.

The picture changes when we recall that preaching is instead a vocation, the call to a particular form of ministry extended through and for a faithful community. Whatever its internal impetus, that vocation is confirmed outside ourselves and therefore is received not to gratify personal desires but to engage the hopes of an assembly that longs to hear the gospel proclaimed. This insight—preaching is a vocation exercised in community—lets us rethink the proper use of pastoral material in what we preach over the span of our ministry. As a part of the community, the preacher is able to attend in sermons to the concrete reality of that common life to encourage more ample witness by all. Speaking from our experience (younger or older, adept or novice) is surely a resource toward that end, but not the only one and sometimes not the best. Even an outstanding ministry can thwart genuine proclamation when it serves merely as a self-referential model for

behavior. More troubling, the minister's experience may connect poorly with listeners or even create an unforeseen hindrance to their discipleship.

To be sure, self-disclosure is an unavoidable part of preaching. Simply how we speak already reveals who we are and how we live. Since the minister's life and work are always on display, therefore, our preaching may be better served by restraint about these, lest it seem that all of life must be filtered through the minister's life before being worthy of consideration. When the aim of the sermon then does truly merit explicit mention of one's own experience, its importance is not to rehearse publicly what the preacher has known or done, but to convey empathy and openness essential to proclamatory credibility. With this in mind, we can now examine a healthier perspective on how reference to a pastoral life that is called into the service of the common life can support and enliven our preaching.

To begin, this perspective challenges three prevalent myths that impede effective use of lived experience from the pulpit. The first is the myth of *more* experience, which treats life as a quantity. In this view, preachers of lower age are less experienced and deficient, while those of greater age are more experienced and mature. This ignores that, for example, being older does not automatically afford insight into the distinctive experience of being young here and now. Related to this, the second myth is that of *improved* experience, which sees life as progress. In this view, preachers naturally or typically become more aware, complex, and altruistic over the course of their lives. This ignores the agelessness of narrow and selfish behavior, let alone the uneven or repetitive way that many lives unfold. The third myth is that of *unique* experience, which regards life as incomparable. In this view, unless a preacher has faced a particular life situation, it is impossible to understand or speak of it. This ignores the power of empathetic identification with others that happens precisely when we acknowledge our particularity and differences. Were these three claims not myth but truth, we could preach only to those like ourselves. The ministry of Jeremiah reminds us, though, that preaching relies on a calling through which one's status, flaws, and limits are used to bear an honest word to a whole people (Jer 1:4-10).

Beyond this, several constructive strategies suggest how experiences relate to preaching. Some pertain to preparation. *Collaboration* during Bible study reveals how those in various stations of life hear God addressing them, and happens through gathering a range of parishioners or mentoring alongside other preachers. *Appreciation* of how diverse people speak of their lives expands our reservoir of language, and is available in ordinary pastoral calling or being a student of public conversations. *Exploration* of experiences far beyond our own can happen through compelling novels, biographical accounts, aesthetic expressions, or even experiential analogues (e.g., events that give insight into how a specific disability feels). Other strategies pertain to performance. *Restraint* in speaking of ourselves paradoxically creates a space for listeners to engage the sermon in their own ways. *Recovery* of what others say about themselves broadens the implications of the sermon and honors many ways of relating to God. *Review* of our preaching over time exposes the experiences we foreground or avoid and serves as a needed corrective. All of these strategies are concrete disciplines for the health of our calling. Better still, they show how that calling can remain lively over the years by drawing upon more than merely ourselves, but especially the labors and lives of those who call us to preach on their behalf. *See* CALL; DEVOTIONAL LIFE/LIFE-STYLE; LEADERSHIP.

COLLABORATION
John S. McClure

Collaboration refers to the process of involving laypersons in sermon brainstorming and feedback, and sometimes in preaching itself. Collaborative preaching incorporates the biblical interpretations and theological wisdom of laity.

A. Background
B. Assumptions
   1. The Proclamatory Vocation of All Believers
   2. The Word of God as Inter-human and Emergent
   3. The Preacher as Host
C. Reasons for Collaborative Preaching
   1. The Postmodern De-centering of Authority
   2. Living an Ethic of Hospitality
   3. Modeling Collaborative Leadership

   4. Teaching the Nature of Proclamation
   5. Teaching the Bible
D. Guidelines for Practice
   1. Forming a Sermon Roundtable
     a. Diversity
     b. Size
     c. Rotation
   2. Location
   3. Group Process
     a. Preparation
     b. Purpose
     c. Organization
   4. Sermon Preparation

A. Background

Browne Barr was the first in the modern context to advocate collaborative preaching. In his 1963 Lyman Beecher Lectures titled *Parish Back Talk*, Barr developed a "sermon seminar" to assist the preacher in sermon preparation. In a later book, *The Ministering Congregation* (1972), Barr developed the sermon seminar into an integral aspect of lay ministry. Collaborative models for preaching were also suggested by Reuel Howe (1963) and Clyde Reid (1963), whose work underscored the importance of dialogue for parish leadership. More recent approaches include my roundtable pulpit model, the conversational preaching models of Lucy Rose (1997) and Wesley Allen Jr. (2005), and various approaches to lay preaching such as those within the United Methodist denomination or the Roman Catholic Dominican Order.

B. Assumptions

1. The Proclamatory Vocation of All Believers
Collaborative preaching assumes that all members of a congregation have vocations as proclaimers of the gospel. Because of this, preachers must find ways to engage in forms of collaboration with laity that will bring their witness to Christ to bear in preaching. Collaboration is not the same as consultation. It is not using the ideas and experiences of others to support or illustrate a preacher's already determined messages. Collaboration means that others may have something to teach the preacher and congregation about the meaning of the gospel. The insights of others may transform the preaching ministry entirely.

2. The Word of God as Inter-human and Emergent

Collaborative preaching assumes that the preached Word of God arrives as an inter-human Word that emerges from the give-and-take of spiritual conversation among human beings who are genuinely seeking to discern God's truth. Typically, an ordained preacher or trained lay preacher preaches a message that emerges from a group conversation about a biblical preaching text. Because of the close relationship between collaborative preaching and spiritual conversation, collaborative preaching is sometimes considered a partner of conversation in homiletics.

3. The Preacher as Host

Instead of viewing the preacher as prophet, evangelist, witness, or herald, the preacher, in a collaborative model, assumes the identity of host. In the 1st cent. house and tenement churches, local religious leaders welcomed seekers of the Way from within and beyond the local community into conversations regarding the meaning of the gospel of Jesus. Itinerant, charismatic preachers such as Paul would visit these churches and were sometimes hosted as a part of these conversations. All with wisdom to share were placed into dialogue so that the Word of God might be discerned.

C. Reasons for Collaborative Preaching

1. The Postmodern De-centering of Authority

In today's postmodern context authority is de-centered and disseminated among a plurality of influences, experts, and resources within a network of connections and relationships. In human terms, this means that people are less willing to accept the authority of hired professionals (academics, clergy, religious leaders), institutions, and traditions. Authority is relocated at the intersection of pluralistic, multiperspectival, situated conversations in which clergy and the institutions and traditions they represent are only one voice. Collaborative preaching works well in this situation because it allows authentic, authoritative norms for faith and practice to emerge within a broad network of relationships and resources, including the complex knowledge represented by educated clergy.

2. Living an Ethic of Hospitality

Collaborative preaching draws upon an ethical framework that emphasizes the ancient biblical concept of hospitality for the stranger. It welcomes "otherness" and "strangeness" into preaching and models a way of being-in-relationship-to-others that moves beyond conflict, persuasion, and even consensus building. It points toward a way of communicating in which elements that might typically be perceived as conflicts of interest are instead discovered as another person's responses to experiences and pressures that one may not yet have experienced or fully understood. The motive for communication shifts from persuasion to understanding difference and "coming to terms" with one another. In an increasingly pluralistic world, this is an important ethic of communication to demonstrate and learn.

3. Modeling Collaborative Leadership

As the focal point of congregational leadership, collaborative preaching models a movement away from sovereign and consultative forms of church leadership toward truly mutual and collaborative models. For this reason, collaborative preaching fits well within newer church leadership models that are more organic, lay-empowering, team-based, and small group-oriented in nature.

4. Teaching the Nature of Proclamation

Many people today gain their only experience of preaching by watching mass evangelists and motivational religious speakers on television. Collaborative preaching re-teaches the nature and purpose of proclamation. As laypersons join with the preacher to study the Bible in order to discern the meaning of the gospel for today's world, they discover what it means to discern and proclaim the good news in the context of a worshiping congregation.

5. Teaching the Bible

Because collaborative preaching grows out of close inductive reflection on the Bible, the Bible is learned in a way that makes it accessible and useful for the day-to-day practice of Christian living. Participants are empowered as readers, interpreters, and practitioners of Holy Scripture.

D. Guidelines for Practice

Although collaborative preaching can be done in a variety of different ways, here are some suggestions and guidelines for practice.

1. Forming a Sermon Roundtable

First, establish a small brainstorming group or sermon roundtable. Several things should be kept in mind when establishing and maintaining this group.

a. Diversity. The group should involve persons of many ages, life-styles, and racial/ethnic backgrounds. The group should involve both believers and non-believing seekers, if possible. Organizers ought to be as creative as possible in group development, inviting newcomers to the church and church neighbors, whether residents or business owners. Roundtables can also use e-mail or chat to receive input from global partners such as missionaries or friends in other countries. E-mail is also a good way to involve persons who cannot regularly attend group meetings.

b. Size. Sermon roundtable groups should be small. It is very difficult to manage the insights and dynamics of large groups. If possible, keep group size at four to six persons.

c. Rotation. The group should change personnel regularly, preferably every six to ten weeks. Doing this ensures that the sermon roundtable does not become a group of insiders. Although the preacher or another designated person can manage group selection and rotation, one of the best ways to keep the group changing is to use a tag-team approach. When members rotate off, they tag others to take their places. This rotation should be staggered, if possible, so that the group changes regularly, but not all at once.

2. Location

It is best if sermon roundtables do not meet in the pastor's study. This can create a somewhat intimidating and pastor-centered experience as group members find themselves surrounded by scholarly commentaries, preaching robes, graduation certificates, and so on. We now know that social location has a great deal to do with how we interpret biblical texts. For this reason, consider moving the sermon roundtable to another room in the church or, better still, beyond the church to a variety of locations: a homeless shelter, public library, coffeehouse, mall, or homes of participants.

3. Group Process

a. Preparation. Participants should know ahead of time the text for the forthcoming Sunday. If the lectionary is used, members should be told which texts to preach. Members can prepare to discuss texts in any way desired. It is a good idea not to force homework on the group. This can distract from the spontaneity of the discussion by luring the group into old patterns of "having the right answer" or "doing the best research." Some members will naturally read commentaries prior to meeting, contributing to the group's scholarly knowledge of the text. Others will meditate on the text devotionally or think about texts in relation to social issues or problems. All of these approaches are useful for group discussion.

b. Purpose. The roundtable is not a Bible study in the usual sense of the term. One ought not let the group get sidetracked into complex historical, textual, or literary issues. Participants should be encouraged to read the biblical text and then reflect honestly and candidly on the meaning of the gospel, in light of that text, for our world and for daily living. Although the preacher usually facilitates this discussion, it is important that the preacher be a participating member of the conversation and not simply a facilitator or bystander. The goal is to have a forthright, mutually respectful, spiritual (not academic or ideological) conversation in which the Bible's witness to the gospel of Jesus Christ is central.

c. Organization. One way to organize the meeting time is as follows:

1. Feedback/feedforward (10 minutes)—Invite participants to reflect on the previous week's sermon. Are there any key ideas for this week's sermon that emerge from last week's effort? What feedback has the group been receiving from family and friends who heard the sermon?

2. Engaging the biblical text (20 minutes)—Read the text aloud and ask if there are any questions about the historical context, words, or authorship of the text. This is not a time to take over the conversation, demonstrating elite knowledge and special powers of discernment, steering the group toward a specific interpretive framework. Focus on providing brief answers to questions and ensuring that the historical, theological, and liturgical backdrop for the text is understood.

3. Engaging one another (60 minutes)—This is the most important part of the meeting for preaching. It is crucial to get participants to lift their heads out of the biblical text and move them into an engagement with one

another about insights, questions, experiences, and issues that arise from the living of life today. When possible, take notes during this conversation.

Here are some types of questions and examples that will help a leader to move the group along:

Opening Questions. Look for something within the text or topic that will help the group get to know each other better, or hear their own voices in the discussion. Look for something that is not necessarily central to the text or topic, but that will lead into a conversation. For example (text: road to Emmaus; Luke 24:13-35): "What are we likely to be thinking about or acting like after we have experienced a great crisis or tragedy in our lives?"

Launching Questions. If the group does not jump in with fervor, the leader will need to have several questions to launch discussion. Create two or three questions that will focus attention on several aspects of the text or a relevant topic. These are simply entry points into conversation around a text or topic. Examples: "What do you make of the fact that they experienced Jesus as a "stranger?"; "What do you think would motivate someone to ask Jesus to stay?"

Guiding Questions. Most well-prepared leaders will need to spontaneously guide discussions at times, and they may try several techniques. (1) Rephrase the question: "You seem to be asking . . ."; "Am I on target?"; "Are you saying . . . ?" (2) Paraphrase or ask "going deeper" questions: "I hear you saying that the story is about the Lord's Supper. What do you think it is saying about the Lord's Supper?" (3) Test for consensus, clarification, or decision. This will tend to draw out differences or contrasts of opinion. "Are we saying that the disciples just thought that this was Jesus, but it was really only a ghost?" or "Would we all want to say . . . ?"

Summarizing Questions. From time to time, it helps the group (and note-taker) if the leader will ask a summarizing question or make a summary response: "So what I hear us saying at this point is, 'Does this sound right?'"

Empowerment Questions. Leaders ought to share the power to generate and interpret ideas. It helps if one uses the name of the person whom one wants to empower. (1) Ask for involvement. Ask those who have not spoken for their thoughts. Try to be specific in your questioning so that they feel addressed by the question: "Nancy, we haven't

heard from you yet. Why do you think the disciples are so preoccupied in this story?" "Is there anyone else here who has ever experienced this kind of preoccupation?" (2) Ask for imagination. Sometimes it helps if you will put them in a hypothetical situation: "If you were on the road to Emmaus, what might you be thinking about?" (3) Ask for feelings: "How do you feel about this encounter with Christ as a stranger on the road?" (4) Ask for stories: "Do any stories come to mind about how you have felt after the death of people you looked up to in your life?"(5) Ask for reframing: "How do you feel about our interpretation of this story of the stranger as only a symbol of the risen Lord? Are there other ways to think about this that might help us see something we might have missed?"

Coming to Terms Questions. These are sometimes called "so what?" questions. (1) Ask for commitment: "What kinds of commitments could we make in light of this discussion?" (2) Ask for scenarios: "What changes in our own lives or in our church could we envision as the result of our discussion tonight?" "What difference could this make to you and me if we really took it seriously?" (3) Ask for application: "What should be done in light of what we've said tonight?"

Practice Questions. These are the nitty-gritty questions. (1) Ask how to get things done: "What practical steps (step) would we have to take . . . ?" (2) Ask how we can change: "What would need to change in order for us to live this way?" (3) Ask what resources are available: "Who could help us? What resources do we need (or already have) that can help us live this way?" (4) Review (5 minutes)—The leader asks members to help review and remember what has been discussed, and how it was discussed. Were there differences of opinions or conflicts of interpretation? How were they addressed? Did they argue? What were the main topics? How were they treated? What stories or experiences were narrated?

4. Sermon Preparation

The collaborative sermon takes its rhetorical shape from the roundtable conversation. Instead of using deductive, inductive, narrative plot, problem-solution, law-gospel, or other stock forms to organize sermon materials, the preacher looks back over the conversation and tries to create a sermon form that will capture at least one central dynamic of the roundtable conversation. The sermon could take the shape of an argument, a group of questions asked and explored, the pursuit of a set of feelings, the resistance to one idea and the encouragement of another, the painting of scenarios, and so on. The richness of any good conversation provides the preacher with a variety of good dynamics with which to work. The preacher may also use stories (with permission, of course), ideas, questions, problems, interruptions, and other elements of the conversation in the sermon. It is up to the preacher, however, to determine how to use these materials, and how to best use his or her perspective and authority in bringing the group's ideas to full sermonic form. On occasion, the preacher may refer to the group, and the group's process explicitly, or even (with permission) refer to the names of group members. If participants allow, it is a good idea to publish the names of group members in the Sunday bulletin. Doing this permits listeners to have a deeper understanding of the sermon's origin and allows for feedback to return to the group from a wide variety of directions.

Over the years, collaborative preachers have developed many variations on the process described here. It is important to create a collaborative preaching practice that reflects the unique characteristics of your congregation. For instance, in one charismatic Episcopal congregation, the roundtable group comes forward prior to the preaching of the sermon and lays hands on the preacher, praying for the illumination of the Holy Spirit. In another context, the preacher uses videotaped testimonials of group members during the sermon. In still another congregation, group members actually come forward and offer portions of the sermon, either retelling stories or repeating ideas or testimonials. No matter what works best, the ultimate goal is for the preaching event to become a communal, participatory, and empowering event. *See* PREACHER'S CREATIVE PROCESS.

Bibliography: O. Wesley Allen Jr. *The Homiletic of All Believers: A Conversational Approach to Proclamation.* (2005); Browne Barr. *Parish Back Talk.* (1964); Browne, Barr. *The Ministering Congregation* (1972); Barbara Bate. *Lay Speakers Preach.* (1998); M. C. Hilkert, O.P., B. Hintersberger, O.P., H. Legrand, O.P., M. O'Driscoll, O.P., and P. Philibert, O.P. "The Dominican Charism of Preaching: An Inquiry." http://www.op.org; Reuel L. Howe. *The Miracle of Dialogue.* (1963); John S. McClure. *The Roundtable Pulpit: Where Leadership and Preaching Meet.* (1995); Clyde H. Reid. "Preaching and the Nature of Communication." *Pastoral Psychology* 14 (1963) 40–49; Lucy Atkinson Rose. *Sharing the Word: Preaching in the Roundtable Church.* (1997).

CRISIS
Joseph R. Jeter Jr.

Most preachers, ordained or lay, have received some schooling in the discipline of sermon preparation and delivery. But that discipline can break down and collapse in the midst of crisis. When the preacher and/or the congregation are in crisis, how is the preacher to respond?

A. Theology and Crisis
   1. Remembrance
   2. Presence
   3. Promise
B. Crises of Decision
C. Some Homiletical Strategies
   1. Naming the Monster
   2. Creative Lamentation
   3. God's Wagons
   4. The Need for Continuity

Generally speaking, people are thrown into crisis when their usual methods of dealing with a problem prove ineffective. A preacher may be faced with crises that are public, congregational, or personal, or that involve all three. Public crises may be political: war, assassination, terrorist attack, riot, and other civic upheavals. They also include natural or other disasters: storm, flood, fire, famine, terrible accidents, and so forth. These may well spill over into congregational crises: untimely deaths by accident or foul play, financial crises, scandals, and crises of dissension or direction. Personal crises strike the preacher directly or indirectly: personal tragedy, family problems, illness, loss of job by being fired, loss of faith, and others.

In the last few years we have seen the balkanization of American politics and religion through the growth of talk radio, blogging, sound bite communication, and direct mail. Congregations that could not have imagined fights over political affiliation, trouble in the Middle East, gay marriage, immigration, stem cell research, and other matters ten years ago are struggling not to fall into internecine hostility or, worse, separation.

A. Theology and Crisis

Ronald Allen divides theological crises into crises of *understanding* and *decision* (Allen 1992, 21–22). Theological concerns attend every crisis situation in which we preach. Does God exist? What is God like? Why did God do or not do this to us? We must approach the sermon as if these questions are present among our people. And if we ignore them because they are hard questions or pretend not to see them because we would rather preach on something else, we make of the preaching ministry less than it can be.

Howard Stone distinguishes between *poetic questions* that express depth of misery, such as, "Why did God do this?" and *harder statements*, such as, "I have had an immense loss and am feeling utterly devastated by it" (Stone 1988, 162). The pastor seeks to determine whether the people in crisis really want to engage in theological dialogue or whether they are simply seeking a way to express their pain. This distinction is critical for the pulpit as well. The painstaking task of reconstructive theology may come later; the more immediate task for the sermon is lament. Some questions that arise in crisis are unanswerable, in a sermon or any other way, but the pastor needs to discover whether these are really the questions being asked.

Assuming that the theological questions are real and serious, here are three theological affirmations that can be made in response: *remembrance, presence,* and *promise.*

1. Remembrance

A crisis may cut us off from memory. The opposite of remember is not necessarily forget; the opposite of remember can be dismember. To re/member is to put back together, to make right again as the people of God, an important response to the dismembering effects of crisis. We need memory to worship. When the present and future have been ripped from the past and bob anchorless on the stormy seas of crisis, what shall we do? We can find our hope in what God has done in the past and bring that to bear on the present.

The Jews in the ghettoes of Europe who celebrated Passover and the Christians who broke bread in catacombs did so because their memories of God's providence were the only things between them and oblivion. Scottish preacher Arthur Gossip put it bluntly in his first sermon after his wife's sudden death, "You people in the sunshine may believe the faith, but we in the shadow must believe it. We have nothing else" (Gossip 1928, 111).

2. Presence

In the past, Christians in crisis searched for the will of God and, when the crisis resulted in tragedy and trauma, sought to yield to that will. When 19th cent. religious leader Alexander Campbell's son drowned in 1847, he bowed to God's will. God was "too wise to err and too kind causelessly to afflict the children of men. . . . We must, and do endeavor, to acquiesce in this affliction, believing that the Lord has done it for some wise and kind, though to us mysterious, purpose." God's actions are mysteries only to us in our weak faith and shallow understanding (Jeter and Lester 1987, 93).

Contrast this with a more recent discussion by Martin Marty. A young woman was killed when a leaf spring broke off a truck and struck her. When she was a youngster, she once said, "I'm not crying; my eyes are just sweating!" Marty concluded: "Was that leaping leaf spring 'the will of God'? I do not know. Picture, only, the eyes of God, sweating" (Marty 1983, 975). An immutable God may be easier to grasp intellectually, but such a God is of little help in our suffering. God as sweaty-eyed cosufferer touches us at our deepest levels.

From beginning to end, the Bible presents to us the possibility of the presence of God. Young Israel sought, awkwardly but persistently, for that presence. Psalmists rejoiced in God's presence and lamented God's absence. And Jesus Christ, God-with-us, promised that he would be with us always, to the close of the age.

3. Promise

God's promise, which reverberates through the pages of Scripture, is that everything will be all right. The problem with that, of course, is that everything is not all right. God does not understand the gravity of the situation, or God knows but is incapable of doing anything about it, or God knows and is at work to this very hour making good on the ancient promise. The latter may be the only response that offers hope. So how is God at work?

When God made a covenant with Abraham in Gen 15, "God walked the bloody path of promise," noted James Wharton (Wharton 1985). The promise "to your descendants" is made in the midst of blood and suffering. And it is worked out in

Scripture and in life the same way. "Can these bones live?" we read in Ezekiel. God says yes (37:1-6). God's beloved son, Jesus, walked the bloody path to Golgotha and paid there the price for the sins of the world. For that reason, we read in Hebrews, Christ "is the mediator of a new covenant" that through his death, people may receive "the promised eternal inheritance" (9:15). According to 2 Peter, the promise is "new heavens and a new earth, where righteousness is at home" (3:13).

Our living is toward that promised future of God, which has been set forth and redeemed in blood. And when we preach to people in crisis, we hold before them the promise of God, the promise that assures us that tomorrow will come. God loves us no less when we have made a mess of things or when the sky falls. God did not make us to be rejected, but to love God and enjoy God forever. And that we shall do so is no vapid, vaporous promise, but one cut in blood and tested by fire.

B. Crises of Decision

Whereas crises of theological understanding may call for sermons on remembrance, presence, and promise, crises of decision may require different approaches. Sometimes crises emerge not because we do not understand what is at issue, but because we do not know what to do in response, in which case the lens of pilgrimage may help. If we are *in* crisis, then we want to get *out*. "What shall we do now?" is another way of saying, "Where shall we go from here?" or "Which direction shall we take now?"

What, then, do we preach in crisis?

When the need is to go on: energy and encouragement.

When the need is to go around: wisdom and discernment.

When the need is to go back: memory and hope.

When the need is to go up: prayer and openness.

When the need is to go down: love and dedication

When the need is to stand: quiet faith.

C. Some Homiletical Strategies

1. Naming the Monster

What homiletical strategies may we name (Jeter 1998, 75–94)? The first task of crisis preaching is naming the monster. To name the monsters that terrify our people is both to assure our people that we appreciate the gravity of the situation and to lay the groundwork for understanding it. The Rumpelstiltskin effect in psychology finds the monster's name to lessen its effect. It also helps escape the pitfall of the too ready identification of tragedy as the will of God, a mistake that preachers make too often, and one that compounds the tragedy, as with AIDS treated as God's punishment.

A word of caution: naming the monster can require theological discernment. The flash point of a crisis is not always its monster. The crisis may seem to be that we cannot read the hymnbooks because the sanctuary is dark, but it is dark because the church has not paid its light bill—and the bill remains outstanding because there has been a failure of faithful stewardship. The base problem, then, may be a lack of faith. To find our way out of this crisis may be where we have to begin.

2. Creative Lamentation

One reason that modern men and women face so many psychological problems is that we have lost our ability to lament. Our funerals are often sterile little recitals, and our sermons, even in the face of disaster, are feel-good enterprises that ignore that people feel bad—shouting, as it were, "peace, peace, where there is no peace!"

I heard my parents talk about the long, slow train that took the body of Franklin D. Roosevelt from Georgia to Washington, D.C., in 1945. I have heard how people gathered by the railroad tracks, how others sat glued to radios, monitoring the progress of the train, and I have seen the haunting photograph of that African American man with the river of tears flowing down his cheeks. Something in lamentation goes beyond the mere naming of the monster.

Consider the book of Lamentations. Its genius lies in the recognition that sometimes there is no substitute for the question: Is there any pain like my pain? The expression of grief and the confession of sin are but a short distance in the economy of God from the expression of hope and the gift of new life. Lamentations is well suited for Christian worship on Maundy Thursday, Good Friday, and Holy Saturday, as well as for other times of fear and grief, but one almost never hears a sermon based on it.

Perhaps the closest thing we have is the pastoral elegy. It is one thing to say, "The president is dead," and it is quite another for Walt Whitman to write his elegy, "When Lilacs Last in the Door-yard

Bloom'd." Ellen Zetzel Lambert wrote, "The pastoral elegy . . . proposes no one solution to the questions raised by death but rather a setting in which those questions may be posed, or better, placed. It offers us a landscape." And this landscape is important, she asserts, "because it can contain pain and suffering. . . . [It] offers us a vision of life stripped not of pain but of complexity" (Lambert 1976, xiii, xv).

The form and function of the pastoral elegy are found in sermons that allow people to lament their pain and unanswered questions, often addressing crises metaphorically, as Stone suggested. Such questions in crisis cannot be answered in propositional language. But they can be "placed in a pain-containing landscape" within metaphors of sufficient size and strength.

Providing this landscape is sometimes difficult because words often seem to fail us. But God tempers the wind to the shorn lamb, shorn of wool or shorn of words. Before entering the pulpit, one might pray, "Remind me, as you did Moses, 'I will give you the words'" (Exod 4:10-17). Lamentation need not be fancy; it needs only to be voiced in faith and hope and love.

3. God's Wagons

Jacob, sitting by his tent, saw a cloud of dust approaching and said, "It is my sons." He rose to greet them, and they hurried to him with the news: "Joseph is alive and is the ruler over all the land of Egypt." Genesis states that Jacob's "heart fainted" because he did not believe them (45:26 KJV). Would you? But then Jacob saw another cloud of dust, and soon the wagons of Pharaoh himself came rolling into camp. When he saw the wagons that Joseph had sent for him, his spirit revived, and he said, "It is enough; Joseph my son is yet alive; I will go and see him before I die" (v. 28 KJV).

The testimony of the messengers in this case was not enough, just as our testimony is sometimes less than convincing. But when Jacob saw Pharaoh's wagons, which could not be sent by order of anyone but Pharaoh himself, he knew that it was true. It was proof positive. The wagons could be believed. Which raises the question: Does God have wagons? Are there assurances that can be given to people in crisis that are compelling in and of themselves, apart from our feeble witness? Yes.

Scripture is a wagon. The eucharist is a wagon. The cross is a wagon, not one that says, "God's in heaven, all's right with the world," but one testifying that God saw the evil in the world and stayed through. The empty tomb is a wagon. An honest, faithful sermon is a wagon. We may not understand all mysteries and be able to open the heavens to our people, but we can lay before them facts such as God loves us; God is not mocked; and God had the first word, God had the second word, and God will have the last word.

4. The Need for Continuity

The fourth suggestion has to do with continuity. When the emperor threatened to destroy Antioch in punishment for a riot, John Chrysostom began what came to be known as the "Homilies on the Statues" by naming the crisis, leading his people in lamenting it, setting before them the steadfast love of God. He then went right ahead to preach on the text for the day and about such things as not swearing and not being a glutton at the dinner table. I thought, *What is he doing? What do table manners have to do with survival?* And the answer came. Chrysostom understood the crucial importance, especially in crisis, of continuity. One of the best ways to deal with the fear that tomorrow might not come is to prepare for tomorrow.

Therefore, do not be too hasty, for example, to discard the lectionary passages for the day. They may be just what you need. Do not even discard your sermon too hastily. Look at it to see if there is a text, a theme, that can be used.

In summary, when the times of crisis come and you climb into the pulpit, seek to name the crisis, the real crisis, and not just its present manifestation. If it is appropriate, express the lamentation of the people of God. Then take courage, set before your people the great eternal truths of the faith, the truths that have led us safe this far, and will, by the grace of God, lead us home. *See* ANTHROPOLOGY; ESCHATOLOGY; FUNERAL; LAMENTS; PREACHER'S WEEK; SIN AND EVIL.

Bibliography: Ronald J. Allen. *Preaching the Topical Sermon.* (1992); Arthur John Gossip. "But When Life Tumbles In, What Then?" *The Hero in Thy Soul.* (1928); Joseph R. Jeter Jr. *Crisis Preaching.* (1998); Joseph R. Jeter Jr. and Hiram J. Lester. "The Tragedy of Wickliffe Campbell." *Lexington Theological Quarterly* 22 (July 1987); Ellen Zetzel Lambert. *Placing Sorrow.* (1976); Martin E. Marty. "God's Will." *Christian Century* (October 26, 1983) 975; Howard Stone. *The Word of God and*

Pastoral Care. (1988); James A. Wharton. Sermon at TCU Ministers Week. Fort Worth, Tex., February 4, 1985.

EXEGESIS OF THE CONGREGATION, DENOMINATION
Stephen Farris

Careful preachers not only read closely the Scripture text for the day. They also read themselves (*see* EXEGESIS OF SELF) and the congregation or other situation in which they will preach. Listeners are not merely passive recipients of sermons, "javelin catchers" according to one memorable phrase. Their reception of a sermon is filtered through a complex web of personal and institutional history or narrative. Indeed, it may be said that listeners not only receive meaning from sermons; they actively create meaning. If this is the case, a thorough reading or exegesis of the situation is vital to effective long-term preaching. In all that follows, it must be remembered that any observer, by the mere act of observing, affects the thing observed. Preachers are therefore best described as participant-observers in the context they are reading. Moreover, their presuppositions and history will materially affect what they are ready and able to perceive in an exegesis of a situation. An exegesis of the situation ought therefore to be done in tandem with an exegesis of the self.

Although a particular sermon may be useful in a considerable range of churches, especially of the same denomination or theological tradition, in extreme cases even the intelligibility and certainly the relevance of the sermon may be at stake. Consider, for example, a sermon preached in a care home for older adults and to a gathering of area youth. The sermons may be preached on the same day, from the same text by the same person, but they must be significantly different from each other if they are to communicate the gospel effectively in their respective settings. An obvious difference is the use of illustrative material. One could reasonably assume, for example, that a reference to D-Day would be grasped immediately in one setting but would require extensive explanation in the other, perhaps so extensive that the preacher might judge it best simply to leave out the reference. More significantly, the main emphasis of the sermon might be very different. For example, if one were preach-

ing that day on the call of Samuel (1 Sam 3), one sermon might reasonably link the listeners to the older Eli but the other to the younger Samuel.

Even in less extreme cases, an exegesis of the congregation is useful. It is part of effective pastoral work, including preaching, to understand the dynamics of the congregation. These include such factors as the age and gender spread of the congregation, its racial or ethnic makeup, the socioeconomic status of the listeners in comparison to the wider community, the general educational level of the listeners, and so forth. A prudent preacher will also explore the power dynamics, both official and unofficial, of the situation. All of this overlaps greatly with the study of congregational dynamics for other purposes.

In addition, preachers must take into account other more nebulous, but nevertheless very real factors. A sense of the history of the congregation or other situation is vital for effective long-term ministry. Listeners will hear whatever the preacher says in light of their perception of that shared history. Specifically, they hear the present preacher in light of their experience of previous preachers from the same pulpit. Most pulpits are haunted by the ghosts of former preachers. There may also be particular issues either in the life of the local situation or in the wider world that for a time affect the listeners' reception of the sermon. Moreover, any group gathered to hear a sermon is likely to have a group personality. The group will turn more easily to the past or to the future. Its members will have characteristic ways of adapting to change and dealing with conflict. As with individuals, it will likely have subjects or emphases that have been absorbed well and others that still need to be learned. There will be subjects that a congregation will hear gladly and others that will be heard only with much resistance. It is not the case that a preacher must either speak only of what is heard easily or of that which is likely to be difficult or painful to hear. Preachers who hope to declare anything approaching the fullness of the gospel are obliged to do both. But, it is better to do this consciously rather than by accident.

Preaching usually takes place in the context of a liturgy. It is therefore also affected by the worship style of the congregation, the choice of music, and the preaching space itself. A sermon preached in a long, narrow Gothic sanctuary, by a preacher in vestments, to longtime worshipers, following an intricate traditional liturgy, will likely need to be different from a sermon preached in a theater-style auditorium to seekers, after contemporary praise songs, by a preacher wearing a tennis shirt and slacks. It is no accident that "worship wars" are fought over these things, for identity is at stake in such symbols, rituals, and activities. Taking note of all this is instinctual in good preachers. A competent exegesis of the situation will, however, raise all this to the level of consciousness.

Such matters might be described as the symbols or codes that make up group identity. Identity is not shaped only by what goes on in church, however. Wise preachers also seek to learn of listeners what books they read, what movies or TV shows they watch, and what music they play. (The latter may be of paramount importance to young people.) All this creates the world of meaning of listeners. Any group of people is shaped by the stories remembered, the songs sung, and even the connotations of widely known words or phrases. All this is likely to be shaped more by the entertainment industry than by the denominational name on the church sign.

The denomination or tradition of the church is also important. Denominational identity often survives in ways that can be hard to specify but are very real. Certain rituals, practices, emphases, and shared values are more likely to be present in some traditions than others. To give but one simple example: the sermon is probably central in a Presbyterian church while the eucharist is likely at the heart of Roman Catholic worship. Similar but more profound observations can be made about other matters. This is particularly the case if one thinks not only of formal denominational labels but also of families of churches. There are churches of various denominations that are seeker sensitive, or define themselves by a thirst for social justice or for evangelism. There is even likely to be a *connection*, to borrow an old Methodist term, among churches that share these emphases. That connection may be stronger than denominational allegiance.

Congregations are not defined by sociology or by a particular shared narrative. They also have a core theology. The theology may be vague and inchoate, but it is certain to be there. The group person of the congregation will have ideas about the nature of God and of humanity and of the relation between God and humanity. It will have an understanding of what the church is and a sense of the central tasks it must undertake (mission). In particular, it will have a doctrine of Scripture. That is to say,

it will have an understanding of the role of Scripture in church life, of the extent of its authority, and of how Scripture ought rightly to be used. Conflict within a church, with church neighbors, or between church and clergy may well be precisely about this doctrine of Scripture. The preacher's task is not merely to affirm this theology; it is to strengthen, deepen, and perhaps even correct it. It is here that denominational identity is potentially of greatest importance. The preacher may exegete the congregation in light of the theological tradition to which the church belongs. This kind of comparative exegesis may well bring more clearly to light the actual theology of the local church. It may also indicate the direction in which that theology ought to be moved and disclose the standards by which it is to be corrected. Enough denominational identity remains in some churches that this process of deepening and correction will be positively received.

It is said that one cannot step into the same river twice, for the river will have changed in the interval. Similarly, one does not step into the same pulpit twice, for the situation will also have changed. An exegesis of the situation is an unending or at least a frequently repeated task. It may be like painting the Golden Gate Bridge. By the time one has finished, it is time to start all over again. *See* ANTHROPOLOGY; CULTURAL HERMENEUTICS; GLOBALIZATION.

Bibliography: Alban Institute. http://www.alban.org; Stephen Farris. *Preaching That Matters: The Bible and Our Lives.* (1998); Leonora Tubbs Tisdale. *Preaching as Local Theology and Folk Art.* (1997); Arthur Van Seters, ed. *Preaching as a Social Act.* (1988).

EXEGESIS OF SELF
Stephen Farris

The great 19th-cent. preacher Phillips Brooks defined *preaching* as "truth through personality" (Brooks, 1889, 8). Whatever else preachers take into the pulpit, they always take themselves. It is always appropriate, therefore, for a preacher to engage not only in an exegesis of the text or of the situation, but also of the self.

In the first place, the preacher's character and personality materially affect the credibility of the message. Aristotle claimed that of the three modes of persuasion—logos, pathos, and ethos—the last, namely, ethos, was likely the most effective (1932, 8–9). Ethos is the perceived character of the preacher. People are more likely to believe preachers whose words cohere with their characters. "Doctrine and life, colours and light, in one / When they combine and mingle, bring / A strong regard and awe: but speech alone / Doth vanish like a flaring thing, / And in the ear, not conscience ring," so wrote the 17th-cent. poet and priest George Herbert (Herbert 1974, 84). This suggests that an examination of one's character would be a wise precaution for preachers, lest our hearers say to us, "Practice what you preach!" In principle, however, this is no different from the self-examination that is required in the spiritual life of any Christian (or for that matter, any spiritually sensitive person). There is, however, an exegesis of the self that is a more direct and specific part of the preaching task.

In such an exegesis the preacher examines the characteristics and tendencies that impinge most directly on the preacher's task. In the first place, what we see in Scripture texts and therefore what we preach is materially affected by our standpoint. This has become a commonplace in biblical interpretation but is no less true for all that. We are likely to see in the texts what our social, economic, racial, gender, and ideological or theological situations enable us to see and remain blind to what they do not permit us to see. One can escape these bounds only partially, but a necessary first step is to examine the self and to name for oneself the factors involved. The preacher can then seek out, either in person or through books and other media, those of differing backgrounds who enable the preacher to view the texts in ways that he or she alone could not achieve. It is not likely and probably not desirable that preachers can entirely escape their settings in life. The myth of the detached and objective reader of Scripture is sometimes a destructive one. It is right and proper for preachers to read Scripture from within their tradition and from their life settings. A careful exegesis of the self, however, may partially liberate the preacher from the worst blindness inflicted by the reality of the limitations imposed by his or her standpoints.

It is probable that most preachers will have doctrines, themes, or subjects that they will tend to overemphasize and others that they will avoid if possible. A preacher's exegesis of the self might

therefore involve a review of sermons for an extended period of time, perhaps six months or a year. The lasting effects of preaching typically lie not in the individual sermon but in the cumulative effects of the preaching over a period of time. This might be compared to eating. Very few individual meals are memorable, and few change a life. A person's health, however, is determined by the nature of one's eating habits over an extended period of time. An exegesis of the self will therefore try to identify long-term tendencies in one's preaching. The truly obsessed may not be able to distance themselves sufficiently from their preoccupations to do this successfully. Most preachers, however, will be able to profit from such an exercise.

Most preachers do their work in particular situations. An exegesis of the self for these preachers will entail a careful comparison of themselves to their listeners. For example, preachers might profitably identify their reading, viewing, and listening habits and compare them to the habits of the listeners. (This presupposes that the preacher also engages in a simultaneous exegesis of the situation.) The results of the comparison may be salutary. Some adjustments are probably necessary, for example, in the preaching style of a supermarket-magazine-reading pastor with a Dostoevsky-reading congregation (or vice versa). Preachers may also compare, as best they can, the way they see themselves with the way others see them. This may involve the use of theological or ideological labels. These labels are often misleading. In particular, a party label such as liberal or evangelical may be especially misleading since the label may say more about the person using the label than the person described by it. Nevertheless, labels can also be handy short forms that enable preachers to compare their stances to those of the people to whom they preach. For most Christian preachers it is particularly important to compare the preacher's understanding of the nature and authority of the Bible to that held by most members of the congregation. A difference in this respect that is not identified and dealt with can disable a ministry.

A few more general observations may be helpful. The exegesis of the self ought not be carried out in isolation. The counsel of trusted advisors is always helpful in this regard. Perhaps this is particularly true with respect to identifying the subjects that we may tend to overemphasize or to avoid and to considering the way that others see us. Furthermore, most preachers are also pastors. The utility of a careful exegesis of the self is not confined to the study or the pulpit. Such a study will strengthen most areas of pastoral ministry. Finally, an exegesis of the self is not a once-in-a-lifetime task. Human beings, even preachers, are growing and changing organisms. A repeated exegesis of the self can help identify those changes and the implications for our preaching. *See* CHARACTER; ETHOS; LOGOS; PATHOS/FEELING.

Bibliography: Aristotle. *The Rhetoric of Aristotle.* Translated by Lane Cooper. (1932); Phillips Brooks. *Lectures on Preaching: Delivered before the Divinity School of Yale College in January and February, 1877.* (1889); Stephen Farris, *Preaching That Matters: The Bible and Our Lives.* (1998) 36–38; George Herbert. "The Windows." *The English Poems of George Herbert.* Edited by C. A. Patrides. (1974); David Schlafer. *Your Way with God's Word: Discovering Your Preaching Voice.* (1995).

GENDER, RACE, AND ETHNICITY
Gary V. Simpson

While the conversations about gender, race, and ethnicity remain some of the most difficult and divisive conversations for the church, it is the preacher's task to facilitate the holy conversations that we have with God and with each other.

A. The Challenges and Complexities of the Conversations of Identity in Larger Cultural Realities
B. Moving Preaching from Mechanization to Meaning
C. Rising Above Public Banter to Holy Conversations of Transformation
D. Some Practical Considerations When Preaching
　1. Who Is the Preacher?
　2. Uncovering Images Fitting for God and Our Human Condition
　3. Considering Whether These Are Words That Everyone Wants or Needs to Sing
　4. Reading the Context of the Hearers
　5. Using the Full Witness of Scripture

A. The Challenges and Complexities of the Conversations of Identity in Larger Cultural Realities

The conversation about gender, race, and ethnicity remains one of the most awkward contemporary conversations within the church. Too often we think that the best way to deal with these questions of identity is simply to ignore them. Yet these matters will never just disappear; they are a necessary part of our conversations as long as our beings are constricted to flesh and blood.

The effects of globalization have made every moment of human interaction a clashing of peoples, cultures, traditions, and postmodern nonconformity. For some, these particular identities are a necessary part of the pain that necessitates gospel salve. In fact, some marginalized people are solely defined by and identify with the value system of the very people who marginalize them. This manifests itself in most destructive self-hatred.

There are women who believe that only men are authentic preachers of the gospel. There are those maligned and abused by racism who can see only the racist's rendering of their reality.

More directly, to speak of gender, race, and ethnicity is a part of what it means to be authentically human. We do not live in a colorless, classless, asexual culture. Even in the most homogeneous congregations with respect to race, there are still many layers of ethnicity, orientation, and class. Perhaps the most dangerous or careless preacher is the one who says, "I don't see color, gender, or ethnicity—I see only people." Of course, race is viewable. Gender is recognizable. Ethnicity is discernible (sometimes!). People do not leave their identities at the church door. They come to hear the Word with their full selves. No one has the privilege of declaring, "Today, I'll just be black, not a black woman." "Today, I'll just be a man, not Japanese."

These three words—words spoken together and individually—represent issues that are so highly charged in our present public discourse that it is impossible to do these issues justice in one setting. This is indeed a most difficult subject to address because of the tendency we all have for oversimplification and gross generalization. The matters of identity and body have been the juggernauts for the faith community since the beginning of time. (See comments on intermarriage [Deut 7:1-4]; Peter's unwillingness to accept the Gentiles [Acts 10:9-33];

Paul's conversations about women and leadership in the church [1 Cor 14:33-35].)

There is no more divisive a place in the world of words and storytelling than the context of identity: gender, race, and ethnicity. In fact, speaking these words together makes the hearers uncomfortable. Why are the issues always lumped together as if none of these categories merits a conversation by itself? We list them almost as a disclaimer at the beginning or the end. We usually intend for the category to be the catchall for everything that is not Caucasian or male, or everything that was not addressed previously.

Whether the circles are politically correct or not, the intentions and integrity of the preacher are called into question as soon as these words, or the issues that are representative of these words, leave the lips. When we raise these identity questions, we are pressed to consider many more questions:

Are we suggesting some ranking order?
Who gets to choose which category is the most significant one for us today?
Are we consciously or subconsciously suggesting that one is far more important than the others?
Are we inferring that any one of these is "the least of these"?
Why is it that marginalized people must always defend and explain themselves on the grand scale of marginality?

As preacher, consider yourself the hearer for a moment: What assumptions are you comfortable with the preacher making about you? For example, take a simple assertion made carelessly by many preachers: "God has come to save man." Since we simply cannot mean that women are outside God's salvific interest, why settle for language that can be interpreted to mean just that?

Preaching is informed, empathetic speech. We owe it to the congregation to be broadly exposed and ever expanding in our view of the kingdom of God. For many people in our congregation, we are the inspired informant.

Those of us who have been in these conversations, discussions, dialogues, and debates are rather weary of discussions that tend to rehash and repackage the age-old unwillingness to "do unto others as you would have them do unto you."

It would be nice if, as preachers, we did not have to deal with such potentially explosive and divisive

categories. Nevertheless, there is no way of avoiding this, and there should not be. Preachers are called to raise the issues and speak the words that pull people—all kinds of people—into holy conversation with God and with each other.

B. Moving Preaching from Mechanization to Meaning

Too often the task of preaching is reduced to the mechanization of the craft. Can we really do art well if we do not ask the deeper questions that give rise to and shape the craft? The preacher is necessarily called into the responsibility of theologian. Anselm described theology as "faith seeking understanding." In the specific work of preaching, this "faith seeking understanding" is in the ministering of the Word. Eugene Peterson has a delightful and delicious rendering of John 1:14: "The Word became flesh and blood, and moved into the neighborhood" (The Message).

Preaching is nonsensical banter if it fails to move into the neighborhood of the listeners. We are called to enlarge the hearts, expand the minds, and invigorate the souls of our hearers. Whereas many who speak rely more on the *what* and *what not* of life, the preacher should never abandon the signal task of addressing the *why*. Because many people who hear us believe we are their first and final interpretation of the world around them, we are to be careful not to paint the world in absolutes. In a world characterized by technologies that give us 256 colors in varying pixel densities, we cannot afford to speak of the world in black and white, recognizing that the preacher's task is actually in the nuance and ambiguity of the varying shades of gray, the creativity of bold and robust colors beyond the monochromatic expression. We really do our work when we are able to describe well enough the patterns—polka dots, herringbones, and plaids—that the congregation begins to see and experience life in its unlimited possibilities.

C. Rising Above Public Banter to Holy Conversations of Transformation

The reality is that church talk and preaching have danced around the questions of identity for years. Our stilted and unimaginative language has dangerous consequences. One might say that all preaching is dangerous. However, the kind of danger I mean is the kind that is nurtured not because the words we speak have caused the hearers to consider something new and bold but because the words we have spoken have caused the hearers to exempt themselves or to be excluded from the whole conversation.

At the same time, the gospel story is not confined to any one person's social location. While faith says that it was birthed into the world in a particular moment in time, through a specific person, a product of a particular heritage and legacy, the message of the gospel is an inclusive one that reaches out to "whosoever will." The "whosoevers" we preach to are made in the image of God, and not the reverse. More important, preachers are made in the image of God, and not the reverse. The great and dangerous dance that the preacher is called to lead recognizes that while we speak most authentically from our knowledge and experience of God, our work is also about liberating the gospel from the confines of language that deny the existence, presence, and participation of those who are not "me." Gardner Taylor has said there is an inescapable and unavoidable word in the Scripture, "Whosoever." No matter how we try to get around it and no matter how many exemptions we attempt to file, the word cannot be ignored. The gospel may be one story, but that story is lifted by a variety of voices and vessels.

D. Some Practical Considerations When Preaching

1. Who Is the Preacher?

Know who you are. It may seem obvious enough, but preachers must first acknowledge their own race, gender, ethnicity, and heritage. What are the lenses through which you view the gospel story? As a man, I recognize that at best I am a recovering sexist. By that I mean that there are times when I benefit from a system that inherently values men over women. I can choose to participate in that if I want, but I live with that reality every day. Honestly, I fail sometimes. The preacher's lack of intentionality, imagination, and compassion can aid and abet the desire of listeners to tune out him or her.

2. Uncovering Images Fitting for God and Our Human Condition

Any discussion of the categories of race, gender, and ethnicity (I want to use another divisive word here, class) must wrestle with the matters of inclusive language.

Endeavoring to make our language as inclusive as possible does not stop with gender inclusion. We must open the conversation about inclusive language to include the classic dark-light dichotomy, particularly in our descriptions of human experience. I have heard many preachers say, "It was a *dark* time in my life." Does that mean, "I was depressed"?

When speaking of outdated ideas, preachers refer to the "Dark Ages." How about choosing instead a seldom-used word, such as arcane?

These words are weighted by a long history of pain and nonbeing. They find their way into our music: "O precious is the flow / *That makes me white* as snow" (author's emphasis).

3. Considering Whether These Are Words That Everyone Wants or Needs to Sing

The voice of the preacher cannot be the proponent for a gospel that files exemptions to every "whosoever will" that Christ utters. The very gospel is a story of inclusion, not exclusion.

4. Reading the Context of the Hearers

As preachers, we are called not only to interpret texts from the Scripture but also to interpret contexts. Know with whom you are speaking this holy conversation. What do you know about these people? Some sermons and images are effective only when shared within a certain cultural context. One can either lose the others with irrelevant discourse or, even worse, defile the moment.

There will be times when we are called to preach cross-culturally. This may include the experience of preaching with an interpreter. In this situation, it is far easier to stay closer to the biblical text. Because so much of our preaching is wedded to context, some of our illustrations and examples are rendered irrelevant in cross-cultural contexts because we do not share the same stories. However as Christian preachers, we do share the common story of Scripture. Speaking outside one's culture renders simple illustrations and customs irrelevant. The story of the sacred text is known and shared. It is the biblical witness with which the listeners are familiar even if they do not know the preacher. Rest in the telling of that story. The more foreign or unfamiliar I am, the more I work inside the story of the Scripture.

Far too often, we make the unnecessary distinction between prophetic and pastoral preaching in unhealthy ways. An experienced sage of the craft told a young colleague of mine: "You have to stop dropping the bombs in your sermons." In the act of preaching, we must move from the tendency of pressing hot buttons and creating controversy to creating the opportunity for the ongoing holy conversation we are called to have as humans radically shaped by the life and event of Christ. Instead of preaching about the matters of gender, race, and ethnicity for their shock value or assumed prophetic character, we should preach about these matters as a part of our normal course. The preacher's handling of them in this way creates an apprehension, an anticipated resistance. We make our listeners defensive when they should be shown how to live fuller, more aware lives. At the conclusion of 1 Cor 12, Paul offers himself as a model for seeing life differently: "I will show you a still more excellent way." This commitment to model the honest, authentic conversation about identity and inclusion is part and parcel of what it means to be human.

5. Using the Full Witness of Scripture

The Bible is an honest account of the struggles of the faith to wrestle with these matters. The preacher cannot be afraid to discover and uncover these tensions for the congregation. Many biblical passages give us a chance to raise the questions of race, gender, and ethnicity.

Here are some texts to be revisited in this context:

Ruth the Moabite. This "half-breed" woman kept the lineage of David, monarch of Israel, alive.

Rahab the prostitute. The actions in Josh 2 and Josh 6.

The good Samaritan. Deal with the sociological oxymoron. Is there such a thing as a "good" Samaritan? Why do we call this person the good Samaritan as if he is the only Samaritan who deserves that modifier?

The book of Acts. As the disciples, now apostles, move to expand the story of the gospel, they are in a clash of cultures. Read especially the listing of the people present at Pentecost "and visitors from Rome."

The conversation between Philip and the Ethiopian eunuch in Acts 8.

The woman at the well. So many cultural taboos are broken by this simple conversation between a rabbi and a woman in the middle of the day.

The black and *beautiful woman who takes the protagonist's voice in Song of Songs.*

The heavenly vision of Revelation. What about that number comprised of "every nation, and kindred, and tongue" (14:6 KJV)?

A guiding image for preaching is John's depiction of the disciples fishing, toiling all night and catching nothing. After following the instructions of Christ, they have great success. The Scriptures declare that they draw their nets filled with "the multitude of fishes" (21:6 KJV). This is the task of preaching, to cast a net as widely as possible so that diverse peoples can find themselves at home in the power of the gospel. It is not sameness but diversity of both identity and gifts that make up the power of the kingdom of God. *See* AFRICAN AMERICAN PREACHING PERSPECTIVES; SUSPICION; WOMEN.

Bibliography: Brian Blount et al. *True to Our Native Land: An African American New Testament Commentary.* (2007); Teresa Frye Brown. *Weary Throats and New Songs.* (2003); Jana Childers, ed. *Birthing the Sermon: Women Preachers on the Creative Process.* (2001); Danna Nolan Fewell. *The Children of Israel: Reading the Bible for the Sake of Our Children.* (2003); Joseph Jeter and Ronald J. Allen. *One Gospel, Many Ears.* (2002); Matthew Kim. *Preaching to Second Generation Korean Americans.* (2007); Cleophus LaRue. *The Heart of Black Preaching.* (1999); Cleophus LaRue. *This Is My Story.* (2005); Henry Mitchell. *Black Preaching: The Recovery of a Powerful Art.* (1990); Eugene Peterson. *The Message.* (1993).

GLOBALIZATION
Arthur Van Seters

Globalization is economics writ large and may be the most critical frontier yet to be engaged by homiletics. In a shrinking world the decisions of any one group have economic and political implications for others. Globalization is a way of acknowledging all God's children as immediate neighbors. Rebecca Peters (2004) points to the different ways in which globalization and its implicit values are defined: neoliberal, developmental, environmental, and neocolonial. The homiletic task is to help congregations discern how the reign of God proclaimed by Jesus exposes and engages our current economic order.

Philip Wogaman believes that most preachers are afraid of economics in general—but not because they consider it unimportant. They are often keenly aware that the Bible gives ample attention to economic matters. Rather, they feel incompetent in this area. The language of global economy seems intimidating, and they wonder how to speak directly to businesspeople who seem to know what works in the economy (1998, 61).

The significant disconnect between pastors and laity when it comes to economics surfaced in a recent study. Many Christians in secular occupations had little difficulty naming ethical challenges in their work lives (such as financial fraud, conflicts of interest, tax evasion, fair pricing, and debt collection). Yet these same people rarely sought pastoral counsel when struggling with such issues. They perceived that pastors lacked business insight and knowledge and believed that the church was indifferent to such matters. They also had a lack of confidence in the church's management of its own business and perceived church culture as one that discourages bringing work-related concerns to a place of worship (Knapp 2005, 47).

Preachers may also feel a tension between preaching locally and preaching globally. Does concentrating on what is near at hand and personal limit the gospel's reach? Some may look at the Great Commission and think that the global is an extension of the local. William Nottingham argues that the reverse should be the case:

> Much preaching lacks interest because it does not contain a local relevance that is shaped by a worldwide concern. It lacks a sense of mission because it lacks an understanding of mission. Christian practice near at hand is an expression of the unlimited nature of the mission of God. (1986, 61)

When economists and theologians do probe ethics and globalization, they often have opposing points of view. In *Having: Property and Possession in Religious and Social Life*, the editors note that, to some, globalization is "an oppressive machine aimed at leveling cultural differences in and through the systematic exploitation of poorer nations and the earth's resources." To others, it is "the harbinger of increased prosperity and with it the possibility that more and more people will take control of their own political and social destinies" (2004, 1). Patrick D.

Miller argues, "The single largest issue or concern of the [Ten] Commandments as a whole is the matter of property and possession" (2004, 21). William Schweiker says greed is an isolating force that undermines the necessary bonds of human community essential to a humane economy (2004, 259).

A number of homileticians offer the following comments on the challenge of preaching in relation to global culture. Preachers need to be culturally critical and to seed countercultural movements that will someday come together to form a new social mind. The reign of God is forever present and coming; it is God's comprehensive coverage of all people, relationships, and issues. Too often, sermons portray God acting with regard only to ourselves. Lacking a God of global reach, faith is diminished. In the expansion of technology and global capitalism, signs of the devouring activity of principalities and powers are evident and call for resistance. Preaching that ventures into this arena is demanding, daring, and dangerous and emerges as an event of transformed imagination in which the world is perceived and voiced differently. These voices provoke a disposition of critical theological reflection and require a process of re-visioning global economic relationships.

Preaching on global economics must be impelled by the Spirit out of theological and biblical insights. The doctrine of creation reminds the preacher that economic realities are related to God's created order; that the earth is gift and that all human beings are made in God's image. The interconnectedness of the world is not ultimately a result of a humanly constructed market or its accompanying cybernetic revolution, but of God's arrangement. Some clues to what this means economically are spelled out in God's covenant with ancient Israel, and they are fundamentally related not to who deserves what in relation to economic endeavor. The covenant is ruled by grace—Katherine Tanner speaks of God's gift-economy. What ideas of God's giving "would appear to most expand the economic imagination of contemporary people?" God's internal relationship and God's relation to the world can be seen as "a complex, multi-staged economy for distributing goods." Unconditional giving, universal inclusion, and noncompetitive possession are all reflected in the language of the Trinity, creation, covenant, redemption, and consummation (Schweiker and Mathewes 2004, 370).

On globalization the Common Lectionary has its limitations. Classic passages on macroeconomics, such as the Sabbatical Year in Deut 15 and the Jubilee Year in Lev 25, are not included. Other texts signal possibilities: Isa 58 connecting true religion with concern for poor people, the economic requirements of the kingdom of God (Matt 25:31-46 and Luke 3:7-17), and the folly of making the acquisition of wealth the ultimate purpose of life (Luke 12:13-21). Perhaps the most provocative biblical reference is the book of Colossians because it invites the church to look at globalization from the perspective of the supremacy of Jesus Christ.

In *Colossians Remixed*, Brian Walsh and Sylvia Keesmaat interpret contemporary globalism as "a religious movement of previously unheard of proportions," one "built on systematic centralizations of power and secured by structures of socio-economic and military control" (2004, 30–31). The gospel of the sovereign Christ exposes the idolatrous nature of this globalization and also offers profound hope that the principalities shall not finally have the last word. This way of approaching the biblical text is one that many preachers will find surprising and perhaps disquieting because they may feel impelled to reexamine post-9/11 developments that have reshaped the entire globe (2004, 35–37).

Will It Preach?

In a passionate sermon on hope a number of years ago, I heard a passionate preacher expose false notions of hope with a rapid-fire catalogue of empty platitudes and myths. He then retold the gospel story as counterpoint. A focus on economic myths could be delivered with the same bold and incisive style. But such preaching can be done only with the help of a congregation truly willing to share such a sermon as it unfolds.

André Resner (2004) would name this the white-hot passion strategy. He also suggests other "paths": irony, indirect parable, identification, "soft sell" justice, and scribal traditioning. While suggestive, the reality of globalization is so pervasive and its power in much of its present form so distorting for life on our planet that homileticians and preachers desperately need a programmatic examination of preaching on globalization. Such an exploration will need to go beyond the liberationist homiletic forms of exposing, naming, and condemning. Nor will it be adequate to reveal the growing corporate social responsibility movement and other promising aspects of an expanding global economy. It will require interdisciplinary

collaboration at least with economists, political scientists, businesspeople, theologians, homileticians, and pastors. Then the emerging homiletic will need to be refined in on-going congregational preaching. The task is daunting but spiritually, socially, and environmentally extremely urgent. *See* CORPORATE ETHICS; ENVIRONMENTAL ETHICS; GEOGRAPHY; LIBERATION CRITICISM.

Bibliography: David Buttrick. *A Captive Voice: The Liberation of Preaching.* (1994); John C. Knapp. "Bridging Christian Ethics and Economic Life: Where Pastors and Laity Disconnect." *Journal for Preachers* 28 (Lent, 2005) 47–54; William J. McElvaney. *Preaching from Camelot to Covenant: Announcing God's Action in the World.* (1989); Patrick D. Miller. "Property and Possession in Light of the Ten Commandments." William Schweiker and Charles Mathewes, eds. *Having: Property and Possession in Religious and Social Life.* (2004); William J. Nottingham. *The Practice and the Preaching of Liberation.* (1986); Rebecca Todd Peters. "The Future of Globalization: Seeking Pathways of Transformation." *Journal of the Society of Christian Ethics* 24 (2004) 105–33; André Resner Jr. "Casting Our Mammon on the Baptismal Waters: Preaching Economic Justice During Lent." *Journal for Preachers* 27 (Lent, 2004) 42–50; Katherine Tanner. "Economies of Grace." William Schweiker and Charles Mathewes, eds. *Having: Property and Possession in Religious and Social Life.* (2004); Brian J. Walsh and Sylvia Keesmaat. *Colossians Remixed: Subverting the Empire.* (2004); Paul Scott Wilson. *The Practice of Preaching.* (1995); J. Philip Wogaman. *Speaking the Truth in Love: Prophetic Preaching in a Broken World.* (1998).

LAY PREACHER
Gregory Heille, O.P.

Lay preaching, in the baptismal context of the church's ministry of the Word, has a rich and demanding heritage of responding to the right of the people of God to have the Word of God preached to them.

Biblical and Historical Context

Such NT notables as the Samaritan woman (John 4) and Mary Magdalene (John 20) witnessed to Jesus and proclaimed the resurrection. Lesser notables such as Priscilla (Acts 18) or the daughters of Philip (Acts 21) ministered the Word of God as evangelists and prophets. Paul's concern for liturgical order (1 Cor 14) and cultural propriety (1 Cor 11) did not exclude or prevent a remarkably open practice of the ministry of the Word in the 1st and 2nd cent. church. Paul indeed acknowledged practices of prayer and prophecy by women in the liturgical assembly—despite the apparent prohibitions of 1 Cor 14:33-35, a later interpolation intended to restrict earlier ecclesial freedom of practice, and 1 Tim 2:11-15, which used a faulty anthropology regarding Eve and the fall to support post-Pauline concerns against giving offense to the surrounding community.

By the 5th cent., when Pope Leo the Great officially prohibited it, lay preaching was no longer practiced. Lay preaching resurfaced with the urban reform movements of the 12th-cent. Beguines and Waldensians and the 13th-cent. Franciscan and Dominican friars, all of whom embraced voluntary poverty while preaching in the spirit of the *vita apostolica* of Luke 10. Although the friars were regularized, the Beguines and Waldensians were not, and lay preaching again was prohibited by the Fourth Lateran Council (1215).

In the years leading to the Reformation, lay preaching was revived. In defiance of Roman Catholic prohibitions, Wycliffe trained lay preachers. Luther first allowed for the right of every Christian to preach, as did the Anabaptists. Zwingli opposed lay preaching, associating this ministry with church office. Luther, too, came to this position. The Catholic Counter-Reformation prohibited the practice even more explicitly at the Council of Trent.

In the North American Great Awakenings of the 1730s to 1770s and 1790s to 1840s a number of noteworthy Puritan, Quaker, Shaker, Baptist, Congregationalist, Methodist, Presbyterian, and AME laywomen, and some laymen, were inspired to evangelize and preach, at great cost to their reputation and, at least at first, without view to ordination. A few most memorable names include Sarah Osborn, Mother Ann Lee, Jarena Lee, Sarah Grimke, Lucretia Mott, Sojourner Truth, Phoebe Palmer, Elizabeth Cady Stanton, and Mother Jones.

Understood as lay apostolate, the Catholic Evidence Guild in England bridged the Atlantic in 1918 to prepare and send street preachers from a number of eastern and northern American cities to foster understanding of Roman Catholicism in the largely Baptist rural South. Not until the new Code of Canon Law in 1983 did the Roman Catholic Church officially assert that "all the Christian faithful have the duty and the right to work so that the divine message of salvation may increasingly reach the whole of humanity in every age and in every land" (#211) and that "lay persons can be admitted to preach in a church or oratory if it is necessary in certain circumstances or if it is advantageous in particular cases" (#766).

Ecclesial Issues

Lay preaching often is framed in terms of the right of the people of God to hear the Word preached and the responsibility of the church to respond. In this understanding, the ministry of the Word is an ecclesial charism in which the Sunday pulpit is the "summit and source" (a Roman Catholic expression) of a ministry of the Word reaching into every aspect of ecclesial life, including catechesis, pastoral care, evangelization, and action for justice. A lively ministry of the Word necessarily requires active participation by well-formed and articulate lay representatives of the Word, as church professionals and volunteers as well as in the workplace and the public square.

Whereas some denominations actively promote lay preaching in the context of worship, the sticking point for other denominations is the expectation that liturgical preaching belongs properly and only to ordained clergy (*see* ORDINATION). As diminishing numbers of clergy are taxed by expanding ministerial demands, many pastors and adjudicatories turn to lay preachers to bridge the gap. Even so, ecclesiastical discipline, as in the case of the Roman Catholic Church, can be exercised ever more restrictively, especially with respect to preaching in the context of worship.

Those who assert the baptismal roots of the preaching ministry make the theological claim that the ministry of the Word is a constitutive dimension of discipleship for all Christians. In this view, the ecclesiastical issue should be one not of exclusion of lay preachers so much as it should be coordination of the ministries of the Word for the sake of the common good.

The marks of a mature and well-formed lay preacher are much the same as for ordained clergy—though training may be in or out of a formal school setting. A well-formed preacher must demonstrate personal, interpersonal, and spiritual maturity; a habit of lifelong learning and critical thinking—with particular attention to biblical hermeneutics, christology, ecclesiology, liturgical theology, spirituality, moral theology, and homiletic and catechetical theory and practice; global perspective and the ability to do social analysis and theological reflection with a view to Christian mission; and, as the case may be, ecclesiastical authorization to preach.

As can be seen from this ambitious list, as well as from an Internet search using the words lay preaching, lay involvement in the ministry of the Word is an arduous responsibility that benefits from both ecclesiastical support and lifelong learning. *See* CALL; CHARACTER.

Bibliography: Catherine A. Brekus. *Strangers and Pilgrims: Female Preaching in America, 1740–1845.* (1999); Sarah Ann Fairbanks. "Displaced Persons: Lay Liturgical Preachers at the Eucharist." *Worship* 77 (2003) 439–57; Nadine Foley, ed. *Preaching and the Non-Ordained: An Interdisciplinary Study.* (1983). Patricia A. Parachini. *Lay Preaching: State of the Question.* (2000).

MISSIONAL PREACHING
Pablo A. Jiménez

Mission is a polyvalent concept. The church uses this term in at least two different ways. First, *mission* is a theological term that refers to God's project for the world and to the role the church plays in the divine project. Second, mission is an ecclesiastical term that refers to the evangelization of peoples and cultures, particularly in countries where Christianity is a minority religion. It is common to use the plural form *missions* to describe the latter term, reserving the singular *mission* for the theological one.

The definition of *missional preaching* thus depends on our definition of mission. On the one hand, missional preaching describes the homiletic endeavors that expound on the Christian mission, calling all institutions and peoples to faith. On the other hand, missional preaching describes the efforts of missionaries who proclaim the gospel in countries deemed fields of mission.

Preaching and Mission: A Theological View

In theological terms, the term *mission* has at least three different uses. First, the church understands that God is the originator, motivator and, ultimately, holder of the mission. The mission belongs to God, who is the first and foremost missionary. Second, as the church participates in God's mission, there is room to talk about the mission of the church (Estrada 1992, 288). However, the church's mission stems from God's mission. The church is not the originator and holder, but a collaborator in the divine mission. Third, as individual believers participate in missionary endeavors, there is also room to talk about the mission of the believer (Floristán 1992a, 289). The church identifies, commissions, and sends believers to participate in missionary endeavors. Again, the mission of an individual believer stems from God's own mission.

The Christian faith understands that both nature and the Bible witness to God's self-revelation to humanity. While the divine revelation through nature is ineffable, the Bible witnesses God's revelation in history through the covenant with the children of Israel and, in particular, through Jesus of Nazareth, whom the church confesses as the Christ (Bosch 1995, 9). God's relationship with the world is both dynamic and inclusive. The inclusive nature of the Christian faith leads necessarily to the proclamation of God's love for the world in general, and for humanity in particular. For this reason, the Christian faith is missionary by its very nature (Bosch 1995, 8–9).

Given that God is the one who loves the world and wants to embrace humanity, the mission is divine; it is *missio Dei* (God's mission). The church has the privilege of collaborating with God in mission. Preaching is one of the many forms in which the church proclaims the gospel of Jesus Christ, calling the world to faith in and reconciliation with the missionary God.

Missional preaching is thus the proclamation of God's love for the world and of the divine offer of salvation to humanity. Such proclamation of love and salvation necessarily leads to the promotion of holistic liberation and human rights, through word and deed (Estrada 1992, 289). The church-in-mission inserts itself in different cultures, dialoguing with the different segments of each society (Floristán 1992a, 290). Ultimately, the goal of missional preaching is the conversion of every nation, tribe, people, and language (see Rev 7:9).

While the Christian faith wants to reach the world as a whole, evangelism is an essential dimension of mission. Bosch defines *evangelism* as "the proclamation of salvation in Christ to those who do not believe in him, calling them to repentance and conversion, announcing forgiveness of sin and inviting them to become living members of Christ's earthly community and to begin a life of service to others in the power of the Holy Spirit" (Bosch 1995, 10–11).

Conversion occurs as a consequence of God's action (Müller 1987, 144–45). Neither the person who proclaims nor the person who listens to the proclamation of the gospel can effect a conversion. God, through the Holy Spirit, transforms the human conscience, leading converts to reject old loyalties. Conversion entails real change as a person adopts values congruent with the kingdom of God; values that usher in new ways of living.

Baptism marks not only a person's initiation in the faith; it is also a call to share the message of the gospel with those who still have not heard (Shelton 1987, 67). To be baptized is to be called to love the world. Those baptized become a "royal priesthood" (see 1 Pet 2:9). They not only preach the gospel but also intercede for the world. Baptism is the link between mission, evangelism, outreach, and worship (González 1995, 27).

Missional preaching witnesses to God's action on behalf of the world (Müller 1987, 23). The term *witness* implies that the church, as an institution, and those who preach, as individuals, demonstrate a commitment to God through a life congruent with the principles of God's mission and the values of the gospel. *Witness* is contrary to *indoctrination*. While indoctrination pushes a partisan point of view with the intention of recruiting new members for a movement, a witness motivated by God's love testifies to an experience with the divine.

In Greek, the word *witness* is *martyr*. Eventually, this word became a technical term to describe those Christians who died for their faith. This reminds us that missional preaching has a sacrificial aspect. As Jesus of Nazareth gave his life, God calls the church and its agents to invest their lives in the proclamation of the gospel, even to the point of martyrdom (Müller 1987, 142). Missional preaching thus requires solidarity with poor, alienated, and deprived persons (Müller 1987, 23).

Carlos Cardoza-Orlandi defines *mission* as "the participation of the people of God in God's action in the world" (2002, 15). Preaching is, thus, one of the myriad ways in which the people of God communicate and participate in God's action on behalf of humanity. Preachers represent the church-in-mission. They fulfill a priestly role, representing the people before God, and a prophetic role, announcing God's message to the world.

In many ways, all preaching has missional aspects. However, missional preaching stresses and conveys God's love for humanity, inviting all peoples to participate and rejoice in God's actions on behalf of the world.

Preaching and Missions: An Ecclesiastical View

Although the church has engaged in missionary activities since its inception, the term *missions* usually describes the missionary endeavors of the church from the late 15th cent. to the middle of the 20th. These dates roughly refer to the conquest of America and the end of the Second World War.

By the late 15th cent., European nations began to explore the world, developing new commercial routes to Africa, India, and China. The conquest of America was an unforeseen consequence of these commercial explorations. The changing geography of the world ushered in the modern era and its political corollary: colonialism. In their efforts to establish hegemony over the new peoples, Europeans launched modern missions. Missionaries, first from Europe and later from the United States, traveled the world preaching to peoples who had never before heard the gospel. Some learned the indigenous languages painstakingly, translating the Bible and establishing new congregations. Others taught European languages to the new peoples, incorporating them into established churches. Some identified with the indigenous peoples, while others identified with the colonial powers. However, they all shared the presupposition that the Anglo-European cultures and peoples were intrinsically superior to the indigenous ones found in the mission fields. To different degrees, they all shared the paradigm of "mission as civilization" (Cardoza-Orlandi 2002, 38ff.), legitimizing Anglo-European hegemony over the world. Therefore, the modern missionary movement implanted a colonial church (Floristán 1992b, 291). Colonial missions produced the following:

1. Poor churches. The mission fields were enclaves of poverty. Even though most countries had rich natural resources, foreigners controlled access to and exploited such resources.
2. Rural churches. While the capitals of the newly conquered countries resembled European cities, most missionaries served in rural and agrarian mission fields.
3. Foreign churches. Given that most missionaries were foreigners, many understood Christianity to be a foreign religion. This perception led many nationalist movements to reject Christianity as a whole, or Protestantism specifically.
4. Clerical churches. As missionaries received monies from their respective metropolis, they became the administrators of all missionary institutions. They dominated institutions because they were the link through which hard currency was funneled from abroad.

In brief, colonial missional preaching legitimized Anglo-European hegemony, focusing on personal salvation and morality. Sadly, it was largely unaware of its social, economic, and political role.

The decolonizing political processes in Africa, Asia, and even South America forever changed traditional colonial missions. Now, the church-in-mission faces an emerging post-colonial paradigm.

1. Europe and the United States are now post-Christian societies and fields of mission in and of themselves. Missional preaching is no longer exclusively tied to foreign missions (Newbigin 1995, 336).
2. The missional preacher has also changed. Instead of foreign missions, most developing countries have national churches led by national leaders. While some Anglo-European missionary agencies still hold to the old paradigm, most now see themselves as partners in mission, particularly in areas such as secular and theological education, advocacy, ecumenism, and health. Some agencies even network with "younger" churches to send preachers from the developing nations as missionaries to Europe and the United States.
3. Missional preaching occurs in pluralistic settings where Christianity, Western-style democracies, and capitalist economies are not the only option. This situation forces the church to develop an intercultural and inter-religious praxis of the faith (Cardoza-Orlandi 1999, 6).
4. The issue of justice is central to missional preaching (Cardoza-Orlandi, 6). Preachers around the world risk their lives denouncing institutional sin, advocating for human rights, combating institutional racism, ministering to victims of pandemics, and helping refugees. In order to preach about justice, the church-in-mission must develop political awareness, establishing strategic alliances with non-governmental organizations (NGOs) dedicated to the promotion of justice and human rights.
5. Missional preaching sees the Bible as a faithful ally in the struggle for liberation and self-determination. Using liberation hermeneutics, it builds on the theological premise that God takes the side of poor and dispossessed persons as they take steps toward justice (Gern 1997, 366). Missional preaching stresses the immediacy of the biblical characters and events, affirming God's solidarity with those who suffer.
6. Missional preaching helps believers to understand their situations and, therefore, themselves on theological terms. In order to reach this goal, missionary preachers must be involved in the conceptual world, the language and culture of the hearers (Newbigin 1995, 335).
7. In summary, missional preaching promotes theological and ecclesiastical decolonization (Gern 1997, 367).

Conclusion

Through missional preaching, the church identifies with the world that God loves (Neill 1971, 492). In brief, missional preaching is proclamation in God's name; proclamation of God's kingdom; and proclamation of God's timely intervention on behalf of a suffering world (Costas 1979, 29–44). See EVANGELISTIC PREACHING; MISSIOLOGY; NEW HISTORICISM; POSTCOLONIAL CRITICISM.

Bibliography: David J. Bosch. *Understanding Mission: Paradigm Shifts in Theology of Mission.* (1995); Carlos F. Cardoza-Orlandi. "What Makes Preaching 'Missional'?" *Journal for Preachers* 22

(1999) 3–9; Carlos F. Cardoza-Orlandi. *Mission: An Essential Guide.* (2002); Orlando E. Costas. *Compromiso y Misión.* (1979); Juan A. Estrada. "Misión de la iglesia." *Diccionario Abreviado de Pastoral.* (1992) 288–89; Casiano Floristán. "Misión del cristiano." *Diccionario Abreviado de Pastoral.* (1992a) 289–91; Casiano Floristán. "Misiones extranjeras." *Diccionario Abreviado de Pastoral.* (1992b) 291–92; Wolfgang Gern. "Preaching." *Dictionary of Mission: Theology, History, Perspectives.* (1997) 362–68; Catherine Gonsalus González. "The Baptismal Lens for Missional Preaching." *Journal for Preachers* 18 (1995) 27–30; Karl Müller. *Mission Theology: An Introduction.* (1987); Stephen Neill. "Preaching for Missions." *Concise Dictionary of the Christian World Mission.* (1971) 492; Lesslie Newbigin. "Missions." *Concise Encyclopedia of Preaching.* (1995) 335–36; Robert M. Shelton. "Mission as a Context for Preaching." *Austin Presbyterian Theological Seminary Bulletin, Faculty Edition* 103 (1987) 67–73.

PREACHING TO CHILDREN
Carolyn C. Brown

Children, like Christians of all ages, need to hear the Word preached in the community of faith. Hearing the Word preached in the intergenerational congregation is very different from exploring Bible stories with peers. Worshipers in the sanctuary gain much more than intellectual concepts. They are knit into the community that retells key texts and ponders their meaning for living. While the church through the years has recognized that children as well as adults need preaching, it has generally treated children as small adults and expected them to be present and listen, or at least be quiet, during preaching targeted to adults.

At the beginning of the 21st cent., we know that children think and hear very differently than adults do. In today's world children, even more than adults, orient to the visual rather than the auditory. Their brains cannot deal with symbols and metaphors in the way that adult brains can. And they have more limited exposure to the world than adults do. But children, especially those between the ages of six and eleven, are also focused on the larger world and want desperately to understand and participate in it. (This focus will fade in adolescence as they pay more attention to their peers than to the larger community.) Therefore, preaching to children within the congregation requires that preachers pay attention to the abilities and needs of children.

Equipped with this knowledge of children, congregations have tended toward three options, each with its own set of assets and drawbacks. When none of the three is pursued, parents as well as children tend to avoid worship, either coming only for church school or searching out a congregation that has a clearer vision of its responsibility to preach to children.

The first option is to send the children out of the sanctuary during the sermon (or for the entire service) for learning activities prepared especially for them. While this meets children's conceptual abilities, it denies them the formative experience of hearing the Word preached in the whole community.

The second option is to include a children's sermon as part of the congregation's worship. Such minisermons are one of the most popular attempts to preach to children. In their favor, children sermons (1) say to children, "You are important, and we are glad you are here," (2) get the children into close physical proximity to the leaders of the congregation, thus building relationships, and (3) give them an opportunity to move their action-oriented muscles as they go to the front of the sanctuary. But it is extremely hard to speak meaningfully to children from the wide age span that appears each week. Bookstores are filled with object lesson sermons for this purpose. An object is presented and its physical properties discussed. The preacher then uses those physical properties to make a spiritual point. The mental ability to do such complex connective thinking does not develop until early adolescence. Although children enjoy the process and understand the concrete meaning of the object, they seldom get the spiritual point. The adults easily understand the point, often find it more memorable than the more complex points of "the real sermon," and enjoy the interaction between the preacher and the children. So, children's sermons generally preach more effectively to the adults than to the children. Last, it must be admitted that there is some exploitation of children for the sake of the adults. It is generally gentle, but adult laughter at a child's sincere comment can deeply embarrass a child. Few adults would willingly put themselves in the position of the children speaking extemporaneously with the preacher in the hearing of the entire congregation.

This said, the pressure to include a children's sermon in the congregation's order of worship is sometimes so great that it is prudent to do so. In such cases, the preacher does well to stick to concrete points that children can understand. Objects used in various parts of the church's life and ministry can be introduced and explained. Parts of the worship service can be explored. Seasonal activities can be discussed. Vocabulary can be introduced or background information provided before the reading of the morning's text. The text can even be read with the children on the steps rather than from the lectern. (See Juengst 1994.)

In the third option the congregation and its leaders work to make the presentation of the Word and the sermon child-accessible. Since the hope is that children will grow into listening to "the real sermon," preachers serve the children better when they invite them to tune in to at least parts of the larger sermon instead of offering them alternatives to listening to that sermon. When this is done, children move from tuning in to the sermon occasionally, to listening to whatever of the sermon they can follow, to hearing the majority of the sermon. As they do this, they hear more and more of the message, and feel more and more part of the congregation.

Preachers wanting to draw children into hearing the preached Word need to pursue some of the following:

Remember the presence of children during preparatory study. Identify vocabulary that will be difficult for children. Choose the biblical translation with consideration for the children's ability to understand it as read. Flag for public explanation objects, customs, and places in the sermon that will be unfamiliar to children. Consider how children will respond to the theme or text. Some biblical stories raise very different questions among children than among adults. For example, the deaths of the Egyptian firstborn at Passover raises questions about why God would kill children to make an obstinate adult pharaoh do what was needed. Also, think about how the text or message applies specifically to the lives of children.

Take note of the ongoing concerns of the congregation's children. Be aware of the beginning and ending of school, report card times, children's community sports, and seasonal activities and events. Keep up with children's literature, movies, and television shows. Mention of any of this during a ser-

mon grabs the attention of children who then stay with the preacher to see what is being discussed.

Remember that sermons are two-way dialogues. At the back door say to young listeners, "I saw you listening." Encourage sermon art—drawings, poems, questions written in response to the sermon. Post such artistic responses on a special bulletin board, use them with the artist's permission in a future sermon, or print them as a worship bulletin cover or as an illustration of an article in another church publication.

Make sure the children hear the text on which the sermon is based. Do not just read it as if it was a newspaper editorial. Choose a reader to match the text, for example, a teenage girl to read the Magnificat (Luke 1:46-55). Honor the poetic format of the Psalms by providing appropriate choral readings by readers of all ages. Involve more than one reader in presenting one of the many dialogues in Scripture. Present complicated stories in a readers' theater format. Vividly presenting the scripture for the day ensures that children at least hear the text and often invites them to listen at least briefly in order to hear what the preacher will have to say about it. Preachers can take responsibility for preparing these presentations or can enlist the aid of a volunteer reader's guild.

Learn some tricks that invite children to listen to the sermon. Begin the sermon by giving children an outline: "I'll be talking about a bear, a basket, and a party in that order." Illustrate the sermon with a visual prop: "Look at this wooden giraffe. I bought it when I was in Jamaica on the youth mission trip. Every time I look at it I remember . . ." Noting that everyone in the sanctuary either is or was a child, illustrate sermon points with stories from childhood (e.g., learning to ride a bike, getting a bad grade, being stuck at home on a rainy day).

Finally, pay attention to parents. Parents need both encouragement and support to help their children listen to sermons. Urge families to discuss the worship service, especially the sermon, in the car on the way home. Each member of a family can identify a "takeaway," an idea, mental picture, even a joke that they want to remember or take away into the coming weeks. Families that include older children and youth can look for "windows," things they heard that led them to crawl out a mental window to explore something important to them. Parents and children can also write notes to each other during the sermon about what is said. When parents talk with their children more about the content of sermons than about their behavior during sermons, children are encouraged to listen. *See* BRIDGING THEN AND NOW; ILLUSTRATIONS AND STORIES; IMAGINATION/CREATIVITY.

Bibliography: Carolyn C. Brown. *Forbid Them Not: Involving Children in Sunday Worship* (Lectionary Years A, B, and C). (1992–94); Carolyn C. Brown. *You Can Preach to the Kids Too.* (1997); Sara Covin Juengst. *Sharing Faith with Our Children.* (1994).

PREACHING TO YOUTH
Kenda Creasy Dean

The term *youth* is seldom a contested term in Scripture. It universally refers to someone, usually male, early in life, situated between infancy and adulthood, or (in its adjectival forms) to qualities associated with this season in life ("youthful vigor" [Job 20:11 NASB]; or "young" stemming from "new" [1 Tim 4:12 NIV]). Neither the Hebrew nor the Christian Scriptures distinguishes youth from childhood, and both use *youth, child,* and *boy* interchangeably to mean someone who has not yet attained adult status in the culture.

Throughout Scripture, God enlists young people in the salvation of Israel (Samuel, David, Jeremiah, Mary, and Timothy are perhaps the best-known examples). God frequently encourages youthful prophets and disciples by urging them to ignore society's dismissive attitude toward the young, and by calling them to trust God instead. In the familiar passage from Jeremiah, the prophet remembers the word of the Lord coming to him, saying:

> Before I formed you in the
>   womb I knew you,
> and before you were born I
>   consecrated you;
> I appointed you a prophet to the
>   nations. (Jer 1:5)

Jeremiah replies:

> "Ah, Lord GOD! Behold, I do not know how to speak, for I am only a youth (na ʿar)!" [*Note:* the NRSV translates na ʿar as "boy."] But the LORD said to me,
> "Do not say, 'I am only a youth,'
> for to all to whom I send you you shall go,
> and whatever I command you you shall speak."
>   (Jer 1:6-7, author's trans.)

Similarly, in the early church Paul admonishes Timothy, who was probably a teenager when he first encountered Paul (Acts 16:1) and whom Paul later sent to lead the church in Ephesus: "Let no one despise your youth (neotētos), but set the believers an example in speech and conduct, in love, in faith, in purity" (1 Tim 4:12). Of course, God's most dramatic enlistment of a young person is described in Luke 1, with Mary's election as the theotokos (God-bearer). Mary's status as a virgin (parthenos, Luke 1:27) fulfills Hebrew prophecy but also confirms Mary as a girl in her early teens, the age of betrothal for women at the beginning of the common era.

The Contemporary Context of Adolescence

Today, childhood and youth are viewed in sharp contrast, a phenomenon that influences preaching with young people. Thanks to youth ministry's persistent emphasis on high school and, after World War II, junior/middle high programming, most churches define *youth* as the ages between twelve and seventeen—though this is an arbitrary, and inaccurate, definition. Social scientists often equate *youth* with mid to late adolescence, referring to young people who are old enough to participate in the workforce or university (compare Friedenburg 1963, 3). Outside the U.S., the term *youth* commonly refers to anyone under the age of thirty or sometimes older, and in some cultures a youth is anyone who is unmarried (Osmer and Dean 2007, 90).

Because adolescence itself emerged as a byproduct of the economies and values associated with the industrialized West (Kett 1978, 7)—and "teenagers" even more so (Hine 2000, 4)—*youth* tends to fluctuate according to its social context. Globalization has expanded the breadth and length of adolescence, as puberty starts earlier and adulthood is increasingly postponed (despite the fact that the age of majority is eighteen in most states) (Herman-Giddens 1997, 505–12; Arnett 2004, 3). Public education has created a culture in which adults and teenagers seldom interact, and age stratification in churches tends to mirror that of society as a whole. This social phenomenon forces teenagers into what Patricia Hersch has called "a tribe apart"—a cohort suspended between both childhood and adulthood in which teenagers, in the absence of adults, increasingly try to raise each other (Hersch 2001, 30).

Preaching and Youth Ministry

Youth ministry has often unwittingly underscored age stratification by maintaining only superficial ties to congregational life and worship. This sometimes leads those in ministry with young people to lapse into one of two errors: to assume that preaching to youth is undesirable, or to approach preaching to youth as a discrete activity unto itself. These misgivings stem from a larger misunderstanding—namely, that proclamation is one-dimensional, and that preaching occurs in only a few ways. In fact, because young people are part of the total congregation and mission of the church, preaching to youth follows the same guidelines for preaching to anybody. Preaching interprets sacred texts for the sake of shaping a community's identity around the living presence of Christ, and therefore may be performed in any way that makes room for the Holy Spirit to do this (see fig. 1). Yet preaching's form—with young people, as with all people—is tethered to what Thomas Long calls its focus (the theme of the text being preached) and its function (the effect the

preacher hopes it will have on the contemporary hearer) (Long 2005, 108–9). This makes preaching to youth, like preaching to adults, a radically contextual form of ministry. It must take into account the context of Scripture and the social and developmental location of the hearers in order to discern which practice of preaching best suits God's purpose with this particular text for this particular (young) flock, in this particular pasture, for this particular moment in time.

Preaching to Youth

Just as children's sermons that reflect on the theological symbolism of concrete objects may be over the heads of children who lack the cognitive schemata that allow them to make such a symbolic leap, youth talks represent another common pitfall when preaching to young people. Youth talks—highly contextualized (and generally humorous) messages designed to present the gospel in a memorable way to bored teenagers—follow most of the rules of preaching to adults, but frequently aim for student interest above developing the focus or function of the text. Like sermons, youth talks vary greatly in homiletical quality. Typically, youth talks

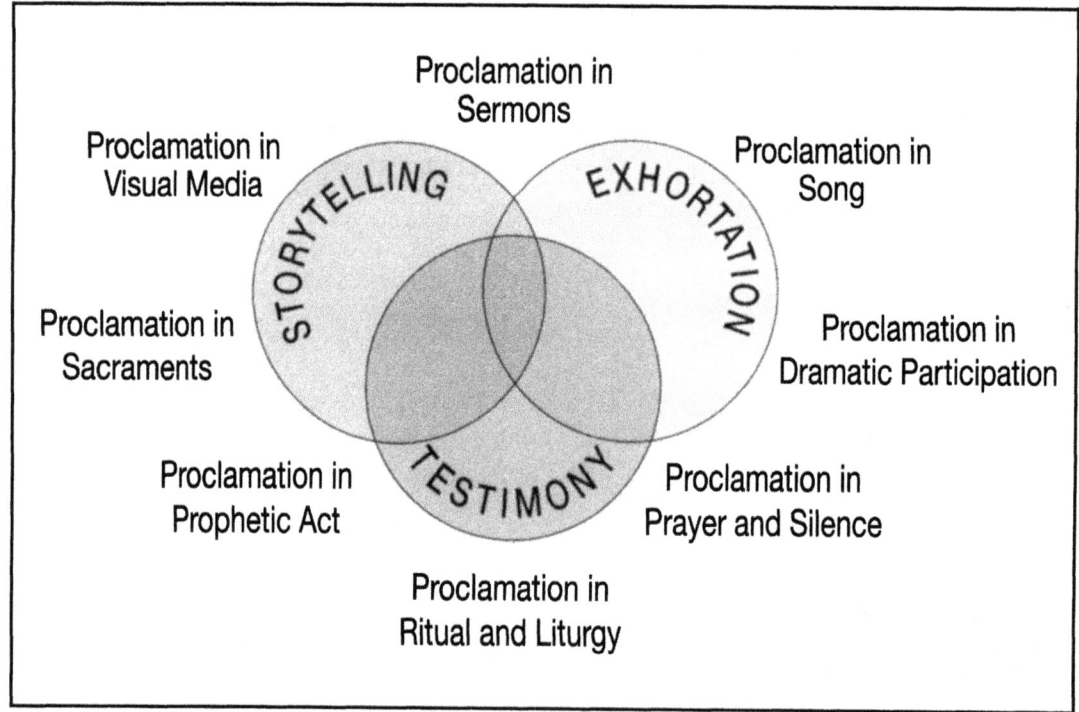

Fig. 1. Some forms of proclamation with young people.

are homilies in disguise, since the assumption is widespread that no self-respecting teenager would listen to a sermon voluntarily.

To be clear, the practice of storytelling remains important during adolescence (and into adulthood). Every culture, Christianity being no exception, maintains its deepest truths embedded in stories. Just because youth can now grapple with the nuances of a text does not mean they are ready to leave storytelling behind. In fact, the importance of stories escalates during adolescence, as movies, literature, and music become primary media that shape and express young people's experience of the world, including their experience of faith. Preachers who contextualize preaching for youth recognize that young people create as well as receive stories, and, therefore, they make room for teenagers to participate in the preaching enterprise as co-creators of proclamation.

At the same time, preaching to youth also takes into account dimensions of human development that adolescence brings to the surface. Chief among these are the increasing interpersonal awareness and relational sophistication that accompany the teen years. As a result, the practice of testimony—the art of sharing how God has come near to us personally—now joins the practice of storytelling as important for preaching to adolescents. Testimony gives everyday language to one's experience of God in and beyond worship. The language made possible by the practice of testimony allows teenagers to recognize faith as more than a feeling, and to describe the ways in which their own life story intersects with God's story.

For example, when young people gather for fellowship or worship, ritualize opportunities to put into words where in the past week they sensed God's nearness, and where they sensed that they were "blocked" from God in some way (this is a very basic form of the Ignatian prayer of examen). Encourage them to tell these experiences as narratives in order to clarify the intersection between the teenager's personal story and the story of the self-giving love of the triune God.

Preaching to Young Adults

As young people approach emerging adulthood, the distinction between the social and developmental contexts of youth and adults becomes nearly imperceptible. Again, the practices of storytelling and testimony remain important to proclamation with all ages; but contextualizing preaching to young adults means taking part in practices of exhortation—namely, those practices that interpret Scripture for the sake of ethical discernment and engagement in the community. Doing this requires the preacher to develop a critical appreciation for cultural materials that function as sacred texts for many young adults, even though they may be devoid of Christian significance (i.e., movies, cultural symbols like Starbucks, or practices like working out). Putting the Christian story in conversation with these materials offers a model for Christian discernment for young adults making their own decisions about their relationship with culture. Exhortation, like testimony, contains a relational element that is important to the developmental location of young adults establishing intimacy; Paul viewed exhortation (from the Greek paraklēsis, "calling to one's side") as the practice of coming alongside someone with words of encouragement, comfort, consolation, and counsel in order to help the community become conformed to Christ and become all that God wants them to be (Rom 12:8).

For example, when young adults form a worshiping community, include time for silence and discernment within the sermon, combined with a meaningful symbolic action, to allow young adults to respond to the claim that the text makes on them personally. (In some traditions, sacraments function as proclamation leading to outreach; in other traditions, the sermon itself moves the hearer from witnessing the good news to bearing this witness to others.) *See* BRIDGING THEN AND NOW; ILLUSTRATIONS AND STORIES; IMAGINATION/CREATIVITY.

Bibliography: Jeffrey Arnett. *Emerging Adulthood.* (2004); Z. Freidenburg. *The Vanishing Adolescent.* (1963); Marcia Herman-Giddens. "Secondary Sexual Characteristics and Menses in Young Girls Seen in Office Practice: A Study from the Pediatric Research in Office Settings Network." *Pediatrics* 99 (April 1997) 505–12; Patricia Hersch. *A Tribe Apart.* (2001); Thomas Hine. *The Rise and Fall of the American Teenager.* (2000); Joseph Kett. *Rites of Passage: Adolescence in America, 1790 to the Present.* (1978); T. Long. *Preaching and the Literary Forms of the Bible.* (1989); T. Long. *The Witness of Preaching.* (2005) Richard Osmer and Kenda Dean. *Youth, Religion and Globalization; New Research in Practical Theology.* (2007).

PULPIT, USE OF
Jana Childers

Although pulpit preaching has been associated historically with literate, thoughtful sermons and a dignified style, in recent years many preachers have been encouraged to "come out of the pulpit." While a number of traditions continue to prize the pulpit as a symbol of the Word's primacy, others have begun to develop a taste for the kind of physical movement and intimacy that can be achieved only in free space. Some preachers wrestle with decisions about when and how much to use the pulpit and when and how much to use the open space around it.

Three key principles guide the preacher's decisions about pulpit use. First, non-verbal messages are far stronger than verbal messages. Stanford University theorist Albert Mehrabian has shown that in face-to-face communication 55 percent of all meaning is conveyed by the face and body and 38 percent by tone of voice. Only 7 percent of all measurable meaning in most public speaking settings is attributable to word content. Second, audiences tend to pay more attention to the content of what is said when it is said from behind a piece of furniture. Audience attention shifts to a more relational focus (i.e., to how listeners feel about the speaker) when a speaker stands in free space. Finally, the fundamental truth of the face-to-face communication event is "the truth will out." In public speaking settings the truth will come out, it will come out non-verbally, and it will be the truth about how the speaker feels.

The decision to move from the pulpit to the open space then must take at least these factors into account. The preacher must be reasonably sure that the verbal and the non-verbal messages cohere, that a relational emphasis is desirable, and that he or she is able to control the non-verbal side of the sermon's delivery—at least enough to minimize unintended messages. In addition, maximizing the strengths of free-space preaching requires numerous delivery skills. The following considerations are recommended:

1. Movement should be disciplined for economy and variety. Excess gesture and foot movement are pruned to minimize distraction. Back-and-forth pacing is eliminated as the visual equivalent of monotone. Large movement on the platform takes the form of a series of triangles.
2. Combining pulpit preaching and free-space preaching in the same sermon often requires a shift in non-verbal styles. Pulpit gestures most often occur in the speaker's "box" (a strike zone in the upper middle of the speaker's body). Gestures in free space are more often fully extended and occur at all levels of reach.
3. The approach-withdraw axis of interaction between preacher and congregation is used judiciously to coordinate with the sermon's shape and peaks of intensity.

See PERFORMING THE MANUSCRIPT; WITHOUT NOTES; WORSHIP ENVIRONMENT; WORSHIP STYLE.

Bibliography: Charles L. Bartow. *Effective Speech Communication in Leading Worship.* (1988); Jana Childers. *Performing the Word: Preaching as Theatre.* (1998); Albert Mehrabian. *Silent Messages: Implicit Communication of Emotions and Attitudes.* (1971); Charles L. Rice. *Embodied Word: Preaching as Art and Liturgy.* (1991); Richard F. Ward. *Speaking of the Holy: The Art of Communication in Preaching.* (2001).

SACRAMENTS, PREACHING AND TEACHING OF
Jennifer Lord

Many Christians understand the preached word and the sacramental word to be of whole cloth: Jesus Christ, the one Word of God, in our midst. And many Christians believe that both ways of encountering Jesus' presence are necessary for every Sunday's assembly: each Lord's Day we eat and drink of God's provision, and this meal is always accompanied by the proclamation of the gospel—the good news of the triune God articulated in our midst.

The timeline of liturgical history is full of examples of the division between spoken word and sacrament, for instance: a certain theology of leadership and a particular theology of atonement contributed to the emphasis on the meal; a wariness about ritual practices and a way of interpreting Scripture contributed to the supremacy of the sermon. Yet some Christians acknowledge a growing ecumenical consensus that the historic, biblical, and ecumenical practice of the church is found in a particular pattern of Sunday worship: gathering, word, meal, and sending. This order is filled out with prayers, water washing, collection of alms, song, and more, but the core of this gathering is preaching and the meal. Many church bodies keep this core for these reasons: scriptural and historical continuity, these worship elements understood as revelation by God and instituted by Christ; both events honored as accommodation by God to human need, both forms known to be means of grace and occasions of the real presence of Christ, both shape the church for service.

In those Sunday assemblies that keep both sermon and eucharist, preachers may or may not refer explicitly to the meal. Sometimes the preacher in a eucharistic context does not speak of the meal because the experience of eucharist is normative: learning is cumulative through participation. However, in the same context some preachers will make associations between the day's texts and the table. And sometimes the preacher refers to the eucharist because the eucharist is central and the sermon builds toward that action. In other contexts the preacher speaks about the meal because the eucharist is not normative. The preacher makes didactic comments to prepare the assembly for the sacramental experience. Or it is believed that the preacher must bring understanding to the sacramental activity. Some preachers even refer to the meal when eucharist is not celebrated, another means of instruction and preparation. The practice of the church is varied.

The sermon may be an occasion for teaching on all sacraments/ordinances. One historic practice of the church has been to teach on the sacraments through a series of sermons (MYSTAGOGICAL PREACHING): instruction on the sacramental experiences of the faithful. Preachers may plan thematic or topical sermons addressing meanings of sacramental practice. Preachers who use the Roman Lectionary or *Revised Common Lectionary* may make connections between images or doctrines in the texts of the day and the sacraments. This can be true for preachers who choose their own lections. *See* SOTERIOLOGY; WORD OF GOD; WORSHIP ENVIRONMENT.

Bibliography: World Council of Churches, Commission on Faith and Order. *Baptism, Eucharist and Ministry.* (1982).

SEXUALITY
See ANTHROPOLOGY.

WAR, PREACHING DURING
Terry W. Eddinger

Carl von Clausewitz, an early 18th-cent. Prussian Army officer and strategist, says war is an act of force to compel an enemy to do one's will (1989, 75). He also says war is "a continuation of political intercourse, carried on with other means" (87). His theory that war is a political instrument is widely accepted, but it is an instrument of the worst kind. Inevitably, people suffer in war, and many of them are innocent of the politics or fighting.

War was a common event in biblical times, so much so that people took it for granted. Instead of being a political instrument of last resort with an internationally recognized cause as is usually the case in modern times, war was often the first choice. The Bible is full of examples, such as Israel's battles in taking the promised land as described in Joshua and Judg 1, Israel's confrontations with the Philistines in 1 and 2 Samuel, or any of the Assyrian or Babylonian campaigns described in 1 and 2 Kings. Yet the absence of war is the biblical ideal, when people will "beat their swords into plowshares and their spears into pruning hooks" (Isa 2:4; Mic 4:3).

Theology of War

How one preaches on war will depend upon whether or not one sees the cause as just. Historically, Christian positions on war range from pacifism (war is never just) to just war (war is sometimes merited, usually in defense) to crusades (holy war or offensive war). The Bible is not always clear about the reason or justification for war. At one extreme, some people fought for taking land, such as the Israelites in Josh 1:6. Deuteronomy 7 and 20 endorse this cause as legitimate, at least for the Israelites. Some battles were raids for plunder, as the Midianites' yearly raid of the Israelites (Judg 6:5). Other wars were simply to exert control over another nation, as Uzziah did to the Philistines, Arabians, and Ammonites (2 Chr 26:6-8). War was also considered a form of punishment, initiated either by a nation or by God. Israel fell to the Assyrians as God's punishment for their sins (2 Kgs 17:6-7). Judah fell to Babylon because Zedekiah rebelled against Nebuchadnezzar (2 Kgs 24:20–25:2).

At the other extreme, Jesus taught, "Love your enemies" (Matt 5:44). Likewise, he taught that one should turn the other cheek when slapped in the face (Matt 5:39). Both sayings suggest a purely pacifist position on war. The difference between the two positions is who is being addressed. Nations or kings are usually the ones being addressed in the OT, and they had to conduct war; but individuals are the ones addressed in the NT, and they are not allowed to conduct war themselves. However, many interpret the NT passages in such a way that allows for an individual to fight for one's country, that is, the individual is under the appointment of the nation.

Preaching about War

After determining whether a war is just, a preacher must consider the sermon's audience, whether it is military members going to battle or family, friends, and citizens staying at home. However, here are two elements common to both audiences the preacher should consider in preaching about war. First, regardless of the war's justification, the pastor must remember that the first priority has to be preaching the gospel of Christ. This includes placing an equal value on human life, even of the enemy. People die in war. God is the Maker of soldiers on both sides of the battle line. Therefore, the pulpit is no place to glorify war, promote patriotism, or push a political agenda. Second, war is a time of crisis. People need to hear that God is present and in control, even when the world seems to be out of control.

1. Preaching to Families, Friends, and Citizens

Preaching to the congregation should emphasize prayer for the safety of military members, divine guidance for leaders, and comfort and support for friends and families. Encourage the congregation to find creative ways to support service members and their families (writing letters, sending care packages, prayer groups, family watch care programs, etc.). Preach that God loves the individual (service member) and the congregation should too, regardless of what it thinks about the cause of the conflict.

2. Preaching to Military Personnel

Deploying military personnel need to hear that God is with them, no matter what lies ahead. A good passage to use is Ps 23 or 46. Emphasize that God is

with them, knows their fears and concerns, and promises to be ever present even when they are in the "valley of the shadow of death." Soldiers in combat need to hear the same message. Do not forget that the military member has a great concern for his or her family while away. Pray for protection of the military member and his or her family and friends.

Soldiers returning from war need to hear that God still loves them, no matter what happened in the war. This is a good time to preach forgiveness for any guilt they may feel and to give thanks to God for their return. Also, it is an excellent opportunity to let them know the church is proud of their service to their country.

3. Preaching a Military Funeral

In preaching a military funeral, take into consideration the background of the deceased—whether he or she wanted to serve in this particular conflict, how the person died, the family's position on the member's military service, and so on. Treat it as any other funeral, except emphasize an appreciation for the service member's service and devotion to one's country. Also, mention that the soldier made the ultimate sacrifice for his or her country and deserves the congregation's highest respect and honor. Perhaps use John 15:13 as a text. Avoid using this event as an opportunity to preach for or against the war. Emphasize the life of the individual, and offer comfort and support for the family. *See* CRISIS; FUNERAL; SIN AND EVIL.

Bibliography: Carl von Clausewitz. *On War.* Edited and translated by Michael Howard and Peter Paret. (1989); Arthur F. Holmes, ed. *War and Christian Ethics: Classic and Contemporary Readings on the Morality of War.* 2nd ed. (2005); Thomas Kennedy. "Can War Be Just?" *From Christ to the World: Introductory Readings in Christian Ethics.* Edited by Wayne G. Boulton et al. (1994) 436–42.

WORSHIP STYLE
Tex S. Sample

Preaching in North America today occurs in a variety of worship styles because the culture settings are quite diverse and the forms of persuasion and terms of engagement vary greatly. This article discusses preaching in terms of three broad cultural formations: traditional oral, literate, and electronic.

The approach here is to characterize briefly each of these cultures, describe their worship styles, and then discuss preaching that best fits these settings.

A. Traditional Oral Culture
1. Worship
2. Preaching
B. Literate Culture
1. Worship
2. Preaching
C. Electronic Culture
1. Worship
2. Preaching
D. Conclusion

A. Traditional Oral Culture

People of a traditional oral culture are a large group in North America and even larger in the world. They tend to be people who live in extended family relationships. They seek out churches and other institutions that are organized like extended families. In North America the great majority of traditional oral people can read and write, but they engage the world in oral practices, especially in worship and preaching. Inhabiting the lower half of the class structure, they tend to be older and vary by race and ethnicity. Because traditional culture is under attack and thus without legitimation in the larger culture, many people in this formation engage in a range of resistances to the dominant culture. These practices are often covert and pose no little challenge to the pastor from a different culture, especially if he or she is insensitive to their lived lives and attempts to impose alien practices on them.

1. Worship

In this cultural setting worship will make use of tradition and oral practices. Well-known practices such as call and response, the lining out of songs and spoken responses, and uses of rhythm and emphasis in liturgical speech characterize oral worship. Since these are not literate people, memorization is very important. Memorization of Bible verses and a host of proverbs will be important. The services will not be "printy," although a bulletin may be used because it is expected. The soul music of the people will be important. By soul music, I mean the music with which they are encoded and that tells their stories. The Bible will, of course, be central, and it will be approached devotionally rather than critically. Biblical stories and sayings will be prominent in the use of Scripture in worship. Testimony remains an important practice in traditional oral worship. Prayer will be dramatic, extemporaneous, and episodic. When done indigenously, worship will be ecstatic and/or expressive, for example, the ecstatic character of serpent handling services, the expressive nature of black worship or Pentecostal services, the emotive and heartfelt worship of Caucasian churches, and so on. This listing is too brief and partial, of course, but perhaps it will suggest a wider range of practices so that a turn to preaching is now appropriate.

2. Preaching

In traditional oral cultures preaching takes on an improvisational and extemporaneous character. Its heartfelt and emotional character testifies not only to its emotional depth but also to its authenticity and truthfulness. What is not felt is not genuine and is not true. Preaching in this culture is not linear discourse leading a congregation through the ins and outs of a developing argument that takes objections into account and arrives at a logical conclusion. Rather, it takes on a dramatic character where words are themselves events. Their semantic meaning, while not absent, is secondary to the power of their impact. The use of story is key to preaching in this culture, and a story does not fundamentally make a point; it is the point. The crystallization of wisdom occurs not only in stories but also in proverbs or other pithy sayings such as biblical verses and wise sayings that people can remember. Because these are people who live in the bottom half of the class structure, preaching will be life based and focused on survival and coping in a world that does not turn out right. For these reasons as well, sermons will address hope. Sermons on social issues and other matters will be best heard and received when preachers think through issues in terms of extended family relationships. Here the appeal is to empathy and hence to raising questions about "how it would make you feel if this happened to members of your family." Sermons on issues will focus not so much on analysis as on display, that is, to show the impact of an issue rather than enter into an extended analysis of it. Sermons, therefore, hone in on the heartache and call forth a morality of empathy. Tradition will be important in these congregations. The preacher will then need to learn the stories of the congregation and to reach back into the tradition to approach issues. To work creatively with a tradition is to bring it forward to address contemporary concerns.

B. Literate Culture

Literate culture is made up primarily of business and professional people. Typically, their families are more nuclear in form and their lives focused more in friendship and affinity groups, with relations at work playing an integral role in private life as well. They tend to be more high-average or affluent in income, and career takes on central importance in their lives. Their training and careers usually require articulate use of language, and insofar as they provide leadership in their occupations, explanation is a significant practice. They are the representatives of the dominant culture. Located most often in suburbia, they are the majority of members in most mainline churches. They live in the tension of being achievement oriented and pursuing self-fulfillment. At the same time they hold their children in high regard, and the education and success of these youngsters play critical roles in family commitments, decisions, and plans.

1. Worship

Literate worship is a print-oriented form of worship. It makes use of creeds, responsive readings, and printed prayers. Hymnals, books of worship, bulletins, and other printed resources form the liturgy. Music is typically high culture when it is not classical. Choirs often have professional and/or trained musicians in solo roles. The worship service is more emotionally restrained and formal. Scripture readings often come from the lectionary but may not include more than one reading, especially in a congregation where the emphasis on preaching is central. As such, the eucharist is not usually celebrated every Sunday in these services unless offered at an earlier time. More typically, the eucharist is celebrated once a month or even once a quarter.

2. Preaching

In literate congregations, preaching is often modeled on print insofar as the sermon attempts to be articulate, well-reasoned, linear, and thought-provoking. The sermon is often read, and competent preachers in this medium do this well. Sermons take on a prose quality with such preachers. Preaching often concentrates on subjective experience, and psychological models like Myers-Briggs and family systems theory are seen as providing more gravity to homiletical efforts.

Increasingly, too, leadership language and talk of selling find their way into preaching, in part a reflection of corporate America and its organizational concerns. Furthermore, literate congregations in the U.S. tend to be individualistic, and the challenge of preaching is to proclaim a more embodied and communal vision of the church and its life, one not limited to psychological models or overly focused on subjective experience or too informed by business and consumerist language. In sharp contrast to electronic culture, as we see below, literate preaching emphasizes meaning in words; that is, careful definition of words, use of clear concepts, and semantic precision attempt to communicate the faith in representative language. Explanation becomes, therefore, very important. Hence getting one's ideas exactly right and being able to convey them in communicative language take on high priority. The use of the biblical text requires careful and informed exegesis by competent preachers in literate congregations. This capacity to take the text and place the worlds of a congregation in God's story is a high skill of the first order. Storytelling in literate culture tends to be illustrative; that is, it tends to be anecdotal. Stories do not so much make the point as they illustrate the point.

C. Electronic Culture

A technological, informational, and communicational transformation is occurring around the globe. Manuel Castells reports that we can now integrate "into the same system . . . the written, oral, and audio-visual modes of human communication" (Castells 1996, 328). Such integration now constructs ecological-like gatherings where image, music, beat, light, move, dance, and word converge into a single reality. Think here of contemporary concerts by artists who perform in multisensory, multimedia settings where "a capsule of reality" is generated by the use of visual, kinesthetic, aural, rhythmic, musical, and lyric forms in a cohesive, ecstatic spectacle. These settings take on an immersive character, and an audience is no longer merely a passive, listening, and viewing collective, but becomes a participating body actually performing with the artist. Members of the audience typically sing, move, and dance and thereby constitute the full, embodied, immersive character of the event.

1. Worship

The suggestion here is not that worship simply ape immersive events of the kind described above, but that the church learn from them because they are the most powerful practice of persuasion and formation indigenous or native to the electronic culture emerging today. Worship will be multisensory and multimedia. It will be immersive and performative. Central to this emerging form of worship, however, is God's story. The approach is not to place God's story in electronic media and practices, but to place these in God's story. The right move is for these immersive practices to glorify and praise God. Therefore, multimedia and multisensory worship will be shaped by the Christian Year, by the lectionary, and by the use of classical structures of worship. The core practice of this worship will be the eucharist. The premium of this worship, however, will be not on talking heads, but on a performing body of Christ immersed in liturgy characterized by the faithful integration of image, music, beat, light, move, dance, and word.

2. Preaching

Obviously, preaching will undergo a transformation in these settings. For one thing, it will be more experiential in approach. Younger generations seek meaning in experience more than they do the meaning in words of literate culture. This, of course, does not mean that there will be no words but that words play a different role as they are integrated into these immersive events. Meaning in experience is emotive and embodied. It does not so much attempt to describe and explain in language that corresponds to a state of affairs; rather, words will connect with the visual, the aural, and the kinesthetic; they will trigger the memories of smell and light, of gesture and move and dance. Preaching will use the language of events, objects, and experiences. Imagery or figure, always important in preaching, takes on added significance. Language that paints a picture or functions like video not only has the capacity to touch or move people but strikes the imaginations of those formed by multimedia and multisensory practices. Preaching of this kind will therefore use language about objects or events rather than intricate conceptualization or words of complex definition. Finally, storytelling is making a comeback in electronic culture, but a significant change now characterizes narrative performance. Mitchell Stephens underscores the importance of scene changes in fast-cut video and maintains that these are now basic to storytelling (Stephens 1998, 178–203). Stories now move through a variety of scenes in their telling in electronic settings.

D. Conclusion

The practices of worship and preaching summarized above require the rich particularity of a congregation and they need the vibrant coloration of racial and ethnic life, but they indicate directions for the preacher who would address the growing diversity of culture in a North American context and the direction of a faithful response in worship and preaching. *See* EMERGING CHURCH PREACHING; EVANGELISTIC PREACHING; MISSIONAL PREACHING; PREACHING TO YOUTH; TECHNOLOGY; TECHNOLOGY AND THE SERMON.

Bibliography: Manuel Castells. *The Rise of the Network Society.* Vol. 1. *The Information Age: Economy, Society and Culture.* (1996); Mitchell Stephens. *the rise of the image the fall of the word.* (1998).

Part 8 Experience. Introduction: Preaching in a Diverse World

Joseph R. Jeter Jr.

The time was when a preacher stood up before a congregation that looked very much alike. The preacher was male and assumed that his listeners had the same worldview that he did, processed reality in the same way that he did, and used language in the same way that he did. It is too facile to say that times simply have changed, although they have. But the time when a congregation's worldview, understanding of language, and processing of reality were uniform never really existed.

We know now that women and men generally do not have the same approach to language. The increasing numbers of women in ministry in some denominations bring new opportunities and challenges for religious communication. To people in those settings even the assumption that a preacher is male may not just be dated, but offensive. Those who refuse to engage diversity creatively will find that minoritized groups will no longer suffer gladly under language, doctrine, and ethos that exclude them. The beloved community is soon fractured.

The woman or man who stands in the pulpit or, more and more, out of the pulpit and on the floor looks at a mixed multitude that can be intimidating. There are differences in gender, in age, in modes of mental process, in physical ability, in sexual orientation, in culture—including race, ethnicity, geography, and other ways of personal identification. Conservatives and liberals sit, sometimes uncomfortably, next to each other. One also encounters people of different economic status, those who are largely silent in a noisy setting, and those who are struggling with displacement (Jeter and Allen 2002; Nieman and Rogers 2001). Different approaches to theology, music, the degree of emotion appropriate to worship, and so forth are evident and often compete with one another for primacy. When it comes to preaching, some people have never listened to an evangelistic, soul-winning kind of preaching, while others know no other kind of preaching.

Realizing the diversities that exist in any congregation, the diverse theological groundings, diverse interpretations of biblical texts, diverse comfort levels with worship styles, diverse views on what is happening in the self, the family, the church, the community, the country, the world, and what should be done about any or all of these, how can the preacher open her or his mouth? The answer, of course, is carefully and courageously. If the preacher expects everyone to agree with everything he or she says, the preacher can only remain mute. But there are some understandings of preaching in an increasingly diverse world that can help preachers and their listeners hear a helpful word. Here are six of them.

1. *Recognition of the neighbor.* Whether a preacher arrives at a small town on the prairie of the Middle Border or the streets of Little Havana or the suburbs of Silicon Valley or anywhere else, she or he will be preaching to a multicultural congregation, whether it is intentionally or unintentionally so. We understand *neighbor* as referring to "how we act toward fellow human beings, particularly those nearby and in need" (Nieman and Rogers 2001, 14). Preachers need to respect and appreciate the neighbor and to be open to the experience of those who have been marginalized, learning more about themselves in the process and gaining insight about relationships they may have to rethink.

2. *Avoidance of words that hurt.* Rabbi Lawrence A. Hoffman has written about "prayers that hurt" (Hoffman 1990, 13), prayers that exclude, for example, women, African Americans, or Jews from the presence of God. One might say the same things about "sermons that hurt," not by prophetic judgment, but by exclusion. For example, Professor Nancy Eiesland has written about the importance of bringing persons with disabilities into "the speaking center" (Eiesland 1994, 81) of the church and the wider world. Her comments about persons with disabilities are true of other groups that make up the congregation. Each group needs to be a part of the speaking center, that is, to know that its concerns are expressed clearly and are understood by others in the community. In a similar way, each group in the congregation needs to be

able to hear and understand others in the community. One way for this to happen is for the pastor to discover the concerns and characteristics of the various listening and speaking groups and take them into account in the sermon. This leads to the third understanding.

3. *The mixed multitude.* Some people resist diversity and cite the "Babelization" of worship and church life as their rationale. But others find a better description in Exod 12. When the Israelites left Egypt, "a mixed multitude also went up with them" (RSV) (Hoffman 1990, 17). Preachers need to become multilingual if they want to be heard by the mixed multitude of 21st-cent. churches. How would women hear this message? Youth? Latinos? African Americans? We live in a world of languages. We function fairly well jumping from one world to another in secular conversation. But when we move to religious language, the problems multiply. We may find ourselves using archaic or outdated language that has lost its meaning for most people today. Words like *justification* are of little innate interest to most of the mixed multitude in churches. And we may also find that meanings often shift between languages and/or generations, as found in words like *bad*.

Because we have many sets of ears in worship that hear language in different ways, there are two basic choices in front of us as preachers. We can find a style that is most comfortable to us and preach that style as best we can. If we are really good at it, some or many may follow us. We may create a church modeled after ourselves, after what we believe and how we speak it. But what happens when we leave? A preacher with a different style may run into significant trouble from those who had been formed in one's own mold. Or the church may fall completely apart. A second choice is to engage the diversities that exist in the community called church. This will require preacher and people to negotiate areas of contention, understanding that change will be inevitable.

4. *Negotiated language.* If the congregation is going to survive as a multicultural community, some things must be negotiated. This does not mean that anything goes. Nor does it mean that we must accept a lowest common denominator approach to being church. What it most likely will mean is that out of these negotiations, new understandings will arise that will lead to different approaches to worship and other aspects of our life together.

An interesting word comes to us from John of Damascus, a 7th-cent. Christian preacher. He described the relationship between the three persons of the Trinity as "perichoresis," which is a kind of circle dance in which the persons move around the circle in a way that implies intimacy, equality, unity yet distinction, and love (Cladis 1999, 4). Perichoretic preaching could function in two ways. First, it could invite a variety of people to be involved in dialogue leading to the sermon. Second, the sermon might move around the theme or text, stopping to provide views from various perspectives. The preacher might say, "From here we can see this, but if we move around to this side, we have a different perspective, a different view." Inviting people to look at a text or theme from a perspective new to them can be energizing.

Another negotiating tool has to do with finding linguistic genres that tend to cut across cultural lines. Among them is *narrative*. People hear stories with both head and heart and draw analogies from their own experience. A closely related tool is *images.* Images can be vivid and impressive. More and more people, especially the young, are visual learners. A third tool is *sayings.* Multiethnic groups have a variety of sayings that permeate their daily lives, and memorable sayings in sermons can live on in people's minds. "God is good . . . all the time! All the time . . . God is good!" Spending time with persons in neighborly occasions leads to learning sayings that open new homiletic doors.

One other tool is *poetic language* (Nieman and Rogers 2001, 44–47). Preaching began in poetry, and great mysteries and truths call for poetry. Poetry not only makes language; it also makes rhythm. It may not offer a template for preaching, but it does offer a spirit—creative, rhythmic, colorful, evocative—that can be received by people in a diverse church and a diverse world. Television portrayed Paul McCartney playing "Hey, Jude" in front of a million young people in Moscow's Red Square who were singing along with him. They will not forget. Those who heard Martin Luther King Jr. say his famous Free at last! will never forget. And the people who gathered in worship after the bombing of the federal building in Oklahoma City remember the closing words of the sermon voiced Andraé Crouch's "Through It All" lyrics, "I've learned to depend upon God's word."

5. *Displacement and distance.* Some people sitting in church do not want to be there. Not just

there in church, but there in the community, even there in the country. Nieman and Rogers enumerate some of the problems that people have with displacement in locale (homesickness), time (nostalgia), and belonging (alienation), any of which can result in severe anomie. They suggest the use of parallel images in sermons can be helpful. People struggling with displacement can identify with biblical persons who knew rejection, like Abraham and the good Samaritan, and biblical actions, like wilderness wandering and persecution (Nieman and Rogers 2001, 86–88, 104–8).

There is another concern that is almost the opposite of displacement. It is rather a disregarding of those who live at a distance. It is a very diverse world, and today's people know that better than any prior generation. Instant news and pictures from faraway places with strange-sounding names leap out of television and computer screens. Two or three generations ago, people in North America would probably have been unaware of tragedies in places like Darfur, Sumatra, and Sri Lanka. But the world is smaller and closer. People and religions and political systems and ecological dangers that were unknown or, if known, could have been ignored a generation ago can no longer be labeled out of sight, out of mind. There is more to outreach and relief now than putting a few dollars in a plate. Preachers in North America and other more fortunate areas need to remind their congregations "from everyone to whom much has been given, much will be required."

6. *An inviting presence.* The preaching event is a compound of text, Spirit, sermon, preacher, audience, occasion, and other factors. We do not have control over all or even most of these factors. But we can do this. Remember that the preacher's presence is often as important as his or her words. Greet people warmly. Speak in a caring voice, and visually include people in the sermon. As for the content of the sermon, even if the text and theme are harsh, assure people that God loves them and that God remembers, even when we forget. Be open to the experiences of others in the message, and make it available through clear thoughts and vivid images. Remind listeners that God has not left anyone ungifted, that we all have gifts we can use for God, God's people, and God's world.

In the book of Revelation we find these words: "Then I saw another angel flying in midheaven, with an eternal gospel to proclaim to those who live on the earth—to every nation and tribe and language and people" (14:6). The angel has passed that task of proclamation to us. Pray that, with God's help, we shall be equal to the task.

Bibliography: George Cladis. *Leading the Team-based Church.* (1999); Andraé Crouch. "Through It All." 1971. Nancy Eiesland. *The Disabled God: Toward a Liberatory Theology of Disability.* (1994); Lawrence A. Hoffman. "Jewish-Christian Services: Babel or Mixed Multitude?" *Cross Currents* (Spring 1990); Joseph R. Jeter Jr. and Ronald J. Allen. *One Gospel, Many Ears.* (2002); James R. Nieman and Thomas G. Rogers. *Preaching to Every Pew: Cross-Cultural Strategies.* (2001).

❖   ❖   ❖   ❖

AFRICAN AMERICAN PREACHING PERSPECTIVES
Cleophus J. LaRue

African American preaching at its best has remarkable strengths. The making of an effective black preacher does not begin with formal studies, but rather in the formative stages of the preacher's life. It is there that the black church molds and shapes a preacher's thought-world in the richness and depth of the black religious experience. Owing to this reality, black preaching is not so much taught as it is caught. It is a way of being in the world that one develops over time by immersing oneself in the culture and norms of black religious life. One does not learn how to become a black preacher, one learns how to become a preacher in the black religious experience.

1. Imitation of the Masters
2. The Hermeneutic of an All-Powerful God
3. The Importance of Wrestling with the Text
4. A Sense of Divine Encounter
5. The Significance of the Waiting Congregation
6. An Astute Awareness of the Culture
7. The Importance of a Manuscript
8. A Fitting Close
9. The Sermon as Continuous Creation
10. The Power of the Living Voice

While the following fundamental features are characteristic of black preaching, that come to fore time and time again in this style of proclamation, preachers in the black tradtions learn them largely by immersion and imitation. Nonetheless, preachers from other traditions can benefit from considering them.

1. Imitation of the Masters

While a majority of contemporary ministers learn to preach through preaching manuals and informed reflection on homiletic texts, many black preachers continue to learn to preach primarily through imitation of the masters. That is, they learn to preach by observation, participation, and an eventual mastery of the "how-tos" of preaching from accomplished artisans of the preaching craft whom they have come to admire and respect.

Learning to preach through imitation of the masters does not imply a mere copying of the style of others. It does suggest learning by means of closely observing and subsequently mastering the dynamics that come together to make black preaching a powerful communicative tool in the hands of a master craftsperson. This preaching pedagogy is deeply embedded in the black religious psyche. In fact, it is so deeply woven into the fabric of black religious life that it becomes a part of the black sacred story—those stories that lie so deeply within human consciousness that one is not always aware of just how forceful they are in shaping belief and behavior.

2. The Hermeneutic of an All-Powerful God

Effective black preaching concerns itself with the extraordinary experiences of a people and their God. It concerns itself with a people's unique way of understanding the Bible and applying those insights in very practical ways. When one considers the historical conditions under which blacks embraced Christianity it is easy to see how their sociocultural experiences would have a profound effect on their understanding of who God is and how God works out God's meaning and purpose in their lives. A central truth blacks quickly came to embrace when they were allowed to read and interpret scripture for themselves is that scripture revealed a God of infinite power who could be trusted to act on their behalf. This direct relationship between black struggle and divine rescue colors the theological perceptions and themes of black preaching in a very decisive manner.

A God who is unquestionably for them is what blacks see when they go to the scriptures. Thus a distinctive characteristic of black preaching is that which blacks believe scripture reveals about the sovereign God's involvement in the everyday affairs and circumstances of their existence. African Americans believe the sovereign God acts in very concrete and practical ways in matters pertaining to their survival, deliverance, advancement, prosperity, and overall well-being. This is the lens through which they interpret the scriptures in preparation for preaching.

The preacher who would preach with a certain sense of authority and accomplishment in the traditional black church must always remember that at its heart the black sermon is about God—God's purposive acts in and for the world. The most effective preaching is preaching that conveys with clarity and insight how God acts in concrete situations in the lives of those who hear the gospel. This is not to suggest that every sermon ought to have the word "God" in it, but each sermon should concern itself with God's essence and actions—God's divine initiative and revelatory activity, especially as that activity is manifested through the work and person of Jesus Christ, biblically witnessed and historically confessed. This all-encompassing hermeneutic is at the core of traditional black preaching.

3. The Importance of Wrestling with the Text

There is in black preaching a high regard for scripture. Black preaching has historically been noted for its strong biblical content. In many black churches, biblical preaching, defined as preaching that allows a text from the Bible to serve as the leading force in shaping the content and purpose of the sermon, is the type of preaching considered to be most faithful to traditional understandings of the proclaimed word. Indeed, it is no secret that the Bible occupies a central place in the religious life of black Americans. More than a mere source for texts, in black preaching, the Bible is the single most important source of language, imagery, and story for the sermon. Though biblical literacy in black churches is greatly diminished from earlier years, it has yet to reach the state where the Bible's primacy as a rich resource for black preaching is no longer the case.

Thus, black preaching is inextricably tied to Scripture. In the eyes of the black church a preacher without Scripture is like a doctor without a black bag. Which is to say, what one needs to get the preaching job done comes with some kind of encounter with Scripture. Any preacher who seeks to be heard on a regular basis in a black church must learn some method of engaging the scriptural text and drawing from that encounter some sense of the Word of God revealed *to* and acting *upon* the present day human situation of the black listeners. Effective preachers recognize that this daunting task of creatively engaging the scriptures and pairing them with black lived experience is at the center of their weekly preparation. Therefore the preacher must be familiar with the Bible. The in-depth knowledge of Scripture required of the preacher cannot simply be a task-oriented familiarity with Scripture, for the Bible does not fully yield its treasures as the Word of God to those who visit it from time to time when fishing for a sermon. One has to live with the Scriptures and walk up and down the streets of the texts in order to have those texts speak forth with power and conviction. Black preachers learn early on to seek this kind of engagement with the text.

4. A Sense of Divine Encounter

Blacks believe they are encountered by God throughout the sermon preparation process and most especially during the initial stages of sermon preparation. This encounter manifests itself in various ways. For some it involves a sitting silent before God, while for others it is a "tarrying" for the Spirit. Something comes from without and buoys the spirit and sparks the creativity of the preacher as he or she embarks upon the sermon creation process. Many attribute this creative spark to something beyond their own subconscious mindset. They refuse to advance the preparation process until they have some sense that a power from beyond them is at work in and through them. Without this in-breaking activity many feel that the sermon will focus too much on process and not enough on purpose.

5. The Significance of the Waiting Congregation

The people for whom the sermon is being prepared are never far from the thoughts of the preachers at the time of preparation. In fact, many blacks speak of their need to maintain a constant focus on those who will hear the message. In a strange way, the preachers seem to anticipate the anticipation of the waiting congregation. Thus, every effort is made to say *for* them and *to* them what they (the congregation) would say if they had the chance. Participatory proclamation not only impacts the rhythm and cadence of their delivery, it also affects the interaction of Scripture and context. Effective preaching can only happen when pulpit and pew are united in conversation with one another. Owing to the prominence of participatory proclamation blacks learn early on the importance of the symbiotic relationship between the pulpit and the pew. Preaching is always done in community—even when the community is not physically present at the time of preparation.

6. An Astute Awareness of the Culture

There was a time in black religious life when some people believed that the truly "spiritual" preachers shut themselves away from the world and descended from the mountaintop of their studies on Sunday morning to deliver a word from on high. Today's preachers warn against such aloofness and detachment from the world. They recognize the need to be in tune and in touch with the world around them. They sharpen their powers of observation by constantly seeking to name God's presence in every aspect of human existence. There is no distinction between the sacred and the secular in black religious life. The most effective preachers are mindful of the happenings in their social, political, educational, and economic surroundings. Many argue, in fact, that such an awareness actually strengthens one's preaching. The best of black preaching seriously engages the whole of God's created order in its beauty and splendor, its disorder and unruliness. There are no areas of human existence where black preaching fears to tread. To this end, black preaching to the uninitiated ear can strike some as harsh, intrusive, and at times offensive. Yet, it is this kind of preaching, that takes every aspect of life seriously, that has the greatest appeal among a large number of the black church-going public.

7. The Importance of a Manuscript

While many black preachers do not carry a manuscript into the pulpit, most will tell you that to preach without a manuscript does not mean one is preaching unprepared. In times past it was believed that a manuscript preacher was an intellectual preacher, and conversely, a preacher without a manuscript was a spiritual preacher. Such distinctions are quickly fading. While preaching without a manuscript gives the impression of immediacy, spontaneity, and anointing by the Holy Sprit, it is becoming more acceptable in black preaching to prepare a manuscript even if one does not intend to preach from it in the pulpit.

Writing the sermon out helps to bring focus and clarity to the sermon, prevents one from rambling, and firms up language written for the ear. A tightly worded manuscript, where each phrase has been carefully considered, helps the preacher to paint the mental picture more effectively. Moreover, a manuscript allows the preacher to get comfortable with the flow and contours of the sermon and thus serves to strengthen the rhythm and cadence of the oral delivery. To have the language of the sermon set down in writing and subsequently clearly set down in one's mind sharpens the oratorical thrust and limits unintended pauses and dead air in the preaching event.

Those who do choose to use a manuscript in the pulpit do so with great effect because the oral nature of the event is never far from their minds even when reading from a prepared text. In black preaching the style of delivery determines, in large part, the success of the oral performer. Blacks learn early on to steer clear of lackadaisical deliveries. Verbal essays that sound like a lecture in the pulpit are a no-no in many black churches. The oral delivery must be dynamic and invigorating. Spontaneity that allows for improvisation and digression even when using a manuscript is not only acceptable, in black preaching it's expected.

8. A Fitting Close

One must learn the importance of closing the sermon in a proper manner. For some the sermon should always end in a joyful celebration, while for others the most important thing is that the sermon end in a manner that is logically consistent with the controlling thought. On some occasions the close should cause one to reflect on faith and life. At other times it should move one to repent and to think more deeply on the mercies of God. At other times the close should call us to some specific action in the larger world in service to others. Sometimes the close should simply issue forth in ceaseless praise to the wonders of a God who is for us. The closing of the sermon should not be a disjointed distraction or some tacked-on ornamental rhetorical flourish intended to whip the congregation into a fevered pitch. Rather it should send the listeners away with a clear sense of what the preacher was attempting to convey throughout the entire message.

9. The Sermon as Continuous Creation

In black preaching circles, sermons are never fully completed. There is always more that could be said and will be said, since blacks have no qualms about preaching the same sermon again. The sermon is never a finished product. After the sermon had been prepared and readied for Sunday service, different ideas and new ways of thinking about it continue to come. Even while preaching the sermons, new thoughts and ideas come pouring out and thus become unexpected additions to the sermon. Many edit their sermons soon after they have been preached in order to take advantage of fresh insights that come to them during its delivery or immediately thereafter. For some, the unplanned additions turned out to be some of the more creative parts of the sermon.

10. The Power of the Living Voice

In black preaching the sermon from beginning to end is viewed as an oral/aural exercise. It is to be spoken and heard. The sermon manuscript is never regarded as an end in itself. What is written is but an "arrested performance" lying dormant on the page that can only be brought to life through the skillful articulation and mastery of the preacher's viva vox (living voice).

People who come from cultures with a high oral residue consider the spoken word to have great power. All oral utterance that comes from inside living organisms is "dynamic." Many black preachers rely on the power of the living voice to bring to full expression what they hope to accomplish in the preaching event. Blacks know intuitively that there has to be a certain energy and conviction to the spoken word when proclaiming the gospel. Ultimately, their ability to evoke, empower, challenge, and change comes not through that which they have written, but through the spoken word–articulated sound. An awareness of the oral nature of the finished product is a key component in the composition of the sermon. The performative component in black preaching is seldom frowned upon by other blacks because of the importance they attach to articulated sound.

While one could argue that these basics are unique to black preaching, they could also be argued to offer valuable perspectives from which preachers in other traditions might view their own preaching. See CALL AND RESPONSE; MANUSCRIPT; ORAL/AURAL COMMUNICATION; SUSPICION.

Bibliography: Gerald L. Davis. *I Got the Word in Me and I Can Sing, You Know: A Study of the Performed African American Sermon.* (1985); Cleophus J. LaRue. *The Heart of Black Preaching.* (1999); Cleophus J. LaRue. *Power in the Pulpit: How America's Most Effective Black Preachers Prepare Their Sermons.* (2002); Paul Oliver. *Songsters and Saints: Vocal Traditions on Race Records.* (1984); Albert J. Raboteau. *Slave Religion: The "Invisible Institution" in the Antebellum South.* (1978); Bruce A. Rosenberg. *Can These Bones Live? The Art of the African American Folk Preacher* (1970)

CALL AND RESPONSE
Robert Smith Jr.

The term *call and response* refers to a pattern of verbal interplay between preacher and congregation that occurs during the sermon and shapes its delivery. This dynamic is strange to some religious traditions and unfamiliar to others. However, in the African American religious tradition, the strange is familiar. German theologian-preacher Helmut Thielicke recalled preaching to a black congregation in Chicago. He remarked: "The congregation responded enthusiastically, kept on interrupting me with loud cries as 'Yes Lord!', 'Hallelujah', 'Amen!' and many other acclamations. That stimulated me so much that I was carried away as if on a crest of a wave" (Thielicke 1995, 360). This dialogical interaction between the preacher and the congregation, though characteristic of this tradition, is not unique to the African American religious experience. Like the African American preacher, the Welsh folk preacher was not a helpless soloist or a liturgical dictator but affirmed and authenticated the hearers as valued partners in the preaching process by dialogically participating with the elders in the "amen corner." If there is one thing preachers who practice call and response have in common, it is this intentionality about providing "sacred space" for the congregation to respond with "sacred sound." (*See* COLLABORATION.)

The roots of call and response are deeply planted in the soil of West African music. The practice was transplanted to the plantations of North America in the American slavery experience. Encountering European church music, the slaves recycled handed-down hymns through a technique called lining out. The slave preacher would sing the first line of the hymn, and the black worshipers would sing it back. This technique provided the basic structure for a kind of responsive improvisation that found its ultimate expression in the preaching event.

Call and response was born of the reaction of slaves to the worship experience of the white church—a church whose preachers engaged the worshipers from the neck up without encountering them from the neck down. By contrast, African American preachers created an opportunity for worshipers to participate in the sermon's emotions—to have a "feel back" experience as a prelude to a "talk back" expression. Such appreciation for the importance of pathos is long-standing in Christian preaching. Even Augustine admitted, "I did not consider I had achieved anything when I heard them applauding me, but only when I saw them weeping. Their applause only showed they were being instructed and delighted, while their tears indicated that they were being swayed" (Augustine 1996, 234). Though the call and response dynamic may be influenced by variations in style and delivery—conversational, lecture, intonation, or the whoop—when it is combined with scriptural substance, it is a powerful tool for engaging the congregation's minds, hearts, and voices in the preaching event. See AFRICAN AMERICAN PREACHING PERSPECTIVES; CELEBRATION; ORAL/AURAL COMMUNICATION.

Bibliography: Augustine. *Teaching Christianity.* Edited by Edmund Hill and John E. Rotelle. (1996); Helmut Thielicke. *Notes from a Wayfarer.* Translated by David R. Law. (1995).

CELEBRATION
Henry H. Mitchell

The best way for preachers to be used of the Holy Spirit, to motivate hearers to grow in grace and do the will of God, is to help them celebrate—to rejoice and be glad about the Word with which they have been led to identify. People remember better and are far more likely to be changed by ser-mons that rise to moving celebration. This is not to be confused with the kind of sermons that arise out of deep, negative feelings. "Fiery mad" is quite the opposite of "fiery glad." The gospel is good news. Although Western culture is suspicious of deep emotion, there are lofty as well as lower emo-tions. Faith, hope, and love are lofty emotions. And preaching devoid of such emotion is lifeless.

There are many examples of the abuse of emo-tions in the pulpit and on the television screen, giv-ing rise to the need for guidelines not only for effective design but also for homiletical integrity:

1. The sermon is designed to bring alive a posi-tive biblical text. While it may be necessary to elaborate on sins of which hearers are inad-equately aware, the major emphasis is on what the will of God is for, not against. One cannot celebrate what is wrong, no matter how fine the rhetoric. We almost always end in the abundant life in Christ, which is counted as and celebrated with all joy.

2. While Paul urges admonition, this is for the main body of the sermon. Celebration is not to be confused with the most beautifully stated challenges, with rare exceptions.

3. Preaching is most effective when contagiously communicated from the very depths of one's own life in Christ. Trust is an emotion more caught than formally taught.

4. As in drama or symphony, preaching orches-trates intensity of feeling. Sermons build to cli-mactic utterance and then subside; sermons are art, not argument. The climactic utterance is celebration.

5. The celebration is the most difficult part of the sermon to design. Once text, behavioral pur-pose, and genre are chosen, it is often wise to design this text's matching celebration. The rest of the sermon builds to this peak.

6. The materials of celebration are many. Biblical narratives, for example, Joseph's declaration in Gen 50:20, provide material for celebration of the providence of God: "You meant evil against me; but God meant it for good" (RSV). Personal testimonies (TESTIMONIAL) of oth-ers are effective, and our own are also, when not too frequent. Great literature offers imagery, stories, words, and phrases. Height-ened rhetoric and poetic language are a good

fit for celebration. Just think of Paul's rhetor-ical tours de force such as, "Who shall sepa-rate us . . . ?" in Rom 8:35 (RSV). Finally, there is poetry from hymns.

7. Celebration occurs only once.

The challenge of these disciplines is worth the effort; it provides the celebration of the text with ecstatic reinforcement.

Bibliography: Henry H. Mitchell. *Celebration and Experience in Preaching.* (1990); Frank A. Thomas. *They Like to Never Quit Praisin' God.* (1997).

EMERGING CHURCH PREACHING
Thomas G. Rogers

The *emerging church* is a collective term for the individuals who see themselves as emerging from a process of deconstruction and reconstruction of Chris-tianity; it also describes Christians who have joined groups being led by such individuals. This movement began sweeping across North America, Western Europe, and the South Pacific in the last decade of the 20th cent. No single organization coordinates the emerging church globally, and there is no assur-ance that the phenomenon will ever be organized for-mally. Nonetheless, participants in this movement (or conversation, as some prefer to call it) are convinced that significant cultural changes, influenced in part by postmodernism and Web-oriented thinking, indicate that a new church is emerging.

While the participants in the movement are quite diverse and the lines marking inclusion are fuzzy at best, emerging church proponents are generally characterized by objecting to what they see as an outdated epistemology of modernism. They view the modern period as a time when it was believed that one could know things certainly and absolutely. Truth was achieved through rationalistic, linear thinking. For the church, this led to an emphasis on propositional truths in relation to faith. Advocates of the emerging church argue that postmodernism's challenge to modernism needs to be reflected in the church. Much of what we can know is not absolute; rather, it is shaped by our culture, emo-tions, and experience. A church in synchronization with the values of postmodern generations should focus on relationships, tolerance in the midst of plu-ralism, integrity in discussions, and stories—the telling of one's own stories to others in the community and the telling of biblical stories in Bible study and preaching. While some argue that this is an oversimplification or misreading of modernism and postmodernism, nonetheless, this assertion that the church must emerge beyond modernistic tendencies unites participants in the emerging church.

Another aspect of the emerging church is its reaction to the seeker-sensitive, mega-church movement that flourished in the 1990s. Some argue that the emerging church is a continuation of the Saddleback/Willow Creek movement, serving as a guide for church leaders in how to go after the post-seeker-sensitive generation. However, some who claim the emerging church label see themselves very differently. While the seeker-friendly approach offers a "come to church" type of evangelism, the dominating slogan in the emerging church is "come to Jesus." Both approaches include a desire to shape the church experience to meet the actual needs of the unchurched, though in different ways. While the seeker-sensitive movement attempts to deliver a polished product to a typically baby boomer target demographic, the emerging church movement focuses more on authentic personal interactions and ongoing reanalysis of the Bible against a variety of contexts.

Leaders in the emerging church movement claim that its role is to continue the mission of Christ. While there is acceptance of a wide range of expressions of what that mission includes, there is common agreement that the Scriptures, with their timeless truths, are to be the center of that mission. Some are eager to compare the emerging church movement to the Reformation, another movement that claimed it wanted to reform the church. The 16th-cent. Reformers wanted to make changes in the church, not because they wanted the church to adapt its approach to evolving cultural changes, but because they perceived that a theology and related practices in the church had developed that contravened Scripture and needed to be reformed by the Word of God. The reform called forth by the emerging church is quite different in that, for the most part, it maintains that it is preserving traditional confessionalism but changing the ways in which the faith is understood and applied because the culture has drastically changed.

The emerging church is also related to the house church movement in that both are challenging traditional notions of how the church should be organized. Each embraces a minimalist and decentralized organizational structure. Not all house churches are as influenced by postmodern philosophy as the emerging church, but many emerging churches are also house churches.

Preaching in the emerging church is centered in storytelling. At first glance one might expect a close connection to the narrative movement that was foundational to the new homiletic in the last quarter of the 20th cent.; however, the emphasis here is not so much on using narrative theory in constructing the design of a sermon, but on connecting hearers with the biblical stories themselves. Emerging church preachers do not assume that their hearers know the stories of Scripture, so they tell the story of God's interaction with humans again and again. There is frequently a great deal of scriptural exposition in a given sermon, but the end of such preaching is to shape a theological worldview for people. The overarching goal is for post-Christian listeners to be able to see the world through a theological, big-picture, scriptural story lens.

The focus of much emerging church preaching is theocentric rather than anthropocentric. To a certain extent, this is another departure from the seeker-sensitive movement, which often offers topical, felt-need messages from the pulpit. While emerging church preachers give attention to kingdom living as a disciple of Jesus, their preaching is rooted in showing how the ancient wisdom of Scripture applies to kingdom living; toward that end, the preacher lifts up the role of God. Teaching concerning the triune God is not avoided, and the central message is rooted in what it means that Jesus is the way to God.

Emerging church preachers critique modern church preaching in which the sermon is sometimes seen as the focal point of the service and the preacher serves as the dispenser of biblical truths to help solve personal problems in modern life. They claim that the sermons of modernism emphasize explanation—*what* the truth is. In the emerging church movement, the preacher seeks to emphasize and explain the experience of *who* the truth is. The sermon is seen as only one part of the experience of the worship gathering. The scriptural message also is communicated through visual arts, silence, and testimonies. Emerging church proclamation seeks to emulate the multifaceted approach to experiencing information common among people raised in a Web-oriented world. *See*

CULTURAL HERMENEUTICS.; SEEKER MESSAGES; WORSHIP STYLE.

Bibliography: Eddie Gibbs and Ryan K. Bolger. *Emerging Churches: Creating Christian Community in Postmodern Cultures.* (2005); Dan Kimball. *The Emerging Church: Vintage Christianity for New Generations.* (2003); Doug Pagitt, *Preaching Re-Imagined.* (2005).

EVANGELISTIC PREACHING
Al Fasol

Evangelistic preaching is a biblically based approach to sharing the good news of the saving grace that God offers through Jesus Christ.

Evangelistic preaching seeks to convince non-Christians to accept Jesus the Christ as their Lord and Savior. The word *evangelistic,* etymologically, means "good news." Evangelistic preaching is the proclamation of the good news that Jesus has provided the way for us to be reconciled to God. The suppositions behind this definition are that Jesus was conceived by the Holy Spirit and birthed by the Virgin Mary (Matt 1:8-25); lived a sinless life (Heb 4:15); was crucified and resurrected (John 19–20); and ascended to heaven with the promise that he will return (Acts 1:9). Jesus' victory over sin and death qualifies him alone to say, "I am the way, and the truth, and the life. No one comes to the Father except through me" (John 14:6).

Evangelistic preaching is *relevant* because "all have sinned and fallen short of the glory of God" (Rom 3:23). The result of sin, which is a rebellion against God, is death, but God has given us the gift of eternal life by accepting God's Son, Jesus, as our Savior (see Rom 6:12-23). A keen awareness of sin and a strong pointing to Jesus as the one who rescues us from our sins are integral to evangelistic preaching.

Evangelistic preaching is *urgent* (see 2 Cor 6:2). This urgency calls for a positive response now rather than later. An immediate response is called for because God may withdraw divine promptings (Gen 6:3a); death is certain (Heb 9:27); and it is an awesome thing to fall into the hands of the living God (Heb 10:31). For these reasons, most evangelistic sermons allow for a time of response by non-believers. Often, this response is called for immediately.

Evangelistic preaching is not limited to a set form. In the Bible, evangelistic preaching was parabolic (Luke 15:11-24), didactic (Rom 10:8-13), testimonial (Acts 6:9–7:60; 26:1-29), in major discourse (Acts 2:1-40), and in a one-on-one setting (Acts 8:26-39). At various times, evangelistic preachers have employed visual aids, dramatic skits, and music within the sermon.

Evangelistic preaching is usually done in corporate worship services in church buildings; in radio or television studios; in temporary locations, such as stadiums, arenas, or tents; and even on street corners. The desire of the evangelistic preacher is to proclaim the message of God's saving grace to as many persons as possible.

Evangelistic Preaching and Biblical Authority

Direct Biblical Authority

Direct biblical authority simply means *what the text teaches, the sermon preaches.* Therefore, the selection of a biblical text for the evangelistic sermon is important. Luke 15, for example, speaks to those who are not followers of Jesus. This passage condemns self-righteousness and portrays God as a father longing for his rebellious (sinful) children to repent and be received. Other passages, such as John 3 (especially vv. 7, 16-17), emphasize that newness of life comes through Jesus. These two passages of Scripture and several others may be preached evangelistically with direct biblical authority.

Secondary Biblical Authority

Occasionally, a preacher may preach with secondary biblical authority. Ephesians 2:8-10 was written to believers and reminds and affirms how our salvation experience not only begins our new life in Christ but also gives direction as we strive to live for him. A direct biblical sermon would be preached in that way. However, an evangelistic sermon could be adapted from that text. The evangelistic sermon would not remind and affirm the saving grace of God, but would proclaim how God's grace can be accepted by the non-believer. Preachers must be cautious in making such adaptations. It is not a good homiletical (or hermeneutical) practice to manipulate a text to serve an evangelistic purpose. For example, a preacher should not say, " 'Blessed are the poor in spirit, for theirs is the kingdom of heaven' [Matt 5:3]. However, you cannot be blessed until you first accept Jesus as your Lord and Savior." This practice amounts to announcing a text, reading that text, and then abandoning that text in order to preach from a prior agenda.

Evangelistic Preaching and Effective Communication

Source Credibility

An elementary rule of communications demands that the source (for our purposes, the source is the evangelistic preacher) must be believable. This credibility is established in three ways:

1. The integrity of the evangelistic preacher is paramount. The greed and adultery of a few so-called evangelistic preachers have made it difficult but not impossible to establish credibility among non-believers. The evangelistic preacher must live in such a way that non-believers will say, "I believe in this preacher and am willing to hear what this preacher has to say."
2. Expertise is important. Listeners also need the confidence of knowing that the message the evangelistic preacher proclaims is trustworthy and accurate. Whether the evangelistic preacher is explaining a biblical text, applying that text, or employing an illustration about that text, the listener should be able to say, "I trust this person to tell me exactly what I need to know."
3. A dynamic speaker communicates a sense of excitement, urgency, passion, and energy. Dynamism convinces the listener that the preacher deeply believes in and is strongly committed to what is being proclaimed. Both extremely high dynamism and extremely low dynamism should be avoided. The highly dynamic speaker will draw more attention to the messenger than to the message. The low dynamism speaker will unwittingly communicate that the message is not urgent or vital. Evangelistic preachers should speak within the context of their personalities and gifts, but all preachers should communicate a sense of vitality and urgency no matter what their style of preaching may be.

Knowing the Listeners

Evangelistic preachers should know as much as possible about their listeners. Some information, such as demographics, can be quickly assessed but varies from one church or community to another. Other information, however, is constant. Listeners receive messages in three ways, and for most listeners, one way is dominant. Therefore, each of the ways of receiving messages is important, and a preacher must use each during the course of an evangelistic sermon.

- *The Information, Please Listener*

Some listeners respond when they are receiving information. In the evangelistic sermon, the information offered is usually an explanation of the biblical text for that sermon. This is where feeding from the Word occurs. The evangelistic preacher will carefully exegete the text, select the most pertinent information, and then share that information in an appealing manner.

- *The What Does It Mean to Me Listener*

Some listeners respond best to the application of the message. These listeners are classic examples of the *What? So what? Now what?* style of thinking. When they hear the subject, or *what*, the preacher is proclaiming, they want to know, "So *what* does that mean to me?" When that question is answered, their next question is, "*Now what* do I do?" The use of second person pronoun works best for these listeners.

- *The Now I See What You Mean Listener*

Most listeners appreciate illustrations. Some people need illustrations to comprehend the message. The evangelistic preacher may well proclaim a logically developed and clearly applied message only to have these listeners say, "I just do not see what you are saying!" These listeners need illustrations. *To illustrate* means "to cast light upon." Illustrative material may consist of a figure of speech or an anecdote. Communication studies frequently conclude that a message with an analogy is always more persuasive than the same message without an analogy. That is why illustrative material is necessary in evangelistic preaching.

Preaching with Impact

Communications experts have found that a strong mental and emotional impact has a direct bearing on how the listener will respond to the message. Consequently, communications experts have developed a negative corollary. Their formula is predictability and distance kill impact.

Predictability may occur in the content of the message; that is, the listener knows or predicts what the speaker will say before the words are said. Predictability may also occur in the delivery of the sermon, especially if the preacher speaks in a set pitch or volume pattern.

Distance has to do with what are called the frames of reference of the listeners. Distance occurs when a preacher departs from the listeners' frames of reference. Jesus always stayed within the frames of reference or the areas of experience of his listeners, as, for example, when he said, "A sower went out to sow" (Mark 4:3), or "There was a man who had two sons" (Luke 15:11). Each of his listeners could readily relate to those words, which were within their frames of reference. There was no distance between the message and the listeners.

Put in positive terms, impact is equal to vital content supported by effective delivery. For the evangelistic sermon, vital content means that the sermon is biblically based and clearly relates to the listeners' needs. Effective delivery means that the preacher speaks in a way that focuses the listener on the message being proclaimed rather than on the messenger doing the proclaiming.

Evangelistic preaching proclaims the good news that "in Christ God was reconciling the world to himself" (2 Cor 5:19). *See* DOCTRINAL; EXEGETICAL; EXPOSITION; THE FOUR PAGES OF THE SERMON; SEEKER MESSAGES; TEACHING.

Bibliography: William J. Abraham. *The Logic of Evangelism.* (1989); Craig A. Loscalzo. *Evangelistic Preaching That Connects: Guidance in Shaping Fresh and Appealing Sermons.* (1995); William H. Willimon and Stanley Hauerwas. *Preaching to Strangers: Evangelism in Today's World.* (1992).

FEMINIST PERSPECTIVES
Christine M. Smith

Feminism is a movement that seeks the equal rights of women, the just treatment of women, and the full inclusion of women in every aspect of human life. This movement offers both serious challenges and life-giving perspectives to preachers in religious communities.

Convictions and Diverse Perspectives

Feminist perspectives on theology, the Bible, the church, and the larger world are as varied and distinct as the women and men who articulate and believe them. Yet within a world of complex and varied feminist perspectives, two fundamental convictions inform most feminist perspectives. One foundational conviction at the heart of feminist perspectives is that in both church and society, women have been and continue to be oppressed by systems of male power and privilege. A historical or modern-day look at economic gender disparity, statistics surrounding violence against women the world over, and the underrepresentation of women in local, national, and worldwide governing bodies and ecclesiastical structures conveys this truth with complete transparency. A second equally important conviction at the heart of feminist thought and action in the church and in the world is the belief that for women to have true equality with men, their distinct voices, their critique of sexism, their lived experience, and their constructive thought must be lifted to a place of equal importance with the thought, experiences, and worldviews of men. Women not only need equal rights, but they also need their lives to be treated as valuable and sacred. How women and male allies have responded to the many layers of systemic gender oppression with critical thought and with constructive action constitutes the feminist movement worldwide.

While there are points of commonality within feminist perspectives, there are also significant differences. These differences reflect the depth of critique one has of sexism and what one believes is of ultimate importance in creating gender justice as a reality. Some feminists believe that securing basic equal rights for women is ultimately at stake. If women had the same human rights as men, we would experience a transformed world. Other feminists believe that the very lives of women—their work, their embodied female experience, their relationships, their worldviews, and their religious and spiritual beliefs and practices—must come to be equally valued and equally represented in church and society. If the real lives of women were honored, valued, and represented as fully as men's lives, we would experience a transformed world. Some feminists insist that the entire systemic structures of human life the world over reflect not only sexism but also racism, classism, ableism, ageism, heterosexism, and militarism. (*See* GENDER, RACE, AND ETHNICITY.) For these feminists, only when all of these systems of oppression are dismantled will we experience a transformed world. This is a vision of profound solidarity in which women understand the fundamental ways that their oppression is linked with the oppression of all other people and creatures of the earth, and a vision that honors the truth that not all women are oppressed in the same way or to the same degree.

Feminist Preaching

Feminist women and their male allies in the Christian church would place themselves within all of these different perspectives. Preachers with a feminist consciousness would certainly lift up the essential task in church and society of granting women their equal and just rights. This might include breaking the silence that still surrounds violence against women and female children in our homes and neighborhoods. Preachers might educate congregations about labor and economic realities that still reveal the exploitation of women's work in the world. Many preachers with a feminist consciousness would also lift up the distinctive female experience of women, and the invisible or marginalized religious and theological voices and witness of women throughout the Christian tradition and in the Bible. These preachers might speak about some of the women in the Bible who are invisible or not well known in most of our congregations. Some of these women might include Jephthah's daughter in Judg 11, the Canaanite woman in Matt 15, the women ministers working with Paul whose names appear in Rom 16, or the life-saving midwives (Shiphrah and Puah) in Exod 1. Preachers recovering women's distinctive perspective in regard to the Christian tradition might lift up the voices of early women preachers, women mystics throughout the ages, and women who have offered a critique of traditional male theology. Other preachers would attempt to help congregations understand the enduring and interdependent links between sexism and all other forms of human and earth oppression. For instance, it is past time for most European American congregations to understand the intersection of race and class and gender in the Hagar, Sarah, and Abraham story in Genesis. Christian churches of privilege might attend to the overarching stories of conquest and imperialism that are embedded in the Exodus liberation story of the Israelites.

Preachers who understand feminism in a systemic way might help congregations understand concrete connections across all forms of oppression.

Each of these perspectives carries with it practical challenges. It is essential that our churches never forget the equal human rights for which women struggle in countless places in the world where these rights are still denied and unrealized. The voices and experiences of women in the Christian tradition, within the Bible, and throughout our contemporary world are still marginalized and disregarded. The radical voices of feminist women, who will not let the church and world forget that all forms of oppression are utterly connected, will keep inviting us to see feminism as a movement for radical social change.

If one focuses on Christianity in particular as a distinct arena of feminist work, then some remaining reflections about that work are crucial. Out of the many challenging tasks that face a preacher who would preach from a feminist perspective, there seem to be three primary tasks that make Christian feminist work so important and so necessary. These tasks are the task of re-membering/remembering, the task of theological deconstruction, and the task of visionary reconstruction.

Re-membering/Remembering

For years now when feminist women and our male allies have gathered for conferences, classes, and special events that have an explicit feminist, African American, womanist, Latina, and/or Hispanic *mujerista* agenda, acts of re-membering/remembering have been central to those gatherings. Because women's voices and experiences have not been at the center of the rehearsal of the Christian tradition, nor have they held a primary place in traditional biblical interpretation and powerful ecclesiastical structures, it is important to speak women's names aloud and remember the body of humanity with women's historical and contemporary lives. Naming women's names, remembering their stories, and honoring their human agency are all a fundamental part of the religious tasks that any feminist preacher will embrace.

Deconstruction

For several decades now feminist women have been involved in the work of deconstruction in relation to the Christian tradition and its theology.

(*See* DECONSTRUCTION.) This is the work of the feminist preacher as well. One must be willing to probe every theological category in Christian theology in an effort to see how it perpetuates the oppression of women, the oppression of other marginalized people, and the oppression of the earth and its creatures. Feminist christological work is a prime example of this work. Christian feminists have waged a thorough critique of traditional atonement theology. They have identified its contribution to the justification of human suffering, to violence against women and all creation, and to an individualistic religious worldview that leaves social systemic injustice virtually intact. Feminist theologians have been asking, "How can sin be pride, arrogance, and rebellion when women continue to be socialized into states of weak ego strength, roles of passivity, and ways of being in the world that conform to male expectations and domination?" Feminist preachers will need to have the courage to deconstruct every aspect of Christian theology that undergirds oppression and injustice.

Visionary Reconstruction

And finally, any preacher who preaches from a feminist perspective cannot escape the task of visionary reconstruction. Feminists have been creating new theological concepts, new ways of interpreting the Bible, and new ways of bringing analyses to our contemporary world of thought and theology. There have been new Christ images created that are non-hierarchical and communal; new images of resurrection articulated that honor women's struggle against the forces of sexist, racist, classist death that surround them; new images of "woman church"; and new images of redemption and salvation. These theological constructions are always about justice and change; they are about a new world, not the repairing of an old world.

Equal rights for women in church and society are essential. Honoring women's voices and lived experiences in the church and society is crucial. Yet if feminism is only about women, as essential as that is, and not about understanding and resisting all other forms of human and earth oppression, it will be reduced to a partial movement that will not lead us into the kind of world transformation that most of creation needs. See CULTURAL HERMENEUTICS; FEMINIST CRITICISM; WOMANIST CRITICISM; WOMEN.

Bibliography: Teresa L. Fry Brown. *Weary Throats and New Songs: Black Women Proclaiming God's Word.* (2003); Anna Florence Carter. *Preaching as Testimony.* (2007); Christine M. Smith. *Weaving the Sermon: Preaching in a Feminist Perspective.* (1989); Christine M. Smith. *Preaching as Weeping, Confession, and Resistance: Radical Responses to Radical Evil.* (1992); Mary Donovan Turner and Mary Lin Hudson. *Saved from Silence: Finding Women's Voice in Preaching.* (1999).

HOLY DAYS AND HOLIDAYS
Linda Lee Clader

Holy days are high points in the Christian Year, usually focused on major theological themes and significant figures and chapters in the history of the church. Christian communities also celebrate a variety of holidays marking national, civic, or cultural events or concerns, as well as secularized versions of some of the holy days of the church. All these events are important because the way a community marks time shapes its identity. Preaching on these occasions, therefore, presents special challenges to preachers to find ways to build bridges between the tradition and contemporary needs, between Scripture and community concerns.

The most ancient holy days of the Christian calendar are those relating to Christ's resurrection. The earliest Christians identified "the first day of the week"—the day that Gentiles named for the sun and Jews designated as the day of the creation—to be the proper day for a weekly commemoration of Christ's resurrection. The oldest annual holy day, attested from the 2nd cent. onward, is Easter itself, originally a celebration of both Jesus' death and resurrection. This event was eventually elaborated to become one liturgy celebrated over three separate days (the *Triduum*) commemorating specific parts of the paschal story: Maundy Thursday (also known as Holy Thursday), remembering the Last Supper; Good Friday, remembering Christ's passion; and Holy Saturday—Easter Eve or the Vigil of Easter—consisting originally of a fast, a vigil of twelve readings from the OT, and the first eucharist of Easter. Different religious traditions have celebrated these days with particular rites, such as the veneration of the cross on Good Friday, or the consecration of sacred oils on Maundy Thursday. From Easter, the designation of particular times of the year was elaborated backward into Lent's forty days of penitent preparation and forward into the celebratory great fifty days of Easter. Today Christ's ascension is commemorated on the fortieth day following Easter, and Pentecost, the celebration of the gift of the Holy Spirit, on the fiftieth. The Eastern church keeps the Sunday after Pentecost as the Feast of All Saints, while many traditions in the Western church celebrate the Feast of the Holy and Undivided Trinity.

Similarly, the earliest celebration of Christ's nativity was the Feast of the Epiphany, which, along with Christmas on December 25, was probably a Christianization of pagan festivals surrounding the winter solstice. Traditions around Epiphany evolved differently in the Eastern and Western churches, with the Eastern church emphasizing the commemoration of Christ's baptism, and the Western church recalling the adoration of the magi. The Western church elaborated the celebration with a time of preparation that came to be known as Advent, and the Eastern church prepared for Christmas with a month-long period of fasting.

Other holy days historically evolved to commemorate particular points in the NT (e.g., the Feasts of the Holy Innocents, Holy Name or Circumcision, the Presentation, the Visitation, the Transfiguration), great saints or prominent figures in the history of the church (e.g., Mary the Virgin, Mary Magdalene, St. Joseph, James of Jerusalem, John the Baptist, Michael and All Angels, apostles and evangelists, and in some traditions other saints), and major theological themes or events (All Saints, Holy Cross, the Immaculate Conception, the Holy and Undivided Trinity, the Assumption of the Virgin). In addition, today many churches consider some national holidays as holy days (e.g., Independence Day in the U.S.; Canada's Victoria Day; Veterans, Memorial, or Remembrance Day; Thanksgiving; birthday of Martin Luther King Jr.), every tradition or cultural group has some special commemorations that are celebrated more or less widely throughout a community (e.g., Earth Day, Our Lady of Guadalupe, Juneteenth, a parish's patronal feast, Chinese New Year, Cinco de Mayo, Mother's and Father's Days, Day of the Dead, Indigenous Peoples Day), and some cultures and traditions honor individuals (or saints) important to their history.

The first concern of the preacher should be to identify how the holy day functions in the life of the church catholic and then turn to the needs and context of the specific congregation. An ancient holy day peculiar to the church may function primarily to remind the gathered assembly of their connection with millennia of Christians, or explicitly with the communion of saints. A sermon or homily on that occasion might appropriately focus on continuity between the ancient story and the present, with translation of the historical event into the current situation. For example, a sermon for the Feast of Pentecost might emphasize how the Spirit teaches the contemporary community languages to communicate with people outside familiar boundaries. A homily for Epiphany might appropriately challenge the assembly to be on the lookout for manifestations of Christ among members of their community, or appearing from sources that might surprise them. A saint's day may call on the preacher to acknowledge the model the individual offers, present some historical material or theological reflection, and ask how the life of the saint challenges current Christians to assess their behavior or respond to God's call to ministry or evangelism.

In the case of a Christian holy day that has been secularized (Christmas or Easter), a preacher might be tempted to emphasize how the Christian message intended by the occasion has been usurped or corrupted by secular society. Before taking that approach, however, it is wise to consider carefully how important the secularized version of the holiday may be to the community. What might be near universal human associations with the festal event (the need for a midwinter celebration of light, or the celebration of the coming spring)? How does the reunion of families for a holiday participate in the Christian assembly's notion of a church family? What does hunting for Easter eggs have to do with the religious foundations of the holiday? Are all the secular trappings mere nostalgia or romantic silliness, or is there a point to accommodating the preaching to some people's emotional attachment to cultural traditions?

At the same time, preaching on holy days offers an opportunity to preach a prophetic word. (See PROPHETIC MESSAGE.) Christians are called to be different, to stand apart in some ways from the secular world. The commercialization of Christmas, in particular, is an easy target: the challenge is to find a word that honors the secular reality of the congregation's lives without sacrificing a proclamation of the faith of the church. Indeed, it is precisely the Christian community's faith in "God with us" that sets it apart, and so a preacher should strive to find a lively way to proclaim the mystery of the incarnation in terms that make sense to people faced with the pressures—and pleasures—of contemporary society. The preacher can use the collision of secular and sacred calendars to help raise a community's awareness of its identity. Faced with decisions about priorities in how they use or mark time, they must necessarily ask questions that clarify for them to whom they belong, or where they stand in relation to God and the world.

Secular or national holidays that are celebrated in church gatherings require a similar strategy. While celebrating the birth of a nation, is the preacher tempted to identify being Christian with being nationalistic? Is dying in defense of one's country the same as dying for one's faith? Are mothers who make sacrifices for their family extolled as Christian saints or held up as examples of the proper ministry of women in the church? Does a preacher romanticize national myths in a manner that perpetuates the marginalization of native people or those conquered in battles of the past? If one preaches in a religious tradition that does not assign readings for the day, it is all the more important to choose scriptural material that both supports and challenges the prevailing cultural pieties associated with the festival.

In churches that use a set Sunday lectionary (*see* LECTIONARY AND THE CHRISTIAN YEAR), many of these events require judicious juggling of the appointed readings for a Sunday and special readings related to a particular feast. In some traditions, Sunday takes precedence over any but the church's most important holy days; similarly, although Mother's Day and Father's Day always fall on Sunday, lectionary-based denominations do not provide special readings for those secular occasions. A preacher must weigh the perceived need to include secular celebrations in the preaching against the requirements of the church's traditions or the use of a common lectionary. Marking these secular holidays during an announcement period, or celebrating them after the service with a special coffee hour, may be a legitimate alternative to focusing the sermon in their direction.

Weekday services focused on one of these special occasions present an unusual opportunity to preachers. Aside from exceptional weekday celebrations (e.g., Christmas or Thanksgiving), many Christians do not attend worship services apart from Sundays, and parishes that offer regular midweek services do not usually schedule them to coincide with special feasts or commemorations of the church. In an environment that does mark particular feasts, therefore, a preacher can expect a congregation of people who are more inclined than most to attend to the church's traditions and who may be particularly interested in the less familiar figures and celebrations of their denomination. The presence of such church members (often in a smaller congregation) can provide a rich environment for homiletical experimentation such as shared or interactive preaching.

Bibliography: Roger Alling and David J. Schlafer. *Preaching through Holy Days and Holidays: Sermons That Work, XI.* (2003); Cheslyn Jones, Edward Yarnold, Geoffrey Wainwright, and Paul Bradshaw, eds. *The Study of Liturgy.* (1992); J. Ellsworth Kalas. *Preaching the Calendar: Celebrating Holidays and Holy Days.* (2004).

HOLY LAND TOURS
Duncan Macpherson

Although the term *Holy Land* can include adjacent *Bible Lands*, it refers primarily to modern Israel-Palestine. Christian visitors to the land are in a special position to appreciate the historical background of the Bible message and to develop appropriate interpretive preaching approaches. These approaches should include engagement with issues of Christian ecumenism, the threat to the survival of the indigenous churches in the Holy Land, and Jewish-Christian and Muslim-Christian dialogue. Crucially, they must also take account of questions of justice and peace in this most politically contested of lands.

The rich background of historical and archaeological material is of great potential value to the preacher. For example, a visit to Megiddo, an archaeological site more than 3,500 years old, supposedly one of the chariot cities of Kings Solomon and Ahab, where King Josiah fell in battle, will certainly clarify its strategic importance in wars ancient and modern. It may also explain the belief of some biblical literalists that it will be the site of the final battle of Armageddon, in which modern Israel will play a decisive role. However, in gathering such impressions it will be important for the preacher to take account of the religious, social, and political realities of the Holy Land itself, subject as it is to rival claims by Israelis and Palestinians.

The religious life of observant Jews in Israel provides numerous reference points for the Christian preacher, but the models of social and cultural life in the peasant society in which Jesus lived also find parallels in Palestinian and other Arab societies. For example, watchtowers and landmarks survive to offer visual echoes of OT symbols. Although modern Arab society is changing dramatically under Western influences, Palestinian peasants farm olive groves, and fig trees are much as they were in the time of Jesus. Palestinian shepherds have changed little, and the fact that they lead rather than drive their sheep, as Western shepherds do, provides valuable preaching insights. Preachers will often discover other parallels with the society in which Jesus lived, yielding insights into the extended family, the patron-client relationship, the status and role of women, and a code of shame and honor. For example, in relation to the last two of these, a sermon about how Mary's fiancé, Joseph, "unwilling to put her to shame, resolved to divorce her quietly" (Matt 1:19), might include the comment that Joseph "lived in an area where even today disgraced women can be rejected from society and become the victims of so called honor killings" (Macpherson 2005, 31–32).

The Land and the Understanding of the Meaning of the Holy

Since all liturgy and preaching take place within, or create, sacred place, the Holy Land of Israel-Palestine can be regarded as sacred space. As the locus of events described in the OT, it has an established importance within Judaism. For Christians, even before the institution of Christian pilgrimage to the Holy Land became generally established in the 4th cent., geographical locations associated with the life of Jesus, in particular Jerusalem, had seminal importance. In the NT and the pre-Nicene fathers, the Land of Promise and the Holy City are symbols for a spiritual eschatology (Wilken 1992, 46–64). Visits to these sites can contribute to understanding of liturgy and the embodiment of tradition.

In addition to informing an understanding of liturgy, Christian pilgrimage to the Holy Land has historically included elements of historical inquiry and preaching. A further, less desirable element of

establishing political and cultural control of the Holy Land and its people needs to be displaced by commitment to encounter between the pilgrim liturgical community and the indigenous Christians, the "living stones" of the land (1 Pet 2:4-5), as well as the believers in Christianity's sister faiths of Islam and Judaism.

Visitors to the Holy Land will discern a variety of often competing Christian communities present in the Holy Land today. Sensitivity to this phenomenon should encourage ecumenical awareness in preaching. So too with the reality that the Holy Land is holy to the three Abrahamic faiths: Christianity, Islam, and Judaism. Frequently one or the other, or both of the other two faiths also revere sites revered by Christians. This can provide rich opportunities for interfaith perspectives in preaching. For example, after a visit to the Cenacle, the traditional place of the Last Supper, the preacher might make a comment like the following: "The room of the Last Supper on Mount Zion in Jerusalem was used for several centuries as a Muslim shrine, and nearby there is the Jewish *Tomb of David*. This reminds me that there is a need for a unity that embraces not only Christians, but everyone. The Eucharist is a sign . . . that Christians are called to be one. It can also be a sign that serves to remind us of the wider unity that God wills for all the people on earth—one family, one body, and one blood" (Macpherson 2004, 24).

The Holy Land and Christian Worship

For Christians, visiting religious sites contributes to the understanding of liturgy as the embodiment of Christian tradition. Ever since the identification of the hill of Golgotha and of the tomb of Jesus by the Empress Helena and the beginning of the building of the church by Constantine in 348, the Church of Holy Sepulcher, built over the site of a temple of Aphrodite, has been a central focus of pilgrimage. With the coming of Islam in 638, Christian pilgrimage continued, and indigenous Christians enjoyed a measure of real, if unequal, freedom. However, from 915 onward, several violent incidents contributed to the emergence of new forms of pilgrimage, known better as military crusades. During the crusader period (1099–1299), old shrines were restored, new shrines were discovered, and local alternative Holy Land sites were developed. All of these provided new homiletic and liturgical opportunities. In the subsequent period of restored Muslim rule, Christian pilgrimage to the Holy Land continued, and the experience of pilgrims helped to keep the Holy Land alive in the imagination of those who preached and prayed at home. Thus, for example, in the 15th cent., the Franciscans set up the Stations of the Cross on the route supposedly taken by Jesus on the way to Calvary, giving rise to innumerable sermons.

In the 19th cent. modern Protestant forms of pilgrimage as lecture tour developed. In response to critical biblical scholarship, these tours were largely concerned with the possibility that archaeology might confirm the truth of Scripture. For the less academically inclined they could be experienced as devotional evocations of the life and times of Jesus. In 1883, General Gordon of Khartoum identified a rival site outside the Ottoman city walls of Jerusalem that became an alternative site for the Church of the Holy Sepulcher for evangelical pilgrims. The historical and archaeological evidence for the authenticity of this site is thin. Although disputed by some scholars, the historical evidence in favor of the traditional site of the Church of the Holy Sepulcher is stronger. However, the contemplative atmosphere of the alternative site's Garden Tomb conforms more readily to the sentimental expectations of many Western pilgrims. By contrast, the awfulness of the traditional site is in keeping with several historical tragedies. Associations with the traditional site suggest a number of preaching strategies. The preacher of the Crucified could emphasize, for example, that a few miles away at Yad Vashem, the deaths of six million Jews are commemorated on land expropriated from Christian Palestinians in 1948, and two hours away, in Gaza, nine hundred thousand Palestinian refugees live in squalor in the most overcrowded place on earth. Far from offering dignity or hope for the future, this dreadful place is a breeding ground for religious fanaticism and violence. Crucifixion did not end on Good Friday. Another example of preaching inspired by travel in the Holy Land is drawn from a visit to one of the possible sites of Emmaus (Luke 24:13-25). The sermon included sympathetic identification (*see* IDENTIFICATION) with the two downcast disciples: "Our hope had been that the peace process in Israel-Palestine would have been going forward like the Northern Ireland peace process that it helped to inspire. It was like that for the two disciples: 'Our hope had been that he would

be the one to set Israel free . . .'—free from the military occupation of the Romans" (Macpherson 2004, 39).

The key to preaching in a Holy Land context is to hang on to the paradox that the place that witnesses to Christian hope is set in a land of ambiguity and calamity. From the favelas of Latin America to the killing grounds of Chechnya or Darfur come the cries of innocent victims. Easter faith is not blind, but to be proclaimed faithfully, it must be preached in the context of fear and of the ambiguity of the empty tomb in Jerusalem that still draws so many pilgrims to the land of the Holy One. *See* ARCHAEOLOGY; GEOGRAPHY; TECHNOLOGY AND THE SERMON.

Bibliography: K. Cragg. *Palestine: The Prize and Price of Zion.* (1997); L. A. Hoffman, ed. *The Land of Israel. Jewish Perspectives.* (1998); Duncan Macpherson. *Pilgrim Preacher: Palestine, Pilgrimage and Preaching.* (2004); Duncan Macpherson. "Living with Uncertainty." *The Preacher* (December 2005) 31–32; J. E. Taylor. *Christians and the Holy Places: The Myths of Jewish-Christian Origins.* (1993); R. L. Wilken. *The Land Called Holy: Palestine in Christian History and Thought.* (1992).

HOLY SPIRIT/PASSION
Luke A. Powery

The experience of the Holy Spirit, the Third Person of the Trinity, is life-giving and holistic, manifesting in individual, communal, and social realms. The Spirit is the *fons vitae*; thus, without the Spirit, there is no life. As the Giver of life, the Spirit is primarily known not through intellectual discussion but through human experience. *Spirit* is an experiential term (*ruakh*) suggesting that one can experience God (Gen 1:2). It means "wind," "breath," "vitality," or "life," leading to two essential OT understandings of the Spirit as God's life-giving presence and power in the world, encompassing every dimension of existence.

Individual Manifestations of the Spirit

On the individual level, the Spirit is the presence of God within a person (Ps 51:11) through justifying grace, which sparks faith and confession in Jesus

Christ (1 Cor 12:3). Professing Christ reveals the presence of the Spirit, and the internal and external call to preach also represents a movement of the Spirit in the life of an individual. This call necessitates piety, especially prayer, an experience of the Spirit (Gal 4:6-7). Prayer fosters a relationship with God, allowing the Spirit to empower preaching. Holy listening to spiritual directors, participating in corporate worship, and partaking the sacraments are some means of grace, along with prayer, that help maintain an openness to the Spirit. Active spirituality nurtures love for God, leading to genuine passion in preaching.

In the Spirit, one's life awakens, fueled by the subject and object of the gospel. Some individuals' bodies are possessed by the Spirit, noticeable in some African American and Pentecostal churches. This indicates that human bodies are temples of the Spirit (1 Cor 6:12-20). However, passion is not just about emotional display of bodies. It is more than emotions. *Passion* stems from a Greek word (paschō), meaning "to suffer" or "to endure," linking it to the suffering Christ and the entire paschal mystery. Passion guided by the Spirit forms one into the gospel pattern and passion of Christ expressed in the sorrowful crucifixion and joyful resurrection. Passion is not about "feeling good" but is about being rooted in the Good Friday–Easter motif of the life of Christ such that one expresses the lament of the cross and the celebration of the empty tomb. The Spirit of Christ groans because of a suffering world (Rom 8) and rejoices because of the future hope found in a resurrected Christ. Spirit-induced passion manifests the full spectrum of human experience by expressing the Spirit as lament and celebration.

Passionate expression is ultimately due to the revelation of God in Christ. The Spirit, an inward teacher, reveals the Word of God, bestows wisdom, gives understanding and insight (1 Cor 2:10-13), and guides our interpretation of the Word. The Spirit's illumination makes the Word effectual, for the Spirit is the power of the Word (1 Cor 2:4-5), a fact that is evident also in the Hebrew prophets. Power is sensed in preaching as well as in other forms of human speech because one may view the Spirit's gift as the gift of speech (Acts 2); thus, glossolalia and singing (Eph 5:18-20) are ways the Spirit fills us individually. However, the work of the Spirit is not limited to individuals but is experienced in congregations.

Communal Manifestations of the Spirit

The movement of the Spirit extends to faith communities. The Spirit gives new life to a people (Ezek 11:19; 37:1-14), even creating a church and filling all with the Spirit (Acts 2; Joel 2:28-30). Each person receives a manifestation of the Spirit for the benefit of the community (1 Cor 12:7), establishing the body of Christ as a charismatic community. The gifts of the Spirit are communal experiences of the Spirit. Likewise, the experience of unity in congregations is a marker of the Spirit's presence (1 Cor 12:4-30), including a common confession and a demonstration of love for each other (1 Cor 12:1-3; 16:14). The practice of individual gifts should foster the experience of the Spirit as unity. This corporate manifestation of the Spirit represents the centripetal work of the Spirit, but the Spirit also moves centrifugally.

Social Manifestations of the Spirit

The Spirit sends people into the world to serve in love. The social dimension of the experience of the Spirit is vital for discerning a life in the Spirit because the Spirit is not self-serving but self-giving. This is seen in Christ, who is empowered by the Spirit to minister (Luke 3:22; 4:1, 14). The messianic way of life serves a hurting world with a sense of hope, granting life instead of death. The Spirit urges hospitality to the other, especially those who are oppressed. In the Spirit, it is impossible to neglect others because the Spirit draws people together into reconciliatory relationships.

The Spirit also resists destructive societal powers by working for the liberation of others. This Spirit of social liberation is present in the work of Christ (Luke 4:18-19), the epitome of a life in the Spirit, as he aims to free people from earthly bondage. Working for human liberation reveals the Spirit. Liberation from oppression is an experience of the Spirit in the world, suggesting that the Spirit is not satisfied with an inward religiosity void of outward relevance but strives for a congruency between inner experience of the Spirit and outer expression of the Spirit. A life in the Spirit is authenticated by the evaluation of one's life in the world because the embodied witness of a person and community ultimately reveals their spiritual nature.

Significant Implications for Preaching

The holistic manifestation and life-giving experience of the Spirit have implications for preaching. The experience of the Spirit through prayer is crucial because prayer stirs passion. However, if authentic passion is to be expressed, the gospel must have significant meaning for the preacher. Effective sermon delivery stems from a rhetoric of the heart that embodies what is proclaimed. The preacher's passion may spark the listeners' passion, so that all passionately worship God through lament and celebration.

Viewing passion as the expression of the passion and pattern of Christ may impact sermon form, especially if one sees LAMENTS and CELEBRATION as manifestations of the Spirit in the actual sermon. With this approach, the sermon moves from lament (crucifixion) to celebration (resurrection). Celebration is noted as a manifestation of the Spirit in African American preaching traditions. Lament is also present, though it does not receive the same attention, in homiletical literature. Celebration is the sermonic climax that ecstatically reinforces the good news about Jesus Christ. Lament is an expression of the Spirit who groans and sighs through humanity (Rom 8:22-23, 26). Lament begins with the declaration of human pain but moves toward hope because of trust in God's power. To lament apart from celebration or vice versa is insufficient for the full experience of the Spirit in preaching.

Furthermore, through the Spirit, the scope of preaching is expanded to impact all areas of human life. If the Spirit manifests in all realms of life, preaching in the Spirit will express this breadth in sermon content, dealing with individual, corporate, and social issues. J. Alfred Smith, in his sermon "Foundations of Our Faith," expresses the Spirit by speaking about varied human issues through lament and celebration. He laments,

> In a century when AIDS seeks to destroy Africa and African Americans, hope is a tiny sprout growing in cracked concrete. In a world where our youth live by the secular gospel of rappers, who profane the holy with cursed speech, hope lives. In a sensate culture where pleasure-intoxicated persons live from their waist down, rather than from their shoulders up, hope in Christ is present for the preservation of the moral fiber of society. In an era of racism, ageism, classism, and homophobism, hope survives in the name of the Living Christ. (LaRue 2002, 143)

During lament, hope and a future celebration rooted in Christ are anticipated. Eventually, Smith moves into a climactic celebration, emphasizing life and not death, resonating with the Spirit of life. He says,

> You can accept his offer of protection today; death did not destroy the Lord Jesus Christ. The grave could not hold him. . . . He is your resurrection and your life. He converts you from corruption. He cleanses you from guilt and self-condemnation. . . . He commissions you to serve him in a compassionate ministry to those who need help and healing. He retrofits your faith for times of trouble, trial, and testing. Through the Holy Spirit, he gives you courage for every challenge, comfort for every crushing earthquake, and in the end when death has brought your early life to a conclusion, Jesus Christ offers your commencement in a place he has prepared for prepared people. (LaRue 2002, 144)

Smith's sermon represents preaching that manifests the Spirit through sermonic lament and celebration while engaging the individual, communal, and social realms. Where there is lament of the absence of life and celebration of the presence of life, there is the Spirit because the Spirit is a giver of life; thus, quenching the Spirit would be the death of Christian preaching.

Bibliography: James Forbes. *The Holy Spirit and Preaching*. (1989); Cleophus J. LaRue, ed. *Power in the Pulpit*. (2002); Jürgen Moltmann. *The Spirit of Life: A Universal Affirmation*. Translated by Margaret Kohl. (1994); Charles H. Spurgeon. *Lectures to My Students: A Selection from Addresses Delivered to the Students of the Pastors' College*, Metropolitan Tabernacle. (1875); Eduard Schweizer. *The Holy Spirit*. Translated by Reginald H. and Ilse Fuller. (1980).

INTERNET PREACHING DATABASES
Robert R. Howard

This article will examine the nature, potential, and problems of Internet preaching databases. Christianity has always danced with technology, whatever its contemporary dress (*see* TECHNOLOGY AND THE SERMON), but the rise of the Internet in the 1990s, and particularly of the World

Wide Web, created unprecedented opportunities for human interaction. Religious organizations were quick to notice the potential for reaching out to uncounted millions of people, both within the church and beyond—and were especially struck with the opportunities offered by Internet capabilities for preaching. As a result, numerous sermon resources are available. These are found in several types of database collections.

Collections of Sermons and Sermon Outlines

Sermons and outlines occur on several sorts of websites and in differing formats. The overwhelming number of sermons on the Internet are electronic versions of print sermons, although an increasing number of sites offer sermons in audio and video formats. In the first decade of the 21st cent., a fairly new, and rapidly growing, format appeared on the scene: the podcast, or compressed package of one or many audio sermon(s), to which one may subscribe (have sent to one's computer via e-mail or feedreader software) and which may be heard at one's leisure. These religious podcasts quickly acquired the appellation Godcasts (e.g., The Godcast Network). Sources for sermons include web portals, or central clearinghouse websites that collect and organize many hyperlinks to various web pages containing sermons (e.g., SermonCentral; Sermon Audio); and religious organizations, denominations, congregations, or individuals whose websites include sermons. At all levels, some websites charge for either basic or premium services, while the majority are free. Electronic versions of printed sermons may also be offered with accompanying graphics, in the form of PowerPoint graphics, picture slides, or movie clips (usually these combination packages are not offered free of charge). The majority of sermons draw upon an evangelical Protestant Christian orientation bespeaking revivalist, fundamentalist, or Pentecostalist roots, but there is certainly a broad representation from Roman Catholic, Orthodox, liberal, African American, Spanish-speaking, Jewish, feminist, Asian-heritage, and gay/lesbian perspectives as well. A bit of time with an Internet search engine will locate representative websites. Recent emergent church initiatives are experimenting with differing models of preaching, a reality that tends to prompt online discussion—blogging—about the nature of preaching itself in the 21st cent., rather than

actual sermon-creation activity. (*See* EMERGING CHURCH PREACHING.) Finally, a growing number of sermons from voices of both genders throughout Christian history may be found on the Internet (e.g., Christian Classics Ethereal Library; Fathers of the Church; Quaker Homiletics).

Preaching Aids

Preaching aids include online Bible study tools; commentaries on biblical books or individual texts; historical, theological, sociocultural, psychological, aesthetic, or visual resources related to the preaching task; collections of illustrations, whether topically organized or related to specific texts; weblogs (blogs); and sermon discussion groups (*see* INTERNET PREACHING FORUMS). The various preaching aids may or may not be lectionary-based, and offered freely or for a fee. Again, the user may visit the website and download material, copy it directly, or subscribe to an e-mail service that will send material regularly (e.g., Living Web Lectionary Project; Aquinas Institute of Theology Online Preaching Resources).

Articles, Essays, Journals, and Bibliographies

These offer a more generalized consideration of the preaching task. Online versions of preaching journals abound, and usually replicate electronically the printed volumes. Some websites offer extra features specific to the online presence, including exclusive articles or opportunities to comment directly on any particular article or sermon. Some web portals provide collections of links to articles and essays from a variety of global sources; others collect the articles themselves. These collections of articles often include those from a variety of theological and confessional perspectives, in multiple languages (e.g., Religion Online; Wabash Center). A growing number of online bibliographies collect resources that explore the many dimensions of preaching from a variety of perspectives (e.g., Notre Dame Center for Liturgy Preaching Bibliography; Vanderbilt University Divinity Library Homiletics Research Bibliography).

Internet Distinctives

As already indicated, the types of preaching databases found on the Internet resemble those in print.

One may look at the glowing computer screen and view a page that looks precisely like one in a book or journal. The radical and global connectivity of the World Wide Web creates a fundamental distinction, however. At the click of a mouse, one may flit from web page to web page, across continents and through time, and collect resources from various places and ages into one's sermon. Further, in combination with computer hardware and software, the resources available on the Internet offer the potential for enhancing the sermon by means of audio and visual features, in seamless ways heretofore unknown.

Advantages

Beyond issues of ease of access and integration of print, audio, and video resources into the sermon, Internet-based preaching databases offer unprecedented opportunities to enhance both congregational life and ecumenical interaction. Members may access sermons from their minister and others, for their own edification. And preachers from all confessional perspectives, ethnic heritages, geographic regions, social locations, and linguistic communities may easily share resources and discuss the craft at any time of the night or day, to the benefit of the entire church. Lectionary preachers have at their fingertips an astonishing wealth of aids to the sermon, many centered on the various lectionaries now available. (*See* LECTIONARY AND THE CHRISTIAN YEAR.) Preachers of all stripes may benefit from the wisdom of the ages, viewing online sermons from historic figures in Christianity, both famous and obscure. And the growing body of bibliographies of online and print resources related to the task of preaching can point inquirers to a wealth of other perspectives now available.

Disadvantages

With regard to sermons themselves, the Internet databases share a chief liability with print versions of sermons: sedimented into print, they become artifacts divorced from the living encounter between God and people. Audio and visual renditions of the sermon modify this reduction, but only slightly. The living human interaction of preacher and people, and the divine presence hovering in the midst of this encounter, cannot be duplicated by a screen, which frames and flattens the event into two dimensions. Further, the very fecundity of the Internet presents a subtle threat of homogenization: whether or not one appropriates another's sermon wholesale, one at the very least will be influenced by the sermons read or heard online. The temptation beckons to create in one's sermon a patchwork quilt from other hands, raising ethical issues of plagiarism. With regard to this particular issue, the Internet does not so much create the temptation as make it much easier, with accountability more difficult. For example, one can download an entire sermon prepackaged with PowerPoint slides. Another temptation presents itself as well: the profusion of lectionary-based aids offers shortcuts for preachers, enabling them to escape doing the hard exegetical and interpretive work that should accompany the preaching task. The growing commercialism of the entire World Wide Web cannot but affect preaching databases, which suffer under consumerist pressures to create inoffensive content marketable to the widest population possible. Socioeconomic factors also influence preaching databases: conservative, white, male, middle-class perspectives predominate. There are indeed a few sites presenting African American, Spanish-speaking, Asian-heritage, and gay/lesbian perspectives—but they are relatively rare. Finally, issues of Internet accessibility threaten to duplicate socioeconomic splits throughout Christianity (its own version of the digital divide), as poorer, more rural congregations may not have access to computers or Internet providers, although aggressive efforts to ameliorate this problem certainly exist (*see* TECHNOLOGY).

In sum, the Internet will continue to influence preaching, providing new opportunities for proclamation of the gospel, embracing the preaching of established denominations, parachurch organizations, and individuals, and offering a host of online sermons and preaching-related resources.

Bibliography: Due to the effervescence of the Internet, the following websites may not be active as time passes from the publication date of this handbook. Web Portals: Aquinas Institute of Theology Online Preaching Resources. http://www.op.org/domcentral/preach; The Godcast Network. http://www.godcast.org; Sermon Audio. http://www.sermonaudio.com; SermonCentral. http://www.sermoncentral.com. Lectionary-Related Websites: Living Web Lectionary Project. http://www.livingweb.com; The Text This Week.

http://www.textweek.com. Historical Sermons: Christian Classics Ethereal Library. http://www.ccel.org; The Fathers of the Church. http://www.newadvent.org/fathers; The Quaker Homiletics Online Anthology. http://www.qh press.org/quakerpages. Online Studies about Preaching: Homiletics Articles at Religion Online. http://www.religion-online.org; Wabash Center Internet Guide: Preaching. http://www.wabash center.wabash.edu. Bibliographies: Notre Dame Center for Liturgy Preaching Bibliography. http://liturgy.nd.edu/bibliography; Vanderbilt University Divinity Library Research Bibliography in Homiletics. http://divinity.library.vanderbilt.edu/bibliographies.

INTERNET PREACHING FORUMS
Robert R. Howard

Wise preachers have always sought conversation about the craft of preaching in order to sharpen their skills, glean ideas from other perspectives, and find new material for inclusion in their sermons. With the advent of the Internet, opportunities for such aids have increased dramatically. This article will examine the nature and types of Internet preaching forums, and some implications of these new resources for preaching.

Types of Internet Preaching Forums

The rise of the World Wide Web in the early 1990s was soon accompanied by web-based religious expressions, many of them related to worship and preaching (White 1994, 47–49; Jewell 2004). Paralleling popular print resources, Internet-related preaching-helps sites took advantage of the new technology (INTERNET PREACHING DATABASES; TECHNOLOGY AND THE SERMON), providing opportunities for conversation among preachers as well as for the sharing of resources. Among the various preaching-related sites, discussion groups and forums became quite popular. These sites occur in three chief types and include various kinds of content.

The first type operates from a centrally located website, which allows preachers (and other interested parties) to share ideas, resources, and perspectives. These websites may be operated by a denomination (for example, the Preaching Ministry Forum of the Churches of Christ, or the United Church of Christ's Lectionary and Preaching) or commercial enterprise (DesperatePreacher.com). The preacher loads the web page and, by clicking on the proper button, may communicate the contribution for all to see. Conversations about a single topic are called threads and may continue intermittently for weeks. Some websites restrict the interaction to electronic conversations, while others allow uploading or downloading of material, such as sermons, sermon outlines, illustrative material, quotations, images, and the like. One advantage of this form of interaction is that preachers may visit this type of site at their leisure, and read or respond to the contributions that appeal to their interests. Also, preachers can often download material from this central site, thus benefiting from others' contributions. Finally, this kind of forum is usually moderated, offering some control over the content. One possible disadvantage is related to this—the gatekeeping moderator may shut down certain types of discussion. Another disadvantage may be that some sites require log-ins and passwords, and some charge a fee. Many such discussion forums may be found at Yahoo's e-groups.com by entering into the search screen sermon or homily or preaching. These preaching forums span the globe and include every confessional orientation imaginable.

A second type of interactive forum is a topical e-mail listserv, such as PRCL-L (Preaching the Revised Common Lectionary), to which interested parties may subscribe (free or for a fee). Submissions are sent to a central computer server, which then passes them along to all subscribers. Contributions are necessarily limited to text, but lively conversations ensue, with advice, correction, insights, ideas, links to web pages, and commentary on the craft of preaching being offered. Again, a number of concurrent topical threads may be created. One advantage of this particular interactive method is that one need not seek out a central web page; one receives the contributions with one's other e-mail. This suggests a potential disadvantage, for popular e-mail discussion lists may provide dozens of contributions daily, threatening to swamp the hapless preacher.

A third type of preaching forum is a weblog, or blog. Gaining popularity in the first decade of the 21st cent., blogs provide an opportunity for anyone to record thoughts on any subject, with the entire wired world as audience. Blogs may be likened to diaries, with electronic versions able to include links and material from anywhere on the World Wide

Web. Preaching blogs are usually individual efforts, though commercial and denominational blogs are available as well. Interested parties may respond by clicking on the appropriate button. Often a topical thread will be created in response to a blog entry. This sort of preaching forum is much more individualized. It bears the stamp of the writer's interests, for good or ill. Preaching-related blogs may be found at blogger.com by searching for key words such as *preaching, sermon,* or *homiletics*.

General Characteristics of Internet Preaching Forums

Electronic preaching forums are backed by three types of sponsors: denominationally related organizations, commercial ventures, and individuals. A number of denominations provide interactive electronic forums for preachers to discuss either ministry in general or preaching in particular (see the Preacher's Exchange). Any number of preaching-related print journals have online websites that feature discussion forums. Individually sponsored websites usually espouse a particular perspective, while maintaining a general openness to other points of view (see, e.g., Working the Angles [emergent church perspective], or A Pomo Pentecostal Lectionary Blog). With regard to the actual content, discussion groups may include sermons and sermon outlines, material useful for creating sermons (illustrations, quotations, images, ideas, PowerPoint® slides, movie clips, and the like), exploration of theological and cultural themes (e.g., Preaching Peace and U2 Sermons), and exegetical studies of the biblical text. Textual studies groups may examine weekly assigned texts of the *Revised Common Lectionary,* or more freely chosen texts or word studies. Some forums will be focused on the craft of preaching itself, such as the Academy of Homiletics' Homiletix e-Forum. The majority of discussion forums seem to espouse either a mainline denominational orientation, with lectionary discussions predominating, or an evangelical or conservative theological orientation. A few African American (see, e.g., HomileticsPortal.com and African American Preaching) forums exist. But as far as gender goes, forums are almost exclusively male-sponsored, and the majority of participants are male as well.

Advantages and Disadvantages

As with any technological innovation, the World Wide Web has brought with it breathtaking new vistas and stubborn new problems. Internet preaching forums offer an astonishing breadth of perspectives, for literally anyone with a computer can participate in any number of conversations simultaneously and, inserting hyperlinks, bring into the discussion an unlimited number of conversation partners. Thus, the conversations surrounding the act of preaching may have innumerable voices, from divergent physical locations, espousing an array of confessional heritages and theological perspectives. Internet availability has spread widely, making available resources, insights, and conversation partners to preachers who may in earlier days have been isolated. Such an expansion of the conversation about preaching was simply impossible to imagine before the arrival of Internet technology. Furthermore, in addition to the preachers, congregations are availing themselves of the opportunity to bring laypeople into the conversation about the sermon, making preaching a truly communal event that endures beyond the final spoken syllable. Finally, the confessional and geographic breadth of such participants fosters relationships centered on the Word that are ecumenical in the finest sense of the word.

On the other hand, a few disadvantages limit the potential of Internet preaching forums. First of all, they require computer hardware, computer literacy, and connectivity to the Internet, the necessity of which precludes many from the discussion. Despite the best efforts of governments, institutions, and business, there still exist geographical areas without Internet accessibility, and demographic cohorts who are not conversant with the new technologies. Furthermore, the overwhelming number of online discussion groups display Eurocentric male perspectives. Although the potential for the widest diversity of voices to join the conversation certainly exists, this potential is as yet unfulfilled. Another drawback in these discussion groups: their presence enables preachers to proclaim the sermons of others instead of creating their own. In predigested biblical exegeses offered electronically and prefabricated outlines or sermon manuscripts, preachers face this temptation from online sources as never before, due to the sheer number of resources and the ease of access. In some cases, the easy availability of others' ideas may stunt the growth of the preacher's creativity. Ironically, the very abundance of resources available may end up impeding the creative task.

Internet preaching forums offer unprecedented help for the preacher, as well as opportunities to converse with other practitioners who love the craft of preaching. These days preachers may connect with others around the clock and across the globe, to discuss techniques, seek insights, and offer suggestions, in ways never before imagined. A wealth of exegetical and confessional perspectives is available through Internet preaching forums. The Internet has become yet one more way for technology to serve the Word of God.

Bibliography: African American Preaching. http://groups.yahoo.com/group/africanamerican preaching; DesperatePreacher.com discussion forum; HomileticsPortal.com. http://www.homilet icsportal.com; Homiletix e-Forum (Academy of Homiletics). http://www.homiletics.org; John P. Jewell. *Wired for Ministry.* (2004); Lectionary and Preaching (United Church of Christ). http://forums.ucc.org; A Pomo Pentecostal Lectionary Blog. http://pomolectionary.blogspot.com; Preacher's Exchange (Roman Catholic Order of Preachers). http://www.opsouth.org; Preaching (Calvin Institute of Christian Worship). http://www.calvin.edu; Preaching Ministry Forum (Churches of Christ). http://cconline.faithsite.com; Preaching Peace. http://preachingpeace.blogs.com; U2 Sermons. http://u2sermons.blogspot.com; Susan J. White. *Christian Worship and Technological Change.* (1994); Working the Angles. http://www.mtsi.org/pat/tag/preaching.

JEWISH/CHRISTIAN PERSPECTIVES
Patricia K. Tull

Christianity stands in a peculiar relationship to its closest sibling faith. Both descend from ancient Israel's religion; both claim many of the same scriptural books as canon; both interpret that Scripture in relation to subsequent writings—for Christians, the NT; for Jews, the Talmud and midrashic literature. Both share many beliefs regarding creation, divinity and humanity, worship, and faithful living. But while Jews stand in a direct line of descent from

Israel, and Judaism's intelligibility stands independent of Christianity, the tenets of Christian theology are largely unintelligible when severed from their Israelite origins. Not only were Judeans the Bible's primary authors, but Christianity's founding figures, Jesus and his apostles, were born and remained faithful Jews. Christian preaching requires a clear-sighted comprehension of relationship to Judaism.

A long history of vituperation and violence against Jews has sullied this close relationship. More than half a century after the Jewish Holocaust, Christian anti-Semitism is still reflected in residual unforgotten—but mostly unconscious—biases rooted in anti-Jewish biblical interpretation. This article will briefly survey the history of Jewish-Christian relations, discuss common interpretive pitfalls, and offer suggestions for preachers wishing to help mend Christianity's self-presentation in an interfaith world.

While members of the first generation of Christians were Jews, by the early 2nd cent. the church was largely constituted of Gentiles relatively new to Israel's traditions. What had begun as an in-house debate between Jesus and other rabbis was gradually replaced by theological and political rivalry between two increasingly distinct groups. Rome's destruction of the Jewish Temple in 70 CE led many Jews to renewed faithfulness. But Christian leaders, anxious to find their place in divine history, saw in the Temple's destruction a sign that God had replaced Abraham's heirs with a new Israel, Gentile Christianity.

Social dynamics changed considerably when the 4th cent. emperor Constantine granted favored status to Christians. Church leaders increasingly gained legal power that sporadically but severely limited Jewish rights—expelling them from towns, burning synagogues, and forbidding intermarriage and even interfaith hospitality. Such actions remained occasional and local until the Crusades began around 1095/96, when violence against Jews as well as Muslims became pervasive in Christendom. Forced conversion, expulsion, ghettoization, seizure of property and children, burning of Talmuds and synagogues, torture, and massacre characterized this time.

In the 18th and 19th cent., a more insidious form of anti-Semitism arose, based not on traditional religion, but on pseudoscientific racial classifications. This ideology, coupled with traditional religious anti-Judaism, eventually facilitated Hitler's slaughter of two-thirds of Europe's Jews, as well as of other people declared inferior. The Holocaust was clearly not a Christian event, but centuries of Christian prejudice were its necessary precondition.

Post-war reflection on the Jewish Holocaust as the horrific outcome of two millennia of anti-Judaism prompted many church leaders to rethink their teachings. Such work gained momentum with the 1965 Vatican II statement titled "Nostra Aetate" and with similar documents drafted in Protestant denominations. Religious anti-Judaism came to be viewed as not only ethically unconscionable, but also theologically unacceptable, since it contradicts Jesus' teachings and portrays God as a breaker of promises.

For most preachers today, the primary issue is not conscious attitude but biases that have infused self-understanding so deeply that their errors elude detection. Historical Christian misinterpretation of Judaism has resulted in confusion over the role of the OT as Scripture, unfamiliarity with its contents, and reluctance to preach its rich and varied themes. Misunderstanding of the Judaism of Jesus and his disciples has also led to misappropriations of the NT.

Many Christians, including preachers, mistakenly dichotomize OT law and NT grace. The Hebrew word *Torah*, traditionally translated as "law," actually means "teaching." Pentateuchal and psalmic discussions of Torah make it clear that God's commands were not dismal burdens through which Israelites expected to earn favor, but were given because God chose to form a nation sensitive to the holiness of daily life. For Jews as for Christians, grace is not freedom from divine rule, but freedom joyfully to seek God's purposes. Careful readers of Scripture recognize divine grace from the beginning of Genesis, and divine command to the end of Revelation.

A second fallacy is supersessionism, the notion that the *Old* Testament can be bypassed for the *New* without diminishing Christian theology. While Christ's life and teachings, and incipient *Christ*ology, are to be sought in the NT, the Hebrew Scriptures inform *theo*logy, as well as anthropology, wisdom, ethics, and worship. Preaching the whole of Scripture's breadth and depth, including the narratives, prophecies, psalms, and proverbs, infuses faith with richness that cannot be derived from the NT alone.

Alongside supersessionist rejection of the Bible's first Scriptures comes the notion of Jews as OT people rather than as contemporary peers who have continued, like Christians, to adapt to cultural change. Modern Jews and Christians have more in common spiritually with one another than either group has with their ancestors of two or three millennia ago. A similar misconstrual is the notion of Israelites (and, by extension, contemporary Jews) as exceptional sinners. Classical prophets such as Hosea, Amos, and Isaiah harshly criticized sin and injustice in ancient society. Stories of patriarchs and kings likewise offered rich portraits of ambiguous human nature. What was criticized was not Jewish wrongdoing, but human sin. Scribes who compiled the Bible are to be commended for retaining, rather than expunging, such embarrassingly frank portrayals of their ancestors, portrayals that remind both Christians and Jews of human finitude and divine grace.

Christian lectionaries unfortunately continue to fuel another misconception, the notion that all of the prophets predicted Jesus' messianic coming, but that his contemporaries, misunderstanding their own Scriptures, failed to recognize him. The prophetic books yield no harmonized messianic story line. Like preachers today, Israel's prophets primarily addressed the fears and hopes of their communities. Portraits of the prophets as heralds of Jesus as Messiah were developed in hindsight, as early Christians searched Scripture to understand his life, death, and resurrection. Through the centuries Jews have reminded Christians that Isaiah's vision of a messianic age, characterized by profound peace, reconciliation between enemies, and spiritual prosperity, still awaits fulfillment.

The NT poses other interpretive challenges. The synoptic Gospel writers take Jesus' Jewishness for granted. (*See* SYNOPTIC GOSPELS.) The Gospel of Matthew, for example, portrays Jesus as a faithful heir to the words and deeds of scriptural figures, proclaiming, "Until heaven and earth pass away, not one letter, not one stroke of a letter, will pass from the law until all is accomplished" (Matt 5:18). From a birth narrative echoing that of Moses, to forty days of testing in the wilderness, to healing stories resembling those of Elijah and Elisha, to prophetic "jeremiads" against his contemporaries, to sufferings interpreted through psalmic laments and a resurrection suffused with divine encounter, Matthew's Jesus recapitulates the narrative of his ancestors.

Jesus' critiques of his contemporaries, which the synoptic Gospels present as in-house rabbinic debates, are often misapprehended as wholesale characterizations of Jews and rejections of Judaism. Tendencies to presume too sharp a contrast between Christianity and Judaism are effectively resisted when Jesus' own Jewishness is taken seriously. Many contemporary preachers rightly see the sins that Jesus criticized as those to which religious leaders in any denomination may be tempted.

Sociological analysis of the particular communities in which each account arose helps clarify the vision of each Gospel writer. Sensitivity is needed especially in sorting out the polemics in John, which arose later than the Synoptics, in a more bitterly divided community, and which strangely characterize Jesus' opponents as "the Jews"—as if Jesus and his disciples were Gentiles—and even as children of the devil (John 8:44). (*See* PASSION NARRATIVES.)

Jewish-Gentile relations reflected in Paul's letters are likewise easy to overinterpret. Paul never left his Judaism behind to convert to Christianity. His questions were not about Judaism but about how Gentiles understood, and were welcomed into, the community of Christ's followers: Must the uncircumcised become Jewish converts to believe in Jesus? Convinced that the end of time was near, and asserting the particularity of Israel's calling, he answered with a resounding no, while vigorously asserting, "God has not rejected his people whom he foreknew" (Rom 11:2). His generous efforts to extend to Gentiles the good news of reconciliation should not be misread as rejections of his heritage.

Anti-Jewish biblical interpretation has recently left deleterious marks on international politics, damaging Western Christian ability to achieve a respectful and nuanced comprehension of the relationship of modern Israel to its Arab neighbors. In some mainline Christian circles, failure to distinguish fairminded support of Palestinians in Israel from old-fashioned anti-Semitism has endangered Christian-Jewish reconciliation. By contrast, the fundamentalist eschatological movement often called Christian Zionism, which arose from millennialist misappropriations of Daniel and Revelation, offers uncompromising support to Israel, ignoring Palestinian claims. Proponents hold that when Israel populates the disputed West Bank, and the Jewish Temple is rebuilt in Jerusalem, a catastrophic war will issue in Christ's second coming. To promote this outcome, Christian Zionists give enormous financial and political support to fundamentalist Jewish groups who, through intimidation and violence, try to remove Palestinians from their land. Eschatological scenarios, in which all humans must either be born again as Christians or burn in hell, display contempt not only for Muslims but also, perplexingly, for Orthodox and Roman Christians still living in Christianity's birthplace and, paradoxically, for the Jewish people central to such scenarios. Since parishioners are both curious about and confused by the political and religious minefield of Middle Eastern politics, preachers must offer nuanced guidance that resists demonizing either Jewish Israel or its Arab neighbors and residents, and that conveys carefully what the Bible says and does not say about the world's future.

All these interpretive pitfalls notwithstanding, this is an exciting generation in which to read and preach Scripture. Broader Christian understanding of Judaism has resulted in a more profound knowledge of our heritage. Collaboration between Jewish and Christian scholars increasingly enriches commentaries, introductory textbooks, educational materials, and worship resources. Pastors wishing to stay abreast should refresh their reference libraries with newer Bible introductions and commentaries such as the *New Interpreter's Bible*, as well as with writings by Jewish scholars, such as the *Jewish Publication Society Torah Commentary Series*. Interfaith worship and community events, as well as scriptural study with local Jewish clergy, can help pastors gain a deeper grasp of the similarities and particularities of the two faiths. The story of God's dealings with Christians and Jews is still unfolding, and this generation's preachers are entrusted with a small but significant part in the shaping of that story. *See* PENTATEUCHAL NARRATIVES; PROPHETIC PREACHING; PSALMS.

Bibliography: Ronald J. Allen and John C. Holbert. *Holy Root, Holy Branches: Christian Preaching from the Old Testament.* (1995); Ronald J. Allen and Clark M. Williamson. *Preaching the Gospels without Blaming the Jews.* (2004); John Gager. *The Origins of Anti-Semitism: Attitudes toward Judaism in Pagan and Christian Antiquity.* (1985); Howard Clark Kee and Irvin J. Borowsky. *Removing Anti-Judaism from the Pulpit.* (1996); Marilyn J. Salmon. *Preaching without Contempt: Overcoming Unintended Anti-Judaism.* (2006).

LECTIO CONTINUA
Ronald J. Allen

Lectio continua is a significant pattern by which preachers can organize the content of sermons over several Sundays. The expression *lectio continua* is Latin for "continuous reading" and refers to the practice of preaching sequentially through a part of the Bible such as a single book (e.g., Gal), an extended portion of a book (e.g., Isa 24–26), or several books from the hand of a single author or community (e.g., the Pentateuch). In recent years, a modified form of *lectio continua* has appeared: semicontinuous readings in which the preacher does not take up every individual passage in a continuous body of material but focuses on key passages and on passages that represent many others.

Many scholars think that a form of *lectio continua* was in use in synagogues by the 1st cent. CE. *Lectio continua* has been characteristic of many preachers across the history of the church (e.g., Augustine and Chrysostom), and was especially influential through the preachers of the Reformation such as Calvin and Zwingli and their descendants. Some preachers continue this practice today.

In the mode of *lectio continua*, worship leaders determine the biblical texts either by freely choosing the material or by following a part of a lectionary that is organized as continuous reading. When developing sermons in the mode of *lectio continua*, the preacher divides the larger body of biblical material into meaningful units and preaches on one or two units a week for a sequence that can range from three or four Sundays to several weeks or even many months.

The following are among the strengths of preaching from *lectio continua*. The preacher can correlate the theological perspective of a book of the Bible with the theological needs of the congregation and can explore that correlation in depth. Given the biblical and theological illiteracy of many congregations today, *lectio continua* offers an excellent opportunity for the congregation to become acquainted with the content and continuity of a large body of biblical material, the historical situation (if known) that gave rise to that material, the literary and rhetorical style(s) of the material, its theological claims, and its intended effects on the community (or communities) in antiquity to which it was addressed.

Through *lectio continua*, congregations become aware of the larger historical, literary, and theological contexts of particular texts. Over the weeks of *lectio continua*, the listening community can begin to inhabit the theological world of the biblical readings. Instead of the congregation encountering tiny elements of a biblical book as the preacher jumps week to week from one book to another, *lectio continua* helps the community engage in sustained critical theological reflection on the fully developed theological themes of biblical books. When the biblical material is narrative in type (e.g., Josh; Judg; 1 and 2 Sam; 1 and 2 Kgs), *lectio continua* helps the congregation develop a sense of the sequence of the biblical narrative and its events.

Sermons based on *lectio continua* texts can easily build from week to week. Preaching in this way simplifies aspects of sermon preparation because the preacher can work for several weeks out of a single body of research into the historical background, literary features, and theological claims of the single book (and does not need to investigate those motifs anew for passages from different books from one week to the next).

In *lectio selecta* (a Latin expression meaning "selected reading"), passages from the Bible are selected because they coordinate with theological themes in an overarching pattern for organizing worship. In the early 21st cent. the most widely used lectionary in North America is the *Revised Common Lectionary* and its cognates. (*See* LECTIONARY AND THE CHRISTIAN YEAR.) This lectionary centers on two great cycles depicting a Christian version of the story of redemption: Advent/Christmas/Epiphany Day and Lent/Easter/Pentecost Day. During these seasons, the Bible readings in the lectionary are chosen because they illuminate the theological themes of the respective seasons. However, in Ordinary Time, modified versions of *lectio continua* appear in this lectionary. In the latter part of Ordinary Time in the Sundays after Epiphany, the readings from the Gospels are continuous, and the readings from the Letters are semicontinuous. On the Sundays of Ordinary Time after Pentecost Day, the Gospel and Letter readings are continuous or semicontinuous. In this long latter season, the lectionary appoints two sets of readings from the First Testament—one set selected to coordinate with the Gospel reading and the other set presenting semicontinuous aspects of the First Testament: the ancestral stories, the exodus and the entry into the promised land (Year A), the monarchy and wisdom literature (Year B), and the prophets (Year C). By following the *Revised Common Lectionary*, the preacher and congregation can have some benefits of both *lectio continua* and *lectio selecta.*

When preaching in *lectio continua* today, the preacher typically needs to take account of the fact that few members of the congregation are in worship every week: (1) while sermons should be thematically connected from week to week, each sermon should also have its own message, and (2) over the course of a continuous series, the preacher needs repeatedly to provide background information on the biblical material.

A popular approach of *lectio continua* preachers has been to interpret texts verse by verse (or, more accurately, segment by segment). However, within *lectio continua* the preacher can structure the sermon in ways that serve such factors as the particular shape of the text, the listening pattern of the congregation, the intended effect of the sermon, and the preacher's style. *See* DOCTRINES AND BIBLICAL TEXTS.

Bibliography: Ronald J. Allen and Gilbert L. Bartholomew. *Preaching Verse by Verse.* (2000); John P. Burgess. "Shaping a Congregation through Lectio Continua." *Reformed Liturgy and Music* 30 (1966) 3–6; Shelley E. Cochran. *The Pastor's Underground Guide to the Revised Common Lectionary.* Vols. 1–3. (1995–97); Hughes Oliphant Old. "Preaching by the Book: Using the Lectio Continua Approach in Sermon Planning." *Reformed Worship* 8 (1988) 24–25; James A. Sanders, "Canon and Calendar: An Alternative Lectionary Proposal." *Social Themes of the Christian Year: A Commentary on the Lectionary.* (1984) 73–81.

LECTIO DIVINA
Brendan Moss, O.S.B.

In the opening words of his *Rule*, St. Benedict invites his monks to incline "the ear of their hearts" (*Rule of Saint Benedict* Prologue 1) and to listen for the voice of God. *Lectio divina* (holy reading) is the ancient monastic practice that may teach the preacher to listen to sacred texts in ways that will inspire the heart and transform preaching. Since the foundation of Western monasticism, monks have spent time each day listening for the voice of God speaking through the Scriptures. St. Benedict taught his monks to pray this way more than fifteen hundred years ago, and Benedictine monks, nuns, and sisters continue the practice of this spiritual discipline to this day. According to Luke Dysinger, a Benedictine monk, *lectio divina* is "a slow contemplative praying of the Scriptures which enables the Bible, the Word of God, to become a means of union with God." Preaching should draw the preacher and hearers into a holy exchange between the heart of God and their own; preaching should also be "a means of union with God" (Dysinger, under "The Process of *Lectio Divina*").

Lectio divina is a practice of praying with the Word of God in four movements: *lectio* (reading), *meditatio* (meditation), *contemplatio* (contemplation), and *oratio* (prayer). Progressing through each movement, one builds upon the other and opens the heart of the one praying for holy transformation. A typical process may be described as follows:

In preparing for *lectio divina*, we find a place apart, quiet, and pleasant, thereby creating a sacred space. Once settled comfortably into our personal chapel, we begin with an epiclesis: an invocation of the Holy Spirit (*see* HOLY SPIRIT/PASSION). While an invocation of the Holy Spirit may be a formal prayer, it may also be improvised. Something as simple as "Come, Holy Spirit, open my heart that I may receive the Word of God" will suffice. Ultimately, the effect of this opening verse is to settle the spirit and open the heart of the preacher. With the Spirit of God summoned, we enter the practice of holy reading.

The first movement of *lectio divina* is reading the Word (*lectio*). Simply stated, we begin by reading the passage aloud from beginning to end. After the first reading, we consider the text and identify the primary elements of the story. Like a good detective, we answer basic questions. We identify the book or letter in Scripture from which the passage comes and its place in the Bible (its Testament). We name the style of writing (i.e., a letter, a monologue, or poetry). We list the characters involved and recognize the principal speaker(s). We recap the major event in the passage and its context. We are cognizant about what precedes and succeeds the text. This investigation serves one fundamental purpose; it familiarizes us with the chosen pericope and prepares us to listen for its latent meaning. As with all textual passages in *lectio divina*, we read the text a second time aloud. This allows the Word to be proclaimed and engages the hearer/reader through multiple learning senses (*see* LEARNING STYLES). The goal of this second proclamation is to tell the story of the text and convey its meaning. In other words, since the text is proclaimed for our own hearing, we announce the good news of the Scripture to ourselves. With the completion of the second reading come a fuller appreciation of the passage at hand and a deeper readiness to allow the Word of God to speak directly to our hearts.

The second movement of *lectio divina* is *meditatio* (meditation). Meditation begins with a third reading of the pericope. However, this careful and attentive reading is performed with the ear of the heart inclined toward the voice of God. As we read the text aloud, we stop to consider the first word, phrase, or image that stands out or seems noteworthy. Trusting the presence of the Holy Spirit previously invoked, we enter into a conversation with God about that particular word, phrase, or image that has captured our attention. Holy exchange begins when we first consider how this word, phrase, or image speaks to our relationship with God, self, and others. We ask why God chose this word. We ponder how this phrase might call us to recognize our own sin or demand our conversion. As preachers, we also focus on how this image, word, or phrase may speak to the community in which we preach. What does the Word ask of our church and community? We explore our word, phrase, or image in whatever way may be helpful and allow God to speak in return. After some time, five to ten minutes, we enter silence and embrace the quiet.

When all is quiet and the spirit is at rest, the third movement has begun. *Contemplatio* (contemplation) is the third movement of *lectio divina*. In this phase, we simply sit and rest with the Divine in sacred silence. Silence is often uncomfortable and, in some cases, frightening. However, by recalling in whose company we are, the silence is welcome, for it provides the space to be in the presence of our eternal lover. Contemplation occurs when our still spirit engages the still Spirit of God. No words are necessary. Now our being is in union with the Divine Presence. Thus, as a result of this time in contemplation, the desire to give praise and thanks to God arises.

Here, the fourth movement of *lectio divina* begins when our hearts are drawn to eucharist: to

giving thanks through prayer. The fourth movement of holy reading is *oratio* (prayer). The prayer of *oratio* is a free expression of gratitude for the holy exchange given in *meditatio* and *contemplatio*. This is spontaneous prayer and need not be complicated. At times a simple "thank you" is enough. With this prayer of thanksgiving—this eucharistic action—*lectio divina* comes to a close.

However, all is not yet complete. For preachers, if *lectio divina* is to bear fruit in our practice, there is more work to be done. Consider the word, phrase, or image given us in our meditation. What might this word, phrase, or image from the scripture passage offer our community, and how might it help understand the Word in a new way? In light of the ways in which this word may speak to the church, preachers may then formulate what the scholar Thomas Long calls a focus statement. (*See* FOCUS AND FUNCTION STATEMENTS.) Preachers answer two questions: What is the gospel about? What must this preaching say? Essentially, our meditation can reveal what is at the heart of the pericope, and potentially what is at the heart of our preaching.

Furthering the work of *meditatio*, the preacher may return again to the word, phrase, or image explored during this phase. This time the preacher considers what this word, phrase, or image asks the faith community to do. What response does this meditation require? Ultimately, the Word of God is dynamic, and its readers are asked to respond. The word, phrase, or image given for the preacher's mediation should also call the church to action. Reconsidering the conversation of the *meditatio*, the preacher formulates what Thomas Long calls the function statement of the sermon or homily. From the fruit of the *meditatio* two questions arise: What does the Word call us to do? What action does this preaching call forth from the community?

The preacher's *lectio divina* gives birth to the focus and the function of the preaching event. Directly from prayer and with the Word of God, preachers reveal the starting place of their preaching. The fundamental question for exegesis is uncovered, and the beginnings of the sermonic or homiletic theme ferment.

How might preachers use the practice of *lectio divina* during their preaching preparation in the course of a week? The following suggestion assumes the use of a lectionary cycle for readings; however, one may pursue *lectio divina* with only one text, multiple times, early in the week, or simply begin the preparation later toward midweek.

Sunday evening:	Use *lectio divina* with the Gospel pericope for the coming week.
Monday:	Use *lectio divina* with the First Reading or Lesson.
Tuesday:	Use *lectio divina* with the Second Reading.
Every day:	Seek points of connection between the community's experience and the focus of your *meditatio*
Wednesday:	Decide which reading will be at the heart of your preaching and pursue study of the chosen text.
Thursday:	Write a draft of the homily.
Friday:	Revise and finalize a draft.

Lectio divina inclines the ear of a preacher's heart and allows him or her to listen closely to the voice of God (*Rule of Saint Benedict* Prologue 1). Given time, this Christian and monastic practice will form and transform the preacher's heart. *Lectio divina* will become the womb in which the focus and function of our sermons/homilies will grow and, ultimately, be birthed. *See* DEVOTIONAL LIFE/LIFE-STYLE; EXEGESIS.

Bibliography: Enzo Bianchi. *Praying the Word: An Introduction to Lectio Divina.* Translated by James W. Zona. (1998); Michael Casey. *Sacred Reading: The Ancient Art of Lectio Divina.* (1995); Luke Dysinger. "Accepting the Embrace of God: The Ancient Art of Lectio Divina." http://www.valyermo.com; Timothy Fry, O.S.B., ed. *The Rule of Saint Benedict in English.* (1982); Thomas Long. *The Witness of Preaching.* (1989); Salvatore Panimolle, ed. *Like the Deer That Yearns: Listening to the Word and Prayer.* (1998); Basil Pennington. *Lectio Divina: Renewing the Ancient Practice of Praying the Scriptures.* (1998).

LECTIONARY AND THE CHRISTIAN YEAR
Laurence Hull Stookey

A lectionary is an organized system of readings (from Latin, *lectio*, an act of reading). Within the church a lectionary is a systematic reading of the Scriptures, usually aloud in the course of corporate worship and related closely to the Christian Year.

A. Forms of Lectionaries
B. The Form of the Christian Year
  1. Easter
  2. Christmas
  3. Ordinary Time
C. Readings in Relation to Calendrical Occasions
D. Concerning Current Three-Year Lectionaries
E. The Design of the *Revised Common Lectionary*
F. Preaching from the *Revised Common Lectionary*
G. Practical and Pastoral Considerations
  1. Comprehensive or Limited Coverage?
  2. Common Objections to Lectionary Preaching
  3. Preparation by All Who Lead Worship and Related Activities
  4. Sustaining Congregational Interaction with the Lections

A. Forms of Lectionaries

The lectionary principle is used in Judaism, and some scholars believe that when Jesus read and interpreted Isa 61:1-2 in the synagogue, he was using a reading assigned for the day, not his own selection. Certainly, the preaching of the ancient church attests the existence of lectionaries in the early centuries. The simplest form of lectionary consists of sequential readings (called *lectio continua*, continuous readings) from one or more biblical books. Thus, one chapter of each Testament might be read in Sunday worship. (*See* LECTIO CONTINUA.) A more complex structure (called *lectio selecta*, or selected readings) organizes the lections for worship around a theme. Most typically, lectionary themes are drawn from the calendar of the Christian Year, in which the Lord's Day (Sunday) is given priority within an annual framework.

B. The Form of the Christian Year

The weekly Lord's Days are organized around three complexes of time by means of which we remember the full saving work of Christ from creation and before to final consummation and beyond.

1. Easter

The Great Fifty Days from Easter through the Day of Pentecost together with its preparatory time of Lent, from Ash Wednesday through the Great Vigil on Easter Eve.

2. Christmas

From Christmas Eve/Day through Epiphany together with its preparatory time of Advent, from the fourth Sunday prior to December 25 to Christmas Eve.

3. Ordinary Time

The periods between the Epiphany (January 6, or the first Sunday in January) and Ash Wednesday, and between Pentecost Sunday and Advent 1. The usual designation of these two periods is not meant to suggest that only unexciting events should be expected to occur. Far from it, since every Sunday is a feast of the Lord's victory over sin and death. *Ordinary* here refers to the ordinal numbers, such that these Sundays are counted as the first/second/third, and so on Sunday after Epiphany or after Pentecost.

A fourth complex of time, the sanctoral cycle, is an independent overlay of days (usually weekdays) in commemoration of the saints. For example, December 26 is given to St. Stephen, the first martyr; December 27 to John the Beloved Disciple; and December 28 commemorates the infants of Bethlehem slaughtered by Herod.

C. Readings in Relation to Calendrical Occasions

At Easter the thematic lections can be drawn from the concluding chapters of the four Gospels, the proclamations of the resurrection in the book of Acts, Paul's discussion of resurrection in 1 Cor 15, and parts of Jer 31, for example. At Christmas, portions of the opening chapters of Matthew and/or Luke can be read along with pertinent verses from Isaiah; and so on.

The Christian Year is a sequence of observances whereby the fullness of the gospel is intended to be annually proclaimed with thanksgiving. Theologically, the complexes of the year begin at the Great Vigil of Easter, for if Jesus is not proclaimed as crucified and risen, then there is no basis for a christocentric year. But formally, in terms of church law and practice, the year begins on Advent 1 (the fourth Sunday before December 25), which looks both backward into history and forward to the eschaton. However, in popular culture the year begins with Christmas, the dating of which, through custom and common practice, may deviate greatly from the church's formal Twelve Days (December 25 to January 6).

D. Concerning Current Three-Year Lectionaries

The Roman lectionary from Trent onward provided only Letter and Gospel readings for each occasion across a single year. Until recently, this pattern was followed also by many Protestant groups that used a thematic lectionary. Vatican II noted the deficiencies of this pattern and in its Constitution on the Sacred Liturgy (paragraph 51) decreed that "the treasures of the Bible are to be opened up more lavishly so that a richer fare may be provided for the faithful at the table of God's Word." An international Vatican commission put together a comprehensive Lectionary for Mass that was spread across three years, with readings from both Testaments. In the light of this, Protestants quickly sensed the anemia of their one-year lectionaries. The *Presbyterian Worshipbook* (1970) adapted the Roman lectionary. Lutherans, Episcopalians, and others followed suit, thereby creating a bewildering array of variants with a common ancestry. The confusion gave rise to the publication in 1983 of the *Common Lectionary*, which sought to lessen the variants but also to answer objections to its predecessors, particularly concerning the use of the OT. In 1992 another consensus version was published under the title *Revised Common Lectionary* (*RCL*), described below.

At this writing (2008) no further alterations are scheduled despite the fact that the term common does not yet mean "universally agreed upon." Some of the difficulty has to do with the sequence of official denominational liturgy books vis-à-vis lectionary versions. Having revised their worship manuals after the content of the *RCL* was known, United Methodists and Presbyterians, among others, have officially adopted the *RCL*. Some Episcopalians follow the *RCL* also, but others prefer to stay with the Book of Common Prayer lectionary version until such time as it is formally updated. The passage of time will, no doubt, bring further change. But because the *RCL* is used widely, if not universally, it is the focus of discussion for the remainder of this article.

E. The Design of the *Revised Common Lectionary*

Before considering how to use the lectionary within the calendar, it is necessary to know how the *RCL* is designed. Readings begin on the fourth Sunday prior to December 25; any Advent whose year is divisible by 3 (2007, 2010, etc.) begins as Year A, which focuses on Matthew's Gospel. Mark and Luke are used in Years B and C, respectively. John is spread across all years, especially during the season of Easter. John also fills out the year of the shortest Synoptic, Mark.

Exceptions to this general design occur at times when the Gospel for the year has little material related to a particular occasion. For example, Mark's lack of a nativity narrative dictates the use of other Gospels during Christmas, Year B. Always a psalm portion and two other readings are specified; readings from the Apocrypha are used as thematically appropriate, with canonical alternatives provided for the traditions that do not use these books.

In the *RCL*, the principles of lectio selecta are followed throughout the Easter and Christmas complexes. To illustrate the relation of lections to liturgical seasons: on an Advent Sunday all readings for the day may share the motif of patient waiting, while on a Lenten Sunday all may deal with covenant faithfulness. The unifying theme may well control not only the sermon's focus but also the selection of music, prayers, and other liturgical elements for the day.

On the counted Sundays of Ordinary Time, the *RCL* reads through the assigned Gospel for that year and through various letters. For the first reading, however, an option is given. Those who prefer a consistent pattern throughout the entire year continue to follow a track in which the Gospel controls the selection of the first reading. For example, if the Gospel reading were about the healing of a person with leprosy, the first reading might be a piece of Levitical legislation about the isolation of persons so diseased, providing background to help interpret the Gospel setting. If on another Sunday Jesus was feeding the multitudes with a few barley loaves and fishes and some remained, the first reading might be the story of Elisha's overly ample multiplication of loaves (2 Kgs 4:42-44). In such an instance, there is an implied typological hermeneutic: the OT is seen as pre-figuration and the NT as fulfillment. (*See* TYPOLOGY.)

The second option is provided in response to two criticisms of earlier three-year lectionaries. (1) A number of critics questioned typological exegesis because it can suggest that the OT books have no integrity of their own and are retained primarily to fill in background for the twenty-seven books of the NT or to serve merely as a pre-figuring of what could be fulfilled only later. (2) Others complained that, typology aside, the first readings hopped around from week to week, with almost no sequential coverage given to specific books.

In response, during Ordinary Time the *RCL* provides two tracks. One, following lectio selecta, links an OT reading to the Gospel as the controlling lesson. The other track, following lectio continua, reads through a book of the Hebrew Bible week by week, independent of the Gospel reading.

On that second track there is, however, a general correlation of the first and Gospel readings, as follows: Torah selections are read during Matthew's year, reflecting the Jewishness of the first Gospel. Readings from the Prophets are found in Luke's year, emphasizing the social justice concerns of the Third Evangelist. Mark's Gospel is accompanied by the Davidic saga because, it is said, Mark is fond of the title "Son of God." Here the logic is strained, however, since Mark actually uses the phrase only in 10:47-48 and less often than in Matthew or even in Luke.

Overall, the *RCL* provides ample scriptural material for the first of the three complexes of time given above. There is no provision for the sanctoral cycle because saints' days usually fall during the week and denominational rosters of the saints vary widely, if they exist at all.

One problem of design cannot be easily solved by any three-year lectionary system. Due to the disparity in the size of the two Testaments, any such lectionary will much more amply cover the second than the first.

F. Preaching from the *Revised Common Lectionary*

Only after understanding the above design can the conscientious preacher safely craft sermons based on the lectionary. Preachers who try to transfer the unifying theme of a lectio selecta occasion to a set of lectio continua readings will become frustrated trying to identify a common motif where none was intended by lectionary framers. Indeed, such preachers can do violence to Scripture. For the sake of physicians of the soul, the opening of the physicians' Hippocratic Oath might well be altered to read: "First, do no harm to the Scriptures." But this is tricky. The Bible has a certain internal consistency, such that there may be a common theme across the day's readings even when the framers of the lectionary intended none. If so, the preacher may be well advised to take advantage of it homiletically.

In general, however, during Ordinary Time the lectionary preacher will need to ask: Do I want to preach my way through this year's Gospel? Or through the letters? Do I instead want to preach from the Hebrew readings—and if so, which of the two tracks? Or do I want to preach from the Psalms? (Often the psalter is overlooked by preachers, who wrongly tend to view it as a set of prayers and acts of praise that hold no homiletical treasure.) Or the preacher will ask, Do I want to hop around from one Sunday to the next according to my own preference, with no implied continuity from week to week? Finally: What are the advantages and drawbacks of each approach in relation to the life and growth of this congregation at this time? How these questions are answered can reveal whether a particular preacher sees the lectionary as a suggestion box to be dipped into on occasion or as a sustained, serious study of Scripture.

G. Practical and Pastoral Considerations

1. Comprehensive or Limited Coverage?

In some denominations, full use of the prevailing lectionary is mandated so that all assigned passages are to be read aloud on each occasion. Where this is not the case, should worship planners jettison some of the readings due to time constraints or congregational sentiment against "having to listen to too much Bible"? If the answer is yes, great care should be taken to see that across time the congregation is given a well-balanced diet of Scripture from both Testaments.

Where time is ample and when no objections to long readings are raised, but when the pastor intends to preach on only one of the day's lections, should the others be read nevertheless? In general, yes, because biblical illiteracy is rampant. If we cannot count on the Bible being read at home, it may be prudent to read it amply in church, even it if is not to be preached upon. But here is a caveat: many passages require careful interpretation if gross misunderstanding is to be avoided. When a difficult passage appears and the preacher does not intend to address the issue, it may be well to omit the public reading until an occasion on which full interpretive attention can be given.

2. Common Objections to Lectionary Preaching

Two objections to lectionary preaching deserve serious comment. First the common query: But what do I do with the lectionary when some crisis arises that must be addressed? Behind this question lurks the suspicion that the Bible really does not have much to do with our daily lives and so is apt to fail us in times of emergency. The answer? Assuming your denomination allows this (some do not), jettison the lectionary for a particular occasion. But look at it very carefully before doing so, for you are likely to discover it addresses precisely the root issues of calamity, human sin and suffering, and divine faithfulness in the time of need.

A case in point: on the Sunday following 9/11/01 the first *RCL* reading was Jer 4:11-12, 22-28, with its haunting words: "I looked, and lo, the fruitful land was a desert, / and all its cities were laid in ruins / before the Lord." And Ps 14 cried out: "O that deliverance . . . would come from Zion! / When the Lord restores the fortunes of [the] people, / Jacob will rejoice." On what better texts could one base a sermon of lament and yet of hope grounded in divine mercy?

The second query comes from the pastor who says, "I would love to explore the riches of the lectionary, but my congregation would have a fit. They are leery of 'high church' practices, such as assigned Scripture readings or the observance of Lent." First, if the congregation uses the International Lesson Series for adult study, it may be pointed out that this is, in fact, a lectionary—biblical readings systematically assigned to give maximum coverage to the canon over several years. Hardly high church stuff! Second, in the weeks before Easter, it is possible to preach on *RCL* passages without ever referring to Lent or related practices that may be viewed with disdain. Lectionaries are simply biblical citations linked to (but somewhat detachable from) calendars, so it is even possible to preach on the readings for the Sunday of the Lord's Baptism in August rather than January if that alleviates free church anxiety but helps the pastor to take advantage of lectionary-based interpretive resources and breadth of biblical coverage.

3. Preparation by All Who Lead Worship and Related Activities

An intentional use of the lectionary obviously allows advance planning not only by preachers but also by church musicians and other leaders of the liturgy. Publishers of periodicals, books, and music often schedule releases to coincide with the lectionary (e.g., a commentary on Luke published several months before the beginning of Year C; a choral setting of certain psalms used in Year B; and so on). A number of Sunday school curricula for both children and adults also are lectionary-based. A multifaceted approach to the Bible within a given parish can provide greater depth and concentration than the scattershot approach often used.

In many locales, ecumenical lectionary study groups have sprung up. Typically, preachers meet for breakfast on Tuesday mornings; the goal is not to produce a sermon written by committee, but to share ideas and resources that aid the individual preachers as they plan their respective sermons throughout the rest of the week. Musicians can similarly share resources, though much farther in advance than preachers are likely to do, in order to accommodate the rehearsal process.

4. Sustaining Congregational Interaction with the Lections

It has become common to announce the lectionary readings for the coming Sunday and to urge those present to study them before returning. Commendable as this seems, it has drawbacks. People who have neglected to do their homework may simply not attend the following Sunday. Those who have done the reading may have decided which passage they want the preacher to address and may be disappointed if a different option is chosen. Or they may firmly decide what a particular passage means and be unreceptive to the preacher who thinks it means something else.

Biblical ignorance is such that we are not far removed from the Reformation situation when printed Bibles were first becoming available and literacy was on the rise. At that time a collect was written as a guide to the appropriate interaction between congregation and lections. This prayer provides an alternative to the "read your homework before you come to church" approach:

Blessed Lord, who hast caused all holy Scriptures to be written for our learning: Grant that we may in such wise hear them, read, mark, learn, and inwardly digest them; that we may embrace and ever hold fast the blessed hope of everlasting life, which thou has given us in our Savior Jesus Christ; who liveth and reigneth with thee and the Holy Spirit, one God, for ever and ever. Amen. (*Book of Common Prayer* 1990, 236)

For our purposes, the force is in that carefully constructed sequence of verbs:

1. Hear the Scriptures as they are read aloud in the service of worship and as they are interpreted in the sermon.
2. Read at home what was read to you in the church, recalling the pastor's application for our time.
3. Mark; take due notice of the meanings set forth by the preacher, underlining in your Bible key phrases or verses highlighted in what you heard.
4. Learn some of what you have underlined, that is, by memorization, so that it is an always accessible resource for you.
5. Inwardly digest what you have heard, read, marked, and learned, not for the sake of impressing others with your knowledge but for the sake of growing in faith and hope.

This pattern seems as appropriate now as it was at the Reformation. It is a means of carrying the force of the Lord's Day service into the following week as the people ponder what they have heard on Sunday and thus grow in grace daily. *See* LECTIO CONTINUA; LONG-RANGE SERMON PLANNIING.

Bibliography: Episcopal Church. *Book of Common Prayer.* (1990); Reginald Fuller. *Preaching the Lectionary.* (1984); Laurence Hull Stookey. *Calendar: Christ's Time for the Church.* (1996); Fritz West. *Scripture and Memory: The Ecumenical Hermeneutic of the Three-Year Lectionaries.* (1997).

RADIO
Thomas G. Long

Almost from the beginning of commercial radio, there has been preaching on the airwaves. In the United States, the first commercial radio station to be established was KDKA in Pittsburgh, Pennsylvania, which began broadcasting in November 1920. People for a thousand miles in every direction from Pittsburgh listened on headphones via homemade crystal radio sets. The first sermon ever broadcast in America, and perhaps in the world, was in January 1921, when KDKA, then three months old, carried live the Sunday service of Pittsburgh's Calvary Episcopal Church.

Struggle for Dominance of the Airwaves

The fact that the first sermon broadcast on the radio in the United States was from an established mainline church is of no small consequence. For nearly a generation, preachers from the traditional Protestant churches—Episcopal, Lutheran, Congregational, Presbyterian, American Baptist, and Methodist—dominated religious radio. By the late 1920s, radio networks were being formed in the U.S., and the first of these, the National Broadcasting Corporation (NBC), as a part of its public service obligations, set aside time free of charge for religious broadcasting. Although NBC made room for Roman Catholic and Jewish programming, Protestants were the most eager to use radio as a vehicle for preaching and evangelization. NBC sought Protestant programming help from the Federal Council of Churches of Christ (later the National Council of Churches). The Federal Communications Commission (FCC) set up the Department of Religious Radio, which established several programs that included preaching, most notably the *National Radio Pulpit*, featuring such well-known Protestant preachers as Methodist Ralph Sockman and American Baptist Harry Emerson Fosdick.

Excluded from this programming, of course, were the independent, evangelical, and fundamentalist churches and their preachers, an increasingly significant force in American religious life. As a result, from the early 1920s until World War II, a progressively contentious battle waged between the mainline churches and the independent churches for control of the airwaves, a struggle that gradually tilted toward the independents. (*See* EVANGELISTIC PREACHING.)

The major radio networks viewed religion as a part of the general public good and desired to carry non-controversial religious programming that would appeal to broad, non-sectarian instincts. The Federal Radio Commission, precursor to the FCC, agreed, and made it clear that, as a part of its protection of the public ownership of the airwaves, the renewal of the licenses of radio stations depended in part upon their being well rounded in regard to religious programming.

The only recourse for the independent churches was to work around the networks and against the will of the Federal Radio Commission by starting their own radio stations and by purchasing time on other independent, mom-and-pop radio stations. By the mid-1920s, 10 percent of all radio stations in the United States were owned by churches, and many of these stations were vehicles for the sermons of fundamentalist and evangelical preachers. These preachers, and the stations on which they appeared, were often supported by contributions from their listeners, which meant that their messages and styles were more in tune with the tastes and beliefs of the broad swath of American Christians than were the broad, generalized sermons of the network-sanctioned preachers. For example, the fiery Pentecostal evangelist Aimee Semple McPherson, who in 1924 became the first woman ever to preach a sermon on the radio, founded her own station, KFSG (Kall Four Square Gospel), in her Los Angeles church. Because of radio skipping, the capacity of AM radio signals to travel long distances at night, McPherson's sermons were heard by thousands of loyal listeners as far away as New Jersey and Australia. Her popularity on the radio helped to draw hundreds of thousands of people to the services in her church, creating massive traffic jams.

The popularity of conservative, independent preaching on the radio garnered both the attention and the alarm of the mainline denominations. Liberal Protestant clergyman Harry Emerson Fosdick named the unease when he said, "Sunday mornings the air will be full of sermons [but] whose sermons will be on the air? It is needless to name those representing a type of Christianity which you and I do not believe in. Ought we to leave the air to their monopoly? I do not believe we should" (Miller 1985, 384).

By the mid-1940s, the battle between mainliners and independents had settled into an uneasy truce: mainline preachers were featured on the major radio networks, and more fundamentalist preachers were featured on the independent radio stations, sometimes stitching together a string of independent stations to create homemade networks.

Programming for Radioland

In the beginning, most preaching on the radio occurred in live broadcasts of services of worship. Listeners would, in effect, overhear what was happening in sanctuaries. It was not long, though, before innovative ministers would recognize that radio as a medium possessed its own untapped communication potential and began to craft sermons for the radio audience.

Perhaps the first to take advantage of this potential was Father Charles Coughlin, a Roman Catholic priest whose parish was in the suburbs of Detroit. Beginning with a Christian radio program for children, Father Coughlin soon realized that his preaching style was made for radio. In the late 1920s, instead of broadcasting services from his church, he began to deliver made-for-radio addresses and sermons that attracted a wide following. His blend of the gospel and a concern for the welfare of workers struck a respondent chord in depression-era America, and by 1930 Coughlin had ten million listeners on the CBS network and received more than eighty thousand letters a week, more than anyone else in the United States, including President Franklin Roosevelt. Part of his appeal was his voice, which seemed crafted for radio listening. Writer Wallace Stegner described it as a "voice of such mellow richness, such manly, heart-warming confidential intimacy, such emotional and ingratiating charm, that anyone tuning past it almost automatically returned to hear it again" (Warren 1996, 25).

Coughlin's sermons became increasingly political, indeed fascist and anti-Semitic. CBS canceled his program in 1931 for being too political, but he pieced together a pastiche of twenty-six independent radio stations and remained on the air. His pro-Nazi views, however, caused his popularity to plummet in the late 1930s. In 1939, the National Association of Broadcasters adopted a strict code of practices for U.S. radio stations that placed prohibitions on the sale of radio time to people with offensive and controversial political views, a policy clearly aimed at Coughlin. In 1942, Coughlin's ecclesiastical superiors ordered him to cease his broadcasts, and today he is remembered as "the father of hate radio."

But Coughlin's genius in using the medium of radio endured. In October 1937, the evangelist Charles Fuller began the *Old Fashioned Revival Hour*, which was a program fashioned explicitly for radio. The last thirty minutes of the hour-long program featured Fuller's radio sermons, which were simple and conversational. Unlike sermons broadcast from live worship services, Fuller's sermons made full use of the intimacy of radio by speaking to listeners one-to-one. Though a fundamentalist, Fuller mainly avoided the harsh language of sin and judgment, preaching a positive message of God's mercies and blessings, and he referred to his listeners in casual and personal terms as "fellow strangers and pilgrims." *The Old Fashioned Revival Hour* drew millions of listeners and stayed on the air until 1968, the year of Fuller's death.

In England during the 1940s, C. S. Lewis was experimenting with a different style of radio preaching, presenting conversational and educational messages on the BBC (eventually collected and published in the 1950s as *Mere Christianity*). In the U.S. in the 1960s, Edmund Steimle, a professor of preaching at Union Theological Seminary in New York, began to preach on the Lutheran series of *The Protestant Hour*, a radio program broadcast on several hundred stations and sponsored by four mainline denominations. He called his presentations "conversations" rather than sermons, indicating his goal of speaking personally and intimately to listeners.

In a way, radio preaching had discovered the power of marketing and communication strategy. As religious cultural historian Tona Hangen has observed, "Just as radio advertisements were designed to awaken consumers' unrecognized desires ('I need a new Buick!'), radio evangelism stimulated people's unspoken fears and longings ('I *am* lonely, I *do* need peace . . .)" (2002, 152).

Radio Preaching Today

Other than the broadcasts of weekly worship services on local stations, there is little mainline preaching on the radio today. *The Protestant Hour*, renamed *Day 1*, continues in a new, sleek format with conversational interviews with the preachers, and a few denominationally based programs continue to be broadcast, but the National Radio Pulpit and similar traditionally Protestant venues have long since ceased. There is still much preaching done by fundamentalists and evangelicals on the radio, especially on the smaller independent and Christian stations, and on shortwave, evangelistic programs are broadcast in a variety of languages around the world. But most of the evangelical world has invested its communicational energies in TELEVISION and in the newer Christian radio formats, which emphasize music, softer messages, and less traditional preaching.

Bibliography: Tona J. Hangen. *Redeeming the Dial: Radio, Religion, and Popular Culture in America.* (2002); Robert H. Lochte. *Christian Radio: The Growth of a Mainstream Broadcasting Force.* (2006); Robert Moats Miller. *Harry Emerson Fosdick: Preacher, Pastor, Prophet.* (1985); Quentin J. Schultze. *Christianity and the Mass Media in America: Toward a Democratic Accommodation.* (2003); Donald I. Warren. *Radio Priest.* (1996).

REVIVALS
James A. Noel

This article discusses the phenomenon of revival from several different and interwoven angles. It focuses on revival as it appeared in the historical context of Christianity while regarding it also as a somewhat universal phenomenon common to all religions and cultures. Hence, revival can be discussed historically, sociologically, psychologically, biblically/theologically, and homiletically. However, the study of this phenomenon may not be as straightforward as it appears on the surface. For one thing, the evaluation of revival is inescapably value-laden because the very nature of revival involves a judgment about what in the society or person requires change, repair, or rehabilitation. In addition, revival tends to assume that whatever outcomes are deemed desirable can be effected through the means of revival. For example, two similarly situated congregations can have the same concern about drug addiction in the community, but one may address the issue through a revival and the other through a drug treatment program. In a case with which I am familiar the former strategy proved more effective; yet the success of the revival in question was not due to the theological factor

alone. It would not be wise to generalize from one anecdote. We should also note how revival involves interrogating the relationship between individual piety and social issues. Among other things, Jonathan Edwards was trying to do this in his *Religious Affections.* The historian does this retrospectively in trying to assess the impact that past revivals have had on particular societies.

Revival is built into the nature of religion itself and occurs when a significant number of a given religion's adherents sense the need to overcome the dichotomy between the ideal and the actual in their religious or social life. Thus, in Christianity revivals must be placed within a long historical trajectory. It is important to connect them to the prophetic admonitions in the OT beginning with Moses' receiving of the Law in Exodus and to all subsequent prophetic denunciations of faithlessness (*see* PROPHETIC PREACHING). King Josiah (620 BCE; 2 Kgs 22–23), though not a prophet, is an exemplary OT reformer or revivalist. It is easy to see, then, that revivalist preaching has a plethora of OT texts at its disposal. Many are texts that explicitly call for reform and repentance. Indeed, a preacher can be oblivious to the necessity for revival only through a very selective type of biblical reading. In the NT, the Synoptics describe Jesus beginning his ministry after undergoing baptism by John the Baptist. Jesus then preaches repentance after a period of testing in the wilderness. In John's Gospel, Jesus explains the necessity of being born again to Nicodemus. Acts describes the church's beginning as a mode of revival and renewal. Paul's letters admonish his congregations to place themselves under the power of the Spirit rather than that of sin, while acknowledging that this is never completely accomplished prior to the eschaton.

Thus, revivals originate in the very core of the biblical message. Yet, as alluded to above, the criteria determining what is personally, sociologically, politically, and historically desirable in revival vary. Here I am referring broadly to the differences between so-called liberal and conservative Christians. Revival can lend itself equally well to conservative/reactionary or liberal/progressive tendencies in church and society. Some church historians have limited our understanding of revivals by focusing only on certain events. The First and Second Great Awakenings in the late 18th and early to mid-19th cent. that invoke the names of Jonathan Edwards, George Whitefield, and later, Charles Finney get attention. Some scholars have added to the First and Second Great Awakenings a third Awakening that occurred between the late nineteenth century and early 20th centuries and a Fourth Awakening that began in the 1960s and may still be underway. But where do we place such historically controversial figures as Nat Turner, Gabriel Prosser, Denmark Vesey, and Tecumseh? Standard historical treatment often excludes the revival-related occurrences of slave rebellions in the United States and the Caribbean. It also excludes the pan-Native American rebellion of Tecumseh whose contours conform to any understanding of revival. Thus, in American religious history textbooks, by the time we get to the 1960s and Martin Luther King Jr. is mentioned, his Baptist church connection is almost incidental to the movement he led. The problem is that civil rights history is not placed in continuity with the history of African American revivalism—a history that is synonymous with African American protest. (See GENDER, RACE, AND ETHNICITY.) Both Euro-American and African American denominations should take note here.

In the United States there are numerous congregations wherein the tradition has been established of conducting yearly revivals that entail evening worship services conducted over three to four consecutive days by a guest evangelist. As implied in the name, revivals are aimed at facilitating spiritual renewal in the host congregation's life. In addition, salvation is offered for the visitors present who have never accepted Jesus the Christ as their Lord and Savior. Thus, there is a very explicit Arminian theological framework within which revival operates and which governs both the style and the content of the preaching conducted in this setting. Consequently, some preachers and some congregations are more suited for conducting revivals than others. Just as Niebuhr once made a correlation between social class and denominational affiliation, it might be possible to make a correlation between theological orientation and preaching style with revivalist worship.

It will be helpful at this point to switch between two different but related terms: *revivals* and *revivalist worship*. The latter term is used to refer to regularly scheduled worship services that incorporate or exhibit prominent features of the classic revival. For example, let us think of an inner-city congregation that has a significant number of people who have come off the streets to attend Sunday worship

service. The preacher may do an altar call every Sunday in which he or she invites people who wish to accept Jesus the Christ as their Lord and Savior to come forward. Or the preacher may invite people to come forward who need special prayer and so on. In these examples, the mix of theological, sociological, existential, and contextual factors that create a sense of urgency for revivals and revivalist worship services is apparent. This is by no means meant to imply that we can reduce the phenomenon of revivals and revivalist worship to socio-economic causes. Some congregations may routinely conduct revivalist worship services due to factors that are more theological than sociological.

We might ask not only how thorough a transformation one expects from a revival but also at what level it is expected to operate. In other words, is revival intended to transform the individual, the church, society, or all of these? Niebuhr's argument in *Moral Man, Immoral Society* and Karl Barth's neo-orthodox critique of liberalism make any response to this question problematic. Nevertheless, it is safe to say that the focus of most revivals is on the individual and the restoration of that individual's relationship with God vertically conceived. Many congregations and denominations struggle but have not yet discovered how to programmatically and organically connect such essential features of Christianity as personal spirituality and social justice. Sadly, the technique of revivalist preaching has been used of late most successfully in a distorted form by the mega-church peddlers of the prosperity gospel. These preachers tend to connect conversion with the guarantee of material wealth while leaving unaddressed the inequities of the political economy. For reasons far too lengthy and complicated to explain here, we have reached a juncture in the church's history when prophetic preaching does not lend itself to revivalist preaching and revivalist preaching does not lend itself to prophetic preaching. If we are to move beyond this morass, homileticians will have to assume the mantle of the prophets. Revivalist preaching will have to be emphasized in a way that conceives it as having less to do with technique and style and more with transformative oratory. Such preaching articulates truth to the powers and principalities of injustice where the oppressed are gathered in protest—for example, Martin Luther King Jr.'s sermons "I Have a Dream" in Washington, D.C.; "Time to Break Silence" at Riverside Church in New York City; and

"I've Seen the Promised Land" in Memphis. These sermons still retain their capacity to revive, inspire, and recommit lives to the cause of God's kingdom and should be classed as revivalist preaching to clarify our understanding of its purpose within the Judeo-Christian heritage of Western culture.

Defining revival is as difficult as defining religion because it pertains to the very essence of Christianity—repentance and conversion. This individual and corporate event must be reenacted repeatedly if the faith is to retain its vitality. The difficulty we face today is how to avoid reducing revival to something that is purely subjective and lacking ethical efficacy on the one hand or, on the other hand, imposing a priori sociological criteria on the phenomenon in such a way that eviscerates its spiritual content by coupling it to our utilitarian purposes. But if it is agreed that revival is necessary for Christianity to retain or recapture its vitality, we must revisit the question that Gilbert Tennent tactlessly asked in 1740 during the First Awakening in his sermon "The Danger of an Unconverted Ministry." Tennent asked, "Is a dead Man fit to bring others to Life?" If revival is advocated, is it because it is something the church does routinely or because some grave prognosis has been made about its moral and spiritual condition? See EVANGELISTIC PREACHING; MISSIONAL PREACHING.

Bibliography: Richard Carwardine. Transatlantic Revivalism: Popular Evangelism in Britain and America, 1790–1865. (1978); Michael J. McClymond, ed. Embodying the Spirit: New Perspectives on North American Revivalism. (2004); William G. McLoughlin. Revivals, Awakenings and Reform. (1978); Iain H. Murray. Revival and Revivalism: The Making and Marring of American Evangelicalism, 1750–1858. (1994); Timothy L. Smith. Revivalism and Social Reform: American Protestantism on the Eve of the Civil War. (2004); Gayraud Wilmore. Black Religion and Black Radicalism. (1998).

SOCIAL JUSTICE NETWORKS
Christine M. Smith

Social justice networks can be community organizations, national organizations, cross-cultural educational experiences, homeless shelters, solidarity movements, denominational committees and structures, local church food banks, and battered women's shelters. There are always more than we can name. Across lines of extensive diversity, these organizations and community expressions are all rooted in a desire to alleviate human suffering, to express social justice commitments in practical and concrete ways, and to offer resources to individuals and institutions that will enable greater social justice work to be done in our world.

The Vision of Social Justice Networks

For individual churches that are concerned about social justice, it is essential for preachers to make connections with social justice networks with the hope that these connections will help keep a religious community socially aware and informed, and offer the possibility that united efforts to respond to human suffering and injustice can often be more effective than isolated, individual responses. For churches less aware of social issues of injustice, connecting to networks of people actively working on justice issues can breathe new life into a religious community and its mission and work in the world. Social justice networks often have within them the prophetic voices and uncompromising visions that can help the members of our religious communities find their own prophetic voices and uncompromising visions about bringing the world closer to the reign or commonwealth of God that was at the heart of Jesus' ministry and work, and is at the heart of Christianity. (See PROPHETIC PREACHING.)

Resources, Spiritual and Religious Transformation, Solidarity

Social justice networks make an impact on the lives of individuals and communities of faith in many significant ways. The following three considerations give a sense of the importance of this work:

1. People working within social justice networks are clear that a part of their work is to help get persons connected to services and resources to sustain life, or to enable life to be more humane and just. For preachers whose congregations include people who need the services offered by these groups and organizations, connecting to social justice networks becomes a part of what is ethically and pastorally required of relevant preaching. As pastors and preachers grow to fully understand the communities they serve, they are sometimes surprised to discover that there are people in most every context

who need social justice resources that are not provided by the church. There are, for example, battered women, children, and men in every congregation who do not know how to stop the violence and change their personal and familial realities. Marie Fortune and the FaithTrust Institute, founded in 1977, are invaluable resources for preachers concerning this issue. Similarly, there may be lesbian/gay/bisexual/transgendered people in every congregation and/or family members of this community who do not have the resources to deal with society's marginalization and oppression. The Human Rights Campaign nationally, or a queer youth support center such as District 202 in Minneapolis, Minnesota, provides useful resources for preachers. Preachers might find the new online "Out in Scripture" project of the Human Rights Campaign helpful in weekly lectionary preaching. (See LECTIONARY AND THE CHRISTIAN YEAR.) And of course, there are people who are unemployed, people who are homeless, people who suffer from mental illness, and people who are hungry within our churches and communities. The Open Door Community in Atlanta has been doing prophetic work around the issue of homelessness for years, and the National Alliance on Mental Illness, founded in 1996, has been educating a large public about mental health issues. To be a responsible and faithful preacher/pastor, one needs to know the social justice networks in the church and community that can help people navigate the difficult and painful realities of their lives, and open to them the concrete possibility of leading new and transformed lives.

2. People working within social justice networks are clear that the society at large is in need of social and systemic transformation. Often these networks and community organizations—including the most radical arms of the Christian church—have helped raise and change the consciousness of our local communities, our nation, and our world. The civil rights movement that changed our nation began as a series of social justice networks struggling against white racism; these networks eventually galvanized. The battered women's movement started out as countless local battered women's shelters, educational experiences, and intervention programs; with time it became a movement that has changed our nation's consciousness about violence in general and violence against women in particular. When preachers help congregations honor and

connect to social justice networks, it behooves us to remember that often secular social justice networks have radicalized our religious communities as to the pervasive reality of social, systemic oppression. (See GENDER, RACE, AND ETHNICITY.) Social justice preaching is difficult work for preachers and religious communities, for in forging deep connections with social justice networks, the church will often have to confront the theology, complacency, and ecclesiastical powers that have contributed in some instances to the very injustices these networks seek to eradicate. There are good reasons, for example, that the battered women's movement has been suspicious of Christian clergy; instead of pastors enabling women to get connected to the networks that would help them stop the violence, many have encouraged them to return to abusive marriages in the name of self-sacrifice and the covenant of marriage. Unfortunately, this list of similar actions by pastors and preachers is a long one. Even though the work of social justice is difficult, and sometimes asks preachers and religious communities to change, making intentional connections with all kinds of social justice networks can literally revitalize the life of a congregation and send it down a path of passionate activism and mission that it could not have otherwise imagined. One of the important impacts, then, that social justice networks can be seen to have on preaching is in the area of social, spiritual, and religious transformation.

3. People working within social justice networks are clear that their work is about solidarity. Social justice networks are made up of people who are trying to move across social, economic, ethnic, age, ability, and national and international barriers that keep people separated from one another and isolated in their experiences of injustice and oppression. Often this work is about trying to build bridges across great human differences. For many of our churches in which people have layers of privilege, this work will involve trying to create ongoing relationships of solidarity with people we ourselves directly oppress. One of the most profound networks working at this level of solidarity involves community educational organizations, grassroots church groups, and community solidarity groups that insist that people of privilege in our churches need to immerse their lives in the lives of poor people. Pastors who travel to Guatemala, Chiapas, Palestine, Colombia, the Philippines, and countless other places both nationally and internationally come back

with their faith, theology, and lives changed. In recent years, seminarians returning from cross-cultural immersion trips have engaged their communities of faith. One school now holds silent auctions to fund projects in Chiapas and Guatemala. The seminarians preach sermons about solidarity and engage congregations with concrete stories and pictures that have influenced whole faith communities to build relationships of solidarity. They have invited communities of faith and individual families to start buying fair trade coffee and fair trade gifts. They have preached in ways that help privileged people from the United States realize their unintentional complicity in the oppression of others, and they have awakened the compassion, global awareness, and humility that are key ingredients to solidarity with poor people of our world. So let there be no doubt that social justice networks both create and cultivate a profound and holy solidarity.

Social justice networks provide resources for the dignity and honor of people's lives, and literally enable people to live instead of die. Social justice networks challenge our churches to a deeper awareness of every form of oppression that dehumanizes people and exploits the earth. Social justice networks help people move from demonizing, trivializing, and exploiting other people's lives, into fragile, holy alliances and solidarity with those same people. A whole world of social justice networks is out there if preachers only have the theological vision, the pastoral discipline, and the faithful courage to utilize, support, and be changed by them. *See* SOCIAL JUSTICE.

Bibliography: The FaithTrust Institute. http://www.faithtrustinstitute.org; The Human Rights Campaign. http://www.hrc.org; The National Alliance on Mental Illness. http://www.nami.org; The Open Door Community. http://www.opendoorcommunity.org; The National Alliance to End Sexual Violence. http://www.naesv.org.

TECHNOLOGY
Quentin J. Schultze

There seems to be little interest, within or beyond the church, in slowing down the pace of technological development. As a result, our ethical and theological understandings almost invariably lag behind the pace of our technological deployment. This lag is obvious in

fields such as genetic engineering and biotechnology, where the emerging ethical dilemmas are particularly baffling. But the lag also becomes clear in discussions about worship, including preaching. Should worship be mediated with high-tech devices? Should preaching make use of new projection technologies, from Power-Point® slides to moving-image DVDs?

A. The World Context for Technology
B. The Twofold Nature of Technology
C. The "Yes, But" of Technological Adoption
D. The Overselling of Technology
E. Putting Purpose before Technology in Preaching
F. The Importance of Congregational Focus During Worship
G. The Preacher as Technological Critic

A. The World Context for Technology

The notion that we live in a high-tech world both overstates and understates reality. Most of the world does not have access to the technologies that many of us take for granted, such as computers, the Internet, and even landline telephones.

By contrast, those of us in the developed world are increasingly dependent upon digital technologies, especially communication systems such as cell phones, e-mail, CDs and DVDs, and the World Wide Web. We are so wedded to computer-based technologies, and the spread of these new technologies is so rapid, that we can hardly make sense of our evolving circumstances. We in the high-tech parts of the world are becoming technological people immersed in technological cultures, where much of our everyday interaction is mediated by computerized devices.

B. The Twofold Nature of Technology

Discussions about using technology faithfully require a basic understanding of the twofold nature of technology. All technologies are both physical things and social practices, including the social values that explicitly or implicitly guide humans' use of the things (sometimes called devices if they are relatively complex). In this perspective, God was the first technologist in the sense that God used vocal practices to create "good" things on earth. The Greek word technē originally meant poetic or, more specifically, linguistic practice.

Worship in general and preaching in particular have always relied upon technological things. For instance, worship requires pastors and other congregants to communicate with things such as larynxes, ears, eyes, books, and sometimes audio amplifiers.

Moreover, these worship-useful things require practices (or techniques) in order for people to employ them. Such social practices are never neutral, since they are based on value-laden purposes and goals, such as entertaining, informing, persuading, and celebrating. The many combinations of devices and techniques, along with the underlying values that direct the techniques, make it difficult to practice technological faithfulness.

Pastors and other worship leaders learn, through unreflective imitation and reflective study, which technological things to use and how to employ them. They might use relatively low-tech practices such as lighting candles or playing recorders, or high-tech practices such as projecting sermon notes and Bible verses on larger screens. Preparing and delivering sermons need not be extremely high-tech, although online research and computerized word processing are extremely common. Some churches employ high-tech devices such as video projectors, PowerPoint® lyrical projections, and musical synthesizers, whereas others use relatively low-tech banners, simple audio amplification, printed hymnbooks, and a cappella singing.

C. The "Yes, But" of Technological Adoption

Throughout history, congregations and Christian traditions have responded variously to the invention of new communication technologies such as the printing press and the video projector. Some have embraced new technologies wholeheartedly, with little discernment or fear. Others have tried to reject novel devices outright, fearing their worldly influence. Yet others have taken a middle ground, slowly and carefully adapting new technologies in tune with good purposes and reasonable outcomes.

Since all of the technologies that humans can use to communicate are gifts from God evident in the cultural unfolding of creation, it makes sense that churches should consider the possible benefits. Nevertheless, not all things and practices are necessarily appropriate for worship. The middle ground, then, is to proclaim a general "yes" to older and newer technologies, but to discern whether, when, and how to use them in worship.

One critically important concept in such discernment is fittingness. For example, when we employ in worship the same technologies that are used outside the church, we have to consider the social practices and underlying values that parishioners might have uncritically adopted from other, sometimes competing, contexts (*see* EXEGESIS OF THE CONGREGATION, DENOMINATION).

Congregants might approach the use of Hollywood film clips during a sermon with an entertainment, consumerist mind-set. Similarly, they might see themselves as students or business colleagues when a pastor "instructs" the congregation with outlines formatted for PowerPoint or other projection software. In some newer churches, congregational seating, architecture, lighting, and interior design are intentionally fashioned after educational, business, and especially theatrical contexts. Sermons can become lecture-like presentations, while worship imitates theatrical and movie consumption.

A second critically important concept for discernment is participation. *Communication*—based from the same root word as *communion*—is shared or, literally, "common" understanding. Communication is not the same as mere transmission, since senders and receivers might not agree on the meaning of the messages. Christians gather in worship in order to remember and believe "as one" in Jesus Christ. In order to foster communal confession and celebration, worship has to be a participatory, back-and-forth dialogue among God and God's people. Worship is not likely to be communication when congregants merely listen and watch what the worship "professionals" are saying and doing. At their best, high- and low-tech communication technologies can draw the congregation into shared, meaningful participation. Since this worship-based, participatory understanding of communication tends to be at odds with the one-way, mass-mediated, manipulative intent of so much public rhetoric in technological societies, it is incumbent upon worship planners, leaders, and pastors to keep in mind the "yes, but" necessary for fitting discernment.

D. The Overselling of Technology

Such discerning use of new technologies in worship is particularly difficult because of the triumphalistic rhetoric that often accompanies technological innovations. News media report on novel technological developments without considering whether or not previous technologies lived up to past hype. Both for-profit and nonprofit institutions are afraid of getting behind and becoming uncompetitive if they do not swiftly adopt the latest devices, especially communication technologies. Even major corporations abandon technological projects during development, while many completed projects fail to live up to organizational expectations.

Various church consultants, worship magazines, and trade books similarly promise more than new technologies can usually deliver. They imply that computers, video projectors, large screens, and enhanced sound systems will solve many church problems, such as declining adult member attendance, youth indifference, and ineffective community evangelism. Used well, some technologies might help a congregation solve such problems, but rarely are there easy technological fixes for complicated issues that actually require much prayer, discernment, study, and conversation across a congregation.

Our response to triumphalistic rhetoric, whether coming from within or outside the congregation, should be tempered by the fact that church life is a highly contextual thing. When it comes to decisions about technology in worship, one size does not fit every church on all occasions. Each congregation needs to figure out which technologies to use, when to use them, and how to use them.

After all, some of the fastest-growing churches in the world are in low-tech areas, including parts of Africa and Latin America. The same is true for some community churches and even megachurches in North America. The idea that technology is the key to church growth, however measured, is simply false.

E. Putting Purpose before Technology in Preaching

Perhaps the biggest mistake that congregations and pastors make with respect to technology is losing track of communicative purpose. Presentational technologies should be fit to worship, not the other way around. For instance, it is essential to fit Power-Point® to the purpose of good preaching rather than allow technology to dictate those decisions.

Within the standards of good preaching (e.g., sound exegesis and clear expression contributing to authentic worship), there are many sub-purposes that high-tech devices might help a preacher fulfill. These include

1. illustrating historical or contemporary images (e.g., Holy Land sites);
2. demonstrating a practice or skill (e.g., how people practice a spiritual discipline);
3. displaying key biblical texts (e.g., primary or related texts);
4. defining an important term or phrase (e.g., a Greek or Hebrew concept);
5. following an outline (e.g., each of three main points);
6. showing congregational faithfulness in action (e.g., youth service projects);
7. exemplifying cultural attitudes and trends (e.g., showing and commenting upon clips from popular movies);
8. encouraging focused, collective reading of creeds or confessional statements.

The issue is whether or not any of these specific sub-purposes are best met with a specific communication technology. A particular skill or practice might be better demonstrated in person by the pastor or another member of the church. Definitions and outlines can be printed and handed out to all worship participants, who can then make notes on them and take them home for reference and distribute copies to others. Presumably, creeds and confessions or other church-unifying documents are already available in printed form.

The main medium in all preaching is the preacher. So the first question to ask is whether the preacher can himself or herself accomplish any of these sub-purposes well. For instance, if the preacher can describe a scene in a Hollywood film, there might not be a reason to show a video clip of this scene. Similarly, some preachers use acronyms or verbally paint visual pictures to help the congregation follow and remember the main points of a sermon. St. Augustine loved to use witty sayings and alliterative expressions to render his sermon points for congregational pleasure and assent.

Much African American preaching uses rich metaphors and engaging storytelling to fulfill some of the same needs for sermon illustration, exemplification, and organization. Perhaps any excessive reliance on presentational technologies today results from pastors being inadequately trained in literary modes of communication, particularly analogy, metaphor, and narrative (RHETORICAL DEVICES). One well-selected, well-presented image can speak volumes in a sermon, but even a plethora of projected texts and images cannot satisfactorily substitute for a preacher's uncreative and inexpressive verbal presentation.

F. The Importance of Congregational Focus During Worship

Today's widespread adoption of computerized presentational technologies during preaching tends to hide a major source of confusion, namely, visual focus. For two millennia the focus was overwhelmingly on the preacher, especially the preacher's body. To listen to a sermon was to concentrate visually on the preacher's non-verbal as well as verbal delivery. In fact, the preacher was the primary medium, conveying the word of God by speaking and showing a tapestry of incarnational expression. A preacher embodied God's speech.

What should a congregation look at during a sermon—and why? Some megachurches understandably need to project the live video image of the preacher on one or more screens in order for many worshipers to see the embodied expression of God's word. But for most smaller and medium-sized churches, the visual movement back and forth between the preacher and the projected text or visual illustration can create congregational confusion. Locating the projection screen near the pastor exacerbates this confusion because the congregation is implicitly asked to look at two images at once. The lack of focus can become even worse when the projected image is never turned off or changes quickly during the sermon.

A preacher can achieve greater focus three ways. First, she or he can indicate in advance to the projectionist when a particular image should be on or off during the sermon. Second, the preacher can encourage those who design projected images to keep them simple and use them in a measured fashion rather than incessantly. Third, a preacher can ask the technologists and interior designers to place screens off to the sides rather than directly next to or over the pulpit area.

G. The Preacher as Technological Critic

The preacher must use technology wisely as part of her or his prophetic witness. In considering the problems of and potential for technological faithfulness, important themes include stewardship, communicative justice, individualism, and pride.

Since technologies are so unevenly distributed around the world, and since North Americans are especially techno-rich, a critical approach to technology should focus significantly on stewardship. Many North American congregations spend extravagantly on worship-related technologies that are used infrequently and contribute little to the overall quality of worship. Sometimes this extravagance is driven by an implicitly competitive spirit—competitive with respect to other churches and to the wider culture, especially the entertainment industry. North American churches tend to be media-rich and relationship-poor, whereas much of the Christian world is fellowship-rich and technologically poor.

In the broader society, public influence often requires media access and skill. Yet within North America as well as the rest of the world, technological "have-nots" typically lack such resources. The result is widespread communicative injustice where the "haves" gain a public voice while the "have-nots" are silenced. This discrepancy places a responsibility on preachers to speak prophetically in church and society on behalf of those who have been essentially excommunicated from public discourse. Many congregants who consume only mainstream media, particularly in the United States, might learn about communicative injustices only via their church communities.

Another important theme for preachers in technological societies is the individualism that pervades technological consumption. New technologies are extolled on the basis of the benefits that they offer the individual, such as greater personal choice and increased privacy in consumption. The domestic ideal seems to be a high-tech home in which each family member has access to her or his resources, such as personal cell phones, radios, computers, and satellite or cable television programming. As a result, cross-generational communication is increasingly problematic, and congregations are becoming smorgasbords of intra-generational church programs.

Finally, preachers might be called to regularly address the prideful spirit of human technological exploitation. In worship as in the rest of society, technology represents the power of human beings to manipulate all aspects of the creation for their own purposes. Technological devices symbolize human conquest of practically every aspect of the fallen world. Prescription drugs and medical diagnostic machinery seem to promise good health even as people fail to eat properly and exercise regularly. New educational technologies such as interactive computer programs and online databases suggest a more informed citizenry, but the gap between accessing information and making wise decisions seems to be growing wider. Europeans and North Americans are rushing to be better connected via cell phones and the Internet, but much of the resulting chat seems frivolous and sometimes publicly disruptive.

The power that human beings gain with new technologies invariably produces both intended and unintended consequences. Nuclear and biogenetic technologies are merely the latest in a long line of humanly crafted innovations that are both powerful and seemingly impossible to control in a world torn apart with conflicting political, cultural, spiritual, and corporate interests.

Yet when Augustine confronted the power of rhetoric to influence church and society, he eventually concluded that he could not release such power to the principalities and powers of his day. Trained as a secular rhetorician, which in his day meant being a deceptive and self-glorifying Sophist, he confronted the ultimate authority of Jesus Christ and decided to renew rather than reject the art of rhetoric. He became a steward of the technology of rhetoric, employing it in the service of church and neighbor rather than self. Such world-engaging humility is probably the most biblical response to the technological disparities, overdone optimism, unstewardly foolishness, and egocentric pride of high-tech societies in a fallen world. See TECHNOLOGY AND THE SERMON; VIDEO CLIPS; WORSHIP STYLE.

Bibliography: Pierre Babin. *The New Era in Religious Communication.* (1991); Richard R. Gaillardetz. *Transforming Our Days: Spirituality, Community, and the Liturgy in a Technological Culture.* (2000); Don E. Saliers. *Worship Come to Senses.* (1996); Quentin J. Schultze. *Habits of the High-Tech Heart: Living Virtuously in the Information Age.* (2002); Quentin J. Schultze. *High-Tech Worship? Using Presentational Technologies Wisely.* (2004); Susan J. White. *Christian Worship and Technological Change.* (1994).

TELEVISION
Ray John Marek, O.M.I.

Television's pervasive influence is detected at all levels of society. Television creates and patterns images of life, depicts historical events, narrates values and morals, prompts viewers to make quick judgments about complex situations, and provides a means of social integration. Today's television-saturated culture challenges preachers to consider their ministry in light of such extensive influence.

Television shapes worldview through its electronic crafting of iconic, sequential, and juxtaposed images. Preachers can often quickly detect the surface messages, themes, and myths depicted in them. More difficult to detect and analyze are the deeper metaphoric images by which viewers come to see and understand reality. Metaphoric images often work unconsciously on the viewer and subtly contribute to a viewer's ideology, values, language, judgments, and roles. For example, in a recent commercial, the images are of a woman feeding rice to her male counterpart directly from a bowl situated near the woman's chest. Subtler than the brand name and the sexual overtones is the metaphoric image that can contribute to and reinforce the subservient role of women. Contemporary reality television on one level emphasizes competition and participant elimination, but on a deeper level evokes metaphoric images. These images can promote an unhealthy individualism and a winner-loser approach to societal functioning rather than support collaboration and care for weaker members of society. This type of metaphoric image may condition and even celebrate social Darwinism. (*See* METAPHOR AND FIGURES OF SPEECH.)

Situations, judgments, dilemmas, and current events projected by the medium are so numerous that audiences often respond unreflectively. Viewers frequently do not question the messages, authorship, rationales, or ethical stances conveyed in the images and narratives they see. Preachers can reawaken viewers' interiority and spirituality by highlighting questionable depictions, exposing television's stances and interests, probing for further illumination, and inviting viewers to relate questions to their spiritual and faith lives.

There are a number of steps that preachers can take to refigure the vision of life that television depicts and narrates. By first exposing the worldview of television programs and then contrasting and comparing that worldview with the alternative script provided by Scripture and church doctrines, preachers help congregations dialogue with events, moral situations, perceived roles, trends, and cultures. Preachers can then lead congregations to respond as disciples.

Preachers can give special attention to the religious and biblical archetypes, themes, plots, characterizations, and motifs that underlie programming. They can establish correlations and provide further development between biblical images and televised images. They can also use the participatory or experiential aspect of television to help raise issues of justice, morality, inclusion, and equality.

Given television's electronic wizardry and star power in capturing audience attention, preachers will want to highlight the radical nature of biblical characters, motivations, and values. Sermons will be strengthened as preachers learn to craft images that illustrate biblical and doctrinal teachings in much the same way that television patterns electronic images. *See* RADIO.

Bibliography: Michael Warren. *Seeing Through the Media.* (1997).

YOUTH MINISTRY
Mark DeVries

Youth ministries seek to nurture the faith of young people and engage them in the life of the church. Though disparate theological views shape the approach and a wide variety of methods are employed, all youth ministries share a common goal and several predictable obstacles.

How can the church effectively engage young people in worship, particularly in an age in which the words *preaching* and *sermon* bear the connotation of *undesirable* and *negative?* Some churches answer this question by excluding teenagers from worship altogether and placing them in a youth church, with a generationally specific message. Others strive to ensure that the message delivered in corporate worship is always appropriate for a youthful audience. But far too many churches simply ignore the question altogether and find themselves sad spectators of the mass exodus of youth from corporate, intergenerational worship, particularly in the mainline church.

A. Youth Ministry in Context
B. Early Youth Ministry
C. Communicating the Gospel to Youth
   1. Storytelling
   2. Third Objects
   3. Youth as Proclaimers
D. Core Components
   1. Worship
   2. Study
   3. Fellowship
   4. Mission
E. Emerging Trends
   1. The Professionalization of Youth Ministry
   2. The Emergent Church
   3. Contemplative Youth Ministry
   4. Beyond Traditional Youth Ministry
F. The Challenge and Opportunity

A. Youth Ministry in Context

To speak of the challenges and opportunities of preaching with sensitivities to youth, one must first begin with the culture context that has given rise to the invention and expansion of youth ministry over the past two centuries. As it is experienced in most North American churches today, youth ministry is itself very young, primarily a post-19th cent. American phenomenon, developed as churches sought to ensure that the proclamation of the gospel hit the mark, specifically with the increasingly hard-to-reach audience of adolescents.

While youth ministry may be a relative newcomer to the ecclesial scene, an emphasis on the spiritual nurture of children is certainly not. Prior to the 20th cent., and even still in many less industrialized nations, youth ministry has happened organically, if somewhat haphazardly, as Christian parents and churches take seriously the ancient injunction for God's people to provide for the spiritual nurture of their children (Deut 6:4-9).

B. Early Youth Ministry

Though theories differ about the earliest antecedents of youth ministry today, a trajectory can be identified as far back as 1727 when Jonathan Edwards began his pastorate in Northampton by intentionally directing his sermons to the youth of his congregation (Brekus 2001, 302). Subsequently, John Wesley described the dramatic role that young people played in the work of the 1779 revival when he wrote in his journal of a "great awakening, especially among youth and children; several of whom, between twelve and sixteen years of age are a pattern to all about them" (Heitzenrater 2001, 296). Five years later, Wesley wrote, "God begins his work with children. . . . Thus the flame spreads to those of riper years; till at length they all know him, and praise him from the least unto the greatest" (Heitzenrater 2001, 296). But it was not until the late 1700s that Robert Raikes began the first Sunday school in England. These original Sunday schools literally were schools where disadvantaged children and youth, who often worked six days a week, were taught math, reading, and the like.

Others interested in tracing youth ministry's roots point to the launching of the YMCA in 1844. With its outreach to young men moving to the cities to find work, the early leaders of the YMCA sought to help them grow into faithful disciples of Jesus Christ, in an urban environment often hostile to the gospel. In both the Sunday school movement and the YMCA, the "preaching" of the gospel came packaged in the form of those who demonstrated the gospel before they proclaimed it, living out St. Francis's counsel about preaching: "Preach the gospel at all times. When necessary, use words."

Most pre-20th cent. youth ministry movements were, by and large, mission movements, designed first and foremost as ministries to those outside the reach of local congregations. But in 1881, with the launch of the Society for Christian Endeavor, youth ministry as most know it today was born. The Society for Christian Endeavor became the first broad-scale, church-based ministry to teenagers, providing a platform for churches to lead their own youth toward endeavoring to live an intentionally Christian life. To make this possible, Christian Endeavor created a replicable process for local churches. Gatherings of young people at Christian Endeavor meetings took place at local churches, typically on Sunday evenings.

Within a few decades, other churches had begun launching their own denominationally distinctive versions of Christian Endeavor. Though these denominational expressions seldom, if ever, garnered the widespread acceptance or the broad national influence of the Christian Endeavor movement, by the early 20th cent., it was undeniable that youth ministry had set up camp in the local church. But by the mid-1940s, when the vast majority of youth were enrolled in school, the social center of gravity for teenagers had made the seismic shift from home and church to school and leisure activities. It was into this cultural context that three national youth ministry organizations were born, all of which where organized around the emerging social networks of a growing national youth culture.

Young Life (est. 1941), Youth for Christ (est. 1944), and the Fellowship of Christian Athletes (est. 1954) built their ministries not around the church campus, but around schools and peer-centered activities outside school. These types of ministries were characterized by creative (sometimes outlandish) programming, led primarily by young adults who often emphasized building relationships with students outside the context of their weekly program.

As the focal point of popular youth ministry began to shift away from a church-based approach, many churches expressed resistance to activities of these organizations. It was not unusual for church leaders to feel threatened by the entrepreneurial aggressiveness of parachurch youth ministries, though many expressed gratitude that the good news of Christ was being proclaimed to youth, regardless of the location of proclamation.

But by the late 1970s and early 1980s, the vast majority of churches had themselves begun adopting many of the same youth ministry methods they had previously resisted. Most youth ministries today still maintain some of the flavor of youth ministry's early antecedents:

1. the emphasis on mission (found in the early Sunday school movement and the YMCA),
2. church-based programming designed primarily to nurture the faith of those within the church (found in the Society for Christian Endeavor), and
3. the ecumenical, entrepreneurial creativity in reaching out to all youth in the name of Christ (found in Young Life, Youth for Christ, and FCA).

C. Communicating the Gospel to Youth

Those charged with preaching the gospel to youth step into a two-hundred-year-old stream. Though the variety of settings, styles, and theological underpinnings of youth ministries may differ widely, those who have effectively communicated the gospel to teenagers have often accessed some of the same core practices. Despite the significant differences between post-millennial youth and those of previous generations, there is a surprising similarity among the practices used by youth workers.

1. Storytelling

Those most effective at communicating the gospel to youth are typically those who, like Jesus, teach most frequently through word pictures and stories. "Once upon a time" has a way of waking up listeners that a predictable, propositional, three-point sermon simply does not.

If we believe that "whoever tells the stories defines the culture," then we should be concerned (Walsh 2000). There is little doubt that young people today need stories that reach beyond the titillating consumerism of the culture. Mary Pipher describes the difference: "The stories that are told are designed to raise profits, not children. Most of the stories children hear are mass-produced to induce them to want good things instead of good lives" (Pipher 1996, 20).

Jesus often preached by painting word pictures and telling stories. His parables were subversive, ordinarily about completely secular topics: sheep, merchants, robbers and victims, and the like. The pedestrian nature of Jesus' stories relaxed his listeners' defenses, often leaving them perplexed. The stories, lodged in listeners' imaginations, like a time bomb, would later erupt in their hearts. Some psychologists have suggested that, apart from narrative structure, concepts simply are not remembered well and are seldom available for further consideration. Sue Monk Kidd was right: "Our stories are the best bread we can offer each other" (Kidd 1990, 154).

2. Third Objects

A second time-tested practice for communicating the gospel to youth is the use of third objects. A third object could simply be an object lesson using items like a set of keys or a machete or an ice cube, though these types of demonstrations can easily feel childish and overdone to teenagers.

Those who preach to young people have found that some youth, particularly boys, have an easier time connecting with each other when they are facing the same direction, with attention focused on an object in front of them (whether that object is a football game, a mission trip, or a sixteen-inch pizza). Third objects can be catalysts for belonging. And there is little question that typical teenagers, with an intense longing to fit in, will be more able to hear a message when they feel that they *belong* to the community in which the message is presented.

Third objects can also include input from the arts—dance, drama, music, photographs, a video clip, or a song that might offer contrast to or convergence with a particular text from Scripture. In an increasingly image-centered culture, third objects can provide a preacher with an accessible resource for awakening the senses of youth to the message of the day.

3. Youth as Proclaimers

At times, the most compelling proclamation of the gospel to young people may come from their peers. Though these expressions may not be as polished or prepared as those that come from the "professional," there is little doubt that teenagers' ears are particularly open to the gospel spoken by persons their own age.

Some churches have found it helpful to include a testimony from a young person in worship periodically throughout the year, sometimes in the form of an edited video in which a teenager is allowed to tell his or her story on camera for the congregation, without the pressure of speaking live in front of the entire church. Other churches choose to set aside a single Sunday of the year for their teenagers to lead the congregation in worship, including the preaching, liturgy, and music.

Whether in the formal setting of worship or in a small group of peers and leaders, youth ministry can provide young people with the chance not only to hear the grand narrative of the gospel but also to discern and tell their stories. And it is often the context of a faith-full community who listens to those stories that best bears witness to the work of God in each young person's life.

D. Core Components

Though the variety of youth ministries may be endless, certain core components are inherent to almost every youth ministry, each component providing a uniquely different context for communicating the message of Christ to youth.

1. Worship

From highly liturgical, ancient worship to hard-rock pyrotechnic praise and everything in between, almost every youth ministry seeks to bring its young people into an encounter with God through worship. The most recent decades have witnessed a dramatic explosion in the variety and the professionalism of worship styles, with many youth naming "praise and worship" as the most meaningful part of their youth ministry experience. The broad ecumenical cross-pollination of the youth worship renewal movement is impossible to ignore, with High Church Anglicans, "decent and in order" Presbyterians, and dancing Pentecostals all singing the same worship music with strikingly similar passion. In addition, there has been a growing introduction of ancient contemplative practices into youth worship, with such practices being embraced across widely divergent theological streams (*see* WORSHIP STYLE).

For many youth and churches, preaching has moved from center stage and has been replaced with a more immediate focus on music and spiritual practices that invite youth, corporately and individually, to encounter God personally. Preaching, in this context, becomes for youth a means for giving language to their experiences discerning God's presence, hearing God's call, and seeking to align their priorities with God's.

2. Study

While many churches continue the traditional design of providing Sunday school for middle school and high school youth on Sunday mornings, some have chosen to focus their efforts away from traditional Sunday school. Whether described as discipleship groups, area Bible studies, or student-led cell groups, most youth ministries make a priority of providing their youth with at least some opportunity for learning about and applying the essentials of the Christian life. It is often in the small group settings, where youth are surrounded by peers and adult leaders, that the gospel is not only proclaimed but also processed and applied specifically to their lives.

3. Fellowship

A focus on fellowship in youth ministry typically involves more than pizza and parties. The most effective youth ministries have become deliberate about building a welcoming climate in which life-long friendships can be made. The two most likely contexts for this community building have proven to be small groups and retreats. Retreats are consistently recognized as the most consistently transformative experience for teenagers, places where the hearts of young people seem to crack open, places where they are able to hear the same messages they have heard at home or church with different ears. Retreats often provide a context in which close peer relationships are formed quickly, and small groups give a context for deepening friendships and Christian accountability. Those who have learned to preach the gospel effectively to students have learned of the profound impact that the emotional and relational context of their messages can have on how well their words are heard.

4. Mission

The majority of youth ministries emphasize service and mission. Most groups participate in a wide variety of local service projects, from helping at the soup kitchen, to visiting persons who are unable to leave their homes, to tutoring inner-city children. A smaller number of youth groups take the emphasis on mission a step further, with some churches training their youth to share their faith through a verbal witness to those outside the church, or with students addressing more systemic causes related to justice and stewardship of the world's resources. In addition to local mission programming, most youth groups now include out-of-town mission experiences (both in country and out of country) in their annual youth ministry calendar. Particularly for the student who has trouble sitting still and simply *hearing* a message, missions provide the opportunity for youth to try on their faith for themselves, to experience the questions of the gospel before hearing its answers.

E. Emerging Trends

Early in the 21ˢᵗ cent., a number of youth ministry trends are appearing on the horizon. The convergence of these trends will likely shape the character of preaching to and with youth in the coming decades:

1. The Professionalization of Youth Ministry

More and more churches and parachurch youth ministries have begun to expect a growing level of expertise from persons they hire to work in their youth ministries. This expectation has led to a dramatic rise in the number of universities, seminaries, and institutes offering specialized theological education in youth ministry. Though historically, youth ministry has been seen as a short-term, entry-level position for those called to pastoral ministry, there seems to be a growing recognition of youth ministry as a terminal profession, not simply a stepping-stone to other forms of ministry.

2. The Emergent Church

Though at this time the emerging church movement, almost by definition, resists definition, there is little doubt that this movement will continue to impact the ways that churches and youth leaders think about the communication of the gospel to youth. (See EMERGING CHURCH PREACHING.) Based on the foundational assumption that a new way of "doing church" is (and, in fact, must be) emerging, the emerging church movement seeks to take seriously the seismic changes that have taken place as the dominant culture has shifted from modern to postmodern. The influence of the emerging church is being experienced (often unconsciously) across denominational and theological lines as a growing generation of young people are less convinced by traditional, propositional apologetics and more persuaded by a transparent presentation of the gospel (e.g., Jones 2001; McLaren 2004; Miller 2003).

3. Contemplative Youth Ministry

In the decades surrounding the year 2000, there has been a growing interest in exploring models of youth ministry built around any number of contemplative Christian practices. This model tends to shy away from more flashy, outrageous programming and seeks instead to provide young people and the adults who work with them with historic Christian practices that invite them into encounters with the living God, both as individuals and as a part of a broader community (e.g., Jones 2003; Yaconelli 2006).

4. Beyond Traditional Youth Ministry

Though youth ministry has, until recent years, been largely a white middle- to upper-class American phenomenon, there is a growing resolve to extend its influence both globally and socially. As a result of the exponential increase in the availability of information, those who previously were excluded from youth ministry training and resources are now gaining access to those resources and establishing networks that are enlivening the possibility of effective, contextualized proclamation of the gospel beyond the limitations of contemporary youth ministry's traditional demographic.

F. The Challenge and Opportunity

Youth ministry has become increasingly accepted as a necessity in local churches, yet some have raised concerns about its effectiveness. In fact, the National Study of Youth and Religion revealed that North American church youth remain "remarkably inarticulate" when it comes to expressing their faith (Smith 2005, 27). This adolescent inarticulateness may represent the greatest single challenge for anyone responsible for effectively communicating the message of Christ to youth.

The dramatic increase in the number of churches choosing to hire professional youth workers is a positive sign, but the historic youth ministry tensions continue to exist: (1) the tension between youth ministry as mission (reaching out to those outside the walls of the church) and youth ministry as Christian nurture (ministry to those already in the church); and (2) the ongoing tug-of-war between youth ministry driven by the distinctives of a particular church or denomination and youth ministry driven by wider, more ecumenical movements and organizations.

It is clear that the most healthy youth ministries simply refuse to accept these unnatural polarizations, choosing to proclaim the gospel to their own youth and to those outside the church, choosing to embrace their unique heritage as well as the movements of the Spirit across theological and cultural lines.

Many have suggested that, for its brief history, youth ministry has served as a seedbed of renewal in the church. Its inherently ecumenical flavor, its inescapable connection to missions, and its persistent search for fresh and engaging expressions of worship and preaching suggest that youth ministry will continue to be a catalyst and harbinger of the hope for the future of the church. See PREACHING TO CHILDREN; PREACHING TO YOUTH.

Bibliography: Catherine Brekus. "Children of Wrath, Children of Grace: Jonathan Edwards and the Puritan Culture of Child Rearing." *The Child in Christian Thought.* Edited by Marcia J. Bunge. (2001) 300–28; Kenda Dean. *Practicing Passion.*

(2004); Richard Heitzenrater. *[Wesley's] Journal and Diaries 6* (February 18, 1779) quoted in "John Wesley and Children." *The Child in Christian Thought.* Edited by Marcia J. Bunge. (2001) 279–99; Richard Heitzenrater. *[Wesley's] Journal and Diaries 6* (June 8, 1784) quoted in "John Wesley and Children." *The Child in Christian Thought.* Edited by Marcia J. Bunge. (2001) 279–99; Tony Jones. *Postmodern Youth Ministry.* (2001); Tony Jones. *Soul Shaper.* (2003); Sue Monk Kidd. *Where the Heart Waits.* (1990); Brian D. McLaren. *Generous Orthodoxy.* (2004); David Miller. *Blue Like Jazz.* (2003); Mary Pipher. *The Shelter of Each Other.* (1996); Christian Smith. *Soul Searching.* (2005); David Walsh. "Whoever Tells the Stories Defines the Culture." http://commerce.senate.gov/hearings/0321wal.pdf. (2000); Mark Yaconelli. *Contemplative Youth Ministry.* (2006).

PART 9 RHETORIC.
INTRODUCTION: SEEKING A RESPONSE

Robert Stephen Reid

In *Design for Preaching*, one of the most influential North American homiletics textbooks of the third quarter of the 20th cent., H. Grady Davis wrote, "The aim of preaching is to win . . . a response to the gospel, a response of attitude and impulse and feeling no less than of thought" (1958, 5). Although many public speaking textbooks at the outset of the 21st cent. would still offer some version of "winning a response" as a purpose for engaging in civic discourse, few homiletics textbooks continue to use this language. Concern to distinguish human purposes from divine, concern to avoid privileging one perspective above another, concern to distinguish efforts to persuade from overt manipulation, and a growing concern to avoid nailing down answers in sermons have converged to problematize the idea of preaching for a response.

Moreover, there is a spectrum of attitudes regarding what preachers expect by way of a response to sermons. For example, some preachers assume the purpose of preaching is to present an argument on behalf of the gospel with a goal to invite convictional assent. Some see preaching's purpose as an advocacy of faith in God with the goal of facilitating a transformative encounter with God. Some see preaching's purpose as a collaborative creation of an experience of coming-to-understanding with a goal of inviting reflective engagement. Still others see preaching's purpose as divine witness and/or a modeling of thinking theologically with a goal of facilitating a formative conversation about the implications of faith in God. These different approaches represent a tension between preaching with a voice of assuredness versus speaking in ways that admit ambiguity. They also represent differences between appeals made to individuals seeking transformation by faith and appeals made to persons as part of a collective community negotiating the meaning of faith (Reid 2006). To explore these different attitudes toward seeking a response necessitates familiarity with the ancient communication theory of rhetoric, contemporary developments in this communication theory, and the implications of these developments for preaching the gospel.

Rhetoric in Ancient Secular and Religious Communication

Since antiquity, the study of rhetoric has been concerned with distinguishing probable reasoning from logical and dialectical reasoning. Aristotle defined rhetoric as a counterpart of dialectic in the task of making productive argument. Where the goal of both logical and dialectical reasoning is to identify and affirm universal truths or at least opinions that are generally accepted by the educated, he maintained that rhetorical reasoning should be recognized as reasoning necessary to arrive at solutions for particular problems or situations that require judgment (*Posterior Analytics* 71a; *Rhetoric* 1355). In other words, probable judgment rather than certain knowledge is the appropriate form of reasoning when argument is contingent on circumstances, when decisions (i.e., about guilt, the expedient, or the honorable) depend on probabilities rather than certainties.

The contingent nature of this approach to reasoning differs from reasoning logically or dialectically in three ways. First, it is public rather than interpersonal communication, speech generally tailored to influence decisions of the citizenry as an audience rather than the kind of speech typical of dialogue. Second, it is persuasive rather than coercive speech, quid pro quo contractual inducements, or imposed rulings (1355b). In contrast to the way that dialogical philosophers like Plato treated language, as if it were a neutral conduit for the representation of reality, rhetorical reasoning recognizes that language functions as a symbolic means of influencing belief and behavior. Aristotle claimed that this ability to influence others is shaped by three human communicative capacities: the effect of ethos or the speaker's character conveyed by words, pathos as the speaker's ability to emotively create identification with and move listeners, and the logos or content of the speaker's actual argument (*Rhetoric* 1356a). Third, it applies to contextual rather than universal situations. Aristotle linked these three universal means of persuasion (*pisteis*) to the specificity of their use in each particular case (1355b–56b)—what contemporary rhetoricians refer to as the "rhetorical situation" (Lucaites and Condit 1999, 2–7). Taken together, these assumptions about the contingent nature of rhetorical reasoning clarify how, from antiquity, trained orators and writers have attempted to employ language strategically to arrive at probable truth and influence specific audiences in civic and cultural matters. Across more than two millennia of Western thought, rhetoric's pre-modern and then modernist fortunes waxed and waned. John Lucaites and Celeste Condit (1999) note,

> The trajectory of Western thought from Plato's Academy through the seventeenth- and eighteenth-century Enlightenment of reason and well into the scientific modernism of the present century spawned an intellectual predisposition for theories of knowledge in which the values of universality and objectivity were privileged over those of particularity, situatedness, and subjectivity or intersubjectivity. (6)

Rhetoric's fortunes in Christian preaching have also waxed and waned across the centuries, but for a different reason. Early church leaders argued that preaching's purpose should be to assert the truthfulness of the gospel claims rather than have listeners judge the merits of a preacher's eloquence or, worse, succumb to the enticement of turning the homily into a dramatic spectacle to be applauded. But this was always a tensional argument. In his treatise *On the Priesthood,* John Chrysostom writes that preachers must combine "contempt for praise [with] the force of eloquence" because "if either is lacking, the one left is made useless through divorce from the other" (*Priesthood* 5.1–2; compare Lischer 2002, 58). Effective teaching should be "seasoned" with rhetoric's "salt," he writes, but only and always with a view to assisting listeners to take the message to heart (5.1–2). When applause broke out during one of his sermons, he responded, "One thing only do I wish, that quietly and intelligently, you should do what is said. This is the applause; this is the panegyric for me" (*Priesthood* 5.37; compare Pelikan 2001, 79–80). Writing about the same time, Augustine also sought to reclaim a place for rhetoric. The church is not well served, he

maintained, if it permits theological "sophists" to persuade listeners in false matters while preachers are charged by their church leaders to remain ignorant of rhetoric's ability to put hearers in a teachable frame of mind (*Doctr. chr.* 4.2). The church has regularly struggled with the relationship between the divine and the human dimensions of preaching.

Rhetoric in Contemporary Communication Theory

Where many scholars credited with reestablishing the importance of rhetoric for 20th-cent. thought (e.g., Richards; Weaver; Burke; Perelman and Olbrechts-Tyteca) recovered the vitality of Aristotle's pre-modern contention that "rhetoric is the faculty of discovering in the particular case what are the available means of persuasion" (*Rhetoric* 1355b), these theorists also generally accepted the culturally dominant and thoroughly modernist conception that persuasion is a philosophically separate category from—or at best only an occasionally overlapping category with—argument. For much of the 19th and 20th cent., this conception also dominated homiletic thought. For example, Broadus followed Whately when he argued that sermons "should be largely composed of argument" and that persuasion was the task of a sermon's "application" (Broadus 1944, xii). Contemporary communication theorists, like those whose seminal essays are collected in Lucaites, Condit, and Caudill's *Contemporary Rhetorical Theory: A Reader,* no longer accept this distinction. They would argue that for persuasion to occur, first, there must be an act of communication in which one person intends to influence another person who has the ability to form a judgment or make a choice in response, whether that first person is speaking to millions or merely knocking on someone's door (e.g., Herbert Simons; Dilip Gaonkar). Second, they would view all rhetoric as communication "called into being" by its contextual exigencies and by the reasoning assumption of the audience for whom the discourse is composed (e.g., Edwin Black; Lloyd Bitzer). In addition, many, if not most, contemporary theorists also believe that rhetoric is epistemic—generative of new knowledge because it is a way of reasoning by which knowledge is created (e.g., Robert Scott; Thomas Farrell).

The argument first uttered in Plato's Academy, that the role of rhetoric is merely one of dressing up communication and that it plays no role in discovering truth, has often been voiced across the centuries by theologians, philosophers, and more recently scientists—communities of people who see their role as discovering and/or protecting timeless truths. In the modernist era this proclivity represented a lust for certitude. It was challenged in the 20th cent. as a new generation of rhetoricians arose who contended that all knowledge in various academic disciplines is socially situated knowledge rather than timeless truth and is maintained by evolving disciplinary arguments that are by nature rhetorical rather than logical or even dialogical. In contemporary academic discourse modernist categorical distinctions between deliberative reasoning, discursive argument, and persuasion tend to collapse into one another. Rhetoric is far from being viewed as a dressed up, eloquent way to communicate ideas, as if the ideas being communicated are somehow persuasively neutral.

Rhetoric in Contemporary Homiletics

Homiletics has been deeply affected by this emerging view of rhetoric's role in its renewed attention to the role of the listener (e.g., Craddock; Buttrick; Long; Allen); the epistemic role of language in creating generative understanding for preaching in community (e.g., McClure; Eslinger; McDaniel); and the role of an embodied-performative evocation of the other (e.g., Childers; Ward; Rice; Troeger). At the same time it is important to note that just as rhetoric has spent two millennia resisting the Platonic tendency to reduce reasoning's purpose to the search for truth rather than a search for good reasons, homiletics regularly struggles with rhetoric over this same issue. Recently, Richard Lischer, James Kay, and William Willimon, much like Karl Barth before them, have argued that concern with persuasion and attending to the concerns of rhetoric places too much attention on the human element of preaching. The result, they claim, becomes preaching that loses God as its subject matter and ceases to function as witness to God's grace. Whenever rhetoric dominates theology in homiletics, this is surely right (compare Kay 2007, 49–75). The question of preaching's starting point matters because it tends to control the possibilities of what one sees. If a preacher begins with the concerns of rhetoric, then the primary concern of preaching likely will be effectiveness, and the distinctiveness of the Christian message will be lost. In an era consumed with technologies of controlling communication, where the deluge of communicated messages may have become an end rather than a means, this concern matters.

Concern over starting points and grounding can become problematic, however, when theologians press what appears to be a "bridge" metaphor too far, treating language as if it were Plato's neutral conduit, as if the language of a sermon moves from a divine location to a human destination rather than moving in the other direction. We do better to imagine the metaphor of rhetoric's relationship to theology in preaching as a "dance," with two partners taking steps to perform a witness of faith—a dance of mutuality in which theology should lead but must partner with rhetoric to perform (Hogan 2006, 6–10). This is a collaborative metaphor of both-and rather than an exclusivist metaphor of either-or. It respects that preaching is a holy calling to name God and to name grace, placing witness to the divine and witness to faith in a reciprocal relationship (Reid 2006, 21). This partnering metaphor can save theologians from asserting, for example, "Why I am not persuasive" (Lischer 1999) or that preaching is better understood as "miracle" than as human witness to the divine (Willimon 2006, 157). Such views tend to reduce rhetoric to a conception of eloquence and miss that its primary role, from antiquity, has been a counterpart to dialectic—one that invites judgment in contingent matters. Homiletic's collaborative dance with rhetoric provides the preacher with a discursive means to express thoughtful reasoning in contingent theological matters while also expressing his or her witness to God's divine revelation in the person of Jesus Christ.

Bibliography: John A. Broadus. "Preface." *On the Preparation and Delivery of Sermons.* Edited by Jesse B. Weatherspoon. (1944); H. Grady Davis. *Design for Preaching.* (1958); Lucy L. Hogan. *Graceful Speech: An Invitation to Preaching.* (2006); James Kay. *Preaching and Theology.* (2007); Richard Lischer. "Why I Am Not Persuasive." *Homiletic* 24 (1999) 13–16; Richard Lischer, ed. *The Company of Preachers: Wisdom on Preaching, Augustine to the Present.* (2002); John L. Lucaites and Celeste M. Condit. "Introduction." *Contemporary Rhetorical Theory: A Reader.* Edited by J. Lucaites, C. Condit, and S. Caudill. (1999);

Jaroslav Pelikan. *Divine Rhetoric: The Sermon on the Mount as Message and as Model in Augustine, Chrysostom and Luther.* (2001); Robert S. Reid. *The Four Voices of Preaching.* (2006); William H. Willimon. *Conversations with Barth on Preaching.* (2006).

❖   ❖   ❖   ❖

ARRANGEMENT
Eugene L. Lowry

Said H. Grady Davis in the first sentence of his remarkable *Design for Preaching:* "Life appears in the union of substance and form." Quickly, he added: "All life, every living thing we know, comes in some organic form," and concluded that "every thought likewise comes in some form. We cannot have a thought without its form." The thought, indeed, "takes shape" (1958, 1). All this, he notes within the first dozen sentences of this classic work. One might observe that we are all capable of poorly shaped thought, but "substance and form" are tied together inextricably; that is the claim. So it is—if one follows this logic—that none of us can prepare a sermon without strategically arranging its shape, even if we may be unaware of, or choose to deny, our underlying strategy.

The subject of arrangement as applied to preaching harks back as far as Aristotle's rhetorical concerns about the "facility of discovering in the particular what are the available means of persuasion" (Loscalzo 1995, 409). (*See* PERSUASION.) It also presses forward to postmodernity's ongoing critique of the Enlightenment's focus on individualism and rationalism. Central to the subject of homiletical shape are the twin questions of human agency and social location.

Fred Craddock put the matter in contemporary terms when he said about the goals of preaching: "The goal is not to get something said but to get something heard" (1985, 167).

Thanks to the Greeks, the Western world has a long history of rhetorical concerns about "the art, study, or skill of using language effectively" (Loscalzo 1995, 409)—or as Paul Scott Wilson puts it: "giving good reasons for people to believe what we are saying" (1995, 75). By the time of Jesus, the five basic principles or norms of classical rhetoric

had been established (although not their relative priority or connection): invention, arrangement, style, memory, and delivery (Loscalzo 1995, 410). And it is helpful to remember that before Augustine's conversion, he was a teacher of rhetoric. That tradition lies behind his articulate plea:

> While the proponents of error know the art of winning an audience to good will, attention and open mind, shall the proponents of truth remain ignorant? While the (sophist) states facts concisely, clearly, plausibly, shall the preacher state them so that they are tedious to hear, hard to understand, hard to believe? While the one attacks truth and insinuates falsehood by fallacious argument, shall the other have too little skill either to define the true or refute the false? (Loscalzo 1995, 411)

This Greek heritage (in various forms) dominated the Western homiletical world for almost a thousand years. Indeed, in recent North American history, no book has enjoyed as long a shelf life as *A Treatise on the Preparation and Delivery of Sermons.* Written by John A. Broadus in 1870, it served as the dominant standard text for nearly seventy-five years. Said Broadus: "[W]e must regard homiletics as rhetoric applied to this particular kind of speaking" (1890, 30).

Not that there were no other views. Both Yngve Brilioth and Paul Scott Wilson trace the development of homiletics, particularly as influenced during the eras of the Middle Ages and the Reformation (Brilioth 1965; Wilson 1992). David Buttrick in 1981 summarized the result regarding sermonic arrangement:

> Since the time of the Protestant Scholastics sermons have been designed according to an aged scheme. . . . Procedurally a text was exegeted, interpreted, and applied in what was a tri-part sermon. . . . An introduction was followed by the text, which in turn was reduced to a propositional topic which was developed in a series of points . . . before the sermon ended in a conclusion. . . . [That] "system . . . is still with us. (1981, 46–47)

Surely, "the purpose of preaching," as Jana Childers has observed, is "broader and deeper than the kind of rational persuasion that is classical rhetoric's goal" (1998, 28).

But two dramatic turns occurred in the 20th cent. Thomas Long described the first:

> Once upon a time, homiletics . . . and rhetoric . . . were a happily married couple. From

Augustine's *On Christian Doctrine* . . . all the way to the big, systematic homiletical textbooks in vogue in the nineteenth century, Christian homiletics looked to the Bible and to theology for the content of sermons and then to the rules and fashions of classic rhetoric for the form and style of sermons. It was a mixed marriage—homiletics being Jewish and rabbinical . . . and thus religious; rhetoric being Greek, gentile and ideologically neutral—and it was a marriage of convenience. . . . Homileticians knew what preachers were supposed to say and rhetoricians knew how they were to say it, so that listeners could hear it and be persuaded by it. (Long 1993, 172–73)

But then, says Long, "Rhetoric suffers a Barth attack," based on the issue of the fall that shattered the *imago Dei.* The result was "complete discontinuity between the Word of God and the existing human condition" (1993, 174). Barth's conclusion caused him to avoid both introductions and conclusions—that would falsely presume a "point of contact." Indeed he regretted ever having mentioned World War I in his own sermons and advised pastors to "aim their guns beyond the hills of relevance" (Barth 1991, 118–19).

All of this is to negate altogether the notion of rhetorical persuasion. "The sermon will be like the involuntary lip movement of one who is reading with great care," he said (Barth 1991, 76). Faithfulness to the text, not pastoral rhetorical strategy, is the key. He warned preachers not to be tempted to even hint at some tragedy that may have befallen the community with "awful impact." That event "belongs to everyday life, but now it is Sunday" (Barth 1991, 118).

The second dramatic North American homiletical turn of the 20th cent. moved the opposite direction. It was biblical scholar Fred Craddock who observed that exegetical work was inductive in arrangement, starting with particulars and specific questions about the text, not with global conclusions as the starting point. Further, he suggested that if the scholar works deductively, chances are great that it is eisegesis, not exegesis, going on. So he asked: Why would preachers conclude their biblical work, move to the pulpit, and begin by announcing the conclusions of their preparatory work? Craddock suggested that people resent arriving at the end of a destination on a trip they have not taken (1974, 146). Moreover, deductive movement of a three-point sermon often reveals three barely related trips downhill—and generally with little suspense or anticipation (1974, 56). How different is the sermon that, following Barbara Brown Taylor's suggestion, "traces the preacher's own process of discovery" (Taylor 1993, 83).

Out of Craddock's groundbreaking work came a movement first labeled the New Homiletic by David Randolph (1969), and quickly picked up by numerous authors with similar concerns. (*See* NEW HOMILETIC.) Whatever differences of view were held, the common thread had to do with commitment to some kind of procedural plot that could involve a strategic delay in the preacher's meaning. The purpose of this strategic delay is to cultivate interest, tension, and even suspense moving toward some kind of resolutional evocation of the, gospel.

Dick Eslinger called this move in North American homiletical work the "Copernican revolution in preaching" (1987, 65). Paul Scott Wilson declared it the most dramatic homiletical shift since the Reformation. Lying at a deeper theological level, the key has to do with the understanding that a sermon is not an object in space but an event in time. The arrangement of ideas is to be calculated toward the evocation of the experience of the gospel—or as James Cone would have it, "The Word is more than words about God . . . it is a poetic happening, an evocation" (1975, 18). Henry Mitchell insists the sermon must have a behavioral aim (1990, 53).

In this sense the closest relative to the sermon is a musical presentation—coming out of silence into the sequence of its timely sound, and then finally dropping back into the silence of history. It goes almost without saying that one does not begin a sonata with the last four bars. This kind of sermon is shaped to move from issue to resolution born of the gospel, or as I often say, "A sermon moves from an itch to a scratch."

Obviously, there are variations, including Charles Rice's story, Buttrick's patterned moves, and Lowry's narrative sermon. Included in these variations of plotted, shaped movement of ideas is the style of African American preaching recommended by Henry Mitchell and others.

Although in many ways Mitchell's kind of sermon initially appears to be a kind of formal, deductively shaped message, there is a different kind of plotted, experiential suspense at work. Though the African American preacher may announce the text and theme up front and then move through what seems to be a traditional form of arrangement, the key difference is a shift toward a final celebration that picks up a decisive center of the rhetorical process and turns it toward an altogether richer form of event.

Involved here is a multilayered form of rationality Mitchell calls *transconsciousness*. Having noted that whereas feelings have been "declared unworthy" by Western culture and that the Enlightenment further exasperated matters by creating a split between reason and feeling, Mitchell observes that "Black culture . . . has not progressed to the level of this lofty mistake" (1977, 12–13). The final celebration is aimed at creating a multilevel appeal for the message.

It is ironic that although through time the legacy of Aristotle's rhetorical writings has influenced one kind of preaching, the legacy of his *Poetics* has influenced another. From Aristotle, we learn the classic western plot line of conflict, complication, peripeteia, and denouement—a process that lies underneath much of the current emphasis upon plotted sermons.

Finally, the bottom line regarding arrangement is that the shape of things said is not separable from the content or substance of things said. When the arrangement of the linear (timely) musical score is shifted, the content of the music is utterly different. It becomes a different song altogether. Likewise, decisions about homiletical form, shape, or arrangement constitute a substantive shift of content. That is why Davis said that we cannot have a thought without form and why Craddock insisted that what is important is not getting something said but getting something heard. *See* DEDUCTIVE; INDUCTIVE; NARRATIVE FORM.

Bibliography: Karl Barth. *Homiletics.* (1991); Yngve Brilioth. *A Brief History of Preaching.* (1965); John A. Broadus. *A Treatise on the Preparation and Delivery of Sermons.* (1890); David G. Buttrick. "Interpretation and Preaching." *Interpretation* 35 (January 1981) 46–47; Jana Childers. *Performing the Word.* (1998); James H. Cone. *God of the Oppressed.* (1975); Fred B. Craddock. *As One Without Authority.* (1974); Fred B. Craddock. *Preaching.* (1985); Henry Grady Davis. *Design for Preaching.* (1958); Richard L. Eslinger. *A New Hearing.* (1987); Thomas G. Long. "And How Shall They Hear?: The Listener in Contemporary Preaching." *Listening to the Word.* Edited by Gail R. O'Day and Thomas G. Long. (1993); Craig A. Loscalzo. "Rhetoric." *Concise Encyclopedia of Preaching.* Edited by William H. Willimon and Richard Lischer. (1995) 409–11; Eugene L. Lowry. *The Sermon: Dancing the Edge of Mystery.* (1997); Henry H. Mitchell. *The Recovery of Preaching.* (1977); Henry H. Mitchell. *Celebration and Experience in Preaching.* (1990); David James Randolph. *The Renewal of Preaching.* (1969); Charles L. Rice. *The Embodied Word: Preaching as Art and Liturgy.* (1990); Barbara Brown Taylor. *The Preaching Life.* (1993); Paul Scott Wilson. *A Concise History of Preaching.* (1992); Paul Scott Wilson. *The Practice of Preaching.* (1995).

COMPARISON
Mike Graves

Comparison is a rhetorical device that finds similarities in different things and manifests itself in at least three distinct ways—comparative language, comparative analogies, and comparative metaphors—each with implications for preachers today.

The erotic poetry of the OT invokes comparative language: "Your lips are like a crimson thread, / and your mouth is lovely" (Song 4:3). Akin to poetic forms of speech, comparative language used to be more popular among preachers who were known for image-rich sermons. John Chrysostom (the Golden Mouth) declared, "Ye have heard the Apostolic voice, that trumpet from heaven, that spiritual lyre. For even as a trumpet sounding a fearful and warlike note, it both dismays the enemy, and arouses the dejected spirits" (Chrysostom, 82–83), and this was only his opening line about the Scripture text. Such language in preaching waxed and waned at various times in church history up until roughly the middle of the 20th cent. but seems to have been neglected of late. Many fine African American preachers are notable exceptions and can function as models.

Comparative analogies include a host of proverbs: "Doing wrong is like sport to a fool, / but wise conduct is pleasure to a person of understanding" (Prov 10:23), or Jesus' comparison of the crowds being "like sheep without a shepherd" (Matt 9:36; Mark 6:34). Analogies are the most common form of comparison among preachers today, perhaps attributable to an overemphasis on the rational aspects of faith. Most commonly enlisted under the all-purpose terms *application* and *illustration*, these analogies seek to help listeners understand the unknown in light of the known (Farris 1998, 2), a device common in ancient rhetoric. In order to help listeners relate to the irony of Jesus' unassuming entry into Jerusalem, for example, the preacher might describe so-called triumphal entries in the ancient Mediterranean world but also compare such events to a military fly-over today. Farris (1998, 80–93) focuses on how persons or groups in the biblical text may correspond with people or groups today (e.g., Israel/the church; Babylonians/unjust institutions; the disciples/the church or individual Christians). Whenever a preacher moves from a biblical text to today, comparison is inevitable. The danger of using too many comparisons in a sermon is that the flow of thought may be lost.

In the synoptic parables, Jesus frequently employs comparative metaphors, such as, "With what can we compare the kingdom of God, or what parable will we use for it? It is like a mustard seed" (Mark 4:30-31). The metaphorical parables of Jesus constitute the rarest form of comparison among contemporary preachers. Rather than seeking to clarify the unknown in light of the known, many, though not all, of Jesus' parables employ the known (bread, seeds, and weddings) only to leave open-ended the implications for the mysterious "kingdom of God." These riddle-like stories place a heavy burden on listeners, "anyone with ears to hear" (Mark 4:9). Ministers familiar with newer approaches to homiletics may recognize the lure, as well as the dangers, of such open-ended preaching styles with an emphasis on experience. *See* BRIDGING THEN AND NOW; METAPHOR AND FIGURES OF SPEECH; PARABLES; PROVERBS.

Bibliography: John Chrysostom. *Nicene and Post-Nicene Fathers.* Cited in O. C. Edwards Jr. *A History of Preaching.* (2004); Stephen Farris. *Preaching That Matters: The Bible and Our Lives.* (1998).

DEFINITION
Teresa Lockhart Stricklen

Definition is useful for clarifying the mystery of God and manifestation of the divine presence in the world. Because the life of faith is often ambiguous and because the gospel is frequently abstract until made plain, preachers often need to define theological language in terms that their hearers can comprehend. Definition is necessary in order to create common ground so that understanding is possible.

For example, a preacher may assume everyone understands the term *salvation,* but because words are associated with our past experiences and the contexts in which we encountered them, some may associate salvation with televangelists peddling faith, not with the goodness of God. It is thus important to clarify what we mean when we use words, especially God-words, keeping in mind that those who control definitions control a whole world of meaningful possibilities. For these reasons, preachers need to be careful with definitions.

There are several ways that preachers can use definition in communicating the gospel. Preachers may briefly define a term like *salvation* with a short parenthetical phrase that provides a simple explanation. They may also utilize stipulative definitions to distinguish a particular way in which a term is used: "When the Bible talks of salvation, it generally means experiencing the whole goodness of God in mind, body, spirit, relationships, and society." Preachers may also use extended definitions that start simple but expand by creating a whole complex of associations with a particular concept in such a way that people can recognize it when they see it. One way that preachers define things is through the use of distinction: "When Paul uses the term *salvation,* he is not talking about what big-haired televangelists sell like snake oil." They may provide examples of salvation in action through analogies (what salvation is like) and stories (how it works). (*See* COMPARISON.) Another way in which we define something is by tracing its origin: "Salvation is from the same root word as salve, a healing balm you put on a wound."

The original biblical language often has no adequate English equivalents, so preachers may need to define a Hebrew, Aramaic, or Greek term so that a fuller meaning may be communicated. For example, people living during the period of the Second Temple who had a background in Hebrew Scripture or Greek versions of the OT understood that *calling* or naming something brings it forth into being, as God does at creation (Gen 1). Therefore, in a sermon about Jesus *calling* Lazarus from the grave (John 11), a preacher can briefly explain the Hebrew and Greek nuances of the word *call,* before showing how we, like Martha and Mary, believe death has the final word. When the preacher then portrays Jesus standing over the face of death's chaos (like the chaos at creation) to *call,* "Lazarus, come out!" our dead faith can be called out into resurrection life. This is the power of definition done well; it can set up the condition for revelation by preparing a way for God's presence to be manifest through a sermon. *See* TEACHING.

ETHOS
André Resner

Ethos is the perceived character of the speaker. Aristotle believed that speakers persuade by three means: logos (the speech), pathos (hearer emotion), and ēthos, which he considered the most potent. In *Christian Instruction*, Augustine agreed: "The life of the speaker has greater weight in determining whether he is obediently heard than any grandness of eloquence" (*Doctr. chr.* 4.27.59). Homileticians through the centuries attributed such power to ēthos that most believed once credibility was established, the heavy lifting of persuasion was done.

Not until Karl Barth was the problem with this thinking clearly exposed: such an attitude makes the preacher's person more powerful than God's logos. Since for Barth Christ himself is the preacher and what is preached is really the WORD OF GOD, the preacher is of no consequence. Only God can make efficacious the Word.

The Apostle Paul struggled with ēthos because his logos of the cross created confusion with his hearers, mainly non-Jews whose expectations were shaped by Greco-Roman rhetoric. To them, Paul himself was at least as much of a stumbling stone as his offensive message. He did not play the rhetoric game correctly. He refused to let his hearers set the conditions for what he said or how his life looked. In Paul's day rhetoric was hearer-driven—the audience was king. But for Paul preaching the gospel was message-driven, the gospel setting the conditions for its delivery and for the preacher's life. His hearers saw his beatings and imprisonments as evidence of his fraud; Cicero said that a truly virtuous life would be ennobled with honor, whereas a cursed life would look like Paul's (compare the peristasis catalogue lists, which ironically validated his calling, e.g., 1 Cor 4:8-13).

When the worlds of rhetoric and the cross collided, ēthos was transformed as much as logos. Cruciform logos as reasoned argumentation bent Greek sensibility. Cruciform ēthos shattered cultural expectations for credibility. Paul's was an ironic or reverse ēthos, one implied in his cruciform logos.

His cruciform life became a vehicle for his logos of the cross. Insofar as his life bore the same witness, it was the power of God, not the character of Paul, that made the difference for hearers. "We preach not ourselves but Christ crucified," but preachers' crucified lives preach the crucified Christ too.

So reconfigured, preaching's purpose shifts from trying to win consumers who think they have market choices, to the confrontation of conflicting worlds of being and value. PERSUASION trades on the preferences of consumers, with the effective preacher adept and chameleon-like—anything to close the deal. Proclamation trusts in the divine efficacy of the logos of the cross: "We are not peddlers of God's logos like so many" (2 Cor 2:17).

It may seem as if ministers spend too much time explaining themselves—what they do, what they say, who they are, and why. Paul helps us see that when identity is shaped by the gospel, such explaining is the ministry of the gospel: "What then is Apollos? What is Paul? Servants through whom you came to believe, as the Lord assigned to each. I planted, Apollos watered, but God gave the growth" (1 Cor 3:5-6).

Preachers' ongoing temptation is to take the easier path, to stop taking pains to live and explain the cruciform life of the preacher and the church, and sell out to the world's standards and lusts. It is easier, and the perks can be nice. But what is lost is the essential—the preacher's and the church's reason for being—to be witnesses (martos), by God's grace, in word and life to the enigmatic logos of the cross. *See* CHARACTER.

Bibliography: Karl Barth. *Homiletic.* (1991); Alexandra Brown. *The Cross and Human Transformation.* (1995); Charles Cousar. *A Theology of the Cross.* (1990); Michael Gorman. *Cruciformity.* (2001); Ronald Osborne. *Creative Disarray: Models of Ministry in a Changing America.* (1991); Andre Resner Jr. *Preacher and Cross: Person and Message in Theology and Rhetoric.* (1999).

IDENTIFICATION
Robert E. Conover

Identification is a rhetorical term developed by Kenneth Burke (1897–1995) whose wide-ranging work includes philosophy, literature, sociology, religion, and rhetoric. In the Burkean system, identification is closely related to other terms: *rhetoric, persuasion,* and *substance* or *consubstantiality.* In order to understand the significance that identification might hold for preaching, all of these terms need to be briefly explored from Burke's perspective.

Identification

Rhetoric and persuasion are often closely associated with each other. A common definition of *rhetoric* is "the art of making persuasive speeches" (*Random House Dictionary*). Burke acknowledges this common association of the two terms. However, rather than use the term *persuasion,* Burke chooses to use the term *identification,* because identification is descriptive of how persuasion occurs: persuasion in its most simple form is identification. Burke says, "You persuade [people] only insofar as you can talk [their] language by speech, gesture, tonality, order, image, attitude, idea, identifying your ways with [theirs]" (1969a, 55).

An additional term Burke uses that is closely related to identification is *consubstantiality.* When people identify with one another, they understand themselves to share a common substance or to be consubstantial with one another. In Burke's words, "To identify A with B is to make A 'consubstantial' with B" (1969a, 21). Identification with another person or group does not imply that the two are identical. Burke states, "A is not identical with his colleague, B. But insofar as their interests are joined, A is identified with B. Or he may identify himself with B even when their interests are not joined, if he assumes that they are, or is persuaded to believe so" (1969a, 20).

Rhetoric is most commonly associated with public speaking, but it is not limited to speaking. Rhetoric encompasses all forms of communication. In this regard, Burke's use of the term *substance* is enlightening: "Substance, in the old philosophies, was an act; and a way of life is an acting-together; and in acting together, [people] have common sensations, concepts, images, ideas, attitudes that make them consubstantial" (1969a, 21).

Identification also helps us understand that human relationships are at the heart of our ability to influence and persuade others. Burke argues that while two people may be joined or consubstantial with each other, they are at the same time distinct from each other. This recognition illumines the natural state of divisions in our human relationships. We hold much in common, and at the same time all individuals or societies are distinctive. This is the natural state of humankind, and it also leads to human divisions. Burke states, "Identification is affirmed with earnestness precisely because there is division. Identification is compensatory to division. If [people] were not apart from one another, there would be no need for a rhetorician to proclaim their unity. If [people] were wholly and truly of one substance, absolute communication would be of [our] very essence" (1969a, 22). But this kind of unity is not the nature of the human community (including the church), thus, we need identification to help hold us together in the midst of all our distinctions. It is noteworthy that in Burke's system, the counterpart to identification is division.

With this brief background in mind, we can say three things: (1) identification helps us see that rhetoric and persuasive power are not limited to speech alone but also include gestures, tonality, order, images, attitudes, ideas, acts, and acting-together; (2) identification helps us see that common interests are a source of both persuasion and unity; persuasion and unity are enhanced by identifying our ways of being with the ways of others, by acting together, and by focusing on the many and various experiences, ideas, and attitudes that we hold in common; (3) identification helps us see that division is a natural state and that distinctiveness in individuals or groups can be maintained while simultaneously fostering a unity between individuals and among larger groups.

Implications for Preaching

As can be seen from the discussion, the implications that identification may hold for preaching are focused in two areas: persuasion and unity.

1. Persuasion

It goes without saying that all speakers want to persuade their hearers, and preachers are no exception. At the very least, preachers want the faithful who gather each week to thoughtfully consider the gospel message they are proclaiming. At best, they hope that the gospel message proclaimed will lead to transformation and a life lived with deeper meaning and service. Responsible preachers work diligently on their sermons. Some weeks they agonize over them and lose sleep over them; the message comes only out of an all-night wrestling match that leaves them with a sore hip. Preachers want to get their words just right and communicate clearly. They want to shape the sermon in a way that will provide the greatest impact. Preachers want to persuade, not in a manipulative way, but in a way that serves as a vehicle to bring the gospel alive in people's living. They take the crafting of their sermons very seriously. However, at times the focus on words and shape can stand in the way of seeing other factors that can enhance a preacher's persuasiveness.

Identification provides preachers with an important reminder of what they already know, that a sermon is only partially about well-crafted words and a well-honed delivery; it is also about non-verbal expression and about the preacher as person. (*See* CHARACTER.) Several of the non-verbal expressions are noted above. Certainly, order receives considerable attention in the homiletical literature, and gesture continues to be acknowledged, though not with the detailed attention it once received. But Burke suggests three items that deserve more of our attention: tonality, attitude, and action.

For our purposes, attitude and tone may be considered as similar characteristics and taken together. We are well aware that the same statement can be said in such a way as to mean two totally different things. When the father says to the older son, "You are always with me," it could express lifelong affection, or it could imply that he was going to be stuck with him living at home forever. Tone or attitude makes all the difference. The question for the preacher is the state of her heart. Is it full of compassion, or is it full of consternation? Regardless of the words on the page, the attitude of the heart will be the sermon the faithful hear.

The actions, the life, of the preacher speak at least as loudly as the words. James gives us a variation on the truth of identification when he says that faith without works "is dead" (2:17). A preacher's words without his or her corresponding action will necessarily suffer in persuasive power. Burke speaks about the relationship between the container and the thing contained (1969a, 41). When they do not correspond to each other, there is some form of cognitive dissonance. When the gospel message and the gospel actions do correspond in the preacher, there is considerable power with the potential to persuade the hearer.

2. Unity

It goes without saying that achieving unity in today's church is an ongoing challenge. Yet we need only recall Corinth to remind ourselves that congregational unity, or the unity between a congregation and preacher, has often been difficult to achieve. Identification instructs us that unity is fostered when we place our attention on those places where we hold things in common. In the context of identification, it is readily seen that these commonalities have at least as much to do with actions and activities as they do with ideas and religious beliefs. Frequently, common work contributes as much, if not more, toward congregational unity than commonly held doctrinal beliefs and biblical interpretations. People will often join together in stocking the homeless food pantry or digging a drainage ditch in a developing part of the world, even though their religious and social beliefs are not in agreement. Theological reflection on what we do together can have power to unify even in the midst of widely differing theological or social perspectives. Experience tells us that acting together is the greenhouse for relational unity, even in the face of widely differing views. Common actions lead to relationship, and relationship builds unity.

Identification also teaches us to keep our attention focused on commonalities and common interests. It is easier to see our differences (because they are fewer and, therefore, more noticeable) than our commonalities. Unity calls for focus on commonalities. A brightly painted house in a neighborhood full of subdued colors will stand out, even though the floor plan and all of the building materials are identical to the homes that surround it. So, too, with our differences. They are much easier to notice and, therefore, receive the majority of our attention. Identification instructs us to keep our attention focused on what we hold in common. In so doing, unity can be enhanced while distinctiveness is maintained. *See* PERSUASION; SHAPING CONGREGATIONAL IDENTITY.

Summary

Identification informs the preacher who seeks to be persuasive to always keep three things in mind while preparing a sermon:

1. attitude of the heart (which will determine the tone of the delivery);
2. correspondence between the preacher's message and actions;
3. emphasis on the places in the congregation where there are actions and interests shared in common.

Bibliography: Kenneth Burke. *A Grammar of Motives.* (1969a); Kenneth Burke. *A Rhetoric of Motives* (1969b); *Random House Dictionary of the English Language.* 2nd ed., s.v. "rhetoric."

LOGOS
André Resner

The term *logos* may be translated as "word," "reason," "logic," "speech," or "message." The backdrop to early church usage of the term is Greco-Roman rhetoric, the OT, and the Jewish conflation of those two streams of thought in Philo. LOGOS was one of Aristotle's three means of rhetorical persuasion (along with **PATHOS** and **ETHOS**), having to do with the reasoned argumentation of a speech. The Stoics regarded logos as the organizing principle of all things. For Philo logos was the intermediary between God and the creation, God's primary means of self-revelation. The first Christians took up the term and used it in a variety of ways, including using it to represent the proclaimed gospel and Jesus Christ incarnate.

According to the Christian Scriptures, God's word (logos) is no mere sound, but is simultaneously an act, a deed, and an occurrence of something concrete in time that God wills. God's word put all things into being, made covenant with Abraham and David, freed Israel from slavery, gave Israel the **Torah** and the prophetic oracles, and made eternal promises—the firstfruit fulfillment of which we see in the Logos incarnate, Jesus Christ.

Post-ascension, the logos is spoken and lived through the human means that God chooses: primarily preachers and the church. Luke and Paul both explain the task of those preachers whom God calls as "guardians" or "assistants" (hypēretēs) of and "witnesses" (sing. martyros) to the logos. By the empowerment of God's Holy Spirit, this logos that we preach is an apocalyptic reenactment of the gospel events. In the speaking and the hearing of it, God's desired deed is done anew.

For Paul the logos was specifically the action of the cross and resurrection event, that moment when the ages turned, salvation was effected, and God inaugurated the new covenant and aeon. A new way of knowing afforded by the logos of the cross effects a new way of being in the world, one that conflicts with age-old ways of knowing and being. Though the flesh (sarx) that logos took on in the person of Jesus was gracious and redemptive, for Paul our flesh (sarx) is at ideological and existential odds with the cross's vision for healthy, just, and redemptive community. As such, the logos of the cross is an offensive and inane word for those who do not understand it within the bounds of its own rules for logic, namely, those of the self-emptying, self-crucifying consciousness and life. This logic of the cross—lived out in cruciform thought and action—is confirmed for the believing community by the reassuring presence and empowerment of the Holy Spirit. As the logos affects the alteration of the faith community's mental, spiritual, and physical landscape, it again becomes flesh in the concrete liturgical and social practices of the people of God. As mere sound or voice, logos is not God's gospel.

Karl Barth's theological project was Word centered and Word driven. (*See* WORD OF GOD.) For Barth everything depends on God's revelation, which takes a threefold form: (1) God's word enfleshed in Jesus Christ, (2) God's word proclaimed, and (3) God's word echoed in Scripture. Though God graciously uses humans to preach the very word of God, humans do not constrain the word to either succeed or fail (1936, 88–124).

Note the odd procession of the word, especially since Jesus: the logos became flesh and dwelt among us, and then flesh became logos again and was preached among us. The divinely verbal became visibly present and then humanly verbal. Oddly, God chose the church's proclamation of the logos as the means for the elongation of the gospel in time. At each point in the procession from divine speech directly given, to divine speech incarnated in Jesus the Son, to divine speech humanly mediated through proclamation, plausibility plummets. Hearers are left to wonder, to be moved by the Spirit, to embrace with faith or be repelled by incredulity or offensiveness.

Preachers, poets, and critics throughout the centuries have pinpointed the great failure of preaching to be the unfleshed, abstracted word of the gospel. The failure of the logos to take on flesh in the lives of the hearers, but especially in the life of the preacher, is preaching's chief contemporary stumbling stone. *Reduplication* was the word that Søren Kierkegaard used to describe the way in which the word is simultaneously spoken and lived in those who preach. For Kierkegaard the reduction of the word to words, articles, lectures, books, and sermons disconnected from life was worse than the ultimate heresy; it signaled the extinction of Christianity: "Christianity not being a doctrine, it is not a matter of indifference, as in the case of a doctrine, *who* expounds it if only (objectively) he says the right thing. No, Christ did not appoint professors, but followers. If Christianity (precisely because it is not a doctrine) is not reduplicated in the life of the person expounding it, then he does not expound Christianity for Christianity is a message about living and can only be expounded by being realized in [people's] lives" (Rohde 1960, 117).

This problem of the "Word preserved from flesh" does not mean that humans—whether preachers or hearers—render logos non-efficacious. That would be a kind of homiletical Donatism, where the potency of the gospel depends on the morality of the preacher. Neither does the life of the obedient hearer make the logos of God efficacious for others. Rather, the lives of faithful preachers and obedient hearers bear witness to the word's efficacy. Rudolf Bultmann argued that it is Jesus Christ himself who takes on flesh again in the preaching and hearing of the word (Bultmann 1954, 307). Thus, the soteriological power manifest in the preacher and hearer is the power of the risen Christ.

But the real problem of homiletical Docetism remains—that problem of no real bodily enfleshment, no human-in-action witness to the logos. This problem raises a serious question: If God's word accomplishes that for which God sends it, does that mean that when it is met with resistance and unbelief, or with apathy and ignorance, that God sent it among a people in order to repel and harden hearts?

Ideally, the two go together—logos richly proclaimed meeting a faith-full hearing with the obvious result of obedient living—lives lived commensurately with the gospel's calling. *See* WORD OF GOD.

Bibliography: Karl Barth. *Church Dogmatics.* Vol. 1, part 1. (1936); Wendell Berry. *A Place on Earth.* (1983); Rudolf Bultmann. *Theology of the New Testament.* 2 vols. (1954); André Resner Jr. *Preacher and Cross: Person and Message in Theology and Rhetoric.* (1999); Peter Rohde, ed. *The Diary of Søren Kierkegaard.* (1960).

MEMORY
Joseph M. Webb

All professional public address since the ancient Greeks, including that of clergy who preach, has been based on the discipline of memory. Public speech and persuasion—the rhetorical arts—were at the heart of Greek culture and learning, and the cultivation of memory was an integral dimension of that educational milieu. The Greeks devised the first mnemonics, or memory aids; in fact, Aristotle is said to have given instruction in mnemonics to Alexander the Great.

While some professional speakers today, notably politicians, read speeches from prepared manuscripts, they tend to do so only when they believe their words might become part of a policy-oriented public record. Most professional speakers, though, value maximum communication over exact word choice. Most know, too, that effective communication is far more complex than word choice itself.

Whatever else clergy are, theologically or pastorally, they are professional public speakers. In pulpit or on platform, they strive to communicate a message, a sermon. Whatever the preacher plans to say, if it is not communicated using the best resources of spontaneous, interactive speech, will have less effect than it otherwise could have. Put another way, the universal expectation of the sermon, however it is theologically understood, is that it will not only capture and hold the complete, undivided attention of those who hear it, but that even the hearing of it will create an emotionally moving experience.

In order to do so, the sermon must be intense, direct, passion-filled, and unmediated. This is particularly true if one is speaking to an audience of young people in a vibrant, music-infused, contemporary worship setting. (*See* EMERGING CHURCH PREACHING; PREACHING TO YOUTH.) These emerging worship environments are unfailingly informal—and all effective preaching in them must be fully informal as well. This becomes possible, though, only when the preacher commits to memory the substance of what he or she wants to say, and then, without prompting, speaks spontaneously and fluidly.

So is the preacher, or any professional speaker, supposed to just wing it and talk off the top of his or her head? The answer is no; and this is where memory plays its decisive role. Professional public speaking, as preaching should be, is always fully and carefully prepared; in fact, hearers can always instinctively tell when it is not. The sermon's prepared content is never to be haphazard or ill thought out. Nor does it arise from a fully written manuscript laboriously committed to memory and then recited. (*See* PERFORMING THE MANUSCRIPT.) That was occasionally done in bygone years, but today's schedules do not allow most preachers to contemplate such a thing; moreover, reciting a memorized piece well requires a level of acting skill that few speakers, including preachers, possess.

The use of memory for today's sermon works best week upon week when the preacher studies fully and carefully, devises what he or she wants to say, and then crafts a simple, sequential outline of the material. At this point, then, as a final step, the preacher commits the sermon's finely tuned outline consciously and deliberately to memory. This is the classic procedure for public address. It allows a preacher to speak from careful preparation and, at the same time, concentrate fully on direct, unimpeded, informal communication of the prepared sermon with hearers.

This procedure, which congregations most often view as the welcome willingness of a preacher to "speak from the heart," requires one to overcome the rather common fear of memorizing. "Others can memorize, I know," one will say, "but my memory is not very good"; or "I was in a play once and forgot my lines—I could not do this." These fears, though, tend not to be justified. Extensive research teaches us that the human powers of memorization are far stronger than we know. Two things are necessary: (1) that we learn how to memorize and (2) that we practice doing it; the more we practice, the better we get at it. Once we learn how to use our memory, and then cultivate that memory by using it, we invariably discover that this extraordinary mental faculty does not let us down. With each sermon, when the studying has been carefully done, the only memorizing required is a seven- or eight-item list, an outline of items that frames everything the preacher wants to say.

Some wonder about memorizing Scripture as a part of this process. While some homileticians advocate that, those who urge speaking from a memorized outline generally advise against it. The contention is that between the informal public speaking and the reading of biblical text, an important balance is at work: reading Scripture gives the biblical text a certain weight of authority; the power of the preacher's words, then, rests not on being read but spoken "from the heart."

Over the past century, the scientific study of memory has intensified, mostly in conjunction with the explosion in educational research. In fact, the questions about how learning and memory are connected have occupied much psychological, sociological, neurological, and even hereditary research. We have learned a number of things about memory in recent years.

We know that there is no one thing that can be called *memory*; instead, there are numerous kinds of memory. The two major kinds are long-term and short-term. Under the heading *long-term memory* is what some scholars call episodic or autobiographical memory; this is the world of personal memories that arise from the ongoing living of life itself. We remember episodes, or experiences, from our past; not all of them, to be sure, but enough to bank year upon year in our memories—all without ever trying to remember them. In addition to the episodic or autobiographical memories are what are often called the *semantic memories*; these are comprised of the thousands of things we are taught at all levels of our schooling—the stories of history, the math formulas, the rules of English, things that serve us throughout our lives via memory.

Long-term memories come into play when a preacher is called on to speak extemporaneously or on the spur of the moment—truly without advance preparation. A church schoolteacher is unexpectedly ill or a guest preacher fails to appear, and the preacher must step forward. Even though this process has seldom, if ever, been explored in homiletical literature, speakers—even preachers—can learn to respond well in such situations by drawing on their own long-term memories.

Clearly, though, what we know as *short-term memory* is that which best serves professional speakers—and preachers. What do we know about short-term memory? We know that despite various mnemonic devices such as acrostics, short-term memory is, most reliably, the art of rehearsal or, more directly, the art of repetition. One repeats a series of items again and again for several short periods of time—the way one studies for an examination. Outlined phrases become burned in the memory, so to speak; and when one repeats the rehearsal process at several intervals spaced a few hours apart, the material sticks.

We know, too, that certain conditions inhibit the ability of the mind to register and remember items during such rehearsals. For example, poor health or tiredness hinders memorization. If one is not particularly interested in the material being memorized, the mind does not hang onto it well. If there are distractions during the time set aside for rehearsal of the material, memory will function poorly. And when the list of items being memorized is organized badly, or does not have a kind of internal logic that the mind can intuitively grasp, memorizing is done only with difficulty.

When these conditions change—that is, when one is feeling well and is rested, when one is deeply interested in the material, when one is able to concentrate on rehearsal without distraction, and when the material is arranged in a well-ordered sequence—then a complex list of items can be memorized within a couple of hours.

All memory research indicates that one can fully trust one's short-term memory, particularly if one goes about the rehearsal process in a disciplined fashion. Can one occasionally forget during speaking something that was committed to memory? Of course, but this usually results from one of two things: either some trauma intervenes between the rehearsal and the speaking, or the mind signals that something in the outline is out of place.

In the first case, which can present a serious problem, the preacher is best advised to preach with the prepared written outline in front of her or him. In the second case, the preacher should simply skip the forgotten point and go to the next one, knowing that the sermon, when completed, will invariably be better than what was originally prepared. Ironically, audiences (and particularly congregations) respond remarkably well even to memory bobbles when preachers are willing to speak to them in the direct, intensively personal way that memorizing the sermon outline makes possible. One has to try the process only once in order to appreciate the unexpected dynamic of it all. *See* ORAL/AURAL COMMUNICATION; WITHOUT NOTES.

Bibliography: Alan Baddeley. *Your Memory: A User's Guide.* (2004); Elizabeth and Robert Bjork, eds. *Memory.* (1996); James L. McGraugh. *Memory and Emotion: The Making of Lasting Memories.* (2003); Endel Tulving and Fergis I. M. Craik, eds. *The Oxford Handbook of Memory.* (2000).

ORAL/AURAL COMMUNICATION
Richard F. Ward

Communication is a process through which human beings employ language, imagery, bodily presence, and gesture to order impressions and information, imbue signs and symbols with significance, and bring persons and objects into relationship in the construction of meaning. Oral and aural communication as it applies to preaching is concerned with the various roles that bodies play in these transactions. Communication is the performance of intentionality through the agencies of voice, body, and enactment.

Communication takes place within social contexts. Within those frameworks for interaction, conventions, styles, codes, and standards are culturally negotiated and mediated and determine how bodies are employed in particular transactions. For example, in one cultural setting maintaining eye contact throughout an exchange of information might gain a desired effect. In another direct eye contact might be read as a sign of disrespect.

Communication studies are organized around models, images, or analogues for the process, each tending in different ways to emphasize speakers, messages, or effect upon receptors. The task of educating men and women for the preaching ministry has tended to favor speaker-based models for studying communication. However, the rapid rise and development of electronic and digital technologies have pushed linear-transmissions models out of the center. (The dynamic interplay between speakers, messages, and receptors, however, still provides an important framework for reflection.) An action that communicates through the use of voice and body is perhaps best imagined these days as taking place within an interactive web wherein speakers, messages, and listeners take turns leading the dance of meaning-making.

When speakers take the lead in the oral/aural communication dance, the body of the speaker goes to work as an instrument of oral communication; the bodies of the listeners become surfaces that reflect their collective and individual responses. We can think of those responses as soundings from the depths of a listener's experience and being. Language about speaker-centered models of communication draws upon linear imagery at some times and elliptical imagery at others. On the one hand, we evaluate a speaker on how well he or she gets a message across the space between the speaker and his or her listener. We sometimes depict this process as an arrow shot from a bow that aims at a target. (You have heard, have you not, of "target audiences"?) On the other hand, we imagine the feedback that a speaker gets from a listener as a loop, or a message that the speaker receives by reading the body language of the listener (and sometimes through auditory cues). The capable speaker is able to adjust what he or she is saying to suit the purpose of the transaction based on his or her interpretation of listeners' responses.

Whether the process is imagined as bows and arrows or as arcs and loops, the speaker's goal in the encounter is to control the flow and interaction initiated and to bring thought and intention into line with vocal and physical behaviors. Obstacles to making sense of the encounter are sometimes described as noise. The speaker's voice and body can often be the source of the noise that interferes with making some sense of the encounter. For example, the attitude or tone of voice that a speaker uses in oral communication may reveal more meaning than what is actually said. Or if there is little congruence between what is said and how it is said, a listener may question its meaning and value. Listeners quite commonly read a gesture or pick up a tone of voice that does not support the flow of thought.

Using linear and elliptical images of communication, a speaker learns the habits and behaviors that will help initiate the task of meaning-making and establish a measure of control over the interaction. Educating speakers using these images involves helping speakers control their voices and bodies and work toward the congruity between thought, movement, and articulation in a way that listeners will call natural.

Of course the point of speaking is to convey a message that is meaningful to both speakers and listeners. Though some messages are rendered in silence, the majority of message-making employs language. Messages intended as written communication sometimes do not translate well into oral communication; language crafted for the eyes of a silent, solitary reader is different from what is suitable for the ear. Oral language privileges imagery over abstraction since it lies in closer proximity to primary human experience. Oral language does not shy away from the colloquial or from idioms. It makes freer use of rhythm, repetition, and refrains because it has a different sense of time. Oral communication is evanescent, that is, it belongs to the moment of utterance. Without access to a written text of a speech, a listener cannot go back over something that a speaker says. Rhythm and repetition give emphasis to a speech, making it easier for the speech to have resonance in the experience of the listener. Concrete imagery also helps the speech take up residence in the listener's memory and imagination.

The purpose of writing changes when its end is oral/aural communication. If there is to be a manuscript or an outline, the speaker will use it as memory aid for the oral event. (*See* MEMORY.) If a speaker places too much emphasis on what is written, neglecting how the words will be said, then the message conveyed will belong more to the medium of print than it will to orality. Such messages are less likely to engage the listener's attention, thought, and imagination. A sermon, for example, is not a typographical object that one delivers to a passive audience. It is, rather, a lively form of human address whose significance is shared within the flow of time by a speaker and his or her listeners. The dynamism of the sermon event defines preaching as dramatic. Preaching is dramatic not because it is marked by a particularly expressive theatrical style but because it takes shape from the different worlds created by language. As the languages of religion, liturgical tradition, and theology are conjoined with the affective language of value and feeling and the colloquial language of everyday experience, they converge, conflate, and collide into oral language the preacher needs for the sermon event.

Communication studies that approach preaching as an aural/oral process may also help a speaker study a biblical text. A text addresses a reader, but outside of any oral/aural context. Writing and print extricate a text out of the fluidity, dynamism, and contested space of orality. The task of interpreting a text may very well be enriched by reoralizing a text. This involves employing the resources of the voice and body to explore, then convey, the affective quality of the text through oral communication. Texts' messages are polyphonic, multivocal, and capable of addressing listeners at different levels of meaning. Voicing and enacting a text's words, gestures, attitudes, and structures inform performed interpretations and open up different fields of meaning for speakers and listeners. Through performance, a text gains a new sense of immediacy, finds new audiences, and gains new futures for interpretation through the performer's body and voice. Oral interpretations, whether through voicing, dramatizing thoughts and actions suggested in a text, or through preparation of performed interpretations, transform written communication into orality and deepen speakers' and listeners' understanding of how a text communicates.

The rapid continuing development of digital and electronic technologies focuses attention on communication studies that emphasize reception (the listener's role) in the making of meaning. What this implies for preaching and proclamation is quite complex. Listeners whose eyes, ears, and even thought have been trained in an age dominated by new technologies have different standards for what makes for good speech than those who were formed in print culture. Of course in the communication world of our congregations and religious communities, there are representatives of both digital and print cultures. Each has different impressions of what would make for effective communication from the pulpit. The latter listener may place a higher priority on what the preacher says, that is, upon (what used to be called) the sermon's content. The digital/electronic listener cannot get thought without its being spoken and presented in a lively, engaging, even conversational style.

However the listeners' eyes, ears, and bodies were trained by whatever communication media dominated their formation, listeners in any communication age respond to these values: authenticity, sincerity, and trust. Good communication depends on the quality of the engagement between the speaker and the listener. No amount of technique or style will displace what the ancients called the ETHOS of the speaker. Ethos refers to the character of the speaker, the identity of that speaker, his or her trustworthiness to speak truth, and the congruity between what is said, who is saying it, and how it is being spoken. It would be hard to overestimate the importance of the role this plays in oral/aural communication. *See* TECHNOLOGY AND THE SERMON.

Bibliography: Jana Childers. *Performing the Word: Preaching as Theatre.* (1998); Donald Davis. *Writing as a Second Language: From Experience to Story to Prose.* (2000); Robert G. Jacks. *Just Say the Word: Writing for the Ear.* (1996); Richard F. Ward. *Speaking of the Holy: The Art of Communication in Preaching.* (2001).

PATHOS/FEELING
John C. Holbert

Pathos is Greek, a noun arising from a verb meaning "to undergo," "to experience," "to suffer." The noun, pathos, preserves this broad range of meanings. In studies of classical rhetoric, three basic divisions of an orator's (or rhetor's) art were catalogued: logos, ethōs, and pathos (LOGOS; ETHOS). Culminating in the work of Aristotle (384–322 BCE), Greek rhetoricians saw clear separations between the three. Logos was used mainly to teach; ethōs was employed to delight; pathos was used to persuade. Such a division could be maintained only if each of the three was sharply identified with one aspect of the speaker's work. Logos was the content of the speech; ethōs was the person of the speaker; pathos was the emotion generated by the first two.

Such a formulation was and is too simplistic, however much it may be used for easy memory. The fact is, as the Greeks and the later Roman rhetoricians recognized, the functions of logos, ethos, and pathos are far more intertwined and far more complex than any simplistic chart might suggest. Listen to Cicero in his *De Oratio* or "On the Character of the Orator" (55 BCE):

> For who is ignorant that the highest power of an orator consists in exciting the minds of men to anger, or to hatred, or to grief, or in recalling them from these more violent emotions to gentleness and compassion? Which power will never be able to effect its object by eloquence, unless in him who has obtained a thorough insight into the nature of mankind, and all the passions of humanity, and those causes by which our minds are either impelled or restrained. (Cicero 1970)

Thus, ethos and pathos may be seen as different degrees of the same thing; a speaker cannot persuade to or away from passion unless he or she has rich insight into human nature and especially those parts of our natures that allow us to be "impelled or restrained." So a speaker must be attentive to his or her ethos as well as to those aspects of the listeners, since the speaker's ethos, as well as the listeners', will determine whether or not they will be moved by the speech. One might say in light of this Ciceronian reflection that ethos, vigorously and thoughtfully expressed, produces pathos. Note, too, that "eloquence" alone, logos by itself, no matter how elegant the argument, may not affect persuasion apart from careful attention to ethos, the nature of the speaker and hearer, and pathos, the possibilities of how the hearers may or may not be persuaded. (*See* PERSUASION.)

The long history of the study of the art of rhetoric has done nothing else than ring interesting changes on these classical formulations, now focusing on one or the other of the three as dominant, now assessing the complexities of the relationships between them. Because of a general ignorance of this history and its complexities, it is fair to say that in the popular mind rhetoric has been reduced to pathos, which in turn has been reduced to persuasion, and more negatively to linguistic manipulation. However, it is crucial that the preacher not make this mistake. Pathos is not merely manipulation nor is it merely a generalized feeling. Augustine was surely correct when, under the influence of Cicero, he said, "These things are required of an Orator. To teach. To delight. And to persuade." (*Christian Instruction*, ch. 12, paragraph 27; Rotelle 1996). Preachers are called to persuade, and because that is true, they must pay the most careful attention to the means by which they do so. Biblical examples are helpful.

In 1 Sam 12 there appears a classic example of persuasion. Samuel, the prophet of God, has shown a consistent desire not to have a king, believing that only YHWH could be king of Israel. Saul, finally anointed secretly by Samuel (10:1), however reluctantly, now wins a huge victory over the Ammonites. Samuel anoints the new military darling of the people in public ceremony. Then he speaks.

He begins by using his own ethos in two ways. He first says that he has done what they requested; he has given them a king (12:1-2*a*). But he quickly adds that, he, Samuel, is "old and gray." He also notes immediately that he has grown old and gray precisely in their service (2*b*). His gray hair has come because of his work for them. In all things, then, Samuel has acted on behalf of his people.

Second, he demands that the people judge him. Has he ever stolen from them? Has he ever defrauded anyone? Has he oppressed anyone or taken a bribe (v. 3)? Samuel stands as a completely blameless and trustworthy man; no one can say otherwise. Thus, he has worked only for the people, and he has done so in a completely righteous way. The people publicly agree with him that his assessment of his ethos is correct (vv. 4, 6).

Now the logos part of the address begins. The content is a lengthy history of Israel, but more particularly the numerous ways in which the people have rejected their God (vv. 6-12). This history is culminated in Samuel's inclusion of himself in a list of the heroes sent by God to rescue the rebellious people time and again. (Many translations choose the Greek version's "Samson" in v. 11, but the Hebrew text plainly reads "Samuel.") Thus is ethos added to logos; the thoroughly righteous and self-sacrificing Samuel was also sent by God in exactly the way that Moses and Aaron and other great figures were sent. Samuel's words are thus given divine force and locus. Verse 12 now turns to accusation; the people's request for a king is nothing less than another example of Israelite rebellion for which they need serious repentance.

After warning the people what will happen to them and their king if they do not obey God, which they clearly have not done by asking for the king in the first place, God's hand will turn against them (v. 15). Then the furious prophet calls down lightning and rain on the harvest. After that demonstration of power, the pathos aspect is demonstrated. The people are terrified and beg Samuel to pray for them, admitting finally that their request for a king was in fact sin (v. 19). He promises to pray for them but warns them again that only righteous behavior will bring favor from God while wicked actions, such as the ones they have done again and again, will earn fury from God and the removal of them and their king.

Here is a wonderful example of logos and ethos leading directly to pathos. The emotion generated is fear and the result conversion to Samuel's view of things, the apparent goal of the speech from the beginning, however mildly it began. One could evaluate this speech as either richly effective in its movement toward change or darkly manipulative, depending upon one's perception of Samuel and his relationship to Saul and God. Pathos, emotions generated in the listener, is a result of a speaker's careful attention to her or his person as the particular one presenting the speech's content (logos). No genuine pathos, for good or ill, may occur without recognition of ethos and logos.

A NT example may prove helpful. Paul has regularly been examined for his use of rhetoric in his letters. His uses of logos and ethos to effect conversion are unforgettable. Compare the two very different ways that he addresses the recipients of his letters to the Galatians and the Philippians. In the former, he starts in a rage. He has heard that those he originally spoke to have very quickly begun to believe later speakers who do not agree with Paul's views. How foolish could they be! Paul has spoken only truth, a truth he did not learn from any human being (1:11). It came from his encounter with the risen Jesus, and if anyone should dare to say anything else than Paul has said, even if he be an angel of God (!), "let him be accursed" (1:8 KJV). This is logos and ethos with a vengeance, designed to shame the hearer (pathos) into admitting error.

Compare Paul in Philippians. Now the apostle, writing from a prison, is sweetness and light as he remembers with great fondness his time in Philippi and the news of the community he founded while there. His continual references to his imprisonment (ethos), his assurances that God is using even that hardship for the spread of the gospel, and his reference to the apparently well-known Christ hymn (2:6-11; logos) urge the Philippians to continue in their good work and love for one another (pathos). Paul thus uses two very different rhetorical strategies in his letters to Galatia and Philippi. It appears certain that his writing to the Philippians is more in tune with his understanding and experience of the matchless grace of Jesus Christ.

These biblical examples, among many others, demonstrate the power of rhetoric to persuade. Historically, preachers have perhaps too often followed Samuel by using fear as a tactic for conversion, bending logos and ethos in the process. But in Philippians we see Paul use ethos and logos for building up a new community, generating hope and joy for a richer future with God. No preacher can stay ignorant of the sheer power of her or his words to offer the joy and demand of the gospel. Attention to that power, and its many possible uses and misuses, remains crucial. See CHARACTER; NEW HOMILETIC.

Bibliography: Cicero. *Cicero on Oratory and Orators.* Translated and edited by J. S. Watson. (1970) 19; O. C. Edwards Jr. *A History of Preaching.* (2004); Lawrence D. Green. "Pathos." *Encyclopedia of Rhetoric.* Edited by Thomas O. Sloane. (2001) 554–69; André Resner Jr. *Preacher and Cross.* (1999); Ronald E. Sleeth. *Persuasive Preaching.* (1956); John E. Rotelle, ed. *The Works of St. Augustine: A Translation for the 21st Century.* Vol. 11. (1996); Jacob Wisse. *Ethos and Pathos from Aristotle to Cicero.* (1989).

PERSUASION
Lucy Lind Hogan

Persuasion is the process by which a person or persons seek(s) to influence the decision making and/or actions of another person or persons by means of language and/or symbolic actions. Unlike coercion or manipulation, which control through physical or emotional force and power disparities, persuasion assumes the free choice of the person or persons to decide or act. Persuasion does not make people do what they do not want to do. It is, as its Latin root, *suasio,* implies, persons urging other persons. In the end, however, the decisions are ultimately the choice of the one being persuaded. These efforts to persuade, engage, and encourage take place in a complex arrangement and interaction of communicators, receivers, ideas, arguments, images, values, contexts, time, and exigencies.

Classical Understanding of Persuasion

The investigation of and training in persuasion are grounded in Greco-Roman civic life. By observing speeches, theorists were able to identify and describe successful persuasive strategies. It was determined that different situations and different audiences required specific rhetorical approaches. The goal was to develop specific strategies that would be effective in the court, legislature, or public ceremonial events.

In his work *Rhetoric,* Aristotle examined the nature of the requirements for each of these primary rhetorical situations. He discussed the principal strategies or means of persuasion that are available to speakers: logos, pathos, and ethos. (*See* PATHOS/FEELING.)

The most obvious means of persuasion are logical arguments. Logos, rational appeals, takes the form of either DEDUCTIVE or INDUCTIVE reasoning. Deductive reasoning begins with a general statement or observation and moves to a specific instance. Aristotle identified the deductive logic appropriate in rhetoric or persuasion as the enthymeme. Unlike the logical syllogism, with its major premise, minor premise, and conclusion, the enthymeme is a truncated syllogism in which only one premise is stated along with the conclusion and the other premise is implied. The other rational appeal available is inductive reasoning or the example. Inductive reasoning begins with observable, verifiable instances and leaps to generalizations about those phenomena.

Clearly, arguments and examples are an important dimension of persuasive strategies, but they are not the only way that speakers persuade an audience. Equally important as a means of persuasion is the emotional state of the listener. Aristotle argued that people make decisions by both their emotions and their reason. Knowledge of an audience's attitudes and values was essential to the speaker seeking to persuade an audience. With that knowledge the speaker was able to employ pathos and craft a speech that would place the listeners in the appropriate emotional frame of mind. If, for example, a speaker wanted to urge people to war, then he or she would need to rouse the audience to anger or fear.

Finally, Aristotle argued that the character of the speaker, ethos, had to be developed in the speech. Listeners were more likely to be persuaded by someone whom they believed to be of good character, someone who demonstrated clear reasoning and knowledge of the topic under question, and seemed trustworthy. Through the arguments the speaker chose, the tone of speech, and delivery, the speaker was able to demonstrate this trustworthiness. Aristotle suggests that ethos may be, in the end, the most potent persuasive appeal.

Following the contributions of the Roman rhetoricians, Cicero (*On the Ideal Orator*) and Quintilian (*The Orator's Education*), discussions of persuasion moved away from lively philosophical discussions into the nature and process of persuasion and became handbooks on how to construct the perfect speech. The understanding of the role of persuasion in preaching contributed to this shift, as did the increasing emphasis on style and eloquence rather than philosophy and dialectic. Nevertheless, the understanding of persuasion as intentional, audience centered, and practical has continued to shape the conversation.

Renewing the Conversation

Contemporary understandings of rhetoric, communication, and the persuasive event have moved far beyond the unidirectional speaker-listener-message model of classical rhetoric. Over the past century, there have been efforts not only to resurrect the classical discussions of rhetoric and persuasion, shaking off the accretions of the centuries that have demeaned and diminished this important dimension of public life, but also to rethink the role that rhetoric and persuasion play in every dimension of life. This has been identified as "the rhetorical turn." In the move to examine the suasory dimension of all forms of human inquiry, even and especially those that purported to operate from a position of so-called neutrality and objectivity, modernist and positivist approaches have been critiqued. Following this turn, reason is understood to some degree as socially constructed and rhetoric and persuasion as the arena where truth and knowledge are explored and developed.

The static and rather limited Aristotelian and Ciceronian approaches to persuasion have given way to a much more fluid, non-linear understanding. Persuasion occurs beyond the traditional arenas of the forensic, deliberative, epideictic. In addition to the individual speaker crafting a speech for an audience, persuasion might be understood to take place at the micro level (i.e., interpersonal) as well as the macro level, the persuasive efforts of a political or advertising campaign. Persuasion occurs in and through speeches, but also in motion pictures, protest rallies, conversation, and dialogue.

There has also been a rethinking of logos. Persuasion occurs through words, but also through a variety of symbolic actions, rituals, and images. The context in which a speech is given adds to the persuasive effort. The oral/aural dimension of persuasion can be enhanced greatly by the visual and kinesthetic. (*See* ORAL/AURAL COMMNUNICATION.) Likewise, the nature of persuasive argument has been revised and expanded. Persuasion cannot rely solely on analytical reasoning. Philosophers Stephen Toulmin, Chaim Perelman, and Lucie Olbrechts-Tyteca have sought to describe persuasive strategies that allow us to negotiate the practical, the contextual, and the contingent. There has also been increased interest in the understanding of narrative as a persuasive strategy. (*See* NARRATIVE PREACHING.) We tell stories not only to teach and delight, as Cicero described in *On the Ideal Orator* 21.69, but also to move.

Over the centuries we have witnessed significant changes in the way people communicate and persuade. First was the move from the oral/aural to the print culture. Now we are witnessing the move from print and mass media to the Internet and digital culture, as well as the shift from oral to the visual. These shifts will have a profound effect on our persuasive efforts.

Preaching and Persuasion

The relationship between persuasion and preaching has been a stormy one throughout the history of the church. Similar tensions had long been part of the political world. Just as many of the church fathers had disparaged and rejected rhetoric, so too had Socrates. In Plato's *Gorgias* 462–466, Socrates declared rhetoric or persuasion a form of flattery that made falsehoods appear to be true. Two primary issues concerning the role of persuasion in preaching have continued to reoccur: the epistemological question (i.e., the nature of truth and revelation) and the anthropological question of human action in collaboration with the divine.

Although many of the early church fathers had been trained in and had been teachers of the rhetorical arts, they rejected the use of rhetoric at their conversion. Preaching was not to be seen as persuasive speech. Such early church preachers did not need to use rhetoric to discover the truth and did not need to persuade others through rational arguments. Faith and conversion were gifts of the Holy Spirit.

By the 4th cent., Augustine of Hippo had come to realize that, in order for the church and preachers to compete in a culture that valued eloquence and persuasion, preachers needed to develop these skills. In Book Four of *Christian Instruction*, Augustine was the first to develop a Christian approach to rhetoric and persuasion employing Cicero's understanding that we are to teach, delight, and move.

Augustine's truce produced only a tentative settlement. The rejection of preaching as suasory discourse has continued in some understandings of the Christian life. A recent example is found in the work of Karl Barth, whose dialectical theology most soundly rejects persuasion. According to Barth, preaching is to be understood solely as proclamation. In the Barthian view, preaching as proclamation is God's word, not human words, and as such is seen as the very antithesis of persuasion. Only God, according to Barth, can persuade, and conversion occurs through the words of Scripture and the actions of the Holy Spirit, not through rhetorical argumentation of the preacher (*The Preaching of the Gospel* 1963).

Such a rejection of the suasory dimension of preaching grew out of a particular theological perspective and an arguably truncated understanding of rhetoric and persuasion. Contemporary understandings open new possibilities for recovering the Augustinian rapprochement between preaching and persuasion. *See* CONVERSATIONAL PREACHING; NEW HOMILETIC; RHETORICAL CRITICISM; RHETORICAL DEVICES.

Bibliography: Aristotle. *Rhetoric;* Augustine. *Christian Instruction;* Karl Barth. *The Preaching of the Gospel.* (1963); Cicero. *On the Ideal Orator;* David S. Cunningham. *Faithful Persuasion: In Aid of a Rhetoric of Christian Theology.* (1991); Lucy Hogan. "Rethinking Persuasion: Developing an Incarnational Theology of Preaching." *Homiletic* 24 (1999) 1–12; Richard Lischer. "Why I Am Not Persuasive." *Homiletic* 24 (1999) 13–16; Chaim Perelman and Lucie Olbrechts-Tyteca. *The New Rhetoric.* (1969); Plato. *Gorgias;* Quintilian. *The Orator's Education;* Herbert W. Simons. *Persuasion in Society.* (2001); Stephen Toulmin. *The Uses of Argument.* (2003).

RHETORICAL DEVICES
Robert S. Reid

Since the time of Aristotle, three kinds of reasoning have been distinguished: logical, dialectical, and rhetorical. Where logical and dialectical reasoning have as their purpose the determination of truth, the purpose of rhetorical reasoning is to influence an audience. Rhetoric shares the concept of argument with logic and dialectic, but rhetorical devices are unique to rhetoric as means that communicators use to make non-cognitive appeals to emotion, the imagination, and the will (motivation). Thus, rhetorical devices refer to non-logical, figurative uses of language employed either to enhance or to change meaning. Traditional divisions are often made between figures of speech (*copia verborum*) and figures of thought (*copia rerum*). Figures of speech typically push use of a word beyond its ordinary meaning (e.g., metaphor, irony, synecdoche, and metonymy) or, conversely, maintain its literal meaning but arrange it in relationship to other words in a way that gives added significance (e.g., alliteration, anaphora, chiasmus, anabasis, and catabasis). (*See* METAPHOR AND FIGURES OF SPEECH.) Figures of thought refer to larger-scale uses of language to accomplish these same ends (e.g., fable, allegory, oracle, parable, and proverb).

From antiquity students have studied principles of rhetoric and mastered distinctions among the rhetorical devices to learn creative ways of developing what to say and how to say it. The goal has always been to build a repertoire of stock ideas and eloquent expressions that could be available for any occasion. Mastery comes when a communicator is able to draw naturally upon the right rhetorical devices at the right moment. For example, in the 1963 March on Washington speech, Martin Luther King Jr. developed six set pieces in the first part of the speech that use the rhetorical device of *anaphora*—the repetition of phrases at the beginning of separate sentences or clauses—to create a litany of images that build to a *climax* of prophetic, biblical hope. King once informed an interviewer that the "Go back" set piece was meant to be his closing *peroration*. Then, "all of a sudden this thing came to me that I have used—I'd used it many times before, that thing about 'I have a dream'— and I just felt that I wanted to use it here" (Garrow 1988, 283). By adding the "I have a dream . . . ," the "With this faith . . . ," and the "Let freedom ring . . ." set pieces, King rhetorically transformed the prepared speech of an eloquent civil rights leader into the inspired words of a national prophet—a transformation that continues to call people in each successive generation to live into its eschatologically anticipated prophetic hope of redemptive justice.

Rhetorical Devices Used in Scripture

Augustine devoted a portion of Book 4 of *Doctr. chr.* to showing scriptural examples of teaching composed in the plain style, of delighting listeners composed in the middle style, and of moving listeners composed in the grand style (4.33–58). And the Venerable Bede (673–735) identified 17 figures of thought and 28 figures of speech in 122 passages of Scripture (*De Schematibus et Tropis*, 96–122). A rich tradition exists that treats the Bible as a treasure trove of examples of every possible rhetorical device, culminating in the one-thousand-page handbook, *Figures of Speech Used in the Bible*, by E. W. Bullinger first published in 1898. Identification of the use of such devices, of course, does not prove that biblical authors were making conscious use of the Greek or Roman rhetorical tradition. Paul may have received training in Greco-Roman rhetoric as a function of schooling required for Roman citizenship. Luke and the writer of Hebrews may also have been schooled in composing argument that would be well received by 1st-cent. Mediterranean readers.

It is doubtful that other biblical authors were formally schooled in this tradition.

The ability to document extensive use of figures in Scripture speaks more to the effort of these various writers to discover myriad ways to make both rational and non-cognitive appeals to the imagination of the community meant to be inspired by these writings. The devices that appear to be most natural to ancient Near Eastern thought tend to involve forms of parallelism in expression. Whether by simple paired parallelism as in, "I will praise the Lord as long as I live; / I will sing praises to my God all my life long" (Ps 146:2), or "Your right hand, O LORD, glorious in power— / your right hand, O LORD, shattered the enemy" (Exod 15:6), the OT is replete with this tendency toward seconding an idea with an echo balance. Christian authors are more apt to report usage of *chiastic* juxtapositions, where significance is heightened by a symmetrical reversal of this tendency to create echo balance:

A   If any want to become my followers,
B   let them deny themselves
B'   and take up their cross
A'   and follow me.
A   For those who want to save their life
B   will lose it,
B'   and those who lose their life for my sake,
            and for the sake of the gospel,
A'   will save it. (Mark 8:34-35)

Preachers wisely attend to the power of such devices because they reveal ways in which the original biblical author worked to create memorable phrases that would capture the hearts and the minds of listeners. If the force of such expressions arises as much from its form as from its content, then preachers would want to exegete the affective function of such rhetorical devices as readily as they exegete for theological meaning. Identification of rhetorical devices at the sentence/phrase level is as important as the identification of the genre at the level of composition as a whole. Preachers concerned with how texts function as inspired literature would treat non-cognitive appeals and cognitive appeals equally in their effort to preach intentions aligned with the original intentions of biblical texts. (*See* HOMILETICAL [THEOLOGICAL] CRITICISM.)

Types of Devices

Device definitions are readily available in Lanham's *A Handlist of Rhetorical Terms* or on the Internet. For preaching they can be usefully distinguished in three ways:

1. Those that create effect:

For some the story is the self. The perpendicular pronoun becomes the Maypole around which the steps of life are danced. These potent egos trade in society's marketplace under the firm name, "Me, Myself, and I, Inc." Ethical decisions are made on the basis of self-interest: What's good for me is right, what's bad for me is wrong. For all such, the world turns on the narrow axis of the self! (Ernest T. Campbell, "What's the Story?" Willimon 2005, 166)

Here *metaphor, irony,* and *metonymy* interplay evocatively and conclude in a profound synecdoche.

2. Those that create emphasis:

[Like Simon from Cyrene] faith calls you out of the crowd: . . . out of the safety of non-involvement into risk; . . . out of hereditary belief into relationship with the suffering Jesus; . . . out of the crowd into a confrontation with the cross, and the person carrying it. That is the powerful pressure of the cross, when it lays hold on you. (Peter Storey, "When the Cross Lays Hold on You." Willimon 2005, 278)

Here a lingering by way of *epimone* and *anaphora* is created that builds through *anabasis* to a *climax* formed by a *chiastic*-like assertion concerning the work of the cross.

3. Those that create epiphany:

Today, the snake's back to see how things are going. He's no less scary, but he still works for God. And this time, in this story, the knowledge he offers is not the forbidden but the saving kind. Hung on a pole, shining in the sun, he is God's own fiery reminder that enemies and angels can look a lot alike. And that the only one who truly knows the difference between them is the one to whom all, all the snakes, belong. (Barbara Brown Taylor, "The Snake Savior." Willimon 2005, 353.)

Here *allegory* is interwoven with contrast (*syncrisis*) and a heaping up of images (*congeries*) to create *parable*-like insight that facilitates coming-to-understanding for listeners.

Rhetorical devices also tend to support different orientations to preaching style. Some preachers present themselves as authorized expositors of scriptural texts or doctrinal beliefs who seek to teach or inform listeners. Such preachers tend to use devices that serve clarity, concision, and directness of language. Other preachers present themselves as wise sages who employ careful word order to push language usage beyond its ordinary meaning. These preachers desire to pique the interest or please the listener who responds to carefully polished sermons. Still other preachers inhabit the dramatic persona of the impassioned speaker who uses ornate or embellished arrangements in language relationships. These preachers want to create memorable ideas and phrases intended to move and inspire listeners to actively respond to the message.

John Henry Newman once wrote, "Matter and expression are parts of one: style is thinking out into language" (1878, 208). The preacher who learns how to make knowing use of different rhetorical devices and different rhetorical styles is mastering the craft of letting sentence form work together with sermon content to effectively name God and name grace in the pulpit. *See* PERSUASION; STYLE.

Bibliography: Augustine. *De doctrina christiana;* Bede. *De Schematibus et Tropis;* David J. Garrow. *Bearing the Cross: Martin Luther King, Jr. and the Southern Christian Leadership Conference.* (1988); Richard A. Lanham. *A Handlist of Rhetorical Terms.* 2nd ed. (1991); Joseph Miller, Michael Prosser, and Thomas Benson, eds. "Bede's De Schematibus et Tropis." *Readings in Medieval Rhetoric.* (1973) 96–122; John Henry Newman. *The Idea of a University.* 1878 (1982); William H. Willimon, ed. *Sermons from Duke Chapel.* (2005).

STYLE
O. C. Edwards Jr.

In ordinary speech, style has a variety of meanings that ranges through the way one speaks or writes (as opposed to the content); the shape or design of something (e.g., a garment); to elegance or distinction in the way one does something. Being in style means being consistent with the latest fashions. Since the ancient Greeks first began to analyze what makes public speaking effective, however, style has had a more restricted meaning in relation to rhetoric. The classical writers saw five tasks that needed to be performed in preparing a speech. The first was invention, figuring out what to say to make a point. Next came disposition, working out the arrangement or outline into which the material would be distributed. Then came what was called **phrasis** in Greek and *elocutio* in Latin, what we call style. It involved putting thoughts into the language that communicates them most effectively. After that came memory, preparation for delivery, and delivery itself.

It was assumed that good style had four virtues. It had to be grammatically correct, it had to be clear in the way it expressed ideas and in the arrangement of the whole, it had to match expression to content appropriately, and it involved the use of figures of sound (like alliteration, see below) or thought to lend emphasis and distinction to what was said, and to make contact with the audience. There has not been a consistent use of technical terms through the ages, but one way to divide the figures is to distinguish between efforts to select the perfect word (figures of speech) and those to combine words in effective ways (figures of thought).

Criteria for selecting the *mot juste* involved consideration of how classical the word was and of its figurative uses (tropes or figures of speech). Tropes include, for example, synecdoche, hyperbole, metaphor, or deliberate misuse of the word. All these tropes and many more are familiar from the Bible. For example, synecdoche, the substitution of a part for the whole, the genus for the species, may be seen in "one does not live by bread alone" (Deut 8:3), when by bread all foods are meant. Hyperbole, of course, is exaggeration, as in Deut 1:28, "The cities are large and fortified up to heaven." Metaphor is saying that one thing is something else, as in Isa 40:6, "All people are grass." Some books attempt to list all the figures of speech in the Bible. (*See* METAPHOR AND FIGURES OF SPEECH.)

When more than one word was involved, the practice was called composition. It includes figures of sound or thought, and groupings of phrases. Examples of figures of sound are anaphora (beginning successive clauses with the same group of words), alliteration (beginning successive words with the same sound), assonance (using words together that have the same or a similar sound in their middle), and homoioteleuton (using similar endings to words, phrases, or sentences). Biblical instances of these figures are observable only in their original languages. An extreme case of alliteration, for example, is Ps 119 in which all the verses of each stanza begin with the same letter of the alphabet, and the stanzas appear in alphabetical order.

Figures of thought, however, depend on the ideas they contain. Among these are antithesis (setting contrasting ideas against one another), rhetorical question, apostrophe (breaking off to address an absent or present person or thing, as "Praise him, sun and moon" [Ps 148:3]), climax (mounting by degrees through linked words or phrases), chiasmus (named after the Greek letter that looks like an x, this figure inverts elements in a reverse pattern, like ABBA; a figure that biblical scholars delight to discover), and the way that words are grouped in periodic sentences.

The classical writers recognized three levels of style and connected them to the three duties of the orator. The plain style was used for proof, the middle for pleasure, and the grand for moving. Many have mistakenly assumed that the grand style was the most ornate, but that is not true. All the bells and whistles were considered to be entertaining and were thus for pleasing the audience. The grand style was used when orators were getting serious about their subjects and wanted to move their audiences to act on what they were saying.

All of the greatest preachers among the post-Nicene Fathers, such as the Cappadocians and Chrysostom, had been trained as professional rhetors before they were ordained, and their oratorical skills were reflexive. This does not mean that their sermons followed all the rules of rhetoric, though. Basing their sermons on passages of Scripture meant that they could not follow the *dispositio*, the arrangement or outline, of any of the classical genres of speaking. Yet it is doubtful that any of them could have told someone the time of day without eloquence, so highly developed were their talents.

The only one of the post-Nicene Fathers to leave a manual on sermon preparation was Augustine. In his *De doctrina christiana*, a title that is best translated as *Teaching Christianity* (however, the standard English title is *Christian Instruction*.), he does not try to summarize all the lore of rhetoric, thinking that if preachers did not learn it in school, they must do so by observing and imitating good preachers. He does, however, talk about the three duties of an orator: to prove, to please, and to move. In doing so, he associates each with the level of style most appropriate to fulfilling it. He does, however, present examples from the Bible of the use of many figures of speech and thought (*Doctr. chr.* 4.6.9–4.8.21).

By the time of the fall of the Roman Empire in the West in 476, the traditional educational system, which was essentially rhetorical, had broken down, and as what used to be called the Dark Ages came on, the number of clergy well educated enough to observe the classical elements of style grew very small. Indeed, for several centuries most clergy felt that it would be presumptuous for them to compose sermons of their own, so they usually managed by re-preaching those of the Fathers. Preaching informed by Greek rhetoric continued in the East, however, and sermons often had a complex style.

Classical rhetoric was not really revived in the West until the Renaissance. In the High Middle Ages a complex sermon form was inaugurated, the thematic sermon, and while it fulfilled complex rules, they generally did not deal with the elements considered to be stylistic in the rhetorical manuals. In the Renaissance and Reformation period there was a great rediscovery of the entire classical heritage, and many of the scholars and clergy at the time thought that Greco-Roman rhetoric ought to furnish the rules for the church's characteristic speech form, the sermon. The difficulty was, as noticed above, that classical speech genres offer no place for the interpretation of a text, which is what patristic preaching had largely been. Thus even someone like Calvin, who was trained as a classicist, did not think rhetorical style appropriate to the pulpit. As time went on, his British disciples, the Puritans, developed their plain style (*see* PURITAN PLAIN STYLE), consciously forswearing the use of many tools of classical style.

Beginning with the neoclassical movement in France, sermons began more and more to take on the form of an essay, to become what are called topical sermons today, and the classical criteria became more relevant. The British incarnation of that movement was the latitudinarian style made popular by Archbishop John Tillotson. Then as the Romantic movement spread, there developed a sense of sermons as a work of the unique genius of the preacher, and style took on the amorphous popular sense that it has today in which it is the earmark of the work of the individual.

Anyone today wishing an excellent contemporary presentation of the resources of style should turn to the work of Karlyn Kohrs Campbell (1982), which reflects the inspiration of the Canadian sage Kenneth Burke. After discussing the stylistic criteria of clarity, vividness, appropriateness, and consistency, she turns to strategies for achieving different aims in speaking. If your purpose is to prove something, then asking rhetorical questions, using the argument *a fortiori*, enumerating things, refuting the other side, and defining terms strengthen your case. If you wish to animate and vivify what you are saying, then use description, depiction, personification and visualization, enactment, and such figures of sound as alliteration, assonance, and rhyme. And if you are trying to change the connotations of something, try labeling, slogans, metaphors, allusion, and identification. Campbell is at one with the classical rhetorical writers in assisting speakers to accomplish what they set out to do. *See* RHETORICAL DEVICES; PERSUASION.

Bibliography: Augustine. *The Works of St. Augustine: A New Translation for the 21st Century.* Part 1, vol. 11: *Teaching Christianity: De doctrina christiana.* Introduction, translation, and notes by Edmund Hill. Edited by John Rotelle. (1996); Karlyn Kohrs Campbell. *The Rhetorical Act.* (1982); O. C. Edwards Jr. *A History of Preaching.* (2004); George A. Kennedy. *Classical Rhetoric and Its Christian and Secular Tradition from Ancient to Modern Times.* (1980).

Technology and the Sermon
Robert R. Howard

This article examines the interface of technology and preaching, identifying contemporary possibilities and problems. The interrelation of technological innovations and the sermon in history is explored, and current permutations and their ramifications are surveyed.

Technology and the Sermon in History

New technologies have always affected preaching in manifold ways. The advent of writing shifted communication from face-to-face oral, dynamic interaction to a more distanced style of discourse. Printing, with its fixed visual ordering, influenced thought by privileging descriptive precision, which, combined with the Protestant desire to teach the faith, resulted in sermons that were much more didactic than previously (see Ong 1982). RADIO evangelism provided an aural encounter with the sermon, but shifted the context from a public space of worship to the intimacy of the listener's home, and language from broadly directed oratory to more intimately focused conversational rhetoric (see Schultze 2003). The advent of TELEVISION only intensified these dynamics, as preaching, influenced by that medium, devolved from oratorical discourse to intimate conversation (see Schultze 1995). The arrival of personal computers and the Internet has affected preaching in numerous ways (*see* INTERNET PREACHING DATABASES; INTERNET PREACHING FORUMS).

Preaching and Technology Today

Contemporary preaching employs many technological devices, with greater or lesser success. First on the list is the television screen. Upon the screen (sometimes wall-sized) may be projected text and images, static or moving. Allied with the visual presentation is a sophisticated sound system for crisp audio clarity. Such audiovisual tools may be built into the worship space in order to enhance the sermon as experienced by a live congregation, or may provide access to sermons by audiences removed from the experience in space or time. Several congregations are currently experimenting with real-time feeds of worship services to satellite locations, such as movie theaters. Second, computers are increasingly employed to arrange the presentations, using programs such as PowerPoint® or presentation software designed specifically for worship (EasyWorship, MediaShout, SongShow Plus, etc.). With these technological tools, preachers may project Scripture quotations, sermon outlines, lists of bulleted points, still images, and clips from motion pictures, or combinations thereof. They are thus able to refer to the scriptures under consideration, trace the progression of the sermon itself, highlight important notions to remember, and use images as visual illustrations of the ideas being presented. A third technology is the Internet, which can provide vast fields of information for the creation of the

sermon as well as a means of storage, transmission, and retrieval of sermons, in print, audio, and video formats.

Advantages

These new technologies offer dramatic benefits for preaching. Preachers may preach sermons with visual and audio clarity to more people, and can make sermons available at all hours of the day, able to be accessed from virtually any point on the globe. In this way, preaching is available as never before. More specifically, the preacher has at hand a wealth of resources with which to create a sermonic experience. Now he or she may combine sensory input in ways heretofore impossible; the sermon may become an enhanced audio and visual experience. Sermons may be stored with greater ease, and retrieved by greater numbers of people. Graphic lists can summarize the sermon's movement so far or offer easily graspable visual contrasts. Creative preachers may include full-motion video of homebound congregants or nursing home residents reading the scripture of the day, and project video of the reading in the worship service, thus making the experience profoundly more inclusive for all. Sermons on missions, for example, might include images of opportunities across the globe, or of this congregation's youth serving others on mission trips. An almost daunting expanse of images, information, and experiences, from innumerable perspectives, lies close to hand for the preacher.

Disadvantages

Technological advances have never been without controversy, however. The very act of writing was accused of murdering the live encounter at the heart of a sermon. Similarly, technologies employed in preaching have their own dangers (see Jewell 2004). First is the initial cost, often prohibitive for all but larger congregations. Mastering the technical details and presenting sound and images without a hitch are often problematic as well. Understanding the tools and clearly communicating goals and timing are key in this regard. Further, the preacher must overcome the split-focus problem. Congregants must already accustom themselves to the intonation, rhythm, and syntax of the preacher's voice, as well as the orientation and content of the thought. Switching representational systems only adds to this burden (see Buttrick 1987, 143–45). Further, there is always the danger that the visual image or film clip may overpower the oral discourse, resulting in the classic situation in which the hearer remembers the illustration vividly, but not what it was meant to illustrate. Associated with this danger is the reality that, in the case of a clip from a popular film, viewers always bring with them the context in which they first saw the film, and this may spark associations and memories divergent from the sermon's aim. To overcome these challenges, wise preachers will assess potential conflicts and provide adequate conceptual context before and after the visual image to weave it seamlessly into the intention of the sermon.

Other pitfalls operate at deeper levels. Images, whether static or moving, frequently trigger unforeseen emotional reactions. Moreover, an overreliance on visual imagery in the sermon can undercut its conceptual progression or simply produce the emotional catharsis of an entertained audience rather than significant growth toward faithful discipleship. Consistent plucking of sentimental heartstrings can create a blandly inert congregation of happy-religion addicts. Furthermore, the uncritical use of visual imagery in preaching may play into a host of entertainment-advertising ideologies embedded in the television and film industries and thus risk turning the gospel into yet one more commodity on the market. The sermon would then function merely to create a need and provide the remedy for the listening consumers (see Schultze 1995).

Visual presentation aided by technological devices may indeed change the nature of the sermon itself. As mentioned before, the development of print influenced Protestant preaching toward the didactic. Visually attractive PowerPoint® images and bulleted lists may sway preachers toward sermons that are heavily didactic. It is already the case that most sermons include elements of teaching and learning. But overreliance upon the technological device of the PowerPoint® presentation may reduce the sermon to a mere transfer of information and nothing more. By their very nature, summaries of information bracket out imaginative leaps, intuitive grasps, oral-rhetorical practices that lead to personal encounters, and of all things, the possibility for awe. The gospel is more than mere information (see Craddock 1978). Related to this final point is another potential pitfall of current technologies employed in the sermon. Overreliance on the visual may adumbrate the orality of the sermon, muting the "word-ness" of the Word. As Ong (1967) has clearly shown, sight presents surfaces and allows visual discrimination among objects through contrast and comparison, but sound reveals interiority—it makes interiors present to others with depth and immediacy (both in the sense of "quickly" and of "directly, without mediation"). Further, sound unites disparate people, and sight divides. As we observe a visual image, we are individuals looking at an object in front of us, from distinct vantage points. As we hear a word, though, we are together immersed in the midst of that sound, brought together by it. If one of the classic understandings of the sermon, crystallized by the Second Helvetic Confession, is that "the preaching of the Word of God is the Word of God," this priority on orality has profound implications for any technological innovation that threatens to divorce the sermon from the distinctly aural nature of the Word. (See ORAL/AURAL COMMUNICATION.) If sound reveals interiority, we dare not risk missing that revelation by looking at what can only be heard (see Ellul 1985).

In sum, discussions about technology and preaching have never been without controversy, whether that technology is the rise of writing on papyrus or the glow of a PowerPoint® slide. On the other hand, the preaching of the gospel has never shrunk from exploring the use of innovative technologies to reach out, touch, and bless lives. *See* TECHNOLOGY; VIDEO CLIPS.

Bibliography: David G. Buttrick. *Homiletic.* (1987); Fred B. Craddock. *Overhearing the Gospel.* (1978); Jacques Ellul. *The Humiliation of the Word.* Translated by Joyce Main Hanks. (1985); John P. Jewell. *Wired for Ministry.* (2004); Walter J. Ong. *The Presence of the Word.* (1967); Walter J. Ong. *Orality and Literacy.* (1982); Quentin J. Schultze. "Television and Preaching." *Concise Encyclopedia of Preaching.* Edited by William H. Willimon and Richard Lischer. (1995); Quentin J. Schultze. *Christianity and the Mass Media in America.* (2003).

PART 10 SERMON.
INTRODUCTION: SEEKING TO BE HEARD

Ronald J. Allen

Some preachers largely regard the sermon as expressing what they want to say. Increasingly, preachers recognize that they need to shape the sermon by taking account of how the congregation *hears* the sermon (while maintaining theological integrity). The preacher cannot ensure that the congregation will enter and remain in the world of the sermon in the way that the preacher intends. Individual and communal circumstances may interfere with listening. The Holy Spirit may not move as the preacher expects (*see* HOLY SPIRIT AND PREACHING). However, the preacher is called to prepare the sermon so that the congregation has opportunities to encounter important theological realities through it. The preacher wants to be as self-aware and critical as possible throughout preparation, preaching, and follow-through (*see* EXEGESIS OF SELF).

Shape the Sermon in Response to the Listening Culture of the Congregation

The preacher can help the congregation want to listen to the sermon by preparing sermons that respect the listening culture of the congregation, that is, ingrained and often unspoken assumptions, values, feelings, preferences, practices, symbolism, and other matters. However, congregations are not cultural monoliths. Within the shared culture, the typical congregation also contains clusters of people who make up subcultures related to factors such as place of origin, gender, race, ethnicity, employment, social class, economic muscle, politics, and religious views, as well as dynamics related to the neighborhood, municipality, nation, and world (*see* CONCERNS OF THE TEXT AND SERMON; CULTURAL HERMENEUTICS; EXEGESIS OF THE CONGREGATION, DENOMINATION). The preacher wants to know, How do these factors combine to become a listening culture in a particular congregation? How can I shape sermons so that the congregation has a good chance of taking them seriously?

To help answer these questions, many preachers use feed forward groups, that is, members of the congregation who meet with the preacher prior to the sermon to discuss where biblical and theological matters intersect with the congregation and the world (*see* COLLABORATION). Congregations are likely to listen to sermons in which they recognize that the preacher is taking account of issues that relate to them.

Name the Purpose of the Sermon

The minister typically has an overarching understanding of the purpose of preaching. Although this understanding may be expressed in the preacher's language, it often derives from the theological family that informs the preacher (e.g., evangelical, revisionary, liberation). In addition, the preacher needs to formulate a purpose for each individual sermon (FOCUS AND FUNCTION STATEMENTS; THEME SENTENCE). Many preachers find it helpful to formulate the purpose of the sermon by stating what they hope will happen in the minds, hearts, and actions of the congregation (LOGOS; PATHOS/FEELING). For instance, the preacher might formulate the purpose of a sermon by completing a statement like the following: "As a result of hearing this sermon, I hope the congregation will (a) understand . . . , (b) feel . . . , and (c) do . . . ." A series of messages (sermon series) sometimes allows more satisfactory treatment of a theme or topic than a single sermon.

Determine the Center Point of the Sermon: Exposition or Topic

Sermons typically have one of two center points—the exposition of a biblical text (or theme) (*see* EXPOSITORY) or the theological interpretation of a topic (*see* TOPICAL). Most sermons rightly center in the exposition of a passage or a theme from the Bible. The aim of the sermon is to offer an exposition of the biblical material that helps the congregation understand what the biblical text or theme asked people in antiquity to believe and do, and to help the contemporary congregation consider what they can believe and do today. The preacher typically selects a biblical text on the basis of a LECTIONARY AND THE CHRISTIAN YEAR, as a part of LECTIO CONTINUA, or free selection from Sunday to Sunday. The preacher helps the congregation enter the text and perceive God and the world from its perspective and also consider how conversation with that perspective can help the community perceive God and the world today (*see* BRIDGING THEN AND NOW; HERMENEUTICS).

In the topical sermon, the preacher helps the congregation interpret a topic from the standpoint of the church's theological convictions that include the Bible but also transcend biblical perspectives (*see* DOCTRINAL). A topic is a subject that the preacher can better address from the perspective of broad theological reflection than by means of the exposition of a biblical text or theme (*see* DOCTRINES AND BIBLICAL TEXTS). Some elements of doctrine, for instance, go beyond any single biblical text or theme. The topical sermon will usually draw on biblical material for illumination, but the sermon is not centered in the exposition of a biblical text or theme.

Because of its proven record for helping congregations encounter the gospel and grow in faithfulness, expository preaching should be the usual basis for preaching. However, the topical sermon may serve particular occasions.

Identify a Pattern of Movement that Will Help the Congregation Follow: Deductive, Inductive, or Combination

With respect to patterns of movement, most sermons are either deductive or inductive, or some combination thereof. While preachers may prefer one approach to the other, preachers need to be able to develop sermons in multiple patterns of movement because the different patterns have their own strengths and weaknesses, and appeal to congregations in different ways. The preacher chooses a pattern that has a good chance of helping the congregation receive the sermon in a positive way. The designations deductive and inductive are quite general.

In the DEDUCTIVE sermon, the preacher announces the major purpose and point of the sermon at the beginning and then develops that notion. The preacher might draw out the implications of the leading point or give arguments that support it. The great strengths of the deductive sermon are clarity and security. The congregation knows immediately what the sermon is about and where it is going. This type of preaching is especially suited to occasions when the congregation has a generally favorable disposition toward the purpose of the sermon. The deductive sermon can reinforce the listeners' favorable inclination, and it can help them specify how to respond to the sermon. A possible downside of the deductive sermon is that, knowing where the sermon is going, the congregation can lose interest. Of course, structure alone does not determine the willingness of the congregation to follow it. If the preacher relates the deductive sermon to important issues in the congregation's life and context, and develops the sermon with verve, the congregation is likely to listen. The sermon in the PURITAN PLAIN STYLE is often deductive.

In the INDUCTIVE sermon, the preacher does not announce the major purpose but helps the congregation discover the subject of the sermon as well as resources that help the congregation reflect theologically on it. After identifying the issue(s) and working through in light of appropriate resources and insights, the preacher comes to a conclusion in the latter part of the sermon. The great strength of the inductive sermon is that it is modeled on more actual life experience; from moment to moment, life tends to have an inductive quality. Moreover, inductive preaching creates tension in a way similar to short stories, novels, movies, or television shows: the listener is hooked on the question at the heart of the sermon and continues listening until the question is resolved. This type of preaching can serve almost any context or situation, but is especially suited to moments when the congregation is disinterested in the subject or resists the theological claim of the sermon. The inductive sermon is especially conducive to creating an experience. The inductive approach allows the congregation to approach the subject matter without feeling immediately threatened. A downside of inductive preaching occurs when the preacher fails to develop the sermon in such a way that the congregation can follow it. A sermon in the style of FOUR PAGES OF THE SERMON is often inductive.

Some sermons combine inductive and deductive qualities. For example, the preacher may begin inductively, reach an important point, and then develop that point deductively. This approach may serve well when the preacher needs to generate interest or overcome relatively minor resistance while also providing sustained guidance in how to respond.

Begin and End the Sermon in Inviting Ways

The beginning and ending of the sermon play special roles. At the beginning (see INTRODUC-TIONS), the preacher invites the congregation into the world of the sermon, usually by helping the congregation identify with the preacher and the focus of the sermon (ETHOS; IDENTIFICATION). The congregation identifies with the sermon when listeners recognize elements of their lives in the life of the preacher and in the sermon. When the listeners do so, they are likely to follow the sermon. The preacher can ask, How can I begin this sermon in a way that invites identification? Preachers often invite identification by referring to congregational life, personal experience, items from the news, life questions, short stories or novels, or the Christian Year.

At the end of the sermon the preacher usually wants the congregation to continue thinking about the message (or feeling aspects of it or taking appropriate actions) after the preacher finishes speaking (see CONCLUSIONS). Ending material that encourages continued interaction with the sermon is often similar to material used in beginnings.

Prepare for the Moment of Preaching

Recent studies of people who listen to sermons show that the congregation is most likely to want to attend to the sermon if the preacher is a lively presence in the pulpit. Listeners want to hear and see the preacher, to feel that the preacher is speaking with them and not reading. They respond positively to eye contact, to vocal inflection, to gestures that are appropriate to the sermon, and to preachers who are themselves in the pulpit. Listeners are discouraged from listening by the opposite characteristics, such as being unable to hear or see the preacher, watching the preacher read the sermon, or having no eye contact. The preacher needs to prepare to embody the sermon so as to be fully present with the congregation in the moment of preaching (see MANUSCRIPT; MEMORY; ORAL-AURAL COMMUNICATION; PERFORMING THE MANUSCRIPT; PULPIT, USE OF; WITHOUT NOTES).

Learn from How Listeners Respond to the Sermon: Feedback

By gathering feedback from the congregation, preachers can identify qualities in preaching to which listeners respond positively and negatively. Preachers can acquire feedback during the pastoral listening that takes place in their everyday ministries. A preacher's well-placed question in a pastoral moment can often evoke thoughtful congregational responses. Listeners are often eager to talk about preaching in individual and small group settings and through written instruments (see LISTENING AND OBSERVATION SKILLS). However, preachers should not mindlessly adjust their sermons according to what parishioners say that they like. The sermon should be faithful to the preacher's theological convictions. Consequently, preachers need to reflect on the degree to which particular adaptations prompted by listener response are theologically appropriate.

Bibliography: Ronald J. Allen. *Interpreting the Gospel: An Introduction to Preaching.* (1998); Ronald J. Allen. *Patterns of Preaching: A Sermon Sampler.* (1998); Ronald J. Allen. *Thinking Theologically: The Preacher as Theologian.* (2008); Stephen Farris. *Preaching that Matters: The Bible and Our Lives.* (1998); Lucy Lind Hogan and Robert Reid. *Connecting with the Congregation: Rhetoric and the Art of Preaching.* (1999); Joseph R. Jeter and Ronald J. Allen. *One Gospel, Many Ears: Preaching and Difference in the Congregation.* (2004); John McClure. *The Roundtable Pulpit: Where Preaching and Leadership Meet.* (1995); Mary Alice Mulligan et al. *Believing in Preaching: What Listeners Hear in Sermons.* (2005); James R. Nieman. *Knowing the Context: Frames, Tools, and Signs for Preaching.* (2008); James R. Nieman and Thomas G. Rogers. *Preaching to Every Pew: Cross-Cultural Strategies.* (2001); Leonora Tubbs Tisdale. *Preaching as Local Theology and Folk Art.* (1997).

❖   ❖   ❖   ❖

CONCLUSIONS
Jerry Carter

The conclusion of a sermon is one of the most critical aspects of preaching; however, it is also one of the most neglected parts. It is the last word, possibly having the most impact. Therefore, the conscientious preacher should pay attention to conclusions, not expecting a sermon merely to "close" itself.

Conclusions should be prepared. Sometimes preachers allow them to be haphazard, causing chaos instead of a clean closure at a sermon's end. John R. W. Stott contends:

> Some preachers seem to be constitutionally incapable of concluding anything, let alone their sermons. They circle round and round, like a plane on a foggy day without instruments, unable to land. Their sermons "are nothing less than a tragedy of aimlessness." Others stop too abruptly. Their sermons are like a play without a finale, like music that has neither crescendo nor climax. (Stott 1982, 245)

Conclusions should be personal. It is not the time for theoretical musing and esoteric pondering. The I-Thou relationship is reaffirmed as the preacher is a person speaking to persons, a "messenger and advocate of God who is beseeching, exhorting, persuading, counseling, guiding, and challenging." "I remind you," "I beseech you," "I plead with you," "I challenge you" are the words of his or her heart (Broadus 1979, 110).

Conclusions should be the natural product of the text/thought that exists at the sermon's core. "Good meat makes its own gravy," as historical African American preachers remark. There is no need to import external conclusions, but allow the text/thought to birth its own conclusion.

The following intentional methods of concluding a sermon are worth considering:

Reflection. Quietly inspire the congregation to meditate beyond the preaching moment by using relevant questions and anecdotal stories.

Application. Work the sermon toward the punch line where the hearer is moved to action. Jesus (Sermon on the Mount) tells the parable of the "wise and foolish" builders, whose foundations differed based on how they applied the word proclaimed. Cicero's dictum, *On the Ideal Orator,* reads "an eloquent man must so speak as to teach (docere), to please (delectare), and to persuade (flectare/movere)" (section 21). The goal is to move the hearer to a point of specific participation in a certain direction.

Celebration. Highlight the positive. Popular in African American preaching, celebration is the conviction that the sermon always ends as good news. The gospel, sometimes being bad news before the good, ultimately culminates in an energetic and lively declaration of good news. It is not mere emotion or histrionics, but it is hope for those who have been "beat up and beat on" all week.

Sermon conclusions are worth the investment to end a sermon with precision and power. *See* RHETORICAL DEVICES.

Bibliography: John A. Broadus. *On the Preparation and Delivery of Sermons.* (1979); John R. W. Stott. *Between Two Worlds: The Art of Preaching in the Twentieth Century.* (1982).

CONVERSATIONAL PREACHING
Ronald J. Allen

Since the 1960s, some preachers have called for out-loud give-and-take between the preacher and the congregation during the sermon. Indeed, some preachers divide the congregation into small groups to talk with one another during the sermon. Some others think of conversational preaching as a style of embodiment (delivery) that is relaxed. However, in the late 1980s and early 1990s, a different notion of preaching as conversation began to take shape in which conversation refers less to style and more to theological method and content. Such sermons are typically monological in form but dialogical in character.

This movement is sparked by multiple factors, including the philosophical hermeneutics of Hans-Georg Gadamer, the recognition that human beings do not have pure and objective perception but that all awareness is interpretive, the awareness that insight is not the bailiwick of specialists (e.g., preachers) but that many non-specialists (e.g., laity) can have insight that specialists miss, a move away from authoritarianism and toward egalitarianism, and the growing realization that encounters with others can often provoke congregations to consider God, the Bible, the church, the world, and ourselves in fresh ways.

Preaching as conversation refers not to the form or genre of the sermon but to its spirit. This movement is diverse (note differences in the sources cited in the bibliography below). Nevertheless, most conversational preachers view the sermon as being centered in listening to voices in the Bible, Christian history, contemporary theology and ethics, the congregation, the personal life of the preacher, and other sources (e.g., arts, philosophy, racial and ethnic analysis, gender analysis, social class analysis). The preacher seeks to respect the integrity (otherness) of these voices.

When preaching in the mode of conversation, the preacher aims to bring such voices into dialogue with one another with the goal of helping the congregation reach an adequate interpretation of God's presence and purposes as well as learning how to respond faithfully. The preacher does not simply apply a biblical text or theological doctrine to today or simply translate the text or doctrine into contemporary categories. The preacher facilitates the congregation's discerning of which voices help identify what God offers and asks. The preacher asks, With respect to God's presence and purposes today, what can we believe and what should we do?

For O. Wesley Allen Jr. a congregation is a matrix of conversations taking place across time involving identity, issues, administrative decisions, and worship. The preacher should think not of a single sermon as an isolated conversational event but of sermons as participating in ongoing conversations. *The Revised Common Lectionary* in the context of the Christian Year can promote sustained conversations that take place across time. *See* COLLABORATION; HERMENEUTICS; NEW HOMILETIC.

Bibliography: O. Wesley Allen Jr. *The Homiletic of All Believers: A Conversational Approach.* (2005); Ronald J. Allen. "Preaching as Mutual Critical Correlation through Conversation." *Purposes of Preaching.* Edited by Jana Childers. (2004) 1–22; Jeffrey Bullock. *Preaching with a Cupped Ear: Hans-Georg Gadamer's Philosophical Hermeneutics as Postmodern Wor(l)d.* (1999); Lucy Atkinson Rose. *Sharing the Word: Preaching in the Roundtable Church.* (1997).

DAILY
Gregory Heille, O.P.

Daily preaching affords preachers of the Word and worshiping communities numerous opportunities to mark the events and situations of daily life in the context of sacred time. Jews, Christians, and Muslims all observe sacred time. As senior religious correspondent Peter Steinfels wrote in the *New York Times* (April 4, 1990), "Religion shapes time as well as ideas and morals. It has its cycles: its yearly seasons and holidays, its weekly worship, its daily prayers, its rites of passage from one stage of life to another. The religious calendar, for those who keep it or try to keep it, is a kind of counter-calendar running alongside—and sometimes across—the one that rules the everyday world." Throughout the week in a number of pastoral celebrations such as baptisms, quinceañeras, weddings, or funerals, Christian preachers minister to other people's once-in-a-lifetime experiences. Meanwhile, in a more quotidian movement of communal worship, preachers and parishioners meet in midweek or daily services to interpret and lift to God the situations of daily life in the context of the scriptural texts of the day and the liturgical time of day, feast day, or season. Whatever one's congregational or denominational practices of weekday worship, daily preaching can afford preachers a priceless pastoral opportunity of anchoring their daily spirituality and that of their congregations in the Word of God and in the liturgy.

The Weekday Lectionary and the Liturgical Year

A lectionary is nothing more than a list or book of biblical pericopes for proclamation on selected Sundays, feasts, special occasions, or days of the year. In 1969, a new post-Vatican II Roman Lectionary departed from the medieval one-year pattern with a carefully considered three-year list of Sunday lections for a Matthew year, a Mark year, and a Luke year—with John interspersed especially during the seasons of Lent and Easter. The lectionary also included an OT first reading chosen in relation to each Sunday's Gospel and a NT letter reading read semi-continuously from week to week. Additionally, a daily lectionary was implemented, with an annual cycle of Gospel readings and a two-year cycle of first readings from the OT, the Acts of the Apostles, and the Letters. The daily lectionary also provided for saints' days and special occasions such as baptisms, weddings, or funerals.

This Roman *Ordo Lectionum Missae* was promulgated in 1969 and soon afterward issued in vernacular translation. Several Protestant communions quickly followed with new denominational lectionaries in this same pattern. In 1983, the ecumenical Consultation on Common Texts published a *Common Lectionary,* a three-year Sunday lectionary adapted to include a semi-continuous first reading of OT texts. The *Revised Common Lectionary,* issued in 1992, is now used by United Methodists, Presbyterians, Disciples of Christ, and the United Church of Christ and provides the basic pattern for Episcopalian and widespread Lutheran usage. The Roman *Lectionary for Mass,* in revision since 1981, has now been issued in the United States in a four-volume chapel edition including one volume of *Readings for Sundays, Solemnities, Feasts of the Lord and the Saints* (1998) and three volumes of *Readings for Weekdays and Other Masses* (2002).

Thanks to the richer biblical fare of the post-Vatican II lectionary, biblical preaching is now normative to Roman Catholic liturgical celebration of Sundays, feasts, and rites of passage. Thanks to the daily lectionary, biblical preaching also has been woven into the daily celebration of the main liturgical seasons and in many local churches throughout the entire liturgical year. This daily lectionary can also be a rich resource for daily and midweek preaching in other Christian churches. Sunday and daily lectionaries are designed to draw upon the broad seasonal themes of the church's liturgical year—early Advent, with its longing for eschatological fulfillment; later Advent and the Christmas season, in their celebration of the incarnation; Lent, with the prophetic and penitential longing of local churches as they accompany their catechumens in preparation for baptism at Easter; Easter, with the daily celebration of the resurrection; and a prolonged meditation on the life of the Christian church during the Easter season leading to Pentecost. The intervening periods between the Christmas season and Lent, and between Pentecost and Advent, give fully half of the church year to Ordinary Time, during which the weekly pattern of Sunday and daily Word and sacrament is celebrated, with emphasis on a daily rhythm of morning praise and petition and evening gratitude and recollection. Throughout the liturgical year, a calendar of saints' days is also observed.

The Practical Matters of Daily Preaching

Whether preaching at daily Word or Communion services, at daily morning or evening prayer, or at regularly scheduled midweek services, daily preaching is by nature an intimate affair between pastoral ministers and a devoted core community of the congregation. Within this circle, daily preaching tends to take a more conversational tone and to be necessarily brief as it accommodates to the busy schedules of parishioner and pastor alike. Seldom will daily preaching strive rhetorically to make more than one succinct point; its most common structure is a three-to five-minute *move* (using David Buttrick's term, 23, 36). Scripture for daily preaching, as assigned by the lectionary or as chosen by the preacher, moves generally in broad sweeps of semi-continuous *lectio continuo.* A busy minister can seldom give more than a brief period to preparing daily preaching, especially in the context of preparation for Sunday. One might form a daily contemplative habit of *lectio divina*, taking the daily texts to prayer and considering the liturgical season and the situations being confronted pastorally in the parish, the neighborhood, and the world. As ongoing daily preaching interprets day-to-day life through the Scriptures, the news, and the liturgy, daily congregants can also become *partners in preaching* (Reuel Howe's term)—willing to join the pastor in weekly Bible and lectionary study, faith sharing, and preparation for and evaluation of Sunday preaching and worship.

The contemplative habit of *lectio divina* can be a huge help to a busy pastor seeking to bring the life-giving resource of the ministry of the Word to the service of pastoral care, catechesis and spiritual formation, neighborhood involvement, parish meetings, and parish retreats or missions. The daily readings and the liturgy always seem to have something to offer to the situation at hand.

Although the predictable ebb and flow of Sunday and weekday preaching enlivens most preachers, they can be burdened by the additional round of parish baptisms, confirmations, weddings, funerals, and neighborhood or global crises. While the lectionary may provide a choice of scriptural readings for each of these events, oftentimes the daily readings themselves come helpfully to the rescue. Here again, a habit of *lectio divina* and a stable rhythm of daily or weekly preaching provide a context and a grounding for preachers called upon to respond pastorally and with preaching to events in parishioners' lives and to crises.

It behooves worshiping communities and their pastors to carefully coordinate the demands of preaching in relation to the other multiple obligations of congregational life. Parishioners can be invited to participate with preachers in the ministry of the Word—through Scripture study, faith reflection, and involvement with preaching preparation and evaluation. Governing councils and pastoral teams can address the necessity of providing competent preachers to meet the diverse needs of the community, and can provide training and current exegetical, liturgical, and preaching resources to assist preachers in their ministry. Ministerial role descriptions can be written to provide adequate time for preaching preparation. The point of daily and weekly preaching is not to overburden pastors. Rather, the goal is to enliven the entire community—pastor and people alike—with the good news of the Word of God on a daily basis. *See* LECTIONARY AND THE CHRISTIAN YEAR.

Bibliography: The Roman Catholic weekday lectionary is issued in NRSV translation in Canada and NAB translation in the United States. For a thorough orientation, see the General Introduction to the Lectionary, 2nd ed. (1981), which can be found online. Weekday chapel lectionaries are published in Canada by CCCB Publications and in the United States by Liturgical Press and Catholic Book Publishing Company. David Buttrick. *Homiletic: Moves and Structures.* (1988); Reuel Howe. *Partners in Preaching: Clergy and Laity in Dialogue* (1967).

DEDUCTIVE
Dave L. Bland

A deductive sermon usually begins with a premise or an accepted truth out of which the preacher unpacks significance for the listeners. That is, the preacher states the main idea near the beginning and then develops that idea through the rest of the sermon. A deductive sermon is logical and linear as it develops a concept. Its reasoning begins with a general proposition and moves to the particulars. In contrast, inductive sermons begin with the particulars, or common human experiences, and out of these discover a truth or a principle. (*See* INDUCTIVE). What deduction and induction have in common is that both develop a theme, concept, or proposition of some kind. One states the theme up front; the other leads the congregation to it at the conclusion. For a good analysis of a theme statement in a sermon see Wilson (2004).

A deductive sermon may build around or develop from a syllogism. When building on syllogistic reasoning, the deductive sermon begins with the major premise accepted by the listeners and then moves with them to discover the minor premises. Whatever the major premise is, the preacher has the freedom to explore it in a variety of ways. The preacher might investigate the implications of the premise, explore its application, examine its limits, consider exceptions, or probe its effects.

In this day and age of narrative preaching, however, deductive sermons have fallen on hard times. Some homileticians and preachers frequently refer to deductive preaching in pejorative terms, pronouncing it terminal. They often stereotype these sermons as being pedantic and lacking new insights. Deductive preaching suffers from a number of misunderstandings. Some characterize it as nothing more than three points and a poem, wooden and mundane. Some accuse it of authoritarianism, asserting that the preacher tells the congregation what they must believe without allowing them to think and decide for themselves. Others complain that deductive preaching reduces the text used in the sermon to nothing more than a proposition. Some have even said that innate to its character is its tendency to misuse Scripture; it easily turns into moralistic preaching. And finally, deductive preaching causes listeners to remain passive. The preacher tells listeners what to believe while the listeners submissively accept. Thus, some homileticians marginalize and even eliminate deductive reasoning.

Though each of the above accusations can be true of deductive preaching, none of the faults is inherent in its nature. When it falls victim to one of these abuses, the problem lies less in the form itself and more in the artless application of it. In other words, the main problem with deductive preaching is the lack of creativity and imagination on the part of the one who employs it. In terms of the form itself, then, the accusations leveled against it have little justification.

Deductive preaching is rooted in the medieval period with the coming of the *artes praedicandi* or *Art of Preaching* manuals. These manuals advocated a thematic approach to the sermon.

Interestingly, however, at least in theory, they viewed the sermon not as static but as alive. For example, one has only to look at the picture of a tree used to visualize the sermon to know that the deductive sermon was viewed organically (Dieter 1965). In these university or thematic sermons, as they were called, preachers began with a theme statement and developed it into three divisions. After dividing the theme into three parts, preachers employed the nine or more standard modes of amplification available to aid in the expansion of the sermon. That they visualized the sermon like a tree implies that they understood the process as a living organism that imitates nature itself. Sermon writing is an art; it appeals to the aesthetic side.

The deductive logic fostered during the medieval period turned more rigid with the arrival of the French humanist Peter Ramus (1515–72). Seeking clarity and simplicity for the sake of establishing certainty, Ramus took deductive reasoning and developed it into a fixed, mechanized system of logic separated from rhetoric. Ramus's approach was fully accepted and incorporated into the Puritans' plain-style sermon, with its simple and direct approach. Such sermons begin with a statement of doctrinal belief, which is followed by an outline of the meaning of the text on which the doctrine is based, and conclude with uses for daily living (Miller 1939). As seen from its origins, the problems of deductive preaching lie less in the form itself and more in how it is used.

Although preachers should not return to the deductive sermon as a staple for preaching, they should not completely excise it. With proper use and creativity, it can play a valuable role. Aristotle, for example, favored the use of the *enthymeme*, a truncated form of syllogistic reasoning. As a creative alternative to the syllogism, the enthymeme leaves out one of its premises. Lloyd Bitzer (1959, 408) says of Aristotle's perspective on enthymemes: "Because they are jointly produced by the audience, enthymemes intuitively unite speaker and audience and provide the strongest possible proof. . . . The audience itself helps construct the proof by which it is persuaded."

Martin Luther King Jr.'s "I have a dream" speech contains a strong deductive component built around an enthymeme. The syllogism of the speech develops like this: major premise, God will reward nonviolence; minor premise, We are pursuing our dream nonviolently; conclusion, God will grant us

our dream. King uses more than half the speech to establish the soundness of the minor premise. The last part of the speech establishes his conclusion offering a vivid image of the dream coming true. He never states the major premise. But he rightly assumes the listeners believe it and therefore engages them in his reasoning. He uses deductive logic moving from abstract principle to specific truth. Interestingly, King mentions only a few examples of discrimination, which inductive reasoning would have employed more predominantly to build toward a general conclusion. (See analysis of this speech by Griffin 2006, 321–23.) Deductive sermons do not automatically create passive listeners. One can develop a deductive sermon in which listeners are quite actively engaged.

Deductive sermons have the ability to manage cognitive principles and concepts. In contrast, inductive, as well as narrative, preaching takes a special interest in the particulars of human experiences. However, sermons cannot and should not dwell exclusively on the particulars. Sermons need also to identify ideas or universal concepts that transcend specific contexts and bring those concepts into new settings. Deductive reasoning serves as a helpful vehicle in transferring a concept of the gospel from one particular setting to another. David Greenhaw (1994, 107) observes, "It is possible to embrace the particular so thoroughly as to be unable to make any claims to the universal." Greenhaw continues, "Without concepts it is not possible to transport what is true in one situation to another situation" (109). The concept, however, does not remain an isolated concept, but is placed in the new context and its cultural trappings. And the preacher unpacks the concept by offering interpretive clues to its meaning and implications in the new context. Scripture itself contains not only the stories and the actions but also the conceptualizations or interpretations of those stories. For example, the parting of the Red Sea story does not reveal its own meaning. Only because of the interpretation that follows do we know how and why it was done (Exod 15:1-5). Thus, the gospel narrative requires conceptualization. Deductive preaching, or various components of deductive reasoning, can aid the preacher in communicating theological concepts.

Where might a preacher find good examples of deductive sermons? In his book *Patterns of Preaching*, Ronald Allen (1998) includes an opening section on traditional patterns of sermons that contains sermons in various forms: "Puritan Plain Style" by Tom Long, "Sermons That Make Points" by R. Scott Colglazier, and "Preaching Verse by Verse" by Fred Craddock.

A deductive strain of reasoning lies embedded in the moves of David Buttrick's homiletic (1987), though not usually acknowledged as such (this observation was made in a personal conversation with Charles Campbell). A series of five or six moves make up the development of a Buttrick sermon. Within each move are a series of stages one must follow beginning by stating the single meaning or idea of that module, followed by imaging the idea, and then closing out the move by restating the single meaning. Thus, Buttrick's moves are a creative way for preachers to integrate deductive movement into the body of the sermon.

Another classic example of the way in which a preacher can use deductive reasoning dynamically is seen in John Tillotson's "Sermon Against Evil Speaking" (1967), which he preached in 1694. He begins with his proposition: we must not speak in an invective way against another person. Tillotson then lays out in summary fashion what the sermon will do and follows with a detailed assessment of the subject. Tillotson playfully interacts with his proposition, exploring it from a variety of angles: How far do we extend this prohibition? What are its limitations and boundaries? Is this an absolute? Are there exceptions? Is there ever a time when we can legitimately criticize another? What is the cause of this sin? What are the consequences of practicing this vice? How does one keep from falling victim to it? Along the way Tillotson offers brief but concrete examples of the various quandaries he explores. His wisdom and insight into the nature of human beings engage the listener (156–72).

Deductive preaching continues to play a role in contemporary preaching, though perhaps not a dominant one. Preachers should take care not to dismiss too quickly the value of deductive reasoning but to use it in creative ways as they seek to communicate God's Word effectively. An approach to preaching that includes both narrative and non-narrative methods is most healthy, allowing listeners to experience the gospel and to understand the gospel. For an excellent treatment of the use of discursive language in preaching, see Campbell (2003). *See* EXPOSITORY; INDUCTIVE; POINT FORM; PURITAN PLAIN STYLE.

Bibliography: Ronald Allen. *Patterns of Preaching: A Sermon Sampler.* (1998); Lloyd Bitzer. "Aristotle's Enthymeme Revisited." *Quarterly Journal of Speech* 45 (1959) 399–408; David Buttrick. *Homiletic: Moves and Structures.* (1987); Charles Campbell. "From Narrative Text to Discursive Sermon: The Challenge of Hebrews." *Preaching Hebrews.* Edited by David Fleer and Dave Bland. (2003) 29–43. Otto Dieter. "Arbor Picta: The Medieval Tree of Preaching." *Quarterly Journal of Speech* 51 (1965) 123–44; David Greenhaw. "As One with Authority: Rehabilitating Concepts for Preaching." *Intersections: Post-Critical Studies in Preaching.* Edited by Richard L. Eslinger. (1994) 105–22; Em Griffin. *A First Look at Communication Theory.* 6th ed. (2006); Perry Miller. *The New England Mind: The Seventeenth Century.* (1939); John Tillotson. "Sermon Against Evil Speaking." *An Historical Anthology of Select British Speeches.* Edited by Donald C. Bryant, Carroll C. Arnold, Frederick W. Haberman, Richard Murphy, and Karl R. Wallace. (1967) 156–72; Paul Scott Wilson. "Biblical Preaching." *Preaching and Homiletical Theory* (2004).

DELIVERY.
See PERFORMING THE MANUSCRIPT.

DOCTRINAL
Duncan Macpherson

All authentic Christian preaching is doctrinal in that it either includes or presupposes fundamental Christian teachings. More specifically, *doctrinal preaching* focuses on teaching the rule of faith rather than on proclaiming the message of a scriptural text or responding to contemporary issues or concerns.

Early Historical Perspective

Christian preaching generally falls into three categories: proclamation, formation, and instruction. Examples of preaching recorded in the Acts of the Apostles are concerned with proclamation (Greek, kerygma) of an event rather than a didactic instruction in doctrine. Systematic catechetical formation (Greek, didachē meaning "doctrine" or "teaching") in the doctrinal and ethical teaching of the church found its place as part of the formation of recently baptized persons. (*See* MYSTAGOGICAL PREACHING.)

In *The Apostolic Preaching and Its Developments* (1936), C. H. Dodd analyzed Peter's speeches in Acts (1:16-22; 2:14-36, 38-40; 3:12-26; 4:8-12, 19, 20; 5:29-32; 10:34-43; 11:5-17; 15:7-11) and discerned the shape of kerygmatic preaching in which Peter proclaims that the new age, foretold by the prophets, has now arrived. This has happened by virtue of the life, ministry, death, and resurrection of Jesus, now exalted to the right hand of God as Lord and Christ, with the outpouring of the Holy Spirit in the church as evidence of his present power. Christ will return in glory as judge, and the hearers are invited to repent. For all that Dodd oversimplifies early church preaching, such a summary still has merit.

Since proclamation, formation, and instruction each find their center in the mystery of Christ, there is an inevitable overlap in their content. However, the doctrinal content of mystagogical preaching typically includes systematic instruction on the creed, the Lord's Prayer, the Ten Commandments, and the sacraments. Doctrinally focused preaching, not subsidiary to either kerygma or baptismal catechesis, developed to meet new historical challenges. The first of these lay in doctrinal disputes challenging the unity of the church, and the second in the large number of uninstructed Christians who had been baptized as infants.

The early church fathers were greatly concerned with engaging doctrinal disputes concerning the divinity and the humanity of Christ; therefore, much of their preaching is directed to combating heresies such as Arianism. Much of the targeted christological content of their sermons appeared under the headings either of mystagogy or of scriptural homilies. Thus, since expositions of the creed were an integral part of preaching to newly baptized persons, the sermons of preachers such as Cyril of Alexandria (d. 444) were packed with doctrinal instruction, often with one eye on heresy.

Gregory of Nazianzus: A Model Doctrinal Preacher

Gregory of Nazianzus (ca. 329–389) is an example of a purely doctrinal preacher. His *Five Theological Orations* (Orationes 27–32) do not develop around a preaching text but stand alone as classical rhetorical exposition of Orthodox faith. Commenting on this, Hughes Oliphant Old recognizes that some people may find such preaching distasteful but attributes this to modern post-Enlightenment "pietistic agnosticism." Gregory's doctrinal preaching includes studied cadences and rhythms, rhymes and alliterations, rhetorical questions, irony, and invective (Old 1998, 67). Taking a series of texts used by the Arians to suggest the subordination of the Son, Gregory meets them with a mixture of sarcasm, logic, and sheer poetry. In his preliminary discourse, Gregory sarcastically describes his opponents as having a tongue "so voluble and clever" and calls them "strange acrobats of words." In the fourth oration, on the union of God and man in Christ, Gregory combines logic and irony, asking how Christ can be divine if he is also created, "for that which is created is not God. . . . I marvel that you . . . did not count up the modes of generation of birds and beasts and fishes, and bring under some one of them the divine and ineffable generation, or even eliminate the Son out of your new hypothesis." However, irony and logic frequently give way to a mystical sense of wonder, as where he is discussing how the Arians used Heb 7:25, "He liveth to make intercession for us," when Gregory suddenly breaks into the argument with the phrase, "O, how beautiful and mystical and kind."

Doctrinal Preaching in the Post-patristic Period

During the early medieval period, preaching was in general decline, and doctrinal preaching, even more than other kinds of preaching, was largely confined to the monasteries. Popular preaching reemerged from the 11th cent. onward, first to promote the Crusades and second to combat the Albigensian heresy. Unlike the Franciscans, whose preaching seems to have been concerned mainly with spiritual renewal of the laity, the Dominican order engaged in doctrinal exposition of the creed, the Our Father, and the Hail Mary as well as moral instruction on the Ten Commandments. All this was with a view to providing a remedial religious education for those who might otherwise be attracted to heresy. These catechetical sermons were often preached in the afternoons at special preaching services, which allowed more time and did not need to be linked with the Mass readings or the season.

Preaching and the Reformations

The Protestant Reformation and the Catholic Reformation that followed brought a revival of preaching in Western Christendom. Since the Protestant

Reformers appealed to Scripture alone for their authority, most of their preaching was based on biblical texts. However, Luther's Catechism (1529) and the Calvinist Heidelberg Catechism (1563) provided systematic teaching and polemical material against controverted Roman Catholic doctrines. Meanwhile in 1554, St. Peter Canisius presented his Roman Catholic Catechism. In addition to the doctrinal content of scriptural preaching, these and other catechisms became the basis for doctrinal preaching.

The Modern Debate on Doctrinal Preaching

Homileticians today are divided on the usefulness of doctrinal preaching. Among Protestant Christians, conservative evangelicals are suspicious of an approach placing doctrine before Scripture, and liberals are unhappy with any emphasis on traditional dogma that ignores the realities of daily life. Friedrich Schleiermacher (1768–1834), the pioneer of liberal Protestantism, saw religion and preaching as being concerned with evoking a "feeling of absolute dependence" rather than with doctrine. In 1928, Harry Emerson Fosdick's article "What Is the Matter with Preaching?" advocated topical preaching as more interesting and relevant than doctrinally or scripturally based sermons. By contrast, William J. Carl III argued that the contemporary church, like the early church, the church of the Reformation, and the church of the two evangelical Great Awakenings (1730s to 1770s; 1790s to 1850s), needed clear doctrinal preaching. Thus, although Scripture texts or topic-centered approaches may constitute starting points for preaching, every sermon has either an explicit or an implicit doctrinal hermeneutic and should move to a focus on one or more Christian doctrines, regardless of its starting point,

Meanwhile, Roman Catholic sermons frequently focused on a doctrine rather than on the readings. However, the Second Vatican Council was responsible for the rediscovery of the biblical homily, identifying the primary purpose of the homily at Mass as providing "a living commentary on the word" and as an integral part of the liturgical action (*Sacrosanctum Concilium*, 56, 7, 33, and 52). The homily might need to be both catechetical and kerygmatic, but the primary purpose would be proclamation, grounded in Scripture and church teaching. Pope John Paul II stressed the importance of the homily not only as liturgical, biblical, and tailored to the needs of the congregation (the description favored by Pope Paul VI in his 1975 encyclical *Evangelii Nuntiandi*), but also as having important "catechetical fruits."

In some parts of the Catholic world, programs of doctrinal instruction, structured around the lectionary (*see* LECTIONARY AND THE CHRISTIAN YEAR), have been suggested. More recently, Proposition 19 of the 2005 Roman Synod of Bishops recommended the preparation of thematic homilies as an aid to clergy, based both on the readings and on the 1992 Catechism of the Catholic Church, covering the creed, sacraments, commandments, and the Our Father. However, such programs might risk the scriptural and liturgical character of the homily being obscured and the texts of Scripture being used as a springboard for talking about unrelated teaching. Other solutions to the need for systematic religious instruction might include provision of a brief religious instruction after the Communion. Alternatively, teaching might emerge naturally from the preaching of biblical and liturgical texts.

Conclusion

Clearly, there are occasions when doctrinal emphasis in sermons is recommended. These include preparation for the sacraments and more general remedial catechesis. Sometimes, too, topical debates over divisive theological issues may require attention. Although preaching in a context remote from our own, the preaching of Gregory of Nazianzus provides a historical model of systematic doctrinal preaching. However, modern congregations are probably not suited to approach doctrinal material in such a didactic fashion. Presentation of Christian doctrine needs to be grounded in Scripture and in the experience of God's people. If the alternative is doctrine-free preaching, all preaching should be seen as doctrinal preaching. *See* DOCTRINES AND BIBLICAL TEXTS.

Bibliography: William J. Carl III. *Preaching Christian Doctrine.* (1984); C. H. Dodd. *The Apostolic Preaching and Its Developments.* (1936); Gregory of Nazianzus. *On God and Christ: The Five Theological Orations and Two Letters to Cledonius* (Orationes 27–32). (2002); Hughes Oliphant Old. *The Reading and Preaching of the Scriptures in the Worship of the Christian Church.* Vol. 2, *The*

Patristic Age. (1998). *Sacrosanctum Concilium: Constitution on the Sacred Liturgy.* (1963).

EXEGETICAL
David A. Davis

An exegetical sermon is intimately connected to a biblical text in both form and content. The descriptive term also implies close association with the preacher's own process of biblical interpretation (exegesis). In a basic understanding of biblical preaching and its relationship to particular biblical texts, one would affirm that all such preaching is in some way exegetical. That is, the preacher's interpretive work with a text influences what is communicated in a given sermon. However, homileticians agree that exegetical preaching stretches the relationship of text and sermon beyond simply what is being communicated to include how that gospel word is being communicated.

The most common form of an exegetical sermon follows a biblical text verse by verse. While not always tagging each verse by number, a preacher may choose to work his or her way through Ps 23 image by image, line by line, verse by verse. Another preacher may attempt to unpack Paul's theology of the resurrection by moving through 1 Cor 15 thought by thought, verse by verse. Still another preacher may choose to pause over every detail, every verse of the OT narrative of Elijah at Mount Horeb (1 Kgs 19), working at every verse to draw the listener into the experience of the still, small voice. Only in the strictest sense of such sermon form would a preacher have to announce "now in verse 4." The imaginative preacher offers exegetical sermons with creativity and variety.

With respect to content, every preacher wrestles with how much exegetical material to bring into the sermon. Most would affirm that there is always more interpretive homework left in the study. The bulk of scholarly material that provides the necessary foundation for a biblically grounded and theologically sound sermon may not show up in the preaching moment. To define a sermon as exegetical, then, is to affirm that sometimes the preacher does bring more of the tools of the trade to the pulpit. A sermon about Uzzah may include a significant explanation of the instructions for handling the ark of God (2 Sam 6). A preacher may spend quite a bit of sermon time sharing the results of a word study on what it meant for the shepherds to be "sore afraid" as the glory of the Lord shone all around them (Luke 2). Some preachers may choose to try to establish the importance of context in First or Second Isaiah, and that context impacts the listeners' understanding of the prophet. Exegetical sermons may simply be the preaching efforts that are heavy on teaching biblical material with less emphasis on attempting to make it all so relevant to the contemporary hearer.

Traditionally, exegetical preaching has also been referred to as expository preaching. Both labels refer to preaching that values a high commitment to the biblical text and bestows an authority on that text. On the one hand, a sermon would not be based on some broad theological theme. On the other hand, neither would it be based on a very brief portion or snippet of a verse. Sermons would presumably be based on selections of texts, narratives, or pericopes as the hearers of the Word are invited to experience for themselves something of the exegetical world too often reserved for the educated preacher.

Some contrasting voices in preaching theory would support a broad understanding of exegetical sermons defined in both form and content. The New Homiletic of Fred Craddock and Thomas G. Long utilizes the language of "executing" biblical texts (Craddock 1985; Long 1989). The intent is to allow a particular text to be heard afresh in the contemporary world of the listener, as if for the first time. In a different homiletical corner, Charles Campbell and others argue for allowing the narrative texts of Scripture to draw the hearer into the biblical world (Campbell 1997). Rather than attempt to translate for the listener, the preacher simply tells the biblical story in a fashion that captures the imagination of the hearer. In both theoretical approaches, a preacher could offer exegetical sermons that stick close to the interpretive homework done in the pastor's study.

A few practical concerns exist for preachers who find themselves drawn to such sermons. There is a real danger in simply broadcasting one's expertise in biblical scholarship week after week. Conversations about power and authority in preaching ought to wrestle with the tendency of some to want to show a congregation how much knowledge they possess. Exegetical material does not equate to the gospel, and average preaching does not simply get better by adding Greek or Hebrew. A second concern relates to a lack of variety in sermon form.

Homileticians will remind us that people hear in different ways and pastors ought to be intentional about diversity of shape and movement in their sermons. A verse-by-verse propositional approach every week lacks imagination. Similarly, a preacher who offers the teaching portion of a sermon in the same shape, size, and place week after week is in a rut. Last, exegetical sermons demand a certain "aha" moment of interpretation where a light bulb goes off and the preacher figuratively runs to share it with the hearers on Sunday. Most preachers know there will be those weeks where no new idea or fresh insight can be found. Other tools in the box may need to come into play when the preacher's exegesis seems far from fresh.

The world of biblical exegesis has been changing in the past few decades. A purely historical-critical approach to exegesis is now balanced by a more literary, cultural approach. Exegesis is widely accepted as more of an art form than a science (see Wilson 2004). If preachers are to keep up with and experience that now changed landscape of biblical exegesis, then one's understanding of an exegetical sermon will have to be reshaped as well. While such preaching must still rest near to the biblical text in content and form, we may no longer simply be talking about a sermon that is shaped verse by verse.

In the essay "The Preacher as Scribe" (2004), Walter Brueggemann explores a fresh image for this intimate connection between preacher, text, and sermon in a post-historical-critical world. For him the preacher is a scribe who engages the text in an "intentional, self-conscious, interpretive editorial process" (13). Preacher-scribes are deeply connected to the text, and they lead their communities in a re-engagement with the texts. As Brueggemann puts it, "the preacher's task . . . is to re-text this community; to turn the imagination and the practice of the community back to its most elemental assurances and claims" (13).

Not surprisingly, Walter Brueggemann's sermons are consistently exegetical. Whether he is unpacking an OT narrative, preaching his way through a psalm, or taking his listeners to the feet of Jesus the Teacher, Brueggemann never strays far from the text in terms of sermon structure and sermon content. Sometimes he will announce this verse or that, but more to the point, with every sermon, he nurtures an encounter between the listener and the text itself while not allowing many illustrations to get in the way. In that fashion, he joins a great company of exegetical preachers in various traditions with diverse theological approaches whose sermons stay close to a biblical text.

In years to come exegetical sermons will be tools for teaching the Bible and drawing the listeners into a biblical world that tells of the kingdom of God. Preachers who yearn to nurture a faith community's deep and abiding connection to the biblical text will continue to explore the many ways that a sermon can best proclaim that kingdom in content and in form. *See* EXEGESIS; EXPOSITORY; SERMON RESEARCH.

Bibliography: Walter Brueggemann. "The Preacher as Scribe." *Inscribing the Text: Sermons and Prayers of Walter Brueggemann.* Edited by Anna Carter Florence. (2004) 5–19; Charles L. Campbell. *Preaching Jesus: New Directions for Homiletics in Hans Frei's Postliberal Theology.* (1997); Fred Craddock. *Preaching.* (1985); Thomas G. Long. *The Witness of Preaching.* (1989); Paul Scott Wilson. "Exegesis for Preaching." *Preaching and Homiletical Theory.* (2004).

EXPOSITORY
Joel C. Gregory

As a description, expository preaching does not define any single mode of preaching in the current context. The term connotes more an attitude toward biblical authority than it defines a homiletic form. By the late 20th cent. the term evoked among evangelicals a general stance toward direct biblical authority in preaching. While some mainliners practiced exposition, they made little use of the term itself. There is pervasive agreement that expository preaching eludes definition.

Expository preaching may be defined by morphology. The expository form usually embraces a biblical unit of thought. That unit may be a single word, phrase, verse, paragraph, chapter, or biblical book. It is typical of exposition that the smaller the text, the more exhaustive the exegetical examination of its details. Atomistic exposition focuses on a meticulous examination of individual words. D. Martyn Lloyd-Jones (1899–1981) exemplified this pain-staking approach. Synthetic exposition embraces larger texts and seeks catalytic verses within an extended passage to explicate. George

Campbell Morgan (1863–1945) represents the synthetic approach in his magisterial expositions of biblical books. Alexander MacLaren (1826–1910) typified the literate exposition of biblical paragraphs, often treating a text of five to ten verses.

Expository preaching may be understood in terms of the agreed historic examples of its incidence. The first consensus patristic expositor, John Chrysostom (347–407) of Antioch, expounded biblical books. John Calvin (1509–1564) embodies the flower of Reformation exposition, although Luther, Zwingli, and Knox demonstrated expository prowess. The Puritan pulpits inherited the expository emphasis of the magisterial Reformers, exemplified by Richard Baxter (1615–1691), although Puritan exposition became cramped with detail. The 19th cent. was the golden era of English language expository preaching. In London, exposition typified the devotional preaching of Frederick Brotherton Meyer (1847–1929) and the oratorical imagination of Joseph Parker (1830–1902). Alexander Whyte (1836–1921) of Edinburgh demonstrated erudite synthetic exposition in the form of biblical biographies, treating the lives of major characters with a now vanished expository erudition. John Albert Broadus (1827–1895) represents the flower of 19th cent. American exposition, although his *On the Preparation and Delivery of Sermons* (1870) introduced generations of American preachers to a Hellenic rhetorical appliqué that made American exposition more argumentative than analytic of the text.

In the latter half of the 20th cent. expository preaching may have been honored in the breach more than in the practice. The very term *expository* became a mantra for a certain ambient approach to the preaching often lauded but seldom achieved. Instances of exposition include academic, pastoral, and popular media expositors. The persons cited are those who identify themselves primarily as expositors, and any list risks being theologically tendentious. For example, Presbyterian Tom Long of Princeton and Emory would not prefer the designation expositor, but he is an excellent example. Among academic expositors, Haddon Robinson in his text *Biblical Preaching* (2001) reached beyond his own evangelical environment to touch preaching nationally. Pastoral expositors predominantly occupied evangelical pulpits. Two Presbyterians crossed over from their pulpits to the media with thoughtful exposition, Lloyd John Ogilvie and James Montgomery Boyce. Popular literary and media expositors included the evangelical Charles R. Swindoll, the authoritarian fundamentalist John MacArthur Jr., as well as pastor, radio personality, and author Warren Wiersbe. London pastor Stephen F. Olford (1918–2004), who later occupied the Calvary Baptist Church pulpit in New York City, exemplified a now vanishing expository technique rooted in the homiletic of William Graham Scroggie (1877–1958).

Expository Strengths

Expository preaching may assure direct biblical authority for the sermon. If the proclaimer takes the canonical, book, and immediate context of a passage seriously, the sermon may resonate with the echo of Scripture. Rugged exegetical examination of each operative word, phrase, and clause both grammatically and syntactically characterizes careful exposition. Most expositors embrace a hermeneutic of singular authorial intent and seek to discover that intent. The expositor attempts to come to the experience of preaching without textual presuppositions. This is not to say that the expositor is a *tabula rasa*. The honest expositor acknowledges presuppositions but seeks to unpack the text only for what the text itself says. When this happens, the preacher may stand with the assurance of direct biblical authority.

Proponents of exposition insist that expository preaching addresses the life situation of postmodern persons more cogently than therapeutic models of preaching. The Bible reflects every human predicament in its rudimentary form. Scripture does not address stem cell research, Internet pornography, or the exploitation of wetlands. More profoundly, it addresses the metanarrative behind each of these contemporary concerns. What is life? What is human sexuality? What is human responsibility for creation? Exposition rests on the conviction that the particulars in Scripture address the universals of human experience. What happened in the confines of ancient Israel does indeed speak today, and speaks with more cogency than a manufactured homiletic relevance.

Expository preaching may protect the preacher from homiletic myopia that misidentifies the human dilemma. Many preachers ride hobbyhorses, tending to analyze the human predicament using their own paradigms. The evangelist sees the need to convert, the social justice preacher the need to rectify wrong, and the eschatological preacher the need to warn of the imminent end. Every situation passes through a peculiar perceptual grid screening out other aspects of rich and complicated human experience. Authentic exposition guards the preacher against this perspectival bias. There in Scripture parades the spectrum of human greed, lust, corruption, altruism, friendship, loyalty, despair, and every other complicated confluence of human drives and obsessions. Biblical exposition hits more of these by accident than contrived relevance hits on purpose. Expository preaching may protect the preacher from nearsighted neglect.

Practically, exposition gives the preacher a competent, secure, and repeatable approach. Striving for a sermon idea haunts the preacher with the hunt for a great idea, a novelty that compels. This produces an encore syndrome in which the preacher lives on the treadmill of always seeking a better idea. The expositor finds the idea in the text. Armed with this confidence, the preacher can approach the weekly task with security. The text beckons. It is a mine, and the preacher is the mine worker. The proclaimer already knows there are more rich veins than can be tapped in a lifetime. Sermon preparation begins with security. Further, exposition is a repeatable process. The preacher who builds Rome anew beginning every Monday morning has a Sisyphean task: how to roll the stone up the hill this week. The expositor need not invent the sermon idea, for it is discovered in the text.

Expository Weaknesses

Yet characteristic weaknesses mark some expository preaching. A mere historicizing of the text weakens exposition. The preacher, who has parsed one verb too many, leads the somnolent congregation on a tour of verbs in *mi*, the archaeology of Asia Minor, and the syntax of the concessive participle. The preacher plays Galilee and could just as well be in a toga at Tiberius. The message reeks of "wasness" rather than "isness." The preacher lives with Elijah in the cave on Horeb rather than in the suburb where his congregants dwell. The historicizing tendency represents the greatest weakness of the expository method.

The opposite of the historicizing tendency is the unwillingness to do the tough, exhausting exegetical work that feeds authentic exposition. Expository preaching that pelts the congregation with obvious commonplaces on the surface of the text dilutes the meaning of exposition. Running commentary of banal commonplaces that any inattentive congregant could observe on the surface of the text is not exposition. Enduring expository preachers live with analytical, exegetical, philological, and critical commentaries as lifetime friends. Their study is a congregation of the voices of the church, from the far-off echo of the patristics to the digitized theological wordbooks on the hard drive of their laptop. Exegesis is the neighborhood where the expositor lives, not a side trip.

Nor does a certain rhetorical structure mark exposition. American evangelical exposition has sometimes been hijacked by alliteration, euphony, or overly clever outlines. God forgive the preacher who outlined an "expository" sermon on the prodigal son "His Madness, His Badness, and His Gladness." Far too often such homiletic circus tricks and shell games substitute for the tedious discipline of exegesis that gives substance to exposition.

Neither is exposition a didactic running commentary on an interminable block of Scripture that oozes over the congregation like an amorphous blob from a horror movie. Exposition does not eliminate the need for intentional rhetorical structure in preaching. The expository sermon calls for a thesis, proposition, central idea, or sermon in a sentence, in a word, unity. The expositor had best state this timeless truth in a present tense, active voice, declarative statement that defines the boundaries.

Expository preaching sometimes disrespects time. For the studied preacher, the art of exposition is the art of elimination. The studied expositor will have much more exegetical matter than the sermon can bear or the congregation can hear. The apt expositor is a sculptor, not a painter. Sculpting is a subtractive art that reduces a mass; painting is an additive art that increases mass. The expositor eliminates a mass of material in sculpting a sermon.

As a generic term, "expository preaching" may apply to any apt homiletic that exposes the meaning of a biblical unit of thought accurately and relates it to the current human situation. *See* BRIDGING THEN AND NOW; SERMON RESEARCH; THE BIG IDEA.

Bibliography: John Albert Broadus. *On the Preparation and Delivery of Sermons.* 4th ed. (1979); Haddon Robinson. *Biblical Preaching.* 2nd ed. (2001).

FALLEN CONDITION FOCUS
See THE BIG IDEA.

THE FOUR PAGES OF THE SERMON
John M. Rottman

The Four Pages of the sermon approach to preaching describes the homiletic of Paul Scott Wilson articulated most fully in his book *The Four Pages of the Sermon: An Approach to Biblical Preaching.* In the broader field of homiletics the Four Pages approach can be classified with those homiletical approaches that prioritize theological considerations, as opposed to rhetorical, in guiding sermon structure (Wilson 2004, 91). The design emphasizes God and gospel as the purpose of preaching. A sermon in the Four Pages mode can be characterized as having four moves (*see* MOVES), two moves that focus upon the biblical text and two moves of application. The first two moves (roughly half the sermon) explore trouble, first moving into the biblical text and then moving into the contemporary world. The final two moves proclaim the good news of the gospel, again first moving into the biblical text and then moving into the world of the listener. Considerations for each of the Four Pages can be characterized as follows:

Page One: The World of the Biblical Text through the Lens of Trouble

Since sin has infected the world, it is both the occasion of God's judgment and the cause of cosmic (including human) brokenness. This first movement of the sermon presents the world of the biblical text as seen through the lens of trouble. The trouble might center on the trouble that occasioned the text's writing or transmission. The trouble might also be seen in the lives of one of the characters as it plays out in a particular biblical narrative. Or the trouble might appear as resistance to the biblical Word voiced. Ordinarily, this presentation of trouble in the Bible will take a narrative form, in that it is part of the historical redemptive story of God's creating and saving action in the world. On the occasions where there seems to be little or no trouble in the text, the broader biblical narrative should provide a trouble focus for Page One.

Page Two: Our World through the Lens of Trouble

This part of the sermon can be thought of as a movement of application that presents the same sort, or a similar sort, of trouble in our day and age as that found in the corresponding world of the biblical text. This movement of the sermon identifies brokenness in our world (horizontal focus) and/or the judgment and displeasure of God against human failure (vertical focus). Ordinarily, this movement will contain a story that exemplifies or embodies the trouble, brokenness, failure, sin, and so on in view. This is the part of the sermon where the preacher challenges the congregation. In this section the preacher need not pull any punches in voicing God's judgment or calling for change. Practical suggestions are also fully appropriate here.

Page Three: The Biblical World through the Lens of Good News

This next part of the sermon presents the good news of the gospel that begins to address the trouble presented in the first two movements of the sermon. This good news is always the saving action of God that enables or empowers God's people in the face of the particular trouble, judgment, brokenness, or sin. The theological assumption here is that we are unable to save ourselves. A sentence that encapsulates this good news might be identified as the theme of the sermon. Since the saving action is first of all God's action, God (Father, Son, and/or Holy Spirit) will be the grammatical subject of the sentence. The preacher will ask what God is doing in the biblical text to lift the burden of trouble from God's people. The last two pages of the sermon preach hope, good news of the sort that stands over against the trouble without necessarily removing it.

Page Four: Our World through the Lens of Good News

This fourth movement of the sermon speaks about the action of God, identical or similar to the action of God in the previous movement of the sermon, but now in our day and age. This part might be thought of as a second movement of application speaking about what God is doing to address trouble in our world of the sort identified in the first half of the sermon. Stories of God addressing that particular brokenness, sin, or trouble in our world will be featured here as the sermon continues to speak of the action of God here and now to save and restore God's fallen world. The examples on Page Four may have the character of testimony that address the question about whether God is doing and saying today the things that God was doing in the biblical text. The preacher might point to what God is already doing or beginning to do in a particular congregation to address that brokenness. Human response pictured in this section speaks of God as the senior partner in our sanctification by grace and in our participation in God's mission in the world.

The Four Pages is rightly thought of as a rudimentary homiletical method, but in another sense also functions as a deeper homiletical grammar, a theoretical shorthand for talking about the necessary features of any sermon. For example, the preacher might linger exclusively in the biblical text while preaching the parable of the Prodigal Son. She might note the trouble evidenced in both sons' estrangement from their father and the good news of his gracious forgiving love. If in so doing the preacher includes little or no application, the sermon could be said to be a Page One–Page Three sermon. If the preacher selected a passage from Amos 4 referencing God's judgment against the "fat cows of Bashan" and moved on to speak judgment against the fat cow in his own nation who ignored the needs of poor people, he or she could be said to have preached a Page One–Page Two sermon.

Wilson specifies the one-through-four order of the pages as normal, but does not shy away from suggesting a variation of order from time to time (Wilson 1996, 243). While both rhetorical and theological considerations will keep the preacher on most occasions from beginning with grace and ending with trouble, switching the order of pages may on some occasions provide a welcome variation. On other occasions when the community expects or requires a longer sermon, the sermon might include six of the four pages, two Page Ones and two Page Twos, or several of each of the pages on the grace side of the sermon.

Sermon introductions and conclusions are important but auxiliary parts of the Four Page sermon. Introductions serve the critical function of inviting the listener to move from hearing the Word read into further engagement with it as the preacher uses that Word to proclaim the good news of the gospel. The introduction might take the form of a story that foreshadows the trouble that the sermon will address, a little Page Two, or it might foreshadow the good news of the gospel in the sermon, a miniature Page Four. Alternatively, it might focus upon a particular aspect or feature of the biblical text that will then serve as an entryway into a fuller presentation of that text. The introduction provides space for the listener to negotiate numerous rhetorical aspects, especially those revolving around issues of ethos. Consequently with all of this rhetorical instability at the outset, the introduction should be "light," long enough, and accessible (i.e., no one should die in the introduction). The conclusion briefly states the trouble once again and then celebrates the grace of God that lifts the burden of that trouble as God responds to it.

Some have suggested that preaching in the style of Four Pages invites predictability. Listeners will begin to time out each page in anticipation of the end or begin to yawn in anticipation of the good news in the second half. But unless the hearer is consciously listening for each page, the Four Page structure seems to operate below the awareness of those who are not specifically looking for sermon structure. The Four Page approach also has proved rather adaptable in handling texts from a variety of theological perspectives and biblical genres.

While Wilson suggests a balance between trouble and grace halves of the sermon, there may be occasions when an imbalance serves the preacher best. Preaching on Good Friday may demand that the sermon dwell to a greater degree upon trouble. Conversely, a funeral sermon may not need to develop trouble very much at all, especially with a coffin in full view of the listeners. In such an instance the preacher may be able to dedicate the lion's share of the sermon toward preaching the hope of the resurrection. See MOVES; PREACHER'S WEEK; SERMON RESEARCH.

Bibliography: Paul Scott Wilson. *The Four Pages of the Sermon.* (1996); Paul Scott Wilson. *Preaching and Homiletical Theory.* (2004); Paul Scott Wilson. *The Practice of Preaching.* Rev. ed. (2007).

FUNERAL
Thomas G. Long

The main purpose of a funeral sermon is not to soothe the brokenhearted or to provide explanations but instead to confront head-on the lies proclaimed by the other preacher at a funeral: Death.

A. Introduction
B. The Purposes of Funerals and Funeral Sermons
C. The Tasks of the Funeral Sermon
   1. Kerygmatic
   2. Ecclesial
   3. Oblational
   4. Eucharistic
   5. Therapeutic
   6. Commemorative
   7. Missional
   8. Educational

A. Introduction

Many issues swirling around funerals and funeral preaching can be seen in the story of a nearly forgotten Christian named Tutaswampe, one of a tribe of Native Americans converted to the faith in the early 1600s by New England Puritans. Tutaswampe and his kin had been schooled in a strict Calvinistic understanding of the gospel, including a fierce prejudice against funeral ceremonies. Considering the funeral practices they had inherited a blasphemous, showy mess, the Puritans attempted to eliminate funerals altogether from the Christian repertoire. So when a certain member of Tutaswampe's tribe died one day, Tutaswampe and others tramped out in silence to the burying place in the woods, intending to inter their friend with neither word nor ceremony, for that was what the Puritans had taught them was the Christian manner. However, after standing for a long while obediently at the grave in mute sorrow, they could no longer abide the barren wordlessness of the occasion. Their borrowed theology dictated silence, but their hearts demanded something more, and so they broke the rules. They walked a little piece from the grave and gathered under a nearby tree, where they asked Tutaswampe to speak a hopeful word, which he did (Stannard 1977, 107).

Funeral preachers today know that, while the Puritans were right in seeing funerals as too often vain, glib, and sentimental, Tutaswampe and those with him rightly sensed that the Puritans were pastorally wrong. The heart comprehends another truth. We discern a deeper wisdom that the gospel always involves human words being pressed beyond their knowing into the void of death to bear witness to a hope visible only through faith. As was the case with Tutaswampe, God continues to stir up hearts to break the silence of death with a hopeful and prayerful word.

B. The Purposes of Funerals and Funeral Sermons

But what to say? When the preacher stands, like Tutaswampe, under whatever tree in whatever corner of a darkened wood, beside whatever grave in whatever cemetery, before the mourners wherever they may be gathered in the face of death, what can one possibly say? Decisions about what to say at funerals depend on how we answer an even more basic question: What in the name of God are we trying to do at a funeral anyway? What exactly is the purpose of a funeral and, thus, of a funeral sermon? Toward what goals are our words flung? Before we can know what to say and how to say it, we must face the question of why we are up there in the first place trying to say anything at all.

Officially, many Christian denominations and movements have tried to make it clear that one thing preachers are not there to do is to eulogize the dead, to compliment and praise the deceased. The rubrics for the current Roman Catholic funeral Mass expressly forbid eulogies: The *Order of Christian Funerals* is quite specific: "A brief homily based on the readings is always given after the gospel reading at the funeral liturgy, and may also be given after the readings at the vigil service; but there is never to be a eulogy" (*OCF*, 27). In the Protestant world, the command of the Lutheran *Manual on the Liturgy* is typical: "The sermon may include a recognition of the life of the deceased, but its purpose is not eulogy *but a proclamation of hope and comfort in Christ*" (Pfatteicher and Messerli 1979, 360, emphasis added).

We know what these rubrics are after—preach the gospel; do not preach the life of the deceased; focus on God and the gospel, not on human beings—but what seems liturgically desirable is often pastorally problematic. Most funerals, by far, include at least some reminiscences about the deceased that would fall within the range of the definition of a eulogy (literally, a good word), and it would seem cold and sterile not to include them. Small wonder pastors are unclear about the shape and aim of a funeral sermon.

What, then, is a funeral (and a funeral sermon) for? Is it to remember fondly the deceased? To comfort the grief-stricken? To proclaim the gospel? To evangelize the living? Many clergy take the high road by working to shape funerals as reverent services of worship in which there are joyful hymns and powerful, upbeat "witness to the resurrection" sermons. Increasingly, these ideal funerals are envisioned as memorial services absent the "distraction" of the body (or the cremated remains), which would have been disposed of previously in a private way. But this approach often collides with the desires of the larger culture, which seems intent on turning funerals into open-mike events in which coaches, nephews, and neighbors flood the room with stories and jokes about the deceased. And so we have a tug-of-war between the quiet, but somewhat abstract, ideal of a worship service reflecting on the joy of the resurrection and a talk show–style carnival of anecdotes and memories.

Actually, both options would be unrecognizable to our early Christian forebears. Woven out of strands borrowed from Jewish and Roman burial practices, distinctively Christian funeral customs had been firmly established by the 5th cent., and they bear little resemblance to what we call a Christian funeral today. In brief, Christians would lovingly wash and anoint the bodies of the deceased, dress them in baptismal garments, and then carry them to the place of burial, singing psalms and hymns as they traveled. The dead were seen as saints traveling on to God. At the place of burial, the faithful would give the kiss of peace to the deceased, and with prayers, words of hope, and tears mingled with alleluias, they would bid farewell to those who had died.

We can see in these early Christian funeral practices a strong response to our question about the purpose of a funeral and a strong corrective to current customs. Put clearly, what we now think of as an optional appendage to the funeral—the journey to the cemetery carrying the body of the deceased—was, for early Christians, not just part of the funeral. It was the funeral. Despite appearances, the funeral sermon is not some prompt to meditation for mourners gathered quietly in a chapel. It is rather a word spoken in the middle of a march, spoken to pilgrim people who are in the middle of a pilgrimage to the place of farewell, singing the songs of Zion and bearing the body of a saint as they travel.

When all is said and done, we do not preach at funerals primarily to provide comfort—though solace and support are, thank God, often given through the sermon. And we are not there to explain why all of this happened—though the hunger for meaning in the face of meaninglessness, thank God, is often addressed in what we say. What is more, we are not there to supply spiritual solemnity to an already somber situation. What we are there to do is to say what Christians want and need to say as we carry a brother or sister on the long journey through the valley of the shadow of death to the place where we release the one we have loved into the arms of the God we trust.

C. The Tasks of the Funeral Sermon

What, in fact, do Christians need and want to say as they walk along the pilgrim way with a saint traveling to God? This gospel story is, of course, many-sided, and funeral preachers would do well to have in mind, as they prepare funeral sermons, a theological checklist of the themes that can and should be sounded at a funeral. The following checklist, inspired by the work of liturgical theologian Paul Hoon (Hoon 1976, 169–81), does not tell us what to say, but it does give us ways to think theologically about each funeral situation. The theological emphasis in each funeral sermon will fall at different places depending upon the circumstances, but here are eight broad categories to consider in the creation of the funeral sermon:

1. Kerygmatic

The first and overarching goal of a funeral sermon is to proclaim the gospel truth, to announce the good news about who God really is and what God is doing in this place. In this regard, funeral preaching is no different from week in, week out sermonizing. The preacher stands in a specific context, a particular moment in time, turns expectantly, attentively, and inquisitively to a passage of Scripture, and then speaks the truth about what is heard there.

The context of a funeral sermon, of course, is death, and implied in this context are doubts about the presence, power, and goodness of God. Even the peaceful death of an aged saint raises these doubts because every particular passing is connected to the general human experience of death. Even "good" deaths remind us of other deaths—tragic deaths, infant deaths, painful deaths.

This means that kerygmatic preaching at a funeral is not merely the gentle sharing of hopeful words but is the unmasking of a lie. Whether we are aware of it or not, there is another preacher present at every funeral, following the funeral procession shouting taunts and jeers, and this preacher is a liar. I refer to Death (capital *D* Death is the final enemy, the power that seeks to destroy all that God intends for human life; little *d* death, biological death, can sometimes come as a friend). Death is the preacher of evil's most convincing lie. Death claims persuasively that the God who promised to be present turned out to be absent, that the God who vowed to give and preserve life would not— or could not—keep that promise, and that all talk of steadfast loving relationships and enduring community is so much empty wind.

Death preaches a sinister sermon, one that leaves us to confess the sad and inescapable creed, "I believe that God, who promised to be with us, turned out, when the chips were down, to be missing in action. We are forced to relinquish the empty promises of God and turn toward the inevitable truth that life is swallowed up in Death. Death is Lord. O Death, here is your victory." What makes Death's story so compelling is that it has all of the evidence on its side. Look at the lifeless body, the empty chair at the table, the unraveled narratives of hope and meaning.

Funeral sermons, then, are not merely gentle messages of comfort; they are words of combat. "Christian hope," maintains Amy Plantinga Pauw, "requires a restless protest against death" (Pauw 1997, 170), and no matter how tenderly we may speak, we should not forget that our task as preachers of the gospel is to engage Death's lies in pitched battle. What we are there to do is to uncover what Death tries with all of its might to conceal and distort, to name the truth that Death struggles to hide with falsehoods. The task of the funeral preacher is to stand and face the same harsh reality, the same seemingly irrefutable evidence, but to tell another story, the gospel story, to tell the faith story that is truer than our senses, deeper than our emotions, more real than the empirical evidence at hand.

2. Ecclesial

Another lie that Death tells is that we are alone; we die alone, and Death teaches us the lesson that, consequently, we live alone since we are always facing Death. As the woman standing at the grave of her husband is supposed to have said, "All good marriages end up here." In combating this lie of isolation, the preacher has no better text than the congregation itself, the communion of saints. Some Latin American congregations, in worship, call out the names of members of the church who have died, some violently. As each name is read, the congregation vigorously exclaims, *"Presente!"* as a sign that the church refuses to accept death as the last and defining word about them. "As a part of the 'great cloud of witnesses' (Heb 12:1), they are declared present to the living community through God's gift of life that triumphs even over the last enemy, death" (Pauw 1997, 171).

The funeral sermon should not take the form of a private counseling session, zeroing in on the individual mourners, as if they were facing this all alone. Instead, the preacher should make audible and visible the great company of saints traveling the last mile of the way with the one who has died.

3. Oblational

Death, that lying preacher, always takes up a collection. Death moves through the pews with the collection plate and demands a toll: "Give me your hopes. Give me your memories. Give me your loved ones. I return nothing."

The church, on the other hand, never takes up a collection but instead receives an offering. A collection is extorted; an offering is freely given. People come to a funeral ready and needing to give, and one of the functions of the funeral sermon is to receive the offering in the name of God. People bring offerings of many kinds—their memories, their sorrows, their stories, the body of the one who has died, their anticipations of their own death— and the sermon is one of the places where those offerings can be named and placed in the loving hands of the God who preserves and saves.

To think of the funeral sermon as the receiving of the offering also allows the preacher to move from the prophetic role to the priestly, and to preach with prayerful arms extended. Sometimes preachers think of funeral sermons only as God's words addressed to the people. That puts the preacher exclusively in the posture of trying to speak God's thoughts, even to the point of making judgments. But sometimes the best funeral sermon comes when the preacher figuratively leaves the pulpit, stands in the pew, lifts up the offering plate, and cries, "O God, we loved this person. Please, O God, receive him and all that we remember of him good and bad as our offering to you."

4. Eucharistic

Another theme of funeral preaching is thanksgiving, but this theme must carefully be distinguished from happiness. We give thanks for many things—from hard work to lessons learned in sorrow—that do not particularly make us happy. This is why the Lord's Table stands at the center of Christian worship. The eucharistic table is, after all, a place of death: we show forth here the Lord's death until he comes. At this table we discover in brokenness, sorrow, loss, and death—not apart from these things—the grace and saving mercy of God. When we get up from the Lord's Table, our vision has been altered. We now see what could not see before: all of life is the theater of the glory of God, and it is our duty and delight to say, "Thank you. Thank you."

So it is at a funeral—and in funeral preaching. We give thanks for the gift of a life—not the parts of the life that we found pleasing or that made us especially happy, but all of it. Every life is a gift of God's grace, and the fact that some lives are transparent to that grace and some are opaque does not prevent our giving thanks to God, even for what we have learned in suffering and loss.

5. Therapeutic

God's presence is a healing presence, and another task of funeral preaching is to speak that healing word. In a therapeutic culture, it is important to discriminate between authentic gospel therapy of the gospel and the smaller, more psychologically defined tasks of bereavement management or coming to terms with the emotions of grief. The therapeutic task is larger than achieving psychic equilibrium; it is to recover the capacity to place the experience of this death into the fabric of the overarching story of God's care for us.

"I don't think people are afraid of death," observed a young man dying of leukemia. "What they are afraid of is the incompleteness of their life." This is why in the wisdom of the classic funeral liturgies, the life of the one who has died is always seen in the context of baptism. This is not because baptism somehow makes a person better than the next, but because baptism connects the brief, fragmented, episodic story of a human being to the larger and whole narrative of Jesus Christ.

When the essayist Anatole Broyard was dying of cancer, he observed, "I would . . . like a doctor who enjoyed me. I want to be a good story for him." In a world without religion, however, Broyard recognized the sad truth that we have to fabricate our own stories. "Once we had a narrative of heaven and hell," he stated, "but now we make our own narratives" (1993, 42, 45). No, counters the gospel preacher, we do not have to make up our own story. We are given a story, and the brief sentence fragment that constitutes any one life, bounded before and after by an ellipsis, is, by the grace of God, incorporated into the full and rich narrative of Christ.

6. Commemorative

The Puritans' negative reaction to the funeral sermon came because many of the funeral preachments they had heard were short on gospel and long on eulogy, full of rhapsodies about the life of the deceased at the expense of descriptions of the life of God. It is a caution worth heeding, of course, not to preach the noble adventures of the dear departed deceased instead of the gospel of the eternally present Christ.

On the other hand, we do not know about any God who can be described apart from the stories of the people with whom this God chooses to get involved. Properly told, God stories are always human stories, and human stories are always permeated by the wonder of God. Good funeral sermons will be enriched by honest memories of the one who has died. The idea here is not to tell stories that act as showcases for the virtues of the deceased but as examples of how this life was a prism, refracting the grace of God.

The telling of stories about those who have died is, in part, how the Christian community is shaped over time in the identity of Christ. The identity we carry in the stories of our lives is, in the deepest sense, the identity of God's image, and it is a task of the funeral sermon to claim and narrate that identity.

7. Missional

One of Death's boldest lies is that the Christian pilgrimage leads to a cul-de-sac. It is a common experience of grief to feel that life has come to an end, not only for the one who has died, but for everyone else as well. Death holds up a stop sign: "Go no farther. This is the end of the road."

The gospel, however, both warns us and reassures us that death, no matter how tragic, and grief, no matter how deep, are pausing places along the way, not stopping places. The message of Easter is not, "Christ is risen! Sit patiently awaiting your own resurrection," but instead, "Christ is risen! Go to work for God in the world!" The funeral sermon can remind those who are traveling with the deceased to the cemetery that in the Christian vocabulary, cemeteries are not final resting places but the places where Christian mission begins, as it did on Easter. The pilgrimage will not stop at the grave; the pilgrims will go into the world to continue their work and witness. The sermon can also announce that the one who has died has not ceased from the labors and vocation of a saint, but has joined that great chorus of praise to God, which is the ultimate human vocation.

8. Educational

Funerals are the worship of God's people in a public place, and there are often people present who do not know or share the Christian faith. The old technique of using the funeral sermon to evangelize people in the narrow sense was a misguided recognition of the presence of strangers in the household of God. A better, and more theologically sound, reaction is to show hospitality, and one sermonic form of that hospitality is to do some gentle, low-key teaching. The preacher can explain in simple terms why we say and confess and pray as we do on such an occasion. In the final analysis, it is the best evangelism of all to bring into view, as clearly as we can, how it is that we see life and death, humanity and God.

"The purpose of Christianity," wrote the great Orthodox scholar Alexander Schmemann, "is not to help people by reconciling them with death, but to reveal the Truth about life and death in order that people may be saved by the Truth" (Schmemann 1973, 99). So it is with funeral sermons. The preacher tells the truth about death and life. But this does not begin, Schmemann reminds us, at the funeral. "It begins every Sunday as the church ascending into heaven, 'puts aside all earthly care' . . . in the joy of Easter" (Schmemann 1973, 101). *See* ANTHROPOLOGY; CRISIS; RHETORIAL DEVICES; SPECIAL OCCASION; WORSHIP STYLE.

Bibliography: Anatole Broyard. *Intoxicated by My Illness: And Other Writings on Life and Death.* (1993); Catholic Church. *Order of Christian Funerals;* Paul Waitman Hoon. "Theology, Death, and the Funeral Liturgy." *Union Seminary Quarterly Review* 31 (Spring 1976) 169–81; Amy Plantinga Pauw. "Dying Well." *Practicing Our Faith: A Way of Life for a Searching People.* Edited by Dorothy C. Bass. (1997); Philip H. Pfatteicher and Carlos R. Messerli. *Manual on the Liturgy: The Lutheran Book of Worship.* (1979); Alexander Schmemann. *For the Life of the World.* (1973); David E. Stannard. *The Puritan Way of Death: A Study in Religion, Culture, and Social Change.* (1977).

INDUCTIVE
Michael A. Brothers

An inductive sermon based on a biblical text leads the hearer through form and movement on a journey of discoveries toward the answer to the question: What does this text mean for us today?

Inductive vs. Deductive

The inductive sermon form has been influenced by inductive argumentation and reasoning. Based on classical rhetoric and philosophy, an inductive argument is often described as one that reasons from specifics to the general, in contrast to a deductive argument that reasons from the general to specifics. Yet a more contemporary understanding of an inductive argument is the testing of less-than-certain inferences through particular cases that leads toward general conclusions. Whereas a deductive argument's validity of the premises guarantees the truth of the conclusion, a conclusion through induction is a discovery that depends on new information introduced in the process. Unlike deduction, induction has an element of uncertainty, for there is the possibility that new information introduced during or after the argument may provide new conclusions.

Similarly, an inductive sermon is often described as a sermon that begins with the specifics of experience and ends with a general conclusion; whereas a deductive sermon begins with a conclusion and supports it with specifics from experience and Scripture. Yet a more dynamic understanding of the inductive sermon is an engagement between text, preacher, and hearer, in which hunches are tested and played out through experiences in a quest for the discovery of a biblical truth. Often this discovery is a surprise! Not unlike the inductive argument, the conclusion may be open-ended, prompting further surprises and discoveries of the gospel in the experiences of the hearers.

Form and Exegesis

Much of the popularity of inductive sermons since the 1970s can be attributed to Fred Craddock with the introduction of his inductive method in *As One Without Authority* (1971). As an alternative to the propositional deductive sermons that dominated the 1950s and 1960s, Craddock proposed that the form of the sermon should have as much anticipation, movement, and excitement of discovery as the preacher's exegesis of the biblical text. Thomas G. Long aptly summarizes:

> In Craddock's view, exegesis is, for the preacher, a potentially thrilling process of discovery. Facing the biblical text, the preacher follows hunches, explores toward interpreting the text. Exegesis is, in short, an exciting adventure that darts first this way, then that way, resisting all reduction to a process of linear logic. (1989, 81)

For Craddock, the problem with deductive sermons was not in their exegetical support, careful preparation, or efforts toward relevance. "It is the movement that is wrong," he claimed, where inductive anticipation of exegesis is replaced by the deductive exhortation. Craddock's solution was for the sermon's movement to regenerate, with the hearers, the inductive adventure experienced by the preacher in exegesis (Craddock 1971, 125; Long 1989, 81). Long continues:

> Craddock proposed that sermons be shaped according to the same process of creative discovery employed by preachers in their exegetical work. When preachers study biblical texts, he said, they do not know in advance what those texts mean; they must search for meanings, putting clues together until meanings emerge at the end. Sermons, therefore, ought to recreate imaginatively this inductive quest so that the listeners can share the preacher's experience of illumination. (1989, 97–98)

Advantages and Limitations

What have been celebrated by some as the inductive sermon's strengths have been challenged by others as its limitations: the engagement of the

hearer on a tensive journey, and the shifting role of authority.

The primary advantage of inductive sermons is the direct engagement of the hearers from the opening to the conclusion of the sermon. There is no need to begin with an attention getter or conclude with a final step of application, since testing, questioning, and the evoking of experiences invite hearers' participation throughout the sermon. The hope is that by the sermon's end, there is the discovery of a biblical truth the hearers have already begun to claim for themselves. Because the inductive form creates tensions regarding yet-to-be-resolved understandings of biblical texts, it can be especially useful in helping the congregation discover new meanings from familiar passages.

Whereas propositional preaching lets the hearer know from the beginning what the sermon is about, an inductive journey's success depends on the craft of the preacher to arrive at a destination, and the tolerance for ambiguity and suspense by the hearer. If one or the other falls short, the sermon is either derailed or missed altogether.

A secondary advantage is in regard to authority. Without an unquestionable proposition based on a foregone conclusion, hearers are encouraged to reach their own conclusions. Here there is a shift in authority from the conclusions of the preacher to the interaction between the congregation and the biblical text. Because of this shift of authority, some homileticians have stated that the inductive form is best for addressing controversial issues when the preacher is at odds with the congregation; whereas others support it as a fitting response to the changing role of authority in the culture at large, thereby providing the best opportunity for the sermon to be heard.

In response to this relocation of authority, Charles L. Campbell warns that inductive preaching's emphasis on human experience and individual response creates a danger that the biblical text will become secondary, where the "real authority" becomes "the experience of individual hearers, which both precedes and verifies the message of scripture" (Campbell 1995, 271).

Example

The inductive sermon's emphasis on movement toward disclosure has fostered sermon structures as diverse as a problem-solving quest, an unfolding narrative plot, and a sequence of clarifying images. In the sermon "Waiting," John W. Vannorsdall leads the hearer during the season of Advent on a quest to understand Ps 130:5-7, "I wait for the Lord, my soul waits . . ." Through testing and exploring common experiences of waiting, the hearer along with preacher searches for an answer to the question: But what does it mean to wait for the Lord? In true inductive form, a surprising twist at the end transforms both the question and the experience.

Vannorsdall begins:

> There was a time when waiting meant that we weren't old enough for something. Since we were confident of our immediate readiness, waiting had no redeeming qualities at all. In fact, the "go-go" temper of American culture turned waiting into a downright bad thing to do.

The impatience of culture and church then challenges the biblical text.

> It was not different in our churches. The imperative laid upon us was that we "decide for Christ," and that the time for doing that was right now, before we left this service or at least before this particular "crusade" was over. What could it possibly mean to "wait for the Lord," and what good could come of it?

With this guiding question, Vannorsdall moves to a hunch about the value of waiting in relationship to human experience and God.

> What the years have taught is not only that waiting is a normal part of the human experience, but that waiting is the arms of welcome half-circled to receive that which has not yet come; arms which describe the shape of that which we desire to receive. . . . But waiting for the Lord is different from other kinds of waiting.

What follows is an exploration of different kinds of human waiting: beginning with the "ordinary waiting" for water to boil, for a taxi, or for the first day of school; moving to the waiting for a person or a relationship; and ending with the waiting for an event like war or Christmas. Each is tested according to its adequacy as an analogy for "waiting for the Lord." With each move we come closer, yet all eventually fall short.

Then in a reversal, our waiting is replaced by the one who waits for us: "The Lord . . . who draws near to wait with those who wait for him." Vannorsdall concludes:

> We may wait a long time, but we know for whom we wait. And our waiting is the most important thing we have to contribute. It is the half-circled arms of our waiting which describe him for whom we wait, as our waiting itself begins to give shape to what we desire to become. "I wait for the Lord, my soul waits, and in his word I hope." (1982, 14–19)

See ARRANGEMENT; DEDUCTIVE; NARRATIVE FORM; NEW HOMILETIC.

Bibliography: Ronald J. Allen, ed. *Patterns of Preaching.* (1998); Donald M. Borchert, ed. *Encyclopedia of Philosophy.* (2006); Charles L. Campbell. "Inductive Preaching." *Concise Encyclopedia of Preaching.* Edited by William H. Willimon and Richard Lischer. (1995); Fred B. Craddock. *As One Without Authority.* (1971); Ralph L. Lewis. *Persuasive Preaching Today.* (1979); Thomas G. Long. *The Witness of Preaching.* (1989); Thomas Mautner. *The Penguin Dictionary of Philosophy.* (2005); John W. Vannorsdall. "Waiting." *Dimly Burning Wicks.* (1982).

INTRODUCTIONS
Henry J. Langknecht

Sermon introductions gratefully acknowledge and respond to an audience's desire to engage and know sermons.

Every sermon has a *beginning.* Whether every sermon must have an *introduction* is debated in the homiletic literature. Barth famously stresses that worship is the sermon's introduction; the preacher provides merely a transition from Scripture to sermon. At another pole are homileticians who are silent about worship context, treating the sermon as a stand-alone event, and counseling the introduction strategies of classical rhetoric: gain attention, arouse interest, and curry favor. Most contemporary homileticians tend toward the middle ground, considering the introduction in light of both the sermon's setting in worship and the overlapping theological and rhetorical functions it serves.

Theological function. Introductions, like all aspects of preaching, have theological implications. Barth prohibited introductions because they risked pretending a non-existent point of contact between the world and God's Word. Most preachers today would acknowledge Barth's point while avoiding the drawing of such a sharp distinction. Christian sermons are rooted in Scripture but draw on other sources of authority (e.g., encounters with the triune God, theological traditions, sacraments, imagination, experience, and reason). A specific theological function of the introduction is to hint at the connections between this sermon, its sources of authority, and the world.

Rhetorical function. Other functions served by the introduction are rhetorical and fall into three closely overlapping spheres: hospitality (introducing audience and preacher); sermon form (introducing audience and sermon as a work in context); and sermon content (introducing audience and sermon topic). Thomas G. Long offers the language of promise: in the introduction the preacher makes promises about style, form, and content.

As hinted above, homiletics and classical rhetoric approach differently the need to gain attention, arouse interest, or curry favor. Attention to the preacher and interest in the Word are gifts given by the sermon audience as a faith response. Also, most audience members have an ongoing relationship with the preacher—a relationship affected, but rarely altered, by the preaching. The preacher extends hospitality in the introduction by retaining the attention, interest, and relationship and by making (and then keeping) promises in the sermon.

One act of hospitality is to evaluate the need for transition from what immediately precedes the sermon. This may be a simple matter of metonymy—picking up words or images from what precedes. However, if the precedent involved movement or heightened emotion, a more strategic transition may be necessary. Hospitality is also shown when the preacher adopts tones of body, face, and voice that are appropriate to the sermon. This communicates a sense of integrity and boosts audience confidence in the preacher's investment and preparedness.

The first few sentences may hint toward the sermon's content, but they also have the important function of introducing hearers to the preacher's—and this sermon's—voice, tone, and style. It is during the introduction that the preacher is also beginning to read and respond to this sermon's audience.

Two inhospitable approaches that squander the initial gift of attention and interest are those that apologize in advance for the sermon and those that focus on the sermon composition process (usually to complain about how hard it was).

The promises the introduction makes about sermon form and content begin before a word is spoken. When the preacher takes and claims his or her space, makes eye contact with the audience, and allows for a brief silence before speaking, the sermon, even in the context of liturgy, is framed as a distinct event inviting audience focus.

As the speaking begins, the introduction, like the introduction to a hymn, orients the hearers and prepares them to participate with confidence by establishing an astounding web of elements: tempo, tone, intensity, genre, mood, style, motifs, images, and point of view. Even minimal introductions like, "Once upon a time . . ." or "Today's topic is . . . ," imply promises about what is to follow. The goal is to facilitate and reward the audience's efforts to engage the preaching and to anticipate where the sermon is headed and how it will unfold. In this sense, a good introduction is both indispensable and non-transferable.

In service to the audience, the preacher composes the introduction while exercising rhetorical and aesthetic discernment about appropriate length, content, tone, and style, always considering the implicit promises and whether the sermon will keep them. For example, introductions using hooks (e.g., provocative questions or statements of hyperbole or paradox) can be effective, but only if the sermon will resolve or respond to them. Introductory anecdotes and jokes will serve the sermon if the characters, images, or plots they introduce are employed and ultimately resolved.

It is more helpful, and more difficult, to compose introductions that anticipate as many multiple aspects and elements of the sermon as possible. For example, an introduction might lift up one element of Scripture, hold it in tension with an image from the liturgy, while simultaneously hinting at its relevance for Christian life.

The use of suspense in the introduction raises interesting issues. Audiences want ultimately to know the sermon, but anticipation and tension are important to plotted works that unfold over time. The introduction needs to securely engage the audience but not reveal all. Too much information revealed about the sermon may result in the audience evaluating its subsequent unfolding ("There are seven points and the first one took ten minutes . . . !"). Too little information about location, time, or point of view (as with introductions that hide all identities behind pronouns) makes it hard for audiences to feel secure in their listening work.

Two other devices that thwart audiences are unprepared, stream-of-consciousness introductions, which make direction and focus hard to discern, and step down introductions. Step down introductions result from a preacher's instinct to ease into the sermon's focus through, for example, telling a copious scriptural back story or filtering a topic down from the general to the specific. The audience attempts to latch on to each element, only to be disappointed as the next element is introduced. *See* RHETORICAL DEVICES.

Bibliography: David Buttrick. *Homiletic: Moves and Structures.* (1987); Thomas G. Long. *The Witness of Preaching.* 2nd ed. (2005); Samuel D. Proctor. *The Certain Sound of the Trumpet.* (1994); Paul Scott Wilson. *The Practice of Preaching.* Rev. ed. (2007).

MANUSCRIPT
Clayton J. Schmit

In preaching, there are typically three modes of preparing for and delivering a sermon: preaching without notes, preaching from prepared notes, and preaching a manuscript. We will deal with each in turn before dealing with how to bring a manuscript to life.

The first of these, in some exceptional cases, may involve extemporization, where the sermon is created as it is spoken. In certain settings, this is highly valued and an expected mode of preaching. It is seen as evidence that the Holy Spirit is actively at work in the preacher. While this gift has certainly been useful in the growth of the church, not many preachers can claim the charism of Peter and Paul for extemporaneous street preaching. More typically—and more appropriately for most preaching occasions—preaching without notes involves deep familiarization with the sermon's prepared shape and movement. It often draws upon the preparation of a fully developed manuscript, which is thoroughly rehearsed. In such cases, the sermon may seem to be memorized, although rote memorization of a script will typically yield a wooden recitation. Preaching without notes is less memorization of a script than it is thorough familiarity with a sermon's logic and language. This can yield a presentation that is fluid and responsive to the listeners.

The second typical mode of sermon delivery is preaching from prepared notes. Whether they are sketchy or complete, preaching with notes also requires thorough familiarization with prepared material. In this case, it is preferable to think of internalizing the material, working with it until the logic and language of the sermon are well in hand. When preaching with notes, the well-prepared preacher uses pulpit materials not as an outline from which one slavishly makes points, but as a series of prompts that guide the preacher in bringing the sermon to life.

Preaching from a manuscript is the third common mode of sermon delivery. As with preaching from notes, the key to use of a manuscript is internalization of the material. A common mistake is to use a manuscript as something from which to read. This usually results in a delivery that is remote and unresponsive to the audience. Ideally, the listener should not to be able to tell whether a person is preaching from a full manuscript, from a set of notes, or without notes. Here again, the goal is not to use the manuscript as an inflexible script, but as prompting material for a message that has been carefully prepared for lively communication. Some preachers may argue that writing a full manuscript stifles the working of the Holy Spirit in the preaching moment. Barbara Brown Taylor takes the opposite view. When asked why she always preaches from a manuscript, she said, "I may diverge [from the manuscript] but I have a wild imagination and when I let that go in the pulpit, I am usually sorry" (Gateway Films 1977).

Whether a preacher elects to preach with or without notes, or from a manuscript, faithful work with preaching texts, diligence in crafting a meaningful message, and careful preparation of sermon delivery are critical.

Bringing the Manuscript to Life

1. Internalization

Internalizing the sermon allows for a fluid and responsive performance of prepared materials. It is achieved in several ways. First, the message begins to be ingrained in the mind of the preacher as he or she develops the sermon's focus and shape. Working and reworking the sermon's logic, searching for apt illustrations and metaphors, and editing the material down to a sharp focus—these activities train the memory and spark the preacher's passion for the message. Second, internalization develops as the preacher rewrites the manuscript, searching for the most accurate words and expressions and adjusting the written language for oral communication. Third, internalization is completed by the oral rehearsal of the message. A surefire rule of thumb is to read the manuscript aloud eight to ten times. Regardless of a person's powers for memory, this amount of rehearsal will assure a well-internalized message. While this may appear to take an extraordinary amount of time, there is no substitute in good sermon delivery for practicing the message aloud.

2. Use of the Manuscript

When the preacher has finished the manuscript, it is good practice to continue to make adjustments as the sermon is spoken in rehearsal. The voice will discover difficulties in the text that the eye cannot; speaking the sermon aloud is also the best test for determining whether one is writing for the ear of the listener.

As revisions are made at this stage, it is a good idea to mark the script. Key words and phrases can be cued to emphasize them or to make them easy to find during the delivery. If words are crossed out and replaced, these corrections serve as a reminder to the eye that a change has been made. While the preacher may be tempted to edit the sermon on a word processor and print a clean copy for use in delivery, it can be more beneficial to rely on a hand-marked copy in the pulpit. The eye has a visual memory that is prompted by the clues that result from the editing process. The eye also knows where things fall on the page; reprinting an edited copy of the manuscript can change the pagination and eliminate the benefit of eye memory.

The placement of the manuscript on the pulpit or lectern can also aid or distract in sermon delivery. If the pulpit has an adjustable platform, the preacher can raise it to a level that allows the head to move minimally up and down when looking between audience and manuscript. This keeps the face in view of the audience, eases and shortens downward glances at the manuscript, allows for better posture and breathing, and keeps the larynx unrestricted. If the platform cannot be adjusted, the speaker can try placing the pulpit materials as high as possible on the lectern's slanted surface. Alternatively, the manuscript can be printed only on the top half or two-thirds of the page.

3. Embodiment

Delivery of a manuscript is enhanced by the use of gesture and body movement when they are care-

fully considered for rhetorical effect. Just as the preacher weighs words, he or she can develop movements that support or reinforce the tone and emphases of the sermon. Because movement is a normal part of human communication, its lack in the delivery usually makes it appear stiff and unnatural. For movement to achieve its greatest effect, it can be choreographed and rehearsed by the preacher. Random or awkward movements can be brought under control by viewing oneself in a mirror as the sermon is rehearsed.

Vocal control is a critical element of sermon delivery. The words of the manuscript, even when well internalized, can come across as flat and rote if the preacher falls into an unmodulated or an exaggerated speaking tone. Such pulpit tones can be overcome by allowing the voice to recapture the vitality it has in normal conversation. Fluctuations in pitch, pace, tone, volume, and rate of speech are typical of all conversations. Allowing these variations to color the words of a manuscript will permit the sermon to speak naturally and communicate effectively.

The eyes also play a critical role beyond memory in bringing the manuscript to life. Preachers can use the eyes to gauge audience reaction to their words and make adjustments in language so as to achieve clear communication. They can also use their eyes to cast thoughts or images. To look off in space, something we do regularly in conversation, suggests that an idea, person, or object is being considered. Finally, preachers use their eyes to keep track of their place in the sermon. A good habit is to train the eyes to sweep in blocks of sermon material at a glance. When the preacher allows the eyes to fall into a reading pace, the delivery simply degenerates into a reading of the script. See MEMORY; PERFORMING THE MANUSCRIPT; PREPARATION; WITHOUT NOTES.

Bibliography: Gateway Films. *Great Preachers: Barbara Brown Taylor.* (1977).

MYSTAGOGICAL PREACHING
Duncan Macpherson

The term *mystagogical preaching* refers to any preaching that invites initiated Christians to reflect on the deeper meaning of their sacramental experience. "You were conducted by the hand to the holy pool of sacred baptism, just as Christ was conveyed to the cross from the sepulcher close at hand." These words of St. Cyril of Jerusalem (Myst. 2.4) are part of his extended instructions to the newly baptized, which is typical of mystagogical preaching in its classical sense. Mystagogy, or teaching about Christian sacraments and liturgical rites, comes from the Greek *mystagogia*, or "interpreting of mystery" (literally, the leading of the initiated), originally referring to initiation in pre-Christian mystery religions. In the early church, it referred to the stages through which new Christians were led to a deeper understanding of their baptism, confirmation, and first Holy Communion. From around the late 2nd cent. *Katecheseis Mystagokikai*, or Mystagogical Catecheses, referred to instruction given to the newly baptized during "the week of white robes," following the night vigil and first eucharist of Easter, when the newly baptized had received white garments symbolizing their new status as sharers in the risen life of Christ. These instructions included explanation of the Scriptures, instruction in prayer, and explanation of the doctrine of the Trinity and the Christian moral life (*see* DOCTRINAL).

Today, mystagogy forms part of community-based initiation in the Roman Catholic Rite for the Christian Initiation of Adults (RCIA). This rite was revived in 1962, partly for the large numbers of adult converts in Africa and elsewhere, and partly because of a new situation in parts of Western Europe where growing numbers of people had not been baptized as children. It also reflected the desire to replace individual instruction of the convert with an experience of learning the faith within the Christian community. Similar processes of initiation have been developing in some Protestant churches, and in 2004, the Synod of the Church of England approved a program titled *Rites on the Way: Reconciliation and Restoration.*

After expressing the desire to become Christians, candidates are enrolled as catechumens and begin a period of intensive instruction, usually coinciding with Lent. Initiation, consisting of baptism, confirmation, and first Holy Communion, takes place at Easter and is followed by a period of mystagogy, which occurs between Easter and Pentecost. Mystagogy provides the opportunity for the new Christians to reflect upon the sacraments that they have received within a context of frequent and full participation in the eucharist and of closer ties of friendship with the rest of the Christian community. In a more general sense, mystagogical preaching refers either to preaching that takes congregants back to their Christian initiation or to homilies that draw on the context of a sacramental celebration. *See* SACRAMENTS, PREACHING AND TEACHING OF; THEOLOGY IN THE SERMON.

Bibliography: Bishops' Committee on the Liturgy, National Conference of Catholic Bishops. "Rite for the Christian Initiation of Adults." *The Rites of the Catholic Church.* Vol. 1. (1990); Cyril of Jerusalem. Lecture XIX. "First Lecture on the Mysteries." *Five Catechetical Lectures to the Newly Baptized.* http://www.ccel.org/fathers2/NPNF2-07/Npnf2 -07-25.htm#P2710_771752; Liturgical Commission. *Rites on the Way.* (2005).

NARRATIVE FORM
Mary Donovan Turner

The decidedly narrative quality of the teaching of Jesus is one rightful starting place for the conversation about narrative and preaching. Jesus himself was steeped in the extended narrative accounts of his Jewish ancestry and had, no doubt, an understanding of the power of story. He turned frequently to the parable for his teaching, fictive, and cursory glimpses into human nature and the hoped for and realized reign of God.

The four canonical Gospel writers also chose narrative as the appropriate form for remembering and sharing the life of Jesus. Formed and fashioned by different contexts, hopes, and needs, the four writers piece together narratives that speak a theological word to their communities about Jesus' life and mission. Teaching and learning in both Jewish and Christian communities have continued throughout the centuries to have some relationship to story.

The early Hebrews, like those in oral cultures everywhere, used story to embody commitments and give voice to cherished values. The stories entertained and instructed and were easy to remember. Thus, they could be told and retold to successive generations. Because of their appeal and their persuasive power, narratives were used in Jewish teaching and proclamation from the earliest days into the Hellenistic era. In the edited Torah, the Former and Latter Prophets and the wisdom writings, narrative in varied forms made significant and varied contributions. In the 1st cent. BCE, interpretations of the Torah, of legal and narrative texts, were offered by respected rabbis. This oral Torah was commentary (midrash) that brought forth God's word into the living present. In the liturgy of the synagogue, midrash developed into homily. The rabbis delighted the community with proverbs, pointed commentary, humor, and their gift for provocative story (Osborn 1999, 77–182).

Although there is yet no comprehensive chronology that documents the use of narrative in Christian preaching history, there are milestones along the way that deserve attention. Two representative examples will be outlined here; they come from ca. 6th cent. CE. In each, we can glimpse historical uses and understandings of narrative that weave their way into subsequent centuries and eventually inform our own.

1. Gregory the Great (540–604) was a preacher to preachers and to the masses. He lived in a time when Christianity was "taken for granted," and his purposes for preaching were to help listeners understand how to live life to the fullest, how to live the Christian life. He is arguably the first great preacher who attempted in a systematic fashion to introduce non-scriptural illustrations into his homilies. Gregory, for instance, told stories of a man who began his deathbed experience "in time" and one who did not. In another sermon he tells of a beggar who has a holy death. In yet another, a monk is one who has formerly been a repentant sinner. Gregory drove home the necessity of repentance with the help of story (Edwards 2004, 140).

2. The *kontakia* or songs of St. Romanos the Melode were homiletic poems sung by their authors. In "On Elijah," Romanos retells the story of Elijah from 1 Kgs 17. With powerful and poetic rhetoric, he paints a compelling picture of the prophet who moves from being God's friend to becoming God's problem. The punitive Elijah becomes the antithesis of the loving God who has called him. The preacher Romanos uses one extended narrative, a retelling of the biblical story, to shock the audience into new recognitions and self-reflection.

These two examples demonstrate that both narrative as illustration and narrative as sermon form have deep and long histories in the Christian tradition.

It is interesting, then, that narrative does not, for the most part, claim a substantial role in Christian preaching until the latter part of the 19th cent.; the emergence of story in preaching coincides with the rise in popularity of the short story and novel. The important exception to this is the use of story in African American preaching, which stayed closer to preaching's ancient oral form. In the African American community, preachers could, with great rhetorical power, retell the biblical story with contextualized dialect and idiom and could also paint pictures of oppression and freedom with vivid extended metaphor and narrative.

In recent decades, disciplines closely related to homiletics have begun to explore the importance and qualities of narrative. In biblical studies, for instance, literary critics have examined the structures and qualities of family ancestral narrative cycles in the Pentateuch. Likewise, the literary qualities of the Gospels have been documented and analyzed. Theologians have explored the incarnational aspects of human experience as the locus for God's revelatory presence. The stories about those experiences, it is thought, hold continuing revelatory power. Ethnographic studies have become a primary research methodology. Educators are using story as a pedagogical tool to promote self and communal learning.

It is out of this ferment that conversations about narrative and preaching have sharply risen. Authors and homileticians have explored the narrative quality of human experience and the limits of story in proclamation. Conversations have shifted from the use of story and narrative as illustrative material to narrative as the primary structure for the sermon itself. Accompanying this shift are conversations about the importance of the listener in preaching and the preacher's authority. Just a few of the significant voices in this still emerging conversation are Fred Craddock and Eugene Lowry, who are recognized as prominent voices in the New Homiletic, which can trace its ancestry to the writings of H. Grady Davis and David Randolph.

In 1971 with the publishing of *As One Without Authority*, Fred Craddock began to question the dominant DEDUCTIVE sermon form. Advocating for the INDUCTIVE, Craddock was searching for form that was much like the unfolding of a good short story. The listener, through the inductive form, was taken on a journey and led to a particular destination. While stories may be a part of the journey and provide the specific, particular concrete steps that take the hearer to a general conclusion, at stake here was the narrative quality of the overarching form, one that created a sense of anticipation on the part of the hearer.

In 1980 Eugene Lowry joined the conversation with his publishing of *The Homiletical Plot: The Sermon as Narrative Art Form*. Lowry also advocated for an overarching narrative form. In his thinking, the sermon has a plot, one that begins with a conflict, tension, or disequilibrium. In *The Homiletical Plot* and then later revised in other writings, Lowry describes a sermon form that leads the hearer from complication to a resolution of that tension, a sudden awakening in understanding, and an eventual unfolding of the consequences of this understanding. Through this movement, Lowry says, we experience gospel.

While there are many other historic and contemporary homileticians who have helped the preaching community think about and evaluate the relationship between narrative and preaching, core principles at stake in the inherent nature of narrative commend its use in proclamation:

1. The ancestors of our faith related to successive generations the experiences of God and God's people through the use of story.
2. An incarnational understanding of faith asserts that God is made known through human experience; human experience is revealed through story. Human experience has narrative shape.
3. Story is memorable.
4. Stories hold a surplus of meaning, and they allow persons from different contexts and locations to enter.
5. Narrative's basic inductive movement creates anticipation for the listening community.
6. Narrative can prompt thinking and feeling, thought and emotion.
7. Through image, metaphor, and story, imagination can be piqued and theological worldviews expanded.
8. Narrative allows for participation and, therefore, transformation of individuals and communities.
9. Narrative allows for varied understandings of the preacher's authority to be at work in the sermon's speaking and hearing.
10. Story provides visual imagery for a sermon; it offers concreteness in sermons that, without it, can suffer from abstractness and lack "meet the world" reality.

Related issues, ethical and practical, are inherent in thinking about the use of story in preaching. Does first-person narrative play an important and helpful role in the sermon? What are its dangers and limitations? What are the ethical issues involved in using others' stories in preaching? How does claiming others' stories as one's own undermine relationship and trust between preacher and community? How is this problem exacerbated by the Internet and the prevalence and ready availability of generic story? How can the preacher bring a global sensitivity to the church community through the use of narrative? What role can narrative play in prophetic preaching? What are the limits of story in relation to bringing a call for justice? *See* LITERARY CRITICISM; NARRATIVE PREACHING; NARRATIVE THEORY; NEW HOMILETIC.

Bibliography: William Countryman. "When God's Friend Becomes God's Problem: The Punitive Elijah and the Loving God According to Romanos the Melode." Distinguished Faculty Lecture. The Graduate Theological Union, November 2006; Fred Craddock. *As One Without Authority*. (1971); Stephen Crites. "The Narrative Quality of Experience." *JAAR* 39 (1971); O. C. Edwards Jr. *A History of Preaching*. (2004); Richard L. Eslinger. *A New Hearing*. (1987); Eugene Lowry. *The Homiletical Plot: The Sermon as Narrative Art Form*. (1980); Ronald E. Osborn. *Folly of God: The Rise of Christian Preaching*. (1999); Edmund Steimle, Morris J. Niedenthal, and Charles Rice. *Preaching the Story*. (1980).

NEW HOMILETIC
Paul Scott Wilson

The New Homiletic (NH) refers to a revolution in homiletics that began in the 1950s. It indicates a departure from the old homiletic that is characterized by point form, mechanical notions of structure, vertical notions of authority, use of the Bible in propositional ways, deductive sermons, stories used as illustrations of points already made, objective ideas of truth, religious experience as universal, and sermons that stressed faith as information. By contrast the NH emphasizes organic form, narrative plot, horizontal notions of authority, recovery of the Bible for the pulpit, inductive sermons, stories making their own points in their own ways, contextual understandings of truth, dynamic and tensive notions of language, and sermons as transformational experience.

A. NH Poetics
  1. Inductive Movement
  2. Organic Development
  3. Narrative, Imagination, and Metaphor
B. Theological Dimensions of the NH
  1. Word as Event
  2. Recovery of the Bible
  3. Narrative and Ethics
C. The NH and the Postmodern

Richard Eslinger coined the term *New Homiletic* when the movement was already well established (1987, 14), and it has since been used in preference to more limited terms such as *narrative* and *inductive* preaching. Both old and NH movements represent matters on which there has been considerable consensus. Some people claim that point form is old and no longer works, or that NH sermons are all narrative, or that evangelical preaching is old and NH preaching is mainline Protestant and Roman Catholic. A more nuanced understanding will recognize that the NH reflects wider cultural changes that affect all denominations in the transition from modernity to postmodernity. The NH began in part as a theological movement, yet arguably some of its theological vision has been lost.

A. NH Poetics

Most artistic aspects of NH derive from the English romantic poets like William Wordsworth and Samuel Taylor Coleridge in the early 1800s. Their ideas on poetry and imagination gained brief homiletical attention through the work of F. W. Robertson and Horace Bushnell in the1850s but were largely lost to the academic world until the 1930s and to the pulpit until much later.

1. Inductive Movement
Inductive movement in sermons begins with various biblical and contemporary experiences that gradually narrow to an insight or understanding. Poetry commonly moves by induction. W. E. Sangster first proposed the inductive sermon (1954), but his idea was neglected until Fred B. Craddock advocated that the sermon proceed in a manner that reflects the preacher's inductive journey with the Bible text

through the week (1979). The hearer is drawn by IDENTIFICATION into an experience of the Bible and its truth. By contrast, a DEDUCTIVE sermon starts with its conclusion and then proceeds to build a logical case, often point by point, with the purpose of communicating information, persuading hearers, and motivating them to change their behavior.

Each kind of sermon has its place, and each, its downfalls. Preachers may misconceive the inductive sermon to be free association when it requires studied movement and direction. Inductive sermons can be too open-ended, and some hearers want more direct communication. On the other hand, deductive sermons can be seen to reduce biblical texts to propositions and the act of faith to acquiring information. Ancient rhetoric understood appeal to be not just from logic (*see* LOGOS), but also from emotion (*see* PATHOS/FEELING) and the hearer's relationship to the character of the speaker and the topics discussed (*see* ETHOS). Arguably both forms need a THEME SENTENCE, whether it appears at the beginning or the end, and hybrid approaches are desirable.

2. Organic Development
Organic theories of sermon development assume that each sermon has its own distinctive life and form, more akin to a plant than to something built mechanically by adding parts. Horace Bushnell (d. 1876) was ahead of his time in identifying many meanings in biblical texts, "even as a stock of corn pushes out leaf from within leaf by a growth that is its unsheathing" (Cherry 1985, 100), but not until H. Grady Davis (1958) was the sermon broadly conceived as being like a tree or "an idea that grows."

The NH adopted the romantic idea that form, content, and function are interrelated. Form is not predetermined like a mold into which content is poured, in the manner of a sonnet, a waltz, or even a three-point sermon. Form and content are related to intended rhetorical purposes, for example, to move people to praise, to alter their attitudes, or to offer hope. Excellence is determined not by conformity to an ideal pre-set form, but by the degree to which a work accomplishes its goals. Sermons in the NH do not conform to exact patterns but make use of whatever forms are effective for their purposes.

3. Narrative, Imagination, and Metaphor
By the time the NH arose, new art forms in literature (e.g., NOVELS) and mass media (e.g.,

FILM) had already reached maturity and appropriated many romantic insights. In some ways the NH was a delayed response. Preaching in the NH came to be conceived as much as an art form as a way of teaching. Parts and whole are interrelated, the removal of any part alters the whole, and the whole affects each part. Davis compared the sermon to art and drama. When Eugene Lowry described the unity and structure of NH sermons, he proposed narrative plot in five stages: upset the equilibrium, analyze the discrepancy, disclose the gospel key to the resolution, experience the gospel, and anticipate the consequences (1980).

Imagination, image, and metaphor became key. Coleridge said imagination brings two dissimilar things into relationship and harnesses the tension between them in an apparent "reconciliation of opposites" (1817, ch. 13). Metaphor is inherently tensive (love is a red rose), it contains poles (love and a rose), and the hearer must enter into the tension in order to find its resolution (e.g., love is delicate and beautiful). In the 20th cent. scholars came to understand that all language is tensive; it contains poles that afford meaning by their interaction, just as good implies bad. The structure of metaphor underlies the use of image, idea, symbol, and story in a sermon. Two things are brought into relationship, a biblical text and our time, judgment and grace, pastor and prophet, or doctrine and story, and creative possibilities emerge (Wilson 1988). The NH values apparent contradiction and paradox, and the ability of language to generate worlds. David Buttrick says sermon language gives shape to consciousness (1987, 294). Knowledge comes through words. Language itself is eventful or performative; it is not merely denotative but invites participation and does things by performing actions such as promising, affirming, forgiving, and dreaming.

B. Theological Dimensions of the NH

1. Word as Event

Such ideas about language have affinity with the Word. In the Bible what God says actually transpires (e.g., Gen 1; Isa 55:11). The word event became a key concept for the New Hermeneutic in the 1960s, a movement led in part by Ernst Fuchs and Gerhard Ebeling. God comes to us in and through the words of Scripture as they are read, interpreted, and proclaimed for our time. In the proclamation of the gospel, Christ is encountered in the power of

the Spirit, and life is changed. Preaching is transformative. The implications of the new hermeneutic filtered to the NH through David James Randolph's *The Renewal of Preaching.* He argued that (1) preaching is contextual, not universal, and God encounters listeners in the precise circumstances of their lives, (2) sermons move to confirm experience rather than to assert axiomatic truth, (3) biblical stories make their own points not through abstraction or as history but by coming to life in the situations of the hearers, and (4) the literary form of a biblical text has a bearing on the shape and message of the sermon (1969, 22–23).

2. Recovery of the Bible

The NH arose in the tumultuous era of the Vietnam War and its aftermath, the death of God movement, and various new challenges to authority, including the authority of the Bible. The NH became part of a larger movement to reclaim the Bible for the pulpit (*see* LECTIONARY AND THE CHRISTIAN YEAR) using the fruits of historical-critical and literary biblical scholarship. The Bible was reclaimed as the source and driving force of the sermon. Scripture was not just mined for propositional statements and universal truths; it was honored for its stories, images, metaphors, characters, and various genres that each communicated in its own way. The rhetorical purpose of biblical texts, combined with notions of the word event, led Craddock to focus the sermon on "what the text is saying" and "what the text is doing" (1985, 122). Thomas G. Long called these the FOCUS AND FUNCTION STATEMENTS of the sermon (1989a, 86). He demonstrated how literary forms of biblical texts can have some impact on the form, content, and function of the sermon (1989b). One impact of the NH has been to allow "the eventfulness of the text" to guide "the eventfulness of the sermon" (2005, 108).

3. Narrative and Ethics

Plain speech modeled on science with an emphasis on "just the facts" had revolutionized use of the English language in the 1800s (Cmiel 1990). The NH helped to retrieve narrative. Interest in the word event as kerygma in the 1960s led to new interest in Jesus and his use of story in parables. The advertising world shifted from didactic commercials to ads that told stories. Scholars came to realize that life as it is lived has a narrative quality to it, seeming to move by plot, character, and emotion. Narrative theology used thick description to deal with the realities of people's lives instead of boiling down situations into propositions. At the same time, liberation, feminist, and black theologies raised the importance of experience and perspective in assessing theological claims. The NH told stories of particular people in particular circumstances as a way of addressing major social ills such as poverty, apartheid, and injustice. By lifting up the stories of individuals before the Word, hearers had the opportunity to identify with them. The worldly process of dehumanizing people and minimizing their needs is reversed. Preaching in former eras understood that generalizations speak to everyone, but the NH argued that generalizations favor the status quo and silence voices of need.

C. The NH and the Postmodern

The postmodern world challenges three key modern notions (Smith 2006, 23), and the NH accommodates each: (1) The text does not refer to objective realities; rather, there is no world beyond what is disclosed by the text (or by language). The NH reclaims the centrality of the Bible and situates the interpretive act within specific communities. (2) Metanarratives, like the Christian story or science as the theory of everything, are subject to SUSPICION and disbelief. The NH recovers the importance of individual stories, biblical and otherwise. It avoids universal truth claims (with the possible exception of those revealed about God) in preference to individual confession or testimony, and values ways of knowing beyond reason. (3) Knowledge and objective truth are not neutral but are determined by forces of power within social systems. The NH uses individual narratives and other ways of knowing to shape community and behavior.

Postmodern forces are decentering, non-hierarchical, and relational. Some of these same forces may also have worked against the NH. While it began with a focus on the gospel and the Word or Christ-event, it has largely evolved to focus on a text event in which the role of the triune God is often unclear. The values of the NH will remain important, but whether it can offer anything new or assist the theological purposes of preaching is now questioned. See METAPHOR AND FIGURES OF SPEECH; NARRATIVE PREACHING; NARRATIVE THEORY.

Bibliography: David Buttrick. *Homiletic: Moves and Structures.* (1987); Conrad Cherry, ed. *Horace Bushnell: Sermons.* (1985); Kenneth Cmiel. *Democratic Eloquence: The Fight Over Popular Speech in Nineteenth-Century America.* (1990); S. T. Coleridge. *Biographia Literaria.* (1817); Fred B. Craddock. *As One Without Authority.* (1979); Fred B. Craddock. *Preaching.* (1985); H. Grady Davis. *The Design of the Sermon.* (1958); Richard Eslinger. *A New Hearing: Living Options in Homiletical Method.* (1987); Thomas G. Long. *The Witness of Preaching.* (1989a, 2005); Thomas G. Long. *Preaching and the Literary Forms of the Bible.* (1989b); Eugene Lowry. *The Homiletical Plot: The Sermon as Narrative Art Form.* (1980); David James Randolph. *The Renewal of Preaching.* (1969); W. E. Sangster. *Craft of the Sermon.* (1954); James K. A. Smith. *Who's Afraid of Postmodernism?: Taking Derrida, Lyotard, and Foucault to Church.* (2006); Paul Scott Wilson. *Imagination of the Heart: New Understandings in Preaching.* (1988).

POETICS

See PART 5 POETICS. INTRODUCTION: POETICS AND THE CONTEXT OF PREACHING.

POINT FORM
Scott M. Gibson

Preachers and listeners typically think that sermons are made of points. But what are points? Points are sub-ideas that support the larger idea the preacher is communicating. The idea of the text is the basis for the idea of the sermon. Once the idea of the sermon is determined, the assertions that explain, prove, or apply the idea become the points. Points comprise the structure of the sermon.

But sermons are not just made of random points or assertions. Good sermons have three elements that hold them together: unity, order, and progress, which are non-negotiable. Sermon unity communicates a sense of completeness. Order—whether deductive, inductive, or a combination of both—shows the listener that the sermon has a flow to it, and the flow makes sense to the listener. Progress conveys to the listener that the preacher has a destination in mind, that from start to finish the sermon is going somewhere, not ambling along or lazily diverted, but with a clear purpose.

With unity, order, and progress in view, the preacher can develop sermons that demonstrate a clear idea with points that support the idea. Yet one may ask, How many points should sermons have? The scholastic sermons of the medieval period appear to be the first to champion the three-part or three-point sermon for the purpose of helping listeners remember the sermon. Yet other medieval sermons, later Puritan sermons, and modern sermons have many more points.

Point form has to do with the organization of that which the preacher intends to communicate. Recent discussion on point form speaks of rhetorical MOVES (David Buttrick), induction (Fred Craddock, Ralph Lewis) (*see* INDUCTIVE), narrative (Edmund Steimle) (*see* NARRATIVE FORM), homiletical "plots" (Eugene Lowry), scenes (as in plays or acts), and "pages" (Paul Scott Wilson) (*see* THE FOUR PAGES OF THE SERMON), all of which suggest some sort of organization. Even though one might want to dispense with the statement of formal points in one's outline, a structure for the preacher and listener is necessary.

There is no one sermon form. The preacher determines which form best communicates the text at hand and addresses the listeners' needs.

The Purpose of Points and Determining Points

The purpose of point form (sermon shape and flow) is to provide coherence for both preacher and listener. The points provide a logical or psychologically pleasing way of maintaining unity, order, and progress. Among the various ways of determining sermon point form are following the flow of the text, deciding the purpose of the sermon, and letting the idea of the sermon shape point form. First, sermon point form may be developed by following the logical flow of the text. The preacher determines the logical development of the author's thought, and the sermon development mirrors the development of the text. A sample of textually determined sermon structure is found in Matt 24:36-51. The homiletical idea is: "Watch for Christ's return by living faithfully and wisely, and you will be blessed."

I. We do not know when Christ is coming back (vv. 36-41).

II. But we are to watch for him (vv. 42-44).
III. If we do, we will be blessed (vv. 45-51).
IV. Watch for Christ's return by living faithfully and wisely, and you will be blessed.

Another way that sermon point form may be developed is from the purpose of the sermon. That is, the intention of the sermon—which is application-oriented—influences the shape of the sermon. One may firmly grasp what the text states but may shape the sermon for the sake of the listeners. The author of the text may have developed his argument deductively, but an inductively shaped sermon may help the listeners more readily embrace the idea. If the purpose of the sermon is, "As a result of hearing this sermon, I want my listeners to know that they can make it in this world if they are obedient to what God wants them to do," then a sermon on 1 John 2:1-17 would look like:

I. These are tough times.
II. Tough times call for tough-mindedness.
III. Tough times call for tender-heartedness.
IV. Tough times call for tough-mindedness and tender-heartedness.

In addition, the preaching idea, also known as the homiletical idea (Robinson 2001, 103–6), may provide the point form for the structure of the sermon. For example, if the idea of Ps 100 is, "Everyone, everywhere is to praise God every day for every thing because God is God," then the point form would be as follows:

I. Everyone, everywhere is to praise God.
II. Everyone, everywhere is to praise God every day for every thing.
III. Everyone, everywhere is to praise God every day for every thing because God is God.

A final approach for determining points is by parallelism. Bryan Chapell (1994, 148) suggests the following point form supporting the central idea, "We must present Christ at every opportunity," with the analytical question, "Why?"

I. Jesus alone purchased salvation.
II. Jesus alone possesses salvation.
III. Jesus alone bestows salvation.

Strength and Weaknesses of Point Structure

Point form provides clear structure for both preacher and listener. Especially in a deductive sermon, a preview of the points gives listeners a clear sense of the direction of the sermon. Repetition or parallelism in the sub-points provides unity to a sermon as the listeners hear the sermon build and support the larger sermon idea. Weaknesses of point form structure include the forcing of the outline on the text (alliteration and key words) and the imposition of one's theological presuppositions on the text.

Insistence on an alliterative point form may result in shaping the sermon into something the text may not or does not say. This may occur when the preacher imposes a fragmented alliteration on the point form:

I. The power of prayer
II. The purpose of prayer
III. The practice of prayer

The three points may be biblical and orthodox, but may not reflect the intention of the text. Such mishandling of the form reflects a mishandling of the text.

Likewise, although a time-tested homiletical device, some key-word preaching may force a homiletical point structure that is not supported by the text. In these cases, the point form methodology becomes more dominant than the thrust of the text. The following is an actual example, the feeding of the five thousand (John 6:1-15), with the key word *things*: "What things does the boy do to set an example for us?" The point form structure appears to steer away from the thrust of the text:

I. He ran with the right crowd.
II. He looked ahead.
III. He dared to be different. [Daniel is introduced here.]
IV. He gave all that he had to Jesus.

Some point form challenges also come with hermeneutical presuppositions that a preacher brings to the text. For example, a preacher who approaches the text with the historical redemptive hermeneutic might insist that every sermon end with Jesus Christ. In this way, OT texts may not be allowed to stand on their own but must be interpreted through a historical redemptive lens. Likewise, a preacher who embraces the New Homiletic comes to the text with the presupposition that what the text says is not as important as what the text does (Rudolph 1969, 19). The thoughtful preacher recognizes how his or her hermeneutical presuppositions affect the development of the sermon.

Induction and Points

Deductive sermons introduce the idea of the sermon in the introduction and explain, prove, and apply the idea throughout. Inductive sermons lead the listeners to the idea. Tension is established in the sermon by raising a question or describing an event that requires resolution. A classic structure for inductive sermons is:

I. Not this.
II. Nor this.
III. But this.

Haddon Robinson in a class on sermon form at Gordon-Conwell Theological Seminary in 2007 suggested that inductive sermons can be mapped out in the following way:

1. The mess someone is in.
2. But look! This personal mess is really part of something larger.
3. Not only that, but this mess didn't start with us.
4. That raises a deeper question: how did any get into this mess?
5. Folks don't go down without a struggle. What solutions have they tried to clean up the mess they were in?
6. Finally, there must be good news. There is a way out of the mess!

Induction appeals to the experiences of life, so one can move from one illustration or image to the other, leading up to the central idea. Ralph Lewis proposes the following outline:

I. Illustration A
II. Illustration B
III. Illustration C
IV. Central Idea and Conclusion (1983, 82)

Eugene Lowry suggests the following for developing the plot of a sermon:

I. Upsetting the equilibrium ("oops")
II. Analyzing the discrepancy ("ugh")
III. Disclosing the clue to resolution ("aha")
IV. Experiencing the gospel ("whee")
V. Anticipating the consequences ("yeah")
 (1980, 25)

Point form is crucial to clear communication, assisting both preacher and listener. *See* DEDUCTIVE; EXPOSITORY; LOGOS; STYLE.

Bibliography: Bryan Chapell. *Christ-Centered Preaching: Redeeming the Expository Sermon.* (1994); Ralph Lewis with Gregg Lewis. *Inductive Preaching: Helping People Listen.* (1983); Eugene Lowry. *The Homiletical Plot.* (1980); Haddon W. Robinson. *Biblical Preaching.* (2001); David Rudolph. *The Renewal of Preaching.* (1969); Keith Willhite and Scott M. Gibson. *The Big Idea of Biblical Preaching.* (1998).

POPULAR PSYCHOLOGY AND PREACHING
Alyce M. McKenzie

Popular psychology can help preachers diagnose and respond to human emotional struggles, but its insights need to be placed in a biblical, theological context that recognizes the human problem as sin and its antidote as Divine Grace.

Psychology is the science that studies human behavior and the physiological and cognitive processes that underlie it. There are many branches of and schools of psychology: cognitive, gestalt, clinical, behaviorism, and functionalism. Applied psychology is concerned with everyday situations, applying the accumulated knowledge of psychology to practical problems. Popular psychology is an approach and a resulting genre of literature, often taking the form of self-help books, that seeks to make the insights of psychology available to a mass audience in terms they can understand and appropriate.

During the first half of the 20th cent., many preachers believed that psychological considerations were antithetical to the proclamation of the gospel. The neo-orthodox school of theology that held sway in preaching during the post World War II period felt that psychological considerations were out of place in the preaching event. Disillusioned with the depth of human sin and liberal optimism that scientific knowledge would lead to a more humane world, these theologians, Karl Barth chief among them, believed that God was wholly Other and radically transcendent. The preacher was a messenger, speaking God's Word, confident that it would make its own hearing. Considerations of human context, and mental and emotional issues were a distraction. (Wilson 1995, 28)

Meanwhile, others took an opposing view. Harry Emerson Fosdick preached from the pulpit of Riverside Church on Morningside Heights in New York City from 1931–46 and is viewed as the greatest liberal preacher of the 20th cent. While Barth grounded preachers in the Word of God, Fosdick urged them to be attentive to the life situations of their parishioners. He criticized the expository preaching of his day which proceeded on a verse by verse explication that, he charged, often remained Bible-bound. He also criticized topical preaching that took up one current issue after another, rarely mentioning the Bible at all. He believed that preaching should begin with the personal problems of the people. He pioneered what he called the 'life situation sermon' in which some problem that challenged, puzzled, or pained his people was brought in contact with Scriptural texts and insights. He defined preaching as pastoral counseling on a group basis. His sermons focused on making moral choices, getting over bad habits, setting right priorities, and dealing with interpersonal conflicts. For him, the preaching event took on the intimacy of a one-on-one counseling session in which each listener felt he or she was being personally addressed. (Long 1989, 32–33).

Fosdick's liberal optimism about human nature's essential goodness and therapeutic, problem-solving approach, in its secular form can be identified in the writings of Dale Carnegie (1936) and Napoleon Hill (1937). Another positive, problem-solving preacher of the second half of the 20th cent. was Norman Vincent Peale, whose best selling *The Power of Positive Thinking*, first published in 1952, remains a popular classic. Robert Schuller's "possibility gospel" message from the Crystal Cathedral in California has, for several decades now, taught a positive evaluation of human nature to build up self-worth and self-esteem. (Aden and Hughes 2002, Chapter 3).

Popular psychological approaches in preaching can offer helpful diagnosis, practical analysis, and concrete recommendations for putting such insights into practice. Such approaches can, however, also tend to suggest that all human problems have solutions or answers. They can be too quick to want to "solve" issues of complex origin and effects in people's lives. Popular psychology tends to leap too quickly to offering definitive advice based on minimal knowledge. Preaching that relies too heavily on popular psychology's approach is in danger of taking on its weaknesses, becoming almost indistinguishable from the approach of the talk show psychologist, the television judge, or the radio therapist on the local call-in show.

One of the weaknesses of preaching that relies heavily on popular psychology is that it tends to use the Bible as proof texts or solution texts to solve the particular problem at hand. The sermon does not grow out of a two-way conversation between the preacher and the text. Instead, the preacher's conclusion about what the text has to say about the problem has been determined before he opens the Bible. The Bible is reduced to a *Farmer's Almanac*, a recipe book, Web MD, or the Help function on our computer. It is often the case that the gospel, the good news of the Bible, destabilizes lives lived with the aim of maintaining the economic, social, or political status quo. Theological shallowness is a symptom of this trivialization of the Bible's role in preaching. Much psychologically driven preaching downplays both the reality of sin and the power of divine grace in addressing it. It can tend to present Jesus as a teacher while discounting his divinity and can focus on personal problems to the neglect of the implications of the gospel for public life.

More recent psychological approaches to preaching are aware of these dangers. Among authors who have addressed issues of psychology in preaching are Randall Nichols (1980), Carol Noren (2001), Donald Capps (1980), Lee Ramsey (2000), Henry Mitchell and Emil Thomas (1994), and LeRoy Aden and Robert Hughes (2002). These authors generally seek to avoid the pitfalls of reducing Scripture to a source of themes to address human problems and the gospel to a message of self-help. They seek to employ psychological insights into human behavior in trying times in crafting sermons that are biblically grounded, theologically sound, and pastorally sensitive. (Aden and Hughes 2002, 35)

Popular psychology has a kinship with a perspective that we also find in the Bible in what is known as the wisdom literature. It consists primarily of Proverbs, Ecclesiastes, Job, the sayings and parables of the synoptic Jesus, although wisdom themes also appear in John, James, and Paul's letters to the Corinthians. Wisdom can be defined as practical guidelines for the living of daily life. As such, everyone is both searching for wisdom and living by a wisdom of sorts. The popularity of self-help literature is evidence of this. Wisdom, whether secular or biblical, takes several similar forms. Insights for daily living come in the form of proverbs (one-sentence, memorable nuggets of advice); moral tales (brief narratives that hold a lesson for living); and reflections, longer musings on some topic with regard to how best to live daily life. Biblical wisdom literature in both the OT and NT contain proverbs, brief narratives, and reflections that are similar in form to self-help works.

It is accurate, then, to say that the advice of popular, self-help psychology and biblical wisdom have the same aim—to help people navigate the winding paths of daily life. It is also accurate to say that they employ similar literary forms. But there the similarity ends. For biblical wisdom believes that guidelines for living in keeping with God's will are a divine gift to the one who persistently asks for wisdom and seeks to live wisely. Popular psychology tends to view problems as having solutions rooted in human determination and to view a productive, fulfilled life as a human achievement.

Preachers and pop psychologists are in partial agreement as to the psychological ills that plague humankind. Both agree that many people suffer from addictions, lack of discipline, unproductive guilt, lack of meaning, and low self-esteem. While pop psychology attributes these ills to ignorance and negativity, Christian preachers identify them as spiritual ills and attribute them to sin and alienation from God.

Both preachers and pop psychologists offer antidotes to these psychological ills. Pop psychology offers strategies to help a person access their inner determination to overcome lack of discipline and to counter their guilt by realizing its unproductive nature. Pop psychology encourages people to counter their low self-esteem with positive self-talk as they move toward the fulfillment of their potential.

While pop psychology offers antidotes rooted in human resources and goals, the preacher offers spiritual antidotes that issue from the presence and power of God. The preacher offers the undisciplined or addicted person the grace of God to overcome the root of the condition as one surrenders to God, rather than to the addictive substance or behavior. The preacher encourages those struggling with guilt to accept divine forgiveness as an unmerited gift, and to then extend it to others. The preacher offers those searching for meaning the opportunity to live as disciples of Jesus Christ. The preacher offers the person suffering from low self-worth a new identity, as a child of a God whose acceptance and love for us trumps the negative messages of any person or group.

In exegetical work, preachers need to distinguish between psychological and exegetical, theological analysis. Just as we need to be careful that we do not use the Bible solely to solve our psychological problems, we need to resist the temptation to fill in all the blanks in the Bible and to solve all its mysteries by applying 21st-cent. psychological explanations. David was suffering from a midlife crisis. Zacchaeus suffered from short man syndrome. Ruth suffered from overattachment to her mother-in-law. We can suggest how we might feel or respond in various situations using psychological language, but we need to avoid psychologizing the text; let what the text does or does not say guide conclusions about motives and actions of biblical characters.

If the preacher approaches popular psychology with a critical eye, it can be quite helpful in preaching. It names the afflictions of contemporary people and how they manifest themselves in daily life. It is then up to the preacher to frame those concerns biblically and theologically so that we can offer our listeners a resource more powerful than human determination and a vision more satisfying, just, and lasting than self-fulfillment. *See* PERSUASION; PREACHING TO CHILDREN; PREACHING TO YOUTH.

Bibliography: LeRoy H. Aden and Robert G. Hughes. *Preaching God's Compassion.* (2002); Donald Capps. *Pastoral Counseling and Preaching: A Quest for An Integrated Ministry.* (1980); Dale Carnegie *How to Win Friends and Influence People.* (1936); Napoleon Hill. *Think and Grow Rich* (1937); Thomas G. Long, *The Witness of Preaching.* (1989); Henry Mitchell and Emil Thomas. *Preaching for Black Self Esteem.* (1994); J. Randall Nichols. *The Restoring Word: Preaching as Pastoral Communication.* (1987); Carol Noren. *In Times of Crisis and Sorrow: A Minister's Manual Resource Guide.* (2001); Norman Vincent Peale. *The Power of Positive Thinking.* (1952); Lee Ramsey. *Care-full Preaching: From Sermon to Caring Community.* (2000); Paul Scott Wilson. *The Practice of Preaching.* (1995).

PREPARATION
Michael Duduit

"If I had eight hours to chop down a tree, I'd spend six sharpening my axe," Abraham Lincoln once observed. Any important task requires preparation, and effective preaching demands it.

Some people, of course, argue that human preparation conflicts with the need for the sermon to be empowered by the inspiration of the Holy Spirit. There are preachers who insist that they must step into the pulpit without any prior preparation, completely open to the leadership of the Spirit in that moment. Most preachers, however, recognize that the Spirit inspires in the study as well as the pulpit, and believe that solid preparation will work in partnership with the Spirit's guidance to produce preaching that moves the minds and the hearts of the listeners.

Any discussion of preparation in the context of preaching must consider two issues: the preparation of the preacher, then the preparation of the sermon.

The Preacher's Preparation

Although the preacher is a public speaker, he or she is more than that. It has long been the judgment of the church that the one who stands to preach must have experienced a divine call to ministry. One does not simply choose to become a preacher; God calls one, sets one aside to this special task. This call to preach is an essential element in the preparation of a preaching minister.

Beyond the initial call, the preparation of the preacher involves continuing spiritual growth—a maturing in one's walk with Christ. The preacher does not simply study the text and assemble an articulate public address. The preacher spends time with God in prayer and study of Scripture, seeking divine leadership in understanding how the truth of God's Word speaks to the needs of God's people today. The preacher seeks the insight and illumination offered by the guidance of the Holy Spirit. Such spiritual preparation enables the minister to preach "out of the overflow" of an intimate and growing relationship with Christ.

In the *Handbook of Contemporary Preaching* (Duduit 1993, 135–41), Frank Pollard talks about preparing the preacher, and he suggests five questions every preacher should answer:

1. Have you bought what you are selling? Do you have a relationship with Christ? Have you experienced the power of God, which you are proclaiming?

2. Can you do without it? Are you divinely called, or is preaching something you can walk away from?

3. Is the main thing the main thing? Is preaching the priority of your ministry, or are you allowing other worthy tasks to take the time you should be devoting to the preaching of the Word?

4. Are you real? Are your Christian life and example authentic, or are they shams? Are you a person of genuine integrity and compassion? As Pollard observes, "We must not play the role of a Christian leader; we must be Christian leaders."

5. Who is in charge of your career? Which more accurately characterizes your life and ministry: ambition or humility? Are you letting Christ direct your ministry wherever *he* leads?

Before the first word of the sermon is written, the preacher must know that he or she has been called to the task, and has entered into an ongoing and growing walk with Christ that empowers and informs the preaching task. We cannot lead people where we ourselves have not gone.

Preparing the Sermon

The preparation of the sermon itself is at the heart of the preacher's task. Too often, the task of preparation is allowed to take a backseat to the pressing issues of the pastor's life—meetings, administrative details, and such—and preaching suffers as a result. It is important for the pastor who is serious about preaching also to be serious about developing a system for sermon preparation.

1. Planning the Preaching Schedule

Few pastoral activities are as stressful and unproductive as the practice of developing individual sermons week to week without a comprehensive plan. The pastor who arrives at the office each Monday morning facing a blank page and the demands of next Sunday's sermon is a pastor who will waste valuable hours—and most likely will wear out many a rug pacing the floor of the study.

The better approach is to develop a preaching plan that covers a period of months or even a year at a time. Such a plan allows the preacher to address vital topics in a more systematic way, to do advance study and stockpile materials for future sermons, and to give other worship leaders the opportunity to plan ahead for more meaningful worship experiences that are linked to the sermon theme.

Preaching plans can take on a variety of forms. Many pastors use a plan that draws sermon texts from the lectionary; this also allows the preacher to benefit from the many published resources that are based on lectionary texts. Other preachers may develop a plan based on systematically moving through a biblical book or section of a book. Some preaching plans are developed around themes or issues. Whatever approach is taken, the use of a plan allows the preacher to be a more effective steward in the use of his or her preparation time. (*See* SERMON SERIES.)

2. Preparing the Sermon

Even with a preaching plan, there comes the time when the individual sermon must be prepared. Pastors often develop their own weekly schedules for sermon preparation, based on their personalities, pastoral demands, and other issues. Henry Ward Beecher would think about the sermon all week, but would not sit down to craft his message until Sunday morning before breakfast. James S. Stewart would spend the first half of the week preparing his Sunday morning message, then on Thursday and Friday would turn to the Sunday evening sermon. W. A. Criswell (still in pajamas) would spend his mornings studying in his home office, then in the afternoon would dress and go into the church office to attend meetings or to do pastoral calls.

In other words, there is no standard schedule for sermon preparation. Whatever the approach adopted, however, establishing some type of schedule and protecting the preacher's study time are necessary. Like a plant, sermons need time to germinate and grow before they are mature and ready for presentation.

There are a variety of methods with which the preacher may craft the sermon. Among the various approaches are these:

a. Manuscripts. A sermon MANUSCRIPT is a full written text of the sermon to be presented. In writing a manuscript, the preacher does well to remember that he or she is not writing an essay or a document to be read; the sermon manuscript must be written with an emphasis on its oral delivery. The sermon should be written for the ear, not the eye.

There are disadvantages to writing a manuscript, particularly the danger that the sermon becomes a literary production rather than a dynamic oral presentation. Even when the preacher writes a manuscript, he or she should be very familiar with the document so that it can be preached rather than read to the congregation. Many well-known and effective preachers use manuscripts in the pulpit, but they are typically so familiar with the text (through frequent review and even oral rehearsal) that listeners are often unaware that a manuscript is present.

The major advantage of a manuscript is that it enables the preacher to think through the words and thoughts to be presented in order to refine them and produce a clear and dynamic message. The manuscript allows the preacher to select in advance the words and phrases that will produce the most effective presentation of the biblical message rather than seek to formulate them in an extemporaneous fashion while engaged in preaching the message before a congregation.

b. Oral manuscripts. Some homileticians argue that a written manuscript offers too much potential for a stiff, formal style unsuited to a dynamic sermon. The oral manuscript is suggested as an alternative preparatory model, created through preaching aloud thoughts and ideas to form the ultimate version of the sermon. While the preacher may produce some written notes, the primary thrust of this approach is to craft the sermon orally.

c. Outlines and notes. Rather than develop a full manuscript of the sermon—written or oral—some preachers prefer to craft the sermon through notes only, without working out the final wording of the sermon until the time when the sermon is preached. Such an approach can offer the potential for a more free and less formal delivery of the sermon; it can also produce sermons in which the arguments and ideas are in less than finished form.

d. Preaching Without Notes. The trend among a growing number of preachers in the contemporary church is the preaching of the sermon with no manuscript or notes brought into the pulpit, though they have been used in the preparation of the sermon. (This method of delivery often leads to the removal of the pulpit itself.) Except for the uniquely gifted, such preaching requires significant additional preparation, but it can also result in very effective communication with today's congregations. Some preachers turn to significant memorization to accomplish this approach. Ed Young, a pastor known for his creative preaching, has popularized the use of "mind mapping" techniques as a memory aid to enable preachers to preach without notes (Young 2006, 107).

The preparation of the sermon may involve an array of methods and techniques on the part of the preacher. What is most important is that it engage the heart and the mind of the preacher through a significant investment of time, inspired and illuminated by the work of the Holy Spirit. The resulting preparation will lead to powerful preaching and changed lives. *See* MANUSCRIPT; MEMORY; PULPIT, USE OF; SERMON RESEARCH; WITHOUT NOTES.

Bibliography: Michael Duduit, ed. *Handbook of Contemporary Preaching.* (1993); Ed Young. *The Creative Leader: Unleashing the Power of Your Creative Potential.* (2006).

PROPHETIC MESSAGE
Marvin A. McMickle

One of the essential needs in every congregation of believers is an occasional sermon rooted in the words and witness of the OT prophets. Preachers need to play a role within the life of their congregation and their community similar to the role that such people as Amos, Jeremiah, and Micah played within the life of the nations of Israel and Judah. James Ward and Christine Ward begin their important book on this subject of prophetic preaching by writing:

> The natural inclination of the Christian community, like all religious communities, is to adapt its witness of faith to its most immediate human needs. In doing this the community always runs the risk of obscuring the wider dimensions of the gospel, particularly the wider implications of God's demand for righteousness and justice. What is needed, therefore, is preaching that recovers these wider dimensions and illuminates the ways in which the community obscures them. (1995, 11)

What Is Prophetic Preaching?

Prophetic preaching shifts the focus of a congregation from what is happening to them as a local church to what is happening to us as a society. Prophetic preaching then asks the question, What is the role or the appropriate response of our congregation, our association, and our denomination to the events that are occurring within our society and throughout the world? Prophetic preaching points out those false gods of comfort and of a lack of concern and acquiescence in the face of evil that can so easily replace the true God of Scripture who calls true believers to the active pursuit of justice and righteousness for every member of the society.

The prophets preached truth to power, attacking the monarchs and the ruling elite for putting more confidence in armies and alliances than they did in the God who had brought them into that land. The prophets challenged the people of Israel who believed that God would never abandon them, no matter how far the nation strayed from the covenant it had established with God back at Sinai. With an urgency that could not be contained and a fervor that could not be controlled, the prophets declared their "Thus says the Lord" despite the ridicule, rebuke, and outright rejection that most of them experienced throughout their lives. It is impossible to imagine the biblical narrative being told without the pronouncements of the prophets.

Why Is Prophetic Preaching Important Today?

It is easy to see the need for prophetic preaching in our churches and throughout our society. Many Christians worship inside immaculately maintained churches that are situated in neighborhoods that look like bombed out war zones. Many Christians drive to church from the suburbs to churches located within a community that has been ravaged by poverty, drug trafficking, the loss of industry through outsourcing and factory closings and underfunded and overwhelmed public school systems. Of course, many Christians never have to see these sights or confront the people and problems in these inner-city communities because they have moved out of the city to pristine outer ring suburbs and have brought their churches to the upscale areas with them.

For those who continue to travel into the crumbling and decaying cities of our nation, a prophetic word is necessary about the problems that surround their church, the social policies that are the root cause of those problems, and what they can do as an expression of their biblical faith to bring about change. For those who live and worship in exurbia and who never get close enough to the grimy side of America for anything to rub off on them, prophetic preaching becomes even more urgent. It is crucial that people with wealth, power, and influence be challenged by a prophetic word that calls upon them to direct their resources not simply for tax advantages for themselves, but for a fairer and more just society for their fellow citizens.

What Are the Issues and Themes of Prophetic Preaching?

The prophets remind Israel, just as we need to be reminded through regular doses of prophetic preaching, that God is the sovereign creator and sustainer of the whole creation. The God who sent Jonah to preach salvation in Nineveh is the same God who used Babylon and Persia as the instruments of God's will. The God who formed Israel into a great nation when they were delivered from bondage in Egypt is the same God who can send Israel back into captivity and cause them to hang their harps upon the willows and weep as they sit along the banks of the River Chebar and remember the life they once lived back in Zion. God's concern is for the whole of creation and for all the people who dwell therein. When the people of God lose sight of the fact and begin acting as if only they and their nation really matter, it is time for a prophet to declare, "Thus says the Lord!" In other words, God does not sing "God Bless America!"

Prophetic preaching focused the people's attention on the issues that were broader than how to worship or where to pray or what it is lawful to eat. The Mosaic covenant included a series of clear commandments to care for the widows, the orphans, and the stranger who was among them. When the people of Israel lost sight of those commandments, the prophets were there to remind them. When contemporary churches become more interested in praise and worship than in justice and righteousness, it is time for prophetic preaching.

Now as then, there is a need to lift up the conditions of widows, orphans, and strangers. Today they take the form of single women, many of them living in great poverty, who have been abandoned by husbands and boyfriends and are raising children by themselves. The world is literally awash with children who have been left orphaned by the unrelenting ravages of HIV/AIDS, as well as by tribal warfare in Africa, ethnic cleansing in the Balkans, and wars in Iraq and Afghanistan that use the methods of terror (shock and awe) to combat acts of terrorism around the world.

The stranger is also among us today, though here too the forms have shifted. Now the strangers are the migrant workers who pick our food, the illegal immigrants who clean our homes and hotels, and the prisoners at Guantanamo Bay (and those who were inside Abu Ghraib prison) who are under U.S. control but are not afforded the protections of the U.S. Constitution, the Geneva Convention, or the common decency that U.S. citizens would expect and/or demand for themselves. The stranger is also that person with an "Arab-sounding name" or that Sikh from India who, because his religion requires him to wear a turban or some other kind of head wrap, is being caught up in the post-9/11 frenzy created and sustained by a government that is always on the lookout for a "person of interest."

How Is the Bible Used in Prophetic Preaching?

Prophetic preaching does not demand or even require the use of a text taken from one of the prophetic books of the OT. Nor does it require any reference to one of the prophets of the classical period that stretched from the 8th to the 5th cent. BCE. Many sermons based upon a passage from a prophetic book have been far more pathetic than prophetic. That is usually the result of a preacher who did not have his or her focus on what constantly occupied the biblical prophets, namely, the fact that God's people were living in disobedience to the covenant that had been established between God and the people.

Prophetic preaching occurs when the preacher seeks to bring the will of God to the attention of the people of God and then, as Elizabeth Achtemeier observes, challenges them "to trust their Lord in all circumstances and to obey him with willing and grateful hearts" (1998, 118–19). Prophetic preaching happens when the preacher has the courage to speak truth to power not only inside the church

building but also in the streets and boardrooms and jail cells of the secular order. We must be willing to do this if we are to be faithful to and worthy of following in the footsteps of Samuel who confronted Saul, Nathan who confronted David, Amos who condemned Jeroboam, Jeremiah who challenged both Jehoiakim and Zedekiah, and John the Baptist who did not grow mute or meek in the presence of Herod Antipas. In a time of "patriot pastors" and the belief that critiquing the leaders of the nation is both ungodly and unpatriotic, it is time for prophetic preaching. It is time to hear the words, "This is what the Lord says." See PROPHETIC PREACHING; REVELATION; SOCIAL JUSTICE; WORD OF GOD.

Bibliography: Elizabeth Achtemeier. *Preaching from the Minor Prophets.* (1998); Walter Brueggemann. *Prophetic Imagination.* (2001); Marvin McMickle. *Where Have All the Prophets Gone?* (2006); Mark Taylor. *Religion, Politics and the Christian Right.* (2005); James Ward and Christine Ward. *Preaching from the Prophets.* (1995); Beverly Zink-Sawyer. *From Preachers to Suffragists.* (2003).

PURITAN PLAIN STYLE
O. C. *Edwards* Jr.

Properly speaking, the Puritan Plain Style refers only to preaching done by English Calvinists in England from the time of Elizabeth through the Restoration, and in America from the time of the original settlement of Massachusetts through the Revolution. Some later and even contemporary preaching shares basic structural features with it, but the differences are greater than the similarities.

Although one can go through church history collecting statements from most major preachers in favor of simplicity, those help little in reconstructing what preaching looked like at the time. Chiefly, the call for plainness was a moral rather than a structural demand; preaching should be in service of the gospel rather than incite admiration for the one who did it. The Puritans' call for plainness was a function of their Calvinism. Calvin called for such modest and earnest preaching, but his reasons for doing so were deeper. They grew out of his doctrine of double predestination and his belief that preaching was the ordinary channel by which election became effective. His high doctrine of Scripture meant that all sound preaching for him was a matter of biblical interpretation and application.

Calvin's English disciples had his theory of preaching packaged for them by William Perkins (1558–1602) in his *Arte of Prophesying*. There were four steps to his homiletical method: (1) reading a passage from the Bible, (2) exegeting it, (3) identifying the doctrine taught in that passage, and (4) applying it to the life of the congregation. In the course of doing this, it was necessary to prove the doctrine by reciting other verses from the Bible that taught the same thing. This was verse-by-verse commentary, and each sermon was a portion of an ongoing effort to preach through an entire biblical book or, at least, a major portion of one.

Although Calvin typically preached on a passage of a number of verses, sometimes Puritans preached on only one. If, however, they took a longer passage, they went through all of Perkins's steps for a verse or connected section and then started all over with the next section, and continued until they ran out of time. This method was called doctrines and uses, and the uses were the applications made of the doctrines; there were usually several uses for each doctrine. These sermons ordinarily had no more introduction than a reference to where the preacher had left off in the previous sermon and had no conclusion beyond the uses.

The Puritan Plain Style was also based on the logic of Pierre Ramus and its rhetorical implications as worked out by Omer Talon. It was assumed that doctrines had to convince by reason and uses must stir emotions, yet election was the work of God rather than the force of human thought or emotional manipulation. Ramist thought made invention, disposition, and memory functions of logic, leaving rhetoric with only the operations of style and delivery. With this chastening of rhetoric Puritans could favor preaching that was reasonable and passionate while still leaving results entirely in the hand of God.

The emotional appeal means that the plain style made uses of at least some figures of sound and thought. The rational appeal means that the preaching was supposed to be scholarly. Thus, plainness was not a lack of art but proceeded on the theory that the best art is that which covers up art. This also means that while Puritan preaching was delivered without manuscript, it was carefully prepared—unlike that of the independents of various sorts who believed in the inspiration of the moment

and who often had little schooling. (Some of them could be eloquent for the gospel, however, as John Bunyan shows.)

Efforts have been made to consider the preaching of John Wesley a continuation of Puritan Plain Style, but it represents a different movement with a different rationale. Wesley follows in the rhetorical tradition of neoclassicism as exemplified in Archbishop John Tillotson, but the style was modified to accommodate the emotional appeal for souls that the Arminian Wesley had learned from the Welsh Awakening.

Some contemporary homileticians use the label of Puritan Plain Style for any preaching that moves from biblical interpretation through theological statement to life application, and they do so with a certain appropriateness, but something closer to the way that Puritans actually preached is the sort of sermon based on verse-by-verse interpretation recommended by Ronald Allen and Gilbert Bartholomew (2000), and even closer is the expository preaching advocated by evangelical writers. *See* EXEGETICAL; EXPOSITORY; HOMILETICAL (THEOLOGICAL) CRITICISM; RHETORICAL DEVICES; STYLE; TEACHING.

Bibliography: Ronald J. Allen and Gilbert L. Bartholomew. *Preaching Verse by Verse.* (2000); Perry Miller. *The New England Mind: The Seventeenth Century.* (1939); Harry S. Stout. *The New England Soul: Preaching and Religious Culture in Colonial New England.* (1992); Michael Warner, ed. *American Sermons: The Pilgrims to Martin Luther King, Jr.* (1999).

RHETORIC
See PART 9 RHETORIC. INTRODUCTION: SEEKING A RESPONSE.

SEEKER MESSAGES
Mary J. Scifres

After the Reformation, the task of preaching centered on educating the converted. On the American frontier, however, preaching developed a new purpose in the Great Awakening of the 17th and 18th cent. and in the Second Great Awakening of the 19th cent.: to convict and to convert people to certain tenets of Christian faith. In the 20th cent., traditional preaching returned to the art of educating the converted. As the 20th cent. closed, however, a new form of conversion preaching has emerged, often referred to as seeker-friendly preaching. Sermons preached in this format are categorized as seeker messages.

The term *seekers* is far from clear in its definition or delineation. However, *seekers* most often refers to people from a non-religious background who are now exploring the Christian faith and church. Seekers may be followers of other religions, spiritual persons without a religious history, people with little experience in formal religion, or even former Christians. To define this huge group of people in a short article is virtually impossible. However, preaching to this broad-based group of people carries common elements that separate seeker messages from traditional sermons.

In seeker-sensitive churches, the sermon is often renamed the message. In most cases, this is nothing more than a title change to avoid language unique to the church. Yet seeker messages also use different forms, approaches, and even content. Churches that design worship with seekers in mind challenge the preacher to rethink the task of delivering the sermon each week. These are not the days of the Great Awakening camp meetings, when preaching was a time for proclaiming God with fire and brimstone, invoking fear of the wrath to come. Seeker messages today are invitational in nature, and inspirational in their honesty and connection with the listener. God's Word is proclaimed in order to invite people onto the Christian journey without coercion or demand. The message is illustrated in ways that show people the relevant connection to their daily lives and ongoing spiritual journeys. The preacher relates to the people in a way that reflects Christ's open care and concern for the world. The seeker message is communicated without requiring the listener to know biblical stories, church language, or religious history. Rather, the message invites people into the Christian story, to join the journey of faith with thousands who have gone before.

Biblical Preaching

The seeker message can still be a biblical sermon. After all, Christians are a people steeped in the tradition of Holy Scriptures. The Bible is a story, first and foremost. The message time is simply one opportunity to share that story with listeners who yearn to enter into the ancient story of God's ongoing activity and presence in the world.

The preacher may incorporate Scripture into the message in many ways, but the seeker message cannot require people to know the story. For instance, to refer to Noah in a joke about a long series of rainy days assumes people know the story of Gen 7–9. Even this ancient and popular story is not known widely in today's culture.

In seeker messages, a non-judgmental, invitational use of Scripture will convey Christ's message most effectively. The seeker message that uses Scripture to manipulate or coerce people into Christian belief will often fail to reach its audience. Biblical preaching that invites people to engage in Scripture study, to enter into the story of God's work, or to question and ponder the message of a given Scripture or sermon is truly seeker-sensitive preaching.

Seeker messages may reflect this invitational and non-judgmental nature by moving out of the pulpit area. Delivering the seeker message at floor level or in the open chancel is a common practice. The body language of the preacher can then convey the open, invitational nature of the Christian message. Even seated on a tall stool, a preacher can preach the message in order to offer a more informal mood to the message time.

Likewise, the art and nature of preaching in a postmodern world incorporate the full range of arts and media into the seeker message. God's never-ending invitation of love and the Christian's ongoing journey of faith are messages beautifully reflected in art, story, song, dance, and drama. Sharing this message in a new and changing world with people from outside the church walls is very effective when multiple senses are engaged. Seeker messages may convey the biblical story with visual images, stained glass, movie clips, popular songs, dancers, actors, or artists. For instance, an artist may throw a pot during the reading of Jer 18:1-6. Seeker messages that convey God's Word through embodiment and the arts address the need for full sensory engagement.

Preaching Styles

Preaching a seeker message can be as varied and diverse as preaching a traditional sermon. Limiting the message delivery to one format week after week is neither necessary nor helpful when ministering with seekers. Exploring a variety of methods and styles may help the preacher to determine how she or he can communicate most effectively with seekers in the worship setting. However, the most important aspect of preaching to seekers is the authenticity and honesty of the preacher. A well-delivered five-point sermon that includes honest reflections and an open approach to Scripture may be the best seeker message in town! Still, alternative styles of preaching can reflect the invitational and open nature of the seeker message.

1. Preaching the Questions

One alternative method of relating to seekers is allowing them to participate in the message time. Designing a message time that allows questions and answers or sermon feedback encourages participation. This may happen immediately following the message or in a small gathering for discussion and dialogue after worship. Or gathering questions on note cards before or during the service to be addressed in the message time can alleviate the time difficulties of a sermon feedback format. For the preacher who is not comfortable with extemporaneous speaking or who needs more preparation time to respond to challenging questions, questions can be gathered as topics for future messages.

To "preach the questions," the preacher will prepare by carefully and diligently studying the Scripture text and related theological themes. Observing similar themes in novels, television, movies, newspapers, and magazines, or discussing them in a small group of seekers and churchgoers, can also be helpful. Finally, the well-prepared preacher will undergird this message time with a great deal of prayer.

Preaching a questioning sermon is a wonderful invitation onto the Christian journey for seekers. It is also a broadening exercise for the preacher and a challenging experience for followers.

2. Preaching the Story

Jesus taught some of the most profound messages through the art of storytelling. Jesus relied upon storytelling, utilizing common images, daily experiences, and believable characters. Jesus then allowed the stories to speak for themselves, permitting the listener to hear and receive God's word in her or his own way.

Retelling the biblical story or preaching a story sermon can be a powerful and effective way of reaching seekers. The story may be retold in a dramatic portrayal of a character or event within the story. The story may be retold in informal or modern-day language, or simply read from a paraphrase like Eugene Peterson's *The Message* (1994). Another story sermon utilizes fictional stories or poetry to illustrate a biblical message or event. Likewise, parables can be reworked using modern images and occurrences to bring home the relevance of Jesus' teachings in contemporary life.

Leaving the pulpit invites people into the story and creates a warmer storytelling atmosphere. When the preacher both tells the story and relates how the story has affected his or her life and ministry, listeners are shown a way of relating the story to their lives.

3. Preaching without Words

For worship planners designing reflective or meditative worship experiences, traditional sermons may be replaced by centering time or meditative reflections. In a meditative sermon, the preacher strives to become unimportant in the worship experience. The seeker is encouraged to connect directly with God and listen for God's message during the time of meditation or reflection. Guided meditation may be used, or Scripture and related readings may be offered prior to a time of reflection on the readings. A method of LECTIO DIVINA can be utilized in which a scripture is read, followed by silence, several times repetitively. Instrumental or vocal music can be intertwined with Scripture to assist in the reflection process.

The challenge in offering a meditative sermon is to overcome stereotypes about the responsibility for preachers to preach the Word. Since the Reformation, this has come to mean the responsibility to exegete and explain certain Scripture passages. In the meditative sermon, the preacher acknowledges that God and God's Word are readily found through ritual, music, liturgy, and silence.

Preaching the Seeker Message

Whatever the preaching style, the preacher's attitude of open acceptance and invitational approach is an important aspect. As with most preaching, the personal connection remains a crucial element in the seeker message. Practical applications of the message to the Christian life can also provide helpful connection points.

The preacher who exudes warmth, offers sincerity, and displays genuine faith and love will reach seekers with almost any preaching style or format. As preachers display Christ's love through the art and nature of preaching, the Holy Spirit is enabled to work in the lives of all who wish to listen and receive God's message. *See* EMERGING CHURCH PREACHING; EVANGELISTIC PREACHING; MISSIONAL PREACHING; TECHNOLOGY AND THE SERMON.

Bibliography: Ed Dobson. *Starting a Seeker Sensitive Service: How Traditional Churches Can Reach the Unchurched.* (1993); Doug Pagitt. *Preaching Re-Imagined: The Role of the Sermon in Communities of Faith.* (2005); Eugene Peterson. *The Message.* (1994).

SERMON AS PROCLAMATION
David J. Lose

Recent interest in the proclamatory nature of preaching stems from biblical and theological work done during the 20th cent. In *The Apostolic Preaching and Its Developments*, for instance, C. H. Dodd distinguished between the proclamation (kerygma) and the teaching (didache) of the early church. The salvific message of the gospel that characterized the preaching of the apostles contrasted their ethical or theological instruction: "Much of our preaching in the church at the present day would not have been recognized by the early Christians as kerygma" (Dodd 1936, 7–8).

While some criticized Dodd's work for drawing too sharply the distinction between teaching and proclamation, it nonetheless resonated with proposals made by Karl Barth, Dietrich Bonhoeffer, Rudolf Bultmann, Gerhard Ebeling, and others. Sermons characteristic of mainline Protestant preaching in Europe and North America had lost their existential edge, often devoting themselves to the historical details of the tradition rather than confessing the historic faith. Preachers had reverted to dogmatic instruction and moral exhortation. Preaching, many concluded, must reclaim its kerygmatic nature in order truly to be the preaching of the church.

Four elements of this turn from *didache* to *kerygma* made during the middle of the 20th cent. remain central to current homiletical theory and practice. Each emphasizes a shift toward actually creating an experience of God in and through the sermon. We define a kerygmatic sermon as the authoritative proclamation of God's decisive saving activity in the person of Jesus Christ as witnessed in Scripture so as to make a claim upon the individual in the present.

First, Christian proclamation must be thoroughly biblical. As Dietrich Bonhoeffer told his students at the confessing seminary in Finkenwald, Christian preaching is "commissioned by and bound by the biblical witness. . . . Its content is the biblical witness alone" (1991, 132–33). The heart of the truly biblical sermon is not simply content—the exposition of the text—but making manifest the dynamic impulse that animates the passage of Scripture at hand. A kerygmatic sermon seeks to bring to expression both the message and the claim that first inspired the biblical text itself. As Gerhard Ebeling wrote, "The Bible bears witness to a proclamation which has taken place and is the impulse to a proclamation which is to take place" (1961, 183).

Second, kerygmatic preaching is inherently eventful. It seeks not only to express the content of a distinct biblical passage but also to manifest the same effect on the hearer. Scripture is, to borrow a category from John Austin, inherently performative, seeking to do something to the hearer. Ebeling says that "we do not get at the nature of words by asking what they contain, but by asking what they effect, what they set going, what future they disclose" (1961, 187). Kerygmatic preaching is interested precisely in doing something rather than simply saying it. Thus, a sermon should not talk about forgiveness, but should forgive, that is, create an experience for the hearer of being forgiven.

Third, there is an inherently objective element to Christian proclamation as it witnesses confidently to a truth that stands beyond both preacher and hearer as its own objective reality. The word *kerygmatic* stems from the Greek kerux, or "herald," someone commissioned to announce the proclamations of the king. Likewise, preachers stand in the stead of another, offering an announcement of what God has done and is still doing, and this proclamation is authorized by no one other than God. As Karl Barth asserted, the authority of the preacher "rests on the authority of him who sends the herald" (1991, 50). Hence, this good news, *gospel*, remains objectively true apart from the wisdom, experience, or personality of the preacher, and remains independent of the changing currents of history. While preaching is expressed in culturally relevant ways, there remains the proclamation of timeless truth beneath its timely expression.

Fourth, Christian proclamation is relational; it establishes and deals with the relationship between God and humans mediated through Jesus Christ. Preaching does not seek to supply hearers with information about God but seeks to draw them into an encounter with God. There is an immediate, or present-tense, character to proclamation that has, borrowing the language of Martin Buber, an "I-thou" character to it. The concern is not primarily with God's activities in the past but is focused on what God is doing here and now, in the lives of the present audience. As Rudolf Bultmann warned, a purely historical or narrative Jesus "does not make any direct demand on us, nor does he condemn us for any deed we have committed against him. . . . For actually he is only seen making demands on others and pronouncing judgment on others. . . . I have done him no wrong and he has nothing to forgive me" (1987, 126–28). For hearers to be encountered by the judgment and promises of God, the preacher must move from the third-person language of description to the first- and second-person language of relationship, thereby drawing the hearer into the biblical witness and sermon.

The kerygmatic turn in theological studies in general took hold of North American homileticians in the late 1960s and early 1970s and continues developing in and up to our own time. In *As One Without Authority*, Fred Craddock harvested the insights of Ebeling and others and applied them to preaching, inviting preachers to imagine that their sermon might actually have an effect on their hearers rather than merely relate information to them. He reminded preachers, first, that one cannot separate form, content, and function and, second, that the forms they had adopted were those of logical and historical analysis rather than proclamation. Theological study, exegesis, and historical analysis must not be undertaken for their own sakes: "exegesis has its natural and proper fulfillment in proclamation" (1979, 123). He urged preachers to move to a more INDUCTIVE form of preaching that would prompt an encounter and experience with the living God. Few contemporary homileticians, and particularly those in traditions descended most directly from the Reformation, would characterize the primary purpose of preaching as didactic.

Preaching is today described as confession, as witnessing or testifying to the ongoing work of the God of Scripture in the lives of contemporary Christians. Thomas Long, for instance, writes, "The preacher as witness is not authoritative because of rank or power but because of what the preacher has seen and heard. . . . The preacher is listening for a voice, looking for a presence, hoping for the claim of God to be encountered through the text" (1989, 44). Anna Carter Florence describes preaching as testimony, asserting that all the preacher has to offer, finally, is her or his testimony of an experience of the God we know in Christ made manifest in the biblical texts and in our lives (2007). Other homileticians have likewise argued that the center of the faith, and therefore of preaching, is neither an argument about the existence of God nor a description of the faith but a confession of God's primary activity in the death and resurrection of Jesus, an event that encounters hearers in and through the proclaimed Word (Lose 2003).

Kerygmatic preaching today resists the trend to place at the center of the sermon the application of the biblical text today. Dietrich Bonhoeffer suggests that application consists of seeking to find some past principle or religious truth to apply to current questions and circumstances. When this is done, the dynamic, kerygmatic element of the apostolic witness is flattened by the didactic concerns of the preacher to answer a contemporary question with a biblical answer. Bonhoeffer advocates interpretation over application; the preacher speaks Scripture into the present on its own terms so as to see what questions and answers, problems and responses it elicits. In the interpretive act, neither the answers nor the questions are presupposed; the task is to see what happens when we stand amid our own circumstances and attempt to listen to the living and active Word.

The primary goal of kerygmatic preaching is to interpret Scripture in order that the witness of past events and deeds may speak into the present and thereby usher hearers into an encounter with the living Lord. Gerhard Forde writes, "In proclamation one not only explains the Word but also one does the Word to the hearers" (1990, 149). Such preaching may provide some information about God and the faith, and describe biblical and contemporary events, but the purpose is eventually and climactically to move hearers to be confronted by the claims of the living God and provoked into living faith. Or as John 20:31 states, preachers proclaim the gospel so that hearers "may come to believe that Jesus is the Messiah, the Son of God, and that through believing you may have life in his name. *See* CHRISTOLOGY; HOLY SPIRIT AND PREACHING; THEOLOGY OF PROCLAMATION; WORD OF GOD.

Bibliography: Karl Barth. *Homiletics.* Translated by Geoffrey Bromiley and Donald Daniels. (1991); Dietrich Bonhoeffer. *Worldly Preaching: Lectures on Homiletics.* Edited and translated, and with critical commentary by Clyde E. Fant. (1991); Rudolf Bultmann. "On the Question of Christology." *Faith and Understanding.* (1987); Fred Craddock. *As One Without Authority.* 3rd ed. (1979); C. H. Dodd. *The Apostolic Preaching and Its Developments.* (1936); Gerhard Ebeling. *The Nature of Faith.* Translated by Ronald Gregor Smith. (1961); Anna Carter Florence. *Preaching as Testimony.* (2007); Gerhard Forde. *Theology Is for Proclamation* (1990). Thomas G. Long. *The Witness of Preaching.* (1989); David J. Lose. *Confessing Jesus Christ: Preaching in a Postmodern World.* (2003).

SERMON SERIES
Michael Duduit

The preaching pastor has two options in regard to selection of a topic and/or text for the Sunday sermon. The pastor can let each Sunday's message be completely independent of other messages—this Sunday a sermon on forgiveness, next Sunday on the family, the next on prayer, and so on.

By contrast, more and more pastors are now recognizing the value of the second option: planning the preaching schedule in series. There is significant value in preaching in series rather than jumping from topic to topic each Sunday.

Why Preach in Series?

One advantage of series is that it simplifies the preparation of the sermon—the preacher can spend less time deciding what to preach and more time focused on what to say about the chosen theme. Rather than pacing the floor each Monday morning wondering what to do the following Sunday, the pastor who preaches in series is able to plan a number of messages at one time. Then when sermon preparation is on the schedule, the preacher can simply turn to the message itself rather than try to determine a topic for the week.

A second advantage is that preaching in series allows the preacher to deal with topics in greater depth and breadth. The time available in a single sermon is limited and offers the opportunity to do little more than touch on the highlights of a major theme if the message is completely autonomous and unrelated to a wider preaching plan. Rather than superficially touching on a significant theme or biblical book and then rushing to the next topic, series allow the preacher to dig deeper and offer more meaningful treatments of major areas of concern. And the preacher can design the series to deal with a variety of issues relating to the theme of the series, thus making preaching moments more valuable to a wide range of listeners. The series can offer the congregation a sense of progress and movement as they gain a greater understanding of the theme being addressed by the series.

Yet another advantage of sermon series is a practical one: because the preacher will spend an extended time with a single biblical book or theme, he or she can afford to invest in more resources (in background study and purchased materials) for study of that book or topic. For example, if the preacher will be preaching from Genesis one week, Luke the next, and Hebrews the next, it is difficult to do the significant background study that is possible when the preacher knows he or she will be spending the next several weeks in the Gospel of Mark. However, spending several weeks in a single book or theme allows time for preliminary study that can yield important insights for preaching. Likewise, because the series will be focused on a single book for an extended period, the preacher can more readily justify purchasing several quality commentaries or studies on the theme of the series, which will aid study and preparation.

Preaching in series simplifies the process of preparing the annual preaching calendar as well. Instead of facing an empty calendar of fifty-two Sundays in search of fifty-two different topics, the series preacher plans for perhaps six to twelve series of varying lengths. Planning a year of preaching becomes a more manageable task when that year is divided into a handful of sermon series rather than a host of individual Sundays.

What Kind of Series?

There are numerous approaches to planning sermon series, and many preachers use several types of series during the course of a year of preaching.

The use of a lectionary can offer one approach. Though a lectionary will guide you through all the sections of the Bible during a period of years, most lectionaries contain textual series composed of multiple weeks dealing with a single book of the Bible, such as one of the Gospels. By selecting and preaching from those selections, the preacher can create a number of biblical sermon series through the year.

A more common type of series in many churches is the LECTIO CONTINUA method—the use of a book of the Bible as the basis for an extended series of sermons. Such series once typically ran for many months and even years; Martyn Lloyd-Jones preached thirteen years from the book of Romans in his Friday evening services, and his series on Ephesians was later published in an eight-volume collection (*Exposition of Ephesians*). However, in the church today such series are the exception rather than the rule.

Nevertheless, sermon series based on biblical books continue to be common. Some preachers use a verse-by-verse format in such preaching, while others select passages. Another approach to this planning model is to develop a series of sermons on a section of a biblical book rather than on the entire book. For example, many sermon series have been developed around the Sermon on the Mount (or more narrowly, the Beatitudes), the Ten Commandments, or the letters to the seven churches in Rev 2–3.

What are the benefits of a sequential approach to preaching the biblical text? There are several: the planning process is simplified, since the preacher knows where he or she will be going the next Sunday; the preacher will inevitably deal with texts that might otherwise be avoided, thus opening to the congregation (and the preacher) new insights from God's Word; the preacher can more readily address controversial or difficult passages as part of a sequence, as opposed to selecting such a passage to deal with as an isolated message; and the congregation can measure their progress through the biblical book.

Another approach is to develop a series thematically rather than base it on a single biblical book. For example, the preacher might develop a series of sermons on the family or on ways to grow as a Christian disciple. Each sermon would be designed to focus on one aspect of the theme. Such sermons, while planned as a progressive series, would not necessarily be based on passages from a single book of Scripture.

As You Prepare Sermon Series . . .

As they plan their preaching, preachers will want to consider that the length of sermon series is growing shorter than it has been in years past. Great preachers of past generations sometimes preached book series that ran for years. Though there are exceptions, today most pastors find that it is nearly impossible to sustain the interest of a congregation in a series for such a sustained period. What is more common today is for series to run from four to eight weeks, sometimes as long as twelve. Often where a series must be longer, the pastor will find ways to break it up with shorter series inserted between. (For example, a short series related to Advent might be inserted into a longer book series, allowing you to spend more time with a single biblical book if that is needed.)

Another caution is to make each sermon independent of the one before and after it. In preaching a series, it is tempting to depend on "As you will remember from last week" and to continue the discussion from there—but what if 20 percent of the congregants were not in attendance last week? In that event, they (and new members or visitors) are lost as the sermon begins. So even as a series allows you to build progressively on a theme, the preacher must avoid making sermons dependent on those that went before.

In planning series, consider how your preaching can reinforce and teach about themes relating to the Christian calendar. Series developed around Advent, Lent, and Easter offer excellent preaching opportunities. Adam Hamilton of The United Methodist Church of the Resurrection in Kansas City, for example, preached a six-part Lenten series called "24 Hours That Changed the World" on the passion of Christ. Rick Warren preached a five-sermon series on "God's Gift for You This Christmas."

Sermon series can be used effectively to lead a church to deal with issues of importance in the life of the congregation. Because the preacher has several messages to deal with a topic, it is possible to establish a solid foundation, discuss the topic in some detail, and motivate to action. No wonder, then, that many pastors have found that sermon series form the bulk of their preaching ministry. *See* EXEGESIS OF THE CONGREGATION, DENOMINATION; HOMILETICAL (THEOLOGICAL) CRITICISM; LONG-RANGE SERMON PLANNING.

Bibliography: Adam Hamilton. *Unleashing the Word: Preaching with Relevance, Purpose, and Passion.* (2003).

SHAPING CONGREGATIONAL IDENTITY
Edwin Searcy

The practice of preaching constitutes a people with a distinctive identity in the world. In congregations that suffer from chronic anxiety, apathy, and fear as well as in those that are tempted by idols of success and security, preachers glimpse symptoms of collective amnesia. Whenever the church is in danger of forgetting who—and whose—it is, the vocation of the preacher is the building up of the church (1 Cor 14:3-4).

Preaching that seeks to shape congregational identity invites the congregation into a world that is being redescribed by the Bible. Hearing such preaching is akin to being immersed in a foreign culture. It assumes that the church exists to be a witness to the odd customs and surprising ways of life in the kingdom of God. Its central concern is how Scripture intends to shape the people of God. The sermon that results does not ask what a text means to individuals or how it speaks to social issues. It is confident that a congregation that learns to live these texts will faithfully address the needs of individuals and the issues it faces in society.

When Jesus says, "You are the salt of the earth" (Matt 5:13), we regularly imagine that he is speaking to individuals. Shaped in a culture of individualism, we often fail to notice that biblical texts like this one are addressed to the community: *you folks.* This shift from the singular you to the plural *you-all* is key when preaching to build up congregational identity. The focus of this preaching is the church as a collective disciple rather than the church as a gathering of individuals. Sermons in this mode are addressed to the congregation as a disciple of Jesus with a particular personality and a unique calling. A sermon on the story of Bartimaeus may now place the congregation in the role of the blind one who, when given the gift of sight, follows Jesus on the way to the cross (Mark 10:46-52). Over time such sermons help to shape a people that assumes its life together is to be a living interpretation of the gospel for the world to see, hear, and enter.

Preaching that intentionally shapes congregational identity places the church between the interpreter and the text. Contemporary culture need not be mined for illustrations so that the Bible can be understood. Instead, the congregation gathered at the font and table is the living illustration of the text. The text addresses the congregation's struggle to believe, its acts of faithfulness, its aching lamentation, and its call to serve. Scripture speaks to the church in the present tense. The preacher does not jump back and forth from the modern world to the ancient world (not "Jesus said to his disciples" but "Jesus says to his disciples"). Now Sarah and Abraham are not ancient ancestors but our contemporaries. Now the exile is not a history lesson but is our story. Now Paul is writing not to the early church but to this congregation. Now this congregation is not a voluntary organization worried about declining membership and roof repairs but is, instead, "a holy nation, God's own people" (1 Pet 2:9).

This emphasis in preaching teaches the congregation to think of the sermon as a corporate act of hospitality. The text comes as a holy visitor with a surprising word to God's people (Gen 18:1-15; Heb 13:2). The preacher invites the congregation to give this visitor a hearing by staying close to the Scripture, paying attention to its twists and turns, not trying to resolve all the problems it raises. The congregation learns to take the time to notice the allusions to its own struggles and calling that inhabit the text. Preaching like this is less an act of translation and more a practice of catechesis (from the Greek katēcheō meaning "to echo"). It is an invitation to the congregation to collectively echo the sound of its source—the Word of God—in its life in and for the world.

While congregational identity is shaped one text and one experience at a time, these texts and experiences are given their place in the common mind of the congregation through underlying figures or types. Preachers can uncover these figures and types by asking: How does this congregation figure things out? What type of a congregation is this? In congregations that are in danger of forgetting what it is to be Christ's cruciform disciple, these power-ful assumptions about the church often reveal the ways in which witnessing to the kingdom of God has been forgotten or abandoned. Figural (or typo-logical) preaching understands that these deeply embedded figures and types are in need of trans-formation by the gospel if the church is to be Jesus' salty, yeasty people. A figural preacher pays atten-tion to the large narratives within which the texts are located: slavery / exodus / promise; judgment / exile / homecoming; repentance / trust / disci-pleship; and Good Friday / Holy Saturday / Easter. The figural preacher locates particular texts within the intratextual world of the Bible. In this way the congregation's story is interwoven with the biblical drama. Now our terrible endings are not the end we imagined because they are our Good Friday entry to the gospel story. Now our long seasons of waiting for God are not outside the faith because they belong on Holy Saturday. Now Easter is not simply the predictable promise of the cycle of life but is the raw, inexplicable reality of God's new cre-ation breaking in upon us when we have all but given up hope. By locating texts and our life within these sustaining figural / typological narratives, preachers offer their congregations the gift of a deep communal memory of God's mercy and faithful-ness. See COLLABORATION; EXEGESIS OF THE CONGREGATION, DENOMINATION; IDENTIFI-CATION; LEADERSHIP; WORSHIP STYLE.

Bibliography: Walter Brueggemann. *Texts Under Negotiation: The Bible and Postmodern Imagina-tion.* (1993); Charles L. Campbell. *Preaching Jesus: New Directions for Homiletics in Hans Frei's Postliberal Theology.* (1997); Justo L. and Catherine G. Gonzales. *The Liberating Pulpit.* (1994).

SPECIAL OCCASION
James A. Wallace, C.Ss.R.

Preaching on special occasions calls a community to focus on, ponder, and discern the theological meaning of a particular celebration or event. It does this primarily through the lens of a biblical text or texts, chosen or appointed, thereby offering a faith perspective on the occasion and evoking a faith response to the God who was and continues to be fully revealed in Jesus Christ.

What Makes an Occasion Special?

Special occasions are usually rooted in events and/or persons of importance and density for the community. These include (a) faith celebrations, either of the great feasts of the Christ-event (Christ-mas, Easter, Ascension, Pentecost) or of lesser feasts dedicated to Mary (Mary, Mother of God, Our Lady of Guadalupe) or to those saints esteemed by a com-munity, or of particular days of communal prayer (Ash Wednesday, the days of prayer for Church Unity); (b) celebrations of special events in the lives of the community (baptisms, weddings, anniver-saries, funerals); (c) civil holidays (Martin Luther King Jr. Day, Fourth of July, Labor Day, Thanksgiv-ing); and (d) extraordinary events in the life of a community or nation, whether joyous or tragic, that call for pastoral attention.

Rationale for Special Occasion Preaching

Special occasion preaching reminds us that while we often think of time as chronos, that is, "clock time" with its steady movement of minutes into hours, days, weeks, months, and years, time may suddenly be transformed into kairos, a moment of grace, touched by God's saving power. Such preach-ing helps the community to recognize that the divide between the civil and the sacred calendars is fluid and the flow of grace often unpredictable, even unnoticed, unless one develops a habit of atten-tiveness. Focusing on the depth dimension of particular occasions helps form a sensitivity to recognizing God at work in all the events of life.

Certain special occasions call for highlighting an aspect of God's grace particular to that occasion. Such preaching is not so much speaking on or about an occasion, but through it, so as to reveal God's gracious action at work. At these times, such preaching can be recognized as an exercise of nam-ing grace in light of the occasion.

Such preaching can also be seen as a response to crisis events that threaten to diminish and destroy faith. Joseph R. Jeter writes, that people in sorrow need a "landscape where the pain of the situation can be placed" (1998 153). Preaching can provide such a landscape when it offers the opportunity to weep over the power of radical evil in our world, confess the truth of its presence, and call the com-munity to active resistance through the power of the gospel at work in us (Christine M. Smith, 1992). Such occasions allow for the movement from despair to hope despite the odds.

Some Practical Suggestions

Preaching on special occasions evolves from the preacher's facilitating a conversation between the particular occasion, the word of God in Scripture, and the community present. The following steps are suggested:

1. Exegete the occasion. What does the event say about life, about being fully human? What are its core meaning and its theological implications?
2. Reflect on the faith community's relation to the occasion. What is its meaning for them at this time? What possible reactions and questions might the community bring?
3. Attend to the Scripture(s): listen to, pray with, meditate on, and exegete the biblical text(s), whether selected or assigned. How can the Scripture readings serve as a lens on this occasion and speak God's life-giving word to the community?
4. Consider what message emerges from this interaction between preacher, community, the Word of God, and the special occasion. Is it possible to offer
   a. a word of grace leading to celebration,
   b. a word of challenge enabling action in the world,
   c. a word of hope in God carrying those present into tomorrow?
5. Recognize that the preaching that marks a special occasion is experiential, biblical, ecclesial, liturgical, and—usually—christocentric.

Some Examples of Special Occasion Preaching

Examples of special occasion homilies on major and lesser feasts and at particular rituals, such as weddings and funerals, can be found in most sermon collections, and offered as examples in whole or in part in most books on preaching. Three resources this author has found helpful and would suggest for both study and inspiration are the sermons in the final chapter of *Crisis Preaching* (Jeter 1998); the sermon given by the musician Bono at the National Prayer Breakfast, February 2, 2006, addressing our political leaders on the grave situation in Africa; and, perhaps most surprisingly, Father Barry's sermon in the 1954 movie *On the Waterfront*, given in the hold of a warehouse on the dock and offering a powerful use of Christ imagery.

Conclusion

No final word is likely to be spoken on these occasions but a revelatory one may be, sometimes evangelizing, sometimes catechizing, sometimes prophetically confronting—all to the end of allowing chronos to mutate into kairos. Preaching on special occasions can strengthen, even restore, the identity of a community as being "in Christ," in light of the great events of the past or the important moments of the present, whether joyful or tragic. Such preaching can lead the community to discern more clearly through the lens of God's Word that indeed God is working and walking with them into the future. *See* CRISIS; EXEGESIS OF THE CONGREGATION, DENOMINATION; FUNERAL; HOMILETICAL (THEOLOGICAL) CRITICISM.

Bibliography: Bono. National Prayer Breakfast, February 2, 2006. http://americanrhetoric.com/speeches/bononationalprayerbreakfast.htm; Joseph Jeter. *Crisis Preaching: Personal and Public.* (1998) 139–66; Haddon Robinson and Craig Brian Larson, eds. *The Art and Craft of Biblical Preaching.* (2005); David J. Schlafer. *What Makes This Day Different? Preaching Grace on Special Occasions.* (1998); Christine M. Smith. *Preaching as Weeping, Confession, and Resistance: Radical Responses to Radical Evil.* (1992); Leonora Tubbs Tisdale. *Preaching as Local Theology and Folk Art.* (1997); James A. Wallace. *Preaching to the Hungers of the Heart: The Homily on the Feasts and Within the Rites.* (2002).

TEACHING
Ronald J. Allen

Teaching can be a significant function of preaching. Teaching is helping the congregation identify and claim the congregation's most important convictions concerning the nature of God, God's purposes for the world, and the way in which the life of the congregation as individuals and community can embody those convictions. Teaching sermons help the congregation learn the content of Christian tradition, reflect critically upon that content, and think creatively about how to relate the tradition, the congregation's beliefs in the contemporary setting. In its fullest manifestation, teaching in the Christian community involves not only helping the mind come to critical clarity but also integrating the life of feeling and the decisions of the will into the self and community.

History

As Deut 6:4-9 makes clear, teaching was a foundational dimension of the life of Israel in the period of the First Testament. The Gospels portray Jesus as a rabbi, a word that means "teacher" (e.g., Mark 2:13; 4:1-2; 6:6, 34). Indeed, rabbis have led synagogues since the 1st cent. CE. Teaching was fundamental to the earliest communities of Jesus' followers (e.g., Rom 12:6-8; 1 Cor 12:8-10, 28-30; Eph 4:11). From the biblical period to the present, many ministers have integrated teaching qualities into preaching (e.g., Gregory the Great, Martin Luther, John Calvin, Richard Baxter, Alexander Campbell). Indeed, in the Reformed tradition, teaching is the raison d'etre of preaching.

Contemporary Need

Some preachers and scholars of preaching believe the time is ripe in the early 21st cent. to reemphasize teaching qualities in sermons. Many congregations in the long-established denominations are not sufficiently familiar with the content of the Bible or Christian theology, nor do they have theological methods for adequately correlating that material to the situation of the world today. Furthermore, many congregations in the long-established denominations do not have a distinctive sense of Christian identity or mission. Sermons with teaching foci could help such congregations develop a more robust sense of theological acuity, identity, and power for mission.

Defining Sermons with Teaching Qualities

Preachers sometimes think of a teaching sermon as the dissemination of information in a lecture-like fashion. A fuller understanding recognizes that teaching in the Christian community is concerned not only with distributing information but also with helping the congregation develop feelings and behaviors consistent with the congregation's deepest theological convictions. From the contemporary point of view, the teaching minister is less one who delivers bricks of biblical, doctrinal, or theological knowledge, and is more one who creates sermons as experiences whose purpose is to help the congregation deepen in discipleship through the integration of information, feeling, and behavior. Teaching seeks to help members of the listening community get in a position in which they can make gospel-shaped discoveries. Some circumstances and sermons, in fact, may call for lecture-like methods, but the teaching dimension of preaching is defined not by a limited method or form (such as lecture) but more by the spirit of the larger purpose just articulated.

All sermons teach. Whether or not the preacher intends them to have teaching dimensions, all sermons lead the congregation to name God and the world. Every week preachers should be careful to help the congregation interpret God and the world consistently with the church's most important theological axioms. Simple questions to ask of every sermon are, What does this sermon teach? Is it teaching the gospel? Similar questions can be asked of preaching about the effects of sermons over time: Across several weeks, months, and years, what are sermons teaching about faith and witness? What does the congregation learn from this sermon (or seasons of sermons) about Christian faith and life?

From time to time, preachers will almost undoubtedly want to develop sermons whose specific purpose is teaching. Some circumstances particularly call for sermons with teaching elements, as, for example, when a congregation does not adequately understand a biblical text, theological theme, Christian practice, or personal or social situation. To take another example, a preacher may want to help the congregation grasp more fully why it is important to continue to believe, feel, and do things that the congregation is already doing.

Preparation of Sermons with Teaching Qualities

The preparation of sermons with a teaching focus might take the following steps: (1) through pastoral listening, the preacher becomes aware of an aspect of the congregation's perception, feeling, or behavior that needs to be addressed by a teaching sermon; (2) the preacher identifies resources from the Bible, tradition, theology, and other sources to help the congregation learn how to think, feel, and behave in theologically appropriate ways in relationship to the topic; (3) the preacher designs the sermon or series of sermons to give the congregation optimum opportunity to make the requisite discoveries; and (4) after preaching the sermon (or series), the preacher reflects on points at which learning appeared to take place, points at which it did not, and what the preacher might do in future sermons to reinforce the positive effects and minimize the negative ones.

Teaching over Time

Three patterns for organizing teaching sermons over several Sundays are prominent. First is to preach seriatim through a book of the Bible (or through a part of a book). A pastor might preach for several weeks, for instance, through the book of Exodus. Second is to put together a series of sermons that explores significant topics in the Christian faith. For example, a minister might devote one sermon a week to the major elements of Christian faith: God, Christ, Holy Spirit, church, world, and world to come. The elements of such a series might derive from an affirmation of faith, such as the Nicene formulation. A slight adaptation might be for the preacher to focus on elements of one part of Christian life. For instance, the preacher could develop messages on the person and nature of Christ, or on the sacraments or ordinances. Third is to create sermons that follow the Christian Year and a lectionary. The Christian Year seeks to teach the congregation fundamental aspects of Christian identity and behavior through the calendar of the two great cycles of redemption, Advent/Christmas/ Epiphany Day, and Lent/Easter/Pentecost Day, as well as through the long seasons of Ordinary Time. The primary readings in the lectionary are chosen because they are supposed to illumine the main theological themes of the seasons in which they appear.

Diverse Genres for Sermons with Teaching Qualities

There is no single formula for the teaching sermon. Ministers can develop sermons that teach in many genres of sermons correlated to the different ways that people learn (some in more linear fashions and others more inductively and associatively).

Teaching often takes place through linear models of preaching such as the PURITAN PLAIN STYLE (with its simple form: beginning, exposition of the text, theological reflection, application, and ending), sermons that make points derived from a body of biblical literature or from a doctrine, or sermons that proceed through a biblical book verse by verse. These approaches are often well received by people whose mental operations are linear. With respect to teaching, the virtues of such approaches are clarity and helping the congregation think logically. However, when used woodenly, such approaches can appeal mainly to the mind (with little consideration for feeling or behavior) and may not connect with people who think in more associative ways. The preacher may misuse such approaches by becoming domineering or oppressively hierarchical.

Recent trends in preaching have moved away from such linear models to more inductive, associative, narrative, imagistic, impressionistic, and intuitive modes of expression. With respect to teaching, these approaches are often well received by people whose patterns of understanding are less analytical and are more associative, narrative, and intuitive. Sermons in these modes are often suited to texts, doctrines, and topics that are controversial, highly emotional, or marked by ambiguity. However, listeners sometimes have difficulty coming away from such sermons with a clear understanding of the content of the message. A steady diet of such preaching does not always develop the congregation's capacity to think clearly and critically about the Bible, doctrine, ethics, and life.

From the perspective of teaching, a promising approach is preaching as conversation. The preacher brings into conversation the Bible, tradition, doctrine, other sources of understanding, and the experience of the congregation as well as people in the larger world. The sermon, usually monological in form but dialogical in tone, seeks to help the congregation converse with these resources to discover an adequate interpretation of a text, doctrine, practice, or personal or social circumstance. This approach teaches the congregation methods for critical theological reflection. *See* DOCTRINAL; EXEGETICAL; HOMILETICAL (THEOLOGICAL) CRITICISM.

Bibliography: Ronald J. Allen. *The Teaching Sermon.* (1995); Ronald J. Allen. *Preaching Is Believing: The Sermon as Theological Reflection.* (2002); Ronald J. Allen. "Preaching as Mutual Critical Correlation through Conversation." *Purposes of Preaching.* (2004) 1–22; Ronald J. Allen, ed. *The Teaching Sermon Series.* 5 vols. (1997–1999); Mary Elizabeth Moore. *Teaching from the Heart: Education and Theological Method.* (1998); Clark M. Williamson and Ronald J. Allen. *The Teaching Minister.* (1991).

Testimonial

Gary V. Simpson

There is a great tension inherent in our preaching. By outward appearances alone, the preacher is active, and the listeners are passive. We are the performers, and the congregation is the audience. We act; they watch. We speak; they listen. We believe that preaching is something we do to the people. After all, we are called "to proclaim, to prophesy, and to tell forth." Too often the preaching enterprise and process is understood solely as a word that proceeds out of the preacher's mouth into the listener's ear. In reality, the sermon is for and with the people who hear it. The weekly struggle is in what ways a sermon speaks truth, life, and challenge into the lives of the listeners. The paradox is that the preacher is listener also, and in order to speak life into a congregation, the preacher, too, must have life spoken into her or him. We perhaps would preach differently if we understood ourselves as part of the congregation to which our sermons are pronounced.

No one would disagree that preaching must be relevant. For the most part we work with a very old tool kit in this technically savvy and seduced world of gadgets and ideas. The Bible is an ancient book. Its customs, mores, and practices are from a time and often a culture that have passed. The preacher is already at a disadvantage because she or he has to bring alive the lives, foibles, and frustrations; the penchants and the promises; the trials and the triumphs of a people whose day is past. Our postmodern culture has an innate aversion to the already, a disdain for the decided, and a disinterest in the dated.

We see this dynamic when we beg the question, Can the preacher tell the story? The story the preacher tells is actually a part of the long procession of Christian witness. The preacher tells only a part of the believing community's story. Preaching is but one piece of the testimony of believers. It is a part of the larger dynamic of "talking ourselves into being Christian," as Tom Long so aptly puts it (Long 2004). At times, the preacher can tell forth with personal passion, intensity, and vigor, yet the people can remain disinterested. Somehow, the capacity for listening is constricted if the entire message is "telling them something."

Asking the First Questions

In some preaching traditions, the preacher longing for connection with the listeners will ask, "Can I get a witness?" Too often this becomes a gimmick for soliciting audible response. Preaching is not pandering for assent with a passive audience. In reality, the question the preacher asks a congregation must first be turned inward. It is not, Can I get a witness? but, Can I be a witness? What am I willing to invest, what am I willing to stake a claim in, what am I willing to risk, or to put it in the language of the calling as disciple, what am I willing to die for in this message? The point here is that preaching is not something done to the people; it is something done among the people. The key word here is *authenticity.*

It is not difficult to speak lofty words about the unconditional love, unmitigated grace, and unobscured mercy of God divine, but the holy conversation that preaching necessitates is that the preacher make a personal investment, stake a claim, add his or her conviction to the word that is declared. The preacher is first witness, Exhibit A in the grace of God. The preacher cannot expect the congregation to be convicted, challenged, charged, or changed if the sermon has no markings of personal investment. Too often the preacher is asking the wrong question. It is not, Will they believe this? but, Do I believe this?

The prophet Ezekiel declares, "I sit where you sit." Harry Emerson Fosdick contended that his sermons were often candid and open conversations he had with himself as the congregation listened (Miller 1995, 333–78).

A word of caution should be inserted here about distinguishing sermon from pure autobiography. Too often the preacher sets up autobiographical insight that suggests to the listener: This is how I have gotten it together. If you want to really experience God as a mature believer, you must become exactly like me. Autobiography is not the same as testimony. The central subject in autobiography is *me.* Testimony is a lens through which to see my life as a witness to the person and presence of God in the world.

Each time the congregation gathers and pauses for the proclamation, it is as if congregants are saying directly to the preacher, "Have *you* seen anything?" If so, "Tell us about it." Barbra Brown Taylor simplifies the task of preaching when she says, "All we have to learn [as preachers] is to say what we see" (Taylor 1993, 83).

The struggle to produce authentic preaching is enhanced by the preacher's authentic struggle to live. I had been working on a sermon about Jesus Christ as our Redeemer. All week I wrestled with the passage, and it seemed that although I understood the concept of redemption in my head, I could not articulate it well enough for a sermon. Remembering Dietrich Bonhoeffer's edict to avoid the temptation of running to a text that may be more "preachable," I fought to no avail (Bonhoeffer 1991, 120–21). That Thursday, I took my two young children to the dentist. Not paying attention to the parking rules, I returned to my car as the tow truck was pulling away.

To spare the details, I learned that day what redemption was all about as a few hours turned into a life lesson and an entry into the lives of the congregation. The sermon began, "I struggled all week long trying to grasp the idea of redemption. . . . Then I got my car towed on Thursday." Telling that story of how I was indeed a part of the world of the listeners gave us all the opportunity to explore the world of the gospel. It was a rather expensive sermon for me, but it was the gospel to each of us who heard it that day. *See* SELF-DISCLOSURE; STORIES, ETHICS IN USE OF; SOTERIOLOGY.

Bibliography: Dietrich Bonhoeffer. *Worldly Preaching: Lectures on Homiletics.* Edited by Clyde Fant. (1991); Anna Carter Florence. *Preaching as Testimony.* (2007); Thomas Long. *Testimony: Talking Ourselves into Being Christian.* (2004); Robert Moats Miller. *Harry Emerson Fosdick: Preacher, Pastor, Prophet.* (1995); Barbara Brown Taylor. *The Preaching Life.* (1993).

THE BIG IDEA
Casey Barton

Haddon Robinson's homiletic focuses on identifying a central or "big idea" gleaned from the biblical text and developed into the central communicative concept of the sermon. Robinson defines *expository preaching:* "Expository preaching is the communication of a biblical concept, derived from and transmitted through a historical, grammatical, and literary study of a passage in its context, which the Holy Spirit first applies to the personality and experience of the preacher, then through the preacher, applies to the hearers" (2001, 21). The biblical text governs the thought and development of the sermon. With this hermeneutic Robinson proposes a philosophy for preaching and not merely a homiletical method.

The sermon explains, proves, or applies a single idea drawn from Scripture. Acknowledging his debt to H. Grady Davis (2001, 14; Davis 1958), Robinson defines an *idea* as the combination of a "subject" and a "complement." An idea's subject is the complete answer to the question, "What am I talking about?" The complement is the full answer to the question, "What am I saying about what I am talking about?" (2001, 41). Together a complete idea is stated. Habakkuk 1:2-4 provides an example:

> *Subject:* Habakkuk laments about the injustice he sees in Judah.
> *Complement:* He wonders why God, who is righteous, doesn't judge the nation for its sin.
> *Idea:* Habakkuk laments that his righteous God does not punish sin in Judah. (2001, 44–45)

This is the text's "exegetical idea."

The exegetical idea is submitted to "developmental questions" to explore its meaning and communication today—What does this mean? Is it true? What difference does it make? It is then converted into a "homiletical idea," a contemporary restatement of the text's idea in clear, memorable language based on listeners' knowledge and experience. For example, from the parable of the Good Samaritan: "Your neighbor is anyone whose need you see, whose need you are in a position to meet" (2001, 105). The sermon develops according to the form the idea demands.

Robinson's central idea shows similarities and differences with other homiletical projects such as Bryan Chapell's and Paul Scott Wilson's. Chapell shares an emphasis on a central idea (1994, 37). His homiletic is explicitly theological in viewing a commonality in the "fallen condition" of humanity as represented in the text and today (Fallen Condition Focus/FCF). In each text God's grace addresses humanity's common fallenness (1994, 42). Wilson also advocates a central theme (2007, 41). With Chapell, Wilson emphasizes a focus on God's grace in text and sermon. While Robinson focused on asking what the text says, Wilson asks, "What is God doing in or behind this text?" (2007, 46). For Wilson the subject of preaching is what the text says plus the action of God in the text and today. The difference is an ultimate focus on gospel. The text remains essential as the grace-filled action of God, then and now, becomes the locus of one's preaching. *See* EXPOSITORY; FOCUS AND FUNCTION STATEMENTS; THEME SENTENCE.

Bibliography: Bryan Chapell. *Christ-Centered Preaching: Redeeming the Expository Sermon.* (1994); H. Grady Davis. *Design for Preaching.* (1958); Haddon Robinson. *Biblical Preaching: The Development and Delivery of Expository Messages.* 2nd ed. (2001); Paul Scott Wilson. *The Practice of Preaching.* Rev. ed. (2007).

TOPICAL
Robert Smith Jr.

Ronald Allen describes the topical sermon as one that "gives a systematic or integrated treatment of a theme considered worthy of discussion" (Lischer and Willimon 1995, 492). The responsible topical sermon interprets the biblical text and provides the insights for the listener to cognitively, affectively, and behaviorally respond to the topic that is corroborated by the text. The topical sermon may or may not be biblical. Topical preaching receives divine approbation only when it remembers its role as a servant of the text and faithfully proclaims the great themes, concepts, and truths of the Bible.

Texts have to speak to people in their own *Sitz im Leben* (situation in life). Preaching that addresses only the what question of the implications of the text without responding to the *so what* question of the application of the text to daily concerns and vice versa is neither authentically expository nor responsibly topical. Responsible topical preaching can serve as a bridge for the kind of topical preaching that has been guilty of searching newspaper articles and television shows for relevant and timely topics without adequately treating the text and the type of preaching that masquerades as expository preaching without sufficiently addressing the human plight. On a televised lecture I once heard, Bishop Fulton Sheen remarked that if he started his ministry over, he would begin in the familiar world of the people and then proceed to take them into the less familiar world of the Bible. Proverbially speaking, the preaching foreparents of the 20th cent. ate the sour grapes of dividing biblical revelation from contemporary relevance, and the teeth of the children of the 21st cent. have been set on edge. To make up for the loss of relevance, present-day homiletics is moving dangerously close to a topic-full/text-less message. Responsible topical preaching does not negotiate between text or topic. What has been joined together must not be separated. It is crucial for the preacher, as Karl Barth recommended, to hold the Bible in one hand and the newspaper in the other, thereby connecting the "was-ness" of the ancient Word with the "is-ness" of the contemporary world.

The responsible topical sermon finds its residence at the intersection where the anthropological question meets the theological answer. In the thought of Fred Craddock (1987), "Lurking in the backwoods of everyone's mind is the question of God; and immediately following is the question of humanity."

Which comes first, the topic or the text? Ultimately, this question has to be answered in the context of *sub specie aeternitatis* (under the aspect of eternity), for in pre-existent eternity, the omniscient God furnished the written Word (the Bible), anticipating humanity's concerns; the spoken word (the gospel), directing humanity's destiny; and the revealed Word (the incarnate Christ), providing humanity with the human face of God. Haddon Robinson appears to support the position that the text of Scripture pre-supposes and anticipates contemporary human interests (Robinson 1980, 20). He says that expository preaching is the communication of a biblical concept transmitted through a historical, grammatical, and literary study of a passage in its context, which the Holy Spirit first applies to the personality and experience of the preacher, then through the preacher to hearers.

Harry Emerson Fosdick's preaching represented a reaction to the proclamation of 19th-cent. discredited liberalism that was sterile and pedantic and emphasized biblical revelation, often detached from contemporary relevance. Fosdick detested preachers who had the penchant for being "bull-dogmatic," having their heads in the Bible and never lifting them out of the Bible to relate the

Scriptures to the life experiences of their hearers. In Fosdick's 1924 Lyman Beecher Lectures, *The Modern Use of the Bible*, he observed that "the preacher deprived of his Bible would be as 'lost as a judge without the Constitution, thrown back upon the bare ideal of Justice without historical content'" (Miller 1985, 348). He believed that preaching was backward and needed to be turned around. In the analysis of the preaching of his times, preachers started with the Bible, which for him was the wrong point of departure, instead of beginning in the milieu of the masses and moving them into the locale of the Bible. He sought to ascertain the congregation's burning questions, perplexing issues, and troubling doubts, and he prayed that God would give him insights into these so that he could meet the people where they were, take them to where God was, and lead them (through the Scripture) to the place where God was going.

On the inside cover of his work *Harry Emerson Fosdick: Preacher, Pastor, Prophet,* Robert Moats Miller (1985) cites Rabbi Stephen Wise's comment that Harry Emerson Fosdick was "the least hated and the best loved heretic that ever lived." Can Harry Emerson Fosdick be rightly criticized for initially addressing the *zeitgeist* (the spirit of the times) before he addressed the spirit of the Word? Did not the greatest preacher in human history employ this sequence and format? Jesus responded to questions put to him by addressing their concerns, whether related to a financial quarrel between two brothers (Luke 12—the parable of the Barn Building Fool), criticism from Jewish leaders for having table fellowship with publicans and sinners (Luke 15—the parables of the Lost Sheep, Lost Coin, and Waiting Father), or a lawyer interrogating him about his definition of neighborliness (Luke 10—the parable of the Good Samaritan). Jesus used the eternal Word to bring clarity to human chaos. In other words, Jesus preached the truth of God's Word as he encountered the topical and thematic contexts of his hearers. Preachers who stand between the two worlds of the text of Scripture and the texture of human life would do well to embrace the homiletical intent of Harry Emerson Fosdick, who stated, "In general, my gospel is to get hold of live issues that really matter in the life of people, to look at them long enough so that I believe something terribly hard, to baptize my conviction in the spirit and truth of the New Testament, and then to put it across to the people as hot as I can"(Miller 1985, 342). *See* DOCTRINAL; HOMILETICAL (THEOLOGICAL) CRITICISM; TEACHING.

Bibliography: Ronald J. Allen. *Preaching the Topical Sermon.* (1992); Fred Craddock. Luncheon dialogue, E. Y. Mullins Lectures on Preaching. Southern Baptist Theological Seminary, Louisville, Ky., March 5, 1987; Richard Lischer and William Willimon, eds. *Concise Encyclopedia of Preaching.* (1995); Robert Moats Miller. *Harry Emerson Fosdick: Preacher, Pastor, Prophet.* (1985); Haddon W. Robinson. *Biblical Preaching: The Development and Delivery of Expository Messages.* (1980).

VERSE BY VERSE
See EXEGETICAL; PURITAN PLAIN STYLE.

WEDDING
Charles L. Rice

The celebration and blessing of a marriage presents the preacher with a unique opportunity. The ambiguity of the marriage ceremony, in which secular and sacred elements combine, challenges the preacher's imagination, pastoral skills, and powers of communication.

A. The Church's Role and Teaching
B. Biblical and Liturgical Resources
    1. Vocation in Marriage
    2. Grace in Marriage
    3. Service in Marriage
    4. Community in Marriage
C. Practical Considerations

A. The Church's Role and Teaching

Christians initially followed Jewish custom and later they adapted Roman practices. Both traditions included betrothal, the procession of the bride to the groom's house, and feasting. The ring, joining of hands, and special garments were Roman; the signing of a contract was Jewish. Christians added the presence of a bishop, substituted Christian prayers and blessings for the pagan ones, and used the Eucharist in place of Roman sacrifices.

In the Middle Ages the church assumed full responsibility for marriage, to the degree that weddings were to be conducted only in sacred precincts. The formal declaration of marriage—the state's interest in this ceremony—was sometimes done on the porch or in the vestibule, the priestly blessing and exhortation within the church proper. In this practice we see what has been the continuing ambiguity of a legal transaction occurring on ecclesiastical territory: weddings occur in church before a priest, but it is the state, finally, that licenses, records, and dissolves marriages. Though there was a period after the Reformation when weddings were performed during the Sunday service, marriage has more often occupied a kind of middle ground, neither fully inside nor outside the rites of the church.

From the earliest days Christian thinkers have struggled with the meaning and practice of marriage. Jesus' view as represented in the Gospels appears clear: the relationship of man and woman is grounded in creation, and this is the basis of a union that ought not to be dissolved (Mark 10:1-11). This view is complicated by Matthew's accommodation to the legalistic casuistry which has led to the intricacies of canon law on marital matters (Matt 5:32, 19:1-12). Paul, in his struggle to accommodate the attachments of marriage in a world that was passing away, sees marriage as both necessary and good, and he guides Christians away from an undue asceticism that disparages or forbids marriage.

Augustine also affirmed the inherent goodness of marriage, but he did so in the context of a basic distrust of human sexuality. As a consequence, sexuality and sin are often linked in the Christian mind, and marriage is considered by many as a concession to the flesh, rather than the joyful and creative reception of a divine gift. Given this bias, it is not surprising the 1549 Book of Common Prayer set forth a threefold purpose for marriage which can be read as a kind of justification of the institution: "the procreation of children," a "remedie against sinne," and for "mutuall societie, helpe, and coumfort."

Luther saw marriage as a Christian vocation. This idea is foreshadowed in John Chrysostom, who urged the men of Constantinople and their wives to give up the pursuit of money and to direct their married life toward true purity and piety. Chrysostom grounded marriage in the analogy of Christ and the church, and Luther elevated marriage as a calling to live a life justified by grace.

B. Biblical and Liturgical Resources

Like most of the available lectionaries, the 1979 *Book of Common Prayer* provides lessons, Gospels, and psalms for reading at weddings. Relying on the lectionary, it is possible to preach biblical sermons that draw also on the marriage rite. The couple can participate by choosing the biblical texts and being drawn into conversation about their choices. The result can be a textual/thematic homily, which draws from scripture, liturgy, and the particular occasion.

Four themes that connect with the ritual and readings for the day emerge from Christian reflection on the meaning of marriage. If the preacher keeps these themes in view while reflecting upon the unique event at hand—this particular couple, their history and vocations, and their spiritual understanding—the homily can connect profoundly with them, their family, and friends. Two simple moves can help with this: Ask the couple to collaborate in selecting the text on which the homily is to be given, and go to the rehearsal dinner. Then, keep these four theological and pastoral themes in view.

1. Vocation in Marriage

"Make their life together a sign of Christ's love to this sinful and broken world, that unity may overcome estrangement, forgiveness heal guilt, and joy conquer despair." (*The Book of Common Prayer,* 1979, 429)

The preacher, following this prayer and the biblical texts, speaks of matrimony as a holy vocation. God calls those who receive the sacramental gift of marriage to reveal the gospel in the way they live together. The 1958 Lambeth Conference affirmed that "marriage is a vocation to holiness, through which men and women may share in the love and creative purposes of God" (Lambeth Conference, 1958, Resolution 113. Cited in Evans and Wright, 1991, 431). Marriage establishes a family with a healing and reconciling vocation.

Readings for the day lend themselves to this theme. Genesis grounds marriage in creation: man and woman are to live in harmony with the One who gives them life, and they are to have a special role in caring for the earth and its creatures. Ephesians asks that Christ may dwell in their hearts, and that they walk in love, sharing Christ's sacrificial life. Matthew calls on them to let their life together be a light shining with good works that glorify God (5:3-16).

At a wedding, high feeling and high calling meet. There lies the preacher's responsibility and opportunity.

2. Grace in Marriage

> "Give them grace, when they hurt each other, to recognize and acknowledge their fault, and to seek each other's forgiveness and yours." (BCP, 429)

Marriage is an extraordinary arena for living out in ordinary ways the grace of God. The Lambeth Conference "calls upon all Church people to have in mind that, since our Lord's ministry gave a new depth and significance to forgiveness, his Church and the families within it must be a forgiving society, and that there are no wrongs done by its members, one to another, that are unforgivable. . . ." (Lambeth Conference, 1958, Resolution 116. Cited in Evans and Wright, 1991, 431.) As much as this may go against popular culture, the opening words of the marriage rite call upon those seeking Christian marriage to approach these vows reverently and deliberately, knowing that it is only by living in grace that they can succeed in their life together.

H. H. Farmer has called preaching the declaration of God's "ultimate demand and final succour" (Farmer, 1942, 70.) Nowhere could a better analogy of that—and school for practice—be found than in marriage. As the teaching of Jesus asserts, marriage springs from the gift of God in creation, the gift of sexuality. Received gratefully as God's gift, and used for the purposes of love, sexuality continues as a constant gift throughout married life. This ground of "final succour"—understanding and healing, comforting and giving joy—becomes a bodily experience of the gospel's power. To be married and stay married is a school of grace.

The nuptial blessing—"Most gracious God, we give you thanks for your tender love in sending Jesus Christ to come among us, to be born of a human mother, and to make the way of the cross to be the way of life. . . ." (BCP, 430)—sets marriage in the context of the incarnation and the cross. It is to this that Christian marriage is consecrated: shared life in the flesh and sacrificial love.

Lections that connect easily with the themes of grace and forgiveness come from Song of Solomon ("Many waters cannot quench love") and Tobit ("That she and I may grow old together"). First Corinthians 13 gives specific examples of what grace looks like in daily life, while Colossians 3 is a call to dwell in Christ so as to live in forbearing harmony. John 15:9-12 calls the couple to love one another as Christ loves. Both the collect of the day and the post-communion prayer speak of relying upon the grace of Christ in order to live in patience, forgiveness, and peace.

3. Service in Marriage

> "Give them such fulfillment of their mutual affection that they may reach out in love and concern for others." (BCP, 429)

The celebration of a wedding can suggest consumerism and a happy life insulated from the needs of the world. This petition prays for marriage as a purposeful life of service. The preacher could draw, for example, on the metaphor of an overflowing vessel, a fountain welling up and flowing out. "My cup overflows" becomes a picture of service, as two joyous people let their life together bless others. In some liturgies, the married couple's first act is to bring forward the bread and wine for the Eucharist, an acting out of this prayer: mutual joy in the service of all.

This is not, of course, a time to carp about materialism and consumerism. The idea is to lead the couple to see their life together as a gift of God to "this sinful and broken world." This will be a gift to the couple, reminding them that God seeks "in holy love to save all people from aimlessness and sin (Statement of Faith, United Church of Christ)." A wedding day is a teachable moment for such proclamation.

Ephesians 5, in its call to walk in love as Christ loved us, calls partners in marriage to serve each other. Matthew 7 calls the couple to live wisely, to build their house on the commandments to love God and neighbor. Setting these texts alongside the marriage rite, the preacher reminds the newly married—and the overhearing congregation—that blessing issues in service.

4. Community in Marriage

> "Grant that the bonds of our common humanity, by which all your children are united one to another, and the living to the dead, may be so

transformed by your grace that your will may be done on earth as it is in heaven. . . ." (BCP, 430)

A wedding creates a new community—the family—and it relies upon a larger community, the congregation that promises to do all in their power "to uphold these persons in their marriage." (BCP, 425) Beyond that, the liturgy reminds this couple, setting out on a new journey together, that their life together—its humanity so frankly recognized in the nuptial blessing upon their work and companionship, sleeping and waking, joys and sorrows, life and death—leads to "that table where your saints feast for ever in your heavenly home." (BCP, 430) The preacher can begin with the simple reminder that two families are brought together and suggest the larger family of faith by pointing to Holy Communion and the eventual baptism of children.

Genesis shows us that first community in Eden—all harmonious among God, humankind, and nature—and also brokenness and separation. Ephesians 3 and 1 John tell of God's love in Christ as the basis of community, easily symbolized in a family saying grace at a shared meal. Colossians 3 sets community in the context of worship. The Beatitudes picture a community mirroring God's reign.

C. Practical Considerations

For the service of the Word the couple and their attendants should be seated for the readings and homily. The preacher can stand on the floor level, close to the couple, making it easy to speak directly to them. There is homiletic advantage in doing this: the congregation will hear much more acutely what they are *overhearing.*

A good rule of thumb for preaching: The bigger the occasion the smaller the sermon. The occasion is itself speaking loudly, and the congregation is likely to be diverse and somewhat distracted. The homily should be "smaller" than usual, 6-8 minutes in length, and in modulated tone and style. Conversational and instructive, the homily is no less profoundly theological and pastoral.

Preaching has not been a significant part of weddings in North America and remains optional. If the preacher can come to the wedding as celebrant, teacher, and pastor, relying on venerable texts, the Word at a wedding can turn water into wine. *See* ANTHROPOLOGY; SPECIAL OCCASION; WORSHIP STYLE.

Bibliography: Perry Biddle, *A Marriage Manual.* (2006); G. R. Evans and J. Robert Wright, editors. *The Anglican Tradition: A Handbook of Sources.* 1991; H. H. Farmer. *The Servant of the Word.* (1942); William Hethcock, "Preaching at Marriages." *Breaking the Word: Essays on the Liturgical Dimensions of Preaching*, Carl Daw, ed. Church Hymnal Corp., 1994, 127-35; Charles Rice, "Preaching at Weddings." *Sewanee Theological Review*, 41:3 (Pentecost, 1998): 228-40.

WITHOUT NOTES
Joseph M. Webb

Preaching without notes refers to the process of thoroughly preparing a sermon, outlining it concisely, memorizing the outline, and then presenting it extemporaneously from behind a pulpit or on an open platform. It is one of three general approaches to public speaking, the other two being the reading aloud of a written manuscript and the memorizing of a manuscript with the words then recited in public. Preaching extemporaneously with notes or without notes is usually considered the same thing, though all professional public speakers, as well as the speech professors and the writers of speech textbooks, emphasize that speaking without notes is always far more effective in communicating with an audience than using them.

Although there are examples of Greek and Roman orators reciting from memorized speeches, even that practice appears to have been rare. Using all of their rhetorical training, the orators of the classic period, including the early Christian era, extemporized their speeches. By all accounts, the sermons of the early church fathers, Chrysostom and Augustine among them, were not just delivered extemporaneously, but without notes. Chrysostom would sometimes follow a week of intense study by deciding what he would preach on his way to church or even as a result of something that would arise during the service itself.

The turbulent 16th and 17th cent., with the Protestant Reformation struggling into existence, particularly in England, brought a major change in the nature of preaching, largely as a result of two factors. First, new Protestant clergy found it prudent not to displease the Crown, since complaints about theology in sermons could easily land one in deep, even mortal, trouble. So with an understandable deep desire not to rile powerful hearers, clergy began to carefully write out and read their sermons. They quickly learned, too, that their reading should not be emotional, lest it produce dangerous emotional responses. Even sermon reading began to be done as flatly and unemotionally as possible, to the point of the preacher keeping head down and making no eye contact from the pulpit. The practice spread throughout all Europe and, strangely, continues in many settings today.

The second factor in the manuscript reading of those days was that countless young clergy were relatively untrained yet in the emerging Reformation theology that had captured their allegiance. Key leaders prepared sets of sermons that were to be read from the growing number of Protestant pulpits. It was the fearless, radical Puritan preachers, though, who kept alive the extremely risky practice of preaching extemporaneously, passionately, and without notes.

By the end of the 18th cent., the dangers associated with state-controlled preaching were largely gone, even in Anglicanism. So was the lack of untrained Protestant clergy who needed someone to write sermons for them. The 19th cent. brought a revival of interest in rhetoric, in crowd-stirring public address, in passionate preaching, particularly among the denominations that thrived on the American frontier. (*See* REVIVALS.) Books on sermon preparation and public speaking began to proliferate, books that emphasized the psychology of audiences and that extolled the ancient processes of oratorical effectiveness. One of the most influential of these books was John Broadus's 1870 volume titled *Preparation and Delivery of Sermons*. No book before—or since—has devoted such keen attention to the dynamic complexity of public speaking in the pulpit. Broadus's was the first full-scale scholarly effort to call the church back from the Reformation-induced reading of manuscripts in the pulpit to the basics of classical public address, particularly preaching without notes.

Broadus contended that "only in extemporaneous speaking, of one or another variety, can [preaching] ever be perfectly natural, and achieve the highest effect" (Broadus 1898, 462). He called preaching without notes "the ideal of speaking," an ideal, moreover, that "cannot be reached in any other way. . . . And while painstaking culture vainly strives to read or recite precisely like speaking, the extemporaneous speaker may with comparative ease rise to the best delivery of which he [or she] is capable" (462). For Broadus, though, preaching without notes was not about just using the voice to "deliver" a sermon; its uniqueness was that it alone brought together the preacher's entire body—voice, movement, countenance, ethos, character, and eye—in a natural harmony, to "attain their full power" (462).

In today's age of new contemporary worship forms, preaching without notes is rapidly becoming the new necessity for speakers of the gospel. The demand is for worship—and its preaching—to be spontaneous, interactive, energetic, passionate, and fluid. The preacher is being called on to respond to the flow of the emergent service, whatever form the worship takes. In these dynamic interplays of music, Scripture, drama, media, and testimony, the preaching situation is expected to become uniquely improvisational—both well planned and directed by the call of the moment. The preacher must know what he or she wants to say, yet, at the same time, be able to think, feel, and interact with congregants from the beginning to the end of the sermon—all the time allowing the Holy Spirit to supply words and unfurl sentences. This is the essence of what it means to preach without notes.

What does it take to preach extemporaneously—without notes? It takes three disciplines. First is the discipline of careful planning and organizing. Preachers know how to exegete biblical texts, gather information, tell their own stories. The discipline that makes preaching without notes possible is knowing how to form a simple, well-constructed outline of no more than seven or eight items, items that, while diverse, are all related to each other in the sermon being prepared. These are the simple guiding phrases that hold the sermon together, leading to a single central idea that will emerge inductively from what the preacher says.

Second is the discipline of using and trusting one's memory. Preaching without notes requires some memorization. The prepared outline of related items or phrases must be committed to memory in the same way that one studies for an examination. It requires up to two hours or so after the outline is crafted. One repeats again and again to oneself the main points of the outline. Our memory faculties work well—far better than we believe they do. The more one practices the art of memorization, the better one's memory works.

Third, preaching without notes requires the discipline of courage in public speaking. Standing before people to speak, no matter how often it is done, is always daunting. When one makes a decision to preach without notes, nervousness always results. What invariably happens, though, is that within moments of beginning, the preacher becomes caught up, along with the congregants, in what more often than not becomes an electrifying experience, an experience, in Broadus's words, "in which the preacher's language rises, without conscious effort, to suit the heightened grandeur and beauty of his conceptions" (Broadus 1898, 460). Courage is required for embodying speech without notes, but the Holy Spirit turns the speech into things often completely unexpected.

This is what today's young people want in one who speaks to them. They want the gospel presented in a way that holds and captivates, that energizes and moves them. And—as odd as it sounds—there is only one kind of preaching that can genuinely and consistently accomplish that in today's new worship environments. It is preaching without script or notes, the gospel embodied in a courageous and well-prepared preacher. It is the ancient form of preaching that has never been newer than it is today. *See* MANUSCRIPT; ORAL/AURAL COMMUNICATION; HOLY SPIRIT AND PREACHING; PERFORMING THE MANUSCRIPT.

Bibliography: John A. Broadus. *A Treatise on the Preparation and Delivery of Sermons.* 37th ed. (1898); Teri Kwal Gamble and Michael W. Gamble. *Public Speaking in the Age of Diversity.* (1998); Charles W. Koller. *Expository Preaching without Notes.* (1962); John J. Makay. *Public Speaking: Theory into Practice.* (1992); Rudolph F. Verderber. *The Challenge of Effective Speaking.* (1994); Joseph M. Webb. *Preaching without Notes.* (2001).

PART 11 THEOLOGY.
INTRODUCTION: BEARER OF THE WORD

F. Gerrit Immink

Practicing Theology

Since preaching has to do with God, doing theology in the pulpit is inevitable. Preachers name God in relation to the world in which we live, and by doing so they construct some form of practice-related theology. This theology is embedded in the local community of faith and in touch with the lived experiences of real people. Sermons, therefore, as they intend to portray God's involvement with our world, always represent some form of local theology. Consequently, theology and pulpit are necessary partners.

Unfortunately, contemporary preachers have become very cautious about doing theology in the pulpit. What are the reasons for this indifference? (1) Preachers often associate theology with deductive preaching and abstract and lifeless doctrines. (2) Narrative and inductive preaching are in vogue, and these modes of discourse may pay less attention to the more reflective dimensions of faith. (3) Contemporary preachers realize that on Sunday morning they are not simply preaching in a framework of common vision. They find themselves in a situation of diverse worldly and ecclesial experiences. Knowing that theological diversity can easily lead to bitter conflict, pastors feel the temptation to remain silent on dogmatic issues.

Theological Competence

However, if one turns one's back on profound theological reflection, one will in the long run weaken one's ministry. Theology in the pulpit is urgently needed in contemporary preaching. Understandably, preachers feel a certain impediment with respect to theological reflection. It takes courage and wisdom to proclaim the grace of God in the midst of human misery. Staying close to one's contextual human situation seems easier in a culture that cherishes lived experiences. Yet preachers also may feel a certain passion for announcing the good news of God's kingdom. How can this be done in an adequate way?

Doing theology in the pulpit requires a practice-related theological competence: the ability to picture a world of faith in which the lived experiences of daily life are intertwined with the God-talk. To meet this challenge, the preacher must not only have a pastoral attitude, but must also be equally competent (professionally and personally) in handling the realities of faith. She must be well trained in theology in order to discern what God's dynamic presence in Jesus Christ means in this specific context. Not to mention the confessional stance, the preacher must be sensitive to the questions, challenges, and expectations that faith evokes in this specific situation. During Lent, for example, the preacher has the task to reflect on the suffering of Jesus in the context of worldwide human suffering.

Doing theology in the pulpit is the vocation of the ministry. As Richard Lischer observes,

> We cannot reverse the massive trends in communication or rescue the profession of the ministry from social decline, but we can embrace our vocation. We can preach. And the vocation, since it comes from God, will make of us a sign in a world unsure of its responsibility and in a culture that treats language with loose indifference. (2005, 41)

This vocation brings joy and tension. Often preachers feel puzzled, and yet they want to speak with passion. Sermons in which life experiences are intertwined with the language of faith need to arrive at some theological truth claim.

Sermon Examples

In terms of theology in the pulpit two negative examples may be most instructive; taken as they are from two excellent preachers, they indicate how pervasive the problem can be. In his sermon "Outrageous God, Season of Decrease" Brueggemann introduces the biblical witness as an almost scandalous voice:

> There is something deeply outrageous about Advent, which is made clear in this poem of Isaiah

65. It is so outrageous that none of us really believes it. Nonetheless, we are the baptized people who have promised to share such a text, such a vision. (1996, 65)

The presumed tension is extremely strong: none of us really believes Advent. Yet the preacher motivates the gathered community right away; the poem of Isaiah 65 is presented as a vision of a new world, wrought by God. It is a world in which there will be no more terrorized folk, no more infant mortality, and so on.

> I told you it was outrageous. It is outrageous because the new world of God is beyond our capacity and even beyond our imagination. It does not seem possible. In our fatigue, our self-sufficiency, and our cynicism, we deeply believe that such promises could not happen here. Such newness is only poetic fantasy, and there are the persistent realities of injustice and grief and terror, and it will never end, not in any future we can conjure. (Brueggemann 1996, 66)

The function of lyrical poetry, according to Brueggemann, is to surpass human cynicism with respect to the everyday world. Hearers are cut free to imagine that new things can enter their world. Is this new world so outrageous that there is not much to do about it, except wait for it? Here the sermon receives the mode of an ethical imperative. Decrease what is old and destructive, and increase life-giving compassion and forgiveness. Advent requires that we attend to both the outrageousness of God and the daily work of decreasing.

How does theology function here? Brueggemann construes a form of *dialectical* relationship: God's new world is wholly other. The antithesis between ordinary life and the kingdom of God is extremely strong. Furthermore, by evoking a narrative perspective and using a high potential of symbolic and poetical eloquence, God's new world almost sounds somewhat fictional. One might ask, To what do these assertions about God's new world refer? What kind of truth claim is involved? It turns out that exactly this outrageous otherness has a critical and transforming power with respect to the life-style in the community of faith: decrease what is destructive. One could argue that this lessens the referential dimension of God-talk and falls short of the good news of the gospel.

In a sermon on Acts 2 Barbara Brown Taylor introduces the Holy Spirit as a power present in the riches

of ordinary experience. The Holy Spirit swoops in and out among us, knitting us together through the breaths we breathe. She constructs her perspective on the Holy Spirit from "below" rather than from "above." The Spirit is as common and near to us as the air we breathe. She suggests that the air we breathe keeps circulating around our planet (and has circulated from creation onward), and using this figure, she connects Jesus' last breath with the rush of a violent wind on the day of Pentecost:

> When Jesus let go of his last breath—willingly, we believe, for love of us—that breath hovered in the air in front of him for a moment and then it was set loose on earth. It was such a pungent breath—so full of passion, so full of life—that it did not simply dissipate as so many breaths do. It grew, in strength and in volume, until it was a mighty wind, which God sent spinning through an upper room in Jerusalem on the day of the Pentecost. God wanted to make sure that Jesus' friends were the inheritors of Jesus' breath, and it worked. (1999, 144)

According to Taylor, divine presence is found in ordinary life. Our problem, however, is this: Do we recognize the Spirit when acting? In her sermon she offers a few focal instances of how the Spirit might be at work. Sometimes, for example, we do not know how to name our experiences. "But just in case you have had some things happen to you that you do not have a name for, I want to suggest some ways I believe the Holy Spirit acts" (147). Or, another example, when someone is estranged from someone and she finds a way back into relationship: "You can call that anything you want. I call it an act of the Holy Spirit" (148).

What kind of theological truth claim is involved? Unlike Brueggemann, Taylor assumes a strong continuity between the ordinary and the holy. The ways of the Spirit are neither ecstatic nor spectacular. Furthermore she describes the manifestations of the Spirit by means of analogical connections. Consequently, the divine presence is suggested to be immanent and intimate. Taylor runs the risk of naming God without accounting for the external, critical divine initiative. This, too, seems to fall short of the gospel.

Criteria for God-talk

In sermons the messy realm of work, love, celebration, and suffering, where human beings dwell, is represented in relationship to God. Preachers have the calling to speak about God's saving involvement in the scary, lovely, hurting life, with all its failures and sadness, with all its sudden bits of joy and happiness. Precisely good theology helps us to generate meaningful God-talk in relation to our-being-in-the-world.

The gospel is not a naive solution to our problems. Yet the preacher as a theologian finds the courage to confess that the dynamic presence of God in Jesus Christ shapes our mode of being-in-the-world. The dogmas and doctrines of the church can offer help; they articulate the depth and richness of salvation and qualify the mystery of God's presence in the world. Dogmas and doctrines can function as guidelines for adequate God-talk. By paying attention to them, preachers can increase theological competence.

Contemporary listeners need some sort of confessional framework to interpret the societal and spiritual quest of our postmodern time. Recovering the more reflective dimensions of faith may help preachers to dig deeper into the mysteries of life and to consider and reconsider both certitudes and unsettled questions. Hence in addition to narrative and inductive preaching, thoughtful reflection and argumentative discourse may help to shape the identities of the communities of faith. Therefore, preachers should not be too afraid to reflect on the dynamic presence of God in Jesus Christ and on the work of the indwelling Spirit. What do the vicissitudes of life look like in a faith relationship? How do we handle the challenges of real life? A preacher has the calling to help the community to come to terms with these issues. Seen from this perspective, the preacher is not only a pastor, but also a reflective co-believer.

God-talk is risky. But the preacher cannot run away; one has to speak about God and the kingdom to come. Sometimes one even speaks a word *of* God. One cannot do so without a solid exegesis of Scripture and a sense of contextual hermeneutics. As a co-believer, the preacher is also aware of the local theology of the community. Since God-talk is experientially and socially embedded in a local community, the preacher should stand in a relation of *fit* to the local community. As a trained theologian, the preacher is also familiar with the broader theological tradition of the church. A Protestant preacher, for example, is aware of the fact that God-talk, as it is enacted in the interaction of preaching and

listening, can become a *Word of God*, that is, an encounter in which people experience salvation and receive renewal.

Precisely this dimension, namely, sermonic interaction becoming a *Word of God*, calls for theological competence. It refers to the external origin of salvation: it is God who initiates the relationship, restores justice, and transforms us in Jesus Christ. It is the preacher's task to enact this divine disclosure and eschatological perspective adequately such that it fits the actual context. It is almost impossible to preach on resurrection, miracles, parables, prophecy, the promised land, and so on without the construction and reconstruction of pulpit theology. Preaching requires a specific theological habit: an open mind and heart for the divine disclosure. *See* AUTHORITY OF THE PREACHER; CALL; SERMON AS PROCLAMATION.

Bibliography: Walter Brueggemann. *The Threat of Life: Sermons on Pain, Power, and Weakness.* (1996); F. Gerrit Immink. *Faith: A Practical Theological Reconstruction.* (2005); Richard Lischer. *The End of Words: The Language of Reconciliation in a Culture of Violence.* (2005); Barbara Brown Taylor. *Home by Another Way.* (1999).

❖   ❖   ❖   ❖

ANTHROPOLOGY
Amy Plantinga Pauw

Theological anthropology is Christian reflection on the nature of humanity before God and the meaning and responsibility of life. Several basic claims may be made concerning human beings. We are (1) good and beloved creatures of God; (2) sinners; (3) redeemed in Jesus Christ by the power of the Holy Spirit; (4) awaiting our promised consummation. Our existence is intrinsically relational. The preacher shares and addresses every aspect of human identity.

A. The Fourfold Human Drama
    1. Creation
    2. Sin
    3. Redemption
    4. Consummation

B. Existence in Relation
  1. Hospitality to the Stranger
  2. Sexuality
C. Preaching the Life Cycle
  1. Baptism
  2. Calling
  3. Marriage
  4. Death

A. The Fourfold Human Drama

Christian anthropology depicts human persons as participants in a fourfold drama. We are good and beloved creatures of God. We are sinners. We are redeemed in Jesus Christ by the power of the Holy Spirit. We await our promised consummation. These human identities, in both their individual and their communal forms, are best seen as simultaneous, not sequential (Jones 2003, 143). We remain sinners, even as we celebrate our redemption. We remain finite creatures, subject to death, even as we anticipate our glorious consummation. Keeping these four identities in view counters the tendency, especially in Western preaching, to collapse the human condition into a sequence of sin and redemption. The fourfold drama also reminds us that the first and last word on us is joy: we were created out of God's overflowing joy, and our consummation is everlasting, joyful communion with this same God.

1. Creation

The psalmist proclaims, "For it was you who formed my inward parts; / you knit me together in my mother's womb. / I praise you, for I am fearfully and wonderfully made" (Ps 139:13-14). Being a creature fearfully and wonderfully made in the image of God (Gen 1:26-27) is the common truth about all human persons. Our many differences complicate and enrich our human unity but do not contradict it. Ignoring the baseline truth of our created goodness falsely narrows preaching and can lead to distorted understandings of human sin and redemption. This is particularly true regarding the goodness of our bodies. Feminist theology rightly affirms bodily existence as a divine gift, while at the same time warning against pigeonholing or devaluing people on the basis of bodily differences. Sermons should not portray our bodily existence primarily as a source of temptation and suffering. Neither should the essence of a person's identity be located in physical characteristics or abilities, such as race or the ability to bear children. Preachers should also be careful about using physical disabilities, such as deafness and blindness, as metaphors for human sin.

To be a creature is to be contingent. Our very existence is a gift of God's grace. Therefore, dependence is the mode of our being. This is not an enslaving or demeaning dependence, but the presupposition for our freedom and agency. Human freedom should be construed neither as utter self-determination nor as simply a matter of rights and entitlements. Our freedom is a gift of God and is meant for God and others. Law and covenant are God's gifts to help us exercise our freedom in right relation with God and neighbor. In a culture that highly values autonomy and self-sufficiency, preachers rightly insist that human beings are not their own makers and keepers and cannot find authentic life except in relation to God, the source of all life.

To be a creature is to be finite. We are embodied beings who change and grow, get sick and die. Our finitude marks us as different from God. But it is not a negative judgment on us and does not contradict our created goodness. Our redemption is not redemption from finitude. Preaching positively on human finitude helps disassociate sickness and death from human sin and divine judgment. Our material needs and desires require that we live in interdependence with other creatures, both human and non-human. Living in a way that sustains the planet is part of our faithfulness as God's creatures. This is the theological root of sermons on ecology.

2. Sin

Being a sinner is another universal truth about human persons. But sin is a corruption of our human identity, not the ultimate truth about us; this means that sin should not be the pivot on which preaching about human existence turns. Sin is best portrayed as a general human condition, not a list of discrete acts, though it can certainly give rise to individual acts that are sinful. Two classical images are helpful in preaching on sin. First, sin is an intruder and a parasite: it feeds on and contaminates our good creatureliness. Second, living contrary to God's intentions for us is intergenerational: we inherit sin, claim it as our own, and pass it on to others. Sermons on sin should avoid one-sidedness: we are victims of sin, yet also responsible for it; sin lurks both in individuals and in the structures and patterns of our corporate life.

Sin incurs God's wrath. God is angry at sin because God wants us to flourish. Whether it takes the form of pride and rebellion or sloth and self-denigration, sin denies what we were made for: to stand in God's glorious presence as holy and whole creatures. One of sin's most pernicious effects is to deceive us about the reality and consequences of our own sinfulness. Jonathan Edwards's famous sermon "Sinners in the Hands of an Angry God" emphasizes the comforting self-deceptions of sinners in the face of their precarious hold on life. Like all good sermons on sin and divine wrath, Edwards ends by reminding his hearers that "Christ has flung the door of mercy wide open." God's grace functions to unmask our sin and show us who we really are. But that same grace also gives us hope for forgiveness and renewal.

Preachers do not escape their own sinful condition even when preaching on sin. Words from the pulpit have tremendous power to bless and to curse, and preachers must be wary of the sin of sin-talk. Sermons on sin should avoid dividing the world into sinners and non-sinners, targeting those with little social power, playing on negative cultural stereotypes, or making sin the essence of a person or group. Humility and penitence are the rule when preaching on sin. Preachers consistently get into trouble when their question is, What is God's word about them and their sin? Naming sin is always for the purpose of seeking God's forgiveness and deliverance.

3. Redemption

Redemption from sin is a central feature of God's dealings with humanity. God "does not deal with us according to our sins, / nor repay us according to our iniquities," but is instead constantly at work redeeming our life "from the Pit" (Ps 103:10, 4). Indeed, wherever in the world we see deliverance from evil and suffering, liberation of the captive, reconciliation among enemies, healing of alienation, there God's redemptive power is at work. But for Christians, the paradigm of all manifestations of redemption is the life, death, and resurrection of Jesus Christ. In most of Western Christianity, Christ's cross and resurrection are the heart of the good news. Eastern Christianity puts special emphasis on the union with God made possible for us through the perfected and glorified humanity of Christ. Pentecostal theology emphasizes the power of the Holy Spirit in releasing us from sin and evil. Human redemption is the work of the whole Godhead, and preachers should avoid systematically neglecting one or more persons of the Trinity or, even worse, setting them in opposition to each other, for example, contrasting an angry Father and a merciful Son. Sermons on redemption should follow the example of Scripture and employ a variety of images to show how we are made "at one" with God. Always falling back on images of Christ paying our debt or taking on our punishment, for example, impoverishes the good news of redemption and makes it hard for some people to hear it.

Redemption is not an individual "afterlife insurance" policy. Redemption transforms us already now, and this transformation is communal as well as personal. The Apostle Paul declares, "So if anyone is in Christ, there is a new creation: everything old has passed away; see, everything has become new!" (2 Cor 5:17). This new creation is both a present gift and a lifelong calling. Theologians have distinguished these two dimensions of redemption by the terms *justification* and *sanctification.* In his powerful sermon "You Are Accepted," Paul Tillich preaches justification, exhorting his hearers to "simply accept the fact that you are accepted!" (Tillich 1987, 201). By contrast, Dietrich Bonhoeffer's famous reflections on "the cost of discipleship" call Christians to ongoing sanctification in community (Bonhoeffer, 2001). Both themes, as well as the links between them, deserve attention in preaching.

Christians differ about the role of human agency in redemption: Is faith primarily a free human response or a divine gift? The renowned preaching of Billy Graham, for example, emphasizes the need for individual human decision in response to God's offer of salvation. To what extent is the church an efficacious mediator of redemption? Sharing sacraments and the Word and acting in mission are central here, though understandings vary. But all Christians agree that redemption is made possible by God's grace, and that redeemed life is lived out in community. What about the redemption of non-Christians? Here the overall message of the Bible is of the "wideness of God's mercy." Christian preachers should witness as best they can to the grace poured out in Jesus Christ through the power of the Spirit, trusting that this is not a narrow or stingy grace, and is in any case not theirs to bestow or to withhold.

4. Consummation

This earthly life, with all its joys and sorrows, is not all there is, and will not last forever. One day it will pass away, and our transient human achievements and failures will pass away with it. This is true on both an individual and a cosmic level. However, Scripture assures us that "love never ends" (1 Cor 13:8), and that assurance should inform our earthly priorities. Consummation invites temporal images: beyond death lie eternity and everlasting life. Consummation also invites spatial images: beyond the chaos and injustice and anguish of this world lies the new Jerusalem, the kingdom of God, the realm where God's will is done. These spatial images depict our hopes for Christ's second coming. In our earthly space and time, consummation is experienced only in glimpses and glimmers. It is the stuff of visions and poetry. Consummation thus poses special challenges and dangers for preachers, and is often preached in ways that contradict Christian convictions about creation, sin, and redemption. For example, consummation has been articulated in individualistic, disembodied ways that deny the goodness of communal and bodily existence. It has been used to justify earthly suffering and injustice by the promise of heavenly compensation. It has been a repository for an unmitigated divine wrath that seems to contradict the gospel message of God's creative and redemptive mercy. Overconfidence in preaching on consummation leads to preoccupation with timetables and metaphysical explanations. Timidity leads to general avoidance of the subject, except for vague platitudes at funerals.

Good sermons on consummation adopt a firm posture of trust and hope, grounded in the conviction of God's faithful and transforming presence. They do not pretend to walk by sight rather than by faith. They are not escapist or vengeful. Martin Luther King Jr.'s preaching is exemplary for the way it aligns present realities with the ultimate promises of faith. His sermons take us "up to the mountain top" and show us "the promised land" in ways that inspire and encourage Christian discipleship down in the valleys.

B. Existence in Relation

Preachers should resist contributing to the pervasive individualism of contemporary culture in their anthropological sermons. Creation, sin, redemption, and consummation are all intrinsically relational: they concern the intricate webs of relationship with God and neighbor that constitute our human identity. Preachers should take special care to avoid individualistic understandings of redemption and consummation. Having a "personal relationship" with God is inseparable from right relation to our neighbor: "Those who say, 'I love God,' and hate their brothers or sisters, are liars" (1 John 4:20). The most profound image of our final hope is feasting together at the eschatological banquet table.

Preaching on our existence in relation raises some of the most inflammatory topics in contemporary culture: differences of race, class, religion, and sexuality.

1. Hospitality to the Stranger

God's all-embracing hospitality is the presupposition for every aspect of our lives—physical, social, and spiritual. God calls us to enter into the interplay of divine hospitality by offering hospitality. While it is tempting to content ourselves with cozy gatherings of the culturally homogeneous, God calls us to defy boundaries of race, class, and religion by offering hospitality to the stranger (Lev 19:33-34). Since most congregations are culturally homogeneous, sermons on hospitality are an invitation to both interior transformation and wider, deeper relations with others.

2. Sexuality

Scripture reflects the ambiguity of human sexuality. Sexual relations are a metaphor for both our union with God (Eph 5:25-32) and our unfaithfulness to God (Hos 1:2-3). Sexual relations are an expression of maximum human openness and vulnerability: in them, persons become "one flesh." They therefore carry the potential for great joy and intimacy, but also great physical and emotional harm. We are both good creatures and sinners in our sexual relations. However, sexuality is not the most fundamental marker of our human identity in the church and before God. Our unity as beloved creatures of God and as those made one in Christ is stronger than any sexual differences.

Sexual mores shift across the span of biblical tradition, from the acceptance of polygamy in ancient Israel to Paul's counsel to celibacy (1 Cor 7:6-9). Biological offspring are a sign of divine blessing (Ps 127:3-5), but their importance is relativized in the teaching of Jesus (Matt 10:37; 12:47-50). Preachers must be honest about the range of biblical teaching on human sexuality, and not present their favorite passages as the biblical view. Homosexual orientation is a modern concept that is not within Scripture's purview. Same-sex activity is a peripheral concern of Scripture. Where it does come up, it is related to other, more crucial communal issues: in the OT, threats to Israel's physical and spiritual survival as a people (Lev 20:13); in the NT, Gentile unworthiness in the context of God's acting "against nature" to graft them into the covenant promises given to Israel (Rom 1:26-27; 11:24). Preachers should assume that persons of homosexual orientation are among their hearers. Thus, any sermon about homosexuality must concern "God's word to us" (see the cautions above regarding the "sin of sin-talk").

C. Preaching the Life Cycle

One of the great privileges of preachers is to be present at pivotal moments in people's lives. Sermons on these occasions should address multiple aspects of the human condition.

1. Baptism
Baptism marks a beginning. In the case of infant baptism, this includes a biological beginning; in other cases, the beginning of a new life of faith. So it is always appropriate at baptism to give thanks for earthly life and for the sustenance and renewal of it by God's grace. Baptism is the beginning of a new life in community, not merely a family ritual. God says to the baptisand and to the gathered witnesses, "You belong to me, and therefore you belong to one another." In baptism we affirm our ties to our Christian brothers and sisters across time and space, most of whom we will never meet. Baptism does not mark the end of life as a sinner. But it is a sacrament of God's promise to wash away our sin, and thus, it is something to cling to throughout our lives, especially when we feel overwhelmed by our sin. Baptism is a death to sin that prefigures our final resurrection with Christ.

2. Calling
Commissioning youth on mission trips, installing church officers, and ordaining new pastors are all times to recognize the generosity of God in calling us as ambassadors of divine reconciliation. In shaping their sermons, preachers should be alert to those in the congregation whose gifts and talents are nei-

ther nurtured nor officially recognized. God's calling does not transcend our creaturely vulnerabilities or our sinfulness; it regularly takes us beyond our boundaries of competence and comfort. Sermons should thus stress that we are called to depend on God's grace and forgiveness, not our own strength and gifts. Consummation is the horizon for divine calling: the love we show to God and others will bear fruit in eternity.

3. Marriage
Marriage is a promise of lifelong faithfulness to another, relying on and echoing God's perfect faithfulness. It presupposes the goodness of embodied life. Marriage is not a shared selfishness: it makes space for more love to flourish. It is thus a gift to the entire community. With so many marriages ending in divorce, it is appropriate to call on the support of the community to help marriages thrive. Preachers should avoid tying the joy and fruitfulness of marriage too tightly to the procreation of children. As theologian Mercy Amba Oduyoye notes, our highest calling is to multiply the fullness of humanity that is found in Christ and to fill the earth with the glory of God.

4. Death
Consummation is not the only appropriate anthropological theme for funerals. Our hope for everlasting life permits no evasion of death's hard reality. Funeral sermons should make room for lament, particularly when the gift of creaturely life has been cut short. After Jesus' famous promise in John 11:25, he weeps with Martha and Mary over the death of their brother, Lazarus. Death is both personal and communal: "We do not live to ourselves, and we do not die to ourselves" (Rom 14:7). It is a great comfort to know that when we die, the community will gather to grieve and to celebrate our lives. By participating in the dying of others, we are preparing for our own deaths. *See* EXEGESIS OF THE CONGREGATION, DENOMINATION; FUNERAL; GOD, ETHICS AND; WEDDING.

Bibliography: Kathleen D. Billman and Daniel L. Migliore. *Rachel's Cry: Prayer of Lament and Rebirth of Hope.* (1999); Dietrich Bonhoeffer. *Discipleship.* Dietrich Bonhoeffer Works. Vol. 4. (2001); Serene Jones. "What's Wrong with Us?" *Essentials of Christian Theology.* Edited by William Placher. (2003) 141–58; Stephen G. Ray Jr. *Do No Harm: Social Sin and Christian Responsibility.*

(2003); Jonathan Sacks. *The Dignity of Difference: How to Avoid the Clash of Civilizations.* (2002); Paul Tillich. "You Are Accepted." *The Essential Tillich: An Anthology of the Writings of Paul Tillich.* Edited by F. Forrester Church. (1987) 194–202.

AUTHORITY (THEOLOGY)
Thomas G. Long

Although Christian preachers do not have "worldly" authority in the usual senses, they do, nevertheless, possess authority in their preaching. This authority comes from being authorized by God to speak and from the capacity of hearers to discern in their sermons a word from God.

A. The Ironic Authority of the Preacher
B. Authority through Authorization and through Reception
   1. Authorization
     a. God
     b. Jesus Christ
     c. The gospel
     d. The church
   2. Reception
     a. Rational-legal authority in preaching
     b. Traditional authority in preaching
     c. Charismatic authority in preaching
     d. The forms of preaching authority in relationship

A. The Ironic Authority of the Preacher

In a deep sense, even to raise the question of the authority of the preacher and of the sermon is to enter the world of irony. Usually, when we speak of someone in authority, we are referring to the possession of a certain kind of recognized and legitimate power, but Christian preachers (and the Hebrew prophets before them) have often insisted that they do not have such power, at least in its conventional forms. Jeremiah shirked the mantle of the "prophet," protesting that he was "only a boy" (Jer 1:6), and Isaiah cowered in the Temple before the smoke-shrouded mystery, exclaiming that he was "lost . . . a man of unclean lips" (Isa 6:5). Amos protested that he was neither a prophet nor the son of a prophet, but a mere "herdsman, and a dresser of sycamore

trees" who had been plucked out of the pasture and thrust, without much say in the matter, into the task of prophecy (Amos 7:15). Pontius Pilate, interrogating the prisoner Jesus of Nazareth, could not believe that Jesus seemed oblivious to the basic structures of power. "Do you not know," he sputtered, "that I have power to release you, and power to crucify you?" (John 19:10) In other words, to ordinary eyes Pilate was the authority figure; Jesus was not. Those who heard the bold preaching of Peter and John were amazed not only by their words but also by the fact that they "were uneducated and ordinary men" (Acts 4:13), in other words, men devoid of the learning and status that were considered typical sources of authority in the ancient world. Paul confessed to the Corinthian church that his sermons were saturated not with worldly wisdom and power but with terror. "I came to you," he said, "in weakness and in fear and in much trembling" (1 Cor 2:3).

In short, any discussion of the authority of the Christian preacher must begin with its negation: the frequency with which biblical models for proclamation distinctly underscore the lack of traditional authority. Before there can be any talk of the power and authority of preaching, there must be an acknowledgment of the lack of power, the loss of authority, involved in preaching. In one of his sermons, Augustine, aware of the fact that as he preached he was seated like a ruler or a judge on a throne-like *cathedra*, the traditional posture of authority in antiquity, took care to undermine the image. "Do not think," he said, "just because we speak to you from this elevated spot—that for that reason, we are your teachers. There is One who is the teacher of all, the One whose *cathedra* is above the heavens" (*Sermo* 301A.2, quoted in Harmless 1995, 167–68).

B. Authority through Authorization and through Reception

On the other hand, preachers, even while rejecting the picture of themselves as authority figures, are much like other orators. They are often in positions of recognized leadership; they address groups of people using ordinary human language; and they both depend upon and utilize the same sources and strategies of authority as any other public speaker. Usually, the authority of a speaker, such as a preacher, can be described in two primary ways: in terms of authorization and in terms of reception. Authorization has to do with where and how preachers and other speakers receive the power, the mandate, the validation, and the motivation to speak. Reception, on the other hand, has more to do with the dynamics of human communication. What is it about a speaker and a message, a preacher and a sermon, that causes those who hear to confer authority on the person who speaks and on what is said? A public schoolteacher, for example, is authorized to teach by the Board of Education. But having a teacher's certificate simply gets one in the classroom door. Once inside, only if the teacher is knowledgeable, personable, and skillful will the second kind of authority come into play and the students receive the teacher as authoritative.

1. Authorization

In terms of authorization, the authority to preach derives from God, from Jesus Christ, from the gospel, and from the church.

a. God. The act of preaching is ultimately a response to the command of God to serve as a witness. A mark of authenticity among the Hebrew prophets was that they did not in any sense volunteer for the role, but were instead commissioned to preach by God, summoned, sometimes against their will, by divine mandate to the task of proclaiming the Word. Jeremiah's description of his call is dramatic, but not atypical:

> "Now the word of the LORD came to me saying, / 'Before I formed you in the womb I knew you, / and before you were born I consecrated you; / I appointed you a prophet to the nations.' / Then I said, 'Ah, Lord GOD! Truly I do not know how to speak, for I am only a boy.' But the LORD said to me, / 'Do not say, "I am only a boy"; / for you shall go to all to whom I send you, / and you shall speak whatever I command you. / Do not be afraid of them, for I am with you to deliver you, / says the LORD" (Jer 1:4-8).

For Jesus, his authority as a preacher also comes from God, but his authorization to preach derives less from a specific call experience and more from his status as divine Son. In the Gospel of Mark, Jesus is baptized, at which a heavenly voice announces him as "my Son, the beloved" (Mark 1:11). The baptism leads immediately to his being tempted in the wilderness, and then, signaled by the arrest of John the Baptizer, Jesus' public ministry begins—a ministry inaugurated by preaching: "Jesus came to Galilee, proclaiming the good news of God, and saying, 'The time is fulfilled, and the

kingdom of God has come near; repent, and believe in the good news'" (Mark 1:14-15). The connection between Jesus' identity as a Beloved Son and his preaching is reaffirmed at the transfiguration, when the divine voice again declares, "This is my Son, the Beloved," and then adds the command, "Listen to him!" (Mark 9:7).

b. Jesus Christ. The disciples, and Christian preachers who follow them, are commissioned by God, too, but their divine mandate to preach comes more particularly from Jesus himself. The proclamation of Christian preachers was understood from the beginning to be both an extension of Jesus' own preaching and a ministry specifically commanded and authorized by Jesus. Jesus sends out the twelve apostles "to proclaim the kingdom of God" (Luke 9:2), and later he sends out seventy others, promising that "whoever listens to you listens to me" (Luke 10:16). In the final words of Matthew's Gospel, Jesus says to the eleven remaining disciples, "All authority in heaven and on earth has been given to me. Go therefore and make disciples of all nations" (Matt 28:18-19). In Acts, when he was preaching at Caesarea, Peter explicitly names the authorization of Jesus when he states, "[Jesus] commanded us to preach to the people and to testify that he is the one ordained by God as judge of the living and the dead" (Acts 10:42). Christian preachers throughout the history of the church have understood themselves to engage in the act of preaching not on their own authority but in obedience to the command of Christ.

c. The gospel. When Peter says that Jesus not only commanded the disciples to preach but also to "testify that he is the one ordained by God" (Acts 10:42), this points to a theological shift that occurred in the formation of the church: from the preaching of Jesus to the preaching about Jesus. Christian preachers not only continue to preach Jesus' message of the kingdom of God; they now begin to proclaim the gospel about Jesus, that the life, death, and resurrection of Jesus the Christ are themselves the constitutive core of that kingdom reality. Much of the authority of Christian preaching comes not through the sheer act of forceful speaking, but in proclaiming a message that is faithful to the gospel. When Paul indicates to the Corinthians that he "handed on" to them "as of first importance" what he "in turn had received: that Christ died for our sins in accordance with the scriptures, and that he was buried, and that he was raised on the third day in accordance with the scriptures" (1 Cor 15:3-4), he is pointing to the fact that the authority of his preaching and teaching was not a matter of originality, but of biblical and kerygmatic fidelity. Since the beginning, Christians have measured the effectiveness and trustworthiness of preaching over against these authorizing norms.

d. The church. The church itself serves as an authorizing agent for preaching in two principal ways. First, it acts on behalf of God in calling and commissioning people to preach. We can almost surely see an early form of this ecclesiastical authorization of preaching in Acts, which describes the Holy Spirit inspiring the church at Antioch to "set apart for me Barnabas and Saul for the work to which I have called them" (Acts 13:2). What follows is essentially an ordination service for Barnabas and Saul (including fasting, prayer, and the laying on of hands), after which they are sent to Cyprus to preach. In short, the Christian community at Antioch listened to the Spirit, heard God calling two people in their community for the work of preaching, and set in motion a process to recognize and authorize that divine call. Just so, employing a variety of means and procedures, the church today continues to call, prepare, ordain, and commission preachers.

The second way in which the church serves as an authorizing agent for preaching is by setting out and enforcing standards for those who preach. Not everybody who waves a Bible in the air and claims to be a preacher sent by God is, in fact, in tune with the Holy Spirit, and it falls to the church to test the spirits and to separate the wheat from the chaff.

2. Reception

While preachers may be authorized by God, faithful to the gospel, and endorsed by the church, none of this is any guarantee that their sermons will actually be received by hearers as authoritative. Jesus' own inaugural sermon in his hometown synagogue was rejected, but the crowd that gathered for the Sermon on the Mount was astonished by his sermon because Jesus "taught them as one having authority, and not as their scribes" (Matt 7:29). The missionary preaching of Paul left the ancient world populated with new Christians and new churches, but it was punctuated by one homiletical failure after another, so much so that his last sermon of which we have a record quotes these pessimistic words from Isaiah: "Go to this people and say, / You

will indeed listen, but never understand, / and you will indeed look, but never perceive. / For this people's heart has grown dull, / and their ears are hard of hearing" (Isa 6:9-10 cited in Acts 28:26-27). As preachers, Jesus and Paul were full of authority in the authorized sense, but only here and there authoritative in the reception sense.

If it is true that authentic witnesses are sometimes denied the status of authority by their hearers, it is also quite possible for a non-authorized preacher, an irresponsible and unfaithful proclaimer, to gather an enthusiastic and receptive crowd. One may hope to find people "pressing in . . . to hear the word of God" (Luke 5:1), as Luke describes the crowd gathering around Jesus beside the Sea of Galilee, but sometimes the crowd simply screams, "Away with Jesus. Give us instead Barabbas!" (John 18:40, author's trans.).

What causes people to hear one preacher with open ears and receptive hearts and to reject another? Why does this sermon catch fire and strike the listeners' ears with great authority, but the next one receives only a shrug and a yawn? In other words, what makes some preachers and sermons authoritative to listeners but others not?

The reasons are complex, of course, but a well-known analysis of authority by the sociologist Max Weber can help us to see some of the categories and factors at work. Weber identified three types of authority: rational-legal, traditional, and charismatic (Weber 1946, 78–79). Rational-legal authority rests on a belief in the legality of certain rules, laws, and regulations and the power of authority figures to enforce them. When the parking lot attendant says, "You are not allowed to park on the first three floors of the garage; those spaces are reserved," most people dutifully receive this news as authoritative and obey the attendant, even if the attendant might not be viewed as an authoritative figure in any other setting. There are rules in this parking lot, and the attendant is the logical person to enforce them. Traditional authority rests upon time-honored traditions and values. In very traditional societies, for example, children look up to adults and obey them as authority figures, not because there is a rule or a law that adults must be obeyed but because of deeply rooted values shaped over time. "In this society," people say, "we honor those older than we; that's just the way it is." Charismatic authority is found where people respond to the extraordinary personal qualities and popular appeal of the one seeking to exert authority—his or her heroism, strong moral character, passion, energy, verbal skills, and so on. When a popular and electric television host recommends a certain book, and the sales of that title suddenly jump by the millions, then charismatic authority has been exercised.

a. Rational-legal authority in preaching. While rational-legal authority is not usually a major factor in preaching, this form of authority is not entirely absent. To a high degree in some Christian traditions, and to at least some degree in almost all Christian traditions, the one who preaches is a legally established authority in a congregation. One Protestant denomination, at the time a new minister is established in a congregation, asks the members to say yes to the preacher's official authority: "Will we listen to the word he or she preaches . . . and honor his or her authority . . . ?" In modern democratic societies, however, where even presidents and prime ministers govern by permission of the people, such rational-legal authority is generally not the main source of receptive authority of the preacher.

b. Traditional authority in preaching. Much more potent for preaching is the traditional basis for authority. In many Christian denominations and groups, the preacher is a living embodiment of the immediacy of God's Word—a symbolic, priestly, in some ways even sacramental, presence. The fact that the preacher is the one who, time and again and at a high moment in the ritual of worship, speaks the sermon imbues the preacher with respect, spiritual power, and authority.

It is in this arena of tradition that some of the more troubling issues of preaching authority have been raised. For example, in the historic Christian traditions, where the clerical offices have been dominated by males, female preachers have often reported the experience, externally caused or internally felt, of feeling silenced in the pulpit. Even when the structures of rational-legal authority are in place, when the rules and laws of a church group permit women to preach, the weight of the tradition can still lean heavily against them.

c. Charismatic authority in preaching. Increasingly today, the most significant form of authority in preaching is the personal skill and magnetism of the preacher. The charismatic dimension of authority, that is, the capacity of preachers to sway congregations by their personal power, has always been present in the Christian movement.

Paul was aware that the Corinthian congregation complained that, while his letters were strong and persuasive, his actual presence and speaking ability were less than desirable (2 Cor 10:10), a sign that the Corinthians desired charisma in their preachers and faulted Paul for his lack in this area. Augustine, Chrysostom, Luther, Wesley, Sojourner Truth, and many other preachers after them have been acclaimed for charismatic preaching power. By the middle of the 19th cent., though, the charismatic authority of preachers began to trump the other forms. In a famous Yale lecture on preaching in the late 19th cent., Boston preacher Phillips Brooks nodded toward charismatic authority in preaching when he underscored the essential personal dimension of the preaching event: "Truth through personality is our description of real preaching" (1893, 8). Today, from the rhetorical savvy of a highly poetic preacher to the "aw shucks" pulpit friendliness of a mega-church charmer, many congregations have come to value the forcefulness of what happens in the moment of preaching over traditional authority and, certainly, over the mandates of rational-legal authority. Preachers are given high marks and granted authority for being "sincere," for "really believing what they say," for "passion" and "energy." The danger in overemphasizing the charismatic dimension of authority is, of course, that the preacher becomes the focus of preaching rather than the gospel.

d. The forms of preaching authority in relationship. Weber readily acknowledged that his three forms of authority were ideal types and rarely, if ever, existed in actual society in pure form (Weber 1946, 79). In fact, every act of preaching customarily finds all three forms—rational-legal, traditional, and charismatic—in operation together. Especially since the Reformation, the history of preaching has been marked by the two strongest forms of authority, the traditional and the charismatic, existing in tension with each other and vying for prominence. Traditional authority tends to emphasize churchly order, orthodoxy, and stability, while charismatic authority emphasizes the power of the laity, innovation, and change and reform. The church needs both, of course, and satisfies its need through a constant tug-of-war over the authority of preaching. Whenever the traditional form of authority begins to dominate, there will arise almost certainly a movement—for example, the Baptists or the Methodists—emphasizing the power of the Spirit to summon the Word in ways and in people no ecclesial tradition or institutional structure can control. On the other hand, when the charismatic form of authority governs preaching, there will inevitably be excesses and deviations from the gospel that prompt the church to look once again to its tradition to ground preaching. *See* AUTHORITY OF THE PREACHER; CALL; ETHOS; EXEGESIS OF THE CONGREGATION, DENOMINATION; ORDINATION; SERMON AS PROCLAMATION; WORD OF GOD.

Bibliography: Phillips Brooks. *Lectures on Preaching.* (1893); Jackson W. Carroll. *As One with Authority: Reflective Leadership in Ministry.* (1991); William Harmless. *Augustine and the Catechumenate.* (1995); Mary Lin Hudson and Mary Donovan Turner. *Saved from Silence: Finding Women's Voice in Preaching.* (1999); Max Weber. "Politics as a Vocation." *From Max Weber: Essays in Sociology.* Translated and edited by H. H. Gerth and C. Wright Mills. (1946).

CHRISTOLOGY
Bryan Chapell

Christology is the study of the person and work of our Lord Jesus Christ. The preacher's christological task is to discern what the Bible says about Jesus and apply this truth so that hearers grow in their relationship with him and their witness to him.

The Apostle Paul underscores christology's importance by writing that our Creator reveals "the light of the knowledge of the glory of God in the face of Jesus Christ" (2 Cor 4:6). Because God reveals his glory to humanity through Jesus, our understanding of God (theology) requires study of Christ (christology). The Apostle John similarly writes that our knowledge of Christ enlightens our understanding of our union with the Father and with each other (1 John 1:1-3; compare John 1:14, 18). Ultimately, the light of all subjects concerning God must pass through the prism of christology to be seen in their full glory (John 14:6-9).

A. Historic Understanding of Christ's Person and Work
B. Historic Understanding of Christ's Person
    1. Controversies Regarding the Humanity of Christ
    2. Controversies Regarding the Divinity of Christ
    3. Councils Regarding the Humanity and Divinity of Christ
    4. Controversies Regarding the Reality of Christ
C. Historic Understanding of Christ's Work
    1. Christ as Prophet
    2. Christ as Priest
    3. Christ as King

A. Historic Understanding of Christ's Person and Work

The glorious mystery of Jesus' divine and human nature has sparked various christological controversies. Knowledge of these past problems can help steer preachers from similar errors in contemporary forms.

Biblical christology teaches that Jesus Christ is the Second Person of the Trinity. The dominant Roman Catholic and Protestant traditions have taught that Jesus is equal in power and glory with the Father, yet as the eternal Son of God, he carries out the will of the Father through the Holy Spirit. According to Scripture, Jesus was conceived by the Holy Spirit in the womb of the Virgin Mary. By his virgin birth and sinless life, Jesus lived without the stain of original sin or the guilt of personal sin. Being fully human, yet without sin, Jesus offered his life in sacrifice upon a cross and then rose from the dead. Through his sinless life, sacrificial death, and victorious resurrection, Jesus provided for human redemption and demonstrated his divine nature. Now he intercedes for his people at the right hand of the Father to further their spiritual nurture and Christian witness through his Word and Spirit. In the future Christ will come again to judge evil, claim for eternity those who have placed faith in him, and renew creation for his eternal kingdom. In all of this redeeming work, Jesus was and continues to be divine and human in two distinct natures and one person forever.

These claims of historic orthodoxy have received many challenges through the centuries, requiring the church to defend and refine its christology.

B. Historic Understanding of Christ's Person

1. Controversies Regarding the Humanity of Christ

The full humanity of Christ has been challenged since the earliest centuries of the NT church. The

Monophysites who followed Eutyches argued that the divine nature of Christ overwhelmed his human nature. The Docetists said that Jesus only appeared (seemed) to be human. The Valentinians denied that Jesus had a human body; it came from heaven. The followers of Apollinaris denied Jesus' human soul.

2. Controversies Regarding the Divinity of Christ

The divinity of Christ is more frequently challenged in secularized and pluralistic societies. The Ebionites were a Jewish sect who wanted to honor Jesus as a prophet, but denied his divinity. The Theodotians, Artemonites, Photinians, and Socinians (in the Reformation era) similarly believed that Jesus was either just a man or a divine representative who had been given special wisdom. An alternative view of Monophysitism (see above) argued that Christ's divine nature had been absorbed by the human.

Various views improperly identified how Christ's human and divine natures interacted. The Apollinarians said that the human and divine nature had coalesced into a unique third nature (*tertium quid*). The Nestorians believed the human and divine natures shared the same body but retained separate personhoods that were morally united. Various forms of Adoptionism taught that Jesus was first human and then became God. Similar to many current misunderstandings, the Sabellians (or Modalists) taught that Father, Son, and Holy Spirit were only different modes/versions (not persons) of the divine. Arians believed that Jesus was divine, but was created by the Father for the purposes of salvation.

3. Councils Regarding the Humanity and Divinity of Christ

Various councils defended biblical christology through the centuries. The First Council of Nicaea (325 CE) responded to Arius with the Nicene Creed that said the Father and the Son are "of one substance" (i.e., *homoousios*; Schaff 1984, 58–59). The Council of Chalcedon (451 CE) said the two natures are in perfect unity "inconfusedly, unchangeably, indivisibly, inseparably" (Schaff 1984, 62–63). Chalcedonian christology asserts that Jesus is fully human and fully divine. His two natures coexist in "hypostatic union," with neither diminishing the other. The natures do not commingle, merge, or replace each other but operate in

accord. Representative of Protestant orthodoxy, the Westminster Confession of Faith (1647) reiterates the Chalcedonian perspective stating that "two whole, perfect, and distinct natures, the Godhead and the manhood, were inseparably joined together in one person, without conversion, composition, or confusion. Which person is very God and very man, yet one Christ" (8.2).

4. Controversies Regarding the Reality of Christ

Differing christological perspectives can be categorized as anthropological or cosmological. An anthropological christology starts "from below" by considering the humanity of Jesus and working toward his divine attributes. A cosmological christology starts "from above," considering first Christ's divine nature. Fundamentalist (and some evangelical) theologies tend to focus on the "from above" and may struggle to affirm Christ's full humanity. Liberal (and some neo-orthodox) theologies tend to focus on the "from below" perspective and may deny the reality (or knowability) of the divine in human history. Such theologians may differentiate "the Christ of history" from "the Christ of faith," claiming that traditional descriptions of the divine/human Christ are artifacts of ecclesiastical or social perspectives on history rather than actual history.

Modern hermeneutical discussions exacerbate christological problems by postulating that the reality/essence of any subject differs from what can actually be communicated about it. Psychological schools of interpretation have approached texts as a combination of subconscious and conscious factors indiscernible by authors. Critical theorists argue the meanings of texts lie in the sociopolitical universe of the texts' past authorship (e.g., Marxist, capitalist, feminist) or present readership (e.g., existentialist, phenomenological, reader-response). As a consequence what we understand the Bible to say about Christ's nature is presumed to be merely a reflection of human circumstance or perception rather than transcendent reality (compare Kant, Schleiermacher, Bultmann). Were these conclusions to remain unchallenged, all assessments of Christ's person and work would be futile (as the more radical existential, phenomenological, and deconstructionist theorists have argued).

The fields of hermeneutics and homiletics have sought haven and continuing purpose in the thought of Hans-Georg Gadamer. He argued that real meaning can be communicated to the extent that there is a "fusion" of a text's and an individual's "horizons" (i.e., the text's meaning and the individual's field of experience). Thus, to the extent that preachers frame their sermons so as to cause listeners to experience what a text does and does not mean, substantial communication can occur. Narrative theorists have seized upon this insight, admonishing preachers to pattern their sermons so that the story of the text and the listener's experience fuse as much as possible for as much meaning transfer as is attainable. The narrative theorists have captured important dimensions of human understanding, but their contributions are incomplete without further insights into Christ's work.

C. Historic Understanding of Christ's Work

In Protestant and Roman Catholic traditions the work of Jesus Christ has been described in terms of the offices he fulfills: prophet, priest, and king.

1. Christ as Prophet

As prophet, Jesus reveals to us by his Word and Spirit the will of God for our salvation. In this role Jesus addresses modern concerns about the need for mutual experience in communication—even of matters divine. Jesus tells Nicodemus that he cannot understand heavenly things because, unlike the Son of Man, the Jewish leader had not experienced heaven (John 3:11-13). Paul similarly writes that just as no one can really understand the thoughts of another person without sharing that person's spirit, so no one can really understand the thoughts of God except the Spirit of God (1 Cor 2:11). However, the Scriptures do not leave us at this communication impasse. Paul writes, "Now we have received . . . the Spirit which is from God, that we might understand the gifts bestowed on us by God. And we impart this in words not taught by human wisdom but taught by the Spirit, interpreting spiritual truths to those who possess the Spirit" (1 Cor 2:12-13 RSV).

The Scriptures teach that Jesus sends the Holy Spirit to indwell those made in the image of God to enable their understanding of God's Word (compare John 15:26; Rom 5:5; 1 Cor 2:10-14; 2 Pet 1:20-21). Because the same Spirit that inspires Scripture indwells Christ's people, shared understanding of his Word is possible. This Word is not merely print upon a page, but the ministry of Christ to which the Scriptures and the Spirit testify (John 5:39; 15:26).

Scripture reveals Jesus as the Incarnate Word, the revelation of God in the flesh. The Apostle John refers to this Christ as the Divine Logos (Word) because he who created the cosmos came into the world to make known the divine (compare John 1:1-4, 9; 1 John 1:1-3). Paul describes Jesus as "the image of the invisible God" (Col 1:15) and says that in Christ "the whole fullness of deity dwells bodily" (Col 2:9), so that we gain "the knowledge of the glory of God in the face of Jesus Christ" (2 Cor 4:6). The writer of Hebrews says that Christ "reflects the glory of God and bears the very stamp of his nature" (Heb 1:3 RSV).

As the prophets of old revealed God's Word to his people, Christ's person and work reveal God. The Spirit that testifies of Jesus in the Scriptures and in our hearts enables us to understand the divine through him. He is the Word of (and about) God. Thus, the preaching of the Word is the continuing ministry of Christ to his people. As the Second Helvetic Confession states, "The preaching of the Word of God is the Word of God." By the proclamation of the truths of God's Word, Christ yet encounters his people. The Spirit who reveals his truth to heart and mind by communicating the inscripturated Word makes known the Incarnate Word by whom God reveals himself. This means that preaching is not merely reflection upon moral precepts taught long ago, but the continuing ministry of the presence of Christ by his Spirit to the people of God.

The preacher speaks for Christ, continuing his prophetic ministry by "re-presenting" (i.e., again presenting) the Word of God. This understanding enables the preacher to proclaim God's Word with authenticity and authority. Because Christ is present, the preacher must honestly acknowledge personal struggle, life's pain, and the need for grace that God's Word is designed to aid. At the same time, because Christ is both author and audience of the message, the preacher must not shy from messages that confront personal, congregational, or societal sin that the Word of God purposes to correct.

2. Christ as Priest

By ministering the presence of Christ to his people, preaching performs a sacramental purpose and helps define Christ's priestly office. Christ serves as a priest (in his incarnate state) by offering himself in example, sympathy, and sacrifice to conquer sin, to instruct us in holiness, and to reconcile us to God, and (in his ascended state) by making continual intercession for us at the right hand of God the Father (Rom 8:34; Heb 4:14-15). The preacher's understanding of Christ's priestly work will largely govern the motivational content of the sermon.

Three main views (often strongly contrasted) have been advanced to explain Christ's priestly work. Each view prioritizes different aspects of human need:

1. The substitutionary atonement view focuses on humanity's fall into sin's guilt that alienates us from a holy God apart from Christ's provision. His sinless life and sacrificial death are understood to provide a substitutionary sacrifice for sinful humans, satisfying the justice of God by receiving the penalty for sin and compensating for the debt of human wrongdoing.

2. The Christus Victor view focuses on humanity's fall under sin's power that enslaves us to forces greater than we can resist apart from Christ's work. His death and resurrection defeat the spiritual forces that hold us captive and enable us to live a life of spiritual freedom that honors God.

3. The moral influence view (originally Abelard; later Ritschl, Harnack, etc.) focuses on humanity's blindness to God's love. Christ's exemplary life and death demonstrate the nature of divine love, convince us of its reality, and guide us in its ethical expression.

Evangelicals and fundamentalists have perceived the substitutionary atonement view as the sine qua non of Christian witness. Neo-orthodox and liberal theologians have viewed it either as an optional expression of the Christian message or as antithetical to it. Modern sensibilities drive concerns that glorifying a Father who would sacrifice a Son to satisfy retributive justice evokes a savage God, impossible to love and in contrast to grace. Feminist, Marxist, and liberation theologians have also claimed the substitutionary atonement encourages oppressed people to accept subjugation and glorifies the redemptive value of violence. Even a few evangelicals have expressed concern that the substitutionary atonement breeds an individualistic faith, primarily concerned for alleviating personal guilt

and ignoring biblical priorities regarding justice and equity for others.

What cannot be denied, however, amid all these concerns is that the Bible teaches atonement through the sacrifice of Christ. Paul speaks of "the redemption which is in Christ Jesus, whom God put forward as an expiation by his blood" (Rom 3:24-25 RSV); and says, "For our sake [God] made him [Jesus] to be sin who knew no sin, so that in him we might become the righteousness of God" (2 Cor 5:21 RSV). Peter writes, "He himself bore our sins in his body on the tree, that we might die to sin and live to righteousness. By his wounds you have been healed" (1 Pet 2:24 RSV). Such scriptures can easily be multiplied (e.g., Rom 3:24-26; 4:25; 1 John 2:2; 4:10). In addition to these direct references to Christ's vicarious atonement, the foreshadowings of the OT sacrificial system presage how the Lamb of God, as our Great High Priest, would sacrifice himself to save his people (see 1 Cor 5:7; Heb 9:11-15; 10:10-14; 1 Pet 1:18-19; Rev 5:8-9).

Ministers who read Scripture plainly, and read well the longings of hearts burdened with guilt, preach that Jesus provides what we cannot: sacrificial reconciliation to God and satisfaction for the penalty/debt of our sin. At the same time, there is no reason to exclude other atonement views that meet other human needs. The Bible also clearly teaches that Christ's death and resurrection defeated the powers of evil (e.g., Eph 4:8), and that Jesus' moral example teaches us how to live (and die) for God and neighbor (e.g., Matt 25:45). By each of these priestly functions, Christ unites his people to himself and prepares them to glorify God (Gal 2:20). Thus, for the guilty, we preach Christ, the crucified, who has made atonement for us; for the despairing, we preach Christ, the Victor over death, who has given us new life; for the callous and uninformed, we preach Christ, the Good Shepherd, who in laying down his life for the sheep has shown us the way to live and love.

3. Christ as King

Not every scriptural text mentions Jesus (nor should be made to do so), but all the scriptures bear some relation to the redemptive message most fully revealed in him (see Luke 24:27). Christ is the King of all the scriptures; they point to him, reveal his grace, and honor his glory—as should all Christian preaching.

No passage is so limited in purpose as only to provide ethical instruction. According to Paul, even the law itself functions as our "schoolmaster to bring us unto Christ" (Gal 3:24 KJV). His story underlies every text. Christ-centered exposition of Scripture does not require us to reveal Jesus by mysterious alchemies of allegory or typology, but identifies how every text furthers our understanding of who Christ is, what the Father sent him to do, and why. Jesus is the apex of all biblical revelation (compare Matt 17:1-13).

Since the promise of Gen 3:15 (the *protoevangelium*), the persons, events, and teachings of Scripture unfold the drama of our redeeming King's progressive establishment of his reign. In addition, as the risen Lord who has conquered sin and death, Christ now advances his kingdom to subdue us by his grace, to establish his lordship, to defend us, and to defeat his (and our) enemies. Preachers maintain this kingdom perspective by demonstrating how all aspects of Scripture predict, prepare for, reflect, and/or result from the person and/or work of Christ.

Such redemptive exposition consistently demonstrates that the Lord Jesus Christ resolves the human dilemma. In union with him who possesses resurrection power, we find freedom from our fallen world and nature (Eph 1:19-23; Gal 2:20). He pardons our unrighteousness, enables our righteousness, provides for our weakness, and establishes us in the covenant and communities of blessing. His glory is always the telos of the sermon; his grace its power.

Sermons marked by consistent adulation of the mercy of God in Christ fill the heart with love for him as the primary motivation and enablement for Christian obedience and witness. We make progress against our sin and the world's corruptions because we are alive in Christ and desire to serve the Lord who saves us. *See* ALLEGORY, ALLEGORESIS; RESURRECTION; SOTERIOLOGY; SYNOPTIC GOSPELS; TYPOLOGY.

Bibliography: Bryan Chapell. *Christ-Centered Preaching: Redeeming the Expository Sermon.* 2nd ed. (2005); Paula Fredriksen. *From Jesus to Christ: The Origins of the New Testament Images of Christ.* 2nd ed. (2000); Sidney Greidanus. *Preaching Christ from the Old Testament.* (1999); Donald MacLeod. *The Person of Christ.* (1998); Klaas Runia. *The Present-Day Christological Debate.* (1984); Philip Schaff. *The Creeds of Christendom.* Vol. 2. Rev. ed. (1984); John Stott. *The Cross of Christ.* (1986); Robert B. Strimple. *The Modern Search for the Real Jesus.* (1995); N. T. Wright. *Jesus and the Victory of God.* (1997).

DOCTRINES AND BIBLICAL TEXTS
James M. Childs Jr.

Biblical preaching and doctrinal preaching are integrally—almost inextricably—related to each other. On the one hand, doctrine helps to provide the preacher with focus for the implications of the text for faith and life. On the other hand, the lively relationship in preaching between text and the human situation helps to ensure that the doctrinal implications are connected to real life; doctrinal preaching should not be simply indoctrination.

A. What Are Doctrines?
B. Doctrinal Differences and Their Significance
    1. Differences on the Basis of Scripture
    2. Differences on the Basis of Relative Importance
    3. A Common Faith
C. Theology, Doctrine, and Preaching
    1. New Insights on Traditional Doctrines
    2. New Insights on the Kingdom of God
    3. New Insights Concerning the Trinity
D. The Intersection of Biblical Text and Doctrine in Preaching
    1. Seasonal Texts and Doctrinal Reflections
       a. An Advent text
       b. An Easter text
       c. A sermon example
    2. Textual Preaching Supported by Doctrine: Sin and Grace
       a. Race: Martin Luther King Jr.
       b. Atonement: Reinhold Niebuhr
       c. Social injustice: Daisy L. Machado
    3. Doctrinal Preaching Enriched by Imagery from Various Biblical Texts
    4. Doctrinal Preaching
       a. Justification by faith
       b. The Holy Spirit

A. What Are Doctrines?

Perhaps the most obvious approach is to say that doctrine refers to the body of teachings that comprise the traditional topics of systematic or dogmatic theology. These include the doctrines of the Word, God, Trinity, creation, anthropology, sin, christology, salvation, the Holy Spirit, sanctification, church, ministry, and sacraments. Some would add prayer and ethics as separate topics. Most topics in this list are embodied in the statements of the ecumenical creeds, the Apostles' Creed, the Nicene Creed, and the Athanasian Creed. They are elaborated upon in catechisms and confessional documents. Calvin saw the concentration of the creeds on the person and work of Christ and the Trinity as the "sum of doctrine" from which all other doctrines are derivative.

B. Doctrinal Differences and Their Significance

1. Differences on the Basis of Scripture

Significant differences will be evident in the interpretation of various doctrines and their scriptural basis among different Christian communions. For example, these differences have been quite evident in teaching on the sacraments. Some insist upon a believer's baptism in which the faith commitment of the baptized is of paramount importance. Others believe in infant baptism and stress the priority of God's gracious initiative in baptism. Still, both traditions, despite these differences, each in its own way, affirm the grace of baptism and the necessity of faith. For some the Lord's Supper is a memorial feast in which Christ is spiritually present as he is in all aspects of the worship experience. For others Christ is really present in the bread and wine. Again, despite the differences noted, Christ is in some sense affirmed as truly present by all parties. As preachers incorporate reflections on baptism and the Lord's Supper into their sermons, the features held in common with other Christian traditions are a reminder of the fact that preaching is a function of the larger Christian community throughout time and space. It is not merely an expression of one's denomination, the culture of one's local congregation, or the subjectivity of the preacher. At the same time the special features of different traditions are a reminder of the particular contribution they seek to make to the larger Christian community.

2. Differences on the Basis of Relative Importance

Noteworthy differences will also be apparent on the relative importance of specific doctrines among various communions. Lutheran and other Protestant preachers are probably more likely than others to speak about justification by grace through faith. Pentecostal preachers will stress the gifts of the Spirit. One may hear echoes of John Wesley's perfectionist teachings when some Methodist preachers turn their attention to sanctification or the Christian life. Some perspectives on salvation in Christ will lead preachers to emphasize God's grace and forgiveness, having faith in the power of the Spirit working through that word to create faith. Others, while certainly affirming salvation in Christ, emphasize the act of faith by calling for people to step forward and make a decision to accept him as their personal Savior.

3. A Common Faith

The doctrines embodied in the creeds and in various confessional and theological traditions, subjected though they are to some diversity of interpretation and emphasis, are still expressive of a common deposit of the faith. They are expressive of the long historical process of the church reflecting on the Scriptures in an effort to give clear and coherent expression to what they tell us about God and the purposes of God for us and our world. This process was always an effort to meet a need: to stem the tide of teachings that seemed destructive of the very core of the biblical witness; to bring about needed biblically based reforms, as in the Reformation; to settle controversies over finer points of mutually accepted doctrine; to respond to new insights; and to meet the challenges of the ever changing cultural context. This intimate relationship between Scripture and doctrinal traditions has clear implications for preaching. That is, it is virtually impossible to preach on a biblical text without being drawn into giving expression to some aspect of the doctrinal heritage of Christianity and/or the special emphases of one's tradition.

C. Theology, Doctrine, and Preaching

1. New Insights on Traditional Doctrines

Theological discussions are continually seeking new insights on traditional doctrines responsive to developments in biblical studies and in response to contextual features of place and time. Biblical scholars and constructive theologians have brought the biblical doctrine of creation into serious dialogue with the scientific view of the world, providing preachers a resource for addressing people's urgent concerns over the relationship between faith and science. Feminist scholars are helping to free us from the incipient patriarchalism of traditional doctrine and practice.

2. New Insights on the Kingdom of God

Modern insights on the biblical symbol of the kingdom of God have had an enormous impact on eschatology and our way of thinking about God's relation to our history and our world. Preaching on peacemaking, justice, and the care of the earth take on new meaning when we see the kingdom of God as the promise of God's future for the whole world of creation in which justice, peace, and the harmony of all creation will reach their perfection.

3. New Insights Concerning the Trinity

Contemporary discussions of the doctrine of the Trinity have emphasized the intimate relationship of love that constitutes the unity in diversity of the persons of the Trinity as a pattern for humanity. It follows that we who are created in the divine image (Gen 1:26) are created for life in a radically inclusive community of love. It is part of the church's vocation to model this reality (John 17:21; 1 Cor 13; Gal 3:28; 1 John 4:7-12). Speaking of the Trinity, then, is more than speaking of a mystery.

D. The Intersection of Biblical Text and Doctrine in Preaching

To bring the text into lively contact with the needs of the people is to do in miniature the very process that has led to the development and interpretation of doctrine. In what follows, then, we look at four examples of how doctrine and biblical text intersect as they address the human situation.

1. Seasonal Texts and Doctrinal Reflections

The seasonal texts lead us into the very center of our understanding of the person and work of the Christ and the implications for Christian faith and life. This is part and parcel of their overarching theme of Emmanuel, God-with-us.

a. An Advent text

In Luke 1:26-38, a text often assigned for the fourth Sunday in Advent, we have the account of the angel Gabriel announcing to Mary that she will bear a son by the power of the Holy Spirit. This lead-up to the nativity of our Lord is the basis of the doctrine of the virgin birth. For some, belief in the truth of this doctrine has become a litmus test for true faith in God's miraculous power and in the inspired truth of the Bible. For others, it is a premodern invention of the early church to safeguard the doctrine of the sinlessness of Jesus. However, rather than ask whether it is true, we can take our clue from the seasonal theme of God-with-us and ask instead, "What if it is true?" This reversal of the question enables the preacher to relate the annunciation text to other implications of the incarnation. Thus, the sermon might build on statements like these, "If it is true that God, who is love (1 John 4:16b), has come to be with us in Jesus, then we are called to love as we have first been loved. If it is true that God was in Christ, reconciling the world to Godself (2 Cor 5:18), then we, too, have a ministry of reconciliation in a world of hostility and conflict. If it is true that God has come to be with us, then the source of all life has entered into our world of death, and we are born again to a new hope." In this manner the preacher delivers the text from doctrinal dispute and opens its deeper meaning.

b. An Easter text

The same question, "What if it is true?" might well be asked at Easter, when the preacher is virtually forced to deal with the doctrine of the resurrection against the backdrop of secular skepticism. It provides an opportunity to lay out the marvelous implications of this linchpin of the gospel and, in so doing, strongly suggests that if it is not true, life would indeed be impoverished (1 Cor 15:12-19).

c. A sermon example

The Christmas texts are a blend of the extraordinary and the ordinary. The announcement in John 1:14 that the Word became flesh, his glory that of the Father's, full of grace and truth, is stunning and magnificent, reflecting the monumental and world-changing nature of the incarnation. The angel's announcement to the shepherds and the song of the heavenly hosts that followed (Luke 2:8-14) are no less suffused with divine glory and gospel hope. Yet Luke goes on to report the very ordinary circumstances of Jesus' birth. Preaching this contrast draws the doctrine deep into our lives as in Christ, God was deep in our flesh.

Here is an excerpt from a sermon I preached at a struggling inner-city church: "Because the Son of God came in love to be born into our ordinary flesh there is hidden in our ordinary lives the mystery of the extraordinary. . . . Ours is a life that is frequently filled with burdens, demands, frustrations, and defeats that seem to tax us beyond our capacities and we want simply to quit. Yet there are some ordinary people here who do not give up but continue in long-suffering care for the church, for the congregation, for the wayward child, for the straying soul, for the troubled spouse, for the ailing parent. And in that long-suffering Christ-like love, the grace of Bethlehem shines through like that star. It is extraordinary." Further illustrations of real-life faith and love follow readily to show how the extraordinary shows through in the ordinary as it did in Bethlehem. Mary Catherine Hilkert has put the matter this way: "Christmas proclaims that 'what we long for is already here,' in ordinary persons. . . . We wanted a God who would take away the darkness; instead we got a God who promised to enter our darkness and to be with us there so that it would not overcome us" (Hilkert 2003, 85).

2. Textual Preaching Supported by Doctrine: Sin and Grace

Teachings on human sin and divine judgment and mercy are throughout the Scripture and at the core of doctrine. Notwithstanding the topic of the text, the sermons we preach on them usually find resolution in the dialectic of sin and grace.

a. Race: Martin Luther King Jr.

In a sermon titled "A Tough Mind and a Tender Heart," Martin Luther King Jr. made application of Matt 10:16 to issues of racial justice but ultimately couched the matter in God's judgment and grace: "On the one hand, God is a God of justice who punished Israel for her wayward deeds, and on the other hand, he is a forgiving father whose heart was filled with unutterable joy when the prodigal returned home" (King 1963, 19).

b. Atonement: Reinhold Niebuhr

Reinhold Niebuhr, while preaching on portions of Matt 27, the mockery of Jesus on the cross, talks of the power and weakness of God as this pertains to justice in our world. However, ultimately, the judgment and grace revealed in the crucifixion move Niebuhr to frame the concerns of the sermon in a doctrine of the atonement: "Yet justice alone does not move men to repentance. The inner core of their rebellion is not touched until they behold the executor of judgment suffering with and for the victim of the punishment. This is the meaning of the 'atonement' as apprehended by faith" (Niebuhr 1946, 147). The various traditional doctrines of the atonement capture judgment and grace in ways that can frame and enrich a variety of textual topics. Moreover, as the Niebuhr excerpt suggests, while preaching to the goal of stimulating concern and action for the good of others involves judgment, it is grace that motivates.

c. Social injustice: Daisy L. Machado

Daisy L. Machado, preaching on Ezek 37:2-5 and Acts 3:5-8, sees in the dry bones and the beggar whom Peter and John met at the gate an indictment of social injustice and a call for the church to be a radically different community. Judgment is there and admonition is there, but the bottom line is, "Can these bones live? The Holy Spirit answers to our hearts: Yes they can!" (Machado 1990, 193).

3. Doctrinal Preaching Enriched by Imagery from Various Biblical Texts

The person and work of Jesus, the Christ, involving as it does some implicit or explicit account of the atonement is a constant doctrinal element in Christian preaching. As suggested above, there is a rich variety of theories of Christ's atoning work. These accounts are enriched by a variety of biblical images. Jesus is understood as the fulfillment of the Suffering Servant of Isa 53, who "was wounded for our transgressions" and "upon him was the punishment that made us whole" (v. 5). Jesus is the "Lamb of God who takes away the sin of the world" (John 1:29). Christ alludes to himself when he says, "No one has greater love than this, to lay down one's life for one's friends" (John 15:13). The person of Christ and his work is captured in Paul's statement that "in Christ God was reconciling the world to himself, not counting their trespasses against them" (2 Cor 5:19). In Christ, then, we are a "new creation" (2 Cor 5:17). In Hebrews we explore the Christ as priest and sacrifice. In Revelation he is the Lamb on the throne, the Alpha and Omega who makes all things new. As the preacher strives to discover ever new ways to communicate the very heart of the faith and thereby open new doors of understanding, the Bible is showing the way.

4. Doctrinal Preaching

There may be times when it seems important and edifying to preach on doctrines central to the Christian faith and/or to a specific tradition within Christianity. At such times the biblical basis for the doctrine may be expounded. This is an occasion to make both doctrine and text come alive in our experience and need.

a. Justification by faith

Doctrinal preaching need not be dry and pedantic. Here is an excerpt of Gerhard Forde's sermon, "Justification by Faith Alone," based on Rom 3:28: "Suppose your child were to ask you, 'Dad, Mom, what do I have to do to be your child?' Is there some law, some deed, some program you could propose? Perhaps the first thing you would have to do would be to weep that the question could ever be raised. But what could you say? What do you have to do to be my child? 'Nothing. Just listen. Believe me. You are my child, I love you, I will never let you go.' So, you see, the child is justified by faith alone without the deeds of the law" (Forde 2005, 89).

b. The Holy Spirit

In preaching on the work of the Holy Spirit in our sanctification the possibilities for touching the hearts of the hearers are manifold. All have ample biblical foundations on which to build. The Spirit is God's gracious power bringing us to faith and schooling us in Christian love. The Spirit is with us when faith is failing and doubt is rising in our hearts and souls. The Spirit is there with us praying with us as we struggle to form the right words of pleading to our merciful God. The Spirit is there with us in times of temptation. The Spirit is with the whole church when we gather around the Word to face tough moral decisions that vex our minds and hearts and threaten to divide the very church that the Spirit has gathered through the gospel. The Holy Spirit is promised by our Lord to keep us in the way of his truth. The Spirit is there to keep us "holy," not yet perfect, but holy as "set apart" for God's mission. Indeed, the Spirit's powerful presence at Pentecost not only reveals our empowerment for mission; the Spirit gives life to an important aspect of the doctrine of the church in pursuit of God's mission, namely, its catholicity. By catholicity is meant the universality of the church. On Pentecost day all the various peoples present were united in the gospel by hearing it proclaimed in their own languages (Acts 2:1-11). This gracious act of divine power reverses the judgment of the Tower of Babel story, reuniting humanity in a new future (Gen 11:1-9). The message of salvation is for all; therefore, the church is global in its outreach and welcomes all without prejudice into its communities. *See* DOCTRINAL; HOLY DAYS AND HOLIDAYS; LECTIONARY AND THE CHRISTIAN YEAR; SYSTEMATIC, CONSTRUCTIVE THEOLOGY; TEACHING.

Bibliography: Gerhard Forde. *The Captivation of the Will.* (2005); Mary Catherine Hilkert. "Two Fingers under the Door." *Just Preaching: Prophetic Voices for Economic Justice.* Edited by André Resner Jr. (2003) 83-85; Martin Luther King Jr. *Strength to Love.* (1963); Daisy L. Machado. "A Powerful Gospel." *And Blessed Is She: Sermons by Women.* Edited by David A. Farmer and Edwina Hunter. (1990) 188–95; Reinhold Niebuhr. *Discerning the Times: Sermons for Today and Tomorrow.* (1946).

ECCLESIOLOGY
William H. Willimon

Preaching is the peculiar public speech that arises out of, is addressed to, and is critical for the formation of the body of Christ, the church.

A. Preaching as God's Word to the Church
B. Preaching as Communal, Embodied, Political Speech
C. Preaching as Critical for the Mission of the Church
D. The Worship of the Church as the Normal Context for Preaching
E. Practical Implications of Ecclesiology for the Preparation of Sermons

A. Preaching as God's Word to the Church

Preaching originates in talk by the triune God who has shown (in Scripture) everlasting determination to be in conversation with the world. Preaching then occurs through the preacher, an official of the church whose major responsibility is to listen for God's word to the people of God, the church. Thus, the Apostles' Creed begins by talking about the creative work of God the Father, and the redemptive work of God in Jesus Christ and, immediately after talking about the Holy Spirit, next speaks of the church as the great culminating, continuing consequence of the communication of the Trinity.

Preaching is specifically Christian when it is biblical, but it is not biblical unless it is ecclesial. The Bible is the communal account of what Israel and the church have heard from God. The Bible's way with the truth is inherently communal and corporate. The peculiarly biblical question is rarely, What should I do?—the preoccupation of contemporary Western society in the grip of individualism and subjectivity. The Bible's ethics are always, What should we do? Therefore, we sometimes speak of the Bible as "the church's book." Scripture's content and purposes tend to be relentlessly communal. Koinonia occurs in various forms thirty-eight times in the NT and is Paul's primary way of speaking about the Christian life. And preaching is faithful to Scripture when it participates in Scripture's essentially communal intent. Preaching is where, in Bonhoeffer's words, the risen Christ is allowed to walk and to talk among his people.

B. Preaching as Communal, Embodied, Political Speech

Community may be contemporary preaching's greatest challenge, at least in the North American context. The American audience is officially schooled in the notion that we are most fully ourselves when we are liberated, autonomous, and on our own, when we have chosen lives that are without external, social determination. Ironically, that we think it desirable or even possible to live our lives without external, social determination is proof that our lives have been externally, socially determined by a culture of rugged individualism and capitalist consumption. None of us came up with the idea that we are sovereign individuals who have no greater purpose in life than to live exclusively for ourselves. This culture has formed us into the narrative that is counter to and at odds with the narrative known as gospel. All lives are externally determined by some story. To be a Christian is to be formed by and answerable to a story (the gospel) that is almost exclusively communal (i.e., ecclesial), and the primary way that communal story comes to us and has its way with us is through preaching.

Therefore, Christian preaching tends to be conflicted speech because preaching is always speech across a linguistic divide that separates communities. One way that a community coheres and survives is through its peculiar speech. A community tends to mobilize against any attempt to intrude into its sanctioned means of describing the world and narrating reality. Whereas the preacher

may think that she is speaking to a conglomeration of open-minded, free-speaking individuals, in reality the preacher is speaking to well-formed communities that have had their discourse determined through the media, years of schooling, hourly assaults by advertising, government spin, and a host of other means that limit their ability to bring some matters to speech. When a member of a congregation responds to a preacher's sermon with, "I do not understand what you are talking about," this is testimonial to the dissonance between linguistic communities.

The line between the church and the world cuts through most congregations, thus the sense among many in the congregation that preachers use strange words. Preachers therefore need to be prepared to take the time patiently to indoctrinate and to inculcate the church's peculiar church speech among their congregations (tasks more traditionally known to the church as catechesis and evangelism). It is difficult to translate the church's theological language into language that appears to be more accessible to non-theological linguistic communities. And yet we preachers must dare. A major means of resistance by the church to the world is through the loving inculcation and training of the church in the church's peculiar speech.

Walter Brueggemann says that preaching involves the nurturance of "alternative modes of speech," and that

> the task and possibility of preaching is to open out the good news of the gospel with alternative modes of speech. . . . Reduced speech leads to reduced lives. Sunday morning is the practice of a counterlife through counterspeech. The church on Sunday morning, or whenever it engages in its odd speech, may be the last place left in our society for imaginative speech that permits people to enter into new worlds of faith and to participate in joyous obedient life. (1989, 3)

The congregation provides the free space whereby things can be said and done that are not always understood or even permitted in the world. Preachers must regularly say things from the pulpit that are so bold, so countercultural, and so strange to ears conditioned to the limits of the world that the church renews its sense of gratitude that God has given us this free space (church) in order to have free speech (preaching).

C. Preaching as Critical for the Mission of the Church

Because the church is "of God," the church is never an assured given, a sustained and solid fact, a perpetual institution. The church is always a gift of God, a speech event, generated afresh and new in every age by the Word of God that loves, in each age, to create something out of nothing. Christ has promised that "where two or three are gathered in my name, I am there among them" (Matt 18:20). The primary way that a trinitarian God creates something out of nothing is through preaching. In every time and place the church is both formed anew and constantly critiqued through sermons. Preaching forms an audience that has the guts to listen to Scripture.

A major difference in much of the preaching of the past century and homiletics today is that preachers—at least in Europe and North America—simply assumed the existence and the social significance of the church. This assumption was related to the old state church mentality in which state and church existed in an easy alliance with each other and the culture provided a sort of prop for the church. It was simply assumed that being Christian was roughly synonymous with being a thoughtful, sensitive citizen. Contemporary preachers seem more aware that the church today finds itself in a more precarious position, having lost some of its previous social significance. Therefore, there is a new sense that preaching ought to make clear the differences between church and world and that preaching is a major means whereby the church is formed and reformed to be a distinctive gathering. There is a heightened awareness of the church as *ecclesia*, those who are called out and called forth from the surrounding cultural context.

In the North American context, some of the most interesting developments in ecclesiology have been initiated through missiology, from a growing recognition that the North American church, once a powerful factor in national life, experiences increased marginalization. There is a new sense of the church's peculiarity and resident alien status, a growing awareness that the church's speech and thought are at odds with the predominant, governmentally subservient and culturally sanctioned speaking and thinking. Therefore, there are a new abrasiveness and friction in the preaching of those who are concerned about the identity and formation of a distinctively different church in a missionary context.

Thus, ecclesiology is a recognition that preaching is always "political" in that it is always about the evocation of a people, a polis. In an incarnational faith, the Word that is preached is meant to be embodied, incorporated, and practiced. A lecture may occur in a thoughtful, detached, reflective setting. Preaching almost never does. Faithful Christian proclamation does not occur in some Docetic vacuum where social embodiment of the Word proclaimed is one option among many. That sermon is effective which makes listeners want to participate in the reality of which the sermon has spoken. Thus, the church is called the body of Christ (1 Cor 12:12). At the heart of all Christian leadership is the political, ecclesial challenge to "equip the saints for the work of ministry, for building up the body of Christ" (Eph 4:12). Preaching is a major purpose of the church because the whole church, not only the preacher, is called to witness, to sign, to signal, and to point to Jesus Christ and invite participation in his coming reign. As Luther stressed, the preacher preaches to the church on Sunday so that the whole church can preach to the world all week long.

D. The Worship of the Church as the Normal Context for Preaching

Ecclesiology reminds us that sermons are normally located within the context of the sacraments. As Augustine said, an act such as washing is made a sacrament when it is done next to the word. Sacraments are visible words and are necessary for preaching to make peculiarly Christian sense. In a sense, every sermon is what is said by the church before coming to the waters of baptism. Some sermons are evangelistic calls to the lost to come forward and be found within the church, while other sermons are a further probing of the significance and implications of our baptism, our initiation into Christ's church. The preached word from the pulpit and the responsive, enacted word at the font belong together.

Every sermon is what is said to the church and by the church before it responds to its Lord's invitation to join the feast at the Lord's Table. At the table, with the family gathered, the church goes beyond the spoken word to the enacted word, reminding itself that this word is meant to be not only said but also done. This holy meal is more than words can say. The sermon is the contemporary, present word; the meal is the eschatological, eternal, enacted word.

Preachers must honestly admit that much of our authorization to preach is bestowed by the congregation. The pastor is called, summoned to preach by a community that lives by the articulated word and privileges the testimony of the pastor. Preaching is therefore rarely a word to humanity in general, or to society as a whole, but to the church in particular, a word delivered by a pastor who is intimately known by, and who knows full well, the congregation. The preacher goes to the biblical text, in service to the congregation, skillfully listening to the text, hoping there to make an invigorating discovery within the text, and then the pastor announces that discovery to the congregation. Sometimes that faithful listening requires the preacher to stand with the Word against the congregation, speaking the truth in love, in order truly to serve the congregation as its preacher.

Preaching is the means whereby God sets the church in motion, and yet, alas, the church is often a means whereby we attempt to stabilize and stagnate the Word. The sociological reality of the church as it is, in all of its sordidness, is part of our sinful resistance to the theological call, heralded from the pulpit, for the church to be all that the Holy Spirit intends to make the church. God has great work in mind for the church, and the church tends to feel fear and consternation in the face of that vocation. Therefore, the church is full of resistance to that Word. Church tends to be not only training in discipleship but also in various techniques of avoiding the Word of God.

Through the Word of God in preaching, the church keeps being prophetically reminded that it is not yet the kingdom of God.

Yet through preaching, the church keeps reminding the world that it is more than the present, visible, sociological reality called church. The church, even at its theological best, is never the whole of God's truth or reality, is never equal to the kingdom of God in its fullness. Preaching keeps the church yearning for more of God's promised reality. Preaching is prior to and superior even to the church. Preaching is the peculiar speech of the church, but preaching is not authorized or dependent upon the church. Preaching may often be experienced as against the church, in order to be for the church. The words of the sermon are not a congregationally derived Word; that Word comes from God to the church. Preachers must be willing to risk conflict, resistance, and rejection by the church in order to be faithful to the church's peculiar vocation: joyful subservience to the Word. Preachers are to serve the Word, not be acquiescent to the congregation.

In a day when pastoral care for and caring about the needs of the congregation have virtually overwhelmed much of Christian ministry, Karl Barth reminds us that the best and most loving service that we clergy can render to our people is utter subservience to the Word. Faithful preachers cannot wait for the church faithfully to embody or to practice the Word of God before they preach the Word of God. The gospel must not be foreshortened to accommodate the alleged limitations of its present audience.

Barth also taught that the church forever faces two threats from within—secularization and sacralization of itself. The greatest threat to the church's faithful service of God is the church. Preaching is the church's greatest means of avoiding these dangers. When the church settles down as just another sociological gathering of people, a helpful means of helping people be better people, preaching points to the theological origins and purposes of the church and its ministry; preaching says, "God has called us for more." When the church idolizes itself, smug in its apostolicity and content in its sacred visibility, preaching has a responsibility to proclaim, "No, not yet."

Preaching preserves the church from drifting off into ethereal, vague spirituality. Preaching saves the church from satisfaction with the present, pointing to the church's vocation to be drawn toward another city whose "architect and builder is God" (Heb 11:10). Barth said that the church is like a bird, constantly beating its wings against its cage, and preaching is the means whereby the church keeps reminding itself that "something bigger is at stake than our bit of preaching . . ."—namely the kingdom of God" (1959).

E. Practical Implications of Ecclesiology for the Preparation of Sermons

A vivid sense of preaching as an ecclesial activity will produce sermons that

1. privilege the use of *we* and *our* over *I* and *mine*, using speech in the first person plural in order to stress the word of preaching as a communally derived, communally addressed word that is more politically, publicly significant than personal, private communication;

2. normally and normatively are preached by a pastor, someone in service to a particular congregation of the body of Christ, someone who appreciates the particularities of the gospel more than its generalities, someone adept at locating the gospel within a specific people who are attempting to embody the Word in their particular lives;

3. are contextualized within a specific time and place, are relevant to the cultures within the congregation, and are therefore more difficult to dismiss;

4. normally and normatively occur within the context of a full celebration of Word and table in which the preached Word is linked to the visible, enacted Word, the sacraments;

5. are preached by pastors who are good listeners, who are adept in analyzing not only the biblical text, but also the congregational context;

6. stress the communally formative aspects of preaching as a corporate act that contributes to the cohesion, the visibility, the survival through time, and the distinctiveness of this human gathering as a part of the body of Christ;

7. take responsibility for prophetic pushing of the church into the world in the name of Christ, prodding the church to be more than a warm and friendly human gathering, refusing to rest in anything less than the full consummation of all that Christ intends his body to be;

8. are constructed by preachers who realize that the most loving service they are called to render their congregations is the weekly, faithful, courageous articulation of the Word;

9. are preached by pastors who love the true and lively Word even more than they love their congregations;

10. demonstrate the pastor's faith that Jesus Christ really does mean to have a visible, tangible, embodied presence in the world, that Christ truly intends to take over the world with this otherwise ragtag conglomeration of redeemed sinners whom, despite their undeniable weaknesses and inadequacies, Christ is unashamed to have as his body.

See PROPHETIC MESSAGE; PROPHETIC PREACHING; SACRAMENTS, PREACHING AND TEACHING OF; WORD OF GOD; WORSHIP STYLE.

Bibliography: Karl Barth. *Dogmatics in Outline.* (1959); Walter Brueggemann. *Finally Comes the Poet: Daring Speech for Proclamation.* (1989); Stanley M. Hauerwas and William H. Willimon. *Resident Aliens: Life in the Christian Colony.* (1989). Lesslie Newbigin. *Foolishness to the Greeks: The Gospel and Western Culture.* (1986).

ESCHATOLOGY
Cheryl Bridges Johns

It is hard to imagine religion without an eschatological dimension. Specifically, Christianity is centered on the belief that God is at work in the created order restoring all things to their intended splendor. This belief in God's power over the end has fueled the passion of Christians for centuries, giving them comfort in times of persecution and hope when evil seems to triumph over good. Yet in spite of the centrality of eschatology for the Christian faith, there is a strange silence among preachers regarding the topic. Moreover, Christianity as a whole is confused over issues surrounding death and the afterlife, the return of Christ, and the nature of the final judgment. This confusion, according to N. T. Wright, "produces quite serious mistakes in our thinking, our praying, our liturgies, our practice and particularly our mission" (2008, 6).

The neglect of last things in preaching is the result of several interweaving factors (see below). These factors have converged to form a perfect storm of resistance to eschatological preaching. In many ways, American Protestant preaching lost its heart when it lost its eschatological vision. Such a loss can be remedied by reapproaching the topic of eschatology as central to the Christian faith. As a result, preaching can once again provide an eschatological vision that is filled with hope and fueled by a passion for the kingdom of God.

A. Biblical/Historical Background
  1. Old and New Testament Images of the End
  2. Preaching Eschatologically in the History of the Church

B. Modern Images of the End
  1. Protestant Preaching
  2. Rise of Dispensationalism
C. Preaching the Eschatological Vision

A. Biblical/Historical Background

1. Old and New Testament Images of the End

For the ancient Hebrews, death was an ambiguous experience. It was the natural ending to life, but it also was viewed as the enemy. The afterlife, known as *sheol*, was the place of the dead and signified absence from the presence of Yahweh (Ps 6:5). However, the ancient book of Job affirmed trust in life beyond the grave:

> I know that my Redeemer lives,
>   and that in the end he will stand upon
>   the earth.
> And after my skin has been destroyed,
>   yet in my flesh I will see God;
> I myself will see him with my own eyes—I,
>   and not another.
> How my heart yearns within me!
>   (Job 19:25-27 NIV)

It was the hope of the righteous that God's power would "ransom" them from the power of the grave (Hos 13:14).

During the exilic period, this hope included an understanding that the wicked would be judged: "Multitudes . . . will awake: some to everlasting life, others to shame and everlasting contempt" (Dan 12:2 NIV).

The OT, beyond its vision of death, conveyed a prophetic message of Yahweh's desire for justice. Israel, with its understanding of linear time, saw history moving forward into the future and not just recycling events. Overlaid upon linear history was an apocalyptic vision, developed by the prophets and later refined between 200 BCE and 100 CE. This vision understood history as a stage of a grand cosmic drama pitting God against the forces of evil. In the end, God would reign over all the kingdoms of the world, and history would culminate with the Day of the Lord. This day would bring about justice and peace, and Israel would be both judged and vindicated.

The NT authors viewed death through the lens of Jesus' resurrection. The resurrection of Christ eliminated all ambiguity; even so, death was still the enemy (Heb 2:14) and was seen as the consequence of sin. Death, according to the Apostle Paul, was the means through which sin reigned in the world (Rom 5:12; 6:23). However, its ultimate power was destroyed through Jesus, who brought eternal life to those who believed in him.

In this sense, for the NT writers, death was a conquered foe. Death no longer held its terror, and "to depart" is to "be with Christ" (Phil 1:23). This is the Christian hope. And it extended to include an apocalyptic vision of history inherited from Israel. For the writers of the NT, human history had entered a special eschatological era. This era was bounded on one end by the advent, life, death, and resurrection and ascension of Jesus and the outpouring of the Holy Spirit. On the other end were the return of Christ and the final judgment.

For NT Christians, the gospel was eschatological, marked by both promise and judgment. The first Christian sermon, preached by Peter on the day of Pentecost (Acts 2:14-36), was framed with apocalyptic images from the prophet Joel. Peter saw the coming of the Spirit as a fulfillment of Joel's prophecy regarding the last days. This sermon not only included the promise of the pouring out of the Spirit upon all flesh; it also made reference to "portents in the heaven above / and signs on the earth below, blood, and fire, and smoky mist" (Acts 2:19). For Peter, the life, death, resurrection, and ascension of Jesus offered both promise and judgment to Israel. Christ's pouring out the Holy Spirit is "for you, for your children, and for all who are far away" (Acts 2:39). Beyond promise is the call to "repent, and be baptized" (2:38) and to "save yourselves from this corrupt generation" (2:40). Thus, hope and judgment are interwoven into the fabric of early Christian preaching.

In a real sense, the NT called for Christians to live faithfully between the times, within the tension of an "already but not yet" kingdom of God. The call to live faithfully involved resisting evil, doing good, and anticipating the coming of Christ. The Sunday worship of early Christians was an eschatological celebration of Christ's resurrection and an offering of hope for the future of Christ's reign.

This worship was a sign of resistance to the forces of evil that were in opposition to the gospel. Just as the kingdom of God was advancing through the preaching of the gospel, so too were the forces of evil at work within the world.

The hope of the NT writers was located in the lordship of Christ who would return, bringing about a climax of human history. Rather than offer a checklist of end-time events that would usher in the coming of Christ, the NT offers hope that it was near (Rev 22:10). This hope sustained Christians during times of persecution. They knew that in the end the powers of the world would be judged by the Lamb of God and that their suffering would be redeemed within the framework of the suffering of Jesus. Thus, the ancient testimony that "Christ has died, Christ has risen, Christ will come again," reflects the basic building blocks of the Christian faith and its eschatological vision.

The return of Christ had implications far beyond the human experience. An often overlooked point is that the eschatological event is for the restoration of all creation, but the Apostle Paul was careful to note this dimension:

> For the creation was subjected to frustration, not by its own choice, but by the will of the one who subjected it, in hope that the creation itself will be liberated from its bondage to decay and brought into the glorious freedom of the children of God. We know that the whole creation has been groaning as in the pains of childbirth right up to the present time. (Rom 8:20-22 NIV)

The transformation of the cosmos is not without judgment that calls for a radical reordering of the elements of the universe (2 Pet 3:10). This reordering of all things liberates creation toward fulfillment of its intended order and beauty.

2. Preaching Eschatologically in the History of the Church

Over the centuries Christian eschatology developed into several streams of thought. In particular, there is diversity of opinion regarding the nature of the coming kingdom. This diversity centers on the placement of the earthly reign of Jesus. Would this reign be prior to the final consummation, or would it come at the end? How one answers this question reflects one's vision of the world as well as one's vision of the nature of the kingdom of Christ.

Those who understand the coming of the earthly reign prior to the final consummation hold to what is known as pre-millennialism. Those who understand the coming of Christ following an earthly golden age are referred to as post-millennialists. Those who understand the time between the two advents as characterized by a mixture of good and evil are known as millennialists. In this belief Christ's appearing will occur in the midst of a final, intense period of persecution of the church.

Pre-Constantinian Christianity, especially during times of persecution, was predominantly pre-millenarian (Justin, Dial. 80; Irenaeus, Haer. 5.30.4; 33.2). It was the Christian hope that earthly powers would be overcome and judged, and there would be a time for the healing and justification of those who had suffered for the cause of Christ. "For it is equitable that in the selfsame creation in which they laboured and suffered tribulation, in all ways tested in endurance, they should also receive the fruits of their patience," wrote Irenaeus (Haer. 5.32).

When Emperor Constantine, in victory over Licinius in 324, restored the unity of the Roman Empire, theologians such as Eusebius of Caesarea understood this event as heralding an era of messianic significance. This era marked the beginning of the imperium christianum. The state was no longer anti-God and anti-Christ doomed for judgment (Rev 13); rather, the state became an instrument of bringing about the kingdom of God. Thus, millenarian hopes were transformed into the reign of the holy empire. After the fall of Rome, these hopes were carried into the reign of the church. It would be the era of the church that executed the rule of Christ on the earth. "The pre-millenarian communities," observes Jurgen Moltmann, "were therefore bound to be condemned as a danger for ecclesiastical rule, just as were the Jews, with their expectation of a future messiah" (1996, 154).

The Reformers understood the millennium as a historical era of the past. They interpreted the pope as a manifestation of the antichrist who brought about the end of this era. For Luther, his struggle with Rome was a struggle with the antichrist. Following this struggle, there would be the resurrection of the dead and the great judgment. The Reformation was followed by Protestant condemnations of what was called Jewish opinions regarding the coming of a golden age prior to the great judgment (Augsburg Confession of 1566, Article 17; Swiss Confession, Article 11).

B. Modern Images of the End

1. Protestant Preaching

The modern era is marked by the resurgence of millennial expectations. The resurgence is tied to the radical Reformers such as the Anabaptists and German Pietists like Jacob Spener and Johann Albrecht Bengel. The period of the 17th cent.

created theologies of hope within Protestant Christianity. This hope was grounded in the belief that humanity could join with the work of Christ to bring about a new messianic era. These longings are most poignantly expressed by Johann Amos Comenius, the last bishop of the Moravian Brethren: "The general amelioration of things will be the work of Jesus Christ, who will renew the condition from which everything has drifted away; in spite of that he requires our assistance, but that will no longer be difficult in the present state of things" (Moltmann 1996, 158). For Pietists such as Comenius, the coming reign of Christ was linked in a positive manner to the radical changes experienced in the Enlightenment.

The Great Awakenings in England and in the United States brought about a renewal of premillennial expectations. In this ferment dispensationalism was birthed. Rooted in the Plymouth Brethren movement and the teachings of John Nelson Darby (1800–1882), dispensationalism divides history into specific periods of time according to the manner in which God works in human history. Dispensationalists argued for seven dispensations of grace that would culminate with the millennium. The Scofield Reference Bible introduced dispensationalism to a wider audience in America, and numerous Bible colleges, such as Moody Bible Institute, helped to educate generations of ministers in dispensational theology.

2. Rise of Dispensationalism

The influence of dispensationalism on American evangelicalism was deep and long lasting. Throughout the 20th cent., dispensational theology was preached with a passion, and it created an ethos characterized by expectations of Christ's soon return (the rapture) and a fascination with modern-day Israel in its role in ending the dispensation of the church. For many dispensationalists the second coming of Jesus would snatch away true believers from the world, and after an interval of ungodliness and tribulation, there would be another return to rule over the world. This belief was popularized in the late 20th cent. by the *Left Behind* series of novels written by Tim LaHaye and Jerry Jenkins. In many circles, preaching dispensational theology was an exercise in timelines and predictions related to current events. Its preachers made extensive use of current events, especially those relating to Israel and the Middle East, as signs of the imminent return of Christ.

In contrast to and often in reaction against dispensationalism, mainline churches of the West offered an approach to eschatology that married post-millennialism with an evolutionary view of history. For the most part, during the latter part of the 19th cent. this marriage worked. Preachers spoke with confidence regarding a time when Christ's kingdom would be made known throughout the whole earth. A spirit of optimism prevailed that placed confidence in the efforts of humankind in the establishing of this kingdom while at the same time recognizing the literal second coming of Jesus.

During the 20th cent. as mainline Protestantism became more in tune with historical criticism, there were attempts to avoid the dramatic and apocalyptic images of the coming of Christ. Instead, its preachers and theologians emphasized a general hope for world renewal. The literal coming of Jesus seemed, for the most part, to be part of a supernaturalism that had disappeared. "The mainstream pulpit," notes Thomas Long, "grew strangely silent about the 'final things'" (2006, 25).

Contemporary preachers are often caught between two extremes. On the one hand, there is the popularity of dispensational theology with its timelines and apocalyptic images of judgment. This extreme reduces reading of the Scriptures as an end-times checklist. It is marked by pessimism regarding the future and sometimes indifference in human initiative for the common good. On the other hand, there is an eschatological void wherein "everything is lodged in the mystical, disembodied present tense" (Long 2006, 26). This extreme offers no real hope or prophetic voice. It ignores the many passages of Scripture that speak of the coming of Christ and judgment of evil and sees little direct supernatural intervention in human history.

C. Preaching the Eschatological Vision

There is a real need for Christianity to recapture its eschatological vision and, as a result, for preaching to recapture its eschatological voice, offering both promise and judgment. When this occurs, Christian communities will be defined as eschatological gatherings that offer to the world a sign of the coming kingdom. Sunday worship will cease to be a disembodied, existential event; rather, it will be seen as an eschatological event, bringing heaven to earth and calling for the day when all creation will join in praise to God.

The task ahead calls for preachers to reread the biblical passages regarding the end times as expressions of hope for the consummation of God's cosmic program. The biblical witness is strong in its assertion that God is at work bringing about the liberation of creation from its present situation (Rom 8:20-22). As Stanley Grenz points out, "God's means of preparing the physical realm for the fellowship he intends to share with creation requires a radical transformation" (1994, 626). Images of judgment, therefore, indicate God's act of transforming the old cosmos into the new, "for the sake of his purposes of establishing the eternal community of a redeemed humankind enjoying the presence of their Redeemer God as they dwell in harmony with the renewed creation" (Grenz 1994, 206).

Preaching eschatologically requires the preacher to be infused with this hope. Such hope is offered not only at funerals, as we preach the promise of the bodily resurrection. It infuses all our preaching. Inasmuch as we preach with the end in sight, our preaching helps establish the tension between the "already" and the "not yet."

Preaching eschatologically is not only preaching about the future hope of new creation; it means bringing that future hope to bear on the present. In that sense, preaching with an eschatological vision means that we preach salvation as more than going to heaven when we die. It means, as N.T. Wright observes, life before death becomes "the essential, vital time, place, and matter into which God's future purposes have already broken in the resurrection of Jesus and in which those future purposes are now to be further anticipated through the mission of the church" (2008, 197). Preaching eschatologically is preaching a hope-shaped mission that calls Christians to participate with God's restoring of all things. Preachers who preach eschatologically call for participation in building *for* the kingdom, knowing, as the Apostle Paul points out in his letter to the Corinthians, "in the Lord your labor is not in vain" (1 Cor 15:58).

Issues such as justice are therefore eschatological in nature. "If we believe," notes Wright, "and pray, as he taught us, for God's kingdom to come on earth as in heaven, there is no way we can rest content with major injustice in the world" (2008, 216). Issues such as "Third World" debt factor into God's judgment of the powers of this world. To preach justice is to announce both judgment and

promise and to call for participation in the restoration of all things to their intended order.

Moreover, the church calendar reflects the Christian eschatological hope. Advent anticipates the second coming of Christ as well as celebrates the first. Lent reenacts the longing and incompleteness of creation for the day when the whole cosmos will be sanctified and made ready for the final resurrection. Easter celebrates the first day of the new creation that is even now among us. And Pentecost shares in the joyful filling of all flesh with the Holy Spirit and anticipates the final filling of the cosmos with the glory of the Lord.

Preaching eschatologically will help bring about the reenchantment of post-Enlightenment Christianity. It will help create what the ancient Celts called "thin places," where the veil between this world and the world to come is nearly transparent. Thus, the preacher can pull back the curtain and call forth the future into the present. *See* CHRISTOLOGY; FUNERAL; LECTIONARY AND THE CHURCH YEAR; SOCIAL JUSTICE; SOTERIOLOGY.

Bibliography: Stanley J. Grenz. *Theology for the Community of God.* (1994); Thomas G. Long. "Imagine There's No Heaven: The Loss of Eschatology in American Preaching." *Journal for Preachers Advent* (2006) 21–28; Jurgen Moltmann. *The Coming of God: Christian Eschatology.* (1996); N. T. Wright. *Surprised by Hope: Rethinking Heaven, the Resurrection and the Mission of the Church.* (2008).

HOLY SPIRIT AND PREACHING
Cheryl Bridges Johns

We may be tempted to ask, "Can anything extraordinary come out of ordinary time, people, and settings in which we live?" By the power of the Holy Spirit the act of preaching can be a most mysterious and extraordinary event. So much so that real transformation takes place and the power of Jesus is manifest on the earth. Yet in order for preaching to be pneumatically constituted, preachers need to overcome what James Forbes labels as "Holy Spirit shyness" (1989, 21). For Forbes inattention to the Holy Spirit has left preachers without the biblical provisions for empowerment, like "unclaimed packages or unopened letters."

The neglect of pneumatology in theology and in preaching is the result of several factors. First,

Protestant Christianity is decidedly Christ-centered when it is not anthropocentric. The preaching of the Word as a witness to Christ Jesus is often a hallmark of Protestant homiletics. Preaching is a means of actualizing the presence of the living Christ. It is the sharing of the good news of the gospel of Jesus. It has been difficult for pastors to maintain this emphasis while at the same time emphasizing trinitarian theology.

Second, stress on the Holy Spirit is often associated with enthusiastic forms of religion and emotive worship over against a more rational and volitional emphasis. Perceived excesses in revivalism and Pentecostalism have fostered an image of Spirit-centered religion as fanatical. As a result, "Holy Spirit shyness" is often preferred over Holy Spirit fanaticism.

Third, preaching is often put over against sacrament. Because of this dichotomy, the act of preaching is stripped of the Spirit-endued mystery found in the liturgy. Preaching in the Protestant principle of prophetic criticism does, as Paul Tillich noted, serve "to make impossible an absolute reliance upon the holy as present" (1948, 109). Tillich warned, however, that "such word cannot do away with the sacramental background; indeed prophetic criticism itself is possible only by virtue of this background" (1948, 109). This neglect of the sacramental nature of preaching and its place within the whole liturgical drama has created an environment conducive to the neglect of the Holy Spirit.

The choice of Christ over Spirit is not necessary. In addition, preachers should not have to choose between Word and Spirit or Word and sacrament. Preaching for the 21st cent. holds promise to be more fully trinitarian and more open to the power of the Holy Spirit in the life of the church. There is rich historical precedent to draw from as well as new homiletical paradigms and a renewal of trinitarian reflection among theologians. There is also an awakening to the sacramental nature of preaching.

A. Historical Precedent
 1. Earliest Christian Preaching
 2. Preaching in the Ancient Church
 3. Medieval Praxis of the Spirit
 4. The Holy Spirit in the Preaching of the Reformers
 5. Modern Dichotomies of Mind and Spirit, Reason and Emotion
 6. The Promise of New Homiletical Paradigms
 7. Renaissance of Trinitarian Theology
B. The Holy Spirit and the Ministry of Preaching
 1. Context: Pneumatically Constituted Community
 2. Gift: Mystery of Christ Revealed
 3. Content: Unity of Word and Spirit
 4. Implications for Preaching

A. Historical Precedent

1. Earliest Christian Preaching

The Luke–Acts (see LUKE/ACTS) corpus portrays Jesus as the one anointed by the Spirit to herald the good news of the kingdom of God. Jesus launched his ministry with reference to the Spirit:

> The Spirit of the Lord is upon me,
> because he has anointed me
> to bring good news to the poor.
> He has sent me to proclaim release to the captives
> and recovery of sight to the blind,
> to let the oppressed go free,
> to proclaim the year of the Lord's favor.
> (Luke 4:18-19, quoting Isa 61:1-2)

Early Christian kerygma built on this claim of Jesus Christ as the Spirit-anointed revelation of God. Peter, speaking on the day of Pentecost, described Jesus as "a man attested to you by God with deeds of power, wonders, and signs that God did through him among you, as you yourselves know" (Acts 2:22). The early Christians prayed to God with references to "your holy servant Jesus, whom you anointed" (4:27). Furthermore, the preaching of the followers of Jesus with power was seen as an extension of the anointing of Jesus. This anointing was the result of the Holy Spirit's being poured out on his followers, empowering them to do the same works as did Jesus.

The Apostle Paul's testimony regarding his ministry to the church at Corinth affirmed his reliance upon the Holy Spirit: "My speech and my proclamation were not with plausible words of wisdom, but with a demonstration of the Spirit and of power, so that your faith might rest not on human wisdom but on the power of God" (1 Cor 2:4-5). Paul, like Luke, understood the reception of the Holy Spirit as empowering believers to both know and speak things learned from God. Believers gained knowledge of "the things freely given to us by God" (1 Cor 2:12 NASB), and they spoke of those things "taught by the Spirit" (1 Cor 2:13).

2. Preaching in the Ancient Church

The patristic writers of the ante-Nicene period spoke of the Holy Spirit in a manner that conveyed the experience of the Spirit as a reality in their lives. Within this context the Holy Spirit was understood as a personal force acting on and through individuals to prepare them for union with God. The work of the Holy Spirit in this preparation was multifaceted and involved driving away evil spirits, healing the mind so that believers could comprehend the truths of God, and sanctifying the entire being. In addition, the Holy Spirit served as an internal guide or trainer (*pedagogue*) who helped believers conform to the image of Christ.

The most pervasive activity of the Holy Spirit in the early church was that of speaking. Early Christians understood that it was the Spirit who spoke through the OT prophets and the apostles. In addition, they viewed the Spirit continuing to speak through pastor-teachers and prophet-teachers. Pastor-teachers were considered gifted of Christ (Eph 4:11-12) and functioning under the leadership of the Holy Spirit. They were the keepers of the truth of the gospel and held authoritative office that evolved into that of the bishop. Their authority was understood as given by the Holy Spirit and recognized by the church. Their words, therefore, were the words of the Spirit to the church. Prophet-teachers were considered to bring instruction directly from the Holy Spirit. Irenaeus wrote in the late 2nd cent. that there were many in the church "who possess prophetic gifts, and who through the Spirit speak all kind of languages, and bring to light for the general benefit the hidden things of men, and declare the mysteries of God" (Irenaeus, *Against Heresies,* 1:531).

In the early 3rd cent. Hippolytus wrote encouraging believers to attend the gatherings where the prophet-teachers ministered: "Let everyone be zealous to go to church, the place where the Spirit abounds" (Dix 1937, 54).

In the ante-Nicene church, preaching and teaching by pastor-teachers and prophet-teachers provided a pedagogy of the Holy Spirit that linked their ministry to both the historical Jesus and the resurrected Lord (Johns 1987).

3. Medieval Praxis of the Spirit

The Middle Ages were not without the benefit of Spirit-inspired preaching. While the office of pastor-teacher resided in the bishop and in the priesthood, there continued the prophetic element in wandering preachers and renewal groups such as the Waldenses. During the latter part of the 12th cent., they preached throughout France, Germany, and Italy. Known as "the Poor in Spirit," the Waldenses stressed biblical patterns of living and understood the Spirit's work to include both women and men. In addition to this group there was an explosion of preaching among the Franciscans and Dominicans. The preaching of St. Francis was especially noted for being "Spirit-filled." Stories abound regarding the conviction and miracles accompanying his sermons.

4. The Holy Spirit in the Preaching of the Reformers

For the Reformers, the revelation of God through the act of preaching depended upon the presence of the Holy Spirit. Noted Calvin: "Outward preaching is vain and useless unless the Spirit himself acts as the teacher. God therefore teaches in two ways. He makes us hear his voice through the words of men, and inwardly he constrains us by his Spirit. These two occur together or separately, as God sees fit" (Commentary on John 14:26, *Calvini Opera* 47:334–35).

For Calvin, the Holy Spirit ratified the sermon to make it the word of God. In addition, the Holy Spirit was the agent of calling the minister.

The radical Reformation saw a flourishing of lay preaching with the strongly held belief in the power of the Spirit to give believers the words to speak. Within this environment, the tension between Spirit and Word created divisions. Excesses of "Spirit-inspired speech" caused many to become suspect of Spirit, favoring Word. In spite of these excesses there was appreciation for the role of the Holy Spirit in enabling preachers to effectively communicate the gospel.

5. Modern Dichotomies of Mind and Spirit, Reason and Emotion

The modern age characterized as the Enlightenment brought about a renewed emphasis on reason. The religious wars following the Reformation left many people skeptical of the supernatural and revelation. With the influence of thinkers such as René

Descartes and John Locke, reason became the avenue for human discourse and progress. The Age of Reason created its own emphasis on logic and reason as the primary means of conveying the gospel. On the other hand, the Age of Reason produced its reactionaries in the form of pietism and revivalism. Modernism thus moved toward dichotomies of mind and spirit, reason and emotion. Preaching took both roads (Edwards 2004, 391–469). Reason became the means of conveying truth, while on the other hand, enthusiasm in religion was dominant among the masses of people who sought a return of the supernatural.

The preaching of John Wesley was noted for many conversions and manifestations among congregants such as shouting and fainting. Wesley's opponents labeled these events as indicators of enthusiasm, even criticizing him as vulgar and common in his appeal to the masses. Preaching in the Great Awakenings in America generated criticism of excesses in emotion. (*See* REVIVALS.) Throughout modernity, there remained skepticism regarding enthusiasm in preaching. Well into the 20th cent. preachers were taught to be skeptical of emotional appeals.

The dichotomies of modernity created a void regarding pneumatology. In order to avoid the excesses of enthusiasm, many Protestant preachers became "Holy Spirit shy."

6. The Promise of New Homiletical Paradigms

The latter part of the 20th cent., with the demise of modernity, saw the field of homiletics experiencing what many described as a "Copernican revolution" in preaching. This turn called into question what Edward Farley calls the "bridge paradigm" in preaching, a more deductive approach in which the preacher attempts to connect rationally the meaning of biblical passages to the world of hearers (Farley). In its place there are emerging new homiletical paradigms that allow for greater emphasis on the inductive and mysterious nature of preaching. Eugene Lowry, in referring to the new homiletic, observes that "it has been suggested that what makes this paradigm shift noteworthy is its turning to homiletical patterns and convictions that had been abandoned or marginalized by modernity" (1997, 19). The space created by the emergence of new paradigms might yet allow for renewed interest in the role of the Holy Spirit in preaching.

7. Renaissance of Trinitarian Theology

In addition to the emergence of new homiletical paradigms, during the last generation there has been a flourishing of trinitarian theological reflection. This reflection spans the Christian tradition involving Orthodox, Roman Catholic, and Protestant theologians. These conversations highlight how the life of the Trinity serves as an icon for the church and its practices. They have potent implications for the field of homiletics. What is common in these discussions is a rejection of the tight separation between the immanent and economic Trinity. In such discussions there is more openness regarding the person of the Holy Spirit and how the Spirit bridges the gap between the life of God and human existence. This *perichoretic* life of God, so often seen as unknowable and distant, is, by the power of the Holy Spirit, brought to us and thus becomes our life.

Emphasizing trinitarian theology does not take away from the christocentric gospel. In reflecting on the implications of the triune life for the church, Miroslav Volf observes that the church, born through the presence of Christ in the Holy Spirit, "presupposes that the exalted Christ himself is acting in the gifts of the Spirit" (1998, 228). Furthermore, "the connection between the charismata and Christ's exalted presence in the church by the Spirit also demonstrates clearly the intimate relation between the charismata and the constitutive activity of confession. Confession of Christ as Savior and Lord is an essential dimension of charismatic activity" (1998, 228–29).

Orthodox theologian Vladimir Lossky (1903–1958) noted that the church is constituted both christologically and pneumatologically: "The Church is not only one nature in the *hypostasis* of Christ: it consists also of multiple *hypostases* in the grace of the Holy Spirit" (1957, 182). This unity of essence (*ousia*) and yet diversity of subsistences (*hypostases*) reflects the life of the Trinity who are one yet exist as three.

B. The Holy Spirit and the Ministry of Preaching

1. Context: Pneumatically Constituted Community

The church as a community of women and men who are endowed by the Spirit with gifts is the primary environment for the task of preaching. The preacher's charismata of office must be integrated into this mutuality. Preaching in such an environment is sacramental in that it has the power to effect transformation and bring the people individually and corporately into the life of God. It recognizes the uniqueness of the preacher and her or his task, but it also stresses that the preacher and the congregation together are being perfected by the grace-filled work of the Holy Spirit.

In the context of the pneumatically constituted community space, time, and people are sacralized. The most ordinary spaces can become sacred, and the most ordinary people are made holy, thereby becoming living icons. Ordinary time becomes *karios* time.

The act of preaching participates in the Holy Spirit's sacralizing of people, time, and space; the sermon has the potential to cross boundaries between the profane and the holy. In this mysterious context the sermon is a sacramental activity, a linguistic symbol of the sacred, which says, "God is here." The spoken words of the sermon make present the reality that it signifies. Yet true to the Protestant ideal of the freedom of the Word, preaching in this pneumatic community offers a fresh word and opposes fixation and objectification of the sacramental.

2. Gift: Mystery of Christ Revealed

The gift of Spirit-empowered preaching is the revelation of the mystery of Christ. The Latin word *sacramentum* is the primary translation for the Greek word *musterion*, which means "that which is revealed." For the early Christians, *musterion* was a technical term they used to reference the mystery of the incarnation of Jesus Christ and the extension of the incarnation in the church (Rom 16:25; 1 Cor 2:7-8; Eph 1:8-10). The recovery of mystery is another characteristic of the New Homiletic in which preaching is understood in terms of an event that evokes presence more than one that explains meaning.

3. Content: Unity of Word and Spirit

Charles L. Bartow points out that it is not only the sermon that actualizes the presence of Christ, but also the reading of Scripture that creates sacred-sacramental space (1997, 20). Scripture should be understood within the context of the ongoing witness of revelation of God by the Spirit. As canon, Scripture is the standard and primary witness of revelation, but revelation should not be collapsed

into Scripture. According to Steven Land, "the Spirit is prior to the written Word of God, but the Spirit inspires, preserves and illumines the Word within the communion of those who are formed, corrected, nurtured and equipped by that Word" (1993, 39). The unity of Word and Spirit creates a multidimensional understanding of the biblical text as Spirit-Word. Thus, the text comes alive, and the Word of God conveys the presence of God. Jesus Christ, the Living Word, dwells richly in the context of a pneumatically constituted community wherein there is the marriage of Spirit and Word.

4. Implications for Preaching

In order to make contemporary preaching more alive to the Holy Spirit, preachers should first seek to place preaching within the context of the mystery of the liturgical drama. Doing so will help to re-enchant the ministry of preaching. Prayerfully, preachers should ask, How can I bring about the sacred presence of the triune life through my sermon? Look for opportunities to open the door or pull back the curtain between the holy and the profane. Preachers should see themselves as working with God to create what the ancient Celts called "thin places," where the curtain between the supernatural world and the natural world was almost transparent.

Second, preachers can learn to dance with the Spirit into the mysterious realm of sacred space, inviting the congregation to join in this dance. Doing so is as simple (yet difficult) as allowing the Holy Spirit to invade all of us: mind, body, and spirit with the elusive presence of the life of God. *See* CALL AND RESPONSE; CELEBRATION; HOLY SPIRIT/PASSION; PREACHER'S CREATIVE PROCESS; TRINITY.

Bibliography: Charles Bartow. *God's Human Speech: A Practical Theology of Proclamation.* (1997); Gregory Dix, ed. and trans. *The Treatise on the Apostolic Tradition of St. Hippolytus of Rome.* (1937); O. C. Edwards. *A History of Preaching.* (2004); Edward Farley. *Practicing Gospel.* (2003); James Forbes. *The Holy Spirit and Preaching.* (1989); Irenaeus. *Against Heresies.* Vol. 6, pt. 1; Jackie D. Johns. "The Pedagogy of the Holy Spirit According to Early Christian Tradition." (Ed.D Thesis Southern Baptist Theological Seminary. 1987); Steven J. Land. *Pentecostal Spirituality: A Passion for the Kingdom.* (1993); Vladimir Lossky. *The Mystical Theology of the Eastern Church.* (1957);

Eugene Lowry. *The Sermon: Dancing on the Edge of Mystery.* (1997); John S. McClure. *Other-Wise Preaching: A Postmodern Ethic for Homiletics.* (2001); Paul Tillich. *The Protestant Era.* (1948); Miroslav Volf. *After Our Likeness: The Church as the Image of the Trinity.* (1998); William H. Willimon. "Overcoming Pentecost in Our Preaching: Proclamation without Spirit" in *Journal for Preachers* (2001), 31.

MISSIOLOGY
Scott M. Gibson

Missionary preaching is the evangelistic proclamation of salvation in Christ as redeemer, calling men and women to repentance as they place their faith in him and become part of the kingdom of God.

A. Preaching as Mission
    1. Preaching as Mission in the Bible
    2. Preaching as Mission in History
    3. Preaching as Mission Homiletically
    4. Denominational Practices
B. Being a Missional Preacher
C. The Practice of Missionary Preaching

A. Preaching as Mission

1. Preaching as Mission in the Bible
New Testament preaching was missionary preaching. Christ's mission and that of the early church were understood missiologically. These sermons are directed not to the household of faith, to those in the Temple courts, or even to the synagogue. Instead, these sermons turn outward to the world. They recount God's redemptive acts in history and are polemical, as displayed in the sermons of Peter, Stephen, and Paul. The sermons in the book of Acts provide examples of the practice and content of missionary preaching.

For the early church, "what begins as a local mission *by* Jews *to* Jews is driven on by its own inner momentum until it embraces the Gentile world and reaches out beyond the borders of the Roman Empire" (Dunn-Wilson 2005, 1). The preaching of the gospel drove the early church beyond local geographical or political boundaries; it was what they were compelled to do—proclaim the good news.

Missionary preaching, then, is preaching that challenges listeners with the promise of the coming Messiah fulfilled in Jesus Christ—it is evangelism. Listeners are to repent from their sins, be forgiven, and know of Jesus' continued presence through the Holy Spirit, thus experiencing the kingdom of God.

2. Preaching as Mission in History
The practice of missionary preaching fans out from Pentecost through the millennia that follow, including various people, languages, geographical locations, ethnic expressions, and cultures. Among these outward-directed preachers were John Chrysostom (347–407); Martin of Braga (ca. 520–580); Celtic missionaries like Columba (ca. 521–597) and Columbanus (ca. 543–615); Boniface (680–754); Benedictine preachers like Julian of Vezelay (1080–ca. 1160); Francis of Assisi (1181–1226) and the Franciscans; Bartolome de las Casas (1484–1566); the Reformers; John Eliot (1604–1690); Jonathan Edwards (1703–1758); Robert Walker (1716–1784); Thomas Chalmers (1780–1847); John Newton (1725–1807); Charles Simeon (1759–1836); William Carey (1761–1834); Adoniram Judson (1788–1850); Samuel A. Crowther (1807–1891); Adoniram Judson Gordon (1836–1895); Sadrach Surapranata (1835–1924); Arthur Tappan Pierson (1837–1911); Phoebe Rowe (1855–1898); Mojola Agbebi (1860–1917); John Mott (1865–1955); and Billy Graham (1918–).

Specific studies on missionary homiletics have emerged that focus on historical periods. Among these are John Foster's study of the first three centuries, David Dunn-Wilson's examination of preaching in the first five centuries, Schutz's work on the 19th cent., Wilhelm Dilger's study on India, and George Sweazy's research on the United States. Missionary preaching gained attention in the later half of the 20th cent. in the writings of Roman Catholics Domenico Grasso and Karl Rahner, and Protestant Hans J. Margull. Hughes Oliphant Old's impressive multivolume study of preaching includes both period and individual research. The above works are expansive, yet more research is needed in the gatheringand analysis of sermons across the centuries and continents.

With the publication of the *Concise Encyclopedia of Preaching* (1995), articles touched on issues of missiological concern: "cross-cultural preaching," "African-American Preaching," preaching in Africa, Asia, India, and Latin America, and missionary preaching. Haddon W. Robinson and Craig Brian Larson edited *The Art & Craft of Biblical Preaching: A Comprehensive Resource for Today's Communicators* (2005), which contains articles on mission and preaching: "Cross-Cultural Preaching," "Hispanic-American Preaching," "African-American Preaching," "Asian-American Preaching," and "Preaching and Pluralism." As for African American preaching, E. K. Bailey and Warren W. Wiersbe collaborated on *Preaching in Black & White: What We Can Learn from Each Other* (2003), a volume that explores what preachers can learn from two cultural perspectives. In an interesting study Jerome Clayton Ross suggests a connection between the Yahwists of the past and African Americans in the present (2000). Cleophus J. LaRue examines the foundations of black preaching by focusing on three crucial dynamics in his work *The Heart of Black Preaching* (1999).

A comprehensive study of missionary preaching from the emerging African, Asian, and South American fronts is warranted. An example of such literature is the fine analysis by John Wesley Zwomunondiita Kurewa. His *Preaching & Cultural Identity: Proclaiming the Gospel in Africa* argues for indigenous communication of the claims of the gospel in the African context. As for Asian preaching, particularly in the American context, Jung Young Lee and Eunjoo Mary Kim have provided analyses of Korean American preaching, as has Matthew D. Kim, "A Bi-Cultural Homiletic: Korean American Preaching in Transition."

However, as a result of missionary preaching, a global church has emerged. Research is beginning to surface, including Timothy C. Tennent's essay, "Evangelical Preaching in the Global Context." Moreover, Philip Jenkins's work, *The Next Christendom: The Coming of Global Christianity*, although not a homiletics study, but a book from which homileticians would benefit, details the changing face of the Christian world. Jenkins demonstrates the gradual shift of Christianity from the white Northern Hemisphere to the multicultural non-white Southern Hemisphere. Indeed, the church has been planted in many of the major cultural regions of the world, and the future will only tell of the advances of the gospel through missionary preaching.

3. Preaching as Mission Homiletically

Missionary preaching grows out of the wider field of homiletics. Wilhelm Leyser (1592–1649)

introduced *homiletics* as the name of the discipline in his *Cursus Homileticus*. Soon thereafter came Sebastian Goebel's *Methodologia Homileticae* (1672), and Friedrich D. E. Schleiermacher used the term in his *Brief Outline of the Study of Theology* in 1830 (Jongeneel 1997, 268).

Gustav Warneck, a 19th cent. missionary statesman, used the terms *mission preaching, mission sermon*, and *missionary sermon*, while Wolfgang Gern used not only the term *mission sermon*, but also *contextual preaching* and *ecumenical preaching*. By the end of the century, Johannes Hesse wrote a book on *mission in the pulpit* with the subtitle "an auxiliary book for mission homiletics." There have been other advances in the field.

As for 20th cent. theologian Karl Barth, Dae Ryeong Kim indicates that Barth "does not attempt to distinguish missionary preaching from preaching in a Christian church service, as it is generally understood." Instead, Kim suggests, "All preaching is a call to repentance and faith. All preaching bears the task of missionary proclamation to the world" (Dae R. Kim 1999, 23).

However, in light of the shifting center of global Christianity, preachers are to be equipped with the requisite tools to engage with this new context. As a result, as Lesslie Newbigin observes, "the Bible can have no privileged status," for it finds itself part of the religious experience of the human race at large. It may be part of our culture, but not part of many others' culture or cultures (Newbigin 1986, 42). Taking the lead from John, the missionary preacher can benefit from the approach used in his Gospel as a "bold and brilliant essay in the communication of the gospel to a particular culture." John used the thought forms of the Hellenistic world so that the Gnostics "in all ages have thought that the book was written especially for them" (Newbigin 1986, 53).

Thus, the missionary preacher calls hearers to a paradigm shift, "traditionally called conversion." These listeners often "inhabit a different plausibility structure" (Newbigin 1986, 62). The gospel is preached as an idea. But more than this, missionary preaching engages the power of language understood by the listeners. This language creates a "world," a cultural framework, in which preachers and listeners live and move and process their experience. Kevin Vanhoozer comments, "The ministry of the Word involves more than communicating a few truths; it involves transmitting a whole way of thinking and experiencing" (Vanhoozer 2005, 74). Missionary preaching requires preachers to understand their hearers by listening, hearing, observing, and speaking. Lesslie Newbigin notes:

> The preacher has, of course, to begin by learning the language, using words that are freighted with meaning, often with profoundly evocative meanings, derived from the mental world of the hearers. The preacher uses, and must use, words that have a meaning for the hearers. The preacher uses and must use words that have a meaning for the hearers different from the preacher's intention. There is no escape from this. Words like God, sin, and salvation derive their Christian content from the entire experience of sharing in the Christian tradition. (Newbigin 1995, 335)

The missionary preacher must understand the mental world of the listeners. Newbigin observes:

> A preacher, for example, who claims to offer eternal life to an audience of Hindus is offering them exactly what they are trying to escape. If he or she offers the gift of salvation in Christ to those who are strangers to the Bible, they will assume that he or she is offering them something like the benefits of the welfare state. (Newbigin 1995, 335)

The homiletical challenges of missionary preaching have remained rather constant throughout the centuries. Like St. John and St. Paul, missionary preachers speak eternal truth into specific contexts. The preacher is challenged to speak to listeners in ways that enable them to embrace the gospel, for preaching is done in community affecting one's behavior. Both the community context and the way in which preaching is lived out, shape Christian character.

4. Denominational Practices

Denominational commitment to mission preaching is demonstrated in two ways. First, preaching on the local level is mission oriented, evangelically driven, to reach men and women with the gospel. Second, like the early church, the gospel is not limited to the local church, but extends to a global witness. Denominations continue to train and send missionaries to proclaim the gospel as mission preachers around the world. Even in North America and Europe, a phenomenon of reverse missionizing is taking place. Missionaries from other countries are going there to preach and teach. Wherever one is preaching, the preacher is sensitive to the geographic, economic, and social context, shaping the sermon for the circumstance, whether it is a North American urban setting or a rural African location. Sermons are influenced by local context expectations of sermon length and language.

Most denominations not only send preachers as missionaries but also provide agricultural and economic development, education, and medical help through people whose mission may not fit the pattern of preaching as discussed in this article.

Although there is a growing sensitivity to beware of not imposing one's culture on others, some denominations may be at risk of not making disciples by the actual, verbal proclamation of the gospel.

The development of missionaries coming to North America to preach and teach is an interesting phenomenon of reverse missions. Whereas the North American West has led the way in the missionary enterprise, now the Two-Thirds World is stepping up to the task of missionary preaching.

B. Being a Missional Preacher

A recent development in understanding the mission of the church is that of being missional. Leaders in this movement critique Western Christendom as fostering an institutionalized church. Darrell L. Guder put it this way:

> In the long and complex process of Christendom, the *mission* of the church was replaced, largely, by the *maintenance* of the church as an institution providing religious services to the citizenry. Absent from this structure was either the theology or the language of mission. . . . Whereas the biblical emphasis is on the people of God, on the community with its shared life and public witness, the preoccupation of Christendom had become the institution—with its structures, traditions, prerogatives, and wealth—and its own preservation. (Guder 2006, 3)

Milfred Minatrea puts it this way: "As mission—the purpose of inviting and equipping individuals to be authentic disciples of Christ—gave way to maintenance of the status quo, people have grown weary of going through the motions of religious trappings without experiencing personal intimacy with God." On the other hand, he asserts, missional people have "caught a glimpse of God and are unwilling to settle for anything less than intimate relationship with [God]." They are "preparing members, and holding each other accountable, to live as representatives for God in their individual spheres of influence, in their world." He concludes, "These are missional churches, reproducing communities of authentic disciples, being equipped as missionaries sent by God, to live and proclaim [God's] Kingdom in their world" (Minatrea 2004, ix–x).

Although the texture of missional churches varies, they typically portray themselves as not just following a restorationist approach to doing church: "The missional church is not a 1st cent. church; it is a 21st cent. church committed to use every means available to accomplish God's missional purpose in the earth. They often use global communication and transportation systems to gain information and extend influence. . . . They are on mission as individuals and as communities of faith" (Minatrea 2004, x). Further, "People in the missional church do pray and give so that others may go and serve; yet for them missions is more centered in 'being and doing' than 'sending and supporting.' The missional church understands that although some may be supported as those sent to other locations, every member of the church is 'sent.' Mission is therefore participative rather than simply representative" (Minatrea 2004, 10–11).

Missional churches often value creativity in preaching, combining content and experience. If the philosophy of mission is consistent with the preaching in missional churches, the future will be the best indicator of success, or they will succumb to the very thing they critique—the status quo.

Developing a philosophy of missionary preaching that captures the best of all movements and visions of the church is the challenge for the preacher who wants to preach with the mission of Christ in mind.

Perhaps a starting place in developing a philosophy of missionary preaching is a reminder of some traditional elements of missionary preaching:

a. proclamation that the kingdom is at hand;
b. a call to repentance;
c. an invitation to faith in Christ, the Messiah;
d. an assurance that believers abide in the presence of the Holy Spirit.

The heart of missionary preaching can be a commitment to the gospel—the good news of salvation in Christ. This means that missionary preaching is essentially evangelistic preaching. Vanhoozer notes, "Preaching and teaching should be 'evangelistic,' then, in the sense of enabling people to indwell the gospel (= *evangel*) as the primary framework for all that they say and do" (Vanhoozer 2005, 74). Does this mean that every sermon is a call to salvation in Christ? The answer is, inherently, yes, but not overtly. That is, every sermon has the spiritual DNA of the evangel in it. Sermons cannot but contain the evangel, for all preaching grows out of the evangel. Evangelism is the source for the good news of salvation in Christ and therefore is at the very center of all preaching.

A missionary philosophy of preaching recognizes the central role of the gospel, and this gospel is then communicated to listeners with sensitivity to their thinking and language thought forms. The goal is that listeners will experience the paradigm shift of conversion from sinner to redeemed sinner.

C. The Practice of Missionary Preaching

Preaching with a missionary mind-set requires the preacher to do the following:

1. Realize that a missionary preacher is an evangelist. A missionary preacher loves the lost and is global, expansive in one's view of the world.
2. Exegete the text—know what the text is saying. A missionary preacher works hard at understanding the biblical text in its historical context.
3. Exegete the culture and/or subculture. A missionary preacher endeavors to know and appreciate the listeners' culture, whether the subculture or popular culture.
4. Speak in the language that engages with the mental world of the listeners. With a love for the listener, an understanding of the biblical text in its context, and an understanding of the listeners' context, the missionary preacher is able to speak to the listeners in a way that demonstrates an ability to appreciate and engage with their world in relation to the gospel.

See EVANGELISTIC PREACHING; GLOBALIZATION; MISSIONAL PREACHING; POSTCOLONIAL CRITICISM.

Bibliography: E. K. Bailey and Warren W. Wiersbe. *Preaching in Black and White.* (2003); David Dunn-Wilson. *A Mirror for the Church: Preaching in the First Five Centuries.* (2005); Whilhelm Dilger. *The Redemption of Man, according to Hinduism and Christianity.* (1902); Scott M. Gibson, ed. *Preaching to a Shifting Culture.* (2004); Domenico Grasso. *Proclaiming God's Message: A Study in the Theology of Preaching.* (1965); Darrell L. Guder. "Leadership in New Congregations: New-Church Development from the Perspective of Missionary Theology." *Extraordinary Leaders in Extraordinary Times.* Edited by. H. Stanley Wood. (2006); Philip Jenkins. *The Next Christendom: The Coming of Global Christianity.* (2002); Philip Jenkins. *The New Faces of Christianity: Believing the Bible in the Global South.* (2006); Jan A. B. Jongeneel. *Philosophy, Science, and Theology of Mission in the 19th and 20th Centuries: A Missiological Encyclopedia. Part 2: Missionary Theology.* (1997); Dae Ryeong Kim. "Karl Barth and a Missiology of Preaching." *Footprints of God: A Narrative Theology of Mission.* Edited by Charles Van Engen, Nancy Thomas, and Robert Gallagher. (1999); Cleophus J. LaRue. *The Heart of Black Preaching.* (1999); Hans J. Margull. *Hope in Action: The Church's Task in the World* (1962); Hans J. Margull, "Presence and Proclamation." *Eye of the Storm: The Great Debate in Mission.* Edited by Donald McGavran. (1972); Milfred Minatrea. *Shaped by God's Heart: The Passion and Practices of Missional Churches.* (2004); Lesslie Newbigin. *Foolishness to the Greeks: The Gospel and Western Culture.* (1986); Lesslie Newbigin. "Missions." *Concise Encyclopedia of Preaching.* Edited by William H. Willimon and Richard Lischer. (1995); Karl Rahner. *Theological Investigations.* (1961); Haddon Robinson and Craig Brian Larson. *The Art and Craft of Biblical Preaching: A Comprehensive Resource for Today's Communicators.* (2005); Jerome Clayton Ross. "The Cultural Affinity Between the Ancient Yahwists and the African Americans: A Hermeneutic for Homiletics." *Born to Preach: Essays in Honor of the Ministry of Henry and Ella Mitchell.* Edited by Samuel K. Roberts. (2000); Werner Schutz. *Geischichte der christichen Predigt.* (1972); George E. Sweazey. *The Church Is the Evangelist.* (1974); Kevin J. Vanhoozer. *The Drama of Doctrine: A Canonical Linguistic Approach to Christian Theology.* (2005); William H. Willimon and Richard Lischer. *The Concise Encyclopedia of Preaching.* (1995).

ORDINATION
Susan Karen Hedahl

Ordination is an ecclesiastical ritual that designates, commissions, and consecrates spiritual leadership in a faith community. Historically, ordination plays a role in specifying who preaches the Word of God and administers the sacraments. Some Christian communities do not require ordination as a prerequisite for preaching, but use other spiritual, ecclesial criteria for designating their preacher. This article discusses the history, theology, and practices associated with ordination in relationship to the preaching of the ordained and the non-ordained.

A. The Biblical Roots of Ordination and Preaching
B. Theologies of Preaching and Contemporary Ordination Practices
C. Practices of Preaching Among the Non-Ordained
D. Ordination: Practical Concerns for Preaching

A. The Biblical Roots of Ordination and Preaching

Preaching plays a central role in the ministry of Jesus and in his primary biblical witness, Paul. Their roles in proclaiming salvation have roots in the prophetic leadership traditions established in the OT. Many listeners recognized their preaching of God's powerful acts as a continuance of these traditions. New Testament passages on preaching, such as the concluding verses of Matthew's Gospel, various comments in Acts, and Paul's statements in Rom 10, testify to the fact that the gospel is presented in preaching and faithful preaching is the gospel's primary expression.

Early church leaders were concerned with matching tasks and human resources and maintaining the basic order of the church. Paul's metaphor of the church as the body of Christ shows that not everyone is equipped for the same tasks. In recognizing the different gifts of Christians preaching was eventually confirmed publicly by communal acclamation, specifically through prayers and laying on of hands.

This process of identifying and setting apart preachers was based on an understanding of the work of the Holy Spirit in the Christian community and in the individual. The call to preach, for ordained and non-ordained alike, has always been biblically centered in the call and confirmation of the Spirit.

Preaching leadership in the NT has three components: the character of the preacher as one called by the Spirit; the nature of the Word preached; and the interaction of the preacher with the listeners. First, the role of the preacher is characterized as subservient to the role of God's Word. Paradoxically, good proclamation and the personality of the preacher are inseparable, yet the preacher's work is derived only from the Word of God. Jesus continually emphasized the reign of God. Paul proclaimed his central mission this way: "For we preach not ourselves, but Christ Jesus the Lord; and ourselves your servants for Jesus' sake" (2 Cor 4:5 KJV).

Preaching is incarnational. The very act of speaking about God influences the demeanor, choices, and acts of the preaching leader. Both Jesus and Paul proclaimed the reign of God through the human realities of life: pain, struggle, sin, and death. The character of the genuine Christian preacher incorporates the preacher's and congregation's life experiences as a genuine mark of Christian proclamation and reflects the Savior's life and the Spirit's work among humanity.

Second, the nature of the preached Word shows its effects in preacher and listeners. According to the Bible, God's Word is on a radically different plane from mere information, philosophical discourse, or practical advice. Rather, the Word has a performative role, creating and causing in receptive listeners what it claims to do and be. As the NT preachers spoke the gospel of the forgiveness of sin and new life in Jesus Christ, this gospel was enacted in the lives of those believers who received it. Things changed. Salvation embodied itself in the lives of listeners.

The NT repeatedly associates this lively gospel with power. The preached Word is the power of God to heal, restore, forgive, enlighten, overcome evil, liberate, and above all, redeem. The privilege of preaching shows itself: as the power of God moving through the preacher's words and personal interaction with the Word himself, Jesus Christ.

Third, interactions between listeners and speakers through preaching offer significant challenges. Pulpit leadership makes clear the aim, purposes, and motives of preaching and elicits a response to the gospel. The Bible is realistic about this task. While the Word's power is independent of the preacher, the preacher nonetheless becomes the recipient of congregational reactions to it. Audiences may happily receive the gospel. They may also reject it and create martyrs out of preachers.

Although the historicity of ordination is often unclear, the NT documents provide sufficient evidence of the marks of the preaching leader, which contribute to today's ordination rites.

B. Theologies of Preaching and Contemporary Ordination Practices

Since ecclesial structures were in flux through the early centuries of the church, this complicates the effort to document the development of liturgical rituals in relationship to the office of preaching. The ordination rite developed historically from a simple act to one that became more complex over time. Early glimpses of the election process for preaching leaders are fragmentary. It is evident, however, that the dual practices of praying and the laying on of hands (see 1 Tim 4:14) were the basic components of the historical roots of ordination. Most faith communities derive ordination from its basic origins in these two actions.

Contemporary ordination practices in Protestant and Roman Catholic services include some mention of the role of speaking the gospel. Mention of preaching tends to be very brief in terms of the overall service, and various words and terms are used for it, including *ministry of the Word, preaching the gospel, Word of God, preach, preach and teach.* In some cases the word *teach* is taken to stand for *preach,* an exchange that has deep roots in the history of the Reformation.

What do all ordination services have in common in terms of the preacher? Following is an outline of what the office of the preacher should look like in relationship to the church, to the sermonic expression of the gospel, and to the personal behavior of the preacher as an ordained leader.

First, the ordinand is linked biblically, ecclesiastically and ritually to certain expectations of preaching. The ordinand is trained within the context of a denomination. Regardless of denomination, there is a general theology of proclamation that emerges in ordination and is characterized by these historical givens: the theology is rooted in biblical expressions of preaching (biblical sermons) and in biblical reflections on the act of proclamation.

Second, the call to preach is mandated by God. A biblically based theology of proclamation repeatedly emphasizes that the primary agency for the call to preach is *God's* call to the individual through the work of Jesus Christ in the power of the Holy Spirit. This is tested and affirmed by the community of faith. Ordination is the final step in a long process that follows the rhythms of God's call and human response.

The ordination ceremony is an affirmation of the experiences, testing, and will of the candidate to respond to God's call to proclaim the gospel. Candidates for ordination do not choose to preach (although they may enjoy preaching); rather, they are called to do so.

Third, as part of the mandated call, the ordinand is specifically designated beforehand as a preacher in a number of possible ways. The theological understanding of vocation and call varies among denominations and may include God's call through the inner, personal workings of the Holy Spirit in the candidate; preparation for ministry through an extended process of theological education; call by lot; communal recognition of certain gifts including preaching abilities for the ordained ministry; and a mystical experience that sometimes includes receiving the call in a dream. Most designations for preaching come about as a result of two or more of these factors.

Fourth, the call to preach is public and corporately based. The call to ministry confirmed through ordination, and ongoing preaching following ordination, are public acts. It means the gospel proclaimed is neither private nor the purview of only a few. Private proclamation results in cults. As Paul repeatedly emphasized, the gospel is not a secret or offered secretively as in Gnostic rites; instead, the public face of proclamation reflects the gospel's intrinsic nature. The gospel of Jesus Christ is inclusive.

Fifth, the primary theological emphasis of ordination parallels that of the biblical emphasis on preaching; both are derived from the Holy Spirit. All theologies of preaching demonstrate that Christian denominations have various ways of speaking about the work and role of the Holy Spirit in ministry and specifically in preaching.

Some use the word *inspiration*. Others use a word such as *gift* or *charism* as the fundamental basis for reflecting the works of the Spirit in preaching. Whether the work of the Spirit is understood as mediated in preaching through the processes of a long theological education and sermon preparation, or the Spirit is felt directly in preaching through the temporal acts of immediate revelation and inspiration, the Holy Spirit inspires true preaching. Most

faith communities strike a balance between these two views.

Sixth, the act of ordination understands preaching as sacramental or quasi-sacramental in nature. The fundamental role of preaching as a channel, response, or experience of God is found in all ordination services. Preaching is never accorded a secondary role, yet views of the nature of proclamation range over a wide theological spectrum. Some Christians have a high or sacramental view of preaching. Martin Luther named preaching as the first of the five means of God's grace, placing it above the sacraments of baptism and eucharist.

In some denominations, preaching may be the central part of the service and act as a spiritual trigger for psychological, emotional, and spiritual experiences of God. Some theological perspectives align preaching with ethics and morals. Preaching in Catholicism tends to link preaching closely to the mysteries of the eucharist. The overall denominational, theological perspectives of a given preacher determine how the listener is to listen to a specific sermon.

Seventh, all ordination rites imply that the candidate will preach true to the denomination's views of what it means theologically to preach the gospel. The gospel comes clothed with perspectives. Obedience to God's call to proclaim the gospel involves an implied consent on the part of the ordinand to preach in accordance with the theological core values of the faith community to which she or he is being called. A Lutheran proclaimer may seek to convey the dynamic of law and gospel. A Roman Catholic priest may preach homilies that honor the eucharist. A preacher in the framework of Spirit-filled language traditions may reflect that in the sermon.

This preacherly obedience to core denominational, theological perspectives guards against the use of the pulpit for heretical proclamation. The rite of ordination shows the assembly and the candidate that choices are being made willingly, corporately, and positively; the ordinand will preach the understanding of the gospel received by that tradition.

C. Practices of Preaching Among the Non-Ordained

The preaching office, viewed through the rite of ordination, roots itself biblically, historically, and theologically in the life of the church. But what does it mean to preach the gospel apart from a rite of ordination? Such preaching occurs among those chosen for the preaching office by other means and by laypeople who do not regularly maintain a type of preaching ministry in the church. Indeed, the work of the Holy Spirit through proclamation is always creative and sometimes even elusive in relationship to the formal structures of the church. Not all proclamation leadership depends on ordination for its structural significance. The case for non-ordained preachers occurs for reasons that have to do variously with worship, community structures, necessity, gender, age, and justice.

Biblically, the act of preaching the gospel is clearly the vocation of all Christians. This is a preliminary step to theologically affirming that Christians do not need an ordination rite to order how they determine their preaching leaders. Some Christians define church structures in ways that do not require formal leadership but share the gospel verbally and in a spirit of egalitarianism. Some forms of Quaker practice witness to the fact that the entire faith community preaches through discernment of the Spirit's promptings.

Gender also plays a role in early church history, which points to evidence that women preached in groups that did not adhere to a "men only" practice of leadership and preaching. Given the church's early social context, women preaching posed a significant challenge or even an outright threat to male preaching leaders. Women preaching on the edge of organized church structures is part of preaching history. Journals and sermons witness to women who preached in public to anyone who would listen or to groups that supported women's preaching leadership apart from the approved and ordained structures of the larger, orthodox denominations.

Less frequent are instances of non-ordained preaching on the part of children. In obedience to the biblical understanding of the manifestation of knowledge "out of the mouths of babes" (Matt 21:16 KJV), this phenomenon exists in some worshiping groups. Some of these child preachers, or child evangelists, are taught the basics in the public use of the Bible and in the speech preaching rhythms characteristic of their worshiping communities. Lay preaching has continued throughout the history of the church in forms that have not necessarily been typed as formal preaching, that is to say, preaching that falls under the rubric of an ordination ritual or even in a church setting. The discourse of the Salvation Army workers on the streets, in the bars, and in their gathered assemblies is a type of lay preaching.

The laity of all denominations also preach in their parishes in forms sometimes described as Temple Talks, in which an articulate congregation leader might speak about pressing concerns. These talks usually do not supplant the service's formal sermon but provide a parallel means of preaching the gospel.

Lay preaching is on the increase because there currently is a crisis in the available numbers of ordained personnel. Efforts are ongoing in Roman Catholic and Protestant judicatories to offer some training for those who are preaching in churches that have no ordained personnel.

Rather than formally recognize such preachers through a service of ordination, some judicatories use language such as licensing or provisional permission for preaching. Others focus on developing lay preacher talent from within their own congregations. All these designations keep alive the tension between laity and ordained. This increase of lay preachers also raises significant theological issues about the relationship of ordained leadership and the office of preaching.

D. Ordination: Practical Concerns for Preaching

The public nature of ordination defines a person as the congregation's preacher. Such a ritual serves a dual function over time. First, preachers may use the memory of the ordination service or the doctrine of ordination to speak about the shared nature of ministry and the congregation's vital connections and responsibilities to the preached Word. The sermon itself can periodically function as a teaching tool to remind listeners of the theology and nature of proclamation, thereby enlivening the entire ministry work of preacher and congregation. This is helpful in communities that get into the habit of thinking that proclamation and ministry are the sole responsibility of the preacher. Second, the congregation can understand any joys or concerns about their minister's preaching against the background of ordination. If the singular, sometimes lonely, nature of preaching tempts the preacher into becoming self-centered, using excessive self-disclosure, or becoming disconnected from the life of the congregation, discussing preaching against the backdrop of ordination may help to refocus both preacher and congregation about the role of proclamation in their shared ministry.

Ego and self-centered preaching can be best held in check with a shared congregational and ministerial sense of the responsibilities, joys, and missional directives of the rite of ordination. Understanding preaching within the ritual structures of ordination enables the church to remain corporate, biblical, accountable, and theologically balanced. *See* AUTHORITY OF THE PREACHER; CALL; CHARACTER; LAY PREACHER; WOMEN; WORD OF GOD.

Bibliography: John Collins. *Deacons and the Church: Making Connections between New and Old.* 2002; Beverly Mayne Kienzle and Pamela J. Walker, eds. *Women Preachers and Prophets through Two Millennia of Christianity.* (1998); Stephen V. Sprinkle. *Ordination: Celebratiing the Gift of Ministry.* (2004).

REVELATION
O. Wesley Allen Jr.

The theological category of revelation refers to the ways that God makes God's self, character, actions, or will (i.e., God's Being) known to humankind. From the under side, the theological category of revelation relates to questions of epistemology within the Christian faith. At issue in debates over the doctrine of revelation, therefore, is the question of how God is known. How is the One who is Mystery, who is Infinite, made known to and understood (albeit partially and imperfectly) by finite human beings?

A. Overview of Issues in Theologies of Revelation
   1. Transcendence vs. Immanence
   2. Christology
   3. Proclamation
B. Theological Models of Revelation
   1. Propositional Doctrine
   2. History
   3. Dialectical Presence
   4. Inner Experience
   5. New Awareness

A. Overview of Issues in Theologies of Revelation

1. Transcendence vs. Immanence
At their core, the above questions involve the inherent tension in a theistic worldview between God's transcendence and immanence. In terms of divine transcendence, the very need for revelation is rooted in God's Otherness. Because humans are finite beings, the eternal reality that is God is essentially hidden from us. God, however, pulls back the curtain that separates heaven from earth to reveal aspects of God's Being to us. Indeed, for theological orientations that stress God's transcendence as a dominant doctrinal motif, God alone can pull back the curtains of Mystery to reveal something of God's self to us. Emphasizing divine transcendence leads to a strong appreciation of Scripture and tradition. Through the Bible and/or church teaching, God speaks a revelatory word to God's people.

However, God is not only in heaven; God is also with us. The Creator is present in and to creation. For theologies that emphasize divine immanence over transcendence, God is so present in the very stuff of creation and human existence that something of God's Being can be discovered by human searching. For theological orientations that stress God's immanence, human reason and experience are invaluable for Christian epistemology. Science, philosophy, and art possess great revelatory potential, as do individual and corporate experiences.

Although obvious, it needs to be asserted explicitly that no theological position holds so strongly to divine transcendence that it completely denies immanence or vice versa. The question is not of choosing one emphasis to the exclusion of the other but of determining the relative weight given to immanence versus transcendence in developing a theological approach to revelation.

2. Christology
Regardless of how different theological stances deal with the paradox of divine immanence and transcendence, within Christianity the Christ-event is viewed as the center of God's revelation. Of course, different christological views of how Jesus Christ addresses this tension interpret this center differently. Suffice it to say generally at this point that, as the Word of God, Christ represents and reveals the fullest (but not the only) expression of God's Being. It is through or over against the Christ-event that all Christian claims about revelation must be judged and interpreted. However, the Christ-event itself comes to us as an already interpreted event and lends itself to multiple interpretations. Different hermeneutical approaches to Scripture, tradition, reason, and experience lead to radically

different interpretations of the revelatory significance of the works (ministry, death, and resurrection) and person of Jesus Christ.

3. Proclamation

Christian proclamation is inherently related to revelation. The nature of that relation, however, is debated. Preachers need to be intentional about shaping their approach to preaching in a manner that coheres with their approach to the tension between divine transcendence and immanence; their valuation of Scripture, tradition, reason, and experience; and the way their christological orientation influences a theological understanding of revelation. They must ask how the work of preaching participates or fails to participate in God's revelation and the church's grasping for knowledge of God. Attending to these questions has practical homiletical implications.

B. Theological Models of Revelation

In an attempt to demonstrate a range of answers to these homiletical questions, we turn to Avery Dulles's *Models of Revelation*. Dulles presents a taxonomy of five primary approaches to revelation that have been influential in Christian theology during the 20th cent. These five models are not exhaustive of every theologian, but instead represent broad movements within modern theology. In what follows we will examine each model that Dulles finds in the theological landscape; analyze the way each model views Scripture, tradition, reason, and experience as potential sources of revelation; discuss the basic understanding of the revelatory weight of the Christ-event inherent in the model; and present the view of preaching implied in the model.

This approach is taken so that readers might locate themselves in this landscape and reflect on their homiletical method in relation to their understanding of revelation. These models are not mutually exclusive, however, and preachers may well find themselves relating to more than one understanding of revelation. They should beware of trying to find affinity with all the different models, for there are serious distinctions between them. It is perhaps helpful to think of the five models as analogous to light dispersed by a prism; it is difficult to tell precisely where one color ends and the next begins. Red bleeds into orange, which bleeds into yellow, and so on and so forth. Preachers might identify the model below with which they most comfortably fit and should then expect to find some theological affinity with models nearest to it; they should also be able to see clear differences with the models that are farther away on the spectrum. The options are presented in an order that flows from emphasizing transcendence to ones that emphasize immanence.

1. Propositional Doctrine

In this first model, revelation is viewed as coming in the form of propositional statements about God's Being that God offers to the church. In other words, divine truth is revealed in logical doctrinal expressions whose very source (perhaps indirectly) is God. God is what God teaches.

Because of God's transcendence and human sin, we humans are unable to know God by our own efforts. Therefore, God must supernaturally "speak" to the fallen world in order to be known. God offers us truths about God's self, about the world, and about human existence that we could not know otherwise or by our own efforts. These doctrinal truths are revealed through Scripture and/or church teaching. While perhaps codified by human hands in Christian community, these expressions of faith are inspired by God and (at least some) are therefore held to be infallible.

Paired with this high view of Scripture and/or tradition is a high christology (i.e., an emphasis on the divine nature of Christ). This means that as the Incarnate Word, Jesus Christ is the very embodiment of God's self-revelation.

Preaching in this doctrinal model has a strong didactic character. Preachers teach doctrine, teach a proper understanding of Christ, and teach the congregation about God. They teach (i.e., pass on to) the congregation Scripture and/or tradition. Therefore, doctrinal preachers will be leery of the dominant conversation in homiletics during the last thirty years, in which there has been a strong movement away from deductive sermons to experiential approaches to preaching. Preachers in the doctrinal model will question how one is to test whether "experiences of the gospel" had during the sermon event are authentic experiences of God or simply emotions stirred by good art. If God makes God's self known through certain claims to which Christians should assent, then preachers should preach deductive, expository sermons that attempt to persuade their hearers of the truth of a doctrine of the church and of the importance of that doctrine for their understanding of God, their relationship with God, and the way they live their Christian life.

2. History

In this model, God is understood to reveal God's self primarily in divine providential and saving acts throughout the course of history. In contrast to the doctrinal model, event is emphasized over teaching. God is what God does.

That said, however, one must be careful not to isolate the specific moments in history as revelatory over against others. The entire span of history is the arena of divine activity—that is, salvation history— that reveals God as *pro nobis* (for us). Still, the biblical canon and church teaching have identified some historical events as paradigmatic for understanding the whole of salvation history. The OT lifts up creation, the Abrahamic covenant, the exodus, the Davidic covenant, prophetic declarations, and the return from exile as such events. For the church, the center of this salvation history is the Christ-event. Through Jesus Christ, God acts to fulfill the past and open up an eschatological future.

While Scripture and tradition are extremely important in this model, they are not viewed as directly revelatory. History is revelatory as the arena of God's salvific activity. Scripture and tradition serve as witnesses to God's revelation in and throughout history.

Preaching in this historical model, put simply, joins Scripture and tradition in witnessing to God's salvation history. This does not necessitate that preachers dive into and report upon such things as research concerning the historical Jesus. It means that preachers must point to Jesus of Nazareth and claim that in this historical person God acted upon the world in a definitive way. As preachers in the doctrinal model reiterate and interpret the doctrines of the faith, in the history model preachers retell and interpret the stories of a God who was and still is active in the world. They rehearse the prophetic, apostolic, and ecclesiastical witness to what God has done and is doing in the world. Indeed, the paradigmatic stories of God's activity in the past serve as means to measure claims concerning God's activity in the present and future. Thus, preachers who view revelation as history offer congregations a view of God's history of which they are beneficiaries, in which they participate, and for which they hope.

3. Dialectical Presence

According to adherents of this model, because God is infinite and humans are not, human language is an inadequate tool for describing the mystery that is God. But one cannot simply claim that God's character and will are ineffable and do theology or proclaim the gospel at the same time. The question is not *whether* to speak but *how* to speak in order to call attention to and minimize the fallibility of language. The answer that dialectical theologians give to this dilemma is that we must constantly place seemingly contradictory theological claims (affirmations and denials, statements and counterstatements) side by side to arrive at deeper truths.

Following this method, dialectical thinkers not only refuse to resolve the tension between divine transcendence and immanence by emphasizing one over the other (as do the other models in this taxonomy), but they claim that holding the tension in place is essential to a proper theological approach to revelation. God is the concealed Revealer.

Although different christological orientations are possible in this model, the dialectical approach is a christocentric model. Adherents claim, in various ways, that the very content of revelation is Christ, the Word in person. Christ is God's self-communication, the Word of God that communicates God to us when, where, and how God pleases. However, because God speaks in and to the human situation, which is by its nature finite and fallen, the very act of revelation continues to conceal God's infinite nature as well.

The revelation of God-in-Christ is not simply a historical revelation of the past. It is also a living, eschatological revelation of God's Being. Revelation is thus objective and subjective at the same time. The Word that was and is incarnate in Christ is also the Word we receive and for which we wait with expectation and hope. Since in revelation God conveys Christ to us, revelation is salvific—it is the freely given word of divine judgment and forgiveness to humankind.

The dialectical presence model views Scripture and tradition (and perhaps experience and reason) as witnessing to God's self-revelation but not as revelatory in and of themselves. God can and will, however, use Scripture, for instance, to reveal God's self whenever God so chooses.

Likewise, God can and does use the church's proclamation to reveal God's self to hearers. This recognition naturally leads to a paradoxical theology of the pulpit. Since every sermon has the potential to be an event in which God communicates God's salvation to God's people, this view has elements of a high theology of preaching. After all, the sermon and the preacher are potentially instruments of divine action! God-in-Christ is not the object of the sermon but is the subject. However, this revelatory potential has nothing to do with the person or skill of the preacher, the form of the sermon, or the emotive potential of the sermonic imagery. God speaks to the worshiping congregation through these means but also in spite of them. Thus, the preacher in this model does not seek to teach correct doctrine, report on history, or exhort congregations on how they should live. The preacher simply proclaims Christ crucified and risen as the core of God's good news and leaves the rest to God and the hearer. In this model, in other words, preaching is always in the form of declaration—it does not involve didactic, hortatory, or experientially oriented forms of rhetoric.

4. Inner Experience

In this theological model, God's revelation is not viewed as something objective and external to the person of faith, whether in the form of a body of propositional truths or historical events. Instead, revelation is the interior experience of God's grace or communion with God. Note that it is not within experience that God reveals truths about God's self. The content of revelation, according to this mode, is simply God's own self. In terms of revelation, God is what God conveys of God's Being to us.

Because God conveys God's Being to us experientially, it is idolatrous to consider Scripture and tradition as themselves expressions of God's revelation. Only God reveals God's self. In this model, therefore, Scripture and tradition are viewed not as revelatory but as expressions of religious experience of the faith communities of the past and thus as measures of authentic religious experience in the present. As such, the primary value of Scripture, tradition, and indeed reason is that they have the potential to awaken spiritual consciousness, to open us to religious experience.

Adherents of this model can hold a range of christological positions. A fairly common position in this model is that all religions, not just Christianity, have the potential to invite awareness of the primordial experience of the divine. Therefore, Christians who hold this model with a higher christology might aver that the God of all human experience is indeed God-in-Christ, whether all humans use that language to name their experience or not. Those with a lower christology, emphasizing the human dimension of Christ's character, would refuse to reduce all experience of the divine to the same experience. Instead of making claims for all humans or for the whole of how God reveals God's Being, they would simply make claims concerning Christian experience—Christians open themselves to revelatory experiences of God by opening themselves to the inner life of Jesus Christ as presented in the NT. In other words, reflection on the person of or the witnesses to Jesus as the Christ leads one to an appropriately Christian awareness of divine immanence (just as, say, a Muslim practice and devotion would lead one to an appropriately Muslim awareness of divine immanence).

Preaching in this experiential model, therefore, strives to join and indeed use Scripture, tradition, and reason to awaken hearers' spiritual consciousness in a specifically Christian manner, in creating in the congregation an openness to the interior experience of God. Preachers will use provocative, artistic modes in the pulpit (such as inductive and narrative sermons) in an attempt to offer hearers an experience of the gospel rather than pointing beyond the worship moment to doctrines or historical events. In this view, preaching has a sacramental function as a potential means of grace. As such, there is a strong emphasis on the individual hearer in this mode of preaching.

5. New Awareness

In this model, the theological understanding of revelation is closest to secular idiomatic use of the word *revelation* in the sense of one discovering or realizing something new. In other words, revelation is not so much a gift from God from outside us as it is new recognition that God generates within us. Thus, this model emphasizes divine immanence but in such a way that is inseparable from the creative potential of human imagination. In this model, God is the ground of what God enables us to imagine.

The content of revelation, therefore, is less God communicating God's self and more a transformation of our understanding of ourselves, our situations, and our world. In other words, revelation sheds light on the human condition, dispelling our illusions and directing us toward potentiality. For the church, Christ is the example and/or bearer of this new awareness, which is salvation.

This model places a high value on human reason as an instrument of new awareness and on experience as reason's companion. It is through reason and experience that the questions of human existence are correlated with biblical and doctrinal expressions of the faith in ways that new awareness and new modes of existence become possible.

The goal of preaching in this model, therefore, is to evoke hearers' existential imagination through the use of the symbols, metaphors, stories, and theological interpretation of the Christian faith so that they might gain a new vision of their lives, their world, and the interaction of the two. Hence, preaching attempts to bring hearers to a moment of clarity about the human condition and their participation in it so that they might strain toward a more significant, meaningful approach to life. *See* CHRISTOLOGY; DEVOTIONAL LIFE/LIFE-STYLE; DOCTRINAL; IMAGINATION/CREATIVITY; METAPHOR AND FIGURES OF SPEECH.

Bibliography: Paul Avis. "Divine Revelation in Modern Protestant Theology." *Divine Revelation.* Edited by Paul Avis. (1997) 45–66; Avery Dulles. *Models of Revelation.* (1982; reissued 1992); Stuart A. Frayne. "Models of Revelation and Models of Preaching: A Review Article." *Theolodite* 8 (1988) 16–27; Mary Catherine Hilkert. "Revelation and Proclamation: Shifting Paradigms." *In the Company of Preachers.* (1993) 113–38.

SIN AND EVIL
Cynthia L. Rigby

In the broadest sense, sin is the situation in which we find ourselves as creatures in relationship to the Creator God. Traditionally put, sin is the separation from God characterizing the relationship between finite and infinite. Classically, Augustine defines evil as "the absence of good" that he sees as the worst thing imaginable. These definitions can be problematic, particularly in connection with suffering. They can be taken either to mean that those who suffer are responsible for their suffering or to deny the reality of suffering. In preaching on sin and evil one seeks to keep in mind those who suffer and at the same time give account for God.

A. Sin, Evil, and the Context of Suffering
B. Sin
C. Evil
  1. Evil and Suffering
  2. Common Misperceptions
  3. Systemic Implications of Sin
D. Sin, Evil, and Preaching to Sufferers
  1. Moral Evil
  2. Natural Evil
  3. Accounting for God

A. Sin, Evil, and the Context of Suffering

One of the rawest questions of human existence concerns the relationship between sin and evil. Even before we ponder what sin is or enter into worthy debates about the character of evil, we struggling, hope-full creatures try to make sense of things by looking for causal relationships. If something evil happens, is sin necessarily in play? we ask. If I am suffering, is it because I have done something wrong?

The first answer to such questions, as all good pastoral caregivers are aware, is no. A person who is suffering has not necessarily done anything wrong. The book of Job refutes at length the assumption that there must be a causal link between suffering and sin. Job and his family suffer despite the fact that Job is righteous. Even when some causal link *can* be made, it is simply not the case that sin can exhaustively account for, or in any way justify, the extent and reality of the suffering we experience. Even if Job *had* sinned, would any sin be terrible enough to merit the deaths of all his children, the loss of all his possessions, and the ruining of Job's own health? Certainly not! we are compelled to argue.

Suffering cannot helpfully be construed as punishment for sinful behavior when so many, so often, sin without suffering or suffer without sinning. Where there is suffering, there is always more operative than the sinful behavior that provoked it, even when sinful behavior *is* in evidence. If I hit someone while driving drunk, for example, there is a relationship between my sin and the suffering that ensues. But my sin cannot explain everything about the suffering that has occurred—why that person crossed the street at that precise moment, for example, or why I happened to choose that route and time to go home. There are inexplicable factors for why horrible things happen, even when a lot can be explained on the basis of sin.

How *is* sin related to evil, if not causally? While most of us rarely preach explicitly on the theme of sin and evil, how we understand their relationship lies always in the background of our proclamation, framing our understanding of the purpose and promise of the gospel itself. In order to answer this question, it will be helpful first to delineate something of what is meant by sin and evil.

B. Sin

To say that sin is separation from God and characterizes finite beings does not mean that to be finite is to be sinful. On the contrary, finite creatures are described by God as "good" on the sixth day of creation. To be finite is, however, to participate in the conditions of historical existence (Tillich 1975), to yearn to bridge the qualitative gap between ourselves and God. Jesus Christ himself participates in sin in this sense. Jesus "in every respect has been tested as we are" (Heb 4:15) and became "sin on our behalf" (2 Cor 5:21 NASB). He was and is "God with us" (Matt 1:23 KJV).

The term *sin* is also used to reference certain problematic behaviors. Used in this way, it acknowledges not only our propensity toward, but also our active resistance to, living in recognition of both our limits and our value as finite creatures. It names our refusal to acknowledge that we stand, as creatures, before the Creator God. In contrast to us, Jesus is one who participates fully in historical existence without resisting his finitude. While he "has been tested as we are," he is "yet without sin" (Heb 4:15). This does not mean Jesus overwhelmed his fully human temptations to sin with his fully divine capacities. Rather, Jesus remained sinless insofar as he steadfastly honored his full humanity, remembering that to be truly human is to recognize one's ultimate dependence on God. Jesus did not deny his finitude, but submitted to the Father God, the infinite one, the Creator of all. He resisted the temptation to attempt infinite behaviors—such as trying to turn stones into bread or jumping off the pinnacle of the Temple—things we sinfully attempt to do when we imagine we can override our finitude rather than worship the one true God.

While Jesus did not commit the sin of pride, neither did he bemoan his finitude, diminishing his creaturely self in the process. He did not say to the tempter, for example: "I cannot turn stones into bread. Therefore, I simply will not eat. Woe is me."

When we understand ourselves to be trapped by our finitude, we commit another kind of sin. Often understood by theologians to be the inverse of pride (Saiving 1992), the sin of self-deprecation is marked by our refusal to accept that we finite creatures are exalted in Christ to participation in the very life of the triune God (Col 3:3). Jesus modeled an alternative to the sin of pride and to the sin of self-deprecation. "Humanity does not live by bread alone," he tells the tempter. He will neither turn the stone into bread nor consider himself deprived. He refuses to engage in sinful behaviors that perpetuate estrangement rather than those that extend trust in God's promised care.

It is living as though our experience of separation from God (our sinful condition) is something we need to override (pride) or to wallow in (self-deprecation) that moves us from the *condition* of sin to the committal of sins. The Scriptures supply lists of them (e.g., Prov 6:6-19; Gal 5:19-21); theologians through the ages have attempted to categorize them (e.g., mortal and venial). While Christian believers have tended to recognize all people as equally mired in the condition of sin, they have made distinctions among sins based upon the degree to which the said sinner is turned toward that which is evil (away from God) rather than toward that which is good (God).

C. Evil

It is at this point in our discussion that evil comes into play. In his *Confessions* (1984), Augustine argues as follows: there is one God, and this God is good. The one, good God created all things "out of nothing" (ex nihilo) with no added, ambiguous ingredients. Because everything that exists or has substance was made out of nothing by the good God, everything that exists must therefore itself be good. The obvious question that then emerges is: Where did evil come from?

One possible response to this question is to reject monotheism and argue that a force or a god other than the God who is good created it. A good God created the good stuff; some demiurge, demon, or not-very-nice, less powerful god created the other stuff. Another option would be to remain monotheists while at the same time acknowledging that God, though mainly good, is not *all* good. God created the evil that exists alongside the good, we could posit.

According to Augustine, neither of these responses honors the Spirit's witness, as evident in our religious experiences and in the book of Genesis, that God is both "one" and "good." After much struggle with the question, he realized evil could be defined, with no compromise to either the divine sovereignty or the divine goodness, if we ceased thinking about it as *something* that had to have come from *somewhere*. Evil came neither from a god other than the one true God or from a God who is not entirely good. Rather, evil names that which we turn toward when we turn away from a good God and the good things God has made, living as though the false reality ("the absence of good") were actually true.

For Augustine, "the absence of good" is the very worst thing imaginable. If good is absent, then God and all God created are absent. Since God and all God created actually exist, evil is, categorically, absolutely *not* what is, the absolutely *not real* (Barth 1970). Evil is, in one sense, the ultimate, incapacitating lie.

1. Evil and Suffering

Unfortunately Augustine's definition of evil has often been used to belittle those who are suffering by denying the ultimate validity of their anguish. The mistake comes when the move is made from understanding evil as the "not real" to suggesting its impact is illusory. Such a move discredits the creaturely experience of suffering. To hold that, because evil is the "not real," things are not as bad as they seem with the intent of being hopeful is to rob those who are suffering of the only hope available in the midst of their pain—that is, the hope inherent in naming the pain for what it is and identifying themselves as subjects in relationship to it. It is the impatient, honest insistence on something other than what actually is that is evident in Job's ardent proclamation: "I know that my Redeemer lives" (Job 19:25), the psalmist's audacious demand: "Rouse yourself . . . O Lord" (Ps 44:23), and Jesus' devastated cry: "My God, my God, why have you forsaken me?" (Matt 27:46). These biblical examples help us understand evil as the bottomless chasm that is the heart of all suffering—the hopeless, hollow, visceral yearning that—in the face of God's promise never to abandon us—leads us to lament our abandonment by the one who never abandons. It is precisely our faith in God's unrelenting presence that makes evil—the absence of God—so utterly shocking, poignant, hopeless.

A related mistake is to identify sin and/or suffering with evil. Neither sin nor suffering can be perfectly correlated with evil precisely because both sin and suffering are, indeed, *something*—that is, distortions of the good. Sin distorts the good by reaching toward the absence that is the antithesis of God's creative and redemptive will. Suffering, as we have mentioned, may or may not be fed by sin, and in varying degrees. Whether sin is involved or not, suffering always includes the never completely accounted for reaching out of absence *to* us. The only answer, from the vantage point of faith, is the answer of Job: to claim the sovereignty and goodness of God despite appearances to the contrary. And the answer of the lament psalmist: to recall God to being who God is. And the answer of Jesus: to insist, as a child desperate to be held by a wayward parent, that the one who forsakes me is "my God."

2. Common Misperceptions

Similarly, to understand evil as the absence of good does not, by necessity, entail denying the existence of Satan and/or demonic beings. Traditionally speaking, Satan is a fallen angel—Lucifer, the angel of light. He was created good—by the good God, with substance. He fought his finite condition, struggling to be on a par with God, and committed sinful behaviors. Contrary to popular understandings that have formed those listening to our sermons, Satan himself is not evil, but the premier manifestation of one who has turned completely away from the reality of the good.

Another common misperception shared by many Western Christian believers is that it is theologically misguided to speak of God's absence precisely because God is omnipresent. Certainly, the reality is that God is with us, whether we go up to the heavens or go down to the depths of Sheol (Ps 139). We often live in ways that ignore, deny, or resist this reality, however. We live as though God is not with us. When we begin living in relation to an absence that is a lie, but so powerful a lie that it operates as truth for us, there are all kinds of detrimental implications. The lie is that God is not here, that God has left us, and that we therefore have to fend for ourselves in whatever way we can. The absence of good is a lie that is more real, in its falsehood, than some of the realest realities. Evil as the absence of good names the fact that we, and this world, turn away from the all-powerful God who created us good, living a lie rather than the true reality of our existence.

To live in this way is, of course, to sin. To sin is to turn away from the real reality of God toward that which is not real—toward emptiness, absence, and denial of goodness. When we sin, we have turned so determinately toward the evil non-real that that which is not substantive exercises real and devastating power over us.

3. Systemic Implications of Sin

Sin has systemic, as well as personal, implications. The sin of individuals hurts others, threatening their perception of the good. Further, when we as individuals turn away from the reality of our existence in relationship to the good Creator, we create systems that perpetuate the unreal reality we claim is antithetical to the character of God's kingdom. The very structure of many institutions, economic systems, and households, developed in the context of our sinful historical existence, supports individuals' commission of pride and self-deprecation, and especially keeping these two sins working in tandem.

As those called to proclaim the good news of the gospel, we are responsible never to tolerate systemic sin with the rationale that it is somehow inevitable in a fallen world. As Gutiérrez so well puts it: "When and where God's reign and demand that we 'do what is right and just' are denied, God is not present" (Gutiérrez 1991, 69). As faithfully as we invite the people of God to the confession and repentance that restore them to right relation to the one who is good, then, we must also insist on the transformation of social structures antithetical to God's creative and redemptive will.

D. Sin, Evil, and Preaching to Sufferers

We have to this point explored sin and evil in relationship to our predicament as finite and sinful creatures. *Sin* is a term we associate with our culpability for suffering, whether our own or the world's. *Evil* references the suffering that cannot exhaustively be accounted for, even if sinful behaviors have contributed to it. When no causal connection between sin and evil can be identified, there is a sense in which we might be relieved. We are not, by virtue of our sinfulness, responsible for the suffering. But we might also be terrified. If there is no causal connection between sin and suffering, we have even less control than we thought. There is no guarantee that we can alleviate suffering by lessening our sin. We must therefore turn to God rather than rely on ourselves, especially in times of pain.

1. Moral Evil

Categorically, theologians speak of *moral evil*—that is, suffering in which sin is definitely in evidence, but cannot simply be allayed. Even when the sinner in question *desires* to reform his or her sinful ways, rehabilitation is easier intended than done. Paul complains, along these lines, "I do not do the good I want, but the evil I do not want is what I do" (Rom 7:19). This description is perhaps especially indicative of individuals insofar as they are complicit in perpetuating sinful systems of which they are unaware, about which they are in denial, or in relation to which they feel powerless to effect change.

2. Natural Evil

Even harder to address than the problem of moral evil, from a theological perspective, is that of natural evil. *Natural evil* is a term used by theologians to describe situations of suffering in which sin is not readily in evidence. The tsunami of 2004 and the Katrina disaster of 2005 are two recent examples of natural evil. Our tendency, as those who want to have some modicum of control, is often to go overboard in attempting to decipher sin rather than to concede to the category of natural evil. In response to the tsunami, for example, some offer discourses on global warming, and our sinful precipitation of it, and its causal influence on natural disasters. While contrition with regard to our complicity in global warming is certainly in order, it must be remembered that repenting from our sins and working to improve the environment are qualitatively different from implying that we can escape tsunamis and Katrinas if only we act properly. When we as preachers concede to the pressure to restore an illusion of control by overemphasizing a causal relationship between sin and evil, we run the risk of conveying to our parishioners that suffering is their, and our, and the sufferers' fault.

3. Accounting for God

As preachers, we know it is even harder to account for God in the face of suffering than it is to account for ourselves. A fundamental truth to which we are ever called to bear witness is that God has to do with everything. As the 16th cent. Reformer John Calvin put it, "Without certainty about God's providence, life would be unbearable"; and "Certainty about God's providence puts joyous trust toward God in our hearts" (Calvin 1960, 1.17.10). When we remember this, we avoid talk of tragedy that substitutes for faithful pondering of God's relationship to evil, whether moral or natural.

Like Calvin and like Job, theodicies are uncompromising in their insistence that God is sovereign over all things. Their purpose is to justify God in the face of suffering. They do this in a variety of ways. They might argue, for example, that suffering is not as bad as it seems; that God is not as powerful as we thought; or that God is not as consistent, in the exercise of God's kindness, as we had hoped. Theodicies are always trying to figure out where God is in relation to the suffering. In so doing, they share in the primary task of the preacher: to get up in the pulpit, week after week, and to reaffirm God's presence even in the face of God's absence.

Preachers have as much difficulty as anyone else seeing God in the midst of suffering. Called upon to bear witness in moments of doubt, we may be tempted to find subtle ways of promoting causal connection between sin and evil. Because we cannot figure out what God is up to, we put the focus on ourselves, instead. To do so relieves those who want to believe we have the power to resolve suffering. But to do so is also, however inadvertently, to absent God from the conversation rather than call God to account.

We, as preachers, *do* have a word of reassurance to offer. It is not reassurance about our capacity to control. Rather, it is reassurance about God's promise to restore, and about our open invitation—as the beloved children of God—to insist that this promise be kept. "Deliver us from evil," Jesus taught us. In our preaching as in our prayer, we insist on the coming of a kingdom where God's presence is always in evidence, where forgiveness of sins is fully realized, and where suffering is no more. *See* CRISIS; FOUR PAGES OF THE SERMON; GOD, ETHICS AND; SOTERIOLOGY; THEOLOGY IN THE SERMON.

Bibliography: Augustine. *Confessions.* Translated by R. S. Pine-Coffin. (1984); Karl Barth. *Church Dogmatics.* Vol. 3, pt. 1. Translated by Geoffrey W. Bromiley. (1970); John Calvin. *Institutes of the Christian Religion.* Edited by John T. McNeill. Translated by Ford Lewis Battles. (1960); James Cone. *God of the Oppressed.* (1975); Gustavo Gutiérrez. *The God of Life.* (1991); Søren Kierkegaard. *Fear and Trembling.* Edited by Edna Hong and Howard Hong. (1983); Gottfried Wilhelm Leibniz. *Theodicy: Essays on the Goodness of God, the Freedom of Man, and the Origin of Evil.* (1985); Valerie Saiving. "The Human Situation: A Feminine View." *Womenspirit Rising.* Edited by Judith Plaskow and Carol Christ. (1992) 25–42; Paul Tillich. *Systematic Theology.* Vol. 2, pt. 3, *Existence and the Christ.* (1975).

SOTERIOLOGY
Sally A. Brown

Soteriology is Christian theological reflection on the ways in which God saves, bringing wholeness to humankind and to creation. The late 20th and early 21st cent. have witnessed lively debates in soteriology, particularly surrounding theories of atonement (specific theological reflection on Jesus' death and resurrection as saving acts of God). Interpreting God's saving work in preaching today requires (1) becoming aware of the history of soteriological reflection; (2) attending to current debates about how Jesus' death and resurrection are interpreted; and (3) creatively employing many different models and metaphors to show how God's saving activity in Jesus' life, death, and resurrection shapes Christian belief, worship, and ethics.

A. Historical Backdrop of Current Debates
   1. Scholasticism
   2. The Reformers
   3. The Twentieth Century
B. Contemporary Soteriology
   1. The Penal Model
   2. Theory as Questionable
   3. Broader Notions of Soteriology
C. Soteriology in Contemporary Preaching
   1. Challenging Narrow or Inadequate Understandings of God's Saving Work
   2. Reclaiming Multiple Metaphors of Salvation
   3. Reading NT Soteriological Metaphors and Images
   4. Sermons Prompted by Different Homiletical Purposes, Occasions, and Cultural Contexts

A. Historical Backdrop of Current Debates

Every religion has its vision of salvation. Christian understandings of salvation embrace the life, death, and resurrection of Jesus as the fulcrum of divine saving activity. God's saving actions toward both human beings and the cosmos as a whole are broader than the events of Jesus' career and passion; yet a distinctively Christian understanding of salvation cannot be separated from these events. Theologians typically have discussed soteriology under the headings of justification (God's work of setting right divine-human relations) and sanctification (God's continuous reordering of human life, individually and collectively, through the Spirit).

Notably, the early church never attempted to arrive at a consensus account of the means and mode of God's saving work comparable to the agreements about the Trinity and christology achieved at the Councils of Nicaea and Chalcedon. Beginning with the NT writings and continuing for several centuries thereafter, various metaphors functioned side by side in concert and complementarity as interpretive frameworks for understanding God's saving work in Jesus' life, death, and resurrection. New Testament writers speak of the freeing of captives (Eph 4:8), propitiation offered to God for sin (1 John 2:2; 4:10), the giving of one's life to avert the death of others (John 18:14), and sacrifice (the book of Hebrews and many other references), to name but a few. Early church theologians felt free to use other metaphors drawn from the local experience of those whose faith they sought to shape.

1. Scholasticism

The rise of Scholasticism in the High Middle Ages prompted more systematic and standardized accounts of God's saving action in Jesus' death, a mode of reflection that later came to be known as atonement theory. A theory of atonement interprets Jesus' death and resurrection using a central concept or metaphor and includes, either explicitly or implicitly, (1) a diagnosis of the human condition (whether bondage to evil powers, sin as a barrier to divine-human fellowship, or guilt as contamination); (2) a portrayal of the way God's nature and motives prompt God's saving action; and (3) an account of the efficacy of Jesus' death and resurrection to overcome the problem (sin, bondage to evil powers, alienation, etc.).

An early and influential atonement account was Anselm of Canterbury's *Cur Deus Homo?* (*Why Did God Become Human?*). Anselm was dissatisfied with the then popular image of Jesus' death as a ransom to free humanity from Satan's clutches. In this view, God permitted the divine Son to fall into Satan's hands through death. Too late, Satan discovered that his victim was in fact not only human, but also divine. Jesus overcame Satan and delivered the entire human race from bondage. Finding this portrayal of God as a trickster beneath the divine dignity, Anselm drew instead upon the feudal system of his day and the relationships between a lord and his vassals to develop an alternative interpretation now known as satisfaction theory. Sinful humanity, said Anselm, is like the vassal guilty of dishonoring his lord. Humanity cannot present adequate restitution for this dishonor, which must be rectified. Only one both human and divine could offer recompense, restoring the human-divine relationship. A point often missed is that at the heart of Anselm's satisfaction theory is not the suffering of a criminal penalty (death), but Jesus' self-offering as restoration of a broken relationship (Green and Baker 2000, 142; Schmiechen 2005, 196–97).

Not all were content with Anselm's explanation. His younger contemporary, Peter Abelard, argued that God cannot be constrained to act by some arbitrary honor code. In Jesus' life and death, said Abelard, God provided a demonstration of divine love so compelling as to move humanity to give up its rebellion against God. Later interpreters of the death of Jesus, notably the Reformers, found Abelard's account of the saving significance of Jesus' death overly subjective (too dependent for its effectiveness on human response).

2. The Reformers

Preferring more objective theories that emphasized God's unilateral action in saving humanity, the Reformers followed Anselm's lead, although they elaborated atonement theory with materials from their historical contexts. Luther emphasized the "happy exchange" in which our sin is borne by Jesus the sinless one, and we are clothed, through faith, with Christ's righteousness. Calvin, trained in law, drew on the framework of criminal law and punishment to develop an interpretation of Jesus' crucifixion in which Jesus pays the death penalty for sin in humanity's place, suffering the full brunt of God's just wrath. Later proponents of the penal atonement tradition have tended to overextend the punitive metaphor, creating an unbiblical portrait of an enraged father appeased by nothing less than the horrible suffering and death of his own son.

3. The Twentieth Century

By the early 20th cent., a form of penal theory juxtaposed with satisfaction and sacrifice motifs had become the dominant explanation for the saving significance of Jesus' death in North American popular Christian discourse. Historically speaking, this standardization of popular atonement theology was an aberration; since NT times, no single metaphor had been allowed to function as the "master" metaphor governing the others.

By the 1930s, it was assumed that atonement could be adequately discussed by means of the threefold typology of ransom, satisfaction/penal substitution, and moral influence (Abelardian) motifs. The publication of Gustaf Aulén's *Christus Victor: An Historical Study of the Three Main Types of the Idea of the Atonement* (1931) served to solidify this consensus. The three-theory approach proved serviceable for teachers and students of soteriology for several decades. However, as the 20th cent. came to a close, a rising chorus of voices began raising questions about the adequacy of the three-theory typology, either as a characterization of the history of soteriological reflection or as a basis for preaching and teaching. Aulén's typology tended to conflate the penal paradigm with Anselmian satisfaction theory, glossing over distinctions between their characterizations of the soteriological problem and the mode for its resolution. The popular three-theory approach also tended to obscure from view the rich variety of metaphors found in the NT and in subsequent theological reflection—metaphors that complemented and balanced one another, calling into play the interpretive resources of many webs of meaning for different cultural and pastoral contexts.

B. Contemporary Soteriology

Critical reassessment and revision have been the hallmarks of contemporary soteriological reflection. Three developments are noteworthy.

1. The Penal Model

First, traditional atonement theories, especially forms of the penal model, have been the focus of searching critique among black, feminist, womanist, and postcolonialist theologians. They point to a dangerous correlation between appeals to some of the most dominant atonement models, especially penal substitution, and abusive uses of power; they focus on the concrete effects of particular atonement doctrines when deployed to shape faith and behavior, especially among socially and politically marginalized persons. Appeals to sacrifice motifs have been used to encourage victims of domestic, social, and political oppression to accept abuse, suppressing victims' capacities to resist their oppressors in domestic, social, and political contexts. Penal substitution theory has sometimes been used to produce moral justification for violence as a good and necessary means of achieving order. Theologians from many perspectives today question the psychologically compelling but biblically questionable penal view of the cross, arguing that this model has been read into many biblical texts that do not support its inner logic or its portrait of God.

2. Theory as Questionable

A second trend in soteriology today is that theologians and biblical scholars question the very notion of atonement theory itself. To speak of theory may imply that it is possible to explain the inner mechanics of God's saving work in an exhaustive and comprehensive manner. The many soteriological images and concepts of biblical and post-biblical Christian tradition function metaphorically. That is, the relationship between Jesus' death, on the one hand, and an image or concept like debt payment, ransom, or sacrifice, on the other, is not one of literal equivalence, but depends on holding together both similarity and difference in creative, semantic tension. For example, Jesus' death is a sacrifice and is not a sacrifice in the OT sense. Jesus' death does not fit neatly into the OT practice and semantics of sacrifice. Jesus died on a cross, not an altar; and he was killed by soldiers, not a priest. His blood was not literally used in the specific ways called for by the OT sacrificial cult. None of this is to say that sacrifice imagery cannot illuminate our understanding of Jesus' life and death today, especially if we are careful to understand the web of meanings it evokes; yet not every element of any metaphorical system bears soteriological significance. Theologians and biblical scholars urge scholars and preachers to recover a diverse metaphorical vocabulary, including neglected biblical metaphors, such as the laying down of life within a friendship paradigm prominent in the Gospel of John (Reid 2004) or the liberation of captives (Ray 1998, 84–145; Weaver 2001, 12–98, 179–228), and testing new ones for their fit with Christian tradition as well as cultural relevance.

3. Broader Notions of Soteriology

Finally, in addition to questioning traditional theories and embracing a wide range of metaphors, theologians are thinking more expansively about God's saving action. Soteriology is broader than atonement theology. A perennial issue in soteriology is how to speak of Jesus' life, death, and resurrection so that their significance is integrated with Christian ethics and with God's ultimate purposes for all creation. Some versions of satisfaction or penal substitution theory, for example, can make the crucifixion appear to be an isolated and arbitrary past event, a forensic transaction struck between God the Father and God the Son with little apparent connection to Jesus' life and ministry or to the ongoing work of the Spirit in sanctification, God's pursuit of justice, the mending of creation (Rom 8:18-23), or the gathering of all things into Christ (Eph 1:9-14, 22-23).

C. Soteriology in Contemporary Preaching

How preachers speak of God's saving work has far-reaching implications today for Christian faith, worship, and public witness. A rich diversity of metaphors deployed for different homiletical purposes, occasions, and cultural contexts is more in keeping with the canonical witness and subsequent soteriological tradition than a single-theory or three-theory approach. The soteriological aspects of preaching can be considered in terms of four dimensions.

1. Challenging Narrow or Inadequate Understandings of God's Saving Work

First, it is important for the preacher to avoid overly narrow views of God's saving work and, by broadening his or her soteriological vocabulary, broaden that of the congregation. Allowing one metaphor of atonement (such as penal substitution) to dominate biblical interpretation and preaching, or speaking of God's saving action in purely individualistic and spiritual terms is a habit that does not take the diversity of biblical atonement language seriously enough.

2. Reclaiming Multiple Metaphors of Salvation

Second, preachers can follow the lead of the church's early preachers and expositors, employing a richly metaphorical (and therefore poetic) soteriological vocabulary, apt to the cultural context and pastoral occasion of preaching. No single metaphor or metaphorical system can be sufficient by itself to interpret God's saving work. Theologians and biblical scholars encourage us to test the considerable range of metaphors that are found in the canon and through the subsequent history of soteriological reflection for contemporary durability and aptness. The language of liturgies and hymn texts, which have a powerful shaping influence on congregational understanding, can be explored and tested in sermons as a means of broadening soteriological vision.

Not surprisingly, the ransom metaphor has enjoyed a renaissance in the late 20th and early 21st cent, since it provides a compelling picture of Jesus' death as an act of divine liberation—a message with sharp cultural pertinence in a world where many are socially, politically, and economically oppressed. Yet important as such an image is for the 21st-cent. context, it would be an error to allow even this metaphor to displace the wealth of other images available in the tradition.

Five questions can be helpful channel markers to test the aptness of chosen metaphors in their homiletical context: (1) What image(s) of God is(are) implied by the metaphor? (2) How is the human condition characterized (bondage to oppressive powers, stained with sin, estranged from God and one another)? (3) What are the practical effects in Christian piety of the metaphorical system at work here, especially for the most vulnerable in domestic, ecclesiastical, social, and political power structures? (4) How does this metaphor demonstrate continuity between Jesus' life, death, and resurrection, on the one hand, and between these events and the ongoing saving work of God in church and world, on the other? (5) How does the metaphor function objectively (as a portrayal of God's effective saving action) and subjectively (as a portrayal of the part human experience or response plays in God's saving work)?

3. Reading NT Soteriological Metaphors and Images

A third dimension of preaching about God's saving work has to do with the preacher's hermeneutic in handling NT texts where soteriological images occur. It is crucial to guard against either consciously or unconsciously accommodating readings of these texts to a pre-set system of atonement thought such as penal substitution or other models. For example, if references to sacrifice so frequently cited in relation to Jesus' death in the NT are read through an assumed penal substitutionary atonement lens, Jesus' death can seem to be a sacrificial payment and the sacrificial animal the victim of punishment. However, these concepts are not in harmony with the OT sacrificial ethos. Old Testament sacrificial practices seem to have been undergirded by basic notions of gift or cleansing rather than payment. The sacrifice represented the willing consecration of one's essential person (represented by an animal, especially its life-blood) to divine purposes. Westerners unfamiliar with sacrificial practices may see only the violent death of a mute victim and mistakenly view the one sacrificed as the substituted object of divine punishment. In fact, the only sacrificial animal that symbolically takes on the sins of the people is the scapegoat (Lev 16:21-22). This sacrificial victim is driven out of the camp; it is not killed. Rehabilitating the metaphor of sacrifice in preaching requires addressing misunderstandings of sacrifice that narrow and obscure its range of meaning. Remarkably, if Jesus dies sacrificially, the handing over of life seems to run in two directions, as an act of both human and divine sacrifice. Jesus hands himself over throughout his life to God—a fidelity that leads to his death. Yet if Jesus is the presence and manifestation of God in human life, God puts God's own life in our hands as well, as the Christian communion in bread and wine implies.

4. Sermons Prompted by Different Homiletical Purposes, Occasions, and Cultural Contexts

A fourth feature of soteriological preaching today will be its pastoral, practical, and context-specific character. To be sure, there may be occasions to devote a single sermon, or even a series of two or three, to exploring one or more metaphors of redemption. Doctrinal sermons of this kind are expected as a regular part of congregational catechesis in some traditions. In others, evangelistic preaching is frequent, and the task is to urge personal response to God's saving action in Jesus Christ. Yet early Christian preachers did not "preach soteriology" as such. Instead, they preached

soteriologically, accessing metaphors of salvation as they sought to explain the sacraments, counteract heresy, comfort the sorrowing, sustain the suffering, and foster in catechumens and believers the practice of Christianity in private and public life. Today's preachers can follow their lead, bringing the news of God's saving work to bear on a great range of preaching tasks and occasions.

Interpreting the sacraments—especially in light of the recovery in many denominations of richer and more regular celebrations of baptism and the Lord's Supper—creates abundant opportunities for exploring soteriological metaphors. Pastoral situations of loss and senseless human suffering require soteriological images such as the identification of God with the human condition and God's going the distance with us to and through death. Metaphors of release from oppressive powers are relevant in sermons that address addiction or injustice. Ethical-formational preaching calls for attention to the ramifications of cross-and-resurrection-shaped existence for both private and public life and creates opportunities to expose the damaging effects of distorted understandings of redemption.

In a sense, all Christian preaching is soteriological since, at its heart, Christian preaching proclaims God's renewal of all things in Jesus Christ. The preacher's weekly task, however, is to bring this saving news to bear on particular times, places, and circumstances. Realities such as individual and social sin, violence, loss, and oppression in a variety of contexts evoke a lively vocabulary of redemption rooted in biblical and historical traditions, yet creatively responsive to occasion and context. *See* CHRISTOLOGY; SACRAMENTS, PREACHING AND TEACHING OF; SERMON AS PROCLAMATION.

Bibliography: Gustav Aulén. *Christus Victor: An Historical Study of the Three Main Types of the Idea of the Atonement.* (1931); Joel B. Green and Mark D. Baker. *Recovering the Scandal of the Cross: Atonement in New Testament and Contemporary Contexts.* (2000); Darby Kathleen Ray. *Deceiving the Devil: Atonement, Abuse, and Ransom.* (1998); Barbara E. Reid. "The Cross and Cycles of Violence." *Interpretation* 58 (2004) 376–85; Peter Schmiechen. *Saving Power: Theories of Atonement and Forms of the Church.* (2005); J. Denny Weaver. *The Nonviolent Atonement.* (2001).

SYSTEMATIC, CONSTRUCTIVE THEOLOGY
David J. Lose

Systematic or constructive theology attempts to give a coherent account of the beliefs of the church and is prompted by the preaching of the church even as it serves to support and assess it. The relationship between preaching and the discipline of constructive, or systematic, theology at times has been fraught with tension, moving between two mutually exclusive poles: on the one side contending that the primary purpose of preaching is to assert the church's theological doctrine, while on the other professing that the best preaching avoids theological language altogether. Neither pole of this false dichotomy, of course, is particularly helpful: preaching is not the tool of theologians, and it cannot flourish in ignorance of disciplined theological reflection. Therefore, to explore the dynamic and positive elements of the relationship between preaching and theology, we need to make three moves.

A. Systematic or Constructive Theology Today
 1. Limitations of a Single System
 2. Avoidance of Any Particular Philosophy
 3. Recognition That All Theology Is Local
B. Preaching as a Particular Kind of Theological Activity
 1. First-order, Second-order, and Third-order Theology
 2. Preaching as an Expression of the Church's Faith Convictions
 3. The Relationship of First- and Second-order Theology
C. The Roles of Theology in Preaching Practice
 1. Descriptive
 2. Normative
 3. Teleological
 4. Formative
 5. Kerygmatic

A. Systematic or Constructive Theology Today

Employing the adjective *constructive* rather than *systematic* to describe theology denotes an important shift in the way theologians view the art and craft of disciplined theological reflection. Whereas *systematic* conveys the desire to organize all the various elements of the church's theological reflection into one ordered whole, or system, *constructive* seeks an equally disciplined but more modest or realistic ambition. Three chief elements have guided this shift in ambition and name.

1. Limitations of a Single System

The first is the awareness that the church's reflections on the mystery of God cannot, finally, be contained in any single system. Noting that both Thomas Aquinas and Karl Barth—perhaps the two greatest theologians of the second millennium of Christianity—intentionally abandoned their respective quests to offer a complete systematics (Aquinas's *Summa Theologica* and Barth's *Church Dogmatics*) in response to their awe at the ultimately incomprehensible mystery of God, modern constructive theologians have advocated relocating their efforts away from comprehensive systems toward offering constructive proposals. In this vein, constructive theologians seek to make a more modest proposal, demurring from speaking for God the way classic systematicians may have ventured and instead striving to speak for the church as it seeks to understand God.

2. Avoidance of Any Particular Philosophy

A second influence is the desire to avoid the unconscious reliance of theology on any particular philosophical school. Because in systematic theology one necessarily needs to unite various and at times diverse biblical and theological themes into a single system, it is difficult not to look beyond the Bible and church tradition to philosophy for a supposedly neutral system by which to organize Christian doctrine. The difficulty, as Barth and his students frequently point out, is that when one seeks a common philosophical language by which to organize Christian reflection, much of the distinctively Christian witness is inevitably lost in translation. Rather than make sense of the whole of Christian thought via external ideologies or philosophical systems, constructive theologians are willing to work on various parts of the Christian tradition on their own terms rather than force them into artificial alignment.

3. Recognition That All Theology Is Local

A third influence prompting the shift from systematic to constructive theology is recognition that all theology, ultimately, is local theology. Abandoning the quest for a unifying system frees the constructive theologian to take seriously the various local and contextual elements of a particular theological tradition. While one can certainly compare and contrast the ways that Christian reflection has emerged from various locales and peoples, one should not flatten the contextual differences of distinct theological traditions by placing them in a unifying system any more than one should flatten the distinct voices of Christian Scripture. One constructs theology from various elements of the Christian tradition as filtered and manifested through the distinct and particular theological, biblical, and cultural frames of reference available.

Although some theologians still prefer the comprehensive goal and heuristic value of systematic theology, the more recently conceived constructive theology serves many theologians and, as we shall see, preachers quite well.

B. Preaching as a Particular Kind of Theological Activity

Typically, when one thinks of the relationship between theology and preaching, one articulates a theology *of* preaching, involving subjects such as the purpose of preaching, hermeneutics, the authority of the preacher, the relationship between the preached word and the Word of God, and so forth. It is, without a doubt, important for preachers to attend to and learn from what various theologians have said about preaching, and equally important for them to articulate their own theology of preaching, if for no other reason than to understand deeply their own conviction of why they stand in the pulpit to preach week in and week out. Yet it is also crucial to realize that preaching is itself a form of theology and to consider intentionally its relationship to the dogmatic tradition we normally associate with theological reflection.

1. First-order, Second-order, and Third-order Theology

Toward this end, it will be helpful to borrow the distinctions that theologians sometimes make between first-order, second-order, and third-order theology. First-order theology is comprised of those utterances that arise in the actual practice of the individual's or community's religious life. Worship, prayer, hymnody, preaching, evangelism, confessing

the faith—all of these constitute first-order theology. Second-order theology, by contrast, is the disciplined reflection on those practices by which the church articulates the norms, or grammar, by which it seeks to understand and articulate its commitments. Third-order theology, which typically has the least bearing on preaching, is the comparison of Christian norms with those of other faith traditions.

2. Preaching as an Expression of the Church's Faith Convictions

From this vantage point, theology is not simply useful for constructing a theory of why we preach, nor is preaching merely the speaking forth of a theological tradition. Rather, preaching itself is a form of theologizing, that is, speaking of God. Preaching, that is, is neither primarily the object nor the subject *of* theology. First and foremost, it is theology. Considered this way, as first-order announcements and confessions, the sermons we offer form the substance of the theology our people learn and, eventually, the church professes. In fact, the sermons preached over the centuries—from those recorded in the Bible itself as well as from significant theologians and less well-known teachers and preachers—are the wellspring from which much systematic and constructive theology has sprung. Preaching itself, then, is a constructive, contextual, and creative act by which the church's faith convictions come to contemporary and concrete utterance addressed to a particular people living at a particular time and place.

3. The Relationship of First- and Second-order Theology

This point places a very high value on the act and art of preaching itself. Preaching has all too often been seen as the end point in a long process of biblical, historical, and dogmatic theology that results in delivering the theological goods to those gathered. Preaching is not simply the communication of truths garnered through other means; rather, it is a creative and even provocative enterprise where the preacher is called upon to articulate the meaning, value, and relevance of the faith in light of the present challenges and opportunities facing the people of God in attendance to hear the sermon. In fact, while noting (as we will see below in greater detail) the important role that second-order theology plays in providing helpful guides and norms for preaching, the primary purpose of second-order theology is not to establish norms for what constitutes faithful first-order speech but to provide the raw materials, resources, and background from which vital, contextual proclamation may take place. Theology, as one theologian has put it, is for proclamation.

C. The Roles of Theology in Preaching Practice

Having established preaching as an act of first-order theology that both prompts and is served by second-order reflection, we can move more productively to ask what roles constructive theology may play in preaching. At least five distinct roles suggest themselves, each of which proposes its own sets of questions and areas for further study and reflection.

1. Descriptive

First, constructive theology can and should be the attempt to order and understand the theological affirmations and confessions regularly made in the practice of preaching. In this sense, constructive theology plays a distinctly *descriptive* role. That is, constructive theologians are called to ask what preachers are actually saying through the course of worship and their sermons. In what way do these utterances shape the larger constructive proposal the theologian offers? How are the contextual aspects of preaching constitutive of the theology that emerges, and how is the theological tradition from which the preacher operates evidenced?

If one engages such questions seriously, one soon discovers that there is no single theology of preaching. Rather, preachers who come from distinct traditions—be they Reformation, feminist, liberation, Roman Catholic, or others—are shaped very much by the theological traditions from which they come. Or put more accurately in light of our discussion thus far, the sermons offered by preachers are contextual and greatly shape the theological positions they inhabit. From Martin Luther to Oscar Romero, theologians have discovered that their sermons do not simply or even primarily reflect their theology, but that their theology often must catch up with their experiences of preaching and parish ministry so as to describe what they have learned and preached in the pulpit.

2. Normative

Second, in addition to functioning descriptively, constructive theology provides doctrinal boundaries within which preaching functions, in this sense playing a *normative* role. In this regard, constructive theology provides criteria for assessing the fidelity of present proclamation. Such criteria may be determined by comparing contemporary preaching with the prevailing grammar that arises from the biblical witness as well as the history of proclamation. It may also arise from a comparison with other forms of contemporary preaching. With this role in mind, constructive theologians may ask whether a particular instance or contemporary tradition of preaching conforms to the norms and convictions of past proclamation. When a contemporary tradition does, in fact, vary from established traditions, one may inquire whether these differences are contextual or confessional and how they reflect and/or arise from current trends in theology and the life of the church. Not surprisingly, while in this regulative role constructive theology sets the boundaries within which faithful proclamation occurs, contemporary preaching is contextual and may also stretch, or even call into question, the norms set by constructive theologians. In this vein, one may ask what the current practices of the worshiping community, and particularly the sermons at the center of that worship, tell us about the theology of the church.

3. Teleological

Third, and as we have noted, constructive theology can aid preachers in constructing a distinct and compelling rationale for their practice. We will describe this function of theology as *teleological*, as it establishes the end, or goal, toward which preaching strives. Constructive theology, from this point of view, does not merely describe the theology the preacher espouses *in* his or her sermons, but articulates a theology *of* preaching, making manifest the reason-for-being of preaching by asking and answering the question, Why do we preach?

While there are a variety of answers to this question, all may be classified in terms of the end—*telos*—toward which they aim. Two broad ends, and therefore patterns, of preaching have often been named. The first arises from the central conviction that in and through preaching God works to justify sinners and that, further, the primary end of preaching is the proclamation of God's justifying word. This pattern stems from the central insights and convictions of the 16th-cent. Protestant Reformation and manifests a very high view of the efficaciousness of the preached word. A second pattern focuses less on the moment or instance of justification but concerns itself with the Christian life, whether individual or corporate, and seeks to instruct, exhort, and encourage the gathered assembly to live into the identity and promise bequeathed through justification. This pattern, which precedes the Reformation, is also taken up by traditions stemming from the Reformation and places its emphasis on sanctification. These two patterns are not mutually exclusive, but each has a distinctive *telos*, or goal, and therefore has a different focus and even tenor. Having established the teleological thrust of one's theology of preaching, constructive theology functioning in this regard can then also provide guidelines and criteria for assessing effective practice. Did the sermon, the constructive theologian may ask, achieve his or her desired end?

4. Formative

Fourth, constructive theology plays a pedagogical or, perhaps better, a *formative* role, as it helps preachers name for the congregation the rules of faith or operative grammar of their tradition. In this way, specific doctrines name the major landmarks of the theological landscape upon which the first-order theological drama is played out. Doctrine, from this point of view, is authoritative not primarily because it has been established by the Christian community as normative but because it furnishes the gathered assembly with reflective categories that help them make sense of their experience. That is, the congregation values the doctrine of the incarnation not because of the views expressed during the Council of Nicaea, but because of the experiential content and force of the confession that in Christ God took on our human lot and life and thereby identifies with us completely. Thus, preachers must constantly ask in what way theological doctrine offers a framework by which to understand and interpret the lived experience of Christian communities, or even makes a proposal concerning it.

5. Kerygmatic

Fifth, and finally, theology plays a *kerygmatic* role as it encourages preachers to hold at the center of worship and their proclamation the work of the God we know most clearly in and through Jesus Christ. Whatever other topics may occupy the attention of the preacher, announcing, proclaiming, and interpreting the work of God in Christ as witnessed to in Scripture and as it relates to our life in this world stands at the center of the preaching enterprise. Further, constructive theology helps to clarify this kerygmatic or evangelical role as the primary reason for the existence of the office of preaching. In this regard, systematic theology, even a more modest constructive theology, may call preachers to speak for God insofar as the preaching office exists to declare and proclaim the Word of God for the people of God. Toward this end, constructive theology seeks to ask preachers about both the evangelical content and the aim of their sermons and offers distinct christological and trinitarian norms by which to assess their proclamation.

Preachers, as has become clear, are always making theological claims, always operating within a theological framework, and always using theology to teach the faith. In order to do these things faithfully and effectively, preachers must regularly engage in disciplined reflection on the norms, content, rationale, and end of their preaching. Toward this end, constructive theology can be a ready ally and reliable support. *See* DOCTRINAL; SERMON AS PROCLAMATION; TEACHING; THEOLOGY IN THE SERMON; TOPICAL.

Bibliography: Ronald J. Allen. *Thinking Theologically.* (2008); Gerhard Forde. *Theology Is for Proclamation.* (1990); Robert G. Hughes and Robert Kysar. *Preaching Doctrine for the Twenty-first Century.* (1997); Serene Jones and Paul Lakeland, eds. *Constructive Theology: A Contemporary Approach to Classical Themes.* (2005); Paul Scott Wilson. *The Practice of Preaching.* (1995).

THEOLOGY IN THE SERMON
James R. Nieman

The sermon should be treated as a fully theological practice of the church that impels faithful witness to Christ's abundant life for the world. To say this, however, calls for bridging the rather recent and unhelpful gulf between preaching and theology, a gulf that also implicitly alienates proclamation from teaching. Further, it calls for affirming theological reflection in and for the church, the main setting where preaching occurs. This connection between sermon and theology, both operating in the ambit of the church, reclaims a more historic role for preaching and enables a more theological engagement with contemporary hearers.

A. Typical Confusions
  1. Faulty Distinctions
  2. Distorted Relations
B. Reclaiming Theology
  1. Adjacent Roles
  2. Proper Relations
C. Sermon Strategies
  1. Prompts for Doing Theology
  2. Ways of Showing Theology

A. Typical Confusions

1. Faulty Distinctions

In common usage, theology has been narrowed to refer to a specialized form of academic scholarship that attends largely to a body of professed religious doctrine. It describes a field of reflection that seeks, among other ends, the internal coherence of beliefs and the external regulation such beliefs can provide. Such reflection is usually seen as abstract and disconnected from everyday life, a view abetted by the technical language in which it is written. We should rightly object that this caricatures theology, reducing it to a shorthand for what actually fits only a few kinds of systematic theology or church dogmatics employed mainly since the Enlightenment. Even so, the rarified stature once allotted to theology as "queen of the sciences" is matched by popular perceptions today of its irrelevance to the local work of churches, and particularly that of preaching.

The sermon has fared no better, however, for related reasons. If the "real truths" of faith are found only through a narrow sort of theology, then the sermon becomes the simplified, if not simplistic, application of these truths in palatable form. Preaching is merely a decorative and persuasive enterprise with low expectations for any actual gravity or impact in relation to the concerns of the day. As sermons become less thoughtful and challenging about beliefs, theology seems ever more remote and sterile. The preacher therefore shuns being thought of as a theologian in the act of preaching, focusing instead on caretaking and entertainment from the pulpit, so that the vocation to speak in the distinctive language of the church is muted. In those rare cases when theology is actually used in preaching, it appears in the untheological guise of promoting right doctrine as an end in itself rather than plainly declaring God's ways for us.

2. Distorted Relations

Separating theology and sermon in this fashion produces several unhelpful relationships. One is sermons about theology, in which preaching is subordinated to a body of dogma and teaching in order to clarify theological topics or provide doctrinal correctives. To be sure, church history has known catechetical sermons that brought valuable theological acumen to matters of worship, Scripture, or behavior. The problem is surely not with theology being an overt focus for the sermon but in its possible disconnection from the life setting. It is one thing to elaborate the riches of baptism among those who have newly undergone that rite (as in 4th-cent. mystagogical catecheses), quite another to expound upon soteriology or sanctification apart from so profound an experience. Moreover, preaching in such cases becomes a functional device for presenting theological ideas, with the sermon as a neutral, inconsequential container for content supplied elsewhere.

It is equally unhelpful to relate the two terms by adopting a single theology of the sermon. Of course, it has been valuable in the history of homiletics to assess the role or aim of preaching in light of larger theological frameworks, such as doctrines of revelation, ministry, or ecclesiology. While this is useful for clarifying what preaching is or can be in broad theological traditions, its particular role in judging the theological legitimacy of specific sermons is more questionable. By treating theology as the master discourse for scrutinizing any ecclesial practice, theology is paradoxically diminished to only evaluative and corrective roles. At the same time, the sermon is positioned as derivative, if not impotent, ignoring those significant periods of church history (as in sermons of medieval and early modern reformers) when preaching challenged and even rejected doctrinal distortions.

The stark separation of theology from sermon, combined with the faulty relations that result, keeps us from imagining more generous ways for theology to be *in* the sermon. We are left with theology either inserted during the sermon to emphasize what was said by other means (thus bringing nothing new) or conjoined to the sermon to authorize what was said with lesser force (thus exerting only coercion). Both theology and sermon are thereby corrupted. Theology becomes a commodity expended in the sermon at a diminishing rate of return, while the sermon becomes a vehicle delivering theological freight to its final destination.

B. Reclaiming Theology

1. Adjacent Roles

This impasse and its liabilities can be overcome by recovering the ancient language of *theologia prima* and *theologia secunda*, primary and secondary theology. A sermon exemplifies theological work in its primary mode. It is one of several practices in which the church is, as Aidan Kavanagh remarked, "caught in the act of being most overtly itself" (1984, 75). When the sermon is spoken and heard, the church is doing the fundamental work of engaging the God who calls it into being and offers lasting life to the world. The most basic theological meaning of the sermon happens in and through the preaching event itself. It is not exhausted there, however, and this is the focus of theological work in its secondary mode. Scholarly, systematic theology (which we noted has unfortunately been conflated with the term *theology* itself) is a response to primary theology. By indirect means, it seeks to illumine the theological meaning of or about a primary expression, like the sermon. For our purposes here, secondary theology (which we might call academic theology) becomes a crucial preparation for and response to what has been uttered in the primary mode of the sermon.

This way of thinking is no ruse for turning the tables on theology by imposing a new hierarchy with the sermon at its peak. Instead, it reclaims a productive, inseparable relation between two ecclesial practices with necessarily distinct tendencies, like the systole and diastole of the heart. The language of preaching is mainly performative, using words that do what they say (as when forgiveness is directly enacted by uttering "I forgive you"). Academic theology is more reflective in form, considering from some measure of remove what has first been said performatively (as when reconciliation is extensively elaborated). The purpose of the sermon and theology also differ. Preaching is mainly discursive, a "telling" that contributes to the witness of the church and models that discourse for others. Academic theology aims more at refinement, a "testing" that draws from the wisdom of a tradition but with an eye toward that same witness. In language and purpose, sermon and theology surely overlap, but more important, each requires the other. Preaching that avoids *theologia secunda* will become careless, if not harmful, while academic theology that yields no *theologia prima* will become

inert, if not ignored. The preacher is the local theologian called to uphold both the primary and the secondary theology of proclamation in the congregation, being a catalyst for witness through the sermon and a conservator of wisdom through theology.

2. Proper Relations

The time-tested connection between theology and sermon provides a more robust and dynamic relationship between the two. This plainly begins with treating the sermon as theology in its own right. Theology is unavoidably at stake from the pulpit. Ignoring this means risking that implicit theological claims accidentally enter and subvert the sermon. For example, careless acceptance of pervasive cultural values will create its own theological tone in the sermon, but one that unhelpfully resonates with social indifference and self-preservation. A fully theological sermon cannot afford this, but stays vigilant and intentional about its claims. This is one reason some sermons from distant times and places seem so bracing, by seriously engaging the depth of human struggle amidst the horizon of divine hope. They never shirk from seeing the sermon as a theological act. We still stand under this proclamatory duty to be theologically responsive to the joys and sorrows facing our world rather than cloyingly palliative. Distilling complex doctrine into clever sayings will not achieve this, however. The preacher must instead journey back and forth between two adjacent terrains: the reflective insights of academic theology and the dynamic expression of theological preaching.

Closely allied with this, we can again learn to appreciate the place of theology *for* the sermon. The disciplined and patient effort required to do academic theology, which sadly drives some away from it, actually becomes a gift when the sermon is its larger aim. There is great advantage in stepping back, slowing down, and resisting the pull to assess the sermon entirely by virtue of its immediate impact. Academic theology provides preaching with valuable tools for discerning a durable theological strategy, deepening connections with a theological heritage, and anticipating the likely theological pitfalls. To recognize and use these scholarly tools do not require that preaching adopt the internal standards of that field as self-evidently good. The technical vocabulary needed within academic theology, along with its drive for deductive logic and structural coherency, can alienate the hearer and be at odds with the aims of the sermon. If we are wary about these things, however, disciplined theological insight will, over time, make our sermons more surefooted and attuned to the deeper wisdom of historic and global Christianity. Nor is the sermon the only beneficiary of this arrangement. When preaching becomes an important horizon for academic theology, it compels such scholarship to stay grounded in the living conversation and mission of the church.

By reclaiming the distinct and crucial contribution that preaching and academic theology make to each other, we develop a healthier sense of theology *in* the sermon. Historic examples sometimes show weighty theological issues accessibly incorporated into the sermon. Ambrose of Milan, for instance, regularly integrated doctrinal matters with subtlety and skill. Recalling the gold, incense, and myrrh given to Jesus by the magi (Matt 2:11), Ambrose declared,

> For the one is a token of a ruler;
> the next an offering to divine power;
> the other an honor to one being buried,
> which does not destroy the dead body, but
>   preserves it.

This was no mere allegory. Ambrose instead used simple objects to gesture toward a sweeping christology that linked the humanity and divinity of Jesus to the larger purpose of his dying. What is more, the very next lines built from this theological gesture to another.

> We also who hear and read these things,
> let us bring forth similar gifts from our treasures;
> for we have treasures in earthen vessels.
> If you therefore regard what you are as not
>   from you but from Christ,
> how much more ought you regard what you
>   own as not yours but Christ's?
> (*Expositio Evangelii secundum Lucam, PL*
> 15.1569.12–21)

In equally plain terms, the doctrine of Christ thus bore implications for the doctrines both of humanity and of creation. With gemlike compression, Ambrose depicted how the nature of the crucified molds the nature of discipleship and stewardship. All of this simply and seamlessly unfolds in but a few sentences because, for Ambrose, theology and sermon were not disjunctive choices but complementary partners. The question for us is how to recognize similar means of integration in sermons today.

C. Sermon Strategies

1. Prompts for Doing Theology

Although the sermon is unavoidably theological, preachers have particular opportunities in which theology can more profitably receive explicit or extended attention. The first of these prompts for theology is situational. For example, profound moments in the human life cycle such as birth, sickness, changed relationships, or death, as well as the Christian rites connected with these, automatically include theological questions about joy, hope, loss, fear, and limits, to name a few. Similarly, significant communal events such as ecclesial festivals, societal crises, or cultural remembrances can be rich moments to interpret our times in relation to God's *kairos* and *eschaton*. Rather than needing to entice listeners to care about doctrinal questions in the abstract, these situations highlight the concrete religious issues where we already have a major stake. Sermons have the opportunity to name those issues honestly, reframe them theologically, and address them compellingly in order to suggest models for faithful thought and speech.

Another prompt is biblical. This opportunity is more challenging, however, since it means resisting the shallow use of Scripture for quaint illustrations or authorizing warrants in preaching. By contrast, when preachers use Scripture to reflect us back to ourselves anew, as people in relationship to a living God, then the sermon can develop genuine theological potential. First, Scripture gives the sermon an opening for theological narrative. The story of our world is not consigned to its own self-contained plot but is retold toward Christ's mercy and promise. Second, Scripture gives the sermon an opening for theological clarification. Revered yet often strange texts will not contribute to our contemporary views without intentional amplification and elaboration. In other words, Scripture prompts the sermon to do the theological work of interpreting the world through God's claim upon it and specifying how we are still part of that sacred story. The strong and accepted sign of Scripture therefore becomes a natural opportunity for the sermon to do theology.

A final prompt is local. Congregations are already replete with theological claims and actions to which sermons can speak theologically, if only we are prepared to notice them. Doing this requires sensitivity to see primary theology throughout church life and not only in preaching or other clergy activities. It also requires not callously converting such theological expressions into moralizing opportunities to tell people how to act. The shrewd preacher instead recognizes that certain communal forms and practices are actually signs of something more, gestures toward transcendent concerns about trust, meaning, worth, hope, or direction that call for a comparably theological response. The theological sermon not only takes note of these signs but also engages them appreciatively, as worthy of theological exploration in public, and responsibly, as demanding theological discernment tethered to a larger tradition. Such local instances thereby are another way that the sermon becomes more theologically vigorous.

2. Ways of Showing Theology

Aware of these prompts, what does such theology actually look like in the sermon? One way to see it is in language forms. We noted that academic theology cannot simply be imported into a sermon without distortion. At the same time, sermons surely must enact theology in more than simplified terms, lest they fail to bear the weight of the mystery proclaimed. Theology in the sermon instead calls for eventful and dynamic language, words that evoke more of an encounter with God than a pondering of concepts. Preaching therefore often uses unfolding narratives, multivalent images, or probing dialogue in order to convey a complex relationship between God and humanity that develops over time. Theology is then heard not as fixed assertions that silence further talk but as a language world we can inhabit because it creates the texture of those actual experiences through which we are able to meet God.

Another and subtler way to see theology in the sermon is by structural patterns. It takes time to detect the recurrent theological themes in a congregation that can be anticipated in future preaching. Similarly, it takes time during any one sermon to create the kind of theological encounter or framing that is fruitful. The point is that preachers learn gradually to appreciate how theology functions at the subterranean level of sermons in patterns that permeate the entire process, from the deep issues we revisit to the mental moves undergirding what we actually say. Over time, preachers profitably reexamine a broad span of sermons and begin to notice these important but often hidden theological structures. Doing so leads to honestly assessing whether those patterns have become stale or trite and need to be reconsidered.

One last and ironic way that theology appears is through disciplined restraint. We cannot address every theological topic in a single sermon or even over time. Preachers must decide which concerns are most pressing or revealing. Such theological restraint thus reflects humility about the place of the sermon as but one catalytic moment in an ongoing faithful conversation. Indeed, what we cannot address in a given sermon may be better engaged theologically elsewhere in congregational life, such as education, counseling, or fellowship. Grounded in the secondary theology of a tradition, preachers are alert for these other occasions to do primary theology beyond the sermon. It thereby becomes more important to conclude any sermon in a way that remains open to further conversation. By so doing, we recognize the place of theology in the discourse of the sermon and restore its value as the language of the church. *See* DOCTRINAL; HOMILETICAL (THEOLOGICAL) CRITICISM; SYSTEMATIC, CONSTRUCTIVE THEOLOGY; TEACHING; TOPICAL.

Bibliography: Ronald J. Allen. *Preaching Is Believing: The Sermon as Theological Reflection.* (2002); Burton Z. Cooper and John S. McClure. *Claiming Theology in the Pulpit.* (2003); Gerhard O. Forde. *Theology Is for Proclamation.* (1990); Aidan Kavanagh. *On Liturgical Theology.* (1984); Leonora Tubbs Tisdale. *Preaching as Local Theology and Folk Art.* (1997); Paul Scott Wilson. "Theology in the Sermon." *The Practice of Preaching.* (1995) 82–97.

THEOLOGY OF PROCLAMATION
James F. Kay

The 20th cent. arguably witnessed the most intense period of theological concentration on Christian proclamation since the Reformation. Reflection on the form and content of the Christian message, attested in Scripture, again became a primary locus of theology as theologians sought to articulate normative criteria to guide Christian teaching and preaching in a time of unprecedented change. The ecumenically influential work of the NT theologian Rudolf Bultmann (1884–1976) and the Swiss Reformed dogmatician Karl Barth (1886–

1968) exercised strong gravitational pulls not only on Protestant homiletics, but also on Roman Catholic preaching textbooks written in the wake of Vatican II. Subsequently, the post-Bultmannian new hermeneutic of Ernst Fuchs (1903–1983) and Gerhard Ebeling (1912–2001) was transposed by David James Randolph and Fred Craddock into a North American New Homiletic, which garnered considerable attention despite the recurring challenges posed to it by various liberation, contextualist, and post-liberal theologians.

A. Proclamation: Preliminary Considerations
B. Consequences of Protestant Liberalism for Proclamation
  1. A Challenge to Biblical Inerrancy
  2. Rejection of Supernatural Divine Agency
  3. Jesus Christ as the Embodiment of the Great Commandment
C. Bultmann's Critique of Liberalism
  1. The Inadequacy of History
  2. Jesus Christ as God's Eschatological Salvation
  3. Demythologization
  4. Crucifixion as Death to the Old Life
D. From the Christ-Event to the Word-Event
  1. The New Hermeneutic
    a. Demythologization taken further
    b. The performative power of the kerygma
    c. Faith as trust in God's Word
  2. The New Homiletic
  3. Dissenting Voices to the New Hermeneutic
    a. The need for social and political pertinence
    b. The role of the Holy Spirit

A. Proclamation: Preliminary Considerations

The English noun "proclamation" comes from the Latin *proclamatio* and its associated verb *proclamare*, "to proclaim." Behind the Latin stands the Greek verb kēryssō, usually rendered "to herald" or "to proclaim" (as in 2 Cor 4:5), and its allied noun kērygma (as in Rom 16:25; 1 Cor 2:4; 15:14), meaning "proclamation" or "preaching." Kērygma can refer either to the act of proclamation (as in 1 Cor 2:4) or to the content of that proclamation (as in 1 Cor 15:14). The term also connotes a

prescribed proclamation entailing authorized messengers, or "heralds" (1 Tim 2:7; 2 Tim 1:11), sometimes called "apostles" or "sent ones" (Rom 16:7; 1 Cor 9:5; 2 Cor 11:5, 13; 12:11-12). Here Paul pictures the preacher as a herald dispatched ahead of the royal entourage to proclaim the monarch's mandates or to announce the sovereign's imminent arrival. As such, heralds "do not proclaim" themselves (2 Cor 4:5); they proclaim only what their sovereign authorizes. Through the mouth of the herald the monarch speaks, much as an envoy conveys authoritative messages from a head of state. For this reason, Paul can declare, "So we are ambassadors for Christ, since God is making his appeal through us" (2 Cor 5:20).

An interchangeable synonym for kēryssō is euangelizō, if you will, "to gospel" (1 Cor 15:1-2). When styling the kerygma as **euangelion**, that is, as "good news" or "gospel," Paul echoes Isa 52:7 (see Rom 10:15) and 61:1-3. Whatever else the Christian message is, it can be characterized as both beneficent and timely. Rightly understood, the proclaimed kerygma can never be taken as either bad or untimely for the creature. The Christian message is urgent (2 Cor 6:2, echoing Isa 49:8); it matters for the good of the hearers and for the good of the world. Moreover, this message is not one that the church invents; it is one that the church has "received" and in which "it stands" (1 Cor 15:1). For this reason Paul employs a genitive of origin: the gospel is "the gospel of God" (Rom 1:1).

B. Consequences of Protestant Liberalism for Proclamation

The nursery for 20th-cent. theological reflection on proclamation was found in the German Protestant liberalism of Albrecht Ritschl (1822–1889), several of whose theological heirs, such as Adolf von Harnack (1851–1930) and Wilhelm Herrmann (1846–1922), were among the teachers of Barth and Bultmann. Liberalism was the attempt, following the Enlightenment, to reconstruct the historical origins of Christianity and to reinterpret the Christian faith in accord with the emerging canons of historical science. This had enormous consequences for preaching.

1. A Challenge to Biblical Inerrancy
The Bible was no longer taken as the inerrantly inspired "Word of God," but as a collection of

religious writings that emerged over time and with variations in outlooks reflecting changing historical circumstances. Literary and historical criticism showed, for example, that the Pentateuch was not authored by Moses, but was the product of several sources whose final redaction occurred only in the post-exilic period.

2. Rejection of Supernatural Divine Agency

In accord with the Enlightenment, liberalism rejected supernaturalist notions of divine agency. A scientific understanding of the world, holding to the impermeable character of immanent causal relations, rendered punctiliar divine interventions in history anomalous and absurd. Nevertheless, unlike Deism, which removed God from the historical process altogether, liberalism understood the historical process itself as the revelation or movement of God in the world. When the Bible is interpreted within the framework of its proper historical chronology, one sees a progressive unfolding of its ideas. Read historically, the Bible reveals a movement from the henotheism of the Israelite tribes, with their god Yahweh and their xenophobic religion, to the magisterial monotheism of Israel's prophets proclaiming one God for all humankind, and culminating in the teachings of Jesus, who alone among Israel's prophets perfectly embodied in his life and ministry the love of God and neighbor as entailed by God's rule over human affairs. Jesus died in fidelity to this message. His resurrection is a way of saying that his incomparable personality continues to exercise undying influence on and within the historical process, guiding it progressively toward the reign of God over all the world.

3. Jesus Christ as the Embodiment of the Great Commandment

In America, the public champion of liberal theology was Harry Emerson Fosdick (1878–1969), founding pastor of the Riverside Church in New York City, whose 1924 Beecher Lectures, *The Modern Use of the Bible*, afforded a classic statement. For Fosdick, the Christian proclamation becomes essentially the Great Commandment to love God and neighbor as oneself, with the historical Jesus serving as the incomparable example and good news that such love is indeed a human possibility. Moreover, as we give ourselves to this ideal embodied by Jesus, we join with our Master in moving the historical process toward the day when the love of God

and neighbor will triumphantly prevail. In this paradigm, what links contemporary Christians to those of the earliest church is not the panoply of orthodox christological formulations, ancient dogmas, and mythical motifs, such as Lord or Christ or Logos. They were all already on the scene in the ancient Near East and Greco-Roman world long before Jesus, and they were subsequently applied to him in quite varied contexts. Thus, the continuity of the Christian message through time stems not from these changing categories, but from the underlying abiding experiences of the incomparable personality of Jesus that prompted them in the first place. For this reason, liberal preaching, such as that of Fosdick and later Martin Luther King Jr. (1929–1968), focused on the life and ministry of Jesus as examples for Christian life and discipleship, engaged freely in moral exhortation, and took its optimism about the future from the visible evidence of God's kingdom of peace, love, and justice taking hold in the world.

C. Bultmann's Critique of Liberalism

Rudolf Bultmann understood liberalism as correct in distinguishing between the historical and the mythical elements in the NT kerygma, but he went on to show where, with the best of intentions, liberalism had foundered (Kay 2000, 84).

1. The Inadequacy of History

The error of liberalism was its failure to recognize that the saving significance of Jesus is never understood by the NT proclamation in a historicist sense, as a fulfillment of the world's latent possibilities; rather, it understands Jesus in an eschatological sense, as one whose coming marks the final judgment or end of the world. This is expressed in the apocalyptic language of Paul's cross-resurrection kerygma sprinkled in summary form throughout his letters (e.g., Rom 6:10; 8:34; 10:9, 14:9; 1 Cor 15:3-5; 2 Cor 5:15; 13:4; Phil 2:6-11;1 Thess 4:14), and which the Synoptic Gospels narrate, and in the Gnostic-derived concepts and framework of the Fourth Gospel, which tell of the divine Revealer who came into the world "from above" (John 1:1-14; 8:23).

2. Jesus Christ as God's Eschatological Salvation

In other words, while the Jewish prophet Jesus of Nazareth, who proclaimed the kingdom of God, is the historical presupposition of Christianity, it is the proclaimed destiny of this Jesus as crucified and risen, or as God's eschatological salvation-event, that is the real source and norm of Christian faith. The proclaimer (of the Kingdom) has become the proclaimed (of the church), and Christian faith only arises from this latter proclamation. Therefore, when the liberals eliminated apocalyptic and Gnostic myths in their portrayals of the historical Jesus and his message, they unwittingly eliminated the eschatological essence of the Christian faith and, hence, the significance of Jesus for salvation. The resultant problem was how the church could continue to proclaim its eschatological message of salvation when that message was first announced in mythological language. This was not simply an academic problem but goes straight to the heart of what it means to preach the gospel. Bultmann's solution was to argue for an existentialist interpretation of NT kerygma, a hermeneutic program known as "demythologization."

3. Demythologization

This program assumes that the real referent of NT mythology is not the objectivized realities of which it literally speaks—an atoning sacrifice, reanimated corpses, or virgin births—but rather the understanding of existence that such mythological constructs symbolize. Thus, preachers must proceed by translating outmoded cosmological categories of the gospel into modern existentialist ones. For example, Paul's mythology of the cosmic powers, which the cross of Christ overcomes (1 Cor 2:6-8; compare Col 2:13-15), is a way of speaking of one's bondage to the norms and patterns of this world, to the past, and to vain attempts to secure existence ever threatened by suffering and death.

4. Crucifixion as Death to the Old Life

Hence, to be "crucified with Christ" (Gal 2:19-20; 5:24; 6:14) means to accept God's judgment on our worldly dependence and to accept God's freedom to embrace the future without fear of death. The word that judges our past and extinguishes our old life is simultaneously the word that re-creates us; it is "the power of God unto salvation" (Rom 1:16). Faith means entering here and now into eschatological existence, into love for our neighbors, and into the freedom of no longer being determined by the power of death. Thus, the resurrection of Jesus is not about the resuscitation of a corpse. It is really a way of saying that when the word of the cross is proclaimed as an appeal for authentic existence, it comes alive in its hearers and effects in them the very judgment and grace it proclaims. By translating cosmological categories into existentialist ones, Bultmann showed how the Christ-myth could still be proclaimed and encountered today as the Christ-event occasioning one's transition into authentic existence. Thus, in the Marburg sermons of Bultmann and those of Paul Tillich (1886–1965) in America we find the apocalyptic dualism of "the two ages" transposed into a dualism of decision, an unequivocal summons to leave behind one's dependence on all temporally conditioned claims demanding our absolute allegiance in order to live a new life of freedom for God and neighbor.

D. From the Christ-Event to the Word-Event

1. The New Hermeneutic

The post-Bultmannian new hermeneutic of the 1950s and 1960s, so formative for recent North American homiletical theory, takes Bultmann's conclusions as the starting points for its reflection on Christian proclamation.

a. Demythologization taken further. For example, the new hermeneutic accepts the need for existentialist interpretation of the Christian kerygma, but it takes Bultmann's program of demythologization even further. When Bultmann identifies the risen Christ with the performative agency exercised by the contemporary proclamation of the gospel, the new hermeneutic finds him still appealing to a supernatural act by God that makes the ordinary language of preaching extraordinarily efficacious. There is thus a mythological remainder in Bultmann amounting to "word magic."

b. The performative power of the kerygma. By contrast, the new hermeneutic, informed by the linguistic meditations of Martin Heidegger (1889–1976), identifies the performative power of the kerygma as inherent in language itself, since language has the natural capacity to make present what is otherwise absent, to reveal what is otherwise hidden, and to trigger a new future. The task of the preacher is not to interpret words; it is to interpret existence by means of words. Indeed, this is the true vocation of language. Thus, there is no need to appeal to a miraculous Christ-event. Rather, the explanation of the power of the Christian message lies in the Word-event in which God, who came to expression in the preaching of the historical Jesus, can again come to expression in our own.

c. Faith as trust in God's Word. What Jesus proclaimed in his parables was the rule of God, not as a future apocalyptic happening, but as the "nearness" or immediacy of God in calling for a way of life not determined by anxiety but by trust in God and love of one's neighbor. To enter onto this path of faith, first trod by Jesus, is what it means to be a Christian; and to proclaim this same message is what it means to be a Christian preacher. On these grounds, the resurrection of Jesus is simply a way of affirming that God's Word, which came to expression in the ministry and message of Jesus, remains victorious even after his death. In this way, the preaching of Jesus, styled the Jesus kerygma, serves to interpret the Christ-kerygma summarized in Paul and narrated in the passion accounts of the Synoptics. Moreover, it replaces the Christ-kerygma as the ultimate source and norm for contemporary Christian proclamation.

2. The New Homiletic

The New Homiletic sought to appropriate the insights of the new hermeneutic for the practice of preaching. In accord with the Heideggerian shift away from an instrumental and denotative understanding of language in favor of language as the site or medium in which Being is disclosed and authentic human existence is thereby illumined, the focus for the New Homiletic is no longer on what sermons say, that is, their propositional or ideational content, but on what sermons do. This reorientation of preaching signals a move from the exposition of the Christian message to its execution as the performative dimensions of communication are given primacy over the cognitive. Here, the preaching of Jesus and his parables, where the kingdom of God came to purest expression, shape new rules of art for preaching. The gap between what a sermon says and what it does disappears when the parables of Jesus are taken as homiletical models; for the parables not only speak of God's kingdom in relation to human existence, but they bring to expression that kingdom as a new possibility, disclosing a new way of life. They show that "concretion" or experiential enfleshment is preferable to intellectual abstractions, that a well-told story need not simply illustrate a point, but can itself be the point, that

indirect, allusive discourse often leads more readily to transformative encounter than logically correct argumentation, and that an invitational tone respecting the listener succeeds better than barking a string of commands. Such perspectives, typical of the New Homiletic, inform the sermonic craft of Fred Craddock and Barbara Brown Taylor.

3. Dissenting Voices to the New Hermeneutic

Despite the overwhelming success of the new hermeneutic in reshaping North American homiletical theory and preaching, a number of issues can be raised about its sufficiency in accounting adequately for Christian proclamation.

a. The need for social and political pertinence. First, the political theologies of Jürgen Moltmann and Dorothee Soelle (1929–2003), the feminist theology of proclamation advanced by Rebecca Chopp, the older dogmatics of Karl Barth, and the newer post-liberal homiletic of Charles L. Campbell all reject, on varying grounds, the existentialist constriction of the gospel typical of Bultmann, the new hermeneutic, and the New Homiletic. There is, for these critics of the Bultmannian and post-Bultmannian tradition, no authentic proclamation of the gospel apart from its social and political pertinence, as well as its power to form and upbuild the church as a countercultural community of emancipatory transformation. When the autonomous individualism of existentialism eclipses the social and political embeddedness of Christian proclamation, as arguably occurs in the preaching promoted by the New Homiletic, the gospel's saving scope and universal vision suffer severe attenuation. For this reason, one encounters in the post-liberal sermons of Walter Brueggemann, with their insistence on the communal forming power of the biblical narratives, and in the sermons of Fleming Rutledge, with their persistent emphasis on the cross of Christ as the touchstone for social ethics, a much stronger emphasis on the political and cultural pertinence of the gospel than is common in North American preaching today.

b. The role of the Holy Spirit. The Barthian tradition, in accord with its trinitarian dogmatics, attributes to the illumination of the Holy Spirit what the new hermeneutic attributes to the natural power of language, namely, to make God a linguistic happening or reality. Thus, the work of hermeneutics so favored by the New Homiletic can be seen as substituting for the gift of the Holy Spirit. For this reason, the question arises whether either a cross-resurrection kerygma alone, or even a Jesus kerygma alone, demythologized or not, can adequately account for the revelatory activity of the Holy Spirit as attested in the Fourth Gospel (e.g., John 14:16-17, 26), in the apostolic preaching summarized in the book of Acts (e.g., 2:14-36), and which is also entailed by the threefold referentiality of the Gospel narratives (Matt 3:13-17; Mark 1:9-11; Luke 3:21-22; John 1:29-34) leading to the identification of the one God as Father, Son, and Holy Spirit. Here the emphasis on the work of the Spirit in preaching found among Pentecostals and prominent in the homiletic of James Forbes may also correct an attenuated understanding of the God in whom the saving proclamation of the gospel finds not only its source and but also its goal. *See* HOLY SPIRIT AND PREACHING; PERFORMATIVE LANGUAGE; SERMON AS PROCLAMATION; WORD OF GOD.

Bibliography: Paul Achtemeier. *An Introduction to the New Hermeneutic.* (1969); Karl Barth. *The Word of God and the Word of Man.* (1957); Rudolf Bultmann. *New Testament and Mythology and Other Basic Writings.* (1984); Charles L. Campbell. *Preaching Jesus: New Directions for Homiletics in Hans Frei's Postliberal Theology.* (1997); Rebecca Chopp. *The Power to Speak: Feminism, Language, God.* (1989); Fred B. Craddock. *As One Without Authority.* Rev. ed. (2001); Harry Emerson Fosdick. *The Modern Use of the Bible.* (1924); James F. Kay. "Bultmann, Rudolf (1884–1976)." *The Oxford Companion to Christian Thought.* Edited by Adrian Hastings, Alistair Mason, and Hugh Pyper. (2000) 83–84; David James Randolph. *The Renewal of Preaching.* (1969); Fleming Rutledge. *The Bible and the New York Times.* (1999).

TRINITY
Michael J. Quicke

Some preachers may view the Trinity as problematical, full of technical, dry theology with little explicit supportive Scripture text and even less practical significance. However, many 20th-cent. theologians have stimulated renewed interest in the Trinity as lively doctrine. Rather than expressing reluctance once a year on Trinity Sunday (when not all lectionary readings seem relevant!), preachers need to think and speak in trinitarian ways in their regular preaching. Trinity in Scripture, and the early church's classic terms and models, continues to impact preaching's language, content, and action. Failure to preach in trinitarian ways falsifies pictures of God, impoverishes understanding of salvation and worship, and misses a vital dynamic for preaching's content and practice.

A. The Trinity in Scripture
B. The Trinity in Church History
    1. Two Models
    2. Key Problems
C. The Trinity Today
D. Preaching the Trinity
    1. Trinity Sunday
    2. Trinity as a Consistent Emphasis

A. The Trinity in Scripture

The word *Trinity* is absent in Scripture, but its concept is woven throughout the NT texture. Out of its post-resurrection conviction that the one and only God of the OT had encountered the apostles in Jesus Christ, the historical Jesus is confessed as divine in the earliest confessions, as in John 20:28, "My Lord and my God," where the Greek translation of the Hebrew *Yahweh* is applied to Jesus. Further, the apostles experienced the person of the Holy Spirit ("another Advocate" [John 14:16]), as the church burst into life at Pentecost (Acts 1:8; 2:1-4, 32-33).

The Gospels record an intimate connection between God's three persons in the ministry of Jesus. See especially the annunciation (Luke 1:35) and baptism (Luke 3:21-22). Jesus spoke about his unique relationship with the Father (Luke 10:22; John 5:18-23) and with the Spirit (Matt 12:28). John's Gospel underlines the unity of Father and Son (10:29-30; 14:9-10) and Jesus' sending of Spirit (16:7-15). Matthew 28:19 offers the clearest trinitarian statement, with each name preceded by the article, emphasizing both singularity and plurality— the Father, the Son, and the Holy Spirit.

New Testament writers directly applied OT passages to Jesus, such as Phil 2:9-11 (Isa 45:23) and Rom 10:11 (Isa 28:16). Within the letters there are occasional explicit references, such as the benediction of 2 Cor 13:13. Father and Son are used with differentiation, as in Col 1:19 and 1 John 1:3. There are longer passages about the work of Trinity, especially in salvation (see Rom 8:3-4, 15-17; 1 Cor 1:4-7; 2:4-5; 6:11; 12:4-6; 2 Cor 1:21-22; Gal 4:4-6;

Eph 1:13-14; 3:16-19; 4:4-7; 1 Thess 1:2-6; 2 Thess 2:13; see also other letters: 2 Pet 1:2; Jude 20-21). Trinitarian implications are to be found everywhere.

Provocative pluralities are also found in the OT, in spite of its rigorous monotheism (Exod 20:2-7; Deut 6:4). Particularly significant is Gen 1:26-27: "Then God said, 'Let us make humankind in our image, according to our likeness. . . .' So God created humankind in his image, in the image of God he created them; male and female he created them." Humanity's creation as male and female somehow reflects God's personal intercommunion, as unity within plurality. Plural language (Gen 3:22; 11:7) is intriguingly personalized, for example, in the role of the Spirit (Gen 1:2), the angel of the Lord (Gen 16:7-14; 22:11; Exod 3:2-6; Judg 13:2-22), the three visitors (Gen 18:1-9), and Wisdom (Prov 8).

The God of Scripture is triune, and Christian faith is trinitarian. Preachers must learn to mine the few specific Trinity texts, paying serious attention to this doctrine (see sermon examples later). Narratives that express the Trinity (e.g., Luke 1:35; 3:21-22) and doctrinal teaching that integrates God's triune action (such as Rom 8) should also be developed intentionally to underline God's triune nature. However, because the trinitarian framework structures Christian understanding of God, no aspect of worship and Christian life should be understood as less than trinitarian. It should exert fundamental influence upon the language of all preachers, whatever text they are preaching from.

B. The Trinity in Church History

Formulating the doctrine of the Trinity out of these Scriptures was a complex and arduous theological process, resulting in the Nicene-Constantinople Creed (381 CE) that emphasized how the eternal relationship between Father and Son is essential to revelation and salvation. Its formulation that God is one in God's essential being (ousia) but subsists eternally in three persons (hypostases), Father, Son, and Spirit, provides the foundation for subsequent reflection. During these church debates, different models and terms emerged that, together with the problems they faced, continue to be of interest to preachers.

1. Two Models

In general, the Western church tended to accentuate God's oneness—the unity or monism of the Godhead. Significant thinkers include Tertullian (160–225 CE), who first used the word *trinity* (Olson and Hall 2002, 29), and Augustine (354–430 CE), who famously likened the Trinity to three aspects of the human mind: memory, understanding, and will. In contrast, the Eastern Orthodox Church began with God's plurality, God's threeness, initially maintaining the full co-presence of two persons—Father and Jesus—and then later adding the person of the Holy Spirit. The Cappadocian fathers were seminal thinkers, comprising Basil the Great (ca. 330–379 CE), Gregory of Nazianzus (329–389 CE), and Gregory of Nyssa (ca. 330–395 CE). Their thinking played a major part in formulating the Nicene-Constantinople Creed.

The tension between monism and plurality gave rise to two models. On the one hand, a model of the immanent Trinity (sometimes called the ontological, psychological, or individual model) described who God is in God's oneness, as triune being. Focusing on the Godhead's essential nature, God's inner dynamics shared by three persons apart from creation, underscores God's freedom and graciousness of salvation.

On the other hand, a model of the economic Trinity expresses how God in three persons is revealed most obviously in relationship to creation—in the act of creation itself, and through the incarnation, crucifixion, resurrection, and Pentecost. By stressing the relationality and participation of three persons, it lays the foundation for a social Trinity model, developed particularly by Richard of St. Victor (d. 1173 CE) (Olson and Hall 2002, 57) that has become highly influential today.

Vitally important to preserve both the unity of the one God and the individuality of the three persons, the patristic doctrine of perichōresis (developed later by John of Damascus in the 8th cent.) held that the persons of the Trinity do not belong as distinct from one another, but that they dwell inside one another (John 10:38; 14:8-11), mutually inhering, drawing life from one another, and therefore only to be experienced because of their relationship to one another. Because of their mutuality, no divine person acts apart from the others. For example, in creation, the Father is Creator, but Jesus is involved (John 1:3), as is the Spirit (Ps 104:30). Or in Eph 1:3-14, the Father elects (vv. 4-5, 11), the Son redeems (vv. 3, 7-8), and the Holy Spirit seals the outcome (vv. 13-14).

The early church fathers called the roles of the Trinity appropriations. Basil the Great defined these: the Father is the origin (first cause) of every divine work, the Son (the efficient cause) carries it out, and the Spirit (the perfecting cause) brings it to completion (Quicke 2003, 58).

It is possible to relate preaching to the Trinity: the Father speaks forth his word in creation and revelation, the Son is the eternally spoken word, and the Spirit causes the word to be heard and preached. Inevitably, preaching has been viewed as an appropriation of the Holy Spirit—making known God in Christ by power (1 Thess 1:5). Echoing the concept of perichōresis, Luther boldly claimed, "There is in the divine Trinity a pulpit. . . . God's triune being is an eternal conversation, and since the Holy Spirit tells us what he hears we are taken into this conversation" (Gunton 2001, 2).

2. Key Problems

Because defining the Trinity involved holding a balance between God's unity and plurality, problems arose whenever one or the other option was stressed. At one extreme, an emphasis on God's unity at the expense of plurality led to modalism. Sometimes called Sabellianism (after the 3rd-cent. thinker Sabellius), it treated Father, Son, and Spirit as modes or successive appearances of a single God. At the other extreme, tritheism understood trinity as three separate gods, each with different responsibilities. Arianism (after Arius 256–336 CE), for example, taught that the Father is fully God, the Son has status of leading creature, though less than fully God, and the Spirit is inferior to the Son.

Extreme though these options are, preachers should be wary of any casual or trite summations of the Trinity that can unsuspectingly repeat them. For example, using simplistic illustrations such as water, ice, and steam immediately falls into modalism. Much more insidious is an unintentional practical unitarianism. While orthodox preachers reject unitarianism, which views God as one person only and denies the divinity of Christ and of the Holy Spirit, they can practice forms of worship and preaching that appear closed to the continuing work of Christ and the Holy Spirit. Preachers need to ensure that the structure of worship and preaching gives due weight to Father, Son, and Holy Spirit.

C. The Trinity Today

Theologians through the last century raised many issues relating to the Trinity. Process theology has questioned the apparent static nature of God's being and persons as classically expressed. Others have criticized the exclusive use of male gender, preferring Creator, Redeemer, and Sustainer. However, the traditional language should be understood not to denote that God is male or analogous to earthly fathers, but should be seen to personalize the God of Scripture, through the particularity of Jesus the Son who enables us to become brothers and sisters.

Several key 20th-cent. theologians, beginning with Karl Barth, and including Karl Rahner, Wolfhart Pannenberg, Jürgen Moltmann, Leonardo Boff, Catherine LaCugna, and John Zizioulas, have worked with the classic trinitarian models and terms, reinterpreting their significance.

Both models have continued to exert influence. The immanent Trinity, expressing love by relationality and mutuality, has been developed with profound anthropological implications. Because God is a plurality-in-unity, the pattern for humankind is not of solitary persons, but persons in relationship grounded in an ethic of love. Humankind made in God's trinitarian image (Gen 1:26-28) is not complete unless it lives in relationships—an emphasis especially significant in the face of Western society's current obsession with individuality.

The economic Trinity, expressing God's perichoretic relationship with humankind in creation and salvation history, has been developed to invite believers' participation within the Trinity's powerful dynamic. Interaction between Father, Son, and Spirit has particularly enlivened views of worship as "the gift of participation through the Spirit in the incarnate Son's communion with the Father" (Torrance 1996, 20). A christology that emphasizes the double movement of Christ acting from "above" as well as "below" enables believers to participate in the double movement of worship and communion: God-humanward from the Father through the Son in the Spirit but also human-Godward, moving to the Father through the Son in the Spirit.

Participation within this double movement has profound implications for the act of preaching itself. A popular metaphor envisages the preacher as bridge builder taking full responsibility for connecting Scripture with hearers. But this trinitarian dynamic suggests that preaching belongs within the bigger dynamic of God's word returning to God (Isa 55:11; 1 John 1:3). The triune God begins and finishes the process of preaching, beginning with God's revelation in Scripture, continuing by Christ's interceding presence and the Spirit's empowering, to impact hearers for God's purpose.

A lively doctrine of the Trinity therefore places a preacher's preparation and sermon delivery within the continuing work of Father, Son, and Holy Spirit. Without such a trinitarian framework, weekly sermon work degenerates into practical unitarianism in which they assume full responsibility. Rather, they should be practical trinitarians, approaching the text open to the Spirit and the gift of participation in God's trinitarian life. Trinitarian preachers are immersed in God's revealed Word and preach under the Son's authority by the Holy Spirit's power.

D. Preaching the Trinity

Lively trinitarian theology therefore influences every part of worship with preaching. Its language should enrich prayer, hymnody, and sermon. Churches with non-liturgical worship must particularly safeguard against incipient practical unitarianism that unwittingly demotes persons of the Trinity, especially the Holy Spirit.

1. Trinity Sunday
The preacher has responsibility to ensure the Trinity is preached as a focused doctrine within the regular pattern of the church year. For liturgical churches, Trinity Sunday offers a strategic opportunity, and non-liturgical churches should make similar opportunities. Unless the Trinity is preached directly, a church will lose sight of this theological doctrine that defends the central faith of Scripture and the church.

Preachers should mine the most appropriate lectionary reading. Presented with Lev 16:1-10; Eph 2:11-22; Mark 10:13-16, Colin Gunton focused on Eph 2:18 (though referring to the other texts): "Through him (Christ) both of us have access in one Spirit to the Father" (Gunton 2001, 55–60). Claiming that the doctrine of the Trinity has concrete and practical implications, he identifies its personal impact upon human community and particularly church community:

> Personal access—access to people, in which we give and receive to and from one another—is the center of what it is to be human in community.

And the doctrine of the Trinity is not about abstract theological theory, but the primacy of the personal. That God is Father, Son and Spirit says that in his innermost being, from and to eternity, God is personal: he is what he is by virtue of what the persons are in their relations to one another. . . . Access to God, the creator of all there is, is not by obeying some law, or by absolute submission to power, or by anything that makes us less than personal. Access to God is through the person of his Son, realized by his Spirit. (Gunton 2001, 59)

But even more important are the implications for the church:

> There is a desperate need in our world for personal values . . . that doesn't come simply from talking about it. The key lies rather in shaping patterns of human community . . . that is to say, in developing what can be called Trinity-shaped communities. This is the church's calling. Our life in the church is shaped by this relationship as week by week we stand under the word and around the table of the Lord. (Gunton 2001, 60)

Note how he uses the immanent Trinity's challenge to be human in community and the economic Trinity's participation through the Son and Spirit that enables Trinity-shaped communities.

Trinity can be approached with contagious excitement. A sermon of my own based on 2 Cor 1:15-22 was titled "God's 'Yes' and our 'Amen.' "

> When Paul is accused of fickleness, of failing to make up his mind, he responds that he is not about a business that is yes/no, on/off, probably/not sure, could be/can't be. For Jesus Christ is never yes/no, on/off, probably/not sure, could be/can't be, but always yes to every one of God's promises.
>
> And when we talk of yes promises, these are not some pleasant spiritual thoughts that make us feel better in church. They are rock solid, life-changing realities of the new creation. "God establishes us together in Christ (note this is a together event—not for individuals only), and has anointed us by putting his seal on us and giving his Spirit in our hearts as a first installment." This is the work of Father, Son and Holy Spirit, not yes/no, on/off, probably/not sure, could be/can't be. Here is the full weight of God's grace and guarantee. The rest of our lives together is saying and living out "Amen" to the glory of God.

The sermon developed the work of God in three persons in the text, and the service ended in Communion.

2. Trinity as a Consistent Emphasis

The entire structure of Christian redemption depends on God's three-in-oneness. When a Scripture text directly mentions Trinity, preachers should ensure its trinitarian dimension is not lost. For example, Matt 28:16-20 is usually preached as a mission call to the Great Commission, but this call should properly be understood only within its trinitarian framework. All trinitarian references, even when less explicit, should be seized on. A baptismal sermon of mine on Luke 3:21-23; 4:1-13 was titled "Baptism and After." Jesus models key spiritual events for believers:

> Praying to the Father. Prayer isn't about technique—it is about relationship.
> Filling by the Spirit. A real experience of God's third person through repentance and faith (as in Acts 2:38).
> Battling with the Enemy. Do not be surprised by the outcome—that after baptism there is a battle to please God and follow God's will.

Keep alert to prepositions, as in Rom 11:36: "for from him and through him and to him are all things," and "above all and through all and in all" (Eph 4:6). When preaching on themes, such as prayer, the preacher needs to highlight the classic pattern of praying to the Father through the Son by the Spirit while encouraging hearers to be aware that prayer may also be offered to Jesus (Rev 5:11-14) and to the Spirit. Preachers have also found value in preaching through the Apostles' Creed, which takes a trinitarian structure (see Van Harn 2004).

No worship should happen without explicit reference to the Trinity—in the call to worship, prayers, creed, and benediction. All preaching also needs to be intentional about this foundational doctrine for Christian life. *See* CHRISTOLOGY; HOLY SPIRIT AND PREACHING; REVELATION.

Bibliography: Colin Gunton. *Theology through Preaching.* (2001); Catherine Mowry LaCugna. *God for Us: The Trinity and Christian Life.* (1991); Roger E. Olson and Christopher A. Hall. *The Trinity.* (2002); Michael J. Quicke. *360-Degree Preaching: Hearing, Speaking, and Living the Word.* (2003); James B. Torrance. *Worship, Community & the Triune God of Grace.* (1996); Roger E. Van Harn, ed. *Exploring and Proclaiming the Apostles' Creed.* (2004).

WORD OF GOD
Charles L. Bartow

The belief of the church and of its preachers and congregants is that Jesus Christ is God's very Word to them. So also the Bible in its attestation to Christ is to be received in the church as the Word of God written. So, following the reading of the lessons in worship, the lector may say, "The Word of the Lord," with congregants responding, "Thanks be to God."

The sermon also is to be heard and received as God's Word, though following delivery of the sermon one does not typically hear preachers say, "The Word of the Lord," expecting congregants to reply, "Thanks be to God." The reason is that the sermon is not canonical, but is, rather, in its witness to Christ Jesus, a word to be received and assessed in terms of its consonance with the witness of Scripture. In other words, the witness of Scripture is warranted in terms of its fidelity to Jesus Christ clothed in his gospel. And the witness of the preacher is warranted in terms of its fidelity to Christ as attested in Scripture. Karl Barth put the matter classically:

> The revealed Word of God we know only from the Scripture adopted by church proclamation or from proclamation based on Scripture. The written Word of God we know only through the revelation which makes proclamation possible, or through the proclamation made possible by revelation. The proclaimed Word of God we know only by knowing the revelation attested through Scripture, or by knowing the Scripture which attests revelation. (1936, 136)

A. Interpretation of God's Word
   1. The Necessity
   2. The Challenge
   3. The Role of the Preacher
   4. The Bible as the Church's Book
B. Practical Implications
   1. Jesus Christ Is Central
   2. Neutrality Is Not Possible
   3. The God Sense of Texts
   4. Other Senses of Scripture
      a. The moral sense
      b. The allegorical sense
      c. The anagogical sense
C. Sermon Outcomes

A. Interpretation of God's Word

It comes, then, to this: How do preachers read, receive, and inwardly digest the written word of the Bible as God's own Word to them and to their congregants? This question has been made poignant because of the distancing, objectivizing stance of historical criticism and the various types of social analysis that followed hard on its heels, for example, Marxist analysis and feminist (and, later, womanist) criticism. These are just two scholarly trajectories that, in keeping with historical studies generally, look for relevant, contemporary significance more in what lies behind the text or in what may be inferred from the text's arguments and stories and expositions to lie hidden in the traditions the text obscures or implicitly or explicitly renounces.

1. The Necessity

David L. Bartlett lucidly has explained what may be gained—and perhaps also lost—in the plethora of historical and liberationist textual studies available to preachers. He also has (1) explored a range of literary methods of biblical interpretation, again noting potential gains and losses, (2) given account of ecclesial-doctrinal responses, such as canonical criticism, (3) advised preachers to avoid facile interpretations that may in some manner appear to speak to immediate, felt needs but that do not at all take account of the complex history of interpretation of biblical texts (1999, 164), and (4) reminded preachers that there is no way around the daunting risk of contemporary, constructive reflection, and engagement with matters of urgent concern in the theological and cultural discourse of the preacher's present moment:

> The Bible provides the source and the criterion of faithful preaching. Sermons start with texts; however, preaching is not just a matter of reading the Scripture in a loud voice, or dramatically. New occasions demand new interpretations, shifted nuances, applications that our forebears never dreamed. (1999, 16)

2. The Challenge

Sandra M. Schneiders deals with ecclesiastical appropriation of Paul Ricoeur's hermeneutic theory (1999). She found in Ricoeur a way to honor, without giving final or exclusive probative value to, the contributions of the varied approaches to critical scrutiny of biblical texts rehearsed and commented

upon by Bartlett. Like Bartlett, she did this with a view to enabling biblically warranted proclamation of the gospel of Jesus Christ in the church catholic. Her own perspective reflects her feminist commitment filtered through her remarkably deep and devout research and teaching in NT and spiritual formation within the Roman Catholic tradition. At the same time, and not coincidentally, her work is ecumenically generous. Therefore, deservedly, it has been given serious attention by Protestant biblical scholars, homileticians, and preachers.

Clearly, it is impossible here to review Schneiders's detailed treatment of the thought of Paul Ricoeur. Suffice it to say that she has traced the history and development of his thought and, in doing so, has highlighted certain of Ricoeur's most enduringly provocative moves: his holding in tensive relationship "ideal meaning" (as opposed to "authorial intent") and emergent meaning (the sense of the text constructed by the reader on the basis of the propositional integrity of sentences); Ricoeur's sense of the textual referent as "the world" projected by the text (which world consists of an ever changing, moving equilibrium of relationships yielding for the reader the experience of orientation, disorientation, and reorientation that signals the text's capacity to interpret the reader-preacher even as the reader-preacher interprets the text); and the goal of "valid" interpretation as opposed to "correct" interpretation. Or to put it in distinctively Ricoeurian terms: if committing a text to writing frees thought from the exclusive intentionality of the author, the text, thus set free, liberates the interpretive imagination of the hermeneut from domination by the context behind the text (as reconstructed by historical criticism) and the hermeneut's own presenting context, her or his ideological proclivities.

3. The Role of the Preacher

The canonical, biblical text thus is a site not of unmitigated constraint but of chastened emancipation. Schneiders therefore can say:

> The work of the exegete and the critic in establishing the ideal meaning of the text is concerned with what I have called the objective pole of interpretation. Establishing what the sentence Jesus "was handed over to death for our trespasses and raised for our justification" means, that is, what it says and what truth claim it makes in terms of the time and place and thought categories in which it was framed, is the prerequisite, the sine qua non,

for all interpretive work. Whatever the theologian, the preacher . . . or the biblical hermeneut elaborates about the full personal and communal meaning of this statement . . . must refer in an intelligible and compatible way to the ideal meaning established by the exegete-critic, or else it must successfully challenge the exegetical claim with an alternative meaning. (1999, 148)

Note here Schneiders's concern for the self-suspicion of the reader, hermeneut, preacher. She or he does not stand in a privileged relationship of judgment upon the text's attestation of Christ. Instead, she or he, along with the text, is made the subject of critique. In other words, critical assessment of biblical texts necessarily entails critical assessment of those interpreting texts. Schneiders herself explains the matter thus:

> Just as feminist interpreters must be not only critical of patriarchal texts but self-critical of feminist premises, so religiously committed interpreters must be not only critical of secularist premises but also self-critical about dogmatic premises or evangelical projects masquerading as faith. (1999, xxxviii)

4. The Bible as the Church's Book

Yet for Schneiders, the Bible is above all the church's book. This can be taken both as historical fact and as interpretive presupposition. Therefore the church, with its liturgy and dogmatic history and missional development (however contested), is relevant to valid exegetical/interpretive inquiry and is the primary locus of such inquiry. In Schneiders's words:

> The most adequate context for the emergence of the full and integral meaning of the Bible . . . is the church, that is, the community of the disciples of Jesus who have been baptized in his paschal mystery and filled with his Spirit and who live faithfully as his body in the world. (1999, 64)

To sum up: Scripture interprets its interpreters (even as they critically interpret it). The Bible also interprets the church, even as the church (in dogmatic history and liturgical practice) interprets the Bible. And those appointed to preach the gospel of Jesus Christ, whatever the nature of their personally held hermeneutical presuppositions or unreflected upon proclivities, and whatever their social location, thus are set firmly within the tensional matrix of this biblical/ecclesial dialectic. The preacher preaches—or in Barth's sense attempts to preach—Jesus Christ as he is attested in Scripture. Moreover, the preacher does this as one held accountable to Scripture by the church, and held accountable by Scripture to the church.

B. Practical Implications

Paul Scott Wilson brings to the preacher's study lessons from the past to help preachers receive scriptural texts as divine word. Wilson seeks to help preachers to interpret Scripture after the manner of Scripture's interpretation of itself. From Wilson's study, "hands on" lessons can be drawn and briefly explicated.

Wilson's approach might be called a neoclassical practical hermeneutic for preaching. In keeping with the trajectory set by Bartlett and Schneiders, this neoclassical practical hermeneutic is critical as much as it is practical. But it is homiletically critical. It is critical in that it means to have preachers attend to texts as persons obligated by ecclesial vocation to preach those texts, and to preach them as written attestation to the incarnate Word of God.

1. Jesus Christ Is Central

The principle of discriminating judgment in interpretation thus is Christ Jesus himself as attested in Scripture and as enthroned on the praises of his people. Presupposed is a strong, governing doctrine of incarnation, namely, that "the incarnation is that event in history which gathers all other revelation into itself" (Jewett 1958, 48). So, with incarnation, a strong view of biblical revelation is implied, which view "is that history is the medium through which the eternal God has revealed himself once for all" (Jewett 1958, 46). And this God "meets [human beings] in the act of revelation not as an Idea, an Unmoved Mover, but as a Person who speaks to us and requires a response from us" (Jewett 1958, 57).

2. Neutrality Is Not Possible

Such a standard of judgment in interpretation proffers no neutrality. But if so-called postmodern thought has taught preachers anything, it has taught them this: there can be no neutral stance in biblical interpretation or proclamation of the gospel. And "the *Deus loquens*, the 'speaking God,' is a foundational experience of both the Christian community of faith and its Jewish matrix" (Fretheim and Froehlich 1998, 9). Further, Luther, for one, "would not have known how to separate the scriptural

Word of God from the one that is proclaimed and heard in the present. . . . The inner word (*verbum internum*) is preceded and mediated by the outer word (*verbum externum*), Scripture and its proclamation. Scripture is the mean" (Fretheim and Froehlich 1990, 9).

3. The God Sense of Texts

Preaching takes place "through faith for faith" (Rom 1:17*a*). The outcome of this, according to Wilson's biblical hermeneutic for preaching, is that the Bible is to be searched by preachers for its "'God sense' . . . [which] may be defined as those dimensions of it that speak of God's nature, acts, and relationship to humanity and creation, and that enable the Bible to be read as Scripture, the book of the church" (Wilson 2001, 68).

This call to read Scripture theologically and ecclesially should not be taken to mean that rigorous historical-critical studies and sociocultural critiques of texts are to be given no account. For, as Colin Brown observed, reflecting upon the work of the Pontifical Biblical Commission:

> Faith and historical study are not mutually exclusive. Indeed they are mutually necessary. But [the commission] warns against the deceptive superficiality of so-called theological ways of reading Scripture that seek to dispense with scholarly study. Facile solutions 'can in no way provide the solid basis needed for studies in biblical theology, even when engaged in with full faith.' (Brown 1991, 70)

4. Other Senses of Scripture

Keeping that caveat in mind, preachers nevertheless are urged by Wilson once again to consider, freshly understood, three classical moves in biblical interpretation: reading texts for their "moral sense," their "allegorical sense," and their "anagogic" or mystical and eschatological sense (Wilson 2001, 159–61).

a. The moral sense. Moral sense should not be understood moralistically. To discover the moral sense of texts is, rather, to grapple with what texts would have people be and do in light of who God is and what God has done in Jesus Christ. Here is found a definition of human being and human doing not autonomously and self-referentially articulated, but articulated christologically. Moral sense, and thus moral conduct, therefore have to do with taking "every thought captive to obey Christ" (2 Cor 10:5).

b. The allegorical sense. So also reading Scripture for its allegorical sense is not an invitation to speculate about texts' hidden significances. It is, rather, to establish settled truths with due regard for the reconstruction of the historical settings in which texts originally were interpreted. Attentiveness to present venues of interpretation also is required (Wilson 2001, 135). Following Northrop Frye, Wilson sees allegory as attaching ideas to poetic images (2001, 140–41). It is no more inventive, nor less imaginative, than striving for what H. H. Farmer long ago called "concreteness" (1964, 66–88), or what J. Randall Nichols labeled "immediacy," a provocation to attentive interest with whatever has to do with textual meaning for human life "at the most immediate pressure point" (1980, 36). Allegory so understood is what Jesus himself is attested as doing in interpreting for his disciples the meaning of his parable of the Seed and Soils (Matt 13:1-23).

c. The anagogical sense. Finally, there is anagogy, which has to do with matters beyond sense and time, but not beyond the purview of God, God's caring and God's justice. In Christ, there is the presence of the future among us (Wilson 2001, 156). This presence, though, does not banish mystery from life. Instead it makes it clear that the future is personal and of consequence. In other words, God is the world's future (Peters 1992, esp. 306–31), God in all the justice and mercy that inheres in God's grace as revealed in Jesus Christ as the Bible bears witness to him. Here the doctrine of eschatology bears upon the doctrine of providence. In other words, who trusts in "God—The World's Future" (Peters 1992) does not live in fear of the next minute.

C. Sermon Outcomes

The practical outcome of the hermeneutic for preaching proposed by Wilson is as follows: if preaching draws upon a neotraditional "moral," "allegorical," and "anagogic" interpretation of Scripture, it will hold being and doing, truth and its poetic resonances, time and eternity in lively tension. Further, in doing so, it will allow the Bible to interpret preachers and their congregants even as preachers, in company with their congregants, interpret the sacred text. Not least, the Bible will be understood to do this not according to its own immanent powers (as if it were a book of magic), but according to the power of the life-giving Spirit that puts Scripture and the preaching of Scripture to a "holy use." To interpret the Bible as God's word is to receive it as a word spoken in the Spirit by Christ Jesus himself, who is the Word of God incarnate and who, beyond any human expectation, fills full of divine significance all history and all prophecy, all prayer and all praise:

> So shall my word be that goes out from my mouth;
>
> > it shall not return to me empty,
> but it shall accomplish that which I purpose.
> > (Isa 55:11)

Helmut Thielicke can be understood to have interpreted Scripture in his own time morally, allegorically, and anagogically, all at one stroke. He spoke to who people truly are to be and how they are to live. He did so with concreteness, specificity, and immediacy. And he did so in the light of an understanding of God as the world's true future and present hope. Even today his preaching seems peculiarly relevant to a world still seemingly set on a course of hell-bent apocalypse. Just so, Thielicke's preaching may be worthy of thoughtful emulation. Thielicke preached thus:

> Even in the pressure zone of mass . . . destruction and growing tyranny, we must have the long view . . . of those who know they have a secure place in . . . God's eternal symphony. For above the battle of the powers . . . above all crises and threats in our personal life there sounds . . . the promise of God. While the earth remains, seedtime and harvest, cold and heat, summer and winter, day and night shall not cease.

Thielicke has God speak the concluding word:

> Don't ever think that anybody will ever break away from serving me! Even in the extreme perversion of authority . . . [people] are compelled . . . to preserve a remnant of my order and they can never succeed in . . . devilizing . . . my world. And . . . shall I not be able to encompass your little life, hear your questions and your groans, and unravel the tangled skein of your need? (Thielicke 1961, 295–96)

One might be tempted, in response to such preaching, to say: "The Word of the Lord" and "Thanks be to God." *See* ALLEGORY, ALLEGORESIS; EXEGESIS; FOUR SENSES OF SCRIPTURE; HERMENEUTICS; TYPOLOGY.

Bibliography: Karl Barth. *Church Dogmatics.* Vol. 1, part 1. Translated by G. T. Thomson. (1936); David L. Bartlett. *Between the Bible and the Church: New Methods for Biblical Preaching.* (1999); Colin Brown. "Scripture and Christology: A Protestant Look at the Work of the Pontifical Biblical Commission." *Perspectives on Christology: Essays in Honor of Paul K. Jewett.* (1991) 39–76; H. H. Farmer. *The Servant of the Word.* (1964); Terrence E. Fretheim and Karlfried Froehlich. *The Bible as Word of God: In a Postmodern Age.* (1998); Paul K. Jewett. "Special Revelation as Historical and Personal." *Revelation and the Bible.* (1958); J. Randall Nichols. *Building the Word: The Dynamics of Communication and Preaching.* (1980); Ted Peters. *God—The World's Future: Systematic Theology for a Postmodern Era.* (1992); Sandra M. Schneiders. *The Revelatory Text: Interpreting the New Testament as Sacred Scripture.* (1999); Helmut Thielicke. *How the World Began.* Translated by John W. Doberstein. (1961); Paul Scott Wilson. *God Sense: Reading the Bible for Preaching.* (2001).

www.ingramcontent.com/pod-product-compliance
Lightning Source LLC
Chambersburg PA
CBHW050637150426

42811CB00053B/969